ABSTRACTS OF THE RECORDS OF THE SOCIETY OF FRIENDS IN INDIANA

VOLUME 1

WHITEWATER AND SPRINGFIELD
MONTHLY MEETINGS
WAYNE COUNTY

Revised edition
by
Ruth Dorrel
and
Thomas D. Hamm

Originally edited by
Willard C. Heiss

Indiana Historical Society
Indianapolis
1996

© 1996 Indiana Historical Society. All rights reserved

Printed in the United States of America

The paper in this publication meets the minimum requirements of American National Standard for Information Sciences—Permanence of Paper for Printed Library Materials, ANSI Z39.48-1984. ∞

Library of Congress Cataloging-in-Publication Data

Abstracts of the records of the Society of Friends in Indiana. —Rev. ed. / by Ruth Dorrel and Thomas D. Hamm.
    p. cm.
    Contents: v. 1. Whitewater and Springfield Monthly Meetings, Wayne County
Vol. 1 originally edited by Willard C. Heiss.
    ISBN 0-87195-113-4
    1. Quakers—Indiana—Wayne County—Genealogy.   2. Society of Friends—Indiana—Wayne County—History—Sources. 3. Wayne County (Ind.)—Genealogy. 4. Wayne County (Ind.)—Church history—Sources. 5. Church records and registers—Indiana—Wayne County. I. Dorrel, Ruth. II. Hamm, Thomas D.
F532.W5A27 1996
929'.3772—dc20   96-18658
                                                                                                                                CIP

TABLE OF CONTENTS

Acknowledgements	i
Introduction	iii
Abbreviations	xiii
Whitewater Monthly Meeting	1
Springfield Monthly Meeting	145
Index	213

ACKNOWLEDGMENTS, 1962

In 1923 Edna Harvey Joseph introduced William Wade Hinshaw, an opera singer, to the possibilities of research in records kept by the monthly meetings of the Religious Society of Friends. Hinshaw, a native of Iowa and a descendant of a long line of Quakers, had an interest in his forebears but did not know how to go about tracing his family history. Miss Harvey was able to fan that small flame of interest into a roaring fire.

Hinshaw engaged Miss Harvey to supply him with all the data about his ancestors that she could find in the various Quaker meetings to which they had belonged. It soon became obvious to Harvey, and she suggested to Hinshaw, that with the money being spent to search scattered material, the entire meeting records could be copied. This suggestion opened a plan of action to Hinshaw. He set out to have **all** the records of **all** the monthly meetings copied with the view of publishing abstracts of the copied records. Not all the records were copied, but hundreds of meetings from the eastern coast to the plains of Iowa and Kansas were copied and sent to Hinshaw.

Thomas W. Marshall shared Hinshaw's interest in publishing Quaker records and in his "spare time" worked tirelessly editing and preparing copy for the printer. The first volume of their monumental work, **Encyclopedia of American Quaker Genealogy**, was published in 1936. It contained the records of the meetings in North Carolina. Up to the time of his death in 1947, Hinshaw published four additional volumes. The Virginia volume, completed after his death, was published by his widow. The Indiana volumes were scheduled to be next in the series, but Mrs. Hinshaw did not feel inclined to proceed with the project. In 1948 the Indiana Historical Society corresponded with Thomas W. Marshall and Mrs. Hinshaw, exploring the possibile publication of the Indiana material by the Society, but after considerable deliberation the matter was dropped. In time, the compiled Indiana material was sent to the Friends Historical Library of Swarthmore College and placed in The William Wade Hinshaw Index to Quaker Meeting Records. This collection consists of Hinshaw's unpublished material.

In the winter of 1960 the Genealogical Section of the Indiana Historical Society became interested in the project again. The Society decided to publish abstracts of the Indiana records. The Friends Historical Library of Swarthmore College has cooperated in making the Hinshaw Indiana abstracts available to the Society. The guidance and suggestions of Dr. Frederick Tolles, Director of the Swarthmore College Library, and Dorothy Harris, Assistant Director, have been invaluable.

Acknowledgment must be given to Mrs. J. E. McMullan, Huntington, Indiana, who did so much work in copying Indiana material for Hinshaw. Many others whose names are unknown to this editor also gave their time.

Indiana and Western Yearly Meetings (Five Years), the Whitewater Quarter of Indiana Yearly Meeting (General Conference), Western Yearly Meeting (Conservative), as well as individual monthly meetings, have unhesitatingly made records available for consultation. Without this cooperation, the project would have been seriously hampered. The various custodians of the record repositories have been most helpful.

Thanks must be given to Hubert H. Hawkins, Secretary of the Indiana Historical Society, who has been tireless in his efforts to promote the project and carry it to completion. Mrs. Irene M. Strieby, Nell W. Reeser, Dorothy Riker, and Carolynne Wendel of the Indiana Historical Society's Genealogical Section have given suggestions and advice on editorial problems. Cecil Beeson, Hartford City, has been of great assistance in supplying materials. Also, without the untiring efforts and diligence of Imogene Brown and particularly Ruth Slevin in searching the original records, the editor would have been helpless. Brenda Bowles, with the patience of Job, was able to interpret our scribbles and jottings and set the copy.

Some of the cost of this publication is being met by contributions from Friends and friends of Friends, namely Paul H. Wolf, F. M. Hadley, Howard E. Henley, B. N. Johnson, Howard Curl, R. N. Hoerner, W. W. Wildman, Carlton B. Edwards, William G. Harter, and William Bray.

Lastly, I have heartfelt thanks for the understanding of my wife and the help of my son, which has made this task easier.

Indianapolis, Eighth month, 1962   Willard Heiss

ACKNOWLEDGEMENTS, 1996

In 1992, when it became apparent that the **Abstracts of the Records of the Society of Friends in Indiana** was soon to be out of print, the Genealogy Publication Committee of the Indiana Historical Society explored options to make this valuable reference work available. The idea of a reprint edition was not acceptable. Records not available at the time of the earlier publication had surfaced, and errors had been found in the early edition. A new edition was planned to include not only new information and corrections but also an every-name index. Most of the original records from which the information was abstracted are in the Earlham College Archives and are available on microfilm. The marriage, birth, and death records and the minutes were checked against the abstracts; corrections and additions were made.

Additions were also made to the list of abbreviations. In this edition, it can be assumed that in most cases if a geographical location is listed without a state, that location is in in Indiana. In a few cases a state is omitted. When there is no concrete evidence of the location (i.e., monthly meetings had duplicate names in several states), the records were again searched to ascertain the state from which the persons came.

Thanks must be given to the Genealogy Publication Committee members: Jane E. Darlington, John German, Thomas D. Hamm, Susan Carter Miller, Mary Morgan, and Thomas Pittman. The encouragement and advice of Thomas A. Mason amd Robert M. Taylor, Jr. is acknowledged. Shirley McCord and Kathleen M. Breen have been patient in the proofreading process.

May 1996   Ruth Dorrel

INTRODUCTION TO 1962 EDITION*
By Willard Heiss

ORIGIN OF THE SOCIETY OF FRIENDS AND ITS SPREAD IN AMERICA

The Society of Friends or Quakers (the terms are synonymous) had its beginning in the middle of the seventeenth century in England. It was in this period of religious and political turmoil and uncertainty that George Fox and others discovered "Truth" as they saw it. Quakerism was but one of the new sects that grew out of those unsettled times. This Society was one that thrived on adversity, grew strong, and left its imprint on subsequent generations. For example, civil rights and religious liberty which we now enjoy can in a small way be attributed to the Quakers firm belief in human equality. The trials, sufferings, and persecutions of these early Friends, that these rights might be established are beyond belief.

Fox swept aside all the clutter and trappings that weighed down the Established Church and put emphasis on personal ethics as they were embodied in the teachings of the original Christians. But he was not content with personal virtues only. Just as Jesus called for a change in the life of a nation, so Fox was concerned with the evil blight that was on England in his day. He urged judges to act justly, protested the low wages paid to laborers, proposed that palaces and manor houses be given to the underprivileged, and that the rich abbeys become orphanages or homes for old people. He demanded that Quaker shopkeepers be honest in weight and measure and that they place a single price on each piece of goods to be sold. He urged abolition of capital punishment and insisted that Friends live a life that took away the occasion for war.

George Fox wrote in his *Journal*, "Some thought I was mad because I stood for purity, perfection and righteousness." Friends believed that with Divine help a man might here and now become perfect, if he were to be wholly obedient to the will of God as "inwardly revealed." Friends held there was no need for priests and others to mediate between man and God but that there is an indwelling Light from God in the heart of every man which can speak to him and guide his actions. Friends live in response to that "Inner Light" which they believe is also to be found within their fellowmen.

One of the central testimonies of the Friends was on the matter of simplicity in all positions of life. The rituals and sacraments (baptism, communion, and the like) of organized religion were discarded as being only "outward forms." The Friends meeting for worship was a gathering of silence and waiting on His presence which might or might not be made vocally manifest.

Quakers first appeared in the American colonies as early as 1656. Within two years monthly meetings were established in Rhode Island and Massachusetts. In 1661, the first yearly meeting in America was opened and held at Newport, Rhode Island. Within the next thirty years, five more yearly meetings were established where there had come to be large centers of Friends. These meetings were New York (1695), Philadelphia (1681), Baltimore (1672), Virginia (1671), and North Carolina (1698). It was one hundred thirteen years after the establishment of North Carolina Yearly Meeting before another yearly meeting was required.

Due mainly to the Appalachian barrier, population stayed on the Atlantic seaboard. The migration pattern of Quakers generally was to move south from Pennsylvania into northwestern Virginia, then farther south into the Carolinas. Due to the decline of the whaling industry, Quakers from Nantucket moved directly to the Carolinas. Prior to the Revolutionary War, a few Friends had started moving westward and had settled in what is now eastern Tennessee. By 1800, there were several settlements of Friends in western Pennsylvania and eastern Ohio; settlements also were being founded in southern and western Ohio. The distance was so great and communications with Baltimore Yearly Meeting were so difficult that in 1813 Ohio Yearly Meeting was set off. It was first held at Short Creek in Jefferson County, Ohio, and later at Mount Pleasant in the same county.

THE SOCIETY OF FRIENDS IN INDIANA

When we now survey the position of Friends in Indiana in relation to an overall pattern of their history, we usually think of them as the link between southern and eastern Friends in their migrations to the West. We almost forget that this was once the West. In the summer and fall of 1806, Jeremiah Cox and family, John Smith and family, Elijah Wright, Frederick Hoover, and perhaps others settled on the Whitewater River at what is now the site of Richmond. Here they cleared land and built cabins that were a great distance, in that unbroken wilderness, from the nearest Friends settlement at West Branch, Ohio. It seems incredible, but that same year the settlement was visited by John Simpson, a minister from Philadelphia. He was traveling under a concern to visit the Indian chief Tecumseh and his followers. Upon leaving the Whitewater settlement, he journeyed some thirty miles north to Fort Greenville.

As the settlement of Friends grew there was a need for a monthly meeting closer than the one at West Branch, Miami County, Ohio. In 1809 Whitewater Monthly Meeting was established and it is from this meeting that all meetings in Indiana descent. While Indiana was yet a territory three monthly meetings were set off from Whitewater, namely **New Garden** (1815), Wayne County; **Lick Creek** (1813), Orange County; and **Blue River** (1815), Washington County.

Following the War of 1812, the migrations of Friends from the Carolinas and Tennessee increased and more monthly meetings came into existence, **Silver Creek** (1817), Union County; **West Grove** (1818) and **Springfield** (1820), Wayne County; **Driftwood** (1820), Jackson County; **Honey Creek** (1820), Vigo County; and **Cherry Grove** (1821), Randolph County. The above named monthly meetings along with some others in Ohio belonged at this time to Ohio Yearly Meeting, which was held at Mount Pleasant, Ohio. It is apparent that if representatives from the Richmond area going to yearly meeting faced a hardship, then those going from the southern and western part of the state were confronted with an even greater hardship. It was concluded to divide the yearly meeting.

*A revision of an article published in *Indiana History Bulletin*, 39:51-82 (March-April 1962), under the title "Guide to Research in Quaker Records in the Midwest."

Indiana Yearly Meeting

On the 8th of 10th Month, 1821, the first sessions of the Indiana Yearly Meeting were held in Richmond, Indiana, with some two thousand Friends in attendance. Women Friends met in a log house used by Whitewater Monthly and Quarterly Meeting and the men used a shed nearby. In the 1820s a large brick meetinghouse was completed, which was used until the present meetinghouse on East Main Street was built.

Besides the meetings named above, all the meetings in southwestern Ohio were also a part of the Indiana Yearly Meeting.

As the central part of the state was opened for settlement, Friends not only continued to arrive from the southern and eastern states, but they also moved on from the previously established settlements. By 1835 there were substantial communities of Friends in Henry, Grant, Morgan, Marion, Hendricks, Hamilton, Montgomery, and Parke counties. The westward expansion stretched the Yearly Meeting to include meetings established in Illinois and Iowa. About seventy monthly meetings were within these limits in the 1850s. Again, the distances representatives were required to travel to attend the yearly meeting at Richmond became a hardship, and a division was made of Indiana Yearly Meeting.

Western Yearly Meeting

Plainfield, Hendricks County, Indiana, was chosen as the location for the new Yearly Meeting. Large numbers of Friends were located in the adjoining counties and Plainfield was geographically somewhat closer to points west. Western Yearly Meeting was established and the first session held on the 29th of the Ninth Month, 1858, with some six hundred Friends in attendance. The meetings in the eastern and northern part of the state remained with Indiana Yearly Meeting. The meetings in the central, western, and southern part were included in Western Yearly Meeting. The meetings in Howard County were at first with Indiana, but later transferred to Western. This arrangement has continued to the present day.

Indiana Yearly Meeting (Hicksite)

In 1827 and 1828, a controversy that involved most of the Society of Friends, with the exception of Friends in the Carolinas and New England, finally caused an irreconcilable split. The names that came to distinguish the two groups after a separation took place were Hicksite and Orthodox. The former label was given to supporters of Elias Hicks (1748-1830), the Quaker minister from Long Island who was at the center of the controversy. The Hicksites, as one historian has put it, "held doctrines, not as essential to Christian faith but as fruits of it." The doctrine of the "Inner Light" continued to be their central belief. Rufus Jones comments that "for a whole generation, the Society had tacked, like a ship sailing against the wind, in a curious zigzag, back and forth from Scripture to Inner Light and from Inner Light to Scripture." The Orthodox group emphasized the centrality of the divinity of Christ and the authority of Scripture. These differences were aggravated by a procession of traveling English Friends who might have served the "Cause of Truth" best by staying in England.

This controversy affected Indiana Friends, splitting many monthly meetings. The Hicksites, the minority, held the first session of their yearly meeting in Waynesville, Ohio, in the last week of Tenth Month, 1828. The annual sessions then alternated between Richmond and Waynesville. Hicksite monthly meetings established in Indiana at the time of the separation were Whitewater and Milford in Wayne County, Honey Creek in Vigo County, and Blue River in Washington County. Hicksites later established other monthly meetings.

A great source of confusion lay in the fact that both groups, Hicksites and Orthodox, continued to call themselves Indiana Yearly Meeting of Friends. In 1975 the Hicksite group changed its name to Ohio Valley. Since 1900 Hicksites have become generally known as General Conference Friends, while the Orthodox have identified themselves as Five Years Meeting or Friends United Meeting Quakers, for associations to which yearly meetings of the two bodies belong.

Indiana Yearly Meeting (Anti-Slavery)

If the separation of 1828 left a divided Society, the next controversy left a mutilated Society. The English Friends continued to avail themselves of the audience of the Orthodox Branch of the Society in America. New England Yearly Meeting had not been seriously affected by the earlier schism but it was here the English Evangelicals widened an incipient crevice. A staunch defender of traditional practices and beliefs of Friends in New England Yearly Meeting was John Wilbur. The leading proclaimer of the new theological approach was Joseph John Gurney of Norwich, England. A separation occurred in New England in 1845.

Indiana Yearly Meeting (Orthodox) was not notably affected by the Gurneyite-Wilburite controversy as it was involved in internal conflict of its own. All members of the Society were, to some degree, committed to the opposition of slavery. Differences came in the application of this belief. There were members who flagrantly violated the Fugitive Slave Law, joined anti-slavery societies that were not under the influence of Friends, and opened meetinghouses to conferences of these societies. To conservative Friends this was unsound and as a consequence the two groups diverged. On 7th of Second Month 1843 Indiana Yearly Meeting of Anti-Slavery Friends was organized and met annually at Newport (now Fountain City), Indiana. In a few years the attitudes of the larger body changed and by 1857 there had been effected somewhat of a reunion of the two groups. The damage was considerable since many valuable members were permanently lost.

Western Yearly Meeting (Conservative)

Following the Civil War, changes in attitudes assumed by some members in the Western Yearly Meeting and to a limited extent in Indiana Yearly Meeting, coupled with an influx of new members into the Society who were not concerned with traditional Quaker doctrines and practices, brought about some startling changes in many of the meetings throughout both yearly meetings. The Society of Friends had become rather static, but a movement by concerned Friends to revitalize the Society had been overwhelmed by the leadership of such ex-Methodists as Frame, Clark, and Updegraff. Esther Frame once implied that the main reason she came to join the Friends was that the Methodists did not allow women in the ministry. In any event, by the 1870s, what might be aptly characterized as the "Wesleyan influence" provoked such questions as conversion, conviction for sin, salvation, and sanctification into heated discussions. All of these were unrelated to the traditional doctrines of Friends.

The contemplative silence of meetings for worship was replaced by hymn singing and programmed church services. The interiors of meetinghouses were gutted as the galleries and partitions were ripped out and rostrums and pulpits installed for the hired ministers. There was no rest on the part of the innovators until the soughs from the reed organ had been added to the off-key harmony of unfamiliar hymns. The final desecration was the introduction of the "revival meeting" and its attendant emotionalism–the singing, shouting, and writhing at the "mourner's bench."

This movement developed rapidly and as more stable members of the Society were unable to stem the tide, most of these retired from the fray and established on 14th of Ninth Month 1877, Western Meeting of (Conservative) Friends which included one meeting from eastern Indiana and two in western Ohio. This Yearly Meeting was held at Sugar Grove, south of Plainfield. If previous separations had been tragedies, this one was a disaster as the Society was divided into two extreme positions, whereas if the division could have been avoided, the leavening effects of both groups would have greatly influenced and helped the Society of Friends in the Midwest. This Yearly Meeting was laid down 3rd of Ninth Month, 1962.

LATER DIVISIONS OF YEARLY MEETINGS

Iowa Yearly Meeting (Orthodox) was established by Indiana Yearly Meeting in 1863. Salem Monthly Meeting had been established in 1838. It is important to note that all certificates of removal for Friends moving to Iowa prior to 1838 were deposited with Vermilion Monthly Meeting, Illinois, that being the nearest monthly meeting to the Iowa settlements. There was a separation in Iowa due to causes similar to those given above, and in 1878 Iowa Yearly Meeting (Conservative) was established.

Kansas Yearly Meeting (Orthodox) was established by Indiana Yearly Meeting in 1872 and met at Lawrence. A separation, due to the same reasons as stated in the sketch of Western Yearly Meeting, brought about the establishment of Kansas Yearly Meeting (Conservative) in 1879. Their annual meetings were held in Emporia, Kansas, the last being in 1929 when the Yearly Meeting was laid down. The surviving members were attached to Iowa Yearly Meeting (Conservative).

In 1892 Wilmington (Ohio) Yearly Meeting was set off from Indiana Yearly Meeting (Orthodox). It included nearly all the meetings in western and southern Ohio.

The Indiana Yearly Meeting (Hicksite) was divided by setting off Illinois Yearly Meeting in 1874, comprising southern Indiana, all of Illinois, and also meetings in Iowa and Wisconsin.

ORGANIZATIONAL STRUCTURE OF THE SOCIETY OF FRIENDS

Yearly Meetings

The final authority for decisions in the Society of Friends rests in the body of the yearly meeting. As the name implies, this is an annual meeting composed of representatives from the quarterly meetings which comprise the yearly meeting. Any member of the Society may attend and is free to express his views, but the representatives are appointed to assure the attendance of some persons from all parts of the yearly meeting. A clerk presides over these sessions, which last for several days, and all decisions are made from a "sense of the meeting." Reports from various committees are read, statistics are compiled, etc. This information, together with the minutes of the meeting, are compiled and published. Collections of these printed minutes are to be found in many libraries: the Friends Historical Library at Swarthmore College and Haverford College Library probably have the most complete sets. Earlham College, of course, has a complete set for Indiana Yearly Meeting, Guilford College for North Carolina, etc.

The original manuscript minutes as they exist are found in the archives of the respective yearly meetings. For the past decades many yearly meetings have been sending minutes and reports directly to the printer and have not compiled a manuscript records–hence in many instances the printed record is all that exists.

The importance of these minutes varies, depending upon the interest of the researcher. From the earliest days there are committee reports of the Indian, Temperance, Education, and other committees. Through these minutes, it is possible to follow the changes of attitudes of the Society on matters of discipline and theology. (Friends do not admit a theology.) These attitudes, advices, and regulations were collected from time to time and published in a "Discipline." Although these advices have existed almost from the beginning of the Society, it was not until the latter part of the eighteenth century that they were put into print. Many revisions have been made since that time.

Of importance to the genealogist are the death notices of ministers and elders which appear in the printed yearly meeting minutes. The number of notices vary; in 1842 there were eight in the Minutes of Indiana Yearly Meeting of Friends; two examples:

Ann Cox, an elder, and member of White River Monthly Meeting, died twelfth
month 4th, 1841; aged 65 years, wanting 5 days.

Exum Elliott, an elder, and member of West Grove Monthly Meeting, died tenth
month 8th, 1841; aged 76 years, 5 months and 29 days.

Before leaving the matter of yearly meeting records, I would like to draw attention to the minutes of the "Meeting for Sufferings." In America, these records exist from the mideighteenth century and consist of a record of the matters that came before a representative body (in effect, an executive committee) that met and functioned for the yearly meeting when it was not in session. These meetings contain much material concerning the resistance of Friends to wars as well as other matters relating to meetinghouses and graveyards.

Quarterly Meetings

These meetings for business were composed of representatives appointed by the component monthly meetings. Reports were brought to this meeting and annual summaries prepared. Problems that were unresolved by the monthly meetings were sent here and decided or, if found "too weighty," were forwarded to the yearly meeting. The quarterly meeting established or "set up" new monthly meetings or "laid down" such meetings as had come to the end of their usefulness. They usually confirmed action in relation to meetings subordinate to the monthly meetings.

In former days (and yet today) these meetings served as an important link in bringing widely scattered Friends together for their spiritual needs and, equally as important, they were a focal point in the Society's social life.

Monthly Meetings

A monthly meeting was usually comprised of several preparative meetings. It is here that the bulk of the business of the Society is transacted and recorded in the minutes. These records will be outlined in another section.

A misunderstanding of the monthly meeting should be clarified. Let us take for an example White River Monthly Meeting (Randolph County, Indiana). In 1840 it consisted of five preparative meetings. To the uninformed it might appear that White River Meeting was the head and the rest of the meetings were subordinate. This is not the case. White River Meeting was a preparative, along with Jericho, Dunkirk,

Sparrow Creek, and Cabin Creek. Together this group of preparatives formed a monthly meeting which went by the name of White River. In fact, the monthly meeting rotated at that time, being held consecutively at White River, Jericho, and Dunkirk.

As settlers came into a community or an adjacent area, the population of a Friends meeting increased. When the monthly meeting became unwieldy, due to increased membership, another monthly meeting was created. For example, in 1824, when White River Monthly Meeting was "set up," there were settlements of Friends only the central and eastern parts of Randolph County. By 1840, the western part of the county had been settled and there was a need for reorganization. In 1841 Sparrow Creek Monthly Meeting was "set off" and was comprised of Sparrow Creek, Dunkirk, and Cabin Creek Preparatives.

Another situation that is a source of confusion, even to persons familiar with Friends, needs to be explored. The following is a fictional situation.

Let us suppose a John Overman and his family, preparing to remove in 1806 from the Carolinas to north of the Ohio River, would request and get a certificate of their membership to Miami Monthly Meeting (Warren County, Ohio). The certificate is received accordingly at Miami Meeting, but when John arrives in Ohio he concludes to settle in Miami County instead of Warren County. Upon his request, the certificate is endorsed by Miami Meeting and sent to West Branch Monthly Meeting. He and his family are then members of West Branch. In 1808 our fictional family moves to Indiana Territory and settles just north of Richmond. The following year, when Whitewater Monthly Meeting is "set off," they become members of that meeting. In 1815, as New Garden Monthly Meeting is "set off" from Whitewater, they become members of New Garden. In 1820 our family moves to near Winchester (Randolph County). They then become members of Cherry Grove Monthly Meeting when it is "set off" from New Garden in 1821. There is a division of Cherry Grove Monthly Meeting in 1824 and the Overmans become a part of White River Monthly Meeting. In 1830 the family moves to Grant County, Indiana, but are still members of White River as that meeting encompassed in its membership all the territory to the north and west of Randolph County. Then, in 1832, Mississinewa Monthly Meeting is "set off." Our Overmans are now members of Mississinewa.

This is a rather far-fetched example but it points up what might have happened when a family you are tracing disappears from the records. The last record of the Overman family appearing in meeting records is the reception of the certificate at West Branch. It is possible that John Overman might never appear in the minutes of any of the above mentioned meetings as serving on a committee or the like. And, it is further possible that he was never recorded in any birth or death record. Yet he was a member of the Society until his death, even though the last recorded evidence of his membership was in 1806 at West Branch.

A similar situation would be possible if a family never moved from its original pioneer homestead. Suppose a family settled in the southwesterly part of Wayne County, Indiana, at an early date. They could have been members of the Whitewater, West Grove, and Milford meetings consecutively. I have dealt with the above problem at length, as I have found it be one of the most perplexing for individuals who come to the "stone wall" in their tracing of families.

A similar situation has occurred in another way. Suppose a family transferred its membership to Duck Creek Meeting in Henry County, Indiana, in 1835 and then apparently disappeared from the records. The answer to this enigma lies in the fact that from 1837 through 1840 Duck Creek Meeting was "laid down" and its membership attached to Spiceland. So if the family in question removed in 1838, its removal certificate would be found in the Spiceland records.

The same situation exists for Cherry Grove Monthly Meeting, Randolph County, Indiana, which was "laid down" from 2nd month through 11th month 1825 and its membership attached to White River, except for Center and Lynn preparatives which were attached to New Garden Monthly Meeting. Blue River Monthly Meeting, Washington County, Indiana, was "laid down" from 1828 through 1829 and its membership attached to Lick Creek for that period of time. Doubtless, other examples exist that do not come to mind.

When a monthly meeting is "laid down," whether temporarily as illustrated above, or permanently, the membership is attached to another monthly meeting. Pleasant Hill Monthly Meeting, Howard County, Indiana, was "set off" from Honey Creek in 1861. In 1891 it was "laid down" as a monthly meeting and its membership attached again to Honey Creek.

A more complex problem is to be found in the matter of Honey Creek Monthly Meeting, Vigo County, Indiana (not to be confused with the above mentioned meeting with the same name). In 1820 this monthly meeting was "set off" from Lick Creek. At the time of the separation in 1829, the meeting was "laid down" by the Orthodox branch and its members attached to Bloomfield (later Bloomingdale) Monthly Meeting. However, the meeting had a large Hicksite membership and as such continued as Honey Creek Monthly Meeting in the Hicksite branch of the Society.

Preparative Meetings (sometimes called *Particular Meetings*)

A preparative meeting, as the name suggests, is a meeting where business is prepared to be presented at the ensuing monthly meeting. This type of meeting and function has almost ceased to exist. Monthly meeting was usually held on Seventh-day (Saturday). The preparative was held earlier in the week; it often followed the midweek meeting for worship. At this meeting complaints against members were brought forward by the overseers, requests for membership were presented and forwarded to the monthly meeting, etc. Most of the trivia was sifted out at these meetings and only business of a worthwhile nature was taken up at the monthly meeting. Very few records of the preparative meetings have survived. Preparatives held meetings for worship each First-day (Sunday) and at midweek.

Meeting for Worship

A meeting for worship was allowed by a monthly meeting where there was a settlement of Friends large enough that it could be maintained in good order but the number of Friends was not large enough to function as a preparative meeting. The meeting for worship met regularly for First-day and midweek meetings and usually advanced to the point of having a meetinghouse. In matters of business, it was attached to the nearest preparative meeting. It might be stated that all Friends meetings, whether for business or otherwise, were in part a meeting for worship.

Indulged Meeting for Worship

On the frontiers, two or three families might have been far removed from a Friends meeting. It was usually inconvenient, if not impossible, for them to attend an established meeting. In this situation the monthly meeting allowed members to meet in a home or in a public place on First-day as an indulged meeting for worship. This meeting was under the care of a monthly meeting committee which visited with the

"Indulgement" regularly to see that "truth was maintained." If the meeting grew, it then became a regular meeting for worship. This type of meeting has not existed since the beginning of this century.

THE FRIENDS MEETING HOUSE

To George Fox the "steeple house" was an abomination. Yet, most Friends churches in the Midwest are indistinguishable from other Protestant churches replete with stained glass windows. The testimony of simplicity, like most other Friends testimonies, has been all but forgotten.

Traditionally, the meetinghouse, the center of a Quaker settlement, was quite plain. But few of these remain. New Garden meetinghouse, near Fountain City, Indiana, appears externally almost as it was built, except for a small belfry. The "white brick" meetinghouse at Waynesville, Ohio, is unchanged, except for the men's side which has been remodeled into rooms for First-day school. Sugar Grove, south of Plainfield, Indiana, is almost unchanged. It is not even electrified.

Most, of not all, meetinghouses were oriented east and west with the doors on the south side. I know of no reason for this practice; it may be more accidental than intentional. The building was rectangular in shape, about twice as long as wide. The interior was divided into two rooms; a partition or shutters that could be raised separated the rooms. A door near the front of the partition gave access to each room. Two sets of doors in the front wall permitted men and women to go into different sides of the building. As one faced the building, the men's side was on the right. The members sat in their respective rooms during business meetings. During worship, the shutters were up; they were lowered during the business session.

The reason for these separate sessions dates back to the beginnings of Quakerism when Friends declared that all persons were equal. Women were given an equal voice in the decisions of the Society. It has been said that the reason for separate sessions was that women were timid and hesitated to express their opinions in the presence of men.

There were separate sessions at preparative, monthly, quarterly, and yearly meetings. There were clerks and assistant clerks and minutes kept for both men's and women's meetings. Beginning in the late nineteenth century this practice was gradually discontinued until by the early 1900s all branches of Friends were holding joint meetings. At First-day or midweek meetings for worship, the men and women usually sat on the men's side of the building, but the women still sat on the left side of the room.

The interior of the meeting rooms had two rows of plain benches on either side. Facing the room, across the front, was a raised "gallery" or platform with two rows of benches where the elders and ministers sat. These benches were sometimes referred to as facing benches. The reason they were elevated was so that if any of these worthies were moved to speak they could be easily heard. This did not preclude any other member from speaking.

Meetings for worship had a member who "sat at the head of the meeting." This member was an Elder and never a woman. How he was chosen is not clear but it appears that he was chosen by the overseers. It was a lifetime appointment. The "head of the meeting" sat on the first bench on the right side of the gallery. When he sensed that it was time to "break" meeting, he would shake the hand of the person nearest him and meeting was over.

The second row of the gallery had a drop-leaf board which was raised for a writing surface for the clerk during business meetings.

The monthly meeting records are the most important Quaker materials for the researcher, whether he be a historian, genealogist, or a person with other interests. The monthly meetings have from almost the earliest times kept minutes, records of births and deaths, marriage records, and removal certificates. Only a few of the older monthly meetings have preserved complete sets of records.

TYPES OF RECORDS

Monthly Meeting Minutes

From the time a monthly meeting was "set up," a minute record was kept by the clerks in which information concerning the affairs of the meeting was written. During monthly meetings, the notes and minutes made by the clerk were written on sheets or scraps of paper and were known as "rough minutes." Later, usually twice a year, these minutes were transcribed into the permanent record book. I make particular mention of this because a minute might be recorded that Joel Kindly, being about to remove with his family, requested a certificate to convey his and his family's membership. The matter was referred to a committee to investigate his affairs to see if he is "clear" to remove. At the time the "rough minutes" are transcribed, by error, the report of the committee and the granting of the certificate might not be recorded.

Information found in the minutes includes removals, disownments, members received, and birthright memberships.

Removals. It is possible to trace a family line from arrival in Pennsylvania in the late 1600s through Virginia, North Carolina, Tennessee, Ohio, and Indiana to Iowa in the 1850s. This is true if the family has not had members disowned in the intervening generations or if the meeting records still exist.

When a family wished to remove to another section of the country, a request was made to the monthly meeting for a certificate of membership to be sent to the monthly meeting nearest the family's new residence. An investigating committee was appointed to determine whether the affairs of the family were in order. This committee usually reported to the next monthly meeting. If all was in order a certificate was granted. The following example is from the minutes of Cherry Grove, Randolph County, Indiana:

    11-12-1831 Joseph Way and family request a certificate to Whitewater Monthly Meeting.

    1-4-1832 A committee reported that it "found obstructions which was out of their premise to remove."

    5-12-1832 Joseph and wife Alice were disowned for "insubordination" two months earlier.

    8-11-1832 Minor children of Joseph Way granted a certificate to Whitewater.

By consulting the Whitewater minutes, it can be learned that the children were Joseph, Obed, Martha, and Rebecca.

Usually, the date of the actual removal of a family will nearly coincide with the date of the request for the certificate and the minutes will state "about to remove." Occasionally, a family moved and then wrote back to the meeting requesting a certificate. The minutes in this case usually appended a note "already removed" to the request. In this situation the member might have migrated six months or more previous to the request. Instances exist where a family removed and never requested its membership be forwarded. Usually the monthly meeting would finally forward a certificate to the monthly meeting nearest the family. In this case, several years may have elapsed. The point here is that simply because a membership certificate is recorded in 5th month 1832, it does not prove that a family settled in a community during that month or the month previous. It is possible that the family arrived a year or more before.

Disownments. The Society of Friends did not profess to hold to any theological forms or creeds, yet did have a set of standards by which members were expected to live. These standards were set forth in their Discipline as adopted by the yearly meetings. Any infraction of these testimonies and advices were reported to the overseer of the preparative meeting who in turn sent it to the ensuing monthly meeting. If the complaint seemed valid, a committee was appointed to visit with the party concerned and attempt to have him acknowledge his error. If he were so moved, he sent an acknowledgment or an offering in the form of a written note to the monthly meeting stating that he was sorry for his misconduct and hoped that Friends would pass it by and that in the future, with God's help, he would do better. In the event he did not admit error the committee continued to visit with him to determine with certainty his guilt. After further "treating" with him, the committee might report that it "had no satisfaction" whereupon the monthly meeting would disown him from being a member. Some of the disownments were for the following reasons:

> for deviating so far as to keep ale to drink and give it to others.
> for refusing to fulfill a marriage contract.
> for leaving the country without settling his outward affairs.
> for deviating from plainness in dress and address.
> for drinking spirituous liquors to excess.
> for deviating from the truth.
> for neglecting to pay his just debts.
> for getting in a passion and fighting his fellow man.
> for unchastity with her who is now his wife.
> for joining another society.
> for using profane language.
> for asking and receiving twenty-five percent on money loaned.
> for neglecting attendance of meeting.
> for accomplishing his marriage contrary to discipline.
> for accomplishing his marriage before the expiration of the time therein
>   proscribed after the decease of a former wife.
> for attending a marriage performed contrary to discipline.
> for marrying a first cousin.
> for marrying contrary to discipline.
> for marrying out of unity.

Regarding the last two items, there is a technical difference between "marriage contrary to discipline" and "marriage out of unity." The former is a situation in which both parties are Friends and married by other than a Friends ceremony. When a Friend married a non-Friend, he married "out of unity."

Received in membership. When an individual desired to become a member of the Society, the overseers of the preparative meeting were informed. They in turn forwarded the request to the monthly meeting. A committee was appointed to "visit with him on occasion" and determine whether he was sincere "and convinced of the truth." After careful consideration by the monthly meeting, the application for membership was approved or returned to the applicant. A person who had been disowned and wished to be reinstated went through the same process.

It was not uncommon for one member of the family to be disowned yet the rest of the family would retain membership. The disowned party might continue to attend meetings for worship but could not participate in business meetings.

Birthright membership. If both parents became members of the Society, all minor children became members. Children born to Quaker parents were birthright members. If a father were disowned and the mother remained in good standing, any further children were birthright members, but that was not the case with children born to a mother who had been disowned and the father was yet a member. When both parents were disowned, the minor children remained members and their membership certificate was forwarded to the nearest monthly meeting in event the family moved. Under these circumstances, their record finally disappears because in reality the children usually followed their parents into another religious society. One will probably not find a record of disownment for the children.

Conclusion. After the 1860s the application of the Discipline to the lives of Friends became increasingly relaxed. Many boys served in the Civil War in complete violation of Friends principles. Some meetings passed this by without comment. A few did disown them. Some, such as White River Monthly Meeting, accepted an "acknowledgment" such as the following by Benoni Hill on 4-7-1866:

> "in an unguarded hour I so gave way as to enlist in the army and bear arms which being contrary to the will of God, and for which I feel regret and ask for your forgiveness as well as God's and pass it by and continue me a member as my conduct may admit."

Disownment for marrying a non-Friend or for marrying by civil ceremony had been abandoned by the 1860s. The member concerned had only to indicate that he wished to retain his membership. By the 1880s the whole matter was ignored. Some Friends churches had paid preachers and the marriage form was soon fashioned after other Protestant ceremonies.

By the late nineteenth century there were few disownments except for serious matters that could not be easily ignored. In the White River minutes appears the following dated 3-3-1877:

> Harry T. Warren was disowned for he "has attended places of Diversion, is intemperate, has abused and mal-treated his family and expressed a disbelief in the Bible."

Except among Conservative and Hicksite branches, little concern was shown about many of the testimonies that had claimed the attention of Friends for generations.

Minutes and records for the later period have often been very poorly kept. Whereas the script of early records was usually excellent, later writing in some cases is almost illegible.

Marriage Records.
From earliest times Friends refused to be married in a civil ceremony or by a "hireling priest." They married themselves. At monthly meeting the couple would announce its intention to marry. Committees were appointed to learn if both persons were "clear of engagements." At the next monthly meeting, the committees reported and if both were "clear" the meetings left them "at liberty to accomplish the marriage." Committees were then appointed to attend the marriage and see "that good order was preserved." Unless a special meeting was appointed, the marriage took place the following midweek meeting for worship. Marriages were not accomplished on First-day until the mid-1800s.

Where marriage records exist, either the original certificates or a copy of them are recorded in the meeting record book. This record contains invaluable information, such as the county of residence of each contracting party, the name of the parents of each, whether the parents are deceased, and the late residence of the parents.

The laws of Indiana, until the 1920s, exempted Friends from the legal requirement to obtain a civil marriage license. Thus marriages performed under the care of a monthly meeting will not be found in courthouse records.

Birth and Death Records.
Friends kept these records because they served two purposes. First, it was a membership record and, secondly, Friends, for many years, were opposed to headstones on graves.

The birth record will vary considerably in makeup from one monthly meeting to another. For example, Dover Monthly Meeting, Wayne County, Indiana, recorded births as follows:

Levi Peacock	b. 5-18-1821
Martha Peacock	b. 3-28-1818
Their children–	
Ruth	b. 5-1-1844
infant daughter	b. 9-19-1846 buried at New Garden

Just a few miles away, at West Grove Monthly Meeting, is found a more complete record with the following entries:

Jonathan Mendenhall	b. 5-6-1782, Wrightsboro, Ga. son of Joseph and Elizabeth
Ann Mendenhall	b. 3-28-1786, Bucks Co. Penna, daughter of John and Ann Phillips
Their children–	
Elizabeth	b. 8-21-1804, Stokes Co., North Carolina
Phebe	b. 11-30-1805, Stokes Co., North Carolina

Even though the minutes usually show that the recorder was regularly admonished to make his records complete and keep them up to date, the fact is that few, if any, of these records are complete.

The birth record is found in the front part of the volume and the death record in the back. The entry for the death gives the name, date of death, and age at death. Usually the place of burial is also given, and in some instances, the place of residence at the time of death. Some examples from Poplar Run Monthly Meeting, Randolph County, Indiana:

Mary Hunt, d. 9-5-1879, ae 77 yr 5 mo 4 da Died at Wesley Hunts, buried at Nettle Creek
Joseph Fisher, d. 3-28-1874 ae 69 yr 9 mo 15 da Died at Robert Fisher's, Delaware County
Mary Lamb, d. 2-17-1877 ae 76 yr 7 mo 2 da Died at E. Bond's, buried at Poplar Run

Removal Certificate Record
This record book is seldom found among the collection of monthly meeting records. It may be that some meetings did not keep removals as a separate record.

As mentioned above, when a membership transfer came to a meeting, it was recorded in the minutes. In White River Monthly Meeting minutes are the following entries:

11-10-1838 (Men's) George Thomas received on certificate from Cherry Grove Monthly Meeting
11-10-1838 (Women's) Asenath Thomas and daughters, Elvira and Anna, received on certificate from Cherry Grove monthly meeting

From the same meeting's minutes is an example of a removal:

3-6-1858 Tilnias Hinshaw and family granted a certificate to Cherry Grove Grove monthly meeting.

By consulting the Book of Removals we learn that Tilnias Hinshaw and wife, Eunice, and children, Nathan, Lindley, James Colwell, William Henry, and Ira were given a certificate.

FRIENDS BURYING GROUNDS AND FUNERALS

Funerals and burying grounds were under the care of a committee appointed by the monthly meeting and continued from year to year. Friends were for many years opposed to any marker on a grave. The grave of George Fox was unmarked for almost two centuries. Acceptance of any marker was very slow in coming. There seems to be have been varying emphasis placed on this practice from one part of the country to another.

Mill Creek burying ground in Hendricks County, Indiana, has a large number of small markers with initials only–a larger percentage than elsewhere. Most of the older burying grounds have rude field stones, some unmarked, and some crudely carved, and some small marble markers which are engraved with the name, date of death, and age of the deceased.

Miami Monthly Meeting (Hicksite), Warren County, Ohio, decided in 1845 to remove all monuments in its graveyard. In 1846, there was reported "compliance." The Discipline at the time admonished that "Friends are also enjoined to maintain our testimony against affixing monuments of any description to graves." So much difference of opinion existed over this subject that in 1869 the Discipline was revised to read, "They are not to erect grave stones higher than ten inches above the level of the ground, nor more than fourteen inches wide, nor three inches thick, entirely plain, with only the necessary name and date thereon."

It would appear that until the 1870s not much care was given to the burying grounds other than keeping them fenced. At this time, there were numerous newspaper accounts of work parties that would spend two or three days cleaning out brambles, setting up headstones, and arranging them in rows.

In an 1880 account of the work on Cherry Grove burying ground, Randolph County, Indiana, it was estimated that more than 200 graves lacked markers. This was probably about half of the burials up to that time.

Friends funerals were very simple. There was a short "sitting" at the home, then another at the meetinghouse. There might or might not be speaking. The casket was then carried to the grave and consigned with no ritual at all. Not even members of the family dressed in mourning.

REFERENCE MATERIAL*

The number of books and pamphlets written by or about Friends is countless. Excellent sources that give considerable details and insight into the practices of Friends are:

Hugh Barbour and J. William Frost, *The Quakers* (1988)
Howard H. Brinton, *Friends for 300 Years* (1952)
Thomas Clarkson, *A Portraiture of Quakerism* (1806)
Thomas D. Hamm, *The Transformation of American Quakerism* (1988)
Willard Heiss, *A List of All the Friends' Meetings . . . in Indiana* (1961)
Gregory P. Hinshaw, *Indiana Quaker Heritage* (1995)
Ezra Michener, *A Retrospect of Early Quakerism* (1860)
John Punshon, *Portrait in Grey* (1985)
Richard P. Ratcliff, *Our Special Heritage: Sesquicentennial History of Indiana Yearly Meeting* (1971)
Elbert Russell, *The History of Quakerism* (1942)
Stephen B. Weeks, *Southern Quakers and Slavery* (1896)

For the genealogist there is the monumental work by William W. Hinshaw, the *Encyclopedia of American Quaker Genealogy* (6 vols., 1936-50), containing abstracts of the following monthly meeting records: Vol. I. The Carolinas; Vol. II. Philadelphia, Pennsylvania, Salem and Burlington, New Jersey, and Falls Monthly Meeting, Bucks County, Pennsylvania; Vol. III. New York City and Long Island, New York; Vol. IV. and V. Ohio and meetings in southwestern Pennsylvania; and Vol. VI. Virginia. Hinshaw's unpublished material is deposited in the Friends Historical Library at Swarthmore College in Pennsylvania. The Hinshaw volumes have been reprinted by the Genealogical Publishing Company. Abstracts of other Quaker records are appearing with increasing frequency.

Quaker Necrology (2 vols., Haverford College Library, 1961) is an index to 60,000 death notes published in Friends periodicals. The periodicals indexed are: *The Friend* (Philadelphia), *The Friends Intelligencer, The Friends Review*, and *The Friends Journal*.

The Christian Worker was established at New Vienna, Ohio, in 1874, later moved to Chicago and combined with the *Gospel Expositor* and was called *Christian Worker and Gospel Expositor*. In 1894 this periodical, combined with *The Friends Review*, was called *American Friend*. (This should not be confused with a periodical of the same name published in Richmond, Indiana, in the 1860s).

Another source of brief biographies is *The American Annual Monitor* (New York: 1858-63) which contains obituaries of Friends in America.

Further sources of information, both historical and genealogical, are the printed histories of various monthly meetings. Some of the better histories of Indiana Monthly Meetings are:

A History of Farmers Institute Monthly Meeting (ca 1951)
Plainfield Friends Mark a Century (1951)
A History of Union Street Meeting of Friends of Kokomo, Indiana (1958)
Booklet about Friends in Orange County, Indiana (1958)
Jericho Friends Meeting (1958)
Memories of New London Community (1936)
Whitewater--Indiana's First Quarterly Meeting (1959)
Early Friends in Grant County, Indiana (1961)

* Updated by Thomas D. Hamm in 1996

LOCATION OF ORIGINAL RECORDS

The following are the major repositories for Indiana Quaker records:

Friends Collection, Lilly Library, Earlham College, Richmond, Indiana.

The repository for the records of Indiana and Western Yearly Meetings of Anti-Slavery Friends and Indiana Yearly Meeting (Hicksite), as well as microfilms of the records of other American yearly meetings.

Quaker Collection, Wilmington College, Wilmington, Ohio

The repository of Ohio Valley Yearly Meeting (formerly the Hicksite Indiana Yearly Meeting).

William Henry Smith Memorial Library, Indiana Historical Society, Indianapolis, Indiana

The repository for the records of Western Yearly Meeting of Conservative Friends. The library also has the largest holdings of any repository of records of Indiana Yearly Meeting of Anti-Slavery Friends.

CRIMP

A portion of the County Records in Indiana Microfilm Project (CRIMP) microfilmed holdings of libraries and individuals in the various counties in Indiana. The collection of Indiana Quaker Records in the Friends Collection, Lilly Library, Earlham College was filmed. These microfilms may be borrowed and viewed at local branches of the Latter-day Saints libraries.

It should be noted that some Indiana Quaker records are still locally held. Those for the old Hicksite Blue River Monthly Meeting, for example, are in the Washington County Historical Society Library. Many records for Friends in Parke County, Indiana, are in a vault in Bloomingdale, Indiana. Similarly, the vault of the New London Friends Church holds records of many monthly meetings in Howard County.

ORTHODOX MONTHLY MEETINGS IN INDIANA PRIOR TO 1850

Date	Name	County	Other information
1828	ARBA	Randolph	set off from New Garden
1838	BACK CREEK	Grant	set off from Mississinewa
1827	BLOOMFIELD	Parke	set off from Honey Creek; later called Bloomingdale
1815	BLUE RIVER	Washington	set off from Lick Creek
1821	CHERRY GROVE	Randolph	set off from New Garden
1823	CHESTER	Wayne	set off from Whitewater
1837	DOVER	Wayne	set off from New Garden
1820	DRIFTWOOD	Jackson	set off from Blue River
1826	DUCK CREEK	Henry	set off from Milford; reestablished in 1840
1826	FAIRFIELD	Hendricks	set off from White Lick
1844	GREENFIELD	Tippecanoe	set off from Sugar River; later called Farmers Institute
1850	HINKLES CREEK	Hamilton	set off from Westfield
1820	HONEY CREEK	Vigo	set off from Lick Creek
1846	HONEY CREEK	Howard	set off from Mississinewa
1841	HOPEWELL	Henry	set off from Milford
1813	LICK CREEK	Orange	set off from Whitewater
1823	MILFORD	Wayne	set off from West Grove
1834	MILL CREEK	Hendricks	set off from Fairfield
1832	MISSISSINEWA	Grant	set off from White River
1815	NEW GARDEN	Wayne	set off from Whitewater
1841	RICHLAND	Hamilton	set off from Westfield; later called Carmel
1846	ROCKY RUN	Parke	set off from Bloomfield
1850	RUSH CREEK	Parke	set off from Bloomfield
1817	SILVER CREEK	Union	set off from Whitewater; later called Salem
1841	SPARROW CREEK	Randolph	set off from White River
1833	SPICELAND	Henry	set off from Duck Creek
1820	SPRINGFIELD	Wayne	set off from New Garden
1840	SUGAR PLAIN	Boone	set off from Sugar River
1830	SUGAR RIVER	Montgomery	set off from White Lick
1836	WALNUT RIDGE	Rush	set off from Duck Creek
1818	WEST GROVE	Wayne	set off from Whitewater
1849	WEST UNION	Morgan	set off from White Lick
1835	WESTFIELD	Hamilton	set off from Fairfield
1823	WHITE LICK	Morgan	set off from Lick Creek
1824	WHITE RIVER	Randolph	set off from Cherry Grove
1809	WHITEWATER	Wayne	set off from West Branch, Ohio

HICKSITE MEETINGS IN INDIANA AFTER SEPARATION IN 1829

Date	Name	County
	BLUE RIVER	Washington
	CAMDEN	Jay
	FALL CREEK	Madison
	HONEY CREEK	Vigo
1854	MAPLE GROVE	Huntington
	MILFORD	Wayne
	WHITEWATER	Wayne

ANTI-SLAVERY FRIENDS MONTHLY MEETINGS IN INDIANA AFTER SEPARATION IN 1843

Name	County
Cabin Creek	Randolph
Cherry Grove	Randolph
Clear Lake	Porter

Deer Creek	Grant
Duck Creek	Henry
Dunkirk	Randolph
Newbury	Howard County
Newport	Wayne County
Salem	Union
Springfield/Nettle Creek	Wayne
Westfield	Hamilton

CONSERVATIVE MONTHLY MEETINGS IN INDIANA AFTER SEPARATION IN 1877

Name	County
BEECH GROVE	Marion
MILL CREEK	Hendricks
PLAINFIELD	Hendricks
WEST UNION	Morgan
WESTFIELD	Hamilton
WHITE RIVER (JERICHO)	Randolph

ABBREVIATIONS

acc	accepted; accomplished	dt	daughter of
ae	age	end	endorsed
altm	at liberty to marry	f	father
apd	attending places of diversion	fam	family
appt	appointed	form	formerly
AR	Arkansas	fr	from
arr	arrived	GA	Georgia
ass	associating; association; assistance	gc	granted a certificate
att	attend; attended	gct	granted a certificate to
b	born	gl	granted a letter
bef	before	glt	granted a letter to
bur	buried	gr	granted
CA	California	grdt	grandaughater
cert	certificate	grs	grandson
ch	child; children; church	h	husband
chm	condemned his/her own misconduct	IA	Iowa
Co	county	inf	informed; information
comm	committee	IL	Illinois
compl	complained of; complaint	j	joined
con	condenmed; confirmed; consent; conduct	jas	joined another society
Cong	Congregational	jASF	joined Anti-Slavery Friends
cons	consideration	jC	joined Conservative Friends
d	died; death; days	jH	joined Hicksites
dec	deceased; decision	KS	Kansas
dis	dismissed; disowned	lt	letter
div	divorced	ltf	letter from
dp	deviation from plainness of dress	m	marry, month, months
dr	drinking spiritious liquors to excess	mbr	member
drpd	dropped		

mbrp	membership	res	residence; resident; residing
mcd	married contrary to discipline	ret	retained; returned
M E	Methodist Episcopal	rocf	received on certificate from
ME	Maine	rolf	received on letter from
mem	memorial	rpt	report; reported
MH	Meeting House	rq	request
min	minor	rst	reinstated in membership
MM	Monthly Meeting	s	son of
MN	Minnesota	SC	South Carolina
mou	married out of unity	sd	said
mtg	meeting	St	Street
na	non-attendance	stepdt	stepdaughter
NC	North Carolina	steps	stepson
NJ	New Jersey	Terr	Territory
NY	New York	TN	Tennessee
o	overseer	tr	treated
OH	Ohio	UB	United Brethren
PA	Pennsylvania	unc	under care of
par	parents	unm	unmarried
perm	permission	upl	using profane language
PM	Preparatory Meeting	w	wife
prcf	produced a certificate from	w/	with
prep	prepared	wc	with consent of
Presb	Presbyterian	WI	Wisconsin
prev	previous	wid	widow; widower
QM	Quarterly Meeting	wthd	withdraw; withdrew; withheld
rec	received; recorder	WY	Wyoming
rel	released	y	year; years
rem	removed		

WHITEWATER MONTHLY MEETING
Wayne County, Indiana

Whitewater Monthly Meeting was set off from West Branch Monthly Meeting, Ohio; its first meeting was held on 30th of Ninth Month 1809. Whitewater was the first monthly meeting to be established in the Indiana Territory. In 1807 West Branch Monthly Meeting had allowed an indulged meeting for worship to be held in what is now the city of Richmond.

The eastern limits of Whitewater Monthly Meeting extended into Ohio. A minute was recorded at a monthly meeting held 24th of Second month, 1810 to clarify "the Boundry between Elk and Whitewater, [as] a line to begin on Twin Creek, and running a Southwesterly direction so as to leave Eaton 3 miles to the East, thence leaving Eli Dixons and Caldwells settlement to Elk, and on said course to the State line, thence with said line to Ohio River and all on the west side to belong to Whitewater monthly meeting."

The following monthly meetings have been set off or set up by Whitewater Monthly Meeting: *Lick Creek* (1813), Orange County, Indiana; *New Garden* (1815), Wayne County, Indiana; *Silver Creek* (1817), Union County, Indiana; *Chester* (1823), Wayne County, Indiana; *West Grove* (1818), Wayne County, Indiana; *Kansas* (1860), Leavenworth County, Kansas; *Chicago* (1866), Chicago, Illinois; *Archer* (1884-98), Florida; *Kerr City* (1886-98), Florida; *West Richmond* (1909), Wayne County, Indiana; and *Dayton* (1909), Dayton, Ohio.

White Water Monthly and Preparative meetings were located on a site north of the old Pennsylvania Railroad Station. In 1865 Richmond Preparative Meeting was established and in 1902 was set off as South Eighth Street Monthly Meeting. In 1878 East Twelfth Street Preparative was established and in 1888 the names was changed to East Main Street Preparative. In 1925 Whitewater Preparative became North Tenth Street Monthly Meeting. At the same time East Main Street Preparative became Whitewater Monthly Meeting and South Eighth Street Monthly Meeting was laid down and the members attached to Whitewater Monthly Meeting. There were two strong preparative meetings in the environs of Richmond that were an important part of Whitewater Monthly Meeting. They were Orange (1819-1921) and Smyrna (1825-1892). Another preparative meeting of importance was Southland (1870-1926) located at Helena, Arkansas. This was at Southland College, a freedmen's school established by Friends after the Civil War.

A detailed history of Whitewater Monthly Meeting is readily found in several sources. *Proceedings of the Celebration of the Establishment of Whitewater Monthly Meeting of the Religious Society of Friends* (Richmond, Indiana: 1909) contains many excellent sketches and reminiscences. *Whitewater, Indiana's First Monthly Meeting 1809-1959*, by Opal Thornburg (Richmond, Indiana: 1959 is a brief but informative account. *Annals of Pioneer Settlers on the Whitewater . . .* by [Macamy Wasson] (Richmond, Indiana: 1875; Indianapolis, Indiana: John Woolman Press: 1962) is filled with delightful sketches of the early settlers. *Pioneer Sketches of the Upper Whitewater Valley*, by Bernhard Knollenberg (Indianapolis: Historical Society Publications, 15:1, 1945) contains information about Quakers in the whole area as well as in the vicinity of Richmond. Not easily available, but well worth the effort to search out, is material published in the "History Scrapbook" a column written by Luther Feeger in the Richmond, Indiana, *Palladium-Item*.

Original Members of Whitewater Monthly Meeting

It may be helpful to add the following lists of members of Whitewater Monthly Meeting. The first is from the memory of Jeremiah Cox, Jr., in a letter to Charles Coffin; the second is compiled from the Minutes.

The Cox letter, which with other Coffin manuscript material is in the archives of Earlham College, is as follows:

Middleborough, Ind[a]. 2nd Mo. 17th 1856

Esteemed friend

Thy letter of Inquiry of the 14th Instant came duely to hand, which I hasten to answer to the best of my recollection, not having much else to build upon, and in order to have the answers as near correct as possible I have consulted my friend Isaac Commons (whose memory I think more reliable than my own). We have undertook to give the names of each family with their numbers as near as we could, several of them we know to be correct, others we gessed at as well as we could from circumstances had in remembrance. Which thee will find on the other side of this sheet, first the names of those who were here at the opening of the meeting in 1807 which we think was only an indulgence until the establishing of the monthly meeting. Secondly the names of the several families residing in reach at the opening of the monthly meeting, we may very posibly have given some names as residing here at the opening of the indulgence who came shortly afterwards, and on the other hand we may have given a few as coming after who were at the first opening of the meeting.

My fathers family was the first family of friends in what is now Wayne County and Robert Smiths the second, then Frederick Hoover, Elijah Wright, next John Smith. There was a few families about the same time, settled at Silver Creek, in what is now Union County.

The names of the friends in the white-water at the opening of the first meeting in 1807.

Jeremiah Cox 10, Robert Smith 4, Elijah Wright 2, Frederick Hoover 2, Jacob Fouts 4, Benjamin Hill 6, Robert Hill 4, Ephraim Overman 9, Benjamin Small 9, Beele Butler 5, John Addington 2, Isaac Commons 1, Andrew Hoover 7, Rebecca Cox 1, James Morrison 1, John Hawkins jr 4, David Bowles 4.

[In 1809] John Townsend 11, Wm Harvey 1, James Townsend 1, Jesse Bond 6, John Morrow 7, Ralph Wright 6, Jacob Jessop 7, John Hawkins 6, Amos Hawkins 6, Joseph Comer and Mother 2, Robert Comer 5, Stephen Comer 4, Rachel Pike 1, Joshua Pickett, Isaace Barker 7, John Clark 7, Rice Price 10, Nathan Pearson 5, David Bailey Mother and Sister 3, Robert Andrew 7, Benjamin Harris 10, Jane Massey 1, Benjamin Cox 1, William Bond 9, Joseph Thornberry 5, John Charles 3, Israel Elliott, 3, Benjamin Morgan 5, Benjamin Modlin 6, Lewis Hosier 1, Wm Hosier 1, William Hastings 4, David Bailey Sr. 7, Sarah Burgess 1, Jasper Koons 7, Nathan Overman 1, Christopher Hill 1, Thomas Hills (deceased) family 6.

The second list of original members was compiled by Eli Jay from the minutes of the Miami and West Branch meetings of those who settled at Whitewater prior to 1809. This list was published in the *Proceedings of the Celebration of the Establishment of Whitewater Monthly Meeting* (1909) and gives the names of the meetings from which the members came.

Piney Grove, South Carolina: Josiah and Naomi Lamb and children John, Esau, Hannah, Jonathan, Reuben, Ruth, and Nancy

Bush River, South Carolina: Jacob and Mary Wisener and children Isaac, Sarah, and Thomas

Cane Creek, South Carolina: John Addington and children Sarah, Elizabeth and James; John and Elvira Townsend and children Jonathan, William John, Mary, Sarah, Hester, Elizabeth, and Barbara

Conteney, North Carolina: Rice and Sarah Price and sons James, Rice, and Robert

Symons Creek, North Carolina: David Bowles and son George Fox; David Bowles Jr; Ephraim Overman Bowles

Spring, North Carolina: Robert Andrews and sons John and William

Cane Creek, North Carolina: Isaac Barker and sons Thomas, Jacob, and Abel; Jeremiah and Catherine Cox and children Mary Jeremiah, Margery, Ruth, Emma, Hannah, Elijah, and Enoch; John and Mary Morrow and children Andrew, Joseph, Hannah, Mary, and Ruth

Springfield, North Carolina: Joshua Piggott and sons Benjamin and Joshua

Back Creek, North Carolina: Ralph and Hannah Wright and sons Ralph and David; David and Catherine Bailey and daughter Caroline; John and Elvey Charles and sons Abraham and Samuel; William and Sarah Hastings and daughters Anna, Catherine, Eunice and Welmet; Jesse and Elizabeth Hill; Robert and Susannah Hill and children Martha, William, and Benjamin; Andrew and Elizabeth Hoover and children Henry, Andrew, Rebecca, Catherine, and Sarah; Gasper and Abigail Koons and children John, Gasper, Jeremiah, William, Hannah, Nathan, Henry, and Samuel; Benjamin and Leah Maudlin and children Wright, Samuel, Thomas, John, and Peninah; Benjamin and Naomi Morgan and children Micajah, Charles, Isaac, and Catherine; John and Elizabeth Pool and son Charles; John and Tiche Smith and children Nathan, John, Rachel, Sarah, Elizabeth, Penninah, and Gulielma.

Lost Creek, Tennessee: Jacob Elliott and Israel Elliott; Ann Elliott and child Olive; Wilmet Elliott and daughters Esther and Edith

Mt. Pleasant, Virginia: Jesse and Phebe Bond and sons Nathan, Robert, and John; Benjamin and Mary Hill and children John, Jacob, Sarah, William, and Joseph; Ephraim and Rachel Overman and children Ephraim, Silas, Reuben, Lydia, and Rachel; Benjamin and Lydia Small and children Aaron, Abner, Jesse, Penninah, Mary, Miriam, and Sarah; Isaac Commons; Jesse Overman; Eli Overman

In 1828 there was separation in Whitewater Meeting due to the Hicksite controversy. Both monthly meetings were located in Richmond and went by the samename. The records for the Whitewater Hicksite Meeting will appear in another volume.

Whitewater Monthly Meeting Records

All of the monthly meeting records extracted in this volume are deposited in Indiana Yearly Meeting Archives in Lilly Library of Earlham College. Listed below are the volumes from which this publication was compiled. The original volumes searched for this publication are marked *. The volume marked ** is in the archives of Earlham College. Items marked *** are available on microfilm at the Indiana Historical Society Library. Items marked **** were filmed by the County Records in Indiana Microfilm Project and are available on interlibrary loan from the Genealogical Society of Utah.

```
Men's Minutes                      Women's Minutes
Vol. I    1809-30 *, ***           Vol I    1809-36 *,**,***,****
Vol. II   1830-43 *,**,***,****    Vol. II  1836-57 *,**,***,****
Vol. III  1843-54 *,**,***,***     Vol. III 1857-81 *,**,***,****
Vol. IV   1855-67 *,**,***,****    Vol. IV  1881-94 **,**,****
Vol. V    1868-74 *,**,***,****    Vol. V   1895-1897 **,****
Vol. VI   1874-83 **,****          Vol. VI  1898-1900 **,****
Vol. VII  1883-93       **,****    Hereafter meetings were held jointly
Vol. VIII 1893-1902 **, ****
```

Vol. I Removal Certificates, 1823-46 *,**,***,****
Vol. II Removal Certificates, 1846-1905 *,***
Vol. I Marriage Records, 1809-52 *,**,***,****
Vol. II Marriage Records, 1853-1911 *,**,***,****
Vol. I Birth and Death Records, 1809-56 *,**,***,****
Vol. II Birth and Death Records, 1856-1900 *,**,****

Whitewater Monthly Meeting Birth and Death Record

ACTON
Harold b 8-4-1894 Eaton OH s Ollie & Nellie

ADAMS
Mahlon h Nevada May b 8-18-1872 dt Jacob & N (**Thomas**) **Elliott** m 4-6-1892
Ch: Edith b 4-28-1896

ADDINGTON
Claudia b 1-7-1882 Winchester dt James & Laura **Brown**

John h Elizabeth
Ch: Joseph b 7-21-1776
    Thomas b 12-1-1778

Joseph b 7-21-1776 s John & Elizabeth h Rachel
Ch: John b 10-18-1800
    Wm b 8-25-1802
    Joseph b 2-27-1804
Selah 2w b 2-22-1785 dt John & Elvira **Townsend**
Ch: Rachel b 3-19-1810
    Thomas b 7-14-1811
    Jonathan b 3-18-1813
    Elvira b 4-20-1815
    Elisha b 9-11-1817

Melvin C s Nathan & Elizabeth m 1-1-1898

Sarah Elizabeth b 8-3-1843 Fountain City dt Nathan & Mary Anne (**Browne**) **Williams** m 3-6-1863 Randolph Co

Thomas b 12-1-1778 s John & Elizabeth
Mary b 2-18-1786 dt Mercy **Smith**
Ch: Hannah b 11-15-1808
    Matilda b 8-29-1810 d 3-15-1811 bur Whitewater
    David Smith b 2-24-1812 d 2-25-1813 bur Whitewater
    Jesse b 6-22-1814
    James b 7-12-1816
    Mercy b 5-21-1819
    Joseph b 12-10-1820
    George b 9-19-1822

AGEE
Martha b 12-3-1869 Washington Co KY dt Nimrod & Melinda **Hendren** m 3-30-1898 Mercer Co KY

ALBERSON
Jesse h Abigail
Ch: Eli
    Eliza
    Milton

ALBERTSON
Benjamin s Joseph & Sarah d 7-18-1824 ae 23y 2m 20d h Millicent
Ch: Alfred b 4-1-1821 d 7-17-1840
    James b 10-12-1822

Eli h Jeanette dt Hannah **Kennedy** d 7-6-1894 m 6-29-1887

ALLBRIGHT
Benjamin F b 12-20-1853 s John & Susan
Susie R b 10-1-1859 dt John H & Fannie (**Coffin**) **Pickitt** m 9-10-1882 Randolph Co
Ch: Mabel b 7-24-1883
    Nona b 12-19-1885

ALLEN
Anna b 3-27-1854 Plainfield dt Fred & Ann **Truckness** m 8-27-1873 Indianapolis

Charles A s Philander John & Rachel (**Boone**)

Charles Francis b 5-10-1849 s Joseph Milton & Charity Williams (**Kersey**) h Deborah (**Butler**)

Harmon h Ann (**Clark**)
Ch: Joseph Milton b 10-16-1822 d 8-20-1899
    Philander John

Joseph Milton b 10-16-1822 s Harmon & Ann (**Clark**) d 8-20-1899
Charity Williams b 8-20-1822 dt Wm & Rachel (**Hiatt**) **Kersey**
Ch: Charles Francis b 5-10-1849
    Annie Eliza b 9-20-1851
    Emma Semyra b 8-25-1853 d 2-21-1899 bur Earlham
    Mary Anna b 10-29-1856
    George C b 10-11-1860
    Miriam Coffin b 8-7-1863

Philander John s Harmon & Ann (**Clark**)

WHITEWATER MONTHLY MEETING
BIRTH AND DEATH RECORD

ALLEN (Philander John cont)
Rachel b 3-4-1821 dt Driver & Anna (**Kersey**) Boone m 12-12-1841
Ch: Naomi Jane b 11-2-1844
    Gulielma b 11-4-1845 d 6-7-1856 bur Whitewater
    Allice b 3-19-1856
    Wm C b 3-19-1856 d 3-27-1856
    Charles A b 9-27-1857
    Mary b 1-2-1860

Rufus Morris b 7-22-1883 s Thomas Clarkson & Ardella B (**Armstrong**)

ALLISON
Cyrus h Ruth A b 11-9-1847 dt Isaac & Ruth **Lockwood** m 1-30-1870 Laurel
Ch: Mattie E b 7-25-1872 Laurel

George Woolsey b 8-1-1878 s Alfred & Edith (**Sherman**)

AMMON
Conrad b 4-25-1858 s John H & Mary
Anna Lee b 5-2-1859 dt Joseph & Elizabeth (**Janes**) **Johnson** m 9-24-1884 Wayne Co
Ch: Louis B b 12-11-1885

ANDERSON
Isaac d 5-20-1831 ae 44y 11m 25d bur Whitewater h Elisabeth
Ch: David b 5-19-1809
    Samuel b 11-5-1810
    Jane Alexander b 9-15-1813
    Thomas Simkins b 9-13-1815
    Hannah b 6-14-1817
    Elisabeth b 11-24-1819
    Mary Townsend b 3-3-1821

John b 9-16-1836 Orange Co NC s Wm & Mary (**Cosans**) d 3-15-1897
Rilla b 3-12-1837 Black Co KY dt James & Rachel (**Varney**) **Webster** m Black Co KY
Ch: Mahala b 11-7-1861 Wayne Co
    James b 12-23-1863 Wayne Co

ANDREW
Mary d 4-9-1835 bur Smyrna

Robert d 3-17-1822 ae 60y 6m 6d bur Smyrna

Wm h Mary dt Jehu & Sarah **Stewart** d 3-17-1826 ae 21y 5m 7d b Smyrna
Ch: Ellwood b 11-22-1821
    Jemima b 8-27-1823
Catherine 2w
Ch: Mary C b 2-29-1828

ANDREWS
John d 9-21-1829

ANSCOMBE
Frances M b 4-19-1884 dt Samuel Allen & Elizabeth (**Wilson**)

Francis b 7-20 ?
Margaret L b 12-15 ?

Margaret b 3-25-1845

ANTRIM
Levi h Anna
Ch: James P b 5-2-1800
    Daniel b 8-25-1802
    Elizabeth b 7-3-1807

Mary Ann b 4-5-1832 dt Daniel & Sarah

APPIARIUS
Zetta A b 11-27-1887 dt Henry & Anna (**Kepper**)

ARMFIELD
Avis Jane dt Henry & Vienna (**Irish**)

ARMSTRONG
Saloma b 2-14-1826

ARNOLD
Sarah b 4-4-1813

ARROWSMITH
Charles M b 9-28-1862 Piqua OH s Miller P & Elizabeth (**Vance**)
Emma C b 9-4-1862 Piqua OH dt Isaac & Elizabeth (**Lee**) **Colbert** m 11-14-1886

ATKINSON
Delia b 2-6-1859 Wayne Co dt Mahlon & Elizabeth **Arnett** m 12-25-1877 Wayne Co

John b 8-31-1855 Wayne Co s Ark
Della b Wayne Co dt Mary **Murphy**

AUSTIN
Wm E b 8-1-1859 Preble Co OH s John & Rebecca
Mary Elizabeth b 8-22-1875 dt Josiah & Ann **Feasel**

AYDLOTT
Stewart h Sarah S d 8-13-1846 ae 36y 2m 30d bur Whitewater

Stewart h Anna
Ch: Joseph Benjamin b 1-9-1850
    Sarah b 12-28-1851
    Mary E b 9-7-1853
    Jehu b 2-20-1855 d 2-22-1855 bur Whitewater

BAILEY
Caroline b 9-7-1791 dt John & Catherine

David b 1-24-1780 s John & Dorcas
Sarah dt Rice & Catherine **Price**

Jesse A b 3-9-1869 Lee Co IA s Moses & Malvina C (**Addleman**)
Viola b 2-5-1875 Wayne Co dt R J & Lydia **Addleman** m 10-11-1894 Wayne Co

Jessie M b 8-21-1896 dt Riley Oscar & Florence E (**Pickett**)

BAILY
George Dillwyn b 10-28-1845 Flushing OH s Jesse & Lydia

H Lavinia b 4-6-1837

BAKER
Grace B b 11-5-1881

James Augustus h Lucretia (**Blanchard**)
Ch: Timothy b 8-24-1850 Perquimans Co NC
    Joseph B b 2-23-1860 Henry Co

Joseph B b 2-23-1860 Henry Co s James Augustus & Lucretia (**Blanchard**) h Lena
Ch: Warren A b 4-16-1892 Wayne Co

Mary Ella d 6-21-1899 ae 45y bur Earlham

Timothy b 8-24-1850 Perquimans Co NC s James Augustus & Lucretia (**Blanchard**)
Mabel b 8-8-1872 Springfield IL dt Charles & Jane E **Wall**

BALDWIN
Albert C b 8-5-1866 s Baily Pine & Elizabeth (**Pollard**)
Marillia C b 7-22-1878 dt Sena & Katherine (**Stump**) **Kaucher** m 9-21-1893

BALDWIN (Albert cont)
Ch: Mary E b 7-12-1894
    Jonathan A b 7-18-1895
    Sena E b 12-15-1899

Baily Pine b 7-31-1840 s Jonathan & Mary Ann (**Albertson**)
Elizabeth b 11-13-1842 dt Samuel & Sarah **Pollard**
Ch: Albert C b 8-5-1866

Enos P d 4-30-1869 h Martha
Ch: Wm H b 12-5-1854
    J Howard b 8-3-1857
    Horace M b 12-25-1859
    Mary Elizabeth
    Benjamin L

James Alpheus b 4-25-1854 Wayne Co s Jonathan & Mary Ann (**Albertson**)
Emma b 6-10-1852 dt Wayne Co James & Lydia (**White**) **Martindale** m 7-31-1875 Wayne Co

Jesse h Catherine d 10-23-1823 bur Center OH

Jonathan b 12-4-1815 s John & Charlotte (**Payne**) d 3-13-1896 bur Earlham
Mary Ann b 8-11-1815 dt Jesse & Ann **Albertson** d 11-22-1891 bur Earlham m 6-22-1836
Ch: Baily Pine b 7-31-1840
    James Alpheus b 4-25-1854 Wayne Co

Nerens B b 4-6-1854 Randolph Co s Jesse F & Pheba

Thomas b 4-26-1813 s Daniel Jr & Christiana

BALLARD
Catherine d 7-6-1848 ae 77y 7m 29d bur Whitewater

Edgar H b 8-4-1871 s Addison & Sarah (**Reeve**)
Mary Adelaide b 1-4-1871 Wayne Co dt Eli & Mahalah (**Pearson**) **Jay** m 8-31-1895
Ch: Juanita b 8-2-1896 Wayne Co
    Eleanor b 10-11-1897 Wayne Co

Jesse h Pheriba d 6-13-1847 ae 39y 11m 19d bur Whitewater
Ch: Jesse H d 7-10-1845 ae 21y 9m bur Whitewater
    Phebe Ann d 7-5-1845 ae 5y 3m 18d bur Whitewater
    George C b 1-22-1845
    Elijah b 5-8-1847 d 6-20-1847 bur Whitewater
    Elisha b 5-8-1847 d 6-9-1847 bur Whitewater

Jesse F d 7-23-1881 ae 78y 28d h Mary
Ch: Lauretta Candace
    Jeremiah d 6-23-1881
    Ida

Samuel b 5-29-1808 s Nathan & Martha (**Bond**)
Millicent H b 11-30-1810 dt Jesse dec & Mary (**Albertson**) **White** m 7-7-1831
Ch: Mary E b 4-18-1832
    David b 6-15-1834
    Cornelius H b 12-26-1836

BALLENGER
Elijah h Melissa (**Morrow**)
Ch: George b 9-28-1879
    Elsie Marie b 5-6-1888 Preble Co OH
    Essie Irene b 5-6-1888 Preble Co OH
    Myrtle

Nathan 1w d 8-16-1880
Martha M 2w b 5-16-1848 dt Jesse & Sarah (**Lamb**) **Morris** m 11-4-1855 Grant Co
Ch: Marguerite H b 1-31-1891

BANNON
Rebecca dt Jacob & Ann (**Grave**) d 9-26-1824 ae 13y 11m 12d

BARGER
Martin J h Margaret H b 3-27-1844 dt Samuel S & Anna (**Shoemaker**) **Richie** d 3-31-1881 bur Smyrna m 1873 IL
Ch: Anna Margaretta b 7-17-1874

BARKER
Isaac b 12-4-1773 s Nicholas & Hannah
Hannah b 5-11-1773 dt John & Mary **Davis** d 8-18-1808 bur Whitewater
Ch: Thomas b 9-1-1798
    Jacob b 10-25-1800
    Phebe b 1-24-1803
    Abel b 1-19-1805
    Mary b l-8-1807
Mary 2w b 4-28-1788 dt Jeremiah & Margery **Cox** m 11-1-1809 Whitewater
Ch: Enoch b 8-20-1810
    Hannah b 2-14-1812
    Jeremiah b 8-5-1814
    Margery b 7-16-1816
    Nicholas b 6-28-1818
    Ruth b 8-16-1820
    Isaac b 2-2-1822

Matthew h Ruth d 12-26-1871 ae 84y bur Earlham
Ch: Elizabeth B b 1-10-1827 d 9-10-1887 bur Earlham

BARNARD
Paul b 7-14-1808 s Wm & Matilda (**Gardner**) d 11-6-1880 bur Earlham
Martha b 9-8-1817 dt Jonathan & Susan B **Wright** m 9-13-1855 Poplar Ridge Salem MM

Susan W d 12-31-1857 ae 22y bur Whitewater

BARNES
Elizabeth b 1-21-1831

Jennie
Ch: Cora d 3-1-1888 ae 14y bur Hopewell
    Ethel May

BARNET
Leola b 1-8-1883 dt James M & Elizabeth (**Kelley**)

BARNETT
Preston b 11-11-1848
Lucy L b 8-21-1845

BARRETT
Don Carlos m 8-3-1892 h Marcia Frances (**Moor**)

BARTON
Alice L b 12-12-1889 Wayne Co dt Harvey L & Elizabeth

BATCHELOR
Russel H b 3-25-1892 Richmond s John L & Mary E

BAUMGARDNER
Sarah D dt Albert & Lydia **Hill**

BAXTER
Wm d 9-6-1886 ae 62y 6m 25d bur Earlham
Mary Ellen (**Barker**) b 8-8-1830
Ch: Sarah M b 12-3-1857
    Mary Ellen b 11-1-1860 Wayne Co
    Maria B b 5-12-1862
    Emily Jane b 6-30-1864 d 12-4-1894
    John Howard b 7-1-1866 d 8-7-1867 bur Earlham
    Lucy Vincent b 6-5-1868
    Wm Herbert b 2-4-1871

WHITEWATER MONTHLY MEETING
BIRTH AND DEATH RECORD

BEALS
Oliver Cromwell h Delphina b 8-19-1861 Hamilton Co dt Henry & Abigail **Mendenhall** m 2-3-1883 New London
Ch: Jesse F b 11-5-1886 Howard Co
Eliza May b 2-25-1890 Howard Co

BEAR
John H b 10-4-1869 s Amos & Mary

BECKMAN
John A h Laura Jennie dt Isaac H & Anna (**Jessup**) **Perkins** m 2-12-1887 Wayne Co
Ch: Barbara Anna

BEEDE
Willis b 9-18-1888 Dawes NE s John Joseph & Alberta F

BEELER
Elsie Marie b 2-27-1885 Richmond dt Peter S & Emma (**Hurst**)

BEERS
James h Lavina b 7-15-1853 South Bend dt Peter & Albertha **Stephens**
Ch: Ralph b 1-27-1897 Dayton OH
Wanetta b 11-14-1898 Dayton OH

BELL
John h Eliza E b 7-23-1831 Wayne Co dt Jonathan & Amelia (**Huff**) **Elliott** m 12-31-1852 Wayne Co
Ch: Harriet A b 7-24-1872 Wayne Co

Ruth b 2-8-1899 Rush Co dt Julius

Wm d 3-5-1871 bur Earlham
Hannah d 2-20-1860 bur Earlham
Ch: John
Wilhelmina
Wm Edmund

Wm Edmund s Wm & Hannah
Elizabeth C b 8-21-1852 dt George & Hannah (**Richie**) **Dilks** d 9-14-1877 bur Earlham m 1-25-1873 Cincinnati OH
Ch: Edmund Herbert b 9-24-1872
Wm Aubrey b 5-13-1874
Ida May 2w dt Henry & Tacy Ann (**Meredith**) **Henley** m 1888

Wm O h Eunice Estell dt Charles & Lucinda **Moffitt** m 12-26-1895

BELLIS
Edward b 10-1-1827 s Samuel & Mary (**Ward**)

Mary Ruth b 5-26-1890 dt Joseph H & Esabella L

Samuel b York England
Mary H b West Elkton OH
Ch: Wm H b 8-5-1853
Mary Winifred b 8-12-1860

Wm H h Emma A (**Brooks**) m 1-1877

BELSHAM
Arthur h Essie
Ch: Charity C
Alden P b 2-3-1875
Bertha M d 4-24-1877 ae 11m

BENBOW
Thomas L b 9-11-1861 Randolph Co s Wm L & Flavia
Clara J b 4-27-1868 West Milton OH dt Isaac & Sarah (**Elleman**) **Burns** West Milton OH
Ch: Walter T b 7-16-1887
Isaac H b 1-2-1890 Randolph Co

BENBOW (Thomas cont)
David A b 2-23-1892 Richmond
Mary
Orville E b 8-29-1893 Randolph Co

BENEDICT
Rachel J b 6-16-1835 dt James & Sarah (**Votaw**) **Johnson**

BENHAM
Wm h Frances
Ch: Fern b 12-29-1894 Preble Co OH
Hazel b 1-25-1896 Wayne Co

BENSON
Daisy b 1-5-1881 Lafayette dt Henry & Cassie

Ephraim B h Amy
Ch: Ida C
Elizabeth A
James H
Grace E
Jennie Mabel b 3-12-1879 d 4-6-1879

Robert b 1-18-1870 Burke Co PA s Josiah & Ruth (**Osborn**)
Martha b 10-25-1869 Burke Co PA dt Seth & Lucinda (**Anthony**) **Kern** m 2-4-1891 Burke Co PA
Ch: Catharine b 6-10-1892 Burke Co PA
Wm b 11-23-1896 Burke Co PA

BENTLEGE
Ethel A dt Addison & Sarah Ann (**Jessup**) **Hough**

BENTLEY
John d 11-21-1834 ae 69y 5m 10d bur Smyrna

BENTON
Robert A h Ellen D b 8-19-1866 Wayne Co dt Allen & Rebecca **Harris** m 8-19-1884 Wayne Co
Ch: Mildred b 1-11-1899 Wayne Co

BETTS
Aaron Homer b 2-6-1845 s Christopher & Lydia (**Huff**)
Margaret H b 9-29-1854 dt John M & Rachel (**Smith**) **Whitacre** m 11-24-1887 Martinsville OH

Homer Madison h Caroline J b 7-30-1839 Martinsville OH dt Joseph & Elizabeth **Janney** m 6-30-1859 Martinsville OH
Ch: Elizabeth R b 6-25-1862 Martinsville OH

BEVAN
Albert R b 7-20-1878 s Stacey & Alice A

BILDERBACK
Hattie b 9-30-1893 Darke Co OH dt Wm & Ellen

BINFORD
Gurney h Elizabeth C dt Phillip & Susan **Schneider**

Levi b 8-18-1843 s Micajah C & Susannah (**Bundy**)
Abigail (**Marshall**) m 1-6-1870
Eve (**Henley**) 2w

Micajah C h Susannah (**Bundy**)
Ch: Levi b 8-18-1843
Micajah M b 12-18-1851
Edward S
Susanna R

Micajah M b 12-18-1851 s Micajah C & Susannah (**Bundy**)
Susannah R (**Binford**) m 3-19-1872
Ch: Edward

BINNS

Amos bur Earlham h Rebecca d 10-13-1868 ae 27y 9m 18d bur Earlham
Ch: Lilla Aurelia
    Charles

Josephine b 5-8-1892 Delaware Co

Richard h Gulielma H
Ch: Mary Emma b 8-27-1856
    Willie A b 1-19-1858
    Horace Mann b 7-7-1857
    Franklin b 10-24-1861
    Anna Laura b 11-21-1864
    John Bertrand b 8-7-1867

BIRDSALL

Charles H h Anna E b 11-7-1852 Clinton Co OH dt Alfred & Phebe **Timberlake** m 3-18-1875 Clinton Co OH
Ch: Mary D b 4-15-1876 Clinton Co OH
    Grace G b 8-3-1877 Clinton Co OH

BITTNER

Abraham h Ida R d 12-22-1892
Ch: Charles

BLAUSETT

Ethel b 8-27-1888 Randolph Co dt Isaac & Anna

BLUE

Nathan h Sarah
Ch: Phebe b 10-3-1882 Wayne Co
    Amanda M b 4-26-1885 Wayne Co

BODE

Willard H b 5-24-1895

BOGUE

Clinton H b 3-18-1870
Ada L b 5-20-1871
Ch: Russell S b 12-26-1892

Jesse b 11-9-1846
Mary M b 3-26-1845
Ch: Leora b 10-3-1879

Joseph h Mary
Ch: Sarah Cassie b 10-11-1889 Wayne Co
    Lucinda b 8-26-1893 Athens AL

BOND

Benjamin s Silas d 11-22-1850 bur Whitewater

Charles Frances b 4-18-1860 s Peter & Martha (**Little/Fulghum**) h Lurana (**Jolly**) m 1888

Cornelius h Ann Elizabeth (**Icombrock**)
Ch: Elma b 9-8-1858 Wayne Co
    Charles T H b 8-24-1862 Wayne Co
    Rebecca Caddie b 11-1-1869
    Jennette b 1-19-1872 Wayne Co

Edward h Ann
Ch: Wm b 12-11-1773
    Anna b 9-19-1776

Erastus C b 10-26-1851 s Peter & Martha (**Little/Fulghum**)
Mary Hortense b 9-5-1852 dt John B & Rachel (**Green**) **Murray** m 5-31-1871 Fountain City
Ch: Louisa G d 10-24-1896 ae 24 bur Earlham
    Mary T
    Edna J b 10-31-1876

BOND (Erastus cont)

    Laura A d 1-13-1895 ae 15 bur Earlham
    Charles Wm b 10-4-1883
    J Elmer b 11-5-1886

Franklin H b 7-19-1861 s Wm & Sarah (**Jessop**) h Mary (**Emmons**) m 5-25-1886 Wayne Co
Ch: Nellie R b 8-3-1887
    Hirschel R b 5-23-1889
    Anna M b 1-19-1890

Hannah d 3-6-1855 dt Benjamin

Jehiel b 1-30-1842 s Levi & Lydia (**Williams**)
Anna Jane dt Evan & Gulielma **Marshall**
Ch: Clara Etta b 11-7-1868 Wayne Co
    J Edgar b 8-1-1876
    Jennie F b 10-24-1878

Jesse s Jessie Sr

Joseph h Sarah
Ch: Aaron b 1-8-1811
    Isaac b 11-4-1812
    Achsah b 12-10-1814
    Dinah b 12-2-1816

Levina dt John d 9-22-1835 ae 25y bur Whitewater

Lindley b 6-27-1845 s Thomas & Ann (**Hawkins**)
Sarah A b 5-16-1847 dt Henry & Sarah (**Strawbridge**) **Jay**
Ch: Wm Albert H b 12-18-1868 Wayne Co

Peter b 10-17-1824 s Joseph & Sarah (**Mendenhall**) d 8-31-1881 bur Earlham
Martha dt Frederick & Piety (**Parker**) **Fulghum**
Ch: Erastus C b 10-26-1851
    Frederica Jane b 6-11-1855 d 11-21-1875 bur Earlham
    Miriam Josephine b 11-1-1851
    Charles Francis b 4-18-1860
    Josiah R b 9-16-1862
    Marianna b 1-4-1866
    Sarah M b 10-27-1870

Pleasant Alma b 10-11-1865 Farmland s Darius & Hannah H
Florence B (**Cowgill**) b 9-6-1867 m 10-12-1882/83 Farmland
Ch: Fred E b 5-2-1884 Farmland
    Olive L b 12-14-1888 Farmland

Silas 2-23-1858 bur Smyrna

Wm b 11-16-1771 s Edward & Ann
Charlotte b 12-11-1773 dt Wm **Hoff** d 12-25-1852
Ch: Ann b 9-23-1793 d 7-11-1794
    Mary b 5-9-1795
    Sarah b 1-22-1796 d 3-17-1815 bur Whitewater
    Lydia b 2-3-1800
    Jesse b 2-14-1803
    Charlotte b 8-9-1806
    Wm b 11-20-1810
    John b 3-3-1813
    Ira b 7-25-1815

Wm b 10-13-1834 s Jesse & Anna (**Cook**)
Sarah b 5-1-1837 dt Thomas & Rebecca (**Binford**) **Jessop** m 9-20-1855
Ch: Franklin H b 7-19-1861
    Mary A b 4-5-1858

Wm A b 8-19-1866 s Dewitt C & Lucy L
Anna M b 1872 dt Abraham & Edith F **Jeffries** m 11-7-1894 Wayne Co

WHITEWATER MONTHLY MEETING
BIRTH AND DEATH RECORD

BOND (cont)
Wm Albert H b 12-18-1868 Wayne Co s Lindley & Sarah (**Jay**)
Cora E b 6-13-1869 dt Peter & Priscilla (**Cox**) **Thomas** m 3-18-1890

BONINE
Daniel h Mary
Ch: Isaac b 3-22-1790
     James d 11-6-1824 ae 27y 10m 13d

David h Prudence
Ch: Clark b 4-22-1814
     John b 6-5-1816
     Betsy b 8-13-1820
     Joshua b 3-18-1824
     Malinda b 1-11-1827
     Maryann b 9-3-1829
     Wm
     Isaac
     Rachel

Isaac b 3-22-1790 s Daniel & Mary
Sarah b 1-31-1791 dt Jacob & Susannah **Talbot**
Ch: Susanna b 5-30-1815
     James E b 9-5-1816
     Samuel b 1-3-1820
     Evan b 9-10-1821
     Daniel b 1-14-1818 d 8-23-1819
     Jacob b 8-21-1823
     Lot b 7-18-1825
     Lydia b 6-14-1827
     Isaac b 10-12-1829
     Sarah b 9-20-1831
     Jonathan B b 11-10-1833

James b 7-18-1825 s James & Hannah

Thomas h Martha
Ch: James b 11-1-1826
     Mary b 11-1-1826
     Sarah b 10-22-1828
     Emily
     John Talbert

BOOMERSHINE
Ruth b 3-12-1899 Preble Co OH dt Allen & Blanche

BOONE
Jonathan C b 8-14-1852 Spiceland s Driver & Elizabeth (**Cooper**)
Mary Anna b 4-19-1860 Wayne Co dt Lyndsey & Irene (**Thornburg**)
Dennis m 8-7-1878/79 Wayne Co
Ch: Myron Lyndsey b 6-21-1885 Henry Co
     Frank Driver b 6-7-1894 Wayne Co
     Orville E b 6-3-1896 Wayne Co

BOSWELL
Ezra h Elizabeth
Ch: Anna b 2-23-1807
     Daniel K b 6-4-1809
     Mary b 8-8-1815
     Rebecca b 6-4-1818
     John K b 12-10-1822
     Sarah b 9-8-1825

BOURADAILE
E M H Irene b 11-13-1860 Putnam Co IL dt Lorenzo & Rebecca (**Mullen**) **Stout** m 10-25 1881 Preble Co OH
Ch: Eva L b 11-9-1887 Preble Co OH

BOWERS
George b 11-10-1859 Bobtot IA s Jacob & Sarah A (**Bear**)
Mary b 8-1-1855 Polk Co IA dt Levi & Lucinda (**Bear/Bayers**)
Crest

BOWMAN
Elizabeth b 12-5-1830

Lucile b 10-1897 dt H S & Laura (**Wright**)

Olive b 12-9-1894 dt Lewis S & Mary A (**Kepler**)

Wm Jr b 9-7-1796 s Wm & Anna (**Bowman**)
Sarah b 12-26-1798 dt John & Martha (**Sanders**) **Hubbard** d 9-11-1825
Ch: Milton H b 9-18-1818
     Martha Ann b 6-14-1820
     Edmond F b 4-20-1823
Elvira 2w
Ch: Sally Jane b 5-18-1827
     Emaline b 10-10-1829

BOWSMAN
Alonzo h Augusta (**Casner**)
Ch: Lucy b 6-18-1890
     Clarissa b 2-17-1897

BOYD
A Orville b 3-2-1872 Wayne Co s John & Celia
Lora A b 7-16-1875 Randolph Co dt Mahlon & Miriam **Little** m 12-24-1896 Wayne Co
Ch: Olive M b 2-4-1898 Wayne Co
     Ruth B b 3-28-1899 Wayne Co

BRADFORD
Ruth Isabell b 3-6-1892 Grant Co dt Benjamin S & Isabell (**Haynes**)

BRADWAY
Effie b 9-5-1873 dt H L & Angelena (**Cartwright**)

BRANNON
Elizabeth b 12-5-1830 d 4-30-1907 ae 76y bur Earlham

BRANSON
Thomas b 1-24-1861 Van Buren Co IA s Wellington & Elizabeth
Mary b 4-17-1876 Miami Co OH dt Francis & Naomi **Thompson** m 10-18-1899 Sidney OH

BRATTAIN
Robert b 10-1-1746 s John & Rachel d 9-8-1824 h Hannah dt John & Ana **Maudlin**

BRAZINGTON
Samuel b 8-16-1797 NJ s Isaac & Susanna
Lydia b 10-8-1798 dt Isaac & Rebecca **Andrews**
Ch: Joseph S b 6-16-1825 Jersey
     Wm A b 9-22-1828 Jersey
     Samuel b 12-31-1831 Jersey
     Hannah Ann b 8-30-1834

BREESE
George A b 9-6-1898 New Westville OH s Alonzo & Mary

BRENIZER
Susanna b 2-23-1830

BREWER
John d 6-5-1847 ae 50y 8m 8d bur Whitewater h Sarah
Ch: Susannah b 2-22-1843
     John Wilson b 12-17-1844 d 5-13-1847 bur Whitewater
     Rebecca b 1-6-1847

BRIGGS
Lucy J
Ch: Mary K b 4-7-1866
     Annie B b 8-25-1870
     Otis Willis b 1-25-1874

WHITEWATER MONTHLY MEETING
BIRTH AND DEATH RECORD

BROOKS
Arthur b 2-10-1841/48 s David & Lydia (**Mendenhall**)
Clara M 2w b 1-18-1870

Jesse H b 11-8-1840 Wayne Co s Wm & Anna
Mary b 5-11-1843 Wayne Co dt Ezekiel & Ruth **Haisley**

Sarah Ellen Lydia b 5-11-1850

BROOMFIELD
Ethel b 10-7-1886 Fayette Co dt A D & Alice

BROWER
Everett V h Lula Hazel b 7-17-1874 Wayne Co dt Wm Henry & Martha Elma (**Cook**) Davenport
Ch: Paul Vernon b 5-8-1898 Richmond

Horace b 7-7-1865
Viola b 1-18-1874

BROWN
Albert Edwin b 10-1-1849

Albert Emmons b 11-22-1877 s Clinton & Hannah (**Pitman**)

Alfred h Effie b 11-22-1857 dt Paul & Eliza (**Horn**) Newbern m 6-5-1888 Miami Co OH
Ch: Russell L b 10-28-1892

Althea b 4-21-1898 dt Albert J & Ada G (**Cosand**)

Bartley h Christiana L (**Friesdorf**) m 8-1898

Benjamin d 10-14-1879 bur Orange
Mary Ann d 7-17-1838 bur Orange
Ch: Clayton P b 10-6-1828
     Isaac b 6-3-1830 d 2-2-1840 bur Orange
     Martha N b 8-20-1832
     Jacob b 3-15-1835 d 2-26-1840 bur Orange
     Elizabeth b 2-17-1838 d 2-29-1838 bur Orange
Naomi (**Taylor**) 2w d 10-14-1888 ae 81y bur Orange
Ch: Hannah E b 11-5-1841 d 3-24-1898 bur Spiceland

Carlos b 8-27-1875

Clarence E b 12-3-1860 Wayne Co s Elam J & Sarah (**Clark**)
Carrie M b 4-5-1864 New Brighton PA dt J M & Christiann **McCullough** m 4-13-1887

Clayton P h Carrie L
Ch: Bessie
     Nellie Maud b 5-25-1887
     Marietta b 10-17-1888

Clayton P b 9-25-1803 d 6-2-1872 bur Earlham
Sarah b 8-25-1803 d 3-4-1875 bur Earlham
Ch: Joseph B

Clayton P b 10-6-1828 s Benjamin & Mary h Phebe R
Ch: Nathan b 5-27-1854 d 5-27-1854 bur Orange
     Mary J b 7-14-1856 d 5-21-1867 bur Orange
     Gurney L b 2-6-1859 d 3-25-1859 bur Orange
     Sarah G b 3-20-1860
     Hannah Elma b 4-21-1863
     Orynthee Lizzie b 3-20-1870
     Wm S b 4-1-1866

E Howard b 3-22-1871 Crawford Co s James & Lucinda
Ruth P b 12-17-1877 Hartland dt Henry & Beulah **Pemberton** m 12-29-1897 Hubbard IA
Ch: Percy P b 12-29-1898 Lynnville IA

BROWN (cont)
Eli b 8-12-1792 s James & Martha d 5-6-1867
Martha dt Amos & Anna **Hawkins** d 9-11-1877 bur Earlham m 9-3-1817 Whitewater
Ch: Anna H b 12-29-1818
     Elam P b 12-19-1821
     Eliza B b 1-9-1823 d 5-31-1840 bur Whitewater
     Alfred H b 1-31-1825
     Jane S b 1-25-1827
     Maryann b 4-24-1829
     Oliver H b 7-15-1831
     Wm S
     Amos James
     Franklin J b 2-12-1839
     Joseph

Enoch h Harriet B
Ch: Harvey D b 2-17-1881 Union Co
     Howard O b 9-4-1884 Union Co

Ethel Etta dt Elmer & Lizzie **Hale**

Gloster b 3-9-1816 d 4-15-1875 bur Earlham
form a slave h Lucretia
Ch: Wm b 1845
     Roxana b 1847
     Fanny b 1849
     Gloster Jr b 1852
     Harriett b 1857

Homer J b 1-6-1862
Amanda Alice b 11-29-1872 Wayne Co dt Lewis & Eliza (**Maudlin**) **Demaree** m 2-15-1898 Wayne Co

Horace b 7-7-1865

Jesse b 11-14-1839

Leola b 1-8-1883

Louise b 4-16-1898 Cuba OH dt Lee & Bertha

Nathan Herbert b 3-27-1871
Janette b 4-28-1874 m 7-28-1892
Ch: Allen Jay b 4-4-1893
     Myrtle b 7-14-1895
     Adell b 6-25-1897

Otis R h Nannie J
Ch: Hattie
     Walter J
     Lizzie
     Charles M

Samuel S d 1-4-1886 bur NE h Susannah L
Ch: Lindley H
     Annie Mary

Seth b 7-23-1830

Seth b 3-13-1836 Wayne Co s Asher & Esther (**Jones**)
Martha Ann b 1-24-1836 Wayne Co dt Harmon & Mary (**Hill**) Hill m 4-4-1855 Wayne Co
Ch: Emma E b 2-10-1856 Wayne Co
     Anna Mary b 9-17-1857
     Marinda
     Naomi R b 2-17-1868

Stacey h Alice Ann dt Reese J & Lydia **Mendenhall** m 5-6-1852
Ch: Albert R b 7-20-1878

Thomas E b 7-24-1850
Susan C b 1-23-1849

WHITEWATER MONTHLY MEETING
BIRTH AND DEATH RECORD

BROWN (Thomas cont)
Ch: Charles b 8-27-1875
    Manona P b 7-6-1879

Viola b 1-18-1874

Wm h Celah
Ch: Cyrus N b 10-9-1824
    Milton D b 11-27-1825
    Mary b 5-6-1829

Zeri H b 10-3-1856 Preble Co OH s Jonathan & Rhoda
Martha A b 8-28-1858 NC dt Daniel & Sarah **Nelson** m 6-4-1882 Greensfork
Ch: Frederick b 3-5-1886 Wayne Co

BRUNSON
Orville b 11-28-1881 s Lee & Delphina (**Myers**)

BUDD
John b 6-14-1812 s John & Mary
Elizabeth b 9-10-1811 dt Jonathan & Phebe (**Coffin**) Hunt
Ch: Calvin H b 1-6-1837
    Albert b 4-22-1839
    Phebe Ann b 5-1-1841

BUELL
Willard Lewis b 6-30-1872 St Joseph Co MO s Willard N & Juliet (**Wright**)
Alice Jennie b 10-7-1862 Wayne Co dt Thomas & Sarah E (**Thornburg**) Dennis m 4-21-1897 Wayne Co
Ch: Bessie Lucille b 11-8-1898

Wm h Ellen M b 8-16-1831 Ashburnham MA dt Samuel & Nancy (**Lawrence**) Barrett m 1884

BUFFUM
David h Marianna b 7-21-1854 dt Timothy & Sarah H (**White**) Nicholson m 9-20-1877

BUFKIN
John A h Esther J
Ch: Wm R
    Elizabeth

BUILER
Charles b 12-13-1853

BULLERDICK
Elizabeth K b 7-12-1849 dt John & Rachel (**Thorne**) Brown

BUNDY
Charles H b 10-22-1872 Rush Co s Thomas H & Adaline
Lestle b 12-23-1879 Madison Co dt Samuel & Matilda **Hancher**

Henry C h Mary E
Ch: Wm H b 10-20-1868
    Nellie b 3-11-1870
    Alsie

J Elwood
Ch: Mary
    Arthur L
    Walter J

Mary b 4-21-1855

BUNKER
Abram b 8-1-1768 s Reuben & Judith
Anna b 9-19-1776 dt Edward & Ann **Bond**
Ch: Kezia b 3-29-1804
    Thomas b 11-20-1805

BUNKER (Abram cont)
Phebe b 12-24-1807
David b 10-23-1810
Anna b 5-13-1812
Daniel b 1-15-1816

BURDETT
Eva J b 10-23-1888 Irvin KY dt Wm T & Mary A

BURGESS
Howard b 6-4-1893

Sarah d 4-29-1841 bur Whitewater

BURK
Esther b 11-13-1878 Williamsburg OH dt Samuel & Maria **Elliott** m 8-10-1898

BURKETT
Russel b 6-6-1889 Darke Co OH s Daniel & Maria

BURNARD
Edith b 2-2-1837 dt Curtis **Grave** d 12-26-1871

BURNETT
Oma b 5-30-1888 Arcanum OH dt Oscar & Leosa (**Willoughby**)

BURRIS
Minnie F b 10-6-1892 dt Harry E & Cora (**Woodhurst**)

BURSON
David S h Margaret E b 88-26-1818 dt Thomas & Hannah (**Pedrick**) Evans
Ch: Edward Thomas b 5-22-1839 d 12-3-1873 bur Earlham
    Ann E b 3-29-1841
    Lydia Ann b 10-22-1843
    H Mary (?) b 2-4-1846
    Jemima S b 11-8-1848
    Isaac E b 12-15-1850 d 5-28-1875 bur Earlham
    Josephine b 1-1-1854
    David S Jr b 8-6-1857
    Benjamin E b 4-13-1860 d 12-27/31-1882 bur Earlham

Jemima d 9-11-1860 ae 81y minister

BURTON
L Ann d 8-16-1882 ae 70y

Mary Emma b 8-27-1856 dt Richard & Gulielma H **Binns**

BUTLER
Ansolm d 8-30-1861 ae 40y 9m 4d

Beale d 6-12-1842 ae 76y 11m bur Whitewater

Charles b 12-13-1853 Farmland s James & Elizabeth
Sarah A b 8-26-1855 Randolph Co dt Wm & Rachel **Stanton** m 9-21-1876 Farmland
Ch: Earl b 4-25-1884 Farmland
    Cecil Clarence b 10-11-1891 Winchester
    Mary E b 9-1-1894 Winchester

Fred S b 10-15-1860 s George P & Ellen E (**Rollins**)
Anna b 6-12-1863 dt Jacob D & Margaret (**Reynolds**) Hampton m 5-22-1883
Ch: Eleanor b 3-3-1884

Mary d 7-17-1837 ae 73y 9m 6d

Susannah d 12-2-1832 ae 87y 2m 16d

CADWALADER
Howard b 1818 d 8-3-1895 bur Earlham
Margaret b 6-13-1820 Columbiana Co OH dt Benjamin &

CADWALDER (Howard cont)
Martha (**Grisell**) **Johnson** m 9-30-1841
Ch: Reese J b 6-27-1842
     Edwin C b 2-13-1844 d 2-26-1865 bur Earlham
     John H b 1-21-1846 d 5-18-1874 bur Earlham
     Benjamin Parry b 8-6-1851 d 11-2-1851
     Mary Emma b 4-6-1854
     Martha Elma b 8-10-1858

Reece d 5-29-1862 ae 71y 8m 25d bur Whitewater
Sarah b 1799

CADWALLADER
M h Rachel b 9-6-1849 dt John H & Kesiah T **Griffith**

Reese J b 6-27-1842 s Howard & Margaret (**Johnson**)
Sarah A (**Elliott**) d 7-16-1893 m 2-21-1867
Ch: Anna E b 10-29-1869 d 12-1-1891 bur Earlham
     Mary Edna b 12-1876 d 7-28-1896
     Martha

CAIL
David s Edgar P & Grace (**Pryfogle**) h Annis (**Crist**)
Ch: Anna N b 9-25-1885 Preble Co OH
     Ethel b 10-29-1888 Preble Co OH
     Blanche M b 9-27-1894 Preble Co OH
     Hazel b 6-30-1895 Preble Co OH
     Edith b 4-11-? Preble Co OH

CALDWELL
Charles h Maud Bertha dt Samuel R & Jane/Jennie **Males** m 11-18-1894

CALLOWAY
Ethel b 11-30-1897 Piqua Co OH dt Wm & Etta

CAMPBELL
Louis B b 2-6-1877 Williamsburg s James H & Lydia
Emma C b 1-27-1876 Lynn dt John & Lydia **Hollingsworth** m 3-5-1898 Lynn
Ch: Roy McKinley b 10-15-1898

CAMPLING
Arthur Edwin b 4-29-1888 Fleet Lincolnshire England s Matthew & Sarah E (**Hallifax**)

CANDLER
Theodore F b 9-1-1844 minister
Sarah Elizabeth b 8-7-1850 dt Benjamin & Susan (**Collins**) **Wickett**
Ch: Susan
     Bessie
     Rosco b 10-6-1895 adopted

CAREY
Clarence L b 4-30-1877 Grant Co s Richard & Mary D
Washtella E b 3-10-1876 Grant Co dt Oliver & Mary R **Haisley** m 10-17-1895 Grant Co

CARPENTER
Charles C b 5-21-1836 Clinton Co OH s Walter L & Susan (**Mabie**)
Elizabeth b 4-25-1843 dt James M & Matilda (**Ong**) **Newlin** m 9-14-1864 Smithfield Jefferson Co OH
Ch: Mary Edna b 11-24-1866 Wayne Co
     Caroline M b 6-14-1872 Richmond

Edwin b 8/10-1825/26 s Nathaniel & Zerniah
Louisa b 6-20-1828 Clinton Co dt Eli & Ann (**Hadley**) **Hale** d 7-13-1879
Ch: Laura Ann b 1-9-1852
     Caroline E b 4-22-1858
     Wm Clifford b 9-26-1860

Rosetta dt Isaac & Deborah

WHITEWATER MONTHLY MEETING
BIRTH AND DEATH RECORD

CARPENTER (cont)
Walter T b 1-1-1811 Schnectady NY s Isaac & Mercy (**Frost**)
Susan M b 12-27-1811 Winchester Westchester Co NY dt John & Elizabeth (**Avery**) **Mabie** m 9-24-1834 Wilmington Clinton Co OH
Ch: Charles C b 5-21-1836 Clinton Co OH
     Caroline b 3-22-1846
     Elizabeth b 4-25-1849

CARR
Preston b 1-15-1862 Frankfort KY s Calvin & Sarah

CARSON
Finley S b 3-31-1881 Springfield OH s James & Viola

Ray S b 11-12-1879 Hamilton Co s Samuel & Harriet (**Charles**)

CARTER
Clinton b 5-21-1864 Sabina OH s John M & Susana F
Mary/May b 6-3-1872 Sabina OH dt John & Ellen **Worley**
Ch: Frank Kenneth b 10-21-1896
     Adebert Jennings b 5-16-1899

CARTRIGHT
Jonathan b 11-13-1842 Adams Co IL s Jesse & Mary (**Haley**)
Hannah b 3-19-1844 Cook Co IL m 12-20-1867 Grant Co
Ch: Murray b 2-10-1869 Grant Co
     Edward b 6-14-1872 Wayne Co

CASE
Clarence Marsh b 1-18-1874 s Elon Ervin & Palemia (**Marsh**)
Katherine b 3-27-1871 dt Walter & Lydia B (**Stanton**) **Moore**

CHALFANT
Wesley Frank b 6-9-1855 Delaware Co s George & Julia Esther (**Hutchins**)
Melissa Jane b 10-28-1857 IL dt David & Minerva (**Hall**) **Taylor** m 11-5-1887 Delaware Co
Ch: Adda b 12-31-1884
     Ora b 11-19-1886
     Rosa L b 7-19-1889 Henry/Delaware Co
     Edna b 9-24-1894 Henry Co

CHAMBERS
Belle b 10-18-1858 Henry Co dt R M & Zurilda

CHAMNESS
Albert N b 8-19-1873 Randolph Co s Mahlon H & Emily J (**Hodgin**)
Rebecca E b 3-15-1877 Economy dt Oliver Lindley & Emma E (**Edwards**) **Hiatt** m Economy
Ch: Vaughn b 4-26-1898 Randolph Co

Fernando Ulysses b 11-4-1868 s Wm & Martha (**Modlin**)

Joseph Allen b 7-8-1860 Dalton s Wm & Martha
Annie M b 1-20-1864 Richmond dt Fred & Barbara **Miller** m 9-12-1888 Mooreland
Ch: Mira E b 4-29-1890 Mooreland

Lemuel C b 9-4-1871 Bloomingsport s Joshua Anthony & Isabell (**Tegal**)

Seth d 3-4-1889 bur Losantville

CHANCE
Orville E b 4-13-1887 Westfield s T L & Clara

CHANDLER
Ann b 2-19-1815 dt Elijah Sr & Susannah **Wright** d 12-15-1892 bur New Paris OH

CHANT
Frank P b 11-7-1898 Wayne Co s Arthur & Lula

WHITEWATER MONTHLY MEETING
BIRTH AND DEATH RECORD

CHAPEL
Martha b 1-11-1836 dt Wm & Margery (**Moffitt**)

CHAPMAN
Elizabeth b 3-11-1845

Pearl M b 3-6-1881 Wayne Co dt Nathan & Eliza S (**Wright**)

CHARLES
Eliza b 10-9-1841

Frederic b 7-13-1868 s Matthew & Eliza D (**Timberlake**) h Cora (**Garwood**)

J Edwin b 4-24-1878 s Wilson & Caroline

James b 5-4-1840 Wayne Co s Daniel & Miriam
Martha (**Horne**) m 9-25-1861 Randolph Co

John b 12-23-1786 s Samuel & Gulielma d 3-18-1826 bur Whitewater
Elvy b 9-22-1785 dt Abraham & Margaret **Peacock** d 8-15-1827
Ch: Abraham b 8-8-1807
     Samuel b 2-11-1809
     Sarah b 1-10-1811
     Jesse b 3-9-1813
     Margaret b 8-5-1815
     Thomas b 2-3-1817
     Mary b 8-28-1819
     Eli b 8-26-1823

Josephine b 8-19-1868 Nashville TN dt Nathan & Anna (**Iredell**) **Garwood** m 10-22-1891 Wayne Co

Leona V b 8-23-1895 Randolph Co dt Roslyn & Virginia

Margaret S b 7-16-1844

Matthew b 6-18-1831 Wayne Co s Nathan & Mary (**Symons**)
Eliza D b 5-9-1843 dt Aquilla & Phebe (**Dean**) **Timberlake** m 10-23-1863
Ch: Caroline b 11-30-1866 d 12-2-1866 bur Whitewater
     Sarah b 11-30-1866 d 12-10-1866 bur Whitewater
     Alfred b 11-30-1866 d 11-30-1866 bur Whitewater
     Frederick R b 7-13-1868 Wayne Co
     Nathan Herbert b 11-28-1870 Wayne Co
     Arthur M 8-28-1873 Wayne Co

Nathan d 1-14-1865 bur Maple Grove h Mary (**Symons**)
Ch: Wilson b 10-31-1829
     Matthew b 6-18-1831 Wayne Co
     Sarah G b 4-7-1833
     Gulielma b 4-9-1835 d 10-18-1837 bur Whitewater
     Samuel H b 6-13-1837 Wayne Co
     Rebecca b 7-23-1839 d 6-14-1870 bur Maple Grove
     Anna Martha b 10-8-1841 d 7-10-1876 bur Maple Grove
     Naomi b 5-21-1844 d 11-29-1844 bur Whitewater
     Ann b 11-19-1846 d 1-5-1852 bur Whitewater
     John S b 3-21-1849 d 5-17-1851 bur Whitewater

Nathan Herbert b 11-28-1870 Richmond s Matthew & Eliza D (**Timberlake**)
M Alice b 10-27-1867 dt Thomas C & Matilda J (**Canaday**) **Brown**
Ch: Edna b 12-15-1893

Samuel h Gulielma d 8-20-1847 ae 85y 10m 13d bur Whitewater
Ch: John b 12-23-1786
     Sarah b 9-24-1789 d 2-25-1872 bur Whitewater
     Gulielma b 7-23-1792 d 12-8-1860 bur Whitewater
     Joseph d 6-23-1825 ae 21y 5m 6d bur Whitewater

Samuel d 8-16-1849 ae 90y 3m 10d bur Whitewater

Samuel H b 6-13-1837 s Nathan & Mary (**Symons**)

CHARLES (Samuel H. cont)
Margaret S b 7-6-1843 dt Robert & Elizabeth (**Graham**) **Simpson**
Ch: Anna Laura b 8-13-1867
     Wm E b 3-26-1872 Richmond
     Robert S b 6-20-1876 Richmond

Wilson b 10-31-1829 s Nathan & Mary (**Symons**) h Caroline **Cockett**

CLANDLER
Elizabeth b Richmond

CLARK
Alexander b 8-8-1854 s Wm
Elizabeth b 11-30-1852 dt Biba & Catherine (**Thurston**) **Vanzant** m 4-16-1889

Anna d 1-2-1833

Calvin b 7-21-1820 Granville OH s John & Anna (**Price**)
Alida b 2-9-1823 dt Wm & Keziah (**Ward**) **Clawson** d 3-14-1892 bur Granville OH
Ch: Semira b 7-22-1845 d 6-6-1865 bur Granville OH
     Eliza b 10-7-1848
     Annie b 6-15-1853 d 5-27-1859 bur Whitewater

Daniel d 3-30-1865 ae 74y 5d bur Orange
Susanna (**Ward**) d 8-14-1853 ae 58y bur Orange
Ch: Enos b 8-5-1816
     Jemima b 5-29-1818 d 6-9-1895 bur Earlham
     Thomas b 8-20-1820
     John F b 7-5-1827
     Cyrus O b 3-15-1831 d 8-13-1848 bur Orange
     Wm b 6-24-1833

Dougan b 5-17-1828 s Dougan & Asenith (**Hunt**) d 10-11-1896 bur Earlham
Sarah J b 4-18-1825 dt Fleming & Unity **Bates** m 4-21-1852
Ch: Charles G b 4-2-1853
     Wm F b 5-12-1855
     Henry H b 5-1-1859

Emma Robinson b 4-26-1850 dt Daniel & Mary R (**Hoag**)

Gertrude Seaman b 3-15-1894 Wayne Co dt Henry & Julia (**Seaman**) **Clark**

Henry T h Christena B b 12-20-1852 dt Levi & Sarah (**Murphy**) **Coffin** m 10-6-1870 Hamilton Co
Ch: Sarah Ethel b 11-21-1875

Jesse b 12-24-1773 NC s John & Margaret d 6-4-1828 bur Whitewater
Hannah d 6-4-1814 ae 40y 6m 22d bur Whitewater
Ch: Margaret b 11-2-1796
     Wm b 8-29-1799
     Nathan b 6-27-1803
     Mary b 12-28-1805
     Eli M b 12-6-1810
Elizabeth 2w b 2-28-1788 dt Mordacai & Rachel **Moore**
Ch: Gulielma b 7-22-1817
     Hannah b 7-2-1819 d 10-5-1825 bur Whitewater
     Jesse Jr b 5-26-1821
     Thomas b 4-4-1823
     Ellwood b 2-17-1826 d 9-9-1832 bur Orange

John b 6-29-1796 s John & Sarah d 8-8-1836 bur Orange
Anna (**Price**) b 1-27-1798
Ch: Calvin b 7-21-1820 Granville OH
     Sarah b 1-9-1822
     Maryann b 11-21-1823
     Alfred b 1-12-1825
     Lydia b 10-2-1829

CLARK (cont)
Luella b 2-4-1861 Wayne Co dt L H & Sarah **Stiggleman** m 7-9-1876 Wayne Co

Margaret d 10-9-1804 ae 1y 11m 7d bur Whitewater

Morris Tracy b 5-10-1890 s Robert Morris & Sarah A (**Davis**)

Thomas b 8-27-1861 s John & Nancy (**Hussy**)
Emily Jane b 7-30-1833 dt Joseph & Rebecca (**Burgess**) **Griffin** d 3-20-1882
Ch: Mary B b Randolph Co NC
    John Gurney b 10-16-1865
    Daniel b 6-19-1868 Hamilton Co
    Anna b 10-12-1873 Hamilton Co

Thomas W d 1-22-1887 ae 67y 2m h Joanna

Wm b 11-14-1793 s John & Sarah
Esther b 4-17-1798 dt Jesse & Hannah **Jones** m 4-3-1816 Whitewater
Ch: Cyntha b 3-26-1817
    Stephen E b 4-3-1818
    Elam b 3-19-1820
    Hannah b 8-23-1821
    Sarah Ann b 2-18-1823
    Emela b 12-26-1825
    Elias b 9-13-1828
    Jemima b 9-13-1828

CLAWSON
Abner d 4-26-1870 ae 75y 9m 3d
Elizabeth d 8-9-1867 ae 62y 7m 19d
Ch: Alfred H

Alfred H s Abner & Elizabeth
Emma (**Ollinger**) m 1869
Ch: Charles C b 1-10-1870
    Eugene b 7-3-1872

Amos h Melinda **Davenport**
Ch: Elizabeth D b 9-16-1827
    Rebecca Ann b 10-29-1829

Josiah h Rebekah b 2-29-1763 d 9-3-1850 bur Whitewater

Malinda d 3-12-1880 ae 79y bur Smyrna

Wm s Josiah & Rebecca d 11-24-1865 bur Richmond
Rebecca 2w b 4-11-1813 dt Caleb Harvey & Sarah **Towel** d 10-2-1883 wid Wm **Pool**

Wm b 6-6-1785/86
Keziah (**Ward**) b 12-19-1794 d 7-25-1839 bur Whitewater
Ch: Susanna W b 5-14-1812
    Sibby S b 6-26-1815
    Naomi B b 12-9-1817 d 7-3-1872 bur Maple Grove
    Josiah b 4-26-1820
    Alida b 2-9-1823 d 3-14-1892 bur Granville OH
    Thomas W b 8-26-1825
    Wm Jr b 10-3-1828
    Ann b 4-10-1831
    Sarah Emlen b 12-14-1838
Rebecca 2w
Ch: Martha Jane b 8-29-1843
    Mary Emma b 2-10-1852
    Alice b 10-6-1853

CLEMENTS
Ira A b 5-23-1811 d 11-30-1892
Eva Elnora b 2-2-1861 dt David Sanders & Lydia F (**Fulghum**) **Pegg** m 2-27-1884

CLEMENTS (Ira cont)
Ch: Leota Martha b 10-23-1886 Randolph Co

CLEVENGER
Emma B b 4-29-1884 Centreville dt F M & M E

CLOUD
Carl s Joel Edgar & Ella H d 3-25-1891

Georgia b 1-9-1890 dt Lewis E & Mary E (**Ratliff**)

Wm d 10-1886 h Katie

COATE
E May (**Alexander**)

Lindley M b 4-16-1854 s Elijah & Rebecca (**Coppock**)
Ella R (**Hodgin**) m 2-7-1878
Ch: Bertha L b 9-14-1879
    Myrtle O b 1-2-1881
    Esther b 8-30-1885

Robert Harris b 10-18-1847 Miami/Montgomery Co OH s Joshua & Adila (**Jenkins**)
Vashti H b 10-1-1848 Miami Co OH dt Wade & Mary B (**Tucker**) **Miles** m 8-15-1867 Miami Co OH
Ch: May Evaline b 7-12-1870 Dayton OH
    Walter J b 3-13-1873
    Martha A b 10-4-1875
    Clarence M b 12-15-1881 Wayne Co

COCKAYNE
Charles h Lilly (**Wolf**)

James Sr d 9-4-1849 ae 78y bur Orange

James Jr b 6-6-1802 s James & Sarah d 3-8-1859 bur Orange
Elizabeth b 2-18-1804 dt Joseph & Rebecca (**Stanley**) **Unthank** d 1-23-1872 bur Orange
Ch: Edwin b 12-15-1826
    July Ann b 11-6-1830
    Wm b 11-7-1832
    Ellen b 11-9-1834
    Charles b 11-18-1836
    Joseph b 3-2-1839
    Rebecca b 6-22-1841
    Mary b 9-25-1843
    Henry b 4-8-1848 d 8-29-1853 bur Orange

COFFIN
Adam h Anna d 12-19-1829 ae 59y 11m 2d bur West Grove
Ch: Obediah d 11-8-1829 bur West Grove

Charles Fisher b 4-3-1823 New Garden NC s Elijah & Naomi (**Hiatt**)
Rhoda M b 2-1-1826 dt John & Judith (**Faulkner**) **Johnson**
Ch: Elijah Jr b 5-3-1848
    Charles Henry b 9-1-1851
    Francis Albion b 10-10-1852/53
    Wm Edward b 1-8-1856
    Mary Amelia b 8-3-1858 d 5-19-1861
    Percival Lincoln b 4-25-1865

Charles Henry b 9-1-1851 s Charles Fisher & Rhoda M (**Johnson**)
Flora (**Howell**) m 1876
Ch: Julius Howell

Elijah b 11-17-1798 NC s Bethuel & Hannah d 1-22-1862
Naomi b 11-15-1797 NC dt Benajah & Elizabeth (**White**) **Hiatt** d 6-14-1866
Ch: Miriam Allinson b 1-9-1821 New Garden NC
    Charles Fisher b 4-3-1823 New Garden NC
    Wm Hiatt b 9-26-1825 Milton

WHITEWATER MONTHLY MEETING
BIRTH AND DEATH RECORD

COFFIN (Elijah cont)
    Eliphalet b 8-25-1828 Milton d 5-5-1831 bur Milford
    Caroline Elizabeth b 6-20-1831 Milton
    Mary b 7-15-1834 Cincinnati OH
    Hannah Amelia b 1-16-1836 Richmond

Elijah Jr b 5-3-1848 s Charles Fisher & Rhoda M (**Johnson**)
Sarah Elma b 7-31-1845 dt Samuel Francis & Elizabeth D (**Hiatt**)
Fletcher m 1869
Ch: Charles Francis b 9-22-1870
      Elizabeth Fletcher b 2-22-1879

Francis Albion b 3-10-1852/3 s Charles Fisher & Rhoda M (**Johnson**) h Flora (**Roberts**) m 9-1873

Frank A b 10-27-1860 s Wm H & Sarah (**Wilson**)
Melissa E b 12-19-1864 dt Christopher & Margaret (**Butler**) **Wilson** m 10-25-1885
Ch: Lena Margaret b 3-8-1887
      Myron F d 8-20-1898 ae 8y bur Earlham
      Irvin H b 8-10-1892

Jesse h Emily
Ch: Edom
      Alpheus
      Adeline
      Wilson
      Elva b 1-4-1855

Percival Lincoln b 4-25-1865 s Charles Fisher & Rhoda M (**Johnson**)
Lucy Vincent b 6-5-1865/68 dt Wm & Mary **Baxter**

Thomas C h Mary b 3-28-1814 dt Wm & Sarah **Harvy** d 3-20-1841 bur Bloomfield

Wm Edward b 1-8-1856 s Charles Fisher & Rhoda M (**Johnson**) Lydia (**Roberts**) m 9-1873

Wm Hiatt b 9-26-1825 Milton s Elijah & Naomi (**Hiatt**)
Sarah (**Wilson**) b 8-8-1824
Ch: Charles F b 12-26-1846 d 12-25-1850 bur Whitewater
      John Wilson b 8-20-1848
      Wm Henry b 4-29-1850
      Albert b 11-24-1851
      Robert B b 2-19-1853

Wm V h Sarah b 7-1-1869 dt Timothy & Mary (**White**) **Nicholson** m 4-28-1897 Whittier CA

COGGESHALL
Allen b 10-18-1843 s John & Nancy (**Baughman**)
Delphina M b 11-13-1854 dt Wm & Mary (**Pegg**) **Fulghum** m 10-18-1877
Ch: Clyde J b 8-14-1880
      Jessie F b 9-15-1882
      Charles A b 7-22-1884
      Preston P b 5-14-1890

John h Nancy (**Baughman**)
Ch: Allen b 10-18-1843
      Martha C b 5-5-1849

Oliver W h Ann M
Ch: infant son b 8-14-1864 d 8-19-1864 bur Centerville
      Nova Elmer b 11-12-1866
      Guy Rowland b 2-4-1869
      Frederick Wharton b 5-28-1871 d 1-8-1874 bur Earlham
      Clarence Dwight
      Eva Millicent b 2-21-1875

COGGSHALL
Esther Jane dt Daniel d 7-19-1885

COLGLAZIER
Ethel b 3-5-1882 dt Abraham & Minnie (**McCoskey**)

COLTER
George b 8-26-1828
Mary d 8-2-1898 ae 63y
Ch: George
      Wm

COLVIN
Elmer G d 4-18-1897 bur Orange
Margaret b 7-27-1877 dt George & Anna (**Davenport**) **Paulson** m 11-18-1895
Ch: Roy Elmer b 10-5-1897

COMER
Amos d 1-26-1885
Mary d 10-27-1881
Ch: S Emily b 1849 Wayne Co

Claudie Lenore b 7-10-1875 dt Addison & Ruth Anna

James h Susannah dt Martha **Crampton** m 1874

Robert d 12-25-1841 ae 70y 8m 8d bur Whitewater
Martha d 1-23-1848 ae 74y 4d bur Whitewater
Ch: Mary b 3-13-1799 Union Co SC d 8-30-1825
      Amos b 11-28-1802 Union Co SC
      Ann b 10-5-1804 d 1-11-1813
      Lydia b 12-9-1810
      Isaac b 1-8-1812
      Elizabeth b 12-28-1813
      Robert b 12-17-1825

Robert b 4-16-1857

COMLEY
Julia E d 1-23-1898 ae 88y bur Earlham

COMMONS
Charles A b 2-13-1863 s Isaac & Keziah (**Stubbs**) d 11-23-1887 bur Piqua m 2-1885 h Cora (**Lee**) m 2-1885

Edwin Lindorf b 6-11-1856 Wayne Co s Isaac & Kiziah (**Stubbs**)
Mary Alice b 7-11-1859 dt Mahlon & Violena (**Garrett**) **Harvy** m 8-28-1876 Wayne Co
Ch: Carlton b 11-29-1894 Wayne Co
Cynthia 2w b 1-1-1865 dt Peter & Priscilla (**Cox**) **Thomas**

Francis Edwin s Robert & Elizabeth (**Cook**)
Elizabeth b 2-28-1859 dt Walter Denny & Rebecca Ann (**Clawson**) **Jay** m 1878

Isaac h Kiziah (**Stubbs**)
Ch: Edwin Lindorf b 6-11-1856 Wayne Co
      Riley O b 6-5-1858
      Charles A b 2-13-1863 d 11-23-1887 bur Piqua
      Mary Anna b 8-3-1869
      Bertha Eleanor b 8-4-1873

J Clinton b 8-28-1851 s Robert & Elizabeth (**Cook**)
Cassie B b 12-13-1860 Appanoose Co IA dt George & Elenor **Swearengen** m 3-13-1884 Greene Co IA

Robert s Isaac & Mary (**Townsend**) h Elizabeth b 2-3-1827 dt Seth & Ruth (**Cook**) **Cook** m 12-4-1845
Ch: Wm Harvey
      Francis Edwin
      J Clinton b 8-28-1851 Wayne Co
      Isaac Newton
      Mary Emily b 8-8-1858
      Elmore Ellsworth b 10-13-1861
      Anna Jane b 1-2-1864

COMMONS (cont)
Wm Harvey s Robert & Elizabeth (**Cook**) h Annie **Smith**

COMPTON
Anna dt Joseph & Christiana d 6-2-1825 ae ca 10y

CONKLIN
Joseph d 2-7-1883

CONLEY
Robert Carl b 3-11-1880 Randolph Co s H C & N A

COOK
Carrie dt Edward & Phebe Ann **Stanton**

Charles W m 1877 h Hannah J (**Ross**)

Clifton L b 10-6-1879 h Rosetta

Elijah b 8-11-1824 s Seth & Ruth (**Cook**) d 7-27-1877 bur Smyrna
Rachel b 10-11-1827 dt Merick Starr & Anna (**Smith**) **Crampton**
Ch: Ruth Anna b 3-1-1852
    Martha Elma b 6-30-1855 Wayne Co
    Sarah Elizabeth b 1-26-1857
    John Wesley b 9-30-1860

Harvey h Angelia
Ch: Leslie
    Lillian

Isaac b 3-9-1822 Miami Co OH s Seth & Ruth (**Cook**)
Mary S (**Reagan**) d 8-7-1847 ae 18y 7m 2d bur Smyrna m 8-29-1845
Ch: Hannah Josephine b 3-26-1847
Martha 2w b 11-10-1829 dt Merick Starr & Anna (**Smith**) **Crampton** m 10-23-1857
Ch: Anna Mary b 4-1-1860

James S b 10-20-1861/62 s Daniel & Lydia (**Knight**)
Nevva L b 4-16-1868 dt John & Angelina (**Shugart**) **Cox** m 1-29-1890 Wayne Co
Ch: Charles Ned b 8-30-1891/92

Jonathan h Emma S b 9-21-1841 dt Edward S & Lydia (**Burcham**) **Knight** m 10-18-1864

Mary C b 11-15-1862 dt David & Esther (**Steddom**) **Pyle**

Samuel h Prudence
Ch: Elijah b 5-22-1828
    Isaac b 7-5-1829
    Mahlon b 11-30-1830
    Philip b 4-1-1832
    Rachel b 7-23-1834

Seth d 4-24-1855 ae 60y 9m 29d bur Smyrna
Ruth (**Cook**) d 10-16-1882 ae 88y
Ch: Amos b 7-29-1819
    Isaac b 3-9-1822 Miami Co OH
    Elijah b 8-11-1824 d 7-27-1877 bur Smyrna
    Elizabeth b 2-3-1827
    Nathan b 12-5-1829 d 5-8-1836 bur Smyrna
    Sarah b 5-25-1833 d 6-19-1834 bur Smyrna
    Mary b 6-23-1835
    Seth b 2-15-1839 d 7-15-1843

Thomas h Mary
Ch: Sarah b 12-12-1772
    Zimri b 2-13-1789

Wm Penn b 3-24-1843 s Cyrus & Phebe (**Smith**)
Gulielma b 3-5-1849 Wayne Co dt Elijah & Mary Ann (**Clawson**) **Harvey** m 3-14-1867 Wayne Co

COOK (Wm cont)
Ch: Jeanette Alice b 7-3-1871 Hamilton Co

Zimri b 2-13-1789 s Thomas & Mary
Lydia b 3-28-1790 dt Valentine & Mary (**Mills**) **Pegg** m 11-3-1813 Whitewater
Ch: Cynthia Ann b 12-4-1814
    Cyrus b 9-4-1818
    Clarkson b 5-17-1821
    Jesse b 8-29-1824
    Cyrene b 7-28-1826
    Joseph P b 10-13-1828
    Calvin b 8-5-1832

COOPER
John s Amy Ann

Joseph E s Isaac & Elizabeth (**Howard**)
Lydia E b 8-13-1816 dt Thomas & Hannah (**Pedrick**) **Evans**

COPPICK
Charles M b 4-19-1863 Howard Co s David J & Ann P
Magdalen b 10-22-1863 Wayne Co dt Thomas & Hannah Ann (**King**) **Eubank** m 2-7-1884 Wayne Co

CORYELL
Osa Francis b 5-13-1887 Brewersville s John A & Lillie

COTTERILL
Clara Currie b 8-26-1873

COUSER
Addison h Ruth Anna b 3-1-1852 dt Elijah & Rachel (**Crampton**) **Cook**

COWGILL
Caleb h Rachel d 1-26-1823 ae 39y 2m 2d
Ch: Henry b 4-18-1811 Columbiana Co OH
    Elizabeth b 4-16-1815 Columbiana Co OH
    Lydia b 4-9-1817 Columbiana Co OH
    Caleb b 1-31-1825
    John b 1-9-1827

COX
Alfred b 11-20-1843 Henry Co
Ruth Anna (**Wickersham**) b 2-15-1850 Henry Co m 9-26-1867
Ch: Neclessen S b 9-19-1873
    Ethel b 2-4-1886

Clare b 1-7-1877 Tipton s James H & Lucy A
Nellie b 12-21-1880 Doylestown OH dt Benjamin & Mary A **Razor**

Elihu h Martha
Ch: John T b 11-30-1834
    Charles b 7-14 1837
    Ann G b 1-21-1839
    Louiza b 4-18-1841
    Enoch b 5-24-1843

Hannah M b 9-18-1855 dt George & Matilda **Anderson** m 10-29-1873

John T h Belle R b 4-7-1876 Wayne Co dt Henry S & Martha (**Charles**) **Roberts** m Wayne Co

Mary d 6-23-1887 ae 83y 20d bur NC

Narcissa b 7-26-1819 dt Henry **Way**

Neclessen S b 9-19-1873 s Alfred & Ruth Anna (**Wickersham**)
Myrtle b 6-23-1871 dt James L & Ann Eliza (**Thomas**) **Smith** m 12-24-1894

WHITEWATER MONTHLY MEETING
BIRTH AND DEATH RECORD

COX (cont)
Rebekah b 1-14-1747 dt Harmon & Jane

Thomas M s Samuel d 11-28-1844 ae 21y 7m 13d bur Whitewater

CRABB
Mildred b 1-8-1895 Wayne Co dt Thomas & Cora A

CRAGG
Levi b 8-7-1864 Montgomery Co OH s Thomas & Katie
Eva A b 10-21-1867 Fayette Co dt A J & Maria **Lawson** m 2-22-1883 Darke Co OH

CRAIG
Elmira b 9-29-1898 Wayne Co dt Sylvester & Emily

Marshall E b 9-26-1869 Hamilton Co s Thomas L & Johan
Mary L b 8-25-1873 Delaware Co dt Aaron & Martha **Oron** m 9-2-1893 Randolph Co
Ch: Mildred M b 3-19-1895 Union Co

CRAMPTON
Isaac h Edith (**Hampton**) m 1878

Joshua Smith b 1-9-1832 Wayne Co s Merrick Starr & Anna (**Smith**)
Margaret E (**Graham**) b 9-26-1833 d 11-8-1898 m 12-18-1853
Ch: Stephen Alva b 5-15-1855 d 10-1898
    Clarinda J b 8-26-1857
    Letitia b 12-15-1859
    Anna Mary b 12-3-1863
    Merrick b 8-29-1865

Merrick Starr h Anna (**Smith**)
Ch: Rachel b 10-11-1827
    Martha b 11-10-1829
    Joshua Smith b 1-9-1832
    Samuel b 8-10-1837

Samuel 8-10-1837 s Merrick Starr & Anna (**Smith**)
Mary b 6-23-1835 dt Seth & Ruth (**Cook**) Cook
Ch: Wm E b 8-2-1859
Adelaid (**Conner**) Stone 2w b 4-27-1848 m 1-1-1896

Stephen Alva h Elizabeth Ann b 9-3-1857 Wayne Co dt Jehu & Hannah **Norris** m 3-12-1875 Wayne Co

Wm E b 8-2-1859 s Samuel & Mary (**Cook**)
Jennie V dt John **Cox**

CRATE
Robert Harris b 10-18-1847 s Joshua & Adila (**Jenkins**)
Vashti E b 10-1-1848 dt Wade & Mary B (**Lucker**) **Miles** m 8-15-1867 Miami Co OH
Ch: Walter J b 3-13-1873
    Martha A b 10-4-1875
    Clarence M b 12-16-1881

CRAWFORD
Charles Wesley b 10-13-1854 s Daniel J & Mary (**Hoover**)
Emily Catherine b 10-28-1855 dt Aaron & Agatha (**Teagle**) **Snyder** m 10-1-1874
Ch: Edwin G b 12-21-1883 Wayne Co

Iva C b 10-1873 MO dt Wm & Mary

CREECH
Sarah L b 10-29-1879 Wayne Co dt Clark B & Emma E (**Brown**) **Lewis** m Wayne Co

CREGAR
Leslie Wasson b 10-16-1893 Wayne Co s Wm H & Rose Emma

CROUCH
Jefferson b 12-15-1886 s Turner & Mary

Mary b 8-12-1867 Estill Co KY dt Jasper & Tobitha **Grey**

CROWE
D Harry b 10-12-1861 Wayne Co s Milton & Jane
Mary Elizabeth b 1866 Randolph Co dt Isaac & Marible **Hollingsworth** m 1886 Wayne Co
Ch: Esther M b 1897 Randolph Co

CRULL
Irene O b 10-23-1895 Wayne Co dt Jacob & Belle

CULBERTSON
Samuel S b 5-25-1893 Darke Co OH s Samuel W & Martha L

CURES
Hazel C b 5-13-1899 Boone Co dt Colvin H & Ida E

CURRY
Bessie b 1-3-1898 Indianapolis dt John & Isa

Isadora b 12-29-1873 dt Henry J & Melissa (**Allison**) **Northern** m 12-16-1892 Fayette Co

DAGGETT
Earl P b 4-6-1885

DALBEY
Viola M b 2-6-1884 Wayne Co dt Wm S & Pheba J

Walter L b 5-20-1869 Richmond s Edw T & Martha J
Jane W b 3-19-1872 Economy dt Jesse B & Susan (**Bowers**) **Underhill** m 7-20-1892 Economy
Ch: Herbert W b 10-16-1896 Richmond
    Raymond B b 3-19-1898 Richmond

DANIELS
Charles b 5-7-1895 s Theodore Marion & Lewvera (**Ridgeway**)

DAVENPORT
Jesse Elwood b 4-21-1853 s Warner & Rebecca (**Crampton**)
Sarah Elizabeth b 1-26-1857 dt Elijah & Rachel (**Crampton**) Cook m 1-1879
Ch: Ruth R
    Bertha R
    Ernest

Myron Warner b 7-15-1896 Wayne Co s Alonzo & Mary D

Rebecca Sr d 4-20-1862 ae 78y 1m 5d bur Orange

Richard Albert b 4-27-1854 s Warner & Rebecca (**Crampton**) h Delphina (**Grimes**)

Warner b 2-5-1826 h Rebecca (**Crampton**)
Ch: Sarah Jane b 3-21-1846 d 11-29-1865 bur Orange
    Anna A b 6-6-1848
    Jesse Elwood b 4-21-1853
    Richard Albert b 4-27-1854
    Wm Henry b 2-22-1856 Wayne Co
    Alonzo b 12-1-1859
    Alice b 6-30-1863
    Franklin b 1-22-1865
    Emma b 1-27-1872 d 1-27-1872

Wm Henry b 2-22-1856 Wayne Co s Warner & Rebecca (**Crampton**)
Martha Elma b 6-30-1855 Wayne Co dt Elijah & Rachel (**Crampton**) Cook m 9-10-1873 Wayne Co
Ch: Lulu Hazel b 7-17-1874 Wayne Co
    George b 12-2-1877

DAVENPORT (Wm Henry cont)
    John
    Rachel Lurena b 2-10-1887 Payton IA

DAVIS
Benjamin d 9-3-1898 ae 42y bur Corning AR
Lizzie G d 2-3-1899 ae 37y bur Corning AR
Ch: Ethel
    Freddie b 8-22-1890

Beryl b 2-23-1889 Wayne Co s Thomas & Nora (**Farmer**)

Clarkson b 1-7-1833 s Wyllis & Ann (**Coggshall**) d 5-26-1883 bur Spiceland
Hannah E b 11-5-1841 dt Benjamin & Naomi (**Taylor**) **Brown**
d 3-24-1898 bur Spiceland m 9-1-1862

David M h Margaret J b 3-13-1862 Wayne Co dt Robert & Luzena **Moorman** m 8-3-1888 Wayne Co
Ch: Martha E b 1-13-1899 Wayne Co

Frederick L h Josephine
Ch: Mable F b 8-22-1891 Wayne Co
    Earnest b 9-15-1894 Wayne Co
    Virginia b 3-28-1898 Wayne Co

Hezekiah b 11-23-1820 h Angelina

Jonah M b 3-2-1824 s Jesse & Alice (**Mace**) d 9-1899 bur Earlham
Ella J b 3-26-1848 dt Benjamin F & Frances C (**Miles**) **Jenkins**
m 11-9-1875 Georgetown IL
Ch: Royal J b 11-29-1878
    Ruby b 8-3-1880
    Ella J b 1-15-1883

Mary B b 8-13-1885 Knightstown dt Rufus H & Mary H

Norton b 4-15-1849 Frankfort OH s Wm & Cynthia
Florence Anna b 11-2-1855 Johnson Co dt John & Perlina **Harrell**
m 8-3-1874 Johnson Co

Wm d 12-20-1847 ae 76y 3m 16d bur Whitewater

Wm H b 7-11-1854 Union Co s Thomas C & Rebecca B
Rebecca b 7-4-1855 Butler Co OH dt Lewis & Martha Ann **Taylor**
m 12-13-1877 Eaton OH

DEEM
Wm J b 9-13-1876 Manchester OH s John Howard & Lydia (**Petry**)

DE LOS RIOS
Alfredo b 2-6-1897 s Pedro & Maria M (**Lavin**)

DENNIS
Abbie L d 2-18-1822 ae 63y

Albert H b 10-17-1861 s Thomas & Sarah E (**Thornburg**)
Clara E b 7-8-1868 dt Joseph & Elizabeth (**Pemberton**) **Thomas** m 5-3-1887
Ch: Howard T b 2-5-1888
    Joseph Forrest b 7-19-1890
    Glenn S b 3-17-1895

Charles C h Caroline b 7-21-1837 dt Achilles & Beulah (**Unthank**) **Williams**

David Worth b 4-8-1849 s Nathan & Evelina (**Worth**)
Martha (**Curl**) m 6-22-1876 Parke Co

Harry S b 3-19-1867 Wayne Co s John & Mary
Elizabeth b 2-6-1869 Richmond dt Jesse & Mary **Brooks** m 3-8-1888 Richmond

WHITEWATER MONTHLY MEETING
BIRTH AND DEATH RECORD

DENNIS (cont)
John d 6-14-1892 ae 71y 3m
Mary b 7-7-1827
Ch: Thomas P
    Harrison
    Eliza May
    Frank

Samuel P b 11-25-1862 Wayne Co s Thomas & Lucy Ann
Minnie B b 5-25-1862 Wayne Co dt James M & Sarah Ann **Borroughs** m 2-18-1885 Wayne Co
Ch: Mabel N b 4-11-1887 Wayne Co
    H Cecil b 3-19-1893 Wayne Co

Susan d 10-16-1867 ae 83y 5m 18d

Thomas h Sarah E (**Thornburg**)
Ch: Albert H b 10-17-1861
    Alice J b 10-7-1862 Wayne Co
    David A b 4-28-1868
    Dempsey E b Warren Co OH
    Grace D Irena b 8-17-1885 Wayne Co

Wilson H b 3-25-1856 Wayne Co s Branson & Elma Millicent b 4-24-1857 Wayne Co dt John D & Huldah **Mills** m 10-4-1881 Henry Co
Ch: Hazel b 12-25-1887 Wayne Co

DEWEESE
James s David d 2-15-1845 ae 2m 7d bur Smyrna

DEXTER
Walter Friar b 11-21-1886 s Harry & Margaret (**Bell**)

DICKINSON
Alice d 10-19-1863 ae 73y bur Earlham

George h Sarah
Ch: Elizabeth b 1-1-1845
    Charles b 11-5-1846
    Wm P b 8-27-1853 d 2-21-1854 bur Whitewater
    John Pool b 9-15-1855
    Minnie Bell b 12-3-1858

James Hunt h Mary J (**Winder**)
Ch Alice Rebecca b 3-10-1865 d 9-6-1865 bur Earlham
    James H d 12-14-1875 bur Earlham
    Mary Jane d 9-8-1870 bur Earlham
    Wm Huntley b 8-25-1866
    Ellen Winder b 2-27-1868

Joseph b 6-10-1820 s Jonathan & Alice H d 8-5-1895 bur Earlham
Esther G b 3-2-1816 dt Banajah & Elizabeth (**White**) **Hiatt** d 2-2-1891 bur Earlham m 10-17-1844 Milford MM
Ch: Hannah b 11-15-1845
    Samuel b 5-29-1848/49
    Maria b 2-3-1851
    Joseph John b 4/11-7-1856

Joseph John b 4/11-7-1856 s Joseph & Esther G (**Hiatt**)
Martha Elma b 8-10-1858 dt Howard & Margaret (**Johnson**) **Cadwallader** m 8-28-1879
Ch: Elma May b 3-2-1883
    Joseph Howard b 11-12-1886

Joshua Ingle b 9-16-1855 s Charles & Hannah F

Otho K b 4-23-1874 s Samuel & Laura F (**Ullrick**) h Hylie W (**Barnes**) m 12-11-1895

Robert B/R h Jane Ann b 7-8-1853 Wayne Co dt Wm & Matilda (**Parker**) **Clawson** m 1-4-1875 Wayne Co

17

WHITEWATER MONTHLY MEETING
BIRTH AND DEATH RECORD

DICKINSON (cont)
Samuel b 5-29-1848/49 s Joseph & Esther G (**Hiatt**)
Laura F b 7-29-1853 dt Fredrick & Urillia (**Schaffer**) Ullrick m 2-18-1873
Ch: Otho K b 4-23-1874
      Irene b 6-9-1877
      Frederick U b 7-10-1884

Wm Huntley b 8-25-1866 s James Hunt & Mary J (**Winder**)
W Sophia b 4-29-1867 dt Wm & Nancy J (**Smoot**) Gause m 12-24-1890
Ch: Ellen Marie b 2-1-1897

DIFFENDORFER
Frederick d 1830
Elizabeth B (**Cranford**) b 6-14-1804 m 1824
Ch: Elizabeth

DILHORN
Robert h Sarah
Ch: George b 5-2-1805 Red Stone PA d 10-11-1805
      Wilson b 9-24-1806 Red Stone PA
      James b 3-26-1809 Red Stone PA
      Ann Eliza b 1-14-1811 Red Stone PA
      Mary Jane b 3-9-1813 Red Stone PA
      George Chalkley b 11-22-1815 Red Stone PA d 8-13-1833 bur Whitewater
      Elenor b 4-7-1818 Red Stone PA
      Joshua W b 9-5-1821
      Wm G b 11-10-1823
      Ann Mariah b 2-18-1826

DILKS
George h Ethel b 1-27-1881/82 dt Leander J & Annie B (**Evans**) **Woodard**

George b 6-8-1808 NJ
Hannah H b 9-29-1816 dt Robert & Sarah **Richie** d 7-5-1880 bur Earlham m Philadelphia PA
Ch: Rachel J b 4-4-1840
      Wm W b 3-25-1841/42 d 9-3-1898 bur Earlham
      Sidney b 4-10-1845 d 2-3-1883
      Hannah H Jr b 4-2-1847 Philadelphia PA
      Sarah Ellen b 3-30-1849
      Elizabeth C b 8-21-1852 d 9-14-1877 bur Earlham
      George Russell b 10-20-1854

George Russell b 10-20-1854 s George & Hannah H (**Richie**)
Anna Jane b 7-6-1854 dt George & Tacy B (**Hibbard**) Hill m 10-31-1876 Pendleton
Ch: Grace R b 9-13-1877
      George H b 8-25-1879
      Harrie R b 1-13-1885
      Annie G b 3-6-1889
      Dorothy E b 2-25-1896

Wm W b 3-25-1841/42 Richmond s George & Hannah H (**Richie**) d 9-3-1898 bur Earlham
Anna B b 5-29-1840 dt Charles & Mary (**Boone**) Shoemaker d 1-22-1880 bur Earlham m 12-30-1863
Ch: Charles S b 11-30-1864
      Wm W Jr b 2-27-1874
Sarah 2w b 2-22-1850 dt Jonathan & Dorcas (**Edwards**) Scarce m 11-3-1881

DILL
Wm h Laura S dt Henry & Tacy Ann (**Meredith**) Henley m 1884

DILLE
Clarkson D b 7-10-1861 s James & Anna (**Morris**)
Lizzie Loretta b 9-6-1869 dt Franklin & Eliza Ellen (**Hagerty**) **Russell** m 9-22-1889 Grant Co

DILLMAN
Wm b 5-21-1878 Preble Co OH s Adam & Mary

DILTS
Phebe dt Lydia **Lane**

DINGLEY
Henry J b 6-4-1830
Lydia Sarah b 7-15-1828 dt John & Ann (**Hudson**) Haines m 7-19-1855
Ch: Elizabeth Ann b 9-1-1858
      Stephen George
      Wm Henry
      Edward Charles

DIXON
J Fulton b 7-15-1873 Gillespieville OH s Mahlon & Rebecca

DOAN
Deborah Elizabeth b 3-20-1839

Harrison J b 11-10-1861 s Joseph & Deborah E (**Taylor**)
Mary F dt Wm G & Eliza (**Matthews**) Conner m 10-30-1884
Ch: Joseph Wayne (adopted)

Isaac b 11-26-1837 s Joseph & Eliza (**Carpenter**)
Priscilla M b 10-7-1845 dt Wm & Phebe **Macy** d 11-25-1881 bur Earlham
Ch: Mary Z b 6-4-1867
      Wilmot M b 3-25-1871 d 9-18-1872 bur Earlham

Joseph b 5-25-1794 NC d 3-1-1861
Eliza b 2-18-1802 dt Jacob & Phebe **Carpenter** d 3-30-1873 bur Center
Ch: Jemima b 9-28-1830
      Mary b 2-26-1833 d 10-8-1887 bur Earlham
      Isaac b 11-26-1837
      Elizabeth b 1-1-1843

Joseph b 5-17-1835 s Joseph & Elya
Deborah E dt Jesse & Deborah **Taylor**
Ch: Harrison J 11-10-1861
      Clifford G b 7-15-1865 d 2-16-1891
      Joseph E b 11-10-1875 d 1-25-1876 bur Earlham
      Wendell P b 8-23-1859 d 1-8-1861
      Allen J d 8-3-1888

Nathan h Anna E (**Downing**)
Ch: Frances E
      Alice J
      Walter J b 2-27-1859

Walter J b 2-27-1859 s Nathan & Anna E (**Downing**)
Emily H b 8-22-1857 dt George & Eliza (**Ogborn**) Coale m 2-19-1880
Ch: Harry C b 3-18-1885
      Anna M b 4-20-1887 Wayne Co

DODD
Helen Lucille b 2-11-1897 Decatur IL dt Frank S & Nellie B

DONLIN
Wm h Cora Mead b 12-15-1870 dt Benjamin & Adaline (**Elmore**) **Lunsford**

DORAN
Milo Verner b 3-11-1879 PA

DORLAND
Margaret H b 9-9-1882 Prince Edward Ontario Canada dt John P & Lavina (**Hubbs**)

DORSEY
Josephine b 7-10-1852 Rush Co dt Agustus & Eliza (**Walker**) **Walker** m 11-7-1874

18

DOUGAN
David H h Rosa b 2-19-1845 dt Isaac & Rebecca **Lamb**

DOUGLAS
Hattie b 4-10-1891 Ripley Co dt Samuel & Etta

DOWLES
Millie b 11-12-1830 Estill Co KY

DOWNING
Harry C h Lula b 12-31-1863 dt Webster W & Emma (**Rissebron**)
Teague m/1 1-4-1882 Edgar J **Ward** m/2 9-8-1890

Otto Forest b 9-3-1884 Darke Co OH s James L & Minnie J

DRAKE
Edgar h Olivia Stevens b 6-6-1858 dt Stephen C & Rachel A
(**Johnson**) **Mendenhall**

DRAPER
Susan Bernice b 7-17-1861 dt David & Lydia J (**Thornburg**)
Nordyke m 1895

Sylvester h Bell b 9-22-1854 Oakland OH dt James & Eunice
(**Howes**) **Ward**
Ch: Homer G
     Charles E b 9-1-1883
     Don H b 3-6-1888

DRULEY
T Hollie W b 1-2-1879 Boston IA s Joseph S & Mary R

DUGDALE
Benjamin h Hannah d 3-4-1842 ae 57y bur Whitewater

Samuel h Susannah
Ch: Hannah Maria b 7-7-1845
     Margaret Annesley b 6-3-1850
     Horace L bur Earlham

Thomas h Elisabeth
Ch: Edward Wm b 7-28-1857
     Harriet Ida b 1-25-1859
     Wm Annesley b 8-2-1864 d 8-28-1867
     Charles Coffin b 7-3-1866 d 8-23-1867
     Rachel Elmira b 10-19-1868

DUKE
James b 2-26-1847 s John & Miriam (**Alred**)
Ruth A b 8-18-1853 dt Phineas & Sarah (**Jones**) **Lamb** m 10-5-1870
Ch: Ora O b 7-5-1871

DUMM
Etta b 4-25-1894 Wayne Co dt Noah & Ann

DWIGGINS
Moses F d 1-20-1890 ae 38y bur Wilmington OH

DYKEMAN
Sarah b 8-8-1899 dt Floyd & Elizabeth

EAST
James h Hannah
Ch: James Milten b 4-7-1825
     John C b 3-6-1827
     Jesse b 6-2-1829
     Martha Jane b 8-30-1831

Joel h Sarah
Ch: Edom b 6-17-1826
     James b 11-14-182?
     Susannah b 10-10-1829
     Martha Ann
     Thomas

WHITEWATER MONTHLY MEETING
BIRTH AND DEATH RECORD

EAST (cont)
Wm Sr b 5-6-1773
Rachel b 8-25-1780
Ch: Hannah b 12-16-1798
     John b 5-31-1800
     Joel b 9-29-1802
     James b 6-1-1804
     Polly b 3-29-1807
     Susannah b 3-6-1809
     Jacob T b 6-12-1811
     Sally b 4-6-1814
     Wm H b 4-5-1817
     Rebeckah b 8-3-1819
     Martha b 10-22-1822
     Isom b 4-4-1826

EDGERTON
Daniel h Rachel
Ch: Calvin b 1-9-1827
     Mary b 2-21-1829
     Margaret b 3-27-1836
     Daniel b 6-5-1840 d 6-5-1840 bur Whitewater

Ellen
Ch: Alice J b 5-28-1850
     Wm b 2-27-1862
     Susan b 8-30-1864
     Mary b 2-9-1867
     Elizabeth b 3-5-1869
     Charles b 12-26-1871

Jonathan b 3-8-1857 s Nathan & Ruth A (**Rogers**)
Lois b 11-27-1867 dt John W & Caroline M (**Clark**) **Weeks** m
6-15-1889
Ch: Charles Roger b 3-18-1891
     Chauncey W b 2-24-1893
     Ruth C b 10-19-1895
     Phillip Russell b 7-13-1897

Owen/Oliver d 2-1-1872 ae 82y 4m 16d bur Whitewater
Elenora L d 5-23-1864 ae 63/67y 3m 23d bur Whitewater

Wm b 9-8-1801 s Samuel & Elizabeth d 5-18-1858 bur Orange
Abigail b 11-18-1813 dt Job & Letitia **Stratton**
Ch: Thomas S b 6-11-1833 Westfield OH d 7-23-1845 bur Orange
     Sarah E b 6-26-1837 Wayne Co
     Mary Elizabeth b 6-26-1840 d 6-3-1857 bur Orange
     Susanna b 2-18-1843
     Eliza Ann b 2-2-1846
     Emily C b 1-26-1851

EDWARDS
John h Anna J b 9-18-1871 Henry Co dt Christopher & Louise
Showalter mar 10-29-1895 Henry Co
Ch: Mildred b 8-6-1896 Middletown
     Evelyn b 4-18-1898 Henry Co
     Marjorie b 9-21-1899 Henry Co

EIDSON
James d 3-24-1875

ELLEMAN
Enos h Margaret (**Ward**)
Ch: Thomas b 5-9-1841
     Isom b 3-15-1846

Isom b 3-15-1846 s Enos & Margaret (**Ward**)
Phebe b 12-1-1846 dt Henry W & Phebe (**Cathran**) **Coate** m
3-25-1864
Ch: Joseph Alton b 7-23-1871 Miami Co OH
     Enos Clifford b 4-27-1880 Wayne Co
     Orpha b 8-4-1888

WHITEWATER MONTHLY MEETING
BIRTH AND DEATH RECORD

ELLEMAN (cont)
Joseph Alton b 7-23-1871 Miami Co OH s Isom & Phebe (**Coate**)
Rosa E b 5-22-1868 Wayne Co dt John & Anna E **Thornton**
Ch: Aidee E b 2-22-1895 Wayne Co
     Ruth b 5-28-1899 Darke Co OH

Thomas b 5-9-1841 s Enos & Margaret (**Ward**)
Lydia Emeline b 5-3-1854 dt John & Sarah (**Jessup**) Hawkins m 6-28-1894 Wayne Co
Ch: John H b 3-13-1896

ELLIOTT
David s Elias & Jane h Hannah (**Cobb**)
Ch: Delphina M b 8-30-1862
     Hattie A b 10-15-1865

Elias h Jane
Ch: Mary Jane b 7-13-1840
     Hettie A b 10-15-1848
     John B b 6-20-1854
     David
Martha (**Sanders**) 2w

Ellen H b 3-10-1851

Exum b 2-10-1765 s Jacob & Zilpha
Katherine b 8-6-1774 dt Jacob & Sarah **Lamb**
Ch: Zilpah b 3-15-1792
     Jacob b 8-22-1793
     Huldah b 6-24-1795 d 8-27-1796 bur Back Creek NC
     John b 2-20-1797
     Elwood b 2-16-1799
     Isaac b 3-16-1801
     Rebeckah b 1-31-1803
     Ursley b 7-7-1805
     Escum b 1-7-1808
     Nathan b 3-15-1810
     Sarah b 10-28-1812
     Mark b 12-28-1813

James h Alluria F b 12-21-1856 Nora IL dt Robert & Rebecca (**Small**) **Morgan** m 10-14-1875 Spartinsburg
Ch: Robert Hill b 9-13-1885 Randolph Co

Joseph b Richmond h Sarah Ellen dt John & Sarah (**Jessup**) **Hawkins**
Ch: Sarah Ellen b 3-10-1851
     John B b 6-10-1854
     Martha M
     Maud M
     J Harry
     E Warren

Stephen d 6-14-1882 ae 82y
Anna d 4-6-1885

Woodgie Ray b 11-17-1891 Randolph Co dt Miles & Caroline

ELLIS
Arthur Wilson b 3-20-1883 s Ellwood O & Ida (**Hussey**)

Chester Johnson b 7-3-1893 TN adopted

Edna b 6-22-1887 OH dt ? **Cook** adopted by J O **Ellis**

Elsworth b 2-15-1882 s W H & Alzina (**Gregg**)

Estella b 3-11-1876 Jefferson Co IA dt Isaac & Martha E (**Roberts**)

Jane b 11-4-1861 Randolph Co dt Jessie & Mary Ann (**Adams**) **Ozbun** m 4-4-1883 Randolph Co

ELMORE
Benjamin d 4-28-1875 ae 65y bur Orange
Elizabeth d 9-19-1873 ae 61y 7m bur Orange
Ch: Mary Almeda d 8-13-1881 bur Orange
     Elihu Arlington
     Adeline

Wm Allen h Keziah (**Gifford**)
Ch: Minnie Jesse b 10-1-1864
     Edgar G b 1-9-1866
     Elvin C b 6-6-1867
     Charles b 6-1-1869
     Sarah E b 7-11-1874

ELTON
Frank b 5-9-1890 Great Britain s Robert W & Clara

EMERY
Herbert Clarke h Louisa Winifred b 1-17-1866 dt Oliver & Mary Caroline (**Cotton**) White m 3-27-1898 m Onanegna Nicaragua

ENGLEBERT
Leonard C b 12-23-1889 Wayne Co s John & Louisa (**Hirshfield**)

ENOCH
Arthur W b 5-15-? Cincinnati OH s James & Elizabeth

ESTES
Lewis A s Thomas & Betsy h Huldah C dt Nathan C & Abigail **Hoag** m 2-4-1848
Ch: Ludovic b 3-4-1849
     Thomas Rowland b 12-14-1851

EUBANK
Wilbur Charles b 4-3-1894 Richmond s Charles & Stella

EVANS
Frederick Charles b 2-26-1895 Washington Co NY s George B & Lela (**Wheeler**)

Isaac P b 3-1-1821 s Thomas & Hannah (**Pedrick**) d 9-28-1882 bur Earlham h Mary Ann dt Timothy & Anne **Buffum** m 5-2-1855
Ch: Annie B b 1-26-1856
     Mary Matilda b 7-25-1861 Wayne Co
     Sarah Charlotte b 6-1-1863 Wayne Co
     Flora B b 9-16-1869 d 9-26-1869 bur Earlham

Jesse Jr b 4-9-1792 s Jesse & Deborah d 1-22-1880 bur on his farm near Richmond
Esther b 2-1-1790 dt Wm & Charity (**Williams**) Hiatt bur on farm near Richmond
Ch: Juretee b 8-21-1812 NC
     Risden b 6-2-1814 NC
     Rian b 11-14-1815 NC
     Pleasant Newby b 3-23-1823 Wayne Co d 5-23-1841 bur Whitewater

Mary b 8-16-1896 dt George H & Edna B (**Pyle**)

Thomas h Hannah (**Pedrick**)
Ch: Lydia E b 8-13-1816
     Margaret E b 8-26-1818
     Isaac P b 3-21-1821 d 9-28-1882 bur Earlham
     Mary E b 8-5-1825

EVES
John E b 7-9-1848
Sadie H b 7-21-1851
Ch: Anna V b 6-4-1885
     Lillian b 4-24-1889

FAHLSING
Lewis Edward b 8-10-1874 Wayne Co s Wm & Caroline

FARLOW
Rachel d 9-25-1880 ae 84y bur Elkhorn

FARMER
Herbert J b 3-7-1874 Adrian MI s Henry & Margaret A

FARNHAM
C h Mary B dt James & Elizabeth **Johnson**

FARRAR
Grace (**Baker**) b 11-5-1881

FAUCETT
Emmett b 10-16-1897 Wayne Co s Thomas & Susan

FAULKNER
Daniel C b 11-7-1839

FEASEL
Jacob D h Sarah I b 7-28-1856 dt Samuel & Elizabeth (**Fres?**) **Lamb** m 1-8-1885
Ch: Charles B b 7-3-1886
Nellie M b 3-5-1888
Laurence McF b 12-24-1889

Josiah b 10-9-1834
Annie S b 3-14-1845
Ch: Ella b 7-26-1869
Mary Elizabeth b 8-22-1875
Anna Lora b 8-24-1884

FEEZER
Erma b 10-26-1884 dt James H & Margaret

FEREE
Edna b 9-16-1883 Marion dt Evan Harvey & Alice (**Carmack**)

FESLER
Mary R dt Addison & Sarah Ann (**Jessup**) **Hough**

FIELDS
Martha F b 9-11-1884 Carmel dt Jesse & Luana

FINLEY
Harry W b 1-14-1878 s Samuel & Eliz (**Stilwell**)

Wade h Mary Belle b 4-10-1865 dt Joel & Sarah B **Horney**

FINNY
Margaret b 10-25-1870 dt Joseph & Elizabeth

FISHER
George h Ruth
Ch: Mahala P b 8-10-1850
Nellie b 7-11-1853

Hattie A b 4-5-1870 dt Francis G & Rachel (**Carey**) **Hockett** m 9-30-1891

FLEMMING
Charles David b 9-24-1843 s Samuel & Sarah G
Hannah D b 11-15-1845
Ch: Lucy b 3-1-1872
Edith b 8-30-1882
Louis Joseph b 6-29-1884
Maria b 8-28-1888

FLETCHER
Albert White b 1-2-1842 s Samuel Francis & Elizabeth D (**Hiatt**)
Elizabeth Dix b 12-10-1840 dt Henry & Mary **Peelle** m 9-10-1868 Milford
Ch: Wilfred b 7-4-1871

FLETCHER (cont)
Edward Bradley b 2-11-1857
Sarah M b 12-3-1857 dt Wm & Mary (**Barker**) **Baxter** m 9-23-1886
Ch: Esther b 9-8-1888
Emily Maria b 2-17-1895

Francis Nixon b 6-19-1854 s Samuel Francis & Elizabeth D (**Hiatt**)
Martha E b 1-19-1854 dt Isaac Cooper & Joanna (**Miles**) **Teague** m 6-1878
Ch: Wm Dixon b 6-1893

Mordecai b 9-18-1849 s Samuel Francis & Elizabeth D (**Hiatt**) m 4-2-1884 h Anna (**Perry**)

Samuel Francis d 4-3-1894
Elizabeth D (**Hiatt**) d 3-20-1891
Ch: Albert White b 1-2-1842
Sarah Elma b 7-31-1845
Wm b 8-29-1847 d 1-27-1897 bur Earlham
Mordecai b 9-18-1849
Rhoda Alice b 11-8-1851
Francis Nixon b 6-19-1854
Edward Bradley b 2-11-1857
Jesse D b 4-15-1860
Charles b 11-22-1862

FLOOD
Orlando E b 4-12-1866 Farmland s Frank & Elizabeth
Lula b 8-25-1865 Winchester dt Nathan & Eliz **Addington** m 1-1-1888 Sherman

FOLGER
Estella L b 8-6-1874 Rush Co dt J W & Rosella

FOULKE
Martha A b 10-4-1875

FRANCISCO
Charles A b 9-24-1843 s Louis & Abigail J (**Casad**)
Hannah b 11-15-1845 dt Joseph & Esther G (**Hiatt**) **Dickinson** m 1-24-1870
Ch: Lucy b 3-1-1872
Amy b 7-28-1875
Edith b 8-30-1882
Louis Joseph b 6-29-1884
Maria b 8-28-1888

FRAZER
Oliver M b 12-10-1867 Jefferson Co IA s James & Ruth (**Whitson**)
Laura E b 9-6-1876 Lake Co IL dt Edwin & Annie (**Young**) **Stewart** m 3-9-1899 Loup Co NE

FRENCH
Oliver P b 4-24-1857 s Howell B & Sarah T (**Flood**)
Sarah A b 12-20-1852 dt James & Mary A **Hardwiage** England m 9-16-1884

FRY
Amos d 12-1869 ae 85y bur Goshen
Keziah d 7-20-1875 ae 69y bur Goshen

Calvin M b 3-24-1856

Josephine H b 8-9-1847 dt James B & Georgeina M (**Jennings**) **Hallinan** m 3-13-1889

Oliver H b 11-12-1833

Roy C b 11-20-1883 Wayne Co s F A & Florence (**Shirley**)

FULGHUM
Albert B b 1-9-1842 s Benjamin & Rhoda
Harriett E b 5-22-1844 dt Samuel & Martha (**Meredith**) **Pitts** m 4-5-1879

WHITEWATER MONTHLY MEETING
BIRTH AND DEATH RECORD

FULGHUM (cont)
Benjamin d 5-10-1877 ae 70y
Rhoda d 1-11-1866 ae 60y 4m 18d
Ch: Martha b 2-26-1829 d 9-4-1832 bur Whitewater
     Franklin B b 10-29-1830 d 9-13-1832 bur Whitewater
     Charles b 8-22-1832 d 9-22-1832 bur Whitewater
     Hannah J b 8-12-1833
     Caroline b 12-29-1835 d 8-4-1869
     Eliza B b 10-20-1837
     Wm A b 3-8-1840
     Albert B b l-9-1842
     Mary b 3-5-1844
     John Allen b 7-17-1846 d 11-5-1847 bur Whitewater
     Naomi b 10-19-1849

Frederick h Piety (**Parker**)
Ch: Frederick C b 12-25-1840
     Martha

Frederick C b 12-25-1840 s Frederick & Piety (**Parker**)
Rebecca E b 1-17-1840 dt Benjamin & Rachel (**Hixon**) **Elliott**
m 1-1-1862 Alba
Ch: Oscar E 10-23-1862
     Franconia L b 6-13-1866 d 9-20-1889 bur Earlham
     Lucy b 11-6-1872 d 3-6-1890 bur Earlham
     Walter B b 4-20-1879

Mary J b 3-10-1852 Randolph Co dt Jeremiah & Ruth

Wm A b 3-8-1840 s Benjamin & Rhoda
Harriett (**White**) b 11-24-1839
Ch: Roscoe W b 4-25-1863
     Benjamin W b 4-11-1865
     Edgar W b 12-25-1867
     Caroline b 6-1-1870
     Elma

FULTON
Samatha b 5-29-1898 Anderson dt Oliver Phillips & Rella

FURSTENBURGER
Albert J b 10-27-1877 Morrow Co OH s Henry & Evaline
Cora B b 9-2-1880 Delaware Co OH dt Benjamin & Ida **Herbert**

FYE
Benjamin h Catherine
Ch: Harry E b 8-7-1881
     Beth Margaret b 1-30-1887 Richmond

GAAR
Ann Eliza b 9-20-1851 dt John Milton & Charity Williams (**Kersey**) **Allen**

Fielding h Mary T b 3-l-1847
Ch: Jonas B b 1-22-1867
     Charley b 7-3-1868
     Andrew b 4-29-1875

Lucile b 2-8-1885 dt Clem A & Fannie (**McMeans**)

GALLAHUE
Pearl b 8-20-1875 dt Isaac Cooper & Joanna (**Miles**) **Teague**

GAMP
Hattie E b 1-17-1878 Louisville KY

GANO
Nixon H s Aaron h Lizzie dt Abraham & Edith F **Jeffries**
Ch: Paul Jefferies b 11-18-1892 d 7-25-1895 bur Earlham
     Mary b 6-5-1898

GARDNER
Alonzo M b 2-3-1860 s Benjamin A & Susannah (**Morgan**)

GARDNER (cont)
Susan Belle b 7-9-1862 dt Harmon & Susan (**Price**) **Clark** m 5-5-1887 Fountain City

GARFIELD
Winfield b 2-22-1881

GARNER
Marvel R b 2-17-1868 s Seth & Martha A (**Hill**)

Marvel R b 10-29-1896 s Elwood H & A Luella (**Rush**)

GARRETT
Wm b 2-28-1801 s Abigail
Anna b 6-5-1806
Ch: Mary Ann b 10-16-1828
     Maddison b 2-18-1830 NC
     Daniel b 10-4-1832

GARVER
Walter B b 4-28-1867 s B C & Ruth A (**Rohrer**)
Georgia L b 7-24-1876 dt Wm O & Lydia J (**Haworth**) **Mendenhall** m 6-10-1896

GARWOOD
David C h Mary E b 1-17-1844 Fayette Co PA dt Joseph & Eliza A **Negus** m 3-18-1869 Clark Co OH
Ch: Bertha M b 12-16-1877 Henry Co

Ralph Stillman h Juanita (**Garza**) b 7-1-1870

GAUSS
S Clarence h Naomi R b 2-17-1868 dt Seth & Martha Ann (**Hill**) **Brown** m 6-6-1899

GIBBONS
Lydia Ann d 3-6-1879 bur Earlham

GIBSON
Wm W b 4-6-1862 Wayne Co s Samuel & Rebecca
Minnie b 2-11-1868 Davis Co MO dt Lot W & Matilda **Martin** m 11-22-1893 Wayne Co
Ch: Grace Rebecca b 9-3-1896 Wayne Co

GIFFORD
Andrew d 5-23-1882 ae 80y
Sarah d 1-18-1872 ae 68y 11m 12d bur Orange

Daniel b 1836 d 11-16-1859 bur Orange
Jessie d 8-15-1860 ae 21y 6d bur Orange

James C b 10-14-1883 Putnam Co s James & Louisa

GILBERT
Jeremiah h Miriam
Ch: Josiah b 8-20-1773
     Thomas b 2-20-1779

Josiah h Elizabeth **Chaffin** b 1-25-1848 dt Warner & Rachel Linetta **Shearon**
Ch: Warner Morris b 1-20-1870
     Harry W b 2-26-1872

Josiah b 8-20-1773 s Jeremiah & Miriam
Dorothy b 4-17-1777 dt John & Jane **Nixon**
Ch: Miriam b 2-17-1798 d 6-18-1819 bur Whitewater
     Sarah b 2-7-1800 d 9-12-1802 bur Marlborough NC
     Elizabeth b 8-3-1802
     Mary b 2-15-1805
     Dorothy b 12-29-1807
     Josiah b 11-30-1809
     Lydia b 4-22-1812
     Achsah b 3-28-1815

GILBERT (Josiah cont)
    Morris b 7-10-1817
    Thomas b 8-18-1818

Thomas b 2-20-1779 s Jeremiah & Miriam
Sarah b 4-14-1788 dt Aaron & Sarah **Hill**
Ch: Phebe b 4-2-1811
    Miriam b 3-7-1813
    Hannah b 3-14-1815
    Mary b 6-8-1817
    Jeremiah b 10-17-1819
    Gulielma b 12-7-1821
    Martha b 2-2-1824 d 6-12-1824

GILMER
J Albert b 4-26-1883 s John D & Ann E (**Swain**)

GLUYS
Marmaduke James b 11-25-1849 s John B & Mildred (**Mendenhall**)
Zelinda Annis b 10-3-1853 dt Oliver & Mary (**Foulk**) **Binford**
m 10-8-1879
Ch: Howard b 9-2-1883
    Mary Susannah b 9-18-1888

GODSEY
Robert b 9-16-1888 Scott Co VA s Wm & Rhoda

GOODRICH
Charles h Hattie dt Otis R & Nannie J **Brown**

GORDEN
Seth b 9-18-1802 d 8-11-1838 bur Whitewater
Sarah b 4-11-1806 dt Joseph & Rebecca (**Stanley**) **Unthank**
Ch: Phebeann b 5-13-1825
    Emeline b 7-3-1829

GORDON
Elsie C b 10-19-1898 Randolph Co dt Carl & Mary

GRACE
Sarah Ann d 9-15-1864 ae 57y bur Smyrna

GRAHAM
George b 2-1-1882 Preble Co OH s Joseph & Mary

Joseph b 9-24-1875 Scioto Co OH s Isaac & Nancy
Minnie b 7-6-1876 Scioto Co OH dt John & Lucina **Morgan** m 4-4-1896 Scioto Co OH

Wm H b 12-24-1891 Wise Co VA s Frank P & Ada P

GRANT
Martha Pearl b 9-2-1875 dt Benjamin & Adaline (**Elmore**) **Lunsford**

GRAVE
Alen h Mary
Ch: Mary Ann b 1-20-1834
    Jonathan L b 1-27-1836
    Lydia H b 9-18-1838
    Rachel T b 6-19-1841
    Charles

Curtis h Eliza d 9-16-1838 bur Smyrna
Ch: Edith b 2-2-1837

David h Eliza
Ch: Lydia Ann b 3-13-1829
    Joseph b 7-15-1830 d 9-9-1832 bur Smyrna
    Esther b 9-10-1832 d ae 17y bur Smyrna
    Elizabeth b 8-14-1834
    Jesse b 7-2-1836
    Henry b 7-1838
    Thomas Clarkson b 9-13-1840
    Hannah Mariah b 11-20-1842

GRAVE (cont)
David P h Sarah Ann
Ch: Allen W b 10-9-1840 Wayne Co
Jane (**Wright**) 2w d 1-11-1843 ae 25y 11m 12d bur Smyrna

Enos b 5-28-1771 DE s Jacob & Rebeckah C
Betsy b 12-19-1775 PA dt John & Betty **Jones**
Ch: Jesse b 7-29-1799 d 7-27-1833 Redstone MM bur Smyrna
    Sarah b 9-6-1801 Redstone MM
    David b 8-11-1803 Redstone MM
    Susan b 11-22-1808 d 4-3-1819 Redstone MM bur Whitewater
    Rebecca J b 4-30-1811 Redstone MM
    Kersey b 11-20-1813 Redstone MM
    Enos b 8-15-1816

Enos h Dorothy
Ch: Martha H b 8-30-1838 d 3-20-1840
    Angelina E b 1-31-1840
    Joseph K b 11-19-1841

Howell h Hannah C b 11-19-1824 dt John & Esther **Nicholson**
Ch: Josephine

Jacob h Rebeckah
Ch: Enos b 5-28-1771 DE
    Jonathan L b 4-14-1774 d 10-8-1824 bur Smyrna
    Nathan b 7-16-1884

Jacob d 4-15-1817 ae 73y 9m 11d bur Whitewater

Jacob h Ann d 6-19-1849 ae abt 70y bur Smyrna
Ch: Rebecca b 10-14-1805 Center MM DE
    Milton b 8-4-1807 Center MM DE
    Rachel b 8-9-1809 Center MM DE d 10-4-1828 bur Smyrna
    Mary b 3-19-1811 Center MM DE
    Curtis b 1-31-1813 Center MM DE
    Levi b 5-2-1814 Center MM DE
    Martha b 7-10-1816 Westland MM PA
    Ruth b 6-30-1818
    Anna b 9-19-1819
    Joseph C b 1-26-1824

Jonathan L b 4-14-1774 s Jacob & Rebeckah d 10-8-1824 bur Smyrna
Lydia b 11-4-1782 dt Stephen & Sarah B **Howell** d 11-6-1846 bur Smyrna
Ch: Israel b 4-3-1803 d 4-21-1826 bur Smyrna
    Sarah Ann b 12-12-1808
    Allen b 1-19-1811
    David b 8-16-1813
    Warner b 3-4-1816
    Howel b 5-12-1818
    Hannah b 2-16-1821

Nathan b 7-16-1784 s Jacob & Rebekah
Hannah b 6-12-1791 dt Stephen & Sarah **Howell** d 2-10-1820 bur Whitewater
Ch: Stephan b 12-15-1809
    John L b 10-20-1811
    Pusey b 11-10-1813
    Ellwood b 3-13-1816 d 1-18-1818 bur Whitewater
    Ann P b 8-10-1818

Sarah Ann d 9-15-1864 ae 57y bur Smyrna

Wm h Elizabeth d 6-30-1893 bur Goshen
Ch: Margaret Rosetta b 3-24-1864

GRAVES
James W h Sarah Ellen
Ch: Mamie May

WHITEWATER MONTHLY MEETING
BIRTH AND DEATH RECORD

GRAVES (James cont)
Mary Alice
    Daisy d 5-30-1886
    Earlham b 10-13-1885

Vernon D h Emma b 10-9-1858/59 dt Alpheus & Elizabeth (**Moffitt**) **Test** m 3-27-1884

GRAY
James h Mary Jane
Ch: James b 9-1854
    Robert Thomas b 1856
    Wm b 7-1857 d 5-1884
    Sarah Jane b 1861
    Hugh Mallory b 1863
    John b 1865
    Samuel Walker b 1869
    Joseph Hillis b 1871

GREEN
Robert h Mahalah d 8-7-1830 bur Wapakoneta OH

GREENSTREET
Thomas A b 8-13-1877 Sycamore IA s Eli & Ruth
Lilian H b Pennville dt Joseph & Ellen **Whitacre** m Muncie

GREER
Lydia d 8-7-1874 ae 8y 2m bur Whitewater

GREY
Emma C dt Thomas & Rebecca **Robinson** d 6-17-1880 ae 23y bur Earlham

GRIFFIN
Jacob b 5-2-1776
Mary b 8-28-1776 dt Joshua & Susanna **Copeland**
Ch: John b 11-5-1801 d 3-18-1802 bur father's plantation Randolph Co NC
    James b 11-5-1801
    Samuel b 1-22-1804
    Joseph b 7-26-1806
    Joshua b 4-13-1808
    Jacob b 12-20-1810
    Wm b 7-12-1813
    Mary b 4-16-1816

Mary Jane b 7-12-1840 dt Elias **Elliott** m/1 ? **Hall**

GRIFFITH
David L h Hannah B b 4-30-1845 dt Charles H & Mary (**Boone**) **Shoemaker**
Ch: Charles J b 9-29-1870
    James Henry b 9-4-1872
    Helen b 4-30-1875

Eli h Rachel P d 11-18-1851 ae 58y bur Whitewater

George D h Martha F (**Hayward**) m 12-9-1891

John W h Keziah T
Ch: Seth S b 11-21-1844
    Rachel b 9-6-1849
    Mary b 2-6-1851 d 5-14-1881 bur Earlham
    Anna J b 11-17-1855
    Alice B b 12-22-1857
    Martha L b 4-3-1860
    Elizabeth B b 12-25-1864

GRUBBS
Wm G b 8-5-1880 Randolph Co s Benjamin

HADLEY
Alfred b 1-5-1834 h Keziah K (**Overman**)

HADLEY (Alfred cont)
Ch: Elmer F b 11-24-1871
    Lelia H

Artemus N h Elizabeth M
Ch: Elsie b 9-13-1864
    Mary b 8-13-1866
    Samuel Lee b 2-16-1868

Benjamin h Mary P (**O'Neal**)

Clark Hinman b 5-8-1849 s John C & Emeline h Mary (**King**)

Edwin b 5-16-1826 s Jonathan & Olive (**Mendenhall**) d 10-9-1890 bur Earlham
Jemima b 9-28-1830 dt Joseph & Eliza (**Carpenter**) **Doan**
Ch: Eliza D b 10-12-1856 Warren Co OH
    Ellen b 6-9-1859 d 6-23-1874 bur Earlham
    Anna M b 10-9-1861
    Edwin Clarence b 5-1-1865
    Joseph Doan b 3-26-1867 d 8-27-1867
    Turner W b 1-24-1871
    Horace Greeley b 9-20-1872
    Jessie C b 2-15-1875

Edwin Clarence b 5-1-1865 s Edwin & Jemima (**Doan**)
Emma b 10-4-1869 dt Daniel & Marth Ann (**Hussey**) **Hill** m 9-2-1891
Ch: Ruth b 10-2-1893

Elmer F b 11-24-1871 s Alfred & Keziah (**Overman**)
Ida M b 12-21-1874
Ch: Gwenaline b 1-1-1895
    Grace b 5-7-1897

Elwood b 11-9-1832
Ann P b 8-16-1838 dt Richard & Susannah B **Pedrick** d 9-24-1875 bur Earlham
Ch: Corilia M b 11-5-1860
    Louis E b 12-20-1867 d 1896

Hiram h Hannah J b 8-12-1833 dt Benjamin & Rhoda **Fulghum**
Ch: Walter C b 9-8-1857
    Caroline E b 2-25-1861
    Francis Lusk b 7-27-1863 d 2-6-1864
    Anna Rhoda

Jeremiah b 11-24-1805 d 12-24-1879 bur Earlham
Esther b 8-7-1819 d 11-29-1861 bur Whitewater
Ch: John Smith b 1-14-1840 d 11-16-1862
    James Williams b 1-14-1840 d 10-20-1865
    Jane Ann b 2-19-1843
    Samuel Smith b 1-23-1845 d 8-25-1890
    Thomas Elwood b 3-21-1849
    Flora Rosetta b 1-24-1857
    Herbert b 4-24-1861
Rebecca C 3w d 2-24-1897

Jesse H h Azonetta
Ch: Alden W
    Ernest B
    Samuel Percy

Jessie Carpenter b 2-13-1876

John C b 3-28-1814 d 12-17-1894 bur Earlham
Emeline b 5-12-1816 d 10-8-1888 bur Earlham
Ch: Wm Sawring b 12-28-1847
    Clark Hinman b 5-8-

Samuel S b Aspen CO d 7-25-1890
Ch: Thomas E
    Herbert

HADLEY (cont)
Wm Bail b 1830 h Elizabeth M
Ch: Elsie b 9-13-1864
   Mary b 8-13-1866
   Samuel Lee b 2-16-1868
   Rebecca Jane d 5-18-1890 bur Earlham

Wm L b 12-28-1848

HAHN
Abner H h Ellen S b 12-1-1849 dt John R & Sarah (**Frame**) **Smith** m 8-10-1876

HAISLEY
Anna d 11-24-1897 ae 70y

Joseph b 5-7-1830
Sarah d 7-15-1888 bur New Garden

HALE
Perry b 8-18-1850 s David F & Salina (**Hunt**)
Addie R b 1-1-1866 dt Jasper N & Mary A **McCarty** m 3-18-1886
Ch: Pearl M b 10-10-1887
   Beulah B b 1-31-1890

HALER
John h Martha
Ch: Lawrence E b 4-20-1885 Greensfork
   Pearl b 3-7-1887 Wayne Co

HALL
Alfred h Mary Jane b 7-13-1840 dt Elias & Martha (**Sander**) **Elliott**

Edwin h Effie b 11-22-1857 dt Paul & Eliza (**Horn**) **Newbern** m/1 Alfred **Brown** m/2 9-20-1899

Emily Melvina b 6-23-1833

John b 11-23-1792 Rich Square MM s John & Miriam
Sarah b 1-10-1790 NC dt Jeremiah & Karen (**Newby**) **Parker**
Ch: Martha b 11-9-1812
   Phinihas b 9-24-1814
   Robert b 1-19-1817
   Moses b 6-18-1819
   Sarah b 1-9-1826
   John b 1-19-1828
   Jeremiah b 4-22-1830 d 7-8-1830 bur Orange

R Willard b 10-8-1854 s Robert & Lydia (**White**)
Alice b 2-12-1853 dt James W & Eliza (**Brown**) **McCoy** m 10-12-1876

HAM
Alice May b 9-27-1885 Alleghany Co NC dt Theo & Manda **Osborn**

Hezekiah b 11-15-1768 s Philip & Priscilla B d 10-15-1832 bur Whitewater
Sarah b 7-25-1762 dt John & Sarah **Stuart**
Ch: Priscilla b 6-12-1799 d 10-4-1823
   Hezekiah Jr b 8-8-1801 d 11-14-1830 bur Whitewater
   Sarah b 5-8-1803
   Emsley b 2-10-1805
   Mary b 12-12-1806 d 1-24-1841 bur Orange
   Jehu b 7-12-1808 d 10-25-1823
   Jason b 4-8-1811 d 4-13-1873 bur Earlham
   Elizabeth b 3-18-1813 d 2-14-1834 bur Orange
   Anna b 9-2-1815 d 3-3-1823

Jason b 4-8-1811 s Hezekiah & Sarah (**Stuart**) d 4-13-1873 bur Earlham
Elizabeth d 7-13-1881 bur Earlham
Ch: Benjamin F b 11-11-1847

HAMMER
John Riley b 7-17-1850 Richland IA s Laban & Rachel
Melinda C b 7-19-1850 Randolph Co NC dt Levi & Mary Ann **McCalum** m 10-9-1872 Hardin Co IA
Ch: Ethel Mary b 2-27-1880 Hardin Co IA
   Esther Grace b 9-11-1883 Hardin Co IA

HAMPTON
Arthur W b 7-24-1862 h Mary (**Clark**)
Ch: Anna Margaret b 7-23-1888
   Harold E b 11-9-1889

Jacob D d 12-1896 bur Earlham
Margaret (**Reynolds**) b 4-9-1823
Ch: Anna b 6-12-1863

Lewis N h Bertha b 4-2-1868 dt John S & Sidney (**Dilks**) **Iredell** m 10-12-1892

Mary V d 4-13-1898 ae 36y bur Earlham

HARLAND
Edna L b 7-30-1878 Wayne Co dt W E & Carla Leota

HARMON
Daisy M b 7-12-1886 Nicholas Co VA dt James & Martha

HAROLD
Herman b 4-28-1841 s Nathan & Betsey
Ruthanna W b 2-20-1842 dt Joseph & Elizabeth **Wilson** m 12-21-1864 Carmel
Ch: Rollo Homer b 12-20-1876
   Eva b 5-2-1879

Isaac S b 1-1-1852 s Nathan & Rebecca (**Hawkins**)
Cordelia B b 11-2-1852 dt Jonathan & Jane (**Millican**) **Hodgin** m 10-14-1874
Ch: Frank L b 5-12-1878
   Halcy J b 6-26-1884

HARPER
George b 6-13-1877 Sims s S P & Percilla

HARRIS
Albanus h Lydia Marie
Ch: Ida Elena
   Wm Henry
   Jesse Frederic b 4-7-1876

Almedia b 6-17-1833

Jesse M h Emily Jane d 1-6-1881 ae 53y bur Earlham
Ch: George W b 1-24-1854
   Jane M b 9-2-1858
   Mary L b 6-6-1862
   Francis F b 12-10-1866

John b 6-17-1854 Jesselman KY s Calldre & Katherine
Mattie b 6-4-1861 Garnett KY dt David & Eliza **Scott** m 3-17-1878 Garnett KY

Joseph Gurney s Wm & Mary
Ch: Lydia
   Anna
   Zeri

Mary P (**Jones**) m 8-1868

HARRISON
Thomas H b 11-16-1860 s Timothy & Naomi W (**Morgan**)
Claribel (**Barrett**) m 6-25-1885
Ch: Isaac Merritt b 9-6-1886
   Raymond T b 1-20-1888

WHITEWATER MONTHLY MEETING
BIRTH AND DEATH RECORD

HARRISON (Thomas cont)
    Julius Paul d 4-22-1891
    Carlos Evans b 3-17-1895
    Wm Henry b 1-2-1897 d 11-16-1899
    Thomas Jr b 11-1898 d 12-5-189?

Timothy b 5-12-1832 d 3-22-1881 bur Earlham
Naomi W b 3-14-1838 dt Charles & Michael (**Butler**) Morgan m 5-5-1852 Raysville
Ch: Mary Emily b 5-30-1859
    Thomas H b 11-16-1860
    Susan R b 11-25-1862
    Lizzie b 5-9-1865 d 9-25-1865 bur Earlham
    Annie R b 8-13-1868
    Timothy b 6-21-1870
    Miriam Alice b 12-16-1871

Timothy b 6-21-1870 s Timothy & Naomi (**Morgan**)
Pearl Adele (**Louden**) b 6-2-1894 Indianapolis
Ch: Anna R b Wayne Co
    Miriam A b Wayne Co

HARTER
Blanch Irene b 11-17-1899 Randolph Co dt Lowell & Etta

Olive b 2-27-1893 North Madison OH dt John & Deliah

Ora V b 12-25-1890 Darke Co OH s James & Margette

Wm b 6-20-1861 Meade KS
Sarah b 1-14-1863 Meade KS

HARTLEY
Edward S b 2-7-1869 Robinson KS s Charles & Mary J
Susie E b 12-6-1869 Henry Co dt Joseph & Cyrenia J ? m 7-19-1891 Middletown

HARVEY
Ada b 5-10-1844

Bertha b 8-5-1877 Darke Co OH dt Lemuel D & Adeline

Charles h Margaret
Ch: Augustus H b 2-7-1868
    Mahlon b 8-8-1871

Elijah h Mary Ann (**Clawson**)
Ch: Daniel Milton b 5-23-1842 d 5-13-1864
    Gulielma b 3-5-1849 Wayne Co
    Elisabeth Ann b 2-10-1852
    Sarah Alice b 6-23-1854 d 4-10-1857
    Abner C b 1-9-1856
    Wm F b 7-1-1858
    George E b 2-4-1861 d 8-31-1861
    Alfred H b 4-14-1862

Wm b 10-25-1788 s Wm & Jemima B d 10-24-1872 bur Whitewater
Sarah b 7-24-1789 dt Samuel & Gulielma **Charles** d 2-25-1872 bur Whitewater
Ch: Mary b 3-28-1814 d 3-20-1841 bur Bloomfield
    Samuel b 9-22-1815
    Elijah b 9-18-1818
    Gulielma b 9-7-1820
    John b 1-9-1823 d 9-10-1847 bur Whitewater
    Mahlon b 4-27-1825
    Milton b 4-27-1825 d 3-21-1841 bur Whitewater
    Wm b 11-4-1827 d 9-5-1847 bur Whitewater
    Charles b 11-27-1832
    George b 6-23-1834 d 1-27-1858 bur Whitewater

HASTINGS
Aaron h Christiana (**Reece**)
Ch: Elias R b 6-25-1835 Henry Co
    John N b 5-10-1841

HASTINGS (cont)
Daniel C h Keziah (**Brown**)
Ch: Rebecca b 4-5-1840
    Eunice C b 7-1-1858

Elias R b 6-25-1835 Henry Co s Aaron & Christiana (**Reece**)
Sarah E b 3-17-1837 Wayne Co dt Wm & Abigail (**Stratton**) **Edgerton** m 1857 Wayne Co
Ch: Wm E
    Mary Emma
    Anna Letitia b 11-11-1886

Jane
Ch: Rebecca Jane d 8-1-1863 ae 29y 6m 26d
    John R d 8-1-1863
    Seth
    Aaron
    Wm Clarkson

John N b 5-10-1841 s Aaron & Christiana (**Reece**)
Jennie/Jane E d 10-27-1898 ae 51y bur Earlham
Ch: Ella M
    Otis L
    Gertrude R

Joshua s John & Sarah d 6-21-1816 ae 1y 4m 4d bur West Grove

Wm b 1-31-1773 s Joshua & Ann
Sarah b 8-23-1781 dt Catharine **Evans**
Ch: Nancy b 8-23-1799 d 2-7-1819 bur Whitewater
    Katherine b 7-30-1801
    Eunice b 2-1-1803
    Welmet b 12-7-1805
    Aaron b 5-2-1808
    Mary b 9-26-1810
    Wm b 3-10-1813
    Daniel C b 2-19-1815
    Sarah b 4-8-1817

HATHAWAY
Alfred C b 9-5-1858 d 4-4-1893 bur Des Moines IA h Minnie R
Ch: Francis W

HAUGHTON
Lewis M h Bertha b 4-2-1868 dt John S & Sidney (**Dilks**) Iredell m 10-12-1882

Richard E b 12-8-1827
Elizabeth C b 11-3-1847 dt Phineas & Ruth Ann **Mather**
Ch: Charles Melville b 3-1871
    Wm Percival b 5-1873

HAWKINS
Amos d 5-1-1834 ae 76y 5m 26d bur Whitewater h Rachel
Ch: Wm b 9-22-1808
    Isaac b 7-27-1810
    Mary b 4-13-1813
    Prudence b 4-29-1815
    Henry b 9-28-1817
    Stephen b 6-4-1820
    Silas b 3-23-1823 d 1-8-1827

Anna d 4-8-1853 ae 89y 3m 9d bur Whitewater

George W h Celena M
Ch: Lella A
    Daisy M
    Alma E

John d 4-26-1890 ae 79y 5 1/2m
Sarah (**Jessup**) d 3-16-1887 ae 73y bur Earlham
Ch: Sarah Ellen b Richmond
    Nathan b 1-27-1842 Richmond

HAWKINS (John cont)
  Oliver b 1-19-1845 Richmond
  Lydia Emeline b 5-3-1854 Richmond

John h Lydia d 10-24-1854 bur Whitewater

John h Christiana (**Guard**)
Ch: Ida b 2-28-1889
     Edna b 8-8-1895

Levi d 8-16-1888 ae 54y bur Earlham h Sarah
Ch: Blanche

Lindly A h Martha b 6-16-1846 dt Mordecai & Guliema **Parry**
Ch: Florence Webster b 7-11-1870

Nathan b 4-15-1808 d 7-14-1890 bur Earlham h Sarah
Ch: Charles N d 9-28-1868 bur Maple Grove
     George W b 1-25-1852
Minnie 2w d 1-4-1884
Ch: Belle b 11-29-1872

Nathan b 1-27-1842 Wayne Co s John & Sarah (**Jessup**)
Naomi b 10-17-1856 Phillipsburg OH dt Wm & Rebecca (**Smith**) **Howard** m 1897 Richmond
Ch: Nellie R b 1898 Wayne Co

Oliver b 1-19-1845 Wayne Co s John & Sarah (**Jessup**)
Emily Jane b 1-31-1861 dt John & Elizabeth **Townsend** m 3-17-1898 West Grove

HAWORTH
James d 3-2-1899 ae 70y h Sarah (**Hawkins**) m 10-9-1895

HEAP
Elizabeth d 3-27-1877

HELSCEL
Myra M b 9-7-1889 Sheffield PA dt John & Mary

HELTON
b 6-17-1883 Benton AR dt Geo & Louise (**Todd**)

HEMINGTON
James h Margaret Susan d 3-7-1867 ae 40y bur Rich Square

HENDERSON
Walter h Bertha b 1-18-1874 dt Isaac P & Lydia **Woodard** m 6-27-1895

HENDRICKS
Ella b 7-20-1869 dt Josiah & Annie S **Fesel**

HENLEY
Edgar h Gertrude (**Parks**) b 3-25-1852
Ch: Walter K b 8-25-1876
     Electa b 8-27-1887 Wayne Co

Henry b 2-20-1826 s Micajah & Gulielma (**Charles**) d 2-5-1883 bur Earlham
Tacy Ann b Richmond dt Jonathan & Nancy (**Purdue**) **Meredith** d 5-19-1889 ae 61y bur Earlham
Ch: Charles F b 3-10-1849
     Emily H b 9-8-1850
     Gulielma
     Micajah C b 6-24-1856
     Ida May
     Cora Ann
     Laura S

Hezekiah h Priscilla b 6-12-1799 dt Hezekiah & Sarah (**Stuart**) **Ham** d 10-8-1823 ae 24y 3m 26d
Ch: Martha L b 2-25-1820 d 7-9-1821
     Sarah H b 7-16-1821

HENLEY (cont)
John b 8-3-1815 s Micajah & Gulielma (**Charles**) d 11-17-1899 bur Earlham
Naomi B b 12-9-1817 dt Wm & Keziah (**Ward**) **Clawson** d 7-3-1872 bur Maple Grove m 9-2-1842
Miriam W 2w b 6-30-1840 dt Robert & Rachel (**Wilson**) **Green** m 11-22-1873
Ch: Robert M b 2-21-1875 Wayne Co

John C b 3-28-1814 d 12-17-1894 bur Earlham
Emeline b 5-12-1816 d 10-6-1888 bur Earlham
Ch: Wm L b 12-28-1847
     Clark H b 5-8-1849

Micajah b 8-6-1785 d 12-13-1857 bur Whitewater
Gulielma b 4-23-1792 dt Samuel & Gulielma **Charles** d 12-8-1860 bur Whitewater
Ch: Mary b 3-17-1813
     John b 8-11-1815 d 11-17-1899 bur Earlham
     Rebecca b 8-30-1817
     Naomi b 7-31-1819
     Martha b 10-10-1821
     Samuel b 3-11-1824
     Henry b 2-20-1826 d 2-25-1883 bur Earlham
     Gulielma b 3-20-1828

Micajah b 6-24-1856 s Henry h Adda (**Williams**)

Samuel b 3-11-1824 s Micajah & Gulielma (**Charles**) d 11-17-1897 bur Earlham
Eliza Ann d 5-21-1898 ae 72y bur Earlham m 4-25-1850 Clinton Co
Ch: Wm Edgar b 5-7-1851
     Mary Eva b 9-13-1853
     Alva J b 12-25-1857 d 10-7-1885 bur Earlham
     Elwood b 10-15-1860 d 10-28-1862 bur Maple Grove

Sarah H d 7-1892

Wm Edgar b 5-7-1851 s Samuel & Eliza Ann h Gertrude **Sparks**

HENSON
Lewis A b 5-29-1877 Randolph Co dt Thomas & Louisa
Flora B b 10-22-1882 Wayne Co dt Isaac & Anna **Revelee** m 5-3-1897 Connersville

HERBERT
Cora S b 2-9-1880 Delaware Co OH dt Benjamin & Ida

HESKETT
Rebecca Mae b 12-21-1882 Jay Co dt James Wm & Sarah J

HIATT
Alfred J b 11-25-1859 s Jesse & Louisa

Asher h Sarah M
Ch: Eleazar B
     Daniel W
     Charles M b 12-29-1846

Benajah h Elizabeth (**White**)
Ch: Naomi b 11-15-1797 NC
     Mordecai b 11-8-1799
     Esther G b 3-2-1816 d 2-2-1891 bur Earlham

Eleazar b 10-2-1783 s Solomon & Sarah B
Anna b 4-17-1789 d 5-21-1819
Ch: Eliza H b 5-2-1812
     Jesse b 9-30-1814
     Daniel b 1-31-1817
Gulielma (**Sanders**) 2w b 12-23-1784
Ch: Martha b 10-16-1822 d 8-8-1823
     John S b 5-12-1825
     Anna Maria b 3-22-1827

**WHITEWATER MONTHLY MEETING
BIRTH AND DEATH RECORD**

HIATT (cont)
Eli h Hannah
Ch: Sidney b 2-12-1822 d 8-17-1822
    Tilney b 5-9-1823
    Thurza b 9-18-1826

Isaac h Shanna
Ch: Daniel W b 9-16-1819 Guilford Co NC
    Phebe b 11-21-1821 Guilford Co NC
    Lydia b 9-11-1824
    Marthajane b 9-17-1827
    Rebecca b 12-6-1829
    Joseph P

James Smith b 7-10-1877 s Wm James & Eliza (**Smith**)
Margaret b 11-20-1875 dt Charles & Elizabeth M (**Stanton**)
Chapman

Jesse d 10-4-1839 bur KS

Mordecai b 11-18-1839 s Mordecai & Elizabeth (**White**) d 11-24-1873 bur Earlham
Rhoda b 5-28-1802 dt Joshua & Elizabeth (**Baldwin**) **Dix** d 12-18-1881 bur Earlham
Ch: Wm James b 12-3-1839

Sarah b 9-29-1747

Wm James b 12-3-1839 s Mordecai & Rhoda (**Dix**)
Eliza Willan b 4-8-1839 dt James & Sarah (**Willan**) **Smith** m 12-26-1865 Cambridge City
Ch: Benjamin b 12-26-1872
    Edgar Fletcher b 10-3-1874
    James Smith b 7-10-1877

HIGHLEY
Edna b 4-3-1889 dt Frank & Louise (**Lester**)

HILL
Arthur J b 5-18-1897 Granett AR

Benjamin h Ann d 4-6-1837 ae 27y bur Orange

Benjamin b 6-22-1770 s Wm & Mary d 2-19-1829 bur Whitewater
Mary d 3-14-1808 ae 31y 8m 2d bur Whitewater
Ch: John b 2-20-1797 Back Creek MM NC
    Sarah b 6-17-1798 Back Creek MM NC
    Jacob b 2-3-1800 Back Creek MM NC
    Wm b 3-18-1802 Mount Olive MM VA
    Joseph b 8-4-1804 Mount Olive MM VA
    Mary b 12-27-1806
Martha 2w b 11-28-1779 dt Benjamin & Rebeckah **Cox** d 12-25-1867
Ch: Benjamin b 9-23-1809
    Harmon b 4-26-1811 d 11-8-1877 bur Maple Grove
    Rebekah b 2-18-1814
    Ezra E b 8-10-1816
    Enos b 9-7-1819

Benjamin C b 1-24-1848 s Thomas T & Nancy (**Davis**)
Mary Esther b 8-5-1848 dt Benjamin & Susan (**Collins**) **Wickett**
Ch: Freddie Reece b 1-24-1872 d 12-5-1873 bur Earlham
    Bertha C b 5-17-1875

Bessie b 1-30-1894 Lynn dt Wm & Virgie

Charles b 5-24-1819 s Robert & Susannah (**Morgan**)
Jemima b 5-29-1818 dt Daniel & Susan (**Ward**) **Clark** d 6-9-1895 bur Earlham
Ch: Daniel C b 9-26-1843
    Elam B b 9-21-1845
    Cyrus W b 6-2-1848 d 8-28-1849 bur Orange
    Robert A b 8-5-1850 d 4-13-1874 bur Orange
    Mary Elizabeth b 1-4-1855
    Wm Franklin b 2-1-1859 d 1-1-1865

HILL (cont)
Daniel h Tamer (**Hussey**) d 5-11-1894
Ch: Emma
    Murray

Daniel Aaron b 11-30-1860 s Joseph B & Rebecca (**Hastings**)
Ella G b 5-8-1861 dt Clark & Susanna (**Baden**) **Green** m 12-24-1884 Richmond
Ch: Cora R b 8-28-1885

Edward Gurney h Eliza (**Stuart**)
Ch: Anna W b 6-19-1879 d 2-7-1880
    Mary Stuart b 6-19-1879
    Joseph H b 3-7-1883
    Flora A

Elijah b 2-17-1827 s Joseph & Martha (**Jay**) d 1-17-1873 bur Smyrna
Rebecca M b 1-28-1826 dt John & Betty (**Compton**) **Mills** d 8-18-1869 bur Smyrna
Ch: John Milton b 9-11-1852
    Joseph H b 9-4-1855
    Wm Edmund b 9-7-1857 d 3-22-1862 bur Sugar Plain
    Enos W b 8-6-1859
    Martha E b 11-29-1861
    Mary Jay b 6-11-1867

Emma C b 7-12-1881 dt Wm & Artalissa (**Bond**)

Harmon b 4-26-1811 s Benjamin & Martha (**Cox**) d 11-8-1877 bur Maple Grove
Mary b 3-17-1813 dt Micajah & Gulielma (**Charles**) **Hill** d 5-30-1881 bur Maple Grove
Ch: Rebecca Jane b 12-7-1831
    Samuel C b 1-7-1834
    Martha Ann b 1-24-1836 Wayne Co
    Gulielma b 8-18-1837
    John Henley b 11-30-1839

Henry b 11-28-1790 s Jesse & Mary
Achsah b 1-2-1793 dt Abraham & Margaret **Peacock**
Ch: Asenath b 8-14-1815
    Daniel b 11-18-1817

John Henley b 11-30-1839 s Harman & Mary (**Hill**) d 5-1892
Phebe A (**Branson**) b 8-21-1841 d 2-23-1870 bur Maple Grove
Ch: Flora Lizzie b 8-7-1862 d 12-23-1864 bur Maple Grove
    Olive A b 12-4-1864
    Cora Bertha b 2-7-1867

Joseph s Benjamin & Mary h Martha b 9-25-1808 Warren Co OH dt John & Mary (**Steddom**) **Jay** d 8-14-1847 bur Smyrna
Ch: Elijah b 2-17-1827 d 1-17-1873 bur Smyrna
    Mary Elisabeth b 9-2-1834
    Sarah Jay b 7-22-1829
Amy 2w
Ch: John J b 9-15-1849
    Martha J b 2-28-1851
    Margaret Elizabeth b 9-16-1853

Joseph B b 2-28-1837 s Aaron & Marion
Rebecca b 4-5-1840 dt Daniel C & Keziah (**Brown**) **Hastings**
Ch: Daniel Aaron b 11-30-1860

Mary J b 8-8-1870

Murray s Daniel & Tamer (**Hussey**) h Anna (**Moffitt**)
Rachel S (**Bailey**) 2w
Ch: Murray b 1-28-1828
Leona B 3w b 5-27-1874 Preble Co OH dt Joseph & Marie (**Young**) **Eikenbury** m 4-19-1897 Preble Co OH
Ch: Emma

Robert b 1-31-1780 s Wm & Mary

HILL (cont)
Susanna b 3-24-1782 dt Charles & Susannah **Morgan**
Ch: Martha b 4-18-1802 d 2-24-1808 bur near Whitewater
     Wm b 10-5-1804
     Benjamin b 1-17-1807
     Samuel b 4-30-1809
     Elizabeth b 7-31-1811
     Mary b 12-7-1813
     Penninah b 2-23-1817
     Charles b 5-24-1819
     Robert b 9-18-1821

Robert b 9-21-1821 s Robert & Susanna (**Morgan**)
Elizabeth D b 9-16-1827 dt Amos & Malinda (**Davenport**) Clawson
Ch: Mary Emily b 11-8-1851
     Edward S b 11-11-1853
     Anna Jane b 8-6-1855
     John C b 2-14-1858
     Mahlon R b 2-5-1863
     Rebecca J b 2-8-1866

Thomas h Sarah
Ch: Hannah b 9-21-1800
     Sarah b 2-6-1803
     Abram b 1-15-1806
     Mordicah b 10-5-1808

Thomas T h Nancy D (**Davis**)
Ch: Benjamin C b l-4-1848
     Miriam Penninah b 6-15-1850
     Eli B b 4-19-1852
     Emma b 2-1-1854 d 10-8-1854 bur NC
     Abbie E b 3-27-1856 Ashelow Co NC
     Asenath E b 4-10-1858
     Maggie M b 5-2-1860

Wm h Mary
Ch: Ruth b 6-13-1808
     Aaron b 3-15-1810
     Hiram b 11-1-1812
     Martha b l-7-1815
     Sarah b 4-27-1817
     Phillip b 5-4-1819
     Rebecca b 11-14-1821

HINKLE
Milo S b 9-9-1883 Miami Co s John H & Julia

HINSHAW
Caroline Mary b 10-14-18? dt Emsley & Pamelia (**Talbott**) **Hamm** m 3-6-1867

H Earl b 4-17-1884 Winchester s S S & Rachel O

Henry h Elizabeth (**Austin**) **Conkle**

Herchel C b 4-29-1893 Randolph Co s Elwood & Samantha

Isaiah b 11-5-1794
Welmet b 12-20-1796
Ch: Benjamin b 5-8-1816
     Susannah b 8-6-1820

Mae b 9-3-1881 Randolph Co dt Elwood S & Sarrah J

HIPPARD
Wm b 5-18-1862 s Marion & Mary (**Maharry**)
Marianna J b 1-4-1866 dt Peter & Martha (**Fulghum**) **Bond** m 11-1-1883
Ch: Vera b 12-23-1886
     Marion N b 1-27-1890
     Wilburn L b 7-26-1899

WHITEWATER MONTHLY MEETING
BIRTH AND DEATH RECORD

HISER
Winfield Scott b 9-20-1865 Wayne Co s Abraham B & Sophia J
Mary Edna b 11-24-1866 Wayne Co dt Charles G & Elizabeth (**Newlin**) **Carpenter** m 5-2-1884/94

HISEY
Kathrine b 7-8-1862 Harveysburg OH dt Robert J & Ann M

HITCH
Laura b 1-28-1862 Westboro OH dt Peter & Amanda (**Dixon**) **Harrison** m 3-27-1880 Westboro

HOAG
Nathan C minister d 11-16-1854 ae 69y 1m 13d h Abigail
Ch: Huldah C

HOBBS
Barnabas C b 1815 d 6-22-1892
Rebecca T d 6-22-1892
Ch: Mary Anne b 5-10-1844
     Lydia b 4-25-1846 d 6-25-1847 bur Whitewater
     Wm Henry b 1-1-1848
     George Tatum b 1-23-1850
     Sibyl Amelia
     Caroline
     Alice Fowler
     Fowel Buxton

Grace Elizabeth b 5-26-1876 dt Marmaduke & Martha (**Nordyke**)

HOBSON
Herman Silas b 7-27-1883 s Orlando & Leanah (**Henderson**)

HOCKETT
Addison b 3-13-1862 Henry Co s Warner M & Sarah G (**Charles**)
Sarah b 11-11-1862 Randolph Co dt Francis & Sarah **Frazier** m 9-1-1883 Wayne Co
Ch: Oliver Clarence
     Carrie May
     Earl Taylor b 2-13-1894 Wayne Co

Francis G b l0-1-1847 s David W & Rebecca (**Hunt**)
Rachel b 3-31-1850 dt Elias & Jane (**Moon**) **Carey** m 8-8-1868
Ch: Hattie A b 4-5-1870
     Homer C b 12-11-1875

Joel d 1-1878 bur West Grove

Sherman h Elizabeth b 11-29-1873 dt Wm & Martha **Study** m 1-29-1895 Bloomingsport

Tamar b 12-2-1823

Warner M h Sarah G b 4-7-1833 dt Nathan & Mary (**Symons**) **Charles**
Ch: Wm N
     Addison b 3-13-1862 Henry Co
     Martha E

HODGIN
Albert L b 6-7-1875 Wayne Co s Milton & Mary M

Charles Elkanah b 8-21-1858 s Tilnias & Rachel (**Hinshaw**)
Sallie E (**Iverman**) m 6-17-1883
Mary E (**Brooks**) 2w m 12-24-1892

Cyrus Wm b 2-12-1842 s Tilnias & Rachel (**Hinshaw**)
Emily Caroline b 4-12-1838 dt Robert & Mary (**Dodd**) **Chandler** m 8-22-1867
Ch: Laura Alice b 4-17-1869

David O b 9-17-1889 s Daniel W & Lydia Elva (**Johnson**)

Elias M b 10-1-1845 s Tilnias & Rachel (**Hinshaw**) d 2-14-1893

WHITEWATER MONTHLY MEETING
BIRTH AND DEATH RECORD

HODGIN (Elias cont)
Rachel E b 8-8-1849 dt Henry & Rachel **Lewelling** m 3-3-1871 Chester
Ch: Martha L b 2-16-1876
　　Mary E b 11-11-1877
　　Amy E b 2-9-1880
　　Grace A b 11-11-1881 d 1-28-1897 bur Earlham
　　Bertha A b 3-6-1884
　　Elva R b 8-19-1889

Joseph N b 1-27-1844 s Tilnias & Rachel (**Hinshaw**)
Martha dt Henry & Rachel **Lewelling** d 6-17-1876 ae 29y 10m bur Maple Grove
Ch: Elizabeth Emma b 5-10-1869
　　Henry T b 11-5-1870
Emma (**Harlan**) 2w m 10-4-1877

Sarah b 11-29-1842 Guilford Co, NC dt Jonathan & Alice (**Stalker**) **Anthony** m 4-1880 Greensboro NC

Tilnias b 6-12-1817 s Joseph & Ruth (**Dix**) d 1-13-1884 bur Earlham
Rachel b 11-18-1820 dt Jacob & Phebe (**Allen**) **Hinshaw** d 6-13-1874 bur Earlham m 3-25-1841
Ch: Cyrus W b 2-12-1842
　　Joseph N b 1-27-1844
　　Elias M b 10-1-1845 d 2-14-1893
　　Phebe Alice b 8-11-1853
　　James Orlando/Lealand b 8-27-1856 d 12-4-1864 bur Whitewater
　　Charles Elkanah Hodges b 8-21-1858
　　Emma Edna/Eldora b 3-24-1860 d 11-29-1864/84 burWhitewater
　　Wm Percival b 1-10-1863
Amy (**Hodgins**) 2w m 9-2-1875

Wm Percival b 1-10-1863 s Tilnias & Rachel (**Hinshaw**) h Elizabeth (**Stewart**) m 6-17-1844

HOEFFER
Charles Foster b 11-24-1879
Blanche May b 5-6-1880

HOLE
Allen David b 8-6-1866 h Mary (**Doan**)

Raymond h Isabel b 8-3-1837 Wayne Co dt David & Sarah (**Cosand**) **Wilson** m Jackson Co m 6-17-1857

HOLLINGSWORTH
Asiph h Ann (**Wickersham**)
Ch: Lydia b 11-11-1830
　　Israel H b 1-1-1843

Charles h Caroline b 12-29-1835 dt Benjamin & Rhoda **Fulghum** d 8-4-1869
Ch: Iola d 3-16-1889 bur New Boston IL

Frank S b 10-15-1853 Warren Co OH s Elias & Lydia
Jennie C b 6-15-1860 Clinton CO OH dt B H & Elizabeth **Vance** m 10-15-1879 Wilmington OH
Ch: Goldie V b 11-1881 Clinton Co OH

Israel H b 1-1-1843 s Asiph & Ann (**Wickersham**)
Rachel W b 4-23-1843 dt Edward & Hannah (**Thorne**) **Wildman** m 9-26-1870 Clark Co OH
Ch: Clarence W b 9-13-1872
　　Mabel b 2-29-1880

Milton d 10-19-1871 ae 47y 1m 11d bur Maple Grove h Susan M
Ch: Joanna Inez b 3-26-1848 d 1-11-1865 bur Maple Grove
　　Clarence b 2-27-1850 d 3-10-1855 bur Maple Grove
　　Ona H b 7-2-1856 d 7-1-1887 bur Brooklin
　　Arabel b 4-14-1858
　　Martha E b 1-26-1860 d 3-29-1884
　　Franklin b 2-18-1862

HOLLINGSWORTH (Milton cont)
　　Elwood Clare b 8-16-1865
　　Joseph Fallas b 1-30-1867 d 12-25-1868 bur Brooklin
　　Milton b 6-28-1869

Rachel A d 7-3-1899 ae 50y bur Ridge
Ch: Homer

HOLLOWAY
Stephen s Amos & Hepsibah h Elizabeth dt John & Tishe **Smith** d 2-2-1825 bur Whitewater m 2-8-1816
Ch: Nathan b 5-5-1818
　　Jason b 2-21-1820
　　Margaret b 6-27-1822 d 8-13-1823
　　John S b 7-24-1824

HOLZAPPEL
Clara Barbara b 11-10-1892 Richmond dt Samuel & Lizzie

HOOPS
Mary Ella b 5-17-1854 dt Samuel & Anna S

HOOVER
Andrew Jr b 9-10-1791 s Andrew & Elizabeth
Gulielma b 8-6-1791 dt Cornelius & Elizabeth (**Saint**) **Ratliff** m 9-30-1812 Whitewater
Ch: Elizabeth b 11-14-1813 d 4-4-1834 bur Hicksite Graveyard Whitewater
　　Mahlon b 1-20-1815
　　James b 8-23-1816
　　Enos b 8-1-1818
　　Thomas b 10-26-1820
　　John b 7-15-1824
　　Mary b 1-22-1827

Frederick b 9-24-1783 s Andrew & Elizabeth
Katherine b 7-15-1788 dt Henry & Mary Ann **Yount**
Ch: Alexander b 1-13-1807
　　Samuel b 5-22-1809
　　Sarah b 8-16-1811
　　John b 10-15-1814
　　Henry b 5-2-1817
　　Mary b 7-12-1819

Henry d 1-23-1868 bur Hoover Burying Ground

Levi C b 9-28-1857 s Henry & Ann (**Cook**)
Emma A b 9-14-1859 dt Levi & Rebecca (**Hunt**) **Cloud** m 9-30-1880
Ch: Helen b 11-26-1881
　　Edna Lois b 10-13-1885

HOPKINS
Richard P d 1833
Elizabeth B b 6-14-1804 dt Frederick & Elizabeth B (**Cranford**) **Diffendorfer** m 1833

HOPPE
Alma Henrietta b 2-20-1881 Richmond dt Harmon & Caroline (**Schumaker**)

HORN
Clyde L b 10-30-1883 Randolph Co s Arthur D & Iona

Emma C b 11-6-1874 Randolph Co dt Josea & Achsah

Hannah J b 5-25-1868 Wayne Co dt Thomas P & Orpha A **White** m 3-26-1892 Wayne Co

Valentine K b 11-2-1846 s Silas & Charlotte (**Knox**)
Annie b 8-31-1853 dt Holly R & Rebecca (**Green**) **Leeds** m 12-18-1872
Ch: Irma C b 12-15-1886
　　Silas H b 10-17-1894

HORNADAY
Paul d 1-28-1887 ae 40y h Olive A
Ch: Martha Ellen b 7-24-1875 d 8-16-1875

Paul d 3-1899 ae 72y

HORNEY
David Sanders b 12-2-1812 s Solomon & Elizabeth (**Sanders**)
d 11-19-1887 bur Earlham h Ann (**Mathews**)
Ch: Elizabeth Longstreth b 7-13-1846
     Martha b 5-6-1849
     Susan b 9-19-1851 d 2-16-1892 bur Earlham
     Samuel b 9-13-1854

Edward
Ch: Clara b 9-15-1879
     Howard Allen b 2-14-1881

Joel b 2-14-1825 s Solomon & Elizabeth (**Sanders**) d 3-10-1866 bur
Whitewater h Sarah B
Ch: Albert b 10-28-1853 d 6-19-1887 bur Earlham
     Hellen b 12-24-1854
     Wm b 3-24-1856 d 7-31-1856 bur Earlham
     Edward b 4-25-1857
     Emily b 1-24-1859
     Richard b 7-25-1862 d 8-13-1863 bur Earlham
     Mary Belle b 4-10-1865

John b 2-22-1806
Prudence b 4-6-1808
Ch: Jane b 10-21-1829
     Jonathan b 12-17-1830
     Elizabeth b 4-12-1832

Jonathan h Susanna L b 5-29-1820 dt Richard & Elizabeth **Mather**
Ch: Richard M b 6-26-1845 d 12-23-1845 bur Whitewater
     Charles b 1-6-1847

Solomon b 2-4-1788 s John & Mary d 4-13-1865 bur Whitewater
Elizabeth b 6-20-1786 dt David & Sarah **Sanders** d 5-29-1844
bur Whitewater
Ch: David Sanders b 12-2-1812 d 11-19-1887 bur Earlham
     John b 2-7-1814
     Samuel b 7-19-1815 d 7-22-1816 bur Whitewater
     Jonathan b 8-8-1817
     Jesse b 9-14-1819
     Eli b 7-25-1821 d 7-19-1822 bur Whitewater
     Philip b 5-31-1823 d 2-27-1824 bur Whitewater
     Joel b 2-14-1825 d 3-10-1866 bur Whitewater
     Daniel Clark b 12-30-1826 d 6-26-1833 bur Whitewater

HORNISH
Jacob B b 10-27-1794
Tamar b 9-24-1792
Ch: Bazabel B b 7-24-1820
     Wm H b 4-14-1822

HORNY
Elijah h Mary
Ch: Samuel Milton b 5-23-1842
     Gulielma b 3-5-1849
     Elizabeth Ann b 10-2-1852

HORRALL
James C b 8-14-1854 s Thomas H & Susan (**Mendenhall**)
Martha E (**Bond**) d 12-11-1897 ae 43y bur Earlham 12-23-1880
Ch: Fannie E b 10-15-1886

HOTCHKISS
Horace h Mary Winifred b 8-12-1860 dt Samuel & Mary K **Bellis**
Ch: Wm Kenworthy b 10-9-1884 d 10-26-1885
     Mary Winifred b 5-8-1886

HOUGH
Addison h Sarah Ann b 11-7-1843 IA dt Jehu & Mary A (**Whitacre**)
Jessup
Ch: Bertha J
     Ethel A
     Mary R
     Eugene B
     Wm Clarence
     Robert B
     Roscoe

Emma b 8-13-1861 dt Moses & Penniah

Hiram h Hannah b 4-1-1814 dt Wm & Martha (**Vickers**) **Milhous**
wid **Mendenhall** m 12-6-1877

Roscoe h Celia b 11-29-1874 IL dt Jos & Rachel J **Cox** m 11-29-1894

HOWELL
Claud W b 5-7-1889 Tipton s John & Bell

Harry C Jr h Laura P b 12-12-1858 dt Isaac Cooper & Joanna
(**Miles**) **Teague**

Samuel C h Deborah Ann (**Starr**) m 8-1876

Stephen h Sarah B
Ch: Lydia b 11-14-1782 d 11-6-1846 bur Smyrna
     Hannah b 6-12-1791 d 2-10-1820

Verdie b 1-26-1895 dt D M & Martha (**Carroll**)

HOZIER
Wm b 10-15-1783 s Ann
Milicent b 3-15-1787 dt John & Catharine **Bailey**
Ch: Mary b 10-15-1803
     Nathan b 12-12-1805
     Henry b 7-29-1809
     Caroline b 3-22-1812

HUBBARD
Henry F h Nellie (**Clark**)
Ch: Louise
     Dorothy Tuttle b 2-7-1897

Jeremiah d 11-23-1849 ae 73y bur New Garden
Martha C d 31-1845 ae 67y bur Whitewater

HUBBELL
H Harriet b 4-3-1894 Richmond dt Franc & Mary E

HUBBS
Margaret b 9-9-1882 Prince Edward Ontario Canada dt John
Frumpour & Lavina

HUNNICUTT
Delitha d 1-16-1866 ae 90y 6m

James d 11-5-1861 ae 91y 9m 6d bur Whitewater

HUNT
Abner b 9-27-1799 s Eleazer & Ann
Susannah b 5-22-1804 dt Richard & Susannah **Williams** d 7-4-1843
bur Whitewater
Ch: Eliza b 9-7-1820 NC
     Alonzo b 10-5-1822 NC
     Albert b 11-13-1824
     Anna Jane b 2-8-1828 d 10-21-1839 bur Whitewater
     Mary Emily b 10-5-1834

Ann d 6-26-1859 ae 72y bur Whitewater

Catharine dt Adam **Coffin** d 11-2-1829 ae 36y 9m 12d bur West Grove

WHITEWATER MONTHLY MEETING
BIRTH AND DEATH RECORD

HUNT (cont)
Charles 8-25-1871 Wayne Co s John & Emily
Jessie b 12-7-1874 Wayne Co dt John A & Martha **Chenoweth** m 10-14-1893 Wayne Co
Ch: J Verlin b 8-24-1894 Wayne Co

Clayton b 6-26-1815 s John & Ann (**Brown**)
Elizabeth dt John & Mary **Starr** d 7-31-1881 ae 67y bur Earlham m 11-29-1837
Ch: John L b 9-13-1838
    Joseph B b 9-11-1840
    Mary L b 6-16-1843
    Clayton B b 11-23-1845
    Esther W b 7-14-1849
    Benjamin b 11-8-1852
    Joshua G b 11-8-1852
Ruth Anna 2w b 6-24-1827 Warren Co OH dt Joseph & Rhoda (**Whitacre**) **Hollingsworth**

Francis/Frank J b 5-21-1866 s Franklin B & Elizabeth M
Anna Laura b 8-13-1867 dt Samuel H & Margaret (**Simpson**) **Charles**
Ch: Margaret b 5-12-1895
    Elizabeth Elanor b 11-5-1898

Franklin B h Elisabeth M d 10-9-1881 bur Earlham
Ch: Phebe Ann b 3-30-1847
    Nelson A b 6-1-1849 d 10-15-1876 bur Earlham
    Orlando B b 5-29-1852
    Viola Eliza b 11-25-1856 d 6-5-1861 bur Whitewater
    Flora Ida b 10-29-1860
    Frank J b 5-21-1866

Joshua G b 11-8-1852 s Clayton & Elizabeth (**Starr**)
Flora H b 4-5-1858 dt Wm B & Rebecca (**Hadley**) **Hadley** m 8-6-1885
Ch: Wilbur H b 2-28-1893

Lewis b 1-18-1847 Randolph Co s Pleasant & Ann
Rhoda b 3-31-1847 dt Benjamin & Elizabeth (**Candler**) **Hodgin** m 5-25-1874 Middletown
Ch: Ida Eldora
    Robbie Benjamin 10-9-1886 ae 12y bur Lynn
    Cora Elizabeth

Nelson A b 6-1-1849 s Franklin B & Elizabeth M d 10-15-1876 bur Earlham
Anna Maria dt Alpheus & Phebe **Test** m 8-1872
Ch: Frederic M b 8-9-1874

Orlando B b 5-29-1852 s Franklin B & Elizabeth M m 2-1876

HURLEY
Cary L b 4-29-1868 North Burlington OH s John & Elizabeth
Bertha b 5-25-1873 College Hill Cincinnati OH dt Harlan & Anna **Edwards**

HUSSEY
John b 2-6-1838 s Stephen & Rachel (**Thornburg**)
Anna R b 10-2-1843 dt John & Anna (**Leedy**) **Fall** m 12-22-1864
Ch: Mary India b 6-17-1876

Rachel B d 5-12-1896 ae 86y 1m 15d bur Earlham

Samuel b 9-13-1854

Sarah b 3-8-1830

HUTCHENS
Owen E b 4-12-1855 Chambersburg OH s Darias & Elizabeth h Alice m 9-29-1879 Chambersburg OH
Ch: Ruth b 6-24-1894 Chambersburg OH

HUTCHINS
Harris h Jemima (**Jenkins**)
Ch: Clifford
    Bessie M H b 12-17-1880

HUTSON
Dorena/Donna b 11-1-1893 Randolph Co dt John & Catherine

HUTTON
Catherine b 6-17-1883 Benton AR dt George & Louise (**Todd**)

Edward h Lydia Alta b 11-6-1867 dt Isaac P & Lydia **Woodard**

IBAUGH
Frank h Jennie S b 7-9-1850 dt Marcus & Rhoda (**Stiddom**) **Mote**
Ch: Fannie Theodora b 8-13-1876

ILIFF
J Edgar h Flora Rosetta b 1-24-1857 dt Jeremiah & Esther **Hadley**
Ch: Wm Edgar b 2-11-1875

INGERSOL
John h Josephine
Ch: Mary Lottie
    Ada Gertrude
    Edwin Dozois b 8-14-1889

INGERSTRODT
Stella Elizabeth b 6-23-1893 Wayne Co dt Edward & Minnie

IREDELL
John S b 7-2-1839 s Samuel E & Marinetta (**Sofrain**)
Sydney/Sidney b 4-10-1845 dt George & Hannah H (**Richie**) **Dilks** d 2-3-1883 m 1-16-1867 New Paris OH
Ch: Bertha S b 4-2 1868
    Mary Ann b 11-4-1869 d 2-21-1896 bur Earlham
    Rachel S b 10-27-1876

Nathan Garwood b 9-2-1873 s Samuel Ellis & Sarah (**Dilks**)
Nora b 10-21-1872 dt James & Elizabeth (**Jefferis**) **Frame** m 6-1-1898

Samuel E h Marinetta Sherman Jones b 11-24-1812 dt John & Eleanor **Sofrain** d 10-2-1896 bur Earlham
Ch: Lizzie
    John S b 7-2-1839
    Samuel Ellis

Samuel Ellis s Samuel E & Marinetta (**Sofrain**) Sarah Ellen b dt George & Hannah (**Richie**) **Dilks** d 3-20-1881 m 1-24-1872
Ch: Nathan Garwood b 9-2-1873
    Mary Starr
    Belle

IRWIN
Cora Ann dt Henry & Tacy Ann (**Meredith**) **Henley**

ISENHOUR
Eva b 6-19-1874 Clinton Co OH dt J F & Rachel **Frazier**

JACKSON
Hazel M b 2-12-1889 Wayne Co dt Zue & Sarah Ann

Lawrence N b 4-18-1879

Tabitha b 9-30-1855 Winchester dt Arthur & Nancy **Hedgpath** m 9-17-1880 Spartansburg

JACOBS
Mabel b 2-24-1896 Noblesville dt Alfred & Ella

JACONA
Martha b 1-24-1873 Wayne Co dt Thomas & Louisa **Henson** m 2-2-1888 Richmond

JAMES
David b 5-11-1803 s Isaac
Mary b 10-30-1804 dt Isom & Margaret **Hunt**
Ch: Ruthann b 10-17-1823 d 12-5-1858 burWhitewater
　　Mary b 2-18-1825
　　Levi E b 10-20-1828
　　Atticus S b 10-16-1830
　　Alfred b 12-19-1832

Isaac P h Susanna
Ch: Sarah Emily b 10-6-1837 d 4-11-1844
　　Caroline b 8-14-1839
　　Lot B b 2-6-1842

JARRETT
Jennie b 9-13-1888 dt R L & Nancy M (**Jones**)

JAY
Allen b 10-11-1831 Miami Co OH s Isaac & Rhoda (**Cooper**)
Martha Ann b 10-22-1833 Greene Co OH dt Buddel & Elizabeth (**Welsh**) **Sleeper** d 4-28-1899 bur Earlham m 4-20-1854 Farmer's Institute
Ch: Wm C 12-22-1860 d 1-10-1898
　　Edwin S b 3-3-1863 Farmers Institute
　　Isaac E b 10-5-1865 Tippecanoe Co

Edwin S b 3-3-1863 Tippecanoe Co s Allen & Martha Ann (**Sleeper**)
Martha Evangeline b 9-3-1868 Wayne Co dt Miles & Rachel (**Bain**) **Moore** m 5-5/25/1892/93
Ch: Allen Jr b 4-14-1893 Mahaksa IA
　　Willard Bain b 8-29-1894 Mahaska IA

Eli b 2-19-1826 Miami Co OH s Walter Denny & Mary (**Macy**)
Mahala b 12-7-1827 Miami Co OH dt Moses & Sarah (**Pearson**) **Pearson** m 10-24-1849 Miami Co OH
Ch: Mary Adelaide b 1-4-1871 Wayne Co

Ethel b 2-17-1885 Miami Co OH dt E A

Henry b 8-13-1813 Warren Co OH s John & Mary (**Steddom**) d 7-26-1891
Leah (**Nicholson**) d 9-28-1838 bur Smyrna m ca 1834
Ch: Elizabeth Hanes b 9-29-1834 d 11-30-1837 bur Smyrna
　　John S b 9-2-1836 d 11-6-1836 bur Smyrna
Sarah 2w dt Joseph & Elizabeth **Strawbridge** d 5-16-1847 37y 6m 6d bur Symrna
Ch: Jesse Walter b 11-30-1841
　　Leah b 3-13-1842
　　Lindley b 4-2-1844 d 3-8-1845 bur Symrna
　　Sarah A b 5-16-1847
Priscilla 3w b 5-9-1827 d/o John & Sarah (**Grave**) **Reed** m 8-31-1848
Ch: Martha b 1850
Alice 4w dt Joseph & Sarry (**Horney**) **Hollingsworth** m 1856

Isaac E b 10-5-1865 Farmer's Institute s Allen & Martha Ann (**Sleeper**)
Anne Daisey b 11-7-1869 Cincinnati OH dt Lewis & Caroline (**Pomeroy**) **Horton** m 5-25-1893 Richmond

John b 2-27-1782 Newberry Co SC s John & Elizabeth (**Pugh**) d 9-1-1844 bur Smyrna
Mary b 9-12-1784 Newberry Co SC dt Henry & Martha (**Pearson**) **Steddom** d 8-17-1843 bur Smyrna m 12-3-1807 Warren Co OH
Ch: Martha b 9-25-1808 Warren Co OH d 8-14-1847
　　Henry b 8-31-1813 Warren Co OH d 7-26-1891
　　John S b 11-3-1816 Warren Co OH d 12-6-1831 bur Smyrna
　　Walter Denny b 6-16-1823 Warren Co OH d 5-5-1882

John A b 12-13-1847 s Walter Denny & Rebecca Ann (**Clawson**)
Sarah R (**Johnston**) m 4-1873 near Paris OH

Joseph Frederick b 11-7-1874 Richmond s Joseph Wareham & Susannah M (**Mather**) h ? (**Griffin**)

JAY (cont)
Joseph Wareham b 1-22-1825 Miami Co OH s Thomas & Eliza (**Wareham**)
Anna O Unthank b 1-21-1831 Raysville dt Samuel & Harriett (**Pickett**) **Pritchard** d 2-27-1867 m 5-2-1856
Ch: Harriet E b 8-13-1858 d 2-8-1874
　　Wm P b 9-27-1863 Raysville
Sarah Jane 2w b 11-25-1835 Raysville dt Samuel & Harriet (**Pickett**) **Pritchard** d 3-31-1869 Raysville m 1-21-1869 Raysville
Susannah M 3w wid **Hawkins** b 9-28-1842 Warren OH Co dt David & Lurena (**Steddom**) **Mather** d 12-21-1881 bur Earlham m 6-25-1872 Fountain City
Ch: Joseph Frederick b 11-7-1874 Richmond
　　Henry Mather b 11-26-1875 Richmond
　　Anna Elizabeth b 12-15-1877 Richmond
　　Mary Lurena b 7-17-1880 Richmond
Jane M 4w b 5-26-1845 Richmond dt Charles & Elizabeth (**Hill**) **Shute** m 10-16-1883 Richmond

Naomi Harrison b 3-17-1838 dt Charles & Michel (**Butler**) **Morgan** m Wayne Co

Russell b 4-20-1890 Bethel s James & Josephine (**Jeffries**)

Walter Denny b 6-16-1823 s John & Mary (**Steddom**) d 5-5-1882 bur Smyrna
Rebecca Ann b 10-29-1829 dt Amos & Melinda (**Davenport**) **Clawson** d 1-24-1877 bur Smyrna m 2-18-1847
Ch: John A b 12-13-1847
　　Mary b 12-9-1852 d 6-23-1854 bur Smyrna
　　Alice b 5-27-1855
　　Elizabeth b 2-28-1859
　　Wm Denny b 6-18-1863
　　Robert d ae 2m bur Smyrna

Wm C b 12-22-1860 s Allen & Martha Ann (**Sleeper**) d 1-10-1898
Anna F b 3-25-1863 dt Thomas & Miriam (**Ratliff**) **Newby** m 5-2-1883 Dublin
Ch: Wm Isaac b 3-22-1884

Wm Denny b 6-18-1863 s Walter Denny & Rebecca Ann (**Clawson**) h Mary Elizabeth (**Macy**) m 10-1892 Henry Co

Wm P b 9-27-1863 Raysville s Joseph Wareham & Anna O Unthank (**Pritchard**) h Mate **Power** m 11-23-1898

JEFFRIES
Abraham S b 11-21-1835 h Edith F
Ch: Lizzie
　　Anna M b 1872

Asa b 9-13-1796
Margaret b 9-17-1798
Ch: Elijah Ware b 12-23-1823
　　Rebecca Roberts b 2-3-1826
　　Wm Darling b 12-13-1827
　　Asa b 4-3-1830
　　John b 8-15-1832
　　Margaret D b 12-15-1836 d 11-3-1841 bur Orange
　　Hannah Ann b 8-8-1838
　　Benjamin E b 7-13-1840 d 12-20-1841 bur Orange

JENKINS
Amasa M b 6-1-1844 Miami Co OH s Robert & Ann (**Pearson**)
Mary Ann b 12-23-1843 Fountain City dt Luke & Mildred (**Fulghum**) **Thomas** m 5-24-1866 Fountain City
Ch: Atwood L b 12-24-1869 Fountain City
　　Olive L b 2-14-1873 Fountain City
　　Alice A b 7-21-1878 Fountain City
　　Alfred Wm b 11-23-1883 Fountain City
　　Charles Francis b 8-22-1867 Montgomery Co OH

Atwood L b 12-24-1869 Fountain City s Amasa M & Mary Ann (**Thomas**)

WHITEWATER MONTHLY MEETING
BIRTH AND DEATH RECORD

JENKINS (cont)
Mary E b 8-24-1868 Wayne Co dt Oliver & Sarah (Dennis) Test
m 10-16-1895 Wayne Co
Ch: Raymond b 6-15-1897 Wayne Co
     Naomi b 5-11-1899 Wayne Co

Charles M b 12-5-1854 s Evans H & Emeline (Lewis) h Ann E
(Dickinson) d 5-6-1890
Ellen H (Dickinson) 2w d 5-10-1897 ae 29y m 1-1-1892
Ch: Wm Wallace b 12-13-1892 d 2-22-1893 bur Earlham
     Alice Atlee b 2-1894 d 12-4-1894 bur Earlham
     Evan C b 5-1895 d 9-1895 bur Earlham
     Russell Lewis b 1-4-1898

Silas Newton b 1-24-1842 s Evans H & Martha (Shepperd) h
Sophia A (Hall) m 4-22-1868
Ch: Wm

JENNINGS
Anna dt John & Rebecca Baker

Bert b 6-15-1876 Wayne Co
Daisy b 1-5-1881 Lafayette dt Henry & Cassie Benson m 2-25-1899
Wayne Co

JESSOP
Abraham h Hannah
Ch: Jane b 9-17-1812
     Hannah b 3-16-1814
     Elizabeth b 12-29-1815
     John L b 9-3-1817
     Rachel Ann b 7-17-1819
     Allen b 11-30-1822 d 1823
     Alfred b 11-30-1822
     Ellis W b 11-15-1824

JESSUP
Albert S b 2-22-1853 s Levi & Mary h Anna (Goodrich)

David d 12-5-1879 ae 71y 7m 26d
Sarah d 10-30-1896

David d 12-10-1895 bur Earlham
Ch   Edna

Grace gdt Sarah

Jonathan b 8-18-1785 s Jacob & Rachel
Elizabeth b 8-2-1789 dt Thomas & Anna Hill
Ch: Mary b 2-5-1810
     Penninah b 9-15-1811
     Thomas b 9-8-1813

Levi b 12-26-1816 s Isaac & Ann (Hawkins) d 4-28-1899 bur Earlham
Mary 3w b 8-21-1814 d 12-26-1868 bur Earlham
Ch: Lindley M b 1-11-1844
     Lydia H b 3-22-1845 d 4-23-1852 bur Whitewater
     Thomas R b 8-7-1847
     Gulielma b 1-23-1849
     Albert S b 2-22-1853
     Eli S b 11-22-1856
Rachel M 4w d 10-21-1878 ae 51y bur Earlham

Lindley M b 1-11-1844 s Levi & Mary h Elma (Hough)
Anne (Maxwell) 2w

Milton H d 11-24-1882 bur Maple Grove

JOHN
James E h Eliza J
Ch: Mabel Claire b 2-4-1894 Jay Co
     Agnes Maria b 9-4-1895 Union City
     James L b 1-18-1898 Union City

JOHNSON
Alfred b 10-28-1825 Warren Co OH s James & Elizabeth (Griffith)
Anna Mary b 1-19-1828 dt John & Elizabeth Thorne m 3-28-1858
Warren Co OH
Ch: Anna Mary b 5-25-1868 Howard Co OH

Allen Clifford h Susan R b 11-25-1862 dt Timothy & Naomi W
(Morgan) Harrison

Benjamin b 1-26-1833 s Benjamin
Elizabeth B b 1-10-1827 dt Matthew & Ruth Barker d 9-10-1887
bur Earlham
Ch: Thomas Edward b 8-9-1859 d 9-9-1859 bur Earlham
     Benjamin Franklin b 6-21-1864 d 2-27-1865
     John Howard b 8-2-1867
     Mary Amy b 2-28-1869

Charles h Mary b 3-13-1799 Union Co SC dt Robert & Martha
Comer d 8-30-1825
Ch: Caleb b 4-8-1819
     Martha b 10-12-1820
     Betsy Ann b 4-13-1823
     Mary b 8-30-1825

Doris Silva b 9-28-1880 Randolph Co dt Wm & Martha

Fran b 7-13-1874 Lynn s George W & Cornelia
Lura b 10-1-1874 dt Wm & Elizabeth Manning
Ch: Edith

George W h Cornelia
Ch: Fran b 7-13-1874 Lynn
     Jean C
     Georgia Mae b 2-2-1887

Howard b 12-24-1871 Metamora s Joseph & Caroline
Gertrude b 8-13-1876 Barthlomew Co dt Frank & Margaret Wright

Irvin b 11-18-1875 Clinton Co OH s Joseph & M B (Bennet)
Mary D b 4-15-1876 Clinton Co OH dt Charles M & Anna E
(Timberlake) Birdsall m 11-14-1894 Wilmington OH
Ch: Harold B b 11-9-1897

James d 1-4-1860
Elizabeth d 3-12-1884 ae 84y bur Earlham
Ch: Hannah M
     Mary B
     Rebecca N
     Amy G
     Suzanne J
     James Brooks

James Brooks s James & Elizabeth h ? (Myrick)

John Howard b 8-2-1867 s Benjamin & Elizabeth (Barker) Eliza b
3-28-1871 dt Timothy & Mary (White) Nicholson m 6-18-1893
Ch: Benjamin Nicholson b 11-1-1894
     Mary Elizabeth b 3-29-1896
     Robert Howard b 12-3-1898

Josiah
Ch: James b 8-9-1812
     Rebeckah b 5-11-1814
     Rachel b 3-22-1816
     Wm b 4-30-1818
     Elijah b 9-24-1820
     Elam b 9-18-1822
     Ashla b 11-27-1824

Lura b 10-1-1764 dt Wm & Elizabeth Manning

Mary b 4-11-1811 d 4-17-1895 bur Earlham

JOHNSON (cont)
Mary J b 7-2-1877 Clinton Co OH dt Joseph & Isabell

Susan E b 4-17-1850 Highland Co OH m 8-23-1882 Clinton Co OH

Wm b 9-6-1862 s James P & Mary (**Cain**)
Mary J b 3-1-1867 dt Alfred & Cynthia (**McWhinney**) **Jones** m 9-6-1888
Ch: Aline K b 8-9-1890

JOHNSTON
Oscar B b 2-11-1848 s Asa Dillwyn & Elizabeth (**Shoaf**)
Alice Caroline b 4-20-1857 dt Windsor & Ann E (**Hartman**) **Wiggs** m 1-1-1874

JONES
Clayburn S h Margaret Jessie b 5-20-1864 Richmond dt Jesse & Mary E (**Evans**) **Kenworthy** m 5-20-1886
Ch: Morris Evans b 3-10-1887
    Jesse Raymond b 7-27-1890
    Clayburn Everett b 1-1-1892
    Howard Kenworthy b 9-9-1894

Clyde O b 12-29-1891 Delaware Co s John V & Sarah E (**Parker**)

Louis T b 7-1-1884 s Thomas & Mary Frances (**Luscomb**)

Louisa K b 9-22-1857 Clinton Co OH dt Dean & Esther (**Carpenter**) **King** m 11-16-1884 Tippecanoe Co

Micajah h Sarah
Ch: Jesse b 2-24-1806
    Ruth b 9-24-1807
    Sylvanus b 10-6-1809
    James b 9-18-1811
    Eli b 3-31-1814
    Jane b 2-19-1816
    Elihu b 5-8-1818

Morgan d 10-20-1882
Ch: Maria
    Mary

Samuel b 1798 d 1849 m 2-23-1826

Walter h Sina A b 10-1852 Clinton Co OH dt Eli & Ruth **Harvey** m 9-11-1874 Spiceland MM
Ch: Alice A b 9-6-1879 Dayton OH
    Gladys b 3-4-1883 Dayton OH
    Mary H b 11-25-1884 Dayton OH
    Edith Emma b 5-15-1886 Dayton OH
    Dona C b 7-16-1891 Dayton OH
    Elizabeth b 8-16-1893 Dayton OH
    Paul b 12-4-1886 Dayton OH
    Percy b 9-20-1895 Dayton OH
    Richard Mack b 1-3-1899 Dayton OH

JORDAN
John R b 10-13-1856
Olinda/Olive B b 3-9-1866 Wayne Co dt Peter & Priscilla E (**Cox**) **Thomas** m 12-16-1897 Middleboro

KAIN
Salt h Mary Anna b 11-25-1850 dt Phineas & Ruth Ann **Mather**
Ch: Ruth Anna b 9-16-1879 d 9-26-1880 bur Williamsburg OH

Wm d 4-18-1893 ae 43y llm h Elizabeth L (**Brown**)
Ch: Henry F d 10-9-1898 ae 19y bur Earlham
    Raymond
    Rachel Manorah b 9-3-1889
    Albert W

KALE
Wm h Martha b 6-17-1839 dt Griffith & Elizabeth **Mendenhall**
Ch: Anna Mabel b 4-7-1874

KAMINSKY
Charles E h Anna E dt Isaac & Eliza Anna (**Ong**) **Lewis** m 9-17-1873
Ch: Olive M b 1-29-1875
    Lillian V b 5-28-1877

KEATES
Harry Rowland b 9-13-1846 s John & Sarah (**Rawson**)
Elizabeth b 11-24-1849 dt John & Martha (**Carruthers**) **Robinson** m 4-15-1869
Ch: Minnie Carruthers b 9-3-1879
    Ellen Carruthers b 10-22-1881
    Lydia Ackers b 1-11-1884
    Catherine Clibborn b 5-22-1886
    Harry Swift b 5-19-1888
    Stonehill b 7-11-1890
    Frank Tabor b 8-11-1895

KELLY
Mary V b 3-3-1878 Ruple OH dt Nicholas & Henrietta

Robert h Anna P b 4-2-1832 Miami Co OH dt Moses & Sarah (**Pearson**) **Pearson** m 3-19-1863 Miami Co OH
Ch: Robert Lincoln b 3-22-1865 Douglas Co IL
    Benjamin Wade b 5-4-1875 Parke Co

Robert Lincoln b 3-22-1865 Douglas Co IL s Robert & Anna (**Pearson**)
Cecilia R dt James & Martha (**Cilley**) **Rifner** m 8-13-1890 Parke Co
Ch: Agnes Rifner b 8-16-1891 Tenason MI
    Lois Anna b 4-22-1895 Hendricks Co

Rose May b 8-30-1877 Randolph Co dt Wm Westley & Caroline (**Potter**)

KEMPTON
John h Jane
Ch: Sarah J b 11-8-1835 New York City
    Joseph Marshall b 12-28-1846 Cincinnati OH
    Alice G b 5-12-1855 Cincinnati OH

KENDAL
Thomas h Elizabeth
Ch: Wm b 8-17-1808 Springfield Guilford Co NC
    Nancy b 7-13-1810 Springfield Guilford Co NC
    Margaret b 2-16-1812 Springfield Guilford Co NC
    David b 7-30-1815
    Hannah b 6-30-1818
    Lydia b 7-11-1820 d 8-8-1844 bur Whitewater
    Cyrus b 9-21-1822
    Amy b 12-24-1823
    Dennis b 6-23-1827

KENDALL
Alsie b 9-26-1844 dt Michael & Martha R

Elizabeth d 6-13-1853 ae 63y 7m 9d bur Whitewater

Margueretta b 1-4-1850 dt Dennis & Rebecca Jane

Wm h Abigail
Ch: Mahlon b 5-2-1834
    Enos b 10-22-1835

KENNEDY
Hannah d 5-11-1884 ae 80y
Ch: Jennette d 7-6-1894
    Louisa d 12-1-1867 ae 26y bur Earlham

WHITEWATER MONTHLY MEETING
BIRTH AND DEATH RECORD

KENSLER
Ann d 1-14-1849 ae 63y 4m 3d bur Smyrna

KENWORTHY
Alice Caroline b 9-3-1853 dt Joseph & Ann

Ann d 10-10-1862 ae 55y minister

David b 11-13-1771
Dinah b 11-13-1772 d 8-28-1821
Ch: David b 11-8-1810
     Amos b 6-13-1813
     Levi b 4-14-1816
Hannah 2w b 11-21-1790
Ch: Susannah b 2-12-1826

Eli h Rachel (**Puckett**)
Ch: Harriett K b 6-6-1872
     Margaret

Jesse J h Mary P b 8-5-1825 dt Thomas & Hannah (**Pedrick**) **Evans**
Ch: Thomas Evans b 10-2-1851 Wayne Co
     Mary Alice b 3-1-1856
     Lydia Matilda b 6-2-1860
     Margaret Jesse b 5-20-1864 Richmond
     Jesse J d 8-29-1864 bur Earlham

John B h Rebecca J
Ch: Lizzie Olive b 2-5-1869
     Charles Frederic b 8-1-1872

Mary b 10-21-1819 Butler Co OH dt Luke & Rebecca (**Roberts**) **Langston**

Thomas Evans b 10-2-1851/52 Wayne Co s Jesse J & Mary P (**Evans**)
Ella b 7-3-1859 Philadelphia PA dt H L & Annie (**Levering**) **Edgar**
m 6-2-1886 Philadlephia PA
Ch: Anna Edna b 9-24-1887 Marion Co
     Mary Grace Lillian b 1-5-1890 Marion Co
     Jesse Henry b 1-15-1892 Preble Co OH
     Thomas Evans Jr b 11-9-1894 Preble Co OH
     Frank Edgar b 1-26-1897 Cass Co

Truman C b 3-17-1863 Sugar Creek IA s Isaac F & Abigail
Marianna b 9-17-1867 Cadiz OH dt Peter C & Mary T **Thomas**
m Oskaloosa IA
Ch: Helen T b 7-8-1890 Hubbard IA
     Mary b 5-31-1892 Des Moines IA
     Richard P b 4-4-1894 Des Moines IA
     Catharine b 1-3-1898 Oskaloosa IA
     Eunice Edna b 10-24-1899 Oskaloosa IA

Wm d 11-17-1877 ae 83y bur Earlham

KENYON
John h Asenith
Ch: Rebecca W b 12-12-1845
     Rodah Jane b 1-30-1849

KEPLINGER
Theodore h Rose
Ch: Carrie Ruby b 10-4-1881/7
     Leslie Martin b 7-15-1890

KERR
Jennie Agnes b 2-14-1880 dt James G & Mary S

KERSEY
Charles h Ruth b 5-16-1844 dt Samuel M H & Levina (**Cox**) **Morris**
m 12-21-1891

Richard M h Verling
Ch: Charles A d 6-1886

KERSEY (Richard M cont)
    Pliny Earl bur CA
    Margaret H

KESSLER
Clifford O b 4-9-1878 New Paris OH s Samuel & Jenus
Kathlyn b 2-5-1879 Warren Co OH dt Charles & Margaret **Collins**
m 10-11-1899 New Paris OH

KIMBLE
Wm h Emma D b 10-8-1855 dt Wm H & Mary (**Stradlin**) **Dennison**
m 8-23-1877

KING
Bertha Elizabeth dt Edward & Mary (**Evans**)

Francis Ann b 12-25-1822

Joseph A h Sarah E d 3-3-1891 ae 50y

Lewis b 5-26-1867 s Richard & Mary (**Whiteman**)
Anna Gertrude b 7-8-1873 dt Orrin S & Martha (**Tyler**) **Mote**
m 4-28-1897 Wayne Co

Thomas h Rebecca (**Clark**)
Ch: Harry E b 5-3-1898 Preble Co OH
    Henry b 5-3-1898 Preble Co OH

KINSEY
Frank b 8-26-1875 s Thomas E & Margaret (**Showalter**) h Susan dt Theodore F & Sarah Elizabeth (**Wickett**) **Candler**

Fremont h Mary Ann (**Wright**)

Isabella Louise b 2-2-1867 dt Reed & Elizabeth (**Conkle**) **Bracken**
m 4-10-1889

Thomas E h Margaret b 8-31-1848 dt Charles & Mary (**Boone**) **Shoemaker** d 9-29-1896 bur Earlham m 5-13-1873 Richmond
Ch: Frank b 8-26-1875
     Mary Alice b 1-1883
     Wm C b 2-13-1888 Richmond

KIRK
Benjamin h Elizabeth d 3-7-1825 ae 44y 10m 17d

Wm s Benjamin & Elizabeth d 7-14-1822 ae 13y 6m 2d

KIRKMAN
Alva h Rebecca (**Werts**)
Ch: James M b 6-16-1857 Guilford Co NC
     Sarah Elizabeth b 2-9-1858 Greensboro NC

Alva b 4-19-1815 Guilford Co NC h Ella May
Ch: Bessie Eveline
     Mattie
     Lula
     Henry

James M b 6-16-1857 Guilford Co NC s Alva & Rebecca (**Werts**)
Flora b 2-1-1855 Wayne Co dt Jacob & Louisa (**Nelson**) **Werts** m 9-20-1875 Wayne Co
Ch: Wm R b 9-18-1894 Wayne Co
     Cyrus Edward b 5-4-1897 Wayne Co

M L h Lela H dt Alfred & Keziah (**Overman**) **Hadley**
Ch: Murel b 9-30-1898 Wayne Co

KITSELMAN
John h Margaret M
Ch: Marietta b 8-9-1867
     Albert Leroy b 6-8-1869
     Franklin E b 4-18-1871
     Alfred W b 5-27-1874

KLEMMANS
Charles h Grace b 4-4-1883 dt John E & Elizabeth/Mary **(Jenkinson) Wolfe**

KNOTT
Wm d 6-1897 ae 60y h Isabel

KOONS
Ghasper d 11-8-1820 ae 61y bur Whitewater
Abigail d 2-16-1850 ae 78y 17d bur Whitewater

Jeremiah d 7-10-1877 ae 78y 17d bur Earlham

Jesse d 1-10-1836 ae 21y 7m 12d bur Whitewater

Wm d 2-28-1838 ae 38y 10m 15d bur Whitewater

KRAMER
Lillian Elizabeth b 11-20-1892 dt Charles G & Mary J d 1-29-1893 bur Earlham

KRICK
Elizabeth May b 10-10-1873 dt Benjamin & Adaline **(Elmore) Lunsford**

LACKEY
Gerold b 7-20-1890 Piketon OH s John

LAFLIN
Wm w Agatha b 12-29-1830 Topeka KS m 12-1878

LAIRD
George Andrew b 3-1-1866 h Sadie **(Brown)**
Ch: Mildred Elizabeth b 5-8-1895 Preble Co OH
Margery (Smith) 2w b 6-20-1879 m 9-19-1899 Preble Co OH

LAMAR
Franklin b 1-13-1870 s Nathan & Alice **(Billheimer)**
Zetelia b 4-29-1873 dt Orange V & Ida **(Morgan) Lemon** m 6-6-1894

LAMB
Hosea h Mary
Ch: Restore b 7-28-1819
    Lydia b 11-24-1821 d 9-4-1823
    Elizabeth b 2-4-1824
    Rhoda b 10-16-1826
    Anna b 1-21-1830
    Sarah b 9-29-1832
    John b 1-18-1835

Isaac h Rebecca **(Jarrett)**
Ch: Vashti b 10-9-1843
    Rosa b 2-19-1845
    Thomas b 3-3-1847
    John b 5-10-1850 d 5-23-1853 bur Whitewater
    Isaac Newton b 1-20-1853
    Ann Rebecca b 1-20-1853 d 2-18-1853 bur Whitewater
    Albert Smith b 9-4-1855

Isaac Newton b 1-20-1853 s Isaac & Rebecca **(Jarrett)** h Angia **(Connaway)**

Josiah b 2-11-1839

Jane C b 2-1-1839

Nellie R b 8-3-1897 dt Franklin H & Mary **(Emmons) Bond**

Thomas h Margaret d 9-22-1845 ae 63y 10m 16d bur Whitewater

Thomas s Phenias & Dorotha h Sarah dt John & Letitia **Smith** d 7-24-1833 ae 42y 14d m 8-4-1813 bur Whitewater

LAMB (Thomas cont)
Ch: John b 2-10-1819 d 4-22-1834 bur Whitewater
    Isaac b 4-21-1821
    Phineas b 9-5-1824
    Henry b 8-18-1826
    Elizabeth b 2-3-1830

LAMM
Flossie L b 2-14-1874 Wayne Co dt Israel & Martha J **(Livengood)**

Iris L b 2-1891 Richmond dt Ullan/Ulin & Sarah

LAMOTT
Gertie P b 1-20-1884 Wayne Co dt Jacob & Emma

LANE
Charles h Corilla M b 11-5-1860 dt Ellwood & Ann P **(Watts) Hadley**

Lydia d 1875 ae 64y
Ch: Phebe

Sarah b 4-23-1852 Warren Co OH dt Theodore & Sarah Ann **(Bower)**

LANGDON
Rhoda Alice b 11-8-1851 dt Samuel Francis & Elizabeth D **(Hiatt) Fletcher** m 4-3-1884 Cincinnati OH

LANNING
Ann M b 12-22-1891 Franklin Co dt Edwin & Jenny M

LAWRENCE
Christopher E b 5-20-1862 h Mary E **(Woolman)**
Ch: Alvin Leroy
    Anna Leota
    Benjamin Otho
    Bertha Mary b 8-13-1896
    Robert

Daniel W h Elizabeth **(Windle)**
Ch: Wm E b 4-15-1883
    Mary W b 5-19-1886

Hannah d 6-23-1899 ae 62y bur Earlham

Henry J h Lottie **(Conner)** m 5-13-1896

LAWSON
Everett b 9-30-1895 Anderson TX s Frank & Maggie

LEBO
Elmer h Mary E b 4-29-1868 dt Robert & Minerva **(Hill) Hodgin** m 12-30-1891
Ch: Willard b 11-12-1899

LEE
Charles F b 11-24-1877 s T Riley & Ruth **(Allen)**

Nathan h Hannah
Ch: Ann b 4-2-1808
    Charlotte b 7-28-1811
    Ishmael b 5-23-1815
    Hiram b 2-12-1818
    Henry b 9-1-1821
    Nathan Jr b 8-19-1825 d 11-21-1832 bur Orange

T Riley h Ada E b 4-15-1856 Jamestown NC dt Aaron & Rhoda **(Mendenhall) Elliott** m 12-4-1890 High Point NC

Wm P b 12-19-1849 s David & Susan **(Paine)**
Margaret E b 12-12-1854 dt Emmanuel & Lottie **(Case) Hubler** m 7-1-1872
Ch: Melva D b 9-12-1873

WHITEWATER MONTHLY MEETING
BIRTH AND DEATH RECORD

LEEDS
Ruby b 7-24-1893 dt George Elsworth & Eliza J (**Ireton**)

Vincent d 12-28-1841 ae 85y 4m 29d bur Whitewater

LeFEVER
Wm M h Rebecca C
Ch: Frederic Smith
     Alfred Henry
     Ellen Maria

LEHMAN
David b 4-14-1837
Harriett B b 4-14-1842

LEWIS
Caroline (**Davenport**) d 1871 bur Lafayette

Charles h Phebe b 10-3-1882 Wayne Co dt Nathan & Sarah **Blue**

Clark E b 4-29-1843 s Jesse & Hannah (**Hussey**)
Emma E b 5-10-1856 Wayne Co dt Seth & Martha Ann (**Hill**) **Brown** m 1-1879
Ch: Sarah T b 10-29-1879
     Esther A b 8-26-1882
     Jesse B b 8-22-1884
     Seth B b 3-16-1886 Wayne Co

Isabella M b 6-19-1889 Wayne Co dt Douglas J & Roxa J (**Minor**)

Nathan h Rachel
Ch: Josiah T b 7-10-1819
     Sarah b 12-10-1820
     Martha .b 3-1822
     Rachael M b 10-6-1823
     Susannah b 12-25-1825
     Stephen b 8-1-1829
     Emmaline b 4-23-1830
     John Milton b 8-25-1831
     Tennison b 12-31-1832

Wm h Ann S d 3-8-1878 ae 72y bur Earlham
Ch: Margaret Ann
     Joseph E
     Lucy J

LINDEMUTH
Victoria b 5-13-1858 dt John & Elenora (**Hoffman**)

LINDLEY
Harlow b 5-31-1875 Parke Co s Mahlon & Martha (**Newlin**)

LIPSEY
J Herbert b 4-27-1873

LISTER
Wm L h Ellen B
Ch: Ethel L b 11-5-1889 Delaware Co
     Josephine b 5-8-1892 Delaware Co

LITTLE
David h Martha dt Frederick & Piety (**Parker**) **Fulgham** wid Peter **Bond** m 1-1-1885

Orlando H h Jennette b 1-19-1872 Wayne Co dt Cornelius & Elizabeth Ann **Bond** m 2-2-1899 Wayne Co

LOCKWOOD
Ruth dt Fred & Ruth

LOHR
Mason h Viretta (**Mendenhall**)
Ch: Ida L b 7-28-1881
     Alma b 2-19-1884

LONG
Frank J b 9-8-1887 Spencerville OH s John & Eliza

Lily J b 12-10-1892 Montgomery Co KY dt Joseph & Lucy

LOSEY
J S h Phebe Ann b 3-20-1847 dt Franklin B & Elizabeth M **Hunt** m 8-1873

LOTT
Louis Everett b 9-12-1886 Greenville OH s Samuel & Harriet

LUNSFORD
Benjamin F h Adaline (**Elmore**)
Ch: Wm W b 3-21-1869 d 10-11-1874
     Cora Mead b 12-15-1870
     Flora Eva b 10-11-1872 d 11-3-1872
     Elizabeth May b 10-10-1873
     Martha Pearl b 9-2-1875
     Nellie H b 8-3-1877
     Charles M b 3-21-1879 Wayne Co
Mattie dt Samuel & Jane **Jones**

McBETH
Donald h Beth Margaret b 1-30-1887 Richmond dt Benjamin & Catherine **Fye**

McCLUER
George F b 4-29-1850 s Samuel & Rebecca (**Roberts**) h Eunice m 2-19-1882
Ch: David N
     Melissa J

McCLURG
Andrew b 6-11-1881 Fleming Co KY s Jack & Rilda

McCOY
Minnie b 8-4-1874 Franklin Co dt John & Melinda **Nabb** m 5-4-1892 Franklin Co

McCULLOUGH
Ella R b 9-3-1854 Butler Co OH dt John H & Martha J **Smith** m 8-6-1881 Butler Co OH

McDONALD
Wm b 7-8-1846 s Enos & Dorcas (**Elleman**)
Caroline b 12-10-1851 dt Wm & Mary (**Rhatchamel**) **Burns** m 8-19-1868
Ch: Orissa b 10-8-1871

McGEE
Emma E b 2-28-1892 Richmond dt Wm & Minnie

McGRAW
George W h Annie M
Ch: Stewart M b 9-16-1868
     Charles F b 11-23-1870
     Martha E b 2-2-1872
     Flora Alice b 2-18-1874

McKEE
Wm d 10-26-1875 bur Earlham h Catharine
Ch: Margaret Ellen b 6-12-1873

McKISSON
Wm Douglas b 8-21-1872 Perrysville OH s J D & Lydia (**Threewits**)

McMATH
Guy b 5-9-1893 Union Co s D H & Anna

McMILLAN
Viola Hanna b 12-23-1882 dt Joshua F & Mary Elizabeth (**Lewis**)

McMILLEN
Jane d 11-7-1850 ae 75y 8m 18d bur Whitewater

McMILLER
Joseph b 4-21-1896 Spartansburg s Andrew & Minnie (**Thay**)

McNUTT
Lemuel C b 2-12-1884 Wayne Co

McPHERSON
Mary Edith b 9-25-1872 Brown Co OH dt Adrian & Louisa

McTAGGERT
Alpheus b 4-7-1842
Caroline b 6-8-1850
Ch: Emma b 4-25-1873
    James R b 1-1-1875
    Anna b 7-15-1878 d 9-21-1879 bur Earlham
    Clara b 2-10-1882

MACKIE
James h Rebecca
Ch: George
    Grace
    Edith d 10-10-1898 ae 21 bur New Paris OH

MACY
Stephen b 12-4-1778 s Enoch & Anna
Rebecca b 6-23-1776 dt Francis & Catharine **Barnard**
Ch: Anna b 6-25-1802 NC
    Catharine b 9-13-1804 NC d 9-13-1804
    John G b 12-28-1806 NC
    Eli b 10-31-1808 OH d 6-14-1830 bur banks Wabash (drowned)
    Francis B b 9-18-1810 OH
    Stephen Jr b 2-18-1813 OH
    Eunice B b 7-13-1822 OH

MADDOCK
John C d 4-19-1889 ae 65y 6m bur Earlham
Rachel H b 8-22-1830
Ch: Anna B d 7-30-1884 ae 16y
    Martha Ellen

Francis b 5-22-1821 Preble Co OH

Mildred Elizabeth b 5-8-1895

MALES
Samuel R b 1-25-1841 h Jennie
Ch: Maud Bertha

MANFORD
Carl Monroe b 3-1-1885

MANLEY
Wm F h Lydia (**Gordon**)
Ch: Herbert H b 9-26-1872
    Esther b 10-24-?
    Lydia b 11-17-?
    Pearl C b 8-2-1888
    Estelle
    Ernest G
    Ruth A

MANN
Earl H h Mary Stuart b 6-19-1879 dt E Gurney & Eliza (**Stuart**) Hill

MARCHARD
Fred h Mary dt Morgan **Jones** m 1875

MARINE
Laura b 9-1882 Randolph Co dt John & Hanna

MARKLEY
F Clindore h Mae b 7-12-1874 Milton dt Edw & Ella **Neff** m 10-12-1892 Cambridge City
Ch: Russel b 6-3-1894 East Germantown
    Ralph Herbert b 1-2-1898 East Germantown

MARMON
Benjamin h Rachel
Ch: David b 3-26-1809 NC
    Lydia b 2-1-1814 NC
    Pricilla b 9-19-1816 NC
    Rebecca b 4-28-1819 NC
    James D b 2-15-1822 NC
    Benjamin F b 8-22-1824 NC
    Melinda b 3-1-1827 NC

Charles M d 10-5-1899 bur Earlham
Anna b 8-27-1842 dt Jonathan & ? (**Morrow**) Hawkins

Daniel W s James W & Hannah C Elizabeth b 4-25-1849 dt Walter F & Susan (**Mabie**) Carpenter m 8-18-1870 Richmond
Ch: Walter Carpenter b 8-25-1872
    Mary Townsend b 12-11-1873 d 7-4-1874 bur Earlham
    Howard C b 5-24-1876

James W d 7-28-1849 bur Whitewater
Hannah C 2w d 8-29-1849 ae 36y 7m 21d bur Whitewater
Ch: Wm d 9-10-1848 ae 21y 6m 2d bur Whitewater
    Daniel H

MAROT
Henry h Lucy A b 10-25-1836
Ch: Jennie M b 2-11-1864
    Bessie L b 12-2-1874

MARQUIS
Mary b 9-25-1843 dt James Jr & Elizabeth (**Unthank**) Cockayne
Ch: Harry
    Charley
    Olive

MARRIS
Elias H s John & Ann d 8-10-1838 bur Whitewater

MARSHALL
Abbie b 3-13-1853 dt Evan & Rachel (**Tolbert**)

Alonzo h Margaret b 2-22-1842 dt Absolom & Susan (**Baldwin**) **Wright** m 1-11-1866
Ch: Elsie M b 6-9-1874 Madison Co

MARTIN
Alice d 2-6-1891 ae 25y bur Earlham

Isaac N h Elizabeth S
Ch: John L b 1-1-1841 d 2-3-1841 bur Smyrna
    Sarah J b 10-17-1842 d 9-9-1845 bur Smyrna
    Ruth Anna b 1-29-1845
    Elmina B b 4-20-1847
    Alpheus d ae 11m bur Smyrna
    Thomas Colwell b 9-18-1851
    Benjamin LeRoy b 1-23-1854

James b 8-25-1876 s Lot W & Matilda

MARTINDALE
James h Lydia (**White**)
Ch: John b 10-10-1849 West Grove
    Emma b 6-10-1852 Wayne Co

John b 10-10-1849 West Grove s James & Lydia (**White**) h Amanda

WHITEWATER MONTHLY MEETING
BIRTH AND DEATH RECORD

MARVEL
Charles b 3-28-1864 s Josiah P & Harriett (**Pepper**)
Mary Amy b 1-28-1869 dt Benjamin & Elizabeth (**Barker**) **Johnson**
m 10-18-1893
Ch: Josiah Phillip b 4-17-1896
     Elizabeth Johnson b 10-5-1897

MASON
Mandus E h Anna Mary b 9-17-1857 dt Seth & Martha (**Hill**) **Brown** m 9-22-1886

MATHER
David L h Lurena (**Steddom**)
Ch: Susan M b 9-29-1842 Warren Co OH d 12-21-1881 bur Earlham
     Samuel b 1-22-1850 Warren Co OH

John P b 3-5-1846 s Phineas & Ruth Ann h Ella (**Hough**)
m Fountain City

Louisa A d 3-19-1898 ae 72 y bur Earlham

Phineas d 2-1886 ae 68y bur Earlham
Ruth Ann d 7-16-1875 ae 48y 4m 8d bur Earlham
Ch: John P b 3-5-1846
     Elizabeth C b 11-3-1847
     Susanna S b 7-9-1849 d 8-18-1880 bur Earlham
     Mary Anna b 11-25-1856

Samuel b 1-22-1850 Warren Co OH s David L & Lurena (**Steddom**) h Lillian
Ch: Irene b Wayne Co

MATIX
John Sr h Mary
Ch: John E
     Mary A
     Laura Arminta
     Alexander Alfred
     Caroline

MATTHEWS
Marie L b 5-15-1848 Fayette Co OH dt Amos & Susannah (**Wright**)
m 12-6-1870 Fayette Co OH

Mary d 1-18-1884 bur Earlham
Ch: Anna d 8-8-1884 bur Earlham
     Mary Grace

MATTOX
Mabel b 5-3-1892 dt John & Carolina

MAUDLIN
Benjamin h Leah
Ch: Wright b 3-26-1797
     Samuel b 3-12-1799 d 5-26-1813 bur Whitewater
     Peninnah b 11-2-1801
     Thomas b 1-23-1804
     John b 1-18-1806
     Sarah b 3-10-1809
     Rachel b 12-16-1812
     Susaner b 2-14-1816

MAULE
Thomas d 1873 bur Maple Grove
Priscilla d 1873 bur Maple Grove
Ch: Benjamin
     John
     Wm
     Isaac d 8-25-1875

MAXWELL
Hugh W b 11-8-1820 s John & Hannah (**Whitlock**)
Ruth Ann b 10-17-1823 dt David & Mary (**Hunt**) **James** d 12-5-1858 bur Whitewater
Ch: Mary b 3-18-1841
     Sarah b 2-15-1843
     Caroline b 5-22-1845
     Emiline b 5-3-1847 d 12-22-1858 bur Whitewater
     Ann b 10-17-1849
     Lindley H b 6-17-1852
     Albert D b 4-1-1857 d 9-9-1880 bur Las Vegas NM
Miriam Allinson 2w b 1-9-1821 New Garden NC dt Elijah & Naomi (**Hiatt**) **Coffin**

John M b 8-17-1826 s John & Hannah (**Whitlock**) h Nancy Jane
Ch: Emily P b 1-27-1857
Mary Anna 2w b 10-9-1839 dt Robert C & Ann (**Rambo**) **Moore** d 8-3-1867 bur West Grove
Ch: Robert Moore b 7-23-1864
     Sarah H b 12-26-1866

John S b 12-31-1878 Grand Blanc MI s Samuel & Amanda

MAY
Edward/Edwin Franklin b 5-2-1880 Lawrence s John C & Sarah E

MAYHEW
John M b 5-7-1873 Wayne Co s Lorenzo & Elizabeth
Maria G b 3-27-1872 Warren Co OH dt Americus B & Emma Y **Gooch** m 6-22-1893 Newport KY
Ch: Margery b 6-1-1895 Wayne Co
     Leah/Leslie C
     John M

MEEK
Elizabeth b 10-23-1854

MENDENHALL
Bertha E b 12-6-1884 dt Allen H & Esther Jane (**Irish**)

Edmund d 9-27-1881 ae 46y 2m 21d bur Smyrna

Edwin h Jeanette J b 8-14-1859 dt Samuel S & Anna (**Davenport**) **Richie** m 2-17-1882

Edwin H h Grace b 3-13-1870 dt Irvin J & Sarah (**McWhinney**) **Brown** m 12-6-1899

Freddy b 12-28-1866

Gardner b 9-16-1804 s Caleb & Susannah (**Gardner**) d 3-18-1875/8
Elizabeth 2w b 5-29-1832 dt Davis & Elizabeth (**Macy**) **Thayer**
m West Milton OH
Ch Alice Thayer b 12-8-1864
    Cora Elisabeth b 10-24-1866
    Adella Gardner b 11-11-1868
    Davis Thayer b 2-25-1872
    Everett F b 3-10-1875

George LaFonte b 8-19-1899 Richmond s Mark & Pearl C

Griffith d 2-13-1878 ae 85y h Elizabeth (**Swindle**)
Ch: Bentley b 3-2-1821
     Reese J b 12-13-1823
     Wm G b 8-19-1825 d 7-20-1849 bur Whitewater
     Caleb S b 5-8-1830
     John A b 10-21-1833 d 2-10-1878 bur Earlham
     Findley H b 9-25-1835
     Martha b 6-17-1839

Henry d 8-14-1891

James b 1-2-1806 s Daniel & Deborah (**Horney**) d 9-12-1893

MENDENHALL (James cont)
Millicent b 11-5-1810 dt Joseph & Hannah (**Ballinger**) **Coffin**
d 3-30-1892
Ch: Stephen C b 8-28-1828
    Rebecca Ann b 2-25-1831
    Susan B b 4-24-1833
    Olinda b 8-22-1836
    Sarah E b 6-4-1839
    Hannah B b 12-4-1841
    Joseph Coffin b 2-20-1845
    James Carver b 8-28-1852

John b 8-19-1806 s Aaron & Lydia (**Richardson**) d 9-7-1868 bur Earlham
Hannah b 4-1-1814 dt Wm & Martha (**Vickers**) **Milhous** m 9-30-1835 Belmont OH
Ch: Wm b 10-12-1836 Columbiana Co OH
    Lydia A b 3-7-1839 d 3-19-1865 bur Earlham
    Martha b 4-15-1842
    Charles H b 8-27-1848 d 11-20-1868 bur Earlham
    Henry W

John A b 10-21-1833 s Griffith & Elizabeth (**Swindle**) d 2-10-1878 bur Earlham h Julia dt Jesse & Mary (**Jones**) **Stubbs**
Ch: Morris H b 10-17-1870

Joseph Edwin b 10-15-1856 Wayne Co s Reese J & Lydia h Janetta (**Richie**)

Kirk h Naomi Jane dt Philander & Rachel (**Boone**) **Allen**

Reese J b 12-13-1823 s Griffith & Elizabeth (**Swindle**)
Lydia b 11-7-1827 d 11-2-1890 bur Fairbury NE
Ch: Wm b 10-6-1850
    Alice Ann b 5-6-1852
    Albert b 9-5-1854
    Joseph Edwin b 10-15-1856 Wayne Co
    Anna Mary b 8-2-1859
    Ellis G b 3-29-1863
    Elizabeth H b 8-8-1865
    John R b 9-19-1868
    Flora Estella b 2-8-1872

Stephen C b 5-11-1828 s James & Millicent (**Coffin**)
Rachel A (**Johnson**) b 10-20-1833 d 2-17-1876 bur Earlham
Ch: Walter L b 8-28-1855
    Emma R
    Olivia Stevens b 6-6-1858
    Rhoda Elma b 11-30-1863
    Herbert b 7-28-1864 d 8-4-1864
Alice (**Vining**) 2w

Wm b 10-12-1836 Columbia Co OH s John & Hannah (**Milhous**)
Eliza D H b 10-12-1856 Warren Co OH dt Edwin & Jemima (**Doan**) **Hadley** m 11-29-1886 Wayne Co
Ch: Olive Jane b 2-28-1888 Richmond
    Wm Edwin b 12-3-1889 Richmond
    Jesse Carpenter b 7-7-1894

Wm b 10-6-1850 s Reese J & Lydia h Mary E (**Jones**) m 9-1876 Marion

Wm O h Lydia J b 2-28-1844 dt Thomas & Margaret (**Dillen**) **Haworth** m 9-15-1860
Ch: Edwin H b 11-11-1868
    Georgia L b 7-24-1876

Wm O'Neil b 4-28-1834 MD

MENKE
Frank H h Bessie Pormelia b 7-20-1872 dt Eli & Sarah (**Ham**) **Endsley** m 3-10-1895
Ch: Sarah Ruth b 3-21-1897
    Glenn Wilson b 6-10-1899

METSKER
Mary A (**Elwood**)

MICHOLLAND
Melissa J b 1-1-1837

MILBY
Anna Mary b 8-2-1859 dt Reese J & Lydia **Mendenhall**

MILES
Charles Homer b 5-2-1877 Boston MA s Cornelius V & Elvira (**Kerr**)

Cornelius h Margaret b 11-3-1846
Ch: Jesse Clark

Rachel E b 8-6-1842 Miami Co OH dt Samuel & Elizabeth (**Neal**) d 2-28-1898 bur Earlham

MILLER
Annie M b 1-20-1864 Richmond dt Fred & Barbara

David h Rebecca b 6-22-1841 dt James & Elizabeth (**Unthank**) **Cockayne**
Ch: Viola b 9-1-1865
    Minnie

Emma J b 5-28-1857 Mahaska Co IA s Samuel & Lydia Jane (**Prickett**) **Jones** m 11-2-1882 Wayne Co

Grace A b 1-21-1883 Wayne Co dt Andrew & Jennie

J C h Margaret b 11-24-1872 dt George & Minerva **Jones** m 1890 Winchester
Ch: Maud b 10-30-1891 MI

John G b 7-26-1856 s James & Nancy (**Harris**)
Esther b 6-27-1868 dt Isaac & Mary (**Randall**) **Wright** m 3-17-1886

Parmelia b 10-12-1832

Paul D h Annie Mary b 6-30-1879 dt Charles & Fannie E **Newman**

MILLS
John h Betty (**Compton**)
Ch: Wm C b 4-9-1821
    Amos b 8-9-1822
    John b 1-27-1824
    Elizabeth b 11-20-1825
    Rebecca M b 1-28-1828 d 8-18-1869 bur Smyrna
    Henry F b 12-5-1829
    Joseph b 8-30-1832
    George

Joseph John b 7-21-1847 s Abner & Hannah (**Furnas**)
Emily W dt Michael **Wanzer** m 8-28-1877
Ch: Gertrude b 10-24-1878 Marion Co

Samuel C b 2-21-1859 Marion Co s Amos & Mary Elizabeth (**Cook**)
Flora P b 5-11-1863 Parke Co dt Lot & Asenath (**Canaday**) **Pickett** m 10-24-1889 Parke Co

Thomas H b 10-30-1819 Miami Co s Hugh & Lydia (**Hasket**) d 3-18-1897 Centreville h Susan (**Merideth**) m 1848

MIRZA
Youel Benjamin b 12-23-1888 s Moshie & Rachel (**Nweeya**)

MITCHELL
Andrew F s Parley & Phebe (**Lewis**) h Martha dt Samuel S & Polly (**Morris**) **Jordan** m 9-10-1874 Parke Co
Ch: Frances H b 3-21-1886
    Martha M b 6-11-1899

WHITEWATER MONTHLY MEETING
BIRTH AND DEATH RECORD

MOFFITT
Abijah b 1-24-1824 s Charles & Elizabeth d 3-30-1891 bur Earlham
Lydia (**Townsend**) d 1-2-1894 bur Earlham
Ch: Charles F b 1-22-1857
    Anna F b 7-8-1860
    Mary Elisabeth b 5-20-1862 d 12-3-1863 bur Whitewater

Charles d 12-23-1845 ae 71y 2m 28d bur Whitewater
Elizabeth d 11-30-1860 ae 76y 6m bur Whitewater
Ch: Hugh b 3-1-1806
    Jeremiah b 8-16-1808
    Tacy b 2-24-1810
    Eunice b 3-19-1811 d 1-31-1880 bur Earlham
    Hannah b 1-8-1813
    John b 8-30-1814
    Mary b 7-19-1816
    Nathan b 11-3-1817 d 10-6-1846 bur Whitewater
    Ruth b 12-22-1819 d 3-24-1892
    Elizabeth b 1-3-1822 d 5-4-1883 bur Earlham
    Abijah b 1-24-1824
    —— b 1-18-1826
    Anna b 9-20-1828

Charles d 1-8-1893 ae 47y 10m 16d s Hugh & Sarah h Lucinda (**Grist**)
Ch: Oliver Chester b 4-24-1869
    Emma Estelle
    Arthur Clyde
    Hugh C
    Herschell P

Hannah d 8-28-1829 ae 35/36y bur Whitewater

Hugh b b 3-1-1806 s Charles & Elizabeth d 8-9-1885 bur Earlham
Sarah b 11-14-1892 ae 84y bur Earlham
Ch: Charles d 1-8-1893 ae 47y 10m 16d
    Ann Elizabeth

Jeremiah d 7-31-1825 ae 53y 10m 2d bur Whitewater h Margery
Ch: David b 1-11-1825
    Hannah b 3-10-1826 posthumous

Oliver Chester b 4-24-1869 s Charles & Lucinda (**Grist**) h Sarah May
Ch: Paul Appleton
    Hugh Charles b 4-1898

MOODY
Olive A b 12-4-1864 dt John Henley & Phebe A (**Branson**) Hill

MOON
Anna Elizabeth b 12-6-1840

Elizabeth b 4-29-1868

Hiram E b 3-7-1830
Almina b 12-11-1832 d 1-21-1876 bur Earlham
Ch: Mary L b 2-22-1854 d 5-28-1874 bur Earlham
    Ossian C b 8-31-1856
    Margaret b 7-6-1864
Ann Elisabeth (**Moffitt**) 2w m 6-19-1877
Ch: Winfred Garfield b 2-22-1881

Ossian C b 8-31-1856 s Hiram E & Almina
Eleanor T b 8-22-1855

Thomas H b 11-12-1888 IN s Larken & Malinda

MOORE
Benjamin b 1-1-1837 h Jennie (**Haisley**)

Benjamin B d 10-23-1857
Lydia d 12-31-1852

MOORE (Benjamin B cont)
Ch: Ann b 7-12-1808 Gloucester Co NJ
    Ira b 1-9-1810 Gloucester Co NJ
    Matilda b 11-8-1811 Gloucester Co NJ
    Chalkley b 10-9-1813 Gloucester Co NJ
    Caroline b 5-28-1816 Gloucester CO NJ
    Rachel b 8-14-1818 Gloucester Co NJ
    Harriet b 1-21-1821
    Hannah b 2-21-1823
    Ruth b 3-3-1825

Charles W b 2-4-1875 Randolph Co s John F & Jane
Martha A b 10-14-1875 Preble Co OH dt F B & Isabell **Bunger**
m 1-12-1897/99 Randolph Co

Elizabeth A b 6-30-1836

Jacob d 4-9-1891 ae 71y 6 1/2m
Jane (**Elliott**) b 10-17-1826
Ch: Hattie Elliott

John F b 3-13-1837/2-9-1838 Montgomery Co s Jacob & Tacy (**Butler**)
Elizabeth A b 6-18-1836 Montgomery Co dt Peter & ? (**Whitacre**) **Binford** m 11-15-1860 Montgomery Co
Ch: Willis b 12-12-1861
    Lineas A b 7-2-1865 Montgomery Co
    Martha/Mary J b 3-5-1867 Montgomery Co
    Otis J b 1-21-1876 Montgomery Co

Joseph b 2-29-1832 Washington Co s John Parker & Martha (**Cadwalader**)
Deborah Ann b 10-8-1837 Warren Co OH dt Joseph & Catharine (**Stanton**) Stanton m 9-6-1863
Ch: Joseph Edward b 7-12-1864 Richmond
Mary T 2w b 8-3-1847 Greene Co OH dt Thos & Ruth (**Greene**) **Thorne** m 3-28-1873 Selma OH
Ch: Anna Mary b 1-5-1873 Wayne Co
    Grace Ella b 5-5-1876 Wayne Co
    Lucy H b 9-1-1879 Wayne Co
    Willard Embree b 8-8-1884 Wayne Co

Joseph b 9-19-1880 s Samuel A & Gulielma

Joshua d 2-2-1843 bur Whitewater

Josiah d 5-27-1853
Elizabeth d 2-14-1854
Ch: Jonathan b 7-6-1806 d 8-27-1884
    Lydia b 12-19-1808
    Isabel b 6-19-1811
    Anne b 11-21-1813
    Susannah b 3-10-1816
    Jesse b 11-13-1817
    Elias b 8-27-1820
    Leah b 2-1-1822 d 2-13-1822
    Miriam b 7-18-1823 d 10-9-1826

Linias A b 7-1-1865 s John F & Elizabeth A (**Binford**) h Margaret (**Steele**) m Richmond

Lydia dt James d 11-1-1884

Martha Evangeline b 9-3-1868 dt Miles & Rebecca (**Bain**)

Melva D b 9-12-1873 dt Wm P & Margaret (**Hubler**) Lee m 9-23-1899

Nathan Andrew b 5-3-1833 s Robert & Ann R (**Rambo**) h Anna G (**Gilbert**)
Ch: Thomas E
    Herbert N
    Mary E
    Catharine G
    Ann E

MOORE (cont)
Robert b 2-13-1808 s Andrew & Ann d 3-30-1887 bur Earlham
Ann R b 7-3-1809 dt Nathan & Elizabeth **Rambo** d 8-2-1891 bur Earlham
Ch: Nathan Andrew b 5-3-1833
    Ann Elizabeth b 1-16-1834 d 8-3-1867 bur West Grove
    Mary Anna b 10-9-1839

Wm h Ann
Ch: Samuel b 6-18-1818
    Thomas b 7-30-1820
    Achasa b 7-18-1822
    Truman b 7-19-1824
    Sarah b 7-3-1827 d 8-6-1827 bur Ridge
    Margaret F b 5-14-1828

Wm A d 12-23-1880 ae 40y bur Earlham h Lydia P
Ch: Amanda b 5-17-1877

Wm E b 6-16-1854 Wayne Co s Jacob & Christina
Ida M b 3-25-1859 dt Joseph & Mary **Long** d Wayne Co m 12-25-1877

Willis b 12-12-1861 s John F & Elizabeth A (**Binford**) h Fannie (**Campbell**) m Montgomery Co OH

MOORMAN
Joel H b 10-18-1861 s Richmond & Mary (**Morris**) m 10-6-1886 Randolph Co

Levi b 5-2-1849 s Richmond & Mary (**Morris**)
Martha C b 5-5-1849 dt John & Nancy (**Bangham**) **Coggeshall** m 2-13-1870

Richmond h Mary (**Morris**)
Ch: Harriett b 9-9-1841
    Sarah b 7-7-1846
    Levi b 5-2-1849
    Peninah b 7-8-1855
    Nancy Hannah b 3-26-1858
    Joel H b 10-18-1861
    Mary Alice b 6-16-1864

MORFIELD
Francis h Alice A dt Amasa & Mary Ann (**Thomas**) **Jenkins**

MORGAN
Benjamin s Charles & Susanna h Naomi d 7-8-1811 ae 37y 11m 14d bur Whitewater
Ch: Micajah b 11-10-1798
    Charles b 2-18-1801
    Isaac b 12-31-1803
    Katherine b 8-10-1806 d 4-18-1808 bur Whitewater
    Susannah b 11-6-1809
Elizabeth 2w dt James & Ruth **Johnson** m 9-2-1812 Whitewater
Ch: Hannah b 4-24-1814

Benjamin F h Anna H
Ch: Naomi W
    Gertrude
    Charles O d 10-11-1882

Charles d 8-7-1864 ae 63y bur Earlham
Michel (**Butler**) d 8-19-1888 ae 86y 4m 19d bur Earlham
Ch: Naomi W Harrison b 3-17-1838
    Benjamin F

Lucille b 7-5-1899 Spartansburg dt Thomas B & Nina

Micajah d 9-12-1860 ae 61y 10m 2d bur Whitewater h Hannah
Ch: George F

Nathan h Beulah d 6-13-1825 ae ca 34y

MORGAN (cont)
Nathan b 11-15-1823 Wayne Co s Nathan & Beulah (**Beetle/Butte**) m 6-29-1846 Baltimore MD

Wm B h Sarah H
Ch: Wm Earl b 9-29-1859
    Jesse Henley b 7-6-1861
    Charles b 11-27-1863 d 4-24-1869
    Thomas Evans b 7-29-1867 d 7-29-1867 bur Earlham
    Rebecca Shinn b 7-29-1867 d 3-6-1868 bur Earlham

MORRIS
Charles E h Ann Elizabeth dt Hugh & Sarah **Moffitt** m 5-1877

Dorian C b 8-13-1856

Elizabeth b 9-17-1842 dt Samuel Moore & Levina (**Cox**) d 12-7-1878

Ellwood b 6-5-1845 s Samuel Moore & Levina (**Cox**)
Esther W b 7-14-1849 dt Clayton & Elizabeth (**Starr**) **Hunt** m 8-24-1876
Ch: Joseph b 8-26-1877
    Ralph Waldo b 3-2-1879
    Howard Clayton b 8-5-1884 d 9-2-1885 bur Earlham
    Elizabeth b 3-2-1892

Jehoshophat s Jonathan & Pennelope h Peninnah dt Benjamin & Sarah **Bundy** d 7-23-1813 ae 26y 3m 26d bur Whitewater 1-1-1813 Whitewater
Ch: Benoni b 2-18-1813 d 7-23-1813
Sarah 2w b 6-17-1798 Back Creek Mm NC dt Benjamin & Mary **Hill** m 8-1-1817

Jesse h Mary
Ch: Margaret b 1-12-1805
    John b 7-15-1806
    Mary b 6-19-1809 d 7-22-1851 bur Whitewater
    Sarah b 11-24-1810
    Miriam b 1-5-1813 d 2-1-1813
    Samuel Moore b 8-16-1815

John d 8-26-1861
Ann E d 5-11-1842 ae 33y 9m 8d bur Whitewater
Ch: Elias H b 10-25-1833 d 8-10-1838 bur Whitewater
    Mary Jane b 8-3-1834
    Nathan b 8-2-1837 d 5-21-1854 bur Whitewater
    David b 8-20-1840
Edith 2w
Ch: Albert C b 5-16-1854
    Jabez W b 10-22-1856 d 12-6-1860
    Ann b 2-13-1858
    Emily b 12-31-1859 d 12-20-1860

Mary Charles d 7-29-1888

Samuel Moore b 8-16-1815 s Jesse & Mary d 5-11-1853 bur Whitewater
Levina (**Cox**) b 12-14-1816
Ch: Elizabeth b 9-27-1842 d 12-7-1871 bur Milton
    Ruth b 5-16-1844
    Ellwood b 6-5-1845
    Samuel Emlen b 12-3-1850

Thomas E h Ernestine J (**Paulus**) m 1-1879

MORRISON
Edwin b 3-5-1861 Parke Co s Eli & Sarah Jane
Mary E b 6-25-1861 Red Cedar Co IA dt Benjamin & Elizabeth (**Bean**) **Miles** m 5-8-1890 Salem OR
Ch: S Elizabeth b 2-1-1891 Henry Co
    Louis A b 2-5-1897 Newberg OR

WHITEWATER MONTHLY MEETING
BIRTH AND DEATH RECORD

MORROW
Albert Theodore b 4-15-1846 s Elihu & Anna H m 12-27-1877 h Alice (**Holmes**)

Andrew bur Maple Grove h Jane d 9-15-1867 ae 56y 10m 15d bur Maple Grove

C L b 3-8-1862 Sabina OH s Wm & Sarah
Netta E b 5-2-1866 Harveysburg OH dt David & Martha **Edwards**
Ch: D Kenneth b 9-7-1897 Sabina OH

Elihu d 9-16-1892 ae 76y bur Earlham h Anna H
Ch: Albert Theodore b 4-15-1846
     Martha Eliza b 3-11-1848 d 9-15-1883
     John Edward b 11-15-1849
     James Wm b 3-10-1855

John b 6-17-1769 s Wm & Rachel d 3-14-1825 bur Whitewater h Hannah
Ch: Elizabeth b 9-12-1793
     Andrew b 5-28-1798
     Joseph b 10-13-1799
     Hannah b 2-6-1802
     Mary b 2-27-1804
     Ruth b 4-19-1806
     John b 9-18-1809
     Jane b 10-18-1811
     Nancy b 10-5-1813
     Elihu b 2-5-1817
Mary 2w b 10-26-1777 dt Joseph & Hannah **Stout** d 5-12-1843 bur Whitewater

MORSE
Kent b 12-2-1894 s N S & Nellie (**Worth**)

MOSS
Pearl M b 10-10-1887 dt Perry & Addie R (**McCarty**) **Hale**

MOTE
Edgar Smith b 1-30-1874 Wayne Co s Elisha Jones & Hannah (**Dickinson**) h Cora May (**Conley**)

Elisha Jones b 9-21-1836 Miami Co OH s Luke Smith & Charity (**Jones**) h Hannah (**Dickinson**)
Ch: Charles Albert b 1-29-1871 d 9-27-1871
     Elbert Linden b 11-30-1872
     Edgar Smith b 1-30-1874 Wayne Co
     Emma Alice b 9-22-1877
     Mabel
     Clarence D b 8-19-1880 Richmond

Henry D s Marcus & Rhoda S (**Steddom**) d 1-14-1882 h Daisy Belle
Ch: Olive d 9-24-1886 ae 14y 2m 24d bur Earlham
     Daisy Belle

Kirk L
Ch: Clarence Leslie b 6-27-1865
     Minnie C

Marcus b 6-19-1817 s David & Miriam (**Mendenhall**) d 2-26-1898 bur Earlham
Rhoda S b 3-10-1821 dt Samuel & Susannah (**Teague**) **Steddom**
Ch: Henry D d 1-14-1882
     Susanna J
     Jennie S b 7-9-1850

Orrin S d 4-16-1898 ae 60y bur West Branch OH
Martha J b 12-15-1845 dt John & Phebe M **Tyler** m 9-21-1871
Ch: Anna Gertrude b 7-8-1872
     John Edgar b 10-8-1875

Wm C b 9-2-1883 Marion Co s John & Emily (**Hadley**)

MOYER
Edith Estella b 7-28-1899 Randolph Co dt Daniel & Martha

MULHOLLAND
John h Rasel
Ch: Charles
     Marjorie b 8-13-1891 Wayne Co

MUNDANE
Jesse h Mary
Ch: Ruth Eliza b 9-22-1809
     Sarah b 1-4-1812 d 9-9-1814 bur Whitewater
     Wm b 1-2-1814

MUNSON
Claud b 3-4-1885 Highland Lake CO s Louis O & Luella

MUSTARD
Alpha R b 1-27-1880 Eaton OH dt Joseph & Amanda Alice

Clyde h Minnie b 1-18-1883

James h Amanda Alice b 9-6-1856 Butler Co OH dt Joseph & Mary ? m 8-10-1877 Covington KY

MYERS
Fred b 12-26-1896 Hartford City s Robert & Helen

Wm T b Franklin Co s Adam & Nellie

MYRICK
Stephen Stanton b 6-24-1875 Wayne Co s Reuben & Alabama (**Hawton/Houston**)

NAPIER
R Aaron b 1-16-1876 Liberty s Wm & Charlotte
Jennie b 3-22-1880 dt John & Mamie **Paddock**

NEFF
Tressa b 5-7-1893 Camden Co OH

NELSON
Leslie W b 9-6-1891 Mattoon IL s Wayne & Clara

NEWBY
Benoni h Jane d 4-4-1838 ae 29y 2m 3d bur Whitewater
Ch: Susannah 10-21-1824
     Wm b 2-5-1827
     Daniel b 9-11-1829
     Albert b 8-25-1832 d 3-10-1836 bur Whitewater

Miriam d 3-1876 bur Earlham

Thomas h Alice
Ch: Wm Hurtley d 1-12-1858 bur KS
     Jonathan D b 7-29-1852
     Cassius Albert b 4-12-1855
     Richard P b 7-21-1857
     Anna Grace b 9-6-1859

NEWLAND
Herman b 4-18-1883 Champaign Co OH s Mary

NEWLIN
Finley b 6-13-1839 s James M & Matilda (**Ong**)
Emma b 9-4-1841 dt Alexander & Sarah (**Charles**) **Mossman** m 7-23-1867 Allegheny PA
Ch: Edgar
     Charles

Hannah
Ch: Viola
     Edward

NEWMAN
Charles E b 9-5-1848 h Frances E dt Nathan & Annie E (**Downing**) **Doan**
Ch: Annie May b 6-30-1879
    Walter H b 6-19-1883
    Alice E b 7-31-1887

NEWSOM
Martha P b 10-16-1830

NICELY
Ora Warren b 2-15-1889 Boone Co s Thomas & Minnie

NICHOLLS
George D h Lydia Matilda b 6-2-1860 dt Jesse J & Mary (**Evans**) **Kenworthy** m 9-17-1887

NICHOLS
Chester b 3-1-1881 Randolph Co s Luke & Esther

James W b 10-8-1827

Kathleen b 5-1899

Mark b 3-15-1824
Sarah b 11-3-1829
Ch: James W b 9-9-1855
    Mary A b 5-18-1858
    Simon L b 5-18-1858
    Abijah b 4-29-1866
    Melinda b 3-6-1869

Nate b 3-18-1830

NICHOLSON
F C h Fannie b 10-8-1876 dt Isaac & Mary (**Dean**) **Davis** m 4-3-1897
Ch: Mary b 2-11-1898

Florence C b 9-5-1873 dt Elmer & ? (**Lamb**) **Nicholson** m 4-3-1897 Wayne Co

Harry b 2-11-1897 Continental OH s Elizabeth Marie (**Peacock**)

John s Josiah & Anna (**Robinson**) Mary B dt Ed & Mary **Winslow**
Ch: Edward W b 10-1-1862
    Ellen b 8-19-1867

John W b 6-25-1857 s Timothy & Sarah N (**White**) h Gertrude (**Brahell**)
Edith (**Bonnell**) 2w

Thomas b 11-18-1860 s Timothy & Sarah N (**White**) h Gertrude (**Kates**)

Timothy b 11-2-1828 Wayne Co s Josiah & Anna (**Robinson**)
Sarah N (**White**) b 4-9-1827 d 9-26-1865 bur Earlham
Ch: Sarah Ellen b 1-9-1863 d 9-10-1864
    Marianna b 7-21-1854
    John H b 6-25-1857
    Josiah H b 4-22-1859
    Thomas b 11-18-1860
    Walter J b 8-29-1865
Mary 2w b 10-29-1839 dt John & Mary (**White**) **White**
Ch: Sarah b 7-1-1869
    Eliza b 3-28-1871

NICKLES
Caroline C dt John Milton **Stanton**

NIXON
Josiah h Mary
Ch: Wm b 4-6-1811
    John b 7-27-1813
    Lydia b 11-3-1815

NORDYKE
David J b 7-27-1815 s Micajah & Charity (**Ellis**)
Lydia J (**Thornburg**) d 8-16-1898 ae 80y bur Earlham
Ch Rhoda Ann b 9-21-1838
    Joseph Thornburgh b 10-4-1840 ae 20y d 10-4-1860 bur Whitewater
    Edward Samuel b 10-7-1842
    Sylvanus Arthur b 1-11-1845
    Micajah Thomas b 4-9-1847 d 9-3-1869 bur Whitewater
    Wm Ellis b 3-18-1850 d 9-9-1852 bur Whitewater
    Lydia Mary b 1-6-1853
    Alice Eliza b 5-14-1855 d 10-21-1860 bur Whitewater
    Sarah Elma b 9-18-1858 d 4-12-1864
    Susan Bernice b 7-17-1861

Micajah Thomas b 4-9-1847 s David J & Lydia J (**Thornburg**)
Sarah Catherine (**Latimer**) b 9-19-1846 d 1-29-1898 bur Earlham m 11-1868 Richmond
Ch: Harry Edward b 7-19-1869 d 9-3-1869 bur Whitewater
    Eva b 7-19-1870 d 7-21-1870 bur Whitewater
    Ella b 6-7-1872 d 7-19-1872 bur Whitewater
    Edith Mabel b 6-15-1873
    Henrietta b 9-6-1874
    Frank Wm b 4-6-1878
    Alice b 7-27-1879
    David John b 9-7-1882

Sylvanus Arthur b 1-11-1845 s David & Lydia J (**Thornburg**)
Clara (**Compton**) m 8-1868 Washington OH
Ch: Wm Byron b 6-11-1869 d 10-14-1870 bur Verona MO
    Lillian b 5-22-1871
    Franklin David b 7-21-1873

NORTH
David h Catharine b 8-18-1850 Wayne Co dt John & Scherin **Allen**

NORTHERN
Isom Ray b 1-28-1893

Melissa b 12-10-1852 dt James & Fannie **Allison** m 12-16-1869 Laurel

NUBBELL
H Warren b 4-3-1894 s Isaac & Mary E

NUSS
Bertha Jane b 6-12-1887 Shelby Co dt John & Mary C **Daulin**

Wilford b 4-2-1875 Fountain City s Jonathan C & Elvira
Elizabeth b 3-18-1877 Spartansburg dt Albert & Talitha **Humphrey** m 11-11-1899 Spartansburg

O'CONNELL
Ethel b 1-31-1894 Richmond dt Eugene & Melinda

ODELL
Daniel h Betty
Ch: Polly b 5-15-1826
    Peter b 7-10-1827
    Amelia Jane b 6-2-1828
    Sarah b 9-21-1829
    Enos b 2-2-1831
    Mary J b 4-15-1832

OELSCHLEGER
Josephine dt Emma **Bogue**

OGBORN
Joseph d 3-27-1870

OGBURN
Rebecca A dt Joseph P d 5-1834 bur Whitewater

**WHITEWATER MONTHLY MEETING
BIRTH AND DEATH RECORD**

O'HARA
John h Eliza J d 1-10-1886 ae 50y Hamilton OH
Ch: Edwin Lee
    Isaac Graham
    Alpha Grace

OHLER
Carrie b Union City dt Reuben & Rhoda

OLIVER
Russell M b 3-7-1873 Anderson s John & Urry

O'NEAL
Clara dt Mary P

OSBORN
John S b 12-17-1870 Wayne Co s E & Agnes B (**Patterson**) m 1-14-1890 Wayne Co
Ch: Agnes B b 1-31-1894 Wayne Co
    J Opal b 9-6-1899 Wayne Co

OSBORNE
Frank h Olive M b 11-27-1876 dt Germaine & Christene (**Carter**) **Vincent** m 3-1-1893
Ch: Gordon b 5-15-1898

OUTLAND
David Amos b 12-12-1851 Rich Square NC s David & Margaret
Rhoda M b 11-24-1854 Wabash dt Lindley & Lydia (**Willets**) **Miles** m 2-18-1853 Dublin
Ch: Lydia Grace b 12-25-1883 d 3-23-1891
    Mary L b 7-11-1885
    Sopha M b 1-27-1888
    Jennie Marie b 3-10-1890
    Verona May b 5-22-1892

Mildred b 4-29-1897 Blackford Co dt Henry L & Leona B

OVERMAN
Albert J b 12-1-1882 s L F & Jennie

Charles J h Anna Mary b 5-25-1868 Howard Co dt Alfred & Anna (**Thorn**) **Johnson**

Jonathan J h Martha J (**Hollingsworth**)
Ch: Nellie F b 1-29-1890
    Clementine b 1-23-1897

Lydia Ann dt Ephraim

Marietta dt Nathan & Rhoda **Mendenhall**

Mildred Edwards b 8-6-1896

Nathan h Elizabeth
Ch: Cornelius b 9-11-1805
    Isaac b 8-8-1807
    Sarah b 10-11-1809
    Cyrus b 5-18-1812

OWEN
Thomas d 10-28-1831 bur Whitewater
Hannah W d 3-19-1826 ae 39y bur Whitewater
Ch: Samuel Stockton b 1-26-1818
    Thomas Mathews b 5-22-1821
    Benjamin Franklin Stockton b 11-26-1823

OWENS
S Emily b 1849 Wayne Co dt Amos & Mary **Comer** m 1878 Wayne Co

OWSLEY
Charles S h Mary E b 1853 dt Timothy & Sarah (**Ratliff**) **Thistlethwaite**

PADDOCK
Clarence G b 4-10-1894 Union Co

PAIGE
George h Anna Josephine d 3-12-1883 ae 37y
Ch: John
    Elisabeth

PAINTER
Elva B b 1-22-1869 Westboro OH dt Warner & Maria **Hinshaw** m 9-10-1889 Wilmington OH

PALIN
Myrtle J b 8-2-1875

PALMER
Louis Clarent h Mary Elizabeth (**Crawford**)

PARKE
Royden Edwin b 5-26-1892 s Wm A & Alma (**Bowerman**)

PARKER
Elisha b 4-18-1832
Martha D b 4-27-1833
Ch: Charles T b 3-17-1866 d 7-16-1866 bur Whitewater
    Edward F b 8-8-1867
    John P b 7-15-1875 d 9-4-1875 bur Earlham

Fidelia Coan b 10-9-1869 dt Elwood & Rachel (**Johnson**)

Jeremiah b 11-25-1767 Rich Square MM NC s Joseph & Sarah
Karen b 2-27-1767 Rich Square MM NC dt Robert & Jemima **Newby**
Ch: Sarah b 1-10-1790 Rich Square MM NC
    Robert b 3-13-1792 Rich Square MM NC
    Jeremiah b 1-27-1795 Rich Square MM NC
    Richard b 10-14-1797 Rich Square MM MC
    Catherine b 6-28-1800 Rich Square MM MC
    Isaac b 9-22-1806 Rich Square MM NC

John h Miriam
Ch: John Oscar
    Walter B

John E b 7-17-1862 s Isaac & Hannah M (**Newby**) h Anna M (**Wildman**)
Ch: Edna b 3-16-1895
    James W b 7-27-1896
    Priscella b 2-14-1899

Oran K h Ollie M b 3-5-1875 dt Philip M & Ellen S (**Swain**) **Horner** m 11-4-1891
Ch: Homer H b 7-18-1896
    Russell b 8-30-1899

Richard d 5-20-1818 ae 20y 7m 6d bur Sullivan Co TN

Wm Francis h Ida b 2-9-1875/76 Wayne Co dt Allen Haines & Ruth H **Thorne** m 10-2-1894 Wayne Co
Ch: Margaret Ruth b 4-4-1897 Wayne Co

Wm M h Evaline
Ch: Lindley Hoag b 8-22-1853 d 1-18-1854 bur Whitewater
    Edward Winslow b 4-11-1855
    Horace G b 8-12-1858
    Mary Alice b 11-11-1860
    Wm B b 7-27-1865
    George F b 10-6-1869

PARKS
Leonides L b 12-26-1854 Wayne Co s Wm & Elizabeth
Jennie F b 3-4-1859 Preble Co OH dt Moore S & Sarah **Randolph** m 6-26-1879 Eaton OH

PARKS (Leonides L cont)
Ch: Clarence E b 10-7-1880 Union Co
　　Ernest E b 3-7-1895 Boston
　　Mary L b 1-10-1898 Boston
　　Flora J b 12-16-1899 Boston

PARRY
Mordecai h Gulielma d 8-5-1849 ae 21y 4m 16d bur Whitewater
Ch: Martha b 6-16-1846
　　Webster b 9-25-1848
Sarah B 2w
Ch: Gulielma b 3-5-1856
　　Thomas b 3-30-1858
　　Annie b 9-19-1863 d 1-27-1865 bur Maple Grove
　　Charles M b 5-30-1865
　　Joseph Edwin b 8-15-1870
　　Sarah Belle b 1-26-1872

Samuel b 3-23-1849 Wayne Co s Wm & Mary
Rhoda E b 10-28-1844 Wayne Co dt Robert & Rachel P **Green**
m 1-9-1884 Wayne Co

PARSHALL
John W h Catharine G b 5-7-1860
Ch: Gussie J b 10-25-1882
　　Elmer E b 10-4-1886
　　Alva A b 10-12-1889
　　Roy b 4-9-1893
　　Jesse A b 5-18-1896/97

PATTEN
Ethel b 5-26-1885

PAULSON
George Fiske h Anna A b 6-6-1848 dt Warner & Rebecca **Davenport**
Ch: Margaret b 7-27-1877
2w
Ch: Richard Adams b 2-25-1890 Wayne Co
　　Lillie b 6-8-1896 bur Orange
　　Anna

PEACOCK
Bernice b 5-27-1892 Winchester dt T C & Alice

John Randolph b 5-6-1893 s Willis D & Cynthia A (**Fries**)

Levi b 5-18-1821 Guilford Co NC s Asa & Dinah (**Rich**)
Martha (**Haisley**) m 2-22-1843 Wayne Co
Sarah 2w b 6-22-1835 Randolph Co dt Peter & Sarah (**Hinshaw**)
Lawrence m 5-27-1863 Henry Co
Ch: Daniel L b 12-9-1872 Wayne Co
　　Mary C b 5-8-1875 Wayne Co
　　Levi C b 10-23-1878 Wayne Co

PEARSON
Calvin W b 5-17-1841 s Isaac & Rachel h Marthanna dt Joshua **Taylor**
Ch: Florence Irena b 7-19-1871
　　Edwin Arthur b 4-6-1878
　　Walter Melville b 11-29-1879

Clinton M b 9-24-1890 Henry Co s Cassius M & Nancy Ann (**Myers**)

Nathan h Mary
Ch: Peter b 4-19-1797
　　John b 5-17-1799
　　Ann b 3-12-1801
　　Levi b 4-1-1803
　　Catharine b 1-30-1805
　　Bailey b 2-24-1807
　　Wm b 9-12-1810
　　Stanton b 5-21-1813

PEARSON (cont)
Sarah Jane b 3-21-1846 dt Warner & Rebecca **Davenport** d 10-5-1865 bur Orange

Thomas B b 2-19-1835
Mary E (**Elliott**) b 4-18-1832
Ch: Charles b 5-1-1856

PEDRICK
Richard d 2-6-1880 ae 81y bur Earlham
Mary d 8-18-1830 bur Whitewater
Susannah B 2w d 11-15-1881 bur Earlham
Ch: Isaac b 11-2-1833 d 2-10-1841 bur Whitewater
　　Wm b 7-10-1836
　　Anna b 8-16-1838 d 9-24-1875 bur Earlham
　　Mary b 7-9-1841 d 7-31-1842 bur Whitewater
　　Mary C b 1-31-1843
　　Isaac H b 1-10-1845
　　Joseph B b 11-15-1846
　　Hannah E b 12-26-1848 d 8-11-1872 bur Earlham
　　Richard R b 4-10-1851

PEELE
Charles A b 10-18/28-1856
Josephine b 4-18-1860 dt Fredrick & Urilla (**Shaffer**) **Ullrick**
Ch: Lillian Ruth Urilla b 7-15-1893

Frances May b 8-3-1892 dt Hardin H & Cynthia (**Hendershott**)

Harley b 8-27-1876 Bloomington OH s John & Dorcas
Bertha b 5-1-1876 Cincinnati OH dt Richard & Amelia **Burken**

Henry b 1-4-1870 Bloomington OH s John & Dorcas
Jeanette b 2-28-1871 Washington Court House OH dt Samuel & Jane H **Hartley** m 1-28-1891 Wilmington OH

Henry E d 10-3-1895 ae 79y bur Earlham
Mary d 3-14-1899 ae 74y bur Earlham

John h Dorcas
Ch: Wm John b 11-14-1867 Clinton Co OH
　　Henry b 1-24-1870 Bloomington OH
　　Harley b 8-27-1876 Bloomington OH

Mark h Zilpah b 3-15-1792 dt Exum & Katherine (**Lamb**) **Elliott** bur Surry Co NC

Wm John b 11-24-1867 Clinton Co OH s John & Dorcas
Gertrude b 5-15-1871 Jamestown OH dt Taylor & Elizabeth **Jenks**
m 4-8-1891 Wilmington OH

PEGG
David Sanders b 5-2-1839 Randolph Co s Davis & Jane
Lydia F b 9-3-1839 Wayne Co dt Michael & Sarah (**Woodard**) **Fulghum** m 3-25-1860 Wayne Co
Ch: Eva Elnora b 2-2-1861

James b 10-24-1768 s Valentine & Mary (**Mills**) d 10-27-1839 bur Whitewater
Elisabeth b 12-16-1782 dt John & Mary **Horney** d 7-1-1822 bur Whitewater

Valentine b 4-19-1744 s Wm & Margaret d 11-24-1828 bur Whitewater
Mary b 1-8-1750 dt John & Sarah **Mills** d 1-16-1820 bur Whitewater
Ch: James b 10-24-1768 d 10-27-1839 bur Whitewater
　　Lydia b 3-28-1790

PEIRCE
Samuel b 9-12-1822 s Samuel & Milly (**Iddings**) h Ann
Ch: Esther b 10-22-1855
　　Milly b 4-17-1860
　　John b 3-14-1863
　　Ann

**WHITEWATER MONTHLY MEETING
BIRTH AND DEATH RECORD**

PENNINGTON
Levi T b 8-21-1875 s Josiah & Mary (**Cook**)
Bertha (**Walters**) m 6-1-1898
Ch: Mary Esther b 6-6-1899

PERCIFIELD
Ira Otis b 1-15-1883 Tipton Co s Sampson S & Sarah A

PERRY
Charles Coffin b 12-15-1857 s Joseph James & Ruth (**Moffitt**)
m 5-1890

Chester b 8-25-1887 Dayton OH s Susannah

Clarence b 1 3-1896 OH s Monroe & Almeda

Joseph James h Ruth b 12-22-1819 dt Charles & Elizabeth **Moffitt**
d 3-24-1892 bur Earlham
Ch: Charles Coffin b 12-15-1857

Mary Elizabeth b 9-20-1843 dt Joseph James & Elizabeth (**Howell**)

PETTIBONE
Francis C b 5-24-1867 Wayne Co s Frederick & Elizabeth
Matilda C b 7-9-1868 Randolph Co dt Thomas & Amy **York**
Ch: Leota b 9-21-1899 Randolph Co

PHILABAUM
James b 1-7-1846 Dayton OH s Daniel & Maria
Sarah E b 5-30-1857 Hagerstown dt Urias & Ann **Stoker** m 2-3-1871 Hagerstown

PHILLIPS
Earl b 9-12-1857 Henry Co s J O & Anna R h Lucinda dt Joseph & Mary **Bogue**

Ida b 6-7-1874 Jefferson Co dt Ephraim & Mary **Brown** m 10-8-1898 Jefferson Co

Josiah h Elvira b 9-13-1835 dt Jonathan & Mary (**Smith**) **Roberts**
d 2-1-1883 m 1877

PICKERALL
Mahlon h Sarah B (**Horney**) m 8-1-1888

PICKERING
Bertha H b 9-12-1881 Lebanon OH dt Wm & Anna B **Snyder** m 2-25-1897 Spring Valley

Erma R b 7-9-1889 dt Burrill A & Alice (**Mendenhall**)

PICKETT
Albert h Katie d 8-27-1889
Ch: Myrtle d 8-19-1889
      Florence
      Deborah

Elma b 9-8-1858 Wayne Co dt Cornelius & Ann Elizabeth (**Icombrock**) **Bond**

Gail Marie b 1-23-1898 Wayne Co dt Emerson & Ida (**Study**)

John F h Nancy A
Ch: Alice C b 11-18-1861 Wayne Co
      Iowa Lilly b 8-11-1863 d 11-30-1863
      Lilly E b 2-24-1871 d 2-26-1871

Lena P b 1-2-1882 Spiceland dt Oliver & Mary

Wm H b 3-12-1831
Hannah E b 6-15-1836
Ch: John Francis b 8-23-1859
      Benjamin Everett b 12-5-1861

PICKETT (Wm H cont)
      Minnie May b 2-17-1865
      Willie Elmer b 2-19-1867

PILCHER
Clarence E b 10-12-1885 Greene Co OH s Orlando & Lottie

PIPER
Marion K b 2-6-1884 Melross MA s George M & Grace (**Kennard**)

PITTS
Benjamin b 5-30-1856 Fountain City s Harmon & Ruth
Ellen b 4-24-1859 Webster dt H J & Ruth C **Baldwin**

PLACE
Naomi b 1-20-1827 dt Wm & Priscilla

PLATT
Sarah E m 8-22-1874 Randolph Co

POOL
Charles h Jane Ann b 2-19-1843 dt Jeremiah & Esther **Hadley**

John d 5-27-1865 ae 89y
Elizabeth d 12-25-1848 ae 64y 4m 3d Richmond bur Whitewater
Ch: Clarkey b 11-15-1801
      Gulielma b 11-9-1804
      Charles b 10-14-1807
      Wm b 8-15-1810 d 10-8-1839 bur Whitewater
      Thomas b 4-2-1813 d 7-16-1839 bur Whitewater
      Rebecca C b 11-5-1815
      Sarah b 7-18-1818
      Elisabeth b 1-15-1821 d 11-18-1825 bur Whitewater
      John b 7-18-1823 d 8-26-1823
      Ruthanna b 3-8-1827

Wm h Rebecca
Ch: Joseph b 7-2-1835
      Elizabeth b 6-5-1837

PORTERFIELD
Alice A b 8-4-1864 dt Philip & Rhoda A **Schneider**

POSTHER
Henry h Minnie
Ch: Loran E
      Paul S

Lila H b 6-8-1870 Wayne Co dt Henry H & Henrietta (**Hietland**)

POTTER
T M h Mary Cox b 1-31-1843 dt Richard & Susannah **Pedrick**

POWERS
George Clarkson h Bertha B (**Schlotte**) m 8-20-1897 Peru

PRICE
Joseph A b 3-2-1887 Milan KS s Charles & Martha J (**McKee**)

PRITCHARD
Samuel h Harriet (**Pickett**)
Ch: Anna Unthank b 1-23-1831 Raysville d 2-27-1867 Richmond
      Sarah Jane b 11-25-1835 Raysville d 5-3-1869 Raysville

PROPST
J Franklin b 10-18-1879 Montgomery Co OH s J A

PROVIANCE
Leroy h Gulielma dt Henry & Tacy Ann (**Meredith**) **Henley**

PRYFOGLE
Sherman h Grace L b 7-17-1865 Wayne Co dt John H & Mary C **McCown** m 8-25-1897 Wayne Co

WHITEWATER MONTHLY MEETING
BIRTH AND DEATH RECORD

PUGH
Wm b 3-15-1868 Lanesville OH s Robert & Melinda

PURCELL
Myrtle b 1-14-1871 dt Isaac Cooper & Joanna (Miles) Teague

PYLE
David d 10-2-1868 ae 43y 8m 16d
Esther b 1-10-1827 dt John & Alice (Teague) Steddom d 11-28-1893 bur Goshen m 3-4-1847
Ch: Joseph S b 2-23-1848 d 5-11-1899 bur Earlham
    David b 5-7-1854
    Mary C b 11-15-1862

David b 5-7-1854 s David & Esther (Steddom)
Elizabeth B dt Daniel & Caroline (Clawson) Bulla m 12-11-1878

Olive S b 3-8-1878 dt Joseph & Cora (Spinning)

QUAINTANCE
Greensburg P b 1-2-1845
Sarah b 3-3-1847
Ch: Charles C b 6-29-1880
    Ethel b 1-15-1884
    Vera b 8-3-1889

QUIGG
Belle b 11-29-1872 dt Nathan & Minnie Hawkins

Wm H b 8-12-1866 s Ira E & Nancy (Frazier)
Laura M b 1-26-1872 dt Wm & Katherine (Ashinger) Kramer m 5-10-1895
Ch: Eugene K b 2-14-1896
    Katherine b 9-16-1897

RAILSBACK
Otho h Isabella Louisa dt Elizabeth (Austin) Conkle

RAMBO
Nathan h Elizabeth d 8-29-1849 ae 58y bur Whitewater
Ch: Ann R b 7-3-1809 d 8-2-1891 bur Earlham

Wm h Miriam
Ch: Edward B
    Naomi C
    Francis H

Wm A b 7-26-1811 d 8-11-1858 bur Whitewater
Sarah M d 9-14-1841 ae 23y 10m 8d bur Whitewater
Ch: Sarah Sylvania b 5-21-1840

RANDALL
Bertha b 6-22-1871 dt Eli W & Mary C (Cooper) Evans m 2-19-1893

Charles E b 9-3-1887 Preble Co OH s Dewitt & Lucy A

Frank T h Martha (Hockett)
Ch: Mildred Lucile b 12-4-1894
    Mary Madalin b 8-22-1898

Robert W b 6-1-1862 s Wm & Gulielma (Baily)
Rowena M b 7-6-1863 dt Wm & Jane (Wheat) Hearn m 9-30-1885

RANKER
Sophia b 6-19-1845

RAPER
Clarence b 10-31-1880 Wayne Co

Oliver d 11-1898 bur Whitcomb WA

RATLIFF
Cornelius b 2-10-1756 s Joseph & Mary d 4-6-1828 bur Whitewater
Elizabeth b 6-27-1759 dt Daniel & Elizabeth Saint d 4-24-1828 bur Whitewater
Ch: Mary b 7-24-1782
    Elizabeth b 3-10-1785
    Joseph b 8-6-1787
    Gulielma b 9-10-1791
    Sarah b 5-27-1794
    Millicent b 1-28-1797
    Cornelius b 12-24-1798
    Abigail b 10-6-1800
    Ruth b 10-16-1802 d 3-22-1803 bur Back Creek Randolph Co NC

Cornelius Jr b 12-24-1798 s Cornelius & Elizabeth (Saint) h Mary
Ch: Edward b 8-20-1823
    Margaret b 4-18-1825
    Joseph b 7-8-1827

Joseph b 8-6-1787 s Cornelius & Elizabeth (Saint)
Sarah b 1-14-1797 dt George & Mary Shugard
Ch: George b 11-13-1816 d 2-1-1821 bur Whitewater
    Millicent b 2-5-1819
    John b 3-1-1822
    Eli b 12-6-1825
    Cornelius S b 5-11-1829
    Mary b 7-18-1832

RAY
Albertice C b 2-22-1879 Preble Co OH s Christian & Elizabeth C

Golden Myrtle b 3-8-1886 Preble Co OH dt James Monroe & Lorene (Mikesell)

RAYMOND
Opal C b 3-23-1887 Johnson Co dt Isaac & Lovey M

REECE
Charles h Eunice
Ch: Edwin b 12-17-1854 d 4-1-1859 bur Whitewater
    Oliver b 7-22-1857 d 10-6-1859 bur Whitewater
    Emma Cora b 7-18-1859

REED
Albert b 8-4-1845 h Ellen Maria dt Wm M & Rebecca C Lefever
Ch: Frank L b 7-17-1871
    Walter Clarence b 12-23-1875
    Hugh b 2-2-1878

Alice b 4-21-1846 dt George W & Hannah (Berriman) Templar m 11-10-1876

Anna M b 10-9-1876 dt Edwin & Jemima (Doan) Hadley m 6-3-1890

Charlotte b 7-24-1878 dt Wm Maston & Anna (McComb)

Jerome W b 4-6-1879 Crawford Co KS s Philander & Lucinda

John h Sarah (Grave) d ae 47y 10m 17d bur Smyrna
Ch: Elizabeth S b 5-15-1820
    Rowland T b 9-15-1822 d 8-10-1878
    Martha Ann b 5-30-1825
    Priscilla b 5-9-1827
    Susanna B b 2-3-1831

John G d 6-1873 bur Earlham
Ann d 9-1-1881 bur Washington

Mary d 1-11-1859 bur Smyrna

Mary Alice b 1-1883 dt Thomas E & Margaret (Shoemaker) Kinsey

WHITEWATER MONTHLY MEETING
BIRTH AND DEATH RECORD

REED (cont)
Rowland T b 9-15-1822 s John & Sarah (**Grave**) d 8-10-1878
Drusilla A b 2-14-1821 dt Wm & Rebecca (**Hiatt**) **Unthank**
Ch: Samuel Albert b 8-4-1845
     Wm Zedru b 4-1-1848
     Sarah Ada Evaline b 10-18-1850 d 10-5-1854 bur Smyrna
     Ida Florence b 7-12-1855 d 8-5-1867
     Anna b 9-26-1863 d 6-5-1874

Wm H h Mary Anna b 10-29-1856 dt Joseph Milton & Charity **Allen** m 12-1879

REEVES
Charles P b 5-2-1844 s Mark

Harry B b 4-20-1872 New Burlington OH s A W & LaBelle (**Blair**)
Eva N b 11-27-1872 New Burlington OH dt Joel T & Susannah (**Dakin**) **Compton** m 1-30-1895 Spring Valley OH
Ch: Manassa b 2-27-1896 New Burlington OH

REIGLE
Clayton G b 4-20-1879 Darke Co OH s George W & Nancy J

REIKER
Wm C b 9-27-1885 Dayton OH s Dixon & Laura

RETZ
Ann Marie b 4-16-1896 Wayne Co dt Mikel & Margarett (**Bailey**)

REYNOLDS
Eric L h Lillian Hayden b 11-7-1852 dt Charles Hayden & Elizabeth (**Keith**) **Brown** m 9-6-1871

Wilson b 11-2-1843 Dalton s Isaac & Tamer Hawkins (**Nicholson**)
Elizabeth D b 2-27-1842 Dalton dt George & Lucinda (**Dennis**) **Nicholson** m 2-14-1867 Hagerstown

RHODES
Oscar M b 5-8-1862 Van Wert OH s Alex & Mary Ann

RHULE
John K b 7-28-1861 s Alfred & Sarah (**Miller**)
Annie b 6-17-1868 dt Thomas & Henrietta (**Conner**) **Hapner** m 9-30-1886

RICH
Esther A dt Howell & Hannah C **Gram**
Ch: Howell AT

Judith Ann d 11-22-1851 ae 20y 11m 29d dt Nathan bur Whitewater

Ruby b 9-25-1884 Wayne Co dt Francis & Emma

RICHARDS
Isaac H h Mary J b 6-16-1841 dt Lewis & Maria **Burke** m 10-26-1869 Richmond
Ch: Burke b 6-30-1873
     Mary Griffith b 10-15-1874
     Maria Moffett b 2-24-1876
     Caroline C b 8-10-1878
     Jane Lydia b 6-12-1880
     Ethel b 1-19-1883

RICHARDSON
James b 10-16-1833

RICHIE
John S b 7-23-1840 s Samuel S & Anna (**Shoemaker**)
Mary A (**Brown**) b 2-21-1841 d 12-22-1894
Ch: Rosalie Anna b 1-24-1866
     Robert Clinton b 8-9-1868 d 12-16-1868 bur Smyrna
     Edward Russell b 9-7-1870
     Arthur Coffin b 6-1-1879

RICHIE (cont)
Robert h Sarah
Ch: Samuel S b 5-11-1814 d 11-18-1888 bur Smyrna
     Hannah H b 9-29-1816 d 7-5-1880 bur Earlham

Robert Annesley b 12-8-1846 s Samuel S & Anna (**Shoemaker**) h Belle (**Lynde**) m 6-1877

Samuel Charles b 9-20-1856 Philadelphia PA s Samuel S & Anna (**Shoemaker**) h Mary H (**Hinckley**) m 5-13-1880

Samuel S b 5-11-1814 s Robert & Sarah d 11-18-1888 bur Smyrna
Anna (**Shoemaker**) b 7-7-1814 d 1-31-1885 bur Smyrna
Ch: Elizabeth S b 9-25-1838
     John S b 7-23-1840
     Sarah M b 4-3-1842
     Margaret W b 3-27-1844 d 3-31-1881 bur Smyrna
     Robert Annesley b 12-8-1846
     Anna Mary b 7-2-1852
     Grace S b 12-16-1854 Bucks Co PA
     Samuel Charles b 9-20-1856 Philadelphia PA
     Jeanette J b 8-14-1859 d 2-17-1882

RICKER
Orian/Owen h Laura b 10-11-1867 OH dt Henry & Hannah **Childers** m 5-8-1885 Montgomery Co OH
Ch: Wm C b 9-27-1885 Dayton OH
     Pearl Parry b 12-7-1887 Dayton OH
     Charles b 10-28-1891

Wm h Sadie b 2-18-1882 dt Albert & Anna ?

RIDGWAY
Mary R b 11-3-1847 Burlington IA dt Angus & Mary **Martin**

RIEGLE
Clayton G b 4-20-1874 Darke Co OH s George W & Nancy J (**Harland**)

RIGGIN
Herschel M b 6-4-1887 Pickaway Co OH s Sanford L & Melissa

RIGHT
Gertrude N b 8-13-1876 Bartholomew Co dt Frank & Margaret

ROBERDS
Henry h Anna M (**Jones**) 4-1880

Thomas Jr d 9-21-1838 ae 33y 2m 3d bur Whitewater
Mary d 11-29-1832 bur Whitewater
Ch: Phebe b 3-13-1829
     Wm b 9-11-1832
Mary 2w
Ch: Nathan b 1-4-1835 d 1-7-1839 bur Whitewater
     Willis W b 11-17-1837

ROBERTS
Albert b 5-12-1859 s Wm & Elizabeth h ? (**Johnson**) m 8-1880

David d 1-13-1861 ae 65y 4m 25d bur Whitewater

David Edward b 4-13-1884 Pittsburgh PA s Robert & Katherine

Eli b 9-22-1833 s Jonathan & Mary (**Smith**) h Mary (**Kinzie/Kinsey**)
Ch: Grace

Eveline d 4-13-1888

Frank C b 12-21-1868 Wayne Co s Henry S & Martha (**Charles**)
Mary E b 10-24-1867 Wayne Co dt Warner & Matilda (**Dennis**) **Hockett** m 6-4-1891/2 Webster

Fred C b 4-1-1873 West Elkhorn OH s James & Lucretia
Verona S R b 12-10-1873 West Elkhorn OH dt Thomas & Rachel **Stubbs** m 12-31-1896 West Elkhorn OH

ROBERTS (cont)
Henry S b 10-25-1842 Wayne Co s Jonathan & Mary (**Smith**)
Martha b 10-8-1841 dt Nathan & Mary (**Symons**) **Charles** d 10-7-1878 bur Maple Grove
Ch: Frank C b 12-21-1868 Wayne Co
     Evaline b 6-18-1871 d 4-13-1888
     Belle b 4-7-1876 Wayne Co
Anna M 2w b Wayne Co dt Samuel & Martha L (**Mather**) **Jones** m 4-8-1880 Wayne Co

Inez b 5-5-1888 Richmond dt John & Alice **Armstrong**

Jonathan b 5-30-1808 s Thomas & Ann (**Whitson**)
Mary (**Smith**) b 3-26-1809 d 8-1-1888 bur Earlham
Ch: Avis Jane b 4-30-1832
     Eli b 9-22-1833 Wayne Co
     Elvira b 9-13-1835 d 1-30-1883
     Henry S b 10-25-1842 Wayne Co

Lindley H b 11-15-1856 s Wm & Elizabeth
Alice J b 5-18-1850 dt Ellen **Edgerton** m 8-1876

Louis M b 6-1-1882 s James G & Adeline (**McIntyre**)

Mary A b 11-29-1860 dt Jacob & Mary A (**Randle**) **Kinsey**

Phinehas h Sarah d 8-26-1814 ae 30y 11m 5d bur Whitewater
Ch: Martha b 10-14-1808
     John b 4-6-1810
     Elijah b 12-1-1812
     Elizabeth b 1-9-1814

Samuel d 1-1897 bur Earlham h Catherine
Ch: India Lizzie b 1875
Sarah E (**Burton/Barton**) 2w
Ch: Mary Anna b 5-1878
     Frederic Warner b 8-24-1879
     Iona Lee b 1-18-1883

Solomon Whitson h Elizabeth
Ch: Esther b 7-11-1818
     Polly b 9-25-1820
     Thomas b 12-16-1822
     Daniel b 11-10-1824
     Milton b 9-13-1826
     Anna b 8-3-1828 d 4-1853

Thomas d 9-25-1840 ae 81y 8m 16d bur Whitewater
Ann d 11-28-1840 ae 73y 11m bur Whitewater

Walter h Mary d 8-22-1814 ae 25y 6m 9d bur Whitewater
Ch: Henry b 8-8-1814 d 8-22-1814

Wm h Elizabeth
Ch: Levi J b 7-14-1854 d 4-5-1858
     Lindley H b 11-15-1856
     Albert b 5-12-1859
     John H b 9-11-1861
     Anna Mary b 10-18-1865
     Emma L b 4-26-1868

ROBINSON
Charles H b 11-5-1865 h Gertrude

Elwood h Ella May b 7-27-1859 dt Isaac P & Lydia **Woodard** m 3-1-1895
Ch: Lydia Marine b 7-23-1895

Jessie B b 3-28-1892 Preble Co OH dt Wm & Mary

Olive M b 1-29-1875 dt Charles E & Anna (**Lewis**) **Kaminsky** m 7-12-1899

WHITEWATER MONTHLY MEETING
BIRTH AND DEATH RECORD

ROBINSON (cont)
Thomas d 4-3-1888 bur Earlham h Rebecca
Ch: Wm H
     Emma C d 11-17-1880 ae 23y bur Earlham
     Elizabeth E d 6-17-1889 bur Earlham
     Lemuel
     Isaac

ROBISON
Mary Emily b 2-4-1858 Preble Co OH dt Charles & Maryann **Ross**

ROCKHILL
Calvin h Lydia H b 11-11-1830 dt Asiph & Ann (**Wickersham**) **Hollingsworth** m 12-5-1853 Clinton Co OH

Ernest b 5-16-1898 Wayne Co s Albert & Louanna

ROE
Sarah Cassie b 10-11-1889 Wayne Co dt Joseph & Mary **Bogue**

Thurman s Wm & Grace B

ROGERS
Anna L b 4-12-1870

Charles H b 12-18-1868 s Oliver & Mary (**Bryant**)
Orissa b 10-8-1871 dt Wm & Caroline (**Burns**) **McDonald** m 9-27-1893

Eunice d 7-13-1895 ae 76y bur Earlham

Jonathan h Anna b 8-27-1843 dt John & Martha ? m 6-30-1875

Olive b 11-29-1880 Hendricks Co dt M C & Sally (**Clay**)

Walter h Olinda B b 8-22-1836 dt James & Millicent (**Coffin**) **Mendenhall**

ROHE
Esther b 8-30-1885 dt Lindley M & Ella R (**Hodgin**) **Coate**

ROPER
Oliver d 11-1898 ae 31y bur Whitcomb WA

ROSECRANS
Maud dt John E & Mary Adaline **Wolfe**

ROSS
John A b 10-2-1860 s Timothy & Susan (**Kenworthy**)
Ida E b 1-23-1869 dt Joseph & Mary A (**Overholtz**) **Howard** m 4-27-1895
Ch: Bertha Omelia b 5-26-1896 Wayne Co
     Everett John b 4-16-1899 Wayne Co

ROWE
Deryl Edward b 10-16-1897 Henry Co s Edward & Laura (**Hinshaw**)

RUBY
Lula E b 10-14-1895 Richmond dt Frank & Francis

RUE
Henry d 9-27-1838 ae 39y 6m 10d bur Orange

Rebeckah b 6-29-1793 dt Jacob & Susanna **Talbot** d 1-8-1858 bur Orange

Richard h Rachel J
Ch: Lydia H b 6-30-1846
     John b 9-29-1850
     Eva b 10-19-1852
     Allice b 1-20-1857
     Ada B b 3-10-1859

WHITEWATER MONTHLY MEETING
BIRTH AND DEATH RECORD

RUE (Richard cont)
    Richard Edgar b 2-28-1861
    Ida Rebecca b 7-1-1855 d 8-16-1856
    Lizzie Martha b 2-1863 d 8-20-1863
    Horace G b 5-14-1865
    Maud Emma b 12-22-1867
    Lewis

RUGG
Sadie b 2-18-1882 Lewisburg dt Albert & Anna

RUSSELL
Bertram B b 2-21-1893 Wayne Co s Wm E & Marinda

Elbert b 8-29-1871 s Wm & Eliza (**Sanders**)
Lienetta b 11-17-1872 dt Theodore & Rachel (**Stuart**) **Cox** m 8-14-1895 West Newton

George h Judith
Ch: Ruth b 4-10-1810
      Sarah b 8-6-1812
      Sinah b 3-19-1814
      Timothy b 4-30-1816
      Josiah b 12-23-1817

Lizzie Hunt b 6-20-1855 m 12-30-1870

RUSSEY
Wm h Mary d 3-22-1835 ae 49y 3m

RYAN
Clyde b 12-29-1882 Wayne Co s Joseph & Viola
Emily Jane dt Benjamin C & Esther Ann (**Thomas**) **Wickett**

SACKETT
Robert Lemuel b 12-2-1867 s Lemuel M & Emily (**Cole**)
Mary Lyon b 2-5-1869 dt John & Lucinda (**White**) **Coggeshall** m 7-22-1896
Ch: Ralph Lemuel b 12-16-1897

SAINT
Daniel d 4-14-1892 ae 72y bur Earlham

SAMPSON
Marie b 3-11-1897 Peru dt George

SAMS
Wm s Sarah

SANDERS
Mary d 4-7-1867 ae 78y 11m 6d bur Earlham

SCANTLAND
Cecil H b 6-19-1896 Wayne Co s Oliver H & Cora M

SCARCE
Earl s Caroline d 11-11-1897 ae 14y bur Orange

Edward d 12-23-1898 ae 58y bur Orange h Caroline
Ch: Howard b 2-4-1861 Lowell

SCHEIBLE
Hannah B b 12-4-1841 dt James Mendenhall & Millicent (**Coffin**)

SCHEPMAN
Homer J b 11-4-1869 s John H & Mary (**Verregge**)
Jennie b 1-23-1870 dt Michael & Anna (**Edwards**) **McDonald** m 6-14-1893
Ch: LaVerne b 4-15-1897
      Arl McDonald b 5-16-1899

SCHISSLER
Louise M b 2-28-1844 dt John & Marie (**Leighman**) **Spangler** m 6-25-1866

SCHNEIDER
Anna b 1-14-1866 dt Joseph & Dorothy (**Schlereth**) **Werner** m 12-17-1890

Philip h Rhoda A d 6-30-1866 ae 27y bur Whitewater
Ch: Alice A b 3-4-1864
Susan 2w bur Earlham
Ch: Elizabeth C
      Martha C
      Phillip
      Fred
      Kate C

Philip b 1-8-1840 s Jacob & Elizabeth
Kate C b 2-3-1859 dt John & Elizabeth (**Woodhurst**) **Miller** m 6-3-1875
Ch: Martha C
      Katherine

SCHOOLEY
Hershel b 8-31-1894 Blanchester OH s Wm & Sadie

SCHURMAN
Henry h Florence dt Charles R & Mary E (**Whitacre**) **Unthank**

SCOTT
Agrippa h Anna
Ch: Ellsworth b 12-27-1865
      Eddie b 1-4-1869
      Eva b 1-4-1869
      Willie H b 12-17-1874

Edith Bell b 5-9-1882 Wayne Co dt Benjamin C & Esther Ann (**Thomas**) **Wickett**

Susanna d 9-24-1835 bur Whitewater

SEAL
Sarah b 3-2-1888 dt Thomas & Angeline (**Cook**)

SEAMAN
John b 5-9-1844 Burlington NJ s Charles I & Elizabeth

SEDGWICK
Richard h Marcia E b 12-28-1860 dt David & Deborah A (**White**) **Sutton** m 10-15-1884
Ch: Deborah W b 1-28-1888

SELL
Elizabeth Ann b 9-1-1858 dt Henry J & Lydia Sarah (**Haines**) **Dingley** m 11-13-1878

SETTLES
Ollie May b 8-31-1881 dt John W & Francis (**Wilson**)

SEWELL
Jack b 3-10-1849 Madison Co KY s Turner & Hannah
Ch: Henry b 6-8-1881 Madison Co KY

Ruby b 11-13-1898 Madison Co KY dt Jack & Phebe

SHAFFER
James h Laura dt Alexander & Alice **Pryfogle**

SHARON
Elizabeth d 9-8-1885

SHEARON
Mary d 9-7-1885 ae 86y bur Maple Grove wid Caleb

Warner h Rachel Linetta d 10-5-1888 ae 66y bur Earlham
Ch: Elizabeth Chaffin b 1-25-1848

SHELEY
Granville Louis b 11-27-1877 Salina OH dt Henry & Emily (**Paton**)
Blanch Anna b 12-17-1877 Hillsboro OH dt Oliver & Margaret **Paton**

SHEPHERD
Rena b 1-14-1884 Millville NJ dt Isaac N & Phebe

SHINN
Anna C
Ch: Newman H
　　James Eddie

Newman H s Anna C h Alice (**Scarce**) m 11-1878

SHOEMAKER
Charles H d 7-22-1897 ae 85y h Mary (**Boone**)
Ch: Wm C b 2-1836 Montgomery Co PA
　　Anna B b 5-29-1840 d 1-22-1880 bur Earlham
　　Hannah b 4-30-1845
　　Margaret b 8-31-1848
　　Isaac J

Wm C b 2-1-1836 Montgomery Co PA s Charles H & Mary (**Boone**)
Rachel J b 4-4-1840 Philadelphia PA dt George & Hannah H (**Richie**) **Dilks** m 4-4-1864 New Paris OH
Ch: Howard b 12-9-1872 d 5-27-1873 bur Montgomery MS
　　Elinor b 5-19-1874 d 7-24-1874 bur Smyrna
　　Sydney D b 1-22-1883 d 5-31-1883

SHOWAN
Henry Clay d 3-1869 ae 25y 10m h Lydia Ann dt Ephraim **Overman**
Ch: Mary Elizabeth b 10-18-1866 d 7-10-1867

SHRIVER
Helen b 12-24-1854 dt Joel & Sarah P **Horney**

SHROYER
John h Nellie Barnard b 1-9-1867 dt Michael & Hanora (**Connell**) **Conner** m 9-12-1889

SHULTZ
Samuel F b 11-1-1855 s Jacob & Mary
Eunice C b 7-1-1858 dt Daniel C & Keziah (**Brown**) **Hastings** m 3-25-1891 Newby OR
Ch: Irvin T b 2-25-1892
　　Carlin H b 6-27-1893
　　Joseph D b 5-27-1895
　　Eva L b 3-15-1897

SHUMARD
Warren h Sarah b 7-5-1850 dt Wm & Mary (**Sanders**) **Burgess** m 12-28-1871

SHUNKWILER
Ch: Mae b 2-1-1899 OH dt Oliver

SHUTE
Aaron h Martha b 10-5-1865 dt Lindley & Lydia G (**Willets**) **Miles** m Wayne Co
Ch: Miles L b 2-13-1890 Richmond

Samuel b 6-30-1778 h Jane
Ch: Nancy H b 12-17-1796
　　Rebeckah b 9-26-1798 d 10-16-1799
Alice 2w
Ch: Harriet b 12-6-1803
　　Charles b 3-31-1805
　　Aaron b 12-5-1806
　　Samuel b 7-13-1808
　　Hiram b 4-13-1810 d 11-3-1818
　　James P b 12-5-1811 d 3-30-1812
Sibyl 3w b 9-9-1787

SHUTE (Samuel cont)
Ch: Robert b 10-5-1816
　　Lydia b 11-13-1818
　　Amos H b 7-12-1820 d 9-18-1822
　　Elizabeth H b 11-19-1822
　　Edward F b 11-9-1825

SIMMS
Richard b 5-17-1846 England s Edward G & Ann (**Marshall**)
Florence E b 10-17-1852 Montgomery Co dt Christian & Elizabeth C **Ray** m 4-29-1879 Chicago IL
Ch: Ruthanna Mary b 6-9-1880 Chicago IL
　　Estella b 12-24-1886 Chicago IL
　　Gertrude Elizabeth b 2-16-1891 Chicago IL

SINGLETON
Arthur B s Flora E

SLEAP
Henry F h Lula R (**Colgrove**)
Ch: Lula Dunster b 11-27-1893
　　Silas Frederick b 12-21-1897
　　Caroline Louise b 10-2-1899

SLORP
Frank b 3-2-1883 s Henry & Elizabeth (**Pitman**)

SMALL
Benjamin d 3-7-1826 h Elizabeth
Ch: Penninah b 10-28-1792
　　Abigail b 7-25-1794
　　Mary b 10-7-1796
　　Miriam b 10-8-1798
　　Aaron b 7-28-1800 d 8-20-1821
　　Abner b 3-19-1802
　　Jesse b 2-27-1804
　　Sarah b 3-6-1807
　　Ephraim b 10-21-1809

SMITH
Albert h Isabelle
Ch: Arthur D b 3-13-1893 Wayne Co
　　John Everett b 8-20-1896/98 Wayne Co

Benjamin b 6-23-1787 s Joseph & Hannah
Tamar b 10-19-1784 dt John & Mary **Hawkins**
Ch: Hannah b 4-14-1809
　　Mary b 7-8-1811
　　John b 6-26-1813
　　Wm b 11-20-1814
　　Sarah b 1-22-1818
　　Lydia b 3-4-1819

Caroline M b 7-28-1872 dt Wm J & Clara (**Hopkins**) **Hicks** m 6-14-1894

Carrie Ruby b 10-14-1881/87 dt Theodore & Rosa **Keplinger**

Charles Curtis h Bertha b 5-17-1875 dt Benjamin C & Mary (**Wickett**) **Hill** m 6-14-1894
Ch: Mary Esther b 8-5-1895
　　Agnes Lucile b 7-22-1899

Charles G h Elmira M (**Pearson/Parson**) m 1872
Ch: Lurianna b 10-31-1875

Esther b 8-7-1819 dt John & Jane

Ethel L b 2-27-1887 dt Joseph P & Malina (**Owen**)

Ina b 3-19-1893 Union Co dt John W & Caroline

WHITEWATER MONTHLY MEETING
BIRTH AND DEATH RECORD

SMITH (cont)
Jacob h Sarah d 5-25-1815
Ch: Anna b 5-3-1804
     Nathan b l-2-1806
     Letitia b 7-22-1807
     Gulielma b 4-7-1809
     Mary b 12-23-1810
     Ezra b 10-25-1812
     Sarah b 3-3-1815 d 10-1819
Martha 2w
Ch: Samuel b 1-6-1818 d 9-13-1821
     James b 4-17-1820
     Elisha b 2-17-1822
     Phebe b 2-18-1824
     Seth b 4-16-1826

James b 4-3-1805 s Joseph & Elizabeth (**Dickinson**) d 1-4-1885 Dublin
Sarah J b 10-31-1814 dt James & Elizabeth (**Fossett**) **Willan** d 12-7-1885 m 12-26-1836 Dewsbury England
Ch: Eliza Willan b 4-8-1839

James b 4-14-1823 s Seth & Mary (**Taylor**) h Susan J (**Parrish**) m 3-29-1855

John h Tishe d 2-18-1817 ae 57y bur Whitewater
Ch: Elizabeth d 2-2-1825 ae 31y 2m 2d

John h Letitia
Ch: Sarah d 7-24-1833 ae 42y 14d
     Peninah

John d 11-1-1838 ae 82y bur Whitewater
Jane d 12-26-1839 bur Whitewater

John C h Lydia Mary b 1-6-1853 dt David & Lydia J **Nordyke**
Ch: Caroline
     Catharine
     Minnie

Letitia b 12-24-1827

Percy B b 7-28-1891 College Corner OH s Albert E & Aloha B

Seth b 4-4-1787 d 4-15-1865
Mary (**Taylor**) d 2-15-1884 ae 89y 1m 15d
Ch: James b 4-14-1823 Loudoun Co NC
     Mary
     Letitia
     Charlotte A

Sylvia Mae b 11-15-1883 dt Joseph & Mary **Johnson**

Wm b 9-23-1874 Wapakoneta OH s David & Mary (**Smith**)
Alice b 7-27-1879 Wayne Co dt Micajah Thomas & Sarah Catharine (**Latimer**) **Nordyke** m 10-31-1899

Willis J b 3-31-1875 s Andrew J & Elizabeth (**Hobbick**)

SNYDER
John W b 7-28-1854 Montgomery Co s George & Amy C
Ch: George b 7-24-1892
     Della May b 4-3-1894 Montgomery Co

SOLEMA
Blanch b 1-17-1897 Preble Co OH dt John & Jennie

SOMMERS
Mary A b 7-11-1859 Wayne Co dt Mahlon & Violena (**Garrett**) **Harvey**

SPAHR
Cora S b 7-2-1894 Centerville dt John R & Mamie/Marie (**Gentry**)

SPAULDING
Charles H b 9-22-1896 Richmond s Wm W & Mary E

SPECKENHIER
Harriett K b 6-6-1872 dt Eli & Rachel (**Puckett**) **Kenworthy**

Margaret dt Eli & Rachel (**Puckett**) **Kenworthy** m 5-5-1891

SPEER
John F b 12-21-1837 Spring Valley OH s James & Mary
Mary E b 12-25-1844 Clinton Co OH dt Thomas & Susanah **Hunnicutt** m 9-12-1878 Port William OH
Ch: Gracie b 2-10-1888 Bowersville OH
     Orisey b 3-27-1890 Bowersville OH

SPINNING
Lida P d 10-1889

SPOTTS
Wm b 12-26-1872 Wayne Co s Wm & Adaline A (**Winters**)
Elizabeth b 4-8-1879 Wayne Co dt Franklin & Charlotte (**Braske**) **Brown** m 4-20-1895 Wayne Co
Ch: Ida Maria b 12-7-1895 Wayne Co
     Alpha Charlotte b 11-25-1898 Wayne Co

SPRINGER
Nettie Clara b 3-18-1872 Indianapolis dt Daniel & Margaret

SPRONG
Otto b 1-9-1871 Hamilton Co OH s Alex M & Agusta (**Meeker**)

SQUIRES
Isadore Bell b 3-12-1856 Waynesville OH dt Joseph & Angelina **Lapsheley** m 9-5-1883 Spring Valley OH

STAFFORD
Samuel s Samuel & Abigail
Nancy b 8-23-1799 dt Wm & Sarah (**Evans**) **Hastings** d 2-7-1819 bur Whitewater m 7-1-1817 Whitewater

STANCOMB
Addie Myrtle b 11-21-1888 Lawrence Co dt John & Charlotte

STANLEY
Abraham b 1-23-1850 s Levi & Susan (**Butler**)
Anna Mary b 4-1-1860 dt Isaac & Martha (**Crampton**) **Cook** m 2-19-1879
Ch: Charles Asa b 2-8-1883
     Isaac Orlow

Isaac h Gulielma b 1-23-1849 dt Levi & Mary **Jessup** m 11-1878

Isaac Orlow h Belle dt Samuel Ellis & Sarah Ellen (**Dilks**) **Iredell**

Jesse h Hannah dt James & Elizabeth **Watson** m 1872
Ch: Marina Loan b 6-6-1873
     Mary Ethel b 5-15-1874

Margaret M b 11-30-1888

Wm h Lucinda E d 7-9-1899 ae 57y bur Elkhorn
Ch: Alva L b 6-4-1863
     Franklin Emmet b 6-22-1865
     Sarah Etta b 10-29-1867
     Ada F b 3-10-1869
     Bertha A b 11-13-1872
     Ota Mitchell b 3-5-1876

STANTON
Caroline C dt John Milton

Edna Elizabeth d 11-4-1863 Suffolk VA

STANTON (cont)
Edward d 12-3-1898 ae 70y bur Earlham h Phebe Ann
Ch: Henry A b 9-5-1854
　　Mary Emma b 4-27-1856 d 11-19-1861 bur Whitewater
　　Ada Esther b 4-3-1858 d 12-3-1898 bur Earlham
　　Carrie
　　Maurice

Frederick h Hannah d 7-4-1856 ae 65y 9m 3d bur Whitewater

Henry A b 9-5-1854 s Edward & Phebe Ann h Etta (**Conner**) m 9-1881

John T b 2-11-1841 Warren Co OH s Joseph & Catherine (**Stanton**)
Emily H b 9-16-1843 Morgan Co dt Hiram & Louisa **Hadley** m 10-18-1866 Morgan Co
Ch: Louisa b 6-15-1875 Morgan Co
　　Mariella b 11-26-1882 Marion Co
　　Wm Edward b 9-2-1883 Marion Co

Joseph h Catherine (**Stanton**)
Ch: Deborah Ann b 10-8-1837 Warren Co OH
　　John T b 2-11-1841 Warren Co OH

Joshua h Jane dt David & Miriam **Beard**

Mahala dt Geraldine O

STARBUCK
Edwin b 2-20-1866 Marion Co s Samuel & Luzena (**Jessup**)
Anna b 8-29-1868 Lancaster Co PA dt Isaac & Anna Margaret (**Frey**) **Diller** m 8-5-1896 Lancaster PA
Ch: Arthur Diller b 7-11-1898 Monterey CO

STARR
Annie E b 12-17-1834

Esther b 4-25-1795 d 5-5-1877 bur Earlham

Esther E dt Henry d 6-3-1887 bur Earlham

John d 6-25-1850 ae 73y 10m 22d bur Whitewater
Mary d 12-30-1865 ae 79y 12d bur Whitewater
Ch: Joshua d 9-28-1841 ae 23y 5m 24d bur Whitewater
　　Phebe d 8-10-1843 ae 23y 6m 2d bur Whitewater
　　Wm d 5-14-1843 ae 20y 8m 20d bur Whitewater
　　James d 6-26-1847 ae 22y 7m 11d bur Muney Lycoming Co PA
　　Sarah d 4-23-1844 ae 17y 1m 21d bur Whitewater

STEDDOM
Abijah b 2-14-1822 s John & Alice (**Teague**) d 11-5-1895 bur New Paris
Deborah M 2w b 10-20-1826 Greene Co OH dt Wm & Betty (**Walton**) **Mendenhall** m 10-31-1855 Greene Co OH
Ch: Edward K b 2-9-1860
　　Martha L b 3-6-1862
　　Ella C b 10-26-1863

Cornelia Adelaide b 1-17-1842 dt Wm N & Adelaide (**Park**) **Cammack** m 12-1-1859

John h Alice (**Teague**)
Ch: Abijah b 2-14-1822 d 11-5-1895 bur New Paris
　　Esther b 1-10-1827 d 11-18-1893 bur Goshen
　　Anna T b 2-28-1829 Warren Co OH

STEDHAM
Jonas d 10-26-1888 ae 80y bur Earlham
Elizabeth d 9-9-1894

STEGALL
Curtis h Susan Hannah b 5-29-1846 Darke Co OH dt Eli & Rachel **Mettler**
Ch: Clara F b 11-14-1874 Randolph Co

WHITEWATER MONTHLY MEETING
BIRTH AND DEATH RECORD

STEGALL (Curtis cont)
　　Irvin Delbert b 7-25-1884 Darke Co OH
　　Noah T

Hilda M b 8-20-1899 Wayne Co dt Milo & Viola

Milo C b 6-7-1880 Darke Co OH s Isaiah C/Ervin & Susan H

STEGLE
Sarah E b 2-25-1835

STEPHENS
Francis W b 4-29-1858 s Jacob & Caroline (**Spear/Speer**)
Pharaba b 6-24-1857 dt Josiah T & Elizabeth (**Wilson**) **White** m 6-1-1893 Wayne Co

Henry h Phebe Alice b 8-11-1853 dt Tilnais & Rachel (**Hinshaw**) **Hodgin** m 8-25-1875

Myra C b 4-22-1890

STEVENSON
Elmer P b 8-1-1885

J Elmer b 9-6-1872 Huntsville s Charles & Emily
Chloe C b 9-19-1872 Bloomingport dt Wm & Julia **Kinsey** m 2-1-1893 Wayne Co
Ch: Francis Charles b 1-31-1896 Spartanburg
　　Charles Ernest b 6-8-1898 Modoc

STEWART
Albert W d 10-30-1883 bur Earlham

Robert b 1-27-1879 Harrison Co OH s John & Mary

Rosetta dt Susannah **Mills** m Lancaster OH

Sidney h Alice E
Ch: Edgar
　　Florence

STIDHAM
Jessie Lois b 4-22-1890 dt Wm A & Lillie F (**Tucker**)

Nora A b 10-5-1875 dt J Dunham & Hannah **Hampton** m 7-4-1893 Wayne Co

STIGGLEMAN
Corwin H h Leona Coreen b 12-30-1872 dt Samuel Charles & Cora (**Zimmer**) **Winder** m Wayne Co
Ch: Nellie Irene
　　Leo Charles

STILLMAN
Ralph h Juanita (**Garza**) b 7-2-1870 m 12-27-1893

STIMMEL
Samuel C b 9-13-1881 Chillicothe OH s John A & Anna E

STONE
Rena Harriett b 11-4-1886 dt Jesse Marvin & Elizabeth (**Binford**)

STRADER
Grace dt Eli & Mary A (**Kinsey**) **Roberts**

STRANAHAN
John Henry b 4-1-1848 s Wm & Mary (**Sarieft**)
Othelia P b 11-29-1849 dt James P & Jane (**Johnson**) **Kemp** m 12-28-1871
Ch: Edgar H b 4-10-1875

STRATE
Harry b 9-6-1888 Iroquois IL s Francis Wesley & Anna

**WHITEWATER MONTHLY MEETING
BIRTH AND DEATH RECORD**

STRATTON
Joseph E h Martha H
Ch: Henry H b 8-31-1847
  Micajah H b 3-4-1850

Katherine Mildred b 1-12-1885 Randolph Co dt Isaac & Emily

Zimri d 1873 bur Earlham h Hannah
Ch: Joseph J d 5-6-1862
  Charles W
  Samuel
  Ella Maria d 9-28-1852 ae 17y 3m 1d bur Whitewater
  Sarah Elizabeth b 10-2-1849

STREET
Lewis h Sarah T
Ch: Edgar L
  Charles F b 4-29-1862

Samuel h Anna
Ch: Jane b 3-2-1833
  John b 9-24-1834

STRETCH
James h Ann
Ch: Elizabeth b 3-12-1809
  James A b 7-15-1817
  Sarah G b 10-24-1819
  Hannah Ann b 2-15-1826

STRONG
Corlis H b 12-18-1886 Grand Rapids MI s Henry & Louisa

STUART
Amos b 6-30-1808 s John & Sarah (**Guyer**)
Melissa E b 6-26-1833 Miami Co OH dt Samuel & Anna (**Kelly**)
Miles m 3-25-1875 Wayne Co
Ch: Mary A

Henry S b 3-24-1862 Stringtown s Benjamin & Elizabeth
Lula b 5-16-1873 Sulphur Springs dt Allen & Sarah Ann **Crandall**
m 9-12-1894 New Castle
Ch: Ova Grace b 7-5-1898 New Castle

Jehu b 11-10-1772 s Jehu & Sarah
Sarah b 12-12-1772 dt Thomas & Mary **Cook**
Ch: Absalom b 3-11-1796
  Jehu b 10-15-1798
  Susanna b 11-10-1800
  John b 10-22-1802
  Mary b 10-10-1804
  Temple b 11-15-1806
  Beauly b 10-14-1808
  Sarah b 7-4-1810
  Anna b 2-9-1813
  Robert b 1-7-1815
  Cyrus b 7-20-1817
  Ithamer b 5-18-1820

STUBBS
Alden h Mary (**Conarre**)
Ch: Amy E b 1-3-1870
  Della M b 4-10-1888 Preble Co OH

Eli b 11-24-1823 Preble Co OH s Elisha & Elizabeth h Anna F
(**Moffett**) m 6-4-1851
Ch: Ruth Emma b 4-20-1852 Preble Co OH
  Mary Anna b 7-27-1854

John F b 4-16-1843
Rachel C b 7-14-1845

Joseph h Maria

STUBBS (Joseph cont)
Ch: Esther
  Margaret

Mary d 10-10-1884 ae 82y 5m

Mary Emily b 12-27-1857 dt Jonathan & Rachel

Rachel b 4-8-1841

STUDY
Addison h Alice J b 1-5-1857 Wayne Co dt Nathan & Anna Eliz
Doan m 9-13-1877 Wayne Co
Ch: Wm A b 9-21-1895 Wayne Co

STUPP
Katherine A b 11-21-1847 Miamisburg OH dt George & Leah
Garrison m 12-14-1865 Miamisburg OH

STYLES
Alfred b 9-27-1871 Corwin OH s Aaron & Sarah
Sarah Ruth b 5-18-1875 Dover OH dt Dean & Luvica **Robinett**
Ch: Frona Elizabeth b 1885 Xenia OH
  Ernest Wm b 2-10-1894 Dayton OH
  George Kermeth b 4-11-1896 Dayton OH
  Luella May b 11-12-1899 Stillwater MN

SUFFRINS
John d 9-7-1875 ae 82y 4m 9d bur Earlham

SUTTON
Caroline b 6-1-1876 dt Aaron Franklin & Anne (**Moore**)

Charles G b 3-17-1863 Jay Co s Charles J & Emeline (**Sutton**)

David b 4-26-1827 s Isaac & Sarah (**Underhill**)
Deborah A dt Aaron & Margaret **White** d 1-29-1888 ae 54y bur Earlham
Ch: Marcia E b 12-28-1860
  Howard b 12-16-1868
  David b 3-4-1880 Middlesex Co MA

Howard b 12-16-1868 s David & Deborah (**White**) m 6-23-1896

John G h Mary Ellen b 11-1-1860 Wayne Co dt Wm & Mary Ellen
(**Barker**) **Baxter** m Wayne Co
Ch: Helena B b 2-25-1888

Mary b 12-6-1846 dt Charles H & Marcia (**White**) **Moore** m 8-1-1890

Mary B dt Aaron & Elizabeth M

SWAIN
Thomas F b 5-8-1843
Elzena b 4-26-1846
Ch: Minnie b 6-29-1877
  Alida
  Ellen

SWEET
Solomon b 7-27-1800 s Judith
Catharine b 9-13-1804 NC dt Stephen & Rebekah (**Barnard**) **Macy**
d 7-11-1835 bur Whitewater
Ch: Anna b 8-18-1822
  Sarah b 9-15-1824
  Rebekah b 11-27-1826
  Louiza Amelia b 5-8-1829
  Charles M b 9-7-1831 d 7-6-1832 bur Whitewater
  Eli M b 5-29-1833

SYMONS
Caleb h Peninnah
Ch: Sarah b 3-13-1807
  Lydia b 11-17-1808

SYMONS (cont)
Jesse h Sarah
Ch: Jesse
Nathan b 10-15-1786

Jesse s Jehosaphat & Lydia d 1-16-1812 ae 56y 11m bur Whitewater

Jesse s Jesse & Sarah h Peninah dt John & Letitia **Smith** m 7-27-1812
Ch: John b 9-2-1814
Alfred b 10-21-1816
Anderson b 3-13-1819
Nathan b 3-8-1821
Lucinda b 6-21-1823
Elizabeth b 12-27-1826
Caleb b 4-7-1828 d 8-5-1829 bur Whitewater
Letitia b 8-5-1830

Jesse h Margaret d 11-12-1839 ae 53y 9m 20d bur Whitewater

John M m 4-30-1856 Spiceland h Lydia M

Josiah b 6-10-1812 s Thomas & Hannah

Nathan b 10-15-1786 s Jesse & Sarah
Jane b 12-28-1793 dt Obadiah & Elizabeth **Small**
Ch: Elizabeth b 3-3-1811
Sarah b 3-12-1813
Jesse b 2-25-1815

Samuel h Ann
Ch: Lydia b 6-22-1825
James b 1-7-1828
John b 10-18-1830
Abraham b 8-31-1832
Henry b 12-22-1834

TAGGART
Alpheus M h Caroline (**Richardson**)

TALBERT
Samuel A h Lydia E
Ch: Jessie
India Ora
Melvin E
Earnest L

TALBOT
Jacob d 12-4-1831 ae 83y 3m 15d bur Orange
Susannah d 4-13-1842 ae 92y 2m 21d bur Orange
Ch: Sarah b 1-13-1791
Rebeckah b 6-29-1793 d 1-8-1858 bur Orange

TAYLOR
Charlotte b 6-22-1817 dt James & Charlotte

Elizabeth d 7-25-1891

Lewis A b 4-13-1876 Colorado Springs CO s Frank & Isabelle (**Greene**)

Lillie May b 6-30-1872 dt David W & Mattie E **Wolfe** d 6-8-1897

Mary F b 10-24-1887 Denver CO dt Isaac & Angeline

TEAFORD
Orville J b 11-1-1895 Darke Co OH s George Henry & Margaret

TEAGUE
Isaac Cooper b 7-13-1826 Montgomery Co OH s Samuel & Prudence (**Cooper**) d 10-25-1897 bur Earlham
Joanna/ Johanna M b 2-14-1835 Miami Co OH dt John & Rebecca (**Jay**) **Miles** m 1-13-1852

TEAGUE (Isaac cont)
Ch: Martha E b 1-19-1854
Laura P b 12-12-1858
Edwin b 2-14-1866
Myrtle b 1-19-1871
Pearl b 8-20-1875

Samuel h Prudence b 10-4-1807 dt Isaac & Elizabeth (**Kennedy**) **Cooper** m 6-2-1825 Montgomery Co OH
Ch: Isaac Cooper b 7-13-1826 Montgomery Co OH d 10-25-1897 bur Earlham

TEAS
Edward S h Sarah A b 2-1-1838 dt Amos & Matilda (**Hadley**) **Stuart** m 7-25-1867
Ch: Mary M b 9-4-1871
Vestal H
Willie S
Frederic

Gibson b 12-16-1809 DE s Charles & Mary
Rebecca b 4-30-1811 Redstone MM dt Enos & Elizabeth (**Jones**) **Grave**
Ch: Charles

Sarah C d 2-5-1871 ae 69y 9m 11d bur Earlham

TEST
Alpheus b 2-6-1821 s Samuel & Sarah (**Maxwell**)
Elizabeth b 1-3-1822 dt Charles & Elizabeth **Moffitt** d 5-4-1883 bur Earlham
Ch: Edward b 12-25-1856
Mary Elisabeth b 7-24-1858 d 11-26-1858 bur Whitewater
Emma b 10-9-1859
Phebe (**Talbert**) 2w d 3-9-1893 bur Earlham
Ch: Anna Maria
Martha/Sarah B (**Little**) **Bond** 3w m 11-28-1895

Edna dt Isaac & Lily (**Hill**) **Moore**

Erastus b 11-12-1836 Union Co s Samuel & Hannah (**Jones**)
Mary b 12-5-1844 dt Joseph & Phebe (**Stanton**) **Taylor** m 8-13-1868 Monrovia
Ch: Frederick Cleveland b 6-14-1869 Richmond
Chas Darwin b 6-18-1874 Dundee IL
Louis Agassiz b 6-18-1874 Dundee IL

Frederick Cleveland b 6-14-1869 Richmond s Erastus & Mary (**Taylor**) h Annabel (**Choclane**) m 9-22-1896 Dundee IL

Josiah b 12-6-1826/36 s Samuel Jr & Hannah (**Jones**) d 1864 h Miriam (**Dennis**)

Lindley M b 3-12-1841 s Samuel Jr & Hannah (**Jones**) h Donna Martha (**Kelly**)
Ch: Herbert E b 5-1-1867
Lina E

Oliver b 7-10-1834 s Samuel Jr & Hannah (**Jones**) h Sarah (**Dennis**) bur Earlham
Ch: Samuel Francis b 10-24-1863 d 10-7-1864
Sarah Elma b 6-22-1865
Hannah Amelia b 10-19-1866
Mary Lenora b 8-24-1868
Margaret (**Striedel**) 2w
Bertha (**Grace**) 3w bur Earlham

Rufus b 1-12-1833 Union Co s Samuel Jr & Hannah (**Jones**) h Margaret (**Stubbs**) m 4-28-1858 New Garden
Ch: Irvin b 12-22-1868
Lydia Symons 2w b 2-18-1833 dt Caleb & Hannah (**Sanders**) **Hall** m 2-4-1890 Spiceland
Ch: Lucile Celmens b 12-2-1885 (adopted)

WHITEWATER MONTHLY MEETING
BIRTH AND DEATH RECORD

TEST (Rufus cont)
Samuel Sr b 1-20-1774 d 9-18-1856 bur Whitewater
Sarah (**Maxwell**) b 1-12-1777 d 3-10-1846
Ch: Samuel Jr b 8-6-1798 d 8-10-1849 bur Whitewater

Samuel Jr b 8-6-1798 s Samuel Sr & Sarah (**Maxwell**) d 8-10-1849 bur Whitewater
Hannah b 6-19-1799 dt Morgan & Hannah **Jones** d 1-15-1871 bur Earlham m 2-23-1826
Ch: Josiah b 12-6-1826 d 10-1864
    Zaccheus b 9-13-1828
    Wm b 4-21-1830
    Rufus b 1-12-1833
    Oliver b 7-10-1834
    Erastus b 11-12-1836
    Lindley M b 3-12-1841

Wm b 4-21-1830 s Samuel Jr & Hannah (**Jones**)
Emily (**Woodard**) d 3-9-1893 m 1859
Ch: Hannah Mary
    Williamenah
    Wm H
    James W

Zaccheus b 9-13-1828 s Samuel Jr & Hannah (**Jones**)
Elizabeth M dt Enos G & Elivana (**Townsend**) **Pray**
Ch: Carrie b 5-3-1858 d 5-9-1858 bur Earlham
    Charles Sumner b 8-25-1860 d 12-15-1860 bur Earlham
    Alice b 12-2-1861
    Martha b 12-30-1864
Sarah P (**Anthony**) 2w

THOMAS
Carlton b 3-24-1890 Fountain City s Marquis & Minerva (**Elliott**)

Charles E h Bertha b 2-2-1874 dt Jacob & Minnia (**Thorne**) **Elliott** m 1-19-1897
Ch: Richard W b 7-23-1898

Ellsworth b 10-9-1863 s Peter & Priscilla E (**Cox**)
Letitia C b 12-15-1859 dt Smith & Margaret (**Grimes**) **Crampton** m 8-27-1884 Middleborough Wayne Co
Ch: Franklin M
    Sarah M
    Bessie
    Maria
    Herbert
    Herschell E b 1-17-1898

Forest F b 4-18-1895 Randolph Co s Wm B & Elizabeth (**Rash**)

John h Lydia
Ch: Polley b 12-19-1792
    James b 8-26-1794
    Jesse b 9-9-1796
    Hannah b 11-4-1798
    Nanney b 10-27-1800
    Lydia b 3-19-1803
    Ruth b 4-1-1805
    Henly b 5-22-1807
    Huldah b 4-7-1809
    John b 7-1-1811 d 1-22-1812 bur Whitewater

Lenna M b 10-22-1885 dt Jesse & Effie M (**Zeek**)

Martin M h Agnes Maria b 2-18-1860 dt Benjamin & Susan (**Collins**) **Wickett** m 8-27-1882
Ch: Laura A b 6-20-1887

Mary T b 5-27-1834 Harrison Co OH dt John & Mary **Green**

Nancy D b 8-14-1896 Union Co dt Wm & Jeanette

THOMAS (cont)
Peter h Priscilla E b 5-14-1840 NC dt Benjamin & Jemima (**Branson**) **Cox**
Ch: Cynthia b 1-1-1862
    Ellsworth b 10-9-1863
    Olinda B b 3-9-1866 Wayne Co
    Cora E b 6-13-1869

Robert s Wm & Jennie

Wm E b 12-24-1869 McArthur OH s Zephaniah & Minerva C
Clara M b 12-18-1872 Athens AL dt Silas & Mathilda **Chapin**
Ch: Eva M b 3-22-1895 Wayne Co

Wm Penn h Phebe Ann d 2-1893 bur Earlham
Ch: Albert R b 8-30-1855 d 10-20-1861
    Benjamin Franklin b 5-29-1857 d 10-7-1861
    Wm Anderson b 7-9-1859
    Martha E b 5-18-1865

Zephaniah h Minerva C
Ch: Wm E b 12-24-1869
    Myrtle Rebecca b 3-31-1876
    Albert Clarence b 12-3-1878
    Mary d 4-23-1885 bur Earlham

THOMPSON
Charles d 2-27-1884 bur Centrrville

Goldie b 5-1-1897 Eaton OH dt Warren & Ada

James M h Luella J

John W b 9-9-1854 s John B & Hannah (**Wilson**)
Mary E b 8-10-1860 dt Webster & Charlotte (**Mark**) **Smith**
Ch: Bessie V b 4-13-1884

THORNBERG
India b 6-30-1890 Randolph Co dt Restore & Annetta

THORNBURG
Abel h Rhoda
Ch: Lydia b 1-7-1819
    Eliza b 10-10-1820
    Maryann b 3-30-1823 d 8-28-1823
    Maryann b 11-14-1824
    Rachel b 12-9-1830
    Wm b 8-1-1837

John M h Sarah (**Foland**) b 5-16-1848
Ch: Bertha Lillian b 7-15-1879

THORNE
Allen Haines h Ruth H
Ch: Ollie M b 3-5-1875
    Ida b 2-29-1876 Wayne Co

TIBBETTS
Charles Albert b 2-15-1826 Dover NH s Philip & Abigail (**Roberts**)
Mary H (**Dean**) m 1-19-1854 Dover NH
Ch: Charles Edwin b 4-25-1855 Muscatine IA

Charles Edwin b 4-25-1855 Muscatine IA s Charles Albert & Mary H (**Dean**)
Imelda A b 10-23-1859 Cutler IA dt John H & Edith (**Dean**) **Painter** m 7-30-1879 Muscatine IA
Ch: Edith Mary b 12-18-1882 Mahaska IA
    Herbert Edwin b 9-19-1887 Los Angeles CA
    J Walter b 11-28-1889 Los Angeles CA

TIMBERLAKE
Benjamin B b 5-4-1870 s Edward & Martha (**Brown**) h Mary O (**Floyd**) m 5-19-1896

TIMBERLAKE (cont)
Edward h Martha N b 8-20-1832 dt Benjamin & Mary Ann/Naomi **Brown**
Ch: Benjamin B b 5-4-1870

TITSWORTH
Abraham D b 7-17-1861 s Abraham
Mary Elizabeth/Emily b 5-30-1859 dt Timothy & Naomi W (**Morgan**) **Harrison** m 1-1-1884 Richmond
Ch: Hellen Bills
     Frederic F/H
     Marey E

TOMS
Joseph d 8-20-1894 bur Dublin
Elizabeth W dt Elias & Elizabeth (**White**) **Henby** bur Earlham m 4-8-1875
Ch: Maud b 1-16-1876
     Wm Henry b 4-16-1877

Linville b 9-1-1891 Warren Co OH s John & Elmira

TONEY
Alice b 6-30-1863 dt Warner & Rebecca (**Crampton**) **Davenport**

TOOKER
Emily H b 8-8-1850

TOWNSEND
James b 12-17-1787 s John & Elvira
Rosanna b 9-16-1787 dt Hannah **Smith**
Ch: Thomas b 12-3-1808
     Rachel b 3-7-1810 d 2-22-1811
     Celah b 11-10-1811
     Charlotte b 7-27-1813

Jesse C b 3-3-1897 Wayne Co s Harvey & Olive

John h Elvira
Ch: James b 12-17-1787
     Wm b 4-10-1795

Jonathan h Mary
Ch: Daniel b 8-22-1815
     John b 12-7-1817 d 1-28-1821 bur Orange
     Mahlon b 9-26-1819
     Amos b 12-13-1821
     Stephen b 4-2-1824
     James b 6-16-1826 d 8-7-1826 bur Orange
     Rebecca b 6-30-1827
     Wm b 10-3-1829

Mary A b 1-22-1838 dt Francis & Anna (**French**)

Wm b 4-10-1795 s John & Elvira
Elizabeth b 9-12-1795 dt John & Hannah **Morrow** m 5-9-1816 Whitewater
Ch: Eli b 4-20-1817
     Mary b 11-10-1818
     Sarah b 7-24-1820
     Elvira b 6-5-1822
     Lydia b 12-1-1823
     John M b 10-7-1825
     Eliza Ann b 1-8-1828
     Esther b 1-4-1830

TRACY
John h Catharine b 12-13-1861 New Madison OH dt Samuel & Elizabeth **Mikesell** m 9-28-1882/83 Eldorado CO

TREFFINGER
John F h Ada B b 10-2-1853 dt Edwin & Martha (**Demime**) **Williams** m 9-14-1887

TROGGETT
Sarah M b 10-27-1870 dt Peter & Martha (**Little**) **Bond**

TRUEBLOOD
Alpheus b 6-14-1849 Salem s Joshua & Esther (**Parker**)
Almeda b 4-6-1849 Jonesboro dt Quincy & Mary (**Jay**) **Baldwin** m 9-2-1869 New Garden

Edwin P b 5-16-1861 Washington Co s Jehu & Louisa (**Pritchard**)
Penina b 6-25-1863 Rush Co dt Robert & Mary (**Newby**) **Henley** m 7-2-1889 Carthage

Francis b 7-1-1841 Washington Co
Amy L b 9-8-1840/41
Ch: Alva b 12-17-1871

Walter L h Almeda P b 3-15-1861 dt Joseph & Margaret (**Reed**) **Finney** m 9-19-1883
Ch: Virgil
     Laura Bessie b 10-15-1886
     Herschel J b 8-18-1891

Wm N b 3-22-1846 s Elias & Elizabeth (**Kelley**)
Ruth Emma b 4-20-1852 Preble Co OH dt Eli & Anna F (**Moffett**) **Stubbs** m 8-8-1877 Wayne Co
Ch: Wilford S b 5-9-1878 Wayne Co
     Inez b 7-31-1879 Wayne Co
     Howard Moffitt b 4-16-1884 Wayne Co
     Ralph Waldo b 11-19-1885 Wayne Co
     Charles Kingsley b 8-20-1893

TURNER
Caroline
Ch: Estella
     Orville Hugh
     Ruth Elizabeth
     Rollin

Elijah H b 10-26-1870 Greene Co OH s John & Margaret E
Nettie B b 7-28-1870 Clinton Co OH dt Gilead & Nancy Jane **Stingley** m 10-24-1895 Clinton Co OH
Ch: Noble E b 9-6-1897 Clinton Co OH

Harry E b 10-23-1890 Dayton OH s Elmer

TUTTLE
Dorothy b 2-7-1897 dt Henry F & Nellie (**Clark**)

TYLER
Charles Henry s Joseph & Sarah (**Ennis**)

ULLRICK
Frederick h Urilla (**Schaffer**)
Ch: Laura F b 7-29-1853
     Josephine b 4-28-1860

UNDERHILL
Jesse B d 5-26-1898 ae 68y bur Earlham
Susan b 7-25-1841/42 Bedford Co PA dt Daniel & Annie (**Hoover**) **Bowers** m 9-6-1866 Hagerstown
Ch: John M b Wayne Co
     Edward F
     Alexander E
     Jane W b 3-19-1872

John M b Wayne Co s Jesse B & Susan (**Bowers**) h Indiana (**Miller**)
Ch: Olive Sylphia b 12-17-1894 Wayne Co

UNTHANK
Charles R b 11-12-1846 Wayne Co s Pleasant & Sarah Ann (**Pitts**)
Mary E b 2-2-1849 Wayne Co dt Milton & Sarah (**Bakehorn**) **Whitacre** m 8-23-1866 Wayne Co

WHITEWATER MONTHLY MEETING
BIRTH AND DEATH RECORD

UNTHANK (Charles R cont)
Ch: Albert
      Pleasant
      Florence

Frank b 12-24-1871 La Bette KS s Wm A & Annie E

John h Mary
Ch: Levicy b 10-4-1804
      Anna b 3-18-1806
      Jonathan b 12-21-1807
      Sally b 12-12-1809
      Betsy b 11-4-1811
      Mary b 8-17-1813
      Joseph b 11-10-1815
      Rebekah b 10-6-1817
      John Allen b 12-18-1819

Joseph h Rebecca b 4-2-1771 dt Wm & Elizabeth **Stanley** d 8-16-1833 bur Whitewater
Ch: Beulah b 11-2-1795 d 4-28-1871 bur Earlham
      Elizabeth b 12-18-1804 d 1-23-1872
      Sarah b 4-11-1806

UTTER
Glen b 7-5-1887 s Dora & Minnie

Walter F b 9-27-1868 Columbia s George & Phebe
Mattie E b 7-25-1872 Laurel dt Cyrus & Ruth **Allison** m 5-26-1898 Covington KY

VALENTINE
John b 4-24-1812 d 8-12-1887 bur Earlham
Martha b 10-18-1816
Ch: Wm Henry b 11-28-1840
      Ann b 8-27-1843
      Cornelia b 7-11-1846 d 6-20-1877 bur Earlham
      Gulielma b 6-26-1849 d 4-14-1871 bur Earlham
      Georgiana b 10-19-1854
      Joseph Edward b 11-15-1860 d 6-3-1863 bur Earlham

Wm Henry b 11-28-1840 s John & Martha
Harriett A (**Morrill**) m 6-26-1866
Ch: Edward J b 6-4-1868
      Fletcher E b 5-27-1870 d 3-31-1893
      Wm H b 6-5-1872
      Warren P b 10-12-1875

VAZEY
Mary E b 7-21-1855 Ross Co OH dt John M & Minerva (**McCarty**) **Williams**

VEREGEE
Frank H b 9-25-1865
Dora b 12-16-1864 m 6-2-1888

VORE
Azel h Elizabeth
Ch: Sarah Ann b 5-30-1852 d 3-1871
      Thomas b 8-20-1854
      Isaac L b 3-17-1858
      Mary Jane b 10-26-1860
      Tacy

Elmer E h Martha Jane
Ch: Alice b 11-19-1892
      Inez b 1-4-1890 Richmond
      Othello b 1-13-1894 Richmond
      Nellie S b 9-1-1899 Wayne Co

John h Mary Jane
Ch: Eva J b 11-8-1886 Wayne Co
      Bell E b 10-4-1890 Bloomingsport

VORE (cont)
Thomas b 8-20-1854 s Azel & Elizabeth
Sadie b 12-13-1851 dt Wm M & Annie **Hodgin**
Ch: Vernon W b 4-5-1881

VOSS
Michael T h Anna A
Ch: Pearl A
      Clarence S
      Blanche
      Carl L

VOTAW
Isaac b 11-17-1817 s Jonathan & Elizabeth (**Hampton**) d 7-9-1897 bur Earlham
Anna Maria b 2-22-1827 Wayne Co dt Eleazar & Gulielma (**Sanders**) **Hiatt** m 1-3-1849
Ch: Clarence G b 11-12-1853 Wayne Co
      Ida M b 10-14-1862 Wayne Co d 10-22-1893 bur Earlham

WAKEFIELD
Jennie dt Joseph J & Mary Ann

WALDO
Ruth b 2-9-1893 dt Henry Clay & Nancy Ann (**Bell**)

WALKER
Elizabeth d 12-19-1878 ae 73y bur Wilmington OH
Ch: Louis C
      Calvin B
      Eliza Ann
      Martha Jane

James C b 8-27-1842 Wayne Co s John S & Sarah (**Clawson**)

Sarah C d 7-1-1899 ae 83y

WALL
Mabel b 8-8-1872 Springfield IL dt Charles & Jane E

WALLACK
David h Sarah

WALTERS
Laura M b 7-14-1856 dt Daniel & Sabina (**Shuman**) **Bolender**

Wm s Belle

WAMPLER
Jacob B b 12-17-1862 Madison Co s Joshua M & Rachel E

WAND
Florence E b 8-1-1886 Patrick dt Ellen J D

WARD
Edgar J h Lula b 12-31-1863 dt Webster W & Emma (**Rissebrow**) **Teague** m 1-4-1882

Elizabeth A
Ch: Mary T
      Almina Jane
      Elizabeth N

Jacob M b 4-9-1858 Henry Co s Jacob M & Martha C h Florence G
Ch: Orvill P
      Grace

WARDER
James h Carrie D (**Newcomb**)

WARING
Wm P d 2-10-1885 h Semira H
Ch: Emma

WARING (Wm P cont)
Percival d 1-19-1877 ae 20y bur Earlham
Gertrude b 8-12-1867

WARNER
Rebecca P
Ch: Fairlamb Harrison
    Ella

WASHBURNE
Paul Valens h Maria b 2-5-1851 dt Joseph & Esther G (**Hiatt**) **Dickinson**
Ch: Florence b 7-7-1875 d 3-29-1883 bur Earlham
    Esther b 8-18-1877
    Winefred
    John

WASSON
Archibald b 8-4-1773 s Joseph & Sarah
Elizabeth b 9-26-1774
Ch: Calvin b 2-14-1798
    Jehiel b 1-16-1800
    Anselm b 3-19-1802
    Abigail b 8-6-1804
    Sally b 9-25-1806
    Macamy b 4-25-1810
    Eliza b 7-24-1812

Calvin b 2-14-1798 s Archibald & Elizabeth h Mary
Ch: Wm b 6-20-1819
    Nathan b 3-14-1821

WATSON
Elizabeth b 8-29-1829
Ch: Idell
    Leah

Harmon C h Lydia Ann (**Overman**) **Showan**
Ch: Charles C b 6-22-1870
    Frank E b 12-22-1872
    Lizzie Bell b 8-30-1874
    Edna

James h Elizabeth
Ch: Hannah
    Ida Howard
    Late G

Wm b 11-3-1869 Barry MI h Emily b 2-27-1868 Barry MI

Wm h Jane d 11-1898 ae 69y bur Whitley Co
Ch: Arthur
    Lewis
    Mary
    Josephine
    Franklin L

WATTER
Betty b 5-22-1889 Jessamine Co KY dt Draper & Mary

WATTS
Leotha b 12-5-1893 Preble Co OH dt Newton & Tilly

Martha (**Lundy**)

WAY
Huldah d 7-27-1860 bur KS

Rodah d 7-25-1860 bur KS

WEBB
Benjamin h Sarah b 4-1-1835 dt Achilles & Beulah (**Unthank**) **Williams**

WHITEWATER MONTHLY MEETING
BIRTH AND DEATH RECORD

WEBB (Benjamin cont)
Ch: Robert Williams b 8-11-1869
    Mary Edith b 7-3-1872 d 3-24-1874 bur Earlham
    Alice C b 10-17-1874

John Richard b 1-9-1874 Frontena Ontario Canada s Wm & Elizabeth A (**Hodgson**)

Rena b 7-1-1875 Wayne Co dt Lewis & Anna (**Vereggee**)

WEBSTER
Ella M b 5-18-1854

WEEKLY
Charles Luther b 11-28-1891 Lawrence Co OH s A V & Mary L

WEEKS
James h Casandra
Ch: Merrick C b 8-23-1831
    Ruth Anna b 1-12-1833
    Jane b 5-22-1834
    John Wesley b 12-12-1835
    Samuel b 8-28-1837 d 10-20-1850 bur Smyrna
    Rachel b 11-12-1840
    Louisa b 3-12-1843
    Mary E b 5-17-1845
    Nathan d 9-3-1850 ae 3m 27d bur Smyrna

John s Wm & Susannah d 12-3-1828 ae abt 56y bur Whitewater
Jane d 8-26-1850/56 ae 75y 10m 8d bur Whitewater
Ch: Lydia b 5-15-1795
    Wm b 9-16-1797
    Benjamin b 12-28-1799
    Anne b 5-16-1802
    James b 11-11-1804
    Ralph b 3-3-1809

John W h Caroline M (**Clark**)
Ch: Lois b 11-27-1867
    Ray C b 9-18-1886

Merrick C b 8-23-1831 s James & Casandra h Hannah Eliza
Ch: Minnie C
    Charles L
    Cora M
    Frank W

Reuben d 11-16-1850 ae 53y 17d

WEHR
Anna b 8-19-1892 Clermont Co OH dt Chris & Lilian

WELLER
Grace R b 9-13-1877 dt George Russell & Alice Jane (**Hill**) **Dilks**

WEST
Wm b 5-6-1844 h Mary
Ch: Raymond
    Gladys

WESTCOMBE
Charles F d 3-1881 bur MO
Priscilla d 8-14-1881 bur Earlham

WHETZEL
Rosella W b 8-14-1871 Wheeling WV dt Frances M & Mary K **Showalter**

WHINERY
James h Mary
Ch: Enos
    Henry
    Alpheus

WHITEWATER MONTHLY MEETING
BIRTH AND DEATH RECORD

WHINERY (James cont)
    Adelaide
    Oliver M

WHITACRE
Jesse b 8-2-1861 Connersville s James & Sarah
Ch: Martha
      James
      Ruth

Margaret b 3-19-1886 Connersville dt Jess/John & Phebe

Martha b 9-12-1857 Henry Co dt Madison & Mary **White**

Philip h Dora (**Brumfield**)
Ch: Mamie b 9-11-1888 Richmond
      James M b 3-5-1893 Wayne Co

Wm h Sarah
Ch: Mary Ann b 11-27-1822
      Bethele b 8-24-1824 d 3-21-1826
      Milton H b 1-7-1827
      Jonathan R
      Louisa

WHITE
Alice d 8-4-1874 bur Maple Grove

Charles h Rosaline Anna b 12-24-1866 dt John S & Mary A (**Brown**) **Richie**
Ch: Henry E
      Benjamin M

David F h Angelina
Ch: Elizabeth H
      Edith
      Rose Elma

Edward h Mary B dt James & Elizabeth **Johnson**

Elizabeth b 9-23-1879 Wayne Co dt David Francis & Elizabeth (**Hough**)

James b 7-18-1825 Wayne Co s Joseph & Alice (**Clawson**)
Anna T b 2-28-1829 Warren Co OH dt John & Alice (**Teague**) **Steddom** m 1-23-1856
Ch: Sarah Josephine b 12-11-1856
      Charles S b 1-11-1859
      Ellen Alice b 8-18-1862
      Joseph Selden b 12-10-1866
      Albert F b 8-19-1870 d 10-19-1870
      Hattie P b 11-30-1873

Joseph h Alice (**Clawson**)
Ch: James b 7-18-1825 Wayne Co
      Wm Irvin b 11-13-1838 Wayne Co
      Joseph C b 11-3-1843 Wayne Co

Joseph b 10-8-1874 h Daisy (**Barnet**) m 8-11-1897 New Paris

Joseph C b 11-3-1843 Wayne Co s Joseph & Alice (**Clawson**)
Hannah H Jr b 4-2-1847 Philadelphia PA dt George & Hannah (**Richie**) **Dilks** m 8-11-1868 Smyrna
Ch: Ellis Clinton b 7-24-1870
      Wm Dilks b 2-6-1872
      George b 10-8-1874 d 8-7-1875 bur Maple Grove
      Joseph b 10-8-1874 Wayne Co
      Mary Alice b 6-10-1879 Wayne Co

Josiah T b 4-3-1824 s David & Elizabeth (**White**)
Elizabeth (**Wilson**) m 1-19-1846 Perquimans Co NC
Ch: Wm W b 11-2-1846
      Pharaba W b 6-24-1857

WHITE (Josiah T cont)
    Josiah T Jr b 9-25-1857
Mary J 2w b 11-14-1841 Delaware Co dt David & Elizabeth (**Thomas**) **Jarrett** m 4-16-1885 Richmond

Josiah T Jr b 9-25-1857 s Josiah T & Elizabeth (**Wilson**) h Lucia (**Ware**)

Mary b 10-13-1800 d 5-8-1878 bur Earlham

Oliver b 8-21-1836
Mary Caroline (**Cotton**) b 2-14-1837
Ch: Louisa Winifred b 1-17-1866
      Esther Griffin b 1-20-1869
      Raymond P
      Robert Fisher b 9-11-1875

Robert F b 11-3-1830
Elizabeth S b 9-25-1838 dt Samuel S & Anna (**Shoemaker**) **Richie** m 3-9-1864 New Paris OH
Ch: George Alexander b 2-8-1865 Preble Co OH
      Samuel Richie b 7-3-1867 Preble Co OH
      Robeson Taylor b 12-8-1870 Preble Co OH

Robeson Taylor b 12-8-1870 Preble Co OH s Robert F & Elizabeth S (**Richie**) h Elizabeth Anna (**Lloyd**) m 9-27-1894 Butte MT
Ch: Eynone b 9-10-1895

Wm Irvin b 11-13-1838 Wayne Co s Joseph & Alice (**Clawson**)
Sarah H b 5-17-1843 dt Benjamin & Hannah (**Gladdin**) **Strawbridge** m 12-25-1866 Indianapolis
Ch: Ora M b 10-23-1867 Wayne Co
      Harry B b 1-23-1871
      J Edwin b 7-22-1874
      Maurice W b 4-3-1879 Wayne Co

Wm W b 11-2-1846 s Josiah T & Elizabeth (**Wilson**)
Mary A b 11-29-1848 dt Thomas N & Lydia (**Parker**) **White** m 1-5-1871 Richmond
Ch: Ray b 6-6-1872
      Thomas Rayburn b 8-30-1875
      Marian E b 12-28-1877
      Lydia Florence b 11-23-1880
      Esther Mary b 12-30-1883
      Helen Dora b 1-25-1888

WICKETT
Benjamin b 7-10-1820 d 5-13-1867 bur Earlham
Susan (**Collins**) b 3-9-1824 d 2-10-1872 bur Earlham
Ch: Mary Esther b 8-5-1848
      Sarah Elizabeth b 3-7-1850
      Thomas Wm b 8-2-1851
      John Emmett b 1-19-1853
      Benjamin C b 3-20-1856
      Margaret Ann b 5-6-1858
      Agnes Maria b 2-18-1860
      Charles Henry b 9-9-1861

Benjamin C b 3-20-1856 s Benjamin & Susan (**Collins**) h Esther Ann (**Thomas**) m 12-1876
Ch: Wm F b 8-14-1877 Wayne Co
      Emily Jane
      Edith Bell b 5-9-1882
      Leroy
      Nathan Clem

Esther d 3-26-1853 ae about 68y bur Whitewater relict Thomas Bradford England

Frederick S s Thomas & Ella E (**Stillwell**) h Maude b 7-12-1878 dt James & Lizzie **Akin** m 11-29-1899 Wayne Co

John Emmett b 1-19-1853 s Benjamin & Susan (**Collins**)

WICKETT (John Emmett cont)
Clarinda b 8-26-1857 dt Joshua Smith & Margaret E (**Graham**) **Crampton** m 12-1877/78
Ch: Mary S
    Edgar S
    Samuel H
    Ora D
    Frederic

Thomas Wm b 8-2-1851 s Benjamin & Susan (**Collins**) h Ella E (**Stillwell**)
Ch: Frederick S
    Nellie S
    Herbert A
    Benjamin F
    Mabel E

WIGGINS
George h Mary Eva b 9-13-1853 dt Samuel & Eliza Ann **Henley**
Ch: Ruth E b 11-22-1882 Wayne co

Jessie b 6-21-1892 dt J L & Emma

John d ae 36y bur Orange
Mary Almeda dt Benjamin & Elizabeth **Elmore** d 8-13-1881 bur Orange
Ch: Ernest b 2-26-1874

John D b 7-26-1824 s Daniel P & Phoebe
Ruth Ann b 2-27-1827 Wayne Co
Ch: Frederick D b 6-28-1881

WILCOX
Martha b 4-26-1889 Scott Co WV dt Sarah & Amos

WILDIG
Raymond Lowe b 8-21-1892 Wayne Co s Wm B & Minnie

WILDMAN
Murray Shipley h Olive dt Henry **Stigleman** m 8-16-1893

Olive M dt Marion/Martin & Almeda M

WILKINSON
Anna d 5-1867

Mary Jane
Ch: Edwin F
    Henry F

Orville A b 4-16-1881 s Alva & Alice (**Jessup**)

WILLIAMS
Achilles b 9-23-1795 s Jesse & Sarah d 9-9-1878 bur Earlham
Beulah b 11-2-1795 dt Joseph & Rebecca **Unthank** d 4-28-1871 bur Earlham
Ch: Susannah b 10-15-1816 New Garden NC
    Joseph b 2-2-1818 Warren Co OH
    Edward b 11-25-1819 d 7-23-1821 bur Whitewater
    Rebekah b 10-8-1822
    Zalinda b 12-16-1824
    Robert b 2-18-1828 d 3-22-1861 bur Whitewater
    ? b 2-18-1829
    Martha Ann b 9-23-1830
    Mary b 4-15-1832 d 3-2-1844 bur Whitewater
    Sarah b 4-1-1835
    Caroline b 7-21-1837

Ada Florence dt Rebecca L

Alfred H h Mary 2w dt Seth & Mary **Smith**
Ch: Mary Alice b 6-13-1875

WILLIAMS (cont)
Alpha Grace b 12-12-1875 dt John & Eliza J (**Graham**) **O'Hara** m 10-1-1896

Anna
Ch: Rosa
    Bertha Minnie
    Ida Mae Pearl

Benjamin F h Elizabeth A
Ch: George Walker
    Serton Converse
    John Wm
    Mattie M

Chester b 5-12-1862 Wayne Co s Elisha & Evaline

Daniel h Mary Evalina b 7-12-1870 Dayton OH dt Robert Harris & Vashti (**Miles**) **Coats** m 9-26-1891 Montgomery Co OH
Ch: Elmer C b 11-29-1893 Wayne Co
    Mildred V b 8-14-1897 Wayne Co

Dora A b 1-22-1875 dt Granville & Elizabeth

Esther b 11-18-1820

George W d 8-1893 bur Earlham h Anna J
Ch: Daniel Walter
    John P

Hezekiah b 4-5-1790 s Wm & Rachel d 12-16-1847
Rebecca b 10-13-1787
Ch: Melinda b 2-4-1816
    Milton b 4-10-1818 d 6-22-1849
    Alfred b 2-24-1820
    Aseneth b 5-11-1822 d 6-2-1823
    Achsa b 5-5-1824

Ida Mary dt J **Dennis**

Jesse d 12-21-1833 ae 80y 11m 8 d bur Whitewater
Sarah d 8-20-1833 ae 69y bur Whitewater
Ch: Achilles b 9-9-1795 d 9-9-1878 bur Earlham

John H b 3-5-1831 h Mary Evelina

King R h Elizabeth (**Haxton**)
Ch: Lula
    Wm D b 5-23-1884
    James Earl

Laura J dt John C & Marietta **Townsend**

Mable b 5-30-1888 Wayne Co dt Oliver & Emma

Mae E b 10-6-1884 Winchester dt W H & Minnie F

Margaret K b 12-26-1880 Princeton dt Daniel Edgar & Mary Frances **Higgenbotham**

Mary b 4-30-1848

Melinda d 1-1835

Nathan b 9-21-1855 New Ross OH s John M & Minerva (**McCarty**) h Barbara J (**Greenbrier**) m 11-5-1882 Ross Co OH
Ch: Earl b 9-24-1883
    John
    Stella
    Minerva

Ora Chalfant b 1886 Delaware Co s Wesley & Melissa Jane (**Taylor**)

WHITEWATER MONTHLY MEETING
BIRTH AND DEATH RECORD

WILLIAMS (cont)
Richard b 9-29-1755 s Richard & Prudence
Sarah b 5-26-1792 dt Timothy & Ruth **Russel**
Ch:　Jesse T b 3-20-1822
　　　Nathan S b 9-23-1824
　　　Ithamer W b 11-20-1826 d 9-20-1827 bur Smyrna

Robert s Jesse d 10-16-1822 ae 20y

Robert T h Almisa
Ch:　Herbert P
　　　David W

Stephen/Steven J b 4-16-1858 Wayne Co s Henry B & Margaret M
Rachel A b 8-23-1862 Clinton Co OH dt Wm L & Sidney E
Shepard m 8-29-1880 Warren Co OH
Ch:　Howard E b 10-24-1894 Clinton Co OH
　　　Goldie M b 12-7-1898 Montgomery Co OH

Walter C b 12-4-1893 Wayne Co s Alpheus & Ruthanne

Wm h Martha
Ch:　John F C
　　　Lillie C
　　　Henry D
　　　Nellie

Wm d 8-25-1824 ae 60y 11m 18d bur Whitewater

WILLIAMSON
Silas h Sarah
Ch:　Anna
　　　Augusta

WILMOTT
R K h A A
Ch:　Robert Renison b 2-15-1878
　　　Edward Stanbrook b 2-19-1879
　　　Elinor b 7-31-1881 d 10-7-1899 bur Lake Kerr FL
　　　Ella Mary b 4-23-1883
　　　Winifred Emily b 11-11-1884

WILSON
Ezekiel L h Mariam Penninah b 6-15-1850 dt Thomas T & Nancy
(**Davis**) **Hill** m 9-26-1893 Marcus IA

Folger Pope b 1-9-1845 Loudoun Co VA
Fannie J b 5-7-1847 Cecil Co MD m 12-5-1871 Fairfax Co VA
Ch:　Isaac b 187? Loudoun Co Va
　　　Theodore Pope b 9-16-1872 Licking Co OH
　　　Harvey T b 11-22-1882 Wayne Co

Harmon C h Ida
Ch:　Homer b 9-22-1884
　　　Lincoln b 8-17-1890
　　　Ethel b 6-30-1893
　　　Letta d 8-1899

J Mark h Eliza A b 4-10-1856 dt Isaac & Rachel (**Brown**)
Mendenhall m 6-8-1892
Ch:　Josephine b 5-11-1895

James h Sarah
Ch:　John b 9-21-1826
　　　Mary b 5-29-1829

John S b 2-19-1859
Fannie (**Weaver**) b 1-21-1859 m 8-2-1880 Wayne Co

Samuel h Ruth
Ch:　Joseph b 12-16-1809 NC
　　　Thomas Thornburgh b 7-12-1811 NC

WILSON (Samuel cont)　　　Sarah b 6-1-1813 NC
　　　Henry b 7-31-1815 NC
　　　Abigail b 4-10-1819 NC
　　　Eliazar b 9-23-1821 NC
　　　John Charles b 2-16-1824 NC
　　　Ezekiah Lassiter b 10-13-1825 NC
　　　Samuel b 2-3-1828 NC

Timothy b 1-20-1832 s John & ? (**White**)
Elmina H b 12-22-1827 dt Joshua & ? (**Hunt**) **Foster** m 8-8-1866?

W R h Mary dt K T **White**

Wm Nicholson h Ella (**Taylor**)
Ch:　Olive d 2-21-1883
　　　Benizette b 10-1892
　　　Wm Taylor
　　　Elizabeth

WINCHESTER
Irwin h Cora Ann dt Henry & Tacy Ann (**Meredith**) Henley

WINDER
Abner h Rebecca d 2-10-1856 ae 40y 2m 15d bur Whitewater
Ch:　Samuel Charles d 5-23-1898 ae 56y bur Earlham
　　　Susan

Samuel Charles s Abner & Rebecca d 5-23-1898 ae 56y bur Earlham
h Cora (**Zimmer**)
Ch:　Leona Coreen b 12-30-1872
　　　Ross Raymond b 1-26-1875
　　　Wayne H d 7-8-1895 bur Earlham
　　　Joseph E d 8-31-1886

WINDLE
Job h Mary (**Evans**) d 1-10-1899 ae 85y bur Earlham
Ch:　Rebecca
　　　Deborah
　　　Emilie

WINSLOW
John b 9-22-1829

WINTROW
Ross b 3-5-1878 s Wm & Rachel (**Draper**)

WIRTS
Jacob C b 1-15-1871 Greenville OH s Adam & Sarah
Cora M b 11-21-1870 New Paris OH dt Isaac & Linda **Bennett**
Ch:　Mary F b 4-28-1894 New Paris OH
　　　Charles I b 5-21-1896 New Paris OH
　　　Dorris L b 4-28-1898 New Paris OH

WISHARD
Lucinda P (**Jessup**)

WOLF
Georgia Edith b 7-3-1886 Darke Co OH dt George & Ella

Wm d 3-31-1884 ae 76 1/2 y

WOLFE
David W b 12-16-1833
Mattie E d 3-8-1897 bur Orange
Ch:　Lilly May b 6-30-1872 d 6-8-1897
　　　Nellie J b 3-19-1874 d 11-22-1875
　　　Daisy Pearl b 6-20-1877 d 12-17-1880
　　　James A Garfield b 11-9-1880
　　　Indiana b 11-26-1881
　　　David Willis b 2-24-1885
　　　Elfreda A
　　　Clayton B
　　　Harry P F

WOLFE (cont)
John E b 5-30-1843
Mary Adaline d 11-1-1878 bur Camden OH
Ch: Maud
Mary Elizabeth (**Jenkinson**) 2w m 1-1880
Ch: Wm Clement b 7-22-1881
    Grace b 4-4-1883/85

WOOD
George h Cora Bertha b 2-7-1867 dt John Henley & Phebe A (**Branson**) Hill

N S h Louanna H b 8-20-1859 dt Richard & Kate (**Meeker**) Haughton m 10-22-1885
Ch: Wyatt Sumner b 3-25-1887
    Ruth Evyline b 1-1-1891

Wm T b 6-18-1846 s Thomas & Elizabeth A (**Crew**)
Mary Alice b 3-1-1856 dt Jesse J & Mary P (**Evans**) Kenworthy
m 8-16-1899

WOODARD
Isaac P b 9-3-1825
Lydia d 1-4-1897 bur Earlham
Ch: Martha Jane b 3-10-1850 d 1-11-1893 bur Earlham
    Rebecca b 10-20-1852 d 8-18-1874 bur Earlham
    Albert M b 4-10-1857 d 6-16/17/18-1879 bur Earlham
    Ella May b 7-27-1859
    Oliver C b 1-18-1864
    Lydia Alta b 11-6-1867
    Lois b 1-18-1871 d 1-25-1871 bur Earlham
    Bertha b 1-18-1874

Leander J b 5-24-1854 s Luke & Elvira (**Townsend**)
Annie B b 1-26-1856 dt Isaac P & Mary Ann (**Buffum**) Evans
m 5-6-1880 Wayne Co
Ch: Ethel b 1-26-1881
    Isaac Evans b 6-1883

Luke h Elvira (**Townsend**)
Ch: Ella
    Alice
    Leander J b 5-24-1854

Oliver C b 1-18-1864 s Isaac P & Lydia
Laura Alice b 4-17-1869 dt Cyrus W & Emily (**Chandler**) Hodgin
m 1-27-1890 Richmond
Ch: Lona Lucile adopted 12-3-1891
    Vera Chandler b 10-22-1893

WOOLAN
Ruby Francis b 4-6-1888 St Marys OH dt Hiram S & Emma S

WOOLLEY
Ashen D b 10-15-1897 Wayne Co s Milton & Mary

Mary Helen b 6-17-1886

Wm Herbert b 7-9-1863 s R H & Martha (**Waggoner**)
Anna B b 10-21-1865 dt Abraham & Mary (**Conner**) Brower
m 8-21-1884
Ch: Harry Herbert b 3-18-1894

WOOLMAN
Elizabeth A b 6-6-1879 Wayne Co dt Uriah & Anna

WOOTEN
Wm S h Docia S
Ch: Elmer O
    Martha
    Mary

WOOTON
Abijah h Naomi d 1874 bur New Garden

WOOTON (Abijah cont)
Ch: Addie T
    Charles Welden
    Waldo Emerson

WORTH
Rueben M d 10-6-1850 ae 53y 17d bur Whitewater

WRIGHT
Benjamin F b 1-11-1833 s Cyrus & Miriam h Mary Emily (**Hawkins**) m 1869

Cyrus d 9-8-1877 ae 75y bur Maple Grove h Miriam
Ch: Enoch b 5-22-1826 d 2-5-1845 bur Whitewater
    Edmund b 2-5-1828
    Eliza Jane b 10-22-1829
    Benjamin F b 1-11-1833
    Nathan C b 8-22-1835
    Charles b 7-13-1837 d 2-10-1879 bur Maple Grove
    Oliver b 9-25-1839 d 5-28-1841 bur Whitewater
    Wm b 3-25-1843 d 5-10-1864 bur Whitewater
    Wilson b 3-25-1843 d 12-31-1843 bur Whitewater

David b 10-17-1790 s Ralph & Hannah d 8-20-1870
Hepsa dt Libni & Hepsa **Coffin** d 12-13-1865 ae 79y m 8-4-1813 Whitewater
Ch: Martin b 7-11-1814 d 11-26-1825 bur Chester
    Jesse b 11-8-1815
    Elijah b 1-27-1817
    Abel b 5-14-1818 d 12-5-1818 bur Whitewater
    Rhoda b 1-23-1820
    Ruth b 4-7-1821 d 11-22-1825 bur Chester
    Samuel b 12-15-1822 d 11-24-1825 bur Chester

Elijah Sr d 12-29-1845 ae 69y 12d bur Whitewater h Susannah
Ch: Ralph b 6-21-1807 d 7-19-1833 bur Whitewater
    Mary b 10-2-1808
    Sarah b 4-12-1811
    Elizabeth b 11-29-1812
    Ann b 2-19-1815 d 12-15-1892 bur New Paris OH
    Jane b 1-30-1817
    Hannah b 10-23-1818
    Andrew b 5-13-1821 d 7-17-1822
    Allen b 5-28-1823 d 12-9-1843 bur Whitewater
    Susannah b 5-30-1825
    Eli b 7-5-1829 d 3-4-1848 bur Whitewater

Henry C b 10-4-1844 s Parvin & Mary Ellen (**Stroud**)
Caroline b 3-22-1846 Cincinnati OH dt Walter T & Susan (**Mabie**) **Carpenter** m 1-28-1868 Richmond
Ch: Ellen Florence b 1-4-1869
    Susan Carpenter b 11-2-1870
    Mary Josephine b 1-2-1873
    Ida Jessamine b 4-1-1876 d 7-19-1876 bur Earlham

Isaac d 7-28-1879 bur Orange
Elizabeth d 4-3-1867 ae 56y 9m 15d bur Whitewater
Mary Ann (**Randall**) 2w
Ch: Esther G b 6-27-1868

Jacob S h Matildah Ann
Ch: Benjamin C b 11-7-1844
    Granville S b 11-21-1847

James d 12-5-1833 ae 62y 3m 26d bur Whitewater

Jonathan h Deborah d 7-1867 ae 70y bur Whitewater
Ch: Edward
    Wm d 5-27-1855 bur Whitewater
    Nathan bur Smyrna

Jonathan
Ch: Evan d 7-11-1849 ae 21y 4m 12d bur Whitewater
    Katherine d 6-18-1849 ae 28y 8m 29d bur Whitewater

WHITEWATER MONTHLY MEETING
BIRTH AND DEATH RECORD

WRIGHT (cont)
Jonathan d 5-28-1862 ae 79y bur Whitewater
Lydia d 7-17-1845 ae 58y 8m 9d bur Whitewater
Ch: Rebecca b 7-13-1810
     James b 10-20-1811
     Hannah b 4-9-1813
     John b 3-20-1815 d 6-9-1844 bur Whitewater
     Jabez b 12-30-1817 d 1-27-1843 bur Whitewater
     Wm b 9-23-1819 d 5-27-1855 bur Whitewater
     Nathan b 9-19-1821 d 6-18-1849 bur Whitewater
     Lydia 4-11-1823
     Lewis b 5-7-1825 d 3-5-1826 bur Smyrna

Mary Ann b 1-29-1831 dt Wm & Elizabeth (**Conoro**) **Randall**

Mary C dt Francis M & Mary E

Morris P b 4-19-1849 s Parvin & Mary Ellen (**Stroud**) m 1875 h Harriet (**Lancaster**)

Nathan C b 8-22-1835 s Cyrus & Miriam m 1-1880 h Eliza Jennie (**Chapman**)
Ch: Pearl M b 3-6-1881 Wayne Co

O H b 3-22-1889 Arba s E D & Ena

Parvin b 1817 d 1899 Indianapolis bur Earlham
Mary Ellen (**Stroud**) b 1825
Ch: Henry C b 4-10-1844
     Morris P b 4-19-1849
     Walter B b 7-27-1851

Ralph d 7-23-1837 ae 90y 11m 30d bur Whitewater
Hannah d 2-28-1826 ae 74y 1m 22d bur Whitewater
Ch: James b 9-9-1771
     Wm b 1-1-1773 d 11-4-1780 bur Springfield NC
     Jane b 10-18-1774
     Elijah b 10-12-1776
     John b 11-7-1778 d 10-27-1780 bur Springfield NC
     Richardson b 11-6-1780
     Hannah b 1-4-1783
     Lydia b 1-6-1785 d 6-27-1785 bur Springfield NC
     Jonathan b 4-25-1786
     Ralph b 8-19-1788
     David b 10-17-1790
     Ruth b 9-9-1792 d 7-28-1797 bur Springfield NC

WRIGHT (Ralph cont)
     Mary b 7-24-1795 d 1-22-1799 bur Springfield NC

Susan Jane b 12-12-1842 dt David P & Jane (**Wright**) **Grave**

Susannah d 3-30-1862 ae 76y

Thadeus h Rebecca b 10-8-1822 dt Achilles & Beulah (**Unthank**) **Williams** d 9-23-1866
Ch: Mary L b 1-12-1845 d 4-4-1847 bur Whitewater
     Emma C b 8-12-1849 d 9-24-1850 bur Whitewater
     Charles Evan b 4-18-1854 d 2-11-1861 bur Whitewater
     Anna C b 7-10-1856
     Wm Arthur b 4-14-1859 d 1-3-1861 bur Whitewater
     Elizabeth F

Theodore h Eliza b 10-7-1848 dt Calvin & Alida (**Clawson**) **Clark**

Thomas h Rebecca b 7-23-1839 dt Nathan & Mary (**Symons**) **Charles** d 6-14-1870 bur Maple Grove

Thomas h Laura Ann
Ch: Joel Kindley b 4-14-1847
     Mary Amanda b 2-2-1849

WYATT
Barton h Mary d 2-25-1883
Ch: Pearl b 2-8-1883

YATKINS
Hiram b 11-3-1842 Meigs TN
Sarah b 3-19-1844 Lyons KY m 1-10-1864 Marion Co
Ch: Wm b 12-18-1864 Starke Co OH
     Marcus b 7-25-1868 Lewis Co NY

YEARYAN
I/J Chester b 1-3-1885 Spiceland s George & Phenetta

YEO
Milton J h Martha Ann b 9-23-1830 dt Achilles & Beulah (**Unthank**) **Williams** d 7-7-1866

YOUNG
Omar H b 5-12-1882 Gratis OH s Amos & Jennie (**Hendrix**)

Susan dt Abner & Rebecca

Whitewater Monthly Meeting Minutes and Marriages

ABBEALY
1-28-1886   Herbert rec in mbrp

ADAIR
3-22-1871   Sarah E (**Clawson**) rel fr mbrp to jas

ADAMS
5-25-1895   Anna rec in mbrp

ADAMSON
1-24-1884   Nathaniel Jackson & w Margaret J rq mbrp
2-28-1884   Nathaniel J & w Margaret J rec in mbrp
11-24-1887   Nathaniel J rel fr mbrp

ADDELL
1-22-1862   Jacob gct Salem MM

ADDINGTON
9-30-1809   John appt to comm
4-28-1810   Selah con for mcd
10-27-1810   James dis for mcd
3-28-1812   Joseph & ch John, Wm, Joseph, Rachel, & Thomas rec in mbrp
9-26-1812   Thomas & ch Hannah & David S rec in mbrp; Mary & dt Hannah rec in mbrp
8-27-1814   John Jr rec in mbrp
10-29-1814   James rst in mbrp after con his mcd

ADEL
8-26-1829   Rachel rocf Chester MM
8-23-1843   Rachel gct Chester MM
7-22-1857   Rachel F & ch John T, Jacob, Mary G, & Howell G rocf Chester MM

ADELL
6-26-1861   Mary G dis for na & dancing
1-22-1862   Rachel & s Howell gct Salem MM IA; Jacob Jr & John gct Salem MM IA

AIRY
12-26-1818   John rocf Redstone MM PA
4-20-1822   John gct West Branch MM OH
10-15-1825   John gct Elk MM OH
11-25-1828   John rocf West Branch MM OH
12-22-1830   Wm, George, & Keziah rocf Elk MM OH

AIRY (cont)
2-22-1832   John & w Keziah & ch Mary Ann, Wm, George, & Lydia gct Elk MM OH

ALBERT
2-25-1893   Hannah rq mbrp; lt fr UB ch
3-25-1893   Hannah not rec in mbrp

ALBERTSON
5-30-1812   Joshua rocf Back Creek MM NC
10-30-1816   Joshua s Josiah & Sarah dec Wayne Co m Abigail dt Cornelias & Elizabeth **Ratliff** Wayne Co at Whitewater MH
12-25-1819   Benjamin rocf Back Creek MM NC
5-31-1820   Benjamin Wayne Co s Joseph & Sarah dec m Millicent dt Cornelias & Elizabeth **Ratliff** at Whitewater MH
8-16-1823   Benjamin & w Millicent & s Alfred & James gct West Grove MM; Joshua & w Abigail & ch Eli, Eliza, & Milton gct West Grove MM
3-20-1824   Benjamin & s Alfred & James rocf West Grove MM; Millicent rocf West Grove MM
5-15-1824   Joshua & s Eli & Wm Milton rocf West Grove MM
2-25-1829   Joshua dis for jas
3-25-1829   Abigail dis for jas
7-22-1835   Elias min rocf Spiceland MM
6-27-1838   Eli, Eliza, Milton, & Benjamin ch Joshua gct West Grove MM
1-22-1845   James dis for na, mcd, & dp
10-25-1883   Eunice M rocf Sugar Plain MM
2-28-1891   Mattie J rec in mbrp
4-27-1895   Mattie J gct evangelical denomination

ALEXANDER
3-23-1882   Mary to be rec in mbrp 12th St PM
4-27-1882   Mary rec in mbrp

ALLEN
12-31-1814   Hugh rocf Newberry MM TN
10-31-1818   Sarah (**Harvey**) con mcd
8-17-1822   Cert rec for Zachariah fr Cane Creek MM NC; end to to Elk MM OH
3-18-1826   Sarah gct Silver Creek MM
2-26-1834   Cert rec for Harmon & fam fr Holly Springs MM NC; end to Chester MM

WHITEWATER MONTHLY MEETING
MINUTES AND MARRIAGES

ALLEN (cont)
5-23-1855 Rachel & ch Naomi Jane & Gulielma rocf Spiceland MM
5-28-1856 Harriet (**Marmon**) dis for mcd
3-25-1857 Joseph M & w Charity & ch Charles F, Anne Eliza, Emma Lemira, & Mary Ann rocf Spiceland MM
8-23-1865 Hannah (**Haworth**) con mcd
11-22-1865 Mary (**Marmon**) dis for mcd
1-24-1866 Hannah A (**Hayworth**) gct New Salem MM
12-25-1867 Joseph Milton & w Charity W & ch Charles F, Ann Eliza, Emma, Mary Ann, George Carter, & Minnie gct Carthage MM
3-24-1869 Joseph M & w Charity & ch Charles F, Ann Eliza, Emma, Mary Anna, George Carter, & Minnie rocf Carthage MM
8-28-1872 Charles & min s Joseph B gct Ash Grove MM IL
6-28-1888 Rachel H gct Cleveland MM OH
1-28-1893 Anna rocf Spiceland MM

ALMOND
9-26-1812 Matthew rocf Piney Grove MM SC; Rebeckah & dt Judith & Elizabeth rocf Piney Grove MM SC

ALSOP
9-28-1836 Maria & s Edward B rocf Philadelphia MM PA
5-27-1840 Maria & ch Edward B & Reiceful gct Philadelphia MM PA

AMMERMAN
4-27-1889 Simon E & w Lillie J & min s John Edwin rec in mbrp

AMMON
6-27-1891 Conrad & w Anna & min s Lewis B rec in mbrp; lt fr Richmond Presb ch

ANDERSON
11-28-1818 Leah rocf Springfield MM NC
5-29-1819 Leah gct West Grove MM
10-25-1826 Isaac & s David Samuel & Thomas rocf Greenwich MM NJ; Elizabeth & dt Jane E, Hannah, Elizabeth, & Mary rocf Greenwich MM NJ
3-27-1833 David dis for na & mcd
5-22-1833 Elizabeth dis for apd
10-23-1833 Samuel dis for jH, na, & dp
8-27-1834 Thomas dis for na
1-28-1835 Thomas gct Sugar River MM
4-22-1835 Hannah dis for na & dp
2-24-1869 Robert Helena AR rec in mbrp

ANDREW
2-28-1821 Wm s Robert & Mary Wayne Co m Mary dt Jehue & Sarah **Stewart** Wayne Co at Whitewater MH
6-27-1835 Abigail gct Sugar River MM

ANDREWS
9-30-1809 Mary appt to comm
1-28-1835 Wm & w Catherine & ch Ellwood, Jemima, & Mary gct Sugar River MM
3-26-1828 Wm dis for mcd
6-24-1829 Wm dis for mcd
9-23-1829 Catherine & dt Mary C rec in mbrp
1-28-1835 Wm & w Catharine & min ch Ellwood, Jemima, & Mary gct Sugar River MM

ANTHONY
6-22-1870 Edward Clark rocf Cincinnati MM OH

ANTRIM
4-28-1821 Daniel & James P rocf Darby Creek MM OH; Ann & dt Elizabeth rocf Darby Creek MM OH

ANTRIM (cont)
12-20-1823 James P gct West Grove MM
3-20-1824 Daniel gct West Grove MM
7-16-1825 James rocf West Grove MM
7-26-1826 James P gct Milford MM
4-25-1827 Daniel con att mcd
1-23-1828 Daniel gct Fall Creek MM OH
9-24-1828 Sarah rocf Fall Creek MM OH
4-22-1835 Daniel & w Sarah & dt Mary Ann gct Mississinewa MM
5-27-1835 Ann gct Mississinewa MM

ARBEALY
1-28-1886 Habeeb rec in mbrp

ARMENT
8-25-1852 Sarah B rocf West Grove MM
2-25-1857 Sarah gct Chester MM
3-25-1868 Sarah rocf Chester MM

ARMFIELD
8-27-1873 Vianna (**Irish**) con mcd
9-24-1873 Vianna gct New Salem MM

ARMSTRONG
4-26-1888 Soloma rec in mbrp

ARNOLD
7-27-1889 Sarah rocf White Lick MM

ATHERTON
1-28-1857 Charles & dt Deborah rocf Burlington MM NJ
4-28-1858 Charles & dt Deborah gct Burlington MM NJ

ATKINS
7-28-1830 Jonathan & fam rocf Deer Creek MM MD; end to Chester MM; Mary & dt Eliza rocf Deer Creek MM
6-25-1834 Eliza & Mary rocf Chester MM
5-27-1835 Joseph rocf Chester MM
2-27-1839 Joseph gct Sugar River MM
3-24-1858 Mary gct Salem MM IA

ATKINSON
9-26-1827 Thomas & s Henry W & Caleb F rocf Burlington MM NJ; Rebecca & dt Sarah C, Rebecca L, Deborah C, & Elizabeth Fisher rocf Burlington MM NJ
2-25-1829 Thomas dis for jas
4-22-1829 Rebecca dis for jas
6-25-1834 Jonathan & fam rocf Chester MM
4-22-1835 Henry W, Caleb F, Sarah E, Rebecca S, Deborah C, & Elizabeth ch Thomas gct Mississinewa MM
3-28-1838 Sarah gct Plymouth MM MI
11-28-1838 Elizabeth P rocf Chesterfield MM
7-22-1840 Elizabeth P gct Chesterfield MM NJ
1-27-1841 Cert for Elizabeth P ret by Chesterfield MM NJ; did not reside within their limits
2-24-1841 Elizabeth P gct Cincinnati MM OH
2-24-1858 Mary gct Salem MM IA

AYDELOTT
5-23-1832 Rebecca rocf New Garden MM NC
9-26-1832 Duck Creek MM rq this mtg treat with Sarah for mcd; made satisfaction
7-24-1833 Sarah rocf Duck Creek MM
3-26-1845 Henry C & ch Henry C, Beulah Ann, & Fleming W rec in mbrp; Beulah Anna dt Stewart rec in mbrp
7-26-1848 Spiceland MM rq aid in treating with Ann (**Stuart**) for mcd; made satisfaction
10-25-1848 Stewart con mcd

AYDELOTT (cont)
4-25-1860	Stuart & w Anna S & ch Joseph B, Sarah S, & Mary E gct Walnut Ridge MM
2-27-1861	Fleming W dis for mcd

AYDELOTTE
12-27-1854	Henry C gct Spiceland MM

AYDLOT
11-10-1823	Rebecca gct West Grove MM
10-11-1843	Rebecca gct West Grove MM

AYDLOTT
4-25-1849	Anne rocf Spiceland MM

BACKMAN
12-22-1887	Laura J rocf New Garden MM

BAILEY
12-28-1809	David con mcd
12-30-1809	Sarah con mcd
2-24-1810	John con mcd
12-29-1810	Ruth & dt Bathsheba & Elizabeth rocf Miami MM OH
11-30-1811	Stanton con his breach of order in going to law without perm of MM
6-27-1812	John con for att muster
11-25-1815	Penninah rec in mbrp
11-30-1816	Stanton grs David rec in mbrp
6-28-1817	Ruth & dt gct New Garden MM; Mary gct New Garden MM
10-31-1818	Pininah gct New Garden MM
3-27-1819	Henry gct New Garden MM
9-28-1831	Lydia (**Comer**) dis for mcd

BAILY
1-11-1815	Stanton s David & Ruth Wayne Co m Mary dt Joshua & Sarah **Piggott** Wayne Co at Whitewater MH
2-25-1815	John dis for mcd
4-26-1817	Henry & s Levi & David rec in mbrp
6-28-1817	David & Stanton & fam gct New Garden MM
8-14-1823	Sarah gct West Grove MM
10-18-1823	David gct Milford MM

BAINE
8-26-1820	John rocf Aberdeen MM Scotland

BAKER
8-20-1880	Mary Ella rocf Milford MM Dublin
4-27-1882	Mary rec in mbrp
10-27-1887	Mary drpd fr mbrp
2-23-1895	John, Rebecca, & Anna rec in mbrp
3-23-1895	Grace B rec in mbrp

BALDWIN
11-30-1811	John & s Joel rocf New Garden MM NC; Dorcas rocf New Garden MM NC
12-28-1811	Thomas rocf New Garden MM NC
11-28-1812	Arcadai rocf New Garden MM NC; Daniel & s Elias & Daniel Jr rocf New Garden MM NC; Mary & dt Mary & Sophia rocf New Garden MM NC
10-30-1813	Charles & s Thomas & Solomon Thomas rocf Piney Grove MM SC; Sarah & dt Susannah & Mary rocf Piney Grove MM SC
6-21-1817	Matilda rocf Lost Creek MM TN
9-29-1821	Jesse & Catherine rocf Fall Creek MM OH; Susannah rec in mbrp
5-16-1826	Jesse gct Milford MM
10-25-1826	John & s Joel & Eli rocf New Garden MM; Dorcas & dt Rhoda & Ann roc

WHITEWATER MONTHLY MEETING MINUTES AND MARRIAGES

BALDWIN (cont)
1-23-1828	John dis for indebtedness
9-13-1829	Jesse s John & Charlotte Wayne Co m Priscilla dt Wm & Elizabeth **Johnson** Wayne Co at Whitewater MH
3-24-1830	Priscilla gct West Grove MM
3-28-1832	Cert rec for Daniel C & fam fr Deep River MM NC; end to Springfield MM
4-22-1835	Joel, Eli, George, Rhoda, Ann, & Eliza ch John gct Mississinewa MM
12-28-1842	Ann rocf New Garden MM
2-22-1843	Betty (**Mills**) dis for mcd
2-28-1843	Rhoda rocf Dover MM
11-24-1847	Ann & Rhoda gct New Garden MM
5-29-1851	Enos P s Wm H & Elizabeth Champaign Co OH m Martha dt Benjamin dec & Lydia **Bond** Wayne Co at Whitewater MH
2-25-1857	Martha & s Wm gct Chester MM
8-25-1858	Enos P & w Martha & ch Wm H & John Howard rocf Chester MM
10-27-1858	Chester MM gct rst John
3-23-1862	Enos & w Martha & min ch Wm H, John Howard, & Horace M gct Chester MM
8-22-1866	Enos P & w Martha & ch Wm, John Howard, Horace, & Mary Lizzie rocf Chester MM
7-26-1876	Baily P & w Elizabeth & s Albert rocf West Grove MM
8-28-1878	Jonathan & w Mary Ann rocf West Grove MM
8-27-1879	Baily P rel fr mbrp
5-26-1881	James Alpheus & w Emma rocf West Grove MM
8-23-1883	Jonathan appt elder
11-25-1893	Merrilla C rocf West Grove MM
11-24-1894	Louisa rocf Springfield MM

BALES
8-29-1812	Wm & s Bowater & Nathan rocf New Garden MM NC; Sarah & dt Elizabeth rocf Center MM NC
4-28-1830	Samuel rocf Chester MM

BALEY
10-18-1823	David gct Milford MM

BALL
10-27-1875	Wm B rec in mbrp

BALLARD
2-26-1827	Rhoda rocf Chester MM
4-28-1830	Samuel rocf Chester MM
5-25-1831	Samuel gct Blue River MM
10-26-1831	Millicent H rocf Blue River MM
2-26-1834	Catharine rocf Chester MM
1-24-1838	Samuel dis
6-26-1839	Millicent H & ch Mary Elizabeth, David, & Cornelius W gct Lick Creek MM
10-23-1844	Jesse F & w Phareba & ch Wm, Phebe Ann, & Jesse W rocf Springfield MM
2-26-1845	Peninah (**Nixon**) dis for na & mcd
11-28-1849	Jesse F gct Chester MM to m Mary **Arnold**
1-23-1850	Jesse F & ch Wm & George C gct Chester MM
2-25-1874	Jeremiah rocf Spiceland MM
1-27-1875	Jesse F & w Mary & dt Laurette Candace roc
3-22-1876	Uriah & w Emiline & ch Franklin A, Otho, & Mary L rocf West Union MM
7-24-1878	Uriah & w Emeline & min ch Franklin, Otho, & Mary Leona gct Back Creek MM
11-24-1881	Mary gct Raysville MM
12-22-1881	Loretta Candace rq cert to Raysville MM
1-26-1882	Jeremiah, Mary, & Lauretta C gct Raysville MM
7-31-1895	Edgar H s Addison & Sarah H Hendricks Co m Mary Adelaide dt Eli & Malialah **Jay** at res of her father Richmond

WHITEWATER MONTHLY MEETING
MINUTES AND MARRIAGES

BALLARD (cont)
11-23-1895	Edgar H rocf Plainfield MM
10-22-1896	Edgar H & w Mary (Jay) & Elizabeth J **Schneider** gct Southland College MM

BALLENGER
11-27-1833	Elizabeth (**Comer**) dis for na & mcd

BALLINGER
10-23-1884	Rachel Ann rocf Elk MM OH
5-23-1896	Elijah, Melissa, George, & Myrtle New Westville OH rec in mbrp
12-23-1897	Viola (**Horn**) rel fr mbrp

BANE
5-14-1825	John dis for mcd

BANNER
6-24-1846	Rebecca dis for jas

BANNON
11-28-1832	Rebecca grdt Jacob & Ann **Grave** rec in mbrp

BARGER
9-25-1873	Martin J s Wm J dec & Elizabeth Vermilion Co IL m Margaret W dt Samuel & Annie **Richie** at res of her father New Paris Preble Co OH (Whitewater Mtg)

BARKER
11-1-1809	Isaac Dearborn Co s Nicolas & Hannah NC m Mary dt Jeremiah & Margery **Cox** Dearborn Co at Whitewater MH
12-30-1820	Thomas con mcd
10-23-1822	Jacob s Isaac & Hannah Wayne Co m Eliza dt John & Hannah **White** Wayne Co at Chester MH
1-27-1851	Matthew & w Ruth & dt Elizabeth rocf Scipio MM NY
4-29-1882	Mary rec in mbrp

BARNARD
2-29-1812	Uriah & s George, Wm, & John rocf Deep Creek MM NC; Elizabeth & dt Love, Hannah, Elizabeth, Anna, & Mary rocf Deep Creek MM NC
11-27-1813	Uriah & s Wm, George, & John gct Fall Creek MM OH; Elizabeth & dt Love, Hannah, Elizabeth, Anna, & Mary gct Fall Creek MM OH
12-26-1855	Paul & w Martha & dt Susannah rocf Milford MM
1-22-1868	Paul & w Martha gct Milford MM
4-27-1870	Paul & w Martha rocf Milford MM
9-23-1886	Martha gct Independence MM KS; Indianapolis MM

BARNES
6-18-1825	Elizabeth & dt Elizabeth W & Martha B rocf Falls MM PA
7-25-1828	Elizabeth dis for jH
1-28-1829	Martha dis for jas & dp
5-28-1885	Jennie & dt Cora & Ethel May rec in mbrp
4-25-1891	John F rec in mbrp
10-24-1891	Julia A rocf Dover MM; Harold S s John & Julia rec in mbrp

BARNS
5-23-1896	John T & w Julia A & ch Harold S & Elmer T gct New Garden MM

BARRETT
8-3-1892	Don Carlos s Isaac M & Mary E Greene Co OH m Marcia Frances dt Charles H & Marcia **Moore** Wayne Co at res David & Mary Sutton Richmond

BARTON
9-18-1824	Cert rec for Edward & s Wm fr Northwest Fork MM MD; end to Chester MM
8-28-1884	Alice C rocf Miami MM OH
11-24-1887	Alice C gct Cincinnati MM OH

BATES
4-26-1817	Charity rocf Lost Creek MM TN

BAXTER
12-3-1856	Wm Philadelphia PA s John dec & Mary York Co England m Mary dt Enoch dec & Sophia **Barker** Boone Co at Whitewater MH
1-28-1857	Mary gct Haddonfield MM NJ
9-21-1864	Wm & w Mary & ch Sarah Moffit, Mary Ellen, & Maria rocf Haddonfield MM NJ

BEACH
5-25-1899	Pearl C (**Owen**) rel fr mbrp

BEAL
12-28-1859	Henrietta P rocf Three River MM IA
4-22-1863	Henrietta gct West Branch MM OH

BEAMAN
5-27-1815	Cornelius rocf Back Creek MM NC

BEARD
3-28-1812	John rocf Springfield MM NC
10-31-1812	Patrick & s John, Abraham, & Patrick rocf Newberry MM TN; Hannah & dt Alice, Martha, Elizabeth, & Rachel rocf Newberry MM TN
11-28-1812	Elizabeth & dt Martha, Rachel, Hannah Jane, Dolly, & Mary rocf Springfield MM NC
10-28-1815	John dis for jas
7-26-1817	Cert rec for Wm & s John fr Center MM NC; end to Silver Creek MM
3-27-1850	Rebecca & ch Levina Jane, Benjamin Franklin, & David W rec in mbrp
4-26-1854	Amos rocf Deep River MM NC
12-31-1856	Wm prc fr Cherry Grove MM; Wm s Paul Sr & Hannah dec Randolph Co m Sarah **Kirk** wid dt Samuel & Sarah **Test** at Whitewater MH
2-25-1857	Sarah K & min niece Elizabeth Test gct Cherry Grove MM
11-25-1857	Susannah (**Pickett**) dis for mcd
10-27-1858	Amos dis for jas
5-25-1859	David & w Miriam & ch Jane rocf Deep River MM NC
4-22-1863	Rebecca & ch Lavina Jane, Benjamin F, & David gct Bridgeport MM

BEAUCHAMP
8-31-1811	Wm Sr & s Russ & Caleb rocf Piney Grove MM NC; Elizabeth & dt Mileah rocf Piney Grove MM SC
11-30-1811	Levi rocf Piney Grove MM SC
9-26-1812	Matthew rocf Piney Grove MM SC
2-27-1813	Ellick & s Jesse rocf Piney Grove MM SC; Alice rocf Piney Grove MM SC
8-26-1815	Wm con for tale bearing
10-28-1815	Mathias con for att mcd
1-27-1816	Russ dis for mcd
2-24-1816	Sarah (**Jessop**) dis for mcd
3-30-1816	Levi dis for mcd
8-31-1816	Mileah dis for mcd
11-30-1816	Ellick & fam gct New Garden MM; Alice gct New Garden MM
4-26-1817	Matthew dis for mcd
10-31-1818	Wm dis for making religious visit without consent of friends
4-28-1821	Elizabeth & Caleb gct West Grove MM

BEESON

2-15-1823	Sally & dt Betsy & Lydia rocf Center MM NC
4-19-1823	Mahlon & Absolam rocf Center MM NC
12-27-1826	Tacy rocf Hopewell MM VA
1-1-1829	Sally & ch Betsy, Absalom, Mahlon, John, & Nancy gct Milford
1-28-1829	Tacy dis for jas

BELL

5-31-1817	John & s Josiah, Thomas, & Jesse rocf Springfield MM NC; Lydia & dt Sarah, Rebecca, Margaret, Abigail, & Lydia rocf Springfield MM NC; Lancelot, Mary, & Miriam rocf Springfield MM NC
5-2-1821	Josiah West Grove MM Wayne Co s John & Sarah dec m Abigail dt Samuel & Gulielma **Charles** Wayne Co at Whitewater MH
9-25-1821	Abigail gct West Grove MM
12-25-1850	John rocf Cincinnati MM OH; Hannah C & ch Isabella Wakefield, Wilhelminia, & Wm Edmund rocf Cincinnati MM OH
2-28-1855	Wm rst
5-26-1858	John gct Cincinnati MM OH
3-27-1861	Isabella dis for na & jas
6-28-1865	John rocf Cincinnati MM OH
4-24-1872	Elizabeth C (**Dilks**) con mcd
6-26-1872	Wm E con mcd
6-28-1876	Wm E rel fr mbrp
8-22-1877	John & w Wilhelmina gct San Jose MM CA
3-26-1892	Ida M & step-s Wm A rel fr mbrp
11-23-1899	Harriett A rocf Dublin MM

BELLIS

7-26-1848	Edward & Samuel rocf Balby MM England
6-2-1852	Samuel Wayne Co s Samuel dec & Mary York England m Mary dt Wm & Alice dec **Kenworthy** Wayne Co at Whitewater MH
9-21-1853	Edward dis for mcd
4-22-1863	Samuel & w Mary K & min ch Wm K & Mary Wynne gct Bridgeport MM
8-24-1864	Samuel & w Mary K & ch Wm K & Mary Wynne rocf Bridgeport MM
8-26-1868	Edward & w Ellen C & adopted s Edward Reed **Bracken** rec in mbrp
4-27-1882	Mary E rec in mbrp
3-26-1885	Mary E gct Indianapolis MM
8-26-1886	Dr E Reed rel fr mbrp
4-28-1894	Samuel & w Mary K & s Wm K gct Indianapolis MM

BELSHAM

5-22-1872	Mary rolf Raysville MM
7-24-1872	Arthur rolf Raysville MM
11-25-1874	Essie rec in mbrp
12-27-1876	Arthur & w Charity C & ch Alden P & Bertha M rec in mbrp
12-26-1891	Essie (**Burgess**) not found

BENBOW

5-30-1812	John & fam rolf New Garden MM NC
11-28-1812	Ann rolf New Garden MM NC
5-27-1815	Cert rec for John & s Evan, Benjamin, Aaron, & Moses fr Center MM NC; end to New Garden MM; Charity & dt Mariam rocf Center MM NC
6-24-1815	Edward & s Evan, Edward, Benjamin, & Powel rocf Miami MM OH; Mary & dt Elizabeth rocf Miami MM OH
4-22-1893	Thomas L & w Clara J & min ch Walter T, Isaac W, & David A rocf Cherry Grove MM; Mary rocf Cherry Grove MM
9-21-1899	Thomas L & w Clara & min ch Walter T, Isaac W, David A, & Orville E gct Cherry Grove MM; Mary gct Cherry Grove MM

BENFORD

9-27-1826	Cert rec for Benajah & s John, Asa, David, Benajah, Nathan, Elijah, & Elisha fr Rich Square MM NC; end to Duck Creek MM; Cert rec for James Ladd & s Robert, Joseph, Benjamin, & Wm Ladd fr Rich Square MM NC; end to Duck Creek MM; Cert rec for Micajah & s Wm & Micajah Crews fr Rich Square MM; end to Duck Creek MM

BENHAM

8-23-1888	Alice ae 11, Walter Pharo ae 9, & Robert Bruce Jr ae 7 ch Robert Bruce & Anna M WY Terr rec in mbrp
4-23-1892	Alice, Walter Pharo, & Robert Bruce Jr min ch of Anna gct Philadelphia MM Western Dist PA
7-23-1892	Cert for ch of Anna ret by PA MM; temp res there

BENNET

10-23-1844	Emily & Louisa gct Redstone MM PA

BENNETT

4-27-1836	Louisa & Emilia ch of Isaac & Maria rocf Redstone MM PA

BENSON

5-27-1874	Ephram B & w Amy & ch Ida C, Elizabeth A, & James H rec in mbrp
3-26-1885	Ephraim B, Amy J, James H, Lizzie S, Ida C, Gracie E, & John G rel fr mbrp

BENTLEY

5-29-1819	John & Susannah rocf Redstone MM PA
5-27-1897	Wm & Charles Providence & Friendship Darke Co OH rec in mbrp

BENTLY

7-19-1823	Sarah (**Hill**) con mcd

BERNARD

7-27-1864	Edith (**Graves**) con her mcd

BERRY

9-25-1813	David rocf Salem MM OH
11-30-1816	Susanna & dt Elizabeth, Hannah, & Eunice rec in mbrp; David, Samuel, & Thomas s David rec in mbrp

BETTLES

11-23-1864	Wm & w Susannah Grounds & s Joseph Barnes rec in mbrp

BEVAN

11-27-1878	Alice A (**Mendenhall**) & s Albert R gct Cherry Grove MM

BICKLE

6-22-1842	Anna (**Leeds**) dis for jas & mcd

BINFORD

9-27-1826	Cert rec for Judith & dt Angeline fr Rich Square MM NC; end to Duck Creek MM; Cert rec for Jane & dt Ann fr Rich Square MM NC; end to Duck Creek MM; Cert rec for Joshua & s Mahel, Joshua, James, & Peter fr Rich Square MM NC; end to Duck Creek MM; Cert rec for Lydia & dt Hannah, Polly, & Sarah fr Rich Square MM NC; end to Duck Creek MM; Cert rec for Miriam & dt Rebecca Anna & Sarah fr Rich Square MM NC; end to Duck Creek MM
9-23-1893	Micajah M & w Susanna & min s Edward rocf Walnut Ridge MM

WHITEWATER MONTHLY MEETING
MINUTES AND MARRIAGES

BINFORD (cont)
12-22-1894	Levi & w Eve H & min ch Marshall D rocf Carthage MM
10-22-1896	Ruth rocf Walnut Ridge MM
10-28-1897	Micajah M minister & w Susannah gct New York MM NY
6-23-1898	Ruth gct Haviland MM KS
6-14-1899	Gurney s Josiah & Margaret F Haviland Kiowa Co KS m Elizabeth Julia dt Philip & Kate **Schneider** Richmond Wayne Co at 8th St Mtg Richmond

BINNS
5-23-1855	Richard rocf Short Creek MM OH
10-31-1855	Richard Wayne Co s Wm & Ruth Harrison Co m Gulielma dt Harmon & Mary **Hill** Wayne Co at Whitewater MH
4-22-1868	Amos & w Rebecca & ch Lilia Aurelia & Charles rocf Short Creek MM OH
3-22-1876	Lillie Aurilla min dt Amos & Rebecca dec gct Columbus MM OH; grd Ruth
9-20-1876	Charles gct Columbus MM OH
7-25-1877	Richard & w Gulielma H & ch Willie A, Horace Mann, Franklin, Anna Laura, & John Bertrand gct Lawrence MM KS

BIRDSALL
7-28-1869	Alvin rec in mbrp
4-23-1873	Alvin rqct Chester MM to m Mattie C Hampton
5-27-1874	Alvin T gct New York MM NY

BISHOP
9-23-1897	Milton & w Mary & ch Charles, George, & Dayton rocf Dover MM

BITNER
1-24-1891	Ida B rec in mbrp

BITTNER
10-28-1886	Abraham & w Ida R & min s Charles rec in mbrp
8-25-1887	Abraham & w Ida & ch rel fr mbrp

BLACK
3-23-1895	Allen rocf Springfield MM OH; Clarissa & s John rocf Springfield MM OH
8-24-1895	Allen drpd fr mbrp

BLIZZARD
3-19-1825	Caroline min under care of Thomas & Ann Roberts rec in mbrp
12-17-1825	Elizabeth rocf Fall Creek MM
7-27-1832	Caroline gct Cherry Grove MM

BLUE
4-27-1831	Hannah P (**Moore**) dis for mcd
6-28-1883	Centreville rec Melvina in mbrp
12-27-1883	Melvina rq PM at Centerville
1-24-1891	Melvina gct West Grove MM

BOGUE
7-31-1813	Aaron, Jesse, Miriam, & Nathan rocf Suttons Creek MM NC
1-24-1822	Stephen Preble Co OH s Joseph & Mary both dec Perquimans Co NC m Elvy dt Benjamin & Sarah **Elliott** Wayne Co at Woodberry MH
7-20-1822	Elvira gct Westfield MM OH
3-3-1831	Stephen s Joseph & Mary both dec Preble Co OH m Hannah **Bonine** dt Wm & Rachel **East** Wayne Co at Orange MH
6-22-1831	Hannah & s James **Bonine** gct Westfield MM
9-27-1890	Emma & dt Josephine rocf Spiceland MM
1-27-1898	Clinton W & w Ada L & min s Russell S gct Marion MM
7-28-1898	Emily J gct Spiceland MM

BOMAN
5-28-1828	Wm & s Milton H & Edward F rocf Dover MM NC

BOMGARNER
5-27-1897	Anna Providence & Friendship Darke Co OH rec in mbrp

BOND
10-28-1808	Charlotte & Phebe appt to comm
1-29-1810	Jesse minister
11-24-1810	Edward, Ann, Joseph, & Sarah rocf Deep River MM NC
11-30-1811	Joshua & s Abijah rocf Mt. Pleasant MM VA; Ruth & dt Anna & Deborah rocf Mt Pleasant MM VA
12-28-1811	Edward Jr & s Daniel, Benjamin, Edward, & John rocf Deep Creek MM NC; Anna & dt Kezia, Elizabeth, & Rachel rocf Deep Creek MM NC
5-30-1812	Joseph & s Darius, John, Mordecai, & Joseph rocf Westfield MM NC; Rachel & dt Eunice rocf Westfield MM NC
11-27-1813	Thomas & s Amos, Jesse, & Thomas rocf Westfield MM NC; Mary & dt Betsy rocf Westfield MM NC
10-29-1814	Ornan rocf Westfield MM NC
12-14-1822	Mary (**Vere**) con mcd
2-15-1823	Jesse con mcd
12-5-1833	Jedidiah s Benjamin & Mary dec Wayne Co m Elmina dt Richard & Abigail **Stanley** Wayne Co at Whitewater MH
5-22-1834	Elmina gct New Garden MM
10-22-1834	Jonathan rocf New Garden MM
7-22-1835	Sarah min rocf Spiceland MM
8-26-1835	Levina rocf Spiceland MM
10-25-1837	Jonathan W gct Milford MM
12-26-1838	Pleasant & w Sally & dt Phebe Ann rocf Westfield MM
5-22-1839	Sarah (**Cook**) con mcd
1-22-1840	Pleasant & w Sally & dt Phebe Ann gct Dover MM
5-27-1840	Sarah & min s Elias A gct Spiceland MM
3-27-1844	Silas not rec in mbrp
12-25-1844	Sarah (**Cook**) dis for na & jas
4-26-1848	Benjamin & w Lydia & min ch Martha, Hannah, Sarah, Elizabeth, Mary, Wm, & Susanna rocf Salem MM
5-24-1848	Sarah gct Cherry Grove MM
12-23-1850	Silas rec in mbrp
1-28-1852	Cyrus rocf Hopewell MM
1-25-1854	Peter & w Martha & ch Erastus C rocf Chester MM
6-25-1856	Cyrus gct Spring Creek MM IA
9-26-1860	Rachel rocf Honey Creek MM
1-22-1862	Rachel A gct Salem MM
3-26-1862	Lydia & ch Mary, Wm, Susan, & Esther gct Chester MM
4-22-1863	Elizabeth gct Chester MM
12-23-1863	Peter & w Martha & min ch Erastus Constantine, Frederika Jane, Miriam J, Charles F, & Isaiah R gct New Garden MM
10-25-1865	Peter & w Martha & ch Erastus Constantine, Frederika Jane, & Charles Francis rocf New Garden MM
5-23-1866	Elizabeth gct Cherry Grove MM
10-27-1875	Thomas F & w Julia A rec in mbrp
2-23-1876	Thomas & w Julia A gct Salem MM
6-23-1881	Wm gct Indianapolis MM
3-23-1882	Mary H & ch Edna J & Laura rec in mbrp
9-23-1893	Wm A H & w Cora E rocf New Garden MM; Lindley & w Sarah A & dt Emma rocf New Garden MM
4-28-1894	Lindley & w Sarah A & dt Emma gct West Grove MM

BOND (cont)
10-28-1897   Jehiel & w Anna J & ch S Edgar & Jennie F rocf Dover MM; Lydia rocf Dover MM

BONIGH
5-28-1814   David & s Wm & Isaac rocf Newberry MM TN

BONINE
5-28-1814   Prudence & dt Rachel rocf Newberry MM TN
4-29-1815   Daniel & s James & Thomas rocf Newberry MM TN; Mary & dt Lydia & Ann rocf Newberry MM TN
6-24-1815   Isaac & Sarah rocf Newberry MM TN
5-17-1823   David & w Prudence & min ch Wm, Isaac, Rachel, Clark, John, & Betsy gct West Grove MM
10-21-1824   James s Daniel dec & Mary Wayne Co m Hannah East wid James dt Wm & Rachel **Bonine** at Orange MH
8-20-1825   David & w Prudence & ch Isaac, Wm, Clark, John, & Joshua rocf West Grove MM; Prudence & dt Rachel & Betsey rocf West Grove MM
5-20-1826   Thomas con mcd
2-27-1828   James s Thomas rec in mbrp; Patsy & dt Mary rec in mbrp
7-23-1828   Wm dis for mcd
9-24-1828   Phebe dis for jas
6-23-1830   Isaac dis for jas
8-5-1830   David & w Prudence & ch Clark, John, Elizabeth, Joshua, Melinda, & Mary Ann gct Fairfield MM
8-16-1830   David & fam ret cert; ret to Whitewater MM
8-25-1830   Prudence gct Fairfield MM
8-28-1833   Clark dis for na, jas, & mcd; Thomas gct White Lick MM
10-12-1842   Isaac & w Sarah & min ch Jacob, Lot, Lydia, Isaac, Sarah, & Jonathan B gct Birch Lake MI MM
12-28-1842   Samuel con mcd
10-25-1843   Samuel gct Birch Lake MM MI
12-25-1844   James E con mcd
9-24-1845   James E gct Birch Lake MM MI; Evans dis for na, mcd, & joining a band
9-28-1848   Isaac & fam gct Birch Lake MM MI

BOOKWALTER
12-23-1897   Erva rec in mbrp

BOON
6-22-1853   Sampson rocf Spiceland MM
10-25-1854   Sampson dis for mcd

BOONE
5-26-1894   Jonathan C & w Anna & ch Myron rocf Kokomo MM

BORTON
6-22-1831   Ann **(Moore)** dis for mcd

BOSWELL
10-30-1813   Hiram rocf Back Creek MM NC; Jane, Delilah, Selah, & Lurainca rocf Back Creek MM NC
5-25-1816   Jane rocf Back Creek MM NC
6-3-1816   Barnabas rocf Back Creek MM NC
11-29-1817   Ezra & s Bethual & Dan rocf Miami MM OH; Elizabeth & dt Anne & Mary rocf Miami MM OH; Miriam & Pharaba rocf Back Creek MM NC; John & Samuel s Miriam rocf Back Creek MM NC
7-25-1818   Celia dis for having ch in unm state
4-22-1829   Dempsy & s John & Jesse rocf Stillwater MM OH; Wm & s Isaac & Joseph rocf Summerset MM OH; Mary & Phebe rocf Stillwater MM OH
2-24-1830   Mary, Rebecca, John K, & Sarah min ch Ezra & Elizabeth gct White Lick MM

BOSWELL (cont)
3-24-1830   Wm & w Rachel & ch Ruth, Elizabeth, Essenith, Rebecca, Isaac, & Joseph gct Milford MM
5-26-1830   Ezra dis for jas
7-28-1830   Demsy & w Mary & ch John & Phebe gct Milford MM; Jesse & Ruth gct Milford MM
4-27-1831   Daniel K dis; Elizabeth dis for na
2-28-1849   John K dis for na & mcd

BOSWORTH
3-25-1868   Eliza Ann rec in mbrp

BOWLES
1-29-1810   David appt elder
1-30-1811   David Sr s David Wayne Co m Bathsheba dt David & Ruth **Baily** Wayne Co at Whitewater MH; Ephraim con mcd
8-29-1818   Josiah & Wm min rocf Clear Creek MM OH
11-27-1819   Ephriam con for dr & upl
5-18-1822   Ephriam con dr
10-15-1825   Ruth & ch Josiah, Wm, George, & Miles gct New Garden MM

BOWLS
5-30-1812   Ruth **(Hoggatt)** rpt mcd by Fairfield MM
8-29-1818   Ruth rocf Clear Creek MM OH

BOWMAN
5-28-1828   Martha Ann & Sally rocf Dover MM NC; Elvira rocf New Garden MM NC
5-25-1831   Wm & w Elvira & min ch Martha, Milton, Edmond, Sarah, Emaline, & Calvin gct Chester MM
3-28-1832   Wm & s Milton H, Edmund F, & Calvin W rocf Chester MM; Elvira & dt Martha Ann, Sally Jane, & Emaline rocf Chester MM
12-26-1832   Edmon & s George rocf Union MM; Sarah & dt Phebe, Anne, Eliza, Martha, & Mary rocf Union MM NC
3-27-1833   Wm & w Elvira & min ch Milton H, Martha Ann, Edmund F, Sally Jane, Emaline, & Calvin W gct West Grove MM
10-25-1833   Edmund & w Sarah & ch Phebe, Anna, George, Eliza, Martha, & Mary gct Duck Creek MM
5-24-1883   Alma rocf Duck Creek MM
2-25-1886   Alma gct Duck Creek MM

BOYD
12-25-1833   Elizabeth gct Sugar River MM
9-27-1837   Elizabeth rocf Sugar River MM
1-23-1839   Elizabeth gct Walnut Ridge MM
7-28-1881   Min Bessie, Emma, & Martha rocf Chester MM

BOZWELL
4-22-1829   Rachel & dt Ruth, Rebecca, Asenath, & Elizabeth rocf Somerset MM OH
6-24-1829   Ruth rocf Stillwater MM OH

BRACKMAN
3-25-1874   John rec in mbrp

BRADBERY
7-27-1816   Lydia **(Murphey)** dis for mcd

BRADFORD
5-27-1897   Joseph & Mary Providence & Friendship Darke Co OH rec in mbrp

BRADWAY
8-31-1816   John & s John, Wm, & Thomas rocf Miami MM OH; Abigail & dt Elisabeth, Abigail, & Sarah rocf Miami MM OH
8-23-1883   Ella rocf Georgtown MM IL

WHITEWATER MONTHLY MEETING
MINUTES AND MARRIAGES

BRADWAY (cont)
9-26-1883   Ella rpt j ME ch; cert ret to Georgtown MM IL; h belongs ME

BRADY
7-16-1825   Mary (Wright) con mcd
3-25-1829   Mary dis for jas

BRAINARD
12-25-1883 Elizabeth rec in mbrp

BRAISINGTON
3-26-1834   Lydia rocf Evesham MM

BRANIZER
12-26-1891 Susannah, Walter Ezra, & Wm B rq mbrp Richmond PM

BRANNON
2-23-1896   Elizabeth rec in mbrp

BRANSON
5-22-1833   Jane (Anderson) dis for mcd
1-26-1859   Isiah & w Sarah & ch Martha, Phebe, & Jacob rocf Chester MM; Rebecca G rocf Chester MM
4-24-1861   Isaiah & w Sarah G & min s Jacob gct Chester MM
7-24-1861   Martha dis for jas

BRASINGTON
3-26-1834   James & s Joseph, Wm, & Samuel rocf Evesham MM

BRATTAIN
9-29-1810   Anna & dt Mary rocf Elk MM
10-27-1810 Mary rocf Deep River MM NC
8-31-1811   Robert appt Clerk
10-26-1816 Robert gct Elk MM OH
8-30-1817   Robert rocf Elk MM OH
12-2-1818   Robert s John & Rachel dec Wayne Co m Hannah dt John & Ann **Maudlin** Wayne Co at Whitewater MH
8-26-1820   Jonathan gct Silver Creek MM; Anna & dt gct Silver Creek MM
10-15-1825 Hannah gct Milford MM

BRAXTON
10-26-1811 Thomas & s Jonathan, Hiram, & Wm rocf Spring MM NC; Hannah & dt Margery rocf Spring MM NC

BRAZILTON
5-30-1812   Sarah rocf Deep River MM NC

BRAZINGTON
11-23-1836 Samuel & Lydia & min ch Joseph, Wm, Samuel, & Hannah Ann gct West Grove MM
3-22-1848   Wm A rocf Spiceland MM
6-27-1849   Wm A dis for na

BRENIZER
12-22-1869 Susannah & ch Ida Mayhill, Anna Susan, Bessie Lincoln, Walter Ezra, & Wm Barr rec in mbrp
5-23-1877   Anna Susan & Bessie rel fr mbrp
4-27-1895   David & Ida rec in mbrp

BREWER
7-27-1842   Sarah & ch Wm H, Elias, Mary, Morris W, & Jason W rocf Duck Creek MM
6-28-1843   John rocf Duck Creek MM
7-27-1848   Elizabeth rocf Duck Creek MM
3-24-1852   Elias dis for j ME

BRICE
2-27-1861   Mary (Way) dis for na & mcd

BRIGGS
10-25-1876 Lucy J rel fr mbrp
4-23-1885   Mary R, Anna B, & Otis W ch of Otis & Lucy rel fr mbrp

BRIGHT
4-19-1823   Abigail (Small) con mcd
8-16-1823   Abigail gct New Garden MM
5-28-1828   Abigail rocf Milford MM
8-22-1832   Abigail gct Duck Creek MM

BRIGHTWELL
11-20-1824 Rhoda (Wright) con mcd
4-22-1829   Rhoda dis for jas

BRINER
11-22-1883 Centreville rq mbrp for Elizabeth
12-27-1883 Elizabeth rec in mbrp

BRITTAIN
9-29-1810   Jonathan & s Solomon rocf Elk MM OH
10-27-1810 Robert rocf Deep River MM NC

BROCK
7-25-1812   Elijah rocf Caesar's Creek MM OH
9-26-1812   Elijah & Mary (Way) dis for mcd
8-27-1892   Anna M & min s Fred M **Hunt** glt Dubuque 1st Cong ch IA

BROCKMAN
3-25-1874   John Orange PM rec in mbrp
2-26-1885   John drpd fr mbrp for na

BROMAGEN
4-25-1891   Electa & dt Mary rec in mbrp

BROOKS
4-26-1817   Hannah rocf Miami MM OH
2-23-1882   Margaret rq mbrp in Richmond PM
5-25-1882   Margaret J drp fr cons for mbrp

BROWER
5-23-1896   Horace & Viola New Westville OH rec in mbrp

BROWN
6-27-1812   Abigail (Spivy) con mcd
8-29-1812   Cert rec for Thomas & fam; end to Elk MM OH
12-28-1816 Eli rocf Deep River MM NC
9-3-1817   Eli s James NC & Martha dec Wayne Co m Martha dt Amos & Anna **Hawkins** Wayne Co at Whitewater MH
1-30-1819   Alice (Thomas) con mcd
2-27-1828   Wm & s Cyrus & Milton rocf Dover MM NC; Selah rocf Dover MM NC
2-25-1829   Frederick, Amiel, Hance, & Thomas rocf Dover MM NC; Rebecca & dt Nancy, Frances, & Elizabeth rocf Dover MM N C
3-25-1829   Frederick gct Duck Creek MM
1-26-1831   John & s Aaron W rocf Miami MM OH; Mary W rocf Miami MM OH
12-28-1831 John & w Mary & s Aaron gct Miami MM OH
1-2-1833   Frederick Rush Co s James & Rebecca Hendricks Co m Sarah dt Jesse & Mary **Morris** Wayne Co at Whitewater MH
4-24-1833   Sarah gct Duck Creek MM
4-22-1835   Wm & w Celia & ch Cyrus N, Millon D, Mary, Rebecca, & Henry gct Duck Creek MM; Rebecca & ch Nancy, Frances, Elizabeth, & Thomas gct White Lick MM

BROWN (cont)

10-28-1835	Anniel dis for mcd
2-24-1836	Juretta (Evans) con mcd
11-23-1836	Benjamin & w Mary Ann & ch Clayton, Isaac, Martha, & Jacob rocf Elk MM OH
9-23-1840	Benjamin gct Salem MM to m Naomi Taylor
6-23-1841	Naomi rocf Salem MM
8-26-1846	Clayton Jr rocf Elk MM OH
10-24-1849	Alfred & Elam J gct Richland MM IA
1-23-1851	Samuel s Asher & Esther J Warren Co OH m Hannah dt Thomas & Hannah dec Evans Warren Co OH at Whitewater MH
7-23-1851	Hannah gct Miami MM OH
7-28-1852	Susanna rocf Richland MM IA
5-4-1853	Clayton s Samuel dec & Sarah E Wayne Co m Phebe dt Thomas & Mary both dec Roberts Wayne Co at Whitewater MH
6-22-1853	John A & w Elizabeth J & dt Mary Emily rocf Miami MM OH; Ann Eliza rocf Miami MM OH
4-4-1855	Seth s Asher & Esther J Warren Co OH m Martha Ann dt Harmon & Mary Hill Wayne Co at Whitewater MH
6-27-1855	Martha Ann gct Miami MM OH
6-25-1856	Samuel C rocf Caesar's Creek MM OH; Clayton & w Sarah rocf Caesar's Creek MM OH
1-28-1857	Seth & w Martha Ann & dt Emma E rocf Miami MM OH
4-28-1858	Seth & w Martha Ann & ch Emma E & Annie Mary gct Miami MM OH; Joseph B nephew Clayton rec in mbrp
8-28-1861	Edgar prc Fairfield MM OH to m Sarah Bond
9-11-1861	Edgar s Edgar & Mary Highland Co OH m Sarah dt Benjamin dec & Lydia Bond Wayne Co at Whitewater MH
1-22-1862	Sarah gct Fairfield MM OH
4-23-1862	John A & w Elizabeth J & dt Mary Emily gct Plainfield MM; Ann Eliza gct Plainfield MM
12-28-1864	Gloster rec in mbrp
1-25-1865	Samuel C dis for mcd
3-19-1866	Gloster (colored slave) m Lucretia (colored slave) Madison Co AL 3-1847
8-28-1867	Samuel A rst; dis by Elk MM OH abt 18y previous for mcd
2-26-1868	Lindley M & Annie Mary ch of Samuel S & Susan L rec in mbrp
6-23-1869	Florence rec in mbrp
10-27-1869	Morris Helena AR rec in mbrp
8-23-1871	Joseph res mbrp to jas
10-23-1872	Seth & w Martha Ann & ch Emma E, Anna M, & Naomi H rocf New Garden MM
2-24-1875	Daniel rec in mbrp
5-23-1877	Oliver H & fam gct Westfield MM
7-25-1877	Amos rel fr mbrp
7-22-1880	Benjamin's death rpt; elder d during previous 3 y
8-26-1880	Clayton & w Phebe R and ch Sarah C, Hannah E, Wm S, & Orintha L gct Walnut Center MM IA
6-23-1881	Martha appt o
7-28-1881	Martha A appt Richmond o
2-23-1882	Rachel rq mbrp Richmond PM
3-23-1882	Albert E & Rachel rec in mbrp
5-25-1882	Daniel gct White River MM
6-28-1883	Otis R & w Nannie & min ch Hattie, Walter J, & Lizzie rocf Georgtown MM IL
2-28-1884	Ida rec in mbrp
2-27-1885	Samuel S, Susannah L, Lindley M, & Annie May gc
11-25-1885	Carrie L & min dt Bessie rec in mbrp
10-25-1888	Mary (Allen) rel fr mbrp; jas
9-21-1889	Delpha K rec in mbrp
6-28-1890	Margaretta (Kendal) gct Miami MM OH Waynesville OH
11-22-1890	Walter rel fr mbrp; j Grace ME ch; par con
4-25-1891	Wesley & w Anna V & min ch Lena M & Orville E rec in mbrp

BROWN (cont)

3-26-1892	John W & w Rosena & min s Clarence R rec in mbrp
8-26-1893	Grace rec in mbrp
1-26-1895	Grace gct to jas
11-23-1895	John W & w Rosena E & s Clarence M rel fr mbrp
7-23-1896	Otis R & w Nancy J & s Charles M gct Farmer's Institute MM
11-26-1896	Elizabeth drpd fr mbrp
4-27-1899	Eli & w Pheba rocf Vanwert MM OH
8-24-1899	Jesse gct Westland MM

BRUMFIELD

10-27-1894	Emma rocf West Grove MM

BRUMMET

3-22-1890	Charlotte rel fr mbrp; jas

BRUMMETT

1-24-1884	Orange PM rpts Cockayne & Charlotte & min ch Wm B, Mary, Virgil, & Luetta Wilson rq mbrp
3-27-1884	Charlotte rec in mbrp

BRYANT

4-27-1895	Arta L rec in mbrp

BUDD

12-25-1839	Elizabeth rocf Milford MM
5-27-1840	John & s Calvin W & Albert rec in mbrp
5-24-1842	John & w Elizabeth & min ch Calvin, Albert, Phebe Ann, & Charles gct New Garden MM

BUELL

5-26-1894	Ellen M rec in mbrp; lt fr Richmond 2nd Pres ch

BUFFKIN

8-23-1883	John rocf Piney Woods MM NC ; Esther J rec in mbrp

BUFFUM

3-28-1855	Mary Ann rocf Berwick MM ME
9-20-1877	David E s Thomas B & Lydia Newport Newport Co RI m Marianna dt Timothy & Sarah W dec Nicholson at res of T Nicholson Richmond
4-24-1878	Marianna gct Rhode Island MM Newport RI

BULLA

10-23-1844	Mary (Fulghum) dis for na & mcd
5-23-1849	Salem MM IA rpt Anna (Crampton) mcd
1-22-1880	Carolina rec in mbrp

BUNCH

6-24-1820	Ann (Pearson) con mcd

BUNDY

10-28-1815	Josiah rocf Symonds Creek MM NC; George & s Samuel More & George rocf Symonds Creek MM NC; Karan & dt Sarah rocf Symonds Creek MM NC; Josiah Jr rocf Springfield MM NC; Mary & dt Huldah rocf Springfield MM NC
3-30-1816	Miriam rocf Lick Creek MM
5-31-1817	Jonathan & Jesse rocf Springfield MM NC
5-29-1819	Christopher & Ephraim min rocf Back Creek MM NC
9-14-1822	Christopher con unjustly accusing mbr of taking property not his own
11-15-1823	Christopher dis for trading in spiritous liquors
7-25-1827	Rachel dis for unchastity
10-28-1829	Ephraim dis for na
8-23-1871	Henry C rocf Walnut Ridge MM
10-23-1872	Mary E rec in mbrp
4-24-1878	Henry C & w Mary E & min ch Wm H, Nellie, & Alsie gct Walnut Ridge MM

WHITEWATER MONTHLY MEETING
MINUTES AND MARRIAGES

BUNKER
12-25-1813	Abraham & s Thomas & David rocf New Garden MM NC; Anna & dt Kazia, Phebe, & Anna rocf New Garden MM NC
9-30-1815	John & s Levi rocf Mill Creek MM; Wellmet & dt Rebecca & Judith rocf Mill Creek MM
12-26-1818	Rueben & s Jesse & Samuel rec in mbrp; Rachel rec in mbrp
11-27-1819	Judith & dt Mary & Lydia rocf New Garden MM
4-28-1821	Cert rec for Phebe fr West Branch MM OH; end to West Grove MM

BURGESS
6-26-1813	Sarah rec in mbrp
11-24-1847	Sarah rocf Spiceland MM
7-28-1898	Edgar M rec in mbrp

BURKE
9-24-1892	Louis rec in mbrp

BURNAN
11-27-1878	Edith & ch rel fr mbrp

BURNS
5-28-1851	John rocf Elk MM OH
9-26-1855	John gct Elk MM OH

BURSON
6-22-1836	Eliza rocf Philadelphia MM North Dist PA
10-11-1843	Eliza gct Milford MM
10-26-1853	Jemima rocf Miami MM OH
12-28-1853	David S & w Margaret & ch Edward Thomas, Ann E, Lydia A, Hannah M, Jemima L, & Isaac C rocf Miami MM OH
1-23-1856	Jemima gct Birch Lake MM MI
7-23-1856	Jemima rocf Birch Lake MI
5-25-1864	David S dis for na & fighting
8-23-1883	Benjamin E d 12-31-1882

BURTON
3-25-1868	Sarah E rec in mbrp
4-22-1868	Levi D rec in mbrp
3-27-1872	L Ann rec in mbrp
7-22-1877	Levi rel fr mbrp
7-25-1877	Mary Emma dt Richard & Gulielma **Binns** gct Lawrence MM KS

BUTLER
11-25-1809	Amos rocf Bradford MM PA
1-27-1810	Bail & s Samuel & Wm rocf New Garden MM NC; Mary & dt Susannah & Mary rocf New Garden MM NC; Susannah rocf New Garden MM NC
5-29-1813	Amos dis for mcd
1-28-1815	Samuel dis for military training
1-18-1823	Lemuel & s Thomas, Durham, Samuel, Pleasant, & Mahlon rocf Gravelly Run MM VA; Jane & dt Mary, Jane, Tacy, & Martha rocf Gravelly Run MM VA
3-19-1825	Lemuel & w Jane & ch Thomas, Durham, Mary, Lemuel, Jane, Tacy, Pleasant, Martha, Mahlon, & Joseph gct Milford MM
7-22-1840	Wm chm & rst
5-27-1846	Oliver rocf Walnut Ridge MM
8-25-1847	Oliver dis for na
4-24-1850	Sarah rocf Hopewell MM
5-22-1850	Wm E rocf Milford MM
6-26-1850	Wm dis for na
10-25-1854	Alfred & w Elisabeth & ch Benjamin M & Lindley H rocf Hopewell MM

BUTLER (cont)
4-25-1855	Alfred & w Elizabeth & ch Benjamin M, Lindley H, & Charles Ervin gct West Union MM
3-26-1856	Anselm B rocf Green Plain MM OH
7-25-1860	Sarah & s Joseph Coridon gct Hopewell MM
2-28-1872	Benjamin M rocf Pipe Creek MM
7-26-1876	Benjamin M & min dt Nettie gct Chicago MM IL
3-22-1890	Anna M rocf Chester MM

CADWALADER
2-26-1851	Howard & w Margaret & ch Reece D, Edwin G, & John H rocf Salem MM OH
4-23-1851	Reece & w Sarah rocf Salem MM OH
2-22-1865	Sarah appt overseer Richmond PM
7-26-1869	Sarah A rec in mbrp

CADWALLADER
11-27-1879	Rachel gct ME ch
6-23-1881	Sarah appt o

CALAWAY
8-30-1817	John rec in mbrp

CALLOWAY
8-30-1817	Letisha rec in mbrp

CALVERT
7-23-1885	Reese Garrett prc fr Green Plain MM OH to m Ann Ethel **Kirk**
7-28-1885	Reese Garret Clark Co OH s Thomas & Elizabeth Philadelphia Co PA m Annie Ethel dt Charles & Rachel **Kirk** at res of Charles W **Kirk** Richmond
9-24-1885	Anna Ethel (**Kirk**) gct Green Plain MM OH

CAMMAC
4-29-1820	Hannah rocf Miami MM OH

CAMMACK
1-15-1825	Hannah & min ch Nathan H & David gct West Grove MM
3-28-1866	George W & w Mary & s Willie rocf Clear Creek MM OH
2-26-1885	George & w Mary, & Willie drpd fr mbrp for na

CAMPBELL
10-27-1875	Kate rec in mbrp
10-25-1876	Anna rec in mbrp

CANADA
6-24-1815	Charles & s Nathan & Charles rocf Lost Creek MM TN; Sarah & dt Margaret, Mary, Phebe, Sarah, Charity, & Matilda rocf Lost Creek MM TN
9-30-1815	Amy & dt gct New Garden MM

CANADAY
4-29-1815	Amy & dt Ann, Abigail, & Sarah rocf Lost Creek MM TN
10-26-1816	Mary & dt Sarah, Jane, Margaret, & Ann rocf Lost Creek MM TN
10-25-1817	John & Margaret rocf Lost Creek MM TN

CANDLER
4-24-1872	Sarah E (**Wickett**) con mcd
8-28-1872	Theodore F rec in mbrp

CANNON
2-24-1869	Anna Helena AR rec in mbrp

CAREY
2-22-1860	John F & w Sarah Jane & ch Emma Jane & Louella E rocf Richland MM IA
12-22-1894	Milton rocf Vermilion MM IL

CAREY (cont)
4-27-1895	Anna (**Barlow**) & ch Leroy J, Arthur E, & Dennis H rocf Wilmington MM OH
3-25-1897	Milton & w Anna & min ch Leroy J, Dennis H, & Arthur E gct Anderson MM

CARMAN
8-25-1894	Wm S & w Mary & min ch Herbert, Leslie, & Roy rec in mbrp

CARPENTER
10-23-1850	Isaac & w Deborah A & dt Rosetta L rocf Farmington MM NY
1-28-1857	Walter T & w Susan M & min ch Charles G, Caroline, & Elizabeth rocf Springfield MM OH
3-24-1858	Nathaniel & w Lemira rocf Springfield MM OH; Anna rocf Springfield MM OH
12-22-1858	Edwin & w Louisa H & ch Laura Ann & Caroline E rocf Springfield MM OH
7-24-1861	Isaac E & w Deborah gct Rochester MM NY
4-22-1863	Nathaniel & w Zeriah gct Bridgeport MM; Anna minister gct Bridgeport MM
7-27-1864	Charles G gct Smithfield MM OH to m Elizabeth A **Newlin**
9-21-1864	Edwin & w Louisa H & min ch Laura Ann & Caroline E gct Bridgeport MM
4-26-1865	Elizabeth N rocf Smithfield MM
7-25-1877	Rosetta rel fr mbrp
8-23-1883	Walter T & Susan M appt o

CAR
8-17-1822	Susannah (**Hunt**) dis for mcd

CARREL
2-15-1823	Ann gct New Garden MM

CARROLL
11-28-1818	Rachel rocf Little Falls MM MD
10-31-1821	Thomas Wayne Co s Edward & Elisabeth Columbiana Co OH m Ann L dt Jesse & Sarah **Williams** Wayne Co at Whitewater MH
2-15-1823	Thomas gct New Garden MM
4-24-1839	Ruth Ann (**Pope**) dis for na & mcd

CARTER
11-26-1828	Cert rec for David fr Cane Creek MM NC; end to White Lick MM
2-26-1873	Samuel C & w Alberteen & ch Lilly May & Claudine rocf Spiceland MM
5-26-1875	Samuel C & w Albertine & min ch Lillie M, Claudine, & Clarence W gct Salem MM
7-22-1886	Nathan P & w Alice rocf West Grove MM
8-24-1888	Nathan P & w Alice & min ch gct Indianapolis MM

CARUTHERS
12-26-1891	Alice F not found
2-24-1894	Alice F rel fr mbrp; jas

CASEY
12-22-1894	Milton rocf Vermilion MM IL

CHAFFANT
10-27-1821	Evan & Ruth rocf Redstone MM PA

CHALFANT
4-28-1821	Evan J dis for mcd

CHALFONT
6-23-1830	Ruth dis for jas

CHALFONTE
2-25-1829	Even dis for jas

CHAMBERS
11-30-1811	Jonathan rocf Spring MM NC; Elinor & dt Sarah & Deborah rocf Spring MM NC

CHAMBLESS
7-27-1811	Charity rocf Springfield MM NC
3-30-1811	Mary dis for mcd

CHAMNESS
7-31-1813	Joseph, Samuel, Joel, & Ruth rocf Center MM NC
4-29-1820	Margaret & step dt Abigail & Sarah rocf Cane Creek MM NC
12-17-1825	Margaret & step dt Abigail & Sarah gct White River MM
7-22-1868	Seth M & dt Lena May rocf Springfield MM
2-26-1885	Seth & Lena May gc
8-23-1888	Seth gct Springfield MM
12-26-1891	Lena May not found

CHANDLER
5-17-1823	Joseph & s Levi, Willis, Jacob, & John rocf Westfield MM NC; Anna & dt Lucy rocf Westfield MM NC
10-18-1823	Joseph & w Anna & min ch Lucy, Levi, Willis, Jacob, John, & Edith gct White Lick MM
5-23-1860	Ann (**Wright**) con mcd

CHAPEL
8-14-1824	Huldah rocf Piney Woods MM NC
8-26-1829	Cert rec for Martha fr Piney Woods MM NC; end to Milford MM
10-28-1831	Jacob H dis for jas
6-26-1833	Cert rec for Martha Ann fr Marlborough MM OH; end to Duck Creek

CHAPIN
2-23-1895	Oliver M rec in mbrp
6-23-1898	O M drpd fr mbrp

CHAPPEL
1-28-1829	Huldah dis for na & jas
10-27-1830	Jacob H rocf Suttons Creek MM NC
6-26-1833	Cert rec for Thomas & Peggy fr Marlborough MM OH; end to Duck Creek MM; Wm rocf Marlborough MM OH
10-23-1833	Sarah rec in mbrp
7-30-1834	Wm Wayne Co s Thomas L & Martha dec Hancock Co m Margery **Moffitt** dt Jeremiah & Margery dec **Cox** Wayne Co at Whitewater MH
3-22-1837	Wm & w Marjery & ch David & Hannah **Moffit** & Martha gct Sugar River MM

CHAPPLE
6-26-1833	Cert rec for Thomas L fr Marlborough MM OH; end to Duck Creek MM

CHARLES
5-30-1812	Samuel & s Samuel, Daniel, Joseph, & Nathan rocf Back Creek MM NC; Gulielma & dt Abigail rocf Back Creek MM NC
6-27-1812	Sarah rocf Back Creek MM NC
10-28-1815	Abigail rocf Springfield MM NC
3-9-1820	Daniel s Samuel & Gulielma Wayne Co m Miriam dt Thomas & Abigail **Moore** Wayne Co at Whitewater MH
6-24-1820	Daniel & Miriam gct New Garden MM
11-1-1821	Samuel s Samuel & Gulielma Wayne Co m Sarah dt Thomas & Sarah **Hill** Wayne Co at Ridge MH
5-18-1822	Samuel Jr & Sarah gct New Garden MM
1-17-1824	John con for dr
3-20-1824	John con for dr
10-24-1827	Nathan gct Milford MM to m Mary Symons
7-25-1828	Mary rocf Milford MM

WHITEWATER MONTHLY MEETING
MINUTES AND MARRIAGES

CHARLES (cont)
12-24-1828	Abraham con mcd
3-23-1831	Jesse gct Arba MM; Margaret gct Milford MM
5-25-1831	Samuel s John dis for jas & distilling fruit
2-26-1834	Jesse rocf Arba MM
12-24-1834	Abraham dis for jas
5-25-1836	Jesse gct Spiceland MM
8-26-1841	Thomas gct Fall Creek MM OH
11-24-1841	Thomas gct Richland MM
5-28-1845	Eli gct Spiceland MM
5-27-1863	Wilson gct Cherry Grove MM to m Caroline D **Hockett**
8-26-1863	Matthew gct Center MM to m Eliza D **Timberlake**
12-23-1863	Wilson gct Richland MM
8-24-1864	Samuel H con mcd
9-21-1864	Margretta rec in mbrp
10-26-1864	Eliza D rocf Center MM OH
8-27-1892	M Alice Brown rocf Vermilion MM IL
8-24-1899	Nathan Herbert & w Alice B & dt Edna gct Marion MM

CHENOWITH
10-25-1890	Stella rec in mbrp; fr Richmond Presb ch

CHESNUT
2-23-1882	Emma A rq mbrp Richmond PM
5-23-1882	Emma drpd fr cons for mbrp

CHILDRE
1-26-1831	Martha & Phebe gct White Lick MM

CHILDRU
9-26-1827	Martha & Sally rocf Stillwater MM OH

CHRASHES
2-14-1824	Susannah dis for mcd

CHRISMAN
3-23-1882	Mary E to be rec in mbrp 12th St PM
5-15-1882	Mary E drpd fr cons for mbrp
1-24-1884	Mary E drpd rq for mbrp

CHURCH
10-26-1899	Eliza A drpd fr mbrp

CLARK
12-30-1809	Sarah & dt Susanna, Jamima, Tamar, & Sarah rocf Cane Creek MM NC
9-29-1810	Jane rocf MM in NC
11-30-1811	Sarah appt to comm
9-25-1813	Jesse & s Wm & Nathan rocf Deep River MM NC; Hannah & dt Mary rocf Deep River MM NC
5-27-1815	Daniel con mcd
4-3-1816	Wm s John & Sarah Wayne Co m Esther dt Jesse & Hannah dec **Jones** Wayne Co
4-27-1816	Jesse gct Elk MM OH
5-25-1816	Jane gct Elk MM OH
9-28-1816	Elizabeth rocf Elk MM OH
10-25-1817	Francis rocf New Garden MM NC
3-28-1818	Israel rocf Gunpowder MM MD; Amy & dt Ruth rocf Gunpowder MM MD; Deborah rocf Gunpowder MM MD
9-9-1819	John s John & Sarah dec Wayne Co m Anna dt Rice dec & Catherine **Price** Preble Co OH at Elkhorn MH
3-25-1820	Deborah con for att mcd
11-28-1821	Israel s Joseph & Elizabeth both dec Wayne Co m Mary dt Reuben & Judith **Bunker** Wayne Co at Chester MH
4-20-1822	Mary dis for unchastity
7-20-1822	John gct Elk MM OH
12-20-1823	Enos & Thomas W s Daniel rec in mbrp

CLARK (cont)
2-14-1824	Susannah & dt Jemima rec in mbrp
2-19-1825	Alida rocf Elk MM OH
7-16-1825	Sarah (**Wright**) con mcd
6-27-1827	Francis dis for upl
4-22-1829	Sarah dis for jas
5-27-1829	Wm & Esther dis for jas
7-29-1829	Rachel (**Marmon**) con mcd
3-28-1832	Wm dis for na
12-24-1834	Jane rocf Duck Creek MM
4-22-1835	Cyntha Ellen, Hannah, Sarah Ann, Emily, Jemima, & Elias Hicks ch Wm gct Mississenewa MM
7-26-1837	Enos B gct White Lick MM
8-23-1837	Jane gct Walnut Ridge MM
2-27-1839	Mary Ann gct Walnut Ridge MM
5-27-1840	Calvin & Alfred min gct Spiceland MM; Lydia & Mary Ann gct Walnut Ridge MM
2-24-1841	Jesse gct Westfield MM
11-23-1842	Thomas dis for mcd
12-27-1843	Elizabeth gct Chester MM
3-27-1844	Gulielma gct Chester MM
6-26-1844	Calvin rocf White Lick MM
9-4-1844	Calvin s John & Anna both dec Wayne Co m Alida dt Tom & Keziah dec **Clawson** Wayne Co at Whitewater MH
12-25-1844	Nathan dis for na & mcd
6-25-1845	Thomas gct Salem MM IA
2-25-1846	Elwood con mcd
4-22-1846	Elwood gct Chester MM
11-28-1849	Daniel rocf Walnut Ridge MM; Sarah rec in mbrp
12-26-1849	Mary R rocf Ferrisburg MM VT
2-22-1851	Daniel & w Mary R & dt Emma Robinson gct West Union MM
5-25-1853	John dis for na & mcd
7-27-1853	Wm dis for na
12-23-1863	Springfield MM rpt Melinda (**Macy**) mcd; mbrp retained
7-27-1864	Melinda rocf Springfield MM
10-24-1866	Dougan & w Sarah J & ch Charles G, Wm F, & Henry H rocf Indianapolis MM
8-26-1868	Wm P rocf West Union MM
7-26-1871	Wm P gct Springdale MM IA to m Martha **Pickering**
1-24-1872	Wm P gct Rocksylvania MM IA
12-24-1873	Joanna rec in mbrp
8-22-1877	Emma & Cora gct Salem MM
2-27-1878	Cert granted Wm to New York MM ret with info that he was not ready to become memb of that mtg
10-28-1880	Alexander & w Laura rocf New Garden MM
2-28-1884	Charles G gct Lurgan MM Ireland
2-26-1885	Alexander, Laura, Henry H, & Wm F gc
4-23-1885	Henry H gct Indianapolis MM
7-23-1885	Thomas rec in mbrp
12-27-1890	Cora gct San Jose MM CA; Emma J gct White Lick MM
2-28-1891	Elizabeth rec in mbrp
12-26-1891	Nellie rec in mbrp
7-22-1897	Dougan's death rpt; ae 71y
8-26-1897	Thomas & ch Mary B & Anna R rocf Dover MM
2-24-1898	Mary B gct Indianapolis MM

CLASAON
10-18-1823	Keziah rec in mbrp

CLAWSON
12-26-1812	Rebeckah rocf Cane Creek MM NC
3-30-1822	Sarah rec in mbrp
10-18-1823	Wm & s Josiah rec in mbrp; Mahlon rec in mbrp
6-24-1829	Mahlon dis for mcd
1-23-1839	Rebecca gct Chester MM
7-27-1842	Wm gct Miami MM OH to m Rebecca **Pool**
4-26-1843	Rebecca & ch Joseph & Elizabeth Ann **Pool** rocf Miami MM OH

CLAWSON (cont)
4-22-1846	Elwood gct Chester MM
8-23-1848	Josiah gct Milford MM to m Sarah N **Fletcher**; Rebecca rocf Chester MM
3-28-1849	Josiah gct Chester MM
10-23-1850	Elizabeth & dt Tabitha Jane rec in mbrp
11-27-1850	Abner & s Wm T & Alfred H rec in mbrp
4-28-1852	Wm Jr dis for mcd
12-27-1854	Thomas W gct West Grove MM
9-22-1858	Malinda rec in mbrp
3-25-1863	Wm T dis for mcd
2-22-1865	Wm & w Rebecca & min ch Mary Emma & Alice gct White Lick MM
7-26-1865	Martha Jane gct White Lick MM
5-24-1871	Alfred con mcd
10-23-1878	Alice rocf White Lick MM
7-22-1880	Elizabeth Ann rocf Lawrence MM KS
12-22-1881	Alfred H & min ch Charles C & Eugene gct Cherry Grove MM
2-26-1885	Alice gc

CLAYTON
4-25-1896	John J & w Laura E rec in mbrp

CLEAVER
12-27-1826	Alice rocf Hopewell MM VA
1-28-1829	Alice dis for jas

CLEMENS
3-23-1882	Emma B & Anna M rec in mbrp
4-27-1882	Caroline rec in mbrp
10-23-1884	Caroline & dt Anna & Emma gct Indianapolis MM

CLIFT
3-24-1881	Mary E rec in mbrp; lt fr Richmond Pearl St ME ch
11-22-1883	Mary A gct Columbus MM OH

CLINE
3-24-1881	James & w Mary C & ch Wm C & Mary L rec in mbrp

CLOUD
11-26-1814	Jonathan & s Joel, Wm, & Mordecai rocf Miami MM OH; Elisabeth & dt Anne & Matilda rocf Miami MM OH
3-7-1827	Wm s Jonathan & Elizabeth Wayne Co m Tacy dt Charles & Elizabeth **Moffitt** Wayne Co at Whitewater MH
4-25-1827	Tacy gct Duck Creek MM
3-28-1832	John T rocf Chester MM
2-24-1836	John dis for j ME & dp
4-26-1883	W H & Kate Centreville rq mbrp
6-28-1883	Wm & Kate Centreville rq mbrp
12-27-1883	Wm H & Kate rq PM at Centreville
3-23-1889	Kate dis; in state prison
10-25-1890	Joel Edgar & w Ella & min s Carl rocf Spiceland MM

COALE
2-26-1839	Gunpowder MM rpt Eliz (**Smith**) mcd

COATE
7-28-1894	Robert Harris & w Vashti E & ch Martha A & Clarence M rocf New Garden MM; Walter J rocf New Garden MM

COATES
5-23-1896	Anson rocf New Castle MM

COCKAYNE
11-28-1827	James rec in mbrp
3-5-1828	James Jr Wayne Co s James Sr & Sarah dec Talbott Co MD m Elizabeth dt Joseph late of Guilford Co NC & Rebecca **Unthank** at Whitewater MH

COCKAYNE (cont)
10-27-1830	James rocf Motherkiln MM DE
9-22-1841	Cert rec for Elizabeth fr Stillwater MM OH; dec
6-25-1851	Julia Ann dis for na, dp, & j ME
4-27-1853	Wm dis for na & mcd
7-27-1853	Edwin dis for na
10-28-1868	Joseph con mcd
3-27-1872	Mary & Lilly rec in mbrp
8-28-1872	Charles con mcd
3-27-1884	Anna M rec in mbrp
6-28-1888	Joseph & Anna M rel fr mbrp; j ME ch

COFFIN
12-28-1811	Hepza rocf Mt Pleasant MM VA
5-27-1815	Samuel minister rocf Mt Pleasant MM VA; Elizabeth & dt Abigail, Anna Mary, Ruth, & Susannah rocf Mt Pleasant MM VA
2-24-1816	Elizabeth & fam gct Blue River MM
5-30-1818	Adam & s Francis, Moses, & Obed rocf Mill Creek MM OH; Anna & dt Catharine, Elizabeth, Jemima, Rebekah, & Anna rocf Mill Creek MM OH
10-18-1823	Cert rec for Libni fr Blue River MM; end to Chester MM
1-17-1824	Francis gct Silver Creek MM to m Susanna **Stanton**; Barnabas & Sarah rocf Driftwood MM
11-10-1825	Rachel gct Chester MM
12-17-1825	Priscilla rocf New Garden MM
5-20-1826	Francis dis for na
3-28-1827	Susanna & dt Alladelppi rocf Silver Creek MM
11-23-1827	Rebecca gct Mill Creek MM OH; Sarah & dt Esther gct Chester MM
5-28-1828	Moses gct West Grove MM
7-22-1829	Susanna & ch gct West Grove MM
3-24-1830	Adam gct Silver Creek MM
9-24-1834	Thomas C rocf New Garden MM NC
1-28-1835	Elijah & s Charles F & Wm H rocf Cincinnati MM OH; Naomi & dt Miriam A, Caroline E, & Mary rocf Cincinnati MM OH
1-27-1836	Mary (**Harvey**) con mcd
3-23-1836	Nathan T gct Niagara MM
8-24-1836	Thomas C & w Mary & dt Gulielma gct Bloomfield MM
9-24-1845	Wm H gct Milford MM
2-25-1846	Sarah rocf Milford MM
2-27-1847	Charles F gct Miami MM OH to m Rhoda M **Johnson**
6-23-1847	Rhoda M rocf Miami MM OH
10-24-1849	Wm H & w Sarah & ch Charles F & John W gct Chester MM
8-27-1851	Wm H & w Sarah & ch John W & Wm Henry rocf Chester MM
12-24-1851	Mary H gdt Wm & Sarah **Harvey** rec in mbrp
10-26-1853	Jesse & w Emily & min ch Edwin, Alpheus, Adaline, & Wilson rocf Newberry MM
5-24-1854	Wm H & w Sarah & ch John Wilson, Wm Henry, Albert, & Robert B gct Milford MM
6-22-1859	Susan (**Ellis**) con mcd
11-23-1859	Susan gct Newberry MM OH
4-26-1865	Elijah memorial pres
7-8-1869	Elijah s Charles F & Rhoda Wayne Co m Sarah Elma dt Samuel F & Elizabeth D **Fletcher** Wayne Co at Richmond MH
3-25-1874	Wm H & w Sarah, & ch Robert & Frank rocf West Grove MM
9-15-1875	Wm Edward s Charles F & Rhoda M Wayne Co m Lydia Mary dt John & Mary A **Roberts** Wayne Co at Richmond Mtg
3-9-1876	Arthur H Grayson Co TX s Shubal G & Laura L Guilford Co NC m Anna Mary dt Samuel S & Anna S **Richey** at res of S S **Richey** Preble Co OH (Whitewater Mtg)
5-24-1876	Jesse & w Emily gct Sugar Plain MM
6-23-1881	Rhoda M appt o

WHITEWATER MONTHLY MEETING
MINUTES AND MARRIAGES

COFFIN (cont)
8-23-1883	Wm H appt elder
9-26-1883	Wm H & w Sarah H gct Lawrence MM KS
2-26-1885	Percival B gct Indianapolis MM
2-27-1885	Edwin gc; Alpheus, Wilson, Adaline, & Elias ch Jessie & Emily gc
7-23-1885	Charles Henry rel fr mbrp
2-25-1886	Charles F dis; Wm Edward & s Tristram Robert rel fr mbrp
3-28-1886	Francis A rel fr mbrp
4-22-1886	Rhoda M gct Chicago MM IL
2-23-1888	Frank s Wm gct Spiceland MM
12-26-1891	Edwin, Alpheus, Adaline, Wilson, & Eva not found
7-28-1894	Frank A & w Melissa & ch Lena Margaret, Myron F, & Irwin W rocf Spiceland MM
4-28-1897	Wm Vestal s Samuel D & Mary A Los Angeles Co CA m Sarah dt Timothy & Mary W **Nicholson** at home of Timothy **Nicholson** Wayne Co
9-23-1897	Sarah **(Nicholson)** gct Whittier MM CA

COGGESHALL
2-26-1885	Daniel & dt Esther Jane rocf Dover MM

COGGSHALL
5-22-1867	Lindley rocf Elk MM OH
7-28-1869	Oliver W rocf Fairfield MM
2-24-1875	Lindley & w Hannah & ch Emily Jane, Wm Albert, & Annuel Harvey gct Poplar Run MM
1-24-1877	Alma M rec in mbrp
6-24-1886	Oliver W & w Anna M & min ch Nora Elma, George R, Clarence D, Eva M, Ralph, & Staca L gct Kansas City MM MO

COGGSHELL
10-24-1866	Hannah & ch Emily Jane, Wm Albert, & Annual Harvey rocf Elk MM OH

COHANE
8-25-1841	Cert rec for Elizabeth fr Stillwater MM OH; d 5-27-1841

COIL
5-23-1896	Edgar P New Westville OH rec in mbrp

COLEMAN
7-25-1877	Maud & s rel fr mbrp

COLL
3-23-1831	Margaret M & fam rec in mbrp

COLLATT
6-24-1854	John gct Salem MM IA

COLLETT
5-25-1853	John rocf Salem MM IA
10-26-1853	John gct Salem MM IA to m Mary R Crew

COLTER
5-23-1896	George E, Mary, George, & Wm New Westville OH rec in mbrp

COLVIN
3-23-1895	Elmer rec in mbrp

COMBER
11-25-1809	Stephen & s John, Joseph, & James rocf Cane Creek MM SC

COMER
1-29-1810	Joseph appt to comm
11-25-1809	Mary & dt Rebeckah rocf Cane Creek MM SC; Elizabeth rocf Miami MM OH; end by West Branch MM OH

COMER (cont)
1-26-1811	Stephen appt Clerk
11-29-1817	John rocf Cane Creek MM SC
7-29-1820	Joseph dis for mcd
6-24-1829	Amos dis for mcd
8-27-1834	Isaac dis for na
2-24-1847	Robert dis for na
12-25-1867	Amos & Mary rst; dis abt 30y previous for mcd
7-26-1876	Charles W rec in mbrp
2-16-1885	Susanna gc
4-25-1886	Charles W & w Hannah Jemima gct Cherry Grove MM
4-27-1887	Joseph T rocf Carthage MM
12-22-1888	Charles & w Hannah rocf Cherry Grove MM
5-23-1896	Robert & Ida New Westville OH rec in mbrp
1-27-1898	Charles W & w Hannah rel fr mbrp

COMLEY
1-24-1866	Julia E rocf Cincinnati MM OH

COMMONS
11-29-1809	Isaac Dearborn Co s Robert & Ruth Grayson Co VA m Mary dt John & Elcy **Townsend** Dearborn Co at Whitewater MH
12-28-1811	Wm rocf Mt Pleasant MM NC
5-30-1812	Robert & s John, Eziekiel, Nathan, & David rocf Mt Pleasant MM VA; Ruth rocf Mt Pleasant MM VA
4-4-1816	Ezekiel s Robert & Ruth Wayne Co m Sarah dt Isaac & Sarah **Julian** Wayne Co at West Grove MH
8-31-1816	Wm con mcd
9-28-1816	John gct New Garden MM
5-31-1817	Elisabeth rocf West Branch MM OH
12-26-1832	Jonathan & w rocf Chester MM; Mary Ann rocf Chester MM
4-22-1835	Jonathan & w Mary Ann & min ch David & Mary gct Chester MM
12-4-1845	Robert s Isaac & Mary Wayne Co m Elizabeth dt Seth & Ruth **Cook** Wayne Co at Smyrna MH
2-25-1846	Elizabeth gct Chester MM
3-25-1857	Elizabeth & ch Wm Harvey, Francis Edwin, Clinton, & Isaac Newton rocf Chester MM
3-23-1870	Isaac & w Kesiah S & ch Edwin L, Riley O, Charlie S & Mary Anna rocf Chester MM
5-28-1879	Elizabeth & Joseph Clinton drpd fr mbrp; jas
7-22-1880	Elmer j Middleboro ME ch
1-27-1881	Francis Edwin & w & ch gct Walnut Center MM IA
4-27-1882	Robert & w Elizabeth rst; j Middletown ME ch
5-28-1885	Isaac N gct Paton MM IA
7-28-1887	Cynthia rocf New Garden MM
8-23-1890	Isaac & w Kesiah S & ch Mariana & Eleanor Bertha rel fr mbrp; j Piqua ME ch OH
6-27-1891	Conrad & w Anna & s Lewis B rec in mbrp
12-26-1891	Cynthia Jane & Joseph rq mbrp East Main St PM
2-22-1896	Robert & w Elizabeth rel fr mbrp

CONKLE
8-25-1875	Elizabeth Austin & dt Isabelle Louise rec in mbrp

CONKLIN
8-23-1883	Joseph d 2-17-1883 Smyrna

CONNER
3-25-1868	Mary Maud rec in mbrp
12-27-1871	Lucinda rec in mbrp
1-24-1872	Alvin rec in mbrp
6-28-1876	Lucinda gct Chester MM
4-28-1887	Joseph T rocf Carthage MM
1-25-1890	Lottie rec in mbrp
8-22-1891	Joseph P drpd fr mbrp

CONNOR
7-28-1821	Cert rec for John fr Caesar's Creek MM OH; end to West Branch MM OH

CONNOR (cont)
10-22-1873 Alvin dis for denying the "Divine Inspiration of the Scriptures & the Divinity of Christ"

COOK
5-26-1810 Thomas & s Isaac, Nathaniel, Eli, & Wright rocf Miami MM OH; Kezia & dt Charity & Rebeckah rocf Miami MM OH
10-27-1810 Andrew & Thomas appt to comm
10-31-1812 Zimri rocf Deep River MM NC
11-3-1813 Zimri s Thomas & Mary Wayne Co m Lydia dt Valentine & Mary **Pegg** Wayne Co at Whitewater MH
11-27-1813 Joseph & s Wm, Jehu, & Zimri & bro Nathan rocf Deep River MM NC; Lydia & dt Mary & Anna rocf Deep River MM NC
3-26-1814 John & s Thomas rocf Mill Creek MM OH; Hannah & dt Lydia & Phebe rocf Mill Creek MM OH
4-30-1814 Zimri Silver Creek con mcd
5-28-1814 Jacob & s Thomas & Ira rocf Caesar's Creek MM OH; Judith & dt Betty, Rebeckah, & Mary rocf Caesar's Creek MM OH
8-27-1814 Isaac & Charity rocf Caesar's Creek MM OH
11-26-1814 Wm rocf Springfield MM NC; Anne & dt Alyelina rocf Springfield MM NC; Thomas s Zimri rec in mbrp; Elizabeth rec in mbrp
11-1-1815 Nathan s Thomas dec & Mary Wayne Co m Anna dt Jehu & Mary **Wickersham** Wayne Co at Whitewater MH
11-30-1816 Isaac & s Samuel & John & dt Rachel, Nancy, Ruth, & Mary rocf Caesar's Creek MM OH
5-31-1817 Wm Jr con dr
6-28-1817 Cert rec for Wright & s Thomas, Isaac, Zachariah, John, Joseph, Henry, & David fr Caesar's Creek MM OH
2-28-1818 Wm & s Isaac, John, & Wm rocf Miami MM OH; Sarah & dt Mary, Martha, & Sarah rocf Miami MM OH
2-26-1820 Wm con dr
10-27-1821 Abraham & s Wm rocf New Garden MM NC; Elizabeth rocf New Garden MM NC
4-20-1822 Abraham & fam gct West Grove MM
6-15-1822 Anna w Wm Jr & ch gct West Grove MM
8-17-1822 Wm gct West Grove MM
8-20-1825 Seth & w Ruth & ch Amos, Isaac, & Elijah rocf Miami MM OH
12-20-1825 Hannah rocf Woodbury MM
1-3-1827 Samuel s Isaac & Elizabeth Union Co m Prudence dt James & Ruth dec **Johnson** Wayne Co at Whitewater MH
11-28-1827 Samuel & Prudence rocf Silver Creek MM
3-4-1830 John, Sarah, Elizabeth, Ruth, & Catharine rocf Cherry Grove MM
12-1-1830 John s Isaac & Elizabeth Union Co m Mary dt Josiah & Dorothy **Gilbert** Wayne Co at Whitewater MH
1-26-1831 Mary gct Silver Creek MM
4-25-1832 John, Sarah, Elizabeth, Nancy, Ruth, & Catharine min ch Mary gct Duck Creek MM
5-28-1834 Cert rec for John fr Spiceland MM; end to Chester MM; Sarah rocf Spiceland MM
11-26-1834 Samuel & w Prudence & ch Elijah, Isaac, Mahlon, Phillip, & Rachel gct New Garden MM
8-26-1835 Zimri & w Lydia & min ch Cyrus, Clarkson, Jesse, Cyrene, Joseph P, & Calvin gct Fairfield MM
1-25-1843 Amos dis for mcd
2-22-1843 Lydia (**Wright**) dis for mcd
7-23-1845 Isaac gct Caesar's Creek MM OH to m Mary S **Ragan**
12-24-1845 Mary L rocf Caesar's Creek MM OH
2-25-1852 Elijah con mcd
6-22-1853 Rachel & dt Ruth Anna rocf New Garden
9-23-1857 Isaac gct New Garden MM to m Martha **Crampton**
1-26-1859 Isaac dis for na & "Not owning the divine authority, authenticity, or credibility of parts of the Old Testament, nor all the documents contained in the New"

COOK (cont)
4-25-1860 Martha rocf New Garden MM
5-27-1863 Hannah Josephine gct Caesar's Creek MM OH
8-23-1865 Caleb rocf Dover MM
4-24-1867 Caleb gct Dover MM
3-24-1881 Angeline & ch Lillian & Leslie rocf Chester MM
7-28-1881 Rachel appt Smyrna o
8-23-1883 Ruth d 12-17-1882 Smyrna
10-25-1890 Emma S rec in mbrp; fr Richmond 1st Pres ch
12-26-1891 Ruthana (**Comer**) not found
10-27-1894 Elizabeth rocf Plainfield MM
1-27-1898 Elizabeth gct Dublin MM

COOPER
8-30-1817 Catherine & dt Rachel rocf Muncie MM; James & Thomas rocf Muncie MM
2-26-1820 Thomas dis for mcd
1-27-1821 James con mcd
11-19-1825 James gct Milford MM; Catherine & s Josiah, Joshua, John, Arthur, & Wm gct Milford MM
1-28-1857 Lydia E rocf Miami MM OH
6-23-1881 Lydia appt o
7-28-1881 Lydia appt Whitewater o
1-27-1898 John & Amy Ann rocf Elk MM OH
2-23-1899 Amy Ann gct New Garden MM

COPELAND
5-28-1814 Susannah & dt Winifred, Leah, & Rachel rocf Back Creek MM NC
12-30-1815 Susannah rocf Contentnea MM NC
5-26-1852 Martha (**Moore**) dis for na & mcd

COPLAND
5-28-1814 John & s Jonathan rocf Back Creek MM NC

CORRUTHERS
6-28-1888 Alice F rocf Chester MM

COSAND
9-14-1822 Samuel & Wm rocf Back Creek MM NC; John, Nathan, & Elias s Mary rocf Back Creek MM NC

COTTON
9-22-1869 Robert Henry & w Ann & min s Robert rec in mbrp
5-24-1876 Robert res mbrp
10-23-1878 Anna & ch Orloff res mbrp

COUGILL
3-24-1824 Caleb s Henry & Ruth both dec Wayne Co m Mary dt Hugh & Hannah **Moffitt** Wayne Co at Whitewater MH

COULTER
3-23-1899 Alexander, Mary Elizabeth, & Estella Mary min New Westville OH rec in mbrp

COVERT
5-27-1897 Earl & Albert Providence & Friendship Darke Co OH rec in mbrp

COWGILL
7-29-1820 Caleb & s Henry rocf Carmel MM OH; Rachel & dt Elizabeth & Lydia rocf Carmel MM OH
6-17-1824 Mary gct Chester MM
3-28-1827 Caleb & w Mary & ch Henry, Elizabeth, Liddia, Caleb, & John gct New Garden MM

COWGLE
2-19-1825 Mary & dt Elizabeth & Lydia rocf Chester MM

COX
9-30-1809 Catharine appt o; Jeremiah appt to comm

WHITEWATER MONTHLY MEETING
MINUTES AND MARRIAGES

COX (cont)

12-6-1809	Benjamin Dearborn Co s Joseph & Dinah NC m Mary dt Rice & Catherine **Price** OH at Whitewater MH
7-27-1811	Jeremiah Jr & Ruth (**Andrews**) dis for fornication
12-26-1812	Jehu & s Edom rocf Fairfield MM OH; Esther rocf Fairfield MM OH
4-27-1816	Joseph & s Joseph & Nathan rocf Cane Creek MM NC; Dinah & dt Dinah & Martha rocf Cane Creek MM NC
4-25-1818	Wm, Herman, & Mary rocf Cane Creek MM NC
5-29-1819	Stephen rocf Clear Creek MM
6-26-1819	Herman dis for mcd to first cousin
8-28-1819	Martha rocf West Grove MM
4-29-1820	Stephen dis for dp & upl
10-28-1820	Elijah gct New Garden MM
11-24-1821	Amy & Susannah rocf Minallen MM PA
4-20-1822	Wm rocf New Garden MM; Ruth G & dt Rebecca & Amy rocf New Garden MM
8-17-1822	Jeremiah Jr rec in mbrp after being dis
2-14-1824	Susannah gct Center MM OH
12-17-1825	Martha & ch Dinah, Thomas, & Joseph gct White Lick MM
4-15-1826	Joel rocf Somerset MM OH; Wm dis for na
7-26-1826	Amy gct Center MM OH
8-23-1826	Jeremiah & w Catharine & ch Enoch, Benjamin, Catharine, Robert, Wm, Samuel, & John gct White River MM
1-28-1829	Ruth dis for jas
2-27-1833	Amy rocf White River MM
7-4-1833	Elihu s Jeremiah & Ruth Wayne Co m Martha D dt Jacob & Ann **Grave** Wayne Co at Smyrna MH
1-27-1836	Wm & Mary & bound girl, Elizabeth **Swartz** gct White Lick MM
3-25-1836	Elihu rocf Chester MM
11-23-1836	Rebecca dis for na & dp
8-28-1839	Samuel & w Edith & ch Thomas, Susannah, & Deborah rocf New Garden MM
4-27-1842	Phebe Ann dis for na & dp
10-11-1843	Elihu dis for jas
3-27-1844	Martha D dis for being active in bringing about a separation & jas
5-28-1851	Edith, Susannah, & Deborah gct East Grove MM IA
1-28-1852	Sarah rocf Walnut Ridge MM
3-24-1852	Samuel & Sarah (**Brewer**) dis for mcd
10-27-1852	Warner L dis for na & mcd
2-23-1853	Deborah & Susannah rocf East Grove MM IA
10-26-1853	Benjamin T rocf Walnut Ridge MM
3-22-1854	Cyrus B rocf Walnut Ridge MM
4-26-1854	Mary rocf Holly Spring MM NC
11-28-1855	John F/T dis for mcd
9-24-1856	Cyrus B gct Walnut Ridge MM
12-23-1857	Jeremiah & w Phebe rocf Chester MM
6-22-1859	Ann & Louisa dis for na, apd, & dancing
12-28-1864	Jeremiah & w Phebe gct Chester MM
4-22-1868	Joseph & w Rachel Jane & ch Elvira, Clayton, Medora, & Russel rec in mbrp
7-28-1869	Jeremiah prc fr Chester MM to m Mary **Doyle**
8-4-1869	Jeremiah s Jeremiah & Margery both dec Wayne Co m Mary W **Doyle** wid dt Samuel & Sarah **Test** both dec Wayne Co at Whitewater Mtg
12-22-1869	Mary W gct Chester MM
10-26-1870	Enoch con mcd
4-23-1885	Medora drpd fr mbrp
11-25-1886	Mary gct Holly Spring MM NC
2-24-1887	Cert for Mary ret by Holly Spring MM NC; she did not intend to remain there
2-28-1891	Addie rec in mbrp; lt fr ME ch
3-28-1891	Grace rec in mbrp; cert fr Grace ME ch
9-26-1891	Joseph & w Rachel & ch Alton & Celia gct Chester MM
4-23-1892	Addie & dt Grace gl
1-26-1895	John N & w Angeline & ch Gurney rocf Chester MM
1-25-1896	Narcissa rec in mbrp

CRABB

2-24-1894	Richmond PM rpts Elizabeth C rq mbrp

CRAFT

5-27-1893	Elizabeth rec in mbrp
11-26-1896	Elizabeth drpd fr mbrp

CRAIG

1-23-1833	Jacob rocf Miami MM OH
1-1-1834	Jacob Wayne Co s Samuel dec & Martha NJ m Hannah dt Charles & Elizabeth **Moffitt** Wayne Co at Whitewater MH
6-25-1862	Mary H (**Coffin**) con mcd
9-22-1875	Mary rel fr mbrp
1-27-1894	Emma rocf West Grove MM

CRAMPTON

2-28-1818	Samuel & s Merrick S & Jacob H rocf Miami MM OH; Anna & dt Mary C, Elizabeth G, Cassandra M, & Ruth H rocf Miami MM OH
6-19-1824	Samuel & s Merrick, Joshua, Jacob, Abraham, Jonathon, & Andrew rocf Chester MM; Anna & dt Elizabeth, Cassandra, & Eunice rocf Chester MM
9-23-1824	Merrick s Samuel & Rachel dec Preble Co OH m Anna dt Jacob & Sarah dec **Smith** Wayne Co at Ridge MH
12-20-1825	Cert rec for Anna minister fr Caesar's Creek MM; d bef cert rec
7-26-1826	Joshua dis for upl & offering to fight
5-23-1827	Jonathan dis by Miami MM OH
11-23-1827	Cassandra gct Chester MM
2-27-1828	Samuel & w Anna & ch Jacob, Abraham, Jonathan, Prudah (Priscilla), & Samuel gct New Garden MM
10-28-1829	Merrick & w Ann & min ch Sarah & Rachel gct New Garden MM
11-26-1845	Samuel & w Anna & ch Samuel & Anna rocf Chester MM; Andrew & Eunice rocf Chester MM
6-24-1846	Samuel & w Anna & min ch Samuel & Anna H gct Chester MM; Andrew H & Eunice A gct Chester MM
6-27-1849	Mississinewa MM given con to rst Joshua
1-28-1852	Samuel rocf Salem MM IA
2-23-1859	Mary (**Cook**) con mcd
7-25-1860	Samuel rocf New Garden MM
6-26-1861	Jonathan rocf New Garden MM
4-22-1863	Jonathan gct New Garden MM
11-22-1871	Martha & ch Franklin R, Isaac, & Susanna rocf Chester MM
2-25-1874	Joshua S & w Margaret E & ch Stephen, Alva, Clarinda J, Letitia, Anna Mary, & Merrick rocf Onargo MM IL
5-22-1878	Joshua S & w Margaret E & min ch Anna Mary & Merrick S gct New Garden MM
7-22-1880	Wm glt j Middleboro ME ch
4-27-1882	Susan J rem
12-28-1882	Martha & s Franklin R gct Mississinewa MM
2-23-1883	Susan rq mbrp Richmond PM
2-27-1885	Isaac rc
4-23-1885	Samuel & w Mary gct Portland MM
5-28-1885	Isaac J gct Mississinewa MM
3-23-1889	Joshua Smith & w Margaret E rocf New Garden MM
11-26-1896	Samuel rocf Portland MM; Adelaide S w Samuel rec in mbrp
2-23-1899	Samuel & w Adelaide S gct Chester MM

CRANSTON

7-24-1861	Alfred rocf Albans MM England
2-26-1885	Alfred drpd fr mbrp for na

CREW

7-29-1820	James rocf New Garden MM OH

CREW (cont)
11-28-1821	James Wayne Co s Littleberry & Huldah Columbiana Co OH m Jane dt Isaac dec & Jane **Pleas** Wayne Co at Whitewater MH
11-15-1823	Jane dis for fornication
2-14-1824	James dis for fornication
11-20-1824	Goshen MM OH given con to rst Jane
6-18-1825	Benjamin rocf Goshen MM OH
6-25-1828	Benjamin con mcd
8-25-1830	Benjamin dis for owing money

CRITCHLOW
4-26-1888	Cynthia J rec in mbrp

CROCKER
5-24-1871	Alvin E rec in mbrp
4-24-1872	Alvin E res mbrp

CUBBYHOUS
2-24-1836	Elizabeth (**Anderson**) dis for mcd & na

CULBERSON
9-26-1832	Mary (**Hoover**) dis for mcd

CULBERTSON
11-25-1840	Martha (**Hoover**) dis for mcd & j ME

CUSHING
7-27-1892	Caroline (**Vale**) rel fr mbrp

DAILY
3-23-1895	Matilda (**Black**) rocf Springfield MM OH

DALBY
8-25-1869	Hannah rec in mbrp
7-25-1877	Hannah rel fr mbrp
7-22-1893	Jennie U rocf Springfield MM

DALEY
8-24-1895	Ruth A drpd fr mbrp

DALLEY
8-25-1869	Hannah rec in mbrp

DARLING
3-23-1889	Almeda (**Deerifield**) rel fr mbrp

DAVENPORT
2-26-1820	Rebecca rec in mbrp
5-23-1866	Anna E rec in mbrp
3-25-1868	Caroline rec in mbrp
4-22-1868	Warner & s Wm Henry, Jesse Elwood, Richard Albert, & Alonzo rec in mbrp
2-24-1869	Wm rec in mbrp
3-24-1881	Jesse Elwood & w Sarah Elizabeth gct Walnut Center MM IA; Wm H & w Martha Elma & min ch Lula A & George P gct Walnut Center MM IA
7-28-1881	Rebecca appt Orange o
2-26-1885	Wm dis for na
2-23-1889	Mary & min ch Earl & Florence rec in mbrp
7-27-1889	Wm H & w Martha Elma & ch Lula S, George, John, Ezra, & Rachel S rocf Payton MM Green Co IA
12-23-1893	Wm & w Ella & min ch Lula, John, & Rachel Lurena gct Payton MM IA
11-26-1896	Jesse Elwood & w Elizabeth & ch Bertha R & Ernest rocf Payton MM IA

DAVIDSON
11-28-1812	Samuel rec in mbrp
7-25-1832	Isaiah rocf Marlborough MM OH
12-24-1834	Josiah gct Fairfield MM

DAVIS
11-30-1811	Adam rocf Center MM NC; Lydia & dt Ruth, Elizabeth, Mary, Phebe, & Jemima rocf Center MM NC
11-22-1826	Cert rec for Henry & s Nathan, Thomas Clarkson, & Cyrus fr New Garden MM NC; end to Silver Creek MM; Cert rec for Tristram & s John & Thomas fr New Garden MM NC; end to Silver Creek MM
5-23-1827	Cert rec for Joseph fr New Garden MM NC; end to Silver Creek MM
9-23-1829	Joseph rocf Somerset MM OH
2-24-1830	Joseph gct Milford MM
11-24-1830	John & fam rocf Springfield MM NC; end to New Garden MM
8-24-1831	Margaret & dt Martha, Margaret, Elizabeth, & Ruth rocf Core Sound MM NC; end to White River MM; Clarissa rocf Core Sound MM NC; end to White River MM
2-28-1838	White Lick MM rpt Mary (**Boswell**) mcd
4-24-1839	Jesse, Samuel, Joseph, & Lewis rocf Londongrove MM PA
10-11-1843	Jesse, Samuel, Joseph, & Lewis ch Samuel gct Mississinewa MM
4-23-1846	Wm Henry Co m Sarah **More** wid Wayne Co at Whitewater MH
8-26-1846	Wm & dt Nancy E rocf Springfield MM
5-24-1848	Sarah gct Milford MM
2-28-1849	Nancy gct Springfield MM
4-28-1858	Clarkson rocf Mississinewa MM
9-4-1862	Clarkson Wayne Co s Wyllys & Ann Grant Co m Hannah E dt Benjamin & Naomi **Brown** Wayne Co at Orange MH
8-23-1865	Clarkson & w Hannah E B gct Spiceland MM
10-27-1875	Amanda rec in mbrp
3-23-1882	Sarah R & ch Joseph Alfred & Wm Harlan to be rec in mbrp 12th St PM
10-26-1882	David H gc
10-22-1885	Wm E rocf Springfield MM
4-22-1886	Clarissa rq mbrp
5-27-1886	Clarissa lt fr Mechanicsburg ME ch ret
2-23-1889	Benjamin & w Lizzie G & min dt Ethel rec in mbrp
12-24-1892	David rocf Dover MM
2-25-1893	Margaret J & min ch Mary Elfleta, Robert James, & Annie Pearl rec in mbrp
2-24-1894	Thomas M rec in mbrp
6-22-1895	Jonah & w Ella J & ch Royal J, Ruby, & Ella J rocf South Wabash MM
5-23-1896	Hezekiah & Angelina New Westville OH rec in mbrp
3-25-1897	Margaret rec in mbrp
8-24-1899	David, Margaret, Mary, Robert, Pearl, Thomas M, & Anna L drpd fr mbrp

DAWSON
8-14-1824	James rocf Northwest Fork MM MD
10-24-1827	James S gct Milford MM

DAY
11-28-1891	Elbert H & w Mary Elizabeth rocf Richland MM
7-23-1896	Elbert H & w Mary Elizabeth gct Carmel MM

DEAN
7-22-1897	Frank rocf West Grove MM

DEERIFIELD
4-22-1886	Almeda rec in mbrp

DELON
2-25-1886	Aubrey D & w Sarah A & min ch Wm, Paul, & Horace J rocf Honey Creek MM
1-26-1889	Aubrey F & w Sarah & ch Wm, Paul, & Horace J gct Kokomo MM

WHITEWATER MONTHLY MEETING MINUTES AND MARRIAGES

DENNIS
9-27-1817	Benjamin rec in mbrp
5- 3-1820	Benjamin s John & Hannah OH m Clarky dt John & Elizabeth **Pool** Wayne Co at Whitewater MH
6-24-1820	Benjamin rocf West Grove MM
4-20-1822	Benjamin & fam gct West Grove MM
11-23-1853	Susannah rocf Scipio MM NY
1-28-1857	Charles C rocf Scipio MM NY
5-20-1858	Caroline (**Williams**) con mcd
7-28-1858	Charles C dis for mcd
9-24-1862	Sarah Ann & ch John & Mary rocf Hopewell MM
2-17-1869	Abbie S rec in mbrp
5-26-1869	John & w Mary & ch Thomas R, Ida May, Harrison S, & Albert rec in mbrp
10-27-1875	David W rocf Springfield MM OH
5-24-1876	David W gct Bloomingdale MM to m Mattie **Curl**
9-24-1879	David W gct Wilmington MM MO
7-28-1881	David W rocf Wilmington MM MO
3-26-1885	David W rocf Bloomingdale MM
11-22-1890	Martha Ann & min ch Jessie W, Willie F, & Albert Oron rocf Dover MM
3-25-1893	Caroline gct Minneapolis MM MN
3-24-1894	Mary gct Muncie MM
4-27-1899	Mary rocf Muncie MM

DENNISON
6-25-1873	Emma rec in mbrp

DENNY
2-28-1818	Cert rec for Lazarus & s Asariah, Wm, John, Shubal, Gordon, & Michael fr Westfield MM NC; end to Elk MM OH; Cert rec for Susanna & dt Sarah, Elizabeth, & Rebecca fr Westfield MM NC; end to Elk MM OH

DEVENPORT
11-26-1845	Rebecca (**Rue**) con mcd

DEWEES
5-28-1845	Hannah (**Hartley**) con mcd & jas
4-22-1846	Hannah F gct Elk MM OH

DICKENSON
9-18-1824	Solomon & s Charles S, Edmund, Isaac L, James P, Solomon Jr, & Elias Hicks rocf Philadelphia MM PA
5-25-1831	Charles dis for na & jas
8-30-1843	George s Jonathan dec & Alice Wayne Co m Sarah dt John & Elizabeth **Pool** Wayne Co at Whitewater MH
7-24-1850	Jane adopted dt Henry & Grace rec in mbrp
8-23-1883	Esther G appt elder

DICKINSON
9-18-1824	Hannah W rocf Philadelphia MM PA
9-24-1828	Solomon dis for jH
2-25-1829	Hannah W dis for jas
1-22-1840	Isaac L dis for mcd & dp
7-22-1840	Edmund dis for jH & na
10-26-1842	George rocf Balby MM England; Cert rec for Joseph fr Balby MM, England; end to Milford MM
11-24-1847	George & w Sarah & min ch Charles & Elizabeth gct Goshen MM
7-26-1848	Henry & w Grace rocf Balby MM England
1-27-1851	Joseph & w Esther G & ch Oliver White, Hannah, & Samuel rocf Milford MM
9-24-1851	Robert B dis for na & mcd; Elizabeth (**Kenworthy**) dis for mcd
4-28-1852	Charles & w Hannah F & ch Henry W & Benajah rocf Milford MM; James Hunt & Jonathan rocf Milford MM
7-28-1852	Alice rocf Milford MM

DICKINSON (cont)
11-24-1852	Jonathan gct New York MM; Henry & w Grace & adopted dt Jane gct New York MM
1-26-1853	George & w Sarah & ch Elizabeth, Charles, Alice Hunt, & Susan P rocf Goshen MM OH
10-26-1853	John rocf Cincinnati MM OH
5-24-1854	George & w Sarah & ch Elisabeth, Charles, Alice Hunt & Susan P gct Chester MM
6-27-1855	George & w Sarah & ch Elizabeth, Charles, Alice, & Susan rocf Chester MM
6-25-1856	James Hunt gct New York MM NY
8-26-1857	James Hunt rocf New York MM NY
5-20-1858	Hannah F appt o of KS PM
7-27-1858	Charles, Hannah, George, & Sarah set off with KS MM KS
10- 7-1863	James Hunt s Jonathan dec & Alice Wayne Co m Mary Jane dt Joseph **Winder** Wayne Co at Whitewater MH
3-25-1874	Benajah H rocf Spiceland MM
2-28-1877	Laura F rec in mbrp
7-25-1877	John rel fr mbrp; Benajah gct Spiceland MM
8-28-1879	Joseph John s Joseph & Esther G Wayne Co m Martha Elma dt Howard & Martha **Cadwallader** at res of Howard **Cadwallader** Richmond
5-28-1885	Phenia rec in mbrp
5-24-1891	Mem for Esther G prep
4-27-1899	Wm Hurtley rel fr mbrp

DICKS
8-29-1812	Nathan s Zacharius rocf Center MM NC; Mary & dt Ruth, Rachel, Mary, Lydia, & Rebeckah rocf Center MM NC
11-28-1812	Peter & ch Zachariah, Wm, Jonathan, Ezekiel, & Elizabeth Peter rocf Center MM NC
1-29-1814	Elizabeth & dt Jemima, Mary, Betty, & Rachel **Vestal** & Lydia rocf Center MM OH
5-27-1815	Jemima (**Vestal**) con mcd
3-26-1845	Nathan dis for na, mcd, & dp
1-28-1846	Mary dis for na & jas

DILHORN
11-27-1819	Sarah & dt Ann E, Mary J, & Elenor rec in mbrp
1-29-1820	Robert W, James G, & George s Robert rec in mbrp
4-29-1820	Robert M rocf Redstone MM PA
8-23-1826	Robert con his taking property not his own in a clandestine manner & for making contradictory statements
11-27-1833	Wilson dis for jH
7-25-1838	Mary Jane dis
7-24-1839	Robert & w Sarah & ch Joshua, Wm, & Anna Maria gct Spiceland MM
6-24-1857	James dis

DILKS
8-26-1863	Hannah H & ch Rachel J, Wm W, Sidney, Hannah H Jr, Sarah S, Elizabeth, & George Russel rocf Frankford MM PA
12-l0-1863	Wm W Preble Co OH s George dec & Hannah H Philadelphia PA m Anna B dt Charles & Mary S dec **Shoemaker** at Richmond MH
7-25-1877	Phebe drpd fr mbrp
11-27-1884	George R gct Indianapolis MM
8-25-1887	George R rocf Indianapolis MM
6-23-1894	Grace R, George H, Harrie T, & Annie G ch George R & Alice J rec in mbrp

DILL
8-22-1891	Laura rel fr mbrp

DILTS
6-18-1872	Phebe (**Lane**) con mcd

DIMMET
3-30-1816	Alice rocf Lost Creek MM TN

DINGLEY
5-26-1869	Henry J rec in mbrp
7-28-1869	Lydia Sarah & ch Elizabeth A, Stephen G, Wm Henry, & Edward Charles rec in mbrp
8-22-1891	Stephen George, Edwin Charles, & Wm Henry drpd fr mbrp

DINGMAN
3-23-1895	Otto rec in mbrp

DIX
6-24-1815	Zachariah con mcd
3-18-1826	Jonathan dis for mcd
4-15-1826	Ezekiel dis for mcd
7-22-1829	Peter & Zachariah dis for na & jH
11-24-1830	Elizabeth & Jemima dis for jas
3-26-1834	John dis for na & mcd
10-28-1840	Elk MM rst Jonathan

DIXON
2-28-1844	Sarah & dt Hannah rocf Springfield MM
10-27-1847	Hannah dis for na & dp
11-28-1877	Calvin & w May & ch Keziah, Janetta S, Rosa Jane, Lutitia Ann, & Elmer P rocf Walnut Ridge MM
7-23-1879	Calvin & w Mary & ch Kezia, Jeannetta S, Rosa Jane, Letitia Ann, & Elmer P gct Walnut Ridge MM

DOAN
7-31-1813	Elizabeth & dt Sarah & Rachel rocf Cane Creek MM NC; Ebenezar & s Wm, Jonathan, & Nathan rocf Cane Creek MM NC
11-26-1824	Cert rec for Ephraim fr Cane Creek MM NC; end to White Lick MM
11-27-1850	Ann Elizabeth (**Downing**) dis for na & mcd
5-27-1868	Joseph & w Deborah & ch Harrison J & Clifford T rocf Center MM OH
7-28-1869	Isaac & w Matilda & dt Mary Kate rec in mbrp
2-23-1870	Fanny E dt Nathan rec in mbrp
11-23-1870	Eliza & dt Mary & Elizabeth rocf Center MM
3-28-1877	Walter J & Alice J rec in mbrp
1-27-1894	Walter J rel fr mbrp
7-22-1897	Joseph's d rpt

DODGE
8-22-1838	Sarah (Lewis) dis for mcd

DOREN
2-23-1889	Louella M rec in mbrp
3-23-1895	Lida & Otto rec in mbrp

DORLAND
7-27-1870	Martha N rocf Salem MM IA
5-22-1872	Martha N gct Salem MM IA

DORSEY
6-27-1891	Sylvester & w Emma & ch Albert & Kizia rec in mbrp; lt fr Fountain City ME ch
7-25-1891	James R & w Josephine rec in mbrp
7-22-1893	Sylvester & w Emma rel fr mbrp to j 5th St ME ch; Emma, Albert, & Kezia ch Sylvester & Emma drpd fr mbrp
2-24-1894	James R & w Josephine gct West Grove MM
8-27-1896	James & Josephine rocf West Grove MM
1-28-1897	Josephine rocf West Grove MM

DOUGHERTY
5-26-1852	Martha Ann rec in mbrp
9-23-1893	Charles rocf West Grove MM; Francis L & w Alice S & min s Raymond rocf West Grove MM

DOUGHERTY (cont)
4-27-1895	Charles gct j evangelical denomination
5-27-1897	John, Anna M, Elmer, & Pearl Providence & Friendship Darke Co OH rec in mbrp
3-24-1898	Alva & w Lizzie rec in mbrp
1-26-1889	Francis drpd fr mbrp for na

DOUGLAS
5-26-1847	Cornelius & w Phebe N & dt Mary rocf Springfield MM OH
1-26-1848	Cornelius & w Phebe & dt Mary gct Springfield MM OH

DOVE
4-28-1847	Isaac rec in mbrp

DOWNING
6-26-1838	Margaret, Eleanor, Jane, Ann Elizabeth, Sarah, & Susan rocf Gwinned MM PA
6-26-1844	Margaret L dis for na & jH
4-26-1848	Sarah dis for na, dp, & jH
6-28-1854	Mary E (**Hunnicutt**) dis for na & mcd

DOYLE
4-24-1850	Mary W rocf Salem MM

DRAKE
10-24-1878	Edgar J Wayne Co s Carlton N & Julia A dec Genessee Co NY m Olivia S dt Stephen & Rachel A **Mendenhall** at res of S C **Mendenhall** Richmond
3-26-1885	Olivia S gct Rose Hill MM KS

DRAPER
7-31-1813	Thomas & s Wm rocf Suttons Creek MM; Mary & dt Achsa, Jemima, & Hannah rocf Suttons Creek MM NC; Peter & Elizabeth rocf Suttons Creek MM NC
9-26-1818	Josiah & s Josiah, John, & Joshua rocf Fall Creek MM OH; Jemima & dt Mary Ann & Rebekah rocf Fall Creek MM OH
5-29-1819	Josiah Jr con for dr & upl
4-9-1822	Josiah Jr gct West Grove MM
5-18-1822	Josiah & fam gct West Grove MM
11-16-1822	John dis for mcd
1-17-1824	Mary rocf Driftwood MM
7-16-1825	Mary gct Milford MM
8-25-1830	Aaron & Oswin wards of John **Powel** rocf Western Branch MM Isle of Wight Co VA
5-25-1831	Aaron & sister Sally min wards John & Mary **Powell** gct Chester MM
6-26-1833	Cert rec for Elizabeth fr Marlborough MM; end to Duck Creek MM
6-22-1895	Susan Bernice N gct Amboy MM
9-23-1897	Sylvester W & w Berneice & ch Homer G, Charles E, & Don H rocf Amboy MM

DRAYER
5-22-1884	Sarah rec in mbrp
1-24-1891	Sarah gct West Grove MM
12-26-1891	Sarah not found

DREW
5-27-1868	Daniel Helena AR rec in mbrp

DRULY
10-27-1830	Rachel (**Bonine**) dis for att mcd, na, & dp

DRURY
8-26-1815	Rachel rec in mbrp
10-28-1815	Wm rec in mbrp

DUGAN
7-26-1869	Rosanna (**Lamb**) dis for mcd

WHITEWATER MONTHLY MEETING
MINUTES AND MARRIAGES

DUGDALE
6-27-1838	James K rocf Chesterfield MM NJ; Hannah & s Samuel rocf Chesterfield MM NJ; Sarah rocf Chesterfield MM NJ
8-23-1843	Eleanor (**Downing**) dis for na & mcd
11-22-1843	James K dis for na & mcd
4-28-1847	Samuel dis for na
10-24-1849	Susannah (**Downing**) dis for na & mcd
7-24-1867	Elizabeth rec in mbrp
11-24-1869	Horace rec in mbrp
12-22-1869	Edward & Ida ch Elizabeth rec in mbrp; Hannah Maria & Margaret Annesly rec in mbrp
2-26-1880	Elizabeth W & ch Elwood W, Harriett Ida, & Rachel Scott gct New York MM; ret by her rq
9-23-1886	Elizabeth W & dt Rachel S gct St Augustine FL ME ch
12-26-1891	Harriet Ida, Hanna Maria, & Margaret Ainsley not found
9-24-1892	Edward W gct New York MM NY
1-28-1893	Cert for Edward W ret by New York MM with rq for letter to Presb ch; drpd fr mbrp

DUKE
9-23-1893	James & w Ruth rocf Chester MM; Ora rocf Chester MM

DWIGGINS
3-24-1881	Moses F rocf Dover MM OH
6-28-1888	James F gct Cincinnati MM OH

DWIGINS
8-29-1812	Mary rocf New Garden MM NC

DYMOND
10-27-1869	Charles Helena AR rec in mbrp

DYSON
11-24-1869	Mason & Wm rec in mbrp
3-22-1871	Eleanor & dt Agnes Ann rocf Kendal MM England
6-26-1872	Mason & w Eleanor & ch Agnes Ann & Sarah Wilhelmina gct Salem MM OH
12-25-1872	Wm gct Salem MM OH
9-22-1881	Mason rocf Brighouse MM England

EARL
2-26-1834	Mary (**Hawkins**) dis for mcd & jas

EAST
4-27-1816	Wm & Rachel rocf Newberry MM TN
9-28-1816	John, Joel, James & Jacob s Wm rec in mbrp
6-24-1824	James s of Wm & Rachel Wayne Co, m Anne dt Jesse & Hannah **Jones** Wayne Co at Orange MH
1-14-1826	Joel con mcd
11-26-1828	Edom & James s Joel rec in mbrp
3-25-1829	Sarah rec in mbrp
10-22-1834	Wm & w Rachel & ch Wm, Rebecca, Martha, & Isom gct Mississinewa MM; James & w Anna & ch James Milton, John, Jesse, & Martha Jane gct Mississinewa MM; Joel & w Sarah & ch Edom, James, Susanna, Martha Ann, & Thomas gct Mississinewa MM; Polly, Susannah, & Sally gct Mississiniwa MM; Ann (**Lee**) con mcd
7-22-1835	John & Jacob T dis for mcd
10-26-1836	Ann gct Mississinewa MM

EDGERTON
4-19-1823	Eleanor rocf Darby Creek MM OH
8-16-1823	Owen rec in mbrp
10-16-1823	Joseph s Daniel rocf Goshen MM OH
5-15-1824	Joseph Jr rocf Darby Creek MM OH
9-17-1824	Martha & dt Martha rocf Goshen MM OH
11-20-1824	Wm & s Eli & Owen rocf OH; Nelly rocf Somerset MM OH

EDGERTON (cont)
11-24-1824	Joseph s Joseph & Martha Wayne Co m Anne dt Daniel & Nellie dec **Frazier** Belmont Co OH at Whitewater MH
8-23-1826	Thomas & s Wm & Samuel rocf Goshen MM OH; Mary & dt Elenora & Mary Ann rocf Goshen MM OH
9-27-1826	Samuel dis for mcd
11-28-1827	Joseph dis for mcd
1-23-1828	Wm dis for att shooting match, staking money, & shooting for a prize
2-27-1828	Daniel dis for mcd
2-25-1829	Nelly & h & ch Owen, Ruthanna, Eliza Ann, & Wm P gct Milford MM; Eli, Owen, & Wm P min gct Milford MM
1-27-1830	Thomas & w Mary & ch Wm Osborn, Elnora, Maryann, & Samuel gct Milford MM
7-28-1830	Daniel rst
8-24-1831	Daniel & w & 2 ch rec in mbrp; Mary dt Daniel rec in mbrp
4-22-1835	Wm minister gct Mississinewa MM
11-23-1836	Wm & w Abigail & s Thomas rocf Elk MM
8-22-1840	Elizabeth & s Joseph rocf Salem MM
1-27-1841	Joseph & w Martha gct Duck Creek MM; Rachel & min ch Calvin, Mary, Margaret, & Daniel gct Milford MM
4-23-1845	West Grove MM gr perm to receive Samuel
11-26-1851	Joseph rst; dis 20y previous
7-28-1852	Wm T, Elizabeth Ann, Samuel, Sarah, Jane, & Susan ch Thomas & Mary rocf Milford MM
12-28-1853	Mary Jane rec in mbrp
5-23-1855	Wm Jr & Ellen (**Cockayne**) dis for mcd
6-27-1855	Joseph gct New Garden MM
8-22-1855	Thomas & w Mary & ch Charles F & Mary C rst; dis by Milford MM
12-26-1859	Abigail & ch Susan M, Eliza Ann, & Emma C gct Milford MM
6-24-1874	Ellen & ch Wm, Susan, & Mary Elizabeth rec in mbrp
3-24-1875	Alice J rec in mbrp
5-25-1882	Ellen & min ch Wm H, Susan L, Mary T, Elizabeth C, & Charles gct Payton MM IA

EDMUNDSON
10-24-1849	Susan (**Wright**) dis for mcd

EDWARDS
9-26-1832	John Jr & w rocf Hopewell MM NC
10-24-1832	Delilah & Beaulah rocf Hopewell MM NC
1-23-1833	John & w Beulah & s Asa gct White Lick MM; Delilah gct White Lick MM
2-28-1838	Elizabeth H rocf Philadelphia MM PA
12-23-1840	Cert rec for Ira fr Hopewell MM NC
5-26-1845	Elizabeth ch of Rebeca Mason gct Mississinewa MM
4-26-1888	Elizabeth J rec in mbrp
12-27-1890	Josiah P rocf Spiceland MM
8-24-1895	Charity rec in mbrp
4-27-1899	Josiah P gct Spiceland MM
7-27-1899	Charity rel fr mbrp

EIDSON
3-24-1875	James rec in mbrp

ELDER
2-24-1869	James & Susannah rocf Marsden MM England
11-24-1869	James & w Susannah gct Chester MM PA

ELIASON
8-24-1899	Emma rec in mbrp

ELLIOTT
6-30-1810	Ruth rocf Lost Creek MM TN
6-27-1812	Jacob dis for joining in military operations

ELLIOTT (cont)

11-25-1815	John rocf Deep Creek MM NC; Axion & s Elwood, Isaac, Axiom, Nathan, & Mark rocf Deep Creek MM NC; Catharine & dt Rebekah, Ursula, & Sarah rocf Deep Creek MM NC
12-30-1815	Jacob & s Jonathan & Absolam rocf Deep Creek MM NC; Mary & dt Gulamy rocf Deep Creek MM NC
8-31-1816	Benjamin & s Abraham rocf Piney Woods MM NC; Sarah & dt Deidea & Elvey rocf Piney Woods MM NC
10-19-1822	Job & s Benjamin rec in mbrp; Mary w Job & dt Mary, Elizabeth, & Sarah rec in mbrp
11-20-1824	Ann & h & ch Olive, Alice, Wellmet, Susannah, Elvira, Melinda, Anna, & Isaiah gct Milford MM
6-27-1866	Elias & w Jane & s John B rocf Raysville MM; Mary Jane rocf Raysville MM
7-28-1869	Stephen & w Anna rec in mbrp
8-25-1869	Henry C & w Kizzie rec in mbrp
9-22-1869	Wm P rec in mbrp
1-25-1871	Henry E & w Kizzie M res mbrp; res Topeka KS
5-24-1871	Avis Jane (Irish) dis for m during life-time of former husband
2-28-1872	Delphina Mendenhall & Hetta Ann ch David & Hannah both dec rocf Back Creek MM
8-26-1873	Wm P dis for failing to comply with engagements & na
11-26-1873	Elias & w Jane & min s John B & grch Delphina M & Hettia A gct Milford MM
8-26-1874	Wm P dis for na; Mary Jane gct Milford MM
10-27-1881	Hettie A rocf Milford MM
2-28-1891	Esther S rec in mbrp; lt fr Church of Evangel Assoc
5-23-1896	Esther S rel fr mbrp
2-25-1897	Joseph rec in mbrp
9-23-1898	John B & w Martha M & ch Maud M, J Harry, & E Warren rocf Spiceland MM

ELLIS

11-28-1855	Susan rocf Back Creek MM
5-27-1897	George A Providence & Friendship Darke Co OH rec in mbrp
9-22-1898	Elwood O & w Ida H & ch Arthur W, Dora M & Cressie rocf Fairmount MM

ELLISON

1-23-1878	Nannie (Kirkman) gct New Garden MM

ELLMORE

11-26-1862	Wm Allen & Adeline ch Benjamin & Elizabeth rocf Salem MM
8-24-1864	Wm Allen dis for mcd

ELMORE

7-23-1862	Benjamin & w Elizabeth & ch Mary Almedia & Elihu Arlington rst with perm Salem MM
8-24-1864	Keziah (Gifford) rpt mcd; drpd fr mbrp
1-27-1881	Wm A & w Keziah & min ch Minnie J, Edgar G, Elvin C, Charles B, Sarah E, & Anna P gct Walnut Center MM IA

ELWOOD

7-23-1896	Mary K rocf West Grove MM

EMERSON

5-27-1897	Edith Providence & Friendship Darke Co OH rec in mbrp

ENDSLEY

10-26-1870	Sarah S rec in mbrp
3-26-1892	Sarah Centreville gct West Grove MM

ENGLE

6-18-1825	Phebe rocf Flushing MM OH

ENGLE (cont)

9-27-1826	Rebecca (Whitacre) con mcd
10-25-1826	Rebecca (Whitacre) gct Elk MM OH

EPPERLY

11-28-1838	Lydia (Dix) dis for na & mcd

ERNEST

2-22-1890	Pearl L rec in mbrp
10-25-1890	Ellen rocf Maple Grove MM IL

ERWIN

9-22-1830	John Jr, George, Samuel Edwin, & Wm Platt ch John & Elizabeth rocf Wilmington MM DE
1-26-1831	George & John dis for jas
1-22-1834	Susanna dis for jH
7-24-1844	Samuel dis for na, jH, & mcd
3-22-1848	Edwin dis for na & mcd

ESTELL

2-28-1891	Richard & w Fanny & min ch Clarabel & Ruth rec in mbrp

ESTES

7-28-1847	Lewis A rocf Durham MM ME
2-24-1848	Lewis A s Thomas & Betsey Cumberland Co ME m Huldah C dt Nathan & Abigail Hoag Chittendon Co UT at meeting of Friends Boarding School near Richmond
2-27-1861	Lewis A & w Huldah C & ch Ludovic & Thomas Rowland gct Honey Creek MM

EVAN

6-26-1833	Elizabeth rocf Baltimore MM MD

EVANS

1-29-1814	John & s Daniel & John rocf Deep River MM NC; Sarah & dt Milly, Rachel, & Achsah, rocf Deep River MM NC
1-25-1817	John dis for not complying with contracts; Sarah dis for dr
2-22-1817	John's ch gct Lick Creek MM; Sarah's ch gct Lick Creek MM
2-24-1821	Jesse & s Resden & Ryan rocf Miami MM OH; Esther & dt Jurettee rocf Miami MM OH
3-18-1826	Owen rocf Miami MM OH
7-28-1830	Mourning rocf Suttons Creek MM NC
8-24-1831	Mourning dis for na & jas
6-26-1833	John rocf Baltimore MM MD
1-27-1841	John dis for na & mcd
7-28-1841	Risdon dis for na, dr, upl, & dp
3-23-1842	Wm Ryan dis for na
10-28-1846	Elizabeth W (Moore) dis for na & mcd
4-26-1848	John rocf Salem MM
11-27-1850	Hannah rocf Miami MM OH
4-28-1852	John gct Springfield MM to m Nancy E Davis
12-28-1853	Isaac P rocf Miami MM OH
1-25-1854	John gct Wabash MM
5-2-1855	Isaac P s Thomas & Hannah dec Wayne Co m Mary Ann dt Timothy & Ann A dec Buffum Wayne Co at Whitewater MH
8-23-1883	Mary Ann appt elder; Isaac d 2-20-1883

EVINS

5-30-1812	Lydia rocf Back Creek MM NC

FARLOW

10-26-1811	Joseph & s Jonathan & Nathan rocf Cane Creek MM NC; Ruth & dt Deborah rocf Cane Creek MM NC
10-31-1812	George & s John, Simon, & Hiram rocf Center MM NC; Ann & dt Alice rocf Center MM NC
5-28-1873	Rachel rocf Lick Creek MM

WHITEWATER MONTHLY MEETING
MINUTES AND MARRIAGES

FARQUAR
11-27-1872   Francis & w Hannah & ch Milton J, Harriet A, & Henry B gct Wilmington MM OH

FARQUHAR
5-26-1869   Francis & w Hannah Ann & ch Milton J, Harriett A, & Henry B rocf Wilmington MM OH

FAULKNER
5-23-1896   Daniel C & Abigail M New Westville OH rec in mbrp

FEASAL
6-26-1878   Vesta Ann & dt Ada rel fr mbrp

FEASEL
3-25-1868   Annie S rec in mbrp
3-24-1874   Jacob & w Vesta Ann rec in mbrp
1-27-1881   Josiah rec in mbrp

FELLOW
3-28-1832   Cert rec for Price fr Contentnea MM NC; end to Arba MM; Cert rec for Robert, John, Mary, Rachel, & Sally fr Contentnea MM NC; end to New Garden MM; Cert rec for Abigail & dt fr Contentnea MM NC; end to New Garden MM

FENIMORE
4-26-1888   Emma Cora gct Fairmount MM

FIELDS
3-28-1891   Rebecca P rec in mbrp

FINNEY
4-26-1871   Elizabeth rocf West Branch MM
6-28-1876   Elizabeth & dt Margaret gct New Garden MM

FISHER
2-28-1818   John & s Robert, Joseph, & Thomas rocf Middleton MM OH; Rachel & dt Elizabeth & Marietta rocf Middleton MM OH
8-14-1824   John & w Rachel & ch Joseph, Elizabeth, Thomas, Maryetta, & John gct Springfield MM; Robert gct Springfield MM
5-23-1833   Isaac Warren Co OH s Joseph & Hannah dec Columbiana Co OH m Eunice dt Aaron & Mary **Street** Wayne Co at Whitewater MH
9-25-1833   Eunice gct Miami MM OH
12-27-1848   George W rec in mbrp
7-25-1849   George W gct White River MM
11-26-1851   George W & w Ruth & dt Mahala P rocf White River MM
11-25-1863   Mary Ann rec in mbrp
8-23-1865   Mary Ann gct Le Grand MM IA
9-20-1876   Mary rel fr mbrp
12-27-1883   Ruth gct Portland MM Jay Co
8-27-1892   Hattie A **(Hockett)** rq lt

FLETCHER
12-23-1840   Samuel Francis & w Elizabeth D rocf Milford MM
5-27-1868   Albert W gct Milford MM
12-23-1874   Albert W & w Elizabeth P & ch Wilfred P rocf Milford MM
5-27-1878   Albert W gct Milford MM
6-5-1878   Francis Nixon s Samuel F & Elizabeth D Wayne Co m Martha Elizabeth dt Isaac C & Joanna **Teague** Wayne Co at Richmond
3-23-1882   Mordecai H gct Cincinnati MM OH
4-2-1884   Mordecai Hiatt Hamilton Co OH s Samuel F & Elizabeth D Wayne Co m Anna Elizabeth dt Benjamin & Elizabeth E R **Perry** Wayne Co at Richmond MH

FLETCHER (cont)
9-23-1886   Edward Bradley New York NY s Samuel Francis & Elizabeth D Richmond Wayne Co m Sarah **Moffitt** dt Wm dec & Mary **Baxter** Richmond Wayne Co at res of Wm **Baxter** Richmond
7-22-1897   Wm H's d rpt; ae 46y

FLICK
12-24-1828   Miriam gct Milford MM

FLIK
11-25-1820   Miriom (**Small**) con mcd

FOGG
12-24-1828   Cert rec for Samuel & fam fr Philadelphia MM PA; end to Cincinnati MM OH

FOLKE
10-25-1826   Judah & s Samuel & Thomas rocf Cincinnati MM OH

FOULK
10-25-1826   Sarah & dt Margaret, Lydia, Sarah, & Mary rocf Cincinnati MM OH

FOULKE
11-25-1829   Judah dis for jH
3-24-1830   Sarah dis for jH
12-23-1835   Samuel dis for na
10-24-1838   Sarah (**Gordon**) dis for na & mcd
1-26-1848   Thomas dis for na & jH

FOUTS
7-24-1810   Jacob Jr dis for training with militia
9-25-1813   Elizabeth rocf Back Creek MM NC
11-19-1825   Jacob & w Eleanor gct Milford MM

FOWLER
12-23-1880   Eliza J rocf Duck Creek MM
3-24-1881   Wm E rec in mbrp
2-26-1885   W E gc
6-25-1885   Wm E C & w Lidie drpd fr mbrp

FRABERT
1-28-1874   Ada rec in mbrp
2-26-1885   Ada drpd fr mbrp for na
12-26-1891   Ada not found

FRAME
4-27-1870   Nathan T & w Esther Ellen & ch Itasca M & Hettie C rocf Dover MM
1-27-1875   Nathan T & w Esther E & ch Itaska M & Hettie C gct Caesar's Creek MM OH

FRANCISCO
7-26-1869   Charles A rec in mbrp
11-24-1870   Charles A s Louis J & Abigail Wayne Co m Hannah dt Joseph & Esther **Dickinson** Wayne Co at res of her par
12-28-1882   Charles A rec as minister
8-23-1883   Hannah M appt elder

FRASURE
11-26-1828   Daniel rocf Somerset MM OH

FRAZIER
10-31-1818   Cert rec for Wm Jr fr Lost Creek MM TN; end to West Grove MM
11-20-1824   Anna rocf Somerset MM OH
9-21-1825   Daniel Wayne Co s Daniel & Elenor dec Belmont Co OH m Martha dt Joseph & Martha **Edgerton** Wayne Co at Whitewater MH
2-25-1829   Daniel & w Martha & ch Sarah Ann & Anna gct Milford MM

FRAZIER (cont)
7-28-1830 Mary Ann dis for jas
1-26-1889 Solomon B rocf Barclay MM KS

FREEMAN
9-23-1893 Daniel rocf Salem MM

FRENCH
4-28-1869 Elizabeth, Anna M, & Levi rocf Chester MM
5-28-1873 Elizabeth F gct Miami MM OH

FRIESDORF
1-24-1884 Christiana A rec in mbrp
12-26-1891 Christiana rq mbrp East Main St PM

FROGGATT
10-27-1894 Sarah M (**Bond**) rel fr mbrp

FROST
11-29-1817 Edward L rocf Westbury MM NY
12-25-1819 Philemon H rocf Westbury MM NY
1-31-1820 Edward L Wayne Co s Caleb & Sarah NY m Ann H dt Samuel & Jane dec **Shute** Wayne Co at Whitewater MH
8-1-1827 Edward L Wayne Co s Caleb & Sarah Queens LI NY m Hannah dt David & Hannah **Holloway** Wayne Co at Whitewater MH
4-22-1829 Edward L & Hannah dis for jas
12-27-1854 Lydia rocf Elk MM
5-28-1856 Lydia gct Western Plains MM IA

FRY
12-22-1869 Amos & Keziah rocf Spring Creek MM IA; Oliver H/A rec in mbrp
7-24-1884 Calvin rocf Oskaloosa MM IA
5-28-1885 Wm & w rec in mbrp

FULGHUM
12-27-1826 Benjamin rocf New Garden MM
3-12-1828 Benjamin s Anthony & Mary dec Wayne Co m Rhoda dt Nathan & Martha dec **Ballard** Wayne Co at Whitewater MH
3-24-1830 Mildred gct New Garden MM
9-28-1831 Piety gct Arba MM
1-2-1833 Joseph s Jesse & Phebe Wayne Co m Rebecca T dt Wm & Ruth **Jessop** at Whitewater MH
4-24-1833 Rebecca T gct Arba MM
4-25-1838 Mary rocf New Garden MM
1-26-1853 Jesse rocf New Garden MM
10-22-1856 Jesse dis for mcd
8-28-1861 Wm A gct Raysville MM to m Harriet **White**
1-22-1862 Harriet W rocf Raysville MM
11-23-1864 Wm A & w Harriet & s Roscoe gct Raysville MM
3-22-1865 Eliza B rel fr mbrp
3-27-1867 Wm A & w Harriet & ch Roscoe W & Benjamin rocf Raysville MM
8-26-1868 Benjamin gct Bloomington MM to m Louisa M **Thompson**
2-22-1869 Benjamin gct Milford MM
11-25-1874 Wm A & w Harriet & ch Roscoe W, Benjamin W, Edgar W, Caroline, & Elma gct Orange MM IL
4-28-1881 Harriett E rocf Dover MM
12-28-1882 Frederick C & w Rebecca C & ch Oscar E, Franconia L, Lucy & Walter B rocf New Garden MM
5-24-1890 Zeri rocf New Garden MM

FULGUM
12-27-1826 Piety & Milfred rocf New Garden MM
12-28-1882 Frederick C & w Rebecca C & ch Oscar E, Franconia L, Lucy, & Walter B rocf New Garden MM
12-24-1885 Richmond PM rpts Mary J rq mbrp
2-25-1886 Mary not rec in mbrp
3-25-1886 Mary J lt fr Grace ME ch ret

GAAR
12-24-1873 Mary J & s Jonas & Charles rec in mbrp

GAIL
5-26-1821 Peninah (**Small**) con mcd

GALE
6-23-1830 Peninah dis for na & dp

GALYAN
1-28-1815 Tabitha (**Warren**) dis for mcd

GAMMON
11-28-1891 Robert rec in mbrp
6-25-1892 Mary E rocf Vandalia MM IA
7-23-1892 Robert W rec as minister
8-27-1896 Robert W & w Mary E gct Chicago MM IL
11-26-1896 Cert for Robert W & w Mary E ret by Chicago MM IL; glt jas

GANO
10-22-1892 Nixon H Louisville KY rec in mbrp
11-25-1893 Nixon H & w Elisabeth E & s Paul Jeffries gct Raysville MM

GANT
5-25-1870 Edward & w Dorcas Angeline & ch Andrew Alfred, Edward Ira, Martha Jane, Perry, & Frances Amelia Helena AR rec in mbrp; gr through IN Missionary Board

GARDE
4-29-1882 Alice rec in mbrp
1-24-1884 Alice E rq for mbrp drpd

GARDENER
6-26-1844 Elizabeth (**Brewer**) dis for mcd

GARDINER
8-27-1814 Sarah & dt Elisabeth rocf Elk MM OH

GARDNER
8-27-1814 Eliab & Wm rocf Elk MM OH
4-6-1815 Wm s Eliab & Sarah Franklin Co m Mary dt James & Sarah **Hollingsworth** Franklin Co at Silver Creek MH
12-30-1815 Isaac rocf New Garden MM NC; Dinah & dt Phebe & Maria rocf New Garden MM NC
11-24-1821 Jesse rocf Deep River MM
12-29-1821 Rhoda & dt Eliza, Dinah, & Susana rocf Deep River MM NC; Judith rocf Deep River MM NC
1-26-1889 Alonzo rocf New Garden MM
3-23-1889 Belle rec in mbrp

GARMAN
3-28-1866 Samuel Normal IL rec in mbrp

GARRET
10-31-1812 Wm min rocf Springfield MM NC
5-20-1826 Wm gct Stillwater MM OH
1-25-1832 Anna & dt Mary Ann rocf Springfield MM NC

GARRETT
8-22-1827 Wm rocf Stillwater MM OH
1-25-1832 Madison s Wm rocf Springfield MM NC
6-25-1834 Wm & w Anne & min ch Mary Ann, Madison, Daniel N, & John M gct Milford MM

GARVER
7-23-1896 Walter B rec in mbrp

WHITEWATER MONTHLY MEETING
MINUTES AND MARRIAGES

GARWOOD
12-27-1893 Ralph Stillman s Spencer & Vashbut D Ann Arbor MI m Juanita dt Guillermo dec & Maria Escoborde **de Garza** Matamoras Tamaultipas Co Mexico at res of Eli & Mahalah **Jay** Richmond

GARZA
10-28-1893 Juanita rocf Matamoras MM Mexico

GATES
5-28-1885 Daniel & Charles rec in mbrp
8-24-1899 Daniel drpd fr mbrp

GAYNOR
6-24-1893 Margaret rq lt to Grace ME ch

GIBBONS
1-26-1831 Josiah rocf New Garden MM NC
9-26-1832 Sophia gct Duck Creek MM
4-22-1863 Lydia Ann rocf Elk MM OH

GIBSON
8-20-1825 Hannah rocf Sadsbury MM PA

GIFFORD
4-27-1831 Jesse gct Elk MM OH
6-22-1853 Andrew & w Sarah E & ch Daniel, Elizabeth, Jesse, & Keziah rocf Elk MM OH
6-24-1863 Edith H rocf Elk MM OH
3-22-1865 Edith H gct Elk MM OH
9-23-1886 Benjamin B rq mbrp
10-28-1886 Benjamin rq for mbrp withdrawn; intends to remove

GILBERT
10-31-1812 Josiah & s Josiah rocf Springfield MM NC; Dorothy & dt Miriam, Elizabeth, Mary, Dorothy, & Lydia rocf Springfield MM NC
10-28-1815 Thomas rocf Springfield MM NC; Sarah & dt Phebe, Miriam, & Hannah rocf Springfield MM NC
11-20-1824 Thomas & w Sarah & ch Phebe, Miriam, Hannah, Mary, Jeremiah, & Gulielma gct Milford MM
12-18-1824 Jeremiah rocf Springfield MM NC
11-23-1831 Josiah Jr gct Milford MM
8-22-1832 Josiah & w Dorothy & ch Elizabeth, Achsah, Moses, & Thomas gct Milford MM
9-2-1841 Joel Jr s Joel & Lydia Henry Co m Hannah dt Thomas & Elizabeth **Kendall** Wayne Co at Smyrna Mtg
12-22-1841 Hannah gct Hopewell MM
1-28-1857 Isaiah B prc fr Hopewell MM to m Ann **Dougherty**
2-4-1857 Isaiah B s Josiah dec & Abigail Henry Co m Martha Ann dt Thomas & Nancy both dec **Dougherty** Warren Co OH at Whitewater MH
4-22-1857 Martha Ann gct Hopewell MM
12-25-1867 Josiah B gct Hopewell MM
9-22-1869 Elizabeth C (**Sharon**) con mcd
3-22-1888 Josiah B dis for na & poor bus practices; Elizabeth C & s Harry W & Warner M rel fr mbrp
4-28-1894 Laura rel fr mbrp

GILLIAM
12-23-1897 Lillie rec in mbrp

GLUYAS
2-26-1880 J Marmaduke & w Zalinda A rocf Carthage MM

GOEHNER
2-28-1891 Margaret F & s John H, Jacob L, & Wm P rec in mbrp
3-28-1891 Christie M rec in mbrp
7-22-1893 Margaret, John R, Jacob L, & Wm P rel fr mbrp

GOODRICH
5-22-1889 Charles C rec in mbrp
2-28-1891 C C rel fr mbrp

GOODWIN
7-26-1890 Harriet L rec in mbrp

GORDEN
4-25-1818 Mary & Anna gct West Grove MM
7-28-1898 Luther B minister gct Pasadena MM CA

GORDON
1-29-1814 Charles & s Richard, James, Seth, & Charles rocf Deep River MM NC; Ruth & dt Mary, Anna, Ruth, & Esther rocf Deep River MM NC
3-25-1815 Richard gct Cane Creek MM NC
4-25-1818 Ruth gct West Grove MM
6-23-1824 Seth s Charles & Ruth Wayne Co m Sarah dt Joseph dec & Rebeckah **Unthank** Wayne Co at Whitewater MH
3-18-1826 Seth rocf West Grove MM
5-22-1833 Cert rec for Thomas N fr Blue River MM; end to Chester MM
6-27-1835 Sarah & dt Phebe Ann & Emaline gct Fairfield MM
3-27-1844 Phebe Ann dis for na, dp, & apd
5-28-1845 Emaline gct Walnut Ridge MM
5-25-1895 Luther B rocf Hopewell MM

GOUGH
6-27-1849 Mary rocf Cincinnati MM OH
10-25-1850 Mary gct Cincinnati MM OH

GOURDON
4-25-1818 Charles & s James, Seth, & Charles gct West Grove MM

GOVE
12-22-1894 Alice C rq cert to Portland MM

GRAVE
10-26-1816 Hannah rocf Center MM DE; end fr Redstone MM PA; Jonathan L & s Israel, Allen, David, & Warner rocf Center MM DE; end fr Redstone MM PA Lydia & dt Sarah Ann rocf Center MM DE; end fr Redstone MM PA
12-28-1816 Enos & s David J, Jesse, Kersey, & Enos rocf Redstone MM; Betty & dt Sarah, Susanna, & Rebecca rocf Redstone MM PA
5-31-1817 Cert rec for Jacob fr Center MM; d bef cert arr
8-30-1817 Jacob & s Milton, Curtis, & Levi rec in mbrp
11-20-1824 David con for fighting
2-18-1826 Nathan dis for fornication
2-28-1827 Milton dis for mcd; Smyrna MM
1-23-1828 David gct Silver Creek MM
6-25-1828 Eliza rocf Silver Creek MM
11-26-1828 Enos dis for jH
3-27-1833 Mary rocf Chester MM
4-24-1833 John L dis for jH
11-5-1835 Stephen s Nathan & Hannah dec Wayne Co m Mary dt Joseph & Elizabeth dec **Strawbridge** Wayne Co at Smyrna Mtg
8-24-1836 Eliza (**Adkins**) dis for mcd
6-28-1837 Curtis dis for mcd
11-22-1837 Pusey dis for na, jH, & mcd
3-28-1838 Stephen & fam gct Sugar River MM; Mary & s Joseph gct Sugar River MM
4-25-1838 Ann P dis for na & jH
6-27-1838 Enos Jr con mcd
10-24-1838 Stephen dis for owing money
5-22-1839 Dorothy & dt Martha H rec in mbrp
9-5-1839 David s Jonathan L dec & Lydia Wayne Co m Jane dt Elijah & Susanna **Wright** Wayne Co at Smyrna MH
9-25-1839 Levi dis for na & mcd
10-11-1843 Allen, David I, & Jacob dis for jas
2-28-1844 David P dis for na & att mcd
3-27-1844 Enos dis for jas; Eliza dis for being active in bringing about a separation & jas

GRAVE (cont)
8-28-1844	Kersey dis for na
5-28-1845	Elizabeth rst by rq
8-27-1845	Mary, Ruth C, & Anna H dis for jas
2-25-1846	Joseph Chandler dis for na & att mcd
10-28-1846	Howell dis for na & mcd; Warner dis for na & jas
8-28-1850	Dorothea & ch Angelina, Daniel F, & Wm D gct White River MM
11-27-1850	Elizabeth gct White River MM
12-25-1850	Elisabeth, Jesse, Henry, Thomas, Clarkson, & Hannah Maria min ch David J gct White River MM
3-26-1851	Lydia Ann gct Elk MM OH
11-24-1852	Elizabeth rocf White River MM
9-26-1860	New Salem MM granted perm to rec Enos
5-27-1863	Elizabeth gct West Union MM
11-25-1863	Hannah rocf New Garden MM
1-27-1875	Margaret Rosetta dt Wm & Elizabeth rec in mbrp
7-25-1877	Mary Ann, Jonathan L, & Charles rel fr mbrp
3-27-1884	Vernon D s Howell & Hannah Richmond Wayne Co m Emma dt Alpheus & Elizabeth A **Test** Richmond Wayne Co at res of Alpheus **Test**
7-26-1888	Vernon & w Emma T & min ch Joseph Edward & Perry gct New Garden MM

GRAVES
10-26-1816	Nathan & s Stephen, John L, Pusey, & Elwood rocf Center MM DE; end fr Redstone MM PA
8-30-1817	Ann & dt Rebecca, Rachel, Mary, & Martha rec in mbrp
2-28-1844	Mary T & Betty dis for jas
8-26-1863	Elizabeth cert to West Union MM canceled
1-27-1864	Sugar Plain MM rpt Elizabeth (**Mills**) mcd; mbrp retained
6-22-1864	Elizabeth rocf Sugar Plain MM
5-28-1885	James & w rec in mbrp
6-24-1897	J W gct jas
12-22-1898	James & w Ella rel fr mbrp

GRAY
4-22-1874	James & w Mary Jane & ch James, Wm, Robert Thomas, Sarah Jane, Hugh, John, Samuel, & Joseph rec in mbrp
7-25-1877	James rel fr mbrp; Mary Jane & ch James, Robert T, Sarah Jane, Hugh, John, Samuel, & Joseph rel fr mbrp

GREEN
10-18-1823	Robert rocf Springfield MM OH
5-18-1825	Robert s Rueben & Rhoda Clinton Co OH m Mahalah dt Joseph dec & Rebecca **Unthank** Wayne Co at Whitewater MH
8-20-1825	Min ch Robert gct Milford MM
8-23-1826	Robert & w Mahala gct Springfield MM OH
12-22-1869	Timothy V rel fr mbrp
8-25-1875	Timothy V dis for carrying unlawful weapons
7-27-1882	Ellen W rec in mbrp
8-25-1894	Wm & w Louella & dt Hazel rocf New Castle MM

GRICE
5-26-1881	Catharine rec in mbrp

GRIER
2-24-1847	Ann J & Lydia rocf Chester MM

GRIFFIN
11-25-1809	Mary appt to comm
3-31-1810	Jacob & s James, Samuel, Joseph, & Joshua rocf Fairfield MM OH; Mary rocf Fairfield MM OH
2-28-1822	James s Jacob & Mary Wayne Co m Ann dt John & Jane **Weeks** Wayne Co at Middle Fork MM
12-29-1822	Ann gct West Grove MM
11-26-1845	Eli & w Rachel gct Cincinnati MM OH
4-28-1852	Mary Elizabeth & Willis ch Mariam **Greer** rocf Spiceland MM

GRIFFIN (cont)
9-26-1855	John W rocf Spiceland MM
3-26-1856	Anna C rocf Duck Creek MM
7-22-1857	Mary Elizabeth gct Raysville MM
3-27-1861	John W & w Anna C & dt Emily gct Spiceland MM
2-26-1885	Seth Smith gct Indianapolis MM; Willis drpd fr mbrp for na
11-24-1887	James C & w Eliza & ch Minnie M, John W, Charles O, James E, Esther B, Dahlia H, & Wm C rocf Fairmount MM
3-23-1895	Thomas rec in mbrp
6-22-1899	Thomas & w Elfleda & min s Earl Leroy gct Indianapolis MM

GRIFFITH
8-20-1825	Thomas & w Christiana rocf Sadsbury MM PA; Charlotte rocf Sadsbury MM PA
12-26-1827	Thomas dis
10-28-1828	Christiana & ch Charlotte & Hannah gct Vermilion MM IL
5-24-1843	Eli & w Rachel & s Collins rocf Chesterfield MM OH
9-24-1845	Collins W gct Cincinnati MM OH
11-26-1845	Eli & w Rachel gct Cincinnati MM OH
6-27-1849	Eli & w Rachel rocf Springborough MM OH
7-27-1853	Eli con mcd
11-27-1861	John W & w Kesiah T & ch Seth S, Rachel, Mary, Anna J, Alice B, & Martha L rocf Radnor MM PA
3-22-1865	Edith H gct Elk MM OH
4-26-1865	David L rocf Hopewell MM VA
6-28-1865	Eli dis for marrying again while his divorced w was still living
5-24-1871	Hannah B (**Shoemaker**) con mcd
12-27-1871	David L con mcd
8-22-1877	David & w Hannah B & min ch Charles, Harry, & Helen gct Ozark MM MO
12-25-1879	Alice B rel fr mbrp
2-26-1885	Seth Smith gct Indianapolis MM
11-25-1886	John W rel fr mbrp
6-23-1887	Keziah & dt Martha L & Elizabeth B gct Indianapolis MM
7-28-1887	Anna J rel fr mbrp
12-9-1891	George Dilks s Joseph C & Mary R Chicago Cook Co IL m Martha F dt Henry J & Harriett M **Hayward** Richmond at Richmond
8-27-1892	Martha (**Hayward**) gct Chicago MM IL

GUIFFORD
5-26-1830	Jesse rocf Elk MM OH

GUYER
10-30-1813	Aron, Axiom, & Jesse rocf Suttons Creek MM NC

GWYN
2-25-1815	Cert rec for Charity fr Lost Creek MM TN; end by Lick Creek MM

HADLEY
11-30-1811	Catharine & dt Mary & Jane rocf Spring MM NC
7-26-1817	Cert rec for Joshua Jr fr Spring MM NC; end to Silver Creek MM
11-27-1819	Cert rec for Jeremiah fr Cane Creek MM NC; end to Elk MM OH
6-18-1823	Jacob s John & Lydia Clinton Co OH m Mary dt Beale & Mary **Butler** Wayne Co at Whitewater MH
10-18-1823	Mary gct Springfield MM OH
12-29-1831	Jonathan D s John & Lydia Clinton Co OH m Susanna W dt Wm & Kesiah **Clawson** Wayne Co at Whitewater MH
4-25-1832	Susanna W gct Springfield MM OH
7-26-1838	Jeremiah s James & Ann Clinton Co OH m Esther dt John & Jane **Smith** Wayne Co at Whitewater MH
11-28-1839	Washington s Jonathan & Ann Parke Co m Naomi dt Micajah & Guielma **Henley** Wayne Co at Whitewater MH

WHITEWATER MONTHLY MEETING
MINUTES AND MARRIAGES

HADLEY (cont)

1-23-1840	Evan s James & Mary Morgan Co m Libby L dt Wm & Keziah dec **Clawson** Wayne Co at Whitewater MH
4-22-1840	Esther & min ch John S & James W gct Center MM
5-27-1840	Naomi gct Bloomfield MM; Libby L gct White Lick MM
6-23-1847	Cert rec for Jeremiah & w Esther & ch John Smith, James Wm, Jane Ann, & Samuel S fr Center MM; end to Cincinnati MM OH
6-28-1854	John C & w Emaline & ch Wm Lawrence & Clark Hinman rocf Center MM OH
4-30-1856	Hiram s John & Ann dec Clinton Co OH m Hannah dt Benjamin & Rhoda **Fulghum** Wayne Co at Whitewater MH
3-25-1857	Hiram & Miriam rocf Springfield MM OH
11-3-1858	Elwood s Jacob & Mary dec Clinton Co OH m Ann dt Richard & Susanna B **Pedrick** Wayne Co at Whitewater MH
4-27-1859	Ann P gct Springfield MM OH
7-23-1862	Elwood & w Anna P & min dt Corilla M rocf Springfield MM
6-22-1864	Jeremiah gct Springfield MM OH to m Rebecca **Hadley**
1-25-1865	Rebecca rocf Springfield MM OH
3-28-1866	Edwin & w Jemima & ch Eliza, Ellen, Annie, & Edwin C rocf Miami MM OH
8-26-1868	Artemus N & w Elizabeth M & ch Elsie Mary & Samuel W rocf Springfield MM OH; Wm B & w Rebecca Jane & ch Flora M & Ada E rocf Springfield MM OH
6-23-1869	Hiram & w Hannah P & ch Walter C, Caroline E, & Anna R gct Chicago MM IL
12-27-1871	Clark H con mcd
2-24-1875	Artemus N & w Elizabeth M & ch Elsie Mary & Samuel Lee gct Indianapolis MM
5-22-1878	Laura rec in mbrp
11-23-1882	James A rec in mbrp
12-28-1882	Lydia F rocf New Garden MM
4-26-1883	Herbert H & Thomas M gct Indianapolis MM
2-25-1886	Laura rel fr mbrp
4-22-1886	Elwood rel fr mbrp
7-28-1887	Cora M rel fr mbrp
11-24-1887	James A rel fr mbrp
9-2-1891	Edwin Clarence s Edwin & Jemima D Richmond Wayne Co m Emma dt Daniel & Martha A **Hill** Richmond Wayne Co at res of Daniel **Hill**
11-26-1892	Emily G rocf Dublin MM
12-28-1895	Clark H rel fr mbrp
2-22-1896	Jesse H & w Anzonetta & ch Alden H, Ernest B, & Samuel Percy rocf West Union MM
4-22-1897	Mary O'Neal gct Westfield MM
7-22-1897	Rebecca's d rpt
9-23-1897	Alfred & w Keziah & s Royal J & Clifton O rocf Dover MM; Elmer Fulgum & w Ida May & ch Guendeline & Grace rocf Dover MM
8-24-1899	Jessie H & w Anzonetta & ch Earnest B & Samuel Percy gct West Union MM; Alden H gct West Union MM

HADLY

11-30-1811	Joshua & s Abraham Noah, Wm, & Joseph rocf Spring MM NC

HAINES

10-28-1846	Elizabeth (**Evans**) dis for jH & mcd
1-27-1898	Arthur rec in mbrp

HAISLEY

3-24-1881	Joseph & w Sarah & ch Anna Lee rec in mbrp
4-25-1884	Anna Lee rel fr mbrp
12-22-1887	Annie & Rachel H rocf New Garden MM
4-26-1888	Jonathan & w Eunice & ch Gulia Elma, Sarah Ann, & Francis rocf Dover MM; Anna Lee rec in mbrp

HAISLEY (cont)

1-24-1891	Jonathan & w Emma S & ch Gulielma, Sarah Ann, & Francis J gct Muncie MM

HALE

2-24-1894	Elmer & w Lizzie & dt Ethel rec in mbrp

HALL

7-29-1815	Elizabeth & dt Rhoda & Anna rocf Center MM NC; Joseph, Benjamin, Caleb, Wm, Stephen, & Branson rocf Center MM NC
2-22-1817	Mary (**Small**) dis for mcd
7-25-1818	John Jr & s Phineas & Robert rocf Rich Square MM NC; Sarah & dt Martha rocf Rich Square MM NC
9-22-1830	John & w Sarah & ch Martha, Phineas, Robert, Moses, Sarah, & John gct Milford MM
2-24-1869	Evaline Helena AR rec in mbrp
10-27-1869	Stephen Helena AR rec in mbrp
7-27-1895	Mary Jane rocf Spiceland MM
10-26-1899	Minnie M rocf Chester MM

HALLENSHADE

11-22-1888	Mary rec in mbrp

HAM

5-29-1819	Sarah & dt Sarah, Mary, Elizabeth, & Ann rocf Deep River MM NC
7-22-1829	Cert rec for Elizabeth & dt Martha, Priscilla, Jane, & Elizabeth fr New Garden MM NC; end to Milford MM
8-27-1845	Jason con mcd
7-22-1846	Elizabeth rec in mbrp
8-24-1870	Emsley rst mbrp; dis 40 yrs previous for mcd; d 9-10-1870
11-25-1874	Mary Elizabeth gct Cincinnati MM OH
5-27-1880	Benjamin F rel fr mbrp

HAMILTON

12-24-1836	Springborough MM rq aid in treating with Caroline (**Dabney**) for mcd; did not make satisfaction
2-25-1897	Edna New Westville OH rec in mbrp
3-23-1899	Ida rec in mbrp

HAMISH

7-29-1820	Jacob B rec in mbrp

HAMM

12-22-1830	Emsley dis for mcd & dp

HAMMOND

5-24-1854	James C rocf Pennville MM OH

HAMPSON

1-23-1828	Abraham rocf Chester MM PA

HAMPTON

2-28-1818	Andrew & Rachel rocf Miami MM OH
7-25-1818	David & Jane rocf Miami MM OH
2-24-1821	Jacob & s Elisha rocf Miami MM OH; Eunice & dt Eleanor rocf Miami MM OH
4-28-1821	Sarah rocf Silver Creek MM
7-20-1822	Elisha gct New Garden MM
4-26-1848	Andrew & w Rachel & nieces Judith Ann & Susanna **Rich** rocf Chester MM
4-28-1852	Jehiel rocf Chester MM
5-25-1853	Jehiel dis for na & mcd
4-26-1854	Andrew & w Rachel gct Chester MM
3-7-1855	Haines s Jehial & Sarah dec Wayne Co m Deborah dt Samuel & Edith dec **Cox** Wayne Co at Whitewater MH
5-23-1855	Deborah gct Dover MM
5-22-1861	Haines & w Deborah & ch Sarah Edith, Thomas Elwood, & Samuel rocf Dover MM

HAMPTON (cont)
12-26-1866	Deborah & ch Sarah Edith, Thomas Elwood, Samuel, & Haines gct Duck Creek MM
2-28-1877	Addison rocf Chester MM
1-27-1881	Susan R rocf Chester MM
11-24-1887	Addison rel fr mbrp
4-25-1891	Elwood rocf Duck Creek MM
4-22-1893	Arthur & w Mary A & ch Anna May & Harold C rocf Chester MM
4-27-1895	Jacob D & w Margaret rocf Chester MM
7-22-1897	Jacob D's d rpt; ae 76y

HANKINSON
5-16-1825	Edward gct New York MM NY

HAPNER
5-27-1897	Emma Providence & Friendship Darke Co OH rec in mbrp

HARDWICK
4-22-1829	Betty (**Trueblood**) dis for mcd

HARE
8-22-1827	Cert rec for David rec dec fr Western Branch MM Isle of Wight Co VA

HARKNESS
10-26-1889	John U & w Charity C & ch Lina R & Beulah E rocf Adrian MM MI
5-25-1899	John U & w Charity C & ch Lina R & Beulah H gct Rollins MM MI

HARLEN
1-27-1816	Sarah (**Hollingsworth**) dis for mcd

HAROLD
2-23-1882	Cyrus M & w Elvira & dt Lura rocf Richland MM
1-27-1894	Isaac S & w Cordelia B & ch Earl J, Frank L, & Halsey J rocf Westfield MM
9-24-1896	Cyrus N & w Ella S & minor dt Lure gct Indianapolis MM
10-26-1899	Herman & w Ruthanna & ch Rollo & Luena rocf Westland MM

HARRELL
11-29-1817	Gabriel & Amy rocf Western Branch MM VA

HARRIS
10-28-1809	Margaret appt to comm
2-24-1810	Benjamin & s Obadiah, Pleasant, James, John, Benjamin, & David rocf Deep River MM NC; Margaret & dt Bathsheba, Rebeckah, & Sarah rocf Deep River MM NC
11-30-1811	Obadiah Sr rocf Deep River MM NC; Miriam & dt Lydia **Mendenhall** rocf Deep River MM NC
5-30-1812	Obadiah 3rd & Pleasant dis for mcd
10-31-1812	Obadiah Jr & s Thomas, David, Jonathan, John, & Obadiah gct Caesar's Creek MM OH; Mary & dt Rachel, Betty, & Susannah rocf Caesar's Creek MM OH
4-24-1813	James dis for taking up arms
7-29-1815	Benjamin & fam gct New Garden MM; Margaret & dts gct New Garden MM
10-28-1815	John dis for getting in a pasaion, upl, & offering to fight
1-29-1820	Jonas & s Wm, Henry Jesse, Jonas, & Jacob rocf Middleton MM OH; Hannah & dt Mary, Charity, & Lydia rocf Middleton MM OH
8-14-1824	Jonas & w Hannah & ch Mary, Charity, Wm, Henry, Jesse, James, Jacob, & Lydia gct Springfield MM
11-27-1833	Benjamin H & fam (s Jonathan) rocf White River MM
1-28-1835	Benjamin & w Abigail gct White River MM
5-25-1842	Lydia (**Weeks**) con mcd

HARRIS (cont)
8-24-1842	Lydia gct White River MM
5-25-1843	Jesse M Henry Co IA s Obadiah & Mary Randolph Co m Gulielma dt Wm & Sarah **Harvey** Wayne Co at Whitewater MH
8-23-1843	Gulielma gct Salem MM IA
3-27-1850	Jesse M & w Gulielma & s Albanus rocf Salem MM IA
10-28-1857	Jesse M gct Chester MM to m Emily Jane **Hampton**
5-26-1858	Jesse M & s Albanus & George W gct New Garden MM
1-26-1859	Wm & w Mary & ch Joseph Gurney, Milton, Anna, Lydia, & Levi rocf Dover MM
3-25-1863	Wm & w Mary & ch Anna, Lydia, Maria, & Zeri gct Poplar Run MM
3-28-1866	Milton gct New Garden MM
9-4-1867	John S Wayne Co s Jonathan & Louisa Guilford Co NC m Mary P dt Samuel & Martha L both dec **Jones** at Whitewater MH
3-25-1868	Mary P gct New Garden MM
1-25-1871	Jesse M & w Emily Jane & ch George W, Jane M, Mary L, & Francis T rocf New Garden MM
10-23-1872	Albanus & w Lydia Maria & ch Ida Elma & Wm Harvey rocf New Garden MM
12-22-1881	Albanus & w Lydia Maria & ch Ida Elma, Wm Harvey, & Jesse Frederick gct Cottonwood MM KS; George W gct Des Moines MM IA
7-27-1882	Albanus & w Lydia & min ch Ida Elma, Wm Henry, & Jesse Frederick rq cert to Cotton MM IA
11-24-1887	Charles B rel fr mbrp
2-26-1885	Jesse M, Frank T, & Mary L gc
5-28-1885	Jesse M gct Cottonwood MM KS
9-26-1891	Frank gct Muncie MM
3-25-1893	Almeda rocf New Garden MM

HARRISON
12-28-1859	Timothy & w Naomi & dt Mary Emily rocf Raysville MM
4-23-1885	Thomas H gct Caesar's Creek MM OH to m Claribel **Barrett**
10-28-1886	Claribel rocf Caesar's Creek MM OH
7-27-1890	Timothy rel fr mbrp
6-24-1893	Lydia A rel fr mbrp

HARROLD
5-30-1812	John rocf Westfield MM NC
2-23-1882	Cert rec fr Richland MM Hamilton Co for Cyrus A & w Elvira & min ch Laura B
1-27-1894	Isaac S & w Cordelia B & ch Earl J, Frank L, & Halsey J rocf Westfield MM

HARTLEY
7-25-1832	Thomas & s Norton P, Elias F, & James S rocf Silver Creek MM; Barbara & dt Sarah T, Rachel L, Rebecca D, & Hannah F rocf Silver Creek MM
5-25-1835	Thomas & w Barbary & ch Norten D, Rebecca, Elias P, & James gct Cherry Grove MM
5-27-1835	Elizabeth rocf Miami MM OH
9-23-1835	Rachel gct Cherry Grove MM
7-24-1839	Hannah F gct Elk MM OH
5-27-1840	Elizabeth gct Bloomfield MM
8-25-1841	Hannah rocf Elk MM OH

HARTMAN
8-27-1885	Phebe rocf Wilmington MM OH
9-24-1885	Phebe removed; cert ret

HARVEY
1-27-1810	Elizabeth (**Fouts**) con mcd
2-24-1810	Caleb & s Robert, John, Henry, Amos, Caleb, & Nathan rocf Spring MM NC; Mary & dt Ann & Sarah rocf Spring MM NC; Isaac & Rachel rocf Miami MM OH; Wm rocf Center MM OH

WHITEWATER MONTHLY MEETING
MINUTES AND MARRIAGES

HARVEY (cont)

9-27-1810	Michale & s Elias rocf Fairfield MM OH; Mary rocf Fairfield MM
6-29-1811	Isaac dis for mcd
9-26-1812	Michael con himself for having been concerned in military action
2-27-1813	Robert dis for acting in warlike manner
8-28-1813	Sarah con for mcd
10-30-1815	Elizabeth con att mcd
10-26-1816	Wm Jr rec in mbrp
12-28-1816	Wm Jr & ch Samuel & Polly rec in mbrp
4-2-1817	Caleb s Isaac & Martha both dec Wayne Co m Rachel **Lewis** dt Isaac & Charity **Cook** Clinton Co OH at Whitewater MH
6-28-1817	Samuel rocf Center MM; Rebekah & dt Margaret, Mary, & Sarah rocf Center MM OH
8-13-1817	Henry gct Center MM OH
10-25-1817	John & s Isham, Benjamin, Aaron, Nathan, & Wm rec in mbrp; Jane & dt Rebecca rec in mbrp
6-27-1818	Samuel gct West Grove MM; Rebeckah & dt gct West Grove MM
7-25-1818	Henry gct West Grove MM
6-26-1819	Elizabeth gct New Garden MM
3-20-1824	Rachel & ch David, Keturah, Elizabeth, & Thomas **Lewis** gct Silver Creek MM
12-22-1824	John s Caleb & Mary both dec Wayne Co m Christiana dt Samuel & Margaret both dec **Hunt** Wayne Co at Whitewater MH
4-16-1825	Henry & s George M & Caleb E rocf Springfield MM OH; Ann & dt Mary rocf Springfield MM OH
4-15-1826	Michael & w Mary & ch Elias, Thomas, Abijah, Sarah Ann, Bohan, Martha Jemima, & Stephen gct New Garden MM
9-27-1826	Henry & w Anne & ch George, Caleb, Mary, & Deborah gct Springfield MM
6-27-1827	Nathan con mcd
7-25-1827	Nathan gct Honey Creek MM
9-26-1827	Amos dis for att mcd
7-25-1838	Samuel gct Bloomfield MM
6—1841	John & w Christiana & min ch Samuel, Caleb, Sarah, Eli, & Mary gct Mississinewa MM
4-27-1842	Elijah con mcd
1-28-1846	Mary Ann & s Daniel Milton rec in mbrp
1-23-1851	Wm P s Eli & Sarah dec Clinton Co OH m Ann dt Wm & Keziah dec **Clawson** Wayne Co at Whitewater MH
9-24-1851	Ann C gct Springfield MM
5-24-1854	Elijah & w Mary Ann & ch Daniel Milton, Gulielma, & Elizabeth Ann gct Dover MM
12-27-1854	Charles con mcd
12-26-1855	Mahlon dis
12-28-1859	Elijah & w Mary Ann & ch Daniel Milton, Gulielma, Elizabeth Ann, Abner Clawson, & Wm Forster rocf Dover MM
12-28-1864	Elijah & w Mary Ann & min ch Gulielma, Elisabeth Ann, Abner C, Wm F, Alfred H, & Mahlon C gct West Grove MM
7-25-1877	Charles & ch Augustus & Mahlon gct Spiceland MM
2-28-1891	Lydia H rocf Miami MM OH
8-27-1892	Ada rec in mbrp
7-28-1898	Lydia gct Miami MM OH

HASKET

1-26-1831	Palen rocf Suttons Creek MM NC
3-23-1831	Palen gct Milford MM

HASKINS

5-24-1843	Priscilla Thomas (**Fry**) dis for mcd

HASTINGS

9-30-1809	Wm appt o
10-27-1810	Joseph rocf Back Creek MM NC
10-28-1815	Joshua & Ann rocf Back Creek MM NC

HASTINGS (cont)

9-3-1857	Elias R s Aaron & Christian Wayne Co m Sarah dt Wm & Abigail **Edgerton** Wayne Co at Orange Mtg
6-23-1858	Elias R rocf Milford MM
4-27-1859	Elias R & w Sarah E gct Milford MM
10-26-1859	John R & Rebecca Jane rocf Hopewell MM; Jane & s Seth, Aaron, & Wm Clarkson rocf Hopewell MM
9-26-1861	John R gct Honey Creek MM to m Phoebe **George**
8-26-1863	Phebe rocf Dover MM
1-27-1864	Phebe gct Hopewell MM
4-26-1865	Elias R & w Sarah E & ch Wm E & Mary Emma rocf Milford MM
9-23-1868	Jane & ch Seth, Aaron, Rebecca J, & Wm C gct Milford MM
4-28-1869	Elias R & w Sarah & ch Wm Edward, Mary Emma, & Anna Letitia gct Milford MM
6-28-1890	Seth G & min ch Alton P, Laura Ellen, Willard S, & Esther Jane rocf Muncie MM
11-22-1890	Alice Vining rocf Penn MM MI
4-25-1891	John N & w Jennie E & ch Ella M, Otis L, & Gertrude R rocf Dublin MM
12-26-1891	Seth G & w Alice V & min ch Alton P, Laura Ellen, Willard S, & Carrie Esther rq cert to Muncie MM
2-27-1892	Seth G & fam gct Muncie MM
7-23-1896	Alton P, Laura Ellen, Willard, & Esther ch S G gct Muncie MM
8-27-1896	Seth G rel fr mbrp
3-25-1897	Otis gct jas
12-28-1899	Otis & w Elizabeth H & s Bayard rec in mbrp

HATFIELD

12-25-1813	Jonas & s Jonas, John, & Nathan rocf Elk MM OH; Rachel & dt Mary, Rachel, & Ann rocf Elk MM OH
10-26-1816	Thomas & s Jonas & Richard rocf Elk MM OH; Sarah & dt Lydia rocf Elk MM OH
12-22-1887	Etta drp fr mbrp for na

HATHAWAY

4-25-1891	Alfred C & w Minnie B & min s Francis W rocf Wilmington MM OH
7-22-1893	Minnie R rel fr mbrp; rq lt to ME ch

HATTAN

4-28-1821	George & s Robert rocf Cincinnati MM OH

HATTON

4-28-1821	Margaret rocf Cincinnati MM OH
7-22-1829	George dis for jas
10-28-1829	Margaret dis for jas
2-28-1838	Robert dis for na, jH, & mcd
12-22-1841	Margaret J rocf Middleton MM OH

HAUGHTON

11-26-1873	Louanna rec in mbrp
5-23-1877	Richard E & w Elizabeth C & ch Luranna, Charles M, & Wm P gct Indianapolis MM

HAVENRIDGE

1-29-1814	John & s Wm Samuel & Isaiah rocf New Hope MM TN

HAWKINS

9-30-1809	Amos & s Jonathan rocf Cane Creek MM SC; Anna & dt Charity, Elizabeth, & Martha rocf Cane Creek MM SC; Benjamin & Amos appt to comm; John & s Wm rocf Cane Creek MM SC
10-28-1809	Mary & ch Ann, Rebeckah, Tamar, & Lydia rocf Cane Creek MM SC; John Jr rocf Cane Creek MM SC; Lydia & dt Tamar & Sarah rocf Cane Creek MM SC

HAWKINS (cont)

1-28-1810	John appt to comm
12-29-1810	Ann appt elder
8-28-1813	Nathan & s Thomas rocf Elk MM OH; Rebecca & dt Ann & Betsy rocf Elk MM OH
11-29-1817	Amos & s Wm & Isaac rocf Elk MM OH; Rachel & dt Mary & Prudence rocf Elk MM OH
6-30-1819	Henry s Nathan & Ann both dec Wayne Co m Phoebe dt Thomas & Ann **Roberds** Wayne Co at Whitewater MH
1-18-1823	Jesse rocf Caesar's Creek MM OH
6-18-1825	Jesse dis
7-25-1827	Jonathan dis for fathering an illegitimate ch
10-22-1828	Mary **(Morrow)** dis for mcd
12-23-1829	Sarah dis
8-25-1830	Sarah **(Wright)** dis for mcd
9-22-1830	Nathan dis for mcd; Wm dis for mcd & na
10-27-1830	Sarah dis for mcd
1-26-1831	Isaac dis for na & mcd
7-24-1833	Prudence, Henry, & Stephen ch of Amos dec gct Sugar River MM
9-24-1834	John Jr dis for mcd
1-28-1835	Sarah **(Jessop)** dis for mcd
12-25-1867	Henry W rec in mbrp; John & w Sarah rst; dis abt 30y previous for mcd; Nathan & ch Charles N & George W rec in mbrp; Nathan dis abt 30y previous for mcd
2-26-1868	Martha **(Parry)** con mcd
2-24-1869	Franklin Helena AR rec in mbrp
6-26-1872	Nathan con mcd
3-28-1877	Sarah Ellen & Lydia Emeline rec in mbrp
11-27-1878	Henry gct Cherry Grove MM
5-26-1881	Celina V w George rec in mbrp; Minnie w Nathan rec in mbrp
6-23-1881	Sarah rec in mbrp
11-24-1881	Levi & w Sarah & min dt Blanche rocf Union MM MN
3-23-1882	Alice to be rec in mbrp 12th St PM
10-27-1894	Ruth Blanche gct; jas
2-22-1896	Lella A, Daisy M, & Alma E drpd fr mbrp
3-28-1896	George W & w Celina M rel fr mbrp
4-25-1896	Ella Ernest & dt Pearl Ernest gct Carmel MM OH

HAWLEY

6-30-1821	Caleb & s Joseph & Benjamin rocf Springfield MM OH; Catharine rocf Sandy Spring MM OH
11-15-1823	Richard & w Rachel & s Eli gct Milford MM
5-15-1824	Caleb & w Catharine & min ch Joseph, Benjamin, & Phoebe Ann gct Carmel MM OH

HAWORTH

7-25-1849	Ira rocf West Grove MM; Peninah & ch Emily, Lot, & Hannah rocf West Grove MM
8-22-1849	Ira gct Duck Creek MM to m Asenath **Hunt**
5-22-1850	Ira gct West Grove MM
7-24-1852	Peninah & ch Emily, Lot, & Hannah gct West Grove MM
2-28-1853	Ira & w rocf Duck Creek MM
4-22-1857	Emily rocf Vermilion MM IL; Peninah & ch Lot & Hannah rocf Vermilion MM IL
1-5-1859	George D s Mahlon & Phebe both dec Clinton Co OH m Sarah **Clark** wid dt Samuel & Mary **Stubbs** both dec Wayne Co at Whitewater MH
5-25-1859	Sarah gct Center MM OH
1-25-1865	Peninah gct Duck Creek MM
8-23-1865	Lot con mcd

HAYNES

12-26-1838	Miami MM OH rpt Judith **(Cadwallader)** mcd; mbrp retained

HAYWARD

9-21-1891	Martha F rec in mbrp

HAYWORTH

12-22-1830	Mary **(Hill)** dis for mcd
1-24-1866	Lott gct New Salem MM

HAZELETT

1-28-1886	Lida W rq cert

HAZLITT

4-26-1883	Lida W rocf Chester MM
2-25-1886	Lida W rel fr mbrp; jas
11-25-1886	Lida W gct Maple Grove MM IL

HEAM

5-29-1819	Hezekiah & s Hezekiah, Emsley, Jehu, & Jason rocf Deep River MM NC

HEAP

7-25-1873	Elizabeth rec in mbrp

HEAVENRIDGE

1-29-1814	Margaret & dt Margaret rocf New Hope MM TN
12-5-1816	Samuel Franklin Co s John & Margaret m Elizabeth dt John & Abigail **Bradway** Wayne Co at Silver Creek MH

HEISS

1-24-1884	Jacob & w Mary rec in mbrp
12-26-1891	Jacob & Sarah not found

HEMINGTON

7-23-1856	James rocf Thaxted MM England
8-27-1856	James gct Hopewell MM to m Margaret Susan **White**
4-22-1857	Margaret S rocf Hopewell MM
7-25-1877	James rel fr mbrp

HENDERSHOTT

6-28-1883	Rebecca & ch Cynthia & John Centreville rec in mbrp
12-26-1891	Rebecca, Cynthia, & John not found

HENDERSON

2-24-1810	Susannah rocf New Garden MM NC
5-26-1815	Richard & s Isaac & Wm rocf Center MM OH
5-27-1815	Rachel & dt Sarah & Kesiah rocf Center MM OH
8-17-1822	Margaret **(Hunt)** dis for mcd

HENLEY

1-26-1811	Jesse dis for mcd
7-31-1813	Sylvanus & s Jesse & Thomas rocf Suttons Creek MM NC; Miriam & dt Mary rocf Suttons Creek MM NC
6-28-1817	Micajah & s John rec in mbrp; Gulielma & dt Mary rec in mbrp
7-29-1820	Hezekiah & Priscilla rocf Deep River MM NC
1-28-1829	Hezekiah gct Springfield MM NC
10-28-1829	Henry rcf Back Creek MM NC
3-31-1830	Henry Wayne Co s Joseph & Penina Randolph Co NC m Ruth dt John dec & Mary **Morrow** Wayne Co at Whitewater MH
7-28-1830	Henry & w Ruth gct Duck Creek MM
8-25-1830	Gulielma appt elder
1-26-1831	Cert rec for Elias & fam fr Back Creek MM NC; end to Duck Creek MM
8-3-1842	John s Micajah & Gulielma Wayne Co m Naomi B dt Wm & Keziah dec **Clawson** Wayne Co at Whitewater MH
1-25-1843	John & w Naomi B gct New Garden MM
3-22-1848	Henry gct New Garden MM to m Tacy Ann **Meredith**
11-22-1848	Tacy Ann rocf New Garden MM
3-27-1850	Samuel gct Springfield MM OH to m Eliza Ann **Hadley**
2-22-1851	Eliza Ann rocf Springfield MM OH
8-25-1852	Henry & w Tacy Ann & ch Charles & Emily gct New Garden MM

WHITEWATER MONTHLY MEETING
MINUTES AND MARRIAGES

HENLEY (cont)
2-26-1868	John & w Naomi B rocf New Garden MM
9-24-1873	John rq cert New Garden MM to m Mariam W **Green**
1-28-1874	Henry & w Tacy Ann & ch Gulielma, Micajah, Ida May, Cora Ann, & Laura S rocf New Garden MM
7-22-1874	Miriam rocf New Garden MM
7-28-1881	Miriam appt Richmond o
7-23-1892	Sarah H's d rpt; teacher Freedman's School Little Rock AR
1-26-1895	Micajah & w Martha C & ch Lora Alice, John Eddie, & Alvin Chawner rocf Plainfield MM
1-27-1898	Micajah & w Martha C & ch Lora A, John Eddy, & Alvin C gct Dublin MM

HENNEMYRE
3-23-1899	Jerry & Rose/Ruth Anne rec in mbrp

HESTON
6-15-1822	Ann rocf Caesar's Creek MM OH
7-17-1824	Ann gct Milford MM

HIATT
8-29-1812	Wm rec in mbrp
9-25-1813	Alice rocf Deep River MM NC
2-25-1815	Catherine rocf Deep River MM NC
9-30-1815	Catherine gct New Garden MM
2-22-1817	Jehu min rocf Center MM OH
6-28-1817	Eli rocf Mt Pleasant MM
10-4-1818	Eli s Jehu & Lydia Wayne Co m Hannah dt John & Mary **Morrow** Wayne Co at Whitewater MH
2-27-1819	Eleazar & s Jesse & Daniel rocf Miami MM OH; Anne & dt Eliza rocf Miami MM OH
3-27-1819	Sarah rocf Miami MM OH
3-30-1822	Gulielma rocf Clear Creek MM
1-17-1824	Isaac & s Daniel Williams rocf New Garden MM NC; George rocf New Garden MM NC
3-18-1826	George & w Sarah gct Milford MM
8-23-1826	Cert rec for Martha & dt Rebecca fr Deep River MM NC; end to White River MM
12-27-1826	Ruth (**Ratcliff**) con mcd; gct Milford MM
3-28-1827	Jehu gct Center MM
8-22-1827	Eleazar & w Gulielma & ch Eliza W, Daniel, John S, & Maria gct New Garden MM
1-23-1828	Cert rec for Absolam & Robert fr Deep River MM NC; end to Cincinnati MM OH
7-23-1828	Eli dis for jH
2-25-1829	Hannah dis for na & jas
4-22-1829	Elijah & s Dempsy & Jehu rocf Stillwater MM OH; Anne rocf Stillwater MM OH
7-28-1830	Elijah & w Anna & ch Demsey & John gct Milford MM
10-27-1830	Isaac con insubordination & att oth societies
11-23-1831	Isaac & w Shannah & min ch Daniel W, Phebe, Lydia, Martha, Jane, & Rebecca gct Elk MM OH
5-24-1832	Asiph s Asher dec & Mary Clinton Co OH m Sarah dt Jonah & Avis **Smith** Delaware Co OH at Whitewater MH
7-27-1832	Sarah gct Newberry MM OH
12-24-1834	Isaac & s Daniel W & Joseph rocf Elk MM OH; Shanna & dt Phebe, Lydia, Martha, Jane, & Rebecca rocf Elk MM OH
4-22-1835	Tilney & Thurza ch Eli & Hannah gct Chester MM
5-26-1841	Daniel con mcd
6-25-1841	Isaac & w Shanny D & ch Phebe T, Lydia, Martha, Jane, Rebecca, & Joseph P gct Miami MM OH
5-25-1842	Mary & dt Louisa Ann rec in mbrp
2-28-1844	Daniel W dis for jas
10-23-1844	Mary & min s Alvin gct Salem MM IA
12-23-1846	Asher & w Sarah & ch Eleazar B & Clarkson rocf Milford MM
2-23-1848	Asher & w Sarah M & ch Eleazar B, Clarkson, & Charles M gct Spiceland MM
5-27-1857	Jesse Dicks rocf Milford MM

HIATT (cont)
9-2-1857	Jesse D s Mordecai & Rhoda Wayne Co m Louisa dt Thomas & Miriam both dec **Woodard** Wayne Co at Whitewater MH
7-27-1858	Jesse D & Louisa W set off with Kansas MM KS
4-26-1865	Eleazar B & w Eunice S & dt Lucy rocf Raysville MM
11-28-1866	Wm J & w Eliza W rocf Milford MM
10-28-1868	Alfred J & mother Louisa **Pool** gct White Lick MM
12-28-1870	Eleazar B & w Eunice & ch Lucy gct Minneapolis MM MN; Mordecai & w Rhoda rocf Milford MM
7-24-1878	Jesse & w Margaret Ann & dt Sarah Anna rocf Milford MM; Francis T rocf Milford MM; Wm F & dt Laura Alice rocf Milford MM
6-23-1881	Eliza W appt o
2-23-1882	Joel rec in mbrp
6-22-1882	Jesse & w Margaret Ann & dt Sarah Ann gct Fairmount MM
7-27-1882	Margaret Ann removed; rel fr mbrp
10-25-1883	James s Thomas rocf Springfield MM
2-26-1885	Wm J & w Eliza W & ch Edgar F & James Smith gct Dublin MM
5-24-1890	Wm J & w Eliza W & ch Edgar F & James Smith rocf Dublin MM
6-22-1895	Wm Fletcher rel fr mbrp

HIBBARD
10-15-1825	Cert rec for Benjamin & fam fr Pipe Creek MM MD; end by Springborough MM OH; Charity & dt Jane, Sarah, & Alice Ann rocf Pipe Creek MM
8-27-1828	Benjamin dis for jH

HIBBERD
2-16-1845	Tacy B dis for jH

HIBBERT
9-23-1829	Charity & Jane dis for jas

HICKS
3-25-1886	Hannah E rel fr mbrp
4-22-1886	Wesley F & w Mary rec in mbrp
10-28-1886	Smyrna PM rpt Sarah Elizabeth (**Roe**) jas
1-25-1890	Wesley F dis
12-27-1890	Mary Ellen drpd fr mbrp for na & unbecoming behavior
5-23-1896	Michael & Elnora New Westville OH rec in mbrp

HIGGS
3-24-1881	Emma rec in mbrp
12-24-1885	Emma R drpd fr mbrp
11-25-1886	Sarah E rel fr mbrp; jas

HILES
1-26-1888	Elijah & w Dora rel fr mbrp

HILL
11-29-1809	Jesse dis for mcd
7-24-1810	Peninah appt to comm
8-25-1810	Susannah appt clerk
5-25-1811	Wm & s Aaron rocf Fairfield MM; Mary & dt Ruth rocf Fairfield MM
2-27-1813	Christopher rocf Back Creek MM NC
1-28-1815	Martha & dt Rebecca rec in mbrp
3-25-1815	Benjamin & s Benjamin & Herman rec in mbrp
10-28-1815	Abraham & Mordecai rocf Back Creek MM NC; Sarah & dt Hannah & Sarah rocf Back Creek MM NC
2-22-1817	John s Benjamin & Mary dec Wayne Co m Dinah dt Joseph & Dinah **Cox** Wayne Co at West Grove MH
11-29-1817	John rocf Back Creek MM NC; Benoney & s Matthew rocf Back Creek MM NC; Axsa & dt Asenath rocf Back Creek MM NC; Mary & dt Rebecca rocf Back Creek MM NC
9-26-1818	Thomas rec in mbrp

WHITEWATER MONTHLY MEETING
MINUTES AND MARRIAGES

HILL (cont)

2-27-1819	Henry & s Daniel gct New Garden MM; Achsa & Asenath gct New Garden MM
4-28-1821	Benoni gct New Garden MM; Mary & dt gct New Garden MM
8-30-1821	Thomas s Thomas & Anna both dec Wayne Co m Tamar dt John & Sarah dec **Clark** Wayne Co at Orange MH
10-4-1821	Jonathan s Thomas & Ann both dec Wayne Co m Zilpha dt Rice dec & Catherine **Price** Preble Co OH at Orange MH
4-24-1822	Wm s Benjamin & Mary dec Wayne Co m Charity dt Amos & Anne **Hawkins** Wayne Co at Whitewater MH
11-16-1822	Thomas & fam gct New Garden MM
2-15-1823	Wm Sr gct New Garden MM; Wm Jr & fam gct New Garden MM; Charity gct New Garden MM
11-15-1823	Jonathan & w Zilphy & dt Anna gct Milford MM; Thomas & w Tamer & s Milton gct Milford MM
2-23-1826	Joseph s Benjamin & Mary dec Wayne Co m Martha dt John & Mary **Jay** Wayne Co at Smyrna MH
10-24-1827	Cert rec for Aaron & fam fr Back Creek MM NC; end to New Garden MM
12-26-1827	Samuel rocf Back Creek MM NC
10-2-1828	Benjamin s Robert & Susanna dec Wayne Co m Ann dt John & Sarah both dec **Clark** Wayne Co at Orange MH
1-28-1829	Benjamin s Robert & W Ann gct Duck Creek MM; Robert dis for jH
12-30-1829	Harmon s Benjamin dec & Martha Wayne Co m Mary dt Micajah & Gulielma **Henley** at Whitewater MH
9-22-1830	Wm dis for att mcd
2-23-1831	Samuel dis for jas
7-25-1832	Thomas gct Sugar River MM
7-23-1834	Benjamin & s Benjamin rocf Duck Creek MM; Ann rocf Duck Creek MM
2-25-1835	Thomas rocf Sugar River MM
12-28-1836	Thomas gct Mississinewa MM
1-24-1838	Peninah dis for na & jH
2-28-1838	Benjamin dis for na
3-25-1840	Benjamin dis for na & mcd
4-24-1841	Charles con mcd
6-23-1841	Jemima (**Clark**) con mcd
2-23-1842	Ezra dis for mcd & na
5-25-1842	Samuel dis for mcd
8-23-1843	Benjamin Franklin s Benjamin gct Salem MM IA
7-23-1845	Elizabeth P (**Kirby**) dis for mcd & na
1-28-1846	Enos dis for na & mcd
2-23-1848	Robert dis for na & mcd
11-2-1848	Elijah s Joseph & Martha dec Wayne Co m Rebecca dt John & Betty both dec **Mills** Preble Co OH at Smyrna MH
11-13-1848	Joseph s Benjamin & Mary both dec Wayne Co m Amy dt Thomas & Elizabeth **Kendall** Wayne Co at Smyrna MH
8-28-1850	Thomas & w Tamar & ch Jane, Owen, & Enos rocf Walnut Ridge MM
7-23-1851	George dis for jH
10-22-1851	Thomas & w Tamer & ch Owen, Enos, & Jane gct Walnut Ridge MM
7-25-1855	Samuel C gct Mill Creek MM OH to m Elizabeth Z **Hutchins**
11-28-1855	Elijah & w Rebecca & ch John Milton & Joseph Henry gct Sugar Plain MM
12-26-1855	Joseph & w Amy & ch Sarah J, John, Martha, & Elizabeth gct Sugar Plain MM
10-28-1857	Samuel C dis for mcd
4-24-1861	Charles A rocf Deep River MM NC
4-23-1862	John & Phebe Ellen (**Branson**) con mcd
4-22-1863	Charles A gct Milford MM
12-23-1863	Robert & w Elizabeth & ch Mary Emily, Edward S, Anna Jane, John C, & Mahlon R rec in mbrp

HILL (cont)

9-21-1864	Elijah & w Rebecca M & ch John M, Joseph H, Enos W, & Martha E rocf Sugar Plain MM
1-22-1868	Nancy & ch Benjamin C, Miriam P, Eli B, Abbie E, Asenath E, & Margaret M rocf Walnut Ridge MM
11-23-1870	Thomas T rocf Walnut Ridge MM
4-27-1871	Benjamin C s Thomas T & Nancy D Wayne Co m Mary Esther dt Benjamin dec & Susan **Wickett** Wayne Co at res of Susan **Wickett**
12-27-1871	John H con mcd
6-26-1872	Daniel C con mcd
7-24-1872	Elijah gct Richland MM to m Elizabeth Ann **Binford**
12-25-1872	Eliza L rocf Spiceland MM
4-23-1873	John Milton & Joseph H ch Elijah & Rebecca dec gct Caesar's Creek MM OH; Enos Wilson, Martha Elizabeth, & Mary J ch Elijah & Rebecca dec gct Sugar Plain MM
12-24-1873	Edmund Gurney rec in mbrp
11-24-1875	Joseph B & w Rebecca & s Daniel rocf Springfield MM KS
11-27-1878	Thomas T & w Nancy D & min ch Eli B, Abigail E, Elizabeth A, & Margaret M gct Carthage MM
4-23-1879	Robert & w Elizabeth D & ch Mary Emily, Edward S, Anna Jane, John C, Mahlon R, & Rebecca Jay gct Carthage MM
2-23-1882	Samuel C & Anne E & ch Charles H & Florence rq mbrp Richmond PM
3-23-1882	Samuel C & w Anna E & ch Florence G rec in mbrp
5-25-1882	Charles H rec in mbrp
12-28-1882	Elizabeth J gct Walnut Ridge MM
6-28-1883	John M & w Mary Ann rocf Caesar's Creek MM OH
7-24-1884	Enos N & Martha E rocf Caesar's Creek MM OH
1-27-1887	Samuel C rel fr mbrp
3-24-1887	Martha E gct Caesar's Creek MM OH
8-25-1887	Charles H gct Chicago MM IL; Mary Elizabeth & Elam B drpd fr mbrp; Daniel & w Tamer & ch Murray & Emma rocf Clear Creek MM
12-22-1887	Madora rocf Caesar's Creek MM OH
5-25-1889	John M & w Mary A gct Caesar's Creek MM OH
1-24-1891	Enos & w Dora & s Ralph J gct Caesar's Creek MM OH
3-26-1892	Anna E & dt Florence G gct Chicago MM IL; Charles H gct Chicago MM IL
10-22-1892	Flora A rel fr mbrp
4-25-1896	Daniel gct Spiceland MM to m Rachel S **Bailey**; Wm & w Elizabeth S & ch Bertha Celia rocf New Garden MM; Mary J rocf New Garden MM
8-27-1896	Rachel (**Bailey**) rocf Spiceland MM
1-27-1898	Ella & Cora rel fr mbrp

HILLES

1-24-1884	Elijah & w Dora rec in mbrp

HINES

2-28-1891	Emma & Lydia rec in mbrp

HINSHAW

11-27-1819	Welmet rocf Cane Creek MM
5-26-1821	Susannah dt Isaiah rec in mbrp
6-30-1821	Jesse & s Benjamin rec in mbrp
12-18-1824	Isaiah & w Wellmet & ch Benjamin, Susannah, & Hannah gct White Lick MM
12-22-1830	Ezra & s Rueben, Abijah, & Zimri rocf Cane Creek MM NC; Phebe & dt Sarah, Rebecca, Lydia, Selina, & Nancy rocf Cane Creek MM NC; cert rec for Simon & fam fr Cane Creek MM NC; end to Vermilion MM IL
5-23-1832	Cert rec for Asenath fr Marlborough MM NC; end to Cherry Grove MM; cert rec for Phebe & fam fr Holly Springs MM NC; end to Cherry Grove MM
1-28-1835	Jesse B rocf New Garden MM
1-27-1836	Jesse B con mcd & rec in mbrp
7-27-1836	Lydia rocf New Garden MM

WHITEWATER MONTHLY MEETING
MINUTES AND MARRIAGES

HINSHAW (cont)
10-26-1836	Jesse B & w Lydia gct Duck Creek MM
5-23-1838	Ezra & w Phebe & fam gct Mississinewa MM
6-26-1839	Rueben dis
1-26-1870	Wm B rocf Springfield MM
6-25-1873	Hannah rocf Springfield MM
11-28-1877	Lizzie A (Conkle) rel fr mbrp
1-22-1879	Henry B rocf Walnut Ridge MM
6-23-1881	Wm B & w Hannah gct Indianapolis MM
2-26-1885	Henry drpd fr mbrp for na
2-25-1886	Philander & w Emma & ch Edwin, Elbert, Carrie, Olla, Laura, Franklin, Mary, & Walter rocf Dublin MM
7-28-1887	Philander & w Emma & ch Edwin, Elbert, Carrie, Olla, Laura, Franklin, Mary, & Walter gct Sterling MM KS
12-24-1892	Zilpha rocf Chester MM
6-23-1894	Albert & dt Ethel M rec in mbrp
10-27-1898	Caroline M rocf Chester MM

HIPPARD
3-27-1884	Wm A rec in mbrp

HISER
5-2-1894	Winfield Scott s Abraham & Sophia J dec Richmond Wayne Co m Mary Edna dt Charles G & Elizabeth N Carpenter Richmond Wayne Co at res of her father

HITCHCOCK
12-28-1811	Wm & s Joshua & Barnabas rocf Springfield MM NC; Hannah & dt Priscilla, Lydia, & Deborah rocf Springfield MM NC

HOAG
1-26-1848	Huldah C rocf Ferrisburg MM
8-25-1852	Nathan C & w Abigail R minister rocf Ferrisburg MM VT
1-24-1855	Abigail R gct Walnut Ridge MM

HOBBS
6-27-1812	Wm & s Samuel & Elisha rocf Back Creek MM NC; Priscilla & dt Mary, Delilah, Deborah, & Peninah rocf Back Creek MM NC
6-28-1843	Rebecca T rocf Upper Springfield MM OH
7-26-1843	Barnabas C rocf Short Creek MM OH
4-24-1844	Wilson rocf Walnut Ridge MM
7-23-1845	Wilson gct Miami MM OH
5-28-1851	Barnabas C & w Rebecca T & ch Mary Anna, Wm Henry, & George Tatum gct Bloomfield MM
8-28-1867	Barnabas C & w Rebecca T & ch Wm Henry, Sibyl Amelia, Caroline, Alice Fowler, & Lowell Buxton rocf Bloomfield MM
4-28-1869	Barnabas C & w Rebecca T & ch Wm Henry, Sibyl Amelia, Caroline, Alice Fowler, & Lowell Buxton gct Indianapolis MM

HOBSON
4-29-1815	George & s Thomas Charles, Joshua, & Jesse rocf Lost Creek MM TN; Rebecca & dt Sarah & Ann rocf Lost Creek MM TN
4-28-1821	Aaron rocf Springfield MM

HOCKET
10-25-1817	David & s Joseph rocf Lees Creek MM OH
10-30-1819	Nathan & s Eleazar & Jabez rocf Clear Creek MM OH; Elizabeth & dt Lydia & Nancy rocf Clear Creek MM OH
12-25-1819	Philip gct Darby Creek MM OH
5-27-1820	Unice rocf Darby Creek MM OH
11-28-1891	Frank & w Rachel & ch Hattie & Homer rocf Dover MM OH

HOCKETT
11-28-1812	Philip con himself for speaking an untruth
5-27-1820	Cert rec for John fr Darby Creek MM OH; end to New Garden MM
2-15-1823	Nathan dis for na, dr, dp, & counterfeiting
6-19-1824	Elizabeth & ch Eliazer, Lydia Ann, & Eliza gct Fairfield MM OH
6-26-1872	Joel rec in mbrp
2-26-1873	Sarah G (Charles) con mcd
6-24-1874	Sarah G gct Dover MM
10-22-1885	Albert C rocf Kokomo MM
6-28-1888	Milliken & w Tamar rocf Spiceland MM
3-26-1892	Warner M & w Sarah G & ch Wm N & Martha E rocf Dover MM

HODGESON
9-26-1818	Henry gct Silver Creek to m

HODGIN
5-28-1862	Tilnias & w Rachel & ch Cyrus W, Joseph N, Elias M, Phebe A, James A, Elkanah B, & Emma rocf Cherry Grove MM
4-24-1867	Tilnias & w Rachel & ch Joseph N, Elias M, Phebe A, Elkanah B, & Wm P gct Chester MM
11-25-1868	Joseph N & w Martha A rocf Chester MM
3-24-1869	Tilnias & w Rachel & ch Phebe Alice, Charles Elkanah, & Wm Percival rocf Chester MM
6-22-1870	Cert rec for Wm Milton fr Center MM NC; end to Chester MM
11-23-1870	Cyrus W & w Emily Caroline & min dt Laura Alice gct Hopewell MM
4-23-1873	Jesse rq cert New Garden MM to m Martha Pitts
8-26-1874	Jesse dis
8-23-1883	Cyrus W & w Carrie & dt Alice rocf Hopewell MM; Ellen M rocf Spiceland MM
8-27-1885	Wm C drpd fr mbrp
9-22-1887	Charles E Albuquerque NM; glt jas
10-22-1885	Albert C rocf Kokomo MM
11-24-1887	Ellen M glt New Garden MM
3-23-1889	Lizzie drpd fr mbrp; Margaret rec in mbrp
11-23-1895	Rachel E & ch Mary E, Amy E, Grace A, Bertha A, & Elva R rocf Cherry Grove MM; Martha L rocf Cherry Grove MM
7-22-1897	Grace's d rpt; ae 15y

HODGINS
2-26-1868	Caroline rec in mbrp
7-26-1869	Jesse rec in mbrp

HODSON
10-25-1817	Henry rocf Clear Creek MM
1-30-1819	Phebe rocf Silver Creek MM

HOGGART
6-30-1810	Ruth rocf Springfield MM NC

HOGGAT
2-24-1810	Moses & s Robert & Aaron rocf Springfield MM NC
7-27-1811	Philip & s John & Philip rocf Fairfield MM OH
10-26-1811	Philip & s Nathan, Joseph, Abner, & Elisha rocf Springfield MM NC
6-26-1813	Philip gct Clear Creek MM OH

HOGGATT
2-24-1810	Deborah & dt Miriam, Rachel, & Juley rocf Springfield MM NC
6-27-1811	Elizabeth & dt Irisgladening rocf Springfield MM NC
10-26-1811	Mary & dt Nancy, Rachel, Martha, Mary, Sophia, & Christiana rocf Springfield MM NC
12-26-1812	Alice gct Miami MM OH
2-17-1813	David & fam rocf Mt Pleasant MM VA

HOGSTON
12-23-1897	Floyd rec in mbrp

HOLADAY
6-27-1812	Robert & s Wm, Jesse, & Aron rocf Center MM NC; Edith & dt Jane & Elizabeth rocf Center MM NC
7-31-1813	Wm & s Samuel & Abraham rocf Spring MM NC

HOLAWAY
10-30-1813	Thomas Sr rocf Contentnea MM NC

HOLIDAY
7-31-1813	Wm Jr rocf Spring MM NC

HOLLENSHAD
11-22-1888	Caroline E Dunsmuir CA rec in mbrp

HOLLENSHADE
12-26-1891	Caroline rq mbrp East Main St PM

HOLLEY
4-28-1821	Rachel & dt Ann rocf Plainfield MM

HOLLIDY
7-31-1813	Jane & dt Nancy, Hannah, & Deborah rocf Spring MM NC

HOLLINGSWORTH
2-24-1810	Joseph & Wm rocf New Garden MM NC
8-25-1810	Isaiah rec in mbrp
10-27-1810	Joseph gct Elk MM OH
11-24-1810	Isaac & s John rocf Miami MM OH; Hannah & dt Susannah, Gulielma, & Phebe rocf Miami MM OH; Jonathan rocf Miami MM OH
5-25-1811	Isaiah gct Elk MM OH
6-29-1811	David appt to comm
8-31-1811	Eber, Abijah, Sarah Miriam, & Rebecca ch Jonathan rec in mbrp
9-28-1811	Wm gct Elk MM OH
4-25-1812	Hannah rocf Elk MM OH
5-30-1812	Jonathan Jr con for att mcd; Joseph, Wm, & Hannah gct Elk MM OH
10-31-1812	Patience rocf Elk MM OH
3-27-1813	Jonathan Jr dis for frolicking & dancing
8-27-1814	Thomas & s James, Henry, & Ira rocf Miami MM OH; Sarah & dt Rachel, Katurrah, & Mary rocf Miami MM OH
9-24-1814	Carter rocf Western Branch MM OH
7-29-1815	George rec in mbrp
11-25-1815	Ezekiel rec in mbrp
7-27-1816	Susannah rocf Western Branch MM
10-29-1817	John s John dec & Rachel Warren Co OH m Mary dt Ira dec & Elizabeth **Vestal** Wayne Co at Whitewater MH
12-26-1818	Mary gct Miami MM OH
12-30-1820	Rachel rocf Miami MM OH
10-27-1821	Isaac rocf Dover MM NC
2-25-1822	Nathan rocf Miami MM OH
2-27-1822	Nathan s John dec & Rachel Warren Co OH m Elisabeth dt John dec & Elisabeth **Vestal** Wayne Co at Whitewater MH
5-18-1822	Isaac gct Dover MM NC
4-19-1823	Nathan & fam gct West Grove MM
1-15-1825	Joseph gct West Grove MM
7-22-1829	Rachel (**Vestal**) dis for mcd
2-26-1851	Milton & w Susan M & ch Joanna Ines & Clarence rocf Salem MM IA
9-20-1854	Milton & w Susan M & fam gct Greenfield MM
3-26-1856	Milton & w Susan M & ch Joanna rocf Greenfield MM
8-27-1856	Caroline (**Fulghum**) dis for mcd
9-26-1860	Caroline & dt Iola rec in mbrp
10-26-1882	Rachel A rec in mbrp
4-26-1888	Homer rec in mbrp
7-23-1896	Susan gct Kansas City MM

HOLLINSHADE
9-20-1888	East Main PM rpt Caroline A rq mbrp

HOLLOPETER
4-22-1874	Mary rec in mbrp
4-24-1878	Zilphia rec in mbrp

HOLLOWAY
1-28-1815	Stephen rocf Marlborough MM NC
2-28-1816	Stephen Franklin Co s Amos & Hepsibah Stark Co OH m Elizabeth dt John & Letitia **Smith** Wayne Co at Whitewater MH
7-19-1823	David & s David & Jesse rocf Cincinnati MM OH; Hannah & dt Hannah & Ruth rocf Cincinnati MM OH; John, Margaret, & Abigail rocf Cincinnati MM OH
5-20-1826	Stephen dis for mcd
6-17-1826	Phebe (**Hodson**) dis for mcd
12-24-1828	David gct Cincinnati MM OH; Jesse gct Duck Creek MM
1-28-1829	Abigail dis for jas
4-22-1829	Hannah & dt Ruth dis for jas
9-23-1829	David dis for jas
11-25-1829	John dis for mcd
5-28-1834	Jesse rocf Duck Creek MM
4-22-1835	Nathan, Jason, & John ch Stephen gct Mississinewa MM
2-26-1885	Jesse drpd fr mbrp for na

HOLLOWEL
5-30-1812	Miriam & dt Mary & Sarah rocf Contentnea MM NC

HOLLOWELL
5-25-1811	Robert & s Smithson, Nathan, & Wm rocf Contentnea MM NC
9-28-1811	Elizabeth & dt Michal, Peggy, Mary, & Abba rocf Contentnea MM NC
3-28-1812	John & s Jesse, Jonathan, & John rocf Contentnea MM NC

HOLLY
4-28-1821	Rueben rocf Plainfield MM
11-15-1823	Richard & w Rachel & s Eli gct Milford MM

HOLMAN
5-25-1811	Lydia dis for mcd

HOLOWAY
10-30-1813	Thomas Sr rocf Contentnea MM NC

HOOPES
6-28-1854	Samuel & w Anna S rocf Chester MM PA
8-22-1855	Samuel & w Anne S & dt Mary Ella gct Goshen MM PA

HOOVER
9-30-1809	Andrew appt to comm
10-28-1809	Elizabeth appt Elder
1-31-1810	Henry s Andrew & Elizabeth Dearborn Co m Susanna dt John & Sarah **Clark** Dearborn Co at Whitewater MH
8-25-1810	Henry appt Register
11-24-1810	Frederick & s Allexander & Samuel rec in mbrp; Catherine rec in mbrp
9-30-1812	Andrew s Andrew & Elizabeth Wayne Co m Gulielma dt Cornelius & Elizabeth **Ratliff** Wayne Co at Whitewater MH
3-28-1826	Samuel con mcd
1-24-1827	Alexander dis for mcd; Duck Creek MM
8-27-1828	Andrew Sr dis for jH
10-22-1828	Frederick dis for jH
4-22-1829	Andrew Jr dis for jH; Samuel dis for mcd; Catherine & Guielema dis for jas
8-26-1829	Henry dis for jas
9-23-1829	Susannah dis for jas
1-27-1830	Sarah dis for jas

WHITEWATER MONTHLY MEETING
MINUTES AND MARRIAGES

HOOVER (cont)
12-22-1830	Jonas & s Jonas M rocf Back Creek MM NC; Mary & dt Catharine rocf Back Creek MM NC
7-24-1833	Jonas M w Mary & ch James, Catharine, & Samuel W gct Fairfield MM
9-24-1834	Alfred dis for na & jas
4-22-1835	Mahlon, James, Enos, Thomas, John, & Mary ch Andrew & Gulielma gct Sugar River MM
7-22-1835	Ann dis for j ME
4-26-1837	Henry dis for na & mcd
7-22-1840	Allen, Daniel C, & Wm H ch Henry gct West Grove MM
2-28-1844	John dis for na, jH, & mcd
5-26-1847	Anna dis for jH
10-26-1859	Phebe Ann (Macy) dis for mcd
10-23-1867	Henry rst; dis for taking part in military operations during war
7-26-1890	Levi & w Emma S & min ch Helen C & Edna L rocf Spiceland MM
3-23-1895	Lula & ch Lula, James W, & Martha Elma rec in mbrp

HOPKINS
1-4-1826	Joseph G rocf Third Haven MM MD
4-2-1828	Joseph G Wayne Co s Thomas & Sarah dec Caroline Co MD m Elizabeth D dt Jesse & Sarah Williams Wayne Co at Whitewater MH
9-22-1830	Elizabeth D dis for jas
5-28-1856	Elizabeth B rocf Baltimore MM MD
9-21-1859	Elizabeth B gct Miami MM OH
5-22-1867	Elizabeth B rocf Miami MM OH
6-24-1874	Sarah A gct Milford MM
8-23-1883	Elizabeth B appt elder

HORN
10-24-1838	Jeremiah & w Mazaney & ch Henry, Matilda, & Anna rocf New Garden MM
8-28-1839	Pharaby & Phebe rocf New Garden MM
7-22-1840	Jeremiah & fam gct New Garden MM
11-25-1840	Pharabe & dt Phebe gct Chester MM
3-22-1883	Valentine R rocf New Garden MM
1-26-1895	Josie & w Achsah & ch Annie, Willie, & Olive rocf Chester MM
2-24-1898	Achsah M & Ollie May rel fr mbrp

HORNADA
12-23-1880	Jacob Worley s Paul & Orilla rec in mbrp

HORNADAY
3-25-1874	Paul & w Olive A rec in mbrp
2-23-1889	Henderson rec in mbrp
2-27-1892	Henderson H glt jas

HORNER
8-26-1857	Samuel & w Beulah S rocf Raysville MM
4-27-1864	Samuel & w Beulah gct New Garden MM

HORNEY
8-29-1812	Solomon & Elizabeth rocf Deep River MM NC; Elizabeth rocf Deep River MM NC
5-28-1814	Solomon con himself for hiring a substitute in the militia
7-25-1832	John rocf Deep River MM NC; Prudence & dt Jane & Elizabeth rocf Deep River MM NC
1-28-1835	John & w Prudence & ch Jane, Elizabeth, James, & Wm gct New Garden MM
7-25-1838	John A dis for fornication, upl, & haughty unbecoming manner
6-25-1845	Ann M & Susan L rocf Miami MM OH
4-28-1847	Deborah D rocf Milford MM
7-28-1847	Jonathan & w Susannah L & s Charles gct Chester MM
10-11-1848	Jesse gct Sugar River MM to m Emily Clark

HORNEY (cont)
6-27-1849	Emily rocf Sugar River MM; end to Dover MM IA
7-25-1849	Jesse gct Dover MM IA
8-22-1849	Susannah L & min s Charles rocf Chester MM
1-22-1851	Susanna L & min s Charles gct Philadelphia MM Western Dist PA
9-24-1851	Ann C gct Springfield MM OH
9-22-1852	Joel gct Miami MM OH to m Sarah B Mather
3-23-1853	Sarah B rocf Miami MM OH
5-23-1860	Charles rocf Philadelphia MM PA
1-22-1868	Deborah D gct Milford MM
5-27-1868	Sarah Helena AR rec in mbrp
2-24-1875	Charles gct Hinkle Creek MM

HORNISH
12-25-1819	Tamar rec in mbrp
2-14-1824	Jacob B con for assisting in getting license for mbr Society to mcd
8-14-1824	Jacob B & w Tamar & ch Bazaleel, Wm W, & Sarah Ann gct Chester MM

HORRELL
7-22-1886	Mattie E rec in mbrp
3-28-1891	James C & dt Fannie E rec in mbrp

HOTCHKISS
4-28-1894	Mary Winifred gct evangelical denomination

HOUGH
10-26-1811	Mary rocf Deep Creek MM NC
3-28-1812	Jonathan & s Wm, Thomas, Israel, & Hiram rocf Deep Creek MM NC; Gulielma rocf Deep Creek MM NC
6-25-1814	Wm & grs John & Ira & s Alfred & Isaiah rocf Deep Creek MM NC; Elisabeth, Mary, & Israel rocf Deep Creek MM NC; Martha & niece Martha Hutchens rocf Deep Creek MM NC
2-25-1822	James & fam gct Fairfield MM OH
8-28-1833	Christe dis for apd, dp, & playing in theatricks
12-26-1860	Sarah Elma rocf New Garden MM
12-6-1877	Hiram s Jonathan & Gulielma Wayne Co m Hannah Mendenhall dt Wm & Martha Milhous Belmont Co OH at res of H Mendenhall; Whitewater Mtg
1-26-1889	Josephine Pearl rocf New Garden MM
7-25-1891	Addison & w Sarah Ann, & ch Roscoe, Wm C, Robert B, Eugene B, Berthe I, Ethel A, & Mary A rocf New Garden MM

HOUGHTON
7-26-1854	Wm & w Sally rocf Salem MM
1-23-1856	Richard E rocf Spiceland MM
10-22-1856	Wm & w Sally gct Spiceland MM
3-30-1870	Richard E Wayne Co s Wm & Sally Henry Co m Elizabeth C dt Phineas R & Ruth Ann Mather Wayne Co at her par res

HOWARD
8-30-1817	Barbara (Julian) con mcd

HOWELL
8-24-1876	Samuel C Selma Clark Co OH s Samuel & Hannah both dec Greene Co OH m Deborah A dt Amos & Ann both dec Steer Jefferson Co OH at res of Hannah Dilks Richmond; Whitewater Mtg
11-22-1876	Deborah dt Amos & Ann (Maule) Steer gct Green Plain MM OH

HOWELLS
2-26-1884	Laura B gc
4-23-1885	Laura T gct Chicago MM IL

HOWES
3-23-1882	Charles B rec in mbrp
11-24-1887	Charles B rel fr mbrp

HOZIER
10-27-1810	Lewis rocf Back Creek MM NC

HUBBARD
11-22-1826	George & s Wm B, John T, Elias, Thomas C, & George M rocf New Garden MM NC
9-28-1831	Wm B gct White Lick MM
11-23-1831	George & w Anna & ch John S, Elias H, Thomas Chalkley, Anna Grace, George H, Louisa Jane, & Mary Melinda gct White Lick MM
9-27-1837	Jeremiah & w Martha rocf Short Creek MM OH
11-28-1838	Miriam rocf Deep River MM NC
5-27-1840	Miriam H gct New Garden MM
11-26-1845	Butler & w Celia & ch Eliza Ann & Delila Caroline rocf Hopewell MM NC
8-26-1846	Butler & w Celia & ch Eliza Ann & Delilah Caroline gct Spiceland MM
9-22-1847	Jeremiah gct New Garden MM
12-27-1848	Jeremiah rocf New Garden MM
12-27-1851	Jehiel L rocf Springfield MM OH
6-22-1853	Jehial L gct New Garden MM
7-22-1857	Richard J & w Sarah & ch Emily, Henry, Joseph B, George, Julietta, & Anna M rocf Milford MM
1-27-1858	Harriet P rocf Milford MM
5-26-1858	Richard J & w Sarah & ch Harriet P, Emily, Henry, Joseph B, George, Julietta, & Anna gct Milford MM
2-24-1869	Cert rec for Wm G fr Wabash MM; end to Clear Creek MM OH
4-27-1889	Wm & w Amanda rocf New Garden MM; Henry F rocf New Garden MM
6-27-1891	Mary Alice rocf New Garden MM
12-26-1891	Nellie Clark w Frank rec in mbrp
5-26-1894	Wm & w Amanda gct New Garden MM
4-27-1899	Mary Alice gct New Garden MM

HUDDLESTON
8-26-1815	Phebe & dt Sarah, Lydia, & Anna rocf Deep River MM NC

HUDDLESTONE
8-26-1815	Jonathan & s David, Wm, John, Jesse, & Eli rocf Deep River MM NC

HUDLESTON
3-28-1860	Esther Ann (Winder) dis for mcd

HUFF
12-30-1820	James rocf Fairfield MM OH; Sidney & dt Mary Ann rocf Fairfield MM OH
8-22-1832	Christe rocf New Garden MM

HUFFMAN
12-27-1883	Jacob & Mary Alice rq PM at Centerville

HUGHES
10-4-1827	John Warren Co OH s Evan & Ann Berks Co PA m Hannah dt Robert & Lydia Cook Gloucester Co NJ at Ridge MH
7-22-1829	John rocf Springborough MM OH
7-27-1836	Phebe dis for jH
2-22-1837	James dis for na
9-25-1844	Eleanor Starr dis for na & jH

HUGHS
4-22-1829	Hannah dis for jas
6-23-1830	Phebe rocf Westfield MM
4-25-1832	Elenor Starr rocf Springborough MM OH

HUNNICUTT
4-24-1839	Joshua Bailey & ch Delitha Ann, James Benjamin, Wm Pearson, & Mary Eliza rocf Springborough MM OH; James & w Delitha rocf Springborough MM OH
11-24-1841	Joshua B con failing to satisfy creditors
3-22-1843	Delitha Ann dis for att mcd & na
1-26-1848	Joshua Baley dis for na
4-26-1848	Wm Pearson dis for na
10-25-1848	James Benjamin dis for na
9-1-1858	George E Rush Co s Ephraim & Margaret dec Prince George Co VA m Mary Amy Winslow dt Matthew & Ruth Barker Wayne Co at Whitewater MH
1-26-1859	Mary Amy & s Robert B Winslow gct Walnut Ridge MM
7-26-1888	Cert rec for Mary Amy fr Honey Creek MM IA; end to Baltimore MM

HUNT
8-31-1811	Margaret & dt Elizabeth, Christiana, Susannah, & Dinah rocf Miami MM OH
9-30-1815	John rocf Clear Creek MM
7-26-1817	Cert rec for John & s Nathan fr Newberry MM TN; end to New Garden MM OH
9-26-1818	Ruth rocf New Garden MM NC
4-28-1819	John s of John & Rachel Wayne Co m Catherine dt Adam & Anna Coffin Wayne Co at Whitewater MH
5-29-1819	John Jr con getting in a passion & upl
7-31-1819	Elizabeth & dt Unice rec in mbrp
8-28-1819	Elihu & John s Wm rec in mbrp
6-24-1820	Catharine & dt gct West Grove MM; John gct West Grove MM
11-25-1820	Wm 2nd rec in mbrp
3-30-1822	Hepsabeth (Swain) dis for mcd
4-20-1822	Margaret & Mary rocf New Garden MM NC
12-14-1822	Catharine & dt Irena & Lucinda rocf West Grove MM
2-14-1824	Abner & s Alonzo rocf New Garden MM NC; Susannah & dt Eliza rocf New Garden MM NC
6-24-1829	Jane rocf Dover MM NC
10-28-1829	Jonathan rocf New Garden MM NC; Margaret & dt Beulah rocf New Garden MM NC
4-28-1830	Irena, Lucinda, Calvin, Franklin B, Melinda, & Milton ch John gct West Grove MM
11-24-1830	Sarah & dt Nancy, Rosilla, & Martha rocf New Garden MM NC
7-27-1831	Jane dis for na & dp
8-24-1831	Beulah gct Chester MM
9-28-1831	Newby & w Sarah & ch Nancy, Rozilla, Nathan, Martha, & Elwood gct White Lick MM
12-28-1831	Huldah rec in mbrp
11-26-1834	Claton & Ann rocf Elk MM OH
4-22-1835	Margaret gct Duck Creek MM
8-25-1836	Reuben s Jacob & Lydia Clinton Co OH m Rebecca dt Micajah & Gulielma Henley Wayne Co at Whitewater MH
11-23-1836	Rebecca gct Newberry MM OH
11-29-1837	Clayton Wayne Co s John dec & Ann Burlington Co NJ m Elizabeth dt John & Mary Starr Wayne Co at Whitewater MH
11-28-1838	Abner dis for kicking a man & suing at law
7-24-1844	Alonzo dis for na & mcd
9-25-1844	Albert gct Cincinnati MM OH
9-26-1855	Franklin B & w Elizabeth, & ch Phebe Ann, Nelson, & Orlando rocf Westfield MM
12-26-1860	John S dis for j ME
3-22-1865	Mary S rel fr mbrp
12-27-1871	David W & w Martha N rocf Milford MM
2-28-1872	Clayton B rel fr mbrp
8-29-1872	Nelson A s Franklin B & Elizabeth M Wayne Co m Anna adopted dt Alpheus & Elizabeth A Test Wayne Co at res of Alpheus Test
5-28-1873	David W & w Martha N gct West Grove MM
2-28-1877	Franklin B rel fr mbrp
3-23-1882	Franklin B rec in mbrp
5-25-1882	Flora rel fr mbrp
3-22-1883	Anna M & Frederic rq cert to Indianapolis MM
4-26-1883	Anna M & min s Fredric rq cert; Anna M denied cert; no mtg in her vicinity; mbrp remains here
8-27-1885	Lewis & w Rhoda L & ch Ida Eldora, Robbie Benjamin, & Cora Elizabeth rocf New Garden MM

WHITEWATER MONTHLY MEETING
MINUTES AND MARRIAGES

HUNT (cont)
3-28-1886	Ruth Anna rocf Miami MM OH
10-26-1889	Franklin B rel fr mbrp
3-28-1891	Lucy rec in mbrp
7-25-1891	Orlando B drpd fr mbrp
8-27-1892	Fred M s Anna **Brock** rel fr mbrp
2-25-1893	Lewis & w Rhoda L & ch Bobbie B & Cora E gct Cherry Grove MM

HUNTER
2-24-1869	Judith Helena AR rec in mbrp

HURST
1-24-1891	Orlando B rel fr mbrp

HUSSEY
8-28-1861	Sarah rocf Berwick MM ME
11-28-1891	Rachel B rocf Clear Creek MM OH
12-26-1891	Homer F & Mary J rocf Clear Creek MM OH
5-28-1892	John M & w Anna R rec in mbrp

HUTCHENS
1-28-1815	Susanna & dt Gulielma rocf Deep River MM NC
4-26-1817	Benjamin Jr rocf Deep Creek MM NC

HUTCHING
9-24-1814	Cert rec for Hezekiah fr Deep Creek MM NC; end to Mill Creek MM OH

HUTCHINGS
1-28-1815	Thomas & s Denson & Jonathan rocf Deep Creek MM NC

HUTCHINS
7-26-1817	Benjamin dis for att mcd

HUTSON
1-17-1824	Cert rec for Nathan & s John, Daniel, & James fr Back Creek MM; end to Milford MM

HUTTON
12-28-1816	Thomas min rocf Redstone MM PA
8-20-1825	Thomas dis for j Free Mason Lodge
10-28-1829	Margaret dis for jas
12-22-1841	John & ch Samuel W, Margaret Jane, & Wm H rocf Middleton MM OH
5-28-1845	John & ch Samuel W, Margaret Jane, & Wm H gct West Grove MM
3-23-1889	Alta (**Woodard**) rel fr mbrp

IBAUGH
11-27-1872	Susanna Jane (**Mote**) con mcd
3-28-1891	Fannie Theodora rec in mbrp

INGERSOLL
1-28-1886	John & w Josephine & dt Mary Lotta rocf Salem MM
2-25-1886	Ada Gertrude dt John & Josephine rec in mbrp
8-27-1896	John & w Josephine & min ch Mary Lottie, Ada Gertrude, & Edward Dozier gct Hopewell MM NC

IREDELL
9-25-1867	Sidney (**Dilks**) con mcd
8-25-1869	John S rec in mbrp; Marionetta & dt Lizzie rec in mbrp
1-24-1872	Samuel E s Samuel E dec & Marinetta L Wayne Co m Sarah S dt George dec & Hannah H **Dilks** Wayne Co at Richmond Mtg
8-23-1883	Sidney D d 2-7-1883
7-22-1897	M's d rpt; ae 84y

IRISH
7-29-1852	Samuel s Israel & Esther Morrow Co OH m Avis Jane dt Jonathan & Mary **Roberts** Wayne Co at Whitewater MH

IRISH (cont)
11-24-1852	Avis Jane gct Dover MM
3-28-1860	Avis Jane & ch Esther Jane & Vienna rocf Richland MM
9-24-1873	Esther Jane gct New Salem MM

IRWIN
7-28-1830	Elizabeth, Lydia, & Elizabeth Jr dis for jas
12-22-1888	Cora Ann gct White River MM

JACKSON
5-27-1868	Sarah Ann Helena AR rec in mbrp

JACOBS
12-27-1817	James gct New Garden MM

JAME
5-25-1842	Isaac & w Leah & s Daniel rocf West Grove MM

JAMES
3-31-1821	Naomi (**Stratton**) con mcd
1-18-1823	David rocf Carmel MM OH
2-19-1823	David Wayne Co s Isaac & Sarah Columbiana Co OH m Mary dt Isom & Margaret **Hunt** Guilford Co NC at Whitewater MH
8-16-1823	Evan & s Jonas, Jesse, & Joshua rocf Short Creek MM OH; Rebecca & dt Hannah, Phebe, & Mary rocf Short Creek MM OH
5-15-1824	David & w Mary & min dt Ruth gct Carmel MM OH
12-18-1824	Evan & w Rebecca & ch Hannah, Phebe, Jonas, Jesse, Joshua, & Mary gct Milford MM
10-28-1829	Naomi gct Duck Creek MM
4-28-1830	David & s Levi C rocf Carmel MM OH; Mary & dt Ruthann & Mary rocf Carmel MM OH
8-22-1832	Isaac & Leah rocf Carmel MM OH
12-26-1832	Isaac & w Leah gct Duck Creek MM
11-26-1834	David & w Mary & min ch Levi C, Atticus S, Ruth Ann, Mary, & Alfred P gct Spiceland MM
8-26-1835	Isaac rocf Carmel MM OH
6-2-1836	Isaac L Wayne Co s Isaac & Sarah dec Henry Co m Susanna dt Isaac & Sarah **Bonine** Wayne Co at Orange MH
6-28-1837	Isaac & w Leah rocf Duck Creek MM
4-22-1840	Isaac & w Leah gct West Grove MM
5-27-1840	John & w Esther rocf Carmel MM OH
11-25-1840	John & w Esther gct Clear Creek MM OH
5-27-1846	Isaac P & w Susannah & ch Caroline, Lot B, Mary, & Lydia Ellen gct Birch Lake MM MI
6-24-1846	Isaac & w Leah gct Goshen MM

JANNEY
4-27-1859	Caroline gct Newberry MM OH
7-25-1877	Susan gct Greenwich MM OH

JANNY
10-21-1853	Caroline rocf Newberry MM OH

JARRETT
2-25-1874	Elizabeth rec in mbrp

JAY
12-3-1807	John s John & Elizabeth (**Pugh**) Waynesville Warren Co OH m Mary dt Henry & Martha (**Pearson**) **Steddom** Waynesville Warren Co OH at Miami Mtg Waynesville OH
1-15-1825	John & s Henry, John, & Walter D rocf Miami MM OH; Mary & dt Martha rocf Miami MM OH
6-26-1833	Henry gct Chester MM to m Leah **Nicholson**
11-27-1833	Leah rocf Chester MM
6-28-1837	John con upl
3-8-1838	Henry s John & Mary Wayne Co m Sarah dt Joseph & Elizabeth dec **Strawbridge** Wayne Co at Smyrna MH

JAY (cont)
2-18-1847	Walter Denny s John & Mary (Steddom) m Rebecca dt Amos & Malinda Clawson
8-31-1848	Henry s John & Mary both dec Wayne Co m Priscilla dt John & Sarah Reed Wayne Co at Smyrna Mtg
8-28-1850	Rebecca Ann rec in mbrp; John A s Walter Denny & Rebecca Ann rec in mbrp
2-23-1853	Henry & w Priscilla & ch Jesse Walter, Leah, Sarah, Martha & Dewit Clinton gct Dover MM
11-25-1868	John A con mcd
9-21-1870	Naomi C (Fulghum) con mcd
12-27-1871	Joseph W rocf Raysville MM
5-23-1872	Joseph W gct New Garden MM to m Susan Mather Hawkins
4-23-1873	John A rel fr mbrp; jas
1-28-1874	Susan M rocf New Garden MM
7-22-1874	Eli & w Mahalah & dt Mary Adelaide rocf Hopewell MM
11-25-1874	Walter D & w Rebecca & min ch Alice Elizabeth & Wm gct Chester MM
3-24-1875	Naomi C rel fr mbrp
8-25-1881	Allen & w Martha A & min ch Wm C, Edwin, & Isaac rocf Providence MM RI
8-23-1883	Eli, Mahalah, & Martha appt elders
2-28-1884	Anna F rec in mbrp
1-24-1891	Wm C & w Anna F & s Wm Isaac gct New Sharon MM IA
5-25-1892	Edwin Sleeper s Allen & Martha Ann Richmond m Martha Evangeline dt Miles & Rachel Moore Wayne Co at res of her par Richmond
2-25-1893	Edwin S & w Evangeline (Moore) gct New Sharon MM IA
9-21-1899	Edwin S & w Evangeline M & ch Allen & Willard Bain rocf New Sharon MM IA

JEALISON
5-25-1836	Priscilla (Marmon) dis for mcd

JEFFERES
2-24-1847	Hannah rocf Chester MM

JEFFERIES
8-14-1824	Anna & dt Martha rocf Bradford MM PA

JEFFRIES
5-26-1821	Joshua rocf Bradford MM
8-14-1824	Wm, Isaac, & Jacob rocf Bradford MM PA
9-18-1824	Abraham con mcd
9-17-1825	Abraham rocf Center MM OH
12-17-1825	Martha gct Miami MM OH
11-22-1826	Isaac dis for mcd
12-26-1826	Abraham dis for att mcd
1-28-1829	Asa & s Elijah & Wm rec in mbrp; Ann dis for jH
3-25-1829	Margaret & dt Rebecca rec in mbrp
11-25-1829	Jacob dis for jas
4-24-1844	Asa & w Margaret & min ch Elijah, Wm, Asa, John, Elizabeth, & Hannah Ann gct Hopewell MM; Rebecca gct Hopewell MM
2-26-1880	Abraham S & w Edith & ch Lizzie E & Annie M rec in mbrp

JENKINS
2-27-1850	Lucinda B & Phebe Ann rocf Springfield MM
6-24-1868	Silas Newton rocf West Branch MM; S Newton con mcd
12-23-1880	Charles M rocf West Branch MM
2-22-1883	Anna rec in mbrp
2-26-1885	Wm drpd fr mbrp for na & disinterest
11-22-1890	Amasa & w Mary Ann & ch Atwood L, Olive L, Alice S, & Alfred W rocf New Garden MM; Charles F rocf New Garden MM
1-1-1892	Charles M Wayne Co s Evans H & Amelia A Montgomery Co OH m Ellen W dt James H & Mary J Dickinson Richmond at res Joseph Dickinson Richmond

JENKINS (cont)
10-16-1895	Atwood L s Amasa M & Mary Anna Richmond Wayne Co m Mary Lenora dt Oliver & Sarah dec Test at res of her par
7-22-1897	Nellie's d rpt; ae 29y

JENNINGS
10-18-1823	Sally (Springer) dis for mcd

JESSOP
5-25-1811	Jacob & s Jacob rocf Mt Pleasant MM VA; Rachel & dt Phebe, Rachel, Sarah, & Susanna rocf Mt Pleasant MM VA
7-27-1811	Abraham rocf Mt Pleasant MM VA
4-25-1812	Thomas & s Jonathan, Richard, & Thomas rocf Deep River MM NC; Abraham con mcd
2-25-1815	Isaac rocf Fairfield MM NJ; Nathan & s Isaac & Thomas rocf Fairfield MM NJ; Sarah & dt Phebe & Mary Jane rocf Fairfield MM NJ
6-24-1815	Jacob con mcd
8-26-1815	Elizabeth rec in mbrp
3-30-1816	Jacob gct Center MM OH
2-22-1817	Nathan & fam gct New Garden MM; Sarah gct New Garden MM; Lydia & dt Esther Hiatt rocf Center MM OH
7-26-1817	Hezekiah rocf New Garden MM NC
10-25-1817	Isaac Jr gct New Garden MM
11-29-1817	Isaac Sr & fam gct New Garden MM; Ann gct New Garden MM
10-28-1820	Jacob Jr & fam gct New Garden MM; Elizabeth gct New Garden MM
6-30-1821	Levi & s Wm rocf Westfield MM NC; Jemima & dt Emily rocf Westfield MM NC
4-19-1823	Sarah & dt Sarah rocf Westfield MM NC
9-20-1823	Cert rec for John & Jacob fr Westfield MM NC; end to White Lick MM
10-18-1823	Levi & w Jemima & min ch Emily & Wm Allen gct White Lick MM
4-15-1826	Hezekiah dis for mcd; copy of proceedings sent him at New Garden MM NC
7-25-1827	Jacob Jr & s Elihu, James, & Mahlon rocf New Garden MM; Elizabeth & dt Rachel rocf New Garden MM
5-26-1830	Jacob Jr & w Elizabeth & min ch Elihu, James, Mahlon, & Rachel gct West Grove MM
7-27-1831	Rebecca T rocf New Garden MM
5-28-1834	Sarah rocf New Garden MM
7-23-1834	Elizabeth, Sarah, & Edith rocf Dover MM NC; Jane dis for unchastity
11-26-1834	Abraham & ch Hannah, Elizabeth, Rachel, John, Alfred, & Eli gct Fairfield MM
4-27-1836	Elihu rocf Springfield MM
5-25-1836	Sarah gct Spiceland MM
3-22-1837	Edith gct White Lick MM
8-23-1837	White Lick MM ret cert for Edith with information she had absconded before they rec it
12-27-1837	Edith dis for absconding with a mar man
12-29-1841	Jehu s Isaac & Ann Wayne Co m Mary Ann dt Wm & Sarah dec Whitaker Wayne Co at Whitewater MH
4-27-1842	Mary Ann gct Dover MM
2-1-1843	Levi s Isaac dec & Ann Wayne Co m Mary Roberds wid dt Ralph & Prudence Myers both dec Wayne Co at Whitewater MH
4-26-1843	Levi rocf Dover MM
4-22-1857	Mary Jane gct White Lick MM
7-29-1868	Lindley M Mahaska Co IA s Levi & Mary Wayne Co m Sarah Elma dt Israel & Lydia both dec Hough Wayne Co at res of his father
9-23-1868	Lindley M & w Sarah Elma gct Spring Creek MM IA
4-26-1871	Rachel M rocf Milford MM
12-24-1873	Milton H rec in mbrp
1-26-1876	Lindley M & w Anna M gct New York MM NY
8-22-1877	Thomas R gct Mill Creek MM

WHITEWATER MONTHLY MEETING
MINUTES AND MARRIAGES

JESSUP

2-24-1810	Jonathan rocf Mt Pleasant MM VA
5-25-1811	Isaac rocf Mt Pleasant MM VA
12-1-1813	Isaac s Jacob & Rachel Wayne Co m Ann dt John & Mary **Hawkins** Wayne Co at Whitewater MH
10-18-1823	Sarah & dt Sarah gct White Lick MM
2-25-1829	Lydia dis for jas
12-3-1856	Elias s Joseph & Charity Hendricks Co m Mary Jane dt John & Ann **Morris** Wayne Co at Whitewater MH
2-22-1871	Levi gct Milford MM to m Rachel M **White**
10-23-1872	Lindley M rocf Cincinnati MM OH
7-25-1873	Albert con mcd
7-25-1877	David & w Sarah rocf West Grove MM
7-22-1880	Rachel's d rpt; elder; d during previous 3y
9-23-1880	Levi gct Cherry Grove MM; Albert S & s Cary Levi gct White River MM; Eli S gct White River MM
4-27-1882	Grace rec in mbrp
8-23-1883	Milton d 11-26-1882
4-22-1886	David B & dt Edna rec in mbrp
7-22-1897	Sarah's d rpt; ae 92y

JEWLIN

6-27-1827	Rebecca gct West Grove MM

JOHNSON

10-26-1811	James & s Charles rocf Deep River MM NC; Miriam & dt Hannah & Prudence rocf Deep River MM NC
11-30-1811	Elizabeth rocf Deep River MM NC
10-31-1812	Sarah rocf Deep Creek MM NC
5-31-1817	Cert rec for Isaac Jr fr Westland MM; end to Silver Creek Mtg
8-30-1817	Josiah & s James rec in mbrp; Polly & dt Rebecca & Rachel rec in mbrp
10-1-1817	Charles s James & Ruth dec Wayne Co m Mary dt Robert & Martha **Combers** Wayne Co at Whitewater MH
10-30-1819	Wm & s Ashley & John H rocf Union MM NC; Elizabeth & dt Priscilla, Anne, & Susannah H rocf Union MM NC
7-29-1820	Mary gct New Garden MM; Charles & fam gct New Garden MM
4-19-1823	Charles & s Caleb rocf New Garden MM; Wm con giving way to passion & upl
12-27-1826	Charles gct Springfield MM to m Nancy **Beeson**
1-24-1827	Ashley gct Short Creek MM OH
6-27-1827	Nancy rocf Springfield MM
9-26-1827	Lydia rocf Short Creek MM OH
10-24-1827	Ashley & w Lydia gct White Lick MM
11-23-1827	Martha **(Hubbard)** con mcd
1-23-1828	Philip con mcd
4-23-1828	Josiah & w Polly & ch James, Rachel, Wm, Elijah, Ashley, & Josiah M gct Springfield MM
1-28-1829	Charles & w Nancy & ch Caleb, Martha, Betsy Ann, & Charles gct West Grove MM
4-22-1829	Philip & w Martha gct White Lick MM
11-25-1829	James & s Caleb rocf New Garden MM NC; Mary & dt Anna Rachel, Elizabeth, & Emily Grace rocf New Garden MM NC
5-26-1830	James & w Mary & ch Anna Rachel, Elizabeth, Caleb, Emily Grace, & John Warner gct Milford MM
4-27-1831	Cert rec for Suchy & dt Almida fr Western Branch MM VA; end to Milford MM
10-26-1831	Wm & w Elizabeth & dt Annajane & Susanna H gct White Lick MM
10-24-1832	John H gct White Lick MM
11-26-1834	James & w Miriam gct New Garden MM
4-22-1835	Ch Thomas A gct Mississinewa MM
3-22-1837	Elizabeth **(Jessop)** con mcd
9-27-1837	Elizabeth gct White Lick MM
7-22-1846	Mary gct Dover MM
3-26-1851	Rachel A rocf Miami MM OH
3-31-1852	Eli s John & Judith both dec Warren Co OH m Mary dt Elijah & Naomi **Coffin** Wayne Co at Whitewater MH
5-26-1852	Mary C gct Miami MM OH

JOHNSON (cont)

1-26-1853	Phebe rocf Miami MM OH
4-26-1854	James & w Elizabeth & ch Hannah M, Mary B, Rebecca N, Amy C, Sylvanus, & James Brooks rocf Miami MM OH
8-22-1855	Wm & w Anna & ch Martitia E, Wm Elwood, Emily, & Mary Ann rocf Deep River MM NC
11-28-1855	Wm G & w Anna & ch Martitia E, Wm Elwood, Emily, & Mary Ann gct Spiceland MM
8-26-1857	Benjamin Jr rocf New Garden MM OH
11-4-1857	Benjamin Wayne Co s Benjamin & Martha Columbiana Co OH m Elizabeth dt Matthew & Ruth **Barker** Wayne Co at Whitewater MH
3-24-1858	Cert rec for Eli & w Mary C fr Miami MM OH; end to Cincinnati MM OH
4-28-1858	David F & w Catharine C & ch Charles Albert, John, Joel W, Ida Caroline, & Eli M rocf Miami MM OH
3-28-1860	John W rec in mbrp with con Spiceland MM
9-26-1860	John W gct Spiceland MM
5-22-1861	David F & w Catherine C & ch Charles Albert, John, Joel W, Ida Caroline, & Eli M gct Plainfield MM
12-24-1862	Evan L & ch Morris & Eva E rocf Wabash MM
7-27-1864	Rebecca N rel fr mbrp to jas
9-21-1864	Evan Louis gct Cincinnati MM OH to m Anna M **Taylor**
11-23-1864	Evan Lewis & ch Morris L & Eva E gct Cincinnati MM OH
4-28-1869	Elmina rocf Springfield MM
12-28-1870	Mary rocf New Garden MM OH
10-22-1873	Jacob J Monroe Co AR s Jacob & Judah Green Co AL m Annie dt John & Laura Ann **Cannon** Madison Co AL at Southland Mtg AR
11-26-1873	Elmina L gct Indianapolis MM
7-25-1877	Amy gct Poughkeepsie MM NY
2-26-1880	Sylvanus T gct Chicago MM IL
7-22-1880	Cert for Sylvanus T ret by Chicago MM IL; dprd fr mbrp; jas
4-26-1883	Susan E gct Spiceland MM
2-25-1886	Sylvanus T rel fr mbrp
1-26-1888	Hannah M glt Richmond First Presb ch
6-14-1893	John Howard s Benjamin & Elisabeth dec Richmond Wayne Co m Eliza dt Timothy & Mary W **Nicholson** Wayne Co at East Main St MH Richmond
10-25-1893	Allen Clifford s J Howard & Sarah H dec Oskaloosa IA m Susan R dt Timothy dec & Naomi W **Harrison** at res of her mother Richmond
5-26-1894	Nettie L w E T & ch Mearl S & Althea B rec in mbrp; lt rf Columbus ME ch
6-23-1894	Elisha T rocf Cherry Grove MM; Susan R H gct Oskaloosa MM IA
5-27-1897	James & Josephine Providence & Friendship Darke Co OH rec in mbrp

JONES

11-30-1811	Micajah & s Jesse & Sylvanus rocf Deep River MM NC; Sarah & dt Ruth rocf Deep River MM NC
4-29-1815	Jesse & s Jesse, Wm C, & John M rocf Lost Creek MM TN; Lydia & dt Esther, Lydia, & Anna rocf Lost Creek MM TN
3-30-1816	Jesse & fam gct New Garden MM; Lydia & dt gct New Garden MM
6-29-1816	Micajah & fam gct New Garden MM; Sarah & dt gct New Garden MM
8-31-1816	Martha rocf Elk MM OH
6-26-1819	Micajah & s Jesse Silvenus, James, Eli, & Elihu rocf New Garden MM; Sarah & dt Ruth & Jane rocf New Garden MM
3-25-1820	Hannah rocf Miami MM OH
12-29-1821	Susanna & Ruthanna dt Morgan rocf Dunnings' Creek MM PA
6-17-1826	Morgan min gct Silver Creek MM
8-23-1826	Isaac E & s Bateman rocf Springborough MM OH; Rachel B & dt Hannah B rocf Springborough MM OH

JONES (cont)
8-26-1829	Isaac E dis for jas
10-28-1829	Robert D dis for jas
1-27-1830	Susannah rocf Westfield MM
3-24-1830	Rachel B Jr dis for jas
4-27-1836	Clarkson & Franklin min rocf Redstone MM PA
7-26-1837	Clarkson dis for na & jH
11-22-1843	Hannah B dis for jH
8-28-1844	Bateman dis for na & jH
5-28-1845	Priscilla gct Cincinnati MM OH
6-27-1849	Daniel H & w Amelia & ch James Branson, Rollin, Byron, Newton, & Luvena rocf West Branch MM OH
11-22-1854	Amelia & min ch Newton S & Luvenia E gct Back Creek MM
12-27-1854	James Branson gct Back Creek MM
4-22-1857	Charles Rollin dis for mcd
3-25-1863	Byron gct Mississinewa MM
5-25-1863	Byron dis for adm oaths
7-22-1863	Byron's cert to Mississinewa MM canceled; complained of by that mtg for adm oaths
5-26-1865	Anna M rocf Miami MM OH
10-24-1866	Mary P rocf Miami MM OH
6-23-1869	Morgan, Maria, & Mary rec in mbrp
4-22-1880	Samuel & w Jane & dt Mattie rocf Chester MM
1-25-1883	Claborn L rec in mbrp
6-28-1883	Sylvester & w Mary A & ch Wm C & Maud rocf Dublin MM
12-27-1883	Samuel N & w Jane gct White River MM
5-20-1886	Clayborne S Vanderburgh Co s Morris & Octavia Wayne Co m Margaret Jessie dt Jesse J dec & Mary **Kenworthy** at res of her mother Richmond
1-27-1887	Sylvester H & w Mary A rel fr mbrp; jas
11-22-1890	Samuel & w Jane rocf Le Grand MM IA
12-16-1891	Wm C & Maud not found
10-22-1892	Samuel & w Jane gct Winchester MM

JULEN
7-29-1815	Isaac rocf Center MM NC

JULIAN
10-23-1809	Rebecca **(Hoover)** con mcd
7-29-1815	Sarah & dt Keziah, Sarah, & Barbara rocf Center MM NC

JULIN
6-17-1826	Rebecca rocf West Grove MM

JUSTICE
12-30-1815	Jonathan & s Benjamin & John rocf West Branch MM; Elisabeth & dt Mary, Sarah, Elisabeth, & Anna rocf West Branch MM OH

KAIN
12-24-1873	Salt rec in mbrp
6-28-1877	Salt Clermont Co OH s Henry C & Rebecca Clermont Co OH m Mary Ann dt Phineas R & Ruth Anna dec **Mather** at res her father Richmond
3-23-1889	Wm E & w Elizabeth L & min ch Albert F, Henry E, & Rachel Mamorah rec in mbrp
11-24-1894	Salt gct jas
11-26-1896	Albert H gct jas

KALE
5-25-1870	Martha M con mcd
8-27-1873	Wm H rec in mbrp

KAMINSKY
11-26-1896	Anna E rocf Smithfield MM OH
12-23-1897	Lillian V & Olive M rec in mbrp

KANNADA
9-30-1815	Robert gct New Garden MM

KEISTER
1-27-1898	May rec in mbrp

KELLEY
4-22-1893	Hannah & min ch Wm B, Edmond J, Myrtle W, & Carl rocf White River MM
4-27-1895	Oliver gct jas

KELLY
2-24-1810	Charity rocf New Garden MM NC
6-27-1827	Rebecca **(Coffin)** con mcd
11-23-1827	Rebecca gct Mill Creek MM OH
7-22-1835	Amy **(Underwood)** dis for mcd
4-27-1895	Oliver J rec in mbrp

KENADA
4-19-1815	Robert & s Joshua & Thomas rocf Lost Creek MM TN

KENDAL
3-27-1833	Wm gct Chester MM to m Abigail **Weisnor**
12-26-1849	Cyrus & w Lydia rocf Duck Creek MM

KENDALL
5-31-1817	Thomas & s Wm & David rocf Springfield MM NC; Elisabeth & dt Nancy & Margaret rocf Springfield MM NC
8-28-1833	Abigail rocf Chester MM
9-28-1836	Wm & w Abigail & min ch Mahlon & Enos gct Chester MM
10-25-1837	David gct Spiceland MM
1-28-1846	Cyrus gct Duck Creek MM
1-3-1849	Dennis s Thomas & Elizabeth Wayne Co m Rebecca Jane dt Harmon & Mary **Hill** Wayne Co at Whitewater MH
5-28-1851	Dennis & w Rebecca Jane & dt Margaretta gct Duck Creek MM
3-24-1852	Cyrus & w Lydia gct Duck Creek MM
1-4-1855	Mahlon s Williford & Abigail Wayne Co m Mary Elizabeth dt Joseph & Martha dec **Hill** Wayne Co at Smyrna MH
3-28-1855	Mary Elizabeth gct Chester MM
12-26-1855	Thomas gct Chester MM
4-26-1871	Margretta rocf Duck Creek MM
8-27-1873	Albert rocf Duck Creek MM
7-28-1881	Albert gct Duck Creek MM
3-23-1899	Albert gr another ct Duck Creek MM; one gr 7-28-1881 not rec

KENNADA
9-30-1815	Robert gct New Garden MM

KENNADY
8-26-1815	Wm rocf Lost Creek MM TN

KENNEDY
10-26-1816	Boater & s John, Wm, Walter, Boater, & Russel rocf Lost Creek MM TN
6-24-1846	Hannah & dt Jennette & Louisa rec in mbrp
2-28-1891	Cassius R & w Ella V & ch Omar R, Charles L, Roxy F, & Clara R rec in mbrp
7-23-1896	Cassius R & w Ella V & min ch Omar R, Charles L, Roxie F, & Clara gct Indianapolis MM

KENWORTHY
7-22-1829	David & s David, Amos, & Levi rocf New Garden MM; Hannah & dt Susannah rocf New Garden MM
7-27-1836	Wm rocf Elk MM OH
4-25-1838	David & w Hannah & dt Susannah gct Cherry Grove MM; David gct Spiceland MM; Martha gct Cherry Grove MM
9-25-1839	Levi gct Cherry Grove MM
5-27-1846	Jesse J rocf Elk MM OH

WHITEWATER MONTHLY MEETING
MINUTES AND MARRIAGES

KENWORTHY (cont)
5-26-1847	Joseph & w Anna rocf Elk MM OH
4-24-1850	Elizabeth & Mary rocf Elk MM OH
4-28-1852	Mary E rocf Miami MM OH
7-27-1853	Ann & dt Lina & Mary Ann rocf Cincinnati MM OH
4-22-1863	Joseph & w Anna & min ch Caroline & Wm gct Fairfield MM
1-27-1869	John R & w Rebecca J rocf Elk MM OH
3-26-1885	John R & w Rebecca J & min ch Lizzie Alice & Charles gct Rose Hill MM KS
8-25-1887	Thomas E rel fr mbrp
11-22-1890	Eli & w Rachel & min ch Elmira, Robert, & Harriet rocf Dover MM

KENYON
7-28-1847	Beriah & w Sarah & ch Charles, Eunice Ann, Mary, & Martha rocf Chester MM
10-27-1847	Hoxie rocf Chester MM
4-26-1848	John & w Asenath & dt Rebecca W rocf Chester MM
6-6-1850	Hoxie G s Beriah & Sarah Wayne Co m Jane S dt Eli & Martha **Brown** Wayne Co at Whitewater MH
11-26-1851	John & w Asenath & ch Rebecca W, Rhoda J, & Isaac Lindley gct Chester MM; Charles gct Chester MM
6-23-1852	Hoxie G & w Jane & s Charles G gct Westfield MM
11-24-1852	Beriah & w Sarah & ch Eunice Ann, Mary H, & Martha gct Westfield MM
3-28-1860	John H & w Asenith W & ch Rebecca W, Rhoda J, Isaac L, Addison G, & Albert M rocf Westfield MM; sent to KS PM

KEPLINGER
1-27-1887	Theodore & w Rosa & min dt Carrie R rocf White River MM
3-28-1891	Edward T rocf White River MM

KERSEY
9-26-1812	Cert rec for Thomas & fam fr Springfield MM NC; end to Center MM OH; cert rec for John, Mary, & Ann fr Springfield NC; end to Center MM OH
1-23-1863	Richard W, Charles S, Pliny Earl, & Margaret W ch Vierling & Mary rocf Milford MM
2-16-1885	Richard & Margaret gc
7-28-1887	Charles A dis for na & failing to comply with Friends' principles

KENSLER
3-22-1837	Ann rocf Mill Creek MM OH

KESSLER
5-23-1896	Hannah B & s Harry Nathan rec in mbrp

KIDD
5-22-1878	Francis A rec in mbrp
2-26-1885	Francis A drpd fr mbrp for na

KING
7-17-1824	John rocf Cincinnati MM OH; Mary & dt Phebe rocf Cincinnati MM OH
12-18-1824	Cert rec for Dean fr Miami MM OH; end to Springborough MM OH
5-14-1825	Thomas W & s John L & Henry D rocf Springborough MM OH; Sally & dt Mary E rocf Springborough MM OH
10-15-1825	Dean rocf Springborough MM OH
8-27-1828	Dean gct Center MM OH to m Esther **Carpenter**
3-25-1829	John dis for jas
6-24-1829	Thomas W dis for jas; Esther rocf Center MM
10-28-1829	Sally dis for jas
5-28-1834	Dean & w Esther & ch Mercy Ann, Mary, & Calvin gct Center MM OH
4-25-1838	Mary gct Center MM OH
12-26-1838	Mary rocf Center MM OH
11-25-1846	Mary gct Center MM OH

KING (cont)
9-24-1873	Ellen & ch Isaac, Rose, Estella, Emery, Zeno, Ruth, & Abner rocf Raysville MM
2-23-1882	Anna rq mbrp Richmond PM
4-27-1882	Anna removed
12-24-1885	Joseph A & Sarah E rec in mbrp; lt fr Grace ME ch
3-22-1888	Whitewater PM rpt Anna E rq mbrp
1-26-1889	Anna E withdraws rq for mbrp
1-26-1895	Almira rocf Chester MM
5-23-1896	G Sherman New Westville rec in mbrp
3-25-1897	Frances New Westville OH rec in mbrp

KINSEY
4-24-1839	Isaac, Thomas W, Sarah, & Abram rocf Baltimore MM MD
9-24-1845	Isaac dis for na jH, & dp; Sarah dis for jH
12-22-1847	Thomas W & Abram min s Oliver gct Cincinnati MM OH
12-27-1848	Abram & Thomas W dis for na & jH
11-22-1865	Thomas E rocf Miami MM OH
5-31-1873	Thomas B Marion Co s Wm E & Ann E dec Jefferson Co OH m Margaret dt Charles H & Mary S dec **Shoemaker** Wayne Co at res of her father
4-25-1884	Thomas E rel fr mbrp; jas
12-23-1886	Margaret glt Richmond 1st ME ch
8-22-1891	J Fremont drpd fr mbrp
4-24-1893	Thomas E & w Margaret S & min s Wm C rec in mbrp; lt fr Grace ME ch
7-22-1897	Maggie's d rpt; ae 48y

KINWORTHY
2-24-1830	David Jr gct Elk MM OH
12-22-1830	Martha rocf Cherry Grove MM
5-23-1832	Agnes gct Elk MM OH

KINZEY
4-24-1839	Sarah dt Oliver & Sarah rocf Baltimore MM MD

KIRBY
4-28-1830	Wm & Edward rocf Wilmington MM DE; Ann, Mary, & Elizabeth ch Mark & Mary rocf Wilmington MM DE
3-27-1833	Ann dis for jas
7-24-1839	Mary H dis for jH
7-24-1844	Edward dis for na & jH; Wm dis for na & mcd

KIRK
8-17-1822	Benjamin & s Wm & Benjamin rocf Alum Creek MM OH; Isiah rocf Alum Creek MM OH
11-15-1823	Isaiah gct Center MM OH to m Sarah W **Kirk**
3-20-1824	Sarah W rocf Center MM OH
3-19-1825	Rebecca con mcd
9-17-1825	Rebecca gct Center MM OH
1-28-1829	Benjamin dis for jH
3-24-1830	Sarah Jr dis for jas
9-22-1830	Isaiah dis for jas
1-26-1831	Sarah W dis for jas
4-22-1835	Mahlon & Hannah Jane ch Isiah & Sarah gct Milford MM
4-26-1848	Charles min nephew Benjamin & Lydia **Bond** rocf Salem MM
4-24-1850	Sarah & min s Samuel **Test** & Israel E & niece Elizabeth **Test** rocf Salem MM
3-24-1858	Samuel T gct Plainfield MM
9-22-1858	Charles W gct Center MM OH to m Rachel **Hollingsworth**
11-23-1859	Israel E gct Plainfield MM
2-22-1860	Charles W gct Plainfield MM
10-23-1884	Charles W & w Rachel & dt Anne Ethel rocf Kokomo MM
1-28-1886	Dr Charles W minister & w Rachel gct Shawneetown MM Indian Terr

KIRKMAN
3-25-1874	Nannie E & Wm H rec in mbrp
4-25-1877	Elizabeth rocf Cherry Grove MM
4-26-1883	Elizabeth, Alonzo, Lule, & Mattie Centreville rec in mbrp
6-28-1883	Alva, Lula, & Mattie Centreville rec in mbrp; Ella May & Bessie Eveline ch Alva & Elizabeth Centreville rec in mbrp; Elizabeth w Alva already mbr
12-26-1891	Elizabeth, Alva, Ella May, Mattie, Lulu, & Bessie Evaline not found
8-26-1893	Ella rec in mbrp
1-27-1894	Ella rel fr mbrp; jas
8-27-1896	James M & w Flora rec in mbrp
8-26-1897	Lelia rocf Dover MM

KIRKPATRICK
1-28-1886	George H & w Ellen M & ch Vernie H, Audra J, & Earl M rec in mbrp
8-24-1889	George & w Ellen H & ch Vernie H, Audra J, Earl H, & Sarah E rel fr mbrp; j UB ch

KISKADDEN
5-25-1889	Sarah J (White) rel fr mbrp; j Detroit MI 2nd Congregational ch

KITSELMAN
5-25-1870	Margaret M (Burns) con mcd
2-26-1885	Margaret M, Marietta, Albert Leroy, Franklin E, & Alfred W drpd fr mbrp

KITTERAL
5-27-1868	Henrietta Helena AR rec in mbrp

KNIGHT
10-29-1814	Thomas & s John, Benjamin, Solomon, & James rocf Piney Grove MM SC; Christian & dt Betsy Rachel & Sarah rocf Piney Grove MM SC

KNOTT
4-22-1886	Wm & w Isabella & min s Arthur rec in mbrp
8-23-1890	Wm rel fr mbrp; Isabelle drpd fr mbrp for na & unbecoming behavior

KOON
4-28-1841	Benjamin dis for na

KOONS
12-29-1810	Gasper Jr rpt for dr & upl
1-26-1811	Gasper con for dr & upl
2-24-1830	Henry & Nathan gct White Lick MM
10-22-1834	Jeremiah dis for na
1-27-1836	Joseph dis for na mcd, & dp
11-22-1837	Hannah dis for na & jas
7-23-1845	Samuel dis for na jas, & dp
8-23-1876	Jeremiah rst
5-27-1897	Sherman & Francis Providence & Friendship Darke Co OH rec in mbrp
7-28-1898	Sherman & w Fannie T gct New Garden MM

KRAMER
10-26-1889	Mary J rocf Clear Creek MM OH
2-28-1891	Charles T rec in mbrp
7-23-1896	Charles T & w Mary J gct Indianapolis MM

KROSHER
3-20-1824	Susannah (Baldwin) dis for mcd

KUTH
2-25-1897	Nicholas New Westville OH rec in mbrp
4-28-1898	Jennie rec in mbrp

LACEY
9-23-1824	Pearson s Peter & Susanna Wayne Co m Margaret dt Jesse & Mary Morris Wayne Co at Ridge MH

LACY
11-9-1814	John s Peter & Susanna Wayne Co m Penina dt Thomas & Anna both dec Hill Wayne Co at Whitewater MH
11-25-1815	Peter & s Pearson & Josiah rocf Back Creek MM NC; Susannah & dt Susannah & Ruth rocf Back Creek MM NC
3-25-1829	Margaret & dt Sarah Ann gct Duck Creek MM

LADD
8-24-1848	Wm H Jefferson Co OH s Benjamin W & Elizabeth dec m Caroline E dt Elijah & Naomi Coffin Wayne Co at Whitewater MH
10-25-1848	Caroline Elizabeth gct Smithfield MM OH

LAIRD
3-23-1899	George Andrew New Westville OH rec in mbrp
5-25-1899	George rocf Van Wert MM OH
10-26-1899	Mildred Elizabeth dt G Andrew rocf Van Wert MM OH

LAMAR
7-28-1898	Franklin & w Zitella rec in mbrp
11-23-1899	Frank & w Zitella gct Wilmington MM OH

LAMB
3-27-1813	Thomas rocf Elk MM OH
8-4-1813	Thomas Wayne Co s Phenias dec & Dorotha NC m Sarah dt John & Letitia Smith Wayne Co at Whitewater MH
3-26-1814	Josiah & s John, Jonathan, Esaw, & Rueben rocf Mill Creek MM OH; Naomi & dt Hannah, Ruth, Nancy, & Elisabeth rocf Mill Creek MM OH
9-29-1814	John s Josiah & Naomi Wayne Co m Lydia dt Aaron dec & Miriam Mendenhall Wayne Co at New Garden MH
11-29-1817	Hosea & Barnaba rocf Piney Woods MM NC
8-29-1818	Josiah rocf Piney Woods MM NC
12-26-1818	Hosea con mcd
6-24-1820	Mary rec in mbrp; Restore s Hosea rec in mbrp
9-30-1820	Josiah gct Piney Grove MM SC
12-30-1820	Eli rocf Piney Woods MM NC
4-28-1821	Barnabas con mcd
7-28-1821	Eli gct New Garden MM
6-18-1823	Miles rocf Piney Woods MM NC
5-23-1827	Miles con mcd
6-27-1827	Miles gct Duck Creek MM
7-25-1827	Rueben rocf New Garden MM
6-23-1830	Willis rocf Piney Woods MM NC
9-22-1830	Willis gct Piney Woods MM NC
1-23-1833	Cert rec for Caleb fr Marlborough MM NC; end to Arba MM
6-26-1833	Barna dis for na
9-23-1835	Hosea & w Mary & min ch Restor, Elizabeth, Rhoda, Anna, Sarah, & John gct White River MM
4-26-1837	Thomas gct Duck Creek MM to m Margaret Ratliff
9-27-1837	Margaret A rocf Duck Creek MM
4-27-1842	Isaac gct Salem MM IA
10-23-1844	Isaac rocf Salem MM IA
8-25-1847	Phineas con mcd
7-26-1848	Rebecca rocf Piney Woods MM NC
12-24-1856	Rebecca & ch Vashti, Rosanna, Thomas, Isaac Newton, & Albert rec in mbrp
11-24-1869	Vashti (Lamb) rpt mcd
1-26-1870	Vashti gct Milford MM
7-25-1877	Phineas drpd fr mbrp; jas
9-20-1883	Elizabeth rec in mbrp
12-27-1883	Clarkey Jane & ch Albert Bernard & Olive Afton rocf New Garden MM
4-23-1885	Isaac rel fr mbrp
12-26-1891	Rebecca & 3 s undecided as to which mtg to att; Thomas, Isaac, Albert S, & Rebecca not found
3-23-1895	Thomas J, Mary, Hannah C, & Eliza E rec in mbrp

WHITEWATER MONTHLY MEETING
MINUTES AND MARRIAGES

LAMB (cont)
6-24-1897 John E & w Leonna & ch Raymond, Catherine M, & Edgar H rocf Springfield MM

LANCASTER
6-25-1845 Hannah (**Rue**) con mcd, na & dp
5-27-1846 Hannah gct Mississinewa MM
6-27-1849 Hannah rocf Mississinewa MM
8-28-1850 Hannah gct Mississinewa MM

LANE
3-18-1826 Isabella (**Trueblood**) dis for mcd
2-28-1866 Lydia & dt Phebe rocf Elk MM OH

LANGDEN
4-3-1884 Frank Warren s Oliver O & Jane D Cincinnati Hamilton Co OH m Rhoda Alice dt Samuel F & Elizabeth D Fletcher Richmond at Richmond

LANGSTOWN
3-28-1877 Emily Quakertown rec in mbrp

LAW
7-27-1870 Jennie (**Marquis**) rpt mcd

LAWRENCE
7-23-1879 Hannah rocf Chester MM
12-28-1882 Hannah rec as minister
5-22-1884 Christopher & fam rocf Chester MM
5-28-1885 Dan & w Mary Jane rec in mbrp
10-26-1889 Dan K & w Mary Jane gct Indianapolis MM
9-24-1892 Mary E & ch Alvin Leroy, Anna Leota, & Benjamin Otho rec in mbrp
11-25-1893 Jesse & w Lucy A & ch Eli Verlin, Lillian M, Alice M, & Thomas Everett rocf Fairmount MM
12-23-1893 Inez Maria inf dt Jesse rec in mbrp

LAWS
12-26-1827 John M rec in mbrp
1-30-1828 John M Wayne Co s Clement dec & Mary Philadelphia PA m Joanna dt Joseph & Susanna dec **Plummer** Wayne Co at Whitewater MH
4-22-1829 John M & Joanna dis for jas
10-27-1830 Cert rec for Melson fr Philadelphia MM PA; not acc because he att Separatist mtgs
7-26-1869 Cornelia rec in mbrp
3-23-1870 Cornelia rel fr mbrp

LAYMAN
10-25-1833 Abraham gct NY MM NY
3-23-1882 Aaron rec in mbrp
10-25-1883 Abraham rocf NY MM NY

LEDBEATER
6-22-1859 Wm rocf Carlow MM Ireland

LEDBETTER
2-25-1829 Phebe rocf Deep River MM NC

LEE
1-23-1833 Nathan & s Ishmael, Hiram, Henry, & Nathan rocf Newberry MM TN; Hannah & dt Anne & Charlotte rocf Newberry MM TN
7-24-1833 Ishmael dis for na & jas
10-26-1836 Nathan & w Hannah & ch Charlotte, Hiram, & Henry gct Mississinewa MM
8-26-1840 Mississinewa MM gr perm to rec Ishmael
5-27-1897 Wm, Margaret, Mary, Pearl, Melva, & Clifton Providence & Friendship Darke Co OH rec in mbrp

LEEDS
10-29-1822 Warner M rocf Miami MM OH; Elizabeth & dt Anna rocf Miami MM OH

LEEDS (cont)
4-16-1825 Warner M & w Elizabeth & ch Anna, Wm B, & Noah S gct Springborough MM OH
7-25-1827 Warner M & s Wm B & Noah L rocf Springborough MM OH; Elizabeth B & dt Anna rocf Springborough MM OH
1-27-1830 Warner M dis for jas
6-23-1830 Elisabeth B dis for jas
4-25-1832 Vencent Augustus & Wm s Noah & Ann rocf Springborough MM
4-25-1832 Ann C rocf Springborough MM
7-25-1832 Vincent rocf New Garden MM OH
9-28-1836 Ann C dis for jH
8-23-1843 Wm s Noah gct Milford MM
1-27-1847 Wm B dis for jH
12-22-1847 Noah dis for na
4-26-1848 Catharine dis for jH

LEFEVER
2-28-1855 Rachel rocf Scipio MM NY
7-25-1881 Alfred gct Indianapolis MM
4-26-1883 Rebecca gct Indianapolis MM

LEFEVERE
7-27-1853 Wm M & w Rebecca & ch Frederick Smith, Alfred Henry, & Ellen Maria rocf Scipio MM NY

LEFEVRE
11-26-1856 Rachel gct Salem MM IA
1-27-1881 Frederick S gct Indianapolis MM
7-27-1882 Alfred H rel fr mbrp to j United Presb ch
2-23-1889 Rebecca gct Indianapolis MM

LEHMAN
3-28-1891 David E & w Harriett B rec in mbrp

LEWALLEN
5-29-1819 Meshack gct New Garden MM

LEWALLIN
9-14-1822 Cert rec for Meshack & s Henry, Henderson, John, Seth, & Wm fr Back Creek MM NC; end to West Grove MM

LEWELLIN
3-28-1812 Meshach rec in mbrp
6-28-1817 Meshach con telling untruths

LEWIS
9-24-1814 Thomas & s Zimri, Wm, Isaac, David, & Thomas rocf Caesar's Creek MM OH; Rachel & dt Martha Sally, Katturah, & Elisabeth rocf Caesar's Creek MM OH
8-30-1817 Zimri con mcd
5-30-1818 Zimri gct Silver Creek MM
8-29-1818 Wm con for telling falsities
10-31-1818 Wm gct Silver Creek MM
2-28-1827 Nathan & s Josiah rocf Cherry Grove MM; Rachel & dt Sarah, Martha Rachel, & Susanna rocf Cherry Grove MM
9-28-1842 Nathan & fam gct Hopewell MM
10-12-1842 Josiah T gct Hopewell MM
10-26-1842 Rachel & min ch Susanna, Stephen, Emaline, & John Milton gct Hopewell MM
2-22-1843 Rachel M gct Hopewell MM
4-24-1844 Martha C gct Hopewell MM
8-28-1844 Nathan dis for not paying debts
9-28-1848 Josiah T gct Hopewell MM
2-23-1853 Ann L & ch Margaret Ann, Joseph T, & Lucy J rocf Cincinnati MM OH
8-25-1869 Joseph T rel fr mbrp
6-22-1882 Clark E rocf Saline MM IL
2-26-1885 Ellen C gc

LEWIS (cont)

7-23-1892	Clark E & w Emma E B & min ch Sarah T, Esther B, Jesse E, & Seth B gct Short Creek MM OH
12-22-1898	Clark E & w Emma B & ch Sarah T, Esther B, Jesse E, & Seth B rocf Short Creek MM OH

LINDEMOTH

7-27-1882	John rec in mbrp

LINDEMUTH

12-22-1894	Victoria E rec in mbrp; lt fr Grace ME ch

LINDLEY

10-26-1811	Jonathan & s Wm & Jonathan rocf Spring MM NC; Owen & s Thomas, Jonathan, Wm, & Aron rocf Spring MM NC; Thomas & s Jacob, Samuel, Abraham, & Wm rocf Spring MM NC; Deborah & dt Deborah, Mary, Esther, Catherine, & Sarah rocf Spring MM NC; Grace & dt Sarah, Hannah, Mary, Elizabeth, & Amy rocf Spring MM NC; Jane & dt Mary & Deborah rocf Spring MM NC
11-30-1811	Wm & s David, James, Owen, Wm, & Jonathan rocf Spring MM NC; Amey & dt Mary, Emmy, Margery, & Grace rocf Spring MM NC
8-29-1812	Wm & Amy appt o at Lick Creek MM; Jonathan gct Fairfield MM OH
12-26-1812	Martha & ch Mary, Rebeckah Henley, Hezekiah, John, Joseph, & Henry rocf Fairfield MM OH
10-30-1813	Cert rec for Thomas fr Spring MM NC; end to Lick Creek MM

LIPPENCOTT

3-27-1844	Samuel R dis for na & mcd

LIPPINCOT

4-27-1842	Samuel R rocf Haddonfield MM NJ

LIPPINCOTT

2-26-1846	Benjamin R rocf Philadelphia MM PA
11-27-1878	Benjamin R drpd fr mbrp; jas

LISTON

7-19-1823	Wm & s James Thomas, Jonathan Allee, & Wm Maurice rocf Sadsbury MM PA; Margaret & dt Jane Reese rocf Sadsbury MM PA
2-25-1829	Wm dis for na; James dis for na; residing in Winchester Randolph Co
3-25-1829	Margaret & Jane dis for jH
4-22-1835	Wm Morris gct Mississinewa MM

LITTLE

8-28-1861	David & ch Miriam, Anna, & Jane rocf White River MM; Mary rec in mbrp
3-23-1864	David & w Mary & ch Miriam, Anna, & Jane gct Chester MM
9-26-1883	David rocf Chester MM
1-1-1885	David wid Wayne Co m Martha **Bond** wid Peter dt Frederick & Piety **Fulghum** Randolph Co at Richmond 12 St MH

LONGSTREET

4-22-1886	Josephine rec in mbrp

LOSEY

8-27-1873	Phebe (**Hunt**) rel fr mbrp to jas; rpt mou

LUNCHFORD

1-27-1869	Adeline (**Elmore**) con mcd

LUNDY

7-23-1896	Martha rocf West Grove MM

LUNSFORD

3-25-1874	Benjamin rec in mbrp
3-25-1897	Mattie Jones gct Chester MM

LYLE

5-23-1838	Amy (**Cox**) dis for mcd

LYNDE

8-23-1843	Sarah (**Dugdale**) dis for mcd

McADAMS

2-23-1882	Maggie rq mbrp Richmond PM
5-25-1882	Maggie drpd fr cons for mbrp
1-24-1884	Maggie rq for mbrp drpd
1-24-1891	Bertha rec in mbrp

McCALL

2-23-1831	Wm, John, Joel, & James s John & Margaret rocf Newberry MM OH
9-28-1831	Susannah & Mary dis for na & dp
7-27-1832	Dorcas dis for na & dp
8-23-1837	Wm dis for na & mcd
10-24-1838	Margaret dis for na & being out of unity
5-22-1839	John dis for na
5-27-1840	Margaret & James min gct White Lick MM
10-28-1840	Cert for Margaret & James ret by White Lick MM; did not res within their limits
11-25-1842	Margaret, James, & Martha Jane ch John & Margaret gct Fairfield MM

McCAY

8-23-1871	Joanna (**McFerran**) con mcd

McCLURE

2-24-1893	Nathaniel D & w Letitia rec in mbrp
3-23-1895	Joseph rec in mbrp
5-27-1897	George & Eunice Providence & Friendship Darke Co OH rec in mbrp

McCOLL

2-23-1831	Margaret & dt Mary, Susanna, Doracas, & Margaret rocf Newberry MM OH

McCRACKEN

5-27-1815	Nathan con for dr
9-30-1815	Nathan given a few lines as he has a prospect of going to NC
2-28-1816	Nathan dis for dr, absconding with debts unpaid
8-27-1885	Mary Jane rocf New Garden MM
9-23-1886	Mary Jane gct Pasadena MM CA

McCRAKEN

3-25-1815	Nathan rocf Center MM NC

McDEVITT

12-28-1882	James H & w Mary J & ch Claude H, Cocoa Blanche, Francis G, & Rocoe C rocf Georgetown MM IL
4-23-1885	James H & fam drpd fr mbrp

McDIVITT

2-26-1885	Mary J, Claude H, Cocoa Blanche, Francis G, & Rosco C gc

McDONALD

2-25-1893	Wm & w Carrie & dt Orissa rocf West Branch MM

McDOWELL

12-22-1869	Andrew rec in mbrp
8-26-1874	Andrew J dis for na

McFERRAN

12-25-1867	Joanna rec in mbrp

WHITEWATER MONTHLY MEETING
MINUTES AND MARRIAGES

McGRAW
5-23-1872   George & w Anna M & ch Steward M, Charles T, & Martha E rec in mbrp
2-23-1876   George M & w Anna M & min ch Stewart Maddison, Charles Thomas, Martha Ellen, & Flora Alice gct Mississinewa MM

McKEE
11-26-1873   Wm rec in mbrp

McLAIN
11-26-1814   John & s Samuel rocf Mt Pleasant MM VA; Margaret rocf Mt Pleasant MM VA
1-17-1824   James con for dr
3-19-1825   John con for dr
4-15-1826   John con dr
2-25-1829   John dis for jas
3-25-1829   Catherine dis for jas

McLANE
4-27-1816   Catherine con mcd

McLAUGHLIN
11-27-1872   Philip & w Asenath rocf Indianapolis MM
4-28-1875   Philip & Asenath rel fr mbrp

McLUCAS
4-23-1862   Emily (**Haworth**) dis for mcd

McMILLAN
6-28-1848   Jane rocf Salem MM

McMULLEN
12-22-1887   Etta **Hatfield** & Ada **McMullen** (or Ada **Mullen**) dt Wm **Stanley** drpd fr mbrp for na

McPHERSON
12-25-1833   John rec in mbrp
4-26-1837   John T gct MM in NC
4-28-1869   John W rocf Fairfield MM OH
4-22-1874   John H rec in mbrp

McTAGGART
8-26-1868   Alpheus rec in mbrp
7-26-1871   Alpheus gct Pickering MM Canada to m Caroline **Richardson**
5-23-1872   Caroline rocf Pickering MM Canada
8-27-1896   Emma drpd fr mbrp
2-24-1898   Alpheus & w Caroline rel fr mbrp

McWHINNEY
4-28-1898   John rec in mbrp

MACKIE
5-27-1897   James, Rebecca, George, & Grace Providence & Friendship Darke Co OH rec in mbrp

MACY
7-25-1818   Cert rec for Wm & s Obed, Tristram, Stephen, John, Jonathan, Rueben, & Franklin fr Center MM NC; end to Silver Creek MM
7-29-1820   Thomas rec in mbrp
4-28-1821   Cert rec for Phebe fr New Garden MM NC; end to West Grove MM
4-22-1824   Nathan s Zackeus & Sarah Union Co m Catherine dt Jeremiah & Keren **Parker** Wayne Co at Orange Mtg
12-18-1824   Catherine gct Silver Creek MM
6-27-1827   Stephen & s Eli, Francis, & Stephen rocf Mill Creek MM OH; Rebecca & dt Anna & Unice rocf Mill Creek MM OH
9-26-1832   John gct Chester MM to m Beulah **Hunt**
12-26-1832   Francis gct Duck Creek MM
3-27-1833   Beulah rocf Chester MM

MACY (cont)
8-28-1833   John & w Mary gct Silver Creek MM
6-4-1834   Francis B Henry Co s Stephen & Rebecca Wayne Co m Huldah B dt Isom dec **Hunt** Guilford Co NC at Whitewater MH
7-23-1834   Huldah B gct Duck Creek MM
8-26-1835   Stephen Jr gct Duck Creek MM
7-27-1836   Stephen Jr rocf Duck Creek MM
5-24-1837   Stephen & w Rebecca & dt Eunice B & grch Rebecca & Eli **Sweet** gct Spiceland MM
3-28-1838   Stephen Jr gct Spiceland MM
5-23-1839   Stephen s Stephan & Rebecca Henry Co m Mary dt John & Elvira both dec **Charles** Wayne Co at Whitewater MH
11-27-1839   Mary gct Spiceland MM
11-26-1851   John M & w Betsy Ann & ch Henrietta Maria, Margaret White, & Wm Allen rocf Spiceland MM
10-26-1853   John M & w Betsy Ann & ch Henrietta Maria, Margaret White & Wm Allen gct Spiceland MM
4-25-1855   Phebe Ann rec in mbrp

MADDEN
4-28-1821   Solomon gct Springfield MM OH
2-28-1827   Susannah gct Springfield MM OH

MADDOCK
12-27-1883   John C & w Rachel H rocf Duck Creek MM
1-24-1884   Martha Ellen & Anna B rocf Elk MM OH; end by Duck Creek MM
1-28-1886   Alma rq cert to Duck Creek MM
9-21-1889   Francis rocf Elk MM OH

MADEN
3-25-1820   Solomon rocf Springfield MM OH
1-3-1827   Hiram s George dec & Elizabeth Clinton Co OH m Susanna dt Jehu & Sarah **Stuart** Wayne Co at Whitewater MH

MAHEW
2-27-1892   Catherine drpd fr mbrp

MALES
4-22-1886   Samuel R & w Jennie & dt Maud Bertie rec in mbrp

MALOTT
3-26-1892   James A rec in mbrp
8-26-1893   James gct Van Wert MM OH

MANIFOLD
7-31-1819   Susannah (**Butler**) con mcd
8-14-1824   Susannah gct Springfield MM

MANLEY
10-25-1890   Wm F & w Lydia G & dt Estella & Pearl Charlotte rocf Westfield MM
2-28-1891   Herbert, Hettie, Lydia, Ernest G, & Ruth ch Wm & Lydia rec in mbrp
2-24-1898   Estella gct Stanford MM NY
9-21-1899   Earnest rel fr mbrp

MARCHANT
8-22-1891   Mary J rel fr mbrp

MARCUS
11-28-1866   Mary (**Cockayne**) con mcd

MARDECK
9-24-1814   Ann & dt Elisabeth & Susannah rocf Newberry MM TN

MARDOCK
9-24-1814   Isaac rocf Newberry MM TN
8-31-1816   James rocf Newberry MM TN

MARINE
7-27-1811	Jonathan & s John & Asa rocf Piney Grove MM SC
5-30-1812	Jonathan appt o at New Garden

MARIS
10-26-1811	John rocf Spring MM NC
11-30-1811	Thomas rocf Center MM NC; Jane & dt Sarah, Elinor, Mary, & Ann rocf Center MM NC
10-30-1813	Eli rocf Symons Creek MM NC

MARLOTT
2-26-1880	Laura B rec in mbrp

MARMON
11-28-1827	Rachel & s David, James, & Benjamin Franklin rocf Marlborough MM NC
9-23-1829	Betsy dis for unchastity
5-28-1834	David dis for mcd, na, & dp
11-26-1840	James W s Martin & Susanna Logan Co OH m Hannah **Craig** dt Charles & Elizabeth **Moffit** Wayne Co at Whitewater MH
4-22-1846	James N & w Hannah C & ch Wm, Ann, Harriet, Mary, Charles Moffitt, & Daniel W rocf Goshen MM OH
9-15-1870	Charles M & Daniel con mcd
9-21-1870	Elizabeth **(Carpenter)** con mcd
11-23-1870	Ann gct Goshen MM OH
5-23-1877	Daniel W & w Elizabeth C & min ch Walter C & Howard C gct Indianapolis MM

MARQUIS
3-25-1868	Jennie rec in mbrp
2-26-1885	Mary, Harry, Charles, Olive, & Jennie drpd fr mbrp

MARSHAL
2-23-1822	Susannah rocf Back Creek MM NC

MARSHALL
2-25-1815	Thomas & s Wm & Miles rocf Lost Creek MM TN; Hannah rocf Lost Creek MM TN
12-30-1815	Miles & s Thomas & Mitchel rocf Lost Creek MM TN
1-27-1816	John & Jacob rocf Lost Creek MM TN
5-31-1817	Miles & fam gct New Garden MM; Martha & ch gct New Garden MM
12-18-1824	Susannah gct Springfield MM
1-26-1831	Jacob dis for mcd & jH
1-25-1896	Margaret rocf Springfield MM
10-28-1897	Abbie rocf Dover MM

MARSHILL
12-30-1815	Martha rocf Lost Creek MM TN

MARTIN
6-26-1819	James & Sarah rec in mbrp
3-15-1823	James & fam gct West Grove MM
8-26-1835	Susannah **(Koons)** dis for na & mcd
3-27-1839	Isaac H rec in mbrp
7-4-1839	Isaac N s John & Ruth Wayne Co m Elizabeth L dt John L & Sarah **Reed** Wayne Co at Smyrna Mtg
9-24-1845	Isaac N dis for na & mcd
7-25-1877	Ruth A, Elmira B, Alpheus, Thomas Caldwell, & Benjamin Leroy drpd fr mbrp
2-23-1889	Alice rec in mbrp

MARTINDALE
10-27-1894	John & w Amanda rocf West Grove MM

MARVEL
10-18-1893	Charles Philadelphia PA s Josiah P & Harriett A Sussex Co DE m MaryAmy dt Benjamin & Elizabeth **Johnson** Wayne Co at Richmond MH
11-26-1896	Dr Charles & s Josiah Philip rec in mbrp

MASON
10-26-1816	Thomas rec in mbrp
7-29-1820	Grizzel & dt Edith rec in mbrp
10-19-1822	Thomas Jr dis
11-16-1822	Grazil dis for dp & na
9-26-1838	White River MM gr perm to rst Thomas
10-24-1838	Mary gct White River MM

MASSEY
11-25-1809	Jane rocf Center MM
6-24-1815	Jane gct New Garden MM

MATHER
8-29-1844	Phineas R s Richard & Elizabeth Warren Co OH m Ruth Ann dt John R & Elizabeth **Pool** Wayne Co at Richmond Mtg
2-26-1845	Ruth Ann gct Miami MM OH
10-24-1849	Phineas R & w Ruth Ann & ch John P & Elizabeth C rocf Miami MM OH
3-23-1870	Hannah gct Chicago MM IL
4-28-1881	Henry rocf Miami MM OH
5-28-1885	John P rel fr mbrp
7-22-1886	Henry rel fr mbrp; jas
2-23-1889	Emma R rel fr mbrp; jas
8-27-1896	Louisa A rec in mbrp

MATHERS
10-28-1863	Hannah G rocf Salem MM IA

MATTHEWS
10-23-1867	Mary & dt Anna rec in mbrp
5-26-1869	Mary Grace rec in mbrp
3-23-1870	Hannah gct Chicago MM

MAUDLIN
9-30-1809	Benjamin appt o
10-28-1809	Leah appt to comm to inquire into Mary **Price**'s clearness in m
10-26-1816	Wm & s John, Levi, Richard, & Wm rocf Deep Creek MM NC; Anne & dt Betty rocf Deep Creek MM NC; Ann & Hannah rocf Deep Creek MM NC
11-30-1816	John & s Charles rocf Deep Creek MM NC; George & s Dillon, & Rueben rocf Deep Creek MM NC; Strah & dt Rhoda A & Nancy rocf Deep River MM NC
3-29-1817	Wright con getting into a passion & fighting
12-4-1817	Wright s Benjamin & Leah Wayne Co m Mary dt Jehu & Mary **Wickersham** Wayne Co at West Grove MH
11-28-1818	Charles gct Deep Creek MM NC
9-25-1819	John gct New Garden MM
3-25-1820	Miriam **(Peacock)** con mcd
7-29-1820	George & fam gct New Garden MM; Sarah & dt gct New Garden MM
8-26-1820	Enoch rec in mbrp
10-16-1824	Enoch & w Miriam & ch Eliza & Henry gct Milford MM
6-28-1883	Nathan Centreville rq mbrp
8-23-1883	Abraham rec in mbrp
12-27-1883	Nathan, Betsy, & John rq PM at Centerville
2-24-1887	Nathan gct West Grove MM

MAUL
7-25-1873	Benjamin, Isaac, & John con mcd

MAULE
11-25-1857	Thomas & w Priscilla & ch Thomas Benjamin, Wm, John, & Isaac rec in mbrp
8-25-1875	Isaac dis for na
8-26-1886	Wm, John, & Benjamin drpd fr mbrp

MAXWELL
12-31-1814	John & stepch James, Dillon, & Richard **Hayworth** rocf Lost Creek MM TN; Hannah & Jacob rocf Lost Creek MM TN

WHITEWATER MONTHLY MEETING
MINUTES AND MARRIAGES

MAXWELL (cont)

2-2-1815	Jacob Franklin Co s Hugh & Elizabeth TN m Margaret dt John & Margaret **Heavenridge** Franklin Co at Silver Creek MH
4-27-1816	Hugh & s Wm, Thomas, Hugh, & David rocf Lost Creek MM TN; Hannah & dt Hannah, Mary, Rachel, Ruth, Matilda, & Lydia rocf Lost Creek MM TN
5-1-1817	Wm s Hugh & Elizabeth Franklin Co m Charity dt Isaac & Susanna **Wright** Franklin Co at Silver Creek MH
10-7-1819	Thomas s Hugh & Elizabeth Franklin Co m Jemima dt John & Sarah dec **Clark** Wayne Co at Elkhorn MH
4-29-1820	Jemima gct Silver Creek MM
1-28-1829	Sarah (**Clark**) dis for mcd
4-22-1829	Sarah dis for jas
4-28-1858	Hugh W & w Ruth Ann & ch Mary, Sarah, Caroline, Emeline Ann, Lindley H, & Albert D rocf West Grove MM
8-29-1860	Benjamin F s Hugh & Anna Union Co m Sarah S dt Wm A & Sarah M both dec **Rambo** Wayne Co at Whitewater MH
12-26-1860	Sarah Sylvania gct West Grove MM
1-1-1862	Hugh W s John & Hannah both dec Wayne Co m Miriam A **Rambo** wid dt Elijah & Naomi **Coffin** Wayne Co at Whitewater MH
6-22-1864	Ann Elizabeth (**Moore**) con mcd
12-28-1864	Ann Elizabeth gct West Grove MM
7-26-1869	Mary Anna (**Moore**) dis for mcd
10-27-1877	Emily rocf West Grove MM
4-28-1881	Hugh W & w Miriam A gct Peace MM KS; Lindley H rel fr mbrp
1-25-1883	Sarah gct Sterling MM KS/MO

MAYE
4-22-1886	Wm rec in mbrp

MAYHEW
10-23-1872 mbrp	Elizabeth & ch Margaret M & Catherine L rec in

MAYS
4-22-1886	Wm min rq mbrp

MEEK
7-27-1816	Gulielma (**Smith**) dis for mcd

MEEKER
5-23-1849	Davis & w Emeline & ch Benjamin, Harriet, Mary, & Louisa rocf Poplar Run MM; Robert B rocf Poplar Run MM
9-24-1851	Robert B gct Poplar Run MM
4-28-1852	Davis & w Emeline & ch Harriet, Mary, & Louisa gct White Lick MM; Benjamin gct White Lick MM

MEEKS
5-28-1892	John Wesley rocf New Garden MM

MENDENHALL
11-30-1811	Isaac & s Stephen & Samuel rocf Springfield MM NC; Mary rocf Springfield MM NC
2-26-1812	Wm White s Isaac rec in mbrp
5-29-1813	Mary rec in mbrp
1-29-1814	Dinah rocf Piney Grove MM SC
2-26-1814	Wm White s Wm rec in mbrp
12-28-1816	Dinah gct New Garden MM
9-26-1818	Cert rec for Mordecai fr Miami MM OH; end to West Grove MM
3-27-1819	John & s Elijah rocf Elk MM OH; Margaret & dt Hannah rocf Elk MM OH
12-25-1819	Griffith rocf West Branch MM OH
5-31-1820	Griffith Wayne Co s Caleb & Susannah OH m Elizabeth **Swindler** dt John **Ary** dec at Whitewater MH

MENDENHALL (cont)

7-20-1822	John & w Margaret & dt Hannah & Mary gct Elk MM OH
10-15-1825	Paris rocf Deep River MM NC
11-19-1825	Elijah & s Joseph Coffin, Daniel, Anderson, & John B rocf Deep River MM NC; Huldah rocf Deep River MM NC
4-15-1826	Elijah & w Huldah & ch Joseph C, Daniel, Anderson, & John B gct West Grove MM
1-24-1827	Cert rec for Wm & s Oliver L fr Deep River MM NC; end to West Grove MM
7-25-1827	Paris gct White Lick MM
3-26-1828	Sarah (**Williams**) dis for mcd
5-23-1832	Cert rec for David fr Deep River MM NC; end to West Grove MM
3-25-1835	Caleb Jr & w & s Lewis & Betsy **Vanhorn** min rocf West Branch MM OH
4-22-1835	Ann rocf West Branch MM OH
8-26-1835	Phebe & s Linus & Enos rocf West Branch MM OH
11-23-1836	Phebe dis for jH
10-24-1838	Susannah rocf West Branch MM OH
2-26-1840	Ann & s Lewis gct Spiceland MM
7-28-1841	Caleb dis for na & not paying debts
2-28-1844	Griffith dis for na & jas
3-25-1846	Bently dis for na, dp, & mcd
5-27-1846	Richard rocf White Lick MM
6-24-1846	Elizabeth dis for jas
4-25-1849	Richard gct Hopewell MM to m Sarah Ann **Nixon**
6-26-1850	Sarah Ann & s Charles rocf Hopewell MM
7-24-1850	Richard & w Sarah Ann & s Charles gct White Lick MM
11-27-1850	Reese con mcd
7-23-1851	Lydia rec in mbrp; Wm s Reese J & Lydia rec in mbrp
6-22-1853	Stephen C rocf West Grove MM
7-27-1853	James & w Millicent & ch Olinda B, Sarah E, Hannah B, Joseph C, & James Carver rocf Sugar Plain MM
5-3-1854	Stephen C s James & Milicent Wayne Co m Rachel A dt John & Judith both dec **Johnson** Warren Co OH at Whitewater MH
7-26-1854	Caleb S gct Sugar Plain MM
3-23-1859	Wm rocf Short Creek MM OH
1-28-1863	Lindley dis for mcd
6-24-1863	John & w Hannah & s Charles W rocf Short Creek MM OH; Lydia A rocf Short Creek MM OH
9-23-1863	Naomi J (**Allen**) con mcd
4-26-1865	Elizabeth M rocf West Branch MM OH
10-23-1867	Henry W rst; dis for taking part in military operations during war
12-26-1867	Wm s John & Hannah Wayne Co m Hannah N dt Wm & Rachel S **Lancaster** at Richmond Mtg
11-24-1869	Henry W gct Cincinnati MM OH
9-15-1870	John A con mcd
5-23-1877	Elizabeth M & min ch Alice F, Cora E, Adella G, Davis F, & Everet F gct West Branch MM
6-27-1877	Mary E rocf Birch Lake MM MI
11-27-1878	Edward & dt Carrie rocf Caesar's Creek MM OH
10-23-1879	Wm & w Mary Esther & min s Charles D gct Birch Lake MM MI
3-9-1880	J Edwin Hempstead Co AR s Reese & Lydia Wayne Co m Jeannette dt Samuel S & Annie S **Richie** Preble Co OH at res father
12-22-1881	Maurice min gct Elk MM OH
7-27-1882	Martha Ann rec in mbrp
8-24-1882	Esther Jane rocf Salem MM IA
11-23-1882	Stephen C consents to m of dt Rhoda E to Levi **Willets** on 11-30-1882 at Richmond MH
12-28-1882	Wm O & w Lydia J & ch Edwin H, Wm O, & George L rocf Georgetown MM IL; Allen H rocf Elk MM OH
2-26-1885	Walter gc
3-26-1885	Walter L gct Indianapolis MM; moved to Cincinnati MM OH

MENDENHALL (cont)
4-23-1885	Allen Harvey & w Esther Jane & min dt Bertha E gct New Salem MM Howard Co
7-23-1885	Tabitha Jane rel fr mbrp
9-23-1886	Martha Ann drpd fr mbrp
10-28-1886	Alice Cary min gct Caesar's Creek MM OH
11-29-1886	Wm s John & Hannah M (Hough) Richmond Wayne Co m Eliza Doan dt Edwin & Jemima Hadley Richmond at res of her par
5-24-1888	Henry rec in mbrp
4-25-1891	John rel fr mbrp
10-24-1891	Reese rel fr mbrp
12-26-1891	Alfred not found
2-27-1892	Flora rel fr mbrp
1-22-1894	Elizabeth H rel fr mbrp
7-23-1896	Ellis G rel fr mbrp

MERADETH
4-22-1835	James H gct Spiceland MM

MEREDITH
12-28-1816	John & s Ithamar, Andrew, & Temple rocf New Garden MM NC; Abigail rocf New Garden MM NC
12-28-1818	John & s Ithamar, Andrew, & Temple gct Blue River MM; Abigail gc
1-26-1831	Mary & ch Roseanna, Joanna, & Susanna, Jefferson, Harvey, Jabez, Jesse, & Wm rocf Dover MM NC
9-26-1832	Mary rocf New Garden MM
2-25-1835	Mary gct New Garden MM
4-22-1835	Mary & ch Jabez, Jesse, Joanna, Rosanna, Susanna, & Wm gct Milford MM
6-28-1837	Esther, Rachel, & David ch David & Rachel rocf Gwinned MM PA
8-24-1842	Thomas Jefferson gct Spiceland MM
10-25-1854	Tabitha Jane (Clawson) con mcd
1-24-1855	Tabitha C gct New Garden MM
11-26-1856	Beulah Anna (Aydelott) dis for mcd
4-25-1860	Tabitha Jane rocf Chester MM
6-25-1885	Tabitha Jane drpd fr mbrp

MIDDLETON
4-25-1827	Cert rec for Samuel & s Elihu & Jeremiah fr Hopewell MM NC; end to New Garden MM
6-25-1873	Sidney gct Back Creek MM

MILBY
2-17-1892	Anna M (Mendenhall) rq lt
3-16-1892	Anna M glt

MILES
12-24-1873	Rachel E & Melissa rocf Chester MM
10-27-1875	Rachel E gct Spiceland MM
12-23-1886	Rachel E rocf Chester MM
3-23-1889	Margaret rocf New Garden MM
5-25-1889	Cornelius V rec in mbrp
6-24-1893	Charles rec in mbrp
12-22-1898	Charles rel fr mbrp

MILIKAN
6-21-1817	Mary rocf Lost Creek MM TN
4-29-1820	Mary gct West Grove MM

MILLER
1-25-1837	Caesar's Creek MM OH rq this mtg to treat with Rebecca (Gilpin) for mcd
11-22-1865	Rebecca (Cockayne) con mcd
12-1-1866	J Newton s Jonathan & Mary Wayne Co m Lydia H dt Richard & Rachel Rue Wayne Co at Orange Mtg
3-27-1872	J Newton & w Lydia & s Truman gct Lawrence MM KS
3-26-1873	David rec in mbrp
4-25-1891	John G rec in mbrp

MILLER (cont)
12-23-1897	Martin M & ch Raymond, Vernon, & Bertha rec in mbrp

MILLESON
3-28-1891	Leon B rec in mbrp

MILLIKAN
9-26-1812	Cert rec for Eli & fam fr Springfield MM NC; end to Center MM OH

MILLS
12-26-1812	Cert rec for Hezekiah fr Deep River MM NC; end to Clear Creek MM OH; cert rec for Joseph & fam fr Deep River MM NC; end to Clear Creek MM OH; cert rec for Hannah & dt Sarah fr Deep River MM NC; end to Clear Creek MM OH; cert rec for Jonathan & fam fr Deep River MM NC; end to Clear Creek MM OH; cert rec for Sarah fr Deep River MM NC; end to Clear Creek MM
4-30-1814	Hezekiah rocf Clear Creek MM OH
10-29-1814	Jonathan & s John & Samuel rocf Clear Creek MM OH; Sarah & dt Ann rocf Clear Creek MM OH
11-26-1814	Henry & s Josiah rocf Lost Creek MM TN; Hannah & dt Anne Maria rocf Lost Creek MM TN; Charity rocf Lost Creek MM TN
12-31-1814	Cert rec for Rachel fr Lost Creek MM TN; end to Lick Creek MM
1-28-1815	Moses & s Milton rocf Lost Creek MM TN; Seth & s Aaron & Kinsey rocf Lost Creek MM TN; Charity & dt Bety Ann & Mary Ann rocf Lost Creek MM TN; Cert rec for Elisabeth & dt Garelda fr Lost Creek MM TN; end to Lick Creek MM
6-24-1815	Aaron rocf Lost Creek MM TN
2-28-1818	Cert rec for Asa & s Zimri, Levi, Asa, & Mahlon fr Lost Creek MM TN; end to Silver Creek MM; cert rec for Mary & dt Ruth & Elizabeth fr Lost Creek MM TN; end to Silver Creek MM
6-27-1818	Hezekiah dis for mcd
12-26-1818	Mary (Thomas) con mcd
5-27-1829	John & s Wm, Amos, & John rocf Caesar's Creek MM OH; Betty & dt Elizabeth rocf Caesar's Creek MM OH
2-22-1832	John dis for na
3-28-1832	Eli, Samuel, Rowlan R, Noah, & Joel T rocf Duck Creek MM; Mary Ann rocf Duck Creek MM
11-27-1833	Elizabeth (Hoover) dis for mcd & jH
3-28-1834	Samuel dis for mcd & na
11-23-1842	Amos & Wm dis for na & training in militia
10-27-1847	Noah dis for na
11-24-1847	Joel T dis for na
3-22-1848	Rowland R dis for na & mcd
1-23-1850	John dis for na, mcd, & jas
4-26-1854	George gct Caesar's Creek MM OH
5-24-1854	Lettice rec in mbrp
6-27-1855	Henry J gct Caesar's Creek MM OH
7-22-1857	Elizabeth gct Sugar Plain MM
1-27-1858	Lettice gct Mississinewa MM
12-26-1860	Joseph dis for mcd & na
7-24-1878	Susanna & dt Rosetta rocf Duck Creek MM
6-28-1883	Thomas Centreville rec in mbrp
12-27-1883	Thomas H & Susanna rq PM at Centreville
10-22-1885	Joseph John & w Gertrude Emily & min dt Gertrude rocf Indianapolis MM
2-24-1887	Thomas gct West Grove MM
12-27-1890	Susan gct West Grove MM
8-27-1896	Samuel C & w Flora P rocf New Castle MM
11-23-1899	Samuel C minister & w Flora P gct Knightstown MM

MODLIN
9-25-1819	Ann gct New Garden MM
4-26-1883	Nathan Centreville rq mbrp

MOFFAT
8-23-1883	Hugh appt elder

WHITEWATER MONTHLY MEETING
MINUTES AND MARRIAGES

MOFFIT
11-28-1818	Jeremiah rocf Fall Creek MM
11-24-1830	Hugh & w Sally gct White Lick MM
8-22-1832	Jeremiah & w Cynthia gct Sugar River MM
1-22-1845	Sarah & Mary Barker min rocf Sugar Plain MM
12-22-1852	Ann Elizabeth & Martha J **Tyler** ch Hugh & Sarah rec in mbrp

MOFFITT
12-28-1811	Charles & s Hugh & Jeremiah rocf Cane Creek MM NC; Elizabeth & dt Tacy & Eunice rocf Cane Creek MM NC
10-31-1818	Hannah & dt Ruth & Mary rocf Fall Creek MM
2-18-1824	Jeremiah s Hugh dec & Hannah Wayne Co m Margery dt Jeremiah & Margery dec **Cox** Wayne Co at Whitewater MH
12-3-1828	Hugh s Charles & Elizabeth Wayne Co m Sally dt Wm & Martha **Childre** Wayne Co at Whitewater MH
8-25-1830	Elizabeth appt elder
1-4-1832	Jeremiah s Charles & Elizabeth Wayne Co m Cynthia Ann dt Zimri & Lydia **Cook** Wayne Co at Whitewater MH
8-28-1839	John dis for scandalous immoral conduct
1-22-1845	Hugh & w Sarah & Mary Barker min rocf Sugar Plain MM
11-23-1853	Abijah gct Sugar Plain MM
5-23-1855	Abijah rocf Sugar Plain MM
1-23-1856	Abijah gct Elk MM OH to m Lydia **Townsend**
9-24-1856	Lydia L rocf Elk MM OH
7-24-1867	Charles gct Sugar River MM to m Lucinda **Griest**
1-22-1868	Lucinda rocf Sugar River MM
2-22-1871	Charles & w Lucinda & s Oliver Chester gct Kansas MM KS
1-27-1875	Eunice gct Sugar Plain MM
10-24-1877	Eunice rocf Sugar Plain MM
12-27-1883	Charles, Lucinda, Eunice, Estell, Arthur Clyde, & Hugh C rq PM at Centreville
11-28-1891	Charles & w Lucinda & ch Chester, Eunice, Estelle, Arthur Clyde, Hugh C, & Herschell P rocf West Grove MM
5-27-1893	Charles F rel fr mbrp
4-27-1895	Edward C rec in mbrp
11-25-1897	Sarah May rec in mbrp

MONDON
7-25-1828	Millicent & dt Peninah rocf Back Creek MM NC

MOON
10-18-1823	Simon & s Joseph, Wm, John, & Riley rocf Cane Creek MM NC; Hannah rocf Cane Creek MM NC
4-25-1826	Simon & w Hannah & ch Joseph, Mary, Wm, John, Riley, Sibbinah, & Simon gct Milford MM
9-22-1869	Hiram E & w Almira & ch Louisa, Oscian, & Margery rocf Newberry MM OH
7-25-1873	Mary T rocf Green Plain MM OH
11-27-1890	Hiram rel fr mbrp; jas
9-24-1892	Elizabeth & s Winfred glt

MOOR
5-31-1817	Elisabeth & dt Lydia, Isabel Anne, & Susanna rocf Fall Creek MM
9-16-1818	Phebe & dt Hannah rocf Elk MM OH
11-22-1826	Joshua rocf Springfield MM NC

MOORE
6-24-1815	Thomas & s Wm & Thomas rocf Fall Creek MM NJ; Abigail & dt Leah Jean & Miriam rocf Fall Creek MM NJ
5-31-1817	Josiah & s Jonathan rocf Fall Creek MM; Samuel rocf Springfield MM NC
9-10-1817	Wm s Thomas & Isabel dec Wayne Co m Ann dt Gideon dec & Sarah **Small** at Whitewater MH
9-26-1818	Alexander & s James & Benejah rocf Elk MM OH

MOORE (cont)
10-28-1820	Benjamin B & s Ira & Chalkley rocf Piles Grove MM NJ; Lydia & dt Ann, Matilda, Caroline, & Rachel rocf Piles Grove MM NJ; David & s Henry W, George, Benjamin, & Elexander rec in mbrp; Mary & dt Maryann & Rachel rec in mbrp
5-18-1822	Benajah & James dis for unchastity
6-15-1822	Alexander con for abusing a neighbor's child
3-20-1824	Susannah (**Jones**) con mcd
1-14-1826	Samuel con mcd
3-18-1826	Samuel gct Milford MM
7-26-1826	John & s Samuel & Joseph rocf Piney Woods MM NC; Margaret & dt Martha & Elizabeth rocf Piney Woods MM NC
8-23-1826	Cert rec for Edith fr Deep River MM NC; end to White River MM
11-22-1826	Margaret rocf Springfield MM NC
11-28-1827	Esther (**Hiatt**) con mcd
1-28-1829	Benjamin B, Esther, & Lydia dis for jH; Wm con att Separatist Mtg
3-25-1829	Thomas Jr dis for jas; Alexander dis for na & jas
4-22-1829	Jonathan M & Josiah dis for jas
7-22-1829	John, Lydia, Elizabeth, & Isabella dis for jas
10-28-1829	Margaret w John dis for jas
11-25-1829	Thomas Sr dis for jas
2-24-1830	Wm & w Ann & ch Samuel, Thomas, Achsah, Truman, & Margaret H gct Duck Creek MM
4-28-1830	Susannah F dis for na & jas
5-25-1831	Phebe gct Chester MM
12-26-1832	Anna dis for jas
10-23-1833	Ira dis for jH
11-27-1833	Margaret & dt Elizabeth rocf New Garden MM
1-28-1835	Hannah (**Hiatt**) dis for mcd
7-22-1835	Matilda & Caroline dis for jH
1-4-1837	Joshua s Samuel & Margaret both dec Wayne Co m Sarah dt Thomas & Sarah both dec **Stokes** Wayne Co at Whitewater MH
9-27-1837	Robert Jr & Anna R & dt Ann Elizabeth rocf Sadsbury MM PA
2-28-1838	Chalkley dis for na & jH
4-25-1838	Richard W rocf New Garden MM NC
11-28-1838	Elizabeth gct Spiceland MM
7-24-1839	Susannah dis for jH
8-24-1842	Richard W con mcd
10-12-1842	Anna rec in mbrp
8-23-1843	Richard & w Anna gct Milford MM
8-28-1844	Mary (**Thorn**) dis for na, jH, & mcd
12-25-1844	Elias dis for na, jH, & mcd
9-24-1845	Hannah dis for jH
10-22-1851	Samuel dis for na & mcd
6-27-1855	Joseph rocf Blue River MM
7-25-1855	Hannah (**Shinn**) dis for na & mcd
7-23-1862	Joseph gct Springborough MM OH to m Deborah **Stanton**
1-28-1863	Deborah A rocf Springborough MM OH
5-27-1868	George S Helena AR rec in mbrp
2-28-1870	Lydia P rocf Bloomfield MM; Wm A h Lydia P rocf Sugar River MM
2-28-1872	Joseph gct Green Plain MM OH to m Mary **Thorne**
7-23-1873	Nathan con mcd; Mary F rocf Green Plain MM OH
2-25-1874	Anna rocf Milford MM
12-4-1879	Jacob Boone Co s Abraham & Susannah both dec Wayne Co m Eunice dt Charles & Elizabeth both dec **Moffitt** at res Alpheus **Test** Richmond
4-22-1880	Jacob rocf Sugar Plain MM
5-26-1881	John G & w Hannah & s Cloyd rec in mbrp
6-23-1881	Jacob rqct Milford MM to m Jane **Elliott**
10-27-1881	Jane (**Elliott**) rocf Milford MM
8-23-1883	John F & w Elizabeth A & ch Lineas A, Martha J, & Otis J rocf Sugar Plain MM; Willis rocf Sugar Plain MM; Mary T appt elder
11-27-1884	Lydia P & dt Amanda gct Kokomo MM

MOORE (cont)

4-23-1885	Joseph minister & w Mary T & ch Mary, Grace, Ella, Lucy H, & Hibbard T gct New Garden MM
4-26-1888	Mary rocf Dublin MM
11-22-1888	Ellen rocf Blue River MM; Joseph & w Mary T & ch Anna M, Grace, Lucy H, & Willard E rocf New Garden MM NC
3-23-1889	Linneas gct Chicago MM IL
9-21-1889	Cert for Linneas ret by Chicago MM IL; unable to find him
2-22-1890	Willis E rel fr mbrp; jas
6-28-1890	Evangeline rec in mbrp
2-27-1892	Marcia Francis rocf Dublin MM
11-25-1893	Ellen gct Pasadena MM CA
2-22-1896	Hannah gct j evangelical denomination
7-23-1896	Jennie H rocf Dover MM
8-27-1896	Benjamin rec in mbrp
7-22-1897	Benjamin & w Ann Jane gct Dover MM
10-28-1897	Anna gct Whittier MM CA

MOORMAN

1-25-1812	Uriah & s John & Enoch rocf Piney Grove MM SC; Hannah & dt Maria rocf Piney Grove MM SC
2-29-1812	Mary & dt Susannah rocf Fairfield MM OH
11-28-1827	Rachel & dt Betty, Lydia, Priscilla, & Rebecca rocf Marlborough MM NC
3-24-1841	Hannah C gct Goshen MM OH
3-26-1856	Henry T rocf Caesar's Creek MM OH
11-23-1859	Henry T gct Dover MM OH
12-26-1866	Ann gct Goshen MM WI
9-21-1895	Frank H & w Martha rocf Dover MM
3-25-1897	Anna rec in mbrp
4-22-1897	Richmond & dt Sarah & Harriett rocf New Garden MM
9-23-1897	Lulu rocf New Garden MM
10-28-1897	Levi & w Sarah rocf New Garden MM
2-26-1899	Peninah, Nancy Hannah, & Mary Alice rocf New Garden MM

MORE

10-22-1851	Joseph dis for na & mcd

MORGAN

11-25-1809	Benjamin appt to comm
1-27-1810	Naomi appt to comm to inquire into Lydia **Hawkin's** clearness in m
9-2-1812	Benjamin s Charles & Susanna both dec Wayne Co m Elizabeth dt James & Ruth **Johnson** Wayne Co at Whitewater MH
3-31-1819	Micajah s Benjamin & Naomi dec Wayne Co m Hannah dt Thomas & Sarah **Hill** Wayne Co at Whitewater MM
5-27-1820	Hannah & dt gct New Garden MM
6-24-1820	Benjamin gct West Grove MM; Elizabeth & dt gct West Grove MM
7-23-1823	Benjamin s Charles & Susanna both dec Wayne Co m Ruth dt Hugh dec & Hannah **Moffitt** Wayne Co at Whitewater MH
9-20-1823	Nathan & Beulah rocf Chester MM NJ
11-15-1823	Ruth gct West Grove MM
1-17-1824	Cert rec for Hugh & s David Bransen, Gerrard Johnson, & John Watkins fr South River MM VA; end to Fairfield MM OH
3-7-1827	Nathan Wayne Co s John & Mary Gloucester Co NJ m Margaret dt David & Hannah **Holloway** Wayne Co at Whitewater MH
3-25-1829	Nathan dis for jas
4-22-1829	Margaret dis for jas
11-26-1856	Wm B rocf Spiceland MM; Sarah H rocf Back Creek MM NC
7-25-1860	Micajah & w Hannah & s George F rocf New Garden MM
11-28-1860	Charles & w Michael rocf Raysville MM

MORGAN (cont)

12-26-1860	Benjamin rocf Raysville MM
11-27-1867	Hannah gct New Garden MM
9-22-1869	Wm B & w Sarah & min ch Wm Earle & Jesse Henley gct Spiceland MM
5-28-1873	Benjamin F con mcd
4-24-1878	Anna W rec in mbrp
8-23-1883	Michel appt elder; ch of Benjamin d 11-20-1882
9-26-1883	Wm B & w Sarah H rocf Spring River MM KS
11-23-1889	Wm B & w Sarah H gct Spring River MM Cherokee Co KS

MORMAN

2-29-1812	Zachariah & grs Eli rocf Fairfield MM OH

MORRIS

10-28-1809	Margaret to visit Silver Creek Settlement
7-27-1811	Jesse & s John rocf Deep River MM NC; Mary & dt Mary, Peggy, & Sarah rocf Deep River MM NC; Jonathan & Jehosaphat rocf Symons Creek MM NC
1-1-1812	Jehosaphat s Jonathan & Peninah dec NC m Peninah **Symons** dt Benjamin & Sarah **Bundy** NC at Whitewater MH
7-31-1813	Dempsey & s Jess, Joshua, Benjamin, & Job rocf Suttons Creek MM NC; Jemima & dt Elizabeth rocf Suttons Creek MM NC
10-29-1814	Jehoshophat to travel to Pasquotank MM NC; given a few lines
5-27-1815	Aaron & s John, Samuel, & George rocf Center MM NC; Lydia & dt Elisabeth rocf Center MM NC
6-24-1815	Isaac & s George & Christopher rocf Springfield MM NC; Phebe & dt Margaret, Ruth, Elisabeth, & Gulielma rocf Deep River MM NC
10-28-1815	Josiah rocf Springfield MM NC
12-30-1815	Rueben & s Benjamin, John, & Joseph rocf Back Creek MM NC; Miriam rocf Back Creek MM NC
12-4-1816	Jonathan s Jonathan & Penelope both dec Wayne Co m Abigail dt Benjamin & Sarah dec **Charles** at Whitewater MH
1-8-1817	Jehosphat s Jonathan & Penelope dec Wayne Co m Sarah dt Benjamin & Mary dec **Hill** Wayne Co at Whitewater MH
1-2-1822	Josiah Wayne Co s Christopher & Gulielma dec NC m Abigail dt Abraham & Mary **Symons** Wayne Co at Whitewater MH
7-20-1822	Abigail gct West Grove MM
12-26-1832	John gct Duck Creek MM
10-23-1833	John & w rocf Duck Creek MM; Ann rocf Duck Creek MM
10-22-1834	Jesse dis for na
8-26-1835	Nelly (**Osborn**) con mcd
2-24-1836	Nelly gct Mississinewa MM
8-26-1840	Samuel M gct Walnut Ridge MM to m Levina **Cox**
10-27-1841	Levina rocf Walnut Ridge MM
7-27-1853	John gct White Lick MM to m Edith **Chamness**
2-22-1854	Sarah (**Townsend**) con mcd
3-22-1854	Edith rocf White Lick MM
7-26-1854	Sarah gct Walnut Ridge MM
4-27-1864	Edith & ch Albert C & Ann gct White Lick MM
9-21-1864	David con mcd
12-28-1864	David gct Honey Creek MM IA
12-24-1873	Josiah prc fr Milford MM to m Mary **Charles**
1-6-1874	Josiah Henry Co s Christopher & Gulielma Pasquotank Co NC m Mary **Charles** dt Mathew & Sarah **Symons** both dec Randolph Co NC at res Matthew **Symons** Whitewater MH
3-25-1874	Mary C (**Charles**) gct Milford MM
11-24-1875	Wm & w Priscilla rocf Cherry Grove MM
10-23-1879	Ernestine P gct Wilmington MM OH
6-22-1882	Mary C rocf Milford MM
10-23-1884	Whitewater rpts Priscilla na
11-27-1884	Wm H dis for na; Priscilla drpd fr mbrp for na
4-28-1887	Hannah rel fr mbrp; jas

WHITEWATER MONTHLY MEETING
MINUTES AND MARRIAGES

MORRISON
6-27-1812	James rocf Miami MM OH
7-25-1812	Robert con for att muster
5-31-1817	Jane & dt Hannah rec in mbrp
3-20-1824	Robert con dr
9-24-1828	Robert dis for JH
4-22-1829	Jane dis for jas
7-22-1829	Hannah dis for jas
10-28-1840	James L dis for na & jH

MORRISSON
5- 6-1811	Robert rocf Spring MM NC
7-29-1812	James Wayne Co s Robert & Hannah NC m Mary dt Wm & Mary **Hough** NC at Whitewater MH

MORROW
11-25-1809	John appt to att m Benjamin **Cox**
3-31-1810	John appt o
6-29-1811	Mary appt to comm
2-25-1815	Elisabeth rocf Cane Creek MM NC
6-24-1829	Joseph dis for mcd
1-27-1830	Letitia (**Smith**) dis for mcd
8-24-1836	New Garden MM gr perm to rec Lutitia
4-13-1845	Elihu s John & Mary both dec Wayne Co m Anna H dt Eli & Martha **Brown** Wayne Co at Whitewater MH
4-28-1847	John dis for na & mcd
8-23-1883	Elihu appt elder
1-26-1899	James W drpd fr mbrp for na

MOTE
6-29-1848	Linus s David & Miriam Miami Co OH m Hannah L dt Jonathan & Lydia both dec **Grave** Wayne Co at Smyrna Mtg
11-22-1848	Hannah L gct West Branch MM OH
4-26-1849	Enos s David & Miriam Miami Co OH m Martha Ann dt John G & Sarah **Reed** Wayne Co at Smyrna Mtg
2-27-1850	Martha Ann gct West Branch MM OH
5-22-1867	Marcus & w Rhoda S & ch Henry D & Susannah J rocf Miami MM OH
3-25-1868	Samuel S rocf Miami MM OH
5-27-1868	Elisha J rocf West Branch MM OH
9-21-1871	Orvin S s Zeno & Deborah Miami Co OH m Martha J dt John & Phebe M dec **Tyler** Wayne Co at res of Hugh **Moffitt**
8-27-1873	Orvan S rocf West Branch MM OH
3-30-1876	L Albert s Zeno & Deborah Miami Co OH m Annie E dt Samuel & Elizabeth **Wallas** Richmond at home of her par
5-22-1884	Kirk L & ch Clarence Leslie & Minnie L rocf Miami MM OH
2-26-1885	Mary gc
3-26-1885	Samuel Steddom & ch Clara E, George H, & Jesse E gct Miami MM OH
4-23-1885	Kirk L gct Miami MM OH
1-28-1886	Kirk L rocf Miami MM OH
1-25-1890	Kirk L & dt Minnie L gct Miami MM OH
2-22-1896	Gertrude rel fr mbrp
3-25-1897	Elbert rec in mbrp
4-22-1897	Emma & Mary Alice rec in mbrp
10-27-1898	Daisy B rel fr mbrp

MOTT
7-28-1887	Alvaretta (**Stubbs**) gct Minneapolis MM MN

MULLEN
12-22-1837	Ada drpd fr mbrp
3-23-1889	John rec in mbrp

MULLINS
6-23-1898	John drpd fr mbrp

MUNDANE
7-27-1811	Jesse rocf Springfield MM NC

MUNDEN
7-27-1811	Mary & dt Ruth Alice rocf Springfield MM NC
7-31-1813	Margaret rocf Suttons Creek MM NC
2-25-1829	Joseph & w Millicent & min ch Peninnah & Thomas gct Duck Creek MM

MUNDIN
7-23-1828	Joseph rocf Back Creek MM NC

MUNTZ
5-22-1833	Lydia (**Marmon**) dis for mcd

MURDICK
6-17-1826	Rachel rocf West Grove MM

MURDOCK
7-19-1823	Rachel (**Jessup**) con mcd
3-20-1824	Rachel gct Union MM OH
1-28-1829	Rachel gct White River MM

MURFREY
12-11-1811	Lydia & Elizabeth rocf Back Creek MM NC

MURPHEY
3-26-1814	Miles rec in mbrp

MURPHY
12-28-1811	Robert, Miles, & Clement rocf Back Creek MM NC
7-29-1815	Margaret rocf Miami MM OH
6-29-1816	Robert dis for military training & att mcd

MURROW
12-27-1837	Phebe rocf New Garden MM
7-25-1838	Phebe dis for j ME

MURRY
8-22-1855	Wm Jr, James, & John rocf Lisburn MM Ireland
10-24-1860	James & John gct New Garden MM

MYERS
5-23-1896	Adam New Westville OH rec in mbrp

NANCE
5-26-1821	Hannah (**Osborn**) dis for mcd

NEAL
12-26-1812	Anna rocf New Garden MM NC
9-17-1824	Anna gct Chester MM

NEGUS
11-23-1859	Albert G & w Martha B & ch Charles, Lillian, & Hannah rocf Red Cedar MM IA

NELSON
3-23-1882	John rec in mbrp
12-25-1884	John dis

NEWBY
7-31-1813	Benjamin rocf Suttons Creek MM NC
9-24-1814	Wm & s Thomas & Cyrus rocf Elk MM OH; Elizabeth rocf Elk MM OH
12-28-1816	Wm & fam gct New Garden MM; Elizabeth gct New Garden MM
1-15-1825	Benoni rocf Springfield MM NC
2-18-1826	John rocf Blue River MM; Jane rocf New Garden MM NC
8-23-1826	Cert rec for Wm & s Thomas & Seth fr Holly Spring MM NC; end to Fairfield MM
11-22-1826	Cert rec for Elias & s Wm fr Back Creek MM NC; end to Duck Creek MM
12-27-1826	Cert rec for Wm & Alfred fr Back Creek MM NC; end to Duck Creek MM
3-28-1827	John gct Blue River MM

NEWBY (cont)

11-26-1828	Cert rec for Exum fr Back Creek MM NC; end to Arba MM
8-1-1838	Thomas Wayne Co s Thomas & Mary Jackson Co m Rebecca dt Benjamin dec & Martha **Hill** Wayne Co at Whitewater MH
9-26-1838	Benoni dis for na
11-28-1838	Rebecca H gct Milford MM
7-28-1847	Cert rec for Phebe fr Back Creek MM NC; end to Cherry Grove MM
1-24-1848	Wm con mcd
10-11-1848	Susannah gct Dover MM
10-24-1849	Daniel & Wm gct Dover MM
10-27-1852	Thomas & w Alice & ch Wm Hurtley & Jonathan D rocf Milford MM
8-24-1853	Susannah W rocf Dover MM
7-27-1858	Thomas & Alice set off with Kansas MM
4-27-1859	Miriam rocf Hopewell MM

NEWCOMB

4-27-1882	Carrie D rec in mbrp

NEWLIN

7-22-1880	Hannah & ch Viola & Edward rocf White Lick MM
2-23-1882	Findley & w Emma & ch Edgar & Charles rec in mbrp; Emma form mem Richmond United Presb ch
2-26-1885	Hannah & Edward gc
3-26-1885	Hannah & min ch Edward & Viola gct Plainfield MM
2-24-1887	Charles rel fr mbrp
5-23-1891	Edgar S gct Dublin MM
1-26-1899	Finley & w Emma gc; jas

NEWMAN

12-27-1817	Mary rocf New Garden MM NC
6-27-1818	Mary gct Mill Creek MM OH
4-25-1827	Millicent (**Albertson**) con mcd
5-27-1829	Millicent dis for jas
5-24-1876	Charles E rec in mbrp
3-23-1899	Elizabeth New Westville rec in mbrp

NEWSON

5-28-1828	Luke rocf Back Creek MM NC

NICHOLDSON

1-31-1818	John & s Samuel rocf Center MM DE

NICHOLS

11-25-1874	Mark & w Sarah & ch James W, Mary A, Simeon L, Elijah, & Melinda rocf Cherry Grove MM; Noah rocf Cherry Grove MM
7-25-1877	Mark & w Sarah & ch James W, Mary H, Simon D, Elijah, & Malinda gct Cherry Grove MM
5-24-1883	Mark & w Sarah & ch Elijah & Malinda J rocf Cherry Grove MM; Simeon L & Mary Ann rocf Cherry Grove MM
6-28-1883	Mark & fam rec in mbrp
6-26-1884	James W rocf Cherry Grove MM
11-24-1887	Mary Ann gct Cherry Grove MM
4-26-1888	Mark & w Sarah & min ch Elijah V & Malinda J gct Cherry Grove MM; Simeon L gct Cherry Grove MM
6-23-1894	Joseph W gct Chicago MM IL

NICHOLSON

6-27-1812	Thomas rocf Back Creek MM NC
1-31-1818	Esther & dt Sarah & Leah rocf Center MM DE
1-26-1859	John rocf Piney Woods MM NC
8-28-1861	John gct Scipio MM NY to m Mary B **Winslow**
9-26-1861	Timothy & w Sarah N W & ch Marianna, John W, Josiah W, & Thomas rocf Radnor MM PA
3-26-1862	Mary B rocf Scipio MM NY
4-30-1868	Timothy Wayne Co s Josiah dec & Anna Perquimans Co NC m Mary S dt John dec & Mary **White** Wayne Co at Richmond Mtg

WHITEWATER MONTHLY MEETING MINUTES AND MARRIAGES

NICHOLSON (cont)

6-25-1873	John & w Mary B & min ch Edward W & Ellen A gct Baltimore MM MD
1-26-1889	John rel fr mbrp

NIXON

5-25-1811	Josiah rocf Springfield MM NC; John & s John & Caleb rocf Springfield MM NC; Jane & dt Jane & Miriam rocf Springfield MM NC
7-27-1811	Jane appt to comm
4-24-1813	John Jr dis for waggoning military stores
7-31-1813	Zachariah & s Joseph, Foster, John, & Thomas roc; Martha & dt Mary & Elisabeth rocf Suttons Creek MM NC
9-24-1814	Josiah con giving way to anger & upl
12-30-1815	Miriam rocf Springfield MM NC
1-25-1817	Caleb dis for att mcd
11-1-1827	John s Zachariah & Martha Washington Co m Gulielma dt John & Elizabeth **Pool** Wayne Co at Ridge MH
12-26-1827	Gulielma gct Blue River MM
11-4-1829	Samuel R Warren Co OH s John & Ann both dec Pasquotank Co NC m Martha N dt Isaac dec & Jane **Pleas** Warren Co OH at Whitewater MH
11-25-1829	Mary rocf Deep River MM NC
3-23-1831	Samuel R rocf Springborough MM OH
4-27-1831	Samuel R & w Martha & dt Margaret Jane gct Milford MM
8-22-1832	John rocf Back Creek MM NC
1-20-1833	Gabriel & w Mary gct Milford MM
2-26-1834	Wm min s Wm rocf Elk MM OH; Rhoda, Peninah, & Martha A rocf Elk MM OH
12-28-1836	John dis for mcd
8-22-1838	Christiana & ch Mary & Pheriba rocf New Garden MM
6-26-1839	Sarah rocf Milford MM
11-27-1839	Wm rq mbrp; refused
4-22-1840	Cert rec for Martha & ch Margaret J, Amos, Alfred, & James fr Salem MM; end to Milford MM
5-27-1840	Wm min gct Cincinnati MM OH
11-25-1840	Wm & Christiana & ch Mary, Pheribe, & Wm gct Chester MM
6-23-1841	Sarah gct Center MM OH
5-28-1856	Asenath H & dt Louisa & Emily rocf Honey Creek MM
11-26-1856	Asenath & ch Louisa & Mary Emily gct Honey Creek MM

NORADYKE

2-24-1864	Elizabeth A & ch Mary Isabel & Clayton B gct Clear Creek MM OH

NORDYKE

11-23-1837	David s Micajah & Charity Clinton Co OH m Lydia J dt Abel & Rhoda **Thornbury** Wayne Co at Whitewater MH
11-28-1838	Lydia J gct Clear Creek MM OH
7-22-1846	David & w Lydia J & ch Rhoda Ann, Joseph T, Elwood S, & Sylvanus A rocf Clear Creek MM OH
10-31-1861	Thomas R s Henry & Phebe Clinton Co OH m Elizabeth A dt Andrew & Sarah **Gifford** Wayne Co at Orange Mtg
4-27-1870	Sarah Catherine rec in mbrp
12-27-1871	Sylvanus L con mcd
7-25-1877	Sylvanus A & ch Lillian May & Franklin David gct Ozark MM MO
12-26-1891	Clayton B rocf Whittier MM CA; Luella E w Clayton B rocf West Union MM
2-24-1894	Clayton B & w Louella E gct Indianapolis MM

NORRIS

7-25-1812	Rebeckah con mcd
5-27-1897	James & Cora Providence & Friendship Darke Co OH rec in mbrp

WHITEWATER MONTHLY MEETING
MINUTES AND MARRIAGES

NORTH
12-31-1814	Daniel rocf Deep Creek MM NC
2-24-1821	Daniel con guilty of a breech of trust & telling a falsehood to support himself therein
10-27-1821	Keziah gct West Grove MM

NORTON
5-23-1832	Edward rocf Union MM NC
6-27-1832	Richard & w rocf Union MM NC; Elizabeth rocf Union MM NC
3-14-1833	Edward s Richard & Elizabeth Wayne Co m Nancy dt Thomas & Elizabeth **Kendall** Wayne Co at Smyrna MH
2-26-1834	Richard & w Elizabeth gct Duck Creek MM
7-23-1834	Edward & w Nancy & ch Dennis R gct Duck Creek MM

OAELSCHLAGEL
7-28-1898	Josephine gct Spiceland MM

ODDIE
6-24-1863	Mary Ann rocf West Lake MM Canada

ODEL
1-23-1828	Daniel rocf West Grove MM

ODLE
11-22-1826	Betty & dt Polly rocf Marlborough MM NC
12-27-1826	Daniel rocf Marlborough MM NC
3-28-1827	Daniel & w Betty & ch Polly gct West Grove MM
1-23-1828	Betty & dt Polly rocf West Grove MM
10-28-1835	Daniel D & w Elizabeth & ch Sarah, Wm L, & Enos C gct Sugar River MM

OGBORN
1-25-1832	Rebecca rocf Miami MM OH
2-22-1832	Joseph P & s Samuel & Isaac A rocf Miami MM OH; Elizabeth & dt Ann & Sarah B rocf Miami MM OH; Hannah rocf Miami MM OH
8-31-1836	Samuel F s Joseph L & Elizabeth A Wayne Co m Eliza B dt Abel & Rhoda **Thornberry** Wayne Co at Whitewater MH
5-24-1837	Joseph P & w Elizabeth & ch Ann E & Sarah B gct West Grove MM
11-27-1839	Samuel & w Elizabeth B & min s Henry M gct Clear Creek MM OH
12-23-1840	Isaac dis for mcd & na
7-23-1845	Lydia (**Foulke**) dis for jH & mcd
10-28-1846	Sarah (**Foulke**) dis for mcd & jH
1-26-1848	Elizabeth rocf West Grove MM
11-24-1852	Elizabeth A gct Chester MM
9-21-1859	Isaac F rocf Springfield MM OH
3-25-1868	Joseph rocf Chester MM
1-27-1875	Isaac & w Cornelia gct Indianapolis MM

OGBURN
1-26-1870	Cornelia rec in mbrp

O'HARA
3-23-1882	John & w Eliza Jane & ch Edwin Lee, Isaac Graham, & Alpha Grace rec in mbrp at Richmond PM
11-26-1896	John drpd fr mbrp

O'HARRA
10-25-1837	Betsy (**Van Horn**) dis for mcd

OLIPHANT
6-22-1859	Mahlon & w Rachel B & ch Horace M & Elizabeth rocf Red Cedar MM IA

O'NEAL
3-28-1891	Mary & dt Clara rec in mbrp

OSBORN
3-25-1815	Anna & dt Hannah, Abigail, Rachel, Anna, & Elisabeth rocf Deep Creek MM NC
4-29-1820	Jesse con mcd
2-25-1822	Jesse dis
4-17-1824	Wm & w Anna & ch Ambrose, Rachel, Anna Elizabeth, Wm, Tamer, Jemima, & Daniel gct West Grove MM
1-14-1826	Eli & Edith rocf Center MM NC
8-23-1826	Eli & w gct New Garden MM
1-26-1831	Thomas & s Owen rocf Springfield MM; Rebecca & dt Mary, Martha, Nelly, Rebecca, Lydia, & Susannah rocf Springfield MM
6-27-1832	Owen dis for na; Thomas dis for taking away a ch he had bound out
6-27-1844	David s David & Anne Delaware Co OH m Susan dt Achilles & Beulah **Williams** Wayne Co at Whitewater MH
10-23-1844	Susan gct Alum Creek MM OH

OSBORNE
11-25-1868	Ellen rec in mbrp

OSBURN
3-25-1815	Wm & s Jesse & Ambrose rocf Deep Creek MM NC

OUTLAND
10-25-1890	David & w Rhoda M & ch Lydia Grace & Jennie Marie rocf Dublin MM

OVERMAN
9-30-1809	Rachel to inquire into Mary **Cox**'s clearness in m
10-28-1809	Nathan to inquire into clearness Isaac **Commons** in m; Rachel appt elder
11-25-1809	Ephriam appt to comm to att opening of Silver Creek Mtg
5-26-1810	Jesse gct Elk MM OH
11-24-1810	Nathan Jr & s Cornelius & Isaac rocf Back Creek MM NC; Elizabeth & dt Sarah rocf Back Creek MM NC
4-25-1812	Huldah dis for mcd
11-4-1812	Eli s Ephraim & Rachel Wayne Co m Polly dt John & Lydia **Thomas** Wayne Co at Whitewater MH
2-27-1813	Jesse & s Henry & Eli gct Elk MM OH
6-9-1816	Nathan gct New Garden MM
5-31-1827	Zebulon s Isaac & Mary both dec Highland Co OH m Elizabeth **Small** dt Stephen & Mary **Sawyer** both dec at Ridge MH
11-23-1827	Elizabeth gct Fall Creek MM
12-31-1845	Ephraim s Jesse & Keziah dec Wayne Co m Lydia dt Henry dec & Rebecca **Rue** Wayne Co at Whitewater MH
2-25-1846	Lydia gct Mississinewa MM
6-28-1848	Ephraim Jr & dt Lydia Ann rocf Mississinewa MM
7-24-1850	Susanna (**Rue**) con mcd
11-28-1850	Charles s Eli & Elizabeth Washington Co m Eliza Jane dt Cyrus & Miriam **Wright** Wayne Co at Whitewater MH
10-22-1851	Ephraim con mcd
11-26-1851	Eliza Jane gct Spiceland MM
2-23-1853	Ephraim gct West Grove MM; Susannah & s Albert gct Mississinewa MM
2-24-1858	Ephraim rocf West Grove MM
2-22-1871	Ephraim & ch gct Cottonwood MM KS

OWEN
8-14-1824	Thomas Jr & s Parker, Charles, Samuel Stockton, Thomas Matthews, & Benjamin F rocf Philadelphia MM North Dist PA; Hannah W rocf Philadelphia MM North Dist PA
1-27-1830	Parker dis for jas
4-22-1835	Samuel S, Thomas M, & Benjamin F min ch Thomas dec gct Philadelpha MM PA

OWEN (cont)
5-27-1840	Samuel Stocton rocf Burlington MM NJ
8-23-1843	Samuel S gct Philadelphia MM PA
11-25-1897	Pearl C rocf Amo MM

OWENS
5-27-1868	Mary Helena AR rec in mbrp
3-23-1895	Wilbur W rec in mbrp
4-27-1895	Pearl C rec in mbrp
1-25-1896	Pearl Constance gct Amo MM

OWSLEY
7-27-1887	Mary (**Thistlethwaite**) rpt mcd

OZBORN
12-24-1834	Rebecca & dt Martha, Rebecca, Lydia, & Susannah gct Mississinewa MM; Mary gct Mississinewa MM

PAGE
1-15-1825	John & s Hance N, John C, Joseph C, & Elias H rocf Philadelphia MM PA; Sarah & dt Betsey & Margaret rocf Philadelphia MM PA
8-23-1826	Wm rocf Philadelphia MM North Dist PA
12-26-1827	Wm dis for dr, upl, & offering to fight
7-23-1828	John dis for jH
2-25-1829	Sarah dis for jas
7-27-1831	Elizabeth dis for na & jas
4-25-1832	Hance N dis for na & jas
10-23-1844	John C dis for na, training with militia, & j ME
2-26-1845	Elias H dis for na & dp
3-28-1860	White River MM rq aid in treating with Sarah (**Votaw**) for mcd
8-25-1869	Elias H rec in mbrp
9-22-1869	Mary Ann w Elias rec in mbrp
11-24-1869	George & w Anna Josephine rec in mbrp
9-23-1874	George dis
5-28-1879	Elias H & w Mary A rel fr mbrp
8-23-1883	Josephine d 3-14-1883
9-24-1885	Elizabeth min gct Walnut Ridge MM

PALIN
10-31-1812	Henry & s Nixon, Henry, & Axiom rocf Springfield MM NC; Sarah & dt Mary rocf Springfield MM NC

PALMER
4-29-1820	Sarah (**Pearson**) con mcd
5-26-1821	Sarah gct West Grove MM

PANES
6-17-1826	Morgan gct Silver Creek MM

PARKER
6-25-1814	Thomas & s Jesse rocf Piney Grove MM SC; Anna & dt Celia & Sarah rocf Piney Grove MM SC
7-25-1818	Jeremiah & s Robert, Richard, & Isaac rocf Rich Square MM NC; s Richard d on the way; Karen & dt Jemima & Catharine rocf Rich Square MM NC
2-20-1823	Robert gct Milford MM to m Miriam **Bell**
3-20-1824	Robert gct Milford MM
7-26-1826	Wm rocf Rich Square MM NC
9-27-1826	Cert rec for Samuel & s Silas, James, & John fr Rich Square MM NC; end to Duck Creek MM; cert rec for Rebecca fr Rich Square MM NC; end to Duck Creek MM
10-25-1826	Wm gct Rich Square MM NC
10-27-1830	Jeremiah & w Caren & s Isaac gct Milford MM
9-27-1837	Cert rec for Martha fr Rich Square MM N C; end to Walnut Ridge MM
11-26-1851	Wm A & w Mary & ch Ira C, Nancy Jane, & Elmira Ann rocf Driftwood MM
11-24-1852	Wm A & ch gct Driftwood MM; Mary & ch Ira C, Nancy Jane, & Elmira Ann gct Driftwood MM
1-26-1853	Wm M rocf New Garden MM

PARKER (cont)
7-27-1853	Evaline rec in mbrp
12-26-1855	Wm A dis for withholding payment of just debts
1-25-1865	Elisha rocf New Garden MM
2-22-1865	Martha D rocf Raysville MM
8-26-1874	Wm & w Emiline C & ch Edward W, Horace G, Mary A, Wm B, & George F gct New Garden MM
2-22-1883	John P & w Miriam J & s John Oscar rocf Walnut Ridge MM
10-23-1884	Rachel & ch Leroy, Alvanus, Rebecca, Milla A, & Jonathan rocf Elk MM OH
1-22-1885	Charles O rocf White River MM
10-22-1885	Rachel rq cert
11-26-1885	John & w Miriam & min s John Oscar gct Walnut Ridge MM
1-27-1887	Rachel & ch Leroy, Alvanus, Rebecca, Milla A, & Jonathan rq cert to Wichita MM KS
2-24-1887	Rachel & ch Leroy, Alvanus, Rebecca, Milla A, & Jonathan gct Rose Hill MM KS
7-23-1892	Jesse F rocf New Garden MM
10-26-1895	Amanda J rec in mbrp

PARRISH
11-25-1893	Frank Jarret & w Maud & infant dt Madge M rec in mbrp

PARRY
5-28-1828	Joseph & s Wm, Robert, Isaac, Mordecai, & George rocf Bradford MM PA; Sarah & dt Grace rocf Bradford MM PA
2-25-1829	Sarah dis for jas
3-25-1829	Joseph dis for jas
3-23-1831	Wm dis for jas
4-23-1834	Mary (**Hill**) dis for jH & mcd
7-22-1840	Robert dis for jH & mcd
10-11-1843	George dis for na & jH
12-27-1843	Isaac dis for na
6-4-1845	Mordecai s Joseph & Sarah Wayne Co m Gulielma dt Micajah & Gulielma **Henley** Wayne Co at Whitewater MM
4-25-1853	Mordecai gct Hopewell MM to m Sarah **Bell**
10-24-1855	Sarah B rocf Hopewell MM held at Rich Square
1-28-1857	Ruth (**Moffit**) rpt mcd; drpd fr mbrp
3-27-1872	Mordecai rel fr mbrp
7-25-1877	Sarah B & ch Elma, Charles M, Joseph E, & Sarah B gct Minneapolis MM MN
1-25-1890	Laura E rec in mbrp

PARSHALL
1-24-1884	Jesse & Henry rec in mbrp
3-24-1887	Jesse drpd fr mbrp
2-23-1895	John & w Catherine & ch Gussie Jane, Wm Elmer, Henry Alva, & Roy J rec in mbrp
6-22-1899	John & w Catharine & min ch Gussie J, Elmer, Alva, Roy J, & Jessie O gct Dover MM

PATTERSON
4-26-1888	Samuel F, Mary M, & dt Della rec in mbrp
5-26-1898	Mary M rel fr mbrp

PATTY
1-28-1835	Harvey, Seth, & Davis min rocf Mill Creek MM; Mary & dt Rebecca & Anna rocf Mill Creek MM
8-26-1835	Lot min rocf Mill Creek MM
10-28-1835	Lot min gct West Branch MM
7-24-1839	Mary & min ch Harvey, Rebecca, Anna, Seth, Davis, Rachel Ella, & Erwin gct New Garden MM

PAULSON
11-25-1868	Anna (**Davenport**) con mcd
2-24-1894	George rec in mbrp
3-23-1895	Lillian & Margaret rec in mbrp

WHITEWATER MONTHLY MEETING
MINUTES AND MARRIAGES

PAULUS
12-24-1873   Earnestine J rec in mbrp

PAYNE
11-24-1869   Simeon rec in mbrp

PEACOCK
9-26-1812   Amos rocf Back Creek MM NC
6-26-1813   Amos gct Back Creek MM NC
11-29-1817   Amos & s Jonah & Aaron rocf Back Creek MM NC; Hannah rocf Back Creek MM NC; Abraham & s John rocf Back Creek MM NC; Anne & dt Miriam & Margaret rocf Back Creek MM NC
2-27-1819   Amos & s Jonah & Wm gct New Garden MM; Hannah gct New Garden MM; Abraham & s John J gct New Garden MM; Margaret gct New Garden MM
1-22-1834   Rachel rocf Arba MM
5-27-1840   Rachel gct West Grove MM
4-28-1887   Levi & w Sarah & ch Daniel L, Mary H, & Levi C rocf New Garden MM

PEAL
11-24-1821   Two dt Mark gct New Garden MM

PEARSON
6-30-1810   Nathan & s Peter, John, Levi, & Bailey rocf Back Creek MM NC; Mary & dt Ann & Katharine rocf Back Creek MM NC
5-11-1815   Robert s Enoch & Ann Miami Co OH m Catherine dt Rice dec & Catherine **Price** Preble Co OH at Elkhorn MH
5-27-1815   Jesse & s Jonathan & Jesse rocf Back Creek MM NC; Polly & dt Sarah, Rachel, Elisabeth, Susannah, & Rebecca rocf Back Creek MM NC
7-29-1815   Ann rocf Deep Creek MM NC
11-25-1815   Jonathan rocf Deep Creek MM NC
12-30-1815   Catherine gct Mill Creek MM
10-26-1816   Huldah & dt Sarah, Catharine, Huldah, & Rhoda rocf Deep Creek MM NC
4-3-1817   Henry s Wm S C & Anna dec Warren Co OH m Abigail dt John & Abigail **Bradway** Wayne Co at Silver Creek MH
2-26-1818   Huldah gct West Grove MM
9-29-1821   John gct New Garden MM
9— 1821   Mary o Orange PM d
8-5-1822   Nathan dis
8-16-1822   Catherine gct Milford MM
5-15-1824   Levi gct Milford MM
4-16-1825   John rocf Mill Creek MM
8-16-1825   John gct Mill Creek MM
10-28-1835   Martha rocf Chester MM
3-23-1836   Solomon & w Martha & s Wm gct Chester MM
9-2-1863   Thomas V s Thomas & Hannah Niagara Co NY m Mary Ann dt John & Jane both dec **Oddie** Warrington England at Whitewater MH
2-24-1864   Mary Ann gct Hartland MM NY
5-24-1865   Sarah J rec in mbrp
12-28-1870   Calvin W rocf Spiceland MM
10-23-1872   Elvira M rocf West Union MM
7-23-1896   Calvin W & w Marthanna rel fr mbrp

PEDRICK
4-20-1822   Phillip & dt Catharine & Elizabeth rocf Miami MM OH
7-17-1824   Richard & Mary rocf Miami MM OH
1-26-1831   Richard gct Miami MM OH
1-25-1832   Richard rocf Miami MM OH
10-24-1832   Richard gct Westfield MM to m Susanna B **Hunt**
3-27-1833   Susanna B rocf Westfield MM
8-23-1865   Mary C rel fr mbrp
6-28-1876   Wm C/H rel fr mbrp
7-25-1877   Isaac drpd fr mbrp; jas

PEDRICK (cont)
7-22-1880   Richard elder rpt d during previous 3y
2-26-1885   Joseph gc
6-25-1885   Joseph B rel fr mbrp

PEEBLES
1-24-1827   Samuel rocf Springborough MM OH
7-25-1827   Deborah rocf Springborough MM OH
8-2-1827   Sarah rocf Upper MM VA
7-25-1828   Lucy rocf Springborough MM OH
9-23-1829   Sarah gct Springborough MM OH
8-24-1831   Lucy dis for na & dp
12-28-1831   Deborah gct Miami MM OH
1-27-1851   Elijah rocf Milford MM
9-22-1852   Elijah chm
1-26-1853   Elijah gct Walnut Ridge MM

PEEL
4-25-1818   Cert rec for Rueben fr Deep Creek MM NC; end to West Grove MM

PEELE
10-26-1816   Rebekah & Zilpah dt Mark rocf Deep Creek MM NC
1-24-1884   Josephine E rec in mbrp
12-25-1884   Charles F rocf Dublin MM
1-26-1888   Deborah rocf Dublin MM
5-24-1890   Henry E & w Mary rocf Westfield MM
9-27-1890   Mary Olive rocf Westfield MM

PEELLE
4-28-1898   Margaret rocf Dublin MM

PEGG
10-31-1812   Valentine, Mary, & Lydia rocf Deep River MM NC
5-28-1814   Margaret & dt Mary, Ruth, Sarah, & Lydia rocf Deep River MM NC; John & s Davis, Valentine, & John rocf Deep River MM NC
11-26-1814   James & Elisabeth rocf Deep River MM NC
4-4-1821   Valentine wid Wayne Co m Sarah wid of Gideon **Small** at Whitewater MH
2-24-1830   Sarah gct Milford MM
4-3-1833   James s Valentine & Mary dec Wayne Co m Leah dt Thomas & Isabella dec **Moore** Wayne Co at Whitewater MH
1-26-1842   Leah gct Cherry Grove MM
5-27-1874   Davis & w Mary Catherine & ch Rachel Ellen & Olive A rocf Cherry Grove MM
1-26-1876   Davis & w Mary & ch Rachel E & Olive A gct Cherry Grove MM

PEIRSON
10-26-1816   Nathan & s Axium, Zeno, Wm, & Aaron rocf Deep Creek MM NC
7-26-1817   Cert rec for Wm Jr fr Springfield MM NC; end to Silver Creek MM
12-26-1818   Nathan & s Zeno, Wm, Aaron, & Joseph gct West Grove MM
5-27-1863   Mary & ch Joseph, John, Jane Ann, & George gct New York MM NY

PENNINGTON
12-18-1824   Cert rec for Jonah & fam fr Miami MM OH; end to Milford MM

PENNY
2-28-1891   Sarah rec in mbrp
4-27-1895   Sarah gct jas

PERCEFIELD
4-27-1895   Otis rec in mbrp

PERCIFIELD
1-27-1894   Sarah rec in mbrp

PERDUE
5-23-1827   Elizabeth (**Spronger**) dis for mcd

PERISHO
4-26-1838   Nathan s Joshua & Elizabeth both dec Hancock Co m Sarah M dt Thomas L & Martha both dec **Chappell** Wayne Co at Whitewater MH
6-27-1838   Sarah M gct Walnut Ridge MM

PERRY
1-28-1857   Ruth (**Moffitt**) dis for mcd
9-21-1859   Ruth & s Charles Coffin rec in mbrp
2-25-1882   Thomas colored rec in mbrp
6-23-1887   Thomas drpd fr mbrp for moving without limits this mtg
11-25-1897   Mary rec in mbrp

PERSON
9-24-1834   Solomon rocf Cherry Grove MM
2-25-1835   Solomon gct Chester MM to m Martha **Cook**

PERSONETT
6-25-1885   Charles & w Elizabeth rec in mbrp
7-28-1887   Charles H & w Elizabeth gct Indianapolis MM

PERVIS
3-24-1852   Rachel rocf Duck Creek MM
1-25-1860   Ann rocf Chesterfield MM OH

PETERSON
11-28-1838   Eliza (**Hunt**) con mcd
10-27-1847   Eliza dis for na

PETRY
5-27-1897   John Providence & Friendship Darke Co OH rec in mbrp

PHILIPS
3-28-1877   Elvira R gct Fairmount MM
8-23-1883   Elvira d 2-1-1883

PHILLIPS
9-26-1891   Grace J gct Winchester MM

PHOUTS
10-29-1814   Levi dis for military training

PICKERELL
8-1-1888   Mahlon s Henry & Achsah both dec Pickerilltown Logan Co OH m Sarah B **Horney** wid Joel at her home Richmond

PICKERING
10-19-1822   Cert rec for Samuel & s James C, Hiram H, & Samuel fr Flushing MM OH; end to West Grove MM
8-16-1823   Jonas & s Abner, Samuel, Jonas, Mahlon, Joseph, & Jordan rocf Flushing MM OH

PICKET
1-31-1818   Joseph & s Joseph rocf Center MM OH; Priscilla & dt Thamer, Anne, Lydia, Mary, & Sarah rocf Center MM OH
12-26-1832   Wm & w Sarah gct Duck Creek MM

PICKETT
9-30-1809   Sarah & Joshua appt to comm
6-27-1832   Wm & w rocf New Garden MM
6-27-1855   Susannah rocf Chester MM
5-26-1869   John D rec in mbrp
7-26-1869   Wm F rst
9-21-1870   Nancy A rec in mbrp
12-27-1871   Alice Carrie rec in mbrp
5-22-1872   Hannah E w Wm H & ch John F, Benjamin E, Minnie M, & Willie E rec in mbrp

PICKETT (cont)
5-28-1879   John rel fr mbrp
9-24-1879   Albert & w Hattie & ch Florence, Deborah, & Myrtle rocf Chester MM
3-22-1883   Benjamin N & w Mary rocf New Garden MM
11-27-1884   Wm H & w Hannah E & min ch Minnie M & Willie E gct Chester MM; John F & Benjamin E gct Chester MM; Nancy A & Clemy Alice gc
1-22-1885   Nancy A minister & dt Clara Alice gct White River MM
12-26-1891   Benjamin M & Mary not found
7-23-1896   Albert & Florence drpd fr mbrp

PICKRELL
10-25-1888   Sarah B gct Westland MM OH

PIEHE
4-25-1891   Wm rec in mbrp
11-26-1896   Wm drpd fr mbrp

PIERCE
9-26-1818   Cert rec for Wm fr Deep River MM NC; end to Clear Creek MM OH
4-25-1860   Isaac M & w Anna & ch Abigail Amanda, Casper G, Alexander R, Sarah E, Martha A, George R, Wm E, Joseph J, Charles E, & Nathan R rocf New Hope MM TN; KS Prep Terr
5-26-1869   Samuel & w Ann & ch Esther, Milly, & John rocf Milford MM
4-23-1873   Samuel & w Ann & min ch Esther, Milley, & John gct Dover MM
7-27-1895   Elmer E rocf New Castle MM

PIERSON
2-26-1818   Nathan & s Zeno, Wm, Aaron, & Joseph gct West Grove MM
4-19-1823   Exum dis for mcd
12-6-1827   Thomas s Wm & Elizabeth Randolph Co m Elizabeth dt Parnel & Elizabeth both dec **Blizzard** Perquimans Co NC
2-17-1828   Elizabeth gct Cherry Grove MM
8-26-1857   Mary & ch Joseph, John, Jane Ann, & George rocf Cincinnati MM OH
12-23-1870   Marthana T rocf Adrian MM MI

PIGGOTT
3-30-1822   Sarah dis for unchastity
6-15-1822   Deborah (**Clark**) con mcd
9-14-1822   Benjamin con mcd

PIKE
12-25-1819   Trustam rocf Clear Creek MM OH
12-30-1820   Trustam gct Clear Creek MM OH

PINKHAM
10-23-1879   Wm P & w Emma C & ch Mary C, Arthur E, Gertrude H, Charles H, & Bertha rocf Lick Creek MM
9-25-1884   Wm P & w Emma C & min ch Gertrude Harriett, Charles Heber, & Bertha gct Spiceland MM; Mary Cornelia gct Spiceland MM
4-27-1889   Arthur E gct Westfield MM

PITTS
12-26-1832   Cert rec for Cadwalender & fam fr Union MM; end to Duck Creek MM

PLACE
2-23-1822   Maurice & s Isaac rocf Alum Creek MM OH; Hannah & dt Eliza rocf Alum Creek MM OH
3-15-1823   Morris gct Alum Creek MM OH
4-19-1823   Wm gct Alum Creek MM OH
6-18-1825   Wm rocf Alum Creek MM OH

WHITEWATER MONTHLY MEETING
MINUTES AND MARRIAGES

PLACE (cont)
4-20-1826	Wm s Isaac dec & Jane Wayne Co m Priscilla dt Levi & Prudence **Coffin** Wayne Co at Smyrna MH
5-23-1827	Wm & w Priscilla & dt Naomi gct Duck Creek MM
8-24-1831	Aaron L & w Lydia & min s Elwood gct Milford MM

PLEAS
6-26-1819	Aaron & Isaac min rocf Alum Creek MM OH; Jane Smith & dt Jane & Martha N rocf Alum Creek MM OH
10-30-1819	Wm rocf Miami MM OH
2-18-1826	Maurice rocf Alum Creek MM OH
12-27-1826	Maurice gct Milford MM

PLUMMER
12-20-1823	Joseph P & John T rocf Cincinnati MM OH; Lydia & dt Mary M, Joann H, & Sarah C rocf Cincinnati MM OH
8-27-1828	Joseph P & Lydia dis for jH
4-22-1829	John L dis for jas
7-22-1829	Mary M dis for jas
6-25-1834	Sarah C dis for jH

POOL
11-25-1809	Elizabeth appt to att m of Mary **Price**
11-30-1811	John to inquire into Jehoshaphat **Morris** clearness in m
1-31-1818	Joshua rec in mbrp
11-22-1826	Joshua gct Fall Creek MM OH
5-26-1830	Charles gct Blue River MM
5-28-1834	Rebecca rocf Miami MM OH
4-26-1837	Thomas gct Blue River MM
1-24-1838	Thomas rocf Blue River MM
12-25-1839	Rebecca H & ch Joseph & Eliza Ann gct Miami MM OH
6-23-1856	Joseph gct White Lick MM
11-23-1864	Jane Ann (**Hadley**) con mcd
7-29-1868	Joseph s Wm dec & Rebekah Morgan Co m Louisa M **Hiatt** wid dt Thomas & Miriam **Woodard** both dec Wayne Co at res of Levi **Jessup**
10-28-1868	Louiza & s Alfred J **Hiatt** gct White Lick MM
10-23-1878	Lillian rocf White Lick MM
2-26-1885	Lillian gc

POOLE
7-22-1886	Jane Ann jas; res Carthage MO
8-26-1886	Jane Ann rel fr mbrp; j Congregational ch
12-22-1894	Lily rq cert to Portland MM
12-24-1896	Lillian gct jas

POPE
12-27-1837	Ruth rocf White River MM

POSEGATE
7-24-1861	Isaac & Ellen rocf South River MM IA
4-22-1863	Ellen gct South River MM IA
7-22-1874	Isaac gct Purchase MM NY

POSTHER
1-24-1884	Henry rec in mbrp
12-22-1894	Minnie & ch Loran E & Paul C rec in mbrp

POTTENGER
9-21-1889	Elmina rocf Elk MM OH

POTTER
1-17-1824	Cert rec for Stephen & s Jehiel fr New Garden MM; end to Springfield MM
6-22-1859	Rebecca (**Branson**) dis for mcd

POTTINGER
12-26-1891	Elmina not found

POTTS
5-27-1820	Samuel & s Edward, Lindley, & John rocf Concord MM OH; Mary & dt Rebecca rocf Concord MM OH; Ruthanna rocf Concord MM OH

POTTS (cont)
7-28-1821	Samuel & w Mary & ch Rebecca, Lindley, & John gct Flushing MM OH; Edward G gct Flushing MM OH

POWELL
11-29-1817	Sally rocf Western Branch MM VA

PRAY
4-24-1819	Mary & dt Mary & min s Joseph & Enos rocf Redstone MM PA
10-31-1819	Rachel rocf Redstone MM PA
10-16-1824	Enos min gct Milford MM
10-15-1825	Joseph gct Elk MM OH
11-22-1826	Mary gct Elk MM OH
10-24-1827	Rachel gct Elk MM OH
12-24-1828	Mary H dt Mary gct Elk MM OH
12-22-1830	Mary rocf Elk MM OH
2-22-1832	Mary gct Elk MM OH

PRESNALL
11-22-1826	Cert rec for John & s John, Jeremiah, Daniel, & Jehu fr Back Creek MM NC; end to Duck Creek MM

PRESNELL
1-18-1823	Cert rec for Daniel & s Benony, Daniel, John, & Nathan; end to New Garden MM

PRETLOW
9-26-1838	Springborough MM OH rq aid in treating with Elizabeth Ann for mcd; made satisfaction
2-27-1839	Elizabeth Ann & Julietta rocf Springborough MM OH
8-23-1843	Elizabeth Ann gct Cincinnati MM OH

PRICE
2-24-1810	Rice appt to comm
5-6-1811	Catharine appt to comm
3-4-1819	James s Rice dec & Catherine Preble Co OH m Lydia dt Jesse & Hannah dec **Jones** at Elkhorn MH
4-20-1822	Rice con mcd
11-15-1823	Rice gct Milford MM
1-17-1824	Lydia & dt Exelina gct Springfield MM
6-19-1824	Catherine & s Robert gct Milford MM
1-27-1830	Francis dis for jas
9-24-1862	Theodore rec in mbrp
3-25-1868	Willimpe Eleanor rec in mbrp
4-22-1868	Emma Jane rec in mbrp
6-26-1872	Theodore T con mcd
7-25-1877	Theodore rel fr mbrp
2-26-1879	Theodore rst
12-26-1891	W Eleanor & Emma Jane not found

PRICHARD
10-28-1829	Cert rec for Samuel fr Spring MM NC; end to New Garden MM

PRICKET
8-26-1829	Cert rec for John fr Middleton MM OH; end to West Grove MM

PRYFOGLE
5-23-1896	Alexander, Alice, Sherman, Grace, Everet, Lawrence, & Laura New Westville OH rec in mbrp

PUCKET
12-25-1819	Daniel & Beulah rocf New Garden MM; Cyrus, Thomas, Greenlie, Mary Catharine, & Levina ch Daniel & Beulah rocf Westfield MM Surry Co NC
5-27-1820	Beulah & dt gct New Garden MM

PUCKETT
4-29-1820	Daniel & fam gct New Garden MM
10-28-1874	Susannah rocf Chestnut Hill MM IA
8-22-1877	Susannah gct Cherry Grove MM

PURDY
10-28-1874	Samuel A & w Gulielma rocf Back Creek MM NC

PURNELL
5-27-1886	Benjamin rec in mbrp
9-26-1891	Jennie & min ch Wm McGriffin & Lizzie S rec in mbrp; Lizzie mbr Grace ME ch

PURVIANCE
7-25-1877	Gulielma gct New Garden MM

PURVIS
12-22-1847	Rachel rocf Pennville MM OH
5-28-1851	Rachel gct Duck Creek MM
3-24-1875	Rachel rel fr mbrp
2-26-1885	Ann drpd fr mbrp for na

PYLE
3-24-1858	Wm L & w Mary T & ch Charles C & Marietta rocf Springfield MM OH
12-26-1860	Wm L & w Mary C & ch Charles C & Marietta gct Springfield MM OH
8-26-1868	David & w Esther & ch Joseph C, Abijah H, & Mary C rocf Springfield MM OH
1-22-1880	Elizabeth B rec in mbrp

QUIGG
9-22-1894	Belle (**Hawkins**) gct Cherry Grove MM

RAILSBACK
7-28-1869	Jehiel rec in mbrp
2-26-1879	Jehiel rel fr mbrp

RAMBO
11-22-1837	Sadsbury MM PA rq aid in treating with Sarah M for mcd; made satisfaction
5-23-1838	Wm rec in mbrp
8-22-1838	Sarah M rocf Sadsbury MM PA
5-31-1843	Wm A s Nathan & Elizabeth Wayne Co m Miriam A dt Elijah & Naomi **Coffin** Wayne Co at Whitewater MH
5-22-1844	Wm A & w Miriam & dt Sarah Sylvania gct Cincinnati MM OH
7-23-1845	Elizabeth Jr rec in mbrp
9-22-1847	Elizabeth rec in mbrp
8-27-1856	Wm A & w Miriam A & ch Sarah S, Edward B, Naomi C, & Francis H rocf Cincinnati MM OH
9-20-1871	Edward B Highland Park IL rel fr mbrp
1-28-1874	Francis H rel fr mbrp

RAMSEY
4-23-1885	Jennie M gct Winchester MM

RANDLE
5-26-1898	Robert W & w Rowena E rocf Portland MM

RANKER
5-23-1896	Sophia New Westville OH rec in mbrp

RATCLIFF
11-25-1815	Elizabeth & dt Elisabeth rocf Deep Creek MM NC
4-27-1816	Sarah rocf New Garden MM
10-27-1821	Letitia & dt Ruth, Mary, & Amelia rocf Deep Creek MM NC
1-28-1829	Cornelius & Mary dis for jas
5-25-1853	Joseph dis for na, mcd, & jH

RATLIF
10-30-1819	Hannah & dt Margaret, Achsah, & Hannah rocf Deep Creek MM NC

RATLIFF
10-27-1810	Cornelius & s Cornelius rocf Back Creek MM NC; Elizabeth & dt Sarah, Milicent, & Abigail rocf Back Creek MM NC; Gulielma & Joseph rocf Back Creek MM NC
3-25-1815	Joseph & s Rueben rocf Deep Creek MM NC; Rebekah & dt Jane, Huldah, & Anna rocf Deep Creek MM NC; Jonathan & s Elias rocf Deep Creek MM NC; Sarah rocf Deep Creek MM NC
11-25-1815	Richard & s Gabriel, Richard, & Cornelius rocf Deep Creek MM NC
12-1-1815	Joseph gct New Garden MM
9-25-1819	Cert rec for John, Thomas, Elias, Jesse, & Enos fr Cane Creek MM NC; end to New Garden MM
10-30-1819	Benjamin & Phinehas rocf Deep Creek MM NC
5-4-1820	Richard s Richard & Elizabeth Wayne Co m Caroline dt John dec & Caroline **Baily** Wayne Co at Orange MH
2-24-1821	Caroline gct West Grove MM
10-27-1821	Joshua & s Thomas, Samuel, Ephraim, & Joseph rocf Deep Creek MM NC
5-18-1822	Cornelius gct Miami MM OH
11-16-1822	Mary rocf Miami MM OH
6-19-1824	Phineas gct Milford MM
12-18-1824	Benjamin gct Milford MM; Hannah & dt Achsah gct Milford MM
9-17-1825	Joshua & w Letitia & ch Mary, Thomas, Samuel, Ephraim, Joseph Branson, & Amelia gct Milford MM
8-22-1827	Margaret gct Duck Creek MM
8-8-1833	Joseph & w Sarah & min ch Milicent, John, Eli, Cornelius, & Mary gct New Garden MM
7-7-1836	Rueben s Joseph & Rebecca Henry Co m Margaret dt Thomas & Elizabeth **Kendall** Wayne Co at Smyrna MM
10-26-1836	Margaret gct Duck Creek MM

RAVALREE
1-24-1891	Katharine gct West Grove MM

RAY
5-23-1896	James, Lusena, & Monroe New Westville OH rec in mbrp
2-25-1897	Mary New Westville OH rec in mbrp
4-28-1898	Myrtle rec in mbrp

READ
9-26-1891	Anna Hadley rq ltr to Fairhaven Presb ch WA

REECE
3-15-1823	Cert rec for John & fam fr Back Creek MM NC; end to West Grove MM
10-22-1856	Charles & w Eunice & s Edwin rocf Walnut Ridge MM

REED
12-26-1818	Sarah (**Grave**) con mcd
3-25-1820	John rec in mbrp
3-19-1825	Anna (**Boswell**) con mcd
5-28-1845	Spiceland MM rq aid in treating with Drucilla A (**Unthank**) for mcd; made satisfaction
6-25-1845	Rowland T con mcd
2-25-1846	Drusella A rocf Spiceland MM
7-27-1853	John con mcd
5-23-1860	John G dis for mcd
2-27-1861	Red Cedar MM IA rq aid in treating with Ann (**Negus**) for mcd
8-27-1862	John G rec in mbrp
9-23-1863	Ann rec in mbrp
3-26-1879	Drusilla A gct Spiceland MM
2-26-1880	Albert S & w Ellen & ch Frank LeFever, Walter, & Hugh gct Spiceland MM
4-23-1885	Albert S & w Ellen M & min ch Franklin, Walter, & Albert gct Indianapolis MM

WHITEWATER MONTHLY MEETING
MINUTES AND MARRIAGES

REED (cont)
5-25-1889	Mary Ann gct White River MM
12-24-1892	Deborah rocf New Garden MM

REEDER
4-23-1885	Charles & w Mary Ellen & min ch Clara A, Mary Alice, & Joseph H rec in mbrp
8-23-1890	Mary Ellen & ch rel fr mbrp
1-24-1891	Mary Ellen rel fr mbrp; Joseph & Samuel ch Charles & Mary Ellen rec in mbrp
6-27-1891	Clara rel fr mbrp
8-24-1899	Charles, Mary, & Joseph drpd fr mbrp

REES
5-25-1859	Hiram & w Rachel & ch Enos, John, Zachariah, Leonard D, Mary, Henry P, & Minetta rocf Westfield MM

REESE
1-24-1866	Charles dis for mcd
7-25-1877	Charles P drpd fr mbrp

REEVES
6-19-1824	Ann rec in mbrp
1-28-1829	Ann dis for jas
7-28-1841	Julietta (**Pretlow**) con mcd
5-28-1845	Julietta gct West Grove MM
10-23-1850	Charles P s Mark E rec in mbrp
7-25-1877	Charles P rel fr mbrp

REICE
4-25-1849	Needham & s Joseph & James rocf Hopewell MM

REID
4-27-1831	Anna dis for na, dp, & jas
6-22-1882	James P & Alice & min ch Nettie, George Andrew, Raleigh Newton, & Emily Myrtle rq mbrp
7-27-1882	James P & w Alice & ch Nettie, George Andrew, Raleigh Newton, & Emily Myrtle rec in mbrp

REIMAN
10-17-1875	Louisa rec in mbrp

REYNOLDS
9-23-1830	Isaac s Anthony & Elizabeth Wayne Co m Tamer dt John & Lydia **Hawkins** Wayne Co at Whitewater MH
7-27-1831	Tamar gct Springfield MM
12-28-1859	Hannah & ch Mary Cornelia, Samuel Clarkson, & Charles Earnest rocf Bridgeport MM; Wm & Margaretta rocf Bridgeport MM
1-24-1866	Hannah & ch Wm, Samuel Clarkson, Mary Cornelia, & Charles Earnest min gct Indianapolis MM
10-26-1882	George L & w Sarah B rocf Greenwood MM
8-27-1885	Charles C & w Mary E & ch Delmer M & Herbert G rocf New Garden MM
9-23-1886	Charles C & w Mary E & ch Delmer M & Herbert C gct Pasadena MM CA
2-23-1888	George & w Sarah gct Earlham MM CA
10-25-1888	Othello E rocf Oskaloosa MM IA
10-24-1891	Othello E glt jas

RHOADES
11-23-1895	Emma rocf Walnut Ridge MM

RHODES
12-25-1839	Moses & w Eleanor & ch David & Susannah rocf Chester MM
3-25-1840	Moses & w Eleanor & min ch David & Susanna gct Chester MM

RICE
10-26-1895	Fidella S & w Rachel A & ch Lillie C, Eva M, Howard S, & Arthur A rocf Cherry Grove MM

RICH
12-14-1822	Nathan rocf Miami MM OH
4-23-1823	Nathan Wayne Co s Samuel & Judith dec Warren Co OH m Mary dt Samuel & Rachel dec **Crampton** Wayne Co at Whitewater MH
8-20-1825	Nathan & w Mary & s Samuel rocf New Garden MM
1-14-1826	Nathan & w Mary & s Samuel gct Chester MM
4-26-1888	Lucetta H rec in mbrp

RICHARDS
11-15-1823	Lydia rocf Cincinnati MM OH
6-27-1877	Mary J w Isaac rec in mbrp
2-26-1880	Isaac H & w Mary Jane & min ch Burke, Mary, Maria M, & Carrie C gct Indianapolis MM
1-22-1885	Mary J & ch Burk, Mary Griffith, Maria Moffatt, Caroline C, Jane Lydia, & Ethan rocf Indianapolis MM

RICHARDSON
4-23-1856	Deborah rocf New York MM NY
2-23-1859	Deborah gct Bloomfield MM
11-26-1862	Deborah rocf New Garden MM
3-28-1866	Deborah gct Northern Dist MM Philadelphia PA
5-23-1896	James & Malinda New Westville OH rec in mbrp

RICHIE
12-28-1859	Samuel S & w Anna S & ch Elisabeth S, John S, Sarah M, Margaret W, Robert Annesley, Anna Mary, Grace L, Samuel Charles, & Jeanette J rocf Philadelphia MM PA
5-27-1868	Mary B rec in mbrp
6-23-1881	Anna S appt o
2-23-1882	Sarah M gct Burlington MM NJ
8-27-1885	Robert A rel fr mbrp
11-23-1889	E Russel rel fr mbrp; j Ellendale Bapt ch Dakota
6-27-1891	Grace L rel fr mbrp; jas
12-22-1894	John S & w Mary B & s Arthur C gct Scotts Mills MM OR; Anne & ch Henry E & Benjamin M gct Scotts Mills MM OR

RITCLIF
10-27-1821	Letitia & dt Ruth, Mary, & Amelia rocf Deep Creek MM NC

ROBARDS
11-25-1846	Thomas dis for na & jH

ROBERDS
10-4-1815	Walter s Thomas & Ann Wayne Co m Hannah dt James & Ruth dec **Johnson** Wayne Co at Whitewater MH
11-1-1815	Phenias s Freeman & Martha Wayne Co m Ruth dt Jeremiah & Margery **Cox** Wayne Co at Whitewater MH
1-27-1816	Walter & fam gct New Garden MM; Hannah gct New Garden MM
10-26-1816	Solomon Whitson gct New Garden MM
3-29-1817	Elisabeth rocf New Garden MM
5-23-1827	Thomas gct Silver Creek MM
8-27-1834	Mary rocf Caesar's Creek MM OH
5-22-1839	Esther & Mary dis for jH

ROBERT
12-22-1830	Jonathan gct Alum Creek MM OH to m Mary **Smith**

ROBERTS
6-29-1811	Phinehas & s John rec in mbrp
7-27-1811	Thomas & s Walter, David, Solomon Whitson, Thomas, & Jonathan rocf Elk MM OH; Ann & dt Phebe & Sarah rocf Elk MM OH; Sarah rec in mbrp
12-26-1812	Walter gct Elk MM OH
9-25-1813	Mary rocf Elk MM OH
2-25-1815	Amy con mcd

ROBERTS (cont)
9-26-1827	Sarah rocf Silver Creek MM
5-25-1831	Mary rocf Alum Creek MM
9-26-1832	Solomon W & Elizabeth dis for jH
1-22-1834	Thomas Jr gct Caesar's Creek MM OH to m Mary **Myres**
10-25-1848	Daniel dis for na & mcd
8-31-1853	Wm s Thomas & Mary both dec Wayne Co m Elizabeth dt Henry dec & Rebecca **Rue** Wayne Co at Whitewater MH
10-22-1856	Edward dis for mcd
5-27-1857	Sarah rocf Milford MM
8-26-1868	Henry & Martha (**Charles**) con mcd
2-24-1869	Jordan Helena AR rec in mbrp
5-25-1870	Lydia C rocf Elk MM OH
3-27-1872	Samuel rec in mbrp
8-31-1876	Lindley H s Wm & Elizabeth Wayne Co m Alice dt Wm dec & Ellen **Edgerton** at Orange MH Wayne Co
6-28-1878	Lydia C gct Elk MM OH
8-26-1880	Wm minister & w Elizabeth & min ch John H, Annie M, & Emma L gct Walnut Center MM IA; Lindley H & w Alice E & min dt Ethel B gct Walnut Center MM IA; Albert B gct Walnut Center MM IA
8-23-1883	Jonathan & Mary appt elders
5-26-1887	Samuel & w Sarah E & min ch Mary Annie, Fredrick Warren, & Jane Lee gct New Garden MM
7-25-1891	Mary E rocf Dover MM
9-24-1896	Samuel & w Sarah E & ch Mary, Frederic, & Ione rocf New Garden MM
6-23-1899	Sarah E & ch Mary, Frederick, & Ione gct Indianapolis MM

ROBERTSON
4-16-1883	Sarah Centreville rq mbrp

ROBINSON
5-25-1842	Jane (**Taylor**) dis for na & mcd
9-24-1856	Thomas & w Rebecca & min ch Martha Ann, Isaac King, Harmon, Wm Henry, & Lorenzo Dow rocf Honey Creek MM
9-25-1861	Thomas & w Rebecca & ch Martha Ann, Isaac King, Harmon, Wm Henry, & Lorenzo Dow gct West Grove MM
7-24-1872	Rebecca & ch Wm H, Emma C, Elizabeth E, & Lemuel rocf Vermilion MM IL
12-25-1872	Thomas & s Isaac rocf Wabash MM
8-25-1875	Eleanora & Fanny rec in mbrp
10-23-1878	Thomas & w Rebecca & min ch Isaac, Emma C, Lorrie E, & Samuel gct Milford MM; ret
12-22-1881	Thomas & w Rebecca & min ch Elizabeth & Lemuel gct West Grove MM
3-22-1883	Jane gct New Garden MM
12-27-1883	Elizabeth rq PM at Centerville
5-26-1887	Thomas & w Rebecca & ch Lemuel & Elizabeth rocf West Grove MM
9-24-1896	Mary Woodard & dt Irene gct White River MM
10-28-1897	Charles & w Gertrude rocf Chester MM

ROCKHILL
2-23-1882	Jane rq mbrp in Richmond PM
2-28-1884	Jane rq for mbrp drpd

RODAMMEL
10-27-1847	Wm rec in mbrp

RODEARMEL
3-28-1849	Wm gct Chester MM

RODEFELD
4-25-1896	Lena E rocf Plainfield MM
11-26-1896	Lina rel fr mbrp

ROE
1-24-1884	Smyrna PM rpt Sarah Elizabeth & Rebecca rq mbrp
2-28-1884	Sarah E & Rebecca rec in mbrp
11-25-1886	Rebecca drpd fr mbrp; jas

ROGERS
8-24-1853	Eunice rocf Mississinewa MM
11-22-1858	Olinda (**Mendenhall**) con mcd
3-28-1860	Ansel & w Cynthia & ch Daniel T, Alonzo, Sarah L, & Arthur C rocf Winneshiek MM IA; sent to KS PM
6-30-1875	Jonathan C s Jacob & Christiana Randolph Co m Annie dt John & Martha **Valentine** Richmond at res her father
9-22-1875	Anna (**Valentine**) gct New Garden MM
7-25-1877	Olinda B drpd fr mbrp; jas
5-27-1893	Charles H rec in mbrp
1-27-1894	Nancy J & min ch Esta, Eddie, Frank, & Gertie rocf Portland MM
1-26-1895	Nancy J & ch Esta, Eddie, & Frank gct Portland MM; Gertie gct Portland MM

ROPER
3-23-1895	Oliver rec in mbrp

ROSE
12-30-1809	Hester con mcd

ROSECRANS
1-28-1897	Maude Wolf rel fr mbrp

ROSS
10-25-1876	Hannah J rec in mbrp
5-25-1889	Susanna rec in mbrp
10-24-1891	John A rec in mbrp
10-26-1895	Ida rec in mbrp

ROTHEMERAL
5-27-1897	Asa Providence & Friendship Darke Co OH rec in mbrp

ROWNTREE
3-25-1863	Wm rocf Brighouse MM England

RUE
3-25-1820	Rebecca (**Talbot**) con mcd
5-24-1837	Henry & ch Richard, Hannah, Lydia, Rebecca, Susannah, & Elizabeth rec in mbrp
4-22-1846	Richard con mcd
1-24-1855	Rachel & ch Lydia H, John, & Eva rec in mbrp
6-26-1872	Richard & w Rachel & ch John, Alice, Ada, Edgar, & Lewis gct Lawrence MM KS

RUHLE
5-27-1897	John R & Anna Providence & Friendship Darke Co OH rec in mbrp

RULON
1-28-1829	Sarah dis at rq of Burlington MM NJ for jas
10-24-1832	Eliza Ann (**Atkinson**) dis for mcd & jas; mbr Burlington MM NJ

RUSSEL
10-26-1811	George rocf New Garden MM NC; Judith & dt Ruth rocf New Garden MM NC
10-22-1834	Susannah gct West Grove MM
7-22-1897	Linetta rec in mbrp

RUSSELL
10-16-1824	George & w Judith & ch Ruth, Sarah, Sina, Timothy, Josiah, George, & James gct West Grove MM
9-3-1834	George s Timothy & Sarah dec Wayne Co m Susanna dt dt Ivan & Mary **Jones** Morgan Co at Whitewater MH
6-22-1870	Henry rocf Sandwich MM MA

**WHITEWATER MONTHLY MEETING
MINUTES AND MARRIAGES**

RUSSELL (cont)
11-22-1871   Henry gct Fall River MM MA
6-24-1897   Elbert rocf Fairfield MM

RUSSEY
10-19-1822   Mary rec in mbrp

RUSSY
10-28-1835   Charity (**Williams**) dis for mcd

RYAN
3-25-1874   Daniel rec in mbrp
6-26-1878   Daniel rel fr mbrp

SACKETT
10-28-1897   Robert S rec in mbrp

SAINT
9-26-1812   Thomas & Mary rocf Back Creek MM NC
7-27-1816   Wm & s Escum & Alpheus rocf Piney Woods MM NC; Achsah M & dt Gulielma & Janette rocf Piney Woods MM NC
6-27-1840   Sarah & Richard ch Thomas rocf Milford MM
10-26-1842   Sarah dt Thomas gct Milford MM
6-23-1852   Daniel rocf Milford MM
4-22-1868   Daniel gct Spiceland MM
4-26-1883   Daniel rocf Spiceland MM

SAMMS
9-22-1858   Joseph & Lewis rocf Salem MM IA
4-27-1859   Elizabeth rocf Salem MM IA
5-24-1883   Orange PM rpt Sarah P & min s W E rq mbrp
3-24-1887   Sarah rel fr mbrp

SAMS
6-25-1885   Sarah P & s Wm rec in mbrp

SANDERS
3-31-1819   Jacob Wayne Co s David & Sarah NC m Sarah dt Andrew & Elizabeth **Hoover** Wayne Co at Whitewater MH
1-15-1823   Abigail (**Osborn**) dis for mcd
3-20-1824   Abigail dis for mcd
3-25-1829   Jacob dis for jas
4-22-1829   Sarah dis for jas
11-28-1833   Thomas M s John & Milley dec Highland Co OH m Sarah dt Hesekiah dec & Sarah **Ham** Wayne Co at Orange MH
1-22-1834   Sarah gct Clear Creek MM OH
1-28-1857   Mary rocf Cincinnati MM OH
9-22-1869   Sarah, Mary Caroline, & Ellen rocf Clear Creek MM OH
8-28-1872   Sarah Sr, Mary C, & Ellen gct Clear Creek MM OH

SANDS
5-28-1885   Whitewater rpt Sarah rq mbrp

SAUNDERS
7-26-1817   Jacob rocf Deep River MM NC

SCARCE
5-23-1866   Sarah E rec in mbrp
4-28-1875   Edward rec in mbrp
8-28-1878   Alice rec in mbrp
6-28-1883   Orange PM rpt Edward addicted to intoxicating liquors; dis
11-24-1894   Caroline & s Earl rec in mbrp

SCHANCK
7-25-1877   Herman F rel fr mbrp

SCHENCK
12-24-1875   Herman F rec in mbrp

SCHENEMON
5-26-1898   Wm rel fr mbrp

SCHINNAMON
5-25-1895   Rachel rec in mbrp

SCHINNEMAN
2-24-1894   Wm rec in mbrp

SCHINNEMON
8-24-1899   Rachel drpd fr mbrp

SCHISSLER
6-25-1896   Laura rocf Dublin MM

SCHNEIDER
12-25-1872   Susan rec in mbrp
4-23-1879   Katie C w Phillip & ch Lizzie J & Mattie C rec in mbrp

SCHOOLEY
10-23-1844   Omri & w Elizabeth & min s Wm H rocf New Hope MM
5-28-1845   Omri & s Wm H gct Center MM

SCHWING
8-26-1893   Sophia rec in mbrp

SCOTT
8-27-1834   Susanna bound girl Wm & Mary **Cox** rec in mbrp
6-27-1838   Eleanor (**Dilhorn**) dis for mcd
10-22-1845   Ann & ch Ann Eliza, John L, & Louisa rocf Center MM OH
3-26-1851   Ann & ch Eliza Ann, John L, & Louisa gct White Lick MM
3-27-1872   Agrippa & w Anna & ch Ellsworth, Eddie, & Eva rec in mbrp
3-22-1876   Anne & ch Elsworth G, Eva B, Eddie D, & Willie H rel fr mbrp
5-23-1877   Agrippa rel fr mbrp
5-27-1880   Anna & ch Ellsworth G, Eva B, Eddie D, & Willie H rel fr mbrp
2-22-1890   Elsworth rel fr mbrp
7-23-1896   Edwin drpd fr mbrp

SEAMAN
7-26-1883   Nellie G rel fr mbrp

SEDGEWICK
10-26-1895   Marcia S rel fr mbrp

SEDGWICK
10-15-1884   Richard S Richmond m Marcia E dt David & Deborah W **Sutton** Richmond at res of her father

SETTLES
3-24-1881   John Wesley rec in mbrp
6-23-1898   John Wesley drpd fr mbrp

SHAFFER
7-28-1894   James M & w Mary A rec in mbrp
3-23-1895   Louis & Olive rec in mbrp

SHANK
5-25-1836   Rachel (**Clarke**) dis for mcd
4-26-1837   Ch of Rachel gct Milford MM; not named in removal certs

SHAW
8-1-1860   Aaron s Noble dec & Cicely Morgan Co m Sarah dt Benjamin & Mary **Cox** Wayne Co at Whitewater MH
10-24-1860   Sarah gct West Union MM

SHEARON
10-23-1844	Caleb & Elizabeth rec in mbrp
3-25-1846	Ruth Ann rec in mbrp
12-22-1847	Rachel Lunetta rec in mbrp
1-26-1848	Warner rec in mbrp

SHERBER
4-25-1891	James rec in mbrp
2-24-1898	James rel fr mbrp

SHERIDAN
10-24-1839	Thomas s John dec & Margaret Henry Co m Hannah dt Elijah & Susanna **Wright** Wayne Co at Smyrna Mtg
7-22-1840	Hannah gct Spiceland MM

SHIBELY
11-26-1862	Hannah B (**Mendenhall**) con mcd

SHIELDS
5-31-1817	Sarah rocf Deep River MM NC
7-29-1820	Sarah gct West Grove MM
8-23-1843	Sarah gct Salem MM IA

SHINAMAN
2-24-1894	Wm rec in mbrp

SHINN
2-26-1840	David & Hannah & ch David & Susan rocf Marlborough MM OH
7-25-1855	David dis for na & mcd
6-24-1874	Newman H rec in mbrp
3-28-1877	James Eddie rec in mbrp
5-23-1877	Anna C rec in mbrp
11-6-1878	Newman H s Miles J & Anna C Wayne Co m Alice A dt Jonathan & Dorcas **Scarce** Richmond at Whitewater Mtg
1-27-1881	Newman H & w Alice & min dt Anna gct Rose Hill MM KS; James Eddy & Anna C gct Rose Hill MM KS

SHOEMAKER
5-28-1862	Wm C rocf Philadelphia MM PA
9-23-1863	Anna B, Hannah, Margaret, & Isaac ch Charles rocf Abington MM PA
7-27-1864	Rachel J (**Dilks**) rpt mcd; drpd fr mbrp
12-28-1864	Wm C rpt mcd; drpd fr mbrp
9-22-1869	Wm & w Rachel rec in mbrp
8-23-1883	Sidney D d 5-31-1883
2-26-1885	Isaac gc
7-22-1897	Charles d rpt; ae 85y

SHORT
5-23-1896	T Edward, Charles M, & Eva New Westville OH rec in mbrp

SHOWAN
10-23-1867	Henry C rst; dis for taking part in military operations during war
3-25-1868	Jennie rec in mbrp
2-26-1885	Jennie drpd fr mbrp for na
12-16-1891	Lydia Ann not found

SHOWEN
5-23-1866	Lydia A (**Overman**) con mcd

SHRIVER
6-25-1892	Helen Horney gct Westland MM OH

SHUGARDS
10-26-1811	Mary & dt Mary, Sarah, & Tamar rocf Deep Creek MM NC

SHUGART
9-28-1814	John s George & Mary Wayne Co m Sarah dt Cornelius & Elizabeth **Ratliff** Wayne Co at Whitewater MH

SHULTZ
8-25-1898	Samuel T & w Eunice C & ch C Irvin, Corlin H, Joseph, & Eva rocf Westland MM

SHUMAN
2-24-1869	Lila Helena AR rec in mbrp

SHUTE
10-30-1819	Samuel & s Charles, Aaron, Samuel, & Robert rocf Piles Grove MM NJ; Siby & dt Harriet H & Lydia rocf Piles Grove MM NJ; Ann H rocf Piles Grove MM NJ
1-28-1829	Samuel dis for jas
7-22-1829	Aaron, Charles, Martha, & Sybal dis for jas
9-23-1829	Elizabeth (**Hill**) dis for jas & mcd
5-23-1832	Samuel Jr dis for jH
6-26-1839	Lydia & Elizabeth dis for jH & na
11-22-1843	Robert dis for na & mcd
8-24-1889	Martha A rocf Dublin MM

SIDDALL
9-25-1819	Atticus & s David rocf Carmel MM OH; Sarah rocf Carmel MM OH
4-28-1827	Atticus & w Sarah & s David J, Jesse P, & Albert A gct Silver Creek MM
5-22-1839	David dis for na & mcd
5-28-1845	Jesse P dis for na, jas, & mcd
5-27-1846	Philemon F & Albert P s Atticus gct Back Creek MM

SIDDLE
6-23-1830	David, Jesse, Albert, & Philemon ch Atticus rocf Silver Creek MM

SIDWELL
2-26-1814	David & Esther rocf Elk MM OH

SILVERS
4-27-1842	Ruth Ann (**Cox**) dis for na & mcd

SIMMON
5-30-1812	Abigail rocf Caesar's Creek MM OH

SINGLETON
3-23-1895	Flora E & s Arthur B rec in mbrp

SKINNER
3-30-1822	Deiduma (**Elliott**) con mcd

SMALL
10-27-1810	Jesse rocf Mt Pleasant MM VA
5-6-1811	Elizabeth appt to comm; Nathan rocf Contentnea MM NC
10-30-1813	Jesse gct Fall Creek MM OH
11-27-1813	Josiah rocf Back Creek MM NC
6-24-1815	Obadiah & Isabel rocf Fall Creek MM OH
10-28-1815	Jonathan, Amos, & Nathaniel rocf Fall Creek MM OH; Sarah & dt Ann Ruth & Sarah rocf Fall Creek MM OH
1-3-1816	Josiah s Obadiah dec & Elizabeth Wayne Co m Jane dt Thomas & Abigail **Moore** Wayne Co at Whitewater MH
8-31-1816	Joshua rocf New Garden MM
10-2-1816	Jonathan s Gideon dec & Sarah Wayne Co m Miriam dt Josiah dec & Miriam **Bundy** Wayne Co at Whitewater MH
3-29-1817	Abraham rec in mbrp
11-29-1817	Obadiah & Jonathan & ch gct New Garden MM; Isabella & Miriam gct New Garden MM
2-28-1818	Samuel min rocf Clear Creek MM OH
1-29-1820	Samuel con mcd
2-26-1820	Joshua con mcd
3-25-1820	Joshua gct New Garden MM

WHITEWATER MONTHLY MEETING
MINUTES AND MARRIAGES

SMALL (cont)
4-28-1821	Elizabeth con allowing mcd at her house; Benjamin con for admitting entertainment contrary to discipline
9-29-1821	Abigail (**Stafford**) con mcd
8-17-1822	Amos con mcd
3-20-1824	Abner dis for getting in a passion, upl, & offering to fight
6-19-1824	Sarah dis for unchastity
1-14-1826	Rachel (**Hawkins**) dis for mcd
3-18-1826	Nathan dis for mcd
12-24-1828	Ephraim gct Fall Creek MM OH
4-28-1830	Minute rec fr White River MM informing of d Jesse

SMELSER
3-23-1899	Frank New Westville OH rec in mbrp

SMITH
9-30-1809	John appt clerk
11-25-1809	Tishe appt to comm
4-28-1810	Tamar con mcd
11-24-1810	Nathan con mcd
2-26-1812	Benjamin & s John rec in mbrp
6-27-1812	Robert dis for military training
10-31-1812	Nathan dis for uniting with men concerned in warlike measures
12-27-1813	John con for purchasing & conveying supplies for use of armies
2-25-1814	Hannah, Mary, & John ch Benjamin rec in mbrp
12-30-1815	John Jr con dr & upl
4-27-1816	John Jr dis for mcd
11-30-1816	Caleb rec in mbrp
6-27-1818	John gct Alum Creek MM OH
6-26-1819	Jane & dt Jane & Martha N **Pleas** rocf Alum Creek MM OH
9-29-1821	Jacob & s Nathan, Ezra, Samuel, & Jacob rocf Flushing MM OH; Martha & dt Anna, Letitia, Gulielma, & Mary rocf Flushing MM OH
6-18-1825	Cornelius, Joseph, & John dis for jas; Mary & dt Elizabeth dis for jas
8-20-1825	Sarah, Ira, Millicent, Abigail, & Mary min ch Robert gct Milford MM
11-22-1826	Samuel S & s Wm B & Henry rocf Baltimore MM MD; Eliza Ann rocf Baltimore MM MD
12-27-1826	Anna rocf Baltimore MM MD
1-4-1827	Samuel W s John & Tishe dec Wayne Co m Elizabeth W dt John & Elizabeth **Barnes** Wayne Co at Ridge MH
9-24-1828	Phebe (**King**) dis for jas
4-22-1829	Elizabeth rec in mbrp
7-22-1829	Martha, Eliza Ann, Gulielma, & Mary dis for jas
8-26-1829	Jacob & Wm dis for jas
11-25-1829	Henry dis for jas
6-22-1831	Samuel W dis for na; Elizabeth dis for att ball & deviating from the truth
7-27-1831	Sarah rocf Goshen MM OH
4-25-1832	Nathan dis for being out of unity with Friends, jas, & mcd
4-23-1834	Alice (**Erwin**) dis for jH & mcd
2-24-1836	Jarah & w Avis & ch John & Phebe rocf Alum Creek MM OH; Anna rocf Alum Creek MM OH
5-25-1836	Jarah & w Avis & ch John & Phebe gct Westfield MM IA
11-23-1836	Anna gct Westfield MM IA
1-25-1837	Margaret (**Foulke**) dis for mcd & jH
1-24-1838	Amy Amanda (**Cox**) dis for na & mcd
7-22-1845	Phebe dis for na & jH
11-28-1848	Elisha & Seth dis for na
7-28-1852	James & Mahlon T rocf Hopewell MM VA
7-27-1853	James con mcd
5-23-1855	Letitia & Mary Jr rocf Hopewell MM at Goose Creek VA
11-28-1855	Mary Sr & dt Charlotte A rocf Hopewell MM VA
5-28-1856	Robert B rocf Hopewell MM VA

SMITH (cont)
2-25-1857	Seth rst; dis by Goose Creek MM VA
6-26-1861	Sarah Jane (**Edgerton**) con mcd
8-28-1861	Sarah Jane (**Edgerton**) gct KS MM
9-21-1864	Robert B rpt mcd; drpd fr mbrp
5-24-1871	Lottie rel fr mbrp to jas
11-29-1872	Charles G Wayne Co s James & Mary dec Warren Co OH m Elvira M dt Isaac & Rachel dec **Pearson** Miami Co OH at res of Clayton **Brown** Whitewater MM
11-27-1872	Charles G rocf Salem MM IA
5-26-1875	John E & ch Caroline, Catherine, & Minnie rocf Cherry Grove MM
2-26-1879	Charles G & w Elvira P & dt Orianna gct Miami MM OH
5-26-1881	Charles G & w Elvira P & dt Oriana rocf Miami MM OH
11-24-1881	Hannah (**Whitall**) & dt Alice **Whitall** rq mbrp
1-26-1882	Hannah (**Whital**) & dt Alice W withdraw rq for mbrp
3-22-1883	Mary rocf New Garden MM
5-24-1883	Mary & h removed to Brownsville
6-28-1883	Mary Ann Centreville rec in mbrp
12-27-1883	Mary A, Katie, Carrie, & Minnie rq PM at Centreville
1-24-1884	James & w Sarah J rocf Indianapolis MM
9-25-1884	Charles G & w Ella & dt Orina gct Harmony MM Dakota Terr
2-26-1885	Sarah J minister gct Dublin MM
2-24-1887	John & w Mary & ch Catharine, Carrie, & Minnie gct West Grove MM
3-23-1889	Emily (**Horney**) gct Westland MM OH
10-26-1889	L Mary rel fr mbrp; glt Richmond Christian ch
1-24-1891	Mary Ann gct West Grove MM
2-27-1892	Mary E rec in mbrp; mbr Eaton OH UB ch
12-23-1893	Wm M & w Alice & min s Walter rocf Dublin MM
2-24-1894	Amanda rec in mbrp
3-23-1895	Albert & w Isabel & s Arthur D rec in mbrp
1-25-1896	Sarah rocf Chester MM
4-28-1898	Margery & Abigail rec in mbrp
1-26-1899	Wm M rel fr mbrp; j Ind Volunteer Infantry in Cuba
6-22-1899	Amanda gct West Grove MM

SMYTH
1-24-1872	Martha & min ch Wm H, Howard J, & Benjamin F **Baldwin** gct Cherry Grove MM

SMYTHE
4-27-1870	Martha (**Baldwin**) con mcd

SNIPES
11-26-1851	Mary rocf Elk MM OH
3-26-1856	Mary gct Chester MM

SNYDER
8-26-1863	Agatha rec in mbrp
6-22-1864	Rhoda Ann (**Nordyke**) con mcd
3-27-1867	Philip rec in mbrp

SPENCER
3-27-1872	Elisha & w Elizabeth Orange PM rec in mbrp
6-22-1882	Alice H withdraws rq for mbrp
10-22-1892	Mary Emma rocf Miami MM OH Wilmington OH

SPIVAH
5-25-1811	Axiom & Ephraim rocf Contentnea MM NC

SPIVY
5-30-1812	Abigail & dt Becca & Aba rocf Contentnea MM NC

SPONSLER
6-28-1848	Sarah (**Boswell**) dis for na, j ME, & mcd

SPRAY
7-30-1814	Phebe rocf Miami MM OH

SPRINGER
10-26-1816	Stephen & s Mathew & Wm rocf Deep River MM NC; Sarah & dt Sally & Elizabeth rocf Deep River MM NC; Abigail & Barnabas rocf Deep River MM NC
5-31-1817	Abigail dis for att mcd
4-24-1819	Stephen & s Matthew & Wm rocf Silver Creek MM; Sarah & dt Elizabeth & Sally rocf Silver Creek MM
4-29-1820	Matthew dis for mcd
7-29-1820	George rocf Springfield MM
5-15-1824	Barnabas dis for mcd
12-23-1829	Wm L dis for jas
6-23-1830	George dis for na & att mcd
4-27-1831	Barnabas rst
9-28-1831	Barnabas gct Duck Creek MM
2-22-1837	Sarah gct Milford MM

SPRONG
4-22-1893	Otto rec in mbrp
10-22-1896	Otto gct Pasadena MM CA

STAFFORD
10-27-1810	Thomas rocf Back Creek MM NC
2-26-1812	Thomas & ch Brantly, Elias, & Eli rec in mbrp
10-30-1813	Samuel rocf Back Creek MM NC; Elizabeth rec in mbrp
2-26-1814	Brantley, Elias, Philany, & Eli ch Thomas rec in mbrp
7-31-1817	Samuel Wayne Co s Samuel & Abigail NC m Nancy dt Wm & Sarah **Hastings** Wayne Co at West Grove MH
10-31-1818	Cert rec for Eli fr Back Creek MM NC; end to West Grove MM
7-28-1821	Abigail rocf Westfield MM
9-22-1830	Henry, Wm, & Elam s Thomas & Elizabeth rocf Chester MM
10-27-1830	Thomas rocf Chester MM
4-27-1831	Thomas & w Elizabeth & min ch Martha, Celia, Henry, Wm, & Elam gct Sugar River MM

STALKER
6-30-1810	Rachel & ch Elizabeth, George, Deborah, & Eli rocf Deep River MM NC
9-23-1835	John rocf Springfield MM OH
8-24-1836	John gct Springfield MM OH

STANLEY
9-25-1819	John & Elizabeth rocf New Garden MM
7-28-1821	John & fam gct Cherry Grove MM
8-25-1821	Elizabeth gct Cherry Grove MM
2-28-1822	George s Samuel & Susanna Clinton Co OH m Jemime dt Jeremiah & Karen **Parker** Wayne Co at Orange MH
3-30-1822	Elizabeth rocf Cherry Grove MM
7-20-1822	Jemima gct Newberry MM OH
11-20-1824	Abel & s Nathan & Wm rocf Hopewell MM NC; Rachel & dt Hannah, Elizabeth, Rebecca, Jane, Sarah, Naomi H, & Mary R rocf Hopewell MM NC; Matthew rocf Hopewell MM NC
3-19-1825	Abel & w Rachel & ch Matthew, Hannah, Nathan, Elizabeth, Rebecca, Jane, Sarah, Wm, Naomi H, & Mary gct White Lick MM
6-23-1830	Samuel & s Harvey, Barclay, & Wm rocf Dover MM NC; Anna & dt Rebekah & Sarah rocf Dover MM NC
5-25-1831	Richard & s Elwood, Joshua, & Nathan Dix rocf Hopewell MM NC; Abigail & dt Elmina & Rebecca rocf Hopewell MM NC
12-28-1831	Anna rocf Union MM NC
1-23-1833	James & fam rocf Springfield MM OH
3-27-1833	Samuel & w Anna & ch Harvey, Barclay, Rebecca, Sarah, Wm, & Cyrus gct White Lick MM
2-26-1834	Temple & w Anna gct Duck Creek MM
10-28-1835	Richard & w Abigail & ch Rebecca, Joshua F, & Nathan D gct Duck Creek MM; Elwood gct Duck Creek MM

STANLEY (cont)
11-25-1835	Millicent & ch Martin, Rachel, & Jacob gct Marlborough MM OH
9-26-1838	Jesse rocf Philadelphia MM PA
9-25-1844	Jesse gct Philadelphia MM PA
3-27-1872	Wm & w Lucinda E & ch Alva L, Franklin E, & Ada rec in mbrp
12-24-1873	Eliza & Isaac rec in mbrp
7-25-1877	Isaac gct Cherry Grove MM; Hannah & ch Mauna Loa & Mary gct Cherry Grove MM
5-28-1879	Gulielma J gct Cherry Grove MM
2-23-1882	Abram & s Isaac Orlo rec in mbrp
9-23-1886	Wm dis
6-23-1887	Emmet drpd fr mbrp for na
8-25-1887	Alva rel fr mbrp
3-26-1892	Margaret Maria ae 2y dt Gere & Mertie dec grdt Cornelius & Margaret **Miles** rocf Barclay MM KS; has been adopted by relatives here

STANTON
3-28-1812	James & s John, Elijah, & Amos rocf Salem MM OH; Mary & dt Hannah & Susannah rocf Salem MM OH
11-28-1812	Aron & s Wm, Alfred, & Elwood rocf Salem MM OH; Lydia & dt Elizabeth rocf Salem MM OH
9-24-1814	Latham & ch Daniel, Wm, Stephen Butler, Hepzibath, & Gulielma rocf Miami MM OH
10-6-1814	Latham Franklin Co m Rachel dt James & Sarah **Hollingsworth** Franklin Co at Silver Creek MH
5-31-1820	John s James & Mary Franklin Co m Elizabeth dt Adam **Coffin** Wayne Co at Whitewater MH
1-2-1822	Samuel s Wm & Catherine Union Co m Jemime dt Adam & Anna **Coffin** at Whitewater MH
12-14-1822	Jemima gct Silver Creek MM
12-22-1824	Elijah s James dec & Mary Union Co m Anna dt Adam & Anna **Coffin** Wayne Co at Whitewater MH
5-23-1827	Elizabeth gct Silver Creek MM
7-22-1829	Anne & dt Rosilla gct Silver Creek MM
2-27-1839	Almedia & ch Joseph Fleming, Oliver Henry, & Edna Elizabeth rocf Springborough MM OH
10-11-1843	Frederick & w Hannah & ch John, Edward, & Charles F rocf Springborough MM OH; David rocf Springborough MM OH
10-11-1848	John dis for na
10-25-1848	David dis for na & mcd
9-21-1853	Charles T dis for na & mcd
2-22-1854	Phebe Ann (**Williams**) con mcd
8-23-1854	Edward con mcd
2-28-1855	Edward & w Phebe Ann & ch Henry gct Birch Lake MM MI
10-24-1855	Joseph dis for na & dp
9-23-1857	Edward & w Phebe Ann & ch Henry & Mary Emma rocf Birch Lake MM MI
6-22-1870	Ruth rocf Minneapolis MM MN
5-22-1872	Ruth gct Indianapolis MM
12-25-1872	Wm, Mahala, & Geraldine A rec in mbrp
2-24-1875	Carrie C rec in mbrp
7-27-1889	Emma rel fr mbrp; jas
2-20-1890	Henrietta drpd rq for mbrp; to Presb ch with h
5-24-1890	Henrietta rec in mbrp

STARBUCK
12-28-1811	Esther & dt Mahala rocf New Garden MM NC
9-24-1814	Mary rec in mbrp
10-26-1816	Wm & ch Elihu Coffin, Abigail, & Asa rec in mbrp

STARR
2-18-1826	Elizabeth rocf Green St MM Philadelphia PA; Charles W & s Wm & James rocf Green St MM Philadelphia PA
7-23-1828	Charles W dis for jH
10-22-1828	Elizabeth dis for jH
6-27-1832	John & s Jesse, Joshua, Wm, & James rocf Westfield MM; Mary & dt Elizabeth, Phebe, & Sarah rocf Westfield MM; Esther & ch Henry, James, John, Charles, Willets, & Jeremiah rocf Westfield MM

WHITEWATER MONTHLY MEETING
MINUTES AND MARRIAGES

STARR (cont)

7-22-1846	James s Esther dis for na & mcd; Henry dis for na & mcd
9-23-1846	James s Charles W dis for na
5-24-1848	Jesse dis for na & mcd
10-11-1848	Willets dis for na
3-28-1849	John Jr dis for na & mcd
6-28-1854	Esther gct New Garden MM
6-24-1857	Charles dis for mcd
5-23-1860	Esther rocf New Garden MM
6-23-1869	Anna rec in mbrp
12-22-1869	Charles rec in mbrp
3-26-1873	Esther E rec in mbrp
7-25-1877	Jeremiah rel fr mbrp
8-23-1883	Anna E appt elder
7-22-1897	Charles d rpt; ae 73y

STAYER

6-28-1883	John & Catherine Centreville rec in mbrp

STEADHAM

10-28-1835	Elizabeth (**Wright**) con mcd
7-24-1867	Jonas L rec in mbrp

STEDDOM

1-26-1876	Abijah & w Deborah M & ch Edward K, Martha L, & Ella C rocf Miami MM OH
7-28-1881	Martha appt Orange o
11-28-1891	Cornelia A rocf Cincinnati MM OH
2-24-1894	Martha & Ella C rel fr mbrp

STEER

2-23-1859	Deborah Ann rocf Red Cedar MM IA

STEPHENS

1-24-1855	Moses C rocf Greenfield MM
6-23-1858	Moses C gct Radnor MM PA
2-26-1873	Eva (**Rue**) con mcd
2-23-1888	Alice drpd fr mbrp; j Rushville ME ch
12-23-1893	Frank M/W rec in mbrp

STEVENSON

9-24-1892	East Main St PM rpt Rebecca rq mbrp

STEWARD

12-20-1823	Hannah rocf Greenwich MM NJ

STEWART

3-27-1813	Jehu & s Absalom, Jehu, John, & Temple rocf Deep River MM NC
12-20-1823	Samuel W rocf Greenwich MM NJ
7-25-1827	John gct Milford MM to m Martha **Stratton**
4-26-1876	John Sidney gct Spiceland MM
7-25-1877	Sidney gct Spiceland MM
2-27-1878	Albert W rec in mbrp
3-23-1882	Lizzie rec in mbrp
11-23-1882	Rose rq cert to Union MM OH
12-28-1882	Rosa (**Mills**) gct Union MM OH
2-26-1885	Jonathan gc
12-28-1889	John Sidney & w Laura Ann rel fr mbrp
3-28-1891	Lizzie gl

STIDHAM

5-28-1885	Mary E gct Cherry Grove MM
6-25-1885	Mary Emma gct Cherry Grove MM

STIGGLEMAN

4-22-1880	Sallie E & ch Carrie Alma, Corwin H, & Wm G rec in mbrp
6-24-1893	Olive rec in mbrp
1-26-1899	Leona H & dt Nellie Irene rec in mbrp

STOKES

5-15-1824	Benjamin & s Alexander rocf Philadelphia MM North Dist PA; Ann & ch Sarah & Martha rocf Philadelphia MM PA
10-22-1828	Benjamin dis for jH
1-28-1829	Ann & Martha dis for jH
3-21-1830	Alexander dis for jas
7-28-1830	Cert rec for Edward fr Philadelphia MM PA; end to Cincinnati MM OH
8-22-1832	Samuel & s Edwin Henry & Albert rocf Philadelphia MM PA; Jane & dt Isabella, Elizabeth, Hannah R, & Susan rocf Philadelphia MM PA
5-27-1835	Samuel & w Jane & ch Isabell, Elizabeth, Hannah R, Edwin, Henry, Susan, & Albert gct Milford MM
11-23-1836	Sarah rocf Philadelphia MM PA
7-26-1837	Benjamin gct Byberry MM PA to m Phebe **Walton**; cert ret 10-4-1837; m not acc

STOREY

3-27-1884	Wm R rec in mbrp
12-24-1885	Wm R drpd fr mbrp

STOUT

8-24-1831	Cert rec for Levi & fam fr Holly Springs MM NC; end to New Garden MM

STRANAHAN

5-23-1891	Edgar rec in mbrp
11-24-1898	Edgar H gct Back Creek MM

STRATTEN

4-22-1829	Joseph P dis for jas

STRATTON

8-28-1819	Benjamin & s Levi, Epharaim, Benjamin, Joseph, & Samuel rocf Middleton MM OH; Amy & dt Jerusha, Martha, & Mary rocf Middleton MM OH; Naomy rocf West Grove MM
9-29-1821	Daniel rocf Salem MM OH
11-24-1821	John rocf Caesar's Creek MM OH
10-19-1822	Ruth (**Crew**) con mcd; Springfield MM OH informed
3-15-1823	Levi con mcd; Ruth rocf Center MM OH
10-18-1823	Daniel gct West Grove MM
8-14-1824	Joseph D min rocf Philadelphia MM North Dist PA
7-16-1825	Benjamin minister & w Amy & min ch Eliz, Benjamin, Jerusha, Martha, Mary, Joseph Samuel, & Levainy gct Milford MM
8-23-1826	Ephraim dis by Milford MM for dr & offering to fight
9-27-1826	Joseph Jr rocf Springfield MM
11-28-1832	Jonathan D & fam rocf Westfield MM; Prudence & dt rocf Westfield MM
12-25-1833	Jonathan D & w Prudence & ch Milicent Ann & Samuel gct Duck Creek MM
1-22-1834	Levi & w Ruth & min ch Lucinda, Albert, Hannah, & Amy gct Duck Creek MM
4-23-1834	Hannah (**Ogborn**) dis for mcd
1-28-1835	Benjamin dis for na & mcd
10-31-1838	Joseph E s Eli & Eunice Wayne Co m Nancy dt John dec & Mary **Morrow** Wayne Co at Whitewater MH
1-23-1839	Nancy M gct West Grove MM
4-24-1839	West Grove MM gr perm to rst Hannah; dis by this mtg
5-22-1844	Joseph E & ch Edward D, Caroline E, & Charles W rocf West Grove MM
3-4-1846	Joseph E Wayne Co s Eli dec & Eunice Henry Co m Martha dt Micajah & Gulielma **Henley** Wayne Co at Whitewater MH
6-24-1846	Joseph E & w Martha H & ch Edward D, Caroline E, & Charles W gct West Grove MM
10-27-1847	Hannah & ch Ella Maria & Charles W rocf West Grove MM
4-26-1848	Zimri & s Joseph I & Samuel F rec in mbrp

STRATTON (cont)

5-23-1849	Joseph E & w Martha H & ch Edward D, Caroline E, Charles W, & Henry H rocf West Grove MM
5-25-1853	Joseph E & w Martha H & ch Edward D, Caroline E, Charles W, Henry H, Micajah, & Albert W gct New Garden MM
1-23-1861	Charles con mcd
1-23-1867	Charles dis for na & m 2nd w during lifetime of 1st
8-25-1869	Laura Amelia rec in mbrp
8-24-1870	Abram con mcd
4-23-1885	Samuel T & w Laura & dt rel fr mbrp

STRAWBRIDGE

2-22-1832	Benjamin, Jesse, Thomas, Elizabeth, Mary, & Sarah rocf Deer Creek MM
4-25-1838	Jesse dis for j ME ch, na, & dp
12-26-1838	Benjamin dis for mcd
8-28-1839	Joseph B rec in mbrp
1-24-1844	Joseph B dis for na & jas
3-27-1844	Thomas Clarkson dis for na & mcd

STREET

3-28-1827	John Jr rocf Salem MM OH
5-2-1827	John Wayne Co s Aaron & Mary Columbiana Co OH m Dorothy Jr dt Josiah & Dorothy **Gilbert** Wayne Co at Whitewater MH
10-24-1827	John & w Dorothy gct Silver Creek MM
1-25-1832	Eunice rocf Miami MM OH
4-4-1832	Samuel S s Aaron & Mary Wayne Co m Anna dt Stephen & Rebecca **Macy** Wayne Co at Whitewater MH
4-22-1835	Samuel & w Anna & min ch Jane & John gct Spiceland MM
1-22-1862	Lewis & w Sarah T & s Edgar Louis rocf Bridgeport MM
1-27-1875	Edgar Louis & Charles Fawcett ch Louis & Sarah gct Bristol & Frenshay MM England
4-23-1879	Charles Fawcett rocf Bristol & Frenshay MM England
6-22-1882	Sarah T Richmond PM removed
7-27-1882	Sarah T removed; rel
1-16-1885	Lewis, Sarah T, & Charles T gc
3-26-1885	Charles F gct Chicago MM IL
5-28-1885	Louis & w Sarah gct Indianapolis MM
8-27-1885	Cert for Lewis & Sarah ret by Indianapolis MM
4-28-1887	Louis & w Sarah gct Indianapolis MM

STREETE

2-22-1832	Samuel S rocf Miami MM OH

STRETCH

8-23-1826	James & s James rec in mbrp; Ann & dt Elizabeth, Sarah, & Hannah rec in mbrp
11-25-1835	James & w Ann & ch Elizabeth, James A, Sarah J & Hannah gct Milford MM

STUARD

3-27-1813	Sarah & dt Susannah, Mary, Buly, Sarah, & Anna rocf Deep River MM NC

STUART

8-28-1819	Absolum con att mcd & mcd
9-20-1823	Absalom gct West Grove MM
9-26-1827	Jehu Jr dis for bad business practices
9-23-1828	John gct Milford MM
5-26-1830	Samuel & w Hannah & ch Mary, Elizabeth, James, Beulah, & Charles gct Milford MM
9-28-1831	Jehue & w Sarah & ch Beulah, Sarah, Anna, Robert, Cyrus, & Ithamer gct Duck Creek
3-28-1832	Temple dis for na & att mcd
7-23-1834	Cert rec for Lornhama fr Deep River MM NC; end to Duck Creek MM
9-20-1865	Mary (**Fulghum**) dis for mcd

STUART (cont)

2-23-1870	Jonathan rocf Raysville MM
2-25-1874	Sidney rocf Spiceland MM
3-25-1875	Amos Henry Co s John & Sarah Guilford Co NC m Melissa E dt Samuel & Anna **Miles** Wayne Co at Richmond Mtg
6-25-1875	Melissa E gct Spiceland MM
12-23-1886	Amos & w Melissa E rocf Chester MM
6-28-1888	Sidney & w Alice E & ch Edgar & Florence rocf Chester MM; Mary A rocf Spiceland MM
11-23-1889	Sydney & w rq lt to Anderson 1st ME ch

STUBBS

5-29-1811	Joseph s John & Esther both dec Preble Co OH m Ann dt Caleb & Mary **Harvey** Wayne Co at Whitewater MH
9-28-1811	Ann gct Elk MM OH
3-1-1815	Wm s Nathan & Elizabeth Butler Co OH m Esther dt John & Elvira **Townsend** Wayne Co at Whitewater MH
6-24-1815	Esther gct Elk MM OH
4-8-1818	Joseph s Nathan & Elizabeth Butler Co OH m Sarah dt John & Elvira **Townsend** Wayne Co at Whitewater MH
2-27-1819	Sarah gct Elk MM OH
12-25-1819	Elizabeth (**Townsend**) dis for mcd
11-28-1832	Elk MM gr perm to rst Elizabeth (**Townsend**)
6-4-1851	Eli s Elisha & Elizabeth Preble Co OH m Anna F dt Charles dec & Elizabeth **Moffitt** Wayne Co at Whitewater MH
3-24-1852	Anna F gct Elk MM OH
11-28-1855	Rebecca & ch Alvin, Enoch, Albert, Elvira, & Elizabeth rocf Elk MM OH
9-24-1856	Jonathan rocf Elk MM OH
10-22-1856	Isaac & w Charlotte & ch Susannah, Wm, Esther, Rosanna, Lindley H, Elizabeth Ann, Elvira, & Jesse rocf Chester MM
4-22-1857	Isaac & w Charlotte & ch Susannah, Wm, Esther, Roseannah, Lindley H, Elizabeth Ann, Elvira, Jesse, & Mary gct Vermilion MM IL
11-25-1857	Lydia H (**Grave**) dis for mcd
5-25-1859	Jonathan & w Rachel & ch Alvan, Enoch, Albert, Elvira, Elizabeth, & Mary Emma gct Milford MM
5-22-1867	Mary rocf Elk MM OH
1-27-1869	Eli & w Anna F & ch Ruth Emma & Mary Ann rocf Elk MM OH
6-24-1880	Joseph H & w Maria C & ch Ethel B rocf Spiceland MM
4-27-1882	Alveretta rec in mbrp
8-23-1883	Eli appt elder
2-26-1885	Joseph H & Maria gc
4-23-1885	Joseph H & w Maria & min ch Ethel & Mary gct Indianapolis MM
12-28-1899	Lydia A & ch Herbert & Bessie rocf Elk MM OH

SUFFRINS

3-1-1820	John s David & Deborah Warren Co OH m Harriett dt Samuel & Alice dec **Shute** Wayne Co at Whitewater MH
9-20-1823	John con for att Free Mason lodge; dressing in uniform, marching in procession at bur, and na
8-22-1827	Harriet & s Samuel & Charles gct Miami MM OH
11-25-1846	Samuel dis for na
12-23-1868	John rec in mbrp

SUGART

10-26-1811	George & s John, George Zachariah, & Isaiah rocf Deep Creek MM NC

SUMNER

6-24-1815	Sarah rocf Lost Creek MM TN
9-28-1816	Sarah gct New Garden MM

WHITEWATER MONTHLY MEETING
MINUTES AND MARRIAGES

SUTTON

2-24-1869	Ann Helena AR rec in mbrp
4-26-1876	David & w Deborah W & ch Marcia E & Howard rocf Milford MM
2-28-1877	Aaron F & w Anna M & ch Mary B, Marcia E, & Caroline rocf Milford MM
4-25-1877	Aaron F & w Anna M & ch Mary B, Maria E, & Caroline gct Mississinewa MM
4-27-1882	John G rocf Milford MM
8-1-1890	David s Isaac & Sarah dec Richmond m Mary dt Charles H & Marcia dec **Moore** at res of groom Richmond
3-28-1891	Caroline H rocf Marion MM
1-25-1896	David rel fr mbrp

SWAIN

8-29-1818	Eunice & dt Hepsabeth, Judith, Rebekah, Mary, & Lydia rocf Caesar's Creek MM OH
6-26-1819	Cert rec for Thomas & s Job, Obed, Zeno, & Charles from Center MM NC; end to New Garden MM (except Job)
4-28-1821	Job dis for att mcd
5-23-1827	Cert rec for Timothy fr New Garden MM NC; end to Elk MM OH
9-25-1850	Elizabeth (**Rambo**) dis for mcd
1-25-1860	Eliza B rocf Farmington MM NY
3-27-1861	Rachel (**Way**) dis for mcd & na
8-24-1864	Eliza Bell gct Minneapolis MM MN

SWAINE

8-29-1818	Paul & s Francis rocf Caesar's Creek MM OH

SWALLOW

9-30-1815	Lydia rocf Mill Creek MM

SWARTS

8-27-1834	Elizabeth bound girl of Wm & Mary **Cox** rec in mbrp

SWEET

8-22-1827	Solomon rocf Mill Creek MM OH; Catherine & dt Anna, Sarah, & Rebecca rocf Mill Creek MM OH
5-25-1836	Solomon & ch Anna M & Sarah gct Spiceland MM
7-25-1838	Louisa Emilia youngest dt Solomon gct Spiceland MM

SWINDLER

10-30-1819	Elizabeth rocf Redstone MM PA

SYDELL

7-27-1831	Esther dis for jas

SYMONDS

11-29-1817	Samuel rocf Back Creek MM NC

SYMONS

7-27-1811	Jesse Sr rocf Symons Creek MM NC; Peninah & dt Sarah & Lydia rocf Symons Creek MM NC
9-28-1811	Thomas rocf Springfield MM NC
10-26-1811	Nathan rocf Springfield MM NC; Jane & dt Elizabeth rocf Springfield MM NC
11-30-1811	Hannah rocf New Garden MM NC
7-29-1812	Jesse Wayne Co s Jesse dec & Sarah m Peninah dt John & Letitia **Smith** Wayne Co at Whitewater MH
12-26-1812	Jesse con for speaking untruth
11-28-1818	Cert rec for Mathew & s Matthew fr Marlborough MM NC; end to West Grove MM; cert rec for Thomas fr Marlborough MM NC; end to West Grove MM
5-29-1819	Abraham & s John, Abraham, Matthew, & Thomas rocf Back Creek MM NC; Mary & dt Abigail, Sarah, Margaret, Gulielma, & Phebe rocf Back Creek MM NC
3-25-1820	Abraham & fam gct West Grove MM; Mary & dt gct West Grove MM

SYMONS (cont)

9-19-1822	Samuel s Abraham & Mary Wayne Co m Ann dt Daniel dec & Mary **Bonine** Wayne Co at Orange MH
3-26-1828	Samuel rocf New Garden MM
6-29-1836	Jesse s Jesse & Sarah both dec Wayne Co m Margaret dt Samuel & Margaret both dec Moore Wayne Co at Whitewater MH
8-28-1839	Samuel & w Ann & min ch Lydia, James, John, Abraham, & Henry gct Milford MM
1-27-1841	Hannah & ch Elijah, Thomas, & Abel rocf Mississinewa MM; Rebecca rocf Mississinewa MM
11-24-1841	Andrew con mcd
2-23-1842	Anderson gct Back Creek MM
1-25-1843	Thomas rec in mbrp
11-27-1844	Jemima H rocf Dover MM
12-25-1844	Alfred dis for mcd & dp
3-26-1845	Nathan dis for na & jas; Thomas Jr gct Mississinewa MM
5-28-1845	Jesse & dt Lucinda & Letitia gct Chester MM
7-22-1846	Jemimah gct Mississinewa MM
10-25-1848	John dis for jas
2-28-1849	Abel dis for na
8-22-1849	Jesse rocf Chester MM
11-27-1850	Springfield MM rq aid in treating with Elenor (**Longshore**) for mcd; made satisfaction
3-26-1851	Thomas & w Hannah & s Elijah gct Richland MM; Eleanor rocf Springfield MM OH

TALBERT

11-26-1814	Wm & s Elihu & Cyrus rocf Elk MM OH; Miriam & dt Anne & Sarah rocf Elk MM OH
10-27-1847	Edward con mcd
6-28-1851	Hannah & ch Elisha, Ann, & Phebe rocf Pennville MM OH
10-23-1884	Samuel & w Lydia Ellen & ch Jesse, Indianora, Melva E, & Earnest L rocf Elk MM OH
7-28-1887	Samuel & w Lydia E & ch Jesse, India Ora, Melvia E, & Earnest L gct Indianapolis MM

TALBOT

5-25-1816	Rebekah rocf Newberry MM TN
6-3-1816	Jacob rocf Newberry MM TN
5-24-1848	Edward gct Birch Lake MM MI

TALBOTT

5-25-1816	Susannah rocf Newberry MM TN
8-27-1861	Hannah & ch Elisha, Ann, & Phebe gct Richland MM

TAYLOR

10-31-1818	George, Elizabeth, & Charlotte ch James rec in mbrp
2-27-1839	Jane rocf Salem MM
4-26-1883	John C & w Beulah W & ch Mary Annie & Charles A rocf Elk MM OH
6-28-1883	Elizabeth Centreville rec in mbrp
7-26-1883	Wm E rocf Elk MM OH
12-27-1883	Elizabeth rq PM at Centreville
4-25-1884	Amanda E rocf Greenwood MM
2-26-1885	John C & Beulah W gc
1-27-1887	Laura M rocf Elk MM OH
2-24-1887	Calvin H rec in mbrp
10-27-1887	Sarah E rocf Spiceland MM
11-24-1887	John C & w Beulah W rq cert to Lincoln Center KS
2-23-1888	John C & w withdraw rq for cert
7-26-1888	Calvin H & w Laura M gct Elk MM OH
1-24-1891	Elizabeth B gct Indianapolis MM
4-25-1891	Cert for Elisabeth ret by Indianapolis MM; ret within limits of this mtg
7-25-1891	Elizabeth gct West Grove MM
5-28-1892	Wm & w Amanda & min s Clarence J gct Sugar Plain MM Boone Co
2-25-1897	Elizabeth rocf West Grove MM
11-24-1898	Lewis A rocf Elk MM OH
12-22-1898	Sarah E gct Indianapolis MM

TEAGUE

8-23-1871	Martha E, Laura P, & Edwin ch Isaac C & Joanna rocf Wabash MM
8-28-1872	Lula Webb rocf Wabash MM
2-26-1873	Prudence rec in mbrp
12-24-1873	Prudence gct Mississinewa MM
7-24-1878	Isaac C & w Joanna M & ch Myrtle & Pearl rec in mbrp
6-24-1884	Isaac C rel fr mbrp
2-26-1885	Lula Webb gc
5-25-1899	Edward Davis/Edwin Dawes gl; contemplated jas

TEAS

6-27-1818	Charles & s Joseph, Charles, Gibson, & John rocf Center MM DE; Mary & dt Mary Rachel & Ann rocf Center MM DE
10-15-1825	Thomas L gct Silver Creek MM
8-24-1831	Gibson rocf Chester MM
1-5-1832	Gibson s Charles & Mary Wayne Co m Rebecca I dt Enos & Elizabeth **Grave** Wayne Co at Smyrna MH
11-28-1832	Thomas A & s John & Edward rocf Westfield MM; Sarah rocf Westfield MM
6-5-1834	Joseph s Charles & Mary dec Wayne Co m Sarah S dt Thomas & Barbara **Hartley** Wayne Co at Smyrna Mtg
7-23-1834	Sarah L gct Chester MM
9-24-1834	John rocf Chester MM
5-27-1835	Thomas S & w Sarah & min ch John C, Edward, & Martha gct Spiceland MM
11-22-1843	Gibson dis for na & jas
2-28-1844	Rebecca J dis for na & jas
9-20-1865	Edward rocf Raysville MM
9-26-1866	Thomas S rocf Raysville MM
6-24-1868	Sallie A & Vestal H **Coffin** rocf Raysville MM
9-22-1869	Sarah C rocf Raysville MM
1-28-1874	Ellen M rec in mbrp; Wm S s Edward Y & Sallie A rec in mbrp
2-24-1875	Thomas S gct Union MM MO; Charles rel fr mbrp
3-28-1891	Lizzie Stewart glt Chattanooga TN ME ch

TEASE

12-30-1820	Thomas rocf Philadelphia MM PA
7-25-1877	Edward Y & w Sarah & ch Ellen, Wm, Frederick, & Mary & steps Vestal H **Coffin** gct Spiceland MM

TEST

9-25-1823	John s Samuel & Sarah Silver Creek MM Union Co m Mary dt Robert & Mary **Andrew** Wayne Co at Smyrna MH
11-15-1823	Mary gct Silver Creek MM
2-23-1826	Samuel s Samuel & Sarah Union Co m Hannah dt Morgan & Hannah both dec **Jones** Wayne Co at Smyrna MH
6-17-1826	Samuel & w Hannah gct Silver Creek MM
2-27-1828	John & Mary rocf Silver Creek MM
4-22-1835	John & w Mary gct Sugar River MM
5-27-1835	Samuel Jr & w Hanna & min ch Josiah, Zacheus, Wm, Rufus, & Oliver rocf Salem MM
4-25-1849	Alpheus rocf Salem MM
1-2-1850	Alpheus Wayne Co s Samuel & Sarah dec Union Co m Elizabeth A dt Charles dec & Elizabeth **Moffitt** Wayne Co at Whitewater MH
4-24-1850	Samuel rocf Salem MM
2-22-1854	Miriam C rocf Springfield MM
3-28-1855	Josiah & w Miriam C gct Springfield MM
8-26-1857	Zacheus gct Milford MM to m Elizabeth M **Pray**
5-26-1858	Elizabeth rocf Cherry Grove MM
8-25-1858	Rufus gct New Garden MM to m Margaret M **Stubbs**
1-26-1859	Elizabeth M rocf Milford MM; Margaret M rocf New Garden MM
7-27-1859	Wm gct New Garden MM to m Emily **Woodard**
2-27-1861	Rufus & w Margaret M gct Springfield MM
6-26-1861	Wm gct Springfield MM

TEST (cont)

8-28-1861	Oliver gct Springfield MM to m Sarah **Dennis**
4-23-1862	John rst with perm Sugar River MM
7-23-1862	Mary rocf Honey Creek MM
1-28-1863	Elizabeth gct Plainfield MM
10-28-1863	Sarah rocf Springfield MM
8-23-1865	John con mcd
1-24-1866	John gct Greenwood MM
10-24-1866	Zacheus & w Elizabeth M & ch Alice & Martha gct Scipio MM NY
5-22-1867	Wm & w Emily & ch Hannah Mary & Wilhelmina rocf Springfield MM
7-22-1868	Erastus gct West Union MM to m Mary **Taylor**
10-28-1868	Mary (**Taylor**) rocf West Union MM
6-23-1869	Donna M rec in mbrp
7-26-1869	Anna M rec in mbrp
5-23-1877	Erastus & w Mary (**Taylor**) & min ch Frederick C, Charles D, & Louis A gct Adrian MM MI
8-27-1879	Zacheus & ch Alice & Mattie rocf Scipio MM NY
2-26-1880	Zacheus rel fr mbrp
7-28-1881	Erastus & w Mary (**Taylor**) & ch Frederick C, Lewis A, & Charles D rocf Adrian MM MI; Elizabeth d rpt
3-26-1885	Charles E gct Indianapolis MM
9-24-1885	Alpheus gct Salem MM to m Phebe H **Talbert**
12-24-1885	Phebe H rocf Salem MM
11-25-1886	Wilhelmina Lois rel fr mbrp
3-23-1889	Lina Estella & Herbert Erastus drpd fr mbrp; jas
9-21-1889	Will H & James W rel fr mbrp
5-24-1890	Alice & Mattie rel fr mbrp
11-28-1895	Alpheus s Samuel & Sarah M both dec Wayne Co m Martha **Bond Little** wid David **Little** & wid Peter **Bond** dt Frederick & Piety **Fulghum** at East Main St Mtg Richmond
6-23-1898	Rufus & w Lydia H & adopted dt Lucile **Clements** rocf Springfield MM
10-26-1899	Rufus & w Lydia gct Spiceland MM

THATCHER

10-23-1844	Elizabeth (**Symons**) con mcd
2-26-1845	Elizabeth gct Springfield MM OH

THEIS

1-26-1882	Mary rocf Chester MM
2-22-1883	Mary rel fr mbrp

THISTLETHWAITE

6-25-1845	Rebecca W (**Symons**) con mcd

THOMAS

7-27-1811	Benjamin rocf Piney Grove MM SC; Ann & dt Guly & Betty rocf Piney Grove MM SC
11-30-1811	John & s Jesse & Hendley rocf Piney Grove MM SC; Lydia & dt Polly, Hannah, Nanny, Lydia, & Huldah rocf Piney Grove MM SC
2-29-1812	Francis & s Luke rocf Contentnea MM NC; end by Fairfield MM OH; Lydia & dt Mary rocf Contentnea MM NC; Lewis rocf Piney Grove MM SC
11-28-1812	Benjamin & s James rocf New Garden MM NC; Ann & dt Mary rocf New Garden MM NC
10-30-1813	John & grs Moses **Mendenhall** rocf Piney Grove MM SC; Molly & grdt Rebekah **Mendenhall** rocf Piney Grove MM SC; Solomon rocf Piney Grove MM SC; Anna & dt Maryann rocf Piney Grove MM SC
5-28-1814	Elijah & s Daniel, Simeon, Samuel, Elijah, Milton, & Henley rocf Piney Grove MM SC; Susannah & dt Mary rocf Piney Grove MM SC; Stephen & s Charles rocf Piney Grove MM SC; Hannah & dt Sarah, Mary, Selah, & Nancy rocf Piney Grove MM SC; Isaac & s John rocf Piney Grove MM SC; Rachel & dt Betty, Molly, Achsa, Rachel, & Sarah rocf Piney Grove MM SC
7-29-1815	Lewis gct Lick Creek MM

WHITEWATER MONTHLY MEETING
MINUTES AND MARRIAGES

THOMAS (cont)

10-26-1816	John rocf Center MM DE; end fr Redstone MM PA; Elizabeth & dt Elizabeth, Sarah Ann, & Lydia rocf Center MM DE; end fr Redstone MM PA; Alice & Mary rocf Center MM DE; end fr Redstone MM PA
11-29-1817	James P rocf Center MM DE; Ann & dt Elizabeth rocf Center MM DE
12-26-1818	Elizabeth con for att mcd
11-3-1819	Jesse s John & Lydia Wayne Co m Hannah dt Jeremiah & Margery dec **Cox** at Whitewater MH
6-24-1820	Hannah gct New Garden MM
3-23-1825	John Wayne Co s Wm & Mary dec m Alida C wid **Harned** & **Clark** dt Robert & Catherine dec **Miller** at Whitewater MH
6-18-1825	Alida C gct Chester MM
7-25-1832	Hiram rocf Springborough MM OH
3-26-1834	Elizabeth (**Strawbridge**) dis for na & mcd
10-22-1834	Hiram dis for na & j ME ch
2-24-1835	John & w Grace & ch Miriam & Elias rocf West Branch MM OH
6-26-1839	Rebecca H & ch Elmira, Charles W, Benjamin F, Albert, Isaac H, & Howard rocf Springborough MM OH
2-24-1841	John & w Grace & min ch Miriam & Elias gct Richland MM; Asenath rocf West Branch MM OH
3-24-1841	Rebecca H & min ch Elmira, Charles W, Benjamin, Albert, Isaac H, Howard D, & Elihu gct Cincinnati MM OH
4-28-1841	Asenath, Nancy, & Priscilla rocf West Branch MM OH
10-12-1842	Asenath dis for na
8-25-1847	Wm Pen rocf Chester MM
7-26-1848	Ann dis for na
6-26-1850	Manlove & w Mary & s Joshua & Cyrus rocf Chester MM
3-26-1851	Manlove & w Mary & s Cyrus gct Chester MM
5-28-1851	Nancy gct West Branch MM OH
11-23-1853	Joshua gct Chester MM
8-30-1854	Wm Penn Wayne Co s Manlove & Mary Boone Co m Phebe Ann dt Wm dec & Lydia **Jenkins** Henry Co at Whitewater MH
6-27-1855	Manlove & w Mary rocf Sugar Plain MM
7-25-1855	Mary (**Witchell**) dis for mcd
5-28-1856	Manlove & w Mary gct White Lick MM
5-25-1859	Wm Penn dis for na & jas
10-23-1872	Wm P & w Jane & s Robert rocf New Garden MM
7-23-1873	Uriah rocf Dover MM
2-24-1875	Zephaniah & w Minerva rocf Cottonwood MM KS
4-28-1875	Martha C, Wm Esker, & Blanche Elsie ch Zephaniah & Minerva rocf Cottonwood MM KS
7-25-1877	Uriah rel fr mbrp
3-24-1881	Sarah C rec in mbrp
8-25-1881	Alice Maud & Maggie May rocf Union MM MO
4-26-1883	Wm P & w Jane R & min s Robison gct New Garden MM
4-23-1885	Sarah C drpd fr mbrp
4-28-1887	Zephaniah dis for na & embracing doctrine of "final restoration and Salvation of all mankind, regardless of their conduct in this life."
11-24-1887	Letitia Crampton min gct New Garden MM
7-26-1888	Martha rel fr mbrp; jas
2-23-1889	Lincoln rec in mbrp
1-24-1891	Minerva & s Wm & min ch rec in mbrp; Elsie, Myrtle, & Clarence ch Wm rel fr mbrp
2-28-1891	Stephen F & w Mary & ch Herbert C & Bessie May rec in mbrp
5-23-1891	Elizabeth M & dt Alice rocf New Garden MM; Wm L & w Margaret Jane rec in mbrp
12-26-1891	Elizabeth M & dt Alice glt Knightstown ME ch
9-23-1893	Priscilla & dt Olinda B rocf New Garden MM
10-28-1893	Ellsworth & w Letitia rocf New Garden MM
10-22-1896	Daisy May rec in mbrp
2-25-1897	Laura Alice dt Agnes M rec in mbrp
2-24-1898	Franklin M & w Sarah M & ch Bessie, Maud, & Herbert rocf New Garden MM
10-26-1899	Lincoln gct Chicago MM IL

THOMPSON

12-24-1828	Abraham dis for mcd
4-26-1883	Charles & Elizabeth Centreville rq mbrp
6-28-1883	Charles & Minerva Centreville rec in mbrp
12-27-1883	Charles W & Minerva W rq PM at Centreville
12-23-1893	Luella Bond rocf Dover MM
1-27-1894	James M rec in mbrp

THOMSON

11-25-1897	James & w Luella & min dt Cora gct Dover MM

THORN

4-22-1835	Ezra & Benjamin ch Benjamin gct West Grove MM
8-28-1839	Cert rec for Ruth dt Benjamin fr Chester MM NJ; end to West Grove MM
8-23-1843	Mary dt Benjamin gct West Grove MM
2-22-1865	Wm G rocf Green Plain MM OH
2-28-1866	Edwin J rocf Green Plain MM OH
11-28-1866	Levi rocf Green Plain MM OH
2-27-1867	Ella A & dt Josephine rocf Sugar Plain MM
12-25-1867	Levi E & w Anna Rosella & ch Josephine gct Cincinnati MM OH
7-25-1877	Wm C drpd fr mbrp; jas

THORNBERRY

3-23-1831	Abel dis for na
10-23-1839	Rhoda & minor ch Mary Ann, Rachel, Susanna, & Wm Johnson gct Mississinewa MM

THORNBOROUGH

11-30-1811	Elizabeth & dt Margaret & Sarah rocf Mt Pleasant MM VA
10-30-1819	Abel rocf Springfield MM OH

THORNBURG

7-29-1815	Joseph & Richard con att mcd
8-26-1815	Sarah dis for att mcd
11-15-1823	Abel con for administering an oath
1-25-1854	Walter & w Rebecca & ch Lydia, Wm, & Rebecca Ann rocf Dover MM
2-23-1882	Jannetta rec in mbrp
12-23-1886	Jeannette glt Richmond 1st ME ch
10-24-1891	Sarah & min dt Lillian rec in mbrp; Sarah mbr UB ch

THORNBURGH

11-30-1811	Joseph & s Joseph & Richard rocf Mt Pleasant MM VA
6-24-1820	Henry & s John & Milton rocf Miami MM OH; Rebecca & dt Elizabeth, Unice, & Hannah rocf Miami MM OH
12-29-1822	Henry & fam gct West Grove MM
2-24-1836	Sarah (**Charles**) dis for mcd
3-27-1839	Walnut Ridge MM rq aid in treating with Sarah (**Clark**) for mcd; made satisfaction
7-24-1839	Sarah gct Walnut Ridge MM
2-24-1841	Rhoda & ch gct Clear Creek MM OH; gct Mississinewa MM; end back
9-20-1854	Walter & w Rebecca & ch Lydia, Wm, & Rebecca Ann gct Dover MM

THORNBUROUGH

10-30-1819	Rhoda & dt Lydia rocf Springfield MM OH

THORNE

11-28-1832	Ezra & Benjamin rocf Chester MM NJ; Mary rocf Chester MM NJ
5-24-1871	Edwin J gct Green Plain MM OH

THORNTON

9-25-1813	Eli rocf Union MM OH
4-29-1815	Uriah, Abiah, Thomas, Caturah, Mary, Elizabeth, Eleanor, & Rebecca ch Eli rec in mbrp; Sarah rec in mbrp

THORNTON (cont)
1-27-1816	Eli dis for dr, upl, & abusing a fellow man
3-26-1845	Vermilion MM IL gr perm to rst Eli
11-28-1860	Jane S (**Beard**) con mcd

TICE
1-24-1866	Margaretta (**Reynolds**) dis for mcd

TILSON
4-20-1822	Luther rec in mbrp

TIMBERLAKE
2-23-1859	Jonathan & w Catherine & ch Amelia, Rebecca, Mary, Ann Eliza, & Arthur rocf Springfield MM OH; Sarah Matilda rocf Springfield MM OH
11-28-1860	Jonathan & w Catherine & ch Matilda, Amelia, Rebecca, Mary, Anna E, & Arthur gct Plainfield MM
7-22-1868	Edward rocf Center MM OH
9-1-1868	Edward Wayne Co s Alfred & Phebe Clinton Co OH m Martha N dt Benjamin & Mary Ann dec **Brown** at res of her father
1-28-1874	Susannah E rocf Center MM OH
6-23-1881	Martha appt o
7-28-1881	Martha appt Orange o
8-23-1883	Edward & Martha appt elders

TIMONS
5-27-1897	John & Emanuel Providence & Friendship Darke Co OH rec in mbrp

TITSWORTH
1-1-1884	Abraham D s Abraham D dec & Mary R Western Springs Cook Co IL m Mary E dt Timothy dec & Naomi W **Harrison** Richmond at res of her mother
7-23-1885	Mary E gct Western Springs MM IL
2-22-1896	Frederick **Harrison** & Helen **Bills** ch A D & Mary E rocf Western Springs MM Chicago IL
3-28-1896	Abraham D & w Mary E rec in mbrp

TOMS
4-28-1881	Joseph & w Elizabeth W & ch Maud & Wm Henry rocf Milford MM

TONEY
5-22-1884	Sarah Jane rec in mbrp

TOWEL
11-30-1811	Henry rocf Center MM NC

TOWNSEND
9-30-1809	John & Elvira appt to comm
5-27-1815	Jonathan con for mcd
6-24-1815	Mary rec in mbrp
5-29-1816	Wm s John & Elvira Wayne Co m Elizabeth dt John & Hannah **Morrow** at Whitewater MH
5-27-1820	Wm & s Eli & Josiah rocf Center MM NC; Nancy & dt Elizabeth & Catherine rocf Center MM NC
2-14-1824	Wm Sr con mcd
3-20-1824	Wm & ch Eli, Elizabeth, & Josiah gct White Lick MM
5-20-1826	John Jr gct Elk MM OH
11-22-1826	John & w Elvira & ch Barbara & Stephen gct West Grove MM
8-28-1828	Eli s Wm & Nancy dec Hendricks Co m Cicily dt Wm & Elizabeth **Johnson** Wayne Co at Whitewater MH
4-22-1829	Cicily gct White Lick MM
3-23-1831	Johnathan & w Mary & min ch Daniel, Mahlon, Amos, Stephen, Rebecca, & Wm gct West Grove MM
3-28-1832	Wm & fam gct West Grove MM
3-26-1845	Sarah rocf Walnut Ridge MM
5-22-1861	Sina dis for departing from good order of Friends in her associations and refusing advice of Friends
4-27-1895	Emma Spencer minister gct Clear Creek MM OH

TRUBLOOD
10-27-1810	Abigail rocf Symons Creek MM NC
6-27-1812	Margaret & dt Elizabeth & Miriam rocf Back Creek MM NC; Mourning & Peggy rocf Back Creek MM NC
7-17-1824	Miriam & dt Isabel & Betsy rocf Symons Creek MM NC
4-25-1827	Miriam rocf Fall Creek MM OH

TRUEBLOOD
2-23-1811	Josiah & s Wm Josiah & Lancaster rocf Symons Creek Pasquotank MM NC; Peggy rocf Symons Creek MM NC
3-30-1811	Josiah rpt "having reduced a black woman into a state of Slavery"; Comm appt
12-28-1811	Comm rpts that Josiah complied "to a good degree of satisfaction; but he not appearing, neither any account from [comm is] appt to visit him & inform him if he doth not condemn his breach of order the meeting will be under the necessity of disowning him"; Comm to visit
6-27-1812	Comm rpts "Josiah appeared to be tender & expressed sorrow for what he had done & that under present circumstances it seemed impossible for him to make suitable satisfaction; He is therefore disowned"; Wm & s Josiah, Joseph, Wm, & James rocf Back Creek MM NC
9-25-1813	Wm & s Jonathan rocf Symons Creek MM NC
10-30-1813	Caleb & James rocf Symons Creek MM NC
8-14-1824	Ephraim Overman rocf Symons Creek MM NC
11-9-1825	Miriam gct Fall Creek MM OH
8-26-1829	Ephraim dis for jas
2-28-1872	Benjamin rocf Adrian MM MI
6-26-1872	Benjamin minister gct Clear Creek MM OH
8-27-1873	Benjamin gct Oskaloosa/Spring Creek MM IA
4-25-1877	Wm N rocf Rocky Run MM
7-27-1889	Edwin P rocf Blue River MM
6-27-1891	Walter L & w Almeda F & ch Virgil & Bessie rocf New Garden MM
4-25-1896	Pennina H rocf Carthage MM

TUCKER
7-27-1864	Mary (**Maxwell**) rpt mcd & drpd fr mbrp
11-22-1865	Caroline (**Maxwell**) dis for mcd
4-22-1874	Caroline M & ch Eva Estella, Orville Hugh, Ruth Elizabeth, & Rollin rec in mbrp
4-26-1883	Caroline & ch Orville Hugh, Eva Estella, Ruth Elizabeth, & Roland gct Sterling MM KS

TYLER
12-22-1852	Martha J ch Hugh & Sarah **Moffit** rec in mbrp
4-27-1870	Joseph Sparkes rocf Devonshire House MM London England
9-20-1871	Joseph S gct Lewes & Chichester MM England
1-28-1874	Joseph Sparkes rocf Devinshire House MM England
12-28-1875	Joseph S gct Columbus MM OH
2-23-1888	Sarah Ennis & s Charles Henry rec in mbrp
6-22-1889	Joseph & w Sally & s Charles Henry gct Chicago MM IL

UMBERHOWER
2-23-1882	Cora & John rq mbrp Richmond PM
5-23-1882	Cora drpd fr cons for mbrp
7-24-1884	Cora rq for mbrp drpd

UNDERHILL
4-30-1814	Cert rec for John dec fr Mill Creek MM OH
9-22-1887	Alfred M rocf Poughkeepsie MM NY
2-22-1896	Emma rocf Springfield MM
7-22-1897	Jesse B & w Susan rocf Springfield MM

WHITEWATER MONTHLY MEETING
MINUTES AND MARRIAGES

UNDERWOOD
11-28-1818	John & s Barclay rocf Baltimore MM MD; Mary rocf Baltimore MM MD
3-19-1825	John & w Mary & ch Amy, Barclay, Harriet, Israel, & Eliza gct Chester MM
4-28-1828	Mary & dt Amy, Mary, Harriet, & Eliza rocf Chester MM
5-28-1828	John & s Barclay & Israel rocf Chester MM
7-22-1829	Mary dis for jas
8-26-1829	John dis for jas
10-11-1843	Barclay, Israel, Naomi, Eliza, & Mary ch John gct Birch Lake MM MI

UNTHANK
7-29-1820	Mary & s Jonathan, Joseph, & John Allen rec in mbrp; Mary & dt Leveicy, Anna, Sally, Betsy Mary, & Rebecca, rec in mbrp
2-15-1823	John rec in mbrp
12-20-1823	Wm rocf New Garden MM NC; Rebecca & dt Mahala, Elizabeth, & Sarah rocf New Garden MM NC
6-23-1830	Rachel (**Williams**) con mcd
11-24-1830	Rachel gct Dover MM OH
6-27-1835	Wm S gct Fairfield MM
2-25-1857	Susan B (**Reed**) dis for mcd
4-25-1891	Sarah Ann & dt Alice & Wm H rocf Dover MM
10-26-1895	Charles B & w Mary E & ch Florence & Pleasant rocf Dover MM

VALENTINE
7-28-1852	George rocf Salem MM
5-23-1860	John & w Martha & ch Wm Henry, Anna, Cornelia, Gulielma, & Georgianna rocf Chester MM
6-26-1867	Wm H con mcd
6-21-1881	Martha appt o
8-23-1883	John appt elder

VAN ETTAN
8-24-1899	Daniel, Florence, Edward, Wm, Bertha, Daniel Jr, & Earl drpd fr mbrp

VAN ETTEN
2-26-1885	Florence rq mbrp
4-23-1885	Daniel L & w Florence & ch Edward C, Wm W, Bertha A, Daniel J, & Herbert H rec in mbrp
9-21-1899	Herbert drpd fr mbrp

VANSANT
12-26-1891	Mary rec in mbrp

VANSCHOIACH
2-23-1889	Leonard rec in mbrp

VANSCHOICK
3-23-1889	Isaac rec in mbrp

VAN ZANT
10-26-1889	Richmond PM rpts Mary M rq mbrp
7-26-1890	Mary M rq for mbrp drpd

VARNEY
2-28-1855	Wm H rocf Providence MM RI
9-24-1856	Wm H gct Windham MM ME

VENARD
6-28-1883	Ruth Centrevillerec in mbrp
12-27-1883	Ruth rq PM at Centreville
2-24-1887	Ruth gct West Grove MM
1-24-1891	Ruth gct West Grove MM

VEREGGE
4-29-1899	Frank H & w Dora rec in mbrp

VESTAL
1-29-1814	Samuel rocf Center MM NC
9-27-1826	Samuel dis for mcd; Center MM OH

VICKERS
2-26-1834	Edwin Nixon & Thomas s Isaac M rocf Elk MM OH
1-24-1844	Edwin dis for na, mcd, & jas
4-23-1845	Thomas dis for na & dp

VINCENT
4-27-1836	Grace (**Parry**) dis for jH & mcd
3-27-1884	Victor rec in mbrp
5-28-1885	Christine & dt Matilda rec in mbrp
6-28-1888	Christina & dt Matilda rel fr mbrp
7-26-1888	Victor drpd fr mbrp

VORE
11-28-1818	Jacob, Mary, & Mary Jr rocf Deer Creek MM MD; Jacob Jr & s Israel C & John rocf Deer Creek MM MD; Elizabeth & dt Anne rocf Deer Creek MM MD; Ruth & dt Mary, Eliza, & Ruth rocf Deer Creek MM MD; Isaac & s Jacob rocf Deer Creek MM MD
1-18-1823	John gct New Garden MM to m Sarah **Ballard**
4-27-1831	Deborah (**Underwood**) dis for mcd
6-23-1852	Elizabeth (**Lamb**) con mcd
11-23-1853	Azel rocf Clear Creek MM OH
3-22-1871	Azel & w Elizabeth & ch Sarah, Ann, Thomas, Isaac, Mary Jane, Tacy, Phinehas, Albert, & Gilbert gct Chester MM

VOSS
3-24-1894	Michael F & w Annie K & ch Pearl A, Clarence S, Blanch, & Carl L rec in mbrp

VOTAW
6-21-1817	Mary & dt Unice & Anne **Smith** rocf Miami MM OH; Elizabeth rocf Miami MM OH
6-28-1817	Daniel & Jonathan rocf Miami MM OH
3-25-1893	Isaac & w Anna M & dt Ida rocf Chester MM
7-22-1897	Isaac d rpt; ae 79y

WADE
6-27-1891	Belle H rel fr mbrp; lt to Findley OH 1st ME ch

WAGNER
11-26-1896	Hannah drpd fr mbrp

WAKEFIELD
12-24-1851	Cincinnati MM OH rq aid in treating with Charlotte W for mcd; did not make satisfaction
12-24-1885	Joseph J & w Mary A & dt Jennie rocf Green Plain MM OH
6-24-1886	Joseph J minister & w Mary A & dt Jennie C gct Green Plain MM OH

WALKER
6-28-1865	Sarah rec in mbrp
4-28-1869	Lewis C & Calvin B rocf Wilmington MM OH
5-26-1869	Elisabeth P, Martha Jane, & Eliza Ann rocf Wilmington MM OH
12-27-1871	Calvin B & w Naomi C rel fr mbrp; jas
4-22-1874	Elizabeth rec in mbrp
2-23-1876	Eliza A & Martha J rel fr mbrp
7-25-1877	Elizabeth rel fr mbrp; Lewis C & dt Cornelia rel fr mbrp

WALLACK
4-29-1882	David & Sarah rec in mbrp

WALLON
10-27-1869	James & Henry Helena AR rec in mbrp

WALTERS
4-22-1886	Mary rq mbrp
4-27-1895	Wm & Belle rec in mbrp

WALTON
3-22-1854	Rebecca (**Wright**) dis for mcd
2-25-1897	George Franklin & w Opal rocf Dublin MM

WARD
12-14-1822	Enos rocf Cane Creek MM
4-16-1825	Isaac & Isaiah s Enos rec in mbrp
7-16-1825	Elizabeth & dt Deborah & Sophia rec in mbrp
1-23-1828	Enos & w Elizabeth & ch Isaac, Deborah, Isaiah, Sapphira, & Hannah gct White Lick MM
11-28-1855	Elizabeth (**Edgerton**) dis for mcd
4-22-1860	Richard G rec in mbrp
8-22-1866	Elizabeth A & ch Mary T, Almira Jane, & Lizzie N rec in mbrp
4-23-1885	Lula W gct Chicago MM IL; Richard G rel fr mbrp
8-27-1885	Chicago MM ret cert for Lula W with info that she did not reside within their limits
3-22-1888	Josiah rocf Hopewell MM
4-26-1888	Florence C & s Orville P rec in mbrp

WARDER
5-28-1892	Carrie D (**Newcombe**) rel fr mbrp

WARING
12-26-1849	Wm P rocf Salem MM
6-23-1852	Wm P gct Milford MM to m Semira **Hiatt**
8-22-1855	Wm P & w Semira H & dt Emma gct Sugar Plain MM
11-27-1861	Wm P & w Semira H & ch Emma & Percival rocf Sugar Plain MM
4-26-1890	Emma gct Spiceland MM
5-24-1890	Gertrude L rel fr mbrp
11-25-1893	Semira H gct Indianapolis MM

WARNER
11-27-1879	Rebecca P & ch Faircomb H & Ella rocf Green Plain MM OH
3-23-1889	Harvey rec in mbrp; Rebecca & ch Harrison & Ella gct Chicago MM IL

WARREN
4-20-1814	James & s, James, David, Henry, Azariah, & John rocf Lost Creek MM TN; Sarah & dt Tabitha, Sarah, Rachel, & Margaret rocf Lost Creek MM TN
2-25-1815	James Jr dis for mcd
8-22-1832	Daniel & w Mary & min ch Andrew L, Hoover, Wm Stewart, Rachel, Susanna, & Zina gct White Lick MM

WARRIN
12-28-1831	May & dt Rachel & Susan rocf Union MM NC

WASBURN
8-23-1883	Helena d 3-29-1883

WASHBURN
9-23-1874	Paul rec in mbrp
9-23-1897	Paul V & w Maria D & ch Esther, John, & Winifred rel fr mbrp

WASHUM
1-25-1837	Rebecca (**Marmon**) dis for na & mcd

WASON
4-22-1835	Jesse, Charlotte, Nancy, & Aseneth ch Jehiel gct Mississinewa MM

WASSON
11-29-1817	Archibald & s Calvin, Jehiel, Anselm, & Macamey rec in mbrp; Elizabeth & dt Eliza rec in mbrp

WASSON (cont)
4-2-1818	Calvin s Archibald & Elizabeth Wayne Co m Mary dt Wm & Charlotte **Bond** Wayne Co at Middle Fork MH
11-29-1820	Jehial s Archibald & Elisabeth Wayne Co m Lydia dt Wm & Charlotte **Bond** Wayne Co at Whitewater MH
8-21-1822	Ansalem s Archibald & Elisabeth Wayne Co m Ruth dt Israel & Amy **Clark** Wayne Co at Chester MH
10-28-1829	Jesse, Charlotte, Nancy, & Asenath rocf Duck Creek MM

WATKINS
5-25-1811	Rachel dis for mcd

WATSON
11-23-1842	Catherine (**Hoover**) dis for na, jH, & mcd
10-25-1865	Harmon C rec in mbrp
9-25-1867	Elizabeth & dt Hannah rec in mbrp; Ida, Howard, & Lake ch James & Elizabeth rec in mbrp
7-27-1870	Harmon C & w Lydia Ann (**Showan**) con mcd
8-28-1872	Wm & w Jane & ch Arthur Lewis, Mary Josephine, & Franklin S rec in mbrp
4-22-1880	David A rec in mbrp
1-26-1889	Lake G rel fr mbrp
7-23-1896	Idell rel fr mbrp
5-27-1897	Lydia A, Lizzie B, & Edgar rel fr mbrp

WATT
6-28-1890	Irene rec in mbrp

WAY
3-28-1812	Henry & s Henry & Wm rocf Caesar's Creek MM OH; Charlotta & dt Maryann & Charlotta rocf Caesar's Creek MM OH
5-30-1812	Seth & s Thomas rocf Center MM OH; Sarah & dt Lydia & Hannah rocf Center MM OH
6-27-1812	Joseph & s Jonathan & Joel rocf Caesar's Creek MM OH; Rachel dt Joseph rocf Caesar's Creek MM OH
6-26-1813	Seth dis for being concerned in military operations
8-28-1813	Joseph con for dr
11-10-1813	Joseph s Henry & Charlotte Wayne Co m Alice dt Isaac & Martha **Hiatt** NC at Whitewater MH
1-26-1822	Henry H & s Manlove rocf Cherry Grove MM; Mary & dt Narcissa rocf Cherry Grove MM
4-19-1823	Henry & fam gct New Garden MM
4-22-1829	Robert rocf Stillwater MM OH
4-27-1831	Lydia & min ch Millicent, Mary Ann, & David L gct Milford MM
5-25-1831	Robert con dr
6-22-1831	Robert gct Milford MM
9-26-1832	Joseph, Obed, Martha, & Rebecca rocf Cherry Grove MM
8-24-1836	Martha, Rebecca, Obed, & Joseph ch Joseph gct Cherry Grove MM
4-26-1854	Anthony & w Rhoda & ch Rachel, Hannah, Hiram, Huldah, Anna Louisa, & Esther rocf Cherry Grove MM
8-25-1858	Mary rocf Salem MM

WEAKS
6-25-1814	John & s Wm, Benjamin, James, & Ralph rocf Springfield MM NC

WEATHERALD
11-26-1834	Henry rocf Muncy MM

WEATHERALL
4-22-1835	Henry dis for jH

WEBB
10-23-1867	Benjamin rst; form dis for taking part in military operations during war
2-16-1868	Sarah (**Williams**) con mcd
8-23-1883	Benjamin appt elder
11-26-1885	Benjamin & w Sarah W & ch Robert W & Alice C gct Minneapolis MM MN

WHITEWATER MONTHLY MEETING
MINUTES AND MARRIAGES

WEBSTER
6-17-1826	Taylor rocf Fairfield MM
8-26-1829	Taylor gct White Lick MM
4-26-1888	Ellen M rec in mbrp
12-23-1893	Hubert rec in mbrp
5-25-1895	Hubert gct; jas

WEEKS
6-25-1814	Jane & dt Lydia & Anna rocf Springfield MM NC
2-29-1816	Benjamin s Wm & Susanna dec Miami Co OH m Margaret dt Joseph & Elizabeth **Thornbrough** Wayne Co at Spring Mtg
3-29-1817	Margaret gct Union MM
5-31-1817	John con upl
10-18-1823	Benjamin gct Milford MM to m Winniford **Copeland**
9-18-1824	Benjamin gct Milford MM
6-23-1830	Wm & James con mcd
11-24-1830	Wm gct Duck Creek MM
9-25-1833	Casandra rec in mbrp
4-26-1854	James & w Cassandra & ch John Wesley, Rachel H, Louisa, & Mary E gct Chester MM; Jane, Merrick C, & Ralph gct Chester MM
6-23-1869	Merrick C & w Hannah Eliza & ch Minnie E, Charles L, Cora M, & Frank W rocf New Garden MM
2-25-1886	Hanna E rel fr mbrp
5-23-1892	John Wesley rocf New Garden MM
7-23-1892	Harry D, George F, Cassie M, & Susan G rocf New Garden MM
8-27-1892	Caroline M & s Ray rec in mbrp

WELSH
9-23-1886	John H & Martha rq mbrp
10-28-1886	John & w withdraw rq for mbrp; intend to remove

WERNER
5-28-1885	Anna rec in mbrp

WEST
2-22-1817	Mary (**Benbow**) dis for mcd
1-28-1897	Wm & w Mary rocf West Grove MM

WESTCOMBE
8-24-1864	Charles Trusted rocf Worcestershire & Shropshire MM England
10-12-1864	Charles Trusted Wayne Co s Samuel Thompson & Elizabeth both dec Worcestershire Co England m Priscilla dt Edmund & Margaret both dec **White** Perquimans Co NC at Whitewater MH

WETHERALD
3-22-1865	Hannah J rocf Lisburn MM, Ireland; res MO
12-22-1869	Hannah Jane gct Lisburn MM Ireland

WHARING
1-26-1853	Semira H rocf Milford MM

WHEELER
10-30-1819	Keziah rocf Deep River MM NC
6-27-1855	Mary P rocf Elk MM OH
1-25-1860	Mary P gct Salem MM

WHINNERY
7-25-1860	James & w Mary & ch Arthur, Enos, Henry, Eva, & Alpheus rocf Center MM OH
3-26-1862	James & w Mary & ch Arthur, Enos, Henry, & Alpheus gct Center MM OH
3-28-1866	James & w Mary & ch Enos, Henry, Alpheus, Adelaide, & Oliver M rocf Center MM OH
9-23-1868	James & w Mary & ch Enos, Alpheus, Henry, & Adelaide gct Bangor MM IA
5-25-1882	Adeline gct Bangor MM IA

WHITACRE
9-30-1820	Mary & dt Elizabeth, Rachel, & Mary rocf Carmel MM OH; Rebecca rocf Carmel MM
1-27-1821	Aquilla s Robert & Patience Warren Co OH rpt m to Ruthanna dt Samuel & Mary **Potts** Wayne Co at Whitewater MH
3-31-1821	Ruth Anna gct Miami MM OH
1-30-1822	Wm s Samuel & Mary Wayne Co m Sarah dt Thomas & Ann **Roberds** Wayne Co at Whitewater MH
10-18-1823	John gct Elk MM OH to m Bethula **Roberds**
10-16-1824	Mary & ch Rachel, Louis, Samuel, Joseph Jonathan, & Mary gct New Garden MM; Elizabeth gct New Garden MM
10-15-1825	John gct Elk MM
1-24-1827	John & s Ephraim rocf Elk MM OH; Bethulah rocf Elk MM OH
6-27-1827	Levi, Samuel, Joseph Jonathan, & Elizabeth rocf Chester MM; Mary & dt Rachel & Mary rocf Chester MM; Elizabeth rocf Chester MM
1-23-1828	Wm & w Sarah & ch Mary Ann & Milton H gct New Garden MM
9-24-1828	John & w Bethuly & ch Ephriam & Christoper gct Elk MM OH
5-26-1830	Mary & ch Elizabeth, Levi, Samuel, Jonathan, Joseph, & Mary gct New Garden MM
6-23-1830	Rachel dis for na & dp
5-28-1834	John & s Ephraim & Christopher rocf New Garden MM; Bethula & ch Susannah, Martha, & Mary rocf New Garden MM
10-28-1835	John & w Bethula & ch Ephriam, Christopher, Susannah, Mary, & Martha gct White River MM

WHITAKER
9-30-1820	Wm, Lewis, Samuel, Joseph, & Jonathan rocf Carmel MM OH
6-14-1823	John rocf Carmel MM OH
7-26-1837	Mary Ann, Milton H, Jonathan R, & Louisa min ch Wm & Sarah rocf Dover MM
5-27-1840	Milton H min gct Dover MM

WHITE
11-26-1814	Jane (**Boswell**) dis for mcd
2-22-1817	Dililah (**Boswell**) dis for mcd
12-27-1817	Wm rec in mbrp
8-29-1818	Wm con for dr
11-28-1818	John rocf Little Falls MM MD
12-26-1818	Joel & Charles s John rec in mbrp; Hannah & dt Eliza, Sarah, Lettisha, & Mary rec in mbrp
4-24-1819	Wm dis for mcd & dr
4-19-1823	Benjamin & s Milton, John, & Jesse rocf New Garden MM NC; Mary & dt Elizabeth rocf New Garden MM NC
8-14-1824	Lewis rocf Piney Woods MM NC
1-14-1826	Benjamin & w Mary & ch Elizabeth, Milton, Jesse, Anna, & Rebecca gct White Lick MM
8-26-1829	Lewis dis for jas
9-26-1855	Alice rec in mbrp
7-22-1857	Priscilla rocf Milford MM
11-3-1858	Mordecai Morris Hamilton Co OH s John T & Susanna dec Henry Co m Hannah Amelia dt Elijah & Naomi **Coffin** Wayne Co at Whitewater MH; Nathan s Nathan & Rebecca both dec Washington Co m Elizabeth Ann dt Wm dec & Rebecca **Pool** Wayne Co at Whitewater MH
12-22-1858	Hannah Amelia gct Cincinnati MM OH
12-28-1859	Elizabeth Ann gct White Lick MM
3-27-1861	James T & w Anna C & ch Sarah Josephine & Charles S rec in mbrp
11-26-1862	Mary & dt Mary S rocf Piney Woods MM NC
3-23-1864	Elizabeth (**Richie**) con mcd
2-28-1866	Oliver con mcd

WHITE (cont)

3-28-1866	Mary Caroline rec in mbrp
8-11-1869	Joseph C s Joseph dec & Alice Wayne Co m Hannah H dt George dec & Hannah H **Dilks** Preble Co OH at Smyrna Mtg
10-23-1872	Mary B J con mcd
5-23-1877	Oliver & w Caroline & ch Winnie L, Esther G, Raymond P, & Robert F gct Milford MM
7-25-1877	Mary B J gct Poughkeepsie MM NY
8-22-1877	Joseph C rec in mbrp; Joseph Jr s Joseph C & Hannah D rec in mbrp
12-26-1877	Wm Irvin & w Sarah & ch Ora M, Harry B, & Edwin J rec in mbrp
9-23-1880	Wm W & w Mary A, & ch Roy, Thomas, Reaborn, & Miriam rocf Milford MM
6-23-1881	Anna T appt elder
8-25-1881	Wm W & w Mary Abigail & ch Roy, Thomas, Reaborn, Miriam E, & Lydia Florence gct Adrian MM MI
7-26-1883	Josiah T & ch Mary I, Pharaba W, & Josiah T Jr rocf Maryville MM TN
8-23-1883	Josiah T appt elder
4-23-1885	Winifred rocf Dublin MM
6-17-1885	Charles A s Richard & Mary U Dickey Co Dakotah Ter m Rosalie Annie dt John S & Mary B **Richie** Dakota Ter
7-23-1885	Mary Jarrett rec in mbrp
5-27-1886	Oliver & w Caroline & ch Esther G, Raymond P, & Robert F rocf Dublin MM; Phariba W gct Duck Creek MM
9-20-1888	Alice rq cert for herself & fam to Muncie MM
10-25-1888	Oliver & w Caroline & ch Esther G, Raymond P, & Robert F gct Muncie MM
1-26-1889	Charles S rel fr mbrp; j Congregational ch
2-22-1890	Phariba rocf New Castle MM
5-24-1890	Oliver & w M Caroline & ch Esther G, Raymond P, & Robert F rocf Muncie MM; Wm J & w Eliza W & ch Edgar F & James Smith rocf Dublin MM
5-28-1892	Harry B rel fr mbrp
8-27-1892	Ellis C gct Chicago MM IL
12-23-1893	Ellen S rel fr mbrp to j Detroit MI 1st Congregational ch
1-27-1894	Wm D rel fr mbrp
2-24-1894	Josiah T Jr rel fr mbrp to j Congregational ch; Esther P & J Seldon rel fr mbrp; jas
12-22-1894	Anna (**Richie**) & min s Henry E & Benjamin M gct Scotts Mills MM OR
6-22-1895	J Edwin rel fr mbrp
2-24-1898	Mary A & ch Marian E, Lydia Florence, Esther Mary, & Helen Dora rocf Hopewell MM
11-24-1898	David F & w Angeline H & ch Elizabeth H, Edith, & Rosa Elma rocf New Garden; Mary A & ch Marion E, Lydia F, Esther M, & Helen D gct Frankford MM Philadelphia PA

WHITELY

2-25-1897	Charles O rocf Kokomo MM
11-24-1898	Charles O gct Union Grove MM

WHITSON

7-27-1811	Willis & s Nathan, Joshua Compton, & Amos rocf Elk MM OH; Rebeckah rocf Elk MM OH

WICKERSHAM

1-29-1814	Mary & Rachel rocf Deep River MM NC
3-26-1814	Caleb & s Abel & John rocf Deep Rive MM NC; Lydia & dt Rhoda, Miriam, Mary, & Sarah rocf Deep River MM NC
10-29-1814	Jehu rocf Deep River MM NC; Mary & dt Anne rocf Deep River MM NC
6-24-1815	Sarah rocf Deep River MM NC
2-24-1816	Wm s Sarah rec in mbrp
2-24-1841	Ann Eliza (**Dilhorn**) dis for mcd

WICKERSHAM (cont)

3-26-1856	Honey Creek MM given perm to rst Ann Eliza
4-22-1880	Catherine rec in mbrp

WICKETT

12-22-1852	Benjamin & w Susan & ch Mary Esther, Sarah Elizabeth, & Thomas Wm rocf Scipio MM NY; Esther rocf Scipio MM NY
4-26-1888	Esther Ann & ch Wm F, Emily Jane, Edith Belle, & Leroy rec in mbrp
5-23-1891	Ella E & ch Fred S, Nellie S, Herbert A, Benjamin L, & Mabel E rec in mbrp

WIDOWS

6-24-1815	Sarah rocf Springfield MM NC

WIGGINS

2-28-1838	White Lick MM rq aid in treating with Rebecca (**Boswell**) for mcd; did not make satisfaction
9-24-1851	Ruth Ann (**Shearon**) con mcd
5-26-1881	Horace & w Laura rec in mbrp
4-25-1891	John D rec in mbrp
7-25-1891	Frederick D grs John D & Ruth A rec in mbrp
12-26-1891	Horace & Laura not found
12-28-1899	George & dt Ruth E rec in mbrp

WILCOX

3-26-1845	Martha Ann (**Nixon**) dis for na & mcd

WILDMAN

8-16-1893	Murray Shipley s John dec & Mary T Selma Clark Co OH m Olive dt Henry & Caroline **Stiggleman** Wayne Co at res of her f
6-23-1894	Olive S gct Spiceland MM

WILKINS

9-14-1822	Amos rocf Cedar Creek MM VA
4-15-1826	Amos dis for deserting fam for 2y

WILKINSON

7-28-1858	Anna rocf Hopewell MM VA
3-28-1882	Mary Jane & min ch Edward & Henry to be rec in mbrp 12th St PM
4-27-1882	Mary J & s Edwin & Henry rec in mbrp
8-27-1896	Henry F & Edwin F drpd fr mbrp

WILLCUTS

10-29-1814	Milly & dt Rachel rocf Piney Grove MM NC
9-21-1882	Rachel rocf Spiceland MM
11-30-1882	Levi M s Jonathan & Mary both dec Wayne Co m Rhoda E dt Stephen & Rachel dec **Mendenhall** at Richmond Mtg

WILLCUTTS

10-29-1814	Thomas & s Jonathan & David rocf Piny Grove MM NC

WILLETS

8-30-1817	Harriet rec in mbrp; Belinda & Maria dt Isaac rec in mbrp
4-19-1823	Joshua con att apd & dancing
11-22-1826	Joshua dis for dancing, upl, & dp
12-22-1830	Ann (**Brown**) con mcd
2-26-1840	Ann gct Exeter MM PA
4-26-1854	Joseph & w Charity P & dt Martha rocf Alum Creek MM OH

WILLETT

11-30-1816	Isaac rec in mbrp

WILLETTS

7-26-1817	Joshua, Rueben & Newton s Isaac rec in mbrp

WHITEWATER MONTHLY MEETING
MINUTES AND MARRIAGES

WILLETTS (cont)

10-29-1817	Isaac s Isaiah & Susanna both dec Wayne Co m Miriam wid Pernias **Nixon** dt Joseph & Mary dec **Nixon** Perquimans Co NC at Whitewater MH
2-27-1856	Lewis & w Charity P & dt Martha Ellen gct Alum Creek MM OH

WILLIAMS

9-25-1813	Sarah rec in mbrp
4-30-1814	Wm minister & s John Boyd, Caleb, Joshua, Josiah, Jesse, & Billey rocf Newberry MM TN; Rachel & dt Rachel rocf Newberry MM TN
5-28-1814	Richard & s Wm & John rocf Newberry MM TN; Rachel & dt Sally & Polly rocf Newberry MM TN
2-25-1815	Hezekiah rocf Newberry MM TN
4-29-1815	Pheba **Bonine** & Charity dt Nathan & Rachel rocf Newberry MM TN
9-4-1816	John s Wm & Rachel Wayne Co m Mary dt Joseph & Lydia **Cook** Wayne Co at Whitewater MH
4-26-1817	Hezekiah rocf New Garden MM; Rebecca & dt Malinda rocf New Garden MM
7-26-1817	Joshua s Wm gct New Garden MM PA; Boyd gct Silver Creek MM to m
8-30-1817	Cert rec for Isaac & s Christopher & Owen; end to New Garden MM
4-1-1818	Caleb s Wm & Rachel Wayne Co m Matilda dt Henry dec & Susanna **Baldwin** Jefferson Co TN at Whitewater MH
10-31-1818	Achilles & s Joseph **Unthank** rocf Miami MM OH; Bulah & dt Susanna rocf Miami MM OH; Joshua rocf New Garden MM
7-31-1819	Boyd con for att mcd
11-27-1819	Boyd gct Silver Creek MM
1-29-1820	Joshua con mcd
3-25-1820	Robert rocf Miami MM OH; Hannah rec in mbrp
8-26-1820	Jesse & s Jesse L rocf Miami MM OH; Sarah & dt Anna Lynce, Sarah, & Elizabeth rocf Miami MM OH
10-28-1820	Sarah gct Caesar's Creek MM OH
11-16-1822	Wm & s Joshua rocf Cane Creek MM NC; Mary & dt Ruth & Susannah rocf Cane Creek MM NC
6-14-1823	Jesse & w Sarah & min s Jesse gct West Grove MM; Sarah, Sarah T, & Elizabeth D gct West Grove MM
12-20-1823	Caleb rocf Darby Creek MM OH
2-14-1824	Richard & s Jesse Turner rocf New Garden MM NC; Sarah rocf New Garden MM NC
1-15-1825	Wm & w Mary & ch Ruth, Joshua, Susannah, & Asenath gct Chester MM
7-16-1825	John dis for na
10-15-1825	Matilda w Caleb & ch Henry, Lezene, Salina, & Merchant gct West Grove MM; Caleb ref cert of removal; Clark & s Cyrus S & Wm rocf Springborough MM OH; Mary rocf Springborough MM OH
11-19-1825	Matilda & s Henry & Merchant gct West Grove MM
12-17-1825	Joshua & w Hannah gct West Grove MM
2-18-1826	Caleb dis for spreading scandal & upl
4-15-1826	Jesse rocf West Grove MM
5-20-1826	Josiah dis for buying, keeping, & playing a fiddle
8-23-1826	Jesse dis for playing fiddle for people to dance
3-28-1827	Elizabeth (**Crampton**) con mcd
4-25-1827	Mary & ch Jehiel, John, & Liddia gct West Grove MM
5-28-1828	Billy dis for mcd; res within Orange PM limits
1-28-1829	Rebecca dis for jas
3-25-1829	Hezekiah dis for jas
6-24-1829	Clark dis for na & jH
2-24-1830	Caleb dis for jas
7-28-1830	Rachel gct Dover MM OH
9-22-1830	Richard & w Sarah dis for jas; Mary dis for jas
1-23-1833	Jesse Jr dis for na, jas, & mcd
8-28-1833	Jesse Jr s Wm rst
12-25-1833	Nathan rec in mbrp
3-26-1834	Rachel rec in mbrp

WILLIAMS (cont)

10-22-1834	Nathan & w Rachel gct Mississinewa MM
4-22-1835	Cyrus M, Wm, Narcissa, & Martha min ch Clark gct Cincinnati MM OH
8-23-1837	Jesse & w Elizabeth & min ch Wm, Phebe Ann, & Matilda gct New Garden MM
12-22-1841	Joseph gct Philadelphia MM PA
5-22-1844	Cert rec for Jesse & w Elizabeth & ch Wm, Phebe Ann, Melinda, Cassandra, & Mary Elizabeth fr Chester MM; end to Milford MM
2-26-1845	Achsa dis for jH
4-23-1845	Alfred dis for na, mcd, & jH; Milton dis for na
5-28-1845	Achilles & w Beulah & ch Robert, Martha, Ann, Caroline, & Sarah gct West Grove MM; Zelinda gct West Grove MM
12-24-1845	Jesse T dis for jas & na
3-24-1847	Nathan dis for na
9-26-1849	Jesse & w Elizabeth & ch Phebe Ann, Melinda, Casandra, Mary Elizabeth, & Wm Albert rocf Milford MM
1-2-1851	Jonathan s Isaac & Sarah dec Wayne Co m Ruth Anna dt James & Cassandra M **Weeks** Wayne Co at Smyrna Mtg
5-28-1851	Ruth Ann gct New Garden MM
1-26-1853	Susannah (**Rich**) con mcd
2-22-1854	Jesse con mcd
11-22-1854	Malinda, Casandra, Elizabeth, & Albert ch Jesse gct Birch Lake MM MI
11-28-1855	Achilles & w Beulah & dt Sarah & Caroline rocf West Grove MM
2-27-1856	Robert rocf West Grove MM
9-24-1856	Susannah gct Chester MM
10-22-1856	Jesse gct Birch Lake MM MI
5-27-1868	Rosetta Helena AR rec in mbrp
7-28-1869	Alfred K rocf Cincinnati MM OH
8-25-1869	Granville T s Alfred K rec in mbrp
3-27-1872	Wm & w Martha & ch John F C, Lillie C, Henry D, Wm S, & Nelly A rec in mbrp
6-3-1873	Alfred K Wayne Co s Micajah T & Hannah J both dec Hamilton Co OH m Mary dt Seth dec & Mary **Smith** Wayne Co at res of her mother
12-24-1873	Ada B rec in mbrp
3-25-1874	John rec in mbrp
5-27-1874	Granville rec in mbrp
3-22-1876	John & Ann rel fr mbrp
10-23-1878	Esther rocf Birch Lake MM MI
7-28-1881	Rebecca L & dt Ada Florence rocf Chester MM
9-22-1881	Alonzo P, Edgar A, & Jesse O rocf Chester MM
3-23-1882	Benjamin F & w Eliza Ann & ch George Walker, Luther Converse, John Wm, & Mattie M rec in mbrp
4-27-1882	Alfred K & Mary S & min ch Granville F & Mary Alice rq cert to Union MM Licking Co KS
5-25-1882	Alfred K & w Mary & ch Granville F & Mary Alice gct Union MM KS
2-22-1883	Elizabeth & ch Harvy & Frederick Wm rec in mbrp
6-28-1883	Elizabeth Centreville rec in mbrp
2-28-1884	George & w Anna & ch Daniel Walter & John P rec in mbrp
9-25-1884	Rebecca & minor dt Ida gct Chester MM
2-26-1885	Wm, Martha, John F C, Lillie, Henry D, Nellie, Benjamin F, Elizabeth A, George W, Lerton, John W, & Mattie M drpd fr mbrp for na; Ada Florence gc
4-22-1885	Alonzo gct Chester MM
4-22-1886	Alonzo rocf Chester MM
4-22-1888	Susan rec in mbrp
12-28-1889	Anna & ch Rosa, Bertie, Minnie, Ida, & May rocf Watseka MM IL
10-24-1891	Emily gct West Grove MM
12-26-1891	Granville, Edgar A, Jesse O, Elizabeth, Henry, & Freddie not found
10-27-1894	King R & w Elizabeth & ch Lula, Willie D, & James Earl rocf West Grove MM

WILLIAMS (cont)

4-25-1896	Robert T & w Almyra & ch Herbert P & Daniel W rec in mbrp
5-23-1896	John H, Mary E, Nathan, & Barbara J New Westville OH rec in mbrp
2-25-1897	Earl, Estella, & Minerva ch Nathan & Barbara New Westville rec in mbrp
2-24-1898	Anna & min dt Ida Pearl gct Chester MM

WILLIAMSON

2-25-1874	Silas & w Sarah & ch Anna & Augustie rocf Chester MM
3-22-1890	Augustine M rel fr mbrp; glt Richmond 1st ME ch
5-25-1899	Anna rel fr mbrp

WILLIS

5-27-1815	David rocf Lost Creek MM TN; Metilda & dt Lucinda rocf Lost Creek MM TN
10-28-1815	Lydia rocf Lost Creek MM TN
3-27-1819	David & fam gct New Garden MM

WILLITS

10-26-1831	Ann rocf Westfield MM
10-11-1843	Ann & min s Wm gct Exeter MM

WILLMET

10-30-1819	Joseph & s Thomas & Charles rocf Bristol MM England

WILLMOT

10-30-1819	Polly & dt Lydia, Elizabeth, & Rebecca rocf Bristol MM England

WILLMOTT

2-18-1826	Thomas rocf New Garden MM

WILLS

11-28-1818	Mary (**Thomas**) con mcd

WILMOT

9-22-1830	Thomas dis

WILMOTT

3-30-1822	Joseph & fam gct New Garden MM

WILSON

8-29-1812	John rocf Back Creek MM NC
7-30-1814	John gct Back Creek MM NC
7-17-1824	Cert rec for Joseph fr Piney Woods MM NC; end to Milford MM; Cert rec for Samuel fr Piney Woods NC; end to Milford MM
8-14-1824	John rocf Nottingham MM PA; Catharine & dt Catharine & Esther Mariah rocf Nottingham MM PA; Nathan & James s John rocf Nottingham MM PA; end by Miami MM OH
9-18-1824	Joseph rocf Piney Woods MM NC; Samuel & s John & Nathan rocf Piney Woods MM NC; Kezia & dt Sarah, Milicent, Elizabeth, Lydia, & Martha rocf Piney Woods MM NC
7-16-1825	Joseph rocf Nottingham MM PA
10-15-1825	Samuel & w Keziah & ch Sarah, Millicent, Elizabeth, John, Lydia, Nathan, Martha, & James gct West Grove MM
11-19-1825	Joseph gct West Grove MM
11-24-1825	Nathan s John & Catherine Wayne Co m Sarah dt Benjamin & Ann **Stokes** Wayne Co at Ridge MH
12-21-1825	James s John & Catherine Wayne Co m Sarah dt Josiah dec & Rebecca **Clawson** Wayne Co at Whitewater MH
10-22-1828	John & w Catharine & ch Catharine & Hester Mariah gct Vermilion MM IL
10-28-1829	Nathan & Sarah dis for jas; Joseph gct Vermilion MM IL

WILSON (cont)

11-25-1829	Samuel & s Joseph Thomas, Henry, Eleazar, Ezekiel, John, Charles, & Samuel rocf New Garden MM NC; Abigail & Sarah rocf Back Creek MM NC
4-22-1835	James & w Sarah & ch John, Mary, Sarah, & Rebecca C gct Vermilion MM IL; Henry, Ezekiel, John, Charles, Eleazar, Sarah, Samuel, Samuel & Abigail ch Samuel & Ruth gct Fairfield MM
4-26-1837	Joseph gct Milford MM
5-24-1837	Sarah P rocf Wilmington MM DE
5-23-1838	Jeffries, Wm Poole, & Sarah ch David rocf Philadelphia MM PA
11-24-1841	Thomas dis for na & mcd
9-22-1858	Elizabeth C & Huldah J rocf Fairfield MM; James C & w Maria & dt Alice Lillian rocf Fairfield MM; Eli & w Mary & ch Thomas Jefferson, Wm Penn, & John rocf Fairfield MM
4-27-1859	Henry & w Mary & ch Esther J, Joseph R, Ellis G, & Martha Ellen rocf Richland MM; settled in KS Prep Terr
5-23-1860	Richland MM granted perm to rec Thomas T
7-25-1866	Mary rec in mbrp
7-22-1874	Mary dis for na & showing no regard for society
6-23-1875	Harmon rec in mbrp
2-23-1876	Wm N rocf Spiceland MM
11-28-1877	Ella Taylor rocf Spiceland MM
2-26-1879	Harmon rel fr mbrp
8-23-1883	Olive d 2-23-1883
3-27-1884	Harmon C & w Ada M & ch Wm B, Mary, Virgil, & Luetta rec in mbrp
3-26-1885	Elizabeth B rocf Raysville MM
5-27-1886	Mary W & dt Irena gct Duck Creek MM
4-26-1888	David & Sarah W rec in mbrp
12-22-1888	Timothy & w Elmina H rocf Marysville MM TN
2-23-1889	Lydia & Benjamin rec in mbrp
2-28-1891	Maurice/Morris E & w M Elizabeth rec in mbrp
3-28-1891	Fanny J & dt Theodate P rec in mbrp
8-27-1892	Eva rocf Spiceland MM
10-22-1892	Folger P rec in mbrp
1-28-1893	Eliza (**Mendenhall**) rocf New Castle MM
11-24-1894	Eva E gct Raysville MM
2-23-1895	M Peninah (**Hill**) gct Albion MM IA
3-23-1895	Isaac & Harvey rec in mbrp
1-27-1898	Charles & Hannah gct Earlham MM IA
8-25-1898	Theodate P gct evangelical denomination
9-22-1898	Dr Wm N & w Ella T & min ch Wm Taylor, Elizabeth, & Benezetti gct Indianapolis MM
6-22-1899	Harmon & w Ida & min ch Wm, Virgil, Louella, Homer, Lincoln, & Ethel gct Dover MM
9-21-1899	David & w Sarah W gct Chicago MM IL
11-23-1899	Morris Edward gct jas

WILT

5-27-1897	Frank & Dora S Providence & Friendship Darke Co OH rec in mbrp

WINDER

12-28-1837	Abner s Abner & Hope Champaign Co OH m Rebecca C dt John & Elizabeth **Pool** Wayne Co at Whitewater MH
6-27-1838	Rebecca C gct Goshen MM OH
1-23-1856	Rebecca C & ch Esther Ann, Samuel Charles, Joseph John, & Susan rocf Goshen MM OH
8-26-1863	Mary Jane rec in mbrp
3-26-1872	Samuel C con mcd
4-27-1882	Cora E rec in mbrp
6-27-1891	Leona C rel fr mbrp

WINDLE

6-25-1892	Mary E & dt Rebecca, Deborah, & Emily rocf Chester MM

WHITEWATER MONTHLY MEETING
MINUTES AND MARRIAGES

WINSLOW

8-17-1822	John gct Back Creek MM NC
10-22-1828	John & s Henry & John Hubbard rocf Back Creek MM NC
11-22-1828	Mary rocf Back Creek MM NC
1-28-1829	John & w Mary & ch Henry & John H gct Duck Creek MM
11-24-1852	Mary Amy & ch Mary Barker, John Milton, & Robert B rocf Scipio MM NY
4-24-1861	Mary B gct Scipio MM NY
10-26-1864	John M dis for na & engaging in military service
12-22-1887	John M rec in mbrp

WINSTON

2-27-1828	Cert rec for Seth fr Back Creek MM NC; end to New Garden MM

WISHARD

7-24-1878	Lucinda B J gct Raysville MM

WITCHEL

8-23-1843	Isaac & Mary gct Duck Creek MM

WITCHELL

6-22-1836	Isaac & Mary min rocf Flushing MM OH
6-27-1855	Isaac dis for mcd

WOLFE

9-21-1859	Mary rec in mbrp
6-27-1866	John E rec in mbrp
1-23-1867	Wm rec in mbrp
12-27-1871	John E con mcd
3-27-1872	David & w Mattie E & ch Elfleela R, Clayton B, & Harry P F rec in mbrp; Mary Adleine rec in mbrp
3-25-1874	Elijah rec in mbrp
4-22-1880	Lizzie rec in mbrp
3-26-1885	Elijah B rel fr mbrp to jas
7-22-1897	Martha's death rpt; ae 53y
6-22-1899	Harry gct Indianapolis MM

WOLFORD

1-27-1898	Harry & w Anna New Westville OH rec in mbrp
3-23-1899	Charles C New Westville rec in mbrp

WOOD

10-19-1822	Jacob & s Simeon rocf Flushing MM OH
3-26-1845	Margaret K (**Ratliff**) dis for na & mcd
9-27-1890	Bertha & dt J Henley **Hill** gc
9-24-1896	Luanna rocf Indianapolis MM
5-25-1899	Elizabeth (**Wilson**) drpd fr mbrp

WOODARD

3-29-1848	Cornelius J s Cadan & Rachel Wayne Co m Sarah dt John & Margaret dec **Burgess** Morgan Co OH at Whitewater MH
5-28-1856	Louisa rocf New Garden MM
1-25-1870	Isaac P & w Lydia & ch Martha Jane, Rebecca, Albert M, Ella May, Oliver C, & Lydia Alta rocf New Garden MM
5-6-1880	Leander J s Luke & Elvira F Fountain City Wayne Co m Annie B dt Isaac P & Mary Ann **Evans** Richmond at res of her father
10-28-1880	Leander J rocf New Garden MM
2-22-1883	Nathan D & w Mary C rocf Coloma MM
1-24-1884	Nathan D & w Mary C gct Indianapolis MM
6-28-1888	Luke & w Elvira & ch Alice & Ella rocf Srens Falls NY
11-23-1889	Luke & w Elvira gct Oskaloosa MM IA
11-28-1891	Ella M & Alice gct Muncie MM
2-27-1892	Catharine Mayhew rel fr mbrp
9-23-1893	Lena Lucile adopted dt Oliver C & Laura H rec in mbrp
7-22-1897	Lydia's d rpt; ae 68y

WOODS

5-25-1889	Angelina rec in mbrp

WOODWARD

5-24-1848	Sarah B gct New Garden MM

WOOTEN

6-26-1867	Wm S rocf Honey Creek MM
12-25-1867	Andrew rec in mbrp
5-25-1869	Abijah & w Naomi T & ch Addie T & Charles Welden rocf New Garden MM
6-23-1869	Docia rec in mbrp
7-26-1869	Lydia rec in mbrp
11-25-1874	Andrew gct Spiceland MM

WOOTON

3-27-1872	Wm S & w Docia S & ch Elmer O, Martha, & Mary gct Indianapolis MM
12-27-1876	Abijah & ch Addie F, Charles Weldon, & Waldo Emmerson gct Mill Creek MM

WORTH

12-31-1814	Keziah rocf Deep Creek MM NC
9-26-1838	Reuben M & w Lydia & ch Laura Ann & Joseph Dewit Clinton rocf Springfield MM
1-28-1852	Lydia S gct White Lick MM
7-28-1852	Joseph Dewit Clinton gct White Lick MM

WORTHINGTON

7-27-1858	Samuel, Sarah, & Elizabeth set off with Kansas MM KS
12-28-1859	Elizabeth W w Henry & ch Samuel, Sarah, Jeremiah Willits, Henry W, & Elizabeth Farnam rocf Philadelphia MM North Dist PA

WRIGHT

9-30-1809	Ralph appt elder
1-29-1810	Jonathan rocf Springfield MM NC
2-28-1810	Jonathan s Ralph & Hannah Dearborn Co m Lydia dt John & Mary **Hawkins** Dearborn Co at Whitewater MH
9-29-1810	James rocf Springfield MM NC; Lydia rpt for having a ch soon after m; chm
11-24-1810	Jonathan dis for fornication
8-29-1812	Cyrus grs Ralph rec in mbrp
8-4-1813	David s Ralph & Hannah Wayne Co m Hepsa dt Libni & Hepsa **Coffin** Wayne Co at Whitewater MH
3-25-1815	John Prior rocf Lost Creek MM TN; Susannah & dt Mary, Sarah, Charity, Elisabeth, Naomi, & Susannah rocf Lost Creek MM TN
2-24-1816	Ralph Jr con mcd
7-26-1817	James & Wm rocf Miami MM OH
2-23-1822	John & s John rocf Philadelphia MM PA; Esther & dt Lydia rocf Philadelphia MM PA
3-19-1825	Mary rocf North West MM MD; Rhoda & dt Rhoda & Lydia rocf North West MM MD
6-18-1825	Cyrus con mcd ; Wm rocf Philadelphia MM PA
12-17-1825	Miriam rocf Chester MM
4-15-1826	Wm gct Milford MM
12-27-1826	John & w Esther gct Milford MM
5-30-1827	Isaac s Hatfield & Lucretia Wayne Co m Mary dt John & Esther **Wright** Wayne Co at Whitewater MH
6-27-1827	Aaron rocf Flushing MM OH; Rebecca rocf Milford MM; Edward rocf North West Fork MM MD; James H rpt dis by North West Fork MM MD; res within Whitewater MM
7-25-1827	Mary H gct Milford MM
1-28-1829	Rebecca dis for jas
2-25-1829	Aaron gct Vermilion MM IL
3-25-1829	Rhoda dis for jas
4-22-1829	Edward & John H dis for jas; Lydia & dt Millicent & Mary Ann rocf Stillwater MM OH
7-22-1829	Lydia dis for jas

WRIGHT (cont)

11-24-1830	Aaron gct Flushing MM OH
1-26-1831	James, John, Jabez, Wm, & Nathan s Jonathan & Lydia rocf Chester MM; Lydia & dt Rebecca, Hannah, & Lydia rocf Chester MM
3-27-1833	James Jr dis for selling horse not his own & left under an alias
1-22-1834	Charity rocf Arba MM
2-26-1834	Aquilla rocf Salem MM
4-22-1835	Aquilla gct Cincinnati MM OH
1-25-1837	Susanna rocf Clear Creek MM OH
8-25-1841	Thaddeus rocf Salem MM
5-3-1843	Thaddeus s Jonathan & Susan dec Fayette Co m Rebecca dt Achilles & Beulah **Williams** Wayne Co at Whitewater MH
8-23-1843	Susannah gct Salem MM
5-28-1845	Thaddeus & w Rebecca & dt Mary gct Milford MM
8-27-1845	Evan rocf Salem MM
4-29-1846	Thomas W s Joel dec & Elizabeth Fayette Co m Laura Ann dt Reuben W & Lydia **Worth** Wayne Co at Whitewater MH
4-28-1847	Jacob T & w Matilda Ann & s Benjamin Corryndo & min brother Jonathan rocf Salem MM; Thomas W rocf Salem MM
9-22-1847	Thadeus & w Rebecca rocf Milford MM
6-28-1848	Jonathan & w Deborah & min ch Micajah, Moses, & Edward rocf Salem MM
3-28-1849	Susannah rocf Salem MM
3-26-1851	Jonathan J gct White Lick MM
5-28-1851	Laura Ann & ch Joel Lindley, Mary Amanda, & Reuben Worth gct White Lick MM; Benjamin Corrydon & Granville L ch of Jacob L gct White Lick MM; Thomas W dis
6-25-1851	Moses min gct Cincinnati MM OH
11-26-1851	Eliza Jane gct Spiceland MM
8-25-1852	Jacob T dis
7-26-1854	Jacob rocf West Grove MM
12-27-1854	Isaac & w Elisabeth rocf Elk MM OH; Edmund gct Sugar Plain MM
3-28-1855	John & w Sarah rocf New York MM
5-28-1856	Isaac & w Elizabeth gct Western Plains MM IA
6-24-1857	Macaijah dis for mcd
1-25-1860	John & w Sarah gct Cincinnati MM OH
5-28-1862	Isaac & w Elizabeth rocf Elk MM OH
4-22-1863	Benjamin Corydon & Granville S s Jacob T gct Bridgeport MM
2-24-1864	Jacob gct West Grove MM
8-24-1864	Eliza gct Minneapolis MM MN
10-23-1867	Mary Ann & ch Fremont & Mary Kinsey rec in mbrp
5-27-1868	Isaac con mcd
8-26-1868	Caroline M (**Carpenter**) & Rebecca (**Charles**) con mcd
10-28-1868	Henry C rocf Short Creek MM OH

WRIGHT (cont)

11-3-1869	Theodore F Philips Co AR s Edwin C & Orlena of Licking Co OH m Eliza dt Calvin & Alida (**Philips**) **Clark** at mtg near Helena AR
4-27-1870	Parvin & w Mary B & ch Morris P & Walter B rocf Short Creek MM OH
1-27-1875	Thaddeus & min ch Mary K & Hannah P gct Milford MM
5-23-1877	Henry C & w Caroline M & ch Ellen Florence, Susan C, & Mary Josephine gct Indianapolis MM
7-25-1877	Edward rel fr mbrp
11-27-1878	Benjamin Franklin rel fr mbrp
1-27-1881	Morris P gct Indianapolis MM
4-28-1881	Charles S & Wilbur S gct Indianapolis MM
5-26-1881	Francis M & w Mary Emily & dt Mary Catharine rocf Indianapolis MM
1-26-1882	Walter G rq lt to Pres ch; rel fr mbrp
2-23-1882	Walter G gr lt to Presby ch
3-23-1882	Parvin & w Mary B gct Indianapolis MM
8-24-1882	Francis & w Emily & min dt Kate rq cert to Lawrence MM KS
9-21-1882	Francis & fam gc
10-26-1882	Frank & w Mary & min dt Kate gct Lawrence MM KS
5-28-1885	Susan Jane rel fr mbrp
6-23-1887	Annie & Elizabeth gct Minneapolis MM MN

WYATT

7-27-1882	Barton rec in mbrp; Mary C & dt Audry J rec in mbrp
8-23-1883	Mary d 2-17-1882 Smyrna

YAGER

3-27-1872	Thomas rec in mbrp
3-24-1881	Rose Anna rec in mbrp

YATES

5-24-1854	Eliza rocf Chesterfield MM NJ
5-27-1857	Eliza gct Cincinnati MM OH

YEAGER

9-26-1883	Anna rel fr mbrp
11-25-1886	Thomas drpd fr mbrp for na

YEATS

7-29-1815	Patrick & Enoch rocf Miami MM OH; Mary & dt Clarke & Elizabeth rocf Miami MM OH

YEO

12-25-1855	Martha Ann rocf Caesar's Creek MM OH
6-27-1891	Wm H rocf Springfield MM OH

YOUNG

7-24-1839	Robert W & w Rebecca & ch Robert W, Hiram, & Edward C rocf Cincinnati MM OH
1-22-1840	Robert W & w Rebecca gct Walnut Ridge MM

SPRINGFIELD MONTHLY MEETING
WAYNE COUNTY, INDIANA

Springfield Monthly Meeting was set off from New Garden Monthly Meeting and first held on the 2nd of Second Month 1820.

Friends first began to settle around the present village of Economy in Perry Township about 1814. Most of them came from Lost Creek Monthly Meeting in East Tennessee, so that the community came to be known as the "Tennessee Settlement." After 1820, most Springfield Friends came from North Carolina.

The minister William Williams (1763-1824), in his *Journal*, described a visit to the community on the 9th of Seventh Month 1815: "Had a meeting at James Warren's, in the New Purchase, in a small settlement of Friends, near the boundry [sic] line. They are members of the New-garden Monthly meeting, and it is likely that they will soon have a meeting amongst themselves." The New Garden Minutes show that in the following month "the meeting was accordingly opened and is henceforth to be known by the name of Springfield."

The first Springfield Meetinghouse is said to have been built of round logs, about half a mile northwest of the present town, at the site of what is now the Economy Cemetery, in 1816. In 1821, a house was built of hewed logs near this one. Many of the members who came from North Carolina and Tennessee had roots on Nantucket Island, and so the name Nantucket, colloquially shortened to "Tucket," was given to the neighborhood around the meetinghouse and burial ground.

The Hicksite Separation had little impact at Springfield. The monthly meeting was, however, badly divided by the Anti-Slavery split in 1842-1843. The radical abolitionist Friends withdrew and formed Springfield Monthly Meeting of Anti-Slavery Friends, the name of which was later changed to Nettle Creek. Only a few pages of fragmentary records of this group have survived, in the Isaac W. and Benjamin B. Beeson Papers in the Indiana State Library.

Six preparative meetings were part of Springfield at one time. Besides Springfield, they included West River (1825) and Nettle Creek (1839) in Dalton Township, Wayne County, and three in Henry County: Flat Rock (1829) in Liberty Township, Westbury (1832) in Stony Creek Township, and Mooreland in Blue River Township. Westbury was laid down in 1848, after nearly all of its members became Anti-Slavery Friends. Flat Rock was attached to New Castle Monthly Meeting in 1886 and laid down in 1914. West River was laid down in 1890, but was revived in 1903. All of these except Mooreland had burying grounds. A listing for the cemeteries for the Wayne County meetings can be found in volume III of Beverly Yount's *Cemetery Inscriptions of Wayne County, Indiana*. The West River listing, however, should be used with caution, since it omits many markers. A more complete listing of markers is in the Friends Collection at Earlham College. Records for the Henry County burying grounds can be found in the volumes of cemetery inscriptions for their respective townships published by the Henry County Historical Society. The Blue River Township volume includes a detailed and annotated listing for Nettle Creek.

In 1911, Springfield Preparative Meeting was detached from the monthly meeting to become Economy Monthly Meeting. Mooreland was set off as a monthly meeting in 1920, leaving Nettle Creek and West River to comprise Springfield Monthly Meeting. The name was changed to Nettle Creek Monthly Meeting in 1937. West River became a monthly meeting in 1959.

MONTHLY MEETING RECORDS

The first volume of Women's Minutes has been lost. The volumes listed below are in the Indiana Yearly Meeting Archives in the Friends Collection at Earlham College. Material searched for this publication is indicated with an asterisk (*). A few pages have been cut from Volume II of the Men's Minutes, causing a loss of the records for Second through Fifth Months of 1838 and the Eleventh and Twelfth Months of 1839.

There are two volumes of birth and death records and four volumes of membership records at Earlham. The oldest birth and death record volume also includes some marriage records. It appears that about 1840 most, but not all, of the material in that volume was copied into a new record volume, which was used until about 1870. Apparently two of the membership record volumess consist only of members of Nettle Creek Meeting. These volumes contain material not found in the other records. Neither was used in previous abstracts. In some of the records, information about parentage, death dates, and burial places has clearly been added in another hand, sometimes decades later. This was almost certainly done by Zimri Hanson (1846-1928), a member of Nettle Creek meeting and well-known as a local historian and genealogist.

Items marked with (**) are available on microfilm in the Indiana Historical Society Library. Items marked (***) were filmed by the County Records in Indiana Project (CRIMP) and are available on interlibrary loan from the Genealogical Society of Utah.

Men's Minutes
Vol. I   2-2-1820 - 10-19-1839*,**,***
Vol. II   1-18-1840 - 12-18-1847*,**,***
Vol. III   1-15-1848 - 6-19-1852*,**,***
Vol. IV   7-17-1852 - 6-18-1859*,**,***
Vol. V   7-16-1859 - 11-21-1868*,**,***
Vol. VI   12-19-1868 - 10-18-1884*,**,***
Vol. VII   1884-1899*,**,***
Joint minutes 11-15-1884-1899*,***
Marriage Record 1820-1895*,**,***
Two Volumes of Birth and Death Records*,***
Four Volumes of Membership Records*

Women's Minutes
Vol. II   12-16-1843 - 3-19-1859*,**,***
Vol. III   4-16-1859 - 2-15-1873*,**,***
Vol. IV   3-15-1873 - 9-17-1892*,**,***
Vol. V   1873-1892*,**,***

Springfield Monthly Meeting Birth and Death Record

ABBOTT
Alexander M h Hettie W b 1-17-1873 Miami Co OH dt Lanson & Jane (**Lockwood**) **Wilkinson** m 6-18-1891 Henry Co
Ch: Hazel b 5-28-1895 Wayne Co

ADAMS
Alva E t b 9-10-1869 Randolph Co s John & Mary A (**Gullet**)
Ollie M b 9-10-1875 Randolph Co dt Walter S & Mary E (**Clear**) **Anders** m 12-23-1893

Alvis D b 1-20-1833 Henry Co s Ebenezer & Rebecca (**Davis**)
Asenath b 11-20-1830 Guilford Co NC dt Daniel & Charity (**Hodson**) **Baldwin** m 12-8-1853
Ch: Lewis H b 8-31-1854 Henry Co
    Irena b 10-7-1855 Henry Co
    Mary Jane b 6-3-1858 Henry Co
    Nelson Perry b 6-29-1861 Henry Co
    Marcus D b 9-20-1862 Henry Co
    Olive b 8-8-1864 Henry Co d 1-11-1867
    Malvina b 3-31-1867 Henry Co
    Luella b 1-27-1870 Henry Co

Ebenezer b 1795 d 8-22-1863 h Rebecca (**Davis**)
Ch: Lucinda b 7-14-1822 Surry Co NC
    Anna b 7-15-1824 d 11-22-1849
    Mary b 9-17-1826
    Joel b 11-30-1828
    Asenath b 10-7-1830
    Alvis D b 1-20-1833

Henry M b 9-4-1852 Henry Co s Elijah & Elizabeth (**Dunbar**)
Malvina b 9-26-1857 Randolph Co dt Wm & Pharaby **Snodgrass** m 3-24-1877

Joel b 11-30-1828 s Ebenezer & Rebecca (**Davis**)
Asenath b 1-6-1830 d 8-26-1855
Ch: Albert Preston b 8-24-1854

John R h Ellen N b 5-4-1867 Wayne Co dt Wm R & Elizabeth Mary (**Spradlin**) **Thornburgh**

Lewis H b 8-31-1854 Henry Co s Alvis D & Asenath (**Baldwin**) h Melissa (**Thompson**) m 4-1879

ADAMS (cont)
Wm b 7-28-1789 d 9-30-1864
Rachel b 8-23-1792 d 4-7-1863
Ch: Ann b 11-24-1824
    Lydia b 2-14-1826 d 10-28-1867
    Mary b 9-25-1831

ADAMSON
Simon d 9-13-1889 ae 82y 10m

ALBERTSON
Mark b 1-10-1891 s Joseph L & Louise (**Cook**)

ALCORN
Charles R b 1-4-1853 Preble Co OH s Finley & Harriet
Huldah b 12-30-1859 Wayne Co
Ch: Fredric I b 4-23-1880 Madison Co OH

Finley h Harriet
Ch: Wm b 1-12-1838 Preble Co OH
    Charles R b 1-4-1853 Preble Co OH

Wm b 1-12-1838 Preble Co OH s Finley & Harriet
Amanda b 2-15-1848 Hamilton Co OH dt John & Mary **McClane** m 6-14-1865

ALLEN
Benjamin F b 9-19-1838 Chatham Co NC s Simon & Hannah (**Woody**)
Sarah Jane b 1-8-1837 Almance Co NC dt Jonathan & Esther **Jobes** m 6-3-186-
Ch: David T b 3-27-1861 Almance Co NC
    John W b 10-23-1863 Almance Co NC
    Jonathan S b 10-2-1865 Chatham Co NC

Joseph C b 6-17-1837 Almance Co NC s Simon & Hannah (**Woody**)
Elizabeth b 7-13-1841 d 4-16-1860
Phebe Jane 2w b 2-4-1847 Wayne Co dt Branson & Elma (**Reynolds**) **Dennis** m 3-12-1863
Ch: Laura Mary b 1-17-1864 Wayne Co
    Emma Jane b 7-26-1865 Wayne Co
    Charley b 3-8-1867 Wayne Co
    Elma b 12-16-1868 Wayne Co
    Sarah Malinda b 2-11-1871 Wayne Co

SPRINGFIELD MONTHLY MEETING
BIRTH AND DEATH RECORD

ALLEN (Joseph C cont)
    Branson b 9-1-1874 Wayne Co d 10-23-1876 bur Nettle Creek
    Harvey b 2-13-1877 Wayne Co - removed to New Albany
    Mary b 12-28-1878 Wayne Co
    Estella b 4-20-1882 Wayne Co
    Freddie b 5-18-1884 Wayne Co

Milton b 12-4-1835 Chatham Co NC s Simon & Hannah (**Woody**) h Hannah
Ch: Sarah J b 2-21-1868
Maggie (**Stevens**) 3w m 5-19-1894

Newton b 8-8-1844 Chatham Co NC s Simon & Hannah (**Woody**)
Asenath b 10-2-1845 Almance Co NC dt Harmon & Luezar **Allen** m 9-24-1865
Ch: Anderson Monroe b 6-24-1866 Almance Co NC
    Hannah Louisa b 12-28-1867 Almance Co NC
    Joseph N b 10-20-1869 Almance Co NC d 3-14-1870 Almance Co NC
    Isabel Jane b 12-10-1870 Almance Co NC d 1-5-1871 bur Almance Co NC
    Mary Ellen b 11-28-1871 Wayne Co d 12-6-1871 bur Nettle Creek
    Wm Jesse b 3-22-1873 Wayne Co d 9-27-1873 bur Nettle Creek
    Benjamin Harmon b 8-29-1874 Wayne Co
    George Thomas b 10-16-1877 Wayne Co
    Franklin Pierce b 4-8-1880 Wayne Co d 10-10-1890 bur Jackson Co AL
    Clifton Ellis b 2-25-1883 Randolph Co
    Lester Otis b 2-28-1886 Randolph Co
    Malinda Myrtle b 4-20-1890 Jackson Co Al d 6-24-1890 bur Jackson Co AL

Simon h Hannah (**Woody**)
Ch: Milton b 12-4-1835 Chatham Co NC
    Joseph C b 6-17-1837 Almance Co NC
    Benjamin F b 9-19-1838 Chatham Co NC
    Newton b 8-8-1844 Chatham Co NC
    Caroline b 12-9-1850 Cane Creek MM Chatham Co NC

Zachariah Westbury b 7-5-1796
Susannah b 9-28-1796
Ch: Nancy b 4-19-1819 d 9-6-1821 bur Springfield
    Sarah b 8-24-1823 d 8-7-1838
    Keziah b 2-21-1827
    Eunice b 12-19-1829
    John b 10-25-1831
    Rebecca b 8-20-1833
    Jesse b 9-20-1835
    Zimri b 5-25-1838
    Wm b 2-21-1840

ALLRED
Abijah b 11-25-1875 Moore Co NC s Eli C & Ruhama (**Lamb**) h Nellie (**Study**) m 6-26-1897
Ch: Essie M b 7-21-1898

ANDERS
Walter S h Mary E (**Clear**)
Ch: Ollie M b 9-10-1875 Randolph Co
    Ira E b 6-6-1886 Randolph Co

ANDERSON
Ernest b 5-4-1876 s Joseph & Elizabeth (**Phillips**)
Amy Bell b 7-3-1875 Randolph Co dt Lewis & Eliza A (**Brown**) **Baldwin** m 12-21-1895
Ch: Lula Fern b 7-18-1896 Wayne Co
    Francis Lee b 4-15-1898 Wayne Co d 8-30-1898 bur Nettle Creek

ANDREWS
Joseph B b 8-27-1848 Randolph Co Barrett & Elizabeth (**Routh**)
Hannah H C b 5-1-1847 Wayne Co dt Wesley Stark & Phebe (**Coffin**) **Ledbetter** m 6-15-1875

ANDREWS (Hannah cont)
Ch: Oscar B b 6-14-1876 Wayne Co
    Olie Bell b 2-4-1878 Wayne Co
    Ethe E b 12-1-1879 Wayne Co
    Edna M
    Lawrence
    Francis Willard

ANTRIM
Thomas h Rachel
Ch: John b 4-24-1809
    Rachel b 1-12-1812
    Thomas b 6-30-1814
    Fanny b 12-24-1816
    Sarah b 3-2-1819

ARNETT
Allen b 3-13-1825 d 4-6-1865

Deborah b 9-8-1829 dt Henry & Hannah **Hollingsworth**

James H b 9-9-1816
Phebe w b 10-24-1819
Ch: Thomas b 6-11-1840 d 9-20-1843
    Jane b 5-3-1842
    Valentine b 1-24-1845
    Charlotte b 9-7-1847
    Waldo b 5-1-1850
    Eunice b 11-16-1852

BAILIFF
Jones h Malinda A b 10-4-1836 Wake Co NC dt John m 7-20-1854
Ch: Newton P b 1-10-1862 Almance Co NC
    Robert W b 4-13-1868
    Jesse E b 3-8-1872

BALDWIN
Alpheus S b 12-8-1861 Wayne Co s Wm & Louisa (**Dennis**) h Ellen (**Bond**) m 9-4-1881

Alvin C b 4-14-1868 Henry Co s Andrew & Eunice (**Coffin**)
Martha M b 2-16-1871 Randolph Co dt Thomas M & Ivy J **Davis** m 11-10-1894

Andrew b 1-21-1816 Deep River Co NC s Daniel & Charity (**Hodson**) d 10-2-1896 bur Nettle Creek
Rhoda b 5-16-1819 dt Charles & Mary (**Stout**) **Howell** d 4-26-1861 bur Nettle Creek m 1-18-1838
Ch: Anna b 12-27-1838
    Mary J b 2-10-1841
    Charles b 5-6-1843 d 2-20-1862
    Lydia b 12-26-1845
    Lewis b 2-19-1849 Henry Co
    Esther Ellen b 4-10-1858
Eunice 2w b 8-1-1829 Marlboro MM Randolph Co NC dt John & Abigail (**Hobbs**) **Coffin** wid Samuel **Lamar** d 10-22-1878 bur Nettle Creek
Ch: Martha Ann b 1-3-1866 Henry Co
    Alvin C b 4-14-1868 Henry Co
Hannah A 3w b 10-30-1836 dt Obadiah & Armella (**Hinshaw**) **Elliott** wid Harmon **Ballenger** bur Nettle Creek m 9-2-1880

Calvin b 8-17-1835 Wayne Co s Daniel & Charity (**Hodson**)
Sarah E b 3-1-1841 Randolph Co NC dt Joseph P & Elizabeth (**Hodson**) **Julian** m 3-14-1863
Ch: Marietta b 9-15-1866 Schuyler Co IL

Daniel b 7-19-1796 d 9-20-1862
Charity (**Hodson**) b 10-9-1795 d 10-25-1860
Ch: Andrew b 1-21-1816 d 10-27-1896 bur Nettle Creek
    John b 4-19-1817 Guilford Co NC
    Cynthia b 12-9-1818 d 8-10-1843
    Jane b 4-11-1820 d 2-21-1832

BALDWIN (Daniel cont)
    David E b 1-18-1822
    Elias b 6-11-1823
    Arreny b 2-8-1825 d 7-5-1826 NC
    Sandford b 5-13-1827
    Elizabeth b 11-21-1828
    Asenath b 11-19-1830 Guilford Co NC
    Amelia b 1-18-1833 Wayne Co
    Calvin b 8-17-1835 Wayne Co
    Irene b 11-15-1839

David E b 1-18-1822 Guilford Co NC s Daniel & Charity (**Hodson**)
Ruth b 3-27-1823 dt Charles & Mary (**Stout**) Howell m 10-8-1843
Ch: Charity Jane b 8-21-1845
    Mary Elizabeth b 7-11-1847 Henry Co
    Asenath Caroline b 6-29-1849
    Larkin Ellis b 5-4-1851
    John H b 10-30-1853 Wayne Co
    Eli D b 8-21-1858 Wayne Co
    Eliza Ellen b 8-21-1858 Wayne Co
    Cynthia E b 4-15-1861 Wayne Co
    David Emory b 8-21-1866 Wayne Co
Eliza 2w b 9-27-1836 Pulaski Co KY dt Pouncey & Tamar **Anderson** wid Thomas **Whittier** d 12-20-1893 m 3-17-1889

David Emory b 8-21-1866 Wayne Co s David E & Ruth (**Howell**)
Amanda M b 11-24-1871 Pulaski Co KY dt Thomas & Eliza (**Anderson**) Whittier d 5-4-1894 bur Nettle Creek m 3-31-1888
Ch: George Elwood b 3-4-1893 Wayne Co d 6-12-1894 bur Nettle Creek

Eli D b 8-21-1858 Wayne Co s David E & Ruth (**Howell**)
Martha J b 8-24-1862 Randolph Co dt Joseph & Nancy **Williams** m 1-31-1880
Ch: Elva A b 1-14-1881 Wayne Co d 4-3-1886 bur Nettle Creek
    Charity b 11-15-1884 Wayne Co

Elwood b 1-10-1829 s Jesse & Margaret (**Beeson**)
Jane b 11-22-1830 dt Ezra & Mary **Reynolds**
Ch: Tilman W b 8-15-1851
    Zimri R b 3-5-1853
    Mary E b 6-22-1854
    George R b 10-16-1850
    Rachel P b 9-15-1860
    Urbane E b 9-22-1862
    Emily L b 10-19-1864

George C b 5-9-1852 Wayne Co s George W & Rachel M
Florence Bell b 6-9-1855 Randolph Co dt John C & Didema **Barnes** m 11-10-1877
Ch: Myrtle M b 8-2-1880 Randolph Co
    Carl C b 1-30-1883 Randolph Co
    Webster W b 3-20-1885 Randolph Co

George R h Asenath C b 5-7-1866 Henry Co dt Milo & Mary (**Chamness**) Reynolds m 3-11-1893

Jabez Newton b 5-23-1851 Wayne Co s Nathan & Malinda (**Hinshaw**)
Ruth b 4-30-1860 Henry Co dt Milo & Mary (**Chamness**) Reynolds m 9-1-1878
Ch: Dillen b 5-11-1879 Wayne Co
    Harvey b 6-13-1881 Wayne Co; inmate of insane hospital more than fifteen years.
    Bertha b 7-5-1883 Wayne Co
    Irving b 7-7-1886 Wayne Co
    Mary Malinda b 11-23-1888 Wayne Co
    Nathan Ernest b 12-14-1890 Wayne Co
    Earl b 1-5-1893 Wayne Co
    Luva Ethel b 4-7-1897 Wayne Co

Jesse b 10-16-1783 s Nathan & Hannah d 11-18-1855 bur Nettle Creek h Hannah
Ch: Nathan b 5-16-1811

BALDWIN (Jesse cont)
    Newton b 11-30-1813 d 12-10-1849
    Chalkley b 10-6-1816
    Judith b 4-11-1819 d 6-7-1852
    Eliza b 11-30-1823
Margaret 2w b 5-21-1799 dt Benjamin & Margaret **Beeson** bur Nettle Creek
Ch: Jesse Franklin b 2-25-1827
    Elwood b 1-10-1829
    Urbane b 5-4-1830
    Isaac b 8-3-1833
    Tilman b 11-16-1835 d 8-8-1847
    Rachel b 12-19-1837 d 5-8-1844
    Nerius b 1-8-1840

Jesse b 3-14-1785 d 1-7-1854
Atiria b 2-14-1785
Ch: Luvina b 3-18-1806 d 1-25-1828
    Dianna b 2-11-1812
    Elizabeth b 10-4-1814
    Sarrah b 1-6-1817
    Phebe b 10-24-1819
    Jane b 2-12-1822
    Levi b 3-9-1825

Jesse Franklin b 2-25-1827 s Jesse & Margaret (**Beeson**)
Phebe A b 9-13-1831
Ch: Nereus B b 4-6-1854
    Lindley b 12-12-1855
    Daniel Sylvester b 12-26-1857

John b 4-19-1817 Guilford Co NC s Daniel & Charity (**Hodson**)
Asenath b 11-21-1819 dt Seth **Hinshaw** d 11-11-1840
Ch Jane b 7-3-1837 d 10-23-1839
    Asenath b 10-21-1840 d 11-11-1840
Susannah 2w b 4-8-1821 dt Charles & Mary (**Stout**) Howell d 9-13-1855
Ch: Elizabeth b 4-22-1843 Wayne Co d 12-12-1877 bur Nettle Creek
Anna Maria 3w b 12-26-1829 Fayette Co dt Samuel & Rachel **Coffin** m 4-10-1859
Ch: Henrietta b 1-16-1860 Wayne Co d 4-12-1883
    Emmaline b 2-1-1864 Wayne Co d 7-28-1880
    John E b 8-24-1866 Wayne Co

John E b 8-24-1864 Wayne Co s John & Anna Maria (**Coffin**)
Cora Alma b 10-5-1876 Randolph Co dt Wm & Hannah (**Burroughs**) Snodgrass m 10-6-1894
Ch: Wava Lorene b 9-17-1897 Wayne Co

John H b 10-30-1853 Wayne Co s David E & Ruth (**Howell**)
Elvaretta b 1-26-1857 Henry Co dt Wm C & Mary (**Canaday**) Chamness m 3-26-1884
Ch: Wm Henry b 2-26-1885 Wayne Co
    Thomas Elwood b 9-14-1888 Wayne Co

Lewis b 2-19-1849 Henry Co s Andrew & Rhoda (**Howell**)
Eliza A b 1-12-1852 Randolph Co dt James & Rachel **Brown** m 10-29-1870
Ch: Evalena b 9-10-1871 Henry Co d 6-28-1890 bur Nettle Creek
    Amy Bell b 7-3-1873 Randolph Co
    Frank L b 7-19-1877 Randolph Co
    Carle A b 9-19-1884 Henry Co
    Fred L b 5-26-1887 Henry Co
    Milton Reed b 6-22-1892 Henry Co d 9-20-1892 bur Nettle Creek

Nathan b 5-16-1811 s Jesse & Hannah
Malinda b 12-22-1811 dt Seth **Hinshaw** d 5-2-1854
Ch: Wm b 10-25-1836
    Henry b 6-3-1838 d 6-3-1856
    Seth b 10-5-1840 d 3-4-1853
    Jesse b 2-6-1843 d 7-19-1844 bur Nettle Creek
    Hannah b 2-21-1845 d 4-26-1867 bur Nettle Creek
    Mary H b 5-11-1848 Wayne Co
    Jabez Newton b 5-23-1851 Wayne Co

SPRINGFIELD MONTHLY MEETING
BIRTH AND DEATH RECORD

BALDWIN (cont)
Newton b 11-30-1813 s Jesse & Hannah d 12-10-1849
Anna b 6-30-1815 dt Joseph & Catherine **Davis**
Ch: Lewis D b 5-14-1843 d 12-6-1843 bur Nettle Creek

Wm b 10-25-1836 s Nathan & Melinda (**Hinshaw**)
Louisa b 5-14-1841 Wayne Co dt Branson & Elma (**Reynolds**) **Dennis** m 10-24-1860
Ch: Alpheus S b 12-11-1861 Wayne Co
    Addie O b 9-3-1866 Wayne Co

BALES
Aaron h Alice (**Manifold**)
Ch: Benjamin b 5-28-1814 Knox Co TN
    Wm b 5-20-1828 Knox Co TN

Aaron b 9-22-1790 Knox Co TN s Wm & Rachel (**Green**)

Albert L b 8-16-1869 Henry Co s Solomon & Lucinda (**Pidgeon**)
Emma Florence b 3-28-1876 Wayne Co dt John Henry & Mary Ann (**Locke**) **Thornburg** m 11-28-1894
Ch: Della Maud b 4-15-1898 Henry Co

Benjamin b 5-28-1814 Knox Co TN s Aaron & Alice (**Manifold**) d 5-9-1844 bur Bales Cem
Nancy b 12-18-1814 Clinton Co OH dt Abraham & Rachel (**Reynard**) **Wrightsman** d 7-16-1875 bur Bales Cem

Dillon h Mary b 5-11-1848 Wayne Co dt Nathan & Malinda (**Hinshaw**) **Baldwin** m 11-12-1871

Jacob b 1-15-1776 d 10-19-1855
Sarah b 10-13-1775 d 7-10-1855
Ch: Lydia b 12-6-1797 Lost Creek TN d 9-13-1798
    Seth b 9-20-1799 Lost Creek TN d 11-4-1822
    Parnel b 2-22-1802 Lost Creek TN
    Rachel b 11-14-1804 Lost Creek TN d 10-30-1870
    John b 10-12-1807 Lost Creek TN
    Mary b 5-28-1811 Lost Creek TN
    Henry b 3-20-1814 Lost Creek TN
    Lewis b 8-27-1817 Lost Creek TN
    Sally Ann b 5-30-1820 Lost Creek TN

Lewis V b 7-22-1874 Wayne Co s George W & Lucy Jane (**Spradlin**) h Surelda (**Jackson**)

Solomon b 6-15-1834 Henry Co s Parnell & Elizabeth (**Koons**) h Elizabeth (**Corey**)
Ch: Ada J b 1-15-1859 Henry Co
Lucinda 2w b 5-24-1837 Henry Co dt David & Rachel (**Wilson**) **Pidgeon** m 12-24-1863
Ch: Wm Henry b 8-9-1865 Henry Co d 4-28-1890 bur Nettle Creek
    Rachel Elizabeth b 8-13-1867 Henry Co
    Albert L b 8-16-1869 Henry Co
    Della F b 1-18-1879 Henry Co d 5-15-1890 bur Nettle Creek

Wm b 5-20-1828 Knox Co TN s Aaron & Alice (**Manifold**)
Mary Melissa 2wb 1-24-1842 Wayne Co dt Isaiah & Fanny (**Dennis**) **Beeson** wid Wm W **Chamness** d 5-7-1893 bur Nettle Creek m 6-18-1878
Mary H 3w b 5-11-1848 dt Nathan & Malinda (**Hinshaw**) **Baldwin** m 3-7-1895

Wm Jesse b 5-7-1881 Henry Co s Benjamin F & Catherine (**Brown**)

BALLENGER
Rebecca b 11-25-1792 d 4-24-1852

BARBER
Lavina Maud b 2-4-1899 Delaware Co dt Thomas Jefferson & Anna (**Hiatt**)

BARNARD
Eli B h Huldah b 5-13-1821 dt Robert & Amy **Canaday** d 4-28-1864
Ch: Edith
    Irena M

Sophia b 12-3-1781 d 6-3-1862

Uriah H b 8-27-1761 s Timothy & Love d 4-9-1844
Elizabeth b 10-14-1763 dt Joseph & Mary **Macy** d 2-5-1848
Ch: Jethro b 12-25-1782 d 8-28-1853
    Joseph b 1784 d "on 16th birthday"
    Love b 12-31-1786 d 7-11-1841
    Hannah b 12- -1788 d 1212-1827
    Elizabeth/Betsey b 3-26-1790 d 2-15-1858
    Anna b 5-28-1794 d 12-28-1868
    George b 9-7-1798 d 1838
    Mary/ Polly b 10-19-1800 d 8-21-1853
    Wm b 6-29-1803 d l-4-1887
    John b 3-2-1806 d 5-3-1888

BEARD
Henry C d 9-26-1877 ae 39y 9m 2ld
Lucinda b 4-12-1839 Wayne Co dt Jonathan B & Matilda (**Pierce**) **Macy** m 1-7-1860
Ch: Lenora C b 12-11-1860 Wayne Co
    Jonathan Seward b 11-5-1864 Wayne Co
    John G Whittier b 11-17-1871 Wayne Co
    Charles Sumner b 7-25-1874 Wayne Co
    Henry Fred b 11-27-1876 Wayne Co

Jonathan Seward b 11-5-1864 Wayne Co s Henry C & Lucinda (**Macy**)
Minnie b 4-10-1865 dt Caspar & Catharine **Cooper** m 3-2-1899 Henry Co

Wm D h Laura A (**Ward**)
Ch: Frank E b 2-13-1887
    Byron b 12-14-1889

BEESON
Benjamin b 1-21-1764 NC s Isaac & Isabel (**Pearson**)
Margaret b 2-13-1769 Center MM Guilford Co NC dt Wm & Hannah (**Beals**) **Hocket** d 10-1-1835 m 6-7-1787 Center MM Guilford Co NC
Ch: Isaac W b 12-19-1789 d 11-26-1871
    Benjamin F b 11-6-1796 d 4-2-1840
    Margaret b 5-21-1799 bur Nettle Creek
    Rachel b 7-8-1801
    Ithamer b 1-5-1808
    Charles b 10-19-1811 d 1-2-1892

Benjamin B b 3-17-1843 s Isaac W & Mary (**Branson**)
Olinda (**Lamb**) m 10-14-1865
Ch: Isaac Francis b 8-13-1866 Wayne Co
    Mary Lenora b 1-23-1868 Wayne Co
    Frederick Leton b 7-3-1877 Wayne Co

Benjamin F b 11-6-1796 s Benjamin & Margaret (**Hocket**) d 4-2-1840
Rachel b 11-14-1804 Lost Creek TN dt Jacob & Sarah **Bales** d 10-30-1870
Ch: Mahlon b 6-12-1830
    Luzena b 10-20-1837
    Benjamin F b 4-1-1840 d 9-6-1842

Charles b 10-19-1811 s Benjamin & Margaret (**Hocket**) d 1-21-1892
Cynthia b 12-9-1818 dt Daniel & Charity (**Hodson**) **Baldwin** d 8-10-1843
Ch: Wm b 1-27-1839
    John b l-1-1841
    Lavina b 9-7-1842

BEESON (cont)
David h Lucinda
Ch: Flora H b 10-25-1864 Vermilion Co IL
    Josephine b 6-29-1867 Vermilion Co IL

Frederick Leton b 7-3-1877 Wayne Co s Benjamin B & Olinda (**Lamb**)
Laura M b 10-29-1878 Wayne Co dt John & Caroline H (**Chamness**) **Davis** m 5-22-1897 Wayne Co
Ch: Herbert Edward b 3-3-1898 Wayne Co

Hezekiah h Mareb b 9-16-1796 d 11-11-1874
Ch: Naomi b 9-12-1816 Randolph Co NC
    Josiah b 1-28-1818 Randolph Co NC
    Eunice H b 2-24-1820 Randolph Co NC d 1-8-1821
    Rachel b 2-16-1823 Springfield
    Benjamin b 8-5-1825 Springfield
    Hannah b 2-24-1828 Springfield
    Salley b 2-19-1831 Springfield
    Matilda b 3-6-1833 Springfield
    Marilla b 11-16-1835 Springfield

Igal h Margret
Ch: Amaziah b 3-9-1820
    Elihue b 3-6-1822
    Allen b 2-22-1827
    Rebecca b 3-5-1829
    Thomas Emry b 5-7-1831 d 12-1-1833
    Lydia b 5-4-1833

Isaac Francis b 8-13-1866 Wayne Co s Benjamin B & Olinda (**Lamb**)
Sarah Catherine b 2-16-1869 Henry Co dt Sylvester H & Margaret (**Bowman**) **Huffman** m 10-6-1888 Henry Co
Ch: Grace B b 9-3-1889
    Marguerite b 10-20-1895 Wayne Co

Isaac K h Rebecca b 2-23-1810 dt Thomas & Amassa (**Adamson**) **Lamb**
Ch: Louisa
    Massa b 3-31-1833
    Thomas b 1-30-1835
    Alice b 10-2-1837
    David b 12-27-1840
    Elizabeth b 9-5-1842
    Mary Hannah b 10-11-1844
    Sarah b 3-7-1847

Isaac W b 12-19-1789 s Benjamin & Margaret (**Hocket**) d 11-26-1871
Mary (**Branson**) b 11-18-1797 d 10-10-1851
Ch: Benjamin B b 3-17-1843

Isaiah h Fanny (**Dennis**) b 9-13-1801 d 4-27-1858
Ch: Mary Malissa b 1-24-1842 Wayne Co d 5-7-1893 bur Nettle Creek
    Narcissa b 6-8-1843 d 9-26-1863

Ithamer b 1-5-1808 s Benjamin & Margaret (**Hocket**)
Mary b 5-28-1811 Lost Creek TN dt Jacob & Sarah **Bales**
Ch: Margret Ann b 7-20-1830
    Sarrah b 5-24-1832
    Oliver H b 1-6-1834
    Lewis Riley b 10-3-1837 Wayne Co
    Cynthia Ellen b 8-28-1840
    John Rufus b 7-4-1843 d 9-15-1843
    Wm Henry b 11-25-1844

John W b 2-18-1841 Wayne Co s Thomas Elwood & Elizabeth
Martha b 3-13-1844 Henry Co dt Cornelious & Lucinda **Murray** m 2-15-1866
Ch: Florin M b 1-29-1867 Wayne Co d 10-20-1880
    Wm F b 12-1-1869 Wayne Co
    Jesse Franklin b 3-29-1873 Wayne Co

BEESON (cont)
Jonathan b 12-28-1836 Wayne Co Thomas Elwood & Elizabeth h Mary
Ch: Elmer E b 9-10-1866 Wayne Co
    Alma Alton b 6-17-1868 Wayne Co
    Clarence C b 6-2-1870 Wayne Co

Leora Ursula b 7-10-1875 dt Samuel

Lewis Riley b 10-3-1837 Wayne Co s Ithamer & Mary (**Bales**)
Julia Esther 2w b 5-3-1851 Lee Co IA dt Harvey & Elizabeth (**Moon**) **Beeson** m 6-18-1877
Ch: Harvey F b 3-29-1878 Washington Co KS
    Harley A b 4-2-1882 Washington Co KS
    George G b 12-22-1884 Washington Co KS
    Mary L b 3-12-1887 Washington Co KS
    Walter A b 3-9-1888 Washington Co KS

Manley b 8-14-1833 s Jesse & Zerua

Mildred b 7-24-1810 Guilford Co NC dt Isaac & Hannah d 9-16-1882 bur West River

Newton h Lydia b 4-3-1821

Samuel W b 10-31-1851 Wayne Co s Thomas & Elizabeth
Julia A b 2-18-1859 Henry Co dt Cornelious & Lucinda **Murray** m 12-24-1874
Ch: Laurence C b 12-1-1875 Wayne Co
    Linnie D b 3-30-1878 Wayne Co

Silas H b 7-6-1803 d 1-31-1843
Charity d 12-1834
Ch: Rachel Malvina b 9-21-1832
    Maria Louisa b 8-5-1834
Nancy E 2w
Ch: James Lauren b 1-17-1840

Thomas h Elizabeth
Ch: Keziah b 9-22-1845 Wayne Co
    Wm b 11-27-1847 Wayne Co
    Samuel W b 10-30-1851 Wayne Co

Thomas b 1-30-1835 s Isaac K & Rebecca (**Lamb**) h Deborah (**Strode**)

Thomas E d 2-29-1879

Thomas Elwood b 1-22-1807 d 3-1-1874 bur West River
Elizabeth b 2-15-1814 d 2-19-1854
Ch: David W b 11-23-1832
    Ursula b 10-22-1834 d 9-15-1850 bur West River
    Jonathan b 12-28-1836 Wayne Co
    Benjamin B b 2-22-1839 d 4-18-1876 bur West River
    John W b 2-18-1841 Wayne Co
    Isaac b 4-24-1843
    Keziah b 9-22-1845
    Wm b 11-21-1847
    Lydia Margaret b 2-25-1850 d 1-17-1851 bur West River
    Samuel b 10-30-1851
Selah 2w b 11-29-1818 d 4-19-1875 bur West River
Ch: Thomas E b 11-12-1858

Virgil b 4-13-1845 Wayne Co s Wade & Maria (**Beeson**)
Louisa b 8-23-1849 Henry Co dt Sophia **Niccum** m 8-23-1869
Randolph Co d 8-1-1896 bur West River
Ch: Ida Esther b 11-5-1895 Wayne Co d 12-4-1895 bur West River

Wm h Hannah d 9-9-1852

Zechariah h Hannah
Ch: Zenoah b 10-23-1823 Springfield
    Rachel b 6-18-1825 Springfield

SPRINGFIELD MONTHLY MEETING
BIRTH AND DEATH RECORD

BEESON (Zechariah cont)
    Lucinda b 3-4-1827 Springfield
    Melinda b 3-4-1827 Springfield
    Edward b 5-27-1829 Springfield
    Keziah b 2-6-1831 Springfield

BENBOW
Wm H b 3-15-1842 Wayne Co s Powel & Rachel
Mary Ann b 3-13-1842 Preble Co OH dt George & Mary **Wilcox** m 5-26-1864
  Ch: Francis Asbury
      Mary Ellen
      Cora Evaline
      Sarah Olive b 9-16-1874 Wayne Co
      Anna Eliza b 8-23-1876 Wayne Co

BENNETT
James h Sarah E b 7-9-1883

BENSON
Emmerson h Zelma b 9-5-1879 Randolph Co dt Charles & Emma Bell (**Veal**) **Harris** m 5-7-1899

BEPLEY
Charles h Pearl B b 3-28-1879 dt Wm & Mary J (**Labcytaux**) **Chamness** m 8-13-1895 Montgomery Co OH

BILLHEIMER
Sylvester h Lydia b 8-14-1848 Wayne Co dt Wilson & Rachel **Dennis** m 8-17-1879

BIRD
Estella O b 10-9-1888 dt Wesley & Laura (**Finch**)

Jerome T h Ellen b 5-20-1866 dt Jesse W & Mary (**Chamness**) **Pidgeon** m 9-15-1886 Henry Co
  Ch: Estella b 9-12-1892
      Bessie B b 9-12-1897

BONAWELL
Curtis b 7-12-1887 Owen Co s George & Nancy (**Philips**)

BOND
John late of Deep Creek NC d 12-5-1860 in 92nd y bur Flat Rock

John b 11-3-1820 d 4-18-1869
Lucinda b 7-4-1822 Surry Co NC dt Ebenezer & Rebecca (**Davis**) **Adams** m 11-25-1841
  Ch: Enos b 10-26-1842 d 4-26-1868
      Levi b 9-29-1844
      Mary b 9-23-1846 Henry Co
      Wm b 3-8-1849 d 3-24-1864
      Semira b 6-21-1851 d 7-26-1875
      Gulielma b 8-4-1853 d 8-17-1875
      Ann b 8-4-1853 d 8-9-1853
      John A b l-3-1856
      Joel E b 7-17-1858
      Alvin P b 12-10-1863
      Sarah E b 1-25-1867

Matilda b 6-1-1834 dt Joseph & Naomi

Mordecai h Rachel
  Ch: Lavina b 10-21-1834
      Elmina b 10-29-1836
      Joseph b 11-5-1838

Wm b 9-18-1793 John & Mary d 6-23-1874
Elizabeth b 12-26-1789 dt Luke & Frances **Wiles** d 6-9-1868
  Ch: John b 11-3-1820 d 4-18-1869
      Amelia b 8-19-1822 Guilford Co NC d 8-22-1890 bur Flat Rock
      Gulielma b 4-15-1824

BOND (Wm cont)
    Frances Belinda b 1-12-1826 d 2-11-1845
    Mary Ann b 12-13-1827 Henry Co
    Asenath b l-6-1830 d 8-25-1855
    Elizabeth b 1-13-1834

BONINE
J D h Sarah S b 2-21-1828 dt Charles & Hannah (**Swain**) **Osborn**

BOOKOUT
James h Ellen (**Lee**)
  Ch: Rosettie b 6-16-1871 Randolph Co NC
      Orpha b 12-18-1873 Randolph Co

Louis E b 10-24-1886 Randolph Co s James Rufus & Julia A (**Bussear**) h Grace b Wayne Co

BOONE
John h Mary Ann w b 4-19-1859 Wayne Co dt Lyndsey & Irena (**Thornburg**) **Dennis** m 8-1-1879

BOWLES
Anna M b 7-14-1831 dt George Fox & Elizabeth (**Bailey**)

BOWMAN
Anna May b 6-18-1897 dt Daniel & Elizabeth (**Hoover**)

BROWN
Aaron D b 12-17-1849 Henry Co s Moses & Delphia (**Dowel**) h Clara (**Loer**) m 2-22-1871 Henry Co
  Ch: Gertrude b 10-25-1873 Henry Co
      Edward b 3-16-1876 Henry Co

Earl b 8-3-1881 s Sylvester & Martha Jane (**Shultz**)
Laura Maud b 3-6-1882 dt Walter & Ellen (**Roe**) **Canaday** m 6-11-1898 Henry Co

Isaac b 9-9-1797 s Jacob & Mary (**Armfield**) d 6-30-1877
Mary b 9-28-1795 dt Joseph & Rachel **Mendenhall** d 2-14-1871
  Ch: Tamer b 10-27-1816
      Moses b 12-1-1819 Preble Co OH
      Rachel b 3-9-1822
      Jacob b 1-17-1824 d 1-21-1849
      Anna b 12-24-1825
      James b 8-7-1827
      Isaac b 2-30-1829
      Maryann b 9-10-1833
      Samuel b 10-8-1834 Henry Co
      Thaddeus b 3-31-1837 Henry Co

Isaac D b 7-3-1843 Henry Co s Moses & Delphia (**Dowel**)
Mariah b 8-5-1847 Henry Co dt Daniel & Catherine **Caphart** m 4-24-1863 Henry Co
  Ch: Etta Jane b 9-5-1873 Henry Co
      Daniel Wilbur b 1-8-1880 Henry Co

Jacob b 1-14-1755 s Thomas & Margaret (**Moon**) d 6-18-1831 bur Flat Rock
Mary (**Armfield**) b 3-29-1759 d 1828 bur Flat Rock mou ca 1776
  Ch: Isaac b 9-9-1797 d 6-30-1877

Jonathan b 9-28-1823
Rhoda b 10-9-1832
  Ch: Zeri b 10-3-1854
      Enos F b 11-2-1856
      Valerie b 11-23-1858
      Wm b 7-4-1860
      Lewis b 3-2-1862
      Amos b 7-3-1866
      Sarah Elma b 12-2-1868

Loring L b 4-5-1877 Delaware Co s Henry P & Mary E (**Loer**)

BROWN (cont)
Nettie A b 5-27-1876 Brown Co dt Charles C & Elizabeth (**Abott**) **Smith** m 8-1-1896 Wayne Co

Moses b 12-1-1819 Preble Co OH s Isaac & Mary (**Mendenhall**)
Delphia b 4-15-1819 Surry Co NC dt Peter **Dowel** m 3-28-1839
Ch: Anna M b 2-29-1840 Henry Co
    Margaret A b 8-21-1845 Henry Co
    Isaac D b 7-3-1843 Henry Co
    Delphia D b 3-8-1864 Henry Co
    Aaron D b 12-17-1849 Henry Co

Samuel b 8-10-1834 Henry Co s Isaac & Mary (**Mendenhall**)
Elizabeth b 1-13-1834 d 5-26-1862
Mary Maria 2w b 7-27-1844 Greene Co OH dt Zimri & Elizabeth **Haines** m 10-20-1864
Ch: Zimri Oston b 12-25-1865 Henry Co
    Clarkson b 8-31-1867 Henry Co
    Clara Eldora b 6-27-1869 Henry Co
    Asaph b 3-15-1871 Henry Co
    Sarah E b 6-22-1873 Henry Co
    Arthur b 10-26-1875 Henry Co
    Arlo b 10-26-1875 Henry Co d 4-11-1876
    Meda b 5-26-1878 Henry Co

Sylvester h Martha (**Schultz**)
Ch: Earl b 8-3-1881
    Rosa Priscilla b 2-1-1885 Delaware Co

Thaddeus b 3-31-1837 Henry Co s Isaac & Mary (**Mendenhall**) h Susan dt Henry & Sarah **Holder** m 2-14-1856
Ch: Elizabeth Alice b 4-19-1866 Henry Co
    Mary Frances b 3-19-1870 Henry Co

BRUNNER
John Alonzo b 6-8-1857 Henry Co s Wm & Catharine (**Myers**)
Sally Jane b 11-12-1859 Champaign Co OH dt Andrew H & Lucy (**Fogle**) **Larrowe** m 9-21-1881 Champaign Co OH
Ch: Emmett W b 10-21-1884 Champaign Co OH
    Blanche Hester 11-27-1886 Delaware Co
    Hubert Roscoe b 7-19-1890 Delaware Co

BUCKINGHAM
Levi h Jane b 10-19-1797 dt Charles & Elizabeth **Pidgeon** d 1-24-1887 bur Nettle Creek

BUNKER
John b 3-2-1782
Welmet b 4-29-1796
Ch: Rebecckah b 12-16-1811
    Judith b 3-2-1813
    Levi b 4-2-1814
    Elizabeth b 3-15-1816 d 8-17-1818
    Abram b 5-29-1817 d 8-18-1818
    Rachel b 1-30-1819
    Rhoda b 10-18-1820 d 9-?-1823
    Macy b 10-7-1822
    Deborah b 7-7-1824
    Mary b 1-31-1826

BURCHAM
Henry L h Amelia (**Wiles**) m Deep Creek MM NC 1826
Ch: Frances Sylvina b 7-2-1831
    Benson Wright b 12-21-1833

BURGESS
Anna May b 11-25-1898 Wayne Co dt Wm & Serepta (**Fulton**)

Wm h Mary Ellen b 6-30-1836 Belmont Co OH dt Jason & Abigail **Williams** d 11-1-1894 bur Spiceland m 2-27-1866
Ch: Anna P b 6-30-1867 Henry Co

BURROUGHS
James b 7-27-1839 Randolph Co s Charles & Jane
Adaliza b 12-3-1844 Madison Co dt Samuel & Nancy **Gilmore** m 2-18-1864

BURTT
Carl Moore b 2-18-1879 s Henry & Elizabeth (**Moore**)

CAIN
Henry P b 3-2-1833 Wayne Co s Jonathan & Elizabeth
Rhoda R b 1-23-1847 Randolph Co NC dt Wm & Louisa (**Worth**) **Clark** m 7-24-1869 Wayne Co
Ch: Minerva Gertrude d 12-2-1872
    Bertha Louisa b 1-11-1873
    Olive I b 11-23-1876 Wayne Co
    Nellie C b 11-24-1878
    Wm Henry b 1-7-1881 Wayne Co
    Frank C b 6-16-1883 Wayne Co
    Joseph Addison b 9-16-1885 Wayne Co

John h Clara (**Clark**)
Ch: Effie
    Martha

CANADAY
Joshua b 11-11-1806 s Robert & Amy
Betsey Ann b 2-28-1807
Ch: Oliver H b 10-18-1830
    Thomas Elwood b 9-29-1833

Lyndsay b 11-8-1829 s Robert & Sarah (**Sumner**) h Mary E (**Gibson**)
Ch: Serena L b 11-20-1865 Wayne Co
    Nannie W b 12-8-1866
    Minnie b 6-1869

Robert b 1-13-1777 d 8-5-1836
Amy b 4-24-1782 d 9-25-1823
Ch: Joshua b 11-11-1806
    Lydia b 5-9-1808 d 6-11-1808
    Ann b 5-2-1809
    Abigail b 5-12-1811
    Thomas b 3-5-1813
    Sarrah b 12-13-1814
    Amy b 3-5-1817
    Irena b 4-14-1819
    Huldah b 5-13-1821 d 4-28-1864
Sarah (**Sumner**) 2w b 5-27-1788
Ch: Lyndsey b 11-8-1829

CARR
Benjamin Westbury PM b 12-28-1792 - removed to Howard Co
Pamelia b 4-14-1801
Ch: Esther b 10-7-1821 d 8-25-1844
    Aaron b 12-5-1823
    Hezekiah A b 1-5-1826
    Cyrus b 8-20-1828
    Evan b 12-10-1830
    Amos b 4-27-1830 [sic]
    Mary J b 10-9-1835
    Lucinda b 12-30-1838 d 7-30-1840
    Benjamin E b 11-3-1842
    Job b 10-18-1844 d 7-5-1845

Thomas h Jamima
Ch: Rachel b 9-13-1818
    Hulda b 10-5-1820
    Amos b 7-17-1822
    Charlotte b 5-5-1825
    Daniel Harris b 7-22-1827
    Martha b 2-15-1831
    Kindley Ankrum b 7-31-1833

SPRINGFIELD MONTHLY MEETING
BIRTH AND DEATH RECORD

CARTER
Esther b 3-8-1861 Hamilton Co OH

Wm B b 12-11-1835
Martecia b 5-1-1839
Ch: Ann Maria b 1-26-1858
　　Millicent b 7-15-1859
　　Mary Elizabeth b 11-5-1860
　　Oliver Wilson b 7-18-1864 d 7-27-1864

CATEY
Orlando h Albina Jane b 7-25-1849 Wayne Co dt James & Mary **Smith** m 9-30-1869

CHAMNESS
Albert N b 8-19-1873 Henry Co s Mahlon & Emily (**Hodgin**)
Rebecca E b 3-15-1877 Wayne Co dt Oliver Lindley & Emma E (**Edwards**) **Hiatt** m 10-9-1895 Wayne Co
Ch: Oliver Vaughn b 5-26-1898

Alonzo Arlistus b 1-3-1859 Wayne/Henry Co s Wm & Martha Ann (**Modlin**)
Melissa Adaline b 5-21-1865 dt Wm O & Vesta (**Downing**) **Adamson** m 7-31-1884 Henry Co d 5-8-1897
Flora A 2w b 3-25-1869 Randolph Co dt Joseph B & Catharine (**Miller**) **Branson** m 4-12-1899 Randolph Co

Elijah b 1-31-1836 Wayne Co s Joseph & Susannah (**Reynolds**)
Mary b 6-26-1837 Wayne Co dt Ezra & Mary (**Wrightsman**) **Reynolds** m 11-13-1855 Henry Co
Ch: Leander b 6-12-1860

Fernando Ulysses b 11-14-1868 Wayne Co s Wm & Martha Ann (**Modlin**)
Magdalene b 12-27-1866 Henry Co dt Alexander & Mary (**Covalt**) **Main** m 8-13-1890 Henry Co
Ch: Zola b 7-18-1891 Henry Co
　　Luva b 7-29-1894 Henry Co
　　Wm Clarence b 10-30-1898 Henry Co

George W b 2-14-1817 s Mary h Catharine H (**Davidson**) m 7-25-1838
Ch: Caroline b 5-1-1840 Chatham Co NC d 8-22-1894 bur Flat Rock

Isaac b 11-19-1804 d 5-23-1867 bur Nettle Creek
Rebecca b 3-26-1805 Dover MM Guilford Co NC d 3-24-1881
Ch: Jonathan b 10-21-1832 d 10-26-1832 bur West River
　　Henry b 11-21-1834
　　Melinda b 5-28-1836
　　Uriah b 2-14-1839 d 6-17-1881
　　Jesse b 10-2-1840 d 12-23-1867 bur Nettle Creek
　　Mary b 2-28-1843 d 3-2-1843 bur Nettle Creek
　　Wm N b 5-25-1846 Wayne Co d 5-4-1876 bur Nettle Creek

Isaac b 5-26-1829 Center MM Randolph Co NC s Joshua & Hannah (**Chamness**)
Elizabeth b 6-2-1828 West Grove MM Wayne Co dt Thomas & Elizabeth (**Wilson**) **Dennis** m 11-21-1850 Wayne Co
Ch: Milton W b 12-13-1851 Henry/Randolph Co
　　Esther M b 6-1-1854 Henry Co
　　Mariam b 1-19-1857 Henry Co
　　Cyrus b 11-14-1859 Henry Co d 10-26-1860 bur Nettle Creek
　　Margaret B b 11-17-1861 Henry Co
　　Elmina E b 4-16-1864 Henry Co
　　Hannah E b 8-26-1867 Henry Co

Jesse b 1-11-1809 Center MM Randolph Co NC s Wm & Isabel (**Beeson**) d 9-1-1892
Ruth b 6-30-1814 Cane Creek MM Chatham Co NC dt Hugh & Mary (**Atkinson**) **Woody**
d 5-1-1882 m 12-15-1831 Chatham Co NC
Ch: Mary b 11-20-1833 Randolph Co NC bur Nettle Creek
　　Wm b 6-24-1838 Wayne Co
　　Hugh b 1-19-1840 Wayne Co d 2-29-1844 bur Nettle Creek
　　Isabel b 1-24-1848 Wayne Co

CHAMNESS (cont)
Joseph Nettle Creek b 4-2-1798
Susannah (**Reynolds**) b 8-2-1799
Ch: Abijah b 8-7-1819 d 11-6-1820
　　Wm C b 2-27-1822 Nettle Creek
　　Ebenezer b 3-31-1824
　　Rueben b 1-31-1826
　　Elizabeth b 4-1-1828 d 2-23-1854
　　Elihu b 9-4-1830
　　Jesse b 5-13-1833 d 7-20-1834
　　Elijah b 1-31-1836
　　Hannah b 2-4-1839 d 5-7-1855

Joseph Allen b 7-8-1860 Wayne/Henry Co s Wm & Martha Ann (**Modlin**)
Anna M b 1-21-1864 dt Frederick & Barbara **Miller** m Henry Co
Ch: Myra Ethel 4-29-1890 Henry Co

Joshua b 3-4-1806 Center MM Randolph Co NC s Wm & Isabel (**Beeson**) d 2-25-1889 bur Nettle Creek
Hannah b 3-17-1809 Chatham Co NC dt Mary **Chamness** d 4-27-1881 bur Nettle Creek m 8-7-1828 Chatham Co NC
Ch: Isaac b 5-26-1829 Center MM Randolph Co NC
　　Mary b 12-3-1831 Center MM Randolph Co NC
　　Isabel b 1-1-1835 Randolph Co
　　Mahlon b 1-24-1840 Randolph Co
　　Rachel b 6-9-1843 Randolph Co

Larkin h Ruth b 10-20-1842 Henry Co dt Miles & Nancy (**Modlin**) **Lamb** m 12-2-1868 Wayne Co
Ch: Oliver Perry b 1-19-1877 Wayne Co

Leander b 6-12-1860 s Elijah & Mary (**Reynolds**)
Lillie E b 4-9-1864 dt Jacob & Nancy (**Barekott**) **Shively** m 12-13-1881 Wayne Co
Ch: Charles Clifford b 2-6-1890 Wayne Co
　　Lewis E b 12-5-1882

Mahlon b 1-24-1840 s Joshua & Hannah (**Chamness**)
Emily b 6-15-1840 dt Nathan & Mourning (**Coffin**) **Hodgin** m 11-22-1862 Randolph Co
Ch: Lorinda b 1-17-1865
　　Mary Alice b 10-13-1867 d 3-4-1872
　　Albert N b 8-19-1873 Henry Co

Marcellus b 5-19-1862 Wayne Co Jehu & Hannah
Laura Alice b 12-30-1867 Henry Co dt Isaiah & Rachel (**Chamness**) **Lamb** d 2-5-1889 bur Nettle Creek m 2-20-1885 Wayne Co
Ch: Earl E b 9-3-1887 Henry Co d 12-15-1887 bur Nettle Creek

Milton W b 12-13-1851 Henry/Randolph Co s Isaac & Elizabeth (**Dennis**)
Isabel A b 1-16-1855 Boone Co dt John & Martha J (**Staton**) **Hough** m 9-30-1875 Tipton

Nathan b 4-25-1794 s Wm & Isabel (**Beeson**) d 4-2-1876
Mary b 4-15-1798
Ch: Martha b 2-26-1820 d 3-16-1856 bur Nettle Creek
　　Abigail b 2-12-1822
　　Wm S b 11-2-1824 Randolph Co NC
　　David b 7-5-1828 Randolph Co NC
　　Unice b 12-3-1831 Randolph Co NC
　　Achsa b 8-5-1835

Pearl B b 3-28-1879 dt Wm

Rebecca b 3-26-1805 dt Michael **Stanley** d 3-24-1881

Riley h Caroline b 5-1-1840 dt George W & Catherine H (**Davidson**) **Chamness** wid John **Davis** d 8-22-1894

Russell b 7-31-1865 Randolph Co NC s Uriah & Sarah (**Tinkle**)

CHAMNESS (Russell cont)
Nora A b 8-22-1866 Randolph Co NC dt Isaac & Elizabeth (**Thornburg**) Gilmore m 8-18-1887 Randolph Co

Seth M b Wayne Co s Wm & Ann (**Reynolds**)
Ch: Lena Mary

Uriah b 2-14-1839 s Isaac & Rebecca d 6-17-1881 h Sarah (**Tinkle**) m 9-29-1864
Ch: Russell b 7-30-1865 Randolph Co NC
　　Ellen b 4-1-1870

Wm h Hannah b 5-19-1817 Montgomery Co OH dt Samuel & Jemima (**Cox**) Jackson d 8-8-1898 m 1854

Wm b 7-21-1766 d 10-2-1852
Isabel (**Beeson**) b 1-15-1771 d 7-26-1840
Ch: Nathan b 4-25-1794 d 4-2-1876
　　Mary b 2-16-1800 d 12-5-1871
　　Joshua b 3-4-1806 Center MM Randolph Co NC d 2-25-1889 bur Nettle Creek
　　Jesse b 1-11-1809 Center MM Randolph Co NC d 9-1-1892

Wm d 9-2-1884
Ann b 5-10-1804 dt Ebenezer & Rachel **Reynolds** d 9-2-1844 bur West River m 10-25-1825
Ch: Jahue b 2-5-1826
　　Riley b 2-24-1827
　　Larkin b 6-19-1829
　　Isam b 9-7-1831 d 8-8-1834
　　Mahela b 10-5-1833
　　Seth M b Wayne Co

Wm b 6-24-1838 Wayne Co s Jesse & Ruth (**Woody**)
Martha Ann b 12-31-1839 Wayne Co dt Wm & Mildred (**Beeson**) **Modlin** m 11-26-1857 Wayne Co
Ch: Alonzo Arlistus b 1-3-1859 Wayne/Henry Co
　　Joseph Allen b 7-8-1860 Wayne/Henry Co
　　Alice Josephine b 8-22-1862 Wayne/Henry Co
　　Mildred Ellen b 8-7-1865 Wayne Co
　　Fernando Ulysses b 11-14-1868 Wayne Co

Wm C Nettle Creek b 2-27-1822 s Joseph & Susannah (**Reynolds**)
Mary b 2-2-1825 dt Walter & Hannah **Canaday** d 10-5-1875
Ch: Lydia b 8-22-1845 d 9-1-1852
　　Cynthia b 6-10-1847
　　Rachel R b 5-15-1849 Henry Co
　　Enos b 6-29-1851 d 1-26-1853
　　Lucinda b 11-5-1853
　　Elvaretta b 1-26-1857 Henry Co
　　Thomas Hervey b 12-26-1859 d 1-13-1868

Wm N b 5-25-1846 Randolph Co s Isaac & Rebecca d 5-4-1876 bur Nettle Creek
Mary Melissa b 1-24-1842 Wayne Co dt Isaiah & Fanny (**Dennis**) **Beeson** d 5-7-1893 bur Nettle Creek m 12-23-1868
Ch: Alma Nora b 9-27-1869 Randolph Co
　　Emma Jane b 4-18-1872 Randolph Co d 4-30-1872 bur Nettle Creek
　　Flora May b 7-13-1874 Randolph Co d 4-26-1875 bur Nettle Creek

Wm S b 11-2-1824 Randolph Co NC s Nathan & Mary
Rebecca b 5-16-1836
Ch: Theodore Elbridge b 3-13-1859
　　Caroline Ruth b 4-12-1861
　　Oscar Luther b 12-6-1862
　　Olinda Florence b 1-18-1868

CHARLES
John b 11-3-1822 Center MM Wayne Co s Daniel & Miriam
Eunice W b 12-14-1820 dt Silvanus & Rhoda **Swain** d 2-13-1855
Nancy J 2w b 5-4-1839 Center MM Randolph Co NC dt Wm & Louisa (**Worth**) Clark
Ch: Wm C b 1-15-1863 d 12-15-1864 Randolph Co

CHARLES (John cont)
　　Eunice M b 9-8-1864 Randolph Co
　　Wm C b 10-13-1866 Randolph Co
　　Rosalyn M b 8-23-1868 Randolph Co
　　Mary E b 1-1-1871 Randolph Co
　　Emma S b 2-2-1877 Randolph Co
　　John b 5-9-1882 Randolph Co

CHEESMAN
Ora May b 10-1882 Wayne Co dt Wallace & America (**Lumpkin**)

CLAPPER
David b 10-5-1849 Henry Co s Jacob & Sarah (**Priddy**)
Alice Josephine b 8-22-1862 Wayne/Henry Co dt Wm & Martha Ann (**Modlin**) Chamness m Wayne Co
Ch: Nellie b 1-23-1885 Henry Co
　　Gertrude b 2-13-1891 Henry Co
　　Ruth b 2-10-1894 Henry Co

Hazel C dt Jacob L & Laura (**Taylor**)

CLARK
Barzilla W b 5-6-1841 Center MM Randolph Co NC s Wm & Louisa (**Worth**)
Emily C b 10-26-1850 Randolph Co dt Wm M & Martha A **Botkin** d 11-11-1878 bur Springfield m 10-6-1870
Charity 2w dt John & Sylvania **Knight** d 7-21-1883
Ch: Albert b 4-21-1883
Ellen H 3w b 10-9-1850 dt Eli & Gulielma (**Charles**) Hanby m 11-3-1887 Wayne Co

George Edward b 11-16-1848 Center MM Randolph Co NC s Wm & Louisa (**Worth**)
A Emma b 9-26-1855 Randolph Co dt John & Nancy (**Smith**) Study m 9-22-1880
Ch: Julia C b 8-28-1881
　　John Everett W b 11-28-1883

John h Malinda d 1-24-1872
Ch: Emily J b 2-18-1864
　　Oliver W b 10-8-1866
　　Cora H b 10-13-1868

John Milton b 3-26-1851 Center MM Randolph Co NC s Wm & Louisa (**Worth**)
Ida M b 12-26-1857 Wayne Co dt Isaac & Luzena **Conley** 9-7-1876
Ch: Charles Herbert b 11-11-1877 Wayne Co

Jonathan B b 6-26-1836 Center MM Randolph Co NC s Wm & Louisa (**Worth**)
Matilda Jane b 12-23-1847 Wayne Co dt Isaac & Luzena **Conley** m 12-25-1867
Ch: Eva Celestia b 11-10-1868 Wayne Co
　　Edmund D b 11-28-1869 Wayne Co
　　Maud L b 12-10-1871 Wayne Co
　　Myrtle b 12-21-1874 Wayne Co

Thomas Elwood b 12-9-1834 Center MM Randolph Co NC s Wm & Louisa (**Worth**)
Nancy M b 11-29-1836 dt Edmund & Mary **Goodrich** d 6-6-1882 m 10-5-1862 Randolph Co
Ch: Mary Louisa b 7-6-1863
　　John Goodrich b 6-4-1867
　　Nellie Goodrich b 10-13-1868
　　Miriam b 8-27-1873 d 11-6-1880 bur Springfield

Wm b 10-22-1808 s Dougan d 5-21-1873
Louisa b 11-7-1815 Center MM Randolph Co NC dt David & Eunice (**Gardner**) Worth d 10-1896 m 1-23-1834
Ch: Thomas Elwood b 12-9-1834 Center MM Randolph Co NC
　　Jonathan B b 6-26-1836 Center MM Randolph Co NC
　　Joseph A b 12-26-1837
　　Nancy J b 5-4-1839 Center MM Randolph Co NC

SPRINGFIELD MONTHLY MEETING
BIRTH AND DEATH RECORD

CLARK (Wm cont)
    Barzilla W b 5-6-1841 Center MM Randolph Co NC
    Eunice R b 11-21-1842
    Mariam Asenath b 4-10-1845 Center MM Randolph Co NC
    Rhoda R b 1-23-1847 Randolph Co NC
    George Edward b 11-16-1848 Center MM Randolph Co NC
    John Milton b 3-26-1851 Center MM Randolph Co NC
    Mary M b 3-8-1853 Center MM Randolph Co NC
    Wm D b 4-13-1856

CLEMONS
Lucile b 12-2-1885 Wayne Co res wt Lydia H **Test**

CLOUD
Jonathan h Esther M b 6-1-1854 Henry Co dt Isaac & Elizabeth (**Dennis**) **Chamness** m 10-28-1882

COFFIN
Barnabas b 3-1-1809
Miriam (**Worth**) b 7-26-1809
Ch: Louisa Jane b 10-17-1830 d 10-10-1831
    Martitia b 4-30-1832
    Abigail b 2-11-1834 d 11-14-1839
    Delphina b 9-1-1835
    Hannah b 4-24-1837
    Eunice b 3-28-1839
    David Worth b 6-24-1841
    Catherine Evaline b 5-12-1844
    Roxanna b 4-11-1846 d 1-16-1849
    Albert Wm b 2-28-1850

John b 7-31-1778- d 12-23-1859
Abigail (**Hobbs**) b 3-18-1786 d 7-3-1858
Ch: Mary b 3-13-1819 d 12-3-1857
    John M b 12-11-1824 Randolph Co NC
    Eunice b 8-1-1829 d 10-22-1878 bur Nettle Creek

John M b 12-11-1824 Randolph Co NC s John & Abigail (**Hobbs**) - removed to KS
Martha D b 10-6-1835
Ch: Louisa J b 11-8-1852
    Abigail S b 8-26-1854
    Thomas N b 8-25-1856

Samuel h Rachel
Ch: Anna Maria b 12-26-1829 Fayette Co
    Eunice b 12-13-1833 Fayette Co

COGGSHALL
Peter d 8-17-1832

CONLEY
Isaac h Luzena
Ch: Matilda Jane b 12-23-1847 Wayne Co
    Ida May b 12-26-1857 Wayne Co

John h Cynthia Emaline b 4-1-1848 Wayne Co dt Lindsey & Irena (**Thornburg**) **Dennis** d 1-15-1895 bur Nettle Creek m 9-11-1873 Wayne Co
Ch: Maxie W b 6-23-1874 Adams Co

CONWAY
Charley h Susan G b 11-8-1871 Wayne Co dt Martha **Conway**

James h Martha b 6-29-1832 dt Peter & Nancy A (**Rinard**) **Smith** m 9-5-1849 Wayne Co
Ch: Nancy Ellen b 2-24-1851 Madison Co

COOK
Ira b 9-7-1812
Irena b 4-7-1815
Ch: Sylvanus J b 7-15-1832
    Elvira b 9-19-1838 d 9-16-1841

COOK (Ira cont)
    Thos C b 5-14-1841
    John b 1-8-1852
    Betsey
    Cyrus

Jane b 2-12-1822

John h Ann b 6-20-1851 dt James & Elizabeth **Money** m 1-6-1869 Yadkin Co NC

Rebecca Emmaline b 8-4-1887 dt John & Sinia Esther (**Money**)

Wright h Anna
Ch: Rebeckah b 12-30-1818
    Wright b 6-28-1821
    Anna b 1-25-1823
    Naomi b 9-11-1825

COOMES
Cida Alice b 5-17-1899 dt John & Polly (**Fields**)

CORY
Adam h Elizabeth b 9-5-1842 dt Isaac K & Rebecca (**Lamb**) **Beeson**

Isaac h Sarah b 3-7-1847 dt Isaac K & Rebecca (**Lamb**) **Beeson**

COVALT
Ferdinand h Nancy Roxanna b 12-23-1856 Wayne Co dt Wm S & Louisa (**Beckerdite**) **Farlow** m 11-1-1881

COX
Benjamin h Jemima (**Branson**) b 1-22-1801 m 1830 Cane Creek MM NC
Ch: Branson b 10-5-1833
    Elihu b 3-29-1835
    Mary b 7-13-1836
    Priscilla b 5-14-1840
    Sarah b 11-7-1843

John h Rachel
Ch: Levi b 10-23-1789
    Rachel b 12-10-1799

Levi b 10-23-1789 s John & Rachel d 6-23-1868
Lydia b 10-5-1808 dt Robert & Sarah **Williams** d 6-14-1845
Ch: Joseph b 5-8-1829 d 8-8-1830
    Rebecca b 6-7-1830 Belmont Co OH
    Nathan W b 1-1-1832 d 12-31-1890
    Elisha b 1-12-1834
    Sarah b 10-16-1835 d 9-19-1862
    Rachel b 4-3-1838 d 9-1850
    Zilpah b 4-1-1840
    Levi b 7-16-1843 Wayne Co d 11-5-1845

Mary b 2-8-1835

Nancy b 9-5-1836

Peter b 2-19-1772 d 1-9-1864 Hamilton Co bur Carmel
Margaret b 4-26-1786 d 1-20-1839

Stephen s Wm & Anna (**Barnes**) h Mary (**Grace**)
Ch: Esther B

Stephen b. 5-7-1794
Elizabeth b 11-1-1794
Ch: Cynthia b 2-11-1821 Belmont Co OH
    Stephen b 9-15-1828
    Jared b 8-5-1830
    Rhoda b 9-10-1832
    Deborah b 5-22-1834

SPRINGFIELD MONTHLY MEETING
BIRTH AND DEATH RECORD

COX (cont)
Thomas b 7-25-1786

Wm b 3-15-1776 d 11-29-1857
Elizabeth b 9-23-1773 d 10-18-1849

Wm I b 4-22-1838

CROSS
Charles A b 7-12-1868 Jay Co s Emanuel & Nancy (**Paul**)
Lucinda E b 9-15-1871 Wayne Co dt Martha Jane **Bundy** m 9-2-1889 Henry Co

DALE
Cora Ellen b 4-17-1883 Tipton Co dt Samuel B & Margaret E (**Koon**)

DANIELS
Harrison h Pheraby (**Pierce**)
Ch: Joanna b 6-24-1830 Surry Co NC
    Pheraby b 5-16-1839 Yadkin Co NC

DAVIS
Alpheus b 1-9-1837
Louisa J b 6-16-1847
Ch: Wm E b 12-13-1864
    James A b 5-13-1873

Amos b 10-4-1842 s Spencer & Amelia (**Bond**)
Esther Ann b 12-3-1846 dt Benjamin J & Levina (**Hill**) **Hill** m 10-31-1867 Henry Co
Ch: Mary Etta b 5-8-1869 Henry Co
    Phebe Catherine b 8-1-1870 Henry Co
    Lavina b 6-1-1872 Henry Co
    Son b 12-4-1873 Henry Co d 6-14-1874
    Omar b 6-12-1875 Henry Co
    John H b 1-13-1878 Henry Co
    Millie b 8-15-1882 Henry Co
    Benjamin S b 1-13-1884 Henry Co

Elihu s John & Jane d 4-10-1875
Love dt Uriah & Elizabeth (**Macy**) **Barnard** d 7-11-1841
Rachel 2w b 8-15-1802 dt Elihu & Sarah **Swain** wid John **Thornburg** d 9-25-1890

George b 5-12-1818 s Joseph & Catherine
Charlotte dt John & Charlotte **Baldwin**
Ch: Eliza Ann b 9-15-1842
    Wm Franklin b 5-30-1844

John b 1790
Ruth b 8-13-1792/7
Ch: Spencer b 6-16-1816 d 9-14-1864
    Kezziah b 5-18-1818
    Wm b 9-17-1820
    Mary b 6-16-1823
Lydia 2w
Ch: Jesse C b 5-11-1834
    John M b 4-4-1836
    Daniel b 3-28-1838
    Hezikiah b 12-25-1839
    Mark S b 11-17-1842
    Lydia Ann b 10-18-1844

John h Caroline b 5-1-1840 Chatham Co NC dt George W & Catherine H (**Davidson**) **Chamness** d 8-22-1894 bur Nettle Creek m 8-16-1863
Ch: Mary L b 10-23-1865 Wayne Co
    Anna L b 2-28-1876 Wayne Co
    Laura M b 10-29-1878 Wayne Co
    Ethel C b 3-29-1881 Wayne Co

John S h Louisa b Henry Co dt Elihu & Elizabeth (**Tate**) **Chamness**

DAVIS (cont)
Joseph h Catharine d 9-12-1870
Ch: Nathan b 6-16-1808
    Wm b 10-6-1810
    Mary b 2-11-1813
    Anna b 6-30-1815
    George b 5-12-1818
    Hannah b 11-16-1820
    John b 5-19-1823
    Edom W b 6-28-1826
    Lewis b 6-26-1830 d 10-30-1840 bur West River

Lewis H h Elma Nora b Randolph Co dt Wm N & Mary **Beeson** m 7-19-1891

Miles b 11-13-1849 Henry Co s Spencer & Amelia (**Bond**)
Nancy Jane b 2-2-1862 dt Elijah & Levine (**Lake**) **Cory** m 11-23-1876 Henry Co
Ch: Lizzie E b 11-13-1885 Henry Co

Neziah b 10-10-1805/8
Tamar b 10-27-1816
Ch: Mary b 3-14-1837
    Serfina b 7-7-1838 d 3-11-1839
    Alfred b 1-31-1840
    Levi b 11-27-1841
    Mahlon b 1-3-1843
    Eunice b 3-8-1845
    Isaac b 11-3-1847
    Caroline b 5-22-1851
    Elizabeth b 6-21-1854

Perry h Maude E b 11-27-1884 dt Elisha & Laura Bell (**Lucas**) **Shaffer**

Rufus H b 2-23-1843 Henry Co s Nathan & Hannah (**Moore**)
Emma b 3-4-1860 Henry Co dt James G & Elizabeth (**Wright**) **Allen** m 9-27-1884 Henry Co
Ch: Ethel b 4-18-1886 Henry Co
    Helen b 7-24-1888 Henry Co
    Clara b 10-12-1890 Henry Co
    Ruth b 10-14-1898 Henry Co

Ruth d 10-1-1824 bur Springfield

Silas b 11-23-1806 d 5-18-1844
Ann b 5-19-1804
Ch: Neziah b 2-21-1833 d 4-16-1833
    Sarah b 6-20-1834
    Leander b 12-5-1835
    Jemima b 8-20-1837
    Susannah b 10-31-1839
    Malinda b 10-13-1841

Spencer b 6-16-1816 s John & Ruth d 9-14-1864
Amelia b 8-19-1822 Guilford Co NC dt Wm & Elizabeth (**Wiles**) **Bond** d 8-22-1890 bur Flat Rock m 4-26-1838
Ch: Wm b 3-22-1839
    John b 10-22-1840 d 2-19-1863
    Amos b 10-4-1842
    Eli b 4-25-1845 d 4-13-1865
    Miles b 11-13-1849 Henry Co
    Joseph S b 3-23-1855 Henry Co
    Elizabeth R b 3-12-1858 Henry Co
    Thomas M b 9-16-1861 Henry Co d 9-24-1864
    John H b 3-19-1863

Wm h Elizabeth d 11-25-1844
Ch: Jordan d 9-20-1843

Wm b 1-23-1839 s Spencer & Amelia (**Bond**)
Martha Ellen b 7-4-1843 dt Jacob & Sarah **Remington** m 3-5-1865 Henry Co

157

SPRINGFIELD MONTHLY MEETING
BIRTH AND DEATH RECORD

DAVIS (Wm cont)
Ch: Viretta b 12-29-1865 Henry Co
    Eliza Jane b 5-5-1871 Henry Co
    Oda b Henry Co

DAVISSON
James A h Rebecca M b 9-14-1854 Wayne Co dt Daniel Williams &
Melinda (**Mendenhall**) **Hiatt** m 9-14-1871
Ch: Ora L b 3-1-1873 Wayne Co

DEARDORF
John h Susan wid John **Hockett**

DENNIS
Absolom b 7-2-1807 s Wm & Delilah
Eunice b 1-3-1808
Ch: Anna T b 3-16-1830 d 10-30-1850 Randolph Co NC
    Delilah M b 10-17-1831 Randolph Co NC
    Flavia S b 10-14-1833 Randolph Co NC
    David b 8-3-1835 d 1-2-1839 Randolph Co NC
    Thomas C b 4-2-1838 West River PM
    Eunice b 1-22-1841 West River PM
    Ruth b 8-3-1843 West River PM

Branson b 5-10-1818 Marlboro MM Randolph Co NC s Thomas &
Elizabeth (**Wilson**) d 6-4-1890 bur Nettle Creek
Elma b 9-21-1820 Center MM Randolph Co NC dt Job & Phebe
(**Hockett**) **Reynolds** m 5-20-1840 Wayne Co
Ch: Louisa b 5-14-1841 Wayne Co
    Sarah b 6-3-1842 Wayne Co
    Phebe Jane b 2-4-1847 Wayne Co
    Margaret b 2-9-1854 Wayne Co d 9-11-1857 bur Nettle Creek
    Wilson H b 3-25-1856 Wayne Co
    Job E b 7-12-1858 Wayne Co

Clarkson b 5-29-1862 Wayne Co s Wilson & Lydia (**Reynolds**)
Rosettie b 6-16-1871 Randolph Co dt James & Ellen (**Lee**) **Bookout**
m 3-17-1893 Randolph Co
Ch: Russell Lee b 7-11-1884

Dempsey Thomas b 5-30-1854 Wayne Co s Lindsay & Irena
(**Thornburg**) h Josie (**Lynn**)

Edwin b 8-25-1844 s Nathan & Mary (**Lamar**)
Ch: Royal A b 8-25-1868
    David A b 3-22-1870 d 11-7-1870

Elisha b 7-11-1796 s Wm & Delilah d 10-12-1836 bur West River h Ruth
Ch: Lindsay b 4-5-1826 d 5-31-1827
    Bartlett b 10-1-1827 d 8-16-1847
    Tilman b 7-4-1829 d 9-2-1865
    Mary Ann b 4-20-1832 d 4-20-1833
    Infant b 4-20-1832 d same day]
    Asenath b 10-2-1833
    Matilde Carolina b 9-16-1835 d 6-29-1868

George Prentice b 12-3-1871 Wayne Co s Osborn & Louisa (**Canaday**)
Jennie b 5-15-1877 Wayne Co dt Aaron & Hannah (**Werking**)
Woolard m 12-4-1897 Henry Co
Ch: Grace Ermadine b 10-31-1898 Wayne Co

Henry C h Cordelia **Chamness** m 9-27-1878

Isaac Lindley b 12-30-1864 Wayne Co s Wilson & Lydia (**Reynolds**)
Viola b 9-27-1873 Wayne Co dt Joseph Henry & Hannah
Thompson m 5-17-1891

Isaac Newton b 11-15-1841 s Mahlon & Louisa
Melinda b 10-27-1844 Wayne Co dt Lindsay & Irena (**Thornburg**)
Dennis
Ch: Alpheus Lindley b 1-24-1865 d 3-26-1870
    John Henry b 1-1-1867

DENNIS (cont)
Jesse b 2-1-1799
Unity b 3-2-1804 d ae 30y
Ch: Maria L b 7-23-1824
    Elizabeth S b 5-4-1826
    Luzena C b 9-9-1828
    Julian b 3-3-1831
    Wm b 4-9-1835
Miriam 2w
Ch: Melinda b 6-1-1844
    Hannah b 9-25-1848

Job E b 7-12-1858 Wayne Co s Branson & Elma (**Reynolds**)
Lizzie Ettie b 3-13-1860 Wayne Co dt Joseph E & Zerelda Ann
(**Thornburg**) **Routh** m 3-11-1880 Randolph Co
Ch: Carrie A b 1-24-1881 Wayne Co
    Frank Vernon b 9-19-1884 Wayne Co d 8-12-1890 bur Nettle Creek
    Joseph Branson b 6-7-1892 Wayne Co
    Anna Routh b 4-19-1897 Wayne Co

Lindsay b 3-8-1822 Marlboro MM Randolph Co NC s Thomas &
Elizabeth (**Wilson**) d 11-22-1894 bur Nettle Creek
Irena b 8-1-1824 Wayne Co dt Dempsey & Jane (**Mills**) **Thornburg**
d near Dalton bur Nettle Creek m 11-24-1842 Wayne Co
Ch: Martha Jane b 9-14-1843 Wayne Co
    Melinda b 10-27-1844 Wayne Co
    Cynthia Emeline b 4-1-1848 Wayne Co d 1-15-1895 bur Nettle
    Creek
    Miriam C b 8-3-1851 Wayne Co d 2-8-1855 bur Nettle Creek
    Dempsey Thomas b 5-30-1854 Wayne Co
    Mary Ann b 4-19-1859 Wayne Co
    Oliver L b 3-13-1862 Wayne Co

Mahlon b 7-2-1811 s Wm & Delilah
Louisa b 8-27-1812 dt Isaac & Hannah **Beeson** m 11-7-1833
Ch: Jesse b 10-25-1834 d 11-20-1834 bur West River
    Orlando W b 7-7-1836 d 11-24-1858 bur West River
    Nathan b 1-5-1839 Wayne Co
    Isaac Newton b 11-15-1841
    Zeruiah b 3-9-1844
    Henry C b 12-6-1846
    John b 4-17-1849
    Rebecca b 1-5-1852 Wayne Co
    Louisa b 8-31-1854 Wayne Co

Mary Esther b 11-7-1860 Anderson Co KS dt Alansan & Anna

Nathan b 3-13-1815 s Wm & Delilah d 1-26-1872
Mary b 8-9-1810 dt Isaac & Hannah **Lamar** d 3-22-1847
Ch: Wm b 6-30-1840 d 12-30-1871
    Osborn b 9-4-1842 Wayne Co
    Edwin b 8-25-1844
    Mary b 3-13-1847 Wayne Co
Evelina 2 w b 9-13-1813 Guilford Co NC dt David & Eunice
(**Gardner**) **Worth** m 5-24-1848
Ch: David Worth b 4-8-1849

Nathan b 1-5-1839 Wayne Co s Mahlon & Louisa (**Beeson**)
Julia Ann b 4-11-1845 Wayne Co dt Isaac & Levina H (**Puckett**)
Reynolds m 5-16-1863
Ch: Sarah Alice b 2-15-1864 Wayne Co
    Flora T b 12-24-1868 Wayne Co

Newton b 6-3-1842 s Wm & Rebecca d 1862

Oliver L b 3-13-1862 Wayne Co s Lindsay & Irena (**Thornburg**)
Susanna b 7-31-1861 Henry Co dt Amos & Nancy (**Bales**) **Main** m
2-10-1881
Ch: Ina Bell b 2-19-1883 Wayne Co
    Daisy Odena b 4-3-1884 Wayne Co
    Charley Walter b 5-27-1890 Wayne Co
    Carl Clinton b 4-7-1892 Wayne Co

DENNIS (cont)
Osborn b 9-4-1842 Wayne Co s Nathan & Mary (**Lamar**)
Louisa b 2-18-1847 Randolph Co dt Jonathan & Susanna (**Moore**)
Canaday m 2-6-1868 Randolph Co
Ch: Mary Evaline b 12-12-1868 Randolph Co
    George Prentice b 12-3-1871 Wayne Co
    Osborn Earl b 3-24-1880 Wayne Co

Samuel P b 11-25-1862 Wayne Co s Thomas & Lucy Ann (**Peebles**)
Minnie b 5-25-1861 Wayne Co dt James M & Sarah A (**Gilmore**)
Burroughs m 2-18-1885 Wayne Co
Ch: Mabel N b 4-11-1887 Wayne Co
    Sylvia L b 8-2-1891 Wayne Co
    Horace Cecil b 4-19-1893 Wayne Co

Thomas b 11-4-1791 s Wm & Delilah d 9-4-1839 bur Nettle Creek
Elizabeth (**Wilson**) b 10-12-1794 d 5-21-1863 bur Nettle Creek
Ch: Wilson b 6-1-1814 Marlboro MM NC bur Nettle Creek
    Lucinda b 1-14-1816 Randolph Co NC d 8-31-1893 bur Nettle Creek
    Branson b 5-10-1818 d 6-4-1890 Marlboro MM NC d 6-4-1890 bur Nettle Creek
    Cynthia b 3-21-1820 Randolph Co NC d 10-16-1892 bur Nettle Creek
    Lindsay b 3-8-1822 Marlboro MM Randolph Co NC d 11-22-1894 bur Nettle Creek
    Miriam b 8-10-1824 Spiceland MM d 4-2-1880 bur Earlham
    Wm b 8-8-1826 d 7-28-1827
    Elizabeth b 6-2-1828 West Grove MM Wayne Co
    Thomas b 1-8-1833 Wayne Co bur Nettle Creek
    Melinda b 10-3-1836 d 9-21-1843

Thomas b 1-8-1833 Wayne Co s Thomas & Elizabeth (**Wilson**) bur Nettle Creek
Lucy Ann b 10-18-1826 Prince George Co VA dt John & Michel (**Bailey**) **Peebles** bur Nettle Creek m 3-22-1860
Ch: Samuel P b 11-25-1862 Wayne Co

Thomas C b 4-2-1838 West River PM s Absolom & Eunice
Sarah E b 3-14-1842
Ch: Albert L
    Alice J b 10-7-1862
    Margaretta b 6-17-1864

Thomas E b 1-17-1855 Wayne Co s Wilson & Rachel (**Thornburg**)
Zenora C b 8-6-1853 Randolph Co dt F H & Fanny (**Blount**)
Davidson d 6-28-1885 bur Nettle Creek m 10-5-1882 Randolph Co
Ch: Fidella F b 5-18-1884 Henry Co
Carrie (**Burroughs**) **Lambert** 2w m Randolph Co
Ch: Arthel J b 8-29-1888
    Hansel B b 3-1-1892 Henry Co

Wm b 12-2-1769 NC d 5-6-1847
Delilah b 5-17-1773 NC d 10-5-1839
Ch: Thomas b 11-4-1791 d 9-4-1839
    Elisha b 7-11-1796 d 10-12-1836
    Jesse b 2-1-1799
    Fanny b 9-15-1801 d 4-27-1858
    Absolom b 7-2-1807
    Wm b 7-12-1804
    Mahlon b 7-2-1811
    Nathan b 3-13-1815 d 1-26-1872

Wm b 6-30-1840 s Nathan & Mary (**Lamar**) d 12-30-1871 h Emily

Wilson b 6-1-1814 Marlboro MM NC s Thomas & Elizabeth (**Wilson**) d near Dalton bur Nettle Creek
Rachel b 6-19-1827 Wayne Co dt Dempsey & Jane (**Mills**)
Thornburg d 1-17-1857 near Dalton m 10-21-1847 Wayne Co
Ch: Lydia b 8-14-1848 Wayne Co
    Wm b 2-11-1850 Wayne Co d 12-24-1851
    Elizabeth b 3-30-1851 Wayne Co

DENNIS (Wilson cont)
Susan b 11-19-1852 Wayne Co d 6-27-1861 bur Nettle Creek
Thomas E b 1-17-1855 Wayne Co
Mary Jane b 12-30-1856 Wayne Co d 2-4-1857 bur Nettle Creek
Lydia 2w b 7-5-1831 Wayne Co dt Isaac & Tamar (**Hawkins**)
Reynolds m 6-23-1858 Wayne Co
Ch: Sarah b 4-19-1859 Wayne Co
    Clarkson b 5-29-1862 Wayne Co
    Isaac Lindley b 12-30-1864 Wayne Co

Wilson H b 5-25-1856 Wayne Co s Branson & Elma (**Reynolds**)
Millicent M b 4-25-1857 Wayne Co dt John D & Huldah (**Mendenhall**) **Mills** m 10-4-1881 Henry Co
Ch: John Warren b 7-14-1882 Wayne/ Randolph Co
    Olive Blanch b 1-22-1885 Wayne Co
    Lora Hazel b 12-25-1887 Wayne Co

DENNY
Shubal b 1-8-1812
Margaret d 10-10-1851 ae 52y 8m 20d bur Flat Rock
Ch: Sarah C b 10-14-1835
    Jacob L B b 12-12-1838
    Delilah Susan b 7-6-1842
Dorothy 2w b 2-18-1822
Ch: Wm Alonzo b 9-7-1853 d 3-8-1854
    Margaret Esther b 1-24-1855 d 12-19-1856
    Lewis Marion b 6-29-1857
    Mary Lucinda b 9-5-1859

DEPOY
Elta A b 9-7-1884 Fayette Co OH dt Solomon & Eleanor

DERING
Austin O b 6-1-1873 Wayne Co s John & Lisetta (**Newman**)
Alice C b 7-26-1875 Wayne Co dt Daniel & Mary J (**Hoover**) **Hay** m 11-10-1898 Wayne Co

John b 3-8-1831 Breslau Germany s Anton & Josiel
Lisetta b 6-14-1833 Mecklenburg Germany dt Fredrick & Sophia
Newman m 8-13-1858
Ch: Elizabeth b 8-24-1861 Wayne Co
    Otto b 12-1-1863 Wayne Co
    Austin O b 6-1-1873 Wayne Co

DEVERS
Hedgman Butler b 4-22-1844 Scott Co KY Wm & Nancy (**Giles**)
Martha Ann b 8-28-1852 Hnery Co dt Jesse & Mary (**Chamness**)
Pidgeon m 2-1-1893 Henry Co

DINES
Silas G s Jackson & Nancy (**Hutchens**) h Elizabeth (**Wadman**) b Wayne Co

DIXON
Sarah b 2-21-1787
Ch: Hannah b 11-9-1823

DOUGHERTY
Alonzo h Exalina b 11-24-1856 dt Jesse B & Mary Ann (**Mendenhall**) **Williams** d 1895
Ch: Raymond b 1-21-1888

DRAKE
Joseph Wilson b 12-2-1858 s Moses & Elizabeth
Ada J b 1-15-1859 Henry Co dt Solamon & Elizabeth (**Corey**) **Bales** m 10-16-1880 Henry Co

EAST
Jacob h Anna b 8-20-1830 dt Charles & Hannah (**Swain**) Osborn

EAVES
John h Mary K d 8-9-1836 removed to KY

SPRINGFIELD MONTHLY MEETING
BIRTH AND DEATH RECORD

EAVES (John cont)
Ch: Wm b 5-11-1831
    Martha b 10-3-1833 d 8-3-1834
    Joel b 10-3-1833
    Richard b 3-23-1836 d 3-26-1836
    Thomas b 3-23-1836 d 5-13-1836
Eliza 2w

EBRITE
Wm B b 3-15/16-1850/51 Adams Co OH
Mary b 3-13-1847 Wayne Co dt Nathan & Mary (**Lamar**) Dennis
m 7-31-1873
Ch: Nathan Erwin b 9-23-1874 Wayne Co
    James O b 1-23-1877 Wayne Co
    David O b 1-23-1877 Wayne Co
    Charles D b 4-20-1881 Wayne Co
    Arthur P b 3-27-1885 Wayne Co

EDWARDS
Henry J b 9-26-1809 VA

Morton h Eva Celestia b 11-10-1868 dt Jonathan B & Matilda J
(**Conley**) **Clark** m 1890 Wayne Co

Rena E b 13-1882 dt Oscar & Alice (**Shaw**)

Temple h Rebecca (**Pierce**)
Ch: Emma E b 1-29-1854 Wayne Co
    Nathan F b 11-25-1856 Wayne Co

ELDER
Eunice E b 6-12-1848 Randolph Co NC

ELLIOTT
Claude C b 5-8-1885 Henry Co s Ola (**Carpenter**)

ELLIS
James h Mary b 7-15-1826

Mordecai West River PM h Ruth d 4-28-1848 wid Samuel **Lee**
Ch: Keziah b 2-12-1832 d 1-1-1837
    Edith b 9-17/23-1833
    Samuel b 8-17-1835 d 2-14-1836
    Mary b 1-14-1837
    Lucinda b 12-24-1839 d 2-17-1842
    Martha b 6-12-1843

Nehemiah b 3-3-1806
Sarah d 7-1-1845 New Hope MM TN
Ch: Rebecca b 9-25-1842
Ruth 2w b 8-7-1823 d 8-9-1849
Ch: Nathan D b 4-2-1848
Delilah 3w b 4-4-1811

Sarah R b 12-18-1837 d 9-20-1851

ENGLE
Thomas S b 4-22-1841 Burlington NJ s Samuel & Edith
Hannah b 8-16-1838 Wayne Co dt Jesse & Margaret **Stetler** m 3-18-1877

EVANS
Wm H b 1-5-1851 Wayne Co s Zenas & Catherine (**Ditch**)
Nancy Ellen b 2-24-1851 Madison Co dt James & Martha (**Smith**)
Conway

EWART
Annie Deweese b 1-12-1866 dt John & Margaret (**Doris**)

FARLOW
David Lindsey b 5-5-1863 Wayne Co s Wm S & Louisa
(**Beckerdite**) h Flora B (**Pierce**) m 9-20-1883

FARLOW (cont)
John Franklin b 3-31-1861 Randolph Co NC s Wm S & Louisa
(**Beckerdite**)
Serena L b 11-20-1865 Wayne Co dt Lyndsey & Mary E (**Gibson**)
Canaday
Ch: Clara E b 8-30-1893 Wayne Co
    Blanche b 8-20-1895 Wayne Co

Schuyler Colfax b 9-13-1866 Wayne Co s Wm S & Louisa
(**Beckerdite**) h Carrie (**Helm**) m 11-14-1891

Wm S b 8-27-1832 Randolph Co NC s Enoch & Mary
Louisa b 1-12-1834 Randolph Co dt Boice & Isabel **Beckerdite**
m 9-5-1852
Ch: Lorenzo D b 12-6-1853 Randolph Co NC
    Arron E b 3-31-1855 Randolph Co NC d 7-18-1861
    Nancy Roxanna b 12-23-1856 Randolph Co NC
    Enoch Lewis b 2-10-1859 Randolph Co NC d 1-15-1863 bur Nettle Creek
    John Franklin b 3-3-1861 Randolph Co NC
    David Lindsey b 5-5-1863 Wayne Co
    Schuyler Colfax b 9-13-1866 Wayne Co
    Wm Edwin b 5-28-1868 Wayne Co
    Henry b 12-13-1871 Wayne Co d 12-13-1871 bur Nettle Creek
    Charley b 8-17-1874 Wayne Co d 8-18-1874 bur Nettle Creek
    Myrtle Lenora b 9-15-1875 Wayne Co
    Claude b 8-3-1880 Wayne Co d 11-6-1884 bur Nettle Creek

FARMER
Albert h Matilda
Ch: Macy A b 12-22-1859 d 9-30-1860
    Charles E b 8-12-1861
    Clarence R b 8-17-1864 d 4-24-1873
    Orpha W b 9-4-1867
    Mary E b 9-7-1870
    Melinda C b 1-25-1872

FEAR
Charles E b 7-31-1867 Grant Co s Wm L & Sarah A
Della M b 12-14-1874 MI dt Solomon & Martha **Cox** m 9-19-1892

FEWELL
Elliott b 1-19-1853 Jefferson Co s Wm & Elizabeth
Mary b 3-16-1854 Jefferson Co dt John & Susan **Lovell** m 11-28-1875 Jefferson Co

FIELDS
Isaac A h Mary U
Ch: Elizabeth Lillian
    Maud Lou

FLEMING
David h Clara Bell b 5-20-1861 Wayne Co dt John & Susan
Hockett

FORD
Oliver b 8-1-1858 Randolph Co s Nathaniel & Hannah (**Phillips**)
Eliza Ellen b 8-21-1858 Wayne Co dt David E & Ruth (**Howell**)
Baldwin m 3-31-1889 Wayne Co
Ch: Everett E b 4-1-1890 Wayne Co
    George Clessie b 8-7-1892 Wayne Co
    Hazel Glenna b 7-15-1897 Wayne Co

FOSTER
Robert J b 8-19-1834 LA s Wm & Lucinda
Patience Ann **Shalley** b 11-15-1830 Warren Co OH dt Daniel & Eve
Doughman m 4-14-1869
Ch: Albert b 2-15-1870 Wayne Co
    Charles Thomas b 11-22-1872 Wayne Co
    Wm b 3-18-1874 Wayne Co
    Walter b 2-18-1876 Wayne Co

FOX
Charles W b 12-25-1866 Wayne Co s David & Deborah (Cox)
Nettie Ann b 7-18-1875 Pulaski Co KY dt Thomas & Eliza (Anderson) Whittier m 8-23-1891
Ch: Oscar b 6-1-1892 Wayne Co

Ruth Etta b 2-9-1899 dt John & Martha (Hubbard)

Thomas h Carlista b 1-22-1871 Wayne Co dt John H & Leannah (Lamb) Lamb

FRAZER
Oliver M b 12-10-1867 Jefferson Co IA s James & Ruth (Whitson)
Laura E b 9-6-1876 Lake Co IL dt Edwin & Anna (Young) Stewart

FRAZIER
Abner b 6-29-1844 Henry Co s Isaiah & Sabra

GIBSON
John h Nannie E b 12-8-1866 dt Lyndsey & Mary (Gibson) Canaday m 1898 Wayne Co

GILBERT
Charles b 8-28-1877 Randolph Co s Thomas & Susan (Hilton)
Grace b 10-15-1882 Randolph Co dt Willard F & Emma J (Gray) Pursley m 12-7-1897 Randolph Co

Charles Ernest b 10-15-1889 s Cyrus & Mary (Black)

GILLAM
Mary E b 9-22-1861 dt Benjamin & Mary

GILLESPIE
Charles h Alice b 8-9-1856 Wayne Co dt Jesse & Rachel (Oxley) ? m 7-8-1873
Ch: Eva b 9-19-1876 Van Buren Co MI

GRACE
Jessie b 1-4-1882 dt Annie

GRAY
Orville H b 5-8-1893 s Elisha & Elizabeth (Simerson)

Wm Pinckney b 9-16-1841 Guilford Co NC s Ithamer & Elizabeth (Beeson)
Julia C b 1-27-1841 Guilford Co NC dt Jane Lamb m 11-26-1864
Ch: Alice Carey b 11-26-1867 Tipton Co
    Benjamin Elijah b 8-14-1869 Randolph Co
    Edith Bell b 4-18-1872 Randolph Co
    Jehu Harlan b 7-14-1873 Wayne Co

GROBLE
Elnora May b 8-16-1881 Blackford Co dt Thomas & Naomi (Clark)

GWIN
Cyrus B b 5-26-1826 Wayne Co s John & Charity (Mills)
Asenath b 4-22-1828 Wayne Co dt Elihu & Mary (Worth) Swain m 2-20-1850 Wayne Co
Ch: Elihu Swain b 1-1-1855 Wayne Co

Elihu Swain b 1-1-1855 Wayne Co s Cyrus B & Asenath (Swain)
E Josephine dt George W & Anna (Hollingsworth) Scantland m 8-26-1878 Wayne Co
Ch: Glennie A b 4-5-1879 Wayne Co
    Freddie Carl b 6-1-1882 Wayne Co
    Oscar S b 10-13-1884 Wayne Co
    Charles O b 1-13-1887 Wayne Co
    Alsie L b 7-20-1891 Wayne Co

John d 10-25-1848 ae 64y 9m 2d
Charity dt Aaron & Charity Mills d 3-19-1876 ae 86y 4m 5d
Ch: Julia Ann b 5-28-1812 Jefferson Co TN

GWIN (John cont)
Pleasant b 10-21-1821 Wayne Co
Cyrus B b 5-26-1826

John D b 2-25-1849 Wayne Co s Pleasant & Hannah (Wimmer)
Rhoda Roxanna b 1-4-1850 Wayne Co dt Wesley Stark & Phebe (Coffin) Ledbetter m 2-29-1872
Ch: Etha Inda b 12-13-1874 Wayne Co d 11-2-1875
    Leitha Myrtle b 8-28-1876 Wayne Co
    Golda Mabel b 8-4-1878 Wayne Co

Pleasant h Hannah (Wimmer)
Ch: Walter T b 10-7-1846
    John D b 2-25-1849 Wayne Co

Pleasant b 10-26-1821 Wayne Co s John & Charity (Mills)
Charlotte b 8-15-1836 Wayne Co dt Jonathan B & Matilda Macy m 1-16-1878

Walter T b 10-7-1846 s Pleasant & Hannah (Wimmer)
Nellie b 2-4-1848 dt Edward & Elizabeth (Dunn) Good m 11-11-1872

HADLEY
Katie R b 9-7-1888 Vermilion Co IL dt Wm & Eva (Lewis)

Thomas P b 4-17-1861 Guthrie Co IA s Amos & Rebecca (Bowles)
Lenora C b 12-11-1860 Wayne Co dt Henry C & Lucinda (Macy) Beard m 4-4-1883 Wayne Co
Ch: Ralph S b 11-16-1883 Wayne Co
    Eva Luzena b 11-7-1884 Wayne Co
    Rebecca Madge b 12-8-1886 Wayne Co
    Mazie Matilda b 9-12-1888 Wayne Co
    Anna Clarice b 10-1-1892 Wayne Co

HAFFNER
James h Mary Elizabeth b 11-12-1868 Wayne Co dt Jesse & Irena (Chamness) Lamar m 2-2-1890

HAISLEY
Charles h Bertha Louise b 1-11-1873 Wayne Co dt Henry P & Rhoda R (Clark) Cain m 12-1894 Wayne Co
Ch: Marion b Wayne Co

Davis h Martha Jane b 9-14-1843 Wayne Co dt Lindsay & Irena (Thornburg) Dennis m 9-24-1862
Ch: Thomas

Isaac E b 8-12-1850 Wayne Co s Jonathan & Susanna
Martha E b 5-9-1854 Henry Co dt Miles & Cynthia (Dennis) Mendenhall m 1-1-1874
Ch: Edwin R b 2-11-1875 Henry Co
    Charles Harrison b 5-17-1878 Henry Co

Thomas s Davis & Martha Jane (Dennis) h Lillie dt John & Priscilla (Mullen) Oler m Wayne Co
Ch: Wilbert

HALL
Joseph h Mary E b 10-5-1839 Henry Co dt George & Lucinda (Dennis) Nicholson m 11-8-1893

HAMMER
Joseph b 1809 s Jesse & Lydia d 1888
Matilda dt Reuben & Lucinda Macy d 4-29-1872

HANSON
Benjamin Franklin b 1-16-1859 Howard Co s Elijah & Mary Ann (Morris) h Alice b Carroll Co

Borden b 3-6-1800 s Elijah & Susanna d 7-18-1846
Rachel b 12-10-1799 dt John & Rachel Cox
Ch: John b 7-10-1820 Springfield PM

SPRINGFIELD MONTHLY MEETING
BIRTH AND DEATH RECORD

HANSON (John cont)
    Ann b 1-22-1822
    Levi b 6-18-1824
    Edwin b 10-8-1826
    Thomas b 11-16-1828
    Elisha b 2-20-1831
    Esther b 2-20-1833
    Elijah b 8-8-1835
    Newton b 1-18-1838
    Allen b 2-28-1840
    Milton b 5-6-1842
    Rachel b 7-25-1844

John b 7-10-1820 Springfield PM s Borden & Rachel (Cox)
Sarah b 11-14-1821
Ch: Clara I b 6-4-1840 d 8-5-1841
    Elwood b 7-3-1842
    Silas b 5-29-1844
    Ellen b 8-27-1846

Levi b 6-18-1824 s Borden & Rachel (Cox)
Delilah (Reece) b 2-20-1828
Ch: Zimri b 4-4-1846 Wayne Co
    Susannah b 1-14-1848
    Esther Ann b 12-18-1849

Zimri b 4-4-1846 Wayne Co s Levi & Delilah (Reece)
Isabel b 1-24-1848 Wayne Co dt Jesse & Ruth (Woody) Chamness
m 6-2-1875 Wayne Co
Ch: Emory Clarence b 5-9-1876 Wayne Co
    Alma Ellena b 4-18-1878 Wayne Co d 4-22-1880 bur Nettle Creek
    Elva Ruth b 5-5-1882 Wayne Co
    Elbert Florence b 6-25-1885 Wayne Co

HARDIN
Horace L h Emma M b Wayne Co m 9-17-1888

HARRIS
Jonas h Hannah
Ch: Henry M b 11-19-1811
    Jesse B b 11-3-1613
    Jonas b 12-23-1815
    Jacob b 2-27-1818
    Lydia Ann b 2-27-1818

HARTER
Francis A b 8-4-1872 Jay Co s John W & Priscilla (Goodson)
Orpha b 12-18-1873 Randolph Co dt James & Ellen (Lee) Bookout
m 12-24-1892
Ch: Eva Ruth b 7-9-1898 Wayne Co

Jesse H b 10-16-1871 Henry Co s Joseph & Pheraby (Daniels)
Gracie P b 6-7-1874 Wayne Co dt Cassius M & Sarah (Neff) Burroughs m 11-12-1891 Wayne Co
Ch: Early Irvin b 8-29-1892 Randolph Co
    Hubert B b 8-9-1894 Randolph Co
    Nona Mabel b 4-9-1897 Randolph Co
    Donald Morton b 2-9-1899 Randolph Co

John W b 5-24-1850 Wayne Co s Levi & Elizabeth (Ulrich)
Priscilla b 11-12-1849 dt Uriah & Anna Goodson m 8-3-1871 Wayne Co
Ch: Francis A b 8-4-1872 Jay Co
    Mary G b 9-27-1881 Wayne Co

Joseph L b 10-9-1834 Henry Co s Joseph C & Catharine h Mary (Pierce)
Ch: Wm b 1-8-1860 Wayne Co
Pheraby 2w b 5-16-1839 Yadkin Co NC dt Harrison & Pheraby (Pierce) Daniels m 10-20-1862 Henry Co
Ch: Morton L b 10-15-1864 Wayne Co
    Leroy b 2-1-1867 Henry Co
    Nancy Ellen b 3-5-1869 Henry Co

HARTER (Joseph L cont)
    Jesse H b 10-16-1871 Henry Co
    Emma Florence b 4-15-1876 Wayne Co
    George W b 6-1-1878 d 12-4-1893 killed by accident/ criminal carelessness bur Nettle Creek

Leroy b 2-1-1867 Henry Co s Joseph L & Pheraby (Daniels)
Hannah M b 5-3-1872 Randolph Co dt Tarver & Margaret (Mulford) Seagrave m 8-19-1889 Randolph Co
Ch: Samantha b 7-10-1891

Morton L b 10-15-1864 Wayne Co s Joseph L & Pheraby (Daniels)
Emma 9-6-1863 Wayne Co dt Eli & Mary Cates m 6-15-1884 Wayne Co

Wm b 1-8-1860 Wayne Co s Joseph L & Mary (Pierce)
Mary L b 10-23-1865 Wayne Co dt John & Caroline H (Chamness) Davis m 10-28-1889 Wayne Co
Ch: Maggie b 5-9-1896 Wayne Co

HASTINGS
Mathew J b 6-26-1857 Rush Co s Samuel & Matilda
Lydia Ann b 6-26-1859 Hendricks Co dt Andrew & Catherine Nichols m 2-14-1878
Ch: Lena Daisey b 6-25-1883 Hendricks Co
    Ercie One b 11-18-1885 Hendricks Co
    Charles H b 4-6-1889 Hendricks Co
    Sylvia b 10-18-1896 Delaware Co

HAWKINS
John b 4-3-1838 s Shenandoah Co VA Aaron & Catharine (Lindamood) h Sarah (Van Matre) m 8-5-1860
Mary 2w b 9-23-1846 Henry Co dt John & Lucinda (Adams) Bond

HAXTON
Myrtle Lucille b 4-21-1889 dt Descum & Nellie (Sansbury)

HEALTON
Albert b 1-27-1856 s Joel & Mary Ann (Bond) h Hannah (Wilkinson)

Artemus E b 8-12-1876 Henry Co s Wm Bond & Mary E (Milliken)
Maggie b 11-16-1878 Henry Co dt Mathew & Sarah L (Fleming) Peckinpaugh m 1-1-1898 Henry Co

Joel b 6-19-1828 Yadkin Co NC s John & Sarah
Mary Ann b 12-29-1827 Henry Co dt Wm & Elizabeth (Wiles) Bond
Ch: Emeline b 12-22-1848
    Wm Bond b 4-17-1851 Howard Co
    John A b 1-29-1854
    Albert b 1-27-1856
    Thomas D b 8-24-1858 d 8-19-1860
    Sarah Elizabeth b 12-5-1860 Howard Co
    Orilla b 4-13-1863 d 8-4-1870
    Nathan M b 3-25-1866 Henry Co
    Mary E b 12-28-1868 Henry Co

John b 7-27-1805
Sarah d 6-29-1840 ae 33y 10m 5d
Ch: Allen b 12-23-1824
    Rebecca b 9-3-1826
    Joel b 6-19-1828 Yadkin Co NC
    Jonathan b 4-28-1830
    Ann b 5-13-1832
    Elwood b 8-29-1835
    Wm b 12-15-1837
Ruth 2w b 7-10-1815
Ch: Rhoda b 10-10-1842
    Nathan b 12-11-1844
    Sarah b 10-14-1846

HEALTON (cont)
Wm Bond b 4-17-1851 Howard Co s Joel & Mary Ann (**Bond**)
Mary E b 5-31-1856 Henry Co dt Eli & Mary M (**Holiday**)
Millikan m 11-20-1875 Henry Co
Ch: Artemus E b 8-12-1876 Henry Co
    Bertha M b 3-6-1878 Henry Co

HEINEY
Hobart b 10-1896 Huntington Co s Samuel & Emma (**Shutt**)

HIATT
Daniel Williams b 1-31-1817 Center MM Clinton Co OH s Eleazer & Ann (**Williams**) d 3-24-1891
Melinda b 5-26-1821 Deep River MM Guilford Co NC dt Wm & Rebecca (**Coffin**) **Mendenhall** m 8-26-1841 Wayne Co
Ch: Edwin W b 9-8-1842
    Eliza Ann b 1-15-1844 d 10-8-1862
    James Addison b 3-23-1846 Wayne Co
    Oliver Lindley b 3-26-1848 Wayne Co
    Linden Cornelius b 6-3-1850 Wayne Co
    Emily R b 8-29-1852 Cherry Grove MM Randolph Co
    Rebecca M b 9-14-1854 Wayne Co
    Esther C b 11-2-1856 Wayne Co

James Addison b 2-17-1846 Wayne Co s Daniel Williams & Melinda (**Mendenhall**) h Martha Jane (**Williams**) m 3-23-1871
Ch: Thomas W b 2-17-1872 Wayne Co

John b 4-9-1791 d 9-10-1859
Charity b 6-22-1790 d 12-24-1863
Ch: Sarah b 6-14-1829

Lawrence b 12-31-1874 Wayne Co s Oliver Lindley & Emma E (**Edwards**) h Nellie (**Frazier**) m 11-1-1898 Henry Co

Linden Cornelius b 6-3-1850 Wayne Co s Daniel Williams & Melinda (**Mendenhall**)
Samantha E b 2-24-1851 Fayette Co PA dt Garrett & Margaret **Morrison** m 11-20-1873
Ch: Wm A b 1-5-1875 Wayne Co
    Ervin M b 12-7-1876 Wayne Co

Mary d 11-17-1855 ae 95y 8m 4d

Oliver Lindley b 3-26-1848 Wayne Co s Daniel Williams & Melinda (**Mendenhall**)
Emma E b 1-29-1854 Wayne Co dt Temple & Rebecca (**Pierce**) **Edwards** d 7-19-1899 m 1-22-1874
Ch: Lawrence b 12-31-1874 Wayne Co
    Rebecca E b 3-15-1876 Wayne Co
    Celia Victoria b 1-24-1884 Wayne Co
Emma 2w b 10-10-1855 Wayne Co dt John C & Elizabeth (**Green**) **Potter**

HILL
Adolph H b 3-27-1860 Delaware Co s Charles & Eunice (**Hill**)
Alice b 8-5-1862 Randolph Co dt Alexander & Elizabeth (**Templin**) **Chalfant** m 5-4-1881 Randolph Co
Ch: Lillian A b 6-26-1882 Delaware Co
    Bertha E b 10-31-1884 Delaware Co
    Orville L b 10-31-1886 Delaware Co

Benjamin J b 3-4-1823 Wayne Co s Jacob & Phebe (**Canaday**) d 7-16-1899
Lavina b 6-3-1827 Monongahela Co VA dt John & Esther (**Davis**) **Hill** m 11-6-1845 Henry Co
Ch: Esther Ann b 12-3-1846

Jacob b 2-3-1800 d 8-29-1862
Phebe (**Canaday**) w b 5-7-1802 d 1-1-1867
Ch: Benjamin J b 3-4-1823 Wayne Co d 7-16-1899
    Mary b 11-10-1824
    Charles b 4-17-1827

HILL (Jacob cont)
Henry b 10-31-1828
Wm C b 7-25-1830 d 8-3-1834
Sarah b 4-19-1832 d 2-13-1869
Aaron b 4-29-1834
John b 2-22-1842

HINSHAW
Edmund R b 9-20-1856 Randolph Co s Edmund & Irena
Ellen (**Huffman**) m 4-1-1876

Seth
Ch: Malinda b 12-22-1881 d 5-2-1854
    Asenath b 11-21-1819 d 11-11-1840

Wm B b 11-29-1808
Hannah (**Coffin**) b 12-3-1814
Ch: James Madison b 5-8-1832
    Emily Jane b 6-10-1834 d 7-6-1834
    Elmina Louisa b 9-3-1835
    Oliver Goldsmith b 7-15-1837 d 1-16-1838
    Barnabas Coffin b 3-7-1841
    Evaline b 2-6-1843
    Henry B b 5-19-1848

HIRST
Catherine b 11-7-1813 d 4-10-1835

HOBSON
David s John & Sarah

George h Deborah
Ch: Isaac b 9-14-1812 NC
    George b 6-1-1814 NC
    Wm b 4-15-1816 NC
    Rachel b 12-30-1817 NC
    Elizabeth b 10-15-1819 NC
    Stephen b 2-12-1820 IN
    Rebecca b 5-12-1824 IN
    John b 1-17-1826 IN
    Deborah Ann b 12-27-1827 IN
    Hannah b 1-7-1831 d 12-29-1832 IN
    Thomas b 11-26-1832 IN
    Easter b 10-23-1834 IN
    Mary Jane b 9-1-1836 IN

George Westbury PM b 5-27-1772 d 3-17-1846
Rebecca b 1-24-1780 d 5-10-1851
Ch: Thomas b 5-20-1803
    Sarah b 4-13-1805
    Anna b 11-14-1806
    Charles b 1-1-1809
    Joshua b 2-23-1812
    Jesse b 10-1-1813
    George b 10-19-1816
    Rebecca b 6-17-1818
    Wm b 10-26-1820
    Margaret b 3-6-1823

HOCKETT
Jesse b 9-29-1816
Gillean b 6-1-1818
Ch: Martha Jane b 4-12-1842
    Wm A
    John W

John b 12-20-1831 Randolph Co NC s John & Hannah d 3-10-1870 h Susan
Ch: Clara Belle b 5-20-1861 Wayne Co
    Sarah Emeline b 2-20-1863 Wayne Co
    Hannah Elizabeth b 9-29-1865 Wayne Co
    Perry Albert b 12-15-1867 Wayne Co

SPRINGFIELD MONTHLY MEETING
BIRTH AND DEATH RECORD

HOCKETT (cont)
Warner M h Matilda C (**Dennis**) b 9-18-1825 d 6-29-1868
Ch: Addison Felton b 3-13-1863
    Martha Ellen b 6-16-1865
    Mary Elma b 10-24-1867

Zimri b 12-13-1834 Randolph Co NCs John & Hannah (**Wilson**)
Malinda b 12-28-1834 Davidson Co NC dt Philip & Susan **Grimes** d 4-27-1882 bur Nettle Creek m 11-25-1855 NC
Ch: Sarah Etta b 8-26-1860 Hendricks Co
Susan 2w b 9-23-1849 Wayne Co dt John & Rachel **Gebhart** m 1-20-1884
Ch: Mary Ethel b 12-13-1888 Wayne Co

HODGIN
Pleasant W b 3-7-1846

HODSON
David b 12-29-1825
Sarah Jane b 1-5-1831
Ch: Wm O b 4-13-1849

Henry b 6-22-1818 s John & Sarah
Elvina b 3-16-1817
Ch: Milo b 5-29-1837 d 10-14-1841
    Sarah Jane b 8-6-1841
    John M b 10-7-1843

Jesse b 9-3-1819 s John & Sarah - removed to Iowa
Jane b 9-6-1821
Ch: Sally Ann b 1-7-1840 Westbury PM
    John W b 12-24-1842 Westbury PM

John b 12-16-1787
Sarah b 2-12-1792
Ch: Delilah b 11-7-1811
    Rhoda b 11-19-1812
    Nathan b 3-26-1814
    Ruth b 7-10-1815
    John b 4-23-1817
    Henry b 6-22-1818
    Jesse b 9-3-1819
    Jonathan b 7-5-1821
    Mary b 8-27-1822
    Richard b 12-15-1823
    David b 12-29-1825
    Sarrah b 6-10-1828
    Zachariah b 8-16-1829
    Rachel b 9-25-1831 d 8-20-1832
    Charlotte b 2-14-1833

John b 9-27-1807

Nathan Westbury b 3-26-1814 s John & Sarah - removed to Howard Co
Elizabeth b 10-13-1822
Ch: Lewis b 12-12-1843 Westbury PM
    Eli b 10-25-1845 d 11-13-1845 Westbury PM

Richard b 12-15-1823 s John & Sarah
Matilda b 3-8-1824
Ch: Julia Ann b 11-11-1845
    Gulielma b 3-16-1847

Solomon h Elizabeth
Ch: Rebeckah b 5-16-1822

Thomas d 12-10-1856 bur Westbury h Anna
Ch: Solomon b 9-16-1829
    Uriah b 1-19-1832
    Ira b 1-18-1834 d 4-10-1834

Zachariah b 8-16-1829 s John & Sarah

HODSON (Zachariah cont)
Ginny b 9-9-1829
Ch. Joel b 6-15-1848
    Rachel b 12-10-1849

HOLADAY
Lena Daisy b Hendricks Co

HOLIDAY
P L h Emma Florence b 4-15-1876 Wayne Co dt Joseph L & Pheraby (**Daniels**) **Harter** m 7-7-1895

HOLLINGSWORTH
Henry b 1-20-1804 d 6-27-1876
Hannah b 9-22-1799
Ch: Elizabeth b 6-3-1828
    Deborah Arnett b 9-8-1829 Wayne Co
    Sarrah b 10-20-1832
    Anna b 4-16-1834/35
    Lucinda b 11-30-1831 d 12-13-1831

HOOVER
George M h Sarah Jane b 9-7-1855 Henry Co dt Wm & Esther (**Russell**) **Bales** m 11-3-1894 Henry Co

Grace E b 9-5-1880 Marshall Co dt Jonathan & Susana (**Brower**)

HOUCK
James h Ellen dt Jethro **Macy**

HOUGH
Ira h Elizabeth
Ch: Jesse b 7-11-1816 New Garden
    Aseneth b 8-19-1819 New Garden
    Huldah b 1-1-1823 New Garden
    Mahlon b 12-11-1826 New Garden
    Nathan b 7-5-1829 New Garden

Isaiah h Elizabeth b 7-24-1811
Ch: Ruth b 11-23-1831 d 1-1-1833
    Anna b 2-2-1834
    Martha b 9-20-1835
    John b 8-12-1839

J Franklin h Hannah E b 8-16-1867 dt Isaac & Elizabeth (**Dennis**) **Chamness** m 6-18-1890

John h Martha J (**Staton**)
Ch: Milton W b 12-13-1851
    Isabel A b 1-16-1855 Boone Co
    Manson Z b 6-22-1870 Boone Co

Milton W b 12-13-1851 John & Martha J (**Staton**)
Isabel A (**Chamness**) b 1-16-1855 m ?-30-1875

Samuel J h Anna D b 5-15-1869 Miami Co OH dt Marmaduke & Priscilla **Hedgecock** m 1-8-1890

HOWELL
Charles b 1-20-1787 d 5-3-1875
Mary (**Stout**) b 8-26-1795 d 5-8-1852 bur West River
Ch: Lydia b 1-26-1814
    Nancy b 5-23-1815
    Wm b 3-3-1817
    Rhoda b 5-16-1819 d 4-26-1861 bur Nettle Creek
    Susanna b 4-2-1821 d 9-3-1855
    Ruth b 3-27-1823
    Sophie b 1-25-1825
    Charles b 11-21-1826
    Enos b 12-11-1828
    Levi b 3-1-1831
    Larkin b 11-20-1833 Wayne Co
    Joseph b 5-29-1836 Wayne Co

HOWELL (Charles cont)
Rachel 2w b 12-22-1790 Orange Co NC dt Adam & Catharine
(**Stover**) **Reynard** wid Abraham **Wrightsman** d 1863 bur White
River

Joseph b 5-29-1836 Wayne Co s Charles & Mary (**Stout**)
Amelia b 1-18-1833 Wayne Co dt Daniel & Charity (**Hodson**)
Baldwin m Wayne Co

Larkin b 11-20-1833 Wayne Co s Charles & Mary (**Stout**)
Lydia b 10-4-1839 Wayne Co dt John & Barbara **Jackson** m 3-21-1858
Ch: John b 5-7-1859 Wayne Co
    Nancy Jane b 7-7-1867

HUFFMAN
Edward H h Ellen (**Crumb**)
Ch: Chester W b 2-16-1883 Augusta Co VA
    Paul Edgar b 5-5-1885

HUNNICUTT
Charles Daniel b 9-17-1852 s John Thomas & Jane (**Charles**)
Aurie b 11-20-1856 dt George W & Anna (**Hollingsworth**)
Scantland m 11-25-1877 Wayne Co
Ch: Earl
    Miriam A b 7-30-1881 Wayne Co
    Annie d 11-?-1899
    Walter A b 11-4-1884
    Mabel E b 8-28-1887
    Myra G b 5-10-1892
    Margaret A b 2-10-1894
    Howard A b 8-17-1895

Daniel b 5-11-1771
Jane (**Walthall**) b 12-18-1780 d 9-7-1859
Ch: Jamima Walthall b 8-17-1812
    Mary Batt b 8-17-1814
    John Thomas b 11-25-1816 VA
    Sarah Jane b 9-21-1820 d 1-5-1884 bur Springfield
    Frances Daniel b 10-27-1822 d 3-21-1851

John Thomas b 11-25-1816 VA s Daniel & Jane (**Walthall**)
Jane (**Charles**) b 4-26-1832 d 3-22-1861
Ch: Charles Daniel b 9-17-1852 Randolph Co
    Gulielma b 10-19-1854 Randolph Co
    Albert C b 1-17-1857 Randolph Co d 1-6-1889
    Wm Penn b 5-19-1859 Randolph Co
    Mary Jane b 3-8-1861 Randolph Co
Deborah Arnett 2w b 9-8-1829 Wayne Co dt Henry & Hannah
Hollingsworth d 3-17-1889 m 2-28-1872 Wayne Co

HUNT
Jesse h Mournin d 1-30-1866 ae 72y bur West River
Ch: Phanuel b 1-18/27-1817/19
    Rebecca b 1-4-1822
    Daniel b 9-19-1824
    Wm b 11-11-1826

Phanuel b 1-18/27-1817/19 s Jesse & Mournin
Eleanor b 1-23-1821
Ch: Emily Ann b 12-3-1842 West River Wayne Co
    Elmarinda b 6-15-1844 West River Wayne Co
    Sarah Jane b 6-16-1846 West River Wayne Co
    Henry Clinton b 2-20-1848 West River Wayne Co

Thomas b 12-2-1797
Lydia b 7-1-1799 d 8-16-1840 bur West River
Ch: Sarah b 11-3-1840
    Uriah W b 8-20-1821
    Pheriba b 9-18-1823
    Susannah b 11-6-1825
    Elizabeth b 2-20-1829

HUNT (Thomas cont)
    Rebecca b 2-26-1831
    Henry b 7-13-1833 d 7-28-1834 bur West River
    Ruth b 6-30-1836
    Bronson D b 1-30-1838
    Wesley W b 1-15-1840
Mary 2w b 4-1-1802

HUTCHENS
Emeline b 10-7-1842/72

Hezekiah b 10-14-1793
Clary b ca 1790 Wake Co NC dt Thomas & Milly **Spain** d 9-12-1879
bur Springfield
Ch: Ira H b 6-2-1815
    Emily b 3-14-1817
    Enos b 2-26-1820 d 11-13-1841
    Sarah b 11-14-1821
    Keziah b 5-25-1823 d 6-13-1844
    Thomas b 2-13-1825
    Moses b 5-29-1827 d 4-11-1832
    James b 5-16-1829

Ira H b 6-2-1815 s Hezekiah & Clary (**Spain**)
Nancy Ann b 5-27-1827 dt Philip & Christena **Allen** m 3-11-1868

John h Ann b 1-22-1822 dt Borden & Rachel (**Cox**) **Hanson**
Ch: Hanson b 6-2-1848

John H h Frances Belinda b 1-12-1826 dt Wm & Elizabeth (**Wiles**)
Bond d 2-11-1845
Ch: Wm F b 2-5-1845

Margaret b 20-6-1880 Delaware Co dt James & Nancy (**Bergdoll**)

Nancy Ann b 5-2-1822

Sarah Alice b 9-19-1852 gdt Hezekiah

HYER
Frank b 12-2-1856 Ross Co OH s Samuel & Catherine
Sarah Etta b 8-26-1860 Hendricks Co dt Zimri & Malinda (**Grimes**)
Hockett
Ch: Earl H b 1-1-1888 Wayne Co
    Pearl b 12-5-1889 Wayne Co

JACKSON
Jacob L b 3-30-1859 Carroll Co s Benjamin & Mary (**Harter**)
Emma Bell b 3-25-1861 Wayne Co dt Wm & Fanny (**Stantz**) **Young**
m 11-9-1879 Henry Co
Ch: Frankie Carl b 12-11-1892 Henry Co

Jemima b 8-16-1795 d 9-6-1861

JENKINS
Anderson H b 2-3-1820 s Wm & Lydia
Elizabeth D b 2-10-1824 d 8-12-1845
Ch: Eliza Ann b 1-27-1842
    Irena b 2-12-1844

Benjamin b 11-27-1823 s Wm & Lydia
Frances Clanton b 4-13-1826 IN dt Luke & Rhoda **Wiles**
Ch: Anderson b 9-17-1844
    Elizabeth b 3-13-1846

Wm b 6-4-1797 d 8-31-1843 bur Flat Rock
Lydia b 10-20-1798
Ch: Eliza Ann b 11-9-1818 d 9-29-1822
    Anderson H b 2-3-1820
    Dorothy b 2-18-1822
    Benjamin b 11-27-1823
    Mary b 9-15-1825

SPRINGFIELD MONTHLY MEETING
BIRTH AND DEATH RECORD

JENKINS (Wm cont)
    Phebe Ann b 3-3-1827
    Lucinda b 3-16-1829
    Esther b 12-19-1830
    Sarah b 12-26-1832
    Wm P b 12-6-1834
    Elisabeth b 5-10-1837 d 3-28-1839
    Melinda b 7-25-1840

JESSUP
Albert S b 2-22-1853 s Levi & Mary (**Myers**)
Gulielma Jones b 10-19-1854 Randolph Co dt John Thomas & Jane (**Charles**) **Hunnicutt** m 10-19-1890 Randolph Co
Ch: Mary b 4-17-1892 Randolph Co
      John b 12-19-1894 Randolph Co

Henry h Mary E b 10-5-1839 dt George & Lucinda (**Dennis**) **Nicholson**
Ch: Sarah Ann b 6-13-1859

JOHNSON
Jesse h Rhoda b Randolph Co NC dt Job & Rhoda **Worth** d 2-27-1837

Josiah h Polly
Ch: Rebecca b 5-11-1814 d 3-30-1827
      Rachel b 8-22-1816 d 2-16-1895
      Elam b 9-18-1822
      Ashla b 11-27-1824
      Josiah b 1-20-1827
      Zerelda M b 1-31-1829 d 7-23-1830
      Walter b 7-26-1831

Rachel d 2-16-1895 dt John

JONES
David b 7-2-1827 s Lydia

Gulielma b 10-19-1854 Randolph Co dt John T & Jane (**Charles**) **Hunnicutt**

Jemima b 12-4-1771

Moses h Eunice
Ch: Thomas Carlton b 4-9-1828
      Hannah b 8-24-1830
      Elizabeth b 5-8-1832
      Mary b 7-24-1834

Nellie b 1-1-1883 dt Ephraim M & Gulielma (**Hunnicutt**)

Sylvester H b 8-22-1853 Wayne Co s John D & Susannah
Mary b 11-25-1847/57 Randolph Co dt Wm & Marticia **Northcutt** m 8-23-1877
Ch: Wm C b 7-1-1878 Wayne Co

JORDAN
W D h Elizabeth b 3-30-1851 Wayne Co dt Wilson & Rachel (**Thornburgh**) **Dennis** m 10-10-1872

JULIAN
Behan T h Mary Elizabeth b 7-11-1847/8 Henry Co dt David E & Ruth (**Howell**) **Baldwin** m 10-10-1871 Wayne Co
Ch: Clella L b 11-29-1873
      Stella Rosalie b 12-25-1875 Randolph Co
      Perry Sherman Wayne Co
      Frank b 11-14-1879
      Clemma Nellie b Henry Co
      Maud b 11-13-1882
      Josie Goldie b Randolph Co
      Pearl b 10-7-1885

KEEVER
John Carver b 8-6-1854 Wayne Co s Moses & Sarah (**Bales**)
Romana b 10-8-1859 Wayne Co dt Caleb & Cecilia (**Locke**) **Lamb** m 11-20-1875 Wayne Co

KEEVER (cont)
Moses h Sarah b 2-2-1834 Wayne Co dt John & Nancy (**McMullen**) **Bales** m 5-28-1852
Ch: John Carver b 8-6-1854 Wayne Co

KENWORTHY
Walter C b 1-6-1878 Hamilton Co s Oliver N & Isabel
Eliza Ellen b 10-30-1879 Wayne Co dt John & Eliza **Bell** m 5-25-1898

KIDWELL
Martin b 6 28-1866 Grant Co s James & Mary (**Keever**) h Rosa (**Howell**) m 12-25-1895 Randolph Co

KIMBALL
Malinda Ella b 10-22-1848 Wayne Co dt Josiah & Nancy Ann **Johnson**

Elmira b 9-3/5-1824 Hartford Co NC dt John & Clarissa **Matthews**

Mary E b 10-6-1851

KINLEY
Joel b 1-16-1811
Rachel b 8-7-1813 d 3-8-1847
Ch: Charles b 8-25-1833
      Margaret b 1-2-1835 d 10-4-1850
      Lydia b 10-31-1836 d 4-2-1852
      Joseph John b 5-15-1839
      Rebecca E b 2-28-1842
Eliza 2w b 2-15-1825
Ch: Alpheus C b 10-7-1849
      Barnabas C b 9-4-1852

KINSINGER
Ernest Clifford b 8-10-1898 Wayne Co s Edward A & Lillian (**Ashbaugh**)

KNIGHT
Benajah b 5-17-1830
Delilah b 10-17-1831
Ch: Nathan D b 4-19-1854
      Absalom b 10-18-1856
      Phebe Ellen b 3-24-1859

KNOX
Esther b 8-22-1897 Owen Co dt James & Lena (**Berkhart**)

KOONS
Thomas Benton h Nevada b 12-15-1862 Wayne Co dt Benjamin & Anna **Conley** m 8-23-1885

KOONSMAN
Alice Vestina b 11-20-1866 dt John & Margaret J (**Widener**) **Disinger**

LAMAR
Isaac h Hannah b 2-2-1790 d 7-13-1847 bur West River
Ch: Mary b 8-9-1810 d 3-22-1847
      Ruth b 8-7-1823 d 8-9-1849

Jesse b 7-23-1847 Henry Co s Samuel & Judith (**Baldwin**) d 5-12-1869
Irena (**Chamness**) b 9-10-1849 Wayne Co m 7-25-1867 Wayne Co
Ch: Mary Elizabeth b 11-12-1868 Wayne Co

Miles W b 12-21-1851 Henry Co s Samuel & Judith (**Baldwin**)
Elizabeth H b 3-4-1850 Wayne Co dt Wm & Osee Ann (**Marshall**) **Haslam** m 10-27-1878 Wayne Co
Ch: Anna Lenora b 8-14-1881 Wayne Co
      Thomas Levi b 8-26-1883 Wayne Co
      Paul Vernon b 5-15-1885 Wayne Co

LAMAR (Miles cont)
    Nathan Samuel b 10-19-1886 Wayne Co
    Everett Wayne b 9-2-1888 Wayne Co
    John Haslam b 4-29-1891 Wayne Co

Nathan S b 9-1-1843 Henry Co s Samuel & Judith (**Baldwin**)
Alice b 10-7-1851 Wayne Co dt Solomon & Margaret **Billheimer** m 8-21-1867 Wayne Co
Ch: Franklin S b 1-10-1870 Wayne Co
    Effie Luella b 12-10-1872 Wayne Co
    Mary Florence b 11-22-1875
    Nellie Maud b 2-17-1881
    Fred C b 2-27-1883

Samuel b 5-14-1819 d 5-10-1860 bur Nettle Creek
Judith (**Baldwin**) b 4-11-1819 d 6-7-1852 bur Nettle Creek
Ch: Nathan S b 9-1-1843 Henry Co
    Luther b 7-25-1845 d 1-12-1867 bur Nettle Creek
    Jesse b 7-23-1847 Henry Co d 5-12-1869
    Osborn b 7-10-1849 d 3-4-1869 bur Nettle Creek
    Miles W b 12-21-1851 Henry Co
Eunice 2w b 8-1-1829 dt John & Abigail (**Hobbs**) **Coffin** d 10-22-1878 bur Nettle Creek
Ch: John Milton b 6-29-1854   d 9-13-1857 bur Nettle Creek
    Wm b 9-30-1856 d 12-1-1880 bur Nettle Creek
    Mary b 10-30-1860 d 12-12-1874 bur Nettle Creek

LAMB
Absolom T b 7-13-1798
Francy b 4-13-1799
Ch: Benj F b 1-28-1824 NC
    Hannah L b NC
    Anna b 11-2-1827 NC
    Henry Milton b 8-10-1829 NC
    Charity b 3-11-1831 NC
    Miriam b 9-6-1833 Westbury PM
    Joab Lewis b 5-16-1836 Westbury PM
    Rachel P b Westbury PM
    Harrison b 10-2-1840 Westbury PM
    Wm C b 8-2-1844 Westbury PM
    Absalom H b Westbury PM
    Elizabeth b Westbury PM

Absalom T b 11-11-1853 Howard Co s Benjimin F & Rebecca (**Healton**)
Marcelia b 6-15-1860 Randolph Co dt Joshua & Malinda (**Chamness**) **Woody** m 7-12-1879 Howard Co
Ch: Charley E b 5-10-1880 Randolph Co
    Ira C b 9-22-1881 Randolph Co
    Laura Frances b 10-15-1883 Randolph Co
    Mary Emily b 7-29-1887 Randolph Co

Alonzo F b 7-29-1861 Randolph Co s John & Caroline (**Grills**)
Dora Ellen b 4-1-1869 Randolph Co dt George E & Susanna (**Thornton**) **Merryweather**
Ch: Paul Alonzo b 4-11-1894

Daniel h Massa b 3-31-1833 dt Isaac K & Rebecca (**Lamb**) **Beeson**

George h Sarah Emeline b 2-20-1863 Wayne Co dt John & Susan **Hockett**

George W b 3-2-1849 Henry Co s Thomas & Elvira (**Finch**)
Dora V 2w b 8-10-1856 Delaware Co dt Joel & Louisa A (**Cain**) **Mills** m 9-1-1880 Delaware Co
Ch: Charlie b 5-23-1893 Wayne Co d 5-27-1893 bur Nettle Creek

Harvey d 5-9-1888 ae 74y 11m 19d
Letty C b 1818

Isaiah h Rachel R b 5-10-1849 Henry Co dt Wm C & Mary (**Canaday**) **Chamness** m 1-19-1867 Henry Co
Ch: Laura Alice b 12-30-1867 Henry Co d 2-5-1889 bur Nettle Creek

SPRINGFIELD MONTHLY MEETING
BIRTH AND DEATH RECORD

LAMB (cont)
Jesse M b 7-13-1846 Guilford Co NC s Harvey & Jane Caroline

John h Amanda (**Hammer**)
Ch: Joseph
    Lula

John H b 2-21-1844 Wayne Co s Milo & Susan
Leanna b 10-15-1848 Wayne Co dt Elias & Susan **Lamb** m 2-12-1870
Ch: Carlista b 1-22-1871 Wayne Co
    Edgar A b 12-1872 Wayne Co
    Moody Raymond b Wayne Co

Joseph s John & Amanda (**Hammer**) h Glennie A b 4-5-1879 dt Elihu Swain & E Josephine (**Scantland**) **Gwin** m 1891 Wayne Co

Martin h Emily J b 11-9-1833 dt Andrew & Avis (**Lamb**) **Starbuck** m 12-29-1864
Ch: Helena b 5-18-1876

Milo h Julia Ann b 5-28-1812 Jefferson Co TN dt John & Charity (**Mills**) **Gwin** d 3-17-1895 bur Friends Cem near Economy m 11-22-1877

Thomas b 2-13-1784 d 2-15-1863
Amassa b 8-18-1787 d 2-1-1877
Ch: Rebecca b 2-23-1810
    Martin b 12-27-1827

Thomas d 10-2-1872
Elvira b 4-2-1818 Surry Co NC dt Hamilton & Tabitha (**Holoman**) **Finch** d 12-6-1899 bur Nettle Creek m 4-9-1837 Wayne Co
Ch: George W b 3-2-1849 Henry Co

Thomas C b 10-14-1839 Wayne Co s Samuel & Susannah
Harriet C b 9-9-1842 Chatham Co NC dt Hugh & Elizabeth (**Chamness**) **Woody** m 9-9-1861
Ch: Flora May b 2-15-1863 Randolph Co
    Lincoln E b 10-18-1864 Grant Co
    Nelson Ulysses b 5-19-1868 Madison Co

Wm h Caroline b 12-9-1850 Cane Creek MM Chatham Co NC dt Simon & Hannah (**Woody**) **Allen** m 2-1-1872 Wayne Co
Ch: Lenora b 6-27-1873 Wayne Co

Wm M h Louisa b 8-31-1854 Wayne Co dt Mahlon & Louisa (**Beeson**) **Dennis** m 5-15-1881

LANGSTON
Jonathan b 9-21-1817
Hannah b 4-22-1818
Ch: Margaret Ann b 2-15-1840 d 9-25-1841
    Wm L b 7-6-1842
    Rebecca R b 4-21-1844
    Mary Eliza b 10-11-18
    Rachel H b 1-4-1849

LARROWE
Joel b 10-16-1793 d 6-11-1850
Susannah b 8-28-1792
Ch: Matilda b 3-8-1824
    Hannah b 7-26-1825
    Jonathan b 2-2-1827
    Janney b 9-4-1828
    Anna b 2-12-1830
    Wm b 10-22-1831
    Elnathan b 6-17-1834

LEDBETTER
Wesley Stark b 6-26-1799 Chatham Co NC d 10-9-1871
Phebe (**Coffin**) b 1-30-1807 d 1-13-1878
Ch: Elizabeth Jane b 4-10-1827 Wayne Co

SPRINGFIELD MONTHLY MEETING
BIRTH AND DEATH RECORD

LEDBETTER (Wesley Stark cont)
    Hannah H C b 5-21-1847 Wayne Co
    Rhoda Roxanne b 1-4-1850 Wayne Co

LEE
Ephraim b 11-7-1823 s Samuel & Ruth
Elizabeth Jane b 4-10-1827 Wayne Co dt Wesley Stark & Phebe (**Coffin**) **Ledbetter** d 1-13-1878

John b 8-20-1806
Hannah b 3-10-1810
Ch: Elizabeth b 11-6-1831
    Jesse b 2-28-1833
    Ann b 11-6-1839
    Anderson b 4-13-1842
    Wm b 5-13-1844
    Jonathan B b 7-21-1846
    Hiram b 5-19-1848
    Alonzo b 2-25-1850

Samuel West River PM d 9-12-1827
Ruth d 4-28-1848
Ch: Margaret b 6-22-1820 d 2-15-1842
    John b 2-6-1822
    Ephraim b 11-7-1823
    Ezra b 10-15-1825
    Hannah b 12-18-1827

LEFFINGWELL
Amos Newton b 9-13-1881 Henry Co s Frank & Lucinda (**Rhodes**)

LEGGETT
Wm h Sarah E b 6-6-1853 Dayton Oh dt Lucy A **Riggle** m 1-16-1878

LEWIS
James W h Cora (**Clark**)

Samuel Nettle Creek PM b 11-22-1802
Lucinda b 9-7-1807
Ch: Margret Ann b 1-28-1828
    Mary b-21-1830 d 8-13-1831
    Susannah b 9-16-1832
    Martha b l-5-1835
    Thomas b 6-4-1837
    Ruth b 5-1-1839 d 10-8-1840
    Hannah b 9-30-1841
    Wm H b 3-14-1844

Wm b 1-1-1807
Delilah b 11-24-1816
Ch: Thomas b 3-13-l846
    Mary Ann b l-5-1848
    Wm b 1-8-1851
    Alvah M b 12-11-1852

LINES
Thomas E b 9-13-1855 Henry Co s Elijah & Elizabeth (**Beabout**)
Sarah Josephine b 3-21-1863 Wayne Co dt Emanuel & Mary (**Heiney**) **Lentz** m 5-1-1881 Henry Co

LLEWELLYN
Jabez h Mary d 11-9-1880

LOCKE
Edgar R b 6-3-1871 Wayne Co s John Albert & Martha E (**Thornburg**)
Dora Alice b 4-25-1869 Randolph Co dt Wm & Edith (**Lumpkin**) **Burrows** m 12-27-1894 Randolph Co
Ch: Chester Paul b 6-11-1895
    Edith Marie b 12-6-1898

Orlando E b 6-6-1897 s Luna D & Mary E (**Holiday**)

LOCKE (cont)
Wm elder b 6-13-1787 d 11-3-1868
Demaris b 4-7-1787 d 11-27-1858
Ch: Lucretia b 4-19-1809
    Charity b 12-13-1810 d 8-7-1826
    Hannah b 12-27-1812
    Elizabeth b 10-13-1814 d 1-29-1835
    Rachel b 5-26-1816
    John Aaron b 5-22-1819
    Maryan b 3-5-1821
    Levi b 8-21-1824 d 9-26-1824
    Demaris M b 7-3-1826 TN d 3-30-1886
    Wm Milton b 12-1-1828 TN
Judith 2w b 1-14-1817

LOGAN
Florence Elizabeth b 8-3-1898 dt Charles L & Mary J (**Koonsman**)

LUCAS
Sherilee Cordelia b 10-24-1883 dt Levi F & Minnie (**Lee**)

LUELLEN
Della Anna b 6-15-1883 Randolph/Henry Co dt Loring W & Margaret (**Huffman**)

Wm Newton b 9-29-1871 Henry Co s Jonathan M & Rebecca M (**Current**)
Clara b 12-30-1877 Henry Co dt Patrick & Rachel (**Jones**) **Conner** m 12-1-1897 Henry Co

LUMPKIN
Dempsey O h Rebecca b 1-5-1852 Wayne Co dt Mahlon & Louisa (**Beeson**) **Dennis** m 7-8-1874

LUNDY
Mary Elwood b 12-28-1857 Blount Co TN dt Wm & Rachel

McALLISTER
Mary E b 11-13-1842

McCOLLUM
Jesse b 6-17-1828 d 1-1-1869
Martha b 8-25-1827 Henry Co dt Aaron & Mary (**Hockett**) **Mendenhall**
Ch: Miles b 6-7-1855 Wayne Co
    Mary Ellen b 10-22-1857 Randolph Co
    John E b 9-14-1861 Randolph Co

McFADDEN
Wm H H h Martha b 3-23-1832 Hocking Co OH dt John T & Nancy **Wiggins** m 2-7-1855 OH

MCGRAW
John W b 7-28-1842 Highland Co OH s Thomas & Elizabeth
Anna J b 5-18-1844 Wayne Co dt Uriah H & Orpha A **Baldwin** m 10-8-1868
Ch: Violetta b 7-25-1869
    Orpha Elizabeth b 10-6-1871
    Margaret Elmina b 10-26-1873
    Minerva Jane b 10-4-1875

McGUNNIGILL
Daisy b 1-23-1883 dt Abraham & Mary (**Retz**)

McINTYRE
Gussie M b 1-6-1886 Randolph Co dt Robert & Anna (**Laflesh**)

MACY
Albert d 5-7-1847 ae 73y 3m 3d

Alvah J b 2-25-1813 West River PM Lost Creek TN s Wm & Hannah
Mary b 1-5-1812 Blount Co TN dt Thomas & Anna **Lewis**

MACY (Alvah J cont)
    Ann b 10-1-1834 d 8-17-1835
    Hannah b 1-9-1836
    Melinda b 4-15-1837
    Minerva b 10-16-1839
    Matilda b 10-16-1839
    Huldah b 9-24-1841
    Larkin b 5-4-1843 Wayne Co
    Wm b 4-24-1845
    Wayne C b 4-1-1847 Wayne Co
    Mary b 10-19-1850

Barachiah elder d 8-27-1832 ae 72y 6m 3d

Harry B b 8-10-1877 s Wayne Co John & Anna Lula (**Wiggins**)
Lillian b 2-12-1880 Wayne Co dt Nathan & Addie (**Catey**) **Parker** m 12-28-1898 Wayne Co

Isaac West River PM h Eleanor b 7-27-1804 Jefferson Co TN dt Henry & Nancy (**Maulsby**) **Thornburg** m 4-5-1825 Wayne Co
Ch: Lydia Ann b l-4-1826 Springfield
    Lewis b 2-10-1828 Springfield
    Elvira b 5-6-1830 Springfield
    Jesse b 6-7-1832 Springfield
    Irena b 3-21-1836
    Wm T b 1-19-1839
    John b 5-8-1841 Wayne Co
    Sylvanus b 11-18-1843

John h Alice b 5-24-1811
Ch: Julia Ann b 4-7-1828
    Mary Jane b 4-17-1830
    Irwin b 4-2-1833

John b 5-8-1841 Wayne Co s Isaac & Eleanor (**Thornburg**)
Anna Lula b 3-26-1857 dt Philemon & Mary (**Burr**) **Wiggins** m 9-26-1876
Cb: Harry B b 8-10-1877 Wayne Co
    Frank b 11-29-1879
    Lawrence b 8-27-1884
    Byran b 6-9-1888
    Forrest b 9-10-1893

John H West River b 11-28-1816 Lost Creek TN s Wm & Hannah d 7-7-1849
Myra b 11-13-1815
Ch: Miles b l-2-1840
    Eustacia Ann b 1-15-1842
    Exaline b 9-17-1843
    Elza b 3-23-1845

Jonathan h Hannah
Ch: Eunice b 9-2-1809
    Azra b 12-19-1811
    Henry b 8-15-1814
    David b 10-22-1816
    Mary b 10-14-1819
    Isaac b 11-16-1823
    Jethro b 6-25-1825
    Wm b 2-24-1827 d 10-20-1827
    Aaron b 9-21-1829

Jonathan B h Matilda (**Pierce**)
Ch: Charlotte b 8-15-1836 Wayne Co
    Lucinda b 4-12-1839 Wayne Co

Joseph h Sarah b 4-13-1805 dt George & Rebecca **Hobson**

Mary Louise b 5-28-1880 Johnson Co KS dt Joseph R & Julia E (**Hendrix**)

Nathan H b 8-16-1811 Lost Creek TN s Wm & Hannah
Susannah L b 5-11-1809

MACY (Nathan H cont)
Ch: Wm Lewis b 10-21-1834 West River PM
    Mary Ann b 4-26-1836 West River PM
    Oliver Clinton b 11-12-1837 West River PM
    Thomas Colman b 8-10-1839 West River PM
    Hannah b 5-4-1841 d 9-28-1850 West River PM
    Margaret Melinda b 3-23-1844 West River PM d 9-21-1850

Perry b 8-19-1825 Springfield s Wm & Hannah
Charity b 4-4-1824
Ch: John Henry b 9-15-1849 d 2-28-1850
    Albert W b 1-18-1853

Reuben h Lucinda d 9-25-1867 ae 84y 11m 20d
Ch: Nancy
    Matilda d 4-29-1872

Wm West River b 10-4-1786
Hannah b 2-8-1789
Ch: Jonathan B b 3-7-1810 Lost Creek TN
    Nathan H b 8-16-1811 Lost Creek TN
    Alvah J b 2-25-1813 Lost Creek TN
    Elihu C b 12-25-1814 Lost Creek TN d 5-23-1816
    John H b 11-28-1816 Lost Creek TN
    Lucinda b 8-30-1818 Springfield
    Wm M b 3-8-1820 Springfield
    Margaret b 3-22-1822 Springfield
    Sarah b 11-3-1823 Springfield
    Perry b 8-19-1825 Springfield
    Ira b 5-28-1828 Springfield
    Ruth b l-9-1830 Springfield
    Mary Ann b 10-1-1831 Springfield
    Lydia b 4-16-1834 Springfield

Wm M b 3-8-1820 Springfield s Wm & Hannah
Julia Ann b 7-3-1829
Ch: Hannah M b 1-26-1853

MARKLE
John b 8-16-1830 Schuyler Co PA s Gideon & Anna (**Hart**)

MARSHALL
Aaron h Nancy dt Reuben & Lucinda **Macy**

John h Anne
Ch: Elizabeth b 7-24-1811 NC
    Stephen b 6-17-1813 NC
    Rachel b 9-22-18l4 NC
    Wm b 11-28-1818 NC
    Evan b 5-25-1821 IN
    Joshua b 6-26-1823 IN d 12-18-1828
    John b 7-6-1830 IN

Miles b 3-18-1789 s Thomas & Ann d 4-19-1868
Martha b 3-14-1793 dt Jesse & Hannah **Jones**
Ch: Thomas b 12-8-1811 TN
    Mitchel b 7-19-1813 TN d 3-11-1846
    Myra b 11-13-1815 White Water
    Mahon b 9-21-1817 Springfield
    Minerva b 2-16-1820 Springfield
    Margaret Ann b 6-11-1822 Springfield d 10-4-1823
    Calvin b 8-22-1824 Springfield
    Collin b 10-17-1826 Springfield
    Miles C b 9-18-1830 Springfield
    Martha Jane b 8-3-1832 Springfield

Orlando b 7-31-1847 s Thomas & Cynthia (**Swain**)
Matilda (**Macy**) m 8-21-1869 Wayne Co
Ch: Luella b 9-16-1873
    Vernon

Stephen b 6-17-1813 NC s John & Anne
Gulana b 10-4-1814

SPRINGFIELD MONTHLY MEETING
BIRTH AND DEATH RECORD

MARSHALL (Stephen cont)
Ch: Mary Ann b 9-20-1833
    Elizabeth b 6-9-1836
    Rhoda b 4-17-1838
    Amelia H b 10-16-1839
    John Elliott b 7-4-1841
    Wm b 8-3-1843
    Jacob b 9-22-1845

Susannah b 7-15-1786

Swain b 10-18-1839 s Thomas & Cynthia (**Swain**)
Cynthia b 3-11-1847 dt Elihu & Mary (**Worth**) Swain d 3-8-1874 bur Dexter IA m 3-4-1871
Ch: Thomas Worth b 3-24-1872
    Harry Swain b 2-28-1874
Lucinda 2w b 4-25-1832 dt Elihu & Mary (**Worth**) Swain m 10-23-1875

Thomas b 2-7-1782 s Thomas & Ann d 8-25-1856
Hannah (**Elliott**) b 2-1783 d 2-7-1851
Ch: Wm b 1-21-1809
    Miles b 9-13-1811
    Osce Ann b 6-5-1814
    Rueben b 12-3-1817
    Betsey b 3-4-1822 d 7-11-1843 bur Nettle Creek
    Rebeckah b 3-4-1822 Wayne Co bur Nettle Creek

Thomas b 12-8-1811 s Miles & Martha (**Jones**)
Cynthia b 1-22-1813 dt Silvanus & Rhoda (**Worth**) Swain d 1-31-1851 m 11-3-1833
Ch: Clayton b 8-31-1835
    Rhoda b 7-21-1837
    Swain b 10-18-1839
    Alonzo b 2-20-1842
    Orlando b 7-31-1847
Elvira 2w b 5-6-1830 Wayne Co dt Isaac & Eleanor (**Thornburg**) **Macy** m 3-19-1854
Ch: Cynthia Ellen b 1-19-1855
    Elmer Ellsworth b 3-21-1861

Wm b 11-28-1818 NC s John & Anne
Keziah b 5-18-1818 dt John & Ruth **Davis**
Ch: Mary b 2-10-1839

MARTIN
Joseph C s Squire & Mary (**Crow**)
Malinda (**Hodgin**) m 1-26-1873 Randolph Co

MASSEY
Betsey Ann d 10-15-1829

MAULSBY
Benjamin s John & Elizabeth h Rhoda
Ch: Rachel Melvina b 12-29-1839

David b 1-1-1788
Mary b 12-17-1788
Ch: Wm b 2-27-1810
    Lucinda b 1-14-1812
    John b 11-9-1814
    Macy B b 12-12-1817
    Ira b 5-15-1819
    Malinda b 5-20-1822
    Lydia b 11-1-1825
    Ezra b 4-3-1828
    Matilda b 12-19-1830

James b 12-15-1812
Ruth b 10-77-1809
Ch: Delphina b 5-14-1832 d 8-16-1833
    Silas B b 2-23-1835

MAULSBY (cont)
Macy B b 2-12-1817 s David & Mary
Sally P b 11-11-1820 d 11-3-1851

Milton b 2-19-1841

Richard J b 12-12-1847 Randolph Co s Thomas & Mary
Ellen E w b 6-7-1852 Randolph Co dt Wm & Nancy **Hunt** m 1-7-1870
Ch: Thomas M b 11-21-1872 Randolph Co
    Mary E b l-7-1871 Randolph Co
    Oliver E b 12-9-1877 Randolph Co
    Wm O b 7-28-1884 Randolph Co

Thomas b 8-7-1829 s John

MEDLER
Ruth b 11-13-1886 Randolph Co dt Joshua & Mary (**Howell**)

MELBERT
Michael b 5-14-1843 Darmstadt Germany s John & Catherine
Phillipena b 6-24-1842 Darmstadt Germany dt Phillip & Elizabeth **Cramer** m 6-14-1866
Ch: Anna b 7-22-1869 Lancaster Co PA/Wayne Co
    Charles b 8-8-1873 Lancaster Co PA
    Blanche b 3-25-1886 Henry Co
    Edgar b 3-25-1886

MENDENHALL
Aaron b 10-17-1797 d 1-20-1835 bur West River
Mary (**Hockett**) b 11-1-1800 d 3-28-1878 bur Nettle Creek
Ch: Miles b 4-25-1821 d 5-23-1880 Cherry Grove MM Henry Co
    Nathan b 2-18-1823
    Silas b 1-21-1825
    Martha b 8-25-1827 Henry Co

A G h Phebe (**Oler**)
Ch: Newman S b 7-31-1873 Wayne Co
    Clara b 7-21-1875 Wayne Co
    Charles b 9-27-1878 Wayne Co

Elijah b 2-6-1797
Huldah (**Coffin**) b 6-6-1799 bur Springfield
Ch: Joseph C b 2-10-1818
    Daniel b 12-12-1819
    Anderton b 6-26-1823 d 6-20-1836
    Brooks J b 6-3-1825 d 7-16-1843
    Wm H b 9-6-1827 d 9-12-1845 bur Jefferson Co IA
    Paris b 7-27-1833 d 7-22-1834
    Cyrus b 1-27-1834
    Hannah C b 8-17-1837
    Barnabas C b 12-27-1843 d 10-17-1844
    Jonathan C b 10-4-1845

Isaac h Rachel b 3-9-1822 dt Isaac & Mary (**Mendenhall**) **Brown**
Ch: Viretta
    Eliza Ann
    Luella
    Valentine M
    Alma

James b 12-21-1792
Mary b 2-4-1791 d 12-5-1853

Jesse W b 7-27-1851 Henry Co s Miles & Cynthia (**Dennis**)
Lucy Ann b 8-20-1856 Wayne Co dt Benjamin & Anna **Conley** m 9-11-1873
Ch: Clyde b 6-17-1880 Wayne Co

Lindley H b 12-15-1856 Henry Co s Miles & Cynthia (**Dennis**)
Mary E b 2-10-1857 Wayne Co dt Wm & Fanny (**Stantz**) **Young** m 3-29-1878

MENDENHALL (Lindley H cont)
Ch: James b 4-23-1881 Henry Co
　　Leora b 4-18-1886 Antelope Co NE
　　Ralph b 3-8-1894 Henry Co

Margaret C b 1-9-1812 Guilford Co NC dt Isaiah & Christiana

Miles b 4-25-1821 Cherry Grove MM Henry Co s Aaron & Mary (**Hockett**) d 5-23-1880
Cynthia b 3-21-1820 Randolph Co NC dt Thomas & Elizabeth (**Wilson**) **Dennis** d 10-16-1892 bur Nettle Creek m 10-21-1841 Wayne Co
Ch: Wilson D b 9-29-1842 Henry Co
　　Mary b 7-11-1845 Henry Co d 2-13-1847 bur Nettle Creek
　　Eliza b 1-17-1848 Henry Co d 5-19-1848 bur Nettle Creek
　　Wm D b 5-28-1849 Henry Co d 10-9-1850 bur Nettle Creek
　　Jesse W b 7-27-1851 Henry Co
　　Martha E b 5-9-1854 Henry Co
　　Lindley H b 12-15-1856 Henry Co
　　Esther Carter b 3-8-1861 Henry Co

Newman S b 7-31-1873 s A G & Phebe (**Oler**)
Luella b 9-16-1873 dt Orlando & Matilda **Marshall** m 10-14-1897 Wayne Co
Ch: Hazel Ellen b 8-3-1898

Rufus A b 1-17-1837 Wayne Co s Wm & Rebecca (**Coffin**) d 12-20-1884 bur Nettle Creek
Emaline b 12-17-1846 Miami Co dt Jesse & Jane **Bond** m 7-30-1863 Miami Co
Ch: Esther L Carter b 12-21-1871

Wm b 9-7-1798 s Daniel & Deborah
Rebecca b 11-13-1801 dt Joseph & Hannah **Coffin** d 10-2-1886 bur West River m 4-8-1819
Ch: Oliver b 1-26-1820
　　Melinda b 5-26-1821 Deep River MM Guilford Co NC
　　Adaline b 9-27-1823
　　Eliza b 2-15-1825
　　Huldah b 12-12-1826
　　Mary Ann b 2-6-1829 Wayne Co
　　Milacent b 3-1-1832
　　Esther b 12-4-1834
　　Rufus A b 1-17-1837 Wayne Co d 12-20-1884 bur Nettle Creek
　　Martitia b 5-1-1839
　　Wm H b 11-13-1841

Wm H b 11-13-1841 Wm & Rebecca (**Coffin**)
Eunice R b 11-21-1842
Ch: Schuyler b 11-25-1862
　　Addison b 6-21-1864

Wilson D b 9-29-1842 Henry Co s Miles & Cynthia (**Dennis**)
Martha Ann b 9-19-1839 Wayne Co dt Isaac & Lavina (**Puckett**) **Reynolds**
Ch: Albert J b 3-21-1869 Henry Co d 4-10-1869
　　Myra R b 5-31-1870 Henry Co

MEREDITH
Isaac H b 12-15-1866 Highland Co OH s Elwood & Elizabeth (**Jones**)
Sarah Bell b 11-11-1867 Henry Co dt Allenson & Angeline (**Conway**) **Frazier** m 8-12-1893 Henry Co
Ch: Basil F b 6-18-1896 Randolph Co
　　Edith L b 10-22-1898 Hancock Co

MILLIKEN
Wm b 9-12-1805
Charity b 9-6-1809 d 10-3-1839 bur Flat Rock
Ch: John b 3-17-1831 Flat Rock
　　Charles b 1-8-1833 Flat Rock
　　Mary E b 10-8-1835 Flat Rock d 1-16-1842

MILLIKEN (Wm cont)
　　Sarah E b 10-8-1835 Flat Rock d 11-24-1842
　　Almeda b 11-19-1838 Flat Rock
2w
Ch: Esther b 4-4-1841
　　Eli F b 8-17-1843
　　Thomas K b 6-26-1846
　　Rebecca Jane b 12-12-1848
　　Wm M b 6-20-1851

MILLS
Benoni h Mary d 8-9-1834 ae 69y

Cassius C b 9-24-1861 Lynn Randolph Co s Joel & Cynthia Ella (**Lumpkin**) m 9-19-1888

Charity d 2-19-1836 ae 82y 1m

Daniel h Elizabeth b 5-25-1788 d 9-13-1843
Ch: Sarrah b 11-22-1810 Lost Creek TN
　　Thomas b 1-24-1813 Lost Creek TN
　　Annis b 11-26-1814 Lost Creek TN
　　Lavinia b 1-3-1817
　　Elijah b 8-26-1819
　　Elizabeth b 9-27-1821
　　Jemima b 2-11-1824
　　Daniel b 1-17-1828

Henry h Hannah
Ch: Josiah b 11-1-1811
　　Anna M b 2-6-1814
　　Wm C b 5-8-1816
　　Betsey Jane b 1-25-1819
　　Aaron b 12-26-1821
　　Charity b 4-4-1824
　　Emily b 2-3-1827
　　Juliann b 7-3-1829

Hugh h Jamima
Ch: Phebe b 5-27-1828 d 9-5-1833
　　Charity b 10-5-1829
　　Hannah b 3-20-1832 d 8-25-1833
　　Elizabeth b 1-20-1834

John b 9-4-1778 d 9-12-1824
Mary b 8-13-1785
Ch: Jane b 7-8-1804 Jefferson Co Tn d 9-24-1880 bur West River
　　Seth b 10-3-1805
　　Betsey Ann b 2-28-1807
　　Charity b 9-3-1808
　　Aaron b 2-5-1810
　　Kerenhappock b 4-4-1812
　　Miles b 3-12-1815 [sic] d 5-31-1814
　　Annamariah b 5-5-1815
　　Sarrah b 9-7-1817
　　John D b 10-19-1819
　　Ira b 9-20-1821
　　Elihue b 11-15-1823

John h Mary b 1-14-1837 dt Mordecai & Ruth (**Hinshaw**) **Ellis**

John B b 10-4-1827
Jane b 5-23-1830
Ch: Moses Albert b 11-15-1851
　　Henry Irwin b 1-15-1854
　　Martha E b 5-18-1858 d 2-9-1859
　　Austin b 1-20-1861

John D b 10-19-1819 s John & Mary
Huldah b 12-12-1826 dt Wm & Rebecca (**Coffin**) **Mendenhall**
Ch: Lorinda b 5-11-1844
　　Martitia b 2-11-1847

SPRINGFIELD MONTHLY MEETING
BIRTH AND DEATH RECORD

MILLS (John D cont)
    Wm b 8-15-1849
    Alonzo b 1-25-1852
    Elihu b 4-23-1854
    Millicent M b 4-25-1857 Wayne Co
    Mary Jane b 4-17-1861
    Arthur B

Moses b 12-4-1787 d 4-14-1828
Elizabeth b 3-12-1792 d 6-2-1877

Oliver b 6-20-1823

Richard b 9-13-1783 h Nancy
Ch: Elizabeth b 3-13-1811
    Jemima b 9-22-1812
    Rachel b 5-21-1814
    Polly b 8-6-1817
    Hester Ann b 5-12-1818
    Nancy M b 6-5-1820
    Anna b 9-10-1822
    Richard b 8-23-1824 d 1-11-1844
    Sarah b 5-21-1827
    Ruth b 2-5-1830
    Dorinda Abigail b 7-17-1833
    Adila b 7-11-1832

Seth h Charity - removed to AR
Ch: Aaron L b 11-19-1812
    Kinsey M b 5-13-1814 d 6-16-1834
    Enos b 2-29-1816
    Henry b 5-22-1817
    Sally b 10-8-1819
    Jacob b 2-6-1822
    Seth b 2-2-1824
    Rachel b 3-1-1826
    Lettie b 12-20-l829
    John Kindley b 12-29-1830 d 3-2-1832
    Betsey Ann b d 10-15-1829
    Lucinda b 3-4-1834

MODLIN
Mahlon b 1-28-1837 Wayne Co
Margaret b 1-4-1840 Wayne Co dt Michael & Eliza **Crull** m 8-25-1860
Ch: Nathan L b 1-18-1863 Wayne Co
    Clara Viola b 4-28-1864 Wayne Co
    Laura E b 1-29-1866 Wayne Co
    Eliza Jane b 9-8-1868 Wayne Co
    Sarah E b 7-12-1873 Wayne Co
    John Sherman b 8-29-1879 Wayne Co

Wm b 8-27-1806 Guilford Co NC d 12-6-1881 bur West River
Mildred B b 7-24-1810 Guilford Co NC dt Isaac & Hannah **Beeson** d 9-16-1882 bur West River
Ch: Calvin W b 11-1-1832 d 6-20-1850 bur West River
    Nathan H b 10-17-1834 d 11-28-1858 bur West River
    Mahlon b 1-28-1837
    Martha Ann b 12-31-1839 Wayne Co
    Louisa b 3-10-1841
    Hannah b 6-22-1843
    Jehu b 6-4-1845 d 7-7-1845 bur West River
    Lydia B b 3-31-1847 d 12-22-1853 bur West River
    Jonathan b 5-8-1849 d 8-15-1850 bir West River
    Rachel N b 10-27-1851

MOORE
Anderson b 8-31-1803
Lydia b 7-17-1800
Ch: Alice b 1-23-1830 d 10-27-1849
    Eli 3-9-1832
    Martha Ann b 10-13-1834

MOORE (cont)
Exelina b 1-3-1820 dt Alice

Squire h Louisa dt Isaac K & Rebecca (**Lamb**) **Beeson**
Alice 2w b 10-27-1837 dt Isaac K & Rebecca (**Lamb**) **Beeson**

MORAN
Michael h Bertha M b 3-6-1878 dt Wm B & Mary E (**Millikan**) **Healton** m Wayne Co

MORGAN
Rueben d 12-13-1821 bur Springfield

MORRISON
Charles A b 11-10-1859 s Joseph & Margaret (**Oler**)

MOYSTNER
Jeremiah b 4-15-1867 s Daniel & Maria (**Arnold**)
Clella L b 11-29-1873 dt Behan T & Mary Elizabeth (**Baldwin**)
Julian m 1-15-1891 Randolph Co
Ch: Bertha b 11-24-1895
    Gladis Maud

MULLEN
Merritt B b 6-17-1850 Wayne Co s Josiah & Elizabeth (**Baldwin**)
Mary C b 8-6-1858 Wayne Co dt Elim & Mary (**Cook**) **Johnson**
m 10-6-1891 Wayne Co

MURPHY
Wm h Mary
Ch: Anna b 4-21-1830
    Rachel

MURRAY
Cornelius h Lucinda
Ch: Martha b 3-13-1844 Henry Co
    Julia A b 2-18-1859 Henry Co

NICHOLSON
George b 4-1-1814 Suttons Creek MM Perquimans Co NC s Nathan & Penina (**Parker**) d 8-20-1896 bur Nettle Creek
Lucinda b 1-14-1816 Randolph Co NC dt Thomas & Elizabeth (**Wilson**) **Dennis** d 8-31-1893 bur Nettle Creek m 8-1-1838 Wayne Co
Ch: Mary E b 10-5-1839 Henry Co
    Elizabeth D b 8-27-1841 Henry Co
    Penninah b 11-24-1843 Henry Co d 3-7-1870
    Thomas D b 4-28-1846 Henry Co d 9-29-1876 bur Nettle Creek
    Henry P b 9-23-1849 Henry Co

Henry P b 9-23-1849 Henry Co s George & Lucinda (**Dennis**)
h Lucinda (**Lamb**) m 7-14-1870
Ch: Oliver b 6-1-1871
    Olinda C b1-5-1872
    Mary Alma b 7-31-1875

Thomas D b 4-28-1846 Henry Co s George & Lucinda (**Dennis**) d 9-29-1876 bur Nettle Creek
Mary E b 12-2-1845 dt John & Elvira **Macy** d 12-1-1875 bur Nettle Creek
Ch: Leora Estella b 7-24-1871 Wayne Co
    Macy b 10-20-1874 Wayne Co

NOBLETT
Thomas Monroe b 3-8-1871 s John & Zilpha
Marcella b 11-20-1872 dt John & Sinia Esther (**Money**) **Cook**
m 9-10-1898 Grayson Co VA

OFTERDENGER
Hannah b 1-16-1818

OSBORN
Charles b 8-21-1775 Guilford Co NC s Daniel & Margaret (**Stout**)
Sarah (**Newman**) b VA d 8-10-1812 m 1-11-1798
Ch: James b 11-10-1798
    Josiah b 3-2-1800
    Jehu b 11-28-1801
    Isaiah b 11-25-1803
    Lydia b 10-6-1805
    Elijah b 11-15-1807
    Elihu b 2-9-1810
Hannah 2w dt Elihu & Sarah (**Mills**) **Swain** m 9-16-1813
Ch: Narcissa b 6-20-1814
    Cynthia b 9-30-1815
    Gideon S b 8-12-1817
    Charles N b 9-20-1819
    Parker B b 10-14-1821
    Jordan b 8-6-1823
    Benjamin b 11-21-1825
    Sarah S b 2-21-1828
    Anna b 8-20-1830

Charles W b 2-8-1833 Wayne Co s Isaiah & Lydia (**Worth**)
Asenath W b 11-20-1838 Wayne Co dt Jacob & Phebe (**Pickering**) **Wood** m 3-25-1858
Ch: Arthur Wendell b 1-7-1859 Wayne Co
    Daniel Worth b 10-19-1860 Wayne Co
    Laura C b 6-4-1865 d 1-26-1877
    Edgar C b 10-25-1872
    Wm E b 6-23-1876 Wayne/Randolph Co
    Caroline b 6-23-1876 d 6-23-1876

Edmund B b 11-4-1836 Wayne Co s Isaiah & Lydia (**Worth**)
Mary E (**Rinehart**) d 10-25-1896 m 12-12-1867
Ch: Charles Austin b 5-14-1869 Wayne Co
    Eldora Lydia b 3-25-1871 Wayne Co

Elim b 12-16-1838 Wayne Co s John & Rachel (**Johnson**)
Agnes b 1-26-1845 Porter Co dt Samuel R & Jane (**Turner**)
Patterson m 1-4-1862
Ch: Frank b Wayne Co
    Ethel b Wayne Co
    Daisy Mabel b 10-4-1883 Wayne Co

Frank b Wayne Co s Elim & Agnes (**Patterson**) h Romania **Mendenhall**

Isaiah b 11-25-1803 s Charles & Sarah (**Newman**)
Lydia (**Worth**) b 11-1-1805
Ch: Caroline b 2-4-1831
    Charles W b 2-8-1833 Wayne Co
    Rhoda b 12-7-1834 d 9-9-1859
    Edmund B b 11-4-1836 Wayne Co
    Laurinda b 10-1-1838
    Narcissa b 10-30-1840
    Martha W b 2-15-1843 d 3-31-1848
    Eunice b 5-4-1845 d 4-7-1848

John s Charles & Sarah d 5-2-1874 ae 72y 5m 4d
Rachel b 8-22-1816 dt Josiah & Polly **Johnson** d 2-16-1895
Ch: Elim b 12-16-1838 Wayne Co
    Josiah d 10-17-1892 ae 46y 3m 28d

Josiah b 3-2-1800 s Charles & Sarah (**Newman**)
Mary b 10-19-1800
Ch: Elison b 10-30-1821
    Jefferson b 1-2-1824
    Leander b 12-27-1825
    Obed b 6-18-1828
    Louisa b 5-13-1830

Wm E b 6-23-1876 Wayne/Randolph Co s Charles W & Asenath W (**Wood**)

OSBORN (Wm E cont)
Achsah C b 1877 Wayne dt Francis & Martha (**Weyl**) **Cain** m 4-1896 Wayne Co
Ch: Eugene Field b 1898 Wayne Co
    Martha A b 11-5-1899 Henry Co

OUTLAND
Jesse b 2-6-1821 Northampton Co NC s Wm & Rachel
Elizabeth 2w b 6-21-1831 Guilford Co NC dt David & Rachel (**Wilson**) **Pidgeon** m 1-11-1877

OWEN
Eddie b 8-8-1862 s Nathan & Sarah (**Parker**)

PARKER
Elisha b 12-27-1833 Wayne Co s Nathan & Sarah d 3-10-1882 bur Nettle Creek h Elmina
Ch: John b 2-21-1864 Wayne Co
Mary E 2w b 10-5-1839 Henry Co dt George & Lucinda (**Dennis**) **Nicholson** wid Henry **Jessup** m 4-24-1867
Ch: Henry J b 6-15-1868
    Elmina b 3-27-1871
    Francis T b 4-8-1873 Wayne Co
    Ulysses b 8-16-1875
    Nathan Earl b 8-3-1880 Wayne Co
    George Irvin b 8-3-1880 Wayne Co

Nathan h Addie (**Catey**)
Ch: Lillian b 2-12-1880 Wayne Co
    Edith Lyle b 10-17-1885

Samuel J b 3-5-1845 Wayne Co s Samuel M & Eliza Jane (**Bond**)

PARSONS
George W h Priscilla R (**Matthews**)
Ch: Amos Walter b 6-30-1868 Wayne Co
    Florence Gertrude b 8-23-1878 Wayne Co
    Benjamin F b 2-20-1884 Wayne Co

PATTY
Clarkson b 9-22-1845
Ellen b 8-27-1846
Ch: Arthur A b 8-10-1863
    Mary E b 10-1-1866
    Oliver L b 1-30-1873

PAUL
Samuel h Mary Etta b 5-8-1869 Henry Co dt Amos & Esther Ann (**Hill**) **Davis**

PEAK
Charles h Mary E b 4-31-1873 Grant Co dt Alanson G & Sarah (**Brown**) **Woody** m 1-26-1891

PEARSON
Charles M h Katie Rachel (**Stubbs**)
Ch: Carrie b 8-2-1890 Blackford Co
    Esther b 7-27-1897 Boone Co

PECKINPAUGH
Clara Lula b 4-4-1883 dt Madison & Laverna

PEELLE
Edmund b 1-14-1823 s Robert & Phariba
Mary Jane b 10-5-1826 dt Jesse & Rachel **Ellis**
Ch: James R b 1-5-1850

PERRY
Albert Hockett b 12-15-1867 s John & Susan

PETTY
Annie b 3-26-1838 d 4-10-1876

SPRINGFIELD MONTHLY MEETING
BIRTH AND DEATH RECORD

PHILABAUM
James B b 1-7-1846 Montgomery Co s Daniel & Mariah
Sarah E b 6-30-1851 Wayne Co dt Urias & Ann **Staher**
Ch: Alonzo b 12-30-1871 Wayne Co

PHILLIPS
Charles b 3-9-1861 Wayne Co s Wm & Sophia
Martha Ann b 1-3-1866 Henry Co dt Andrew & Eunice (**Coffin**) **Baldwin**
Ch: Freddie A b 6-11-1885 Wayne Co d 6-15-1885 bur Nettle Creek
    Alta b 5-1-1877 Wayne Co

PICKERING
Samuel b 11-30-1807
Cynthia b 11-23-1808
Ch: Macy b 6-10-1842

PIDGEON
Charles C b 2-7-1834 Henry Co s David & Rachel (**Wilson**)
Emeline b 6-11-1858 Randolph Co dt Jackson & Martha A **Howell**
m 8-11-1881
Ch: Wm Harlan b 12-2-1884 Henry Co d 12-20-1886 bur Nettle Creek
    Mary Alice b 11-30-1886 Henry Co d 7-10-1887 bur Nettle Creek
    Lydia Ethel b 11-23-1887 Henry Co
    Benjamin Harrison b 1-28-1892 Henry Co

David b 9-23-1802 d 5-6-1874
Rachel (**Wilson**) b 4-21-1802 d 10-31-1865
Ch: Jesse W b 12-1-1827 Dover MM NC
    Wm C b 9-11-1829 Dover MM NC d 3-5-1844 bur Nettle Creek
    Elizabeth b 6-21-1831 Guilford Co NC
    Charles C b 2-7-1834 Henry Co
    Lucinda b 5-24-1837 Henry Co
    Isaac W b 6-14-1839
    Miriam C b 7-3-1844
Hannah 2w b 8-20-1812 Guilford Co NC dt Michael & Mary **Stanley** d 11-31-1882 bur Nettle Creek

David L b 4-2-1857 Henry Co s Jesse W & Mary (**Chamness**) h Lizzie (**Hardman**)

Isaac W b 6-14-1839 s David & Rachel (**Wilson**) h Elizabeth
Ch: Mary Alice b 3-24-1866
    Albert Lindley b 10-14-1867

Jesse W b 12-1-1827 Dover MM NC s David & Rachel (**Wilson**) d 3-5-1885
Mary b 12-3-1831 Center MM Randolph Co dt Joshua & Hannah (**Chamness**) **Chamness** m 12-19-1849
Ch: Elizabeth b 9-27-1850 Henry Co d 12-7-1868 bur Nettle Creek
    Martha Ann b 8-28-1852 Henry Co
    Wm C b 3-22-1855 Henry Co
    David L b 4-2-1857 Henry Co
    Isabel C b 6-6-1859 Henry Co
    Wilson b 9-10-1862 Henry Co
    Ellen b 5-20-1866 Henry Co
    John Henry b 1-2-1872 Henry Co

John Henry b 1-2-1872 Henry Co s Jesse W & Mary (**Chamness**)
Levine b 6-1-1872 dt Amos & Esther Ann (**Hill**) **Davis** m 6-15-1892 Henry Co

Wilson b 9-10-1862 Henry Co s Jesse W & Mary (**Chamness**) h Florene (**Marshall**)
Margaret (**Gable**) 2w

Wm C b 3-22-1855 Henry Co s Jesse W & Mary (**Chamness**) h Carrie (**Benedict**)
Ch: Edna Theresa b 4-18-1883

PIERCE
Elizabeth b 12-3-1803 d 5-16-1847

Exalina b 1-3-1820 dt Lydia

John b 6-25-1788 d 6-4-1873
Anna b 1-5-1795
Ch: Jamima b 7-14-1812
    Ruth b 4-13-1814 d 9-17-1824
    Matilda Osborn b 9-22-1816
    Charlotte D b 1-29-1819 d 10-12-1822 bur Springfield
    Daniel b 9-12-1821 d 10-27-1822
    Susannah b 8-23-1823
    Armina b 7-24-1826
    Delila b 1-4-1828 d 6-6-1831
    John Wilson b 2-21-1831
    Jonathan Lewis b 11-13-1833
    Moses b 12-12-1836
    Stephen J b 9-9-1838

PITMAN
Frank A b 5-5-1881 Wayne Co s Morris & Nancy J (**Smith**)

PITTS
Mary b 2-16-1800 dt Wm & Isabel (**Beeson**) **Chamness** d 12-5-1871

POTTER
Stephen h Keziah d 12-6-1826
Ch: Elizabeth b 10-18-1819 d 12-16-1826
    Jehiel W b 4-13-1822
    Benjamin P b 12-30-1824
    Hezekiah b 9-18-1826
Phebe 2w
Ch: Isaac B b 1-26-1831
    Martha b 6-13-1833

RAKESTRAW
Samuel A b 9-18-1852 Clark Co OH

RATLIFF
Elias b 1-27-1807 s Job & Tamar
Achsah b 10-24-1804
Ch: Eli b 6-21-1829

Isaac b 2-6-1820 s Job & Tamar
Huldah b 10-5-1820
Ch: Mary Elizabeth b 11-8-1842 Westbury PM
    Wm Elias b 1-28-1845 Westbury PM
    Jemima b Westbury PM

Isom b 1-7-1846 Henry Co s Elias & Miriam (**Bogue**)
Sarah Etta b 5-27-1869 Howard Co dt Elnathan & Susanna (**Finch**) **Larrowe** m 6-23-1897 Henry Co

Job h Tamar b 8-3-1780
Ch: Elias b 1-27-1807
    Mary b 7-2-1817
    Isaac b 3-6-1820
    Sarah b 8-12-1825 d 5-17-1848
    Elizabeth b 10-13-1822

Thomas h Susannah b 5-11-1804
Ch: Wm b 3-20-1827
    Stephen T b 10-17-1828 d 11-18-1828
    Mary Ann b 9-21-1829
    John b 1-5-1832
    George b 3-18-1834

RETZ
Frank h Emma Florence b 4-15-1876 Wayne Co dt Joseph L & Pheraby (**Daniels**) **Harter** m 7-7-1895

REYNOLDS
Anthony b 7-31-1769 d 11-30-1852 bur Nettle Creek
Elizabeth b 12-19-1767 d 11-4-1842 bur Nettle Creek
Ch: Isaac b 9-26-1795 NC d 5-2-1860 bur Nettle Creek
    Rachel b 9-5-1797 NC
    Susannah b 9-12-1799 NC d 8-18-1838 bur West River
    Mary b 4-1-1802 NC
    Levi b 3-22-1805 NC
    Sarah b 10-20-1807 NC d 9-7-1830 bur West River
    Ruth b 3-20-1810 NC

Edwin b 11-4-1834 Wayne Co s Isaac & Sarah (**Hinshaw**)
Phebe Jane b 8-23-1842 d 11-2-1875
Ch: Martha A b 7-15-1811 Wayne Co
Elmira (**Star**) 2w m 4-1-1877

Elijah b 4-25-1800 - removed to Miami Co 1835
Deborah b 4-5-1805
Ch: Azariah b 9-10-1825
    Ebenezer b 3-29-1827 d 12-13-1833
    Nancy Ann b 8-5-1829 d 8-21-1834
    Sarrah Jane b 8-12-1831
    Rachel Demaris b 10-31-1833

Ezra b 2-10-1809
Mary b 9-12-1810 dt Abraham & Rachel (**Reynard**) **Wrightsman** d 7-3-1837 bur West River
Ch: Rachel b 1-19-1829
    Jane b 11-22-1830
    John b 10-7-1832 d 12-17-1832
    Isaac b 10-7-1832 d 12-17-1832
    Zimri b 11-5-1834
    Mary b 6-26-1837

Harvey b 1-13-1858 Wayne Co s Isaac & Levina H (**Puckett**)
Cynthia E b 4-14-1861 Wayne Co dt David E & Ruth (**Howell**) **Baldwin** m 1-17-1885
Ch: Nellie b 11-8-1885 Wayne Co
    Isaac Herbert b 10-15-1887 Randolph Co
    Bertha F b 3-10-1891 Wayne Co

Henry Lindley b 11-20-1852 s Isaac & Levina H (**Puckett**) h Josie (**Hockett**)

Isaac b 9-26-1795 s Anthony & Elizabeth d 5-2-1860 bur Nettle Creek
Tamar b 2-19-1802 dt John **Hawkins** d 11-27-1864
Ch: Lydia b 7-5-1831 Wayne Co
    Sarah b 11-15-1832 d 2-29-1844 bur Nettle Creek
    Anna b 3-22-1835
    Amos b 4-1-1837 d 4-3-1837 bur Nettle Creek
    John b 6-18-1838 d 2-25-1844 bur Nettle Creek
    Elizabeth b 7-13-1841 d 4-16-1860 bur Nettle Creek
    Wilson b 10-2-1843 Wayne Co

Isaac b 1-24-1805 s Francis & Margaret
Sarah (**Hinshaw**) m 3-15-1827 Marlborough MM NC
Ch: Clarkson b 7-7-1828
    Milton b 12-18-1829
    Francis b 2-8-1832
    Edwin b 11-4-1834 Wayne Co
Levina H 2w b 12-15-1814 dt Daniel & Celia **Puckett**
Ch: Albert b 10-8-1837 d 2-3-1865
    Martha Ann b 9-19-1839 Wayne Co
    Julia Ann b 4-11-1845 Wayne Co
    Mary Ellen b d 11-15-1875
    Henry Lindley b 11-20-1852
    Harvey b 1-13-1858 Wayne Co

Jesse W b 10-21-1855 Henry Co s Milo & Mary (**Chamness**) h Rachel A (**Metsker**)

REYNOLDS (cont)
Levi b 3-22-1805 NC s Anthony & Elizabeth - removed to La Porte Co
Hannah b 2-13-1808
Ch: Thomas C b 6-16-1827 Springfield
    Maria Jane b 2-19-1829 Springfield

Milo b 10-27-1823 Center MM Randolph Co NC s Wenlock & Susanna (**Lee**) d 2-4-1892 bur Nettle Creek
Mary b 11-20-1833 Center MM Randolph Co NC dt Jesse & Ruth (**Woody**) **Chamness** bur Nettle Creek m 11-22-1854
Ch: Jesse b 10-21-1855 Henry Co
    Wenlock b 3-22-1857 Henry Co
    Isaac b 4-30-1860 d 10-11-1861
    Ruth b 4-30-1860 Henry Co
    Susannah b 4-3-1862
    Isobel b 3-7-1864 d 4-25-1893 bur Nettle Creek
    Asenath C b 3-7-1866 Henry Co
    Daniel W b 2-7-1869
    Mary Ellen b 4-22-1872
    Cyrus Lindley b 2-29-1876

Wenlock b 3-22-1857 Henry Co s Milo & Mary (**Chamness**)
Rebecca Ellen (**Poer**) b 6-10-1855 m Henry Co

Wilson b 10-2-1843 Wayne Co s Isaac & Tamar (**Hawkins**)
Elizabeth D b 8-27-1841 Hnery Co dt George & Lucinda (**Dennis**) **Nicholson** m 2-14-1867 Wayne Co

RICH
Everett h Nellie dt John & Mary A (**Locke**) **Thornburg**

RICHWINE
Wesley h Anna b 7-22-1869 Lancaster Co PA dt Michael & Philapena (**Cramer**) **Melbert** m 8-25-1896 div

RIGGLE
Lucy A b 2-9-1831 Clinton Co OH dt Alvis & Elizabeth
Ch: Sarah E b 6-6-1853 Dayton OH

RITTENHOUSE
Wm Walter b 10-13-1857 Ross Co OH s Levi & Nancy
Marietta b 9-15-1866 Schuyler Co IL dt Calvin & Sarah E (**Julian**) **Baldwin** m 6-10-1882 Wayne Co

ROBOSON
James C b 9-18-1842
Sina b 8-10-1843
Ch: Margaret Ellen b 11-2-1866
    Wm Lewis b 2-28-1868 d 4-3-1868
    Ida Jane b 5-3-1869
    John Franklin b 2-25-1872

ROGERS
George h Eva (**Coates**)
Ch: John Ores
    Roscoe
    Paul
    Franz

ROOT
Wm M h Clara B (**Keever**) m Wayne Co
Ch: Everett E b 12-23-1884 Wayne Co
    John Carl b 3-15-1890

ROUTH
Anna Miller b 5-29-1895 dt Alvis & Laura (**Bobo**)

Joseph E h Zarilda Ann b 10-28-1828 dt Dempsey & Jane (**Mills**) **Thornburg** wid Ezra **Lee**
Ch: Cynthia E b 5-26-1858
    Lizzie Etta b 3-13-1860 Wayne Co

SPRINGFIELD MONTHLY MEETING
BIRTH AND DEATH RECORD

SANDERS
Emma J b 5-13-1898

Joseph M b 11-29-1849 Henry Co s Wright & Carolina (**Ratliff**) d 5-2-1893 bur Nettle Creek h Althea
Ch: Frankie L b 11-23-1877 Henry Co
Mary H 2w b 5-11-1848 Wayne Co dt Nathan & Malinda (**Hinshaw**) **Baldwin**

Seth O b 2-4-1883

SCANTLAND
Elmer s George W & Anna (**Hollingsworth**) h Mary Jane b 3-8-1861 Randolph Co dt John Thomas & Jane (**Charles**) **Hunnicutt** m 2-20-1882 Wayne Co
Ch: Edith May b 12-16-1886 Butler Co NE

George W b 6-18-1831 Culpepper Co VA s George W & Catherine (**Burdett**)
Anna b 4-16-1834/35 dt Henry & Hannah **Hollingsworth**
Ch: Aurie b 11-20-1856
    Elmer
    E Josephine

SCHELL
Wm h Hannah dt Samuel **Pierce**
Ch: David R b 10-8-1867 Laura OH
    Henry Alvador b 8-7-1867 [sic] Wayne Co
    John Franklin b 4-27-1873 Wayne Co
    Clarkson E b 4-2-1876 Wayne Co
    Harry Morton b 5-20-1880 Wayne Co
    Wm H b 2-10-1885 Wayne Co

SCHENCK
Murray h Cordelia b 12-3-1863 Wayne Co dt Rufus & Margaret (**Stubbs**) **Test** m 6-26-1895

SCHWENNESSON
Jacob h Lucinda b Wayne Co dt Phillip & Rachel (**Cox**) **Replogle**

SEAGRAVE
Luther b 1-13-1880 s Tarver & Margaret (**Mulford**)

SHAFFER
Daniel h Sarah b 11-30-1830 Henry Co dt Elisha & Mariam **Ogle** m 4-20-1849
Ch: Elisha b 1-5-1857 Henry Co

Elisha b 1-5-1857 Henry Co s Daniel & Sarah (**Ogle**)
Laura Bell (**Lucas**) b 9-1-1867
Ch: Maude E b 11-27-1884 Henry Co
    Guy M b 3-30-1886 Henry Co
    Frances C b 2-2-1888 Henry Co
    Flossie L b 12-16-1893 Henry Co
    Charley G b 10-4-1898 Henry Co

SHAWLEY
Daniel C b 11-17-1857 Wayne Co s George & Patience Ann h Rachel L (**Bunnell**) m 6-27-1897

SHEPARD
Rachel
Ch: Alvah C b 7-31-1874
    Alpha M b 7-31-1874

SHIELDS
Abraham Lincoln b 12-4-1864 Yadkin Co NC s Wm B & Joanna (**Daniels**)
Ophelia Troy b 10-4-1878 Delaware Co dt Elvira **Dowell** m 11-4-1894 Delaware Co
Ch: Leo Winston b 10-31-1895 Delaware Co
    Wilbur Branson b 2-18-1897 Delaware Co
    Gladys Merritt b 1-25-1899 Delaware Co

SHIELDS (cont)
Wm B b 4-8-1829 Guilford Co NC s Benjamin & Mary
Joanna b 6-24-1830 Surry Co NC dt Harrison & Pheriba **Daniels** m 1-29-1856
Ch: Martha Jane b 11-22-1856 Surry Co NC
    Julia F b 1-30-1858 Surry Co NC
    Levi L b 5-16-1861 d 8-22-1876 Davidson Co NC
    John B b 9-22-1862 Yadkin Co NC
    Abraham Lincoln b 12-4-1864 Yadkin Co NC
    Isaac F b 10-4-1866 Yadkin Co NC
    Rachel C b 4-22-1868 Wayne Co
    Sarah E b 6-4-1870 Montgomery Co MO
    Lenora A b 5-16-1872 Wayne Co
    Wm H b 2-28-1814 Wayne Co
    Ophelia Troy b 10-4-1878 Delaware Co

SHOEMAKER
Charles b 8-18-1818
Margaret Ann (**Ellis**) b 1-24-1819
Ch: Ezekiel b 10-2-1840
    Elijah b 10-3-1842
    Tacy b 11-11-1844
    Sophia b 9-11-1845
    Martha Ellen b 6-23-1847 d 5-16-1849
    Thomas Ellis b 9-2-1849

SICKLES
Peter E b 11-20-1859 Henry Co s Cornelius & Sophia (**Niccum**)

SIGGERFOOSE
Cynthia b 9-30-1815 dt Charles & Hannah (**Swain**) **Osborn**

SMILEY
George h Mary Hannah b 10-11-1844 dt Isaac K & Rebecca (**Lamb**) **Beeson**

SMITH
Abraham h Mary (**Barr**)
Ch: Jenettie b 4-15-1865 Wayne Co
    Adam Rinard b 11-3-1861 Wayne Co
    Clarence A b 12-21-1865 Wayne Co

Adam Rinard b 11-3-1861 Wayne Co s Abraham & Mary (**Barr**)
Flora B b 8-11-1869 Henry Co dt Richard & Polly Emily (**Pitts**) **Shepherd** m 4-29-1888

Anna L b 1-28-1876 Wayne Co dt John & Caroline (**Chamness**)

Arthur h Mary Evaline b 12-12-1868 Randolph Co dt Osborn & Louisa (**Canaday**) **Dennis**

Clarence A b 12-21-1865 Wayne Co s Abraham & Mary (**Barr**)
Mary E b 9-22-1864 Wayne Co dt Freeman & Dinah (**Hinshaw**) **Nelson** m 2-14-1890 Wayne Co
Ch: Omer F b 8-30-1891 Wayne Co
    Bertha M b 12-11-1893 Wayne Co
    Nellie J b 9-27-1896 Wayne Co

Elizabeth d 3-30-1854 ae 87y 9m 24d

Jackson h Eunice b 12-13-1833 Fayette Co dt Samuel & Rachel **Coffin** m 5-6-1856 Wayne Co
Ch: Rebecca Ann b 4-22-1858

SMITHSON
Clayton M b 12-22-1886 Randolph Co s Michael & Carlista (**Barnes**)

SOWERWINE
George Albert b 5-5-1869 Delaware Co s Isaac & Susanna (**Clevenger**)

SPRADLIN
Lewis W b 7-7-1836
Mary Jane b 9-10-1834
Ch: Susan Alwilda b 3-23-1860
    Lilly B b 10-13-1861
    Elwood H b 1-2-1863
    Ethalinda b 7-25-1864
    Irena J b 8-3-1866

STANLEY
Agnes b 6-24-1768

Elizabeth b 1-7-1834 d 1-15-1835

James b 12-9-1808
Jemima b 9-22-1812
Ch: Elmina b 4-1-1830
    Nancy b 12-11-1831
    Martha b 3-9-1833
    Sarah b 11-11-1835
    Huldah b 5-8-1837
    Clarkanna b 4-5-1839

Jemima b 4-5-1763

Jesse b 3-16-1803 d 3-16-1855
Anna b 5-30-1809 d 3-21-1855
Ch: Elizabeth b 1-12-1831
    Zebidee b 10-6-1832 d 9-28-1834
    Mary b 9-19-1834
    Sarah b 12-29-1835
    Lewis b 6-24-1838
    Wm b 12-15-1840 d 8-23-1846
    Jesse b 5-14-1843
    Thomas E b 6-7-1846

Joseph h Naomi
Ch: Abigail b 8-19-1829
    Rachel b 2-20-1831
    Rebecca b 8-14-1832
    Elizabeth b 11-27-1834 d 7-27-1836
    Jesse b 7-5-1836
    Martha b 4-3-1838
    Irena b 10-18-1840
    Solomon b 9-1-1842
    Naomi b 4-24-1845
    James
    Nancy Ann b 9-12-1850
    Thomas

Mary b 1-22-1837

Strangeman b 12-26-1811

Wm b 1-16-1839

STANTON
Aaron h Lydia
Ch: Thomas W
    Lillie A
    Wm A

David b 10-25-1837
Penninah b 11-24-1843 dt George & Lucinda (Dennis) Nicholson d 3-7-1870
Ch: Edwin M b 10-26-1864 Randolph Co
    Henry F b 8-31-1866 d 11-3-1869
    Lucinda A b 5-13-1868 d 3-15-1870
2w
    Wm Ellis b 1-15-1872

STANTON (cont)
Edwin M b 10-26-1864 Randolph Co s David & Penninah (Nicholson)
Mattie A b 1-26-1861 Wayne Co dt George G & Elizabeth Mettert d 9-7-1892
Ch: Jennie Opal b 4-13-1892 Wayne Co

STEVENSON
Elzie D b Randolph Co s James

STEWART
Elton h Margaret b 1-17-1861 Henry Co dt Isaac K & Elizabeth (Dennis) Chamness m 9-28-1882

STOUT
Ephraim h Ruth
Ch: James b 1-29-1816
    Charles b 11-11-1817
    Robert b 2-7-1820
    Elias b 4-17-1822
    Enoch b 2-17-1824 d 2-19-1824
    Anna b 3-12-1825
    Ruth b 1-14-1827
    Ephraim b 6-3-1829

Irena b 9-10-1849 Wayne Co dt Ebenezer & Mahala Chamness

STRICKLER
Elnora b 1-7-1883

STRODE
Essie May b 12-21-1876 Bourbon Co KS dt Thomas J & Malinda A (Routh)

SWAIN
Elihu b 1-25-1759 Nantucket s Nathaniel & Bethiah d 9-2-1848
Sarah b 11-7-1765 Guilford Co NC dt John & Sarah Mills d 5-13-1843
Ch: Hannah
    Elihu b 1-1-1800 d 9-14-1847
    Rachel b 8-15-1802 d 9-25-1890

Elihu b 1-1-1800 s Elihu & Sarah (Mills) d 9-14-1847
Mary dt Job & Rhoda Worth d 8-30-1874 m 12-20-1826 Springfield
Ch: Asenath b 4-22-1828
    Thomas b 6-7-1830
    Lucinda b 4-25-1832
    Job b 8-12-1834 Wayne Co
    Minerva M b 5-17-1837
    Lorenzo b 6-10-1840
    Hannah b 8-21-1842
    Cynthia b 3-11-1847 d 3-8-1874 bur Dexter IA

George b 10-29-1805
Margret b 10-10-1793
Ch: Useba b 7-10-1832
    Almira b 1-1-1835

Samuel b 10-24-1792
Elizabeth b 3-26-1792
Ch: Jethro b 11-17-1816 d 2-5-1823
    Julia b 11-22-1818
    Sarah b 9-7-1820
    Elza b 3-27-1822
    John b 2-6-1825
    Mary b 2-4-1827
    Anna b 8-27-1831

Silvanus h Rhoda
Ch: Cynthia W b 1-22-1813 d 1-13-1851
    Eunice W b 12-14-1820
    Eliza M b 3-12-1823

SPRINGFIELD MONTHLY MEETING
BIRTH AND DEATH RECORD

SWAIN (cont)
Thomas h Elzena (Williams)
Ch: Wm F b 12-27-1873
　　Lindley

Zeno h Lucinda b 1-4-1812 dt David & Mary Maulsby
Ch: Rhoda Jane b 9-27-1833/4

SYMONS
Jehu b 7-16-1832
Lydia (Hall) b 2-18-1833
Ch: Elma b 12-15-1859
　　Alfred H b 11-17-1870

TATE
Octa b 10-4-1875 Wayne Co dt Charlotte "of African descent"

TAYLOR
Henry h Minerva b 10-16-1839 dt Alvah J & Mary Macy
Ch: Mabel Odell b 5-17-1871
　　Ledante

James C h Mary Lenora b 1-23-1868 Wayne Co dt Benjamin B & Olinda (Lamb) Beeson m 1-23-1889 Wayne Co
Ch: Benjamin Willard b 1-14-1890 Wayne Co

John h Mareb
Ch: Wilson b 4-24-1838
　　Rebecca b 7-9-1839
　　Elizabeth b 7-26-1841
　　Jinnetha b 4-24-1843
　　Malinda b 10-31-1844
　　Elwood b 5-15-1847
　　Lucinda b 5-3-1850 d 10-3-1851
　　Macy M b 4-23-1852
　　Barnabas C b 2-17-1854

Nathan h Rebecca (Covalt)
Ch: Alonzo b 5-29-1877 Henry Co
　　Archibald b 9-3-1879 Henry Co

TEST
Josiah b 6-12-1826 b d 10-1-1864 bur Earlham
Miriam C b 8-10-1824
Ch: Mary Ellen b 12-1-1856
　　Samuel Edwin b 4-20-1859
　　Almira b1-27-1862 d 7-7-1865 bur Earlham

Oliver h Sarah b 6-3-1842 Wayne Co dt Branson & Elma (Reynolds) Dennis m 9-25-1861

Rufus b 1-12-1833 Wayne Co s Samuel & Hannah
Margaret M b 5-7-1839 Wayne Co dt Joseph & Sarah (Townsend) Stubbs d 8-7-1888 bur Earlham m 9-23-1858 Wayne Co
Ch: Cordelia b 12-31-1863 Wayne Co
　　Zaccheus b 10-9-1865 Wayne Co
　　Emma b 10-12-1867 Wayne Co
　　Irvin b 12-22-1868 Wayne Co
Lydia (Hall) 2w b 1-18-1833 Spiceland Henry Co

Wm h Emily (Woodard) b 11-26-1837
Ch: Hannah b 6-12-1860
　　Wilhemina b 7-27-1863

Zaccheus b 10-9-1865 Wayne Co s Rufus & Margaret M (Stubbs) h Eliza Jane (Baldwin) m 3-29-1888

THALLS
John h Isabel b 6-6-1859 Henry Co dt Jesse & Mary (Chamness) Pidgeon m 9-25-1898

THOMAS
Charity dt Henry & Hannah Mills

THOMAS (cont)
Nathan H b 9-27-1870 Miami Co s Simeon & Mary (Arnold)
Amanda C b 1-16-1868 Delaware Co dt Wm Thomas & Margaret (Jones) Ladd m 1-3-1889 Delaware Co
Ch: Sherman b 5-6-1890 Delaware Co
　　Everett E b 12-11-1892 Grant Co
　　Mary Ruth b 6-5-1895 Grant Co
　　Albert W b 8-15-1897 Grant Co

Ross B b 4-10-1858 Fayette Co s Gilbert & Sarah J (Allen)
Phebe Ellen b 6-22-1861 Henry Co dt Thomas & Mary (Hill) Hewit m 10-21-1885 Henry Co
Ch: Jesse b 11-22-1887 Henry Co
　　Paul b 12-23-1888 Henry Co

THORNBURG
Dempsey b 10-27-1801 Wayne Co s Walter & Mary d 4-7-1885 bur West River
Jane b 7-8-1804 Jefferson Co TN dt John & Mary Mills d 9-24-1880 bur West River
Ch: Irena b 8-1-1824 Wayne Co bur Nettle Creek
　　John b 9-17-1825 Wayne Co d 11-9-1838
　　Rachel b 6-19-1827 Wayne Co d 1-17-1857
　　Zerelda Ann b 10-28-1828 Wayne Co
　　Walter b 5-18-1830 Wayne Co
　　Seth b 11-26-1832 Wayne Co
　　Mary Jane b 9-10-1834 Wayne Co
　　Wm R b 6-3-1836 Wayne Co
　　Elwood b 5-10-1838 Wayne
　　Dempsey Carver b 6-20-1840 Wayne Co
　　Sarah Emeline b3-14-1842 Wayne Co
　　James Riley b 6-15-1844 Wayne Co d 7-6-1845

Dempsey Carver b 6-20-1840 Wayne Co s Dempsey & Jane (Mills)
Ethalinda L b 5-20-1846 dt Jesse & Anna Williams m 9-17-1867 Wayne Co
Ch: George L b 8-31-1869
　　Frank V b 12-31-1871 Wayne Co
　　Harry C b 1 6-1884

Elvin d 8-11-1897 ae 75y 11m 9d
Damaris M b 7-3-1826 dt Wm & Demaris Locke d 3-30-1886

Elvin Pleasant b 11-8-1839 Wayne Co s Walter & Julia (Gwin)
Electa (Patterson) b 10-27-1846
Ch: Effie May b 12-9-1870 Wayne Co
　　Ottawa b Wayne Co
　　Walter R b 7-4-1883 Wayne Co

George L b 8-31-1869 Wayne Co s Dempsey Carver & Ethalinda L (Williams) h Abbie B b Randolph Co dt Wm Botkin m 12-25-1893
Ch: Crozier B

Henry b 6-26-1773 d 6-11-1862
Ann b 11-22-1772 d 10-25-1867

Henry h Sarah b 10-20-1807 d 9-7-1830
Ch: Sarah b 6-24-1830

John b 12-28-1805 s Walter & Mary
Rachel b 8-15-1802 dt Elihu & Sarah (Mills) Swain d 9-25-1890
Ch: Sarrah Jane b 11-12-1826
　　Mary Eliza b 3-19-1829
　　Milton Erwin b 8-7-1831
　　Orlistus Winston b 1-8-1834
　　Martha E b 5-22-1836
　　Elihu S b 7-14-1838 d 9-4-1839
　　Cynthia E b 7-6-1840

John b 3-30-1809
Elizabeth (Hunt) b 12-7-1812 d 6-23-1850 bur West River
Ch: Wilson H b 2-13-1834 d 2-13-1834

**SPRINGFIELD MONTHLY MEETING
BIRTH AND DEATH RECORD**

THORNBURG (John cont)
   Madison b 10-24-1835
   Henry b 9-25-1837 d 1862
   Jesse b 9-18-1839
   Sophia B b 10-24-1842
   Joseph W b 10-15-1844
   Larkin W b 2-2-1847 d 10-11-1862
   Emily R b 7-19-1849 d 1-3-1865

John Henry b 10-13-1839 Wayne Co s Lewis & Lydia (**Macy**) h
Mary Ann (**Locke**) m 1-1-1861 Wayne Co
  Ch: Lenora F b 11-17-1862 Wayne Co
    Lewis Marion b 6-10-1865 Wayne Co
    Laurence D b 5-5-1867 Wayne Co
    Nellie
    Elsie
    Emma Florence b 3-28-1876 Wayne Co

John R b 1-25-1864 s Thomas Elwood & Mary A (**Foutz**)

Jonathan b 2-6-1793 d 1-9-1875
Elizabeth b 1-4-1795 d 6-18-1880

Joseph b 4-16-1742 d 8-6-1823 bur Springfield
Rebecca b 4-30-1744 d 9-20-1821 bur Springfield

Lewis h Lydia (**Macy**)
  Ch: Coleman b 1-21-1830
    Elmarinda b 7-18-1831 d 12-14-1841 bur West River
    Lorenzo b 5-10-1833
    Orlando b 3-20-1835
    Macy M b 3-6-1837 d 9-1-1849
    John Henry b 10-13-1839 Wayne Co
    Larkin b 7-17-1841 d 12-5-1841 bur West River
    Lucinda Ann b 11-9-1842 d 3-5-1850

Seth b 11-26-1832 s Dempsey & Jane (**Mills**)
  Ch: John Henry b 2-9-1866 Wayne Co
    Ida May b 8-27-1868 d 6-21-1870

Walter h Mary
  Ch: Dempsey b 10-27-1801 Wayne Co d 4-7-1885 bur West River
    John b 12-28-1805

Walter b 3-26-1811 d 1-15-1851
Julia Ann (**Gwin**) b 5-20-1812
  Ch: Mary Jane b 1-25-1838
    Elvin Pleasant b 11-8-1839 Wayne Co

Wm R b 6-3-1836 Wayne Co s Dempsey & Jane (**Mills**)
Elizabeth Mary b 2-26-1841 Wayne Co dt Wright & Fanny **Spradlin**
m 4-27-1856
  Ch: Rachel R b 6-26-1856 Randolph Co
    Emma J b 5-4-1862 Randolph Co
    Ellen N b 5-4-1867 Wayne Co
    Walter M b 3-19-1869 Wayne Co
Surelda (**Harris**) 2w

TILSON
Isaac F h Anna b 7-22-1869 Lancaster Co PA dt Michael &
Philipena (**Cramer**) **Melbert** m 5-1-1898

TINKLE
Wm Harvey b 10-18-1856 Wayne Co s Samuel & Catharine
(**Hughes**)
Rebecca Ann b 4-22-1858 Wayne Co dt Jackson & Eunice **Smith** m
3-29-1878 Wayne Co
  Ch: Samuel Clifford b 3-14-1881 Wayne Co
    Cordelia Maud b 6-12-1883 Wayne Co
    Blanche Amy b 2-19-1885
    Jesse Luther b 12-27-1889 Henry Co
    Eunice Marie b 3-27-1895 Henry Co

TOWNSEND
Harvey b 11-11-1873 Wayne Co s John & Elizabeth (**Edgerton**)
Olive Jane b 8-21-1876 Wayne Co dt Jesse C & Eliza (**King**)
Stevens

UNDERHILL
Jesse Butler b 10-9-1829 Springfield Wayne Co s John & Jane
Susan b 7-25-1841 Bedford Co PA dt David & Anna **Bowers** m 9-6-1866
  Ch: John M b 9-5-1867 Wayne Co
    Edward F b 1-27-1869 Wayne Co
    Alfred C b 2-17-1870 Wayne Co
    Anna Jane b 3-19-1872 Wayne Co
    Emma Arminta b 5-2-1873 Wayne Co

John b 8-15-1775 d 9-1-1837
Jane b 3-13-1787
  Ch: Hannah b 2-13-1808 Lost Creek TN
    Lemuel b 12-4-1809 Lost Creek TN
    Alfred b 5-2-1811 Lost Creek TN
    Belinda b 4-8-1813 Lost Creek TN d 3-15-1825
    Emily b 2-2-1815 Lost Creek TN d 3-11-1845
    Elvira b 3-16-1817 Lost Creek TN
    Clarkson b 2-4-1819 Lost Creek TN
    Armina b 3-3-1821 Springfield
    Juliana b 12-4-1822 Springfield
    John E b 10-17-1824 Springfield
    Jane b 7-18-1827 Springfield
    Jesse Butlar b 10-9-1829 Springfield

John E b 10-17-1824 Springfield s John & Jane
Anna b 4-21-1830
  Ch: Mary b 7-11-1850

John M b 9-15-1867 Wayne Co s Jesse Butler & Susan (**Bowers**) h
Ida (**Miller**) m 12-1891

VARDAMAN
Mollie Elnora b 11-24-1891 Randolph Co dt Wm & Mary (**Davis**)

VEAL
Cynthia b 2-11-1821 Belmont Co OH dt Stephen & Elizabeth **Cox**

VORES
James M b 6-30-1871 Henry Co s James & Mary J (**Davis**)

WADMAN
Wm H b 3-15-1843 s Charles & Jane (**Elliott**)
Sarah b 12-15-1850 dt Jesse & Lydia (**Elliott**) **Sykes** m 3-15-1869
Wayne Co

WAGNER
Robert h Mary E b 1-1-1871 Randolph Co dt John & Nancy J
(**Clark**) **Charles** m 7-15-1897

WALTER
Roscoe S b 1-10-1856 s Samuel & Elizabeth (**Stephens**)
Ida M b 6-11-1870 dt C B & Mary Elizabeth (**Wilson**) **Abshire** m
10-3-1884 Wells Co
  Ch: Daisy Dale b 1-20-1890 Wells Co
    Venus A b 11-25-1894

WALTZ
Elmer b 2-5-1892 Henry Co s Edward & Mary Ann (**Heller**)

WARD
George F b 8-21-1841 Union Co s Cyrus & Mary
Christena M b 4-18-1842 Union Co dt John & Sarah (**Ide**) **Brown**
m 9-23-1863 Union Co
  Ch: Laura A b 8-7-1864 Union Co
    Lida Alice b 1-29-1874 Union Co
    Leona A b 3-14-1878 Wayne Co
    Hattie

SPRINGFIELD MONTHLY MEETING
BIRTH AND DEATH RECORD

WARD (cont)
Timothy b 9-4-1806 d 12-9-1843 h Mahala Ann (**Wright**)
Ch: Wm b 4-5-1834
　Joshua b 2-20-1836
　Obed b 3-31-1838
　Triall b 5-13-1840
　Manual b 11-12-1842 d 10-10-1845

WEAVER
George h Rachel R b 6-26-1856 Randolph Co dt Wm R & Elizabeth
Mary (**Spradlin**) **Thornburg** m 11-27-1874

John h Emma J b 8-4-1862 Randolph Co dt Wm R & Elizabeth
Mary (**Spradlin**) **Thornburg** m ?-1-1879

WEBER
Bessie b 6-25-1886 Delaware Co dt Charles & Sarah (**Hoover**)

WHITE
Edgar T h Miriam b 1-19-1851 Henry Co dt Isaac K & Elizabeth
(**Dennis**) **Chamness** m 1-29-1881

Silas b 3-31-1833 s Davis

WHITTIER
Thomas h Eliza b 9-27-1836 Pulaski Co KY dt Pouncey & Tamar **Anderson**
Ch: Amanda M b 11-24-1871 Pulaski Co KY d 5-4-1894 bur Nettle Creek
　Levi b 4-23-1873
　Nettie Ann b 7-18-1875 Pulaski Co KY

WICKER
Noland b 12-11-1889 s Albert Elmore & Louisa Gazzeal (**White**)

WILES
Luke b 3-19-1765 d 6-4-1850
Frances b 1-5-1767 d 12-29-1849
Ch: Elizabeth b 12-16-1789 d 6-9-1868

Luke b 12-17-1797
Rhoda b 5-24-1804 d 2-27-1853 bur Flat Rock
Ch: Elizabeth D b 2-10-1824 d 8-12-1845 NC
　Francis Clanton b 4-13-1826 IN
　Wm Davis b 2-5-1828 IN
　Keziah K b 8-5-1829 IN
　Daniel H b 3-25-1831 IN
　Martha Ann b 12-11-1832 IN d 12-19-1854
　Thomas b 8-15-1834 IN d 5-28-1851
　Nathan H b 2-12-1837 IN
　Rhoda Jane b 1-29-1839 IN
　Luke b 9-18-1841 IN
　Nancy E b 5-7-1843 IN
　Esther G b 11-14-1845 IN
　Anna Mariah b 6-17-1847 IN

Thomas h Elizabeth
Ch: Wm b 6-12-1817
　Luke b 2-5-1819
　Francis b 3-15-1821
　Rachel b 9-11-1823
　Stephen b 1-25-1826
　Nancy b 4-12-1828
　Isaac b 10-25-1830
　Rebeckah b 1-20-1833

WILKINSON
Myrtle Loretta b 9-12-1892 Wayne Co dt Wm & Martha (**Wood**)

WILLIAMS
Azariah b 4-15-1775
Sarah b 1-5-1775
Ch: Thomas Patten b 3-21-1819

WILLIAMS (cont)
Caleb h Matilda
Ch: Henry b 2-1-1819
　Luzena b 2-23-1821
　Salina b 1-14-1823
　Merchant b 3-19-1825

Daniel B b 8-19-1849 Wayne Co s Jesse B & Mary Ann (**Mendenhall**)
Marilla C dt Thomas & Louisa (**Lewis**) **Craner** m 9-11-1873 Wayne Co
Ch: Charles A b 10-5-1875 Wayne Co

Harvey Alonzo b 6-10-1865 s Obed & Christena (**Covalt**) h Mary
Alice (**Lamb**) m 7-12-1884

Henry b 10-2-1800
Nancy b 8-1799 dt Willis & Mary **Biggs** d 1-1-1892 bur West River
Ch: Emsley b 7-27-1827 West River PM Wayne Co
　Oliver b 6-1-1829
　Joseph b 6-27-1831
　Sophia b 9-3-1834
　Obed b 9-11-1836
　Matthew b 8-8-1838
　Henry b 9-2-1840

Jesse B b 9-22-1825 Plymouth MM Bucks Co PA s Daniel & Margaret d 5-24-1879 but Fairfield
Mary Ann b 2-6-1829 Wayne Co dt Wm & Rebecca (**Coffin**) **Mendenhall** m 8-21-1845 Wayne Co
Ch: Caroline b 6-9-1847 Wayne Co d 9-12-1870
　Daniel B B-19-1849 Wayne Co
　Joseph C b 10-21-1851 Wayne Co d 10-14-1856
　Rufus b 7-17-1854 Wayne Co
　Exalina b 11-24-1856 Wayne Co d 1895

John b 11-9-1802
Deborah b 7-27-1806

John Mills b 10-24-1812 Newbury MM Blount Co TN s Richard & Rachel (**Mills**) d 9-5-1895
Sophia b 1-12-1833 Jefferson Co TN dt John & Rachel (**Pierce**) **Cates** d 9-15-1894 bur Springfield

Jonathan b 6-17-1803
Jane b 7-28-1808
Ch: Abraham b 2-24-1827
　Azariah b 6-19-1828
　Deborah Ann b 2-26-1830
　Mary b 2-10-1832
　David b 3-9-1834

Obed b 9-11-1836 s Henry & Nancy (**Biggs**)
Christena b 2-19-1845 Henry Co dt Cheniah & Elizabeth **Covalt** d 1-13-1890 bur West River m 2-16-1864 Henry Co
Ch: Harvey Alonzo b 6-10-1865

Richard b 12-30-1786 s Wm & Rachel
Rachel b 8-25-1786 dt John & Sarah **Mills**
Ch: Sally b 8-16-1806 Lost Creek Sevier Co TN
　Wm b 6-1-1808 Newbury MM Blount Co TN
　Polly Ann b 4-31-1810 Newbury MM Blount Co TN
　John Mills b 10-24-1812 Newbury MM Blount Co TN
　Clarkson b 6-2-1815 Springfield MM
　Rhoda b 2-15-1818 Springfield MM
　Alfred b10-28-1820 Springfield MM
　Elim b 2-20-1823 Springfield MM
　Millican b 1-29-1826
　Rachel b 11-14-1828

Rufus b 7-16-1854 Wayne Co s Jesse B & Mary Ann (**Mendenhall**)
Lydia Ann b 6-9-1852 dt Thomas & Sarah (**Judd**) **Olet** d 1895 m 12-21-1874 Wayne Co
Ch: Jennie b 8-27-1880
　Lester b 6-9-1884

WILLIS
Isaac b 3-27-1787
Anna b 9-15-1793 d 8-2-1841 bur West River
Ch: David b 1-27-1812
    Mary b 3-31-1814 d 4-6-1814
    Rachel b 8-4-1815
    Henry b 5-29-1818
    Lydia b 4-3-1821
    John b 9-7-1823
    Jonathan b 10-19-1826
    Hanah b 1-18-1829 d 8-10-1841 bur West River
    Harvey b 4-15-1831
    Lindsey b 5-30-1834
    Cynthia Ellen b 3-8-1839 d 8-3-1841 bur West River

John b 10-16-1789
Lydia b 12-14-1796
Ch: Eliza Ann b 5-14-1829

Mark R b 3-1-1852 Wayne Co s Jesse & Sarah
Margaret J (**Wright**) b 11-14-1855 Grant Co m 7-16-1784
Ch: Cora Violet b 3-22-1875 Wayne Co
    Dollie Robertha b 6-17-1876 Wayne Co

Wm b 8-24-1784 d 10-4-1850

WILMORE
Jesse W b 12-25-1842
Martha Jane b 4-12-1842
Ch: Mary A b 10-6-1862

WILSON
Isabel b 3-9-1821

Jabez h Hannah b 2-21-1845 Wayne Co dt Nathan & Malinda (**Hinshaw**) **Baldwin** d 4-26-1867 bur Nettle Creek
Ch: Nathan E b 5-6-1865 Wayne Co

Jesse b 7-9-1803
Zeruah b 11-14-1804 dt Isaac & Hannah **Beeson** d 9-27-1847
Ch: Manliff b 8-14-1833
    Hannah b 8-26-1835
    Elizabeth b 8-20-1837

WINDSOR
Alfred b 9-13-1841 Caswell Co NC s Ned & China
Charlotte (**Tate**) b 10-4-1875 Wayne Co m 1-25-1879
Nettie E (**Smith**) 2w (colored)

WISE
Charles B b 7-18-1862 Henry Co s Joseph & Mary (**Wright**)
Malvina b 3-21-1867 Henry Co dt Alvis D & Asenath (**Baldwin**) **Adams** m 10-18-1882 Henry Co

David h Viretta b 12-29-1865 Henry Co dt Wm & Martha Ellen (**Remington**) **Davis**

WOLFORD
John b 1-16-1873 Wayne Co s John W & Asenath C (**Baldwin**) h Dora (**Landick**) m 9-25-1892

John W h Asenath C (**Baldwin**)
Ch: John b 1-16-1873 Wayne Co
    Della May b 5-24-1885 Henry Co

WOOD
Joseph L h Mary Ann b 5-2-1828 Randolph Co dt Thomas & Sarah **Davis** m 8-21-1848
Ch: Sarah E b 9-28-1851
    Margaret J b 6-5-1854

Stephen Albert b 2-14-1863 Henry Co s John & Emmaline (**Featherling**) h Elva b Wayne Co

WOODARD
Alice J b 7-14-1866 Wayne Co dt Luke & Elvira (**Townsend**)

WOODY
Alanson Gray b 5-26-1845 Cane Creek MM Chatham Co NC s Hugh & Elizabeth (**Chamness**) h Sarah (**Brown**) m 9-23-1867
Ch: George L b 8-3-1868 Grant Co
    Mary E b 4-31-1873 Grant Co
Jennettie E 2w b 4-15-1856 Wayne Co dt Abraham & Mary (**Barr**) **Smith** m 4-2-1887 Wayne Co

Hugh b 10-22-1770 s James & Mary d 10-6-1825
Mary b 4-5-1771 dt Thomas & Ruth **Atkinson** d 8-31-1848
Ch: Ruth b 6-30-1814 Cane Creek MM Chatham Co NC

Hugh h Elizabeth (**Chamness**)
Ch: Joshua b 5-27-1835
    Anthony C b 3-14-1838
    Polly C b 7-7-1840
    Harriett b 9-8-1842 Chatham Co NC
    Alanson Gray b 5-26-1845 Cane Creek MM Chatham Co NC

Joshua b 5-27-1835 s Hugh & Elizabeth (**Chamness**)
Malinda (**Chamness**) b 5-28-1836
Ch: Marcelia b 6-15-1860 Randolph Co
    Lavia A b 1-7-1862

WOOLARD
Aaron h Hannah (**Werking**)
Ch: Jennie b 5-15-1877 Wayne Co
    Edith b 7-6-1884

WORTH
David h Eunice (**Gardner**)
ch: Eveline b 9-13-1813 Guilford Co NC
    Louisa b 11-7-1815 Center MM Randolph Co NC

Job h Rhoda
Ch: Rhoda d 2-27-1837 Randolph Co NC
    Mary d 8-30-1874

Thomas d 12-21-1863 ae 6ly 8d h Nancy dt Reuben & Lucinda **Macy** wid Aaron **Marshall**

WRIGHT
Sarah (**Norris**) d 1899

Wm h Hannah
Ch: Wm b 2-26-1831
    Hannah b 4-30-1832

WRIGHTSMAN
Abraham h Rachel b 12-22-1879 Orange Co NC dt Adam & Catherine (**Stover**) **Reynard** d 1863 bur West River
Ch: Mary b 9-12-1810 d 7-3-1837 bur West River
    Nancy b 12-18-1814 d 9-16-1875 bur Bales Cem

James h Rachel Elizabeth b 8-13-1867 dt Solomon & Lucinda (**Pidgeon**) **Bales** m Henry Co

YOUNG
Wm h Fanny (**Stantz**)
Ch: Mary E b 2-10-1867 Wayne Co
    Emma Bell b 3-25-1861 Wayne Co

YOUNTS
Oliver U h Edith Bell b 4-16-1872 Randolph Co dt Wm Pinckney & Julia C (**Lamb**) **Gray**

ZIMMERMAN
David E b 8-26-1876 Wayne Co s Wm & Levine h Elta b Fayette Co OH

Springfield Monthly Meeting Minutes and Marriages

ABBOTT
6-20-1885   Alice rec by rq of Flat Rock PM

ADAMS
6-16-1824   Wm & ch Jonathan, Jacob, Wm, & Joel rocf Westfield MM
12-17-1831   Ebenezer & fam (ch Joel) rocf Deep Creek MM NC
3-16-1833   Jonathan dis for dr, na, & dp
2-17-1838   Jacob rpt dp, na, & att mcd
7-21-1838   Wm Jr dis for mcd, dp, & na; Jacob dis
3-15-1845   Joel dis for j Baptist ch
10-20-1853   Joel s Ebenezer & Rebecca Henry Co m Asenith dt Wm & Elizabeth **Bond** Henry Co at Flat Rock
6-17-1854   Alvis rpt mcd
7-15-1854   Alvis chm
7-18-1857   Joel gct Back Creek MM to m Rachel **Davidson**
4-17-1858   Joel & min s gct New Salem MM

ADAMSON
6-21-1828   John & ch Simon, Nathaniel, John L, & Samuel rocf Marlborough MM NC
8-15-1829   Simon dis for mcd
5-31-1831   Charlotta dis
7-19-1834   Ann dis
9-16-1837   Seth rec by rq w/perm Duck Creek MM
7-20-1839   Aaron rec by rq of f Seth
8-17-1839   Ann (**Hiatt**) dis for mcd; Seth & fam gct Spiceland MM
12-10-1843   Ruth dis for j UB ch
4-18-1857   Sarah dis for mcd

ALBERTSON
12-15-1832   Thomas P rocf Milford MM
12-19-1832   Thomas P Wayne Co s Nexon & Easter Delaware Co PA m Hannah dt Harmon & Hannah **Davis** Wayne Co at Springfield MH
8-17-1833   Thomas P & w gct Milford MM
6-19-1869   Plainfield MM rpt Calvin mcd
7-17-1869   Calvin chm
10-19-1872   Calvin rocf Plainfield MM
3-20-1886   Joseph L & w Louisa C & min ch Jane **Plummer** & Bessie rec by rq
4-20-1889   Calvin drpd fr mbrp

ALBON
10-15-1898   Sonora rel by rq of Nettle Creek PM

ALCORN
2-17-1883   Charles & w Huldah & min s Freddie Ishmael rec by rq of West River PM
2-16-1884   Wm & w Amanda rec by rq
4-17-1886   Wm & w Huldah gct Duck Creek MM
10-17-1891   Charles & fam gct Rose Hill KS

ALLEN
6-15-1825   Zachariah & fam rocf Elk MM OH
8-20-1853   Zachariah & fam gct Three Rivers MM IA
3-19-1859   Cynthia E (**Thornburg**) rpt mcd; drpd fr mbrp
9-17-1859   Joseph G rocf Cane Creek MM NC
11-19-1859   Joseph G & Elizabeth (**Reynolds**) Nettle Creek PM rpt mcd
12-17-1859   Elizabeth (**Reynolds**) mbrp ret
1-21-1860   Joseph G mbrp ret
5-16-1863   Phebe Jane (**Dennis**) rpt mcd; mbrp ret
6-20-1863   Joseph G rpt mcd
7-18-1863   Joseph G mbrp ret
11-17-1863   Hannah J (**Modlin**) rpt mcd; drpd fr mbrp
5-18-1867   Hannah J rpt mcd to div man
12-21-1867   Hannah J dis
2-16-1868   Hannah J appeals dis to QM
6-15-1872   Newton & w Asenath & ch Anderson M & Hannah L rocf Cane Creek MM NC
4-17-1880   Franklin & w Sarah Jane & ch David J, John W, & Jonathan L rocf Cane Creek MM NC; Elizabeth rocf Cane Creek MM NC
11-21-1885   Joseph G & w Phebe Jane & ch Laura May, Emma Jane, Charles B, Elma, & Sarah Melinda rel by rq; j Buena Vista Christian ch Randolph Co
2-21-1891   Anderson M & Newton dis; jas
3-18-1893   Mattie Ethel rec by rq
4-20-1895   Benj & George drpd fr mbrp
10-15-1898   Mary, Harvey, Estella, & Freddie rel by rq of Nettle Creek PM; rq lt Albany Christian ch

ALLRED
3-16-1895   Abijah rec by rq of Nettle Creek PM

ANDERSON
2-21-1891   Hannah L dis; jas
3-16-1895   Earnest rolf Mt Zion UB ch

SPRINGFIELD MONTHLY MEETING
MINUTES AND MARRIAGES

ANDES
5-18-1833	Peter rocf West Grove MM
8-19-1837	West River MM rpt Peter for immoral conduct w/his dt; dis

ANDREWS
3-17-1877	Joseph B & s Osker rec by rq
12-20-1884	Joseph B appt West River o

ANTRIM
5-4-1821	Thomas & fam (ch Benjamin, Aldon, John, & Thomas) rocf Lees Creek MM
5-14-1823	Benjamin rpt for dr & upl
6-11-1823	Benjamin chm
4-13-1825	Benjamin dis for fighting
1-27-1827	Aden dis for fighting
6-18-1831	Thomas dis for jH; Rachel dis
4-21-1832	John dis for j separatists

ANTRUM
7-18-1835	Thomas Jr dis for dp & na

ARNET
7-15-1854	Elizabeth gct Westfield MM

ARNETT
10-?-1839	James rq mbrp
7-20-1850	Deborah (**Hollingsworth**) rpt mcd
8-17-1850	Deborah (**Hollingsworth**) chm
12-21-1850	Allen rocf Dover MM
11-19-1853	Elizabeth rocf Westfield MM
10-21-1854	James H & fam gct Honey Creek MM
10-16-1858	Minerva (**Swain**) rpt mcd; drpd fr mbrp
1-19-1867	Deborah appt o

BAILIFF
9-18-1880	Malida & min ch Newton J, Robert W, & Jesse E rocf Cane Creek MM NC
7-16-1881	Vandelia rocf West Grove MM
5-20-1882	Jones rocf Cane Creek MM NC
10-20-1883	Jones & fam gct West Grove MM Hamilton Co
12-15-1883	Jones West Grove MM Hamilton Co con fighting, "carrying a revolver for self-defense, and concealing himself for a number of days to shun the action of the civil laws."
3-15-1884	West Grove MM rpt Jones chm
3-16-1884	West Grove dealt w/Jones

BAILY
10-19-1839	Eliza dis for j M E ch

BALDWIN
10-12-1825	Jesse & Isaac rocf Milford MM
3-22-1826	Jesse s John & Charlotte West Grove Wayne Co m Levine dt Jesse & Ann **Baldwin** Springfield MM Wayne Co at Springfield MH
11-18-1826	Miriam appt elder
9-15-1827	Jesse & w gct Fall Creek MM
9-17-1831	Eli dis for na & dp
1-21-1832	Jesse & fam (ch Newton, Chalkley, Jesse Franklin, & Elwood) rocf Deep River MM NC
3-17-1832	Nathan rocf West Grove MM
2-25-1835	Newton s Jesse & Hannah Wayne Co m Anna dt Joseph & Katherine **Davis** Wayne Co at Nettle Creek MH
3-21-1835	Jesse Morgan Creek dis for na
10-28-1835	David s John & Charlotte West Grove MM Wayne Co m Mary dt Joseph & Katherine **Davis** Wayne Co at Nettle Creek MH
2-20-1836	Nathan & fam gct Duck Creek MM
5-21-1836	John gct Duck Creek MM to m Asenith **Hinshaw**
5-20-1837	Nathan & fam (s Wm) rocf Duck Creek MM

BALDWIN (cont)
8-18-1838	Andrew chm
1-15-1842	Chalkley rpt m to Mary Ann **Thornburg**
8-20-1842	Nettle Creek PM rpt John mcd; dis
12-10-1843	Chalkley dis for j separatists
2-17-1844	Jesse & Margaret dis for j separatists; Nettle Creek rpt Ruth (**Howel**) mcd
4-20-1844	Ruth (**Howel**) chm
5-18-1844	David E rpt mcd
6-15-1844	David E chm; Nancy Ann dis for j separatists
6-20-1846	Jesse rec by rq
11-21-1846	Levi dis for dp, j M E ch, & mcd
12-16-1848	Elias dis for getting angry & upl
7-21-1849	Jesse & Margaret rec by rq after being dis
3-15-1850	Sarah (**Mills**) rpt mcd
4-20-1850	Sarah (**Mills**) chm
8-17-1850	Sanford dis for mcd
4-19-1851	Jane (**Reynolds**) rpt mcd
5-11-1851	Jane (**Reynolds**) chm
5-17-1851	Elwood dis for mcd
5-25-1854	Phebe Ann rocf Poplar Run MM
8-18-1855	Isaac rpt mcd; drpd fr mbrp
5-17-1856	Daniel & fam gct Western Plain MM IA
9-20-1856	Nathan & Rachel (**Reynolds**) rpt mcd; drpd fr mbrp
10-20-1858	Rebecca gct Western Plain MM IA
5-21-1859	Jesse F dis for na
7-16-1859	Daniel & Charity rocf Western Plain MM IA
3-17-1860	Margaret Nettle Creek PM compl for disunity, na, & j Wesleyan M E ch
5-19-1860	Compl against Margaret dis
10-24-1860	Wm s Nathan & Melinda Wayne Co m Louisa dt Branson & Elma **Dennis** Wayne Co at Nettle Creek Mtg
1-17-1863	Andrew & Eunice (**Lamar**) rpt mcd
2-21-1863	Andrew & Eunice (**Lamar**) mbrp ret
3-18-1865	Elwood & ch Tilman W, Zimri R, Mary E, George R, Rachel P, Urbane E, & Emily rec by rq
4-20-1867	Jesse F & fam gct Cherry Grove MM; Margaret gct Cherry Grove MM
7-20-1867	Elwood & fam gct Cherry Grove MM
7-16-1870	Nettle Creek PM rpt Lewis mcd
10-21-1870	Andrew rq rel fr mbrp
1-16-1872	Andrew wthd rq for rel fr mbrp
4-20-1872	Eunice appt o
9-19-1874	Eunice rq rel fr mbrp
11-21-1874	Larkin E con "certain immoral conduct in the past"
12-19-1874	Larkin E's case referred to Nettle Creek o
6-19-1875	Larkin dis for dr, fornication, and refusing to provide for fam
3-18-1876	Elizabeth, Emma, & Retta rec by rq of Nettle Creek PM
6-15-1878	Sarah rec by rq
1-15-1881	Hannah A rocf Raysville MM
3-18-1882	Ann, Calvin, & Elisa A rec by rq of Nettle Creek PM
2-20-1886	Martha Jane & min ch Elva & Charity J rec by rq of Nettle Creek PM
1-21-1888	Elias & w & min dt rocf New Garden MM
4-20-1889	Elvaretta & Wm, David, John, Eli, & David Emory drpd fr mbrp
5-17-1890	Frank rec by rq of par Lewis & w
2-21-1891	Addie dis; jas
3-21-1891	David E & w Eliza rec by rq
4-18-1891	Alvin rq rel fr mbrp
5-16-1891	Alvin wthdr rq for rel fr mbrp
2-20-1892	Dr G C, John Sr, David Emory, Amanda, John Jr, Elvaretta, Thomas E, Wm H, Belle, Myrtle, Carl, & Wister rec by rq of Nettle Creek PM
6-18-1892	Lydia & dt Mary gct Muncie MM
4-15-1893	Bell rel by rq to j Mooreland Disciples ch
5-19-1894	Nettle Creek PM rpt Eli rq mbrp
9-15-1894	Louisa gct Whitewater MM
4-20-1895	George C drpd fr mbrp; jas

BALDWIN (cont)
1-18-1896	Alvin & w Mattie gct Muncie MM
2-20-1897	John E & w Cora rec by rq
8-20-1898	John H & Elvaretta & s Wm H & Thomas E rel by rq of Nettle Creek PM; Martha J & Charity rel by rq of Nettle Creek PM
10-15-1898	Emory, Martha J, & Charity rel by rq of Nettle Creek PM

BALES
4-6-1820	Seth rpt for dancing
11-1-1820	Seth chm
9-11-1822	Jacob appt o
12-11-1822	John rpt for fighting, dr, & upl
1-15-1823	Asa rocf Westfield MM NC
3-12-1823	John chm
11-12-1823	Asa & w gct White Lick MM
1-14-1824	Boater & fam gct White Lick MM
12-15-1824	Jacob appt to comm
9-15-1827	Dilwin & fam gct White Lick MM
3-15-1828	Jacob rocf Cherry Grove MM
7-17-1830	Jacob Jr & fam gct Cherry Grove MM
3-21-1835	Aaron dis for mcd less than 12 mo after d of former w & apd
7-20-1844	Jacob Jr dis for j separatists
8-17-1844	Rebecca dis for j separatists
7-16-1853	Ann (Pierce) dis for mcd & na
10-15-1864	Lucinda (Pidgeon) Nettle Creek PM rpt mcd
12-17-1864	Lucinda (Pidgeon) mbrp ret
3-16-1878	Ada J rec by rq of Nettle Creek PM
3-18-1882	Solomon & Wm rec by rq of Nettle Creek PM
8-17-1889	Sarah Jane rec by rq
2-20-1892	Lewis rec by rq
3-16-1895	Florence rec by rq of Nettle Creek PM
8-20-1898	Mary rel by rq of Nettle Creek PM

BALLARD
12-10-1843	Jesse F & fam (ch Thomas C, Wm, & Jesse Wilson) rocf Springfield MM OH; Pheraby & dt Phebe Ann rocf Springfield MM OH
7-20-1844	Jesse F & fam gct Whitewater MM

BALLENGER
8-2-1820	Jesse & ch James & Joshua rocf West Branch
5-31-1831	Jesse dis for na & dp
6-17-1837	James dis for na, dp, & mcd
7-17-1847	Nancy (Patty) dis for j M E ch & mcd

BARNARD
8-14-1822	George dis for dancing
2-12-1823	Wm rpt for att mcd
4-16-1823	Wm chm
10-21-1826	Wm dis for dealing in spirituous liquors & offering to fight
8-23-1827	Obed Wayne Co s Wm & Mary Nantucket MA m Sophia **Williams** dt Henry & Rachel **Thornburg** Wayne Co at West River Mtg
5-15-1830	John dis for att mcd, gaming, & dp
5-18-1844	Anna dis for j separatists
10-16-1847	Huldah (Canaday) dis for mcd & na
6-3-1862	Sophia elder d ae 81y
9-15-1866	Edith rec by rq
6-20-1868	Sophia (Williams) West River PM rpt mcd
7-28-1868	Sophia (Williams) mbrp ret
4-20-1895	Rena rec by rq of Springfield PM

BARNES
3-15-1850	Eunice (Allen) rpt mcd; chm
4-20-1850	Eunice (Allen) chm

BARNETT
6-19-1858	Huldah rec by rq

BEALL
6-20-1885	Andrew J, John, & Thomas rec by rq of Flat Rock PM
1-16-1886	Charles B & Carrie Dell rec by rq of Flat Rock PM

BEALS
8-14-1822	Seth rpt mcd; con mcd
9-22-1822	Parnel rpt mcd
10-6-1822	Parnel con mcd
10-16-1822	Seth con mcd
1-15-1823	Boater & Henry Wilson rocf Westfield MM NC
6-11-1822	Nathan rocf Lost Creek MM TN
9-19-1829	Parnel dis for na & dp
8-21-1830	John dis for na & dp
6-20-1835	Henry dis for na, dp, & mcd
11-21-1835	Charity dis
5-20-1837	Lewis dis for offering to fight, upl, & dp
8-18-1838	Jacob & fam (ch Jesse, Joel, & Jonathan) rocf White River MM
9-15-1855	Jesse rpt mcd; drpd fr mbrp

BEARD
6-15-1861	Lucinda (Macy) Springfield PM rpt mcd
7-20-1861	Lucinda (Macy) mbrp ret
4-15-1882	Henry F rec by rq of mother Lucinda; Lenora C rec by rq of Springfield PM
12-16-1899	Frank & Byram rec by rq of par Rufus & Laura (Williams)

BEASON
8-16-1828	Jesse dis for mcd

BECKTOL
10-20-1849	Nancy M (Mills) rpt mcd to 1st cousin
1-19-1850	Nancy M (Mills) chm

BECKUM
1-15-1842	Anna (Holaday) dis for mcd & na

BEESON
7-17-1822	Zechariah rocf Center MM NC
10-6-1822	Zachariah gct Cherry Grove MM
7-16-1823	Benjamin rocf Deep River MM NC
6-16-1824	Zechariah rocf Cherry Grove MM
2-15-1826	Jesse rocf Center MM NC
2-15-1826	Isaac rocf Center MM NC
6-14-1826	Amaziah rocf Green Plain MM OH; Isabela & fam (ch Zenos & Allen) rocf Green Plain MM OH
11-21-1826	Zenas s Amaziah & Isabel Randolph Co m Betsy dt Richard & Nancy **Mills** at Springfield MH
11-23-1826	Amaziah s Amaziah & Isabel Randolph Co m Anna dt John & Rachel **Lee** at West River MH
1-20-1827	Wm min rocf Marlborough MM NC
4-19-1828	West River PM rpt Jesse for dr, upl, & mcd
10-10-1828	Ithamar rocf Deep River MM NC
11-15-1828	Silas & w rocf Deep River MM Guilford Co NC
12-20-1828	Benjamin B rocf Center MM NC
4-18-1829	Wm's min ch (s Seth) rocf Center MM NC; Isabel & fam gct West Grove MM
6-20-1829	Elwood & Isaac Newton ch Hannah rocf Center MM NC
8-20-1829	Benjamin B s Isaac & Hannah Wayne Co m Rachel dt Jacob & Sarah **Bales** at West River Mtg
10-22-1829	Ithamer s Benjamin & Margaret Wayne Co m Polly dt Jacob & Sarah **Bales** Wayne Co at West River
1-16-1830	Zenos rpt for upl
4-17-1830	Zenos chm
6-19-1830	Jesse W rst after being dis
7-17-1830	Igle & fam (ch Amaziah, Elihu E, & Allen) rocf White River MM
8-21-1830	Zechariah rpt for immoral conduct towards a young woman, undervaluing our Saviour by saying that he was liable to err & fall while personally on earth, & not being in unity with friends

SPRINGFIELD MONTHLY MEETING
MINUTES AND MARRIAGES

BEESON (cont)

10-16-1830	Isaac rocf Center MM NC; Zechriah dis for not being in unity with Friends
11-20-1830	Benjamin & fam (s Charles) rocf Deep River MM NC
12- ?-1830	Rachel & Isaac **Macy** adm of estate of Benjamin B **Beeson** dec rq leave to have a matter in dispute with a mbr of this mtg tried by law; Comm appt to try to settle it
1-15-1831	Benjamin B's estate matter settled without recourse to law
7-16-1831	Isabell & fam & Rachel & Lydia prcf West Grove MM; their temporal affairs were not settled; cert ret to West Grove MM
10-15-1831	Allen min s Isabel rocf West Grove MM
12-17-1831	Thomas Ellwood gct West Grove MM to m Elizabeth **Wilson**; mcd; Silas H rpt mcd
2-18-1832	Thomas chm for mcd
4-21-1832	Amaziah rpt for na, for getting into a passion with his fellow man, & offering to fight
7-21-1832	Hannah Jr dis
8-13-1832	Igal rpt for going to law with a friend so far as to inf in case of an arrest by West River PM; rpt changed to inf against a mbr before civil authority in a state case w/out being necessisted [sic] so to do
8-18-1832	Wade & Samuel min ch Isabel rocf Milford MM
12-15-1832	Case against Igal dis
8-18-1832	Thomas Elwood rpt for mcd, charging a friend with a matter he could not support, for not keeping to the truth, & for telling untruth in a boastful manner
9-15-1832	Rpt against Thomas Elwood changed to mcd, getting into a passion, offering to fight, & upl against a neighbor
12-15-1832	Thomas Elwood chm
10-19-1833	Allen rpt mcd
12-21-1833	Allen chm
10-18-1834	Seth gct Elk MM OH
11-15-1834	Lydia dis
1-17-1835	Isabella dt Isabella dis; Zenas dis for fighting & using unbecoming language
8-15-1835	Jesse & fam gct Mississinewa MM
6-18-1836	Isaac rocf Center MM NC
7-16-1836	Flat Rock PM rpt Igle for getting angry & upl
8-20-1836	Igle rq comm to investigate charges against him; Allen dis for fighting
12-17-1836	Case drpd against Igle; not supportable
2-18-1837	Hezikiah dis for vending liquors; Silas H rpt mcd & dp
3-18-1837	Benjamin F rpt mcd
4-15-1837	Benjamin F chm; Silas H chm
7-15-1837	Benjamin F min s Miriam gct White Lick MM
11-18-1837	Isaac gct Cherry Grove MM to m Mary **Mathews**
1-20-1838	Igal & fam gct Bloomfield MM
2-17-1838	Amaziah & fam rq cert to Mississinewa MM
8-18-1838	Benjamin rq privilege of going to law with mbrs
9-15-1838	Benjamin's rq refused
3-16-1839	Charles rpt mcd; Mariah dis
4-20-1839	Isaac Newton dis for upl; Wade dis for fornication
5-18-1839	Charles chm
7-18-1840	Mareb & ch gct Salem MM IA
6-19-1841	West River PM rpt Thomas Elwood for attempting to fight
9-18-1841	Elizabeth & ch gct Salem MM IA
10-15-1841	Thomas Elwood chm; Benjamin F min rocf White Lick MM
12-18-1841	Anna (**Mills**) dis for mcd & j UB ch
3-19-1842	Emily & ch rq cert to Salem MM IA
8-20-1842	Lydia (**Willis**) rpt for mcd & att mcd
9-17-1842	Lydia (**Willis**) chm
10-15-1842	Josiah dis for mcd
9-16-1843	Rachel dis for j separatists
10-12-1843	Mary dis for j separatists
12-10-1843	Charles & Isaac W dis for j separatists
2-17-1844	Ithamer dis for j separatists
5-18-1844	Salem MM IA Terr dis Benjamin living here for na & upl

BEESON (cont)

11-16-1844	Isabella gct Salem MM IA
1-18-1845	Marsh & ch Hannah, Sally, Matilda, & Marilla rocf Salem MM IA
3-15-1845	Lucinda & Malinda dis for att mcd
5-17-1845	Zenoah dis for na & mcd
7-19-1845	Wm M dis for mcd & j separatists
6-20-1846	Wm rec by rq w/perm of Center MM NC
9-19-1846	Benjamin F dis for mcd & j separatists
4-17-1847	Lydia dis for att mcd
7-15-1848	Rebecca & ch Massey, Alice, Elizabeth, Mary Hannah, Sarah, Thomas, & David rocf Bloomfield MM
10-21-1848	Sarah dis for unchastity
11-18-1848	Elizabeth dis for j M E ch
7-21-1849	Charles & Rachel rec by rq
12-15-1849	Mary dis for j separatists
1-18-1851	Flat Rock PM rpt Wm dis for m in less than 12 mos after d of 1st w
3-1-1851	Wm rec by rq
6-21-1851	Hannah (**Canaday**) rpt mcd
9-19-1851	Hannah (**Canaday**) chm
12-20-1851	Keziah dis for att mcd
1-17-1852	Polly & Sarah dis for att mcd & j UB ch
6-19-1852	Charles dis for j Spiritualists
4-16-1853	Mahlon dis for mcd, att mcd, na, & dp
7-16-1853	Elizabeth & ch Isaac N, Job, Wm N, Mary, & Ellen rocf Westfield MM
1-21-1854	David dis for na
5-25-1854	Oliver dis
8-16-1856	Wm gct Western Plain MM IA
9-20-1856	Thomas E gct Milford MM to m Celia **Hunt**
5-16-1857	Celia rocf Milford MM
4-17-1858	Rachel dis for j Spiritualists
7-20-1861	Elizabeth & fam gct Bangor MM IA
8-17-1861	Lewis rpt mcd; drpd fr mbrp
10-19-1861	Thomas dis for jas
9-17-1864	Baraboo MM WI gr perm to rst Wm M
4-15-1865	Celia appt o
11-17-1866	Benjamin B rpt mcd; mbrp ret
10-21-1876	Thomas C West River PM compl "guilty of going into gambling show and wagering money"
12-16-1876	Compl against Thomas C drpd
1-17-1880	Florin M, Wm F, & Jesse F rec by rq of f John W; Flora H & Martha E rec by rq of West River PM
4-17-1880	Julia Ann & ch Laurence Clay & Linnie D rec by rq; Josephine rec by rq
3-18-1882	Louisa & Virgil rec by rq of Nettle Creek PM
4-15-1882	Louisa & Virgil's ch rec by rq of par
6-17-1882	John W & fam & niece Flora gct Dublin MM; Samuel & fam & niece Josephine gct Dublin MM
3-16-1889	Alma A dis
4-20-1889	Jonathan, Elmer E, Alma A, & Clarence G drpd fr mbrp
2-20-1892	Sarah Catherine rec by rq of Nettle Creek PM
3-17-1894	Thomas & Caroline rec by rq of Mooreland PM
3-16-1895	Frederick rec by rq of Nettle Creek PM
3-19-1898	George & Mary rec by rq of par Lewis R & Julia; Harvey F, Harley, & Walter A rec by rq

BEESONS

2-17-1855	Asenath (**Adams**) dis for mcd

BEKTEL

12-18-1834	Annis (**Mills**) dis for mcd & j UB ch

BELL

3-15-1884	Charles & Eliza E rec by rq of Flat Rock PM

BENBA

1-15-1881	Francis Asbury, Mary Ellen, & Cora Evaline rec by rq of f Wm

BENBO
6-20-1874	Mary Ann rec by rq of White River PM

BENBOW
9-20-1860	Wm L s Benjamin & Rachel Randolph Co m Flavia S dt Absalom & Eunice **Dennis** Wayne Co at West River Mtg
2-16-1861	Flavia S gct Cherry Grove MM
3-21-1874	Wm rec by rq of West River PM
8-21-1886	Wm rel by rq; Francis Asbury, Mary Ellen, & Cora Evaline rel by rq of par Wm & Mary Ann; jas

BENNETT
3-18-1876	Elizabeth rec by rq of Nettle Creek PM
4-21-1883	Elizabeth gct White River MM

BILLHEIMER
9-17-1887	Lydia drpd fr mbrp for jas & na
8-16-1828	Jesse dis for mcd

BOGUE
1-15-1841	Flat Rock PM rpt Joseph for cursing, na, dp, & mcd
5-15-1841	Joseph A mbr Vermillion MM; this mtg rq to treat w/him & rpt
12-18-1841	Vermillion MM dis Joseph

BOND
4-20-1826	Robert s Jesse & Phebe Wayne Co m Rachel dt Henry & Ann **Thornburg** Wayne Co at West River MH
6-16-1827	Wm & fam rocf Deep Creek MM NC
8-18-1827	Jesse rocf Deep Creek MM NC
3-31-1831	Mordicai s Joseph & Rachel m Rachel dt John & Anna **Marshall** at Flat Rock Mtg
6-18-1831	Jesse dis for dp, na, dr, & training w/militia; Hannah dis
1-17-1835	Joseph & w rocf Deep Creek MM NC; end by White Lick MM
5-16-1835	Nancy dis
11-19-1836	Joseph & fam gct Bloomfield MM
4-15-1837	Mordecai & fam rocf White River MM
12-18-1841	John rpt m to Lucinda **Adams**
10-21-1843	Rachel dis for j separatists
11-18-1843	Mordecai dis for j separatists & setting up mtgs contrary to discipline
10-21-1848	Salem MM IA gr perm to rst Mordecai & Rachel
6-21-1851	Rachel's min ch gct Salem MM IA
11-19-1853	Millicent (**Mendenhall**) rpt mcd
11-17-1860	John minister & w Anna rocf Deep Creek MM NC
11-16-1861	Anne gct Walnut Ridge MM
12-16-1865	Millicent gct Wabash MM
4-26-1866	Jehiel s Levi & Lydia Wayne Co m Anna Jane Henry Co dt Evan & Gulielma **Marshall** Lee Co IA at Flat Rock
6-16-1866	Anna Jane gct Dover MM
8-15-1868	Elizabeth Flat Rock PM rpt dec
5-21-1870	Levi Flat Rock PM dis for mcd & jas

BOON
5-21-1881	Mary Ann gct Spiceland MM

BRANSEN
9-16-1843	Rachel dis for j separatists

BRANSON
6-11-1823	Isaac rocf Lost Creek MM TN
11-17-1832	Isaac dis for na, getting in a passion, offering to fight, & upl
3-20-1841	Rachel & ch rocf Mississinewa MM

BREWER
8-16-1862	Mary C (**Woody**) Nettle Creek PM rpt mcd; drpd fr mbrp

BREWER (cont)
3-19-1881	Morris W & w Eliza & min ch Clarence A, Otas J, Eva N, Nettie C, Jennie F, Alta A, & Della E rocf Walnut Ridge MM

BROOKS
7-19-1834	Rachel dis

BROWN
6-16-1824	Isaac & ch Moses & Jacob rocf Westfield MM
6-16-1827	Deep Creek NC rpt Moses for failing to have w's signature affixed to land title
7-21-1827	Moses chm; rec by rq
9-13-1827	Jacob rocf Westfield MM
6-21-1828	West River rpt Moses for dr
7-19-1828	Moses chm
8-20-1831	Flat Rock PM rpt Moses for dr
9-17-1831	Moses chm
8-17-1833	Moses dis for being intoxicated & denying
8-17-1839	Moses dis for dp & mcd
3-21-1846	Delphia rec by rq
5-15-1852	James dis for dp, mcd, & na
6-17-1854	Isaac Jr dis for mcd
1-17-1856	Elizabeth (**Bond**) rpt mcd
2-16-1856	Elizabeth (**Bond**) chm
3-15-1856	Samuel rpt mcd; Thaddeus rpt mcd; drpd fr mbrp
4-19-1856	Samuel chm
2-20-1858	Elk MM OH gr perm to rst Rhoda
1-18-1862	Moses rec by rq
1-21-1865	Samuel rpt mcd
3-18-1865	Samuel mbrp ret
1-20-1866	Mary Maria rocf Center MM OH
8-15-1868	Delphia appt Flat Rock PM o
12-17-1870	Anna M rec by rq; Samuel appt o
9-16-1871	Jonathan rocf Dover MM; Rhoda & ch Valteria & Sarah E M rocf Dover MM
10-21-1871	Isaac D rec by rq
4-20-1872	Mary Mariah appt o
6-10-1874	Samuel appt o
1-18-1874	Sarah rocf Poplar Ridge MM
7-15-1874	Isaac appt elder
8-18-1877	Sarah gct Poplar Ridge MM Hamilton Co
3-16-1878	Susan, Margaret Ann, & Maria rec by rq of Flat Rock PM
5-17-1879	Samuel appt elder
1-27-1882	Thaddeus & fam rq cert to Deer Creek MM
10-20-1883	Moses d rpt
3-16-1884	Mary rec on rq of Flat Rock PM
6-20-1885	Sarah C rec by rq of Flat Rock PM
1-16-1886	Aaron D, Francis M, Edward S, & Etta J rec by rq of Flat Rock PM
6-16-1894	Maria & min ch Etta & Wilbur rocf New Castle MM
9-15-1894	Aaron D & min ch Gertrude & Edward rocf New Castle MM
3-19-1898	Loring L & Nettie A rec by rq
5-17-1899	Samuel appt elder

BUCKINGHAM
9-19-1874	Jane rocf Elk MM OH

BURGESS
4-16-1892	Mary Ellen & dt Anna rocf Spiceland MM
12-16-1899	Sarah glt Hagerstown Christian ch

BUROUGHS
1-17-1891	James & w Addie glt M E ch Daviess Co

BURROUGHS
2-16-1884	James & w Ada Lizzie rec by rq
11-15-1890	James & w rq lt Plainfield M E ch; John D **Hartsook** pastor

BUSAN
2-20-1892	Sarah Catharine rec by rq

SPRINGFIELD MONTHLY MEETING
MINUTES AND MARRIAGES

CAIN
10-15-1870	Rhoda (**Clark**) rpt mcd
8-21-1880	Jemima rec by rq
2-16-1884	Henry P & ch Ollie J, Nellie C, Wm H, & Frankie rec by rq (h & ch of Rhoda)
3-17-1888	Clara E rec by rq of Springfield PM
8-16-1890	Effie Lillian & Martha Jennie rec by rq of mother Lizzie

CANADA
6-7-1820	Henry & ch Benjamin, John, Frederick, & Wm rocf Lost Creek MM TN

CANADAY
2-2-1820	Robert & John appt to comm
3-1-1820	John proposed as elder
9-6-1820	Henry Jr rpt for dancing
11-1-1820	Henry Jr dis for dancing
8-1-1821	John Jr rpt mcd; chm
1-2-1822	Henry & fam gct Honey Creek MM
5-15-1822	Hermon chm
1-14-1824	Benjamin res Honey Creek MM rpt for mcd; that mtg rq to treat w/him
8-11-1824	Robert appt o
11-16-1825	Harman dis for complying w/military requisitions, fighting, & dp
4-12-1826	Wm rocf West Grove MM
7-15-1826	John gct Honey Creek MM
11-22-1826	Joshua s Robert & Ammy Wayne Co m Betsy Ann dt John & Mary **Mills** Wayne Co at Springfield MH
3-17-1827	West River PM rpt Wm for na, disunity with Friends, & dp
5-19-1827	Wm dis
3-15-1828	R rpt mcd
4-19-1828	R dis
5-17-1828	Sarah dis
6-21-1828	Elihu dis for using unbecoming language
8-16-1828	John gct Vermilion MM IL
10-17-1828	Thomas rpt for upl & offering to fight
2-20-1830	Thomas chm on 1st charge; 2nd not substantiated
11-20-1830	Walter & fam rocf Center MM NC
12-12-1830	Thomas dis for fighting, upl, & dp after prev dis
2-19-1834	Robert rec in mbrp
8-15-1840	Joshua & fam gct Mississinewa MM
8-20-1842	Walter & fam (ch Jonathan, David, & Wm) rocf West Grove MM
6-17-1843	Jonathan dis for mcd
12-10-1843	Sarah dis for j separatists
12-21-1844	David dis for att mcd
6-17-1848	Wm rpt mcd
10-21-1848	Wm chm
1-19-1850	Bloomfield MM gr perm to rst Harmon
10-17-1835	Lindsey rec by rq
1-14-1837	Robert's d rpt
10-21-1854	Wm gct Poplar Run MM
12-16-1854	Lyndsey dis for na
6-16-1855	Karen H gct Vermillion MM
3-16-1861	Esther R Flat Rock PM rpt mcd; drpd fr mbrp
9-19-1863	Amy gct Mill Creek MM
11-19-1864	Amyrilla rocf Mill Creek MM
3-18-1882	Lyndsey rec by rq of Springfield PM
4-15-1882	Livonia S & Nannie E rec by rq of Springfield PM
12-16-1899	Minnie rec by rq of Springfield PM

CARR
8-17-1839	Benjamin & fam (ch Aaron, Hezikiah A, Cyrus, Evan, & Amos) rocf Fairfield MM OH
3-16-1844	Thomas dis for j separatists
4-17-1847	Daniel dis for j separatists & mcd
7-15-1848	Thomas & fam gct Honey Creek MM; Rachel & ch Kindley & Miles gct Honey Creek MM
6-16-1849	Benjamin & fam gct Honey Creek MM
8-18-1849	Aaron dis for mcd
6-19-1858	Honey Creek MM IA gr perm to rst Thomas

CARTER
7-?-1855	Elihu rpt mcd to Esther B **Mendenhall**
3-21-1857	Marticia C (**Mendenhall**) rpt mcd; drpd fr mbrp
5-19-1860	Wm B & fam rocf Dover MM OH
12-17-1870	Wm B & fam gct Poplar Run MM
3-18-1876	Esther rec by rq of Nettle Creek PM
10-19-1878	Elwood & w Mariah rocf Westfield MM
11-15-1879	Elwood minister & w Maria gct Westfield MM
4-21-1888	Esther rel by rq; j Franklin M E ch
1-18-1890	Esther gct New Castle MM

CARY
8-20-1898	Allice rq lt to Franklin M E ch

CATEY
5-15-1875	Albina Jane rocf New Garden MM

CATY
6-16-1883	Albina Jane gct White River MM

CAVALT
7-16-1892	Roxanna rel fr mbrp; j M E ch

CHAMNESS
6-14-1826	Wm rocf Center MM NC
2-17-1827	West River PM rpt Wm mcd
4-21-1832	Isaac & ch Andrew, John, David, Elwood, Sanford, & Elisa rocf Center MM Guilford Co NC; end by Whitewater MM
8-13-1832	Wm rpt for getting into a passion w/his fellow man & upl
9-15-1832	Wm chm
3-16-1833	Joshua & fam (ch Isaac) rocf Center MM NC; end by Cherry Grove MM
4-20-1833	Nathan & fam (ch Wm & David) rocf Cherry Grove MM
12-20-1834	Jesse & fam rocf Center MM NC
10-20-1838	Wm & w Isabel rocf Center MM NC
6-19-1841	West River PM rpt Wm Jr for threatening to kill his fellow man provided he laid violent hands upon him & upl
9-18-1841	Wm Jr chm
8-9-1843	Wm Jr rpt mcd
9-16-1843	Wm Jr chm
1-20-1844	Wm s Wm dis for j separatists
11-16-1844	Nettle Creek PM rpt Ebenezer mcd; dis
12-21-1844	Reuben dis for att mcd
5-17-1845	Mahala (**Lamb**) dis for mcd & j separatists
11-15-1845	Wm appt elder
2-17-1849	George W rocf Cane Creek MM NC
10-20-1849	Hannah (**Beeson**) dis for mcd to 1st cousin
3-16-1850	Jehu dis for dp, mcd w/his 1st cousin, & na
11-20-1850	Isaac s Joshua & Hannah Randolph Co m Elizabeth dt Thomas & Elizabeth **Dennis** at Nettle Creek Mtg
5-15-1852	Larkin dis for dp, dancing, & upl
10-21-1854	Riley dis for dp & na
12-16-1854	Elihu dis for mcd
7-21-1855	Mary (**Reynolds**) dis for mcd
2-21-1857	David rpt mcd; drpd fr mbrp
11-26-1857	Wm s Jesse & Ruth Wayne Co m Martha Ann dt Wm & Mildred **Modlin** Wayne Co at West River
1-16-1858	Henry rpt mcd; drpd fr mbrp
6-19-1858	Wm S rpt mcd; drpd fr mbrp
9-18-1858	Acsa dis for att mcd
8-17-1861	Ruth appt o
2-15-1862	Susanna dis for sueing a mbr
10-18-1862	Mahlon gct Poplar Run MM to m Emily J **Hodgin**
6-20-1863	Emily J rocf Poplar Run MM
10-15-1864	Wm S & w Rebecca Jane & ch Theodore E, Carrie R, & Oscar L rec by rq
1-21-1865	Uriah rpt mcd
2-18-1865	Uriah mbrp ret
8-18-1866	Seth M rpt mcd

CHAMNESS (cont)
12-15-1866	Seth M mbrp ret
5-16-1868	Seth M & min ch Lena May gct Whitewater MM
2-19-1870	Mary Melissa (**Beeson**) rpt mcd
4-16-1870	Mary Melissa (**Beeson**) mbrp ret
7-16-1870	Wm W Nettle Creek PM rpt mcd
12-17-1870	Mahlon appt o
1-21-1871	Susannah rq "to be joined into membership with Friends again"
3-18-1871	Susannah rec by rq
4-20-1872	Wm S & fam gct Spiceland MM
8-17-1872	Emily appt o
6-20-1874	Mahlon rec as minister; Isaac appt o
3-18-1876	Isabel A rec by rq of Nettle Creek PM
2-17-1877	Mary & dt Abigail gct Spiceland MM
5-17-1879	Emily appt elder
3-21-1885	James M rec by rq of White River PM
2-20-1886	Marcellus & w Alice S rec by rq of Nettle Creek PM
1-21-1888	Adaline rec in mbrp
10-20-1888	Seth rocf Whitewater MM
2-16-1889	Elijah & w Mary rec by rq; Leander & w Lillie & ch Lewis E, Carrie Etta, & Charles C rec by rq
4-20-1889	Russel & Ellen drpd fr mbrp; Pearl B rec by rq
8-16-1890	Sylvester & w Rebecca rec by rq of Mooreland PM
1-17-1891	Annie rec by rq
2-21-1891	Louisa rec by rq of Mooreland PM
2-20-1892	Russel, Nora, Ruth, & Perry rec by rq
9-17-1892	Hannah rec by rq
10-9-1895	Albert N s Mahlon H & Emily J Henry Co m Rebecca E dt Oliver & Emma **Hiatt** at Economy
8-20-1898	Marcellus rel by rq of Nettle Creek PM
3-16-1889	Ellen dis; Pearl B rec by rq of Mooreland PM
2-15-1899	Sylvester & w Rebecca rec in mbrp
11-18-1899	Maggie & Fernando rq mbrp for ch Zola, Luna, & Clarence W

CHARLES
6-18-1842	John Cherry Grove MM rpt m to Eunice **Swain**
12-21-1850	John rec by rq w/perm of Cherry Grove MM
1-18-1851	Eunice rec by rq w/perm of Cherry Grove MM
2-26-1862	John s Daniel & Miriam Wayne Co m Nancy J dt Wm & Louisa **Clark** Wayne Co at Economy
11-21-1863	Narcissa (**Osborne**) rpt mcd
2-20-1864	Narcissa (**Osborne**) mbrp ret
12-16-1865	Narcissa gct New Garden MM
7-15-1874	John appt elder

CLAPPER
6-17-1882	David rec by rq of Nettle Creek PM
3-20-1897	David C & w Alice & ch Nellie, Gertie, & Ruth gct Farmland MM

CLARK
10-20-1860	Wm & w Louisa & ch Thomas E, Jonathan B, Joseph A, Barzilla W, George E, John M, Wm D, Nancy J, Eunice R, Miriam A, Rhoda R, & Mary rocf Marlborough MM NC
2-21-1863	Thomas E rpt mcd
3-21-1863	Thomas E mbrp ret
11-21-1863	Malinda (**Macy**) Springfield PM rpt mcd; rq Whitewater MM to treat w/her
2-20-1864	Melinda (**Macy**) chm
4-19-1864	Wm Springfield PM appt elder
5-19-1866	Joseph A gct Greenfield MM
6-15-1868	Louisa appt Springfield PM o
12-17-1870	Wm appt o
12-16-1871	Nancy P rec by rq
1-20-1872	Emily C & Matilda Jane Springfield PM rec by rq
3-16-1872	Barzilla W rpt mcd
3-16-1878	Ida M & s Herbert Charles rec by rq; she fr Hagerstown M E ch
5-17-1879	Louisa appt elder

SPRINGFIELD MONTHLY MEETING MINUTES AND MARRIAGES

CLARK (cont)
3-20-1886	Milton & w & ch rel by rq; j Economy M E ch; J M & w Ida & min ch Charles Herbert, Solon North, & Irena May glt Economy M E ch
3-17-1888	A Emma, Julia E, & Everett W rec by rq of Springfield PM
5-19-1888	Ellen (**Hanby**) rocf Dublin MM
7-20-1889	S Ella w Wm D & ch George Hershall, John Paul & Will Carlton rec by rq of Springfield PM
2-19-1898	Matilda rel by rq; jas
8-20-1898	Wm D & w L Ella & ch George Hershel, John Paul, Wm Carleton, & Jesse Cates gct Winchester MM

CLEMENS
7-19-1890	Lucile min rec by rq of Cordelia **Test**

CLOUD
6-16-1883	Esther M gct West Grove MM

CLYEDENS
6-19-1858	Eunice W (**Chamness**) rpt mcd; drpd fr mbrp

COFFIN
11-17-1838	Stephen rocf Deep River MM NC
4-18-1840	Stephen rpt mcd
5-20-1840	Stephen chm
6-20-1840	Joseph rocf Deep River MM NC
11-21-1840	Joseph & w gct West Grove MM
8-21-1841	Stephen & fam gct West Grove MM
8-20-1842	Martitia, Delphina, Hannah, Eunice, & David rec on rq of f Barnabas
11-19-1842	Barnabas rec by rq w/perm of Deep River MM NC after being dis
10-16-1852	John & w Abigail rocf Marlborough MM NC; John M & Eunice W rocf Marlborough MM NC
5-21-1853	Martha D & dt Louisa Jane rec by rq
8-20-1853	Joseph rocf West Grove MM
11-17-1855	Mary rec by rq w/perm of Marlborough MM NC
3-19-1859	John M & fam gct Three River MM IA
9-17-1864	Barnabas & fam gct Bridgport MM

COGGESHALL
12-15-1827	Gayer rocf Deep Creek MM NC; Peter & fam rocf Deep Creek MM NC
8-15-1829	Jonathan rocf Deep Creek MM NC
9-19-1829	Geyer gct Milford MM
5-19-1838	Jonathan gct Mississinewa MM

COGGSHALL
10-17-1835	Jonathan rpt mcd
11-21-1835	Jonathan chm

COLBURN
9-16-1848	Elizabeth dis

CONLEY
9-17-1859	Martha Ellen (**Thornburg**) rpt mcd; drpd fr mbrp
4-20-1895	Maxie rel fr mbrp; jas

CONLY
3-18-1882	Nevada rec by rq of Nettle Creek PM

CONWAY
1-19-1884	Martha rec by rq of Nettle Creek PM
3-16-1889	Susan Gertrude rec by rq of Springfield PM
10-15-1898	Susan G rel by rq of Nettle Creek PM
11-18-1899	Wm rec by rq of Mooreland PM

CONYER
11-18-1837	Julia (**Swain**) dis for dp, mcd, & att mcd

COOK
2-12-1823	Jesse rocf Westfield MM NC

SPRINGFIELD MONTHLY MEETING
MINUTES AND MARRIAGES

COOK (cont)
9-15-1832	Wright & fam (ch Henry, David, & Wright) rocf Silver Creek MM
7-18-1835	David dis for dp & na
7-15-1837	Wright & fam gct Duck Creek MM
3-16-1844	Ira dis for j separatists
7-19-1845	Irena dis for j separatists
7-21-1849	Ira rec by rq
9-21-1850	Irena rec by rq
9-21-1850	Betsy & Cyrus rec by rq of f Ira
1-15-1853	Ira & fam gct Duck Creek MM; changed to Richland MM IA

COONS
6-20-1896	Samuel & Elma rel fr mbrp; jas

CORDLE
3-18-1854	Cert rec for Elizabeth fr Deep Creek MM NC; end to Spring Creek MM IA

CORNUTT
5-17-1856	Hannah (Macy) rpt mcd; drpd fr mbrp

CORY
11-15-1856	Rebecca (Beeson) rpt mcd; drpd fr mbrp
6-19-1858	Elizabeth (Beeson) rpt mcd; drpd fr mbrp

COUCH
2-19-1853	West River PM rpt Hannah (Wilson) mcd
3-19-1853	Hannah (Wilson) dis

COX
3-1-1820	Jonathan & ch John & Joseph rocf Mill Creek MM
4-14-1824	Wm & ch Wm, Thomas, & Joseph rocf West Branch MM
5-12-1824	Jonathan rpt for practicing fraud & untruthfulness; West Branch PM rq to treat w/him
7-24-1824	Thomas & fam (s Amos) rocf Fairfield MM
4-13-1825	West Branch MM rpt no satisfaction with Jonathan
5-11-1825	Jonathan dis for practicing fraud & untruthfulness
8-17-1825	Charity gc
7-18-1829	Wm Jr rpt mcd
10-11-1829	Wm Jr chm
5-15-1830	Judith dis
10-16-1830	Wm s Peter dis for making unnecessary use of spirituous liquors, att mcd, & dp
5-31-1831	Wm Jr dis for na & att mcd
10-15-1831	Stephen & fam (ch Stephen & Jared) rocf Somerset MM OH; Thomas & Levi rocf Stillwater MM
11-17-1832	Sarah dis
6-15-1833	Thomas dis for mcd
9-20-1834	Levi rq mbrp for ch Nathan & Elisha
10-18-1834	Peter & fam gct West Grove MM
11-24-1834	Joseph s Wm & Elizabeth Randolph Co m Hester Ann dt Richard & Nancy Mills at Springfield Mtg
3-21-1840	Cynthia dis for att mcd & dp
10-17-1840	Joseph dis for j Christian Friends
1-16-1841	Hester Ann dis for j Christian Friends
1-15-1842	Zimri dis for na, dp, & dr
9-20-1845	Elizabeth rec by rq
6-21-1851	Jemimah & ch Mary, Priscella, Sarah, Branson, & Elihu rocf Holly Spring MM NC
3-20-1852	Thomas gct Honey Creek MM
6-19-1852	Wm rpt mcd
7-19-1852	Wm chm
9-18-1852	Deborah & Rhoda dis for att mcd & na
10-16-1852	Stephen dis for mcd & na
12-18-1852	Jared dis for att mcd & na
9-17-1853	Jemima & fam gct Poplar Run MM
1-20-1855	Elisha dis for na, ass w/evil companions, & fighting
2-15-1862	Rebecca (Ellis) rpt mcd; New Salem MM Howard Co rq to treat w/her

COX (cont)
4-19-1862	Rebecca (Ellis) mbrp ret
5-27-1862	Rebecca (Ellis) gct New Salem MM
3-19-1892	Elisha rec by rq of Springfield PM

CRUMPTON
12-17-1853	Dirinda dis for mcd & na; dec before cert delivered to New Garden MM
10-18-1856	Sarah (Denny) rpt mcd; drpd fr mbrp

CURRENT
9-18-1847	Deborah Ann (Hodson) dis for mcd

DAILY
1-21-1898	Lena rec by rq of Nettle Creek PM

DALBEY
7-15-1893	Jennie (Underhill) gct Whitewater MM

DAVIS
7-5-1820	John appt to comm
2-6-1822	John appt o
4-17-1822	Simeon & fam gct New Garden MM
5-15-1822	Tristram rocf New Garden MM NC
7-17-1822	Tristram rpt mcd; chm
9-17-1823	Joseph & ch Nathan, Wm, & George roc
10-12-1825	Love & ch gct Milford MM
4-19-1826	John gct New Garden MM to m Lydia Farmer
6-16-1827	Tristam & fam gct Silver Creek MM
12-29-1828	Silas rocf Westfield MM NC
7-21-1832	Silas rpt mcd; chm
11-17-1832	Joseph & fam rocf West Grove MM
12-15-1832	Harmon & fam rocf Milford MM
6-15-1833	Harmon & fam gct West Grove MM
8-17-1833	Joseph & fam gct West Grove MM
2-15-1834	Wm dis for na, dp, & att mcd
5-17-1834	Nathan dis for na & dp
9-20-1834	Jesse & Neziah rocf Deep Creek MM NC
10-18-1834	Katharine dis; John rq cert to Mississinewa MM
11-15-1834	Katharine appeals fr the judgment of MM to QM
2-21-1835	Owing to lack of evidence QM reversed MM dec against Katharine
6-23-1836	Neziah Henry Co s Wm & Elizabeth Grayson Co VA m Tamer dt Isaac & Mary Brown Henry Co at Flat Rock Mtg
3-18-1837	Jesse & fam gct Walnut Ridge MM
4-26-1838	Spencer s John & Ruth Henry Co m Amelia dt Wm & Elizabeth Bond Henry Co at Flat Rock
1-19-1839	Rebecca & ch gct Mississinews MM
3-21-1840	David & s Robert rocf Deep Creek MM NC
11-20-1841	George gct West Grove MM to m Charlotte Baldwin
2-19-1842	David & f gct Sugar Plain MM IA
9-22-1842	Wm s John & Ruth Henry Co m Huldah dt Ira & Elizabeth Hough at Flat Rock Mtg
4-15-1843	Maria L dis for mcd
6-17-1843	Jordan R rocf Deep Creek MM NC; Wm & fam rocf Deep Creek MM NC
8-19-1843	Rachel (Thornburg) dis for j separatists & mcd
10-21-1843	Joseph dis for j separatists
12-10-1843	Katherine dis for j separatists
3-16-1844	Rachel dis for j separatists
5-17-1845	John s Joseph dis for j separatists & att mcd
3-21-1846	Wm s John & fam gct Salem MM IA
7-11-1846	Wm & dt gct Whitewater MM
6-19-1847	Lydia (Maulsby) dis for mcd & na
11-18-1848	John & fam gct Mississinewa MM; Keziah (Bales) dis for mcd
12-16-1848	George & fam gct Mississinewa MM
1-20-1849	Edom dis for mcd
5-19-1849	Nancy rocf Whitewater MM
8-18-1849	Ruth (Mills) dis for mcd
10-19-1850	Joseph gct Mississinewa MM
2-18-1854	Ann & fam gct Honey Creek MM

DAVIS (cont)
1-19-1856	Neziah & fam gct Red Cedar MM IA
9-15-1860	New Salem MM gr perm to rst Mariah S
4-20-1861	Baraboo ME gr perm to rst Rachel
3-21-1868	Amos rpt mcd
4-18-1868	Amos mbrp ret
8-15-1868	Joseph & w Katharine Nettle Creek PM rec by rq
12-19-1868	Esther Ann (Hill) rpt mcd
2-20-1869	Flat Rock PM rpt Esther Ann (Hill) mcd; mbrp ret
9-17-1870	Wm Flat Rock PM chm for fighting
6-17-1871	Wm rel by rq
9-16-1871	Alpheus & fam rocf Sugar Plain MM; Louisa rocf Sugar Plain MM
3-16-1878	Wm rec by rq
12-20-1879	Martha Ellen rec by rq of Flat Rock PM
9-19-1885	Wm E gct Whitewater MM
11-16-1889	Hannah M rec by rq
2-20-1892	Anna, Caroline, Ethel, Laura, & Mattie rec by rq of Nettle Creek PM
3-19-1892	James Arthur glt Richmond Grace M E ch
6-16-1894	Miles rocf New Castle MM; Martha Ellen & min ch Eliza Jane & Oda rocf New Castle MM
6-20-1896	Mary Etta rel by rq; jas
2-20-1897	Alma N rel by rq; jas
11-18-1899	Mooreland PM rpt Rufus & Emma rec in mbrp

DEARDORF
2-15-1879	Susan rel by rq; jas

DEARING
3-18-1876	Otto H, Linetta, Austin O, & Elizabeth rec by rq of Nettle Creek PM

DEERING
3-21-1885	John rec by rq
4-20-1889	Ottoway & Elizabeth drpd fr mbrp
7-15-1899	Alice rolf Church of God Chicago IL

DENNA
7-20-1850	Delila Susan rec by rq
12-21-1850	Shubal s Jacob L B rec by rq w/perm Elk MM

DENNING
1-20-1844	Sarah (Mills) dis for mcd

DENNIS
11-6-1822	Thomas & ch Wilson, Branson, & Lindsey rocf Marlborough MM NC
12-11-1822	Thomas & fam rq cert to West Grove MM
2-12-1823	Thomas & fam gct West Grove MM
6-18-1831	Elisha & fam (ch Bartlet & Tilman) rocf West Grove MM
10-15-1831	Thomas & fam (ch Wilson, Branson, & Linsey) rocf West Grove MM
11-17-1832	Wm & s Nathan rocf Marlborough MM NC
4-18-1835	Jesse & fam (ch Wm & Alison) rocf New Garden MM NC
10-15-1836	Absalom & fam (ch David) rocf Marlborough MM NC
11-19-1836	Mahlon rec by rq w/perm of Marlborough MM NC
9-18-1838	Jesse chm
2-15-1840	Orlando rec by rq of f Mahlon
4-18-1840	Branson gct New Garden MM to m Elma Reynolds
9-19-1840	Wm Jr rec by rq
11-24-1842	Lyndsey s Thomas & Elizabeth Wayne Co m Irena dt Dempsey & Jane Thornburg Wayne Co at West River Mtg
1-21-1843	Absalom & fam rq cert to New Garden MM
1-20-1844	Miriam & Jesse dis for j separatists
2-17-1844	Absalom & w Eunice & ch Anna, Delilah, Flavia, Thomas, Clarkson, Eunice, & Ruth rocf New Garden MM
4-20-1844	Wm Jr dis for j separatists.
5-18-1844	Wm dis for j separatists
4-18-1846	Wm rec by rq

DENNIS (cont)
5-15-1847	Nathan & Mary appt elder; Mary d
10-21-1847	Wilson s Thomas & Elizabeth Wayne Co m Rachel dt Dempsey & Jane Thornburg Wayne Co at West River
5-24-1848	Nathan s Wm & Delilah Wayne Co m Evalina dt David & Eunice Worth Guilford Co NC at Springfield Mtg
1-20-1849	Mahlon & fam gct Dover MM; Tilmon dis for dp & upl
3-17-1849	Lyndsey dis for dp & offering to fight
5-19-1849	Lyndsey appeals dis to QM
9-1-1849	QM reversed judgment in Lyndsey's case
11-16-1850	Elizabeth appt elder
3-18-1854	Mahlon & fam (ch James, Orland W, Nathan, Isaac Newton, Henry Carver, & John) rocf Dover MM; Louisa & ch Zeruah & Rebecca rocf Dover MM
6-16-1855	Anna (Baldwin) dis for mcd
10-18-1856	Jesse rec by rq; living in WI; rst
11-15-1856	Melinda C & Hannah M dt Jesse rec in mbrp
12-20-1856	Jesse & fam gct Winneshiek MM IA
6-23-1858	Wilson s Thomas & Elizabeth Wayne Co m Lydia dt Isaac & Tamar Reynolds Wayne Co at Nettle Creek Mtg
9-17-1859	Lyndsey dis for getting angry, threatening to strike with a shovel, & using unbecoming language
2-18-1860	Thomas gct Dover MM OH to m Lucy Ann Peebles; West River PM rpt Matilda C for att mcd
4-21-1860	Matilda C chm
10-20-1860	Lucy Ann rocf Dover MM OH
11-22-1860	Thomas C s Absalom & Eunice Wayne Co m Sarah E dt Dempsey & Jane Thornburg Wayne Co at West River
4-20-1861	Lydia appt o
4-18-1863	Tilmon rec by rq
5-21-1863	Elizabeth elder d ae 68y 7m 9d
7-18-1863	Nathan D rpt mcd
8-15-1863	Nathan D mbrp ret
9-19-1863	Wm rpt mcd
10-17-1863	Wm mbrp ret; Evelina appt o; Dover MM OH rpt Emily (Peebles) mcd; rq this mtg to treat w/her
11-2-1863	Emily (Peebles) chm; Dover MM OH inf
4-16-1864	Emily rocf Dover MM OH
2-18-1865	Isaac N rpt mcd
3-18-1865	Isaac N mbrp ret; Melinda rpt mcd; West River PM rpt Zeruiah W guilty of unchastity; Nettle Creek PM rpt Melinda for unchastity & mcd
4-15-1865	Zeruiah W chm; Melinda mbrp ret
2-17-1866	Absalom & fam gct Cherry Grove MM; Thomas C & fam gct Cherry Grove MM
3-21-1868	Osborn rpt mcd; chm
11-19-1870	Mahlon & fam gct White River MM
12-17-1870	Osborn & Branson appt o
3-18-1871	Louisa West River PM rec by rq
2-17-1872	Edwin rpt mcd; chm; j M E ch
8-17-1872	Lyndsey chm for upl and "threatening violence to a brother member"
11-12-1872	Mahlon & w Louisa & ch Henry C, Rebecca, & Louisa rocf White River MM
3-20-1875	Edwin & min s gct Wabash MM
10-16-1875	David W gct White Water MM
4-21-1877	Dempsey T Nettle Creek PM compl fighting
10-20-1877	Dempsey T dis for fighting
3-16-1878	Mary E rec by rq of Nettle Creek PM
8-17-1878	Thomas appt o
5-17-1879	Osborn, Branson, Louisa, & Lucy Ann appt elder
7-16-1881	Royal Arlistes rocf Wabash MM
3-18-1882	Susan rec by rq of Nettle Creek PM
3-17-1883	Milicent & min s John Warren rocf Hopewell MM
4-21-1883	Henry C gct Spiceland MM
6-?-1884	Osborn rec as minister
2-21-1885	Zenora C & dt Fidella F rec by rq
12-19-1885	Malinda dis for murderous assault upon her h
11-17-1888	Isaac N glt Franklin M E ch
3-16-1889	Mary E dis

SPRINGFIELD MONTHLY MEETING
MINUTES AND MARRIAGES

DENNIS (cont)
4-20-1889	Mary E drpd fr mbrp
8-17-1889	Minnie rec by rq
10-19-1889	Lizzie E rocf Cherry Grove MM
11-16-1889	Hannah M rec in mbrp
9-20-1890	Melinda rec by rq
2-20-1892	Viola (**Thompson**) rec on ltf Franklin M E ch
1-21-1893	Viola T glt Franklin M E ch
3-?-1894	Job E rec minister
3-16-1895	Rosa rec by rq of Nettle Creek PM
4-17-1897	Oliver & w & ch rel by rq
10-15-1898	Nellie M, Lydia, & W H rel by rq of Nettle Creek PM
11-18-1899	Jennie & dt Grace E rec by rq; Rufus & w Emma rec by rq

DENNY
1-19-1850	Margaret rocf Elk MM
4-19-1851	Sarah C rec by rq
11-25-1852	Shubal Henry Co s Lazarus & Susannah Preble Co OH m Doritha **Huff** dt Wm & Lydia **Jenkins** Henry Co at Flat Rock
10-18-1856	Mary T dis for mcd
2-16-1861	Jacob B rpt mcd; drpd fr mbrp
12-21-1861	Shubal & fam gct Duck Creek MM
1-16-1886	Jacob B rec by rq of Flat Rock PM

DERING
3-18-1876	Lisetta, Elizabeth, Otto H, & Austin O rec by rq
4-15-1876	John rec by rq
3-21-1885	John rec by rq

DICK
8-20-1898	Gurney H rocf Spiceland MM

DILLINGER
5-16-1885	Eric rec by rq
6-20-1885	Eric's d rpt

DINES
3-15-1851	Nancy (**Hutchens**) dis for mcd
3-17-1888	Silas G rec by rq of Springfield PM

DOAN
6-17-1891	Enos L s Amos & Martha Marion Co m Mary Louisa dt Thomas Elwood & Nancy (**Goodrich**) **Clark** at Economy
12-18-1897	Louisa rel by rq; j Christian ch

DOHERTY
3-15-1834	Mary dis

DOLBY
5-20-1893	Jennie M rq cert to Whitewater MM

DOUGHERTY
2-18-1899	Raymond rec by rq of Springfield PM

DRAKE
3-19-1898	Joseph W rec by rq of Nettle Creek PM

DUKE
6-16-1855	New Salem MM rpt Marila (**Beeson**) for dp & mcd; that mtg rq to treat w/her & rpt
10-20-1855	Marila (**Beeson**) dis

EAVES
9-16-1837	Chester MM rpt John mcd; rq this mtg to treat w/him
10-21-1837	John did not make satisfaction; rpt to Chester MM
9-15-1838	Chester MM rpt John dis

EBRIGHT
3-21-1874	Wm B rec by rq of West River PM

EBRITE
9-15-1883	Wm appt o
4-18-1891	Wm & fam gct Muncie MM

ECHELBARGER
3-15-1873	Christena E rec by rq of West River PM

EDGERTON
1-17-1852	Caroline (**Osborn**) dis for mcd

EDWARDS
5-19-1860	Henry J rec by rq
4-17-1875	Nathan rec by rq of Springfield PM
2-16-1884	Henry J West River dis for na & disunity
3-15-1884	Henry J dis for na

ELDER
4-17-1869	Eunice E Nettle Creek PM rec by rq
3-16-1889	Eunice E dis
4-20-1889	Eunice E drpd fr mbrp

ELLIOTT
12-16-1875	Flat Rock PM rpt Martha (**Carr**) mcd
5-19-1849	Martha (**Carr**) dis for mcd
4-17-1875	Buffum rec in mbrp

ELLIS
8-18-1832	Mordecai rocf Newberry MM TN
1-19-1833	Samuel rocf New Hope MM Green Co TN
6-15-1844	Samuel dis for j separatists
1-16-1847	James A & w Mary rocf New Hope MM Green Co TN; Nehemiah prcf New Hope MM Green Co TN to m Ruth **Lamar**
1-21-1847	Nehemiah s Samuel & Keziah Wayne Co m Ruth dt Isaac & Hannah **Lamar** Wayne Co at West River Mtg
1-15-1848	Nehemiah & dt rocf New Hope MM Green Co TN; Rebecca min rocf New Hope MM Green Co TN
11-18-1848	James dis for dp, att mcd, & na
11-15-1850	Mary dis for att mcd
1-18-1851	Nettle Creek PM rpt Nehemiah mcd
3-15-1851	Nehemiah chm; Mississinewa MM rpt Delilah (**Runnels**) mcd; rq this mtg to treat w/her & rpt
4-19-1851	Delilah (**Runnels**) chm
7-19-1851	Delilah rocf Mississinewa MM
10-18-1851	Susannah (**Lewis**) rpt mcd
11-15-1851	Susannah (**Lewis**) chm
8-18-1855	Susannah & min ch gct Three River MM
6-19-1858	New Salem MM gr perm to rst Mary
7-21-1860	New Salem MM gr perm to rst Samuel & James A
3-15-1862	Nehemiah & fam gct New Salem MM

ELLOT
3-20-1875	Ruffin rec by rq

ELMORE
11-16-1844	Salem MM rpt Benjamin na & j separatists; rq help in treating w/him
1-18-1845	Rpt to Salem MM that Benjamin did not make satisfsction
9-20-1845	Benjamin dis by Salem MM

EMMAL
7-19-1834	Mary dis

ENGLE
3-17-1894	Thomas & w rec by rq

EVANS
2-15-1845	Sarah Jane (**Thornburg**) dis for j separatists & mcd
5-27-1852	John s James & Martha Wayne Co m Nancy dt Wm & Elizabeth **Davis** Wayne Co at Flat Rock Mtg
9-18-1852	Nancy E gct Whitewater MM; d bef cert arr
10-18-1884	Laura A gct New Salem MM
2-16-1889	Wm & w Nancy Ellen rec by rq of Nettle Creek PM

FARIS
6-20-1891	Lydia M glt Terre Haute M E ch

FARLOW
7-21-1866	Luezer & ch Lorenzo, Nancy, Roxanne, John Franklin, & David Lindsey Nettle Creek PM rec by rq
2-19-1887	Edwin & Lorenzo rel by rq; jas
4-18-1891	Colfax rq rel fr mbrp; S C rel fr mbrp
5-16-1891	S C wthd rq for rel fr mbrp
6-18-1892	Wm S rel fr mbrp
7-16-1892	W S rel by rq
11-17-1894	David L rel fr mbrp
4-20-1895	Lewezer & Myrtle rel by rq
5-21-1898	Sarah V rel by rq; jas
10-15-1898	John F & dt Clara E & Blanch L rel by rq of Nettle Creek PM; Schuyler Colfax rel by rq of Nettle Creek PM

FARLOWE
1-20-1866	Wm S rocf Marlborough MM NC

FARMER
1-2-1822	Nathan, Moses & John gct Cherry Grove MM
5-19-1832	Jemima dis
11-18-1848	Luzena gct Cincinnati MM
8-18-1860	Springfield PM rpt Matilda (Macy) mcd
10-20-1860	Matilda (Macy) mbrp ret

FARQUHAR
2-20-1886	Josie rec by rq
8-21-1886	Frank rec by rq
11-17-1888	Frank & w Josie gct Muncie MM

FIELDER
3-18-1882	Anna rec by rq of Springfield PM

FISHER
9-22-1824	John & fam (ch Joseph, Thomas, & John) rocf Whitewater MM
9-22-1824	Robert rocf Whitewater MM
6-20-1829	John & fam gct White River MM

FLEMING
11-18-1871	Mary Ellen rocf White River MM
3-16-1889	Clara Bell dis

FLEMMING
4-20-1889	Clara Bell drpd fr mbrp

FORD
8-18-1860	West River rpt Gennetta (Taylor) mcd; drpd fr mbrp
12-16-1882	Hannah S & s Jessie Alford rec by rq
2-17-1883	Nathaniel rec by rq
4-17-1886	Oliver rocf Cherry Grove MM
4-20-1889	Jesse A drpd fr mbrp

FORKNER
6-16-1849	Armina (Pierce) dis for mcd

FORSYTHE
2-19-1831	Ruth dis

FOSTER
3-18-1876	Robert J & fam roc
11-17-1883	Patience Ann & ch gct Dublin MM

FOUTZ
3-18-1893	Ella rec by rq

FOX
1-16-1886	Melissa rec by rq of Flat Rock PM
2-20-1892	Charlie & Nadia/Neaty rec by rq
10-15-1898	Charles W & Nettie S & s Oscar rel by rq of Nettle Creek PM

SPRINGFIELD MONTHLY MEETING MINUTES AND MARRIAGES

FRAZIER
8-19-1826	Wm rocf West Grove MM
10-19-1850	Springfield MM Clinton Co OH rpt Rebecca (Millikan) mcd; rq this mtg to treat w/her & rpt
11-16-1850	Rpt to Springfield MM Clinton Co OH Rebecca (Millikan) did not make satisfaction
2-15-1851	Springfield MM Clinton Co OH rpt Rebecca dis
7-17-1852	Wm dis for being out of unity with Friends & na
2-21-1885	Abner rec by rq of Flat Rock PM
3-21-1885	Hannah & min ch Albert T, Bartley E, Charley L, Dallas E, Elvin F, & Freddie E rec by rq of West River PM
10-17-1885	White River PM rpt Abner dr
2-19-1887	Abner & fam gct Cherry Grove MM
2-18-1893	Eldora rocf Duck Creek MM
3-18-1893	Eldora rel by rq to jas

FREEMAN
4-18-1846	Naomi dis for j UB ch

FRENCH
11-17-1894	Eunice glt Horton M E ch KS

GALLION
4-18-1857	Matilda (Beeson) rpt mcd; drpd fr mbrp

GALYEAN
10-15-1853	Edith dis for mcd

GAMBER
2-16-1884	Jacob, Abbe, Michael, & Lucy rec by rq
3-15-1884	Charley A rec by rq of par Jacob & Ada
8-15-1885	Jacob & w Ida & min s Charles glt Decatur First M E ch IL

GIBSON
8-18-1827	Rachel dis

GILESPIE
11-17-1894	Eva rel fr mbrp

GILLESPIE
2-20-1892	Eva rec by rq of Nettle Creek PM
6-18-1892	Alice gct Muncie MM

GLASPIE
8-16-1890	Alice rec in mbrp

GOODE
7-17-1847	Lydia Ann (Macy) dis for mcd

GRACE
2-16-1895	Annie rolf Economy M E ch
3-16-1895	Jessie rec by rq of Springfield PM

GRAY
5-17-1826	Margaret & ch Davis & Jonathan rocf New Garden MM
3-18-1882	Wm P & w Julia & min ch Alice, Benjamin E, Edith B, & John H rec by rq of Nettle Creek PM
2-21-1891	Julia C dis; jas
3-19-1898	Julia C rec by rq
6-18-1898	Julia rel by rq
9-17-1898	Alice (Cary) glt Franklin M E ch

GREEN
6-20-1885	Wm & Luella rec by rq of Flat Rock PM

GREY
3-18-1882	Wm R & w Julia C & ch Alice C, Benjamin E, Edith B, & Jehu rec by rq

GWIN
10-21-1843	Irene (Canaday) dis for mcd

SPRINGFIELD MONTHLY MEETING
MINUTES AND MARRIAGES

GWIN (cont)
4-19-1851	Asenith (**Swain**) dis for mcd
3-15-1873	John D & w Rhoda R rec by rq of West River PM
7-20-1878	Pleasant rec by rq; form M E
5-17-1879	Pleasant appt o
11-17-1883	Pleasant & w Charlotte gct Farmland MM Randolph Co
12-20-1884	John D & fam gct White River MM
3-17-1888	Cyrus B & Asenith rec by rq of Springfield PM
10-20-1894	Elihu Swain & ch Glennie Allice, Freddie Carl, Oscar Swain, Charles O, & Alsie Lena rec by rq
3-16-1895	Nellie rec by rq of Springfield PM

GWINN
11-15-1890	Walter T rec by rq

HADLEY
9-19-1851	Ruth (**Macy**) rpt mcd
11-15-1851	Ruth (**Macy**) chm
8-20-1853	Mary Ann (**Macy**) rpt mcd
1-21-1854	Mary Ann (**Macy**) chm
5-25-1854	Maryann gct White Lick MM
6-16-1888	Thomas P rocf White Lick MM Morgan Co

HAISLEY
9-24-1862	Davis s Joseph & Sarah Wayne Co m Martha Jane dt Lyndsey & Irena **Dennis** Wayne Co at Nettle Creek
2-21-1863	Martha Jane gct Dover MM
8-19-1876	Martha & s Edwin R gct Hopewell MM
1-19-1878	Isaac rocf Hopewell MM
10-15-1881	Isaac & fam gct New Garden MM
3-18-1882	Isaac & fam gct Dover MM to replace lost cert to New Garden
4-16-1887	Isaac & w Martha & 3 min ch rocf Dover MM
4-19-1890	Isaac E & fam gct Muncie MM

HALER
2-20-1897	Joseph & w Maggie rec by rq of Nettle Creek PM
11-20-1897	Joseph & w Maggie gct West Grove MM
8-20-1898	Joseph & Maggie gct West Grove MM

HALL
6-18-1836	Wm G rq mbrp
8-20-1836	Wm G rec in mbrp
2-18-1843	Wm G dis for mcd & j M E
4-21-1894	Mary & min ch Irvin & Earl **Parker** gct Spiceland MM

HAMMER
5-15-1830	Nathan rocf Lost Creek MM TN
8-26-1830	Nathan s Isaac & Hannah m Ruth dt John & Rachel **Lee**
3-16-1833	Nathan & fam gct Duck Creek MM

HANES
12-19-1840	Susannah dis for j Christian ch

HANSEN
1-16-1836	Borden dis

HANSON
10-15-1831	Borden & fam (ch John, Levi, Edwin, Thomas, & Elisha) rocf Somerset MM OH
2-17-1838	Borden chm
12-19-1838	John s Borden & Rachel Wayne Co m Sarah dt Hezekiah & Clary **Hutchens** at Springfield Mtg
10-15-1841	Borden rpt for wthd just debts
1-15-1842	Borden's debts rpt settled; case dismissed
5-22-1845	Levi s Borden & Rachel Wayne Co m Delilah dt Daniel & Sarah **Reece** at Springfield
9-15-1849	John & fam gct Honey Creek MM
4-19-1851	Rachel & ch gct Honey Creek MM
5-17-1851	Edwin gct Honey Creek MM

HANSON (cont)
8-16-1851	Levi rpt for fighting
9-20-1851	Levi chm
11-15-1851	Levi & fam gct Honey Creek MM
4-16-1853	Thomas gct Honey Creek MM
6-2-1875	Zimri s Levi & Delilah Howard Co m Isabel W dt Jesse & Ruth **Chamness** Wayne Co at Nettle Creek
2-17-1877	Zimri rocf Pleasant Hill MM

HARDIN
2-16-1889	Emma (**Test**) gct Duck Creek MM

HARRIS
9-22-1824	Jonas & fam (ch Wm, Henry, Jesse, Jonas, & Jacob) rocf Whitewater
4-17-1830	West River PM dis Wm for mcd & dp
7-21-1832	Jonas dis for na
3-16-1833	West River PM dis Jesse for mcd, na, & dp
4-20-1833	West River PM dis Henry for mcd, na, & dp
8-15-1835	Hannah & fam gct Mississinewa MM
3-21-1885	Julia A & dt Flora **Dennis** gct Farmland MM
4-20-1895	Esther (**Carter**) rocf New Castle MM
11-21-1896	Esther rel by rq to jas

HARTER
2-20-1892	Richard, Jesse, Gracie, John W, Priscilla, Frank, Mary, Joseph L, Pheraby, Emma, Ella, & George rec by rq
3-16-1895	Wm & w Mary rec by rq of Nettle Creek PM
2-15-1896	Orpha rec by rq of Nettle Creek PM
10-15-1898	Richard rel by rq of Nettle Creek PM
1-21-1899	Leroy & Hannah rec by rq of Nettle Creek PM

HARTY
1-17-1856	Mira (**Macy**) rpt mcd; drpd fr mbrp

HASKET
9-20-1884	Zimri rel fr mbrp
6-20-1885	Zimri & w Susan rq mbrp

HASTINGS
1-21-1899	Ercie Ona rec by rq of Nettle Creek PM

HEALTON
11-20-1830	John & fam (ch Allen, Joel, & Jonathan) rocf Deep Creek MM NC
4-20-1839	Sarah (**Swain**) dis for mcd, dp, & apd
10-20-1841	John Henry Co s Abraham & Rebecca Surry Co NC m Ruth dt John & Sarah **Hodson** Henry Co at Westbury Mtg
12-25-1845	Allen s John & Sarah Henry Co m Elizabeth dt Stephen & Elizabeth **Cox** Wayne Co at Springfield Mtg
12-23-1847	Joel s John & Sarah Henry Co m Mary Ann dt Wm & Elizabeth **Bond** at Flat Rock
7-15-1848	John & fam gct Honey Creek MM
2-16-1850	Joel & fam gct Honey Creek MM
9-16-1854	Allen & fam rq cert to Honey Creek MM
11-16-1861	Joel & fam (ch Wm B, John A, & Albert) rocf New Salem MM
12-17-1870	Joel appt o
3-15-1884	Mary E rec by rq of Flat Rock PM
6-20-1885	Hannah rec by rq of Flat Rock PM
1-16-1886	Artemas E rec by rq of Flat Rock PM
5-18-1889	Wm & w Mary E & min s Artemas E rocf New Castle MM
1-21-1899	Maggie rec by rq of Nettle Creek PM

HEFNER
10-21-1843	Mary Ann dis for mcd

HELTON
3-20-1858	Allen dis for na
3-18-1893	Bertha rec by rq of Mooreland PM

HENLEY
9-16-1826	Jacob & fam (ch John L, Isaac, & Wm) rocf Lees Creek MM OH

HERL
12-19-1868	Flat Rock rpt Sarah (Hill) mcd; d bef comm visited her
3-20-1869	Sarah dec

HEYER
2-21-1891	Frank & Sarah Etta rel by rq; jas

HIATT
2-7-1821	John & fam (s Jesse) rocf Center MM Clinton Co OH
12-5-1821	Gideon rocf Center MM OH
7-17-1822	Jesse chm
8-14-1822	John & fam & Jesse gct Cherry Grove MM
8-21-1841	Daniel W prcf West Grove MM to m Melinda **Mendenhall**
9-18-1841	Daniel W rpt m to Melinda **Mendenhall**
8-17-1844	Daniel W & w Melinda & min ch Eliza Ann & Edwin W rocf Dover MM
9-19-1846	Eliza Jane (**Baldwin**) dis for mcd & na; Elizabeth & Luzena dis for j Christian ch
8-21-1847	Sarah rec by rq
10-20-1849	Daniel W & fam gct Cherry Grove MM
7-20-1850	Flat Rock PM rpt Sarah guilty of unchastity
8-17-1850	Sarah chm
2-15-1851	John & Charity rec by rq w/perm of Clear Creek MM OH
3-15-1851	Macy & Mary rocf Fairfield MM
7-16-1853	Daniel W & fam (ch Edwin W, James Addison, Oliver Lindley, & Lyndon Cornelius) rocf Cherry Grove MM; Melinda & ch Eliza & Emily rocf Cherry Grove
7-15-1865	Edwin W gct Wabash MM
3-20-1875	Emma rec by rq
1-19-1878	Samantha Ellen & s Ervin M rec by rq fr UB ch; h Linden C
10-20-1883	James & min s Thomas gct Whitewater MM
7-18-1891	Linden C & Samantha Ellen gct Harmony MM KS

HILL
4-12-1826	Jacob & fam (s Benjamin J) rocf West Grove
4-17-1847	Benjamin rpt mcd
5-15-1847	Benjamin chm
5-17-1851	Charles dis
7-17-1852	Henry dis for mcd
11-17-1855	Aaron rpt mcd; drpd fr mbrp
3-19-1864	John rpt mcd; drpd fr mbrp
9-15-1866	Lavina & dt Esther Ann Flat Rock PM rec by rq
5-17-1879	Benjamin J appt o

HINSHAW
11-17-1838	Wm B & fam (s James) rocf Spiceland MM
6-19-1852	James M dis for mcd, dr, & upl
8-21-1869	Springfield MM compl Wm B wthd payment debts; Ret to Whitewater MM to treat w/him
11-20-1869	Whitewater MM rpt compl against Wm B unfounded
12-18-1869	Wm B gct Whitewater MM
6-21-1873	Hannah gct Whitewater MM

HOBSON
3-1-1820	George & ch Isaac, George, & Wm rocf Deep Creek MM NC
4-18-1829	Thomas gct New Garden MM to m Mary **Thomas**
3-16-1833	Charles & Joshua dis for dp & na
3-2-1835	Flat Rock PM rpt George Jr dp, na, & upl
8-15-1835	Flat Rock PM rpt Isaac for being out of unity, na, dp, & giving his work hands ardent spirits
7-16-1836	George Jr dis for mcd & dp; Matilda dis
5-18-1839	Jesse dis for na, dp, & mcd
7-20-1839	George dis for na, dp, & mCd
10-17-1835	Isaac dis

SPRINGFIELD MONTHLY MEETING
MINUTES AND MARRIAGES

HOBSON (cont)
6-17-1843	Stephen dis for j M E
11-21-1846	Wm dis for mcd & na
9-16-1848	John dis for mcd & att mcd

HOCKET
9-20-1862	Gila Ann Nettle Creek PM rec by rq
1-21-1865	Wm A & John W rec by rq of f Jesse
4-16-1865	Jesse & fam gct Poplar Run MM
6-20-1885	Zimri & w Susan rec by rq
12-15-1894	Perry Allen drpd fr mbrp
4-20-1895	Lizzie drpd fr mbrp

HOCKETT
3-16-1861	Warner M rocf Center MM NC
4-25-1861	Warner M s Wm & Hannah Guilford Co NC m Matilda C dt Elisha & Ruth **Dennis** Wayne Co at West River
8-17-1861	Warner N & w Matilda C gct Raysville MM
6-21-1862	Jesse rocf Cherry Grove MM
12-16-1865	John rocf Center MM NC
6-15-1867	Warner M rocf Raysville MM
10-15-1870	Susan & ch Clara Belle & Sarah Emiline Nettle Creek PM rec by rq
2-15-1873	Warner M rpt mcd
6-20-1874	Warner M & min ch gct Dover MM
3-18-1876	Zimri, Malinda, & Sarah E rec by rq of Nettle Creek PM
3-15-1884	Zimri rel by rq
2-21-1891	Emma rel by rq to j Richmond English Lutheran ch
2-20-1897	Susan J rel by rq; jas

HODGEN
8-17-1833	Samuel gct Cherry Grove MM

HODGSON
7-22-1847	Zechariah s John & Sarah Henry Co m Janney dt Joel & Susannah **Larrowe** Henry Co at Flat Rock

HODSON
8-16-1828	Thomas dis for mcd w/one too near kin
5-15-1830	John rpt mcd
7-17-1830	John chm; Samuel rocf Center MM NC
5-18-1833	Zechariah rec by rq w/perm Center MM NC after dis
6-15-1833	Isaac rpt mcd
8-17-1833	Isaac chm
9-21-1833	Franklin, James, & Isaac & 1 dt ch Zechariah rec by rq
9-21-1833	Thomas rst after dis
11-16-1833	Solomon & Uriah rec by rq of f Thomas
1-18-1834	John dis for dp, mcd, & att mcd
9-19-1835	Thomas & ch gct Vermillion MM
11-19-1836	Henry rpt mcd & dp
2-18-1837	Henry chm
11-19-1836	Jacob rocf Chester MM
4-20-1839	Westbury PM rpt Henry for fighting
7-20-1839	Henry chm
5-18-1839	Deborah dis for being out of unity & na
8-17-1839	John Jr rpt for na & mcd; chm; John gct Sugar River MM
1-18-1840	John Jr moved back; ret cert; John dis for dp, att mcd, & mcd
2-15-1840	Jacob gct Mississinewa MM
3-21-1840	Henry & fam gct West Grove MM
4-18-1840	Jesse rpt mcd; Zechariah dis for dr
5-16-1840	John chm
6-20-1840	Franklin gct Salem MM
9-18-1841	Elizabeth & ch gct Salem MM IA
12-1-1841	Nathan s John & Sarah Henry Co m Elizabeth dt Job & Thamer **Ratcliff** Wayne Co at Springfield; Jonathan rpt m Mary **Allen**
1-15-1842	Henry & fam rocf West Grove MM
6-17-1843	Henry & fam gct Salem MM IA

SPRINGFIELD MONTHLY MEETING
MINUTES AND MARRIAGES

HODSON (cont)
1-20-1844	Elizabeth dis for j separatists
3-16-1844	Solomon dis for j separatists; Henry & fam ret cert
6-17-1843	Henry & fam gct to Salem MM IA; end by that mtg
5-18-1844	Elvira & dt Sarah Jane rocf Salem MM IA
12-21-1844	Thomas & Anna dis for j separatists
8-16-1845	Richard rpt mcd
9-20-1845	Richard chm
12-20-1845	Matilda (**Larue**) rpt mcd
12-25-1845	Matilda (**Larue**) chm
9-19-1846	Westbury PM rpt Henry had taken false affirmation helping a mbr mcd
10-17-1846	Salem MM IA rq to treat w/Henry after compl altered
4-17-1847	David rpt mcd
5-15-1847	David chm
8-21-1847	Sarah Jane rec by rq
7-15-1848	Richard & fam gct Honey Creek MM
1-20-1849	Rhoda rocf Mississinewa MM
6-16-1849	Jonathan dis for j separatists
9-15-1849	Nathan & fam gct Honey Creek MM
1-18-1851	Solomon dis for j separatists & mcd
2-15-1851	Uriah dis for mcd & na
4-19-1851	John & fam gct Honey Creek MM
6-21-1851	Spiceland MM rpt Mary (**Baldwin**) mcd; rq this mtg to treat w/her & rpt
8-16-1851	Spiceland MM rpt Mary (**Baldwin**) did not make satisfaction
9-20-1851	Zachara & fam gct Honey Creek MM
10-16-1852	Rodah gct Honey Creek MM
7-16-1853	Richard & fam rocf Honey Creek MM; Matilda & ch Juliann & Gulielma rocf Honey Creek MM
8-20-1853	John & fam rocf Honey Creek MM; Sarah & dt Charlotte rocf Honey Creek MM; Zechariah & fam (s Joel) rocf Honey Creek MM; Geney & dt Rachel rocf Honey Creek MM
6-17-1854	Zechariah & fam gct Spring Grove MM IA
10-21-1854	John & fam gct Spring Creek MM IA; Richard & fam gct Spring Creek MM IA
10-20-1855	Thomas rec by rq
9-19-1857	Jane dis for jas in IA
10-17-1857	Jesse dis for jas in IA
3-20-1858	New Salem MM gr perm to rst Solomon Jr
7-17-1858	David & fam gct Honey Creek MM; Jesse's min ch gct Honey Creek MM
8-21-1858	Cynthia gct New Salem MM
9-18-1858	Ann rec in mbrp by New Salem MM w/con of this mtg

HOFFNER
2-21-1891	Mary E gc

HOLADAY
12-10-1843	Samuel & fam gct Lick Creek MM

HOLIDAY
1-18-1840	Samuel & fam rocf Springfield MM NC

HOLLINGSWORTH
5-11-1825	Joseph rec in mbrp
2-30-1830	Henry rocf Miami MM OH
5-19-1838	Joseph gct Fairfield MM
1-20-1844	Henry dis for j separatists
3-16-1844	Hannah dis for j separatists
11-21-1857	Henry rec by rq

HOLLOWAY
7-21-1827	Wm & fam rocf Lees Creek MM OH
9-13-1827	John & fam (ch Jacob & John W) rocf Plainfield MM OH
8-16-1828	Wm & fam gct White River MM; John & fam gct White River MM

HOLLOWAY (cont)
6-20-1829	Wm Jr rpt mcd
7-18-1829	John chm
9-19-1829	Wm Jr & fam gct White River MM

HOLLYDAY
5-21-1859	Almeda (**Milliken**) rpt mcd; drpd fr mbrp

HONEYCUTT
4-19-1851	Jane C rocf Cherry Grove MM

HONNEYCUTT
3-21-1829	Daniel & fam rocf Milford MM

HOOKER
9-15-1838	Lydia dis

HOOVER
4-17-1830	Charity dis
8-16-1884	John H chm for "dissipation"

HOUCK
3-17-1894	Ellen rec by rq of Mooreland PM

HOUGH
4-17-1830	Ira & fam (ch Isaiah, Jesse, Mahlon, & Nathan) rocf New Garden MM
11-25-1830	Isaiah s Ira & Elizabeth Henry Co m Elizabeth dt John & Anna **Marshall** Henry Co at Flat Rock
10-20-1832	Elizabeth & fam gct New Garden MM
12-21-1833	Jesse min rocf New Garden MM
9-21-1838	Jesse min dis
6-19-1841	Mahlon & Nathan min rocf Dover MM; Mahlon d bef cert rec
5-16-1846	Isaiah & fam gct Salem MM IA
2-20-1892	Manson rec by rq
3-17-1894	Manson Z rq lt to Windfall M E ch
4-21-1894	Elmina gct Muncie MM
7-17-1897	Anna rocf Amboy MM
1-21-1899	Anna gct New Hope MM

HOWEL
12-12-1830	Charles rec by rq
3-17-1832	Wm, Charles, Enos, & Levi ch Charles rec by rq
11-21-1835	Wm dis for mcd & dp
5-20-1843	Anna rpt j M E; dis
5-19-1849	Levi dis for j M E
7-21-1849	Charles Jr dis for j M E
10-20-1849	Enos dis for j M E
5-19-1855	Joseph & Amelia (**Baldwin**) rpt mcd; drpd fr mbrp
1-21-1865	Charles Jr rec by rq
3-18-1865	Larkin rec by rq
2-16-1884	Larkin, Lydia, & John rec by rq
2-20-1892	Joseph & Amelia rec by rq of Nettle Creek PM

HOWELL
7-15-1854	Rachel (**Rightsman**) rpt mcd
8-19-1854	Rachel (**Rightsman**) chm
4-21-1855	Larkin rpt mcd; drpd fr mbrp
5-15-1880	Larkin dis for having dance at his house, att shooting matches, wagering, & na
8-16-1884	John H chm for dissipation
8-21-1886	John rel by rq; jas

HOWELS
7-20-1844	Sophia dis for j UB ch

HUIT
4-17-1858	Mary (**Hill**) rpt mcd; drpd fr mbrp

HUNNICUTT
1-20-1844	Daniel dis for j separatists
7-20-1844	Jane dis for j separatists
10-17-1846	John dis for j separatists

196

HUNNICUTT (cont)
10-21-1850	John T rec by rq
12-21-1850	John T gct Cherry Grove MM to m Jane **Charles**
5-21-1870	Wm H rocf Raysville MM
2-28-1872	John T s Daniel & Jane Randolph Co m Deborah **Arnett** dt Henry & Hannah **Hollingsworth** Wayne Co at Springfield
6-20-1874	John T appt o
4-17-1875	Deborah rec in mbrp
7-17-1875	Wm P rec in mbrp
3-16-1895	Earl, Mariam, & Anne rec by rq of Springfield PM

HUNNYCUTT
5-20-1848	Mary gct Milford MM

HUNT
3-17-1832	Thomas & fam (s Uriah) rocf West Grove MM; Jonathan, Phanuel, & Wm ch Mourning rocf West Grove MM
2-15-1834	Jonathan gct Chester MM
3-21-1840	West River PM rpt Phanuel for dp, na, att mcd, & upl
5-20-1840	Phanuel chm
11-20-1841	Thomas rpt m to Mary **Reynolds**
1-15-1842	Sarah Jane dis for unchastity
6-18-1842	Phanuel rpt mcd
7-16-1842	Phanuel chm
3-20-1847	West River PM rpt Uriah for dp & mcd; now living within the verge of Springfield MM OH; that mtg rq to treat w/him & rpt
8-21-1847	Springfield MM rpt Uriah did not make satisfaction
9-18-1847	Uriah dis for mcd & dp
9-16-1848	Thomas & fam gct Poplar Run MM
12-16-1848	Wm dis for mcd, na, & dp
1-19-1850	Phanuel dis for j M E ch
12-21-1850	Eleanor dis for j M E
9-15-1855	Edward L prcf Green Plain MM OH to m Delphina **Coffin**; Edward L s Isaiah & Rebecca Clark Co OH m Delphina dt Barnabas & Miriam **Coffin** Wayne Co at Springfield Mtg
8-16-1856	Edward L rocf Green Plain MM OH
6-20-1857	Edward L & fam gct Green Plain MM OH
10-22-1873	Wm s Barnabas & Hannah Randolph Co m Milly dt Nathan & Sarah **Parker** Wayne Co at Nettle Creek
11-15-1873	Milly gct New Garden MM
3-21-1874	Wm rec by rq of West River PM
10-20-1883	Wm gct Portland MM

HUSKING
8-17-1844	Louisa (**Lamb**) dis for mcd

HUTCHEN
2-17-1855	Clara gct Honey Creek MM

HUTCHENS
1-19-1833	Ira rpt mcd, na & dp
2-16-1833	Ira chm
10-19-1833	Nicholas gct Deep Creek MM NC
6-18-1842	Enos rpt mcd
7-16-1842	Enos chm
1-21-1843	Ira dis for j M E ch
7-15-1843	Susannah dis for j M E ch
8-19-1843	Hezekiah dis for separating fr church & setting up mtg contrary to discipline
11-18-1843	John prcf Mill Creek MM OH to m Frances Melinda **Bond**
11-23-1843	John s Benjamin & Hannah Montgomery Co OH m Frances M dt Wm & Elizabeth **Bond** Henry Co at Flat Rock
11-15-1845	Thomas dis for j separatists
6-19-1847	John prcf Mill Creek MM OH to m Ann **Hutchens**
4-15-1848	John & min s Wm Frances rocf Mill Creek MM OH
3-16-1850	James rpt mcd
4-20-1850	James chm

HUTCHENS (cont)
6-15-1850	Mary rec by rq
7-17-1852	John & fam gct Honey Creek MM
8-19-1854	James dis for na & j 2 secret organizations
9-16-1854	Mary dis for na & j 2 secret organizations called Dts of Temperance & Good Tempers
6-20-1863	Clara rocf Honey Creek MM
7-20-1872	Nancy rec by rq
2-17-1877	Zerilda A & min ch Cynthia Emmiline & Lizzie Etta **Routh** gct Cherry Grove MM
10-20-1883	Wm gct Portland MM

HUTCHINS
3-17-1832	Nicholas rocf Deep Creek MM NC; end by Cherry Grove MM
6-23-1847	John s Benjamin & Hannah Miami Co OH m Ann **Hutchens** dt Borden & Rachel **Hansen** Wayne Co at Springfield Mtg OH

HYRE
6-17-1882	Frank rec by rq of Nettle Creek PM
2-21-1891	Frank dis; jas

JACKSON
10-20-1832	Phebe dis
6-18-1842	Rachel dis for j Christian Friends
2-20-1892	Jacob L & Emma B rec by rq

JEFFERIS
12-18-1880	Emily R gct Hopewell MM

JEFFREY
12-17-1853	Sarah (**Jenkins**) dis for mcd

JEFFRIES
11-20-1880	Emily A H rq cert to Hopewell MM

JENKINS
1-18-1840	Wm & fam (ch Anderson Hutchens, Benjamin, & Wm Penn) rocf Mill Creek MM OH
5-15-1841	Anderson H rpt m to Elizabeth D **Wiles**
11-23-1843	Benjamin s Wm & Lydia Henry Co m Frances C dt Luke & Rhoda **Wiles** Henry Co at Flat Rock Mtg
3-18-1848	Benjamin & fam gct Mississinewa MM
10-20-1849	Phebe Ann & Lucinda gct Whitewater MM
5-17-1851	Anderson H dis for mcd & dp
9-16-1854	Line min rocf Dover MM
12-18-1858	Lydia & dt Malinda gct Wabash MM
6-20-1868	Wm P gct Wabash MM

JESSOP
1-21-1832	Jacob & ch Elihu, Mahlon, & James rocf West Grove MM
5-18-1833	Jacob dis for wthd debts
6-15-1833	Elizabeth & ch rq cert to White River MM; not gr
6-20-1835	Elihu gct New Garden MM
1-19-1839	James rpt mcd
3-16-1839	Elizabeth & ch gct White River MM
6-15-1839	James chm
7-26-1839	James gct White River MM
7-21-1849	Back Creek MM gr perm to rst Jacob

JESSUP
4-20-1833	Elihu rpt for getting angry, offering to strike a fellow man, & upl
5-18-1833	Elihu chm
3-20-1858	Henry prcf Dover MM to m Mary E **Nicholson**
3-24-1858	Henry s Thomas & Ann Wayne Co m Mary E dt George & Lucinda **Nicholson** Henry Co at Nettle Creek Mtg
6-19-1858	Mary E gct Dover MM
8-20-1859	Mary E & dt Sarah Ann rocf Dover MM
5-16-1896	Albert S rocf Cherry Grove MM
10-17-1896	Gulielma & min ch rocf Van Wert MM OH

SPRINGFIELD MONTHLY MEETING
MINUTES AND MARRIAGES

JESTER
12-15-1883	John rec by rq

JOHNSON
1-22-1827	Charles s James & Ruth Wayne Co m Nancy dt Amizia & Isabel **Beeson** Randolph Co at West River MH
5-17-1828	Josiah & fam (ch James, Wm, Elijah, Elam, Ashly, & Josiah) rocf Whitewater MM
10-22-1828	Jesse Randolph Co s Jesse & Hannah Chatham Co NC m Rhoda dt John & Rhoda **Swain** Randolph Co at Springfield MH
6-16-1832	James dis for dp
2-16-1833	Charles & fam (ch Caleb, Charles Alexander, & Isaac Kindley) rocf West Grove MM
5-17-1834	Charles & fam gct Whitewater MM
8-16-1834	Josiah dis for promoting mcd & j M E ch
8-16-1834	Polly dis
4-18-1835	Wm dis for na & dp
11-16-1839	Elam & Elijah dis for na & dp
12-27-1842	Mill Creek MM OH gr perm to rst Elam
5-18-1844	Elam rocf Mill Creek MM OH
7-19-1845	Elam rpt mcd
9-16-1845	Elam chm
4-21-1849	Josiah dis for na, j M E, & mcd
10-19-1850	Alfred rocf Miami MM OH
2-15-1851	Alfred gct Wabash MM
5-17-1851	Elam dis for na
1-17-1852	Ashley dis for mcd & na
9-15-1855	Joseph C prcf OH MM to m Elmina **Hinshaw**
9-19-1855	Joseph C s Micajah & Rebecca Warren Co OH m Elmina L dt Wm B & Hannah **Hinshaw** Wayne Co at Springfield Mtg
6-21-1856	Elmina L gct Miami MM OH
8-15-1863	Elmina L rocf Miami MM OH
4-17-1869	Elmina gct Whitewater MM
3-16-1895	George W rec by rq of Springfield PM

JONES
2-2-1820	Jesse appt to comm
3-1-1820	Lydia proposed as elder
11-1-1820	Richard, Moses, & Daniel rocf Mill Creek MM
3-7-1821	Richard con mcd
3-12-1823	R chm after New Garden MM treated w/him; gc
5-14-1823	Francis & s Richard rocf Mill Creek MM
1-14-1824	Francis & fam gct Mill Creek MM
3-16-1825	Lydia removed as elder for slapping an adult step-dt
5-19-1827	Richard & fam (s Daniel) rocf New Garden MM
5-23-1827	Moses s Daniel & Jemima Wayne Co m Eunice dt Jonathan & Hannah **Macy** Wayne Co at Springfield Mtg
7-21-1827	Daniel gct New Garden MM to m
4-19-1828	Richard & fam gct New Garden MM
11-21-1829	Richard & fam gct White River MM
6-18-1831	Jesse dis for att Hicksite Mtg & aiding in appt mtg for them
2-15-1834	Daniel & fam gct Mississinewa MM
3-15-1834	Moses dis for na
7-16-1836	Lucinda dis
9-17-1836	John dis for na, dp, & bearing arms in taking a fellow man
7-21-1838	Wm dis for mcd, dp, & na
8-15-1840	Ruth (**Bailey**) dis for mcd, dp, & j M E
9-19-1840	Sally Ann dis for att mcd
11-21-1840	Pleasant dis for dp, na, & mcd
2-17-1844	Lydia dis for j separatists
5-18-1844	Eunice dis for j separatists
5-16-1846	Lydia rec by rq after dis
8-19-1848	Simpson prcf Mississinewa MM to m Keziah **Wiles**
8-22-1848	Simpson s Stephen & Mary Wabash Co m Keziah K dt Luke & Rhoda H **Wiles** Henry Co at Flat Rock
11-18-1848	Keziah gct Mississinewa MM
3-15-1850	Esther (**Jenkins**) rpt mcd; Mississinewa MM rq to treat w/her

JONES (cont)
6-15-1850	Esther (**Jenkins**) chm
7-20-1850	Esther gct Mississinewa MM
12-21-1850	David dis for mcd, dp, & na
3-19-1859	Lydia gct Rocksylvania MM IA
12-16-1876	Sylvester rocf Spiceland MM
3-16-1878	Mary rec by rq of Springfield PM
5-21-1881	Sylvester H & fam gct Milford MM
11-17-1883	Geula Elma gct Van Wert MM OH
1-16-1886	Emma rec by rq of Flat Rock PM

JORDAN
8-19-1876	Elisabeth rel by rq; j M E ch

JULIAN
3-21-1863	Mary Jane (**Baldwin**) Nettle Creek PM rpt mcd
5-16-1863	Mary Jane (**Baldwin**) mbrp ret
6-17-1871	Charity L (**Baldwin**) rpt mcd; chm; mbrp ret
8-16-1884	Mary J & ch gct Rose Hill MM KS
3-16-1889	Charity & Mary E dis
4-20-1889	Charity & Mary E drpd fr mbrp
2-20-1892	Mary E, Stella Rosalia, Perry S, Frank C, Nellie Maud, & Josie Pearl rec by rq of Nettle Creek PM

KEEVER
5-21-1836	Fanny dis

KEMP
6-17-1837	Sally dis

KENWORTHY
9-19-1857	Cert rec for Amos & fam fr Lynn Grove MM; end by Raysville MM; Phebe rocf Sugar Grove MM IA

KERR
11-18-1842	Thomas gct Spiceland MM to m Rachel **Stout**

KIDWELL
3-18-1893	Martin rec by rq

KIMBALL
3-17-1855	David N rocf Marlborough MM NC
1-16-1858	David N rpt mcd; drpd fr mbrp
3-16-1872	Elmira Springfield PM rec by rq
8-17-1872	Melinda E & Mary E Springfield PM rec by rq
3-20-1875	Wm rec by rq
2-15-1879	Wm rel by rq
4-21-1883	Malinda Ellen rel by rq

KINLEY
9-20-1845	Joel & fam (ch Charles & Joseph John) rocf Milford MM; Rachel & dt Margaret, Lydia, & Rebecca rocf Milford MM
6-22-1848	Joel s John & Betty Wayne Co m Eliza dt Wm & Rebecca **Mendenhall** Wayne Co at West River
9-20-1856	Charles W & fam gct Western Plain MM IA; Joel & fam gct Western Plain MM IA

KISER
3-16-1895	James & Minnie rec by rq of Nettle Creek PM

KIZER
10-15-1898	James & Minnie rel by rq of Nettle Creek PM

KNIGHT
11-20-1852	Benejah prcf Dover MM to m Delilah **Dennis**
11-25-1852	Benajah s John & Phebe Wayne Co m Delilah M dt Absalom & Eunice **Dennis** Wayne Co at West River
8-20-1853	Benajah rocf Dover MM
12-16-1854	Benajah & fam gct Dover MM
3-15-1856	Benajah & w Delilah & min s Nathan rocf Dover MM
10-18-1862	Benajah & fam gct Dover MM
3-16-1878	Charity rec by rq of Springfield PM

KOONS
8-15-1835	Whitewater PM rpt Joseph for na, dp, & mcd
3-18-1893	Elmer & Samuel rec by rq
10-15-1898	Nevada rel by rq of Nettle Creek PM

KOONTZ
3-16-1889	Mildred Ellen dis
4-20-1889	Mildred Ellen drpd fr mbrp

LAMAR
8-20-1842	Samuel rocf Center MM OH
11-23-1842	Samuel s Isaac & Hannah Wayne Co m Judith dt Jesse & Hannah **Baldwin** Wayne Co at Nettle Creek Mtg
9-22-1853	Samuel s Isaac & Hannah Henry Co m Eunice W dt John & Abigail **Coffin** Wayne Co at West River Mtg
2-20-1868	Nathan chm for military service
2-20-1869	Jesse rpt mcd
4-17-1869	Irena rec by rq
2-16-1884	Alice & min ch Mary F, Nelly Maud, & Freddie Clyde (fam of Nathan) rec by rq
2-21-1885	Miles W & w Elizabeth H & ch Anna Lenora & Thomas Levi rec by rq
1-21-1888	Margaret E rocf Spiceland MM
7-16-1892	Effie L rel fr mbrp; j M E ch
1-20-1894	Frank S glt to Richmond 1st M E ch
1-15-1895	Alice glt to Richmond 1st M E ch; Mary F jas
8-20-1898	Nathan gct Whitewater MM; Nellie Maud & Fred rel by rq of Nettle Creek PM

LAMB
3-15-1834	Samuel rocf Center MM NC
6-18-1836	Thomas & fam (ch Martin E & Thomas) rocf Center MM NC
6-18-1836	Kendal rocf Center MM NC
6-17-1837	Thomas Jr rpt mcd
9-16-1837	Thomas Jr chm
11-18-1837	Kendal dis for mcd
6-19-1841	Benjamin F rec by rq; Frances & dt Elizabeth rec by rq
7-17-1841	Absalom T rec by rq w/perm Deep River MM NC; Hannah L, Anna, Henry M, Charity, Hiram, Josh C, Rachel P, & Absalom R rec by rq of par Absolom & Frances
10-18-1845	Benjamin F & Keziah (**Allen**) rpt mcd; Keziah (**Allen**) chm
1-16-1846	Benjamin F chm
12-16-1848	Benjamin F rpt mcd;
5-19-1849	Honey Creek MM rpt Benjamin F chm
6-16-1849	Benjamin gct Honey Creek MM
9-15-1849	Martin rpt mcd
10-20-1849	Martin chm
10-20-1849	Frances w Absalom & ch gct Honey Creek MM; Absalom's wthd
1-19-1850	Flat Rock PM rpt Absalom for wthd debt; res within limits Honey Creek MM; that mtg rq to treat w/him
4-19-1851	Absalom gct Honey Creek MM
10-18-1851	Massa (**Beeson**) rpt mcd
11-15-1851	Massa (**Beeson**) chm
4-16-1859	Massey dis for j Christian ch
7-20-1861	Martin E dis for jas
11-16-1861	Harriett (**Woody**) Nettle Creek PM rpt mcd
12-21-1861	Harriett (**Woody**) mbrp ret
7-20-1867	Rachel (**Chamness**) rpt mcd; dis; jas
9-21-1867	Rachel (**Chamness**) Nettle Creek PM dis for mcd & jas
9-21-1872	Caroline rocf Cane Creek MM NC
8-16-1873	Thomas C & ch Lincoln, Flora Mary, & Ulysses rec by rq of Nettle Creek PM
3-18-1876	Elvira rec by rq of Nettle Creek PM
2-16-1878	John H & w Lannah & min ch Carlistie & Edgar A rec by rq of Springfield PM
7-17-1880	Absalom T & w Marcella rocf New Salem MM

LAMB (cont)
4-21-1883	Louisa gct Spiceland MM
9-15-1883	Thomas C appt o
11-15-1884	Emily rq rel fr mbrp
12-20-1884	Emily w/draws rq for rel fr mbrp; rq cert to Dublin MM
2-21-1885	Emily gct Dublin MM
10-17-1885	Thomas Clarkson & fam gct Back Creek MM; Mary gct Back Creek MM
2-20-1892	George W rec by rq; Dora rec by rq of Nettle Creek PM
3-18-1893	Emily Jane & dt Helena rec by rq of Springfield PM
5-16-1897	John W & w Leanna gct Whitewater MM
8-21-1897	John W & w Leanna gct Whitewater MM

LANDERS
1-21-1899	Belle rec by rq of Nettle Creek PM

LANGSTON
10-16-1852	Jonathan & fam gct Dover MM

LANSTON
12-15-1849	Jonathan & fam (s Wm) rocf Salem MM IA; end by Fairfield MM; Hannah & ch Mary Eliza & Rachel rocf Salem MM IA

LARROWE
7-15-1837	Joel & fam (ch Jonathan, Wm, & Elnathan) rocf Deep Creek MM NC
10-16-1852	Susannah & fam gct Honey Creek MM
9-16-1854	Jonathan dis for dp, upl, & apd

LEDBETTER
4-15-1854	Westley S rec by rq
5-25-1854	Hannah H C & Rhoda Roxana rec by rq of f Westley
4-18-1863	Henry B rec by rq
2-20-1864	Lydia (**Baldwin**) Nettle Creek PM rpt mcd
3-19-1864	Lydia (**Baldwin**) mbrp ret
8-20-1864	Henry gct Poplar Run MM to m Abigail **Hunt**
2-18-1865	Henry gct KS MM; cert not acc
5-18-1867	Rhoda J chm "unchastity through a marriage contract"
3-16-1872	Henry B gct Deer Creek MM
4-20-1872	Henry W gct Deer Creek MM
3-16-1889	Lydia dis
4-20-1889	Lydia drpd fr mbrp

LEE
11-7-1821	Samuel & Wm rocf Newberry MM TN
12-11-1822	Wm rpt mcd
1-15-1823	Wm con mcd
11-12-1823	Samuel appt o
6-16-1824	John & ch John & Nathan rocf Newberry MM TN
4-18-1829	West River rpt John for dr; chm but not acc
7-7-1829	John chm
6-19-1830	John gct New Garden MM to m Hannah **Morris**
7-16-1831	Hannah dis
8-20-1831	John Jr dis for mcd & dp
10-18-1834	Rebecca dis; Wm dis for mcd
3-21-1835	John & fam gct Mississinewa MM; West River PM rpt Nathan for na, dp, & mcd; res within Mississinewa MM; that mtg rq to deal w/him & rpt
3-19-1836	Diana dis
2-18-1843	West River PM dis John for mcd
5-18-1844	Ephraim dis for na, att mcd, & dp
12-18-1847	Rachel rocf Back Creek MM
8-19-1848	Zerilda Ann (**Thornburg**) rpt mcd
2-17-1849	Zerilda Ann (**Thornburg**) chm
12-16-1848	Ezra dis for mcd & dp
4-21-1849	Rachel gct Back Creek MM
7-21-1849	Hannah rec by rq
8-18-1849	Jesse, Anderson, Wm, Jonathan B, & Hiram rec by rq of par John & Hannah

SPRINGFIELD MONTHLY MEETING
MINUTES AND MARRIAGES

LEE (cont)
7-16-1853	John & fam gct Three Rivers MM IA; Elizabeth gct Three Rivers MM IA
5-16-1868	Ephraim & w Elizabeth Jane West River PM rec by rq
10-17-1868	Ephaim res Randolph Co
12-17-1870	Ephraim appt o
12-15-1883	Ephraim & Jane dis for na; mbrp ret
2-16-1884	Ephraim & w Jane West River dis for na & disunity
3-15-1884	Dec on Ephraim & w Jane reversed; mbrp ret

LEGGETT
3-15-1879	Sarah B rec in mbrp

LESH
10-15-1853	Elizabeth (**Baldwin**) dis for mcd

LEVELL
5-19-1838	Sarah Ann dis

LEWELLEN
3-17-1894	Jabez rec by rq of Mooreland PM

LEWELLYN
8-16-1873	Jabez & w Mary rec by rq of Nettle Creek PM

LEWIS
7-20-1844	Samuel dis for j separatists
8-17-1844	Lucinda dis for j separatists
6-19-1858	Bear Creek MM IA gr perm to rst Samuel & w Lucinda
9-18-1858	Margaret Ann gct Bear Creek MM IA after chm
3-17-1866	Wm rocf Newberry MM TN; Delila Springfield PM rec by rq
11-17-1866	Martha gct Bear Creek MM IA after chm; Thomas, Mary A, Wm, & Alvah M rec by rq of father Wm
6-17-1867	Martha rocf Bear Creek MM IA
5-15-1869	Wm & fam gct Plainfield MM

LINDLEY
7-16-1842	Rebecca (**Hobson**) dis for mcd

LITTLE
3-19-1859	Mary Jane (**Thornburg**) rpt mcd; drpd fr mbrp

LOCK
2-17-1859	Wm gct Dover MM OH to m Judith F **Carter**

LOCKE
11-18-1826	Wm appt to comm
7-21-1838	John Aaron dis
8-19-1843	Wm & Demaris dis for separating fr church & setting up mtgs contrary to discipline
6-20-1846	Wm & Demaris rec by rq
1-19-1850,	Wm M dis for mcd
5-19-1860	Judith F rocf Dover MM OH
6-16-1860	Judith appt o
5-20-1871	Judith F gct Poplar Run MM

LOVE
10-19-1833	Charity dis

LOWRY
11-18-1899	Nelson rec by rq

LUCAS
4-18-1857	Sarah (**Cox**) rpt mcd; drpd fr mbrp

LUELLING
3-16-1844	Mary dis for j separatists

LUMPKIN
5-20-1843	Sarah (**Maulsby**) dis for mcd
4-21-1883	Rebbecca gct Poplar Run MM

LUNDY
12-15-1827	Lot rocf Deep Creek MM NC
3-18-1882	Elizabeth R gct West Grove MM
3-15-1884	James G rec by rq of Flat Rock PM
4-19-1884	Mordecai E & w Elizabeth & min s Martin S rocf West Grove MM
2-15-1890	Mordecai & fam rocf New Castle MM
2-20-1897	Mordecai E & w Elizabeth & ch Martin L & Ira S rel by rq; jas

LYONS
12-10-1843	Levine (**Mills**) dis for mcd

McALISTER
5-21-1881	Samuel & w gct White River MM

McALLISTER
8-17-1872	Mary E Springfield PM rec by rq
3-20-1875	Samuel rec by rq

McCOLLUM
3-16-1889	Martha & Mary E dis
4-20-1889	Martha, Miles, Mary E, & John E drpd fr mbrp

McCRACKEN
2-16-1833	Robert & fam (ch David & Thomas Clarkson) rocf Marlborough MM NC
2-15-1834	Robert & fam gct Mississinewa MM

McGRAW
6-21-1879	John W & w Anna Jane & min ch Violetta, Orpha Elizabeth, Margaret Elmina, & Manerva Jane rocf Chester MM
3-19-1887	John & fam gct Cherry Grove MM

McKINNEY
12-21-1850	Jane (**Underhill**) dis for mcd & telling falsehoods

MACOLLIM
4-19-1862	Jesse rec by rq
10-18-1862	Miles, Mary Ellen, & John rec by rq of f Jesse

MACY
6-7-1820	Wm & ch Jonathan, Nathan, Alva, John, & Wm rocf Lost Creek MM TN
7-4-1821	Jonathan & ch Ezra, Henry, & David rocf Lost Creek MM TN
2-6-1822	Wm appt clerk
5-17-1826	Isaac rocf Lost Creek MM TN
8-19-1826	West River PM rpt Isaac mcd
9-16-1826	Isaac chm
11-15-1828	Elihu rocf Lost Creek MM Jefferson Co TN
12-20-1828	Barakiah & fam (steps Jesse **Woodard**) rocf Lost Creek MM Jefferson Co TN
3-1-1830	Barachiah appt elder
6-19-1830	Ezra dis for mcd, dp, & upl
9-13-1830	Pamela dis
5-18-1833	Jonathan Jr rpt mcd
6-15-1833	Jonathan Jr chm
1-18-1834	Nathan rpt mcd
3-15-1834	Nathan chm
6-21-1834	Alvah P rpt mcd
7-19-1834	Alvah P chm
4-18-1835	Henry dis for na, dp, & mcd
7-18-1835	Delila dis
4-15-1837	David rpt mcd & dp
5-20-1837	David chm
10-20-1838	Isaac appt rec of certs in room of David **Maulsby** dec
1-18-1840	John chm
1-16-1841	Jonathan & fam gct Mississinewa MM
11-18-1843	Jonathan B dis for j separatists
12-10-1843	Isaac dis for j separatists

MACY (cont)

1-20-1844	David dis for promoting mtgs contrary to discipline & att such mtgs
5-18-1844	Matilda dis for j separatists
6-15-1844	Eleanor dis for j separatists
4-19-1845	Alvy dis for na
12-19-1846	Lewis rpt for att mcd
1-16-1847	Case against Lewis min dis
7-17-1847	Nathaniel prcf Hopewell to m Rhoda **Farmer**
7-22-1847	Nathaniel s Obed & Lydia Henry Co m Rhoda H dt Michael & Lydia **Farmer** Wayne Co at Flat Rock
6-17-1848	Nathaniel rocf Hopewell MM
8-19-1848	Nathaniel gct Mississinewa MM
6-16-1849	West River rpt Perry mcd
7-21-1849	Perry chm
12-15-1849	White Lick MM rpt Julian (**Mills**) & Charity mcd; rq this mtg to treat w/them
1-19-1850	Julian (**Mills**) & Charity chm
4-20-1850	Wm Jr rpt mcd
5-18-1850	Wm Jr chm; Charity & Julia Ann rocf White Lick MM
11-15-1850	Mary Ann dis for unchastity
4-15-1854	West Union MM rpt Achsah (**Johnson**) mcd; rq this mtg to treat w/her & rpt
5-25-1854	Achsah (**Johnson**) chm
8-19-1854	Asenith (**Baldwin**) rpt mcd
9-16-1854	Asenith (**Baldwin**) chm
11-18-1854	Ira rpt mcd
12-16-1854	Ira mbrp ret
5-19-1855	Achsah rocf West Union MM
6-16-1855	Jesse dis for na, j secret society, & dp
5-17-1856	Perry & fam gct White Lick MM
6-21-1856	Wm M & fam gct White Lick MM
9-20-1856	Lewis rpt mcd; drpd fr mbrp
10-18-1856	Wm & fam gct White Lick MM
5-16-1857	Ira C gct White Lick MM
10-20-1860	Eleanor rec by rq
11-17-1866	Susan gct Bear Creek MM IA
6-17-1867	Susan rocf Bear Creek MM IA
7-20-1867	John gct Indianapolis MM
6-15-1868	Eleanor appt West River PM o
6-20-1868	Wm T rpt mcd
7-18-1868	Wm T mbrp ret
10-15-1870	Miriam C (**Pidgeon**) Nettle Creek PM rpt mcd; mbrp ret
12-17-1870	Miriam C gct Hopewell MM
3-21-1874	Evie G & min dt Emma Bertha rec by rq of West River PM
3-20-1875	Oliver & min s gct Union MM MO
8-21-1880	Larkin gct Milford MM
7-15-1882	John rocf Indianapolis MM
12-19-1885	Lula & min ch Harry B, Frank W, & Laurence G rec by rq
4-18-1891	Wayne C & ch Earl L, Murry H, Howard W, Nellie M, & Edward Earl gct Lone Elm MM AR

MAHONY

7-17-1847	Sarah (**Hodson**) dis for mcd

MALSBY

2-16-1884	Richard J & w Ellen & min ch Mary Elisabeth, Thomas Monroe, & Oliver E rec by rq of Nettle Creek PM

MARIS

8-19-1854	Benjamin L rocf Deep River MM NC

MARKLE

2-20-1892	John rec by rq

MARRIS

1-16-1886	Sarah M rec by rq of Flat Rock PM

MARSHALL

2-2-1820	Thomas appt to comm

MARSHALL (cont)

1-3-1821	Miles appt recorder
1-2-1822	John & ch Stephen, Wm, & Evan rocf Deep Creek MM
11-13-1828	John appt elder
6-19-1830	Aaron rpt mcd & dp
7-17-1830	Aaron chm
10-16-1830	Thomas III produced offering expressing that he had been guilty of fighting, for which he was sorry; offering read & acc
2-19-1831	Whitewater MM rpt Jacob dis for mcd & holding doctrines in sympathy with the Hicksites; testification sent to this mtg w/rq that he be notified
11-17-1832	Stephen gct Milford MM to m Gulana **Elliott**
2-21-1835	Wm dis for na, dp, & mcd
1-20-1838	Mabin rpt for dp & mcd
1-25-1838	Wm s John & Anna Henry Co m Keziah dt John & Ruth **Davis** Henry Co at Flat Rock MH
11-17-1838	Anna appt elder
10-21-1841	Evan s John & Anna m Gulielma dt Wm & Elizabeth **Bond** Henry Co at Flat Rock Mtg
4-20-1844	Wm dis for j separatists
6-15-1844	Keziah dis for j separatists
9-21-1844	Cynthia dis for j separatists
5-17-1845	Mitchell dis for na
8-16-1845	John & fam gct Salem MM Henry Co IA
3-21-1846	Evan & fam gct Salem MM Henry Co IA; Stephen & fam gct Salem MM Henry Co IA
7-18-1846	Calvin dis for na
1-15-1848	Collins dis for dp & training with militia
5-20-1848	Reuben dis for mcd & na
10-19-1850	Miles rpt for solemizing mcd of 2 mbrs
11-16-1850	Miles chm
5-17-1851	Salem MM IA gr perm to rst Keziah & Wm
6-21-1851	Min ch of Wm gct Salem MM Henry Co IA; Wm & Mary gct Salem MM Henry Co IA
9-20-1851	Martha Jane dis for att 2 mcd
12-16-1854	Elvira (**Macy**) dis for na & mcd
1-17-1857	Miles gct Bear Creek MM IA
2-21-1857	Elam rpt mcd; drpd fr mbrp
3-17-1866	Anna Jane rocf Salem MM Henry Co IA
1-17-1880	Margarett Ann rec by rq
11-16-1895	Maggie E gct Whitewater MM

MARSHILL

3-1-1820	Thomas proposed as elder
9-21-1833	Miles Nettle Creek s Thomas & Hannah dis for selling grain for distillation, dp, & na
5-17-1834	Thomas Jr dis for mcd & dp
6-21-1834	Osee Ann dis by judgment of women friends
8-17-1861	Susannah rq cert to Pipe Creek MM
9-21-1861	Comm rpt Susannah not mbr this mtg

MARTIN

2-21-1874	Melinda rocf Chester MM
4-17-1875	Elihu & w Minerva rec by rq of Springfield PM
1-20-1883	Malinda gct Poplar Run MM
4-21-1883	Elihu & w Minerva rel fr mbrp for absconding & leaving debts
1-16-1886	Elmira gct Bloomingdale MM
6-16-1888	Joseph C & w Melinda rocf Poplar Run MM
3-16-1895	Arthur & Eva rec by rq of Springfield PM

MASSEY

8-1-1824	James rocf White River MM
11-11-1826	Mary Ann dis
6-21-1828	Betsey Ann dis
4-16-1831	James dis for na, being out of unity with Friends, & dr
2-15-1845	Rachel (**Beeson**) dis for mcd
3-16-1895	Murrell rec by rq of Springfield PM
3-18-1899	Murrel gct Chicago MM IL

SPRINGFIELD MONTHLY MEETING
MINUTES AND MARRIAGES

MAUDLIN
12-21-1860	Delilah (**Denny**) Flat Rock PM rpt mcd
2-21-1861	Delilah S (**Denny**) rpt mcd; drpd fr mbrp

MAULSBY
2-2-1820	David appt to comm
2-6-1822	David appt ass clerk
1-11-1826	Wm dis for att mcd
2-16-1825	Lemuel rpt for fighting
3-16-1825	Lemuel chm
4-26-1827	Lemuel s John & Elizabeth Wayne Co m Ruth dt Anthony & Elizabeth **Reynolds** at West River
10-20-1831	James Wayne Co s John & Elizabeth Randolph Co m Ruth dt Benjamin & Margaret **Beeson** at West River MH
4-21-1832	Lemuel rpt for immoral conduct; David Jr dis for mcd & dp
2-16-1833	John Jr dis for dp & att mcd
5-17-1834	Wm dis for mcd & dp
8-15-1835	John & fam gct Mississinewa MM; Lemuel & fam gct Mississinewa MM
6-16-1838	John & fam rocf Mississinewa MM
10-20-1838	David dec
7-20-1839	Benjamin rpt mcd
8-17-1839	Benjamin chm; Ira rpt for mcd
9-21-1839	Benjamin dis
1-15-1842	Benjamin & fam gct Birch Lake MM MI
3-18-1843	Birch Lake MM MI gr perm to rst Wm
9-16-1843	James & Ruth dis for j separatists
10-12-1843	Lucinda dis
11-18-1843	Mary dis for j separatists
6-15-1844	Wm dis for j separatists; rst
1-18-1845	Minerva & Zerilda dis for j separatists
6-19-1847	Macy rpt mcd
10-16-1847	Macy chm
11-20-1847	Melinda dis; j Wesleyan M E ch, apd, carried a flag at celebration, att mcd, na, & dpl
10-21-1848	Sally F rocf Duck Creek MM
11-18-1848	Keziah (**Bales**) dis for mcd
7-21-1849	James & Ruth rec by rq
3-16-1850	Mary Eliza dis for mcd & j separatists
9-20-1851	Matilda dis for att 2 mcd; Rachel (**Patty**) dis for mcd
10-18-1851	Ezra dis for mcd & na
6-19-1852	James dis for j Spiritualists
10-18-1856	Rachel M (**Beeson**) dis for mcd
11-15-1856	Macy B gct Bear Creek MM
2-21-1857	Silas rpt mcd; drpd fr mbrp
12-19-1857	Ruth dis for j Spiritualists
10-17-1891	Richard J & fam gct Rose Hill MM KS

MAXWELL
9-15-1860	Salem MM gr perm to rst Lydia
4-21-1883	Lydia rocf Spiceland MM

MEEK
3-20-1869	Susan (**Thornburg**) Nettle Creek PM rpt mcd; drpd fr mbrp

MELBERT
2-20-1892	Michael, Philipena, & Anna rec by rq
3-19-1892	Charles rec by rq; Blanche & Edgar rec by rq of par Michael & Phillippina

MENDENHALL
12-17-1823	Aaron & ch Miles & Nathan rocf Cherry Grove MM
4-21-1834	Wm & fam (s Oliver) rocf West Grove MM
12-17-1836	John C rocf West Grove MM
5-20-1837	Elijah & fam (ch Joseph, Daniel, Brooks, Wm, & Cyrus) rocf West Grove MM
2-15-1840	Huldah appt elder
3-21-1840	Joseph dis for upl & dp
6-19-1841	John C dis for dp, na, & mcd

MENDENHALL (cont)
10-20-1841	Miles s Aaron & Mary Henry Co m Cynthia dt Thomas & Elizabeth **Dennis** Wayne Co at Nettle Creek
3-19-1842	Daniel dis for mcd & j UB ch
6-18-1842	Susannah (**Pierce**) dis for mcd & j UB ch
5-20-1843	Nathan dis for j Christian ch
9-26-1843	Nathan rec by rq
5-18-1844	Rebecca appt elder
7-19-1845	Oliver dis for mcd
12-20-1845	Silas rpt mcd
2-21-1846	Silas chm
11-21-1846	Nathan dis for na & upl
5-20-1848	Wm appt elder
10-21-1848	James & w Mary rocf Elk MM
11-14-1848	Hannah (**Larrowe**) rpt mcd
12-16-1848	Hannah (**Larrowe**) chm
3-17-1849	Flat Rock PM rpt John guilty of fighting; mbr Elk MM; that mtg rq to treat w/him
7-21-1849	Elk MM rq this mtg to treat w/John
3-16-1850	Rachel (**Brown**) dis for mcd w/her lst cousin
8-17-1850	Flat Rock PM rpt Isaac for mcd; mbr Elk MM; that mtg rq to treat w/him
10-19-1850	Elk MM rq this mtg to treat w/Isaac; did not make satisfaction
10-16-1852	Elijah & fam gct Sugar Plain MM
6-16-1855	Elam & Margaret rocf New Garden MM
2-16-1856	Silas dis for j German Baptist ch
8-20-1859	Hannah gct Western Plains MM IA
11-19-1859	Rachel Flat Rock PM rec in mbrp
5-17-1862	Wm H rpt mcd
6-21-1862	Wm H mbrp ret; Eunice (**Clark**) West River PM rpt mcd
7-19-1862	Eunice (**Clark**) mbrp ret
10-17-1863	Rufus rpt mcd
1-16-1864	Rufus mbrp ret
8-20-1864	Rachel gct Duck Creek MM
3-18-1865	Rufus A gct Wabash MM
12-15-1866	Wm H & fam gct Poplar Run MM
2-16-1867	Wilson D rpt mcd; mbrp ret
10-16-1869	Isaac & w & ch Viretta, Eliza Ann, Luella, Valentine M, & Alma rec by rq
12-17-1870	Isaac & min ch gct Duck Creek MM
2-17-1872	Rufus & w Emilene rocf Wabash MM
10-18-1873	Rufus A appt o
7-15-1874	Wm, Rebecca, & Cynthia appt elder
3-18-1876	Lucy A rec by rq of Nettle Creek PM
9-20-1879	Wilson D & w Martha A rel by rq
5-23-1880	Miles minister d in 58th y
3-18-1882	Ella rec by rq of Nettle Creek PM
3-?-1884	Rufus A rec minister
5-19-1888	Jesse W & w Lucy A glt Franklin M E ch
1-18-1890	Emmeline/Emaline gct New Castle MM
2-21-1891	Clyde dis; jas
4-20-1895	Myra drpd fr mbrp
2-20-1897	Newman S rec by rq of Springfield PM
3-20-1897	Clara rec by rq of Springfield PM
9-17-1898	Lindley H & w Mary E & min ch gct Muncie MM

MIDDLETON
9-17-1881	Sidney & w Sarah L rocf White River MM
11-19-1881	Sidney & Sarah gct White River MM

MILICAN
9-19-1840	Flat Rock PM rpt Wm mcd
2-20-1841	Wm chm
4-15-1843	Flat Rock PM rpt Wm mcd
5-20-1843	Wm chm
3-16-1884	Eli & Mary Melinda rec on rq of Flat Rock PM

MILIKAN
3-16-1867	Eli F rpt mcd
5-18-1867	Eli F rpt mcd

MILLICAN
3-15-1884	Eli & Mary Malinda rec by rq

MILLIKAN
3-18-1837	Wm & fam (ch John & Charles) rocf Springfield OH
9-18-1852	Charles dis for upl & offering to fight
2-18-1854	Esther, Eli F, Thomas K, Rebecca Jane, & Wm M rec by rq of f Wm
10-21-1854	John dis for mcd & na
10-18-1856	Wm rpt mcd; drpd fr mbrp
4-16-1865	Rebecca Jane, Thomas K, & Wm M min ch Wm gct Spiceland MM
10-20-1866	Eli F gct Spiceland MM
8-18-1866	Eli F chm for enlisting in Army
7-18-1868	Eli F & min s Lewis gct Spiceland MM
2-16-1884	Richard J & w Ellen & ch Mary Elizabeth, Thomas Monroe, & Oliver E rec by rq

MILLIKEN
1-16-1886	Permelia A rec by rq of Flat Rock PM

MILLS
3-1-1820	Charity proposed as elder; Moses chosen ass clerk; John chosen o
9-11-1822	Daniel chosen o
12-15-1824	Benoni & w & s Hugh rocf Deep Creek Surry Co NC
9-11-1822	James rocf Deep Creek MM NC
4-26-1826	James s Benoni & Mary Wayne Co m Hannah dt Job & Thamer **Ratcliff** Wayne Co at Springfield MH
3-21-1827	Seth s John & Mary Wayne Co m Rebeccah dt John & Julatha **Canaday** at Springfield Mtg
8-23-1827	Hugh s Benoni & Mary Wayne Co m Jemima dt Solomon & Elizabeth **Hodson** at Flat Rock Mtg
2-16-1828	Aaron dis for mcd
8-16-1828	Seth gct Vermilion MM IL
6-20-1829	Hezekiah dis for upl
12-19-1829	Henry & fam gct White Lick MM
5-15-1830	Jesse & Isaac min rocf White River MM
5-19-1832	Aaron s Seth dis for fighting & dp
6-16-1832	Seth dis for being out of unity w/Friends & na
10-20-1832	Aaron dis for dp
3-16-1833	James & fam gct White River MM
4-20-1833	Thomas rpt mcd
6-15-1833	Thomas chm
8-17-1833	Silver Creek MM rpt Asa for dp & mcd; this mtg rq to treat w/him; mbr Silver Creek MM; resides within the verge of this mtg
10-19-1833	Milton dis for att mcd & dp
5-17-1834	Thomas gct Cherry Grove MM
1-16-1836	Walter dis for mcd & j M E
2-19-1836	Charity elder d ae 82y lm
5-21-1836	James & fam (ch David & Osom) rocf White River MM; Mary dt Elizabeth dis
8-20-1836	Jesse gct Cherry Grove MM
6-17-1837	Henry dis for mcd & dp
8-19-1841	Mary & fam gct Vermilion MM IL
6-19-1841	Elizabeth Jr dis for unchastity
3-18-1843	James & fam gct Sugar River MM
5-20-1843	West River PM rpt John D mcd; mbr Vermilion MM IL; that mtg inf
1-20-1844	Vermilion MM IL rpt John mcd; rq ass fr this mtg in treating w/him
2-14-1844	John chm
3-16-1844	Hugh & Jemima dis for j separatists
7-20-1844	Elizabeth dis for j separatists
10-19-1844	John D rocf Vermillion MM
2-21-1846	Anna dis for j Wesleyan M E
3-21-1846	Nancy dis for j separatists; Rufus dis for mcd
4-18-1846	Elijah dis for upl & offering to fight
7-17-1847	Oliver dis for dp & na
3-18-1848	John D & fam gct Poplar Run MM
4-21-1849	Daniel dis for upl
7-21-1849	Elizabeth rec by rq

MILLS (cont)
4-20-1850	John B rpt for na & mcd
9-21-1850	Jane rec by rq
9-17-1853	Mary (**Ellis**) rpt mcd
11-19-1853	Mary (**Ellis**) mbrp ret
6-16-1855	Elihue rocf Bloomfield MM
3-15-1856	John D & w Huldah & ch Larinda, Martitia, Wm, Alonzo, & Elihu rocf Poplar Run MM
6-19-1858	Three River MM IA gr perm to rst Jemima
3-17-1860	Cyrus gct South River MM IA
5-19-1860	Bloomfield MM gr perm to rst Aaron
11-21-1863	Elihu rpt mcd
3-19-1864	Elihu mbrp ret
4-16-1864	Elihu gct Bloomfield MM
12-16-1865	John D & fam gct Wabash MM
5-20-1878	Mary rel by rq; she is remote fr any Friends mtg; jas
2-16-1889	Mary rec by rq of Springfield PM
10-19-1889	Cassius C rocf Cherry Grove MM
10-15-1898	Cassius C rel by rq of Nettle Creek PM

MITCHELL
1-18-1871	Alson E rocf New Garden MM
12-21-1872	Alson E rpt mcd
2-15-1873	Alson E gct Oak Ridge MM

MODLIN
12-1-1831	Wm s Joseph & Violet Henry Co m Mildred dt Isaac & Hannah **Beeson** Wayne Co at West River Mtg
6-21-1834	Wm & fam (s Calvin) rocf Duck Creek MM
10-20-1860	Mahlon rpt mcd
11-17-1860	Mahlon mbrp ret
10-15-1864	Mildred appt o
6-18-1870	Nathan L & Clara Viola rec by rq of f Mahlon; Margaret & ch Clara Viola, Laura Etta, & Eliza Jane rec by rq
6-17-1882	Mahlon & fam gct Dublin MM
4-21-1883	Louisa gct Poplar Run MM
5-18-1883	Louisa gct Poplar Run MM

MOORE
11-15-1834	Rachel dis
7-20-1844	Alice dis for j separatists
1-17-1846	Anderson rec by rq
10-21-1848	Alice & Martha Ann rec by rq
6-19-1852	Anderson gct Back Creek MM to m Rachel **Lee**
11-19-1853	Rachel rocf Back Creek MM
1-21-1854	Anderson & fam gct Three Rivers MM IA
3-18-1854	Eli dis for mcd & na

MORE
1-17-1856	Alice (**Beeson**) rpt mcd; drpd fr mbrp

MORRIS
2-23-1831	John s Reuben & Mariam m Rachel dt Obed & Mary **Ward** Wayne Co at Springfield Mtg
2-21-1835	Rachel & 2 s gct Spiceland MM
9-21-1844	Rachel rpt for div fr h & unchastity
3-15-1845	Spiceland MM rq this mtg to treat w/Rachel
5-17-1845	Spiceland MM rpt no satisfaction w/Rachel
1-17-1846	Rachel dis
9-17-1864	Rachel (**Chamness**) Nettle Creek PM rpt mcd; mbrp ret
3-18-1865	Rachel gct Honey Creek MM IA
1-21-1882	Wm rocf Poplar Run MM
1-16-1886	Sarah M rec by rq of Flat Rock PM

MULLEN
10-19-1850	Elizabeth gct West Grove MM
3-15 1851	Elizabeth's cert ret
7-19-1851	Elizabeth dis for j UB ch
7-20-1895	Merrit B & Mary C rocf Dover MM

MULLENIX
10-20-1832	Elizabeth dis

SPRINGFIELD MONTHLY MEETING
MINUTES AND MARRIAGES

MUMBOWER
3-17-1888	Thomas & w Eunice & ch Cora & James rec by rq of Springfield PM
5-19-1894	Thomas & w Eunice & min ch Cora & James gct Cherry Grove MM

MURPHEY
5-21-1836	Martha dis

MURPHY
10-22-1828	Wm s Joshua & Margaret Wayne Co m Betsy dt Peter & Margaret **Cox** at Springfield
3-17-1832	Miles rq mbrp after dis by Duck Creek MM
8-13-1832	Miles refused mbrp
4-21-1832	David min s Miles rocf Duck Creek MM
1-17-1835	Miles rq mbrp; refused
5-21-1836	David dis for na & dp
9-20-1845	Anna rec by rq

MYERS
4-20-1889	Elizabeth (**Deering**) drpd fr mbrp

MYRES
3-16-1889	Elizabeth (**Deering**) dis

NEWLIN
12-12-1830	Eli & w rocf Springfield MM OH
5-19-1832	Eli & fam gct Springfield MM OH

NICHOLSON
8-1-1838	George Rush Co s Nathan dec form Perquimans Co NC & Peninah m Lucinda dt Thomas & Elizabeth **Dennis** Wayne Co at Nettle Creek Mtg
3-16-1839	George rocf Walnut Ridge MM
10-15-1870	Mary E rec by rq
7-15-1871	Henry rpt mcd
7-15-1871	Thomas rpt mcd
7-15-1874	George & Lucinda appt elder
2-20-1886	Henry & min ch Oliver, Olinda C, Mary, Alma, & Thomas rel fr mbrp
2-21-1891	Leora E dis; jas
10-15-1898	Macy rel by rq of Nettle Creek PM

NORDYKE
9-20-1828	Thomas & John min ch Martha rocf Union MM NC; end by Whitewater
3-21-1829	Thomas dis for training with militia & dp
6-19-1830	John dis for training with militia & dp

NORTH
7-15-1837	Daniel & w gct West Grove MM
3-16-1889	Ellen dis
4-20-1889	Ellen drpd fr mbrp

OSBORN
6-7-1820	David appt to comm; Jonathan rpt mcd
8-2-1820	Jonathan chm
9-6-1820	Josiah & John rocf Short Creek MM
12-13-1820	Josiah Wayne Co s Charles & Sarah m Mary dt Uriah & Elizabeth **Barnard** Wayne Co at Springfield MH
9-11-1822	Elizabeth dis
8-13-1823	Jesse rpt for fornication
11-17-1824	John gct Plainfield MM OH
6-15-1825	Thomas & fam (s Owen) rocf Goshen MM OH
7-13-1825	Jonathan dis for jas
6-14-1826	James gct West Grove MM to m
3-17-1827	Charles & fam gct Springfield MM OH
10-20-1827	James gct West Grove MM
5-16-1829	Elijah gct Chester MM
6-24-1829	Isaiah s Charles & Sarah Wayne Co m Lydia dt Job & Rhoda **Worth** at Springfield Mtg
4-17-1830	Elijah dis for dp & na

OSBORN (cont)
12-12-1830	Charles & fam (ch Gideon S, Charles N, Jordan, Parker Jordan, & Benjamin) rocf Miami MM OH
1-15-1831	Thomas & fam gct Whitewater MM
6-18-1831	Charles liberated to visit Friends in Great Britain
12-17-1831	Wm rocf Center MM NC
9-21-1833	Charles ret cert gr for service in Europe
3-15-1834	Miriam dis
11-15-1834	Wm gct Mississinewa MM
2-20-1836	Josiah & fam gct Mississinewa MM
8-20-1836	Memorial to Narcissa read & approved
2-16-1839	Wm prcf White Lick MM to m Rachel **Hodson**
2-20-1839	Wm s Richard & Rachel Morgan Co m Rachel dt Zecheriah & Elizabeth **Hodson** Wayne Co at Springfield Mtg
5-18-1839	Charles Newman gct Dover MM OH after chm
2-15-1840	Gideon S dis for dp & mcd
2-14-1840	Isaiah appt elder
2-1-1842	New Garden MM rpt Jordon for na & dancing; that mtg rq to treat w/him & rpt
3-19-1842	Jordan denies charge
6-18-1842	Charge against Jordan dismissed; this mtg thinks him guilty
9-17-1842	Charles & fam gct Birch Lake MM MI
11-19-1842	Jordan dis for fighting & na
9-16-1843	Isaiah dis for j separatists
11-18-1843	Lydia dis for j separatists
4-19-1851	Mary M gct Cherry Grove MM
7-16-1859	Charles W rpt mcd
8-20-1859	Charles W mbrp ret
12-21-1867	Asenith W & ch Arthur Wendell & Daniel Worth rec by rq
5-21-1870	Laurinda gct Spiceland MM
12-17-1870	Charles W appt o
7-15-1874	Charles W appt elder
6-17-1876	Charles W rec minister
5-17-1879	Asenath W appt elder
12-17-1887	Worth gct Cherry Grove MM
7-20-1888	Charles W minister & w Asenath an elder gct labor at Southland College AR
11-15-1890	Agnes rec by rq
3-16-1895	Frank & Daisy rec by rq of Springfield PM
1-16-1897	Achsah rec by rq
3-20-1897	Elam rec by rq; Ethel rocf Economy M E ch
8-20-1898	Charles W rel by rq of Nettle Creek PM
3-18-1899	Arthur W gct Spiceland MM

OSBUN
9-20-1850	Jesse prcf Cherry Grove MM to m Mary M **Adams**

OUTLAND
5-19-1877	Jesse rocf Cherry Grove MM
5-17-1879	Jesse appt o
12-15-1888	Jesse & w Elizabeth gct Cherry Grove MM
11-19-1898	Jesse & Elizabeth rc

OWENS
10-17-1829	Chester MM rpt Elijah for dp & na
11-29-1829	Elijah's cert ret; Chester MM rq to deal w/him on behalf of this mtg
3-18-1876	Edward rec by rq of Nettle Creek PM
4-20-1889	Edward drpd fr mbrp

OZBUN
2-16-1845	Isaac prcf Cherry Grove MM to m Mary **Davis**
2-20-1845	Isaac s John & Rebecca Randolph Co m Mary dt John & Ruth **Davis** Henry Co at Flat Rock Mtg
8-18-1845	Mary gct Cherry Grove MM
9-16-1850	Jesse s John & Rebecca Randolph Co m Mary M dt Ebenezer & Rebecca **Adams** Henry Co at Flat Rock
4-22-1869	Elkanah H s John & Rebecca Randolph Co m Mary Jane dt Ezra & Zerilda **Lee** Wayne Co at West River
9-17-1870	Mary Jane rec by rq; gct Cherry Grove MM

PARKER
4-24-1867	Elisha s Nathan & Sarah Wayne Co m Mary E **Jessup** dt George & Lucinda **Nicholson** Wayne Co at Nettle Creek
7-20-1867	Mary E & min ch Sarah Ann **Jessup** gct Dover MM
6-21-1873	Elisha & w Mary E & ch Sarah Ann **Jessup**, John, Henry J, & Elmina **Parker** rocf Dover MM; Milley E rocf Dover MM
4-21-1883	Mary E & fam gct Dover MM
1-16-1886	John rel by rq; jas; Mary & min ch rocf Dover MM
1-16-1892	Mary G min ch rocf Dover MM
12-15-1894	Frances drpd fr mbrp

PARSONS
7-16-1831	Elizabeth dis

PATTEE
6-16-1887	Clarkson W rel by rq

PATTERSON
10-20-1883	Sarah E gct Stanton MM IL

PATTY
11-15-1845	Nancy rocf Dover MM
4-19-1851	Rachel rocf Poplar Run MM
9-20-1851	Rhoda (**Swain**) dis for mcd
3-18-1865	Ellen rocf Winneshiek MM IA
12-16-1865	Clarkson rpt mcd
1-20-1866	Clarkson mbrp ret
11-15-1873	Ellen & ch gct Sioux Rapids MM IA

PEAK
10-15-1898	Mary E rel by rq of Nettle Creek PM

PEARCE
2-16-1867	John rpt mcd; mbrp ret

PEELE
6-15-1850	Mary Jane rocf New Hope MM TN
12-21-1850	Edmond & fam gct Honey Creek MM

PERKINS
7-19-1834	Joseph rocf Hopewell MM NC

PETTY
11-15-1834	Elizabeth dis
11-16-1861	James rocf White Lick MM
3-18-1876	Anna rec by rq of Springfield PM

PHILABAUM
12-16-1876	James B & Sarah E & s Alonzo rec by rq
2-18-1882	James & w Sarah & ch Alonzo & Lura rel by rq; j UB ch

PHILLIPS
2-16-1884	Charles rec by rq
1-16-1897	Charley & w Martha & min dt Alta gct Anderson MM

PICKERING
12-21-1829	Samuel s Jonas & Ruth Henry Co m Cynthia dt John & Elizabeth **Maulsby** Wayne Co at West River Mtg
3-21-1835	Benjamin & fam (ch Nathan & Miles) rocf Lost Creek MM TN
7-15-1837	New Hope MM TN rpt Elisha for dp & mcd; this mtg rq to treat w/him
9-16-1837	Elisha chm
1-20-1844	West River PM rpt Elisha for mcd, dp, & na; dis
5-18-1844	Sarah dis for na & being out of unity with Friends
9-21-1844	Benjamin dis for na
4-19-1851	West River Pm rpt Enos for dp & mcd
7-19-1851	Enos dis
9-20-1856	Benjamin & w Sarah rec by rq; res WI; rst
12-20-1856	Benjamin & fam gct Winneshiek MM IA

PICKERING (cont)
5-15-1858	Henry min s Elisha gct New Salem MM
1-19-1861	Samuel & w Cynthia minister & s Macy rocf Bear Creek MM IA
4-19-1862	Samuel & Cynthia gct Duck Creek MM
5-17-1862	Macy rpt mcd
9-20-1862	Macy mbrp ret
10-18-1862	Macy gct Duck Creek MM; Nathan gct Baraboo MM WI

PICKET
9-19-1863	Huldah M gct West Union MM

PICKETT
2-21-1863	Huldah M (**Macy**) Springfield PM rpt mcd
5-16-1863	Huldah M (**Macy**) mbrp ret

PIDGEON
12-15-1832	David & fam (ch Jesse & Wm) rocf Dover MM NC
12-19-1849	Jesse s David & Rachel Henry Co m Mary dt Joshua & Hannah **Chamness** Henry Co at Nettle Creek
12-16-1865	Isaac W rpt mcd; mbrp ret
6-16-1866	Elizabeth rocf Dover MM OH
10-19-1867	David gct Spiceland MM to m Hannah **Stanley**
3-21-1868	Hannah rocf Spiceland MM
12-19-1868	Hannah appt o
3-20-1869	Isaac W & fam gct Hopewell MM
3-18-1882	Lizzie rec by rq of Nettle Creek PM
4-15-1882	Carrie J rec by rq of Nettle Creek PM
12-15-1883	Emeline rec by rq of Nettle Creek PM
3-15-1890	Wm C & fam gct Hiawatha MM NE
8-18-1890	David & fam gct Spiceland MM
8-20-1898	Emeline rel by rq

PIERCE
10-15-1823	John rocf Union MM
6-21-1834	John rpt gave con to mcd
8-16-1834	John chm
5-17-1856	Wilson rpt mcd; drpd fr mbrp
1-16-1858	Lewis rpt mcd; drpd fr mbrp

PIKE
10-21-1854	Elam prcf New Garden MM to m Anna **Reynolds**
10-25-1854	Elam s Nathan & Mary Wayne Co m Anna dt Isaac & Tamar **Reynolds** Wayne Co at Nettle Creek Mtg
2-17-1855	Anna gct New Garden MM

PITTS
11-16-1844	Kadwalader prcf Duck Creek MM to m Mary **Chamness**
11-27-1844	Cadwaladar s Samuel & Elizabeth Henry Co m Mary dt Wm & Isabel **Chamness** at Nettle Creek Mtg
3-15-1845	Mary gct Duck Creek MM
1-17-1857	Mary rocf Duck Creek MM
3-17-1877	Sarah Ann gct Dover MM

POARCH
2-20-1897	Catherine (**Cain**) rocf Marion MM
1-21-1899	Catherine C rel by rq to j Evanston 1st Cong ch IL

POTTER
1-12-1825	Stephen appt to comm
1-11-1829	Stephen gct Chester MM to m Phebe **Barker**
9-18-1847	Benjamin F dis for mcd & dp
10-16-1847	Rebecca (**Hobson**) rpt mcd
11-20-1847	Rebecca (**Hobson**) chm
11-20-1852	Stephen & fam gct East Grove MM IA

PRESNALL
12-19-1846	James prcf Duck Creek MM to m Anna **Brown**
12-24-1846	James s Stephen & Hannah Henry Co m Anna dt Isaac & Mary **Brown** Henry Co at Flat Rock
3-18-1848	Anna gct Duck Creek MM

SPRINGFIELD MONTHLY MEETING
MINUTES AND MARRIAGES

PUCKETT
6-21-1834	Cyrus & fam (ch Daniel & Levi C) rocf Duck Creek MM
5-19-1838	Cyrus & fam gct New Garden MM

RATCLIFF
12-5-1821	Thamar & ch Thomas, Elias, Jesse, Enos, & Isaac rocf New Garden MM
4-17-1822	John rpt mcd
10-6-1822	John chm
8-17-1825	Mill Creek MM rpt John for threatening to strike a man, up, & na; that mtg rq to deal w/him
10-19-1825	Elias s Job & Tamer Wayne Co m Achsah dt Benoni & Mary **Mills** Wayne Co at Springfield Mtg
4-19-1826	Thomas s Job & Thamer Wayne Co m Susanna dt Obed & Mary **Ward** Wayne Co at Springfield Mtg
11-20-1830	Jesse dis for dp & making vessels to hold spirituous liquors
8-20-1831	Enos dis for dp
4-21-1832	Thomas dis for concealing property not his own & denying it
10-20-1832	Joel rocf Newberry MM OH
8-19-1837	Susannah & ch gct Mississinewa MM
2-19-1842	Isaac rpt mcd
5-21-1842	Isaac chm

RATLIFF
10-20-1849	Elias & fam gct Honey Creek MM
10-18-1851	Isaac gct Honey Creek MM

REECE
3-15-1845	Delilah rec by rq

REYNOLDS
6-7-1820	Ebenezer appt to comm
7-4-1821	Ebenezer con elder
6-11-1823	Anthony & ch Isaac & Levi & nephew Newby **Wilson** rocf Center MM NC
8-18-1824	Elijah s Ebenezer & Rachel Wayne Co m Deborah dt Azariah & Sarah **Williams** Wayne Co at Springfield Mtg
7-15-1826	Elijah appt ass clerk
8-19-1826	Levi s Anthony & Elizabeth Wayne Co m Hannah dt John & Jane **Underhill** at Springfield Mtg
6-21-1828	Ezra rpt mcd & upl
8-16-1828	Ezra chm
9-18-1830	Isaac gct Whitewater MM to m Tamar **Hawkins**
11-19-1831	West River PM rpt Zimri for apd, dr, & dp; dis
8-15-1835	Levi & fam gct Mississinewa MM
9-19-1835	Elijah & fam gct Mississinewa MM
4-20-1839	Ezra dis for mcd
7-15-1848	Isaac's min ch (Clarkson, Milton, Francis, Edwin, & Albert) rocf New Garden MM
8-19-1848	Martha Ann min dt Isaac rocf New Garden MM
1-18-1851	Delilah rq mbrp fr Mississinewa MM; refused; mcd
8-21-1852	Milo rocf Center MM NC
5-21-1853	Clarkson dis for mcd, fighting, upl, & na
11-22-1854	Milo Wayne Co s Wenlock & Susannah Randolph Co NC m Mary dt Jesse & Ruth **Chamness** Wayne Co at Nettle Creek Mtg
9-15-1855	Francis rpt mcd; drpd fr mbrp
2-20-1858	John rpt mcd; drpd fr mbrp
4-17-1858	John dis for mcd & na
8-18-1866	Isaac & w Lovina & ch Ellen, Henry, Lindley, & Harvey rec by rq w/perm New Garden MM
2-16-1867	Martha Ann Nettle Creek PM rpt mcd; mbrp ret
4-20-1867	Wilson rpt mcd; mbrp ret
4-20-1867	Elizabeth D rpt mcd; mbrp ret
12-18-1869	Lavina appt o
3-18-1871	Phebe Jane rocf Dover MM
7-15-1871	Edwin rpt mcd
7-20-1872	Isaac appt o
7-21-1877	Jesse rel by rq

REYNOLDS (cont)
10-15-1881	Edwin & dt gct Hopewell MM
1-21-1888	Rebecca E rocf Spiceland MM
4-20-1889	Henry L drpd fr mbrp
9-17-1898	Harvey & w Cynthia & min ch gct Hopewell MM

RICHARDS
10-20-1883	Margaret J gct Stanton MM IL

RIGGLE
1-18-1879	Lucy A & dt Sarah E **Leggett** rocf Wilmington MM OH

RIGGLES
3-21-1891	Lucy A rocf New Castle MM

RILEY
4-21-1877	Ellen (**Fleming**) gct New Garden MM

RINARD
3-18-1893	James W rec by rq

RITTENHOUSE
8-20-1898	Wm W & Marietta rel by rq of Nettle Creek PM

ROBBINS
3-15-1856	Marticia (**Coffin**) rpt mcd; drpd fr mbrp

ROBERTSON
4-20-1867	James C rec by rq
5-18-1867	Levine (**Jenkins**) rpt mcd; chm; mbrp ret
6-19-1886	Flat Rock PM rpt James C jas
8-21-1886	James rel by rq; jas

ROBINSON
6-19-1886	Sina T & Maggie rpt na

ROE
6-18-1842	Mary Ann (**Lamb**) dis for mcd

ROGERS
7-20-1889	George rec by rq of Mooreland PM
8-17-1889	Eva H w George & min ch John O, Charles R, & Paul D rec in mbrp

ROUTH
3-15-1873	Cynthia E & Lizzie Etta rec by rq of West River PM
5-15-1886	Wesley & w Marticia rec by rq of Springfield PM; form mbr Bridgeport Circuit UB ch
12-17-1887	Wesley & w Marticia rel by rq; j Economy UB ch

SANDERS
2-16-1889	Joseph M rolf New Castle M E ch
2-20-1892	Frank rec by rq
1-20-1894	Seth & Emma rec by rq of mother Mary

SAVERY
9-5-1894	Wm H Wilmington MM DE s Thomas H & Sarah Pim New Castle Delaware Co m Nellie **Clark** dt Elwood & Nancy **Goodrich** at Economy
7-17-1897	Nellie (**Goodrich**) rel by rq to jas

SCANTLIN
5-15-1858	Ann (**Hollingsworth**) rpt mcd; drpd fr mbrp
3-18-1899	Jannie & dt Edith May roc

SCHENCK
7-17-1897	Cordelia (**Test**) rel by rq to j Middletown 1st Presb ch OH

SCHWENNESUN
2-21-1891	Lucinda & s Eustace Sherman **Young** rec by rq

SHAFER
6-19-1852	Luzena (**Beeson**) dis for mcd

SHAFFER
9-15-1866	Cynthia (**Chamness**) Nettle Creek PM rpt mcd; drpd fr mbrp
3-16-1878	Sarah rec by rq of Flat Rock PM
4-20-1889	Elisha & w Laura B & min ch Maud E, Guy M, & Francis C rec by rq of Mooreland PM
6-20-1896	Lorinda rel by rq; jas
7-18-1896	Mooreland PM rpt Elisha na

SHAWLEY
8-19-1893	Daniel C rocf Dover MM
10-16-1897	Daniel C gct Dover MM

SHEDLTNECK
11-17-1855	Mary (**Adams**) dis for mcd

SHELL
5-16-1891	Wm & w Hannah & min ch John Franklin, Clarkson E, Harry Merton, & Wm H rocf New Garden MM

SHEPHERD
3-15-1873	Rachel rocf Cherry Grove MM
4-20-1889	Rachel gct Muncie MM

SHIELDS
9-21-1844	Springfield MM OH rpt Phebe (**Hunt**) mcd; this mtg rq to treat w/her & rpt
10-19-1844	Springfield MM OH inf Phebe (**Hunt**) did not make satisfaction
8-15-1846	Susanna (**Hunt**) rpt mcd
9-19-1846	Susanna (**Hunt**) chm
6-19-1869	Wm B rocf Deep Creek MM NC
7-17-1869	Joanna & ch Martha J, Julia F, Andrew L, John B, Abraham L, Isaac F, & Rachel K rec by rq
6-17-1882	Wm B & fam gct Back Creek MM
3-16-1889	Martha J dis
4-20-1889	Martha J drpd fr mbrp
10-19-1889	Abram rocf New Hope MM TN
4-19-1890	Abram gct Jonesboro MM

SHIVELY
12-16-1848	Sarah (**Thornburg**) dis for mcd

SHOEMAKER
4-17-1841	Charles & fam (s Ezekiel) rocf West Grove
9-21-1844	Charles & fam gct West Grove MM
5-20-1848	Charles & fam (ch Elijah & Ezekiel) roc; Margaret Ann & ch Tacy, Sophia, & Martha E rocf West Grove MM
6-18-1853	Charles & fam gct Vermilion MM IL

SHUELY
7-20-1850	Anna (**Swain**) dis for mcd

SIGERFOUSE
4-16-1842	Cynthia (**Osborn**) dis for mcd

SIMONS
6-15-1861	Lydia & dt Elma rocf Spiceland MM
8-20-1892	Alfred H rocf Spiceland MM

SMALL
8-24-1880	Jesse s Joseph & Clarky Grant Co m Jemima **Cain** dt Daniel & Jemima **Jones** at public mtg in her res Economy
9-15-1880	Jemima (**Cain**) rec in mbrp
1-15-1881	Jemima gct Mississinewa MM

SMITH
11-15-1828	Wm & fam (s Nathan) rocf Lost Creek MM Jefferson Co TN
4-18-1829	Wm rpt for fighting
7-18-1829	Wm chm
1-16-1836	Wm dis for na
11-16-1844	Ann dis for j separatists
7-11-1846	Lydia & ch gct Pleasant Plains MM IA
11-17-1849	Ann (**Adams**) dis for mcd
3-15-1873	Rebecca Ann rec by rq of West River PM
8-16-1873	Eunice rec by rq of Nettle Creek PM
2-15-1896	Adam rec by rq; Omer F & Bertha M min ch rec by rq of par Clarence & w; Clarence, Mary, & Flora rolf Franklin M E ch
1-16-1897	Adam & Flora gct Muncie MM

SMITHY
10-6-1822	Mary dis
3-15-1873	Rebecca Ann rec by rq

SPRADLIN
3-15-1856	Mary Jane (**Thornburg**) rpt mcd; drpd fr mbrp
11-19-1859	Louis & Mary Jane rec by rq

SQUIRES
5-15-1886	Rebecca rocf West Grove MM

STANLEY
12-15-1824	Archelaus & fam (s Isaac) rocf Deep Creek MM NC
12-16-1826	James & fam (ch James & Joseph) rocf Deep Creek MM NC; Jesse rocf Deep Creek MM NC
1-19-1828	Wm & fam (s Jonathan) rocf Deep Creek MM NC
9-25-1828	Joseph s James & Agatha Wayne Co m Naomi dt Solomon & Elizabeth **Hodson** at Flat Rock Mtg
3-25-1829	James s James & Agatha Wayne Co m Jemima dt Richard & Nancy **Mills** at Springfield
9-18-1830	Jesse rpt for mcd & dp; chm
10-16-1830	Jemima & s Strangeman insane person rocf Fairfield MM OH; their maintenance for life secured by Jacob **Horton** of sd mtg
7-20-1833	Wm & fam gct White River MM
10-19-1833	Jonathan rpt mcd
5-18-1834	Jonathan chm
12-21-1833	Archolas & fam gct White River MM
7-19-1854	Wm & fam rocf White River MM
8-20-1836	Archelas & fam (ch Isaac & James) rocf White River MM
8-18-1838	Naomy (**Beeson**) dis
8-17-1839	Wm's w & dt gct Back Creek MM; Wm's wthd
2-15-1840	Wm rpt withholding debts & refusing to settle w/creditors; res in limits of Back Creek MM; that mtg rq to treat w/him & rpt
7-18-1840	Wm dis for wthd debts
6-19-1841	Jonathan dis for j Christian Friends
7-17-1841	Sarah dis for j Christian Friends
3-18-1843	Archelaus & fam gct Sugar River MM
3-16-1844	James dis for j separatists
6-15-1844	Joseph dis for j separatists
7-15-1845	Joseph rst after chm
7-19-1845	Jemima & Naomi dis for j separatists
2-20-1847	Margaret rocf Back Creek MM
8-19-1848	Joseph rec in mbrp
7-21-1849	Naomi rec by rq
6-21-1851	Jesse rpt for na; compl ret to PM
10-18-1851	Joseph & fam gct Pleasant Plain MM IA; James rec by rq of par Joseph
4-20-1861	Baraboo MM gr perm to rst James
1-16-1864	Joseph minister & w Naomi & ch Rachel, Naomi, James, Nancy Ann, Sarah Jane, & Mary Ellen rocf Honey Creek MM
8-20-1864	Joseph & fam gct Honey Creek MM IA
10-15-1864	Baraboo MM WI gr perm to rst Jemima
2-16-1889	Joseph M rec by rq

SPRINGFIELD MONTHLY MEETING
MINUTES AND MARRIAGES

STANTON

5-15-1841	Cert rec for Nathan & fam fr Center MM NC; end to New Garden MM
4-19-1864	Penninah (**Nickleson**) rpt mcd
11-19-1864	Peninah (**Nicholson**) rpt mcd
1-21-1865	Peninah (**Nicholson**) mbrp ret
3-18-1865	Peninah & min s Edwin Murray gct Poplar Run MM
10-20-1866	David & w Penina & min s Edwin M rocf Poplar Run MM
9-21-1872	David rpt mcd
11-16-1872	David & min ch gct Poplar Run MM
1-17-1874	Aaron & w Lydia & min ch Thomas W, Lillie A, & Wm A rocf Poplar Run MM
10-17-1874	Aaron & fam gct Poplar Run MM
11-15-1890	Edwin M rocf Poplar Run MM
1-17-1891	Mattie rolf Bethel UB ch
10-15-1898	Edwin M & dt Jennie Opal rel by rq of Nettle Creek PM

STATE

5-17-1845	Westbury PM rpt Charlotte (**Carr**) mcd
6-21-1845	Charlotte (**Carr**) rpt mcd
7-20-1845	Charlotte (**Carr**) chm

STEARNS

9-20-1862	Exalina C (**Hinshaw**) Springfield PM rpt mcd
10-18-1862	Exalina C (**Hinshaw**) mbrp ret
9-17-1881	Exalina gct Indianapolis MM

STEPHENSON

5-15-1880	Elizabeth (**Allen**) roc
6-19-1880	Reuben rec by rq
3-21-1896	Elza rec by rq of Springfield PM

STEVENSON

9-17-1887	Reuben & w Lizzie & ch rel by rq; jas

STEWART

6-16-1883	Margaret B gct Hopewell MM
11-15-1890	Esther glt M E ch; J O **Bills** pastor

STONEMAN

6-17-1843	Cert rec for Mark D fr Deep Creek MM NC; end to Duck Creek MM

STORMS

7-16-1842	Mary Ann (**Locke**) dis for dp & mcd

STOUT

5-3-1820	Jesse rocf New Garden MM
2-7-1821	Jesse & fam gct New Garden MM
11-18-1826	Ephraim & ch James, Charles, Robert, & Elias roc
2-16-1828	Charles & ch Jesse & Noah rec by rq
1-15-1831	Ephraim gct Duck Creek MM to m Mary **Sheridan**
5-31-1831	Ephraim & fam gct Duck Creek MM
4-21-1834	Jesse rpt mcd
6-21-1834	Jesse chm
12-19-1835	Noah dis for mcd, na, & dp
3-21-1840	Charles gct Westfield MM
11-21-1840	Jesse dis for dp, offering to fight, & administering an oath while acting as justice of the peace
3-16-1889	Irena dis
4-20-1889	Irene drpd fr mbrp

STUDY

8-15-1846	Mahala Ann (**Ward**) dis for mcd & j separatists
6-19-1869	David Springfield PM rec by rq

SWAIN

2-2-1820	Thomas & Elihu appt to comm
3-1-1820	Thomas chosen clerk
6-7-1820	Samuel rpt for dancing

SWAIN (cont)

9-6-1820	Samuel dis
1-12-1825	Obed dis for dancing & att mcd
7-13-1825	Elihu Jr rpt for dancing & dp
8-17-1825	Elihu Jr dis
6-11-1825	Job dis for dancing & dp
1-20-1827	Elihu rpt m to Mary **Worth**
5-15-1830	Ira dis for att mcd
8-21-1830	Sarah L appt elder
1-19-1831	Zeno s Thomas & Lydia m Lucinda dt David & Mary **Maulsby** at Springfield Mtg
9-17-1831	George & w rocf Silver Creek MM
5-17-1834	Charles dis for att mcd
3-19-1836	George & w & fam gct Walnut Ridge MM
8-20-1836	Elihu appt rec of births, death & m
7-16-1842	Elzy dis for unchaste conduct with young woman
11-18-1843	Lucinda dis for j separatists
1-20-1844	Elihu Jr dis for j separatists & refusing to give up the record books of births, deaths, & m
3-16-1844	Mary dis for j separatists
5-18-1844	Elizabeth dis for j separatists
6-19-1847	Mary dis for na, dancing, & apd
7-15-1848	John dis for mcd, dp, & na
2-21-1852	Thomas dis for na
3-16-1895	Job rec by rq of Springfield PM

SYMONS

2-19-1898	Alfred H rocf North Branch MM KS

TALBERT

1-16-1886	Alice glt Westfield M E ch Hamilton Co

TATE

9-17-1853	Mariah Louisa dis for mcd & j UB ch
4-17-1856	Cynthia Ellen (**Beeson**) rpt mcd; drpd fr mbrp
2-21-1891	Octa rec by rq of Nettle Creek PM

TAYLOR

8-20-1836	John rq mbrp
9-11-1836	John rec in mbrp
12-22-1836	John s Wm & Lydia Wayne Co m Mareb dt Isaac & Hannah **Beeson** Wayne Co at West River
4-15-1854	John dis for drinking & giving liquor to others & na
7-16-1859	Elizabeth & Rebecca dis
8-18-1860	Wilson rpt mcd; drpd fr mbrp
1-21-1899	Archie rec by rq of Nettle Creek PM
2-18-1899	Alonzo rec by rq of Nettle Creek PM

TEST

9-21-1853	Josiah s Samuel & Hannah Wayne Co m Miriam C dt Thomas & Elizabeth **Dennis** Wayne Co at Nettle Creek
1-21-1854	Miriam gct Whitewater MM
5-19-1855	Josiah & w Miriam C rocf Whitewater MM
1-20-1860	Emily rocf New Garden MM
4-20-1861	Rufus & w Margaret M rocf Whitewater MM
8-17-1861	Wm rocf Whitewater MM
9-25-1861	Oliver s Samuel & Hannah Wayne Co m Sarah dt Branson & Elma **Dennis** at Nettle Creek
9-19-1863	Sarah gct Whitewater MM
4-20-1867	Wm & fam gct Whitewater MM
8-15-1868	Miriam appt Nettle Creek PM o
8-21-1869	Miriam & ch Mary Ellen & Samuel Edwin gct Spiceland MM
7-20-1872	Rufus appt o
5-17-1879	Rufus appt elder
1-18-1890	Rufus gct Spiceland MM to m Lydia H **Symons**
6-21 1890	Lydia H rocf Spiceland
11-27-1897	Zaccheus rq rel fr mbrp
12-18-1897	Zaccheus wthd rq for rel fr mbrp
5-21-1898	Rufus & w Lydia H & adopted dt Lucile **Clemens** gct Whitewater MM

THOMAS

9-19-1840	Charity dis for mcd
10-21-1848	Elmina (**Stanley**) dis for mcd & j separatists; Ruth rocf West Branch MM
1-15-1859	West Branch MM gr perm to rst Esther Ann

THORNBURG

2-2-1820	Henry appt to comm
3-1-1820	Henry chosen o
6-7-1820	Walter & ch Dempsey, Jesse, John, & Walter rocf Lost Creek MM TN
8-14-1822	Jesse rpt for mcd
9-11-1822	Jesse chm
3-12-1823	Dempsey rpt for fornication & mcd
9-17-1823	Dempsey chm
5-14-1823	Jesse dis for mcd
6-11-1823	Peggy dis
7-16-1823	Thomas rocf Caesers Creek MM
10-12-1825	John & fam (ch Isaac & Wm) rocf Lees Creek MM OH
10-25-1825	Wm dis for att mcd
1-18-1826	John s Walter & Mary Wayne Co m Rachel dt Elihu & Sarah **Swain** Wayne Co at Springfield Mtg
10-21-1826	Job & John rocf Lost Creek MM TN
11-11-1826	Dempsey dis for fornication
11-18-1826	Henry appt elder
8-16-1828	John, Joab, & Job gct White River MM
10-18-1828	Edward & fam rocf Cherry Grove MM
11-20-1828	Henry s Henry & Ann Wayne Co m Sarah dt Anthony & Elizabeth **Reynolds** at West River Mtg
3-25-1829	Lewis s Henry & Ann Wayne Co m Lydia dt Barachia & Lucinda **Macy** at Springfield
6-20-1829	Edward & fam gct Cherry Grove MM
12-19-1829	West River PM rpt Larkin for dp
1-16-1830	Thomas & w gct White River MM
10-13-1831	Walter rpt for mcd & dp
11-19-1831	Walter chm
6-21-1832	John s Henry & Ann Wayne Co m Elizabeth dt Jesse & Mournen **Hunt** Wayne Co at West River Mtg
10-19-1833	John rpt for getting in a passion & offering violence to fellow man
11-16-1833	John chm
4-21-1834	Walter dis for na
4-16-1836	Henry Jr dis
2-18-1837	Lydia (**Howell**) dis
12-16-1837	John dis for disorderly con with a female & denying it
5-19-1838	Walter dis for mcd & dp
3-21-1840	Nathan rocf White River MM
5-16-1840	Dempsy rec by rq
2-20-1841	Walter rec by rq after being dis
12-10-1843	Lewis dis for j separatists
2-17-1844	Phebe dis for j separatists
3-16-1844	Lydia dis for j separatists
4-20-1844	Nathan dis for j separatists
1-18-1845	Demaris (**Locke**) dis for mcd
12-19-1846	Coleman rpt for att mcd
1-16-1847	Coleman's case dis; min
1-19-1850	Mary Jane & Elvin Pleasant rec by rq of father Walter
3-16-1850	Julia Ann rec by rq
12-21-1850	Coleman dis for mcd, dp, & na
4-19-1851	Walter rpt mcd
5-17-1851	Walter mbrp ret
1-17-1852	Margaret (**Beeson**) dis for mcd
8-19-1854	Milton dis for swearing & na
6-16-1855	Lorenzo dis for mcd, dp, & na
5-17-1856	Wm rpt mcd; drpd fr mbrp
1-16-1858	Wilson dis for dp & na
2-20-1858	Madison rpt mcd; drpd fr mbrp
5-15-1858	Anna (**Baldwin**) rpt mcd; drpd fr mbrp
6-19-1858	Thomas E rpt mcd
7-11-1858	Thomas E mbrp ret
5-21-1859	John rpt mcd
7-16-1859	John mbrp ret

THORNBURG (cont)

3-16-1861	John Henry rpt mcd
4-20-1861	John Henry mbrp ret; Seth rpt mcd
5-18-1861	Seth mbrp ret
5-17-1862	Susan Nettle Creek PM rec by rq
8-11-1862	Henry elder d ae 90y
7-18-1863	Rachel & ch Lindon H, Lydia Ellen, & Martha Ann West River PM rec by rq w/consent of New Garden MM
8-15-1863	Joseph W min s John gct Bear Creek MM IA; John's withheld
9-19-1863	Rachel rec by rq w/perm of New Garden MM
2-20-1864	John dis for being out of unity w/Friends
5-21-1864	Elvin P dis for being out of unity w/Friends; Susan Nettle Creek compl for obtaining a div
7-16-1864	Walter M dis for obtaining a div
8-19-1864	Thomas E dis for threatening the life of a fellow man & throwing stones at him
12-17-1864	Orlando rpt mcd; mbrp ret
11-15-1865	Orlando gct Bear Creek MM IA
6-16-1866	Dempsey C dis
7-16-1870	John Henry chm for fighting & upl
2-17-1872	Seth & min ch gct Hopewell MM
3-15-1873	Dempsey C & w Ethalinda T & min ch George G & Frank V rec by rq of West River PM; Elizabeth M & min ch Rachel E, Emma, Ella, & Walter M rec by rq of West River PM; John H rec by rq of West River PM
6-20-1874	Dempsey appt o
3-18-1876	Electa rec by rq of West River PM
3-17-1877	Wm R rec by rq
2-16-1878	Effie rec by rq
10-18-1884	Wm R rel by rq

THORNBURGH

3-20-1886	Elvin Pleasant & min s Ottie rec by rq
4-19-1890	Walter R rec by rq of mother Electa
3-19-1892	Wm R rec by rq

TINKLE

5-20-1882	Harvey rec by rq of Nettle Creek PM
1-17-1891	Clifford rec by rq

UNDERHILL

3-1-1820	John & ch Lemuel, Alfred, & Clarkson rocf Lost Creek MM TN; end by New Garden MM
12-6-1820	John selected clerk
3-20-1830	Lemuel dis for using unbecoming language
9-20-1834	Alfred gct West Grove MM
12-9-1846	John rpt mcd & dp
4-17-1847	John chm
10-16-1847	Clarkson rpt for dp & suing a mbr at law
12-18-1847	Clarkson's case dis
2-20-1847	Anna (**Murphey**) rpt mcd
3-20-1847	Anna (**Murphey**) chm
2-19-1848	Jesse B dis for dp & upl
8-20-1853	John & fam rq cert to Honey Creek MM; wthd; rem to IL
3-18-1854	Clarkson dis for mcd
1-20-1855	John rq cert for himself & fam to Honey Creek MM; bef issued he moved back to Springfield MM
6-16-1855	Cert gr for Anna & ch to Honey Creek MM
7-21-1860	John gct Honey Creek MM
8-17-1872	Susan Springfield PM rec by rq
9-20-1873	Jesse B & ch John M, Edward D, Alfred C, & Anna Jane rec by rq
2-15-1896	Alfred C rel by rq to j Richmond 2d Presb ch; Emma gct Whitewater MM
6-19-1897	Jesse B & w Susan gct Whitewater MM

UPTON

9-17-1836	Samuel rocf Stanford MM NY
11-16-1839	Samuel G dis for offering violence to a civil officer

**SPRINGFIELD MONTHLY MEETING
MINUTES AND MARRIAGES**

VAN HORN
11-19-1836	James refused mbrp; guilty of upl & justifying bearing of arms
1-20-1838	James rocf Miami MM OH
8-18-1838	James dis for offering to fight

VEAL
1-20-1872	Cynthia Springfield PM rec by rq

VORIS
3-17-1894	James rec by rq of Mooreland PM

WADMAN
5-15-1858	Hannah (**Swain**) rpt mcd; drpd fr mbrp

WALTZ
11-18-1899	Lena rec by rq of Mooreland PM

WARD
11-12-1823	Obed & ch Timothy & George rocf West Grove MM
3-16-1833	George rpt mcd
4-20-1833	George chm
5-29-1833	Timothy s Obed & Mary Wayne Co m Mahala Ann dt Joshua & Elizabeth **Wright** Randolph Co at Springfield Mtg
6-15-1844	George dis for j separatists
9-21-1844	Mary & Patience dis for j separatists
2-16-1878	George F & w Margaret C & ch Laura Ann & Lida A rec by rq of Springfield PM

WARREN
4-17-1822	Henry rpt for dancing
7-17-1822	Henry dis
7-13-1825	James dis for jas
8-17-1825	Sarah dis for na
9-19-1829	Azariah dis for mcd
6-16-1832	Seth dis for dp

WATKINS
7-20-1839	Sarah (**Antrum**) dis for mcd

WEAVER
6-17-1882	Rachel & Emma J gct Dublin MM

WEBSTER
9-21-1889	Joseph & w Linda Myra rocf S Wabash MM
6-20-1891	Joseph rpt for not complying w/contracts & making false statements
7-18-1891	Myra gct Marion MM
9-19-1891	Joseph dis & rel fr mbrp

WEYL
10-16-1830	Jemima dis

WHINERY
3-15-1834	Thomas & fam rocf New Garden MM
12-20-1834	Thomas & fam gct Cherry Grove MM

WHITE
7-21-1838	Silas rec by rq of Henry **Hollingsworth** to whom he was bound
5-21-1881	Miriam T (**Chamness**) gct Hopewell MM

WHITTER
2-20-1892	Levi rec by rq
4-20-1895	Levi drpd fr mbrp

WILES
9-11-1822	Thomas & ch Wm, Luke & Frances rocf Cherry Grove MM
7-13-1825	Luke Jr & fam rocf Deep Creek MM NC
8-15-1835	Thomas & fam gct Mississinewa MM
10-20-1838	Luke Sr rec by rq w/perm of Deep Creek MM NC
7-15-1843	Susannah dis for mcd

WILES (cont)
5-7-1851	Wm D gct Hopewell MM to m Deborah Jane **Butler**
7-15-1854	Deborah J & ch Orlando & Lenora rocf Hopewell MM
4-21-1855	Wm & fam gct Hopewell MM; Daniel gct Hopewell MM
11-15-1856	Luke gct Spiceland MM to m Jane **Davis**
2-21-1857	Jane D rocf Spiceland MM
10-16-1858	Nathan dis for dp, fiddling, dancing, & upl
9-21-1861	Luke & fam gct Spiceland MM

WILLETS
2-15-1826	Ruben rocf Milford MM

WILLIAMS
3-1-1820	Azariah appt to comm
1-3-1821	James & ch George, Isaac, Boaz, & Jared rocf New Garden MM
9-11-1822	James & fam gct Honey Creek MM
7-16-1823	Caleb & Martin min rocf Derby Creek MM Goshen
1-12-1825	Richard appt clerk
6-15-1825	Wm rocf Derby Creek MM OH
10-12-1825	Charles dis for mcd
11-16-1825	Mathew rpt mcd by West River PM
4-12-1826	Mathew chm
5-17-1826	West River rpt Joseph mcd
6-14-1826	Joseph chm
8-19-1826	Charles rst after being dis
1-20-1827	Jonathan con mcd
5-19-1827	Wm & fam gct Duck Creek MM
6-16-1827	Wm dis for drinking & upl
9-13-1827	Henry & Marchant min ch Matilda rocf West Grove MM
10-20-1827	Henry rpt mcd
12-15-1827	Henry chm
12-19-1829	West River PM rpt Joseph for gaming
1-16-1830	Joseph chm
8-21-1830	David dis for upl & dp
9-13-1830	Alexander dis for upl & dp
10-15-1831	John & w rocf Somerset MM OH; Mathew dis for dp & na
6-16-1832	Azariah Jr dis for dp
8-18-1832	Matilda dis
2-21-1835	Emsley T, Oliver, & Joseph ch Henry rec in mbrp
3-21-1835	Abraham & Azariah ch Jonathan rec in mbrp
12-9-1835	Jonathan dis for mcd Mississinewa MM
4-15-1837	John M dis for bearing arms in taking a fellow man
6-17-1837	Azariah & fam gct Mississinewa MM
7-15-1837	Richard & fam gct Mississinewa MM
9-15-1838	Charles dis for na & vending spirituous liquors
4-20-1839	Ann (**Hobson**) dis for mcd
10-19-1839	Luzene dis for j M E
5-20-1840	Salina dis for j M E & dp
3-16-1844	Joseph dis for j separatists
5-18-1844	Deborah appt elder
6-15-1844	Ruth dis for j separatists
8-16-1845	Jesse B prcf West Grove MM to m Mary Ann **Mendenhall**
8-21-1845	Jesse B s Daniel & Margaret Wayne Co m Mary Ann dt Wm & Rebecca **Mendenhall** Wayne Co at West River
7-18-1846	Merchant dis for na & upl
12-19-1846	Nancy E (**Beeson**) dis for mcd
3-17-1849	Joseph dis for upl & na
10-20-1849	Stillwater MM rpt Rachel (**Atkinson**) for mcd; rq this mtg to treat w/her
11-17-1849	Rachel (**Atkinson**) chm
2-16-1850	Rachel rocf Stillwater MM OH
4-20-1850	Somerset MM OH rpt Isaac C for mcd; rq this mtg to treat w/him & rpt
5-18-1850	Isaac C chm; Somerset MM OH inf
2-15-1851	Oliver dis for na, dp, & att mcd
8-16-1851	John & fam gct Honey Creek MM

210

WILLIAMS (cont)
10-18-1851	Isaac & fam gct Honey Creek MM
5-21-1853	Jesse B & fam (ch Daniel B & Joseph C) rocf Poplar Run MM; Maryann & dt Caroline rocf Poplar Run MM
3-19-1864	Mathew rpt mcd; drpd fr mbrp
7-16-1864	Mary Ann appt o
8-20-1864	Obed rpt mcd; drpd fr mbrp
9-17-1864	Mary Ann appt elder
10-20-1866	Henry C dis for bearing arms, volunteering for military service, & mcd
3-15-1873	Christena & min s Harvey Alonzo rec by rq of West River PM
1-17-1880	Sophiah rec by rq of Springfield PM
3-17-1888	Marilla, Louie Pearl, Lydia A, Jennie, & Lester rec by rq of Springfield PM
2-21-1891	Harvey A dis; jas
5-21-1898	Pearl gct Marion MM

WILLIS
2-2-1820	David appt to comm
6-7-1820	Jesse rpt mcd
7-5-1820	Jesse chm
9-6-1820	Isaac & s David rocf Lost Creek MM TN
7-16-1823	John rec in mbrp after having been dis by NC MM
12-16-1826	West River PM rpt Jesse for na
2-17-1827	Jesse dis
5-19-1827	Wm gct Duck Creek MM
7-18-1829	David dis for m one who had been div
6-16-1832	David Jr dis for dp
5-21-1836	Rachel dis
4-15-1837	John dis for getting angry & upl
6-20-1840	Henry dis for dp, na, & upl
12-27-1842	Isaac rpt m to Ruth **Dennis**
12-10-1843	Eliza Ann, Loucinda, & Sarah Levine min ch John & Lydia rocf Milford MM
1-20-1844	Isaac dis for j separatists
12-19-1846	John dis for na & dp; Jonathan dis for na, dp, & upl
2-20-1847	Waldo dis for na & dp
10-16-1847	Hannah (**Lee**) dis for mcd
10-16-1847	Ruth rec by rq
6-16-1860	Ruth appt o
5-19-1877	Ruth gct Dover MM; not acc
2-20-1892	Marcus, Maggie, Viola, & Bertha rec by rq
10-15-1898	Mark R, Margaret J, Cora V, & Dottie R rel by rq of Nettle Creek PM

WILLITS
2-23-1826	Rueben s Isaac & Rachel Wayne Co m Mary dt James & Hannah **Harris** Wayne Co at West River MH

WILLMORE
8-16-1862	Jesse W & Martha Jane rec by rq

WILLSON
3-21-1829	Jesse & w rocf Center MM NC

WILMORE
6-18-1864	Jesse & fam gct Poplar Run MM

WILSON
4-16-1836	Newby dis for mcd
5-18-1844	Christian gct Lick Creek MM
11-17-1849	Jesse dis for promoting mcd at his res
6-19-1852	Manlove dis for dp & upl
5-19-1855	Asenath (**Dennis**) dis for mcd; Isabel (**Beason**) rpt mcd
6-16-1855	Isabel (**Beason**) mbrp ret
3-19-1859	Elizabeth dis for j M E
8-20-1864	Hannah (**Baldwin**) Nettle Creek PM rpt mcd
9-17-1864	Hannah (**Baldwin**) chm
12-15-1883	Isabel dis for dr & na
11-17-1894	Nathan L rel fr mbrp

SPRINGFIELD MONTHLY MEETING MINUTES AND MARRIAGES

WINDSOR
2-21-1885	Alfred rec by rq

WINSER
2-21-1891	Octie rec in mbrp

WISE
3-15-1884	Charles rec by rq of Flat Rock PM

WOLFORD
3-16-1889	Asenith dis
4-20-1889	Asenath drpd fr mbrp
2-20-1892	Johnie rec by rq
4-21-1894	Milton rq mbrp
5-19-1894	Milton mbrp rq drpd
10-15-1898	John H rel by rq of Nettle Creek PM
1-21-1899	Della May rec by rq of Nettle Creek PM

WOOD
4-20-1872	Sarah E & Margaret rec by rq
5-20-1878	Mary Ann rec by rq
1-15-1881	Joseph rec by rq
10-20-1883	Joseph L & Mary Ann gct Stanton MM IL

WOODARD
11-17-1855	Thomas & w Mary Ann & ch Emily Jane, Alpheus Lindley, Vestal, Adaline, & Alice rocf Spiceland MM
7-19-1856	Thomas & fam gct New Garden MM

WOODWARD
6-20-1835	Jesse rpt mcd
2-20-1836	Jesse chm
3-19-1836	Jesse gct White Lick MM

WOODY
6-19-1847	Mary rocf Cane Creek MM NC
6-19-1847	Joshua, Anthony, Alson, Mary, & Harriett min ch Hugh rocf Cane Creek MM NC
7-16-1859	Joshua & Melinda (**Chamness**) rpt mcd
8-20-1859	Joshua & Melinda (**Chamness**) mbrp ret
12-19-1868	Joshua & fam gct New Salem MM
2-17-1877	Anthony gct Salem MM
7-17-1880	Laura Alice rocf New Salem MM
2-18-1882	Anthony rocf New Salem MM
4-15-1893	George glt Galveston UB ch Cass Co
3-16-1895	Genetta rec by rq of Nettle Creek PM

WORTH
8-16-1828	Rhoda appt elder
10-15-1831	Thomas rpt mcd to 1st cousin & dp; mbr Center MM NC; that mtg inf
11-17-1832	Wm & fam rocf Center MM NC
12-15-1832	Obed rocf Center MM NC; Reuben M & fam (s Joseph Clinton) rocf Center MM NC
7-24-1833	Wm Randolph Co s Job & Rhoda NC m Sarah L **Swain** dt Joseph & Pheobe **Leonard** at Springfield Mtg
5-17-1834	Wm & fam gct Duck Creek MM
1-21-1837	Obed rpt for bearing arms in taking his fellow man
2-18-1837	Obed chm
6-16-1838	Obed B rpt for dp & mcd; res in verge of Walnut Ridge MM; that mtg rq to treat w/him & rpt
9-15-1838	Obed B chm
8-18-1838	Reuben & fam gct Whitewater MM
10-20-1838	Obed B gct Walnut Ridge MM

WRIGHT
3-12-1823	Luke, James, & Jesse min rocf Cherry Grove MM
2-16-1825	Wm min s Elizabeth rocf West Branch MM OH
5-17-1826	Wm dis for mcd, dancing, & offering to fight
8-19-1826	Betsey dis
10-20-1827	James & fam (ch George, Allen, David, & Joel) rocf Green Plain MM OH

SPRINGFIELD MONTHLY MEETING
MINUTES AND MARRIAGES

WRIGHT (cont)

6-21-1828	James dis for dealing in spirituous liquors & mcd
11-21-1829	Mahala dis
7-17-1830	Judith dis
11-19-1831	West River PM rpt Luke for dp; dis
2-16-1833	James & fam gct White River MM
5-17-1834	James dis for na & dp
7-19-1834	Lucinda dis
2-21-1835	Duck Creek MM rpt George mcd; rq that mtg to treat w/him & rpt
7-18-1835	George dis
1-1-1840	Jesse dis for na, dp, & training with the militia
3-21-1840	Abegail dis for j M E

WRIGHT (cont)

8-15-1840	Ann dis for j M E
1-16-1841	John E prcf Duck Creek MM to m Jemima **Hunnicutt**
2-20-1841	John E rpt m to Jemima W **Hunnicutt**
6-16-1849	Elizabeth & Eliza dis for j separatists & mcd
6-19-1858	Duck Creek MM gr perm to rst Eliza M
10-19-1861	Mary S (**Beeson**) rpt mcd
3-18-1862	Mary S (**Beeson**) chm
4-19-1862	Mary S gct South River MM IA
12-15-1888	Sarah rec by rq

WRITTENHOUSE

3-16-1895	Walter & Mary Etta rec by rq of Nettle Creek PM

INDEX

ABBEALY, Herbert, 67
    see also **ARBEALY**
ABBOTT, Alexander M, 147
    Alice, 183
    Hazel, 147
    Hettie W (Wilkinson), 147
    see also **ABOTT**
ABOTT, Elizabeth, 153
    see also **ABBOTT**
ABSHIRE, C B, 179
    Ida M, 179
    Mary Elizabeth (Wilson), 179
ACTON, Harold, 3
    Nellie, 3
    Ollie, 3
ADAIR, Sarah E (Clawson), 67
ADAMS, Anna, 67
    Asenith (Bond), 183
    Albert Preston, 147
    Alva E, 147
    Alvis, 183
    Alvis D, 147, 181
    Ann/Anna, 147,207
    Asenath, 147,186
    Asenath (Baldwin), 147,181
    Ebenezer, 147,152,183,204
    Edith, 3
    Elijah, 147
    Elizabeth (Dunbar), 147
    Ellen N (Thornburgh), 147
    Henry M, 147
    Irena, 147
    Jacob, 183
    Joel, 147,183
    John, 147
    John R, 147
    Jonathan, 183
    Lewis H, 147
    Lucinda, 147,152,162,187
    Luella, 147
    Lydia, 147
    Mahlon, 3
    Malvina, 147,181
    Malvina (Snodgrass), 147
    Marcus D, 147
    Mary, 147,207
    Mary A (Gullet), 147
    Mary Ann, 20
    Mary Jane, 147
    Mary M, 204
    Melissa (Thompson), 147
    Nelson Perry, 147
    Nevada May (Elliott), 3
    Olive, 147
    Ollie M (Anders), 147
    Rachel, 147
    Rebecca, 183,204
    Rebecca (Davis), 147,152
    Wm, 147,183
    Wm Jr, 183
ADAMSON, Aaron, 183
    Amassa, 151
    Ann, 183
    Ann (Hiatt), 183
    Charlotta, 183
    John, 183
    John L, 183
    Margaret J, 67
    Melissa Adaline, 154
    Nathaniel, 183
    Nathaniel J, 67
    Nathaniel Jackson, 67
    Ruth, 183
    Samuel, 183

ADAMSON, Sarah, 183
    Seth, 183
    Simon, 147,183
    Vesta (Downing), 154
    Wm O, 154
ADDELL, Jacob, 67
    see also **ADEL, ADELL**
ADDINGTON, Claudia (Brown), 3
    David Smith, 3
    Davis S, 67
    Elisha, 3
    Eliz, 21
    Elizabeth, 2,3
    Elvira, 3
    George, 3
    Hannah, 3,67
    James, 2,3,67
    Jesse, 3
    John, 1,2,3,67
    John Jr, 67
    Joseph, 3,67
    Lula, 21
    Mary, 67
    Mary (Smith), 3
    Matilda, 3
    Melvin C, 3
    Mercy, 3
    Nathan, 3,21
    Rachel, 3,67
    Sarah, 2
    Sarah Elizabeth (Williams), 3
    Selah, 67
    Selah (Townsend), 3
    Thomas, 3,67
    Wm, 3,67
ADDLEMAN, Lydia, 4
    Malvina C, 4
    R J, 4
    Viola, 4
ADEL, Howell G, 67
    Jacob, 67
    John T, 67
    Mary G, 67
    Rachel, 67
    Rachel F, 67
    see also **ADDELL, ADELL**
ADELL, Howell, 67
    Jacob Jr, 67
    John, 67
    Mary G, 67
    Rachel, 67
    see also **ADDELL, ADEL**
ADKINS, Eliza, 90
    see also **ATKINS**
AGEE, Martha (Hendren), 3
AIRY, George, 67
    John, 67
    Keziah, 67
    Lydia, 67
    Mary Ann, 67
    Wm, 67
    see also **ARY**
AKIN, James, 62
    Lizzie, 62
    Maude, 62
ALBERSON, Abigail, 3
    Eli, 3
    Eliza, 3
    Jesse, 3
    Milton, 3
    see also **ALBERTSON**
ALBERT, Hannah, 67

ALBERTSON, Abigail, 67
    Abigail (Ratliff), 67
    Alfred, 3,67
    Ann, 5
    Benjamin, 3,67
    Bessie, 183
    Calvin, 183
    Easter, 183
    Eli, 67
    Elias, 67
    Eliza, 67
    Eunice M, 67
    Hannah (Davis), 183
    James, 3,67
    Jeanette (Kennedy), 3
    Jesse, 5
    Joseph, 3,67
    Joseph L, 147,183
    Joshua, 67
    Josiah, 67
    Louisa C, 183
    Louise (Cook), 147
    Mark, 147
    Mary, 5
    Mary Ann, 5
    Mattie J, 67
    Millicent 3,67,117
    Millicent (Ratliff), 67
    Milton, 67
    Nexon, 183
    Sarah, 3,67
    Thomas P, 183
    Wm Milton, 67
    see also **ALBERSON**
ALBON, Sonora, 183
ALCORN, Amanda, 183
    Amanda (McClane), 147
    Charles, 183
    Charles R, 147
    Finley, 147
    Freddie Ishmael, 183
    Fredric I, 147
    Harriet, 147
    Huldah, 147,183
    Wm, 147,183
ALEXANDER, E May, 13
    Mary, 67
ALLBRIGHT, Benjamin F, 3
    John, 3
    Mabel, 3
    Nona, 3
    Susan, 3
    Susie R (Pickitt), 3
ALLEN, Allice, 4
    Anderson M, 183
    Anderson Monroe, 148
    Ann (Clark), 3,4
    Ann/Anne/Annie Eliza, 3,22,68
    Anna, 68
    Anna (Truckness), 3
    Ardella B (Armstrong), 4
    Asenath, 148,183
    Asenath (Allen), 148
    Benj, 183
    Benjamin F, 147,148
    Benjamin Harmon, 148
    Branson, 148
    Caroline, 148,167
    Catharine, 45
    Charity, 50,68
    Charity W, 68
    Charity Williams (Kersey) 3,22
    Charles/Charley, 68,147

ALLEN, Charles A, 3,4
   Charles B, 183
   Charles F, 68
   Charles Francis, 3
   Christena, 165
   Clifton Ellis, 148
   Cynthia E (Thornburg), 183
   David J, 183
   David T, 147
   Deborah (Butler), 3
   Elizabeth, 147,183,208
   Elizabeth (Reynolds), 183
   Elizabeth (Wright), 157
   Elma, 147,183
   Emma, 68,157
   Emma Jane, 147,183
   Emma Lemira/Semyra, 3,68
   Estella, 148,183
   Eunice, 148,185
   Franklin, 183
   Franklin Pierce, 148
   Freddie, 148,183
   George, 183
   George C, 3
   George Carter, 68
   George Thomas, 148
   Gulielma, 4,68
   Hannah, 148
   Hannah (Haworth), 68
   Hannah (Woody), 147,148,167
   Hannah A (Hayworth), 68
   Hannah J, 183
   Hannah J (Modlin), 183
   Hannah L, 183
   Hannah Louisa, 148
   Harmon, 3,4,67,148,
   Harriet (Marmon), 68
   Harvey, 148,183
   Hugh, 67
   Isabel Jane, 148
   James G, 157
   Jesse, 148
   John, 45,148
   John Milton, 22
   John W, 147,183
   Jonathan L, 183
   Jonathan S, 147
   Joseph B, 68
   Joseph C, 147,148
   Joseph G, 183
   Joseph M, 68
   Joseph Milton, 3,50,68
   Joseph N, 148
   Keziah, 199
   Laura Mary, 147,183
   Lester Otis, 148
   Luezar, 148
   Maggie (Stevens), 148
   Malinda Myrtle, 148
   Mary, 4,75,148,183,195
   Mary (Marmon),68
   Mary Ann/Anna, 3,50,68
   Mary Ellen, 148
   Mattie Ethel, 183
   Milton, 148
   Minnie, 68
   Miriam Coffin, 3
   Nancy, 148
   Nancy Ann, 165
   Naomi J, 112
   Naomi Jane, 4,41,68
   Newton, 148,183
   Phebe, 30

ALLEN, Phebe Jane, 183
   Phebe Jane (Dennis), 147,183
   Philander, 41
   Philander John, 3,4
   Philip, 165
   Rachel, 68
   Rachel (Boone), 3,4,41
   Rachel H, 68
   Rebecca, 148
   Rufus Morris, 4
   Ruth, 37
   Sarah, 67,148
   Sarah (Harvey), 67
   Sarah J, 148,178
   Sarah Jane, 183
   Sarah Jane (Jobes), 147
   Sarah Malinda, 147,183
   Scherin, 45
   Simon, 147,148,167
   Susannah, 148
   Thomas Clarkson, 4
   Wm, 148
   Wm C, 4
   Wm Jesse, 148
   Zachariah, 67,148,183
   Zimri, 148
ALLISON, Alfred, 4
   Cyrus, 4,60
   Edith (Sherman), 4
   Fannie, 45
   George Woolsey, 4
   James, 45
   Mattie E, 4,60
   Melissa, 16,45
   Ruth, 60
   Ruth A (Lockwood), 4
ALLRED, Abijah, 148,183
   Eli C, 148
   Essie M, 148
   Nellie (Study), 148
   Ruhama (Lamb), 148
   see also **ALRED**
ALMOND, Elizabeth, 68
   Judith, 68
   Matthew, 68
   Rebeckah, 68
ALRED, Miriam, 19
   see also **ALLRED**
ALSOP, Edward, 68
   Edward B, 68
   Maria, 68
   Reiceful, 68
AMMERMAN, John Edwin, 68
   Lillie J, 68
   Simon E, 68
AMMON, Anna, 68
   Anna Lee (Johnson), 4
   Conrad, 4,68
   John H, 4
   Lewis/Louis B, 4,68
   Mary, 4
ANDERS, Ira E, 148
   Mary E (Clear), 147,148
   Ollie M, 147,148
   Walter S, 147,148
ANDERSON, Amy Bell (Baldwin), 148
   David, 4,68
   David Samuel, 68
   Earnest, 183
   Elisabeth/Elizabeth, 4,68,83
   Eliza, 149,161,180
   Elizabeth (Phillips), 148
   Ernest, 148

ANDERSON, Francis Lee, 148
   George, 15
   Hannah, 4,68
   Hannah L, 183
   Hannah M, 15
   Isaac, 4,68
   James, 4
   Jane, 74
   Jane Alexander, 4
   Jane E, 68
   John, 4
   Joseph, 148
   Leah, 68
   Lula Fern, 148
   Mahala, 4
   Mary, 68
   Mary (Cosans), 4
   Mary Townsend, 4
   Matilda, 15
   Pouncey, 149, 180
   Rilla (Webster), 4
   Robert, 68
   Samuel, 4,68
   Tamar, 149,180
   Thomas, 68
   Thomas Simkins, 4
   Wm, 4
ANDES, Peter, 184
ANDREW, Abigail, 68
   Catherine, 4
   Ellwood, 4
   Jemima, 4
   Mary, 4,68,133
   Mary (Stewart), 4,68
   Mary C, 4
   Robert, 1,4,68,133
   Wm, 4,68
   see also **ANDREWS**
ANDREWS, Barrett, 148
   Catharine/Catherine, 68
   Edna M, 148
   Elizabeth (Routh), 148
   Ellwood, 68
   Ethe E, 148
   Francis Willard, 148
   Hannah H C (Ledbetter), 148
   Isaac, 8
   Jemima, 68
   John, 2,4
   Joseph B, 148, 184
   Lawrence, 148
   Lydia, 8
   Mary, 68
   Mary C, 68
   Olie Bell, 148
   Oscar B, 148
   Osker, 184
   Rebecca, 8
   Robert, 2
   Ruth, 82
   Wm, 2,68
   see also **ANDREW**
ANSCOMBE, Elizabeth (Wilson), 4
   Frances M, 4
   Francis, 4
   Margaret, 4
   Margaret L, 4
   Samuel Allen, 4
ANTHONY, Alice (Stalker), 30
   Edward Clark, 68
   Jonathan, 30
   Lucinda, 6
   Sarah, 30
   Sarah P, 58

ANTRIM, Aden, 184
 Aldon, 184
 Ann/Anna, 4,68
 Benjamin, 184
 Daniel, 4,68
 Elizabeth, 4,68
 Fanny, 148
 James, 68
 James P, 4,68
 John, 148,184
 Levi, 4
 Mary Ann, 4,68
 Rachel, 148,184
 Sarah, 4,68,148
 Thomas, 148,184
 see also **ANTRUM**
ANTRUM, Sarah, 210
 Thomas Jr, 184
 see also **ANTRIM**
APPIARIUS, Anna (Kepper), 4
 Henry, 4
 Zetta A, 4
ARBEALY, Habeeb, 68
 see also **ABBEALY**
ARMENT, Sarah, 68
 Sarah B, 68
ARMFIELD, Avis Jane, 4
 Henry, 4
 Mary, 152
 Vianna, 68
 Vianna/Vienna (Irish), 4,68
ARMSTRONG, Alice, 51
 Ardella B, 4
 Inez, 51
 John, 51
 Saloma/Soloma, 4,68
ARNET, Elizabeth, 184
 see also **ARNETT**
ARNETT, Allen, 148,184
 Charlotte, 148
 Deborah, 184
 Deborah (Hollingsworth), 148,184, 197
 Delia, 4
 Elizabeth, 4,184
 Eunice, 148
 James, 184
 James H, 148,184
 Jane, 148
 Mahlon, 4
 Minerva (Swain), 184
 Phebe, 148
 Thomas, 148
 Valentine, 148
 Waldo, 148
 see also **ARNET**
ARNOLD, Maria, 172
 Mary, 69,178
 Sarah, 4,68
ARROWSMITH, Charles M, 4
 Elizabeth (Vance), 4
 Emma C (Colbert), 4
 Miller P, 4
ARY, Elizabeth, 112
 John, 112
 see also **AIRY**
ASHBAUGH, Lillian, 166
ASHINGER, Katherine, 49
ATHERTON, Charles, 68
 Deborah, 68
ATKINS, Eliza, 68
 Jonathan, 68
 Joseph, 68

ATKINS, Mary, 68
 see also **ADKINS**
ATKINSON, Ark, 4
 Caleb F, 68
 Deborah C, 68
 Delia (Arnett), 4
 Della (Murphy), 4
 Eliza Ann, 125
 Elizabeth, 68
 Elizabeth Fisher, 68
 Elizabeth P, 68
 Henry W, 68
 John, 4
 Jonathan, 68
 Mary, 68,154,181
 Rachel, 210
 Rebecca, 68
 Rebecca L, 68
 Ruth, 181
 Sarah, 68
 Sarah C, 68
 Sarah E, 68
 Thomas, 68,181
AUSTIN, Elizabeth, 29,49,80
 John, 4
 Mary Elizabeth (Feasel), 4
 Rebecca, 4
 Wm E, 4
AVERY, Elizabeth, 11
AYDELOTT, Ann (Stuart), 68
 Anna S, 69
 Beulah Ann/Anna, 68,113
 Fleming W, 68,69
 Henry C, 68
 Joseph B, 69
 Mary E, 69
 Rebecca, 68
 Sarah, 68
 Sarah S, 69
 Stewart/Stuart, 68,69
 see also **AYDELOTTE, AYDLOT, AYDLOTT**
AYDELOTTE, Henry C, 69
 see also **AYDELOTT, AYDLOT, AYDLOTT**
AYDLOT, Rebecca, 69
 see also **AYDELOTT, AYDELOTTE, AYDLOTT**
AYDLOTT, Anna/Anne, 4,69
 Jehu, 4
 Joseph Benjamin, 4
 Mary E, 4
 Sarah, 4
 Sarah S, 4
 Stewart, 4
 see also **AYDELOTT, AYDELOTTE, AYDLOT**

BACKMAN, Laura J, 69
 see also **BECKMAN**
BADEN, Susanna, 28
BAILEY, Bathsheba, 69
 Caroline, 2,4
 Catharine/Catherine, 2,4,31
 David, 1,2,4,69
 David Sr, 1
 Dorcas, 4
 Elizabeth, 69,152
 Florence E (Pickett), 4
 Henry, 69
 Jesse A, 4
 Jessie M, 4
 John, 4,31,69

BAILEY, Lydia (Comer), 69
 Malvina C (Addleman), 4
 Margarett, 50
 Mary, 69
 Michel, 159
 Milicent, 31
 Moses, 4
 Peninah/Penninah, 69
 Rachel, 97
 Rachel S, 28,97
 Riley Oscar, 4
 Ruth, 69,198
 Sarah, 69
 Sarah (Price), 4
 Stanton, 69
 Viola (Addleman), 4
 see also **BAILY, BALEY**
BAILIFF, Jesse E, 148,184
 Jones, 148,184
 Malida, 184
 Malinda A, 148
 Newton J, 184
 Newton P, 148
 Robert W, 148,184
 Vandelia, 184
BAILY, Bathsheba, 73
 Caroline, 123
 David, 69,73
 Eliza, 184
 George Dillwyn, 4
 Gulielma, 49
 H Lavinia, 4
 Henry, 69
 Jesse, 4
 John, 69,123
 Levi, 69
 Lydia, 4
 Mary (Piggott), 69
 Ruth, 69,73
 Sarah, 69
 Stanton, 69
 see also **BAILEY, BALEY**
BAIN, Rachel, 33
 Rebecca, 42
 see also **BAINE, BANE**
BAINE, John, 69
 see also **BAIN, BANE**
BAKEHORN, Sarah, 59
BAKER, Anna, 34,69
 Grace, 21
 Grace B, 4,69
 James Augustus, 4
 John, 34,69
 Joseph B, 4
 Lena, 4
 Lucretia (Blanchard), 4
 Mabel (Wall), 4
 Mary, 69
 Mary Ella, 4,69
 Rebecca, 34,69
 Timothy, 4
 Warren A, 4
BALDWIN, Addie, 184
 Addie O, 150
 Albert, 69
 Albert C, 4,5
 Almeda, 59
 Alpheus S, 148,150
 Alvin, 184
 Alvin, 185
 Alvin C, 148
 Amanda, 184
 Amanda M (Whittier), 149

BALDWIN, Amelia, 149,165,196
  Amy Bell, 148,149
  Andrew, 148,149,174,184
  Ann/Anna, 69,148,184,191,209
  Anna (Davis), 150,184
  Anna J, 168
  Anna Maria (Coffin), 149
  Arcadai, 69
  Arreny, 149
  Asenath/Asenith, 147,149,181,201
  Asenath (Hinshaw), 149
  Asenath C, 181
  Asenath C (Reynolds), 149
  Asenath Caroline, 149
  Atiria, 149
  Baily P, 69
  Baily Pine, 4,5
  Bell/Belle, 184
  Benjamin F, 128
  Benjamin L, 5
  Bertha, 149
  Betty (Mills), 69
  Calvin, 148,149,175,184
  Carl, 184
  Carl C, 149
  Carle A, 149
  Catherine, 5,69
  Chalkley, 149,184
  Charity, 149,184,185
  Charity (Hodson), 147,148,149,150,
    165
  Charity J, 184
  Charity Jane, 149
  Charity L, 198
  Charles, 69148
  Charlotte, 69,157,184
  Charlotte (Payne), 5
  Christiana, 5
  Cora, 185
  Cora Alma (Snodgrass), 149
  Cynthia, 148,150
  Cynthia E, 149,175
  Daniel, 69,147,148,149,150,165,184
  Daniel C, 69
  Daniel Jr, 5,69
  Daniel Sylvester, 149
  David, 184
  David E, 149,160,166,175,184
  David Emory, 149,184
  Dianna, 149
  Dillen, 149
  Dorcas, 69
  Earl, 149
  Eli, 69,184
  Eli D, 149
  Elias, 69,149,184
  Elisa A, 184
  Eliza, 149,184
  Eliza (Anderson) Whittier, 149
  Eliza A (Brown), 148,149
  Eliza Ellen, 149,160
  Eliza Jane, 178,195
  Elizabeth, 28,69,149,172,184,200
  Elizabeth (Pollard), 4,5
  Ellen, 48
  Ellen (Bond), 148
  Elva, 184
  Elva A, 149
  Elvaretta,184,185
  Elvaretta (Chamness), 149
  Elwood, 149,184
  Emily, 184

BALDWIN, Emily L, 149
  Emma,69,184
  Emma (Martindale), 5
  Emmaline, 149
  Emory, 185
  Enos, 69
  Enos P, 5,69
  Esther Ellen, 148
  Eunice, 184
  Eunice (Coffin), 148,174
  Eunice (Lamar), 184
  Evalena, 149
  Florence Bell (Barnes), 149
  Frank, 184
  Frank L, 149
  Fred L, 149
  G C, 184
  George, 69
  George C, 149,184
  George Elwood, 149
  George R, 149,184
  George W, 149
  H J, 48
  Hannah, 149,150,181,184,199,211
  Hannah A, 184
  Hannah A (Elliott), 148
  Harvey, 149
  Henrietta, 149
  Henry, 140,149
  Horace M, 5
  Howard J, 128
  Irene, 149
  Irving, 149
  Isaac, 149,184
  J Howard, 5
  Jabez Newton, 149
  James Alpheus, 5,69
  Jane, 148,149
  Jane (Reynolds), 149,184
  Jesse, 5,69,149,150,184,199
  Jesse F, 5,184
  Jesse Franklin, 149,184
  Joel, 69
  John, 5,69,148,149,157,184
  John Jr, 184
  John Sr, 184
  John E, 149,185
  John H, 149,185
  John Howard, 69
  Jonathan, 5,69
  Jonathan A, 5
  Judith, 149,166,167,199
  Larkin, 184
  Larkin E, 184
  Larkin Ellis, 149
  Levi, 149,184
  Levine/Luvina, 184
  Levine (Baldwin), 184
  Lewis, 148,149,184
  Lewis D, 150
  Lindley, 149
  Louisa, 69,184
  Louisa (Dennis), 148,150,184
  Luva Ethel, 149
  Lydia, 148,184,199
  Malinda/Melinda (Hinshaw),
    149,150, 176,181
  Margaret, 184
  Margaret (Beeson), 149
  Marietta, 148,157
  Marillia C (Kaucher), 4
  Martha,5,69,128

BALDWIN, Martha (Bond), 69
  Martha Ann, 148,174
  Martha J, 185
  Martha J (Williams), 149
  Martha Jane, 184
  Martha M (Davis), 148
  Mary, 69,150,184,196
  Mary (Davis), 184
  Mary (Jay), 59
  Mary Ann, 69
  Mary Ann (Albertson), 5
  Mary Ann (Thornburg), 184
  Mary E, 5,149,184
  Mary Elizabeth, 5,149,166,172
  Mary H, 149,150,176
  Mary J, 148
  Mary Jane, 198
  Mary Lizzie, 69
  Mary Malinda, 149
  Matilda, 69,140
  Mattie, 185
  Melinda, 184
  Merilla C, 69
  Milton Reed, 149
  Miriam, 184
  Myrtle, 184
  Myrtle M, 149
  Nancy Ann, 184
  Nathan, 149,150,176,184
  Nathan Ernest, 149
  Nerens/Nereus B, 5,149
  Nerius, 149
  Newton, 149,150,184
  Orpha A, 168
  Pheba/Phebe, 5,149
  Phebe A, 149
  Phebe Ann, 184
  Priscilla, 69
  Priscilla (Johnson), 69
  Quincy, 59
  Rachel, 149
  Rachel (Reynolds), 184
  Rachel M, 149
  Rachel P, 149,184
  Rebecca, 184
  Retta, 184
  Rhoda, 69
  Rhoda (Howell), 148,149
  Ruth (Howel/Howell), 149,160,166,
    175,184
  Ruth (Reynolds), 149
  Ruth C, 48
  Sandford/Sanford, 149,184
  Sarah/Sarrah, 69,149,184
  Sarah (Mills), 184
  Sarah E (Julian), 148,175
  Sena E, 5
  Seth, 149
  Solomon Thomas, 69
  Sophia, 69
  Susan, 39
  Susanna/Susannah, 69,107,140
  Susannah (Howell), 149
  Thomas, 5,69
  Thomas E, 184,185
  Thomas Elwood, 149
  Tilman, 149
  Tilman W, 149,184
  Urbane, 149
  Urbane E, 149,184
  Uriah H, 168
  Wava Lorene, 149
  Webster W, 149

BALDWIN, Wister, 184
  Wm, 69,148,149,150,184
  Wm H, 5,69,128,184,185
  Wm Henry, 149
  Zimri R, 149,184
BALES, Aaron, 150,185
  Ada J, 150,159,185
  Albert L, 150
  Alice (Manifold), 150
  Ann (Pierce), 185
  Asa, 185
  Benjamin, 150
  Benjamin F, 150
  Boater/Bowater, 69,185
  Catherine (Brown), 150
  Della F, 150
  Della Maud, 150
  Dillon, 150
  Dilwin, 185
  Elizabeth, 69
  Elizabeth (Corey), 150,159
  Elizabeth (Koons), 150
  Emma Florence (Thornburg), 150
  Esther (Russell), 164
  Florence, 185
  George W, 150
  Henry, 150
  Jacob, 150,151,185
  Jacob Jr, 185
  John, 150,166,185
  Keziah, 190,202
  Lewis, 150,185
  Lewis V, 150
  Lucinda (Pidgeon), 150,181,185
  Lucy Jane (Spradlin), 150
  Lydia, 150
  Mary, 150,151,195
  Mary (Baldwin), 150
  Mary H (Baldwin), 150
  Mary Melissa (Beeson) Chamness, 150
  Nancy, 158
  Nancy (McMullen), 166
  Nancy (Wrightsman), 150
  Nathan, 69
  Parnel/Parnell, 150
  Polly, 185
  Rachel, 150,185
  Rachel (Green), 150
  Rachel Elizabeth, 150,181
  Rebecca, 185
  Sally Ann, 150
  Samuel, 69
  Sarah, 69,150,151,166,185
  Sarah Jane, 164,185
  Seth, 150,185
  Solamon/Solomon, 150,159,181,185
  Surelda (Jackson), 150
  Wm, 69,150,164,185
  Wm Henry, 150
  Wm Jesse, 150
  see also **BEALS**
BALEY, David, 69
  see also **BAILEY, BAILY**
BALL, Wm B, 69
BALLARD, Addison, 5,69
  Catharine/Catherine, 5,69
  Cornelius H, 5
  Cornelius W, 69
  David, 5,69
  Edgar H, 5,69,70
  Eleanor, 5
  Elijah, 5

BALLARD, Elisha, 5
  Emeline/Emiline, 69
  Franklin, 69
  Franklin A, 69
  George C, 5,69
  Ida, 5
  Jeremiah, 5,69
  Jesse, 5
  Jesse F, 5,69,185
  Jesse H, 5
  Jesse W, 69
  Jesse Wilson, 185
  Juanita, 5
  Lauretta C, 69
  Lauretta/Laurette/Loretta Candace, 5, 69
  Martha, 89
  Martha (Bond), 5
  Mary, 5,69
  Mary (Jay), 70
  Mary Adelaid (Jay), 5,69
  Mary E, 5
  Mary Elizabeth, 69
  Mary L, 69
  Mary Leona, 69
  Millicent H, 69
  Millicent H (White), 5
  Nathan, 5,89
  Otho, 69
  Peninah (Nixon), 69
  Phareba/Pheraby/Pheriba, 5,69,185
  Phebe Ann, 5,69,185
  Rhoda, 69,89
  Samuel, 5,69
  Sarah, 136
  Sarah (Reeve), 5
  Sarah H, 69
  Thomas C, 185
  Uriah, 69
  Wm, 69,185
BALLENGER, Elijah, 5
  Elizabeth (Comer), 70
  Elsie Marie, 5
  Essie Irene, 5
  George, 5
  Hannah (Elliott), 148
  Harmon, 148
  James, 185
  Jesse, 185
  Joshua, 185
  Marguerite H, 5
  Martha M (Morris), 5
  Melissa (Morrow), 5
  Myrtle, 5
  Nancy (Patty), 185
  Nathan, 5
  Rebecca, 150
  see also **BALLINGER**
BALLINGER, Elijah, 70
  George, 70
  Hannah, 41
  Melissa, 70
  Myrtle, 70
  Rachel Ann, 70
  Viola (Horn), 70
  see also **BALLENGER**
BANE, John, 70
  see also **BAIN, BAINE**
BANGHAM, Nancy, 43
BANNER, Rebecca, 70
BANNON, Ann (Grave), 5
  Jacob, 5
  Rebecca, 5,70
BARBER, Anna (Hiatt), 150

BARBER, Lavina Maud, 150
  Thomas Jefferson, 150
BAREKOTT, Nancy, 154
BARGER, Anna Margaretta, 5
  Elizabeth, 70
  Margaret H (Richie), 5
  Margaret W (Richie), 70
  Martin J, 5,70
  Wm J, 70
BARKER, Abel, 2,5
  Eliza (White), 70
  Elizabeth, 40,70,104
  Elizabeth B, 5,34
  Enoch, 5,70
  Hannah, 5,70
  Hannah (Davis), 5
  Isaac/Isaace, 1,2,70
  Jacob, 2,5,70
  Jeremiah, 5
  Margery, 5
  Mary, 5,21,70
  Mary (Cox), 5,70
  Mary Amy, 101
  Mary Ellen, 5,56
  Matthew, 5,34,70,101
  Nicholas, 570
  Phebe, 5,205
  Ruth, 5,34,70,101,104
  Sophia, 70
  Thomas, 2,5,70
BARLOW, Anna, 77
BARNARD, Anna, 70,150,185
  Betsy/Elizabeth, 70,150, 204
  Catharine, 39
  Edith, 150,185
  Eli B, 150
  Elizabeth (Macy), 150,157
  Francis, 39
  George, 70,150,185
  Hannah, 70,150
  Huldah (Canaday), 150,185
  Irena M, 150
  Jethro, 150
  John, 70,150,185
  Joseph, 150
  Love, 70,150,157
  Martha, 70
  Martha (Wright), 5
  Mary/Polly, 70,150,185,204
  Matilda (Gardner), 5
  Obed, 185
  Paul, 5,70
  Rebecca/Rebekah, 39,56
  Rena, 185
  Sophia, 150,185
  Sophia (Thornburg) Williams, 185
  Susan W, 5
  Susannah, 70
  Timothy, 150
  Uriah, 70,157,204
  Uriah H, 150
  Wm, 5,70,150,185
  see also **BERNARD, BURNARD**
BARNES, Anna, 156
  Carlista, 176
  Cora, 5,70
  Didema, 149
  Elizabeth, 5,70,128
  Elizabeth W, 70128
  Ethel May, 5, 70
  Eunice (Allen), 185
  Florence Bell, 149
  Harold S, 70
  Hylie W, 17

219

BARNES, Jennie, 5,70
    John, 70,128
    John C, 149
    John F, 70
    Julia, 70
    Julia A, 70
    Martha, 70
    Martha B, 70
    see also **BARNS**
BARNET, Daisy, 62
    Elizabeth (Kelley), 5
    James M, 5
    Leola, 5
    see also **BARNETT**
BARNETT, Huldah, 185
    Lucy L, 5
    Preston, 5
    see also **BARNET**
BARNS, Elmer T, 70
    Harold S, 70
    John T, 70
    Julia A, 70
    see also **BARNES**
BARR, Mary, 176,181
BARRETT, Claribel, 25,93
    Don Carlos, 5,70
    Ellen M, 10
    Isaac M, 70
    Marcia Frances (Moor), 5
    Marcia Frances (Moore), 70
    Mary E, 70
    Nancy (Lawrence)
    Samuel, 10
BARTON, Alice C, 70
    Alice L, 5
    Edward, 5
    Elizabeth, 5
    Harvey L, 5
    Sarah E, 51
    Wm, 70
BATCHELOR, John L, 5
    Mary E, 5
    Russel H, 5
BATES, Charity, 70
    Fleming, 12
    Sarah J, 12
    Unity, 12
BAUGHMAN, Nancy, 14
    see also **BOWMAN**
BAUMGARDNER, Sarah D (Hill), 5
    see also **BOMGARNER**
BAXTER, Emily Jane, 5
    John, 70
    John Howard, 5
    Lucy Vincent, 5,14
    Maria, 70
    Maria B, 5
    Mary, 70,88
    Mary (Barker), 21,70
    Mary Ellen, 5,56,70
    Mary Ellen (Barker), 5,56
    Sarah, 88
    Sarah M, 5,21
    Sarah Moffit, 70
    Wm, 5,21,56,70,88
    Wm Herbert, 5
BAYERS, Lucinda, 8
BEABOUT, Elizabeth, 168
BEACH, Pearl C (Owen), 70
BEAL, Henrietta, 70
    Henrietta P, 70
    see also **BEALL, BEALS**

BEALL, Andrew J, 185
    Carrie Dell, 185
    Charles B, 185
    John, 185
    Thomas, 185
    see also **BEAL**
BEALS, Boater, 185
    Charity, 185
    Delphina (Mendenhall), 6
    Eliza May, 6
    Hannah, 150
    Henry, 185
    Henry Wilson, 185
    Jacob, 185
    Jesse F, 6
    Joel, 185
    John, 185
    Jonathan, 185
    Lewis, 185
    Nathan, 185
    Oliver Cromwell, 6
    Parnel, 185
    Seth, 185
    see also **BALES, BEAL, BEALL**
BEAMAN, Cornelius, 70
BEAN, Elizabeth, 43
BEAR, Amos, 6
    John H, 6
    Lucinda, 8
    Mary, 6
    Sarah A, 8
BEARD, Abraham, 70
    Alice, 70
    Amos, 70
    Benjamin F, 70
    Benjamin Franklin, 70
    Byram/Byron, 150/185
    Charles Sumner, 150
    David, 55,70
    David W, 70
    Dolly, 70
    Elizabeth, 70
    Frank, 185
    Frank E, 150
    Hannah, 70
    Hannah Jane, 70
    Henry C, 150,161
    Henry F, 185
    Henry Fred, 150
    Jane, 55,70
    Jane S, 135
    John, 70
    John G Whittier, 150
    Jonathan Seward, 150
    Laura (Williams), 185
    Laura A (Ward), 150
    Lavina Jane, 70
    Lenora C, 150,161,185
    Levina Jane, 70
    Lucinda, 185
    Lucinda (Macy), 150,161,185
    Martha, 70
    Mary, 70
    Minnie (Cooper), 150
    Miriam, 55,70
    Patrick, 70
    Paul Sr, 70
    Rachel, 70
    Rebecca, 70
    Rufus, 185
    Sarah (Test) Kirk, 70
    Sarah K, 70

BEARD, Susannah (Pickett), 70
    Wm, 70
    Wm D, 150
BEASON, Isabel, 211
    Jesse, 185
    see also **BEESON**
BEAUCHAMP, Alice, 70
    Caleb, 70
    Elizabeth, 70
    Ellick, 70
    Jesse, 70
    Levi, 70
    Mathias, 70
    Matthew, 70
    Mileah, 70
    Russ, 70
    Sarah (Jessop), 70
    Wm, 70
    Wm Sr, 70
BECKERDITE, Boice, 160
    Isabel, 160
    Louisa, 156,160
BECKMAN, Barbara Ann, 6
    John A, 6
    Laura Jennie (Perkins), 6
    see also **BACKMAN**
BECKTOL, Nancy M (Mills), 185
    see also **BEKTEL**
BECKUM, Anna (Holaday), 185
BEEDE, Alberta F, 6
    John Joseph, 6
    Willis 6
BEELER, Elsie Marie, 6
    Emma (Hurst), 6
    Peter S, 6
BEERS, James, 6
    Lavina (Stephens), 6
    Ralph, 6
    Waneeta, 6
BEESON, Absalom/Ansolam, 71
    Alice, 151,172,186,203
    Allen, 151,185,186
    Alma A, 186
    Alma Alton, 151
    Amaziah/Amizia, 151,185,186,198
    Anna (Lee), 185
    Anna (Mills), 186
    Benjamin, 149,150,151,185,186,202
    Benjamin B, 150,151,178,185,186
    Benjamin F, 150,186
    Betsy, 71
    Betsy (Mills), 185
    Caroline, 186
    Celia, 186
    Charity, 151
    Charles, 150,186
    Clarence C, 151, 186
    Cynthia (Baldwin), 150
    Cynthia Ellen, 151,208
    David, 151,186
    David W, 151
    Deborah (Strode), 151
    Edward, 152
    Elihu E, 185
    Elihue, 151
    Elizabeth, 151,156,161,186,190
    Elizabeth (Moon), 151
    Ellen, 186
    Elma Nora, 157
    Elmer E, 151,186
    Elwood, 185
    Emily, 186

BEESON, Eunice H, 151
   Fanny (Dennis), 150,151,155
   Flora, 186
   Flora H, 151,186
   Florin M, 151,186
   Frederick, 186
   Frederick Leton, 150,151
   George, 186
   George G, 151
   Grace B, 151
   Hannah, 51,158,172,181,195,186, 203,208
   Hannah (Canaday), 186
   Hannah Jr, 186
   Harley, 186
   Harley A, 151
   Harvey, 151
   Harvey F, 151,186
   Herbert Edward, 151
   Hezekiah, 151,186
   Ida Esther, 151
   Igal/Igle, 151,185,186
   Isaac, 150,151,158,172,181,185,186, 203,208
   Isaac Francis, 150,151
   Isaac K, 151,156,167,172,176
   Isaac N, 186
   Isaac Newton, 185,186
   Isaac W, 150,151,186
   Isabel/Isabela/Isabella, 154,155,174, 185,186,198
   Isabel (Pearson), 150
   Isaiah, 150,151,155
   Ithamar/Ithamer, 150,151,185,186
   James Lauren, 151
   Jesse, 151,185,186
   Jesse F, 186
   Jesse Franklin, 151
   Jesse W, 185
   Job, 186
   John, 71,150
   John Rufus, 151
   John W, 151,186
   Jonathan, 151,186
   Josephine, 151,186
   Josiah, 151,186
   Julia, 186
   Julia A (Murray), 151
   Julia Ann, 186
   Julia Esther, 151
   Julia Esther (Beeson), 151
   Keziah, 151,152,186
   Laura M (Davis), 151
   Laurence C, 151
   Laurence Clay, 186
   Lavina, 150
   Leora Ursula, 151
   Lewis, 186
   Lewis R, 186
   Lewis Riley, 151
   Linnie D, 151,186
   Louisa, 151,158,167,168,172,186
   Louisa (Niccum), 151
   Lucinda, 151,152,186
   Luzena, 150,207
   Lydia, 71,151,186
   Lydia (Willis), 186
   Lydia Margaret, 151
   Mahlon, 71,150,186
   Malinda, 186
   Manley, 151
   Mareb, 151,186,208

BEESON, Margaret/Margreat, 149, 150, 151, 185, 202, 209
   Margaret (Hocket), 150,151
   Margret Ann, 151
   Marguerite, 151
   Maria/Mariah, 151,186
   Maria (Beeson), 151
   Maria Louisa, 151
   Marila/Marilla, 151,186,192
   Marsh, 186
   Martha (Murray), 151
   Martha E, 186
   Mary, 151,157,186
   Mary (Bales), 151
   Mary (Branson), 150,151
   Mary Hannah, 151,176,186
   Mary L, 151
   Mary Lenora, 150,178
   Mary Malissa/Melissa, 150,151,155, 189
   Mary S, 212
   Massa/Massey, 151,167,186,199
   Melinda, 152
   Mildred, 151,155,203
   Mildred B, 172
   Miriam, 186
   Nancy, 71,104,198
   Nancy E, 151,210
   Naomi/Naomy, 151,207
   Narcissa, 151
   Newton, 151
   Olinda (Lamb), 150,151,178
   Oliver, 186
   Oliver H, 151
   Polly, 186
   Polly (Bales), 185
   Rachel, 150,151,186,201
   Rachel (Bales), 150,185
   Rachel M, 202
   Rachel Malvina, 151
   Rebecca, 151,186,190
   Rebecca (Lamb), 151,156,167,172, 176
   Ruth, 202
   Salley/Sally, 71,151,186
   Samuel, 151,186
   Samuel W, 151
   Sarah/Sarrah, 151,156,186
   Sarah Catherine, 186
   Sarah Catherine (Huffman), 151
   Selah, 151
   Seth, 186
   Silas, 185
   Silas H, 151, 186
   Tacy, 71
   Thomas, 151,186
   Thomas C, 186
   Thomas E, 151,186
   Thomas Ellwood/Elwood, 151,186,
   Thomas Emry, 151
   Ursula, 151
   Virgil, 151,186
   Wade, 151,186
   Walter A, 151,186
   Wm, 150,151,185,186
   Wm F, 151,186
   Wm Henry, 151
   Wm M, 186
   Wm N, 157,186
   Zenas/Zenos, 185,186
   Zenoah, 151,186
   Zerua/Zeruah, 151,181
   see also **BEASON, BEESONS**

BEESONS, Asenath (Adams), 186
   see also **BEESON**
BEETLE, Beulah, 43
BEKTEL, Annis (Mills), 186
   see also **BECKTOL**
BELL, Abigail, 71
   Abigail (Charles), 71
   Charles, 186
   Edmund Herbert, 6
   Eliza, 166
   Eliza E, 186
   Eliza E (Elliott), 6
   Eliza Ellen, 166
   Elizabeth C (Dilks), 6,71
   Eunice Estell (Moffitt), 6
   Hannah, 6
   Hannah C, 71
   Harriet A, 6,71
   Ida M, 71
   Ida May (Henley), 6
   Isabella, 71
   Isabella Wakefield, 71
   Jesse, 71
   John, 6,71,166
   Josiah, 71
   Julius, 6
   Lancelot, 71
   Lydia, 71
   Margaret, 17,71
   Mary, 71
   Miriam, 71,119
   Nancy Ann, 60
   Rebecca, 71
   Ruth, 6
   Sarah, 71,119
   Thomas, 71
   Wilhelmina/Wilhelminia, 6,71
   Wm, 6,71
   Wm A, 71
   Wm Aubrey, 6
   Wm E, 71
   Wm Edmund, 6,71
   Wm O, 6
BELLIS, E Reed, 71
   Edward, 6,71
   Ellen C, 71
   Emma A (Brooks), 6
   Esabella L, 6
   Joseph H, 6
   Mary, 71
   Mary (Kenworthy), 71
   Mary (Ward), 6
   Mary E, 71
   Mary H, 6
   Mary K, 31,71
   Mary Ruth, 6
   Mary Winifred, 6,31
   Mary Wynne, 71
   Samuel, 6,31,71
   Wm H, 6
   Wm K, 71
BELSHAM, Alden P, 6,71
   Arthur, 6,71
   Bertha M, 6,71
   Charity C, 6,71
   Essie, 6,71
   Essie (Burgess), 71
   Mary, 71
BENBA, Cora Evaline, 186
   Francis Asbury, 186
   Mary Ellen, 186
   Wm, 186
   see also **BENBO, BENBOW**

BENBO, Mary Ann, 187
   see also **BENBA**, **BENBOW**
BENBOW, Aaron, 71
   Ann, 71
   Anna Eliza, 152
   Benjamin, 71,187
   Charity, 71
   Clara, 71
   Clara J, 71
   Clara J (Burns), 6
   Cora Evaline, 152,187
   David A, 6,71
   Edward, 71
   Elizabeth, 71
   Evan, 71
   Flavia, 6
   Flavia S, 187
   Flavia S (Dennis), 187
   Francis Asbury, 152,187
   Isaac H, 6
   Isaac W, 71
   John, 71
   Mariam, 71
   Mary, 6,71,138
   Mary Ann, 187
   Mary Ann (Wilcox), 152
   Mary Ellen, 152,187
   Moses, 71
   Orville E, 6,71
   Powel, 71,152
   Rachel, 152,187
   Sarah Olive, 152
   Thomas L, 6,71
   Walter T, 6,71
   Wm, 187
   Wm H, 152
   Wm L, 6,187
   see also **BENBA**, **BENBO**
BENEDICT, Carrie, 174
   Rachel J (Johnson), 6
BENFORD, Asa, 71
   Benajah, 71
   Benjamin, 71
   David, 71
   Elijah, 71
   Elisha, 71
   James Ladd, 71
   John, 71
   Joseph, 71
   Micajah, 71
   Micajah Crews, 71
   Nathan, 71
   Robert, 71
   Wm, 71
   Wm Ladd, 71
   see also **BINFORD**
BENHAM, Alice, 71
   Anna, 71
   Anna M, 71
   Fern, 6
   Frances, 6
   Hazel, 6
   Robert Bruce, 71
   Robert Bruce Jr, 71
   Walter Pharo, 71
   Wm, 6
BENNET, Emily, 71
   Louisa, 71
   see also **BENNETT**
BENNETT, Cora M, 64
   Elizabeth, 187
   Emilia, 71
   Isaac, 64,71

BENNETT, James, 152
   Linda, 64
   Louisa, 71
   M B, 34
   Maria, 71
   Sarah E, 152
   see also **BENNET**
BENSON, Amy, 6,71
   Amy J, 71
   Cassie, 6,34
   Catharine, 6
   Daisy, 6,34
   Elizabeth A, 6,71
   Emmerson, 152
   Ephraim/Ephram B, 6,71
   Grace/Gracie E, 6,71
   Henry, 6,34
   James H, 6,71
   Jennie Mabel, 6
   John G, 71
   Josiah, 6
   Lizzie, 71
   Martha (Kern), 6
   Robert, 6
   Ruth (Osborn), 6
   Wm, 6
   Zelma (Harris), 152
BENTLEGE, Ethel A (Hough), 6
BENTLEY, Charles, 71
   John, 6,71
   Susannah, 71
   Wm, 71
   see also **BENTLY**
BENTLY, Sarah (Hill), 71
   see also **BENTLEY**
BENTON, Ellen D (Harris), 6
   Mildred, 6
   Robert A, 6
BEPLEY, Charles, 152
   Pearl B (Chamness), 152
BERGDOLL, Nancy, 165
BERKHART, Lena, 166
BERNARD, Edith (Graves), 71
   see also **BARNARD**, **BURNARD**
BERRIMAN, Hannah, 49
BERRY, David, 71
   Elizabeth, 71
   Eunice, 71
   Hannah, 71
   Samuel, 71
   Susanna, 71
   Thomas, 71
BETTLES, Joseph Barnes, 71
   Susannah Grounds, 71
   Wm, 71
BETTS, Aaron Homer, 6
   Caroline J (Janney), 6
   Christopher, 6
   Elizabeth R, 6
   Homer Madison, 6
   Lydia (Huff), 6
   Margaret H (Whitacre), 6
BEVAN, Albert R, 6,71
   Alice A, 6
   Alice A (Mendenhall), 71
   Stacey, 6
BICKLE, Anna (Leeds), 71
BIGGS, Mary, 180
   Nancy, 180
   Willis, 180
BILDERBACK, Ellen, 6
   Hattie, 6
   Wm, 6

BILLHEIMER, Alice, 37,167
   Jesse, 187
   Lydia, 187
   Lydia (Dennis), 152
   Margaret, 167
   Solomon, 167
   Sylvester, 152
BILLS, Helen, 135
   J O, 208
BINFORD, —— (Whitacre), 42
   Abigail (Marshall), 6
   Angeline, 71
   Ann, 71
   Edward, 6,71
   Edward S, 6
   Elizabeth, 55
   Elizabeth A, 42,43
   Elizabeth Ann, 97
   Elizabeth C (Schneider), 6
   Elizabeth Julia (Schneider), 72
   Eve (Henley), 6
   Eve H, 72
   Gurney, 6,71
   Hannah, 71
   James, 71
   Jane, 71
   Joshua, 71
   Josiah, 72
   Judith, 71
   Levi, 6,72
   Lydia, 71
   Mahel, 71
   Margaret F, 72
   Marshall D, 72
   Mary (Foulk), 23
   Micajah C, 6
   Micajah M, 6,71,72
   Miriam, 71
   Oliver, 23
   Peter, 42,71
   Polly, 71
   Rebecca, 7
   Rebecca Anna, 71
   Ruth, 72
   Sarah, 71
   Susanna/Susannah, 71
   Susanna/Susannah R, 6
   Susannah (Bundy), 6
   Susannah R (Binford), 6
   Zelinda Annis, 23
   see also **BENFORD**
BINNS, Amos, 7,72
   Anna Laura, 7,72
   Charles, 7,72
   Franklin, 7,72
   Gulielma, 76
   Gulielma (Hill), 72
   Gulielma H, 7,10,72
   Horace Mann, 7,72
   John Bertrand, 7,72
   John Bertrand, 72
   Josephine, 7
   Lilia/Lilla/Lillie Aurelia/Aurilla, 7,72
   Mary Emma, 7,10,76
   Rebecca, 7,72
   Richard, 7,10,72,76
   Ruth, 72
   Willie A, 7,72
   Wm, 72
BIRD, Bessie B, 152
   Ellen (Pidgeon), 152
   Estella, 152
   Estella O, 152

BIRD, Jerome T, 152
    Laura (Finch), 152
    Wesley, 152
BIRDSALL, Alvin, 72
    Alvin T, 72
    Anna E (Timberlake), 7,34
    Charles H, 7
    Charles M, 34
    Grace G, 7
    Mary D, 7,34
BISHOP, Charles, 72
    Dayton, 72
    George, 72
    Mary, 72
    Milton, 72
BITNER, Ida B, 72
    see also **BITTNER**
BITTNER, Abraham, 7,72
    Charles, 7,72
    Ida, 72
    Ida R, 7,72
    see also **BITNER**
BLACK, Allen, 72
    Clarissa, 72
    John, 72
    Mary, 161
    Matilda, 83
BLAIR, LaBelle, 50
BLANCHARD, Lucretia, 4
BLAUSETT, Anna, 7
    Ethel, 7
    Isaac, 7
BLIZZARD, Caroline, 72
    Elizabeth, 72,121
    Parnel, 121
BLOUNT, Fanny, 159
BLUE, Amanda M, 7
    Hannah P (Moore), 72
    Melvina, 72
    Nathan, 7,38
    Phebe, 7,38
    Sarah, 7,38
BOBO, Laura, 175
BODE, Willard H, 7
BOGUE, Aaron, 72
    Ada L, 7,72
    Clinton H, 7
    Clinton W, 72
    Elvira, 72
    Elvy (Elliott), 72
    Emily J, 72
    Emma, 45,72
    Hannah, 72
    Hannah (East) Bonine, 72
    Jesse, 7,72
    Joseph, 7,48,51,72,187
    Joseph A, 187
    Josephine, 45,72
    Leora, 7
    Lucinda, 7,48
    Mary, 7,48,72
    Mary M, 7
    Miriam, 72,174
    Nathan, 72
    Russell S, 7,72
    Sarah Cassie, 7,51
    Stephen, 72
BOLENDER, Daniel, 60
    Laura M, 60
    Sabina (Shuman), 60

BOMAN, Edward F, 72
    Milton H, 72
    Wm, 72
    see also **BAUGHMAN, BOWMAN**
BOMGARNER, Anna, 72
    see also **BAUMGARDNER**
BONAWELL, Curtis, 152
    George, 152
    Nancy (Philips), 152
BOND, Aaron, 7
    Abijah, 72
    Achsah, 7
    Alvin P, 152
    Amelia, 152,157,190
    Amos, 72
    Ann/Anna/Anne, 7,10,72,152,187
    Ann (Hawkins), 7
    Ann Elizabeth (Icombrock), 7, 48
    Anna (Cook), 7
    Anna J, 73
    Anna Jane, 187
    Anna Jane (Marshall), 7,187
    Anna M, 7
    Anna M (Jeffries), 7
    Artalissa, 28
    Asenath/Asenith, 152,183
    Benjamin, 7,69,72,106
    Betsy, 72
    Charles F, 72
    Charles Frances/Francis, 7,72
    Charles T H, 7
    Charles Wm, 7
    Charlotte, 7,72,137
    Charlotte (Hoff), 7
    Clara Etta, 7
    Cora E, 72
    Cora E (Thomas), 8
    Cornelius, 7,38,48
    Cyrus, 72
    Daniel, 72
    Darius, 7
    Deborah, 72
    Dewitt C, 7
    Dinah, 7
    E, ix
    Eather, 72
    Edgar, 73
    Edna J, 7,72
    Edward, 7,10,72
    Edward Jr, 72
    Elias A, 72
    Eliza Jane, 173
    Elizabeth, 72,152,183,187,190,194, 197,201
    Elizabeth (Wiles), 152,157,162,165
    Elizabeth Ann, 38
    Ellen, 148
    Elma, 7,48
    Elmina, 72,152
    Elmina (Stanley), 72
    Emaline, 171
    Emma, 72
    Enos, 152
    Erastus C, 7,72
    Erastus Constantine, 72
    Eunice, 72
    Florence B (Cowgill), 7
    Frances Belinda, 152,165
    Frances M, 197
    Frances Melinda, 197
    Franklin H, 7,37
    Fred E, 7

BOND, Frederica/Frederika Jane, 7,72
    Gulielma, 152,201
    Hannah, 7,72,187
    Hannah H, 7
    Hirschel R, 7
    Ira, 7
    Isaac, 7
    Isaiah R, 72
    J Edgar, 7
    J Elmer, 7
    Jane, 171
    Jedidah, 72
    Jehiel, 7,73,187
    Jenette/Jennette, 7,38
    Jennie F, 7,73
    Jesse, 1,2,7,72,152,171,187
    Jessie Sr, 7
    Joel E, 152
    John, 2,7,72,152,162,187
    John A, 152
    Jonathan, 72
    Jonathan W, 72
    Joseph, 7,72,152,187
    Joshua, 72
    Josiah R, 7
    Julia A, 72
    Kezia, 72
    Laura, 72
    Laura A, 7
    Lavina, 152
    Levi, 7,152,187
    Levina, 7,72
    Lindley, 7,8,72
    Louisa G, 7
    Lucinda (Adams), 152,162
    Lucy L, 7
    Lurana (Jolly), 7
    Lydia, 7,69,72,73,75,106,137,187
    Lydia (Williams), 7
    Marianna, 7
    Marianna J, 29
    Martha, 5,69,72
    Martha (Fulghum), 7,29,38,109,133
    Martha (Little) 7,57,59
    Martha E, 31
    Mary, 7,72,137,152,162
    Mary (Emmons), 7,37
    Mary (Vere), 72
    Mary A, 7
    Mary Ann, 152,162,163,194
    Mary H, 72
    Mary Hortense (Murray), 7
    Mary T, 7
    Matilda, 152
    Millicent, 187
    Millicent (Mendenhall), 187
    Miriam J, 72
    Miriam Josephine, 7
    Mordecai/Mordicai, 72,152,187
    Nancy, 187
    Naomi, 152
    Nathan, 2
    Nellie R, 7,37
    Olive L, 7
    Ornan, 2
    Peter, 7,29,38,59,72,109,133
    Phebe, 2,72,187
    Phebe Ann, 72
    Pleasant, 72
    Pleasant Alma, 7
    Rachel, 72,152,187
    Rachel (Marshall), 187

BOND, Rachel (Thornburg), 187
    Rachel A, 72
    Rebecca Caddie, 7
    Robert, 2,7,187
    Ruth, 72
    Sally, 72
    Sarah, 7,72,75
    Sarah (Cook), 72
    Sarah (Jay), 8
    Sarah (Jessop), 7
    Sarah (Mendenhall), 7
    Sarah A, 72
    Sarah A (Jay), 7
    Sarah E, 152
    Sarah E (Little), 57
    Sarah M, 7,59,89
    Semira, 152
    Silas, 7,72
    Susan, 72
    Susanna, 72
    Thomas, 7,72
    Thomas F, 72
    Wm, 1,7,72,37,152,157,162,165,183, 187,190,194,197,201
    Wm A, 7
    Wm A H, 72
    Wm Albert H, 7,8
BONIGH, David, 73
    Isaac, 73
    Wm, 73
BONINE, Ann, 73,132
    Betsey/Betsy, 8,73
    Clark, 8,73
    Daniel, 8,73,132
    David, 8,73
    Emily, 8
    Evan/Evans, 8,73
    Hannah, 8,73
    Hannah (Bonine) East, 73
    Hannah (East), 72
    Isaac, 8,73,102
    J D, 152
    Jacob, 8,73
    James, 8,72,73
    James E, 8,73
    John, 8,73
    John Talbert, 8
    Jonathan B, 8,73
    Joshua, 8,73
    Lot, 8,73
    Lydia, 8,73
    Malinda/Melinda, 8,73
    Martha, 8
    Mary, 8,173,132
    Mary Ann/Maryann, 73
    Patsy, 73
    Pheba/Phebe, 73,140
    Prudence, 8,73
    Rachel, 8,73,85
    Samuel, 8,73
    Sarah, 8,73,102
    Sarah (Talbot), 8
    Sarah S (Osborn), 152
    Susanna, 8,102
    Thomas, 8,73
    Wm, 8,73
BONNELL, Edith, 45
BOOKOUT, Ellen (Lee), 152,158,162
    Grace, 152
    James, 152,158,162
    James Rufus, 152
    Julia A (Bussear), 152

BOOKOUT, Louis E, 152
    Orpha, 152,162
    Rosettie, 152,158
BOOKWALTER, Erva, 3
BOOMERSHINE, Allen, 8
    Blanche, 8
    Ruth, 8
BOON, Mary Ann, 187
    Sampson, 73
    see also **BOONE**
BOONE, Anna, 73
    Anna (Kersey), 4
    Driver, 4,8
    Elizabeth (Cooper), 8
    Frank Driver, 8
    John, 152
    Jonathan C, 8,73
    Mary Ann (Dennis), 8,152
    Myron, 73
    Myron Lyndsey, 8
    Orville E, 8
    Rachel, 3,4,41
    see also **BOON**
BORROUGHS, James M, 17
    Minnie B, 17
    Sarah Ann, 17
    see also **BUROUGHS, BURROUGHS, BURROWS**
BORTON, Ann (Moore), 73
BOSWELL, Anna/Anne, 8,73,123
    Barnabas, 73
    Bethual, 73
    Celia, 73
    Dan, 73
    Daniel K, 8,73
    Delilah/Dililah, 73,138
    Dempsy/Demsy, 73
    Elizabeth, 8,73
    Essenith, 73
    Ezra, 8,73
    Hiram, 73
    Isaac, 73
    Jane, 73,138
    Jesse, 73
    John, 73
    John K, 8,73
    Joseph, 73
    Lurainca, 73
    Mary, 8,73,83
    Miriam, 73
    Pharaba, 73
    Phebe, 73
    Rachel, 73
    Rebecca, 8,73,139
    Ruth, 73
    Samuel, 73
    Sarah, 8,73,128
    Selah, 73
    Wm, 73
    see also **BOZWELL**
BOSWORTH, Eliza Ann, 73
BOTKIN, Abbie B, 178
    Emily C, 155
    Martha A, 155
    Wm, 178
    Wm M, 155
BOURADAILE, E M, 8
    Eva L, 8
    Irene (Stout), 8
BOWER, Sarah Ann, 37
    see also **BOWERS**

BOWERMAN, Alma, 46
BOWERS, Anna, 179
    Annie (Hoover), 59
    Daniel, 59
    David, 179
    George, 8
    Jacob, 8
    Mary (Crest), 8
    Sarah A (Bear), 8
    Susan, 16,59,179
    see also **BOWER**
BOWLES, Anna M, 152
    Bathsheba (Baily), 73
    David, 1,2,73
    David Jr, 2
    David Sr, 73
    Elizabeth (Bailey), 152
    Ephraim/Ephriam, 73
    Ephraim Overman, 2
    George, 73
    George Fox, 2,152
    Josiah, 3
    Miles, 73
    Rebecca, 161
    Ruth, 73
    Wm, 73
    see also **BOWLS**
BOWLS, Ruth, 73
    Ruth (Hoggatt), 73
    see also **BOWLES**
BOWMAN, Alma, 73
    Anna/Anne, 8,73
    Anna (Bowman), 8
    Anna May, 152
    Calvin, 73
    Calvin W, 73
    Daniel, 152
    Edmon/Edmund, 73
    Edmond/Edmund F, 8,73
    Eliza, 73
    Elizabeth, 8
    Elizabeth (Hoover), 152
    Elvira, 8,73
    Emaline, 8,73
    George, 73
    H S, 8
    Laura (Wright), 8
    Lewis S, 8
    Lucile, 8
    Margaret, 151
    Martha, 73
    Martha Ann, 8,73
    Mary, 73
    Mary A (Kepler), 8
    Milton, 73
    Milton H, 8,73
    Olive, 8
    Phebe, 73
    Sally, 73
    Sally Jane, 8,73
    Sarah, 73
    Sarah (Hubbard), 8
    Wm, 8,73
    Wm Jr, 8
BOWSMAN, Alonzo, 8
    Augusta (Casner), 8
    Clarissa, 8
    Lucy, 8
BOYD, A Orville, 8
    Bessie, 73
    Celia, 8
    Elizabeth, 73

BOYD, Emma, 73
    John, 8
    Lora A (Little), 8
    Martha, 73
    Olive M, 8
    Ruth B, 8
BOZWELL, Asenath, 73
    Elizabeth, 73
    Rachel, 73
    Rebecca, 73
    Ruth, 73
    see also **BOSWELL**
BRACKEN, Edward Reed, 71
    Elizabeth (Conkle), 36
    Isabella Louise, 36
    Reed, 36
BRACKMAN, John, 73
BRADBERY, Lydia (Murphey), 73
BRADFORD, Benjamin S, 8
    Isabell (Haynes), 8
    Joseph, 73
    Mary, 73
    Ruth Isabell, 8
BRADWAY, Abigail, 73,95,120
    Angelena (Cartwright), 8
    Effie, 8
    Elisabeth/Elizabeth, 73,95
    Ella, 73,74
    H L, 8
    John, 73,95,120
    Sarah, 73
    Thomas, 73
    Wm, 73
BRADY, Mary, 74
    Mary (Wright), 74
BRAHELL, Gertrude, 45
BRAINARD, Elizabeth, 74
BRAISINGTON, Lydia, 74
    see also **BRAISINGTON, BRAZINGTON**
BRANIZER, Susannah, 74
    Walter Ezra, 74
    Wm B, 74
    see also **BRENIZER**
BRANNON, Elizabeth, 8,74
BRANSEN, Rachel, 187
    see also **BRANSON**
BRANSON, Catharine (Miller), 154
    Elizabeth, 8
    Flora A, 154
    Isaac, 187
    Isaiah/Isiah, 74
    Jacob, 74
    Jane (Anderson), 74
    Jemima, 58,156
    Joseph B, 154
    Martha, 74
    Mary, 150,151
    Mary (Thompson), 8
    Phebe, 74
    Phebe A, 28,42,65
    Phebe Ellen, 97
    Rachel, 187
    Rebecca, 122
    Rebecca G, 74
    Sarah, 74
    Sarah G, 74
    Thomas, 8
    Wellington, 8
BRASINGTON, James, 74
    Joseph, 74
    Samuel, 74

BRASINGTON, Wm, 74
    see also **BRAISINGTON, BRAZINGTON**
BRASKE, Charlotte, 54
BRATTAIN, Anna, 74
    Hannah, 74
    Hannah (Maudlin), 8,74
    John, 8,74
    Jonathan, 74
    Mary, 74
    Rachel, 8,74
    Robert, 8,74
BRAXTON, Hannah, 74
    Hiram, 74
    Jonathan, 74
    Margery, 74
    Thomas, 74
    Wm, 74
BRAZILTON, Sarah, 74
BRAZINGTON, Hannah Ann, 8,74
    Isaac, 8
    Joseph, 74
    Joseph S, 8
    Lydia, 74
    Lydia (Andrews), 8
    Samuel, 8,74
    Susanna, 8
    Wm, 74
    Wm A, 8,74
    see also **BRAISINGTON, BRASINGTON**
BREESE, Alonzo, 8
    George A, 8
    Mary, 8
BRENIZER, Anna Susan, 74
    Bessie, 74
    Bessie Lincoln, 74
    David, 74
    Ida, 74
    Ida Mayhill, 74
    Susanna/Susannah, 8,74
    Walter Ezta, 74
    Wm Barr, 74
    see also **BRENIZER**
BREWER, Alta A, 187
    Clarence A, 187
    Della E, 187
    Elias, 74
    Eliza, 187
    Elizabeth, 74,89
    Eva N, 187
    Jason W, 74
    Jennie F, 187
    John, 8,74
    John Wilson, 8
    Mary, 74
    Mary C (Woody), 187
    Morris W, 74,187
    Nettie C, 187
    Otas J, 187
    Rebecca, 8
    Sarah, 8,74,82
    Susannah, 8
    Wm H, 74
BRICE, Mary (Way), 74
BRIGGS, Anna/Annie B, 8,74
    Lucy, 74
    Lucy J, 8,74
    Mary K, 8
    Mary R, 74
    Otis, 74
    Otis W, 74
    Otis Willis, 8

BRIGHT, Abigail (Small), 74
    Abigial, 74
BRIGHTWELL, Rhoda, 74
    Rhoda (Wright), 74
BRINER, Elizabeth, 74
BRITTAIN, Jonathan, 74
    Robert, 74
    Solomon, 74
BROCK, Anna, 102
    Anna M, 74
    Elijah, 74
    Mary (Way), 74
BROCKMAN, John, 74
BROGAMEN, Mary, 74
    Electa, 74
BROOKS, Anna, 9
    Arthur, 9
    Clara M, 9
    David, 9
    Elizabeth, 17
    Emma A, 6
    Hannah, 74
    Jesse, 17
    Jesse H, 9
    Lydia (Mendenhall), 9
    Margaret, 74
    Margaret J, 74
    Mary, 17
    Mary (Haisley), 9
    Mary E, 29
    Rachel, 187
    Sarah Ellen Lydia, 9
    Wm, 9
BROOMFIELD, A D, 9
    Alice, 9
    Ethel, 9
BROWER, Abraham, 65
    Anna B, 65
    Everett V, 9
    Horace, 9,74
    Lula Hazel (Davenport), 9
    Mary (Conner), 65
    Paul Vernon, 9
    Susana, 164
    Viola, 9,74
BROWN, Aaron, 74
    Aaron D, 152,153,187
    Aaron W, 74
    Abigail (Spivy), 74
    Ada G (Cosand), 9
    Adell, 9
    Albert E, 75
    Albert Edwin, 9
    Albert Emmons, 9
    Albert J, 9
    Albert R, 9
    Alfred, 9,25,75
    Alfred H, 9
    Alice (Thomas), 74
    Alice Ann (Mendenhall), 9
    Allen Jay, 9
    Althea, 9
    Amanda Alice (Demaree), 9
    Amiel, 74
    Amos, 75,152
    Amos James, 9
    Ann/Anna, 32,139,152,205
    Ann Eliza, 75
    Anna H, 9,116
    Anna M, 75,153,187
    Anna/Annie Mary/May, 9,40,75
    Anna V, 75

BROWN, Anniel, 75
Arlo, 153
Arthur, 153
Asaph, 153
Asher, 9,75
Bartley, 9
Benjamin, 9,17,59,75,83,135
Bertha, 9
Bessie, 9,75
Carlos, 9
Carrie L, 9,75
Carrie M (McCullough), 9
Catherine, 150
Celah/Celia, 10,74
Charles, 10
Charles Hayden, 50
Charles M, 9,75
Charlotte (Braske), 54
Christena M, 179
Christiana L (Friesdorf), 9
Clara (Loer), 152
Clara Eldora, 153
Clarence E, 9
Clarence M, 75
Clarence R, 75
Clarkson, 153
Claudia, 3
Clayton, 75,128
Clayton Jr, 75
Clayton P, 9
Clinton, 9
Cyrus, 74
Cyrus N, 10,74
Daniel, 75
Daniel Wilbur, 152
Delpha K, 75
Delphia, 187
Delphia (Dowel), 152,153
Delphia D, 153
E Howard, 9
Earl, 152,153
Edgar, 75
Edward, 152,187
Edward S, 187
Effie (Newbern), 9,25
Elam J, 9,75
Elam P, 9
Eli, 9,74,75,106,116
Eliza, 25
Eliza A, 148,149
Eliza B, 9
Elizabeth, 9,54,74,75,153
Elizabeth (Bond), 187
Elizabeth (Keith), 50
Elizabeth Alice, 153
Elizabeth J, 75
Elizabeth K, 10
Elizabeth L, 35
Emma E, 9,16,38,75
Enoch, 9
Enos F, 152
Ephraim, 48
Esther (Jones), 9
Esther J, 75
Ethel Etta (Hale), 9
Etta, 187
Etta J, 187
Etta Jane, 152
Fanny, 9
Florence, 75
Frances, 74
Francis M, 187

BROWN, Franklin, 54
Franklin J, 9
Frederick, 10,74
Gertrude, 152,187
Gloster, 9,75
Gloster Jr, 9
Grace, 40,75
Gurney L, 9
Hance, 74
Hannah, 75
Hannah (Evans), 75
Hannah (Pitman), 9
Hannah E, 9,17,75,83
Hannah Elma, 9
Harriet B, 9
Harriett, 9
Harvey D, 9
Hattie, 9,23,75
Henry, 74
Henry P, 152
Homer J, 9
Horace, 9
Howard O, 9
Ida, 48,75
Irvin J, 40
Isaac, 9,75,152,153,170,187,190
Isaac Jr, 187
Isaac D, 152,153,187
Jacob, 9,75,152,187
James, 3,9,74,149,152,187
Jane S, 9,106
Janette, 9
Jesse, 9,75
John, 10,74,179
John A, 75
John W, 75
Jonathan, 10,152,187
Joseph, 9,75
Joseph B, 9,75
Juretta (Evans), 75
Keziah, 26,28,53
Laura, 3
Laura Maud (Canaday), 152
Lee, 9
Lena M, 75
Leola, 9
Lewis, 152
Lillian Hayden, 50
Lindley H, 9,75
Lizzie, 9,75
Loring L, 152,187
Louise 9
Lucinda, 9
Lucretia, 9,75
M Alice, 12,78
Manona P, 10
Margaret (Moon), 152
Margaret A, 153
Margaret Ann, 187
Margaretta (Kendal), 75
Maria, 187
Mariah (Caphart), 152
Marietta, 9
Marinda, 9
Martha, 9,58,74,75,106,116
Martha (Hawkins), 9,74
Martha (Hill), 40
Martha (Schultz), 153
Martha A, 75
Martha A (Nelson), 10
Martha Ann, 75
Martha Ann (Hill), 9,22,38,75

BROWN, Martha Jane (Shultz), 152
Martha N, 9,59,135
Mary, 9,10,48,74,75,187,190,205
Mary (Allen), 75
Mary (Armfield), 152
Mary (Mendenhall), 152,153,170
Mary A, 50,62
Mary Ann/Maryann, 9,59,75,135,152
Mary E (Loer), 152
Mary Frances, 153
Mary J, 9
Mary Maria/Mariah, 187
Mary Maria (Haines), 153
Mary W, 74
Matilda J (Canaday), 12
Meda, 153
Millon/Milaton D, 10,74
Milton, 74
Morris, 75
Moses, 152,153,187
Myrtle, 9
Nancy, 74, 75
Nancy/Nannie J, 9,23,75
Naomi, 59,75,83
Naomi (Taylor), 9,17
Naomi H, 75
Naomi R, 9,22
Nathan, 9
Nathan Herbert, 9
Nellie Maude, 9
Nettie A, 187
Nettie A (Smith), 153
Oliver H, 9,75
Orintha L, 75
Orville E, 75
Orynthee Lizzie, 9
Otis R, 9,23,75
Percy P, 9
Pheba, 75
Phebe (Roberts), 75
Phebe R, 9,75
Rachel, 64,75,149,152,170,202
Rachel (Thorne), 10
Rebecca, 74
Rhoda, 10,152,187
Rosa Priscilla, 153
Rosena, 75
Rosena E, 75
Roxana, 9
Russell L, 9
Ruth P (Pemberton), 9
Sadie, 37
Samuel, 75,152,153,187
Samuel A, 75
Samuel C, 75
Samuel S, 9,75
Sarah, 9,74,75,173,181,187
Sarah (Bond), 75
Sarah (Clark), 9
Sarah (Ide), 179
Sarah (McWhinney), 40
Sarah (Morris), 74
Sarah C, 75,187
Sarah E, 75,153
Sarah E M, 187
Sarah Elma, 152
Sarah G, 9
Selah, 74
Seth, 9,22,38,40,75
Stacey, 9
Susan, 187
Susan (Holder), 153

BROWN, Susan C, 9
　Susan L, 75
　Susanna, 75
　Susannah L, 9,75
　Sylvester, 152,153
　Tamer, 152,190
　Thaddeus, 152,153,187
　Thomas, 74,152
　Thomas C, 12
　Thomas E, 9
　Valerie, 152
　Valteria, 187
　Viola, 10
　Walter, 75
　Walter J, 9,75
　Wesley, 75
　Wilbur, 187
　Wm, 9,10,74,152
　Wm S, 9,75
　Zeri, 152
　Zeri H, 10
　Zimri Oston, 153
　see also **BROWNE**
BROWNE, Mary Anne, 3
　see also **BROWN**
BRUMFIELD, Dora, 62
　Emma, 75
BRUMMET, Charlotte, 75
　see also **BRUMMETT**
BRUMMETT, Charlotte, 75
　Cockayne, 75
　Luetta Wilson, 75
　Mary, 75
　Virgil, 75
　Wm B, 75
　see also **BRUMMET**
BRUNNER, Blanche Hester, 153
　Catharine (Myers), 153
　Emmett W, 153
　Hubert Roscoe, 153
　John Alonzo, 153
　Sally Jane (Larrowe), 153
　Wm, 153
BRUNSON, Delphina (Myers), 10
　Lee, 10
　Orville, 10
BRYANT, Arta L, 75
　Mary, 51
BUCKINGHAM, Jane, 187
　Jane (Pidgeon), 153
　Levi, 153
BUDD, Albert, 10,75
　Calvin, 75
　Calvin H, 10
　Charles, 75
　Elizabeth, 75
　Elizabeth (Hunt), 10
　John, 10,75
　Mary, 10
　Phebe Ann, 10,75
BUELL, Alice Jennie (Dennis), 10
　Bessie Lucille, 10
　Ellen M, 75
　Ellen M (Barrett), 10
　Juliet (Wright), 10
　Willard Lewis, 10
　Willard N, 10
　Wm, 10
BUFFKIN, Esther J, 75
　John, 75
　see also **BUFKIN**

BUFFUM, Ann A, 87
　Anne, 20
　David, 10
　David E, 75
　Lydia, 75
　Marianna, 75
　Marianna (Nicholson), 10,75
　Mary Ann, 20,65,75,87
　Thomas B, 75
　Timothy, 20,87
BUFKIN, Elizabeth, 10
　Esther J, 10
　John A, 10
　Wm R, 10
　see also **BUFFKIN**
BUILER, Charles, 10
BULLA, Anna (Crampton), 75
　Carolina, 75
　Caroline (Clawson), 49
　Daniel, 49
　Elizabeth B, 49
　Mary (Fulghum), 75
BULLERDICK, Elizabeth K (Brown), 10
BUNCH, Ann (Pearson), 75
BUNDY, Adaline, 10
　Alsie, 10,75
　Arthur L, 10
　Benjamin, 43,115
　Charles H, 10
　Christopher, 75
　Ephraim, 75
　George, 75
　Henry C, 10,75
　Huldah, 75
　J Elwood, 10
　Jesse, 75
　Jonathan, 75
　Josiah, 75,127
　Josiah Jr, 75
　Karan, 75
　Lestle (Hancher), 10
　Lucinda E, 157
　Martha Jane, 157
　Mary, 10,75
　Mary E, 10,75
　Miriam, 75,127
　Nellie, 10,75
　Peninah/Peninnah, 43,115
　Rachel, 75
　Samuel More, 75
　Sarah, 43,75,115
　Susannah, 6
　Thomas H, 10
　Walter J, 10
　Wm H, 10,75
BUNGER, F B, 42
　Isabell, 42
　Martha A, 42
BUNKER, Abraham/Abram, 10,76,153
　Anna, 76
　Anna (Bond), 10
　Daniel, 10
　David, 10,76
　Deborah, 153
　Elizabeth, 153
　Jesse, 76
　John, 76,153
　Judith, 10,76,78,153
　Kazia/Kezia, 10,76
　Levi, 76,153
　Lydia, 76
　Macy, 153

BUNKER, Mary, 76,78,153
　Phebe, 10,76
　Rachel, 76,153
　Rebecca/Rebecckah, 76,153
　Reuben/Rueben, 10,76,78
　Rhoda, 153
　Samuel, 76
　Thomas, 10,76
　Wellmet/Welmet, 76,153
BUNNELL, Rachel L, 176
BURCHAM, Amelia (Wiles), 153
　Benson Wright, 153
　Frances Sylvina, 153
　Henry L, 153
　Lydia, 15
BURDETT, Catherine, 176
　Eva J, 10
　Mary A, 10
　Wm T, 10
BURGESS, Anna, 187
　Anna May, 153
　Anna P, 153
　Edgar M, 76
　Essie, 71
　Howard, 10
　John, 142
　Margaret, 142
　Mary (Sanders), 53
　Mary Ellen, 187
　Mary Ellen (Williams), 153
　Rebecca, 13
　Sarah, 1,10,53,76,142,187
　Serepta (Fulton), 153
　Wm, 53,153
BURK, Esther (Elliott), 10
　see also **BURKE**
BURKE, Lewis/Louis, 50,76
　Maria, 50
　Mary J, 50
　see also **BURK**
BURKEN, Amelia, 47
　Bertha, 47
　Richard, 47
BURKETT, Daniel, 10
　Maria, 10
　Russel, 10
BURNAN, Edith, 76
BURNARD, Edith (Grave), 10
　see also **BARNARD, BERNARD**
BURNETT, Leosa (Willoughby), 10
　Oma, 10
　Oscar, 10
BURNS, Caroline, 38,51
　Clara J, 6
　Isaac, 6
　John, 76
　Margaret M, 107
　Mary (Rhatchamel), 38
　Sarah (Elleman), 6
　Wm, 38
BUROUGHS, Addie, 187
　James, 187
　see also **BORROUGHS, BURROUGHS, BURROWS**
BURR, Mary, 169
BURRIS, Cora (Woodhurst), 10
　Harry E, 10
　Minnie F, 10
BURROUGHS, Ada Lizzie, 187
　Adaliza (Gilmore), 153
　Carrie, 159
　Cassius M, 162

BURROUGHS, Charles, 153
   Gracie P, 162
   Hannah, 149
   James, 153,176
   James M, 159
   Jane, 153
   Minnie, 159
   Sarah (Neff), 162
   Sarah A (Gilmore), 159
   see also **BORROUGHS,**
      BUROUGHS, BURROWS
BURROWS, Dora Alice, 168
   Edith (Lumpkin), 168
   Wm, 168
   see also **BORROUGHS,**
      BUROUGHS, BURROUGHS
BURSON, Ann E, 10,76
   Benjamin E, 10,76
   David S, 10,76
   Davis S Jr, 10
   Edward Thomas, 10,76
   Eliza, 76
   H Mary, 10
   Hannah M, 76
   Isaac C, 76
   Isaac E, 10
   Jemima, 10,76
   Jemima L, 76
   Jemima S, 10
   Josephine, 10
   Lydia A, 76
   Lydia Ann, 10
   Margaret, 76
   Margaret E (Evans), 10
BURTON, L Ann, 10,76
   Levi, 76
   Levi D, 76
   Mary Emma (Binns), 10,76
   Sarah E, 51,76
BURTT, Carl Moore, 153
   Elizabeth (Moore), 153
   Henry, 153
BUSAN, Sarah Catherine, 187
BUSSEAR, Julia A, 152
BUTLER, Alfred, 76
   Amos, 76
   Anna (Hampton), 10
   Anna M, 76
   Anselm B, 76
   Ansolm, 10
   Bail/Beale/Beele, 1,10,76,91
   Benjamin M, 76
   Cecil Clarence, 10
   Charles, 10
   Charles Ervin, 76
   Deborah, 3
   Deborah Jane, 210
   Durham, 76
   Earl, 10
   Eleanor, 10
   Elisabeth/Elizabeth, 10,76
   Ellen E (Rollins), 10
   Fred S, 10
   George P, 10
   James, 10
   Jane, 76
   Joseph, 76
   Lemuel, 76
   Lindley H, 76
   Mahlon, 76
   Margaret, 14
   Martha, 76

BUTLER, Mary, 10,76,91
   Mary E, 10
   Michael/Michel, 26,33,43
   Nettie, 76
   Oliver, 76
   Pleasant, 76
   Samuel, 76
   Sarah, 76
   Sarah A (Stanton), 10
   Susan, 54
   Susannah, 10,76,110
   Tacy, 42,76
   Thomas, 76
   Wm, 76
   Wm E, 76
BUTTE, Beulah, 43

CADWALADER, Benjamin Parry, 11
   Edwin C, 11,76
   Howard, 10,76
   John H, 11,76
   Margaret, 76
   Margaret (Johnson), 10
   Martha, 42
   Martha Elma, 11
   Mary Emma, 11
   Reece, 11,76
   Reece D, 76
   Reese J, 11
   Sarah, 11,76
   Sarah A, 76
   see also **CADWALLADER**
CADWALLADER, Anna E, 11
   Howard, 11,17,84
   Judith, 95
   M, 11
   Margaret (Johnson), 11,17
   Martha, 11,84
   Martha Elma, 17
   Martha Elma, 84
   Mary Edna, 11
   Rachel, 76
   Rachel (Griffith), 11
   Reese J, 11
   Sarah, 76
   Sarah A (Elliott), 11
   see also **CADWALADER**
CAIL, Anna N, 11
   Annis (Crist), 11
   Blanche M, 11
   David, 11
   Edgar P, 11
   Edith, 11
   Ethel, 11
   Grace (Pryfogle), 11
   Hazel, 11
CAIN, Achsah C, 173
   Bertha Louisa, 153,161
   Catherine, 205
   Clara (Clark), 153
   Clara E, 188
   Effie, 153
   Effie Lillian, 188
   Elizabeth, 153
   Francis, 173
   Frank C, 153
   Frankie, 188
   Henry P, 153,161,188
   Jemima, 188,207
   Jemima (Jones), 207
   John, 153
   Jonathan, 153

CAIN, Joseph Addison, 153
   Lizzie, 188
   Louisa A, 167
   Martha, 153
   Martha (Weyl), 173
   Martha Jennie, 188
   Mary, 35
   Minerva Gertrude, 153
   Nellie C, 153,188
   Olive/Ollie I, 153,188
   Rhoda (Clark), 188
   Rhoda R (Clark), 153,161
   Wm H, 188
   Wm Henry, 153
   see also **KAIN**
CALAWAY, John, 76
   see also **CALLOWAY**
CALDWELL, ——, 1
   Charles, 11
   Maud Bertha (Males), 11
CALLOWAY, Ethel, 11
   Etta, 11
   Letisha, 76
   Wm, 11
   see also **CALAWAY**
CALVERT, Annie Ethel (Kirk), 76
   Elizabeth, 76
   Reese Garrett, 76
   Thomas, 76
CAMMAC, Hannah, 76
   see also **CAMMACK**
CAMMACK, Adelaide (Park), 55
   Cornelia Adelaide, 55
   David, 76
   George, 76
   George W, 76
   Hannah, 76
   Mary, 76
   Nathan H, 76
   Willie, 76
   Wm N, 55
   see also **CAMMAC**
CAMPBELL, Anna, 76
   Emma C (Hollingsworth), 11
   Fannie, 43
   James H, 11
   Kate, 76
   Louis B, 11
   Lydia, 11
   Roy McKinley, 11
CAMPLING, Arthur Edwin, 11
   Matthew, 11
   Sarah E (Hallifax), 11
CANADA, Amy, 76
   Benjamin, 188
   Charity, 76
   Charles, 76
   Frederick, 188
   Henry, 188
   John, 188
   Margaret, 76
   Mary, 76
   Matilda, 76
   Nathan, 76
   Phebe, 76
   Sarah, 76
   Wm, 188
   see also **CANADAY, KANNADA,**
      KENADA, KENNADA,
      KENNADY

CANADAY, Abigail, 76,153
    Ammy/Amy, 76,150,153,188
    Amyrilla, 188
    Ann, 76,153
    Asenath, 41
    Benjamin, 188
    Betsey Ann, 153
    Betsy Ann (Mills), 188
    David, 188
    Elihu, 188
    Ellen (Roe), 152
    Esther R, 188
    Hannah, 155,186,188
    Harmon/Hermon, 188
    Henry Jr, 188
    Huldah, 150,153,185
    Irena, 153,193
    Jane, 76
    John, 76,188,203
    John Jr, 188
    Jonathan, 159,188
    Joshua, 153
    Joshua, 153,188
    Julatha, 203
    Karen H, 188
    Laura Maud, 152
    LindseyLyndsay/Lyndsey, 153,160, 161,188
    Livonia S, 188
    Louisa, 158,159,176
    Lydia, 153
    Margaret, 76
    Mary, 76,149,155,167
    Mary (Gibson), 161
    Mary E (Gibson), 153,160
    Matilda J, 12
    Minnie, 153,188
    Nannie E, 161,188
    Nannie W, 153
    Oliver H, 153
    Phebe, 163
    R, 188
    Rebeccah, 203
    Robert, 150,153,188
    Sarah/Sarrah, 76,153,188
    Sarah (Sumner), 153
    Serena L, 153,160
    Susanna (Moore), 159
    Thomas, 153,188
    Thomas Elwood, 153
    Walter, 152,155,188
    Wm, 188
    see also **CANADA, KANNADA, KENADA, KENNADA, KENNADY**
CANDLER, Bessie, 11
    Elizabeth, 32
    Elizabeth (Wickett), 36
    Rosco, 11
    Sarah E (Wickett), 76
    Sarah Elizabeth (Wickett), 11
    Susan, 11,36
    Theodore F, 11,36,76
CANNON, Anna/Annie, 76,104
    John, 104
    Laura Ann, 104
CAPHART, Catherine, 152
    Daniel, 152
    Mariah, 152
CAR, Susannah (Hunt), 77
    see also **CARR**

CAREY, Anna, 77
    Anna (Barlow), 77
    Arthur E, 77
    Clarence L, 11
    Dennis H, 77
    Elias, 29
    Emma Jane, 76
    Jane (Moon), 29
    John F, 76
    Leroy J, 77
    Louella E, 76
    Mary D, 11
    Milton, 76,77
    Rachel, 21,29
    Richard, 11
    Sarah Jane, 76
    Washtella E (Haisley), 11
    see also **CARY**
CARMACK, Alice, 21
CARMAN, Herbert, 77
    Leslie, 77
    Mary, 77
    Roy, 77
    Wm S, 7
CARPENTER, Anna, 77
    Caroline, 11,65,77
    Caroline E, 11,77
    Caroline M, 11,143
    Charles C, 11,29,77,98
    Deborah, 11,77
    Deborah A, 77
    Edwin, 11,77
    Eliza, 18,24
    Elizabeth, 11,77,111
    Elizabeth (Newlin), 11,29
    Elizabeth N, 77,98
    Esther, 35,106
    Hannah C Elizabeth, 39
    Isaac, 11,77
    Isaac E, 77
    Jacob, 18
    Laura Ann, 11,77
    Lemira, 77
    Louisa (Hale), 11
    Louisa H, 77
    Mary Edna, 11,29,98
    Mercy (Frost), 11
    Nathaniel, 11,77
    Ola, 160
    Phebe, 18
    Rosetta, 11,77
    Rosetta L, 77
    Susan (Mabie), 11,39,65
    Susan M, 77
    Susan M (Mabie), 11
    Walter F, 39
    Walter L, 11
    Walter T, 11,65,77
    Wm Clifford, 11
    Zeriah/Zerniah, 11,77
CARR, Aaron, 153,188
    Amos, 153,188
    Benjamin, 153,188
    Benjamin E, 153
    Charlotte, 153,108
    Cyrus, 153,188
    Daniel, 188
    Daniel Harris, 153
    Esther, 153
    Evan, 153,188
    Hezekiah A, 153,188
    Hulda, 153

CARR, Jamima, 153
    Job, 153
    Kindley, 188
    Kindley Ankrum, 153
    Lucinda, 153
    Martha, 153,192
    Mary J, 153
    Miles, 188
    Pamelia, 153
    Rachel, 153,188
    Thomas, 153,188
    see also **CAR**
CARREL, Ann, 77
    see also **CARROLL**
CARROLL, Ann L (Williams), 77
    Edward, 77
    Elisabeth, 77
    Martha, 31
    Rachel, 77
    Ruth Ann (Pope), 77
    Thomas, 77
    see also **CARREL**
CARRUTHERS, Martha, 35
    see also **CARUTHERS, CORRUTHERS**
CARSON, Calvin, 11
    Finley S, 11
    Harriet (Charles), 11
    James, 11
    Preston, 11
    Ray S, 11
    Samuel, 11
    Sarah, 11
    Viola, 11
CARTER, Adebert Jennings, 11
    Alberteen/Albertine, 77
    Alice, 77
    Ann Maria, 154
    Christene, 46
    Clarence W, 77
    Claudine, 77
    Clinton, 11
    David, 77
    Elihu, 188
    Elwood, 188
    Esther, 154,188,194
    Esther B (Mendenhall), 188
    Frank Kenneth, 11
    John M, 11
    Judith F, 200
    Lillie M, 77
    Lilly May, 77
    Maria/Mariah, 188
    Martecia, 154
    Marticia C (Mendenhall), 188
    Mary/May (Worley), 11
    Mary Elizabeth, 154
    Millicent, 154
    Nathan P, 77
    Oliver Wilson, 154
    Samuel C, 77
    Susana F, 11
    Wm B, 154,188
CARTRIGHT, Edward, 11
    Hannah, 11
    Jesse, 11
    Jonathan, 11
    Mary (Haley), 11
    Murray, 11
    see also **CARTWRIGHT**
CARTWRIGHT, Angelena, 8
    see also **CARTRIGHT**

CARUTHERS, Alice F, 77
    see also **CARRUTHER, CORRUTHERS**
CARY, Alice/Allice, 188,193
    see also **CAREY**
CASAD, Abigail J, 21
CASE, Clarence Marsh, 11
    Elon Ervin, 11
    Katherine (Moore), 11
    Lottie, 37
    Palemia (Marsh), 11
CASEY, Milton, 77
CASNER, Augusta, 8
CATES, Eli, 162
    Emma, 162
    John, 180
    Mary, 162
    Rachel (Pierce), 180
    Sophia, 180
    see also **KATES**
CATEY, Addie, 169,173
    Albina Jane, 188
    Albina Jane (Smith), 154
    Orlando, 154
    see also **CATY**
CATHRAN, Phebe, 19
CATY, Albina Jane, 188
    see also **CATEY**
CAVALT, Roxanna, 188
    see also **COVALT**
CHAFFANT, Evan, 77
    Ruth, 77
    see also **CHALFANT, CHALFONT, CHALFONTE**
CHAFFIN, Elizabeth (Shearon), 22
CHALFANT, Adda, 11
    Alexander, 163
    Alice, 163
    Edna, 11
    Elizabeth (Templin), 163
    Evan J, 77
    George, 11
    Julia Esther (Hutchins), 11
    Melissa Jane (Taylor), 11
    Ora, 11
    Rosa L, 11
    Wesley Frank, 11
    see also **CHAFFANT, CHALFONT, CHALFONTE**
CHALFONT, Ruth, 77
    see also **CHAFFANT, CHALFANT, CHALFONTE**
CHALFONTE, Even, 77
    see also **CHAFFANT, CHALFANT, CHALFONT**
CHAMBERS, Belle, 11
    Deborah, 77
    Elinor, 77
    Jonathan, 77
    R M, 11
    Sarah, 77
    Zurilda, 11
CHAMBLESS, Charity, 77
    Mary, 77
CHAMNESS, Abigail, 77,154,189
    Abijah, 154
    Achsa/Acsa, 154,188
    Adaline, 189
    Albert N, 11,154,189
    Alice Josephine, 155
    Alice S, 189
    Alma Nora, 155

CHAMNESS, Alonzo Arlistus, 154,155
    Andrew, 188
    Ann (Reynolds), 155
    Anna/Annie M (Miller), 11,154
    Annie, 189
    Caroline, 154,157,176
    Caroline (Chamness), 154
    Caroline H, 151,162
    Caroline Ruth, 155
    Carrie Etta, 189
    Carrie R, 188
    Catharine/Catherine H (Davidson), 154,157
    Charles C, 189
    Charles Clifford, 154
    Clarence W, 189
    Cordelia, 158
    Cynthia, 155,207
    Cyrus, 154
    David, 154,188
    Earl E, 154
    Ebenezer, 154,177,188
    Elihu, 154,157,188
    Elijah, 154,189
    Elisa, 188
    Elizabeth, 154,167,181
    Elizabeth, 167
    Elizabeth (Dennis), 154,156,164,177,180,188
    Elizabeth (Tate), 157
    Ellen, 155,189
    Elmina, 154
    Elvaretta, 149,155
    Elwood, 188
    Emily, 189
    Emily (Hodgin), 154
    Emily J, 188,189
    Emily J (Hodgin), 11
    Emma Jane, 155
    Enos, 155
    Esther M, 154,156
    Eunice W, 189
    Fernando, 189
    Fernando Ulysses, 11,154,155
    Flora A (Branson), 154
    Flora May, 155
    George W, 154,157,188
    Hannah, 154,174,188,189,205
    Hannah (Beeson), 188
    Hannah (Chamness), 154
    Hannah (Jackson), 155
    Hannah E, 154,164
    Henry, 154,188
    Hugh, 154
    Irena, 161,166,177
    Isaac, 154,155,164,188,189
    Isaac K, 177,180
    Isabel, 154,162,188,205
    Isabel (Beeson), 154,155,174
    Isabel (Tegal), 11
    Isabel A, 164,189
    Isabel A (Hough), 154
    Isabel W, 194
    Isam, 155
    Jahue/Jehu, 154,155,188
    James M, 189
    Jesse, 154,155,162,175,188,194,206
    Joel, 77
    John, 188
    Jonathan, 154
    Joseph, 77,154,155
    Joseph Allen, 11,154,155

CHAMNESS, Joshua, 154,155,174,188,205
    Joshua Anthony, 11
    Larkin, 154,155,188
    Laura Alice (Lamb), 154
    Lemuel C, 11
    Lena Mary, 77,155,189
    Lewis E, 154,189
    Lillie, 189
    Lillie E (Shively), 154
    Lorinda, 154
    Louisa, 157,189
    Lucinda, 155
    Luna, 189
    Luva, 154
    Lydia, 155
    Magdalene (Main), 154
    Maggie, 189
    Mahala/Mahela, 155,177
    Mahala (Lamb), 188
    Mahlon, 154,188,189
    Mahlon H, 11,189
    Malinda/Melinda, 154,167,181,211
    Marcellus, 154,189
    Margaret, 77,177
    Margaret B, 154
    Mariam/Miriam, 154,180
    Martha, 11,154
    Martha (Modlin), 11
    Martha Ann (Modlin), 154,155,188
    Mary, 149,152,154,155,159,174,175,178,189,205,206
    Mary (Canaday), 149,155,167
    Mary (Reynolds), 154,188
    Mary J (Labcytaux), 152
    Mary Melissa (Beeson), 150,155,189
    Melissa Adaline (Adamson), 154
    Mildred Ellen, 155
    Milton W, 154
    Mira E, 11
    Miriam T, 210
    Myra Ethel, 154
    Nathan, 154,155,188
    Nora, 189
    Nora A (Gilmore), 155
    Olinda Florence, 155
    Oliver Perry, 154
    Oliver Vaughn, 154
    Oscar L, 188
    Oscar Luther, 155
    Pearl B, 152,154,189
    Perry, 189
    Rachel, 154,199,203
    Rachel R, 155,167
    Rebecca, 154,155,189
    Rebecca (Stanley), 154
    Rebecca E (Hiatt), 11,154,189
    Rebecca Jane, 188
    Reuben/Rueben, 154,188
    Riley, 154,155,188
    Russel/Russell, 154,155,189
    Ruth, 77,188,189,194,206
    Ruth (Lamb), 154
    Ruth (Woody), 154,155,162,175
    Samuel, 77
    Sanford, 188
    Sarah, 77
    Sarah (Tinkle), 154,155
    Seth, 11,189
    Seth M, 77,155,188,189
    Susanna/Susannah, 188,189
    Susannah (Reynolds), 154,155
    Sylvester, 189

CHAMNESS, Theodore E, 188
    Theodore Elbridge, 155
    Thomas Hervey, 155
    Unice, 154
    Uriah, 154,155,188
    Vaughn, 11
    Wm, 11,152,154,155,174,188,205
    Wm Jr, 188
    Wm C, 149,154,155,167
    Wm Clarence, 154
    Wm N, 154,155
    Wm S, 154,155,188,189
    Wm W, 150,189
    Zola, 154,189
CHANCE, Clara, 11
    Orville E, 11
    T L, 11
CHANDLER, Ann (Wright), 11,77
    Anna, 77
    Edith, 77
    Emily, 65
    Emily Caroline, 29
    Jacob, 77
    John, 77
    Joseph, 77
    Levi, 77
    Lucy, 77
    Mary (Dodd), 29
    Robert, 29
    Willis, 77
CHANT, Arthur, 11
    Frank P, 11
    Lula, 11
CHAPEL, Huldah, 77
    Jacob H, 77
    Margery (Moffitt), 12
    Martha, 12,77
    Martha Ann, 77
    Wm, 12
    see also **CHAPPEL, CHAPPELL, CHAPLE**
CHAPIN, Clara M, 58
    Mathilda, 58
    O M, 77
    Oliver M, 77
    Silas, 58
CHAPMAN, Charles, 28
    Eliza Jennie, 66
    Eliza S (Wright), 12
    Elizabeth, 12
    Elizabeth M (Stanton), 28
    Margaret, 28
    Nathan, 12
    Pearl M, 12
CHAPPEL, Huldah, 77
    Jacob H, 77
    Margery (Cox) Moffitt, 77
    Marjery, 77
    Martha, 77
    Peggy, 77
    Sarah, 77
    Thomas, 77
    Thomas L, 77
    Wm, 77
    see also **CHAPEL, CHAPPELL, CHAPLE**
CHAPPELL, Martha, 77
    Sarah M, 77
    Thomas L, 77
    see also **CHAPEL, CHAPEL, CHAPLE**

CHAPPLE, Thomas L, 77
    see also **CHAPEL, CHAPPEL, CHAPPELL**
CHARLES, Abigail, 71, 77,115
    Abraham, 2,12,78
    Alfred, 12
    Alice B, 78
    Ann, 12
    Anna Laura, 12,32
    Anna Martha, 12
    Arthur M, 12
    Benjamin, 115
    Caroline, 12
    Caroline (Cockett), 12
    Cora (Garwood), 12
    Daniel, 12,77,155,189
    Edna, 12,78
    Eli, 12,78
    Eliza, 12
    Eliza D, 78
    Eliza D (Timberlake), 12
    Elvey, 2
    Elvira, 110
    Elvy (Peacock), 12
    Emma S, 155
    Eunice, 189
    Eunice (Swain), 189
    Eunice M, 155
    Eunice W (Swain), 155
    Frederic, 12
    Frederick R, 12
    Guilelma/Gulielma, 12,26,27,28,71, 77,155
    Harriet, 11
    J Wilson, 12
    James, 12
    Jane, 165,166,176,197
    Jesse, 12,78
    John, 12,78,110,155,179,189
    John S, 12
    Joseph, 12,77
    Josephine (Garwood), 12
    Leona V, 12
    M Alice (Brown), 12,78
    Margaret, 12,78
    Margaret (Simpson), 32
    Margaret S, 12
    Margaret S (Simpson), 12
    Margretta, 78
    Martha, 15,50,51, 125
    Martha (Horne), 12
    Mary, 12,77,110,115
    Mary (Symons),12,29,51,66,115
    Mary C, 115
    Mary E, 155,179
    Matthew, 12,78
    Miriam, 12,15,77,189
    Miriam (Moore), 77
    Nancy J (Clark), 155,179,189
    Naomi, 12
    Narcissa, 189
    Narcissa (Osborne), 189
    Nathan, 12,29,51,66,77
    Nathan Herbert, 12,78
    Rebecca, 12,66,143
    Robert S, 12
    Rosalyn M, 155
    Roslyn, 12
    Samuel, 2,12,26,27,71,77,78
    Samuel Jr, 77
    Samuel H, 12,32,78
    Sarah, 12,26,44,77,115,134

CHARLES, Sarah (Hill), 77
    Sarah G, 12,29,98
    Thomas, 12,78
    Virginia, 12
    Wilson, 12,78
    Wm C, 155
    Wm E, 12
CHEESMAN, America (Lumpkin), 155
    Ora May, 155
    Wallace, 155
CHENOWETH, Jessie, 32
    John A, 32
    Martha, 32
    see also **CHENOWITH**
CHENOWITH, Stella, 78
    see also **CHENOWETH**
CHESNUT, Emma, 78
    Emma A, 78
CHILDERS, Hannah, 50
    Henry, 50
    Laura, 50
CHILDRE, Martha, 78,114
    Phebe, 78
    Sally, 114
    Wm, 114
    see also **CHILDRU**
CHILDRU, Martha, 78
    Sally, 78
    see also **CHILDRE**
CHOCLANE, Annabel, 57
    see also **COCKAYNE**
CHRASHES, Susannah, 78
CHRISMAN, Mary E, 78
CHURCH, Eliza A, 78
CILLEY, Martha, 35
CLANDLER, Elizabeth, 12
CLAPPER, Alice, 189
    Alice Josephine (Chamness), 155
    David, 155,189
    David C, 189
    Gertie/Gertrude, 155, 189
    Hazel C, 155
    Jacob, 155
    Jacob L, 155
    Laura (Taylor), 155
    Nellie, 155,189
    Ruth, 155,189
    Sarah (Priddy), 155
CLARK, ——, iv
    A Emma, 189
    A Emma (Study), 155
    Albert, 155
    Alexander, 12,78
    Alfred, 12,78
    Alida, 78
    Alida (Clawson), 12,66,78
    Alida (Philips), 143
    Alida C (Miller) Harned, 134
    Amy, 137,78
    Ann/Anna/Annie, 3,12,13,78,97
    Anna (Price), 12
    Anna R, 78
    Asenith (Hunt), 12
    Barzilla W, 155,156,189
    Calvin, 12,66,78,143
    Caroline M, 19,61
    Charity (Knight), 155
    Charles G, 12,78
    Charles Herbert, 155,189
    Christena B (Coffin), 12
    Clara, 153
    Cora, 78,168

CLARK, Cora H, 155
    Cyntha, 13
    Cyntha Ellen, 78
    Cyrus O, 12
    Daniel, 12,13,28,78
    Deborah, 121
    Deborah Anna (Price), 78
    Dougan, 12,78,155
    Edmund D, 155
    Elam, 13
    Eli M, 12
    Elias, 13
    Elias Hicks, 78
    Eliza, 12,66,143
    Elizabeth, 78
    Elizabeth (Moore), 12
    Elizabeth (Vanzant), 12
    Ellen (Hanby), 189
    Ellen H (Hanby), 155
    Ellwood, 12,78
    Emela, 13
    Emily, 78
    Emily C, 189
    Emily C (Botkin), 155
    Emily J, 155
    Emily Jane (Griffin), 13
    Emma, 78
    Emma J, 78
    Emma Robinson, 12,78
    Enos, 12,78
    Enos B, 78
    Esther (Jones), 13,78
    Eunice, 202
    Eunice R, 156,189
    Eva Celestia, 155,160
    Everett W, 189
    Francis, 78
    George E, 189
    George Edward, 155,156
    George Hershall/Hershel, 189
    Gertrude Seaman, 12
    Gertrude Seaman (Clark), 12
    Gulielma, 12,78
    Hannah, 12,13,78
    Harmon, 22
    Henry, 12
    Henry H, 12,78
    Henry T, 12
    Herbert Charles, 189
    Ida, 189
    Ida M, 189
    Ida M (Conley), 155
    Irena May, 189
    Israel, 78,137
    J M, 189
    Jamima/Jemima, 12,13,28,78,97,112
    Jane, 78
    Jesse, 12,78
    Jesse Jr, 12
    Jesse Cates, 189
    Joanna, 13,78
    John, 1,12,13,78,97,99,112,155
    John Everett W, 155
    John F, 12
    John Goodrich, 155
    John Gurney, 13
    John M, 189
    John Milton, 155,156
    John Paul, 189
    Jonathan B, 15,160,189
    Joseph, 78
    Joseph A, 155,189

CLARK, Julia (Seaman), 12
    Julia C, 155
    Julia E, 189
    L Ella, 189
    Louisa, 189
    Louisa (Worth), 153,155
    Luella (Stiggleman), 13
    Lydia, 12,78
    Malinda/Melinda, 78,155
    Malinda/Melinda (Macy), 78,189
    Margaret, 12,13
    Mariam Asenath, 156
    Mary, 12,25,78,189
    Mary (Bunker), 78
    Mary Ann/Maryann, 12,78
    Mary B, 13,78
    Mary Louisa, 155,192
    Mary M, 156
    Mary R, 78
    Mary R (Hoag), 12
    Matilda, 189
    Matilda J (Conley), 160
    Matilda Jane, 189
    Matilda Jane (Conley), 155
    Maud L, 155
    Milton, 189
    Miriam, 155
    Miriam A, 189
    Morris Tracy, 13
    Myrtle, 155
    Nancy (Goodrich), 192
    Nancy (Hussy), 13
    Nancy J, 155,179,189
    Nancy M (Goodrich), 155
    Nancy P, 189
    Naomi, 161
    Nathan, 12, 78
    Nellie, 31,59,78
    Nellie (Goodrich), 155,206
    Oliver W, 155
    Rachel (Marmon), 78
    Rebecca, 36
    Rhoda, 188
    Rhoda R, 153,156,161,189
    Robert Morris, 13
    Ruth, 78,137
    S Ella, 189
    Sarah, 9,12,13,78,97,99,112
    Sarah (Stubbs), 95
    Sarah (Wright), 78
    Sarah A (Davis), 13
    Sarah Ann, 13,78
    Sarah Ethel, 12
    Sarah J, 78
    Sarah J (Bates), 12
    Semira, 12
    Solon North, 189
    Stephen E, 13
    Susan (Price), 22
    Susan/Susanna (Ward), 12,28
    Susan Belle, 22
    Susanna/Susannah, 78,99
    Tamar, 78,97
    Thomas, 12,13,78
    Thomas E, 189
    Thomas Elwood, 155,192
    Thomas W, 13,78
    Will Carlton, 189
    Wm, 12,13,78,153,155,189
    Wm Carleton, 189
    Wm D, 156,189
    Wm F, 12,78

CLARK, Wm P, 78
    see also **CLARKE**
CLARKE, Rachel, 126
    see also **CLARK**
CLAWSON, Abner, 13,79
    Alfred, 79
    Alfred H, 13,79
    Alice, 13,62,79
    Alida, 12,13,66,78
    Amos, 13,29,33,103
    Ann, 13,94
    Caroline, 49
    Charles C, 13,79
    Elizabeth, 13,79
    Elizabeth Ann, 79
    Elizabeth D, 13,29
    Elwood, 79
    Emma (Ollinger), 13
    Emma Mary, 13
    Eugene, 13,79
    Jane Ann, 17
    Josiah, 13,78,79,141
    Kesiah/Keziah, 78, 91,92,94,95
    Keziah (Ward), 12,13,27
    Libby L, 92
    Mahlon, 78
    Malinda, 13,79,103
    Malinda/Melinda (Davenport), 13,29, 33
    Martha Jane, 13,79
    Mary Ann, 15,26
    Mary Emma, 79
    Matilda (Parker), 17
    Naomi B, 13,27,95
    Rebecca/Rebekah, 13,78,79,103,141
    Rebecca (Towel) Pool, 13
    Rebecca Ann, 13,14,33
    Sarah, 60,78,141
    Sarah E, 67
    Sarah Emlen, 13
    Sibby S, 13
    Susanna W, 13,91
    Tabitha Jane, 79,113
    Thomas W, 13,79
    Tom, 78
    Wm, 12,13,17,78,79,91,92,94,95
    Wm Jr, 13,79
    Wm T, 79
CLAY, Sally, 51
CLAYTON, John J, 79
    Laura E, 79
CLEAR, Mary E, 147,148
CLEAVER, Alice, 79
CLEMENS, Anna, 79
    Anna M, 79
    Caroline, 79
    Emma, 79
    Emma B, 79
    Lucile, 208
    Lucille, 189
    see also **CLEMENTS, CLEMONS, KLEMMANS**
CLEMENTS, Eva Elnora (Pegg), 13
    Ira A, 13
    Leota Martha, 13
    Lucile, 133
    see also **CLEMENS, CLEMONS, KLEMMANS**
CLEMONS, Lucile, 156
    see also **CLEMENS, CLEMENTS, KLEMMANS**

CLEVENGER, Emma B, 13
    F M, 13
    Susanna, 176
CLIFT, Mary A, 79
    Mary E, 79
CLINE, James, 79
    Mary C, 79
    Mary L, 79
    Wm C, 79
CLOUD, Anne, 79
    Carl, 13,79
    Elisabeth/Elizabeth, 79
    Ella, 79
    Ella H, 13
    Emma A, 30
    Esther M, 189
    Esther M (Chamness), 156
    Georgia, 13
    Joel, 79
    Joel Edgar, 13,79
    John T, 79
    Jonathan, 79,156
    Kate/Katie, 13,79
    Levi, 30
    Lewis E, 13
    Mary E (Ratliff), 13
    Matilda, 79
    Mordecai, 79
    Rebecca (Hunt), 30
    Tacy, 79
    Tacy (Moffitt), 79
    W H, 79
    Wm, 13,79
    Wm H, 79
CLYEDENS, Eunice W (Chamness), 189
COALE, Eliz (Smith), 79
    Eliza (Ogborn), 18
    Emily H, 18
    George, 18
COATE, Adila (Jenkins), 13
    Bertha L, 13
    Clarence M, 13,79
    E May (Alexander), 13
    Elijah, 13
    Ella R (Hodgin), 13,51
    Esther, 13,51
    Henry W, 19
    Joshua, 13
    Lindley M, 13,51
    Martha A, 13,79
    May Evaline, 13
    Myrtle O, 13
    Phebe, 19,20
    Phebe (Cathran), 19
    Rebecca (Coppock), 13
    Robert Harris, 13,79
    Vashti E, 79
    Vashti H (Miles), 13
    Walter J, 13,79
    see also **COATES**, **COATS**
COATES, Anson, 79
    Eva, 175
    see also **COAT**, **COATS**
COATS, Mary Evalina, 63
    Robert Harris, 63
    Vashti (Miles), 63
    see also **COAT**, **COATES**
COBB, Hannah, 20
COCKAYNE, Anna M, 79
    Charles, 13,79
    Edwin, 13,79
    Elizabeth, 79

COCKAYNE, Elizabeth (Unthank), 13, 39, 41,79
    Ellen, 13,86
    Henry, 13
    James, 13,41,79
    James Jr, ,13,39,79
    James Sr, 13,79
    Joseph, 13,79
    Julia/July Ann, 13,79
    Lilly, 79
    Lilly (Wolf), 13
    Mary, 13,39,79,110
    Rebecca, 13,41,113
    Sarah, 13,79
    Wm, 13,79
    see also **CHOCLANE**
COCKETT, Caroline, 12
COFFIN, Abigail, 79,156, 189,199
    Abigail (Hobbs), 148,156,167
    Abigail S, 156
    Adaline, 79,80
    Adam, 13,31,79,101,129
    Adeline, 14
    Albert, 14,79
    Albert Wm, 156
    Alladelppi, 79
    Alpheus, 14,79,80
    Anna,13,79,129
    Anna Maria, 149,156
    Anna Mary, 79
    Anna Mary (Richey), 79
    Arthur H, 79
    Barnabas, 79,156,189,197
    Bethuel, 13
    Caroline E, 79,107
    Caroline Elizabeth, 14
    Catharine/Catherine, 31,79,101
    Catherine Evaline, 156
    Charles, 1
    Charles F, 14,79,80
    Charles Fisher, 13,14
    Charles Francis, 14
    Charles Henry, 13,80
    Christena B, 12
    David, 189
    David Worth, 156
    Delphina, 156
    Delphina, 189,197
    Edom, 14
    Edwin, 79,80
    Edwin, 80
    Elias, 80
    Elijah, 13,14,40,79,104,107,112,123, 138
    Elijah Jr, 13,14
    Eliphalet, 14
    Elizabeth, 79,129
    Elizabeth Fletcher, 14
    Elva, 14
    Emily, 14,79,80
    Esther, 79
    Eunice, 148,156,167,174,176,189
    Eunice W, 189,199
    Eva, 80
    Fannie, 3
    Flora (Howell), 13
    Flora (Roberts), 14
    Francis, 79
    Francis A, 80
    Francis Albion, 13,14
    Frank, 79,80
    Frank A, 14,80

COFFIN, Gulielma, 79
    Hannah, 13,156,163,171,189
    Hannah (Ballinger), 41
    Hannah Amelia, 14,138
    Hepsa/Hepza, 65,69,142
    Huldah, 170
    Irvin H, 14
    Irwin W, 80
    Jemima/Jemime, 79,129
    Jesse, 14,79,80
    John, 148,156,167,189,199
    John M, 156,189
    John M, 189
    John W, 79
    John Wilson, 14,79
    Joseph, 41,171,189
    Julius Howell, 13
    Laura L, 79
    Lena Margaret, 14,80
    Levi, 12,13
    Libni, 65,79,142
    Louisa J, 156
    Louisa Jane, 156,189
    Lucy Vincent (Baxter), 14
    Lydia (Roberts), 14
    Lydia Mary (Roberts), 79
    Martha D, 156,189
    Marticia/Martitia, 156,159,206
    Mary, 14,79,104,156,189
    Mary (Harvey/Harvy), 14,79
    Mary A, 80
    Mary Amelia, 13
    Mary H, 79,82
    Melissa, 80
    Melissa E (Wilson), 14
    Millicent, 41,51,52
    Miriam, 197
    Miriam (Worth), 156
    Miriam A, 79,112,123
    Miriam Allinson/Allison, 13,40
    Moses, 79
    Mourning, 154
    Myron F, 14
    Myron F, 80
    Naomi, 79,104,107,112,123,138
    Naomi (Hiatt), 13,14,40
    Nathan T, 79
    Obed, 79
    Obediah, 13
    Percival B, 80
    Percival Lincoln, 13,14
    Phebe, 10,148,161,167,168
    Priscilla, 13,79
    Prudence, 13
    Rachel, 79,149,156,176
    Rebecca/Rebekah, 79,105,163,171, 180
    Rhoda, 79
    Rhoda M, 79,80
    Rhoda M (Johnson), 13,14
    Robert, 79
    Robert B, 14,79
    Roxanna, 156
    Ruth, 79
    Samuel, 79,149,156,176
    Samuel D, 80
    Sarah, 79
    Sarah (Murphy), 12
    Sarah (Nicholson), 14,80
    Sarah (Wilson), 14
    Sarah Elma (Fletcher), 14,79
    Sarah H, 80

COFFIN, Shubal G, 79
    Stephen, 189
    Susan, 79
    Susan (Ellis), 79
    Susanna/Susannah, 79
    Thomas, 14
    Thomas C, 79
    Thomas N, 156
    Tristram Robert, 80
    Vestal H, 133
    Wilson, 14,79,80
    Wm, 80
    Wm Edward, 13,14,79,80
    Wm H, 14,79,80
    Wm Henry, 14,79
    Wm Hiatt, 13,14
    Wm V, 14
    Wm Vestal, 80
COGGESHALL, Allen, 14
    Ann M, 14
    Charles A, 14
    Clarence Dwight, 14
    Clyde J, 14
    Daniel, 80
    Delphina M (Fulghum), 14
    Esther Jane, 80
    Eva Millicent, 14
    Frederick Wharton, 14
    Gayer/Geyer, 189
    Guy Rowland, 14
    Jessie F, 14
    John, 14,43,52
    Jonathan, 189
    Lucinda (White), 52
    Martha C, 14,43
    Mary Lyon, 52
    Nancy (Bangham/
      Baughman), 13,14
    Nova Elmer, 14
    Oliver W, 14
    Peter, 189
    Preston P, 14
    see also **COGGSHALL,**
      COGGSHELL
COGGSHALL, Alma M, 80
    Ann, 17
    Anna M, 80
    Annuel Harvey, 80
    Clarence D, 80
    Daniel, 14
    Emily Jane, 80
    Esther Jane, 14
    Eva M, 80
    George R, 80
    Hannah, 80
    Jonathan, 189
    Lindley, 80
    Nora Elma, 80
    Oliver W, 80
    Peter, 156
    Ralph, 80
    Staca L, 80
    Wm Albert, 80
    see also **COGGESHALL,**
      COGGSHELL
COGGSHELL, Annual Harvey, 80
    Emily Jane, 80
    Hannah, 80
    Wm Albert, 80
    see also **COGGESHALL,**
     COGSHALL

COHANE, Elizabeth, 80
COIL, Edgar P, 80
COLBERT, Elizabeth (Lee), 4
    Emma C, 4
    Isaac, 4
COLBURN, Elizabeth, 189
COLE, Emily, 52
COLEMAN, Maud, 80
COLGLAZIER, Abraham, 14
    Ethel, 14
    Minnie (McCoskey), 14
COLGROVE, Lula R, 53
COLL, Margaret M, 80
COLLATT, John, 80
    see also **COLLETT**
COLLETT, John, 80
    see also **COLLATT**
COLLINS, Charles, 36
    Kathlyn, 36
    Margaret, 36
    Susan, 11,28,58,62,63
COLTER, George, 14,80
    George E, 80
    Mary, 14, 80
    Wm, 14,80
COLVIN, Elmer, 80
    Elmer G, 14
    Margaret (Paulson), 14
    Roy Elmer, 14
COMBER, James, 80
    John, 80
    Joseph, 80
    Stephen, 80
    see also **COMBERS**
COMBERS, Martha, 104
    Mary, 104
    Robert, 104
    see also **COMBER**
COMER, Addison, 14
    Amos, 14,46,80
    Ann, 14
    Charles, 80
    Charles W, 80
    Claudia Lenore, 14
    Elizabeth, 14,70,80
    Hannah, 80
    Hannah Jemima, 80
    Ida, 80
    Isaac, 14,80
    James, 14
    John, 80
    Joseph, 1,80
    Joseph T, 80
    Lydia, 14,69
    Martha, 14,34
    Mary, 14,34,46,80
    Rebeckah, 80
    Robert, 1,14,34, 80
    Ruth Anna/Ruthanna, 14,81
    S Emily, 14,46
    Stephen, 180
    Susanna, 80
    Susannah (Crampton), 14
COMLEY, Julia E, 14,80
COMMONS, Anna, 80
    Anna Jane, 14
    Annie (Smith), 15
    Bertha Eleanor, 14
    Carlton, 14
    Cassie B (Swearengen), 14
    Charles A, 14
    Charlie S, 80

COMMONS, Clinton, 80
    Conrad, 80
    Cora (Lee), 14
    Cynthia, 80
    Cynthia (Thomas), 14
    Cynthia Jane, 80
    David, 80
    Edwin L, 80
    Edwin Lindorf, 14
    Eleanor Bertha, 80
    Elisabeth/Elizabeth, 80
    Elizabeth (Cook), 14,15,80
    Elizabeth (Jay), 14
    Elmer, 80
    Elmore Ellsworth, 14
    Ezekiel/Ezikiel, 80
    Francis Edwin, 14,80
    Francis Edwin, 80
    Isaac,1,2,13,14,80
    Isaac N, 80
    Isaac Newton, 14,80
    Isaac Newton, 80
    J Clinton, 14
    John, 80
    Jonathan, 80
    Joseph, 80
    Joseph Clinton, 80
    Kesiah S, 80
    Kiziah (Stubbs), 14
    Lewis B, 80
    Mariana, 80
    Mary, 80
    Mary (Townsend), 14,80
    Mary Alice (Harvy), 14
    Mary Ann/Anna, 14,80
    Mary Emily, 14
    Nathan, 80
    Riley O, 14, 80
    Robert, 14,15,80
    Ruth, 80
    Sarah (Julian), 80
    Wm, 80
    Wm Harvey, 14,15,80
    Wm Harvey, 80
COMPTON, Anna, 15
    Betty, 28,41
    Christiana, 15
    Clara, 45
    Eva N, 50
    Joel T, 50
    Joseph, 15
    Susannah (Dakin), 50
CONARRE, Mary, 56
CONKLE, Elizabeth, 36
    Elizabeth (Austin), 29,49,80
    Isabella/IsabelleLouise, 49,80
    Lizzie A, 98
CONKLIN, Joseph, 15,80
CONLEY, Anna, 166,170
    Benjamin, 166,170
    Cora May, 44
    Cynthia Emaline (Dennis), 156
    H C, 15
    Ida M, 155
    Ida May, 156
    Isaac, 155,156
    John, 156
    Lucy Ann, 170
    Luzena, 155,156
    Martha Ellen (Thornburg), 189
    Matilda J, 160
    Matilda Jane, 155,156

CONLEY, Maxie, 189
    Maxie W, 156
    N A, 15
    Nevada, 166
    Robert Carl, 15
    see also **CONLY**
CONLY, Nevada, 189
    see also **CONLEY**
CONNAWAY, Angia, 37
    see also **CONWAY**
CONNELL, Hanora, 53
CONNER, Adelaide, 16
    Alvin, 80
    Clara, 168
    Eliza (Matthews), 18
    Etta, 55
    Hanora (Connell), 53
    Henrietta, 50
    Joseph P, 80
    Joseph T, 80
    Lottie, 37,80
    Lucinda, 80
    Mary, 65
    Mary F, 18
    Mary Maud, 80
    Michael, 53
    Nellie Barnard, 53
    Patrick, 168
    Rachel (Jones), 168
    Wm G, 18
    see also **CONNOR**
CONNOR, John, 80
    see also **CONNER**
CONORO, Elizabeth, 66
CONWAY, Angeline, 171
    Charley, 156
    James, 156,160
    Martha, 156,189
    Martha (Smith), 156,160
    Nancy Ellen, 156,160
    Susan G, 156,189
    Susan G (Conway), 156
    Susan Gertrude, 189
    Wm, 189
    see also **CONNAWAY**
CONYER, Julia (Swain), 189
COOK, Abraham, 81
    Alvin, 81
    Alyelina, 81
    Amos, 15, 81
    Andrew, 81
    Angelia, 15
    Angeline, 52,81
    Ann/Anna/Anne, 7, 30,81,156
    Ann (Money), 156
    Anna (Wickersham), 81
    Anna Mary, 15,54
    Betsey/Betsy, 156,190
    Caleb, 81
    Calvin, 15,81
    Carrie (Stanton), 15
    Catharine, 81
    Charity, 81,94
    Charles Ned, 15
    Charles W, 15
    Clarkson, 15,81
    Clifton L, 15
    Cynthia Ann, 15,114
    Cyrene, 15,81
    Cyrus, 15,81,156,190
    Daniel, 15
    David, 81,190

COOK, Edna, 20
    Eli, 81
    Elijah, 15,16,81
    Elizabeth, 14,15,80,81
    Elvira, 156
    Emma S, 81
    Emma S (Knight), 15
    Gulielma (Harvey), 15
    Hannah, 81,101
    Hannah, 81
    Hannah J (Ross), 15
    Hannah Josephine, 15,81
    Harvey, 15
    Henry, 81,190
    Ira, 81,156,190
    Irena, 156,190
    Isaac, 15
    Isaac, 54,81,94
    Jacob, 81
    James S, 15
    Jane, 156
    Jeanette Alice, 15
    Jehu, 81
    Jesse, 15,81,189
    John, 156
    John, 81,172
    John Wesley, 15
    Jonathan, 15
    Joseph, 81,140
    Joseph P, 15,81
    Judith, 81
    Kezia, 81
    Leslie, 15,81
    Lillian, 15,81
    Louise, 147
    Lydia, 81,101,114,140
    Lydia (Knight), 15
    Lydia (Pegg), 15,81
    Lydia (Wright), 81
    Mahlon, 15,81
    Marcella, 172
    Martha, 13,81
    Martha (Crampton), 15,54
    Martha Elma, 9,15,16
    Mary, 15,16,48,56,81,82,140,172
    Mary (Gilbert), 81
    Mary C (Pyle), 15
    Mary Elizabeth, 41
    Mary L, 81
    Mary S (Reagan), 15
    Nancy, 81
    Naomi, 156
    Nathan, 15,81
    Nathaniel, 81
    Nevva L (Cox), 15
    Phebe, 81
    Phebe (Smith), 15
    Philip/Phillip, 15,81
    Prudence, 15,81
    Prudence (Johnson), 81
    Rachel, 15,81,94
    Rachel (Crampton), 15,16
    Rebecca Emmaline, 156
    Rebeckah, 81,156
    Robert, 101
    Rosetta, 15
    Ruth, 14,15,16,80,81
    Ruth (Cook), 14,15,16
    Ruth Anna, 15, 81
    Ruthana (Comer), 81
    Samuel, 15,81
    Sarah, 15,56,72,81

COOK, Sarah Elizabeth, 15,16
    Seth, 14,15,16,80,81
    Sinia Esther (Money), 156,172
    Sylvanus J, 156
    Thomas, 15,56,81
    Thomas C, 156
    Wm, 81
    Wm Jr, 81
    Wm Penn, 15
    Wright, 81,156,190
    Zachariah, 81
    Zimri, 15,81,114
COOMES, Cida Alice, 156
    John, 156
    Polly (Fields), 156
COONS, Elma, 190
    Samuel, 190
    see also **KOON**, **KOONS**, **KUNTZ**
COOPER, Amy Ann, 15,81
    Arthur, 81
    Caspar, 150
    Catharine/Catherine, 81,150
    Elizabeth, 8
    Elizabeth (Howard), 15
    Elizabeth (Kennedy), 57
    Isaac, 15
    James, 81
    John, 15,81
    Joseph E, 15
    Joshua, 81
    Josiah, 81
    Lydia, 81
    Lydia E, 81
    Lydia E (Evans), 15
    Mary C, 49
    Minnie, 150
    Prudence, 57
    Rachel, 81
    Rhoda, 33
    Thomas, 81
    Wm, 81
COPELAND, Joshua, 24
    Leah, 81
    Martha (Moore), 81
    Mary, 24
    Rachel, 81
    Susanna/Susannah, 24,81
    Winifred, 81
    Winniford, 138
COPPICK, Ann P, 15
    Charles M, 15
    David J, 15
    Magdalen (Eubank), 15
    see also **COPPOCK**
COPPOCK, Rebecca, 13
    see also **COPPICK**
CORDLE, Elizabeth, 190
COREY, Elizabeth, 150,159
    see also **CORY**
CORNUTT, Hannah (Macy), 190
CORRUTHERS, Alice F, 81
    see also **CARRUATHERS**, **CARUTHERS**
CORY, Adam, 156
    Elijah, 157
    Elizabeth (Beeson), 156,190
    Isaac, 156
    Levine (Lake), 157
    Nancy Jane, 157
    Rebecca (Beeson), 190
    Sarah (Beeson), 156
    see also **COREY**

CORYELL, John A, 15
    Lillie, 15
    Osa Francis, 15
COSAND, Ada G, 9
    Elias, 81
    John, 81
    Mary, 81
    Nathan, 81
    Samuel, 81
    Sarah, 30
    Wm, 81
COSANS, Mary, 4
COTTERILL, Clara Currie, 15
COTTON, Ann/Anna, 81
    Mary Caroline, 20,62
    Orloff, 81
    Robert, 81
    Robert Henry, 81
COUCH, Hannah (Wilson), 190
COUGILL, Caleb, 81
    Henry, 81
    Mary (Moffitt), 81
    Ruth, 81
    see also **COWGILL, COWGLE**
COULTER, Alexander, 81
    Estella Mary, 81
    Mary Elizabeth, 81
COUSER, Addison, 15
    Ruth Anna (Cook), 15
COVALT, Cheniah, 180
    Christena, 180
    Elizabeth, 180
    Ferdinand, 156
    Mary, 154
    Nancy Roxanna (Farlow), 156
    Rebecca, 178
COVERT, Albert, 81
    Earl, 81
COWGILL, Caleb, 15,81
    Caleb, 81
    Elizabeth, 15
    Elizabeth, 81
    Florence B, 7
    Henry, 15,81
    John, 15,81
    Liddia/Lydia, 15,81
    Mary, 81
    Rachel, 15,81
    see also **COUGILL, COWGLE**
COWGLE, Elizabeth, 81
    Lydia, 81
    Mary, 81
    see also **COUGILL, COWGILL**
COX, Addie, 82
    Alfred, 15
    Alton, 82
    Amos, 190
    Amy, 82,109
    Amy Amanda, 128
    Angelina (Shugart), 15
    Angeline, 82
    Ann v,82
    Ann G, 15
    Anna (Barnes), 156
    Belle R (Roberts), 15
    Benjamin, 1,28,58,82,116,126,156
    Betsy, 204
    Branson, 156,190
    Catharine/Catherine, 2,81,82
    Celia, 31,82
    Charity, 190
    Charles, 15

COX, Clare, 15
    Clayton, 82
    Cynthia, 156
    Cynthia, 179,190
    Cyrus B, 82
    Deborah, 82,92,156,161,190
    Della M, 160
    Dinah, 82
    Dinah, 96
    Edith, 82,92
    Edom, 82
    Elihu, 15,82,156,190
    Elijah, 2,82
    Elisha, 156,190
    Elizabeth, 156,157,179,190,194
    Elvira, 82
    Emma, 2
    Enoch, 2,15,82
    Esther, 82
    Esther B, 156
    Ethel, 15
    Grace, 82
    Hannah, 2,134
    Hannah M (Anderson), 15
    Harmon/Herman, 16,82
    Hester Ann, 190
    Hester Ann (Mills), 190
    James H, 15
    Jane, 16
    Jared, 156,190
    Jehu, 82
    Jemima/Jemimah, 155,190
    Jemima (Branson), 58,156
    Jennie V, 16
    Jeremiah, iii,1,2,5,70,77,81,82,114,
        124,134
    Jeremiah Jr, 1,82
    Joel, 82
    John, 15,16,82,156,161,189
    John F/T, 15,82
    John N, 82
    Jonathan, 190
    Jos, 31
    Joseph, 82,96,156,190
    Judith, 190
    Levi, 156,190
    Levina, 36,43,115
    Lienetta, 52
    Louisa/Louiza, 15,82
    Lucy A, 15
    Lydia (Williams), 156
    Margaret, 156,204
    Margery, 2,5,70,77,82,114,118,124,
        134
    Martha, 15,28,82,160
    Martha D, 82
    Martha D (Grave), 82
    Mary, 2,5,15,70,82,126,132,156,190
    Mary (Grace), 156
    Mary (Price), 82
    Mary W, 82
    Mary W (Test) Doyle, 82
    Medora, 82
    Myrtle (Smith), 15
    Nancy, 156
    Narcissa, 82
    Narcissa (Way), 15
    Nathan, 82,190
    Nathan W, 156
    Neclessen S, 15
    Nellie (Razor), 15
    Nevva L, 15

COX, Peter, 156,190,204
    Phebe, 82
    Phebe Ann, 82
    Priscella/Priscilla, 8,14,156,190
    Priscilla E, 35,58
    Rachel, 82,156,161,162,165,176
    Rachel (Stuart), 52
    Rachel J, 31
    Rachel Jane, 82
    Rebecca/Rebechak/Rebekah, 1,16,28,
        82,156
    Rebecca (Ellis), 190
    Rhoda, 156,190
    Robert, 82
    Russel, 82
    Ruth, 2,82,124
    Ruth (Andrews), 82
    Ruth Ann, 127
    Ruth Anna (Wickersham), 15
    Ruth G, 82
    Samuel, 16,82,92
    Sarah, 82,126,156,190,200
    Sarah (Brewer), 82
    Solomon, 160
    Stephen, 82,156,170,179,190,194
    Susannah, 82
    Theodore, 52
    Thomas, 157,190
    Thomas M, 16
    Warner L, 82
    Wm, 82,126,132,156,157,190
    Wm I, 157
    Wm Jr, 190
    Zilpah, 156
    Zimri, 190
CRABB, Cora A, 16
    Elizabeth C, 82
    Mildred, 16
    Thomas, 16
CRAFT, Elizabeth, 82
CRAGG, Eva A (Lawson), 16
    Katie, 16
    Levi, 16
    Thomas, 16
CRAIG, Elmira, 16
    Emily, 16
    Emma, 82
    Hannah (Moffit/Moffitt), 82,111
    Jacob, 82
    Johan, 16
    Marshall E, 16
    Martha, 82
    Mary, 82
    Mary H (Coffin), 82
    Mary L (Oron), 16
    Mildred M, 16
    Samuel, 82
    Sylvester, 16
    Thomas L, 16
CRAMER, Elizabeth, 170
    Philapena/Philipena/Phillipena,
        170,175,179
    Phillip, 170
    see also **KRAMER**
CRAMPTON, Abraham, 82
    Adelaide (Conner) Stone, 16
    Adelaide S, 82
    Alva, 82
    Andrew, 82
    Andrew H, 82
    Ann/Anna, 75,82
    Anna (Smith), 15,16,82

CRAMPTON, Anna Mary, 16,82
   Cassandra M, 82
   Clarinda, 63
   Clarinda J, 16,82
   Edith (Hampton), 16
   Elizabeth, 82,140
   Elizabeth Ann (Norris), 16
   Elizabeth G, 82
   Eunice, 82
   Eunice A, 82
   Franklin R, 82
   Isaac, 16,82
   Isaac J, 82
   Jacob, 82
   Jacob H, 82
   Jennie V (Cox), 16
   Jonathon, 82
   Joshua, 82
   Joshua S, 82
   Joshua Smith, 16,63,82
   Letitia, 16,82
   Letitia C, 58
   Margaret (Grimes), 58
   Margaret E, 82
   Margaret E (Graham), 16,63
   Martha, 14,15,16,54,81,82
   Mary, 124
   Mary (Cook), 16, 82
   Mary C, 82
   Merick/Merrick Starr, 15,16
   Merrick, 16
   Merrick S, 82
   Priscilla, 82
   Prudah, 82
   Rachel, 15,16,82,124
   Rebecca, 16,59
   Ruth H, 82
   Samuel, 16,82,124
   Sarah, 82
   Smith, 58
   Stephen, 82
   Stephen Alva, 16
   Susan, 82
   Susan J, 82
   Susanna/Susannah, 14,82
   Wm, 82
   Wm E, 16
   see also **CRUMPTON**
CRANDALL, Allen, 56
   Lula, 56
   Sarah Ann, 56
CRANER, Louisa (Lewis), 180
   Marilla C, 180
   Thomas, 180
CRANFORD, Elizabeth B, 18,30
CRANSTON, Alfred, 82
CRATE, Adila (Jenkins), 16
   Clarence M, 16
   Joshua, 16
   Martha A, 16
   Robert Harris, 16
   Vashti E (Miles), 16
   Walter J, 16
CRAWFORD, Charles Welsey, 16
   Daniel J, 16
   Edwin G, 16
   Emily Catherine (Snyder), 16
   Iva C, 16
   Mary, 16
   Mary (Hoover), 16
   Mary Elizabeth, 46
   Wm, 16

CREECH, Sarah L (Lewis), 16
CREGAR, Leslie Wasson, 16
   Rose Emma, 16
   Wm H, 16
CREST, Levi, 8
   Lucinda (Bayers/Bear), 8
   Mary, 8
CREW, Benjamin, 83
   Elizabeth A, 65
   Huldah, 83
   James, 82,83
   Jane (Pleas), 83
   Littleberry, 83
   Mary R, 80
   Ruth, 130
CRIST, Annis, 11
CRITCHLOW, Cynthia J, 83
CROCKER, Alvin E, 83
CROSS, Charles A, 157
   Emanuel, 157
   Lucinda E (Bundy), 157
   Nancy (Paul),157
CROUCH, Jefferson, 16
   Mary, 16
   Mary (Grey), 16
   Turner, 16
CROW, Mary, 170
   see also **CROWE**
CROWE, D Harry, 16
   Esther M, 16
   Jane, 16
   Mary Elizabeth (Hollingsworth), 16
   Milton, 16
   see also **CROW**
CRULL, Belle, 16
   Eliza, 172
   Irene O, 16
   Jacob, 16
   Margaret, 172
   Michael, 172
CRUMB, Ellen, 165
CRUMPTON, Dirinda, 190
   Sarah (Denny), 190
   see also **CRAMPTON**
CUBBYHOUS, Elizabeth (Anderson), 83
CULBERSON, Mary (Hoover), 83
   seee also **CULBERTSON**
CULBERTSON, Martha, 83
   Martha L, 16
   Samuel S, 16
   Samuel W, 16
   see also **CULBERSON**
CURES, Colvin H, 16
   Hazel C, 16
   Ida E, 16
CURL, Martha, 17
   Mattie, 84
CURRENT, Deborah Ann (Hodson), 74
   Rebecca M, 168
CURRY, Bessie, 16
   Isa, 16
   Isadora (Northern), 16
   John, 16
CUSHING, Caroline (Vale), 83

DABNEY, Caroline, 92
DAGGETT, Earl P, 16
DAILY, Lena, 190
   Matilda (Black), 83
   see also **DALEY**
DAKIN, Susannah, 50
   Edw T, 16

DAKIN, Herbert W, 16
   Jane W (Underhill), 16
   Jennie (Underhill), 190
   Martha J, 16
   Pheba J, 16
   Raymond B, 16
   Viola M, 16
   Walter L, 16
   Wm S, 16
DALBY, Hannah, 83
   Jennie U, 83
DALE, Cora Ellen, 157
   Margaret E (Koon), 157
   Samuel B, 157
DALEY, Ruth A, 83
   see also **DAILY**, **DALLY**
DALLEY, Hannah, 83
   see also **DAILY**, **DALEY**
DANIELS, Charles, 16
   Harrison, 157,162,176
   Joanna, 157,176
   Lewvera (Ridgeway), 16
   PherabyPheriba, 157,162,164,174,176
   Pheraby (Pierce), 157,162
   Theodore Marion, 16
DARLING, Almeda (Deerifield), 83
DAULIN, Bertha Jane, 45
   John, 45
   John, 45
   Mary C, 45
DAVENPORT, Alice, 16,59
   Alonzo, 16,83
   Anna, 14,40,119
   Anna A, 16,47
   Anna E, 83
   Bertha R, 16,83
   Caroline, 38,83
   Delphina (Grimes), 16
   Earl, 83
   Elizabeth, 83
   Ella, 83
   Emma, 16
   Ernest, 16,83
   Ezra, 83
   Florence, 83
   Franklin, 16
   George, 16,83
   George P, 83
   Jesse Elwood, 16,83
   John, 17,83
   Lula, 83
   Lula A, 83
   Lula/Lulu Hazel, 9,16
   Lula S, 83
   Malinda, 13,29,33
   Martha Elma, 83
   Martha Elma (Cook), 9,16
   Mary, 83
   Mary D, 16
   Myron Warner, 16
   Rachel Lurena, 17,83
   Rachel S, 83
   Rebecca, 47,83
   Rebecca Sr, 16
   Rebecca (Crampton), 16,59
   Richard Albert, 16,83
   Ruth R, 16
   Sarah Elizabeth, 83
   Sarah Elizabeth (Cook), 16
   Sarah Jane, 16,47
   Warner, 16,47,59,83
   Wm, 83
   Wm H, 83
   Wm Henry, 9,16,83
   see also **DEVENPORT**

DAVIDSON, Catharine H, 154,157
  F H, 159
  Fanny (Blount), 159
  Isaiah, 83
  Josiah, 83
  Rachel, 183
  Samuel, 83
  Zenora C, 159
  see also **DAVISSON**
DAVIS, Adam, 83
  Alfred, 157
  Alice (Mace), 17
  Alma N, 191
  Alpheus, 157,191
  Amanda, 83
  Amelia (Bond), 157,190
  Amos, 157,173,174,191
  Angelina, 17,83
  Ann/Anna, 83,150,157,184,190,191
  Ann (Coggshall), 17
  Anna L, 83,157
  Annie Pearl, 83
  Benjamin, 17,83
  Benjamin S, 157
  Beryl, 17
  Caroline, 157,191
  Caroline (Chamness), 154,157
  Caroline H (Chamness), 151,162
  Catharine/Catherine, 150,157
  Charlotte (Baldwin), 157
  Clara, 157
  Clarissa, 83
  Clarkson, 17,83
  Cynthia, 17
  Cyrus, 83
  Daniel, 157
  David, 83,190
  David H, 83
  David M, 17
  Earnest, 17
  Edom, 190
  Edom W, 157
  Eli, 157
  Elihu, 157
  Eliza Ann, 157
  Eliza Jane, 158,191
  Elizabeth, 83,157,190,192
  Elizabeth R, 157
  Ella J, 17,83
  Ella J (Jenkins), 17
  Elma Nora (Beeson), 157
  Emma, 191
  Emma (Allen), 157
  Esther, 163
  Esther Ann (Hill), 157,173,174,191
  Ethel, 17,83,157,191
  Ethel C, 157
  Eunice, 157
  Fannie, 45
  Florence Anna (Harrell), 17
  Freddie, 17
  Frederick L, 17
  George, 157,190
  Hannah, 5,157,183
  Hannah (Moore), 157
  Hannah E (Brown), 17,83
  Hannah E B, 83
  Hannah M, 191
  Harman/Harmon, 183,190
  Helen, 157
  Henry, 83
  Hezekiah, 17,83,157

DAVIS, Huldah (Hough), 190
  Isaac, 45,157
  Ivy J, 148
  James A, 157
  James Arthur, 191
  Jane, 157,210
  Jemima, 83,157
  Jesse, 17,190
  Jesse C, 157
  John, 5,83,151,154,157,162,170,190,
    201,204
  John H, 157
  Jonah, 83
  Jonah M, 17
  Jordan, 157
  Jordan R, 190
  Joseph, 83,150,157,184,190,191
  Joseph Alfred, 83
  Joseph S, 157
  Josephine, 17
  Katharine/Katherine, 184,190,191
  Keziah/Kezziah, 157,170,201
  Keziah (Bales), 190
  Laura, 191
  Laura M, 151,157
  Lavina/Levine, 157,174
  Leander, 157
  Levi, 157
  Lewis, 83,157
  Lewis H, 157
  Lizzie E, 157
  Lizzie G, 17,83
  Louisa, 191
  Louisa (Chamness), 157
  Louisa J, 157
  Love, 190
  Love (Barnard), 157
  Lydia, 157
  Lydia, 83
  Lydia (Maulsby), 190
  Lydia Ann, 157
  Mable F, 17
  Mahlon, 157
  Malinda, 157
  Margaret, 83
  Margaret J, 83
  Margaret J (Moorman), 17
  Maria L, 190
  Mariah S, 191
  Mark S, 157
  Martha, 83
  Martha E, 17
  Martha Ellen, 191
  Martha Ellen (Remington), 157,181
  Martha M, 148
  Mary, 5,83,157,179,184,204
  Mary (Boswell), 83
  Mary (Dean), 45
  Mary Ann, 181
  Mary B, 17
  Mary Elfleta, 83
  Mary Etta, 157,173,191
  Mary H, 17
  Mary J, 179
  Mary L, 157,162
  Mattie, 191
  Maude E (Shaffer), 157
  Miles, 157,191
  Millie, 157
  Nancy, 18,64,83,190,192
  Nancy D, 29
  Nancy E, 83,87

DAVIS, Nancy Jane (Cory), 157
  Nathan, 83,157,190
  Neziah, 157,190,191
  Nora (Farmer), 17
  Norton, 17
  Oda, 158,191
  Omar, 157
  Pearl, 83
  Perry, 157
  Phebe, 83
  Phebe Catherine, 157
  Rachel, 190,191
  Rachel, 191
  Rachel (Swain) Thornburg, 157
  Rachel (Thornburg), 190
  Rebecca, 147,152,190
  Rebecca (Taylor), 17
  Rebecca B, 17
  Robert, 83,190
  Robert James, 83
  Royal J, 17,83
  Ruby, 17,83
  Rufus, 191
  Rufus H, 17,157
  Ruth, 83,157,170,190,201,204
  Ruth (Mills), 190
  Sarah, 83,157,181
  Sarah (More), 83
  Sarah A, 13
  Sarah R, 83
  Serfina, 157
  Silas, 157,190
  Simeon, 190
  Spencer, 157,190
  Susannah, 157
  Tamar, 157
  Tamer (Brown), 190
  Thomas, 17,83,181
  Thomas C, 17
  Thomas Clarkson, 83
  Thomas M, 83,148,157
  Tristam/Tristram, 83,190
  Viretta, 158,181
  Virginia, 17
  Wm, 83,17,157,181,190,191,192
  Wm E, 83,157,191
  Wm Franklin, 157
  Wm H, 17
  Wm Harlan, 83
  Wm Henry, 83
  Wyllis/Wyllys, 17,83
DAVISSON, James A, 158
  Ora L, 158
  Rebecca M (Hiatt), 158
  see also **DAVIDSON**
DAWSON, James, 83
  James S, 83
DAY, Elbert H, 83
  Mary Elizabeth, 83
DE LOS RIOS, Alfredo, 17
  Maria M (Lavin), 17
  Pedro, 17
DEAN, Edith, 58
  Frank, 83
  Mary, 45
  Mary H, 58
  Phebe, 12
DEARDORF, John, 158
  Susan, 191
  Susan (Hockett), 158
DEARING, Austin O, 191
  Elizabeth, 191

DEARING, Linetta, 191
   Otto H, 191
   see also **DEERING, DERING**
DEEM, John Howard, 17
   Lydia (Petry), 17
   Wm J, 17
DEERIFIELD, Almeda, 83
DEERING, Alice, 191
   Elizabeth, 191,204
   John, 191
   Ottoway, 191
   see also **DEARING, DERING**
DELON, Aubrey D, 83
   Aubrey F, 83
   Horace J, 83
   Paul, 83
   Sarah, 83
   Sarah A, 83
   Wm, 83
DEMAREE, Amanda Alice, 9
   Eliza (Maudlin), 9
   Lewis, 9
DEMINE, Martha, 59
DENNA, Delila Susan, 191
   Jacob L B, 191
   Shubal, 191
   see also **DENNY**
DENNING, Sarah (Mills), 191
DENNIS, Abbie L, 17
   Abbie S, 84
   Absalom/Absolom, 158,159,187,191,198
   Alanson, 158
   Albert, 84
   Albert H, 17
   Albert L, 159
   Albert Oron, 84
   Alice J, 17,159
   Alice Jennie, 10
   Alison, 191
   Alpheus Lindley, 158
   Anna, 158,191
   Anna (Baldwin), 191
   Anna Routh, 158
   Anna T, 158
   Arthel J, 159
   Asenath, 158,211
   Bartlet/Bartlett, 158,191
   Benjamin, 84
   Branson, 17,147,150,158,159,178,184, 191,208
   Carl Clinton, 158
   Caroline, 84
   Caroline (Williams), 17,84
   Carrie (Burroughs), 159
   Carrie A, 158
   Charles C, 17,84
   Charley Walter, 158
   Clara E (Thomas), 17
   Clarkson, 158,159,191
   Clarky (Pool), 84
   Cordelia (Chamness), 158
   Cynthia, 159,161,170,171,202
   Cynthia Emaline/Emeline, 156,158
   Daisy Odena, 158
   David, 158,191
   David A, 17,158
   David W, 84,191
   David Worth, 17,158
   Delilah, 158,159,191,198
   Delilah M, 158,198
   Dempsey E, 17,191
   Dempsey Thomas, 158

DENNIS, Edwin, 158,191
   Elisha, 158,159,191,195
   Eliza May, 17
   Elizabeth, 154
   Elizabeth, 156,159,164,166,177,180,188, 191,202,204,208
   Elizabeth (Brooks), 17
   Elizabeth (Wilson), 154,158,159,171,172
   Elizabeth S, 158
   Elma, 184,208
   Elma (Reynolds), 147,150,189,159,178
   Elma Millicent, 17
   Elma Millicent (Mills), 17
   Emily, 159,191
   Emily (Peebles), 191
   Emma, 192
   Eunice, 158,159,187,191,198
   Evalina/Evelina (Worth), 117,158,191
   Evelina, 191
   Fanny, 150,151,155,159
   Fidella F, 159,191
   Flavia, 191
   Flavia S, 158,187
   Flora, 194
   Flora T, 158
   Frank, 17
   Frank Vernon, 158
   George Prentice, 158,159
   Glenn S, 17
   Grace D Irena, 17
   Grace E, 192
   Grace Ermadine, 158
   H Cecil, 17
   Hannah, 84,158
   Hannah M, 191,192
   Hansel B, 159
   Harrison, 17
   Harrison S, 84
   Harry S, 17
   Hazel, 17
   Henry C, 158,191
   Henry Carver, 191
   Horace Cecil, 159
   Howard T, 17
   Ida Mary/May, 63,84
   Ina Bell, 158
   Irena, 194
   Irena/Irene (Thornburg), 8,152,156, 158, 161,191
   Isaac Lindley, 158,159
   Isaac N, 191
   Isaac Newton, 158,191
   J, 63
   James, 191
   Jennie, 192
   Jennie (Woolard), 158
   Jesse, 158,159,191
   Jessie W, 84
   Job E, 158,192
   John, 17,84,158,191
   John Henry, 158
   John Warren, 159,191
   Joseph Branson, 158
   Joseph Forrest, 17
   Josie (Lynn), 158
   Julia Ann (Reynolds), 158
   Julian, 158
   Lindsay/Lindsey/Linsey/Lyndsey, 8, 152, 156,158,159,161,191,194
   Lizzie E, 192
   Lizzie Ettie (Routh), 158
   Lora Hazel, 159

DENNIS, Louisa, 148,150,158,167,184,191
   Louisa (Beeson), 158,167,168
   Louisa (Canaday), 158,159,176
   Lucinda, 50,159,161,166,172,173,175, 177,204
   Lucy Ann, 17,191
   Lucy Ann (Peebles), 159,191
   Luzena C, 158
   Lydia, 152,159,191,192
   Lydia (Reynolds), 158,159,191
   Mabel N, 17,159
   Mahlon, 158,159,167,168,191
   Margaret, 158
   Margaretta, 159
   Maria L, 158
   Martha (Curl), 17
   Martha Ann, 84
   Martha Jane, 158,161,194
   Mary, 17,84,158,160,191
   Mary (Lamar), 158,159,160
   Mary Ann/Anna, 8,152,158
   Mary E, 191,192
   Mary Esther, 158
   Mary Evaline, 159,176
   Mary Jane, 159
   Matilda, 50
   Matilda C, 164,191,195
   Matilde Carolina, 158
   Melinda, 158,158,191,192
   Melinda (Dennis), 158
   Melinda C, 191
   Milicent, 191
   Millicent M (Mills), 159
   Minnie, 192
   Minnie (Burroughs), 159
   Minnie B (Borroughs), 17
   Miriam, 57,158,159,191
   Miriam C, 158,208
   Nathan, 17,158,159,160,191
   Nathan D, 191
   Nellie M, 192
   Newton, 158
   Olive Blanch, 159
   Oliver, 192
   Oliver L, 158
   Orland/Orlando W, 158,191
   Osborn, 158,159,176,191
   Osborn Earl, 159
   Phebe Jane, 147,158,183
   Rachel, 152
   Rachel (Thornburg/Thornburgh), 159, 166,191
   Rebecca, 158,168,191
   Rosa, 192
   Rosettie (Bookout), 158
   Royal A, 158
   Royal Arlistes, 191
   Rufus, 192
   Russell Lee, 158
   Ruth, 158,191,195,211
   Samuel P, 17,159
   Sarah, 34,57,133,158,159,178,208
   Sarah Alice, 158
   Sarah Ann, 84
   Sarah E, 159
   Sarah E (Thornburg), 10,17,191
   Susan, 17,159,191
   Susanna (Main), 158
   Susannah, 84
   Sylvia L, 159
   Thomas, 10,17,154,158,159,171,172, 188,191,202,204,208

DENNIS, Thomas C, 158,159,191
    Thomas E, 159
    Thomas P, 17
    Thomas R, 84
    Tilman/Tilmon, 158,191
    Unity, 158
    Viola (Thompson), 158,192
    Viola T, 192
    W H, 192
    Willie F, 84
    Wilson, 152,158,159,166,191
    Wilson H, 17,158,159
    Wm, 158,159
    Wm Jr, 191
    Zenora C, 191
    Zenora C (Davidson), 159
    Zeruah/Zeruiah, 158,191
    Zeruiah W, 191
DENNISON, Emma, 84
    Emma D, 36
    Mary (Stradlin), 36
    Wm H, 36
DENNY, Asariah, 84
    Delilah, 202
    Delilah S, 202
    Delilah Susan, 159
    Doritha (Jenkins) Huff, 192
    Dorothy, 159
    Elizabeth, 84
    Gordon, 84
    Jacob B, 192
    Jacob L, 159
    John, 84
    Lazarus, 84,192
    Lewis Marion, 159
    Margaret, 159,192
    Margaret Esther, 159
    Mary Lucinda, 159
    Mary T, 192
    Michael, 84
    Rebecca, 84
    Sarah, 84,190
    Sarah C, 159,192
    Shubal, 84,159,192
    Susanna/Susannah, 84,192
    Wm, 84
    Wm Alonzo, 159
    see also **DENNA**
DEPOY, Eleanor, 159
    Elta A, 159
    Solomon, 159
DERING, Alice C (Hay), 159
    Anton, 159
    Austin O, 159,192
    Elizabeth, 159,192
    Fredrick, 159
    John, 192
    Josiel, 159
    Lisetta, 192
    Lisetta (Newman), 159
    Otto, 159
    Otto H, 192
    see also **DEARING, DEERING**
DEVENPORT, Rebecca (Rue), 84
    see also **DAVENPORT**
DEVERS, Hedgman Butler, 159
    Martha Ann (Pidgeon), 159
    Nancy (Giles), 159
    Wm, 159
DEWEES, Hannah (Hartley), 84
    Hannah F, 84
    see also **DEWEESE**

DEWEESE, David, 17
    James, 17
    see also **DEWEES**
DEXTER, Harry, 17
    Margaret (Bell), 17
    Walter Friar, 17
DICK, Gurney H, 192
    see also **DICKS**
DICKENSON, Alice, 84
    Charles, 84
    Charles S, 84
    Edmund, 84
    Elias Hicks, 84
    Esther G, 84
    George, 84
    Grace, 84
    Henry, 84
    Isaac L, 84
    James P, 84
    Jane, 84
    Jonathan, 84
    Sarah (Pool), 84
    Solomon, 84
    Solomon Jr, 84
    see also **DICKINSON**
DICKINSON, Alice, 17,84
    Alice H, 17
    Alice Hunt, 84
    Alice Rebecca, 17
    Ann E, 34
    Benajah, 84
    Benajah H, 84
    Charles, 17,84
    Edmund, 84
    Elisabeth/Elizabeth, 17,54,84
    Elizabeth (Kenworthy), 84
    Ellen H, 34
    Ellen Marie, 18
    Ellen W, 103
    Ellen Winder, 17
    Elma May, 17
    Esther, 88
    Esther G, 84
    Esther G (Hiatt), 17,18,21,61
    Frederick U, 18
    George, 17,84
    Grace, 84
    Hannah, 17,21,44,84,88
    Hannah F, 17,84
    Hannah W, 84
    Henry, 84
    Henry W, 84
    Hylie W (Barnes), 17
    Irene, 18
    Isaac L, 84
    James H, 17,103
    James Hunt, 17,18,84
    Jane, 84
    Jane Ann (Clawson), 17
    John, 84
    John Pool, 17
    Jonathan, 17,84
    Joseph, 17,18,21,61,84,88,103
    Joseph Howard, 17
    Joseph John, 17,84
    Joshua Ingle, 17
    Laura F, 84
    Laura F (Ullrick), 17,18
    Maria, 17,61
    Martha Elma (Cadwallader), 17,84
    Mary J, 103
    Mary J (Winder), 17,18

DICKINSON, Mary Jane, 17
    Mary Jane (Winder), 84
    Minnie Bell, 17
    Oliver White, 84
    Otho K, 17,18
    Phenia, 84
    Robert B/R, 17,84
    Samuel, 17,18,84
    Sarah, 17,84
    Solomon, 84
    Susan P, 84
    W Sophia (Gause), 18
    Wm Huntley/Hurtley, 17,18,84
    Wm P, 17
    see also **DICKENSON**
DICKS, Elizabeth, 84
    Ezekiel, 84
    Jemima (Vestal), 84
    Jonathan, 84
    Lydia, 84
    Mary, 84
    Nathan, 84
    Peter, 84
    Rachel, 84
    Rebeckah, 84
    Ruth, 84
    Wm, 84
    Zachariah/Zacharius, 84
    see also **DICK, DIX**
DIFFENDORFER, Elizabeth, 18
    Elizabeth B (Cranford),18,30
    Frederick, 30
DILHORN, Ann E, 84
    Ann Eliza, 18,139
    Ann Mariah, 18,84
    Eleanor/Elenor, 18,84,126
    George, 18,84
    George Chalkley, 18
    James, 18,84
    James G, 84
    Joshua, 84
    Joshua W, 18
    Mary J, 84
    Mary Jane, 18,84
    Robert, 18,84
    Robert M, 84
    Sarah, 84
    Wilson, 18,84
    Wm, 84
    Wm G, 18
DILKS, Alice J, 84
    Alice Jane (Hill), 61
    Anna B (Shoemaker), 18,84
    Anna Jane (Hill), 18
    Annie G, 18,84
    Charles S, 18
    Dorothy E, 18
    Elizabeth, 84
    Elizabeth C, 6,18,71
    Ethel (Woodard), 18
    George, 6,19,32,53,62,84,102,139
    George H, 18,84
    George R, 84
    George Russel/Russell, 18,61,84
    Grace R, 18,61,84
    Hannah, 100
    Hannah (Richie), 6,32,62
    Hannah H, 84,102,139
    Hannah H (Richie), 18
    Hannah H (Richie), 32,53
    Hannah H Jr 18,62,84
    Harrie R, 18

DILKS, Harrie T, 84
    Phebe, 84
    Rachel J, 18,53,84,127
    Sarah, 32,54
    Sarah (Scarce), 18
    Sarah Ellen, 18,32
    Sarah S, 102
    Sarah S, 84,102
    Sidney/Sydney, 18,25,26,32,84,102
    Wm W, 18,84
    Wm W Jr, 18
DILL, Laura, 84
    Laura S (Henley), 18
    Wm, 18
    see also **DILLE**
DILLE, Anna (Morris), 18
    Clarkson D, 18
    James, 18
    Lizzie Loretta (Russell), 18
    see also **DILL**
DILLEN, Margaret, 41
DILLER, Anna, 55
    Margaret (Frey), 55
    Isaac, 55
DILLINGER, Eric, 192
DILLMAN, Adam, 18
    Mary, 18
    Wm, 18
DILTS, Phebe (Lane), 18,84
DIMMET, Alice, 85
DINES, Elizabeth (Wadman), 159
    Jackson, 159
    Nancy (Hutchens), 159,192
    Silas G, 159,192
DINGLEY, Edward Charles, 18,85
    Elizabeth A, 85
    Elizabeth Ann, 18,52
    Henry J, 18,52,85
    Lydia Sarah, 85
    Lydia Sarah (Haines), 18,52
    Stephen G, 85
    Stephen George, 18
    Wm Henry, 18,85
DINGMAN, Otto, 85
DISINGER, Alice Vestina, 166
    John, 166
    Margaret J (Widener), 166
DITCH, Catherine, 160
DIX, Elizabeth, 85
    Elizabeth (Baldwin), 28
    Ezekiel, 85
    Jemima, 85
    John, 85
    Jonathan, 85
    Joshua, 28
    Lydia 87
    Peter, 85
    Rhoda, 28
    Ruth, 30
    Zachariah, 85
    see also **DICKS**
DIXON, Amanda, 29
    Calvin, 85
    Eli, 1
    Elmer P, 85
    Hannah, 85,159
    J Fulton, 18
    Janetta/Jeanetta S, 85
    Kezia/Keziah, 85
    Letitia/Lutitia Ann, 85
    Mahlon, 18
    Mary, 85

DIXON, Rebecca, 18
    Rosa Jane, 85
    Sarah, 85,159
DOAN, Alice J, 18,56,85
    Allen J, 18
    Amos, 192
    Ann Elizabeth (Downing), 85
    Anna E (Downing), 18
    Anna Eliz, 56
    Anna M, 18
    Annie E (Downing), 45
    Clifford G, 18
    Clifford T, 85
    Deborah, 85
    Deborah E (Taylor), 18
    Deborah Elizabeth, 18
    Ebenezar, 85
    Eliza, 85
    Eliza (Carpenter), 18,24
    Eliza (Hadley), 113
    Elizabeth, 18,85
    Elya, 18
    Emily H (Coale), 18
    Enos L, 192
    Ephraim, 85
    Fanny E, 85
    Frances E, 18,45
    Harrison J, 18,85
    Harry C, 18
    Isaac, 18,85
    Jemima, 18,24,41,49
    Jonathan, 85
    Joseph, 18,24,85
    Joseph E, 18
    Joseph Wayne, 18
    Louisa, 192
    Martha, 192
    Mary, 18,30,85
    Mary F (Conner), 18
    Mary Kate, 85
    Mary Louisa (Clark), 192
    Mary Z, 18
    Matilda, 85
    Nathan, 18,45,56,85
    Priscilla M (Macy), 18
    Rachel, 85
    Sarah, 85
    Walter J, 18,85
    Wendell P, 18
    Wilmot M, 18
    Wm, 85
DODD, Frank S, 18
    Helen Lucille, 18
    Mary, 29
    Nellie B, 18
DODGE, Sarah (Lewis), 85
DOHERTY, Mary, 192
    see also **DOUGHERTY**
DOLBY, Jennie M, 192
DONLIN, Cora Mead (Lunsford), 18
    Wm, 18
DORAN, Milo Verner, 18
    see also **DOREN**
DOREN, Lida, 85
    Louella M, 85
    Otto, 85
    see also **DORAN**
DORIS, Margaret, 160
DORLAND, John P, 18
    Lavina (Hubbs), 18
    Margaret H, 18
    Martha N, 85

DORSEY, Albert, 85
    Emma, 85
    James, 85
    James R, 85
    Josephine, 85
    Josephine (Walker), 18
    Kezia, 85
    Sylvester, 85
DOUGAN, David H, 19
    Rosa (Lamb), 19
    see also **DUGAN**
DOUGHERTY, Alice S, 85
    Alonzo, 159
    Alva, 85
    Ann, 90
    Anna M, 85
    Charles, 85
    Elmer, 85
    Exalina (Williams), 159
    Francis, 85
    Francis L, 85
    John, 85
    Lizzie, 85
    Martha Ann, 85,90
    Nancy, 90
    Pearl, 85
    Raymond, 85,159,192
    Thomas, 90
    see also **DOHERTY**
DOUGHMAN, Daniel, 160
    Eve, 160
    Patience Ann, 160
DOUGLAS, Cornelius, 85
    Ettam 19
    Hattie, 19
    Mary, 85
    Phebe, 85
    Samuel, 19
DOVE, Isaac, 85
DOWEL, Delphiam 152,153
    Peter, 153
    see also **DOWELL**
DOWELL, Elvira, 176
    Olephia Troy, 176
    see also **DOWEL**
DOWLES, Millie, 19
DOWNING, Ann Elizabeth, 85
    Anna/Annie E, 18,45
    Eleanor, 85,86
    Harry C, 19
    James L, 19
    Jane, 85
    Lula (Teague), 19
    Margaret, 85
    Margaret L, 85
    Mary E (Hunnicutt), 85
    Minnie J, 19
    Otto Forest, 19
    Sarah, 85
    Susan, 85
    Susannah, 86
    Vesta, 154
DOYLE, Mary, 82
    Mary W, 85
    Mary W (Test), 82
DRAKE, Ada J (Bales), 159
    Carlton N, 85
    Edgar, 19
    Edgar J, 85
    Elizabeth, 159
    Joseph W, 192
    Joseph Wilson, 159

DRAKE, Julia A, 85
    Moses, 159
    Olivia S, 85
    Olivia S (Mendenhall), 85
    Olivia Stevens (Mendenhall), 19
DRAPER, Aaron, 85
    Achsa, 85
    Bell (Ward), 19
    Berneice, 85
    Charles E, 19,85
    Don H, 19,85
    Elizabeth, 85
    Hannah, 85
    Homer G, 19,85
    Jemima, 85
    John, 85
    Joshua, 85
    Josiah, 85
    Josiah Jr, 85
    Mary, 85
    Mary Ann, 85
    Oswin, 85
    Peter, 85
    Rachel, 64
    Rebekah, 85
    Sally, 85
    Susan Bernice (Nordyke), 19
    Susan Bernice N, 85
    Sylvester, 19
    Sylvester W, 85
    Thomas, 85
    Wm, 85
    Sarah, 85
    Daniel, 85
DRULEY, Joseph S, 19
    Mary R, 19
    T Hollie W, 19
    see also **DRULY**
DRULY, Rachel (Bonine), 85
    see also **DRULEY**
DRURY, Rachel, 85
    Wm, 85
DUGAN, Rosanna (Lamb), 85
    see also **DOUGAN**
DUGDALE, Benjamin, 19
    Charles Coffin, 19
    Edward, 86
    Edward W, 86
    Edward Wm, 19
    Eleanor (Downing), 86
    Elisabeth/Elizabeth, 19,86
    Elizabeth W, 86
    Elwood W, 86
    Hanna/Hannah Marie/Maria, 19,86
    Hannah, 19,86
    Harriet Ida, 19,86
    Horace, 86
    Horace L, 19
    Ida, 86
    James K, 86
    Margaret AinsleyAnnesley/Annesly, 19, 86
    Rachel Elmira, 19
    Rachel S, 86
    Rachel Scott, 86
    Samuel, 19,86
    Sarah, 86,109
    Susannah, 19
    Susannah (Downing), 86
    Thomas, 19
    Wm Annesley, 19

DUKE, James, 19,86
    John, 19
    Marila/Marilla (Beeson), 192
    Miriam (Alred), 19
    Ora O, 19
    Ruth, 86
    Ruth A (Lamb), 19
DUMM, Ann, 19
    Etta, 19
    Noah, 19
DUNBAR, Elizabeth, 147
DUNN, Elizabeth, 161
DWIGGINS, James F, 86
    Moses F, 19,86
    see also **DWIGINS**
DWIGINS, Mary, 86
    see also **DWIGGINS**
DYKEMAN, Elizabeth, 19
    Floyd, 19
    Sarah, 19
DYMOND, Charles, 86
DYSON, Agnes Ann, 86
    Eleanor, 86
    Mason, 86
    Sarah Wilhelmina, 86
    Wm, 86

EARL, Mary (Hawkins), 86
EAST, Ann/Anna, 86
    Ann (Lee), 86
    Anna (Osborn), 159
    Anne (Jones), 86
    Edom, 19,86
    Hannah, 19,72
    Hannah (Bonine), 73
    Isom, 19,86
    Jacob, 86,159
    Jacob T, 19,86
    James, 19
    James, 86
    James Milten/Milton, 19,86
    Jesse, 19,86
    Joel, 19,86
    John, 19,86
    John C, 19
    Martha, 19,86
    Martha Ann, 19,86
    Martha Jane, 19,86
    Polly, 19,86
    Rachel, 19,72,86
    Rebecca/Rebeckah, 19,86
    Sally, 19,86
    Sarah, 19,86
    Susanna/Susannah, 19,86
    Thomas, 19,86
    Thomas, 86
    Wm, 72,86
    Wm Sr, 19
    Wm H, 19
EAVES, Eliza, 160
    Joel, 160
    John, 159,192
    Martha, 160
    Mary K, 159
    Richard, 160
    Thomas, 160
    Wm, 160
    see also **EVES**
EBRIGHT, Wm B, 192
    see also **EBRITE**
EBRITE, Arthur P, 160
    Charles D, 160
    David O, 160

EBRITE, James O, 160
    Mary (Dennis), 160
    Nathan Erwin, 160
    Wm, 192
    Wm B, 160
    see also **EBRIGHT**
ECHELBARGER, Christena E, 192
EDGAR, Annie (Levering), 36
    Ella, 36
    H L, 36
EDGERTON, Abigail, 86,94
    Abigail (Stratton), 19,26
    Alice, 125
    Alice J, 86
    Anne (Frazier), 86
    Calvin, 19,86
    Caroline (Osborn), 192
    Charles, 19,86
    Charles F, 86
    Charles Roger, 19
    Chauncey W, 19
    Daniel, 19,86
    Eleanor/Elenora/Elnora, 86
    Elenora L, 19
    Eli, 86
    Eliza Ann, 19,86
    Elizabeth, 19,86,137,179
    Elizabeth Ann, 86
    Elizabeth C, 86
    Ellen, 19,51,86,125
    Ellen (Cockayne), 86
    Emily C, 19
    Emma C, 86
    Jane, 86
    Jonathan, 19
    Joseph, 86,88
    Joseph Jr, 86
    Lois (Weeks), 19
    Margaret, 19,86
    Martha, 86,88
    Mary, 19,86
    Mary Ann/Maryann, 86
    Mary C, 86
    Mary Elizabeth, 19,86
    Mary Jane, 86
    Mary T, 86
    Nathan, 19
    Nelly, 86
    Oliver, 19
    Owen, 19,86
    Phillip Russell, 19
    Rachel, 19,86
    Ruth A (Rogers), 19
    Ruth C, 19
    Ruthanna, 86
    Samuel, 19,86
    Sarah, 86,94
    Sarah E, 19,26
    Sarah Jane, 128
    Susan, 19,86
    Susan L, 86
    Susan M, 86
    Susanna, 19
    Thomas, 86
    Thomas S, 19
    Wm, 19,26,86,94,125
    Wm Jr, 86
    Wm H, 86
    Wm Osborn, 86
    Wm P, 86
    Wm T, 86

EDMUNDSON, Susan (Wright), 86
EDWARDS, Alice (Shaw), 160
    Anna, 32,52
    Anna J (Showalter), 19
    Asa, 86
    Beaulah/Beulah, 86
    Bertha, 32
    Charity, 86
    David, 44
    Delilah, 86
    Dorcas, 18
    Elizabeth, 86
    Elizabeth H, 86
    Elizabeth J, 86
    Emma E, 11,154,160,163
    Eva Celestia (Clark), 160
    Evelyn, 19
    Harlan, 32
    Henry J, 160,192
    Ira, 86
    John, 19,86
    John Jr, 86
    Josiah P, 86
    Marjorie, 19
    Martha, 44
    Mildred, 19
    Morton, 160
    Nathan, 192
    Nathan F, 160
    Netta E, 44
    Oscar, 160
    Rebecca (Pierce), 160,163
    Rebecca Mason, 86
    Rena E, 160
    Temple, 160,163
EIDSON, James, 19,86
EIKENBURY, Joseph, 28
    Leona B, 28
    Marie (Young), 28
ELDER, Eunice E, 160,192
    James, 86
    Susannah, 86
ELIASON, Emma, 86
ELLEMAN, Aidee E, 20
    Dorcas, 38
    Enos, 19,20
    Enos Clifford, 19
    Isom, 19,20
    John H, 20
    Joseph Alton, 19,20
    Lydia Emeline (Hawkins), 20
    Margaret (Ward), 19,20
    Orpha, 19
    Phebe (Coate), 19,20
    Rosa E (Thornton), 20
    Ruth, 20
    Sarah, 206
    Thomas, 19,20
ELLIOTT, Aaron, 37
    Abraham, 87
    Absolam, 87
    Ada E, 37
    Alice, 87
    Alluria F (Morgan), 20
    Amelia (Huff), 6
    Ann/Anna, 2,20,87
    Armella (Hinshaw), 148
    Avis Jane (Irish), 87
    Axiom/Axion, 87
    Benjamin, 22,72,87
    Bertha, 58
    Buffum, 192

ELLIOTT, Caroline, 20
    Catharine, 87
    Claude C, 160
    David, 87
    Davis, 20
    Deidea/Deiduma, 87,127
    Delphina M, 20,87
    Delphina Mendenhall, 87
    E Warren, 20,87
    Edith, 2
    Elias, 20,24,25,87
    Eliza E, 6
    Elizabeth, 87
    Ellen H, 20
    Elvey/Elvy, 72,87
    Elvira, 87
    Elwood, 20,87
    Escum/Exum, v,20,47
    Esther, 2,10
    Esther S, 87
    Gulamy/Gulana, 1,87
    Hannah, 87,148,170
    Hannah (Cobb), 20
    Hattie A, 20
    Henry C, 87
    Henry E, 87
    Hetta Ann, 87
    Hettia/Hettie A, 20,87
    Huldah, 20
    Isaac, 20,87
    Isaiah, 87
    Israel, 1,2
    J Harry, 20,87
    Jacob, 2,3,20,58,86,87
    James, 20
    Jane, 20,42,87,114,179,114
    Job, 87
    John, 20,87
    John B, 20,87
    Jonathan, 6,87
    Joseph, 20,87
    Katherine (Lamb), 20,87
    Kizzie, 87
    Kizzie M, 87
    Lydia, 179
    Maria, 10
    Mark, 20,87
    Martha (Carr), 192
    Martha (Sander/Sanders), 20,25
    Martha M, 20,87
    Mary, 87
    Mary E, 47
    Mary Jane, 20,24,25,87
    Maud M, 20,87
    Melinda, 87
    Miles, 20
    Minerva, 58
    Minnia (Thorne), 58
    N (Thomas), 3
    Nathan, 20,87
    Nevada May, 3
    Obadiah, 148
    Ola (Carpenter), 160
    Olive, 2,87
    Rachel (Hixon), 22
    Rebecca E, 22
    Rebeckah/Rebekah, 20,87
    Rhoda (Mendenhall), 37
    Robert Hill, 20
    Ruth, 86
    Samuel, 20
    Sarah, 20,72,87

ELLIOTT, Sarah A, 11
    Sarah Ellen, 20
    Sarah Ellen (Hawkins), 20
    Stephen, 20,87
    Susannah, 87
    Ursley/Ursula, 20,87
    Wellmet/Wilmet, 2,87
    Wm P, 87
    Woodgie Ray, 20
    Zilpah/Zilpha, 20,47
    see also **ELLOT**
ELLIS, Alzina (Gregg), 20
    Arthur W, 87
    Arthur Wilson, 20
    Charity, 45
    Chester Johnson, 20
    Cressie, 87
    Delilah, 160,192
    Delilah (Runnels), 192
    Dora M, 87
    Edith, 160
    Edna (Cook), 20
    Ellwood/Elwood O, 20,87
    Elsworth, 20
    Estella, 20
    George A, 87
    Ida (Hussey), 20
    Ida H, 87
    Isaac, 20
    J O, 20
    James, 160,192
    James A, 192
    Jane (Ozbun), 20
    Jesse, 173
    Keziah, 160,192
    Lucinda, 160
    Margaret Ann, 176
    Martha, 160
    Martha E (Roberts), 20
    Mary, 3,160,171,192
    Mary Jane, 173
    Mordecai, 160,171,192
    Nathan D, 160
    Nehemiah, 160,192
    Rachel, 173
    Rebecca, 160,190,192
    Ruth, 160
    Ruth (Hinshaw), 171
    Ruth (Lamar), 192
    Ruth (Lee), 160
    Samuel, 160,192
    Sarah, 160
    Sarah R, 160
    Susan, 79,87
    Susannah, 192
    Susannah (Lewis), 192
    W H, 20
ELLISON, Nannie (Kirkman), 87
ELLMORE, Adeline, 87
    Benjamin, 87
    Elizabeth, 87
    Wm Allen, 87
    see also **ELMORE**
ELLOT, Ruffin, 192
    see also **ELLIOTT**
ELMORE, Adaline/Adeline, 18,20,23,37,
      38,109
    Anna P, 87
    Benjamin, 20,63,87,192
    Charles, 20
    Charles B, 87
    Edgar G, 20,87

ELMORE, Elihu Arlington, 20,87
    Elizabeth, 20,63,87
    Elvin C, 20,87
    Keziah, 87
    Keziah (Gifford), 20,87
    Mary Almeda/Almedia, 20,63,87
    Minnie J, 87
    Minnie Jesse, 20
    Sarah E, 20,87
    Wm A, 87
    Wm Allen, 20
    see also **ELLMORE**
ELTON, Clara, 20
    Frank, 20
    Robert W, 20
ELWOOD, Mary A, 41
    Mary K, 87
EMERSON, Edith, 87
EMERY, Herbert Clarke, 20
    Louisa Winifred (White), 20
EMMAL, Mary, 192
EMMONS, Mary, 7,37
ENDSLEY, Bessie Pormelia, 41
    Eli, 41
    Sarah, 87
    Sarah (Ham), 41
    Sarah S, 87
ENGLE, Edith, 160
    Hannah (Stetler), 160
    Phebe, 87
    Rebecca (Whitacre), 87
    Samuel, 160
    Thomas S, 160,192
ENGLEBERT, John, 20
    Leonard C, 20
    Louisa (Hirshfield), 20
ENNIS, Sarah, 59
ENOCH, Arthur W, 20
    Elizabeth, 20
    James, 20
EPPERLY, Lydia (Dix), 87
ERNEST, Ellen, 87
    Pearl L, 87
ERWIN, Alice, 128
    Edwin, 87
    Elizabeth, 87
    George, 87
    John, 87
    John Jr, 87
    Samuel, 87
    Samuel Edwin, 87
    Susanna, 87
    Wm Platt, 87
ESTELL, Clarabel, 87
    Fanny, 87
    Richard, 87
    Ruth, 87
ESTES, Betsey/Betsy, 20,87
    Huldah C, 87
    Huldah C, 20,87
    Ludovic, 20,87
    Thomas, 20,87
    Thomas Rowland, 20,87
EUBANK, Charles, 20
    Hannah Ann (King), 15
    Magdalen, 15
    Stella, 20
    Thomas, 15
    Wilbur Charles, 20
EVAN, Elizabeth, 87
    see also **EVANS**

EVANS, Achsah, 87
    Annie B, 18,65,142
    Bertha, 49
    Catharine, 16,26
    Catherine (Ditch), 160
    Daniel, 87
    Deborah, 20
    Edna B (Pyle), 20
    Eli W, 49
    Elizabeth, 92
    Elizabeth W (Moore), 87
    Esther, 87
    Esther (Hiatt), 20
    Flora B, 20
    Frederick Charles, 20
    George B, 20
    George H, 20
    Hannah, 75,87
    Hannah (Pedrick), 10,15,20,36
    Isaac, 87
    Isaac P, 20,62,87,142
    James, 192
    Jesse, 20,87
    Jesse Jr, 20
    John, 87,192
    Juretee/Jurettee/Juretta, 20,75,87
    Laura A, 192
    Lela (Wheeler), 20
    Lydia E, 15,20
    Margaret E, 10,20
    Martha, 192
    Mary, 20,36,45,64
    Mary Ann, 87,142
    Mary Ann (Buffum), 20,65,87
    Mary C (Cooper), 49
    Mary E, 20,35
    Mary Matilda, 20
    Mary P, 36,65
    Milly, 87
    Mourning, 87
    Nancy (Davis), 192
    Nancy E, 192
    Nancy Ellen, 192
    Nancy Ellen (Conway), 160
    Owen, 87
    Pleasant Newby, 20
    Rachel, 87
    Resden/Risden/Risdon, 20,87
    Rian/Ryan, 20,87
    Sarah, 26,54,87
    Sarah Charlotte, 20
    Sarah Jane (Thornburg), 192
    Thomas, 10,15,20,36,75,87
    Wm, 192
    Wm H, 160
    Wm Ryan, 87
    Zenas, 160
    see also **EVAN**, **EVINS**
EVES, Anna V, 20
    John E, 20
    Lillian, 20
    Sadie H, 20
    see also **EAVES**
EVINS, Lydia, 87
    see also **EVANS**
EWART, Annie Deweese, 160
    John, 160
    Margaret (Doris), 160

FAHLSING, Caroline, 20
    Lewis Edward, 20
    Wm, 20

FALL, Anna (Leedy), 32
    Anna R, 32
    John, 32
FARIS, Lydia M, 193
FARLOW, Alice, 87
    Ann, 87
    Arron E, 160
    Blanch L, 193
    Blanche, 160
    Carrie (Helm), 160
    Charley, 160
    Clara E, 160,193
    Claude, 160
    Colfax, 193
    David L, 193
    David Lindsey, 160,193
    Deborah, 87
    Edwin, 193
    Enoch, 160
    Enoch Lewis, 160
    Flora B (Pierce), 160
    George, 87
    Henry, 160
    Hiram, 87
    John, 87
    John F, 193
    John Franklin, 160,193
    Jonathan, 87
    Joseph, 87
    Lewezer/Luezer, 193
    Lorenzo, 193
    Lorenzo D, 160
    Louisa (Beckerdite), 156,160
    Mary, 160
    Myrtle, 193
    Myrtle Lenora, 160
    Nancy, 193
    Nancy Roxanna, 156,160
    Nathan, 87
    Rachel, 21,87
    Roxanne, 193
    Ruth, 87
    S C, 193
    Sarah V, 193
    Schuyler Colfax, 160,193
    Serena L (Canaday), 160
    Simon, 87
    W S, 193
    Wm Edwin, 160
    Wm S, 156,160,193
    see also **FARLOWE**
FARLOWE, Wm S, 193
    see also **FARLOW**
FARMER, Albert, 160
    Charles E, 160
    Clarence R, 160
    Henry, 21
    Herbert J, 21
    Jemima, 193
    John, 193
    Luzena, 193
    Lydia, 1,190
    Macy A, 160
    Margaret A, 21
    Mary E, 160
    Matilda, 160
    Matilda (Macy), 193
    Melinda C, 160
    Michael, 1
    Moses, 193
    Nathan, 193
    Nora, 17

FARMER, Orpha W, 160
   Rhoda, 1
   Rhoda H, 1
FARNHAM, C, 21
   Mary B (Johnson), 21
FARQUAR, Francis, 88
   Hannah, 88
   Harriett A, 88
   Henry B, 88
   Milton J, 88
   see also **FARQUHAR**
FARQUHAR, Francis, 88
   Frank, 193
   Hannah Ann, 88
   Harriett A, 88
   Henry B, 88
   Josie, 193
   Milton J, 88
   see also **FARQUAR**
FARRAR, Grace (Baker), 21
FAUCETT, Emmett, 21
   Susan, 21
   Thomas, 21
   see also **FOSSETT**
FAULKNER, Abigail M, 88
   Daniel C, 21,88
   Judith, 13
FEAR, Charles E, 160
   Della M (Cox), 160
   Sarah A, 160
   Wm L, 160
FEASAL, Vesta Ann, 88
   see also **FEASEL, FESEL**
FEASEL, Ann, 4
   Anna Lora, 21
   Annie S, 21,88
   Charles B, 21
   Ella, 21
   Jacob, 88
   Jacob D, 21
   Josiah, 4,21,88
   Laurence McF, 21
   Mary Elizabeth, 4,21
   Nellie M, 21
   Sarah I (Lamb), 21
   Vesta Ann, 88
   see also **FEASAL, FESEL**
FEATHERLING, Emmaline, 181
FEEZER, Erma, 21
   James H, 21
   Margaret, 21
FELLOW, Abigail, 88
   John, 88
   Mary, 88
   Price, 88
   Rachel, 88
   Robert, 88
   Sally, 88
FENIMORE, Emma Cora, 88
FEREE, Alice (Carmack), 21
   Edna, 21
   Evan Harvey, 21
FESEL, Annie S, 27
   Ella, 27
   Josiah, 27
   Mary R (Hough), 21
   see also **FEASAL, FEASEL**
FEWELL, Elizabeth, 160
   Mary (Lovell), 160
   Wm, 160
FIELDER, Anna, 193

FIELDS, Elizabeth Lillian, 160
   Isaac A, 160
   Jesse, 21
   Luana, 21
   Martha F, 21
   Mary U, 160
   Maud Lou, 160
   Polly, 156
   Rebecca P, 88
FINCH, Elvira, 167
   Hamilton, 167
   Laura, 152
   Susanna, 174
   Tabitha (Holoman), 167
FINLEY, Eliz (Stilwell), 21
   Harry W, 21
   Mary Belle (Horney), 21
   Samuel, 21
   Wade, 21
FINNEY, Almeda P, 59
   Elizabeth, 88
   Joseph, 59
   Margaret, 88
   Margaret (Reed), 59
   see also **FINNY**
FINNY, Elizabeth, 21
   Joseph, 21
   Margaret, 21
   see also **FINNEY**
FISHER, Elizabeth, 88
   Eunice, 88
   Eunice (Street), 88
   George, 21
   George W, 88
   Hannah, 88
   Hattie A (Hockett), 21,88
   Isaac, 88
   John, 88,193
   Joseph, ix,88,193
   Mahala P, 21,88
   Marietta/Maryetta, 88
   Mary, 88
   Mary Ann, 88
   Nellie, 21
   Rachel, 88
   Robert, ix,88,193
   Ruth, 21,88
   Thomas, 88,193
FLEMING, Clara Bell, 193
   Clara Bell (Hockett), 160
   David, 160
   Ellen, 6
   Mary Ellen, 193
   Sarah L, 162
   see also **FLEMMING**
FLEMMING, Charles David, 21
   Clara Bell, 193
   Edith, 21
   Hannah D, 21
   Louis Joseph, 21
   Lucy, 21
   Maria, 21
   Samuel, 21
   Sarah G, 21
   see also **FLEMING**
FLETCHER, Albert W, 88
   Albert White, 21
   Anna (Perry), 21
   Anna Elizabeth (Perry), 88
   Charles, 21
   Edward Bradley, 21,88
   Elizabeth D, 79,88,108

FLETCHER, Elizabeth D (Hiatt), 14,21,37
   Elizabeth Dix (Hiatt), 21
   Elizabeth Dix (Peelle), 21
   Elizabeth P, 88
   Emily Maria, 21
   Esther, 21
   Francis Nixon, 21,88
   Jesse D, 21
   Martha E (Teague), 21
   Martha Elizabeth (Teague), 88
   Mordecai, 21
   Mordecai H, 88
   Mordecai Hiatt, 88
   Rhoda Alice, 37,108
   Samuel F, 79,88,108
   Samuel Francis, 14,21,27,88
   Sarah (Baxter) Moffitt, 88
   Sarah Elma, 14,21,79
   Sarah M (Baxter), 21
   Sarah N, 79
   Wilfred, 21
   Wilfred P, 88
   Wm, 21
   Wm Dixon, 21
   Wm H, 88
FLICK, Miriam, 88
   see also **FLIK**
FLIK, Miriom (Small), 88
   see also **FLICK**
FLOOD, Elizabeth, 21
   Frank, 21
   Lula (Addington), 21
   Orlando E, 21
   Sarah T, 21
FLOYD, Mary O, 58
FOGG, Samuel, 88
FOGLE, Lucy, 153
FOLAND, Sarah, 58
FOLGER, Estella L, 21
   J W, 21
   Rosella, 21
FOLKE, Judah, 88
   Samuel, 88
   Thomas, 88
   see also **FOULK, FOULKE**
FORD, Eliza Ellen (Baldwin), 160
   Everett E, 160
   Genetta (Taylor), 193
   George Clessie, 160
   Hannah (Phillips), 160
   Hannah S, 193
   Hazel Glenna, 160
   Jesse A, 193
   Jessie Al, 193
   Nathaniel, 160,193
   Oliver, 160,193
FORKNER, Armina (Pierce), 193
FORSYTHE, Ruth, 193
FOSSETT, Elizabeth, 54
   see also **FAUCETT**
FOSTER, —— (Hunt), 64
   Albert, 160
   Charles Thomas, 160
   Elmina H, 64
   Joshua, 64
   Lucinda, 160
   Patience Ann, 193
   Patience Ann (Doughman) Shalley, 160
   Robert J, 160,193
   Walter, 160
   Wm, 160

FOULK, Lydia, 88
   Margaret, 88
   Mary, 23,88
   Sarah, 88
   see also **FOLKE, FOULKE**
FOULKE, Judah, 88
   Lydia, 20
   Margaret, 128
   Martha A, 21
   Samuel, 88
   Sarah, 20,88
   Sarah (Gordon), 88
   Thomas, 88
   see also **FOLKE, FOULK**
FOUTS, Eleanor, 88
   Elizabeth, 88,93
   Jacob, 1,88
   Jacob Jr, 88
   see also **FOUTZ, PHOUTS,**
FOUTZ, Ella, 193
   Mary A, 179
   see also **FOUTS**
FOWLER, Eliza J, 88
   Lidie, 88
   W E, 88
   W E C, 88
   Wm E, 88
FOX, Carlista (Lamb), 161
   Charles W, 161,193
   Charlie, 193
   David, 161
   Deborah (Cox), 161
   John, 161
   Martha (Hubbard), 161
   Melissa, 193
   Nadia/Neaty, 193
   Nettie Ann (Whittier), 161
   Nettie S, 193
   Oscar, 161,193
   Ruth Etta, 161
   Thomas, 161
FRABERT, Ada, 88
   Elizabeth (Jefferis), 32
   Esther, iv
   Esther E, 88
   Esther Ellen, 88
   Hettie C, 88
   Itasca/Itaska M, 88
   James, 32
   Nathan T, 88
   Nora, 32
   Sarah, 25
FRANCISCO, Abigail, 88
   Abigail J (Casad), 21
   Amy, 21
   Charles A, 21,88
   Edith, 21
   Hannah (Dickinson), 21,88
   Hannah M, 88
   Louis, 21
   Louis J, 88
   Louis Joseph, 21
   Lucy, 21
   Maria, 21
FRASURE, Daniel, 88
   see also **FRAZER, FRAZIER**
FRAZER, James, 21,161
   Laura E (Stewart), 21,161
   Oliver M, 21,161
   Ruth (Whitson), 21,161
   see also **FRASURE, FRAZIER**

FRAZIER, Abner, 161,193
   Albert T, 193
   Allenson, 171
   Angeline (Conway), 171
   Anna/Anne, 86,88
   Bartley E, 193
   Charley L, 193
   Dallas E, 193
   Daniel, 86,88
   Eldora, 193
   Elenor, 88
   Elvin F, 193
   Eva, 32
   Francis, 29
   Freddie E, 193
   Hannah, 193
   Isaiah, 161
   J F, 32
   Martha, 88
   Martha (Edgerton), 88
   Mary Ann, 89
   Nancy, 49
   Nellie, 86,163
   Rachel, 32
   Rebecca, 193
   Rebecca (Millikan), 193
   Sabra, 161
   Sarah, 29
   Sarah Ann, 88
   Sarah Bell, 171
   Solomon B, 89
   Wm, 193
   Wm Jr, 88
   see also **FRASURE, FRAZER**
FREEMAN, Daniel, 89
   Naomi, 193
FRENCH, Anna, 59
   Anna M, 89
   Elizabeth, 89
   Elizabeth F, 89
   Eunice, 193
   Howell B, 21
   Levi, 89
   Oliver P, 21
   Sarah A (Hardwiage), 21
   Sarah T (Flood), 21
FRES, Elizabeth, 89
   see also **FRIES**
FREY, Anna Margaret, 55
   see also **FRY**
FRIES, Cynthia A, 47
   see also **FRES**
FRIESDORF, Christiana, 89
   Christiana A, 89
   Christiana L, 9
FROGGATT, Sarah M (Bond), 89
FROST, Ann H (Shute), 89
   Caleb, 89
   Edward L, 89
   Hannah, 89
   Hannah (Holloway), 89
   Lydia, 89
   Mercy, 11
   Phileman H, 89
   Sarah, 89
FRY, Amos, 21,89
   Calvin, 89
   Calvin M, 21
   F A, 21
   Florence (Shirley), 21
   Josephine H (Hallinan), 21
   Keziah, 21,89

FRY, Oliver A/H, 21,89
   Priscilla Thomas, 94
   Roy C, 21
   Wm, 89
   see also **FREY**
FULGHUM, Albert B, 21,22
   Anthony, 89
   Benjamin, 21,22,24,30,89,92
   Benjamin W, 22,89
   Caroline, 22,30,89,99
   Charles, 22
   Delphina M, 14
   Edgar W, 22,89
   Eliza B, 22,89
   Eliza B, 89
   Elma, 22,89
   Franconia L, 22,89
   Franklin B, 22
   Frederick, 7,22,38,109,133
   Frederick C, 22,89
   Hannah, 92
   Hannah J, 22,24
   Harriet, 89
   Harriet W, 89
   Harriett (White), 22
   Harriett E, 89
   Harriett E (Pitts), 21
   Jeremiah, 22
   Jesse, 89
   John Allen, 22
   Joseph, 89
   Lucy, 22,89
   Lydia F, 13,47
   Martha, 7,11,29,38,109,133
   Mary, 22,75,89,131
   Mary (Pegg), 14
   Mary J, 22
   Michael, 47
   Mildred, 33,89
   Naomi, 22
   Naomi C, 103
   Oscar E, 22,89
   Phebe, 89
   Piety, 89,109,133
   Piety (Parker), 7,22,38
   Rebecca C, 89
   Rebecca E (Elliott), 22
   Rebecca T, 89
   Rebecca T (Jessop), 89
   Rhoda, 21,22,24,30,92
   Rhoda (Ballard), 89
   Roscoe, 89
   Roscoe W, 22,89
   Ruth, 22
   Sarah (Woodard), 47
   Walter B, 22,89
   Wm, 14
   Wm A, 22,89
   Zeri, 89
   see also **FULGUM**
FULGUM, Frederick C, 89
   Lucy, 89
   Mary, 89
   Mary J, 89
   Milfred, 89
   Oscar E, 89
   Piety, 89
   Rebecca C, 89
   Walter B, 89
   see also **FULGHUM**
FULTON, Oliver Phillips, 22
   Rella, 22

FULTON, Samatha, 22
    Serepta, 153
FURNAS, Hannah, 41
FURSTENBURGER, Albert J, 22
    Cora B (Herbert), 22
    Evaline, 22
    Henry, 22
FYE, Benjamin, 22,38
    Beth Margaret, 22,38
    Catherine, 22, 38
    Harry E, 22

GAAR, Andrew, 22
    Ann Eliza (Allen), 22
    Charles/Charley, 22, 89
    Clem A, 22
    Fannie (McMeans), 22
    Fielding, 22
    Jonas, 89
    Jonas B, 22
    Lucile, 22
    Mary J, 89
    Mary T, 22
GABLE, Margaret, 174
GAIL, Peninah (Small), 89
    see also **GALE**
GALE, Peninah, 89
    see also **GAIL**
GALLAHUE, Pearl (Teague), 22
GALLION, Matilda (Beeson), 193
    see also **GALYAN, GALYEAN**
GALYAN, Tabitha (Warren), 89
    see also **GALLION, GALYEAN**
GALYEAN, Edith, 193
    see also **GALLION, GALYAN**
GAMBER, Abbe, 193
    Ada, 193
    Charles, 193
    Charley A, 193
    Ida, 193
    Jacob, 193
    Lucy, 193
    Michael, 193
GAMP, Hattie E, 22
GANNON, Mary E, 89
    Robert, 89
    Robert W, 89
GANO, Aaron, 22
    Elisabeth E, 89
    Lizzie (Jeffries), 22
    Mary, 22
    Nixon H, 22,89
    Paul Jefferies, 22,89
GANT, Andrew Alfred, 89
    Dorcas Angeline, 89
    Edward, 89
    Edward Ira, 89
    Frances Amelia, 89
    Martha Jane, 89
    Perry, 89
GARDE, Alice, 89
    Alice E, 89
GARDENER, Elizabeth (Brewer), 89
    see also **GARDINER, GARDNER**
GARDINER, Elisabeth, 89
    Sarah, 89
    see also **GARDENER, GARDNER**
GARDNER, Alonzo, 89
    Alonzo M, 22
    Belle, 89
    Benjamin A, 22
    Dinah, 89

GARDNER, Eliab, 89
    Eliza, 89
    Eunice, 155,158,181
    Isaac, 89
    Jesse, 89
    Judith, 89
    Maria, 89
    Mary (Hollingsworth), 89
    Matilda, 5
    Phebe, 89
    Rhoda, 89
    Sarah, 89
    Susan Belle (Clark), 22
    Susana/Susannah, 40,89
    Susannah (Morgan), 22
    Wm, 89
    see also **GARDENER, GARDINER**
GARFIELD, Winfield, 22
GARMAN, Samuel, 89
GARNER, A Luella (Rush), 22
    Elwood H, 22
    Martha A (Hill), 22
    Marvel R, 22
    Seth, 22
GARRET, Anna, 89
    Mary Ann, 89
    Wm, 89
    see also **GARRETT**
GARRETT, Abigail, 22
    Anna/Anne, 22,89
    Daniel, 22
    Daniel N, 89
    John M, 89
    Maddison/Madison, 22,89
    Mary Ann, 22,89
    Violena, 14,54
    Wm, 22,89
    see also **GARRET**
GARRISON, George, 56
    Katherine A, 56
    Leah, 56
GARVER, B C, 22
    Georgia L (Mendenhall), 22
    Ruth A (Rohrer), 22
    Walter B, 22,89
GARWOOD, Anna (Iredell), 12
    Bertha M, 22
    Cora, 12
    David C, 22
    Josephine, 12
    Juanita (de Garza), 90
    Juanita (Garza), 22
    Mary E (Negus), 22
    Nathan, 12
    Ralph Stillman, 22,90
    Spencer, 90
    Vashbut D, 90
GARZA, Guillermo de, 90
    Juanita, 22,55,90
    Juanita de, 90
    Maria de Escobordeda, 90
GATES, Charles, 90
    Daniel, 90
GAUSE, Nancy J (Smoot), 18
    W Sophia, 18
    Wm, 18
    see also **GAUSS**
GAUSS, Naomi R (Brown), 22
    S Clarence, 22
    see also **GAUSE**
GAYNOR, Margaret, 90
    see also **GOEHNER**

GEBHART, John, 164
    Rachel, 164
    Susan, 164
GENTRY, Mamie/Marie, 54
GEORGE, Phoebe, 94
GIBBONS, Josiah, 90
    Lydia Ann, 22,90
    Sophia, 90
GIBSON, Grace Rebecca, 22
    Hannah, 90
    John, 161
    Mary, 161
    Mary E, 153,160
    Minnie (Martin), 22
    Nannie E (Canaday), 161
    Rachel, 193
    Rebecca, 22
    Samuel, 22
    Wm W, 22
GIFFORD, Andrew, 22,90,117
    Benjamin, 90
    Benjamin B, 90
    Daniel, 22,90
    Edith H, 90
    Elizabeth, 90
    Elizabeth A, 117
    James, 22
    James C, 22
    Jesse/Jessie, 22,90
    Keziah, 20,87,90
    Louisa, 22
    Sarah, 22,117
    Sarah E, 90
GILBERT, Abigail, 90
    Achsah, 22,90
    Anna G, 42
    Charles, 161
    Charles Ernest, 161
    Cyrus, 161
    Dorothy, 22,81,90,131
    Dorothy Jr, 131
    Dorothy (Nixon), 22
    Elizabeth, 22,90
    Elizabeth (Shearon) Chaffin, 22
    Elizabeth C, 90
    Elizabeth C (Sharon), 90
    Grace (Pursley), 161
    Guilielma, 23,90
    Hannah, 23,90
    Harry W, 22,90
    Isaiah B, 90
    Jeremiah, 22,23,90
    Joel, 90
    Joel Jr, 90
    Josiah, 22,81,90,131
    Josiah Jr, 90
    Laura, 90
    Lydia, 22,90
    Martha, 23
    Martha Ann, 90
    Martha Ann (Dougherty), 90
    Mary, 22,23,81,90
    Mary (Black), 161
    Miriam, 22,23,90
    Morris, 23
    Moses, 90
    Phebe, 23,90
    Sarah, 22,90
    Sarah (Hill), 23
    Susan (Hilton), 161
    Thomas, 22,23,90,161
    Warner M, 90
    Warner Morris, 22

GILES, Nancy, 159
GILESPIE, Eva, 193
   see also **GILLESPIE, GLASPIE**
GILLAM, Benjamin, 161
   Mary, 161
   Mary E, 161
   see also **GILLIAM**
GILLESPIE, Alice, 161,193
   Charles, 161
   Eva, 161,193
   see also **GILESPIE, GLASPIE**
GILLIAM, Lillie, 90
   see also **GILLAM**
GILMER, Ann E (Swain), 23
   J Albert, 23
   John D, 23
GILMORE, Adaliza, 153
   Elizabeth (Thornburg), 155
   Isaac, 155
   Nancy, 153
   Nora A, 155
   Samuel, 153
   Sarah A, 159
GILPIN, Rebecca, 113
GLADDIN, Hannah, 62
GLASPIE, Alice, 193
   see also **GILESPIE, GILLESPIE**
GLUYAS, J Marmaduke, 90
   Zalinda A, 90
   see also **GLUYS**
GLUYS, Howard, 23
   John B, 23
   Marmaduke James, 23
   Mary Susannah, 23
   Mildred (Mendenhall), 23
   Zelinda Annis (Binford), 23
   see also **GLUYAS**
GODSEY, Rhoda, 23
   Robert, 23
   Wm, 23
GOEHNER, Christie M, 90
   Jacob L, 90
   John H, 90
   John R, 90
   Margaret, 90
   Margaret F, 90
   Wm P, 90
   see also **GAYNOR**
GOOCH, Americus B, 40
   Emma Y, 40
   Maria G, 40
GOOD, Edward, 161
   Elizabeth (Dunn), 161
   Nellie, 161
   see also **GOODE**
GOODE, Lydia Ann (Macy), 193
   see also **GOOD**
GOODRICH, Anna, 34
   C C, 90
   Charles, 23
   Charles C, 90
   Edmund, 155
   Elwood, 206
   Hattie (Brown), 23
   Mary, 155
   Nancy, 192,206
   Nancy M, 155
   Nellie, 206
GOODSON, Anna, 162
   Priscilla, 162
   Uriah, 162
GOODWIN, Harriet L, 90

GORDEN, Anna, 90
   Emeline, 23
   Luther B, 90
   Mary, 90
   Phebeann, 23
   Sarah (Unthank), 23
   Seth, 23
   see also **GORDON, GOURDON**
GORDON, Anna, 90
   Carl, 23
   Charles, 90
   Elsie C, 23
   Emaline, 90
   Esther, 90
   James, 90
   Luther B, 90
   Lydia, 39
   Mary, 23,90
   Phebe Ann, 90
   Richard, 90
   Ruth, 90
   Sarah, 88,90
   Sarah (Unthank), 90
   Seth, 90
   Thomas N, 90
   see also **GORDEN, GOURDON**
GOUGH, Mary, 90
GOURDON, Charles, 90
   James, 90
   Seth, 90
   see also **GORDEN, GORDON**
GOVE, Alice C, 90
GRACE, Annie, 161,193
   Bertha, 57
   Jessie, 161,193
   Mary, 156
   Sarah Ann, 23
GRAHAM, Ada P, 23
   Eliza J, 63
   Elizabeth, 12
   Frank P, 23
   George, 23
   Isaac, 23
   Joseph, 23
   Margaret E, 16,63
   Mary, 23
   Minnie (Morgan), 23
   Nancy, 23
   Wm H, 23
GRAM, Esther A, 50
   Hannah, 50
   Howell, 50
GRANT, Martha Pearl (Lunsford), 23
GRAVE, Alen/Allen, 23,90
   Allen W, 23
   Angelina, 91
   Angelina E, 23
   Ann/Anna, 5,23,70,82
   Ann P, 23,90
   Anna H, 91
   Betsy (Jones), 23
   Betty, 90
   Charles, 23,91
   Clarkson, 91
   Curtis, 10,23,90
   Daniel F, 91
   David, 23,90
   David I/J, 90,91
   David P, 23,66,90
   Dorothea/Dorothy, 23,90,91
   Edith, 10,23
   Elisabeth/Elizabeth, 23,91,133

GRAVE, Eliza, 23,90
   Eliza (Adkins), 90
   Elizabeth (Jones), 57
   Ellwood, 23
   Emma (Test), 91
   Emma T, 91
   Enos, 23,57,90,91,133
   Enos Jr, 90
   Esther, 23
   Hannah, 23,90,91
   Hannah (Howell), 23
   Hannah C (Nicholson), 23
   Hannah L, 6
   Hannah Maria/Mariah, 23,91
   Henry, 23,91
   Howell, 23,91
   Israel, 23,90
   Jacob, 23,70,82,90
   Jane (Wright), 23,66,90
   Jesse, 23,90,91
   John L, 23,90
   Jonathan, 116
   Jonathan L, 23,90,91
   Joseph, 23,90
   Joseph Chandler, 91
   Joseph Edward, 91
   Joseph K, 23
   Josephine, 23
   Kersey, 23,90,91
   Levi, 23,90
   Lydia, 90,116
   Lydia (Howell), 23
   Lydia Ann, 23,91
   Lydia H, 23,131
   Margaret Rosetta, 23,91
   Martha, 23
   Martha D, 82
   Martha H, 23,90
   Mary, 23,90,91
   Mary (Strawbridge), 90
   Mary Ann, 23,91
   Milton, 23,90
   Nathan, 23,90
   Perry, 91
   Pusey, 23,90
   Rachel, 23
   Rachel T, 23
   Rebecca/Rebeckah, 23,57,90,133
   Rebecca J, 23
   Rebeckah C, 23
   Ruth, 23
   Ruth C, 91
   Sarah, 23,33,49,50,90,123
   Sarah Ann, 23,90
   Stephan, 23,90
   Susan, 23
   Susan Jane, 66
   Susanna, 90
   Thomas, 91
   Thomas Clarkson, 23
   Vernon, 91
   Vernon D, 91
   Warner, 23,90,91
   Wm, 23,91
   Wm D, 91
   see also **GRAVES**
GRAVES, Ann, 91
   Betty, 91
   Daisy, 24
   Earlham, 24
   Edith, 71
   Elizabeth, 91

GRAVES, Elizabeth (Mills), 91
    Ella, 91
    Elwood, 91
    Emma (Test), 24
    J W, 91
    James, 91
    James W, 23
    John L, 91
    Mamie May, 23
    Martha, 91
    Mary, 91
    Mary Alice, 24
    Mary T, 91
    Nathan, 91
    Pusey, 91
    Rachel, 91
    Rebecca, 91
    Sarah Ellen, 23
    Stephen, 91
    Vernon D, 24
    see also **GRAVE**
GRAY, Alice, 193
    Alice (Carey/Cary), 161,193
    Benjamin E, 193
    Benjamin Elijah, 161
    Davis, 193
    Edith B, 193
    Edith Bell, 161,181
    Elisha, 161
    Elizabeth (Beeson), 161
    Elizabeth (Simerson), 161
    Emma J, 161
    Hugh, 91
    Hugh Mallory, 24
    Ithamer, 161
    James, 24,91
    Jehu Harlan, 161
    John, 24,91
    John H, 193
    Jonathan, 193
    Joseph, 91
    Joseph Hillis, 24
    Julia, 193
    Julia C, 193
    Julia C (Lamb), 161,181
    Margaret, 193
    Mary Jane, 24,91
    Orville H, 161
    Robert T, 91
    Robert Thomas, 24,91
    Samuel, 91
    Samuel Walker, 24
    Sarah Jane, 24,91
    Wm, 24
    Wm P, 193
    Wm Pinckney, 161,181
    see also **GREY**
GREEN, Clark, 28
    Elizabeth, 163
    Ella G, 28
    Ellen W, 91
    Hazel, 91
    John, 58
    Louella,Luella, 91
    Mahala/Mahalah, 24,91
    Mahalah (Unthank), 91
    Mariam/Miriam W, 27,96
    Mary, 58
    Mary T, 58
    Rachel, 7,150
    Rachel (Wilson), 27
    Rachel P, 47
    Rebecca, 30

GREEN, Reuben, 91
    Rhoda, 91
    Rhoda E, 47
    Robert, 24,27,47,91
    Robert, 27
    Robert, 47
    Susanna (Baden), 28
    Timothy V, 91
    Wm, 91,193
    Wm, 91
    see also **GREENE**
GREENBRIER, Barbara J, 63
GREENE, Isabelle, 57
    Ruth, 42
    see also **GREEN**
GREENSTREET, Eli, 24
    Lilian H (Whitacre), 24
    Ruth, 24
    Thomas A, 24
GREER, Lydia, 24
    Mariam, 91
    see also **GRIER**
GREGG, Alzina, 20
GREY, Alice C, 193
    Benjamin E, 193
    Edith B, 193
    Emma C (Robinson), 24
    Jasper, 16
    Jehu, 193
    Julia C, 193
    Mary, 16
    Tobitha, 16
    Wm R, 193
    see also **GRAY**
GRICE, Catharine, 91
GRIER, Ann J, 91
    Lydia, 91
    see also **GREER**
GRIEST, Lucinda, 114
GRIFFIN, ——, 33
    Ann, 91
    Ann (Weeks), 91
    Anna C, 91
    Charles O, 91
    Dahlia H, 91
    Earl Leroy, 91
    Elfleda, 91
    Eli, 91
    Eliza, 91
    Emily, 91
    Emily Jane, 13
    Esther B, 91
    Jacob, 24,91
    James, 24,91
    James C, 91
    James E, 91
    John, 24
    John W, 91
    Joseph, 13,24,91
    Joshua, 24,91
    Mary, 24,91
    Mary (Copeland), 24
    Mary Elizabeth, 91
    Mary Jane (Elliott) Hall, 24
    Minnie M, 91
    Rachel, 91
    Rebecca (Burgess), 13
    Samuel, 24,91
    Seth Smith, 91
    Thomas, 91
    Willis, 91
    Wm, 24
    Wm C, 91

GRIFFITH, Alice B, 24,91
    Anna J, 24,91
    Charles, 91
    Charles J, 24
    Charlotte, 91
    Christiana, 91
    Collins, 91
    Collins W, 91
    David, 91
    David L, 24,91
    Edith H, 91
    Eli, 24,91
    Elizabeth, 34
    Elizabeth B, 24,91
    George D, 24
    George Dilks, 91
    Hannah, 91
    Hannah B, 91
    Hannah B (Shoemaker), 24,91
    Harry, 91
    Helen, 24,91
    James Henry, 24
    John H, 11
    John W, 24,91
    Joseph C, 91
    Kesiah/Keziah T, 11,24,91
    Keziah, 91
    Martha (Hayward), 91
    Martha F (Hayward), 24,91
    Martha L, 24,91
    Mary, 24,91
    Mary R, 91
    Rachel, 11,24,91
    Rachel P, 24
    Seth S, 24,91
    Thomas, 91
GRILLS, Caroline, 167
GRIMES, Delphina, 16
    Malinda, 164,165
    Margaret, 58
    Philip, 164
    Susan, 164
GRISELL, Martha, 11
GRIST, Lucinda, 42
GROBLE, Elnora May, 161
    Naomi (Clark), 161
    Thomas, 161
GRUBBS, Benjamin, 24
    Wm G, 24
GUARD, Christiana, 27
GUIFFORD, Jesse, 91
GULLET, Mary A, 147
GUYER, Aron, 91
    Axiom, 91
    Jesse, 91
    Sarah, 56
GWIN, Alsie L, 161
    Alsie Lena, 194
    Asenath/Asenith (Swain), 161,194
    Asenith, 194
    Charity (Mills), 161,167
    Charles O, 161,194
    Charlotte, 194
    Charlotte (Macy), 161
    Cyrus B, 161,194
    E Josephine (Scantland), 161,167
    Elihu Swain, 161,167,194
    Etha Inda, 161
    Freddie Carl, 161,194
    Glennie A, 161,167
    Glennie Allice, 194
    Golda Mabel, 161

GWIN, Hannah (Wimmer), 161
   Irena (Canaday), 193
   John, 161,167
   John D, 161,164
   Julia, 178
   Julia Ann, 161,167,179
   Leitha Myrtle, 161
   Nellie, 194
   Nellie (Good), 161
   Oscar S, 161
   Oscar Swain, 194
   Pleasant, 161,194
   Rhoda R, 194
   Rhoda Roxanna (Ledbetter), 161
   Walter T, 161
   see also **GWINN**, **GWYN**
GWINN, Walter T, 194
   see also **GWIN**, **GWYN**
GWYN, Charity, 91
   see also **GWIN**, **GWINN**

HADLEY, Ada E, 92
   Alden H, 92
   Alden W, 24
   Alfred, 3,24,36,92
   Amos, 161
   Ann/Annie, 11,91,92
   Ann (Pedrick), 92
   Ann/Anna P, 92
   Ann P (Pedrick), 24
   Ann P (Watts), 37
   Anna Clarice, 161
   Anna M, 24,49
   Anna R, 92
   Anna Rhoda, 24
   Anzonetta/Azonetta, 24,92
   Artemus N, 24,92
   Benjamin, 24
   Caroline E, 24,92
   Catharine, 91
   Clark H, 92
   Clark Hinman, 24,92
   Clifton O, 92
   Cora M, 92
   Corilia M, 24,37,92
   Earnest B, 92
   Edwin, 24,41,49,92,113
   Edwin C, 92
   Edwin Clarence, 24,92
   Eliza, 92,113
   Eliza Ann, 95
   Eliza D, 24,41
   Elizabeth M, 24,25,92
   Ellen, 24,92
   Ellwood/Elwood, 24,37,92
   Elmer F, 24
   Elmer Fulghum, 92
   Elsie, 24,25
   Elsie Mary, 92
   Emaline/Emeline, 24,92
   Emily, 44
   Emily G, 92
   Emily H, 55
   Emma (Hill), 24,92
   Ernest B, 24,92
   Esther, 24,32,48,92
   Esther (Smith), 91
   Eva (Lewis), 161
   Eva Luzena, 161
   Evan, 92
   Flora H, 32
   Flora M, 92

HADLEY, Flora Rosetta, 24,32
   Francis Lusk, 24
   Grace, 24,92
   Guendeline/Gwenaline, 24,92
   Hannah (Fulghum), 92
   Hannah J (Fulghum), 24
   Hannah P, 92
   Herbert, 24
   Herbert H, 92
   Hiram, 24,55,92
   Horace Greeley, 24
   Ida M, 24
   Ida May, 92
   Jacob, 91,92
   James, 91,92
   James A, 92
   James W, 92
   James Wm, 92
   James Williams, 24
   Jane, 91
   Jane Ann, 24,48,92
   Jemima, 92,113
   Jemima (Doan), 24,41,49
   Jemima D, 92
   Jeremiah, 24,32,48,91,92
   Jesse/Jessie H, 24,92
   Jessie C, 24
   Jessie Carpenter, 24
   John, 91,92
   John C, 24,92
   John S, 92
   John Smith, 24,92
   Jonathan, 24,91
   Jonathan D, 91
   Joseph Doan, 24
   Joshua Jr, 91
   Katie R, 161
   Keziah, 92
   Keziah (Overman), 36
   Keziah K (Overman), 24
   Laura, 92
   Lela/Lelia H, 24,36
   Lenora C (Beard), 161
   Libby L (Clawson), 92
   Lilly L, 92
   Louis E, 24
   Louisa, 55
   Lydia, 91,92
   Mary, 24,25,91,92
   Mary (Butler), 91
   Mary (King), 24
   Mary Ann (Macy), 194
   Mary O'Neal, 92
   Mary P (O'Neal), 24
   Maryann, 194
   Matilda, 57
   Mazie Matilda, 161
   Miriam, 92
   Naomi, 92
   Naomi (Henley), 91
   Olive (Mendenhall), 24
   Ralph S, 161
   Rebecca, 32,92
   Rebecca (Bowles), 161
   Rebecca (Hadley), 32,92
   Rebecca C, 24
   Rebecca Jane, 25,92
   Rebecca Madge, 161
   Royal J, 92
   Ruth, 24
   Ruth (Macy), 194
   Samuel Lee, 24,25,92

HADLEY, Samuel Percy, 24,92
   Samuel S, 24,92
   Samuel Smith, 24
   Samuel W, 92
   Susanna W, 91
   Susanna W (Clawson), 91
   Thomas E, 24
   Thomas Elwood, 24
   Thomas M, 92
   Thomas P, 161,194
   Turner W, 24
   Walter C, 24,92
   Washington, 91
   Wm, 161
   Wm B, 32,92
   Wm Bail, 25
   Wm L, 25
   Wm Lawrence, 92
   Wm Sawring, 24
   see also **HADLY**
HADLY, Abraham Noah, 92
   Joseph, 92
   Joshua, 92
   Wm, 92
   see also **HADLEY**
HAFFNER, James, 161
   Mary Elizabeth (Lamar), 161
   see also **HEFNER**, **HOEFFNER**
HAGERTY, Eliza Ellen, 18
HAHN, Abner H, 25
   Ellen S (Smith), 25
HAINES, Ann (Hudson), 18
   Arthur, 92
   Elizabeth, 153
   Elizabeth (Evans), 92
   John, 18
   Lydia Sarah, 18,52
   Mary Maria, 153
   Zimri, 153
   see also **HANES**, **HAYNES**
HAISLEY, Anna/Annie, 25,92
   Anna Lee, 92
   Bertha Louise (Cain), 161
   Charles, 161
   Charles Harrison, 161
   Davis, 161,194
   Edwin R, 161,194
   Emma S, 92
   Eunice, 92
   Ezekiel, 9
   Francis, 92
   Francis J, 92
   Gulia Elma/Gulielma, 92
   Isaac, 194
   Isaac E, 161,194
   Jennie, 42
   Jonathan, 92,161
   Joseph, 25,92,194
   Lillie (Oler), 161
   Marion, 161
   Martha, 47,194
   Martha E (Mendenhall), 161
   Martha Jane, 194
   Martha Jane (Dennis), 194
   Mary, 9
   Mary R, 11
   Oliver, 11
   Rachel H, 92
   Ruth, 9
   Sarah, 25,92,194
   Sarah Ann, 92
   Susanna, 161

HAISLEY, Thomas, 161
    Washtella E, 11
    Wilbert, 161
HALE, Addie R (McCarty), 25,44
    Ann (Hadley), 11
    Beulah B, 25
    David F, 25
    Eli, 11
    Elmer, 9,92
    Ethel, 92
    Ethel Etta, 9
    Lizzie, 9,92
    Louise, 11
    Pearl M, 25,44
    Perry, 25,44
    Salina (Hunt), 25
HALER, John, 25
    Joseph, 194
    Lawrence E, 25
    Maggie, 194
    Martha, 25
    Pearl, 25
HALEY, Mary, 11
HALL, Alfred, 25
    Alice (McCoy), 25
    Anna, 92
    Benjamin, 92
    Branson, 92
    Caleb, 57,92
    Edwin, 25
    Effie (Newbern) Brown, 25
    Elizabeth, 92
    Emily Melvina, 25
    Evaline, 92
    Hannah (Sanders), 57
    Jeremiah, 25
    John, 25,92
    John Jr, 92
    Joseph, 92,161
    Lydia, 178
    Lydia (White), 25
    Lydia Symons, 57
    Martha, 25,92
    Mary, 194
    Mary (Small), 92
    Mary E (Nicholson), 161
    Mary Jane, 92
    Mary Jane (Elliott), 24,25
    Minerva, 11
    Minnie M, 92
    Miriam, 25
    Moses, 25,92
    Phineas/Phinihas, 25,92
    R Willard, 25
    Rhoda, 92
    Robert, 25,92
    Sarah, 25,92
    Sarah (Parker), 25
    Sophia A, 34
    Stephen, 92
    Wm, 92
    Wm G, 194
HALLENSHADE, Mary, 92
    see also **HOLLENSHAD, HOLLEN-SHADE, HOLLINSHADE**
HALLIFAX, Sarah E, 11
HALLINAN, Georgeina M (Jennings), 21
    James B, 21
    Josephine H, 21
HAM, Alice May (Osborn), 25
    Ann/Anna, 25,92
    Benjamin F, 25,92

HAM, Elizabeth, 25,92
    Emsley, 25,92
    Heskiah/Hezekiah, 25,27,126
    Hezekiah Jr, 25
    Jane, 92
    Jason, 25,92
    Jehu, 25
    Martha, 92
    Mary, 25,92
    Mary Elizabeth, 92
    Philip, 25
    Priscilla, 25,27,92
    Priscilla B, 25
    Sarah, 25,42,92,126
    Sarah (Stuart), 25,27
    see also **HAMM**
HAMILTON, Caroline (Dabney), 92
    Edna, 92
    Ida, 92
HAMISH, Jacob B, 92
HAMM, Caroline Mary, 29
    Emsley, 29,92
    Pamelia (Talbott), 29
    see also **HAM**
HAMMER, Amanda, 167
    Esther Grace, 25
    Ethel Mary, 25
    Hannah, 194
    Isaac, 194
    Jesse, 161
    John Riley, 25
    Joseph, 161
    Laban, 25
    Lydia, 161
    Matilda (Macy), 161
    Melinda C (McCalum), 25
    Nathan, 194
    Rachel, 25
    Ruth (Lee), 194
HAMMOND, James C, 92
HAMPSON, Abra, 92
HAMPTON, Addison, 93
    Andrew, 92
    Anna, 10,25
    Anna Margaret, 25
    Anna May, 93
    Arthur, 93
    Arthur W, 25
    Bertha (Iredell), 25
    David, 92
    Deborah, 92,93
    Deborah (Cox), 92
    Edith, 16
    Eleanor, 92
    Elisha, 92
    Elizabeth, 60
    Elwood, 93
    Emily Jane, 93
    Eunice, 92
    Haines, 93
    Hannah, 55
    Harold C, 93
    Harold E, 25
    J Dun, 55
    Jacob, 92
    Jacob D, 10,25,93
    Jane, 92
    Jehiel, 92
    Lewis N, 25
    Margaret, 93
    Margaret (Reynolds), 10,25
    Mary (Clark), 25

HAMPTON, Mary A, 93
    Mary V, 25
    Mattie C, 72
    Nora A, 55
    Rachel, 92
    Samuel, 92,93
    Sarah, 92
    Sarah Edith, 92,93
    Susan R, 93
    Thomas Elwood, 92,93
HANBY, Eli, 155
    Ellen, 189
    Ellen H, 155
    Gulielma (Charles), 155
HANCHER, Lestle, 10
    Matilda, 10
    Samuel, 10
HANES, Susannah, 194
    see also **HAINES, HAYNES**
HANKINSON, Edward, 93
HANSEN, Ann, 197
    Borden, 194,197
    Rachel, 197
    see also **HANSON**
HANSON, Alice, 161
    Allen, 162
    Alma Ellena, 162
    Ann, 162,165
    Benjamin Franklin, 161
    Borden, 161,162,165,194
    Clara I, 162
    Delilah, 194
    Delilah (Reece), 162,194
    Edwin, 162,194
    Elbert Florence, 162
    Elijah, 161,162
    Elisha, 162,194
    Ellen, 162
    Elva Ruth, 162
    Elwood, 162
    Emory Clarence, 162
    Esther, 162
    Esther Ann, 162
    Isabel (Chamness), 162
    Isabel W (Chamness), 194
    John, 161,162,194
    Levi, 162,194
    Mary Ann (Morris), 161
    Milton, 162
    Newton, 162
    Rachel, 162,194
    Rachel (Cox), 161,162,165
    Sarah, 162
    Sarah (Hutchens), 194
    Silas, 162
    Susanna/Susannah, 161,162
    Thomas, 162,194
    Zimri, 162,194
    see also **HANSEN**
HAPNER, Annie, 50
    Emma, 93
    Henrietta (Conner), 50
    Thomas, 50
HARDIN, Emma (Test), 194
    Emma M, 162
    Horace L, 162
HARDMAN, Lizzie, 174
HARDWIAGE, James, 21
    Mary A, 21
    Sarah A, 21
HARDWICK, Betty (Trueblood), 93
HARE, David, 93

HARKNESS, Beulah E, 93
    Beulah H, 93
    Charity C, 93
    John U, 93
    Lina R, 93
HARLAN, Emma, 30
    se also **HARLAND**, **HARLEN**
HARLAND, Carla Leota, 25
    Edna L, 25
    Nancy J, 50
    W E, 25
    see also **HARLAN**
HARLEN, Sarah (Hollingsworth), 93
    see also **HARLAN**
HARMON, Daisy M, 25
    James, 25
    Martha, 25
HARNED, Alida C (Miller), 134
HAROLD, Betsey, 25
    Cordelia B, 93
    Cordelia B (Hodgin), 25
    Cyrus M/N, 93
    Earl J, 93
    Ella S, 93
    Elvira, 93
    Eva, 25
    Frank L, 25,93
    Halcy/Halsey J, 25,93
    Herman, 25,93
    Isaac S, 25,93
    Luena, 93
    Lura/Lure, 93
    Nathan, 25
    Rebecca (Hawkins), 25
    Rollo, 93
    Rollo Homer, 25
    Ruthanna, 93
    Ruthanna W (Wilson), 25
    see also **HARROLD**
HARPER, George, 25
    Percilla, 25
    S P, 25
HARRELL, Amy, 93
    Florence Anna, 17
    Gabriel, 93
    John, 17
    Perlina, 17
HARRIS, Abigail, 93
    Albanus, 25,93
    Allen, 6
    Almeda/Almedia, 25,93
    Anna, 25,93
    Bathsheba, 93
    Benjamin, 1,93
    Benjamin H, 93
    Betty, 93
    Calldre, 25
    Charity, 93
    Charles, 152
    Charles B, 93
    David, 93
    Ellen D, 6
    Emily Jane, 25,93
    Emma Bell (Veal), 152
    Esther, 194
    Esther (Carter), 194
    Francis F/T, 25,93
    Frank, 93
    Frank T, 93
    George W, 25,93
    Gulielma, 93
    Gulielma (Harvey), 93

HARRIS, Hannah, 93,162,194,211
    Henry, 194
    Henry Jesse, 93
    Henry M, 162
    Ida Elena/Elma, 25,93
    Jacob, 93,162,194
    James, 93,211
    Jane M, 25,93
    Jesse, 194
    Jesse B, 162
    Jesse Frederic/Frederick, 25,93
    Jesse M, 25,93
    John, 25,93
    John S, 93
    Jonas, 93,162,194
    Jonathan, 93
    Joseph Gurney, 25,93
    Julia A, 194
    Katherine, 25
    Levi, 93
    Louisa, 93
    Lydia, 25,93
    Lydia (Weeks), 93
    Lydia Ann, 162
    Lydia Maria/Marie, 25,93
    Margaret, 93
    Maria, 93
    Mary, 25,93,211
    Mary L, 25,93
    Mary P (Jones), 25,93
    Mattie (Scott), 25
    Milton, 93
    Miriam, 93
    Nancy, 41
    Obadiah, 93
    Obadiah Jr, 93
    Obadiah Sr, 93
    Obadiah 3rd, 93
    Pleasant, 93
    Rachel, 93
    Rebecca/Rebeckah, 66
    Sarah, 93
    Surelda, 179
    Susannah, 93
    Thomas, 93
    Wm, 25,93,194
    Wm Harvey, 93
    Wm Henry, 25,93
    Zelma, 152
    Zeri, 25,93
HARRISON, Amanda (Dixon), 29
    Anna/Annie R, 26
    Carlos Evans, 26
    Claribel, 93
    Claribel (Barrett), 25
    Frederick, 135
    Isaac Merritt, 25
    Julius Paul, 26
    Laura, 29
    Lizzie, 26
    Lydia A, 93
    Mary Elizabeth/ Emily, 26,93
    Miriam A, 26
    Miriam Alice, 26
    Naomi, 93
    Naomi W, 104
    Naomi W (Morgan), 25,26
    Pearl Adele (Louden), 26
    Peter, 29
    Raymond T, 25
    Susan R, 26,34,104
    Thomas Jr, 26

HARRISON, Thomas H, 25,26,93
    Timothy, 25,25,34,59,93,104,135
    Wm Henry, 26
HARROLD, Cordelia B, 93
    Cyrus A, 93
    Earl J, 93
    Elvira, 93
    Frank L, 93
    Halsey J, 93
    Isaac S, 93
    John, 93
    Laura B, 93
    see also **HAROLD**
HART, Anna, 169
HARTER, Blanch Irene, 26
    Catharine, 162
    Deliah, 26
    Donald Morton, 162
    Early Irvin, 162
    Elizabeth (Ulrich), 162
    Ella, 194
    Emma, 194
    Emma (Cates), 162
    Emma Florence, 162,164,174
    Etta, 26
    Eva Ruth, 162
    Francis A, 162
    Frank, 194
    George, 194
    George W, 162
    Gracie, 194
    Gracie P (Burroughs), 162
    Hannah, 194
    Hannah M (Seagrave), 162
    Hubert B, 162
    James, 26
    Jesse, 194
    Jesse H, 162
    John, 26
    John W, 162,194
    Joseph, 162
    Joseph C, 162
    Joseph L, 162,164,174,194
    Leroy, 162,194
    Levi, 162
    Lowell, 26
    Maggie, 162
    Margette, 26
    Mary, 165,194
    Mary (Pierce), 162
    Mary G, 162
    Mary L (Davis), 162
    Morton L, 162
    Nancy Ellen, 162
    Nona Mabel, 162
    Olive, 26
    Ora V, 26
    Orpha, 194
    Orpha (Bookout), 162
    Pheraby, 194
    Pheraby (Daniels), 162,164,174
    Priscilla, 194
    Priscilla (Goodson), 162
    Richard, 194
    Samantha, 162
    Sarah, 26
    Wm, 26,162,194
HARTLEY, Barbara/Barbary, 93,133
    Charles, 26
    Edward S, 26
    Elias F, 93
    Elias P, 93

HARTLEY, Elizabeth, 93
  Hannah, 84,93
  Hannah F, 93
  James, 93
  James S, 93
  Jane H, 47
  Jeanette, 47
  Mary J, 26
  Norten D, 93
  Norton P, 93
  Rachel, 93
  Rachel L, 93
  Rebecca, 93
  Rebecca D, 93
  Samuel, 47
  Sarah S, 133
  Sarah T, 93
  Susie E, 26
  Thomas, 93,133
HARTMAN, Ann E, 35
  Phebe, 93
HARTSOOK, John D, 187
HARTY, Mira (Macy), 194
HARVEY, Aaron, 94
  Abijah, 94
  Abner C, 26,94
  Abner Clawson, 94
  Ada, 26,94
  Adeline, 26
  Alfred H, 26,94
  Amos, 93,94
  Ann/Anne, 93,94,131
  Ann (Clawson), 94
  Ann C, 94
  Augustus, 94
  Augustus H, 26
  Benjamin, 94
  Bertha, 26
  Bohan, 94
  Caleb, 93,94,131
  Caleb E, 94
  Charles, 26,94
  Christiana, 94
  Christiana (Hunt), 94
  Daniel Milton, 26,94
  Deborah, 94
  Eli, 35,94
  Elias, 94
  Elijah, 15,26,94
  Elisabeth/Elizabeth Ann, 26,94
  Elizabeth, 94
  Elizabeth (Fouts), 93
  George, 26,94
  George E, 26
  George M, 94
  Gulielma, 15,26,93,94
  Henry, 93,94
  Isaac, 93,94
  Jane, 94
  Jemima B, 26
  John, 26,93,94
  Lemuel D, 26
  Lydia, 94
  Lydia H, 94
  Mahlon, 26,54,94
  Mahlon C, 94
  Margaret, 26,94
  Martha, 94
  Martha Jemima, 94
  Mary, 26,79,93,94,131
  Mary A, 54
  Mary Ann, 94

HARVEY, Mary Ann (Clawson), 15,26
  Michael, 94
  Milton, 26
  Nathan, 93,94
  Polly, 94
  Rachel, 93,94
  Rachel (Cook) Lewis, 94
  Rebecca/Rebeckah/Rebekah, 94
  Robert, 93,94
  Ruth, 35
  Samuel, 26,94
  Sarah, 67,79,93,94
  Sarah (Charles), 26
  Sarah Alice, 26
  Sarah Ann, 94
  Sina A, 35
  Stephen, 94
  Thomas, 94
  Violena (Garrett), 54
  Wm, 1,26,79,93,94
  Wm Jr, 94
  Wm F, 26,94
  Wm Forster, 94
  Wm P, 94
  see also **HARVY**
HARVY, Mahlon, 14
  Mary, 14
  Mary Alice, 14
  Sarah, 14
  Violena (Garrett), 14
  Wm, 14
  see also **HARVEY**
HASKET, Lydia, 41
  Palen, 94
  Susan, 194
  Zimri, 194
HASKINS, Priscilla Thomas (Fry), 94
HASLAM, Elizabeth H, 166
  Osee Ann (Marshall), 166
  Wm, 166
HASTINGS, Aaron, 26
  Aaron, 94
  Alice V, 94
  Alice Vining, 94
  Alton P, 94
  Ann/Anna, 2,26,94
  Anna Letitia, 26,94
  Bayard, 94
  Carrie Esther, 94
  Catherine, 2
  Charles H, 162
  Christian, 94
  Christiana (Reece), 26
  Daniel C, 26,28,53
  Elias R, 26,94
  Elizabeth H, 94
  Ella M, 26,94
  Ercie Ona/One, 162,194
  Esther, 94
  Esther Jane, 94
  Eunice, 2,26
  Eunice C, 26,53
  Gertrude R, 26,94
  Jane, 26,94
  Jane/Jennie E, 26,94
  John, 26
  John N, 26,94
  John R, 26,94
  Joseph, 94
  Joshua, 26,94
  Katherine, 26
  Keziah (Brown), 26,29,53

HASTINGS, Laura Ellen, 94
  Lena Daisey, 162
  Lydia Ann (Nichols), 162
  Mary, 26
  Mary Emma, 26,94
  Mathew J, 162
  Matilda, 162
  Nancy, 26,54,129
  Otis, 94
  Otis L, 26,94
  Phebe, 94
  Rebecca, 26,28
  Rebecca J, 94
  Rebecca Jane, 26,94
  S G, 94
  Samuel, 162
  Sarah, 2,26,94,129
  Sarah (Edgerton), 94
  Sarah (Evans), 26,54
  Sarah E, 94
  Sarah E (Edgerton), 26
  Seth, 26,94
  Seth G, 94
  Sylvia, 162
  Welmet, 2,26
  Willard, 94
  Willard S, 94
  Wm, 1,2,26,54,94,129
  Wm C, 94
  Wm Clarkson, 26,94
  Wm E, 26,94
  Wm Edward, 94
HATFIELD, Ann, 94
  Etta, 94,110
  James, 94
  John, 94
  Jonas, 94
  Lydia, 94
  Mary, 94
  Nathan, 94
  Rachel, 94
  Richard, 94
  Sarah, 94
  Thomas, 94
HATHAWAY, Alfred C, 26,94
  Francis W, 26,94
  Minnie B, 94
  Minnie R, 26,94
HATTAN, George, 94
  Robert, 94
  see also **HATTON**
HATTON, George, 94
  Margaret, 94
  Margaret J, 94
  Robert, 94
  see also **HATTAN**
HAUGHTON, Bertha (Iredell), 26
  Charles M, 94
  Charles Melville, 26
  Elizabeth C, 94
  Elizabeth C (Mather), 26
  Kate (Meeker), 65
  Lewis M, 26
  Louanna/Luranna, 94
  Louanna H, 65
  Richard, 65
  Richard E, 26,94
  Wm P, 94
  Wm Percival, 26
  see also **HAWTON, HOUGHTON**

HAVENRIDGE, Isaiah, 94
    John, 94
    Wm Samuel, 94
    see also **HEAVENRIDGE**
HAWKINS, —— (Morrow), 39
    Aaron, 162
    Alice, 5
    Alma E, 26,95
    Amos, 1,9,26,74,94,95,97
    Ann/Anna/Anne, 7,9,26,34,39,74,94, 97,104
    Belle, 27,49
    Benjamin, 94
    Betsy, 95
    Blanche, 27,95
    Catharine (Lindamood), 162
    Celena/Celina M, 26,95
    Celina V, 95
    Charity, 94,97
    Charles N, 27,95
    Christiana (Guard), 27
    Daisy M, 26,95
    Edna, 27
    Elizabeth, 94
    Ella Ernest, 95
    Emily Jane (Townsend), 27
    Florence Webster, 27
    Franklin, 95
    George, 95
    George W, 26,27,95
    Henry, 26,95
    Henry W, 95
    Ida, 27
    Isaac, 26,95
    Jesse, 95
    John, 1,20,26,27,53,94,95,104,124, 142,162,175
    John Jr, 95,194
    Jonathan, 39,94,95
    Lella A, 26,95
    Levi, 27,95
    Lindly A, 27
    Lydia, 27,94,115,124,142
    Lydia Emeline, 20,27,95
    Martha, 9,74,94
    Martha (Parry), 27,95
    Mary, 26,53,86,94,95,104,142
    Mary (Bond), 162
    Mary (Morrow), 95
    Mary Emily, 65
    Minnie, 27,49,95
    Naomi (Howard), 27
    Nathan, 26,27,49,95
    Nellie R, 27
    Oliver, 27
    Pearl Ernest, 95
    Phoebe (Roberds), 95
    Prudence, 26,95
    Rachel, 26,95,128
    Rebecca/Rebeckah, 25,94,95
    Ruth Blanche, 95
    Sarah, 27,94,95
    Sarah (Jessop/Jessup), 20,26,27,95
    Sarah (Van Matre), 162
    Sarah (Wright), 95
    Sarah Ellen, 26,95
    Silas, 26
    Stephen, 26,95
    Susan Mather, 103
    Susannah M (Mather), 33
    Tamar/Tamer, 53,94,124,159,175,206
    Thomas, 95
    Wm, 26,94,95

HAWLEY, Benjamin, 95
    Caleb, 95
    Catharine, 95
    Eli, 95
    Joseph, 95
    Phoebe Ann, 95
    Rachel, 95
    Richard, 95
HAWORTH, Emily, 95,110
    George D, 95
    Hannah, 68,95
    Ira, 95
    James, 27
    Lot, 95
    Lydia J, 22,41
    Mahlon, 95
    Margaret (Dillen), 41
    Peninah, 95
    Phebe, 95
    Sarah, 95
    Sarah (Hawkins), 27
    Sarah (Stubbs) Clark, 95
    Thomas, 41
    see also **HAYWORTH**
HAWTON, Alabama, 44
    see also **HAUGHTON, HOUGHTON**
HAXTON, Descum, 162
    Elizabeth, 63
    Myrtle Lucile, 162
    Nellie (Sansbury), 162
HAY, Alice C, 159
    Daniel, 159
    Mary J (Hoover), 159
HAYNES, Isabell, 8
    Judith (Cadwallader), 95
    see also **HAINES, HANES**
HAYWARD, Harriett M, 91
    Henry J, 91
    Martha, 91
    Martha F, 24,91,95
HAYWORTH, Dillon, 111
    Hannah A, 68
    James, 111
    Lott, 95
    Mary (Hill), 95
    Richard, 111
    see also **HAWORTH**
HAZELETT, Lida W, 95
    see also **HAZLIT, HAZLITT**
HAZLIT, Lida W, 95
    see also **HAZELETT, HAZLITT**
HAZLITT, Lida W, 95
    see also **HAZELETT, HAZLIT**
HEALTON, Abra, 194
    Albert, 162,194
    Allen, 162,194
    Ann, 162
    Artemas/Artemus E, 162,163,194
    Bertha M, 163,172
    Elizabeth (Cox), 194
    Elwood, 162
    Emeline, 162
    Hannah, 194
    Hannah (Wilkinson), 162
    Joel, 162,163,194
    John, 162,194
    John A, 162,194
    Jonathan, 162,194
    Maggie, 194
    Maggie (Peckinpaugh), 162
    Mary Ann (Bond), 162,163,194
    Mary E, 162,194

HEALTON, Mary E (Millikan/Milliken), 162,163,172
    Nathan, 162
    Nathan M, 162
    Orilla, 162
    Rebecca, 162,167,194
    Rhoda, 162
    Ruth, 162
    Ruth (Hodson), 194
    Sarah, 162,194
    Sarah (Swain), 194
    Sarah Elizabeth, 162
    Thomas D, 162
    Wm, 162,174
    Wm B, 172,194
    Wm Bond, 162,163
HEAM, Emsley, 95
    Hezakiah/Hezekiah, 95
    Jason, 95
    Jehu, 95
HEAP, Elizabeth, 27,95
HEARN, Jane (Wheat), 49
    Rowena M, 49
    Wm, 49
HEAVENRIDGE, Elizabeth (Bradway), 95
    John, 95,112
    Margaret, 95,112
    Samuel, 95
    see also **HAVENRIDGE**
HEDGECOCK, Anna D, 164
    Marmaduke, 164
    Priscilla, 164
HEDGPATH, Arthur, 32
    Nancy, 32
    Tabitha, 32
HEFNER, Mary Ann, 194
    see also **HAFFNER, HOEFFNER**
HEINEY, Emma (Shutt), 163
    Hobart, 163
    Mary, 168
    Samuel, 163
HEISS, Jacob, 95
    Mary, 95
HEITLAND, Henrietta, 48
HELLER, Mary Ann, 179
HELM, Carrie, 160
HELSCEL, John, 27
    Mary, 27
    Myra M, 27
HELTON, Allen, 194
    Bertha, 194
    George, 27
    Louise (Todd), 27
HEMINGTON, James, 27,95
    Margaret S, 95
    Margaret Susan, 27
HENBY, Elias, 59
    Elizabeth, 59
    Elizabeth (White), 59
HENDERSHOTT, Cynthia, 47,95
    John, 95
    Rebecca, 95
HENDERSON, Bertha (Woodard), 27
    Isaac, 95
    Kesiah, 95
    Leanah, 29
    Margaret (Hunt), 95
    Rachel, 95
    Richard, 95
    Sarah, 95

HENDERSON, Susannah, 95
   Walter, 27
   Wm, 95
HENDREN, Martha, 3
   Melinda, 3
   Nimrod, 3
HENDRICKS, Ella (Fesel), 27
   see also **HENDRIX**
HENDRIX, Julia E, 169
   see also **HENDRICKS**
HENLEY, Adda (Williams), 27
   Alva J, 27
   Alvin C, 96
   Alvin Chawner, 96
   Charles, 95
   Charles F, 27
   Clark H, 27
   Cora Ann, 27,32,64,96
   Edgar, 27
   Electa, 27
   Elias, 95
   Eliza Ann, 27,63,95
   Elwood, 27
   Emeline , 27
   Emily, 95
   Emily H, 27
   Eve, 6
   Gertrude (Parks/Sparks), 27
   Gulielma, 27,48,91,95,96,97,101,130
   Gulielma (Charles), 27
   Henry, 6,18,27,32,48,64,95,96
   Hezekiah, 27,95
   Ida May, 6,27,96
   Isaac, 195
   Jacob, 195
   Jesse, 95
   John, 27,95,96
   John C, 27
   John Eddie/Eddy, 96
   John L, 195
   Joseph, 95
   Laura S, 18,27,96
   Lora A, 96
   Lora Alice, 96
   Martha, 27,130
   Martha C, 96
   Martha L, 27
   Mary, 27,95,97
   Mary (Newby), 59
   Mary Eva, 27,63
   Micajah, 27,91,95,96,97,101,130
   Micajah C, 27
   Miriam, 95,96
   Miriam W (Green), 27
   Naomi, 27,91
   Naomi B, 95,96
   Naomi B (Clawson), 27,95
   Penina, 59,95
   Priscilla, 95
   Priscilla (Ham), 27
   Rebecca, 27,101
   Robert, 59
   Robert M, 27
   Ruth, 95
   Ruth (Morrow), 95
   Samuel, 27,63,95
   Sarah H, 27,96
   Sylvanus, 95
   Tacy Ann, 95,96
   Tacy Ann (Meredith), 6,18,27,32,48
   Thomas, 95
   Walter K, 27

HENLEY, Wm, 195
   Wm Edgar, 27
   Wm L, 27
HENNEMYRE, Jerry, 96
   Rose/Ruth Anne, 96
HENSON, Flora B (Revelee), 27
   Lewis A, 27
   Louisa, 27,32
   Martha, 32
   Thomas, 27,32
HERBERT, Benjamin, 22,27
   Cora B, 22
   Cora S, 27
   Ida, 22,27
HERL, Sarah, 195
   Sarah (Hill), 195
HESKETT, James Wm, 27
   Rebecca Mae, 27
   Sarah J, 27
HESTON, Ann, 96
HEWIT, Mary (Hill), 178
   Phebe Ellen, 178
   Thomas, 178
   see also **HUIT**
HEYER, Frank, 195
   Sarah Etta, 195
   see also **HYER, HYRE**
HIATT, Absolam, 96
   Alfred J, 27,96
   Alice, 96,137
   Alvin, 96
   Ann/Anna/Anne, 27,96,150,183
   Ann (Williams), 163
   Anna Maria, 27,60
   Asher, 27,96
   Asiph, 96
   Banajah, 13,17,27
   Benjamin, 28
   Catherine, 96
   Celia Victoria, 163
   Charity, 163,195
   Charity (Williams), 20
   Charles M, 27,96
   Clarkson, 96
   Daniel, 27,96
   Daniel W, 27,28,96,195
   Daniel Williams, 96,163
   Dempsy/Demsy, 96
   Edgar F, 96
   Edgar Fletcher, 28
   Edwin W, 163,195
   Eleazar/Eleazer, 27,60,96,163
   Eleazar B, 27,96
   Eli, 28,96
   Elijah, 96
   Eliza, 96,195
   Eliza (Smith), 28
   Eliza Ann, 163,195
   Eliza H, 27
   Eliza Jane (Baldwin), 195
   Eliza W, 96
   Eliza Willan (Smith), 28
   Elizabeth, 195
   Elizabeth (White), 13,17,27,28
   Elizabeth D, 14,21,37
   Elizabeth Dix, 21
   Emily, 195
   Emily R, 163
   Emma, 189,195
   Emma (Potter), 163
   Emma E (Edwards), 11,154,163
   Ervin M, 163,195

HIATT, Esther, 20,114
   Esther C, 163
   Esther G, 17,18,21,27,61
   Eunice, 96
   Eunice S, 96
   Francis T, 96
   George, 96
   Gideon, 195
   Gulielma, 96
   Gulielma (Sanders), 27,60
   Hannah, 28,96,114
   Hannah (Morrow), 96
   Isaac, 28,96,137
   James, 96,195
   James Addison, 163,195
   James Smith, 28,96
   Jane, 96
   Jehu, 96
   Jesse, 27,28,96,195
   Jesse D, 96
   Jesse Dicks, 96
   Joel, 96
   John, 96,163,195
   John S, 27,96
   Joseph, 96
   Joseph P, 28,96
   Laura Alice, 96
   Lawrence, 163
   Linden C, 195
   Linden/Lyndon Cornelius, 163,195
   Louisa, 27
   Louisa (Woodard), 96
   Louisa Ann, 96
   Louisa M (Woodard), 122
   Louisa W, 96
   Lucy, 96
   Luzena, 195
   Lydia, 28,96
   Macy, 195
   Margaret (Chapman), 28
   Margaret Ann, 96
   Maria, 96
   Martha, 27,96,137
   Martha Jane (Williams), 163
   Marthajane, 28
   Mary, 96,163,195
   Melinda, 195
   Melinda (Mendenhall), 158,163,195
   Mordecai, 27,28,96
   Naomi, 13,14,27,40
   Nellie (Frazier), 163
   Oliver, 189
   Oliver Lindley, 11,154,163,195
   Phebe, 28,96
   Phebe T, 96
   Rachel, 3
   Rebecca, 28,50,96
   Rebecca E, 11,154,163,189
   Rebecca M, 158,163
   Rhoda, 96
   Rhoda (Dix), 28
   Robert, 96
   Ruth (Ratcliff), 96
   Samantha E (Morrison), 163
   Samantha Ellen, 195
   Sarah, 28,96,163,195
   Sarah (Smith), 96
   Sarah Ann/Anna, 96
   Sarah B, 27
   Sarah M, 27
   Semira, 137
   Shanna/Shannah, 28,96

HIATT, Shanny D, 96
    Sidney, 28
    Solomon, 27
    Thomas, 96,195
    Thomas W, 163
    Thurza, 28,96
    Tilney, 28,96
    Wm, 20,96
    Wm A, 163
    Wm F, 96
    Wm Fletcher, 96
    Wm J, 28,96
HIBBARD, Alice Ann, 96
    Benjamin, 96
    Charity, 96
    Jane, 96
    Sarah, 96
    Tacy B, 18
    see also **HIBBERD, HIBBERT, HIPPARD**
HIBBERD, Tacy B, 96
    see also **HIBBARD, HIBBERT, HIPPARD**
HIBBERT, Charity, 96
    Jane, 96
    see also **HIBBARD, HIBBER**D, **HIPPARD**
HICKS, Caroline M, 53
    Clara (Hopkins), 53
    Elnora, 96
    Hannah E, 96
    Mary, 96
    Mary Ellen, 96
    Michael, 96
    Sarah Elizabeth (Roe), 96
    Wesley F, 96
    Wm J, 53
HIGGENBOTHAM, Daniel Edgar, 63
    Margaret K, 63
    Mary Frances, 63
HIGGS, Emma, 96
    Emma R, 96
    Sarah E, 96
HIGHLEY, Edna, 28
    Frank, 28
    Louise (Lester), 28
HILES, Dora, 96
    Elijah, 96
HILL, Aaron, 28,29,96,97,163,195
    Abbie E, 29,97
    Abigail E, 97
    Abraham/Abram, 29,96
    Achsa/Axsa, 96,97
    Achsah (Peacock), 28
    Adolph H, 163
    Albert, 5
    Alice (Chalfant), 163
    Alice Jane, 61
    Amy, 28,97
    Amy (Kendall), 97
    Ann/Anna, 28,34,97,107
    Ann (Clark), 97
    Anna (Moffitt), 28
    Anna/Anne E, 97
    Anna Jane, 18,29,97
    Anna W, 28
    Artalissa (Bond), 28
    Arthur J, 28
    Asenath, 28,96,97
    Asenath E, 29,97
    Asenath E, 97
    Benjamin, 1,2,28,29,53,97,115,117, 195

HILL, Benjamin C, 28,29,53,97
    Benjamin Franklin, 97
    Benjamin J, 157,163,195
    Benoney/Benoni, viii,96,97
    Bertha, 53
    Bertha C, 28
    Bertha Celia, 97
    Bertha E, 163
    Bessie, 28
    Charity, 97
    Charity (Hawkins), 97
    Charles, 28,29,97,163,195
    Charles A, 97
    Charles H, 97
    Christopher, 1,96
    Cora, 97
    Cora Bertha, 28,65
    Cora R, 28
    Cyrus W, 28
    Daniel, 24,28,92,97
    Daniel Aaron, 28
    Daniel C, 28,97
    Dinah (Cox), 96
    Dora, 97
    E Gurney, 39
    Edmund/Edward Gurney, 28,97
    Edward S, 29,97
    Elam B, 28,97
    Eli B, 29,97
    Elijah, 28,97
    Eliza (Stuart), 28,39
    Eliza L, 97
    Elizabeth, 2,29,33,34,97,127
    Elizabeth D (Clawson), 29
    Elizabeth J, 97
    Elizabeth P (Kirby), 97
    Elizabeth S, 97
    Ella, 97
    Ella G (Green), 28
    Emma, 24,28,29,92,97
    Emma C, 28
    Enos, 28,97
    Enos N, 97
    Enos W, 28,97
    Enos Wilson, 97
    Esther (Davis), 163
    Esther Ann, 157,167,173,174,191,195
    Eunice, 163
    Eunice (Hill), 163
    Ezra, 97
    Ezra E, 28
    Flora A, 28,97
    Flora Lizzie, 28
    Florence, 97
    Florence G, 97
    Freddie Reece, 28
    George, 18,97
    Guilelma (Charles), 28
    Gulielma, 28,72
    Hannah, 29,96,115
    Harmon, 9,28,72,75,97,105
    Henry, 28,97,163,195
    Herman, 96
    Hiram, 29
    J Henley, 142
    Jacob, 2,28,97,163,195
    Jane, 97
    Jemima (Clark), 28,97
    Jesse, 2,28,96
    John, 2,28,42,65,96,97,163,195
    John C, 29,97
    John H, 97

HILL, John J, 28
    John M, 97
    John Milton, 28,97
    Jonathan, 97
    Joseph, 2,28,97,105
    Joseph B, 28,97
    Joseph H, 28,97
    Joseph Henry, 97
    Lavina/Levina, 157,163,195
    Lavina/Levina (Hill), 157,163
    Leona B (Eikenbury), 28
    Lillian A, 163
    Lily, 57
    Lydia, 5
    M Peninah, 141
    Madora, 97
    Maggie M, 29
    Mahlon R, 29,97
    Margaret Elizabeth, 28
    Margaret M, 97
    Marion, 28
    Marth Ann (Hussey), 24
    Martha, 2,29,40,96,97,105,117
    Martha (Cox), 28
    Martha (Jay), 28,97
    Martha A, 22,92
    Martha Ann, 9,22,28,38,75
    Martha E, 28,97
    Martha Elizabeth, 97
    Martha J, 28
    Mary, 2,9,18,29,43,72,75,95,96,97, 105,115,163,178,196
    Mary (Henley), 97
    Mary (Hill), 9,28,97
    Mary (Wickett), 53
    Mary A, 97
    Mary Ann, 97
    Mary Elisabeth/Elizabeth, 28,97,105
    Mary Emily, 29,97
    Mary Esther (Wickett), 28,97
    Mary J, 28,97
    Mary Stuart, 28,39
    Matthew, 96
    Micajah, 28
    Milton, 97
    Minerva, 37
    Miriam P, 97
    Miriam Penninah, 29,64
    Mordecai/Mordicah, 29,96
    Murray, 28,97
    Nancy, 97
    Nancy (Davis), 28,64
    Nancy D, 97
    Nancy D (Davis), 29
    Olive A, 28,42
    Orville L, 163
    Owen, 97
    Penina/Peninah/Penninah, 29,96,97, 107
    Phebe (Canaday), 163
    Phebe A (Branson), 28,42,65
    Phebe Ellen (Branson), 97
    Phillip, 29
    Rachel (Bailey), 97
    Rachel S (Bailey), 28
    Ralph J, 97
    Rebecca/Rebekah, 28,29,96,97,117
    Rebecca (Hastings), 28
    Rebecca (Mills), 97
    Rebecca J/Jay, 29,97
    Rebecca Jane, 28,105
    Rebecca M, 97

HILL, Rebecca M (Mills), 28
    Robert, 1,2,28,29,97
    Robert A, 28
    Ruth, 29,96
    Samuel, 29,97
    Samuel C, 28,97
    Sarah, 2,23,28,29,43,71,77,96,115,
      163,195
    Sarah D, 5
    Sarah J/Jay, 28,97
    Susanna/Susannah, 2,95,97
    Susanna/Susannah (Morgan), 28,29
    Tacy B (Hibbard), 18
    Tamar (Clark), 97
    Tamer, 97
    Tamer (Hussey), 28
    Thomas, 1,29,34,77,96,97,107,115
    Thomas T, 28,29,64,97
    Virgie, 28
    W Ann, 97
    Wm, 2,28,29,96,97
    Wm Jr, 97
    Wm Sr, 97
    Wm C, 163
    Wm Edmund, 28
    Wm Franklin, 28
    Zilpha (Price), 97
    Zilphy, 97
HILLES, Dora, 97
    Elijah, 97
HILTON, Susan, 161
HINCKLEY, Mary H, 50
HINES, Emma, 97
    Lydia, 97
HINKLE, John H, 29
    Julia, 29
    Milo S, 29
HINSHAW, Abijah, 97
    Albert, 98
    Armella, 148
    Asenath/Asenith, 97,149,163,184
    Barnabas Coffin, 29,97,163
    Caroline M, 98
    Caroline Mary (Hamm), 29
    Carrie, 98
    Dinah, 176
    Edmund, 163
    Edmund R, 163
    Edwin, 98
    Elbert, 98
    Elizabeth (Austin) Conkle, 29
    Ellen (Huffman), 163
    Elmina, 198
    Elmina L, 198
    Elmina Louisa, 163
    Elva B, 46
    Elwood, 29
    Elwood S, 29
    Emily Jane, 163
    Emma, 98
    Ethel M, 98
    Eunice, ix
    Evaline, 163
    Exalina C, 208
    Ezra, 97,98
    Franklin, 98
    H Earl, 29
    Hannah, 97,98,195,198
    Hannah (Coffin), 163
    Henry, 29,98
    Henry B, 98,163
    Herchel C, 29

HINSHAW, Ira, ix
    Irena, 163
    Isaiah, 29,97
    Jacob, 30
    James, 195
    James Colwell, ix
    James M, 195
    James Madison, 163
    Jesse, 97
    Jesse B, 97,98
    Laura, 51,
    Laura, 98
    Lindley, ix
    Lizzie A (Conkle), 98
    Lydia, 97,98
    Mae, 29
    Malinda/Melinda, 149,150,163,181
    Maria, 46
    Mary, 98
    Nancy, 97
    Nathan, ix
    Oliver Goldsmith,, 163
    Olla, 98
    Phebe, 97,98
    Phebe (Allen), 30
    Philander, 98
    Rachel, 29,30,55
    Rachel O, 29,97
    Rueben, 97,98
    Ruth, 171
    S S, 29
    Samantha, 29
    Sarah, 47,97,175
    Sarrah J, 29
    Selina, 97
    Seth, 149,163
    Simon, 97
    Susannah, 29,97
    Tilnias, ix
    Walter, 98
    Warner, 46
    Wellmet/Welmet, 29,97
    Wm B, 98,163,195,198
    Wm Henry, ix
    Zilpha, 98
    Zimri, 97
HIPPARD, Marianna J (Bond), 29
    Marion, 29
    Marion N, 29
    Mary (Maharry), 29
    Vera, 29
    Wilburn L, 29
    Wm, 29
    Wm A, 98
    see also **HIBBARD**, **HIBBERD**,
      HIBBERT
HIRSHFIELD, Louisa, 20
HIRST, Catherine, 163
    see also **HURST**
HISER, Abraham, 98
    Abraham B, 29
    Mary Edna (Carpenter), 29,98
    Sophia J, 29,98
    Winfield Scott, 29,98
HISEY, Ann M, 29
    Kathrine, 29
    Robert J, 29
HITCH, Laura (Harrison), 29
HITCHCOCK, Barnabas, 98
    Deborah, 98
    Hannah, 98
    Joshua, 98

HITCHCOCK, Lydia, 98
    Priscilla, 98
    Wm, 98
HIXON, Rachel, 22
HOAG, Abigail, 20,29,87
    Abigail R, 98
    Huldah C, 20,29,87,98
    Mary R, 12
    Nathan, 87
    Nathan C, 20,29,98
HOBBICK, Elizabeth, 54
HOBBS, Abigail, 148,156,167
    Alice Fowler, 29,98
    Barnabas C, 29,98
    Caroline, 29,98
    Deborah, 98
    Delilah, 98
    Elisha, 98
    Fowel/Lowell Buxton, 29,98
    George Tatum, 29,98
    Grace Elizabeth, 29
    Lydia, 29
    Marmaduke, 29
    Martha (Nordyke), 29
    Mary, 98
    Mary Anna/Anne, 29,98
    Peninah, 98
    Priscilla, 98
    Rebecca T, 29,98
    Samuel, 98
    Sibyl Amelia, 29,98
    Wilson, 98
    Wm, 98
    Wm Henry, 29,98
HOBSON, Aaron, 98
    Ann/Anna, 98,163,210
    Charles, 163,195
    David, 163
    Deborah, 163
    Deborah Ann, 163
    Easter, 163
    Elizabeth, 163
    George, 98,163,169,195
    George Jr, 195
    Hannah, 163
    Herman Silas, 29
    Isaac, 163,195
    Jesse, 98,163,195
    John, 163,195
    Joshua, 98,163,195
    Leanah (Henderson), 29
    Margaret, 163
    Mary Jane, 163
    Matilda, 195
    Orlando, 29
    Rachel, 163
    Rebecca, 98,163,169,200,205
    Sarah, 98,163,169
    Stephen, 163,195
    Thomas, 163,195
    Thomas Charles, 98
    Wm, 163,195
HOCKET, David, 98
    Eleazar, 98
    Elizabeth, 98
    Frank, 98
    Gila Ann, 195
    Hannah (Beals), 150
    Hattie, 98
    Homer, 98
    Jabez, 98
    Jesse, 195

HOCKET, John W, 195
    Joseph, 98
    Lizzie, 195
    Lydia, 98
    Margaret, 150,151
    Nancy, 98
    Nathan, 98
    Perry Allen, 195
    Philip, 98
    Rachel, 98
    Susan, 195
    Unice, 98
    Wm, 150
    Wm A, 195
    Zimri, 195
    see also **HOCKETT**
HOCKETT, Addison, 29
    Addison Felton, 164
    Albert C, 98
    Caroline D, 78
    Carrie May, 29
    Clara Bell, 160,163,195
    David W, 29
    Earl Taylor, 29
    Eliza/Eliazer, 98
    Elizabeth, 98
    Elizabeth (Study), 29
    Emma, 195
    Francis G, 21,29
    Gillean, 163
    Hannah, 163,195
    Hannah (Wilson), 164
    Hannah Elizabeth, 163
    Hattie A, 21,29,88
    Homer C, 29
    Jesse, 163,195
    Joel, 29,98
    John, 98,158,160,163,164,167,195
    John W, 163
    Josie, 175
    Lydia Ann, 98
    Malinda, 195
    Malinda (Grimes), 164,165
    Martha, 49
    Martha E, 29,98
    Martha Ellen, 164
    Martha Jane, 163
    Mary, 168,170,171
    Mary E, 50
    Mary Elma, 164
    Mary Ethel, 164
    Matilda (Dennis), 50
    Matilda C, 195
    Matilda C (Dennis), 164,195
    Milliken, 98
    Nathan, 98
    Oliver Clarence, 29
    Perry Albert, 163
    Phebe, 158
    Philip, 98
    Rachel (Carey), 21,29
    Rebecca (Hunt), 29
    Sarah (Frazier), 29
    Sarah E, 195
    Sarah Emeline/Emiline, 163,167,195
    Sarah Etta, 164,165
    Sarah G, 98
    Sarah G (Charles), 29,98
    Sherman, 29
    Susan, 158,160,163,167,195
    Susan (Gebhart), 164
    Susan J, 195

HOCKETT, Tamar, 29,98
    Warner, 50
    Warner M, 29,98,164,195
    Wm, 195
    Wm A, 163
    Wm N, 29,98
    Zimri, 164,165,195
    see also **HOCKET**
HODGEN, Samuel, 195
    see also **HODGIN**
HODGESON, Henry, 98
    see also **HODGSON**
HODGIN, Albert C, 98
    Albert L, 29
    Alice, 98
    Amy (Hodgins), 30
    Amy E, 30,98
    Annie, 60
    Benjamin, 32
    Bertha A, 30,98
    Carrie, 98
    Charles E, 98
    Charles Elkanah, 29,98
    Charles Elkanah Hodges, 30
    Cordelia B, 25
    Cyrus W, 30,65,98
    Cyrus Wm, 29
    Daniel W, 29
    David O, 29
    Elias M, 29,30,98
    Elizabeth (Candler), 32
    Elizabeth (Stewart), 30
    Elizabeth Emma, 30
    Elkanah B, 98
    Ella R, 13,51
    Ellen M, 98
    Elva R, 30,98
    Emily, 154
    Emily (Chandler), 65
    Emily Caroline, 98
    Emily Caroline (Chandler), 29
    Emily J, 11,188
    Emma, 98
    Emma (Harlan), 30
    Emma Edna/Eldora, 30
    Grace, 30,98
    Grace A, 98
    Henry T, 30
    James A, 98
    James Orlando/Leland, 30
    Jane (Millican), 25
    Jesse, 98
    Jonathan, 25
    Joseph, 30
    Joseph N, 30,98
    Laura Alice, 29,65,98
    Lizzie, 98
    Lydia Elva (Johnson), 29
    Malinda, 170
    Margaret, 98
    Martha (Lewelling), 30
    Martha A, 98
    Martha L, 30,98
    Mary E, 30,37,98
    Mary E (Brooks), 29
    Mary M, 29
    Milton, 29
    Minerva (Hill), 37
    Mourning (Coffin), 154
    Nathan, 154
    Phebe A, 98
    Phebe Alice, 30,55,98

HODGIN, Pleasant W, 164
    Rachel, 98
    Rachel (Hinshaw), 29,30,55
    Rachel E, 98
    Rachel E (Lewelling), 30
    Rhoda, 32
    Robert, 37
    Ruth (Dix), 30
    Sadie, 60
    Sallie E (Iverman), 29
    Sarah (Anthony), 30
    Tilnais/Tilnias, 29,30,55,98
    Wm C, 98
    Wm M, 60
    Wm Milton, 98
    Wm P, 98
    Wm Percival, 30,98
    see also **HODGEN**, **HODGINS**
HODGINS, Amy, 30
    Caroline, 98
    Jesse, 98
    see also **HODGIN**
HODGSON, Elizabeth A, 61
    Janney (Larrowe), 195
    John, 195
    Sarah, 195
    Zechariah, 195
    see also **HODGESON**
HODSON, Ann/Anna, 164,196
    Charity, 147,148,149,150,165
    Charlotte, 164,196
    Cynthia, 196
    David, 164,196
    Deborah, 195
    Deborah Ann, 190
    Delilah, 164
    Eli, 164
    Elizabeth, 148,164,195,196,203,204, 207
    Elizabeth (Ratcliff), 195
    Elvina, 164
    Elvira, 196
    Franklin, 195
    Geney/Ginny, 164,196
    Gulielma, 164,196
    Henry, 98,164,195,196
    Ira, 164
    Isaac, 195
    Jacob, 195
    James, 195
    Jane, 164,196
    Jemima, 203
    Jesse, 164,195,196
    Joel, 164,196
    John, 164,194,195,196
    John Jr, 195
    John M, 164
    John W, 164
    Jonathan, 164,195,196
    Julia Ann/Juliann, 164,196
    Lewis, 164
    Mary, 164
    Mary (Allen), 195
    Mary (Baldwin), 196
    Matilda, 164,196
    Matilda (Larue), 196
    Milo, 164
    Naomi, 207
    Nathan, 164,195,196
    Phebe, 98,99
    Rachel, 164,196,204
    Rebeckah, 164

HODSON, Rhoda/Rodah, 164,195,196
   Richard, 164,196
   Ruth, 164,194
   Sally Ann, 164
   Samuel, 195
   Sarah/Sarrah, 164,194,195, 196, 201
   Sarah Jane, 164,196
   Solomon, 164,195,196,203,207
   Solomon Jr, 196
   Thomas, 164,195,196
   Uriah, 164,195
   Wm O, 164
   Zachara/Zachariah/Zechariah/ Zecheriah, 164,195,196,204
   see also **HODGEN**
HOEFFER, Blanche May, 30
   Charles Foster, 30
   see also **HAFFNER, HEFNER**
HOFF, Charlotte, 7
   Wm, 7
HOFFMAN, Elenora, 38
HOFFNER, Mary E, 196
HOGGART, Ruth, 98
HOGGAT, Aaron, 98
   Abner, 98
   Elisha, 98
   John, 98
   Joseph, 98
   Moses, 98
   Nathan, 98
   Philip, 98
   Robert, 98
   see also **HOGGATT**
HOGGATT, Alice, 98
   Christiana, 98
   David, 98
   Deborah, 98
   Elizabeth, 98
   Irisgladening, 98
   Juley, 98
   Martha, 98
   Mary, 98
   Miriam, 98
   Nancy, 98
   Rachel, 98
   Ruth, 73
   Sophia, 98
   see also **HOGGAT**
HOGSTON, Floyd, 98
HOLADAY, Abraham, 99
   Anna, 185
   Aron, 99
   Edith, 99
   Elizabeth, 99
   Jane, 99
   Jesse, 99
   Lena Daisy, 164
   Robert, 99
   Samuel,99,196
   Wm, 99
   see also **HOLIDAY, HOLIDY, HOLLYDAY**
HOLAWAY, Thomas S, 99
   see also **HOLLOWAY, HOLOWAY**
HOLDER, Henry, 153
   Sarah, 153
   Susan, 153
HOLE, Allen David, 30
   Isabel (Wilson), 30
   Mary (Doan), 30
   Raymond, 30

HOLIDAY, Emma Florence (Harter), 164
   Mary E, 168
   Mary M, 163
   P L, 164
   Samuel, 196
   Wm Jr, 99
   see also **HOLADAY, HOLIDY, HOLLYDAY**
HOLLENSHAD, Caroline E, 99
   see also **HALLENSHADE, HILLINSHADE, HOLLENSHADE,**
HOLLENSHADE, Caroline, 99
   see also **HALLENSHADE, HILLINSHADE, HOLLENSHAD**
HOLLEY, Ann, 99
   Rachel, 99
   see also **HOLLY**
HOLLIDY, Deborah, 99
   Hannah, 99
   Jane, 99
   Nancy, 99
   see also **HOLADAY, HOLIDAY, HOLLYDAY**
HOLLINGSWORTH, Abijah, 99
   Alice, 33
   Ann/Anna, 161,164,165,176,206
   Ann (Wickersham), 30
   Arabel, 30
   Asiph, 30,51
   Caroline, 99
   Caroline (Fulghum), 99
   Carter, 99
   Charles, 30
   Clarence, 30,99
   Clarence W, 30
   David, 99
   Deborah, 148,184
   Deborah Arnett, 164,165
   Eber, 99
   Elias, 30
   Elisabeth (Vestal), 99
   Elizabeth, 164
   Elwood Clare, 30
   Emma C, 11
   Ezekiel, 99
   Frank S, 30
   Franklin, 30
   George, 99
   Goldie V, 30
   Gulielma, 99
   Hannah, 99,148,164,165,176,196,197
   Henry, 99,148,164,165,176,196,197, 210
   Homer, 30,99
   Iola, 30,99
   Ira, 99
   Isaac, 16,99
   Isaiah, 99
   Israel H, 30
   James, 89,99,129
   Jennie C (Vance), 30
   Joanna, 99
   Joanna Ines/Inez, 30,99
   John, 11,99
   Jonathan, 99
   Jonathan Jr, 99
   Joseph, 32,33,99,196
   Joseph Fallas, 30
   Katurrah, 99
   Lucinda, 164
   Lydia, 11,30

HOLLINGSWORTH, Lydia H, 51
   Mabel, 30
   Marible, 16
   Martha E, 30
   Martha J, 46
   Mary, 89,99
   Mary (Vestal), 99
   Mary Elizabeth, 16
   Milton, 30,99
   Nathan, 99
   Ona H, 30
   Patience, 99
   Phebe, 99
   Rachel, 99,106
   Rachel (Vestal), 99
   Rachel A, 30,99
   Rachel W (Wildman), 30
   Rebecca, 99
   Rhoda (Whitacre), 32
   Ruth Anna, 32
   Sarah/Sarrah, 89,93,99,129,164
   Sarah Miriam, 99
   Sarry (Horney), 23
   Susan, 99
   Susan M, 30,99
   Susannah, 99
   Thomas, 99
   Wm, 99
HOLLINSHADE, Caroline A, 99
   see also **HALLENSHADE, HOLLENSHAD, HOLLENSHADE**
HOLLOPETER, Mary, 99
   Zilphia, 99
HOLLOWAY, Abigail, 99
   Amos, 30,99
   David, 89,99,115
   Elizabeth (Smith), 30,99
   Hannah, 89,99,115
   Hepsibah, 30,99
   Jacob, 196
   Jason, 30,99
   Jesse, 99
   John, 99,196
   John S, 30
   John W, 196
   Margaret, 30,99,115
   Nathan, 30,99
   Phebe (Hodson), 99
   Ruth, 99
   Stephen, 30,99
   Wm, 196
   Wm Jr, 196
   see also **HOLAWAY, HOLOWAY**
HOLLOWEL, Mary, 99
   Miriam, 99
   Sarah, 99
   see also **HOLLOWELL**
HOLLOWELL, Abba, 99
   Elizabeth, 99
   Jesse, 99
   John, 99
   Jonathan, 99
   Mary, 99
   Michal, 99
   Nathan, 99
   Peggy, 99
   Robert, 99
   Smithson, 99
   Wm, 99
   see also **HOLLOWEL**
HOLLY, Eli, 99
   Rachel, 99

HOLLY, Richard, 99
    Rueben, 99
    see also HOLLEY
HOLLYDAY, Almeda (Milliken), 196
    see also HOLADAY, HOLIDAY,
        HOLIDY
HOLMAN, Lydia, 99
HOLMES, Alice, 44
HOLOMAN, Tabitha, 167
HOLOWAY, Thomas Sr, 99
    see also HOLAWAY, HOLLOWAY
HOLZAPPEL, Clara Barbara, 30
    Lizzie, 30
    Samuel, 30
HONEYCUTT, Jane C, 196
    see also HONNEYCUTT,
        HUNNICUTT, HUNEYCUTT
HONNEYCUTT, Daniel, 196
    see also HONEYCUTT,
        HUNNICUTT, HUNEYCUTT
HOOKER, Lydia, 196
HOOPES, Anna S, 99
    Anne S, 99
    Mary Ella, 99
    Samuel, 99
    see also HOOPS
HOOPS, Anna S, 30
    Mary Ella, 30
    Samuel, 30
    see also HOOPES
HOOVER, Alexander/Allexander, 30,99
    Alfred, 100
    Allen, 100
    Andrew, 1,2,30,99,100,126
    Andrew Jr, 30,99
    Andrew Sr, 99
    Ann/Anna/Annie, 59,100
    Ann (Cook), 30
    Catharine/Catherine, 3,99,100,137
    Charity, 196
    Daniel C, 100
    Edna L, 100
    Edna Lois, 30
    Elizabeth, 2,30,99,113,126,152
    Emma A (Cloud), 30
    Emma S, 100
    Enos, 100
    Enos, 30
    Frederick, ii,1,30,99
    George M, 164
    Grace E, 164
    Guielema/Gulielma, 99,100
    Gulielma (Ratliff), 30,99
    Helen, 30
    Helen C, 100
    Henry, 2,30,99,100
    James, 30,100
    John, 30,100
    John H, 196
    Jonas, 100
    Jonas M, 100
    Jonathan, 164
    Katherine (Yount), 30
    Levi, 100
    Levi C, 30
    Lula, 100
    Mahlon, 30,100
    Martha, 83
    Martha Elma, 100
    Mary, 16,30,83,100
    Mary J, 159
    Phebe Ann (Macy), 100

HOOVER, Rebecca, 2,105
    Samuel, 30,99
    Samuel W, 100
    Sarah, 2,30,99,126,180
    Sarah Jane (Bales), 164
    Susana (Brower), 164
    Susanna (Clark), 99
    Susannah, 99
    Thomas, 30,100
    Wm H, 100
HOPKINS, Caroline (Williams), 100
    Clara, 53
    Elizabeth B, 100
    Elizabeth B (Diffendorfer), 30
    Elizabeth D, 100
    Joseph G, 100
    Richard P, 30
    Sarah, 100
    Sarah A, 100
    Thomas, 100
HOPPE, Alma Henrietta, 30
    Caroline (Schumaker), 30
    Harmon, 30
HORN, Achsah, 30,100
    Achsah M, 100
    Anna/Annie, 100
    Annie (Leeds), 30
    Arthur D, 30
    Charlotte (Knox), 30
    Clyde L, 30
    Eliza, 9,25
    Emma C, 30
    Hannah (White), 30
    Henry, 100
    Iona, 30
    Irma C, 30
    Jeremiah, 100
    Josea, 30
    Josie, 100
    Matilda, 100
    Mazaney, 100
    Olive, 100
    Ollie May, 100
    Pharabe/Pharaby, 100
    Phebe, 100
    Silas, 30
    Silas H, 30
    Valentine K, 30
    Valentine R, 100
    Viola, 70
    Willie, 100
    see also HORNE
HORNADA, Jacob Worley, 100
    Orilla, 100
    Paul, 100
    see also HORNADAY
HORNADAY, Henderson, 100
    Henderson H, 100
    Martha Ellen, 31
    Olive A, 31,100
    Paul, 31,100
    see also HORNADA
HORNE, Martha, 12
    see also HORN
HORNER, Beulah S, 100
    Buelah, 100
    Ellen S (Swain), 46
    Ollie M, 46
    Philip M, 46
    Samuel, 100
HORNEY, Albert, 31
    Ann (Mathews), 31
    Ann C, 100

HORNEY, Ann M, 100
    Charles, 31,100
    Clara, 31
    Daniel Clark, 31
    David Sanders, 31
    Deborah, 40
    Deborah D, 100
    Edward, 31
    Eli, 31
    Elisabeth/Elizabeth, 31,47,100
    Elizabeth (Sanders), 31
    Elizabeth Longstreth, 31
    Emily, 31,100,128
    Emily (Clark), 100
    Helen/Hellen, 31,53
    Howard Allen, 31
    James, 100
    Jane, 31,100
    Jesse, 31,100
    Joel, 21,31,53,100
    John, 31,47,100
    John A, 100
    Jonathan, 31,100
    Martha , 31
    Mary, 31,47
    Mary Belle, 21,31
    Philip, 31
    Prudence, 31,100
    Richard, 31
    Richard M, 31
    Samuel, 31
    Sarah/Sarry, 33,100
    Sarah B, 21,31,58,100
    Sarah B (Mather), 100
    Sarah P, 53
    Solomon, 31,100
    Susan, 31
    Susan L, 100
    Susanna L (Mather), 31
    Susannah L, 100
    Wm, 31,100
    see also HORNY
HORNISH, Bazabel B, 31
    Bazaleel, 100
    Jacob B, 31,100
    Sarah Ann, 100
    Tamar/Tamer, 100
    Wm H, 31
    Wm W, 100
HORNY, Elijah, 31
    Elizabeth Ann, 31
    Gulielma, 31
    Mary, 31
    Samuel Milton, 31
    see also HORNEY
HORRALL, Fannie E, 31
    James C, 31
    Martha E (Bond), 31
    Susan (Mendenhall), 31
    Thomas H, 31
    see also HORRELL
HORRELL, Fannie E, 100
    James C, 100
    Mattie E, 100
    see also HORRALL
HORTON, Anne Daisey, 33
    Caroline (Pomeroy), 33
    Jacob, 207
    Lewis, 33
HOSIER, Lewis, 1
    Wm, 1
    see also HOZIER

HOTCHKISS, Horace, 31
  Mary Winifred, 31,100
  Mary Winifred (Bellis), 31
  Wm Kenworthy, 31
HOUCK, Ellen, 196
  Ellen (Macy), 164
  James, 164
HOUGH, Addison, 6,21,31,100
  Alfred, 100
  Anna, 164,196
  Anna D (Hedgecock), 164
  Aseneth, 164
  Bertha J, 31
  Berthe I, 100
  Celia (Cox), 31
  Christe, 100
  Elisabeth/Elizabeth, 62,100,164,190, 196
  Elizabeth (Marshall), 196
  Ella, 40
  Elma, 34
  Elmina, 196
  Emma, 31
  Ethel A, 6,31,100
  Eugene B, 31,100
  Gulielma, 100
  Hannah (Milhous) Mendenhall, 100
  Hannah E (Chamness), 164
  Hannah M, 113
  Hiram, 31,100
  Huldah, 164,190
  Ira, 100,164,190,196
  Isabel A, 154,164
  Isabel A (Chamness), 164
  Isaiah, 100,164,196
  Israel, 100,103
  J Franklin, 164
  James, 100
  Jesse, 164,196
  John, 100,154,164
  Jonathan, 100
  Josephine Pearl, 100
  Lydia, 103
  Mahlon, 164,196
  Manson, 196
  Manson Z, 164,196
  Martha, 100,164
  Martha J (Staton), 154,164
  Mary, 100,116
  Mary A, 100
  Mary R, 21,31
  Milton W, 164
  Moses, 31
  Nathan, 164,196
  Penniah, 31
  Robert B, 31,100
  Roscoe, 31,100
  Ruth, 164
  Samuel J, 164
  Sarah Ann, 100
  Sarah Ann (Jessup), 6,21,31
  Sarah Elma, 100,103
  Thomas, 100
  Wm, 100,116
  Wm C, 100
  Wm Clarence, 31
  see also **HUFF**
HOUGHTON, Elizabeth (Mather), 100
  Richard E, 100
  Sally, 100
  Wm, 100
  see also **HAUGHTON, HAWTON**

HOUSTON, Alabama, 44
HOWARD, Barbara (Julian), 100
  Elizabeth, 15
  Ida E, 51
  Joseph, 51
  Mary A (Overholtz), 51
  Naomi, 27
  Rebecca (Smith), 27
  Wm, 27
HOWEL, Amelia, 196
  Amelia (Baldwin), 196
  Anna, 196
  Charles, 196
  Charles Jr, 196
  Enos, 196
  John, 196
  Joseph, 196
  Larkin, 196
  Levi, 196
  Lydia, 196
  Ruth, 184
  Wm, 196
  see also **HOWELL**
HOWELL, Amelia (Baldwin), 165
  Bell, 31
  Charles, 148,149,164,165
  Claud W, 31
  D M, 31
  Deborah (Steer), 100
  Deborah A (Steer), 100
  Deborah Ann (Starr), 31
  Elizabeth, 48
  Emeline, 174
  Enos, 164
  Flora, 13
  Hannah, 23,31,100
  Harry C Jr, 31
  Jackson, 174
  John, 31,165,196
  John H, 196
  Joseph, 164,165
  Larkin, 164,165,196
  Laura P (Teague), 31
  Levi, 164
  Lydia, 23,31,164,209
  Lydia (Jackson), 165
  Martha (Carroll), 31
  Martha A, 174
  Mary, 170
  Mary (Stout), 148,149,164,165
  Nancy, 164
  Nancy Jane, 165
  Rachel (Reynard), 165
  Rachel (Rightsman), 196
  Rhoda, 148,149,164
  Rosa, 166
  Ruth, 149,160,164,166,175
  Samuel, 100
  Samuel C, 31,100
  Sarah B, 23,31
  Sophie, 164
  Stephen, 23,31
  Susannah, 149,164
  Verdie, 31
  Wm, 164
  see also **HOWEL**
HOWELLS, Laur B, 100
  Laura T, 100
  see also **HOWELS**
HOWELS, Sophia, 196
  see also **HOWELLS**
HOWES, Charles B, 100
  Eunice, 19

HOZIER, Ann, 31
  Caroline, 31
  Henry, 31
  Lewis, 101
  Mary, 31
  Milicent (Bailey), 31
  Nathan, 31
  Wm, 31
  see also **HOSIER**
HUBBARD, Amanda, 101
  Anna, 101
  Anna Grace, 101
  Anna M, 101
  Butler, 101
  Celia, 101
  Deliah/Delila Caroline, 101
  Dorothy Tuttle, 31
  Elias, 101
  Elias H, 101
  Eliza Ann, 101
  Emily, 101
  Frank, 101
  George, 101
  George H, 101
  George M, 101
  Harriet P, 101
  Henry, 101
  Henry F, 31,101
  Jehiel L, 101
  Jeremiah, 31,101
  John, 8
  John S, 101
  John T, 101
  Joseph B, 101
  Julietta, 101
  Louisa Jane, 101
  Louise, 31
  Martha, 101,104,161
  Martha (Sanders), 8
  Martha C, 31
  Mary Alice, 101
  Mary Melinda, 101
  Miriam, 101
  Miriam H, 101
  Nellie (Clark), 31,101
  Richard J, 101
  Sarah, 8,101
  Thomas C, 101
  Thomas Chalkey, 101
  Wm, 101
  Wm B, 101
  Wm G, 101
HUBBELL, Franc, 31
  H Harriet, 31
  Mary E, 31
HUBBS, John Frumpour, 31
  Lavina, 18,31
  Margaret, 31
HUBLER, Emmanuel, 37
  Lottie (Case), 37
  Margaret, 42
  Margaret E, 37
HUDDLESTON, Anna, 101
  Lydia, 101
  Phebe, 101
  Sarah, 101
  see also **HUDDLESTONE, HUDLESTONE**
HUDDLESTONE, David, 101
  Eli, 101
  Jesse, 101
  John, 101

HUDDLESTONE, Jonathan, 101
    Wm, 101
    see also **HUDDLESTON,**
    HUDLESTONE
HUDLESTON, Esther Ann (Winder), 101
    see also **HUDDLESTON,**
    HUDDLESTONE
HUDSON, Ann, 18
HUFF, Amelia, 6
    Christe, 101
    Doritha (Jenkins), 192
    James, 101
    Lydia, 6
    Mary Ann, 101
    Sidney, 101
    see also **HOUGH**
HUFFMAN, Chester W, 165
    Edward H, 165
    Ellen, 163
    Ellen (Crumb), 165
    Jacob, 101
    Margaret, 168
    Margaret (Bowman), 151
    Mary Alice, 101
    Paul Edgar, 165
    Sarah Catherine, 151
    Sylvester H, 151
HUGHES, Ann, 101
    Catharine, 179
    Eleanor Starr, 101
    Evan, 101
    Hannah (Cook), 101
    James, 101
    John, 101
    Phebe, 101
    see also **HUGHS**
HUGHS, Elenor Starr, 101
    Hannah, 101
    Phebe, 101
    see also **HUGHES**
HUIT, Mary (Hill), 196
    see also **HEWIT**
HUMPHREY, Albert, 45
    Elizabeth, 45
    Talitha, 45
HUNNICUTT, Albert C, 165
    Anne/Annie, 165,197
    Aurie (Scantland), 165
    Charles Daniel, 165
    Daniel, 165,196,197
    Deborah, 197
    Deborah (Hollingsworth) Arnett, 197
    Deborah Arnett (Hollingsworth), 165
    Delitha, 31,101
    Delitha Ann, 101
    Earl, 165
    Earl, 197
    Ephraim, 101
    Frances Daniel, 165
    George E, 101
    Gulielma, 165,166
    Howard A, 165
    James, 31,101
    James Benjamin, 101
    Jamima Walthall, 165
    Jane, 196,197
    Jane (Charles), 165,166,176
    Jane (Walthall), 165
    Jemima, 212
    Jemima W, 212
    John, 196
    John T, 197

HUNNICUTT, John Thomas, 165,166,176
    Joshua B, 101
    Joshua Bailey/Baley, 101
    Mabel E, 165
    Margaret, 101
    Margaret A, 165
    Mariam, 197
    Mary Amy, 101
    Mary Amy (Barker) Winslow, 101
    Mary Batt, 165
    Mary E, 54,85
    Mary Eliza, 101
    Mary Jane, 165,176
    Miriam A, 165
    Myra G, 165
    Sarah Jane, 165
    Susanah, 54
    Thomas, 54
    Walter A, 165
    Wm H, 197
    Wm P, 197
    Wm Pearson, 101
    Wm Penn, 165
    see also **HONEYCUTT,**
    HONNEYCUTT, HUNNYCUTT
HUNNYCUTT, Mary, 197
    see also **HUNEYCUTT,**
    HONNEYCUTT, HUNNYCUT
HUNT, ——, 64
    Abigail, 199
    Abner, 31,101
    Albert, 31,101
    Alonzo, 31,101
    Ann, 31,32,101
    Ann (Brown), 32
    Anna (Test), 101
    Anna Jane, 31
    Anna Laura (Charles), 32
    Anna M, 101
    Anna Maria (Test), 32
    Asenath/Asenith, 12,95
    Barnabas, 197
    Benjamin, 32
    Beulah, 101
    Bobbie B, 102
    Bronson D, 165
    Calvin, 101
    Catharine, 101
    Catharine/Catherine (Coffin), 31,101
    Celia, 186
    Charles, 32
    Christiana, 94,101
    Claton/Clayton, 32,43,101
    Clayton B, 32,101
    Cora E, 102
    Cora Elizabeth, 32,101
    Daniel, 165
    David W, 101
    Delphina (Coffin), 197
    Dinah, 101
    Edward L, 197
    Eleanor, 165,197
    Eleazer, 31
    Elihu, 101
    Eliza, 31,101
    Elizabeth, 10,101,165,178,209
    Elizabeth (Starr), 32,43,101
    Elizabeth Elanor, 32
    Elizabeth M, 32,38,101
    Ellen E, 170
    Elmarinda, 165
    Elwood, 101

HUNT, Emily, 32
    Emily Ann, 165
    Esther W, 32,43
    Flora, 101
    Flora H (Hadley), 32
    Flora Ida, 32
    Francis/Frank J, 32
    Franklin B, 32,38,101,102
    Fred M, 74,102
    Frederic, 101
    Frederic M, 32
    Hannah, 197
    Henry, 165
    Henry Clinton, 165
    Hepsabeth (Swain), 101
    Huldah, 101
    Huldah B, 110
    Ida Eldora, 32,101
    Irena, 101
    Isaiah, 197
    Isom, 33,102,110
    J Verlin, 32
    Jacob, 101
    Jane, 101
    Jesse, 165,209
    Jessie (Chenoweth), 32
    John, 32,101
    John Jr, 101
    John L, 32
    John S, 101
    Jonathan/Jonthan, 10,101,197
    Joseph B, 32
    Joshua G, 32
    Lewis, 32,101,102
    Lucinda, 101
    Lucy, 102
    Lydia, 101,165
    Margaret, 32,33,94,95,101,102
    Martha, 101
    Martha N, 101
    Mary, ix,33,44,101,102,165
    Mary Emily, 31
    Mary L, 32
    Mary S, 101
    Melinda, 101
    Milly, 197
    Milly (Parker), 197
    Milton, 101
    Mournen/Mournin/Mourning, 165, 197,209
    Nancy, 101,170
    Nathan, 101
    Nelson, 101
    Nelson A, 32,101
    Newby, 101
    Orlando, 101
    Orlando B, 32,102
    Phanuel, 165,197
    Phebe, 109,107
    Phebe (Coffin), 10
    Phebe Ann, 32,38,101
    Pheriba, 165
    Pleasant, 32
    Rachel, 101
    Rebecca, 29,30,101,165,197
    Rebecca (Henley), 101
    Reuben, 101
    Rhoda (Hodgin), 32
    Rhoda L, 101,102
    Robbie Benjamin, 32,101
    Rosilla/Rozilla, 101
    Ruth, 101,165

HUNT, Ruth Anna, 102
    Ruth Anna (Hollingsworth), 32
    Salina, 25
    Samuel, 94
    Sarah, 101,165
    Sarah Jane, 165,197
    Susanna/Susannah, 77,101,165,207
    Susanna B, 120
    Susannah (Williams), 31
    Thomas, 165,197
    Unice, 101
    Uriah, 197
    Uriah W, 165
    Viola Eliza, 32
    Wesley, ix
    Wesley W, 165
    Wilbur H, 32
    Wm, 101,165,170,197
    Wm 2nd, 101
HUNTER, Judith, 102
HURLEY, Bertha (Edwards), 32
    Cary L, 32
    Elizabeth, 32
    John, 32
HURST, Emma, 6
    Orlando B, 102
    see also **HIRST**
HUSKING, Louisa (Lamb), 197
    Anna R, 102
    Anna R (Fall), 32
    Hannah, 38
    Homer F, 102
    Ida, 20
    John, 32
    John M, 102
    Marth Ann, 24
    Mary India, 32
    Mary J, 102
    Rachel (Thornburg), 32
    Rachel B, 32,102
    Samuel, 32
    Sarah, 32,102
    Stephen, 32
    Tamer, 28
HUSSY, Nancy, 13
HUTCHEN, Clara, 197
    see also **HUTCHENS**
HUTCHENS, Alice, 32
    Ann, 197
    Ann (Hansen/Hanson), 165,197
    Benjamin, 197
    Benjamin Jr, 102
    Clara/Clary, 194,197
    Clary (Spain), 165
    Darias, 32
    Elizabeth, 32
    Emeline, 165
    Emily, 165
    Enos, 165,197
    Enos, 197
    Frances Belinda (Bond), 165
    Frances M (Bond), 197
    Gulielma, 102
    Hannah, 197
    Hanson, 165
    Hezekiah, 165,194,197
    Ira, 197
    Ira H, 165
    James, 165,197
    John, 165,197
    John H, 165
    Keziah, 165

HUTCHENS, Margaret, 165
    Martha, 100
    Mary, 197
    Moses, 165
    Nancy, 159,192,197
    Nancy (Bergdoll), 165
    Nancy Ann, 165
    Nancy Ann (Allen), 165
    Nicholas, 197
    Owen E, 32
    Ruth, 32
    Sarah, 165,194
    Sarah Alice, 165
    Susanna/Susannah, 102
    Thomas, 165,197
    Wm, 197
    Wm F, 165
    Wm Frances, 197
    Zerilda A, 197
    see also **HUTCHEN, HUTCHINS**
HUTCHING, Hezekiah, 102
    see also **HUTCHINGS**
HUTCHINGS, Denson, 102
    Jonathan, 102
    Thomas, 102
    see also **HUTCHING**
HUTCHINS, Ann (Hansen), 197
    Benjamin, 102,197
    Bessie M H, 32
    Clifford, 32
    Elizabeth Z, 97
    Hannah, 197
    Jemima (Jenkins), 32
    John, 197
    Julia Esther, 11
    Nicholas, 197
    see also **HUTCHENS**
HUTSON, Catherine, 32
    Daniel, 102
    Donna/Dorena, 32
    James, 102
    John, 32,102
    Nathan, 102
HUTTON, Alta (Woodard), 102
    Catherine, 32
    Edward, 32
    George, 32
    John, 102
    Louise (Todd), 32
    Lydia Alta (Woodard), 32
    Margaret, 102
    Margaret Jane, 102
    Samuel W, 102
    Thomas, 102
    Wm H, 102
HYER, Catherine, 165
    Earl H, 165
    Frank, 165
    Pearl, 165
    Samuel, 165
    Sarah Etta (Hockett), 165
    see also **HEYER, HYRE**
HYRE, Frank, 197
    see also **HEYER, HYER**

IBAUGH, Fannie Theodora, 32,102
    Frank, 32
    Jennie S (Mote), 32
    Susana Jane (Mote), 102
ICOMBROCK, Ann Elizabeth, 7
    see also **ICONBROCK**

ICONBROCK, Ann Elizabeth, 48
    see also **ICOMBROCK**
IDDINGS, Milly, 47
IDE, Sarah, 179
ILIFF, Flora Rosetta (Hadley), 32
    J Edgar, 32
    Wm Edgar, 32
INGERSOL, Ada Gertrude, 32
    Edwin Dozois, 32
    John, 32
    Josephine, 32
    Mary Lottie, 32
    see also **INGERSOLL**
INGERSOLL, Ada Gertrude, 102
    Edward Dozier, 102
    John, 102
    Joseph, 102
    Josephine, 102
    Mary Lotta/Lottie, 102
    see also **INGERSOL**
INGERSTRODT, Edward, 32
    Minnie, 32
    Stella Elizabeth, 32
IREDELL, Anna, 12
    Belle, 32,54
    Belle, 54
    Bertha, 25,26
    Bertha S, 32
    John S, 25,26,32,102
    Lizzie, 32,102
    M, 102
    Marinetta (Sofrain), 32
    Marinetta L, 32
    Marionetta, 102
    Mary Ann, 32
    Mary Starr, 32
    Nathan Garwood, 32
    Nora (Frame), 32
    Rachel S, 32
    Samuel E, 32,102
    Samuel Ellis, 32,54
    Sarah (Dilks), 32,54
    Sarah Ellen (Dilks), 32
    Sarah S (Dilks), 102
    Sidney/Sydney (Dilks), 25,26,32,102
    Sidney D, 102
IRETON, Eliza J, 38
IRISH, Avis Jane, 87,102
    Esther Jane, 40,102
    Henry, 4
    Vianna/Vienna, 4,68,102
IRWIN, Avis Jane (Roberts), 102
    Cora Ann, 102
    Cora Ann (Henley), 32
    Elizabeth, 102
    Elizabeth Jr, 102
    Esther, 102
    Israel, 102
    Lydia, 102
    Samuel, 102
ISENHOUR, Eva (Frazier), 32
IVERMAN, Sallie E, 29

JACKSON, Barbara, 165
    Benjamin, 165
    Emma B, 197
    Emma Bell (Young), 165
    Frankie Carl, 165
    Hannah 155
    Hazel M, 32
    Jacob L, 165
    Jacob L, 197

JACKSON, Jemima, 165
  Jemima (Cox), 155
  John, 165
  Lawrence N, 32
  Lydia, 165
  Mary (Harter), 165
  Phebe, 197
  Rachel, 197
  Samuel, 155
  Sarah Ann, 32,102
  Surelda, 150
  Tabitha (Hedgpath), 32
  Zue, 32
JACOBS, Alfred, 32
  Ella, 32
  James, 102
  Mabel, 32
JACONA, Martha (Henson), 32
JAME, Daniel, 102
  Isaac, 102
  Leah, 102
  see also **JAMES**
JAMES, Alfred, 33
  Alfred P, 102
  Atticus S, 33,02
  Caroline, 33,102
  David, 33,40,102
  Esther, 102
  Evan, 102
  Hannah, 102
  Isaac, 33,102
  Isaac L, 102
  Isaac P, 33,102
  Jesse, 102
  John, 102
  Jonas, 102
  Joshua, 102
  Leah, 102
  Levi C, 102
  Levi E, 33
  Lot B, 33,102
  Lydia Ellen, 102
  Mary, 33,102
  Mary (Hunt), 33,40,102
  Naomi, 102
  Naomi (Stratton), 102
  Phebe, 102
  Rebecca, 102
  Ruth Ann/Ruthann/Ruthanna, 33,40, 102
  Sarah, 102
  Sarah Emily, 33
  Susanna/Susannah, 33,102
  Susanna (Bonine), 102
  see also **JAME**
JANES, Elizabeth, 4
JANNEY, Caroline, 102
  Caroline J, 6
  Elizabeth, 6
  Joseph, 6
  Susan, 102
  see also **JANNY**
JANNY, Caroline, 102
  see also **JANNEY**
JARRETT, David, 62
  Elizabeth, 102
  Elizabeth (Thomas), 62
  Jennie, 33
  Mary J, 62
  Nancy M (Jones), 33
  R L, 33
  Rebecca, 37

JAY, —— (Griffin), 33
  Alice, 33
  Alice (Hollingsworth), 33
  Alice Elizabeth, 103
  Allen, 33,103
  Allen Jr, 33
  Anna Elizabeth, 33
  Anna F, 103
  Anna F (Newby), 33
  Anna O Unthank (Pritchard), 33
  Anne Daisey (Horton), 33
  Dewit Clinton, 103
  E A, 33
  Edwin, 103
  Edwin S, 33,103
  Edwin Sleeper, 103
  Eli, 2,5,33,60,90,103
  Eliza (Wareham), 33
  Elizabeth, 14,33
  Elizabeth (Pugh), 33,102
  Elizabeth Hanes, 33
  Ethel, 33
  Evangeline (Moore), 103
  Evangeline M, 103
  Harriet E, 33
  Henry, 7,33,102,103
  Henry Mather, 33
  Isaac, 33,103
  Isaac E, 33
  James, 33
  Jane M (Shute), 33
  Jesse Walter, 33,103
  John, 28,33,97,102,103
  John A, 33,103
  John S, 33
  Joseph Frederick, 33
  Joseph W, 103
  Joseph Wareham, 33
  Josephine (Jeffries), 33
  Leah, 33,103
  Leah (Nicholson), 33
  Lindley, 33
  Mahala/Mahalah (Pearson), 5,33
  Mahalah/Malialah, 69,90
  Martha, 28,33,102,103
  Martha A, 103
  Martha Ann, 103
  Martha Ann (Sleeper), 33
  Martha Evangeline (Moore), 33,103
  Mary, 33,59,70,79,102,103
  Mary (Macy), 33
  Mary (Steddom), 28,33,102,103
  Mary Adelaid/Adelaide, 5,33,69,103
  Mary Elizabeth (Macy), 33
  Mary Lurena, 33
  Mate (Power), 33
  Naomi C, 103
  Naomi C (Fulghum), 103
  Naomi Harrrison (Morgan), 33
  Priscilla, 103
  Priscilla (Reed), 33,103
  Rebecca, 57,103
  Rebecca (Clawson), 103
  Rebecca Ann, 103
  Rebecca Ann (Clawson), 14,33
  Rhoda (Cooper), 33
  Robert, 33
  Russell, 33
  Sarah, 8,103
  Sarah (Strawbridge), 7,33,102
  Sarah A, 7,33
  Sarah Jane (Pritchard), 33

JAY, Sarah R (Johnston), 33
  Susan M, 103
  Susannah M (Mather), 33
  Susannah M (Mather) Hawkins, 33
  Thomas, 33
  Walter D, 102,103
  Walter Denny, 14,33,103
  Willard Bain, 33,103
  Wm, 103
  Wm C, 33,103
  Wm Denny, 33
  Wm Isaac, 33,103
  Wm P, 33
JEALISON, Priscilla (Marmon), 103
JEFFERES, Hannah, 103
  see also **JEFFERIES, JEFFERIS, JEFFREY, JEFFRIES**
JEFFERIES, Anna, 103
  Martha, 103
  see also **JEFFERES, JEFFERIS, JEFFREY, JEFFRIES**
JEFFERIS, Elizabeth, 32
  Emily R, 197
  see also **JEFFERES, JEFFERIES, JEFFREY, JEFFRIES**
JEFFREY, Sarah (Jenkins), 197
  see also **JEFFERES, JEFFERIES, JEFFERIS, JEFFRIES**
JEFFRIES, Abraham, 7,22,103
  Abraham S, 33,103
  Ann, 103
  Anna/Annie M, 7,33,103
  Asa, 33,103
  Benjamin E, 33
  Edith, 103
  Edith F, 7,22,33
  Elijah, 103
  Elijah Ware, 33
  Elizabeth, 103
  Emily A H, 197
  Hannah Ann, 33,103
  Isaac, 103
  Jacob, 103
  John, 33,103
  Josephine, 33
  Joshua, 103
  Lizzie, 22,33
  Lizzie E, 103
  Margaret, 33,103
  Margaret D, 33
  Martha, 103
  Rebecca, 103
  Rebecca Roberts, 33
  Wm, 103
  Wm Darling, 33
  see also **JEFFERES, JEFFERIES, JEFFERIS, JEFFREYS**
JENKINS, Adila, 13,16
  Alfred W, 103
  Alfred Wm, 33
  Alice A, 33,43
  Alice Atlee, 34
  Alice S, 103
  Amasa, 43,103
  Amasa M, 33,103
  Amelia A, 103
  Anderson, 165
  Anderson H, 165,197
  Anderson Hutchens, 197
  Ann (Pearson), 33
  Ann E (Dickinson), 34
  Anna, 103

JENKINS, Atwood L, 33,103
  Benjamin, 165,197
  Benjamin F, 17
  Charles F, 103
  Charles Francis, 33
  Charles M, 34,103
  Doritha/Dorothy, 165,192
  Elisabeth/Elizabeth, 165,166
  Eliza Ann, 165
  Elizabeth, 165
  Elizabeth D, 165
  Elizabeth D (Wiles), 197
  Ella J, 17
  Ellen H (Dickinson), 34
  Ellen W (Dickinson), 103
  Emeline (Lewis), 34
  Esther, 166,198
  Evan C, 34
  Evans H, 34,103
  Frances C (Miles/Wiles), 17,197
  Frances Clanton (Wiles), 165
  Irena, 165
  Jemima, 32
  Levine, 206
  Line, 197
  Lucinda, 166,197
  Lucinda B, 103
  Lydia, 134,165,192,197
  Malindia/Melinda, 166,197
  Martha (Shepperd), 34
  Mary, 165
  Mary Ann/Anna, 103
  Mary Ann (Thomas), 33,43
  Mary E (Test), 34
  Mary Lenora (Test), 103
  Naomi, 34
  Nellie, 103
  Olive L, 33,103
  Phebe Ann, 103,135,166,197
  Raymond, 34
  Robert, 33
  Russell Lewis, 34
  S Newton, 103
  Sarah, 166,197
  Silas Newton, 34,103
  Sophia A (Hall), 34
  Wm, 34,103,134,165,192,197
  Wm P, 166,197
  Wm Penn, 197
  Wm Wallace, 34
JENKINSON, Elizabeth/Mary, 37
  Mary Elizabeth, 65
JENKS, Elizabeth, 47
  Gertrude, 47
  Taylor, 47
JENNINGS, Anna (Baker), 34
  Bert, 34
  Daisy (Benson), 34
  Georgeina M, 21
  Sally (Springer), 103
JESSOP, Abraham, 34,103
  Alfred, 34,103
  Allen, 34
  Ann, 103
  Anna M, 103
  Edith, 103
  Eli, 103
  Elihu, 103,107
  Elizabeth, 34,103,104,197
  Ellis W, 34
  Emily, 103
  Esther Hiatt, 103

JESSOP, Hannah, 34,103
  Hezekiah, 103
  Isaac, 103
  Isaac Jr, 103
  Isaac Sr, 103
  Jacob, 1,103,197
  James, 103
  Jane, 34,103
  Jehu, 103
  Jemima, 103
  John, 103
  John L, 34
  Jonathan, 103
  Levi, 103
  Lindley M, 103
  Lydia, 103
  Mahlon, 103,197
  Mary, 103
  Mary (Myers) Roberds, 103
  Mary Ann, 103
  Mary Ann (Whitaker), 103
  Mary Jane, 103
  Milton H, 103
  Nathan, 103
  Phebe, 103
  Rachel, 103
  Rachel Ann, 34
  Rachel M, 103
  Rebecca (Binford), 7
  Rebecca T, 89,103
  Richard, 103
  Ruth, 89
  Sarah, 7,70,95,103
  Sarah Elma (Hough), 103
  Susanna, 103
  Thomas, 7,103
  Thomas R, 103
  Wm, 89,103
  Wm Allen, 103
  see also **JESSUP**
JESSUP, Albert, 104
  Albert S, 34,104,166,197
  Alice, 63
  Ann/Anna, 6,197
  Ann (Hawkins), 34,104
  Anna (Goodrich), 34
  Anne (Maxwell), 34
  Cary Levi, 104
  Charity, 104
  David, 34,104
  David B, 104
  Edna, 34,104
  Eli S, 34,104
  Elias, 104
  Elihu, 197
  Elizabeth (Hill), 34
  Elma (Hough), 34
  Grace, 34,104
  Gulielma, 34,54,197
  Gulielma (Hunnicutt) Jones, 166
  Henry, 166,173,197
  Isaac, 34,104
  Jacob, 34,104
  Jehu, 31
  John, 166
  Jonathan, 34,104
  Joseph, 104
  Levi, 34,54,104,122,166
  Lindley M, 34,104
  Lucinda P, 64
  Luzena, 55
  Lydia, 104

JESSUP, Lydia H, 34
  Mary, 34,54,166
  Mary (Myers), 166
  Mary A (Whitacre), 31
  Mary E, 197
  Mary E (Nicholson), 166,173,197,205
  Mary Jane (Morris), 104
  Milton, 104
  Milton H, 34
  Penninah, 34
  Rachel, 34,104,116
  Sarah, 20,26,27,34,104
  Sarah Ann, 6,21,31,166,197,205
  Thomas, 34,197
  Thomas R, 34
  see also **JESSOP**
JESTER, John, 198
JEWLIN, Rebecca, 104
  see also **JULEN, JULIAN**
JOBES, Esther,147
  Jonathan, 147
  Sarah Jane, 147
JOHN, Agnes Maria, 34
  Eliza J, 34
  James E, 34
  James L, 34
  Mabel Claire, 34
JOHNSON, ——, 50
  —— (Myrick), 34
  Achsah, 201
  Alfred, 34,46,198
  Aline K, 35
  Allen Clifford, 34,104
  Almida, 104
  Althea B, 104
  Amy, 104
  Amy C, 104
  Amy G, 34
  Anna/Anne, 104
  Anna (Thorn), 46
  Anna Lee, 4
  Anna Mary, 34,46
  Anna Mary (Thorne), 34
  Anna Rachel, 104
  Annajane, 104
  Annie (Cannon), 104
  Ashla/Ashley/Ashly, 34,104,166,198
  Benjamin, 10,34,40,104,111
  Benjamin Jr, 104
  Benjamin Franklin, 34
  Benjamin Nicholson, 34
  Betsy Ann, 34,104
  Caleb, 34,104,198
  Caroline, 34
  Catharine C, 104
  Charles, 34,104,198
  Charles Albert, 104
  Charles Alexander, 198
  Cicily, 135
  Cornelia, 34
  David F, 104
  Doris Silva, 34
  E T, 104
  Edith, 34
  Elam/Elim, 34,166,172,198
  Eli, 104
  Eli M, 104
  Elijah, 34,104,198
  Elisabeth/Elizabeth, 21,34,43,62,69,
    104,111,115,135
  Eliza (Nicholson), 34,104
  Elizabeth (Barker), 40,104

JOHNSON, Elizabeth (Griffith), 34
  Elizabeth (Janes), 4
  Elizabeth (Jessop), 104
  Elizabeth B (Barker), 34
  Elmina, 104,198
  Elmina L, 104,198
  Elmina L (Hinshaw), 198
  Emily, 104
  Emily Grace, 104
  Eva E, 104
  Evan L, 104
  Evan Lewis, 104
  Fran, 34
  George W, 34,198
  Georgia Mae, 34
  Gertrude (Wright), 34
  Hannah, 104,124,198
  Hannah M, 34,104
  Harold B, 34
  Howard, 34
  Ida Caroline, 104
  Irvin, 34
  Isaac Jr, 104
  Isaac Kindley, 198
  Isabell, 35
  J Howard, 104
  Jacob, 104
  Jacob J, 104
  James, 6,21,34,43,62,81,104,124,198
  James Brooks, 34,104
  James P, 35
  Jane, 55
  Jean C, 34
  Jesse, 166,198
  Joel W, 104
  John, 13,112,166
  John H, 104
  John Howard, 34,104
  John W, 104
  John Warner, 104
  Joseph, 4,34,35,54
  Joseph C, 198
  Josephine, 104
  Josiah, 34,104,166,173,198
  Josiah M, 104
  Judah, 104
  Judith, 104,112
  Judith (Faulkner), 13
  Lura (Manning), 34
  Lydia Elva, 29
  M B (Bennett), 34
  Malinda Ella, 166
  Margaret, 10,11,17
  Martha, 34,104
  Martha (Grisell), 11
  Martha (Hubbard), 104
  Martitia E, 104
  Mary, 34,54,104
  Mary (Cain), 35
  Mary (Coffin), 104
  Mary (Combers/Comer), 34,104
  Mary (Cook), 172
  Mary Amy, 34,40,111
  Mary Ann, 104
  Mary B, 21,34,62,104
  Mary C, 104,172
  Mary D (Birdsall), 34
  Mary Elizabeth, 34
  Mary J, 35
  Mary J (Jones), 35
  Mearl S, 104
  Micajah, 198

JOHNSON, Miriam, 104
  Morris, 104
  Morris L, 104
  Nancy, 104
  Nancy (Beeson), 198
  Nancy Ann, 166
  Nettie L, 104
  Phebe, 104
  Philip, 104
  Polly, 104,166,173,198
  Priscilla, 69,104
  Prudence, 81,104
  Rachel, 34,46,104,166,173
  Rachel A, 19,41,104,112
  Rachel J, 6
  Rebecca/Rebeckah, 34,104,166,198
  Rebecca N, 34,104
  Rhoda (Swain), 198
  Rhoda (Worth), 166
  Rhoda M, 13,14,79
  Robert Howard, 34
  Ruth, 43,81,104,115,124,198
  Sarah, 104
  Sarah (Votaw), 6
  Sarah H, 104
  Suchy, 104
  Susan E, 35,104
  Susan R (Harrison), 34,104
  Susan R H, 104
  Susanna/Susannah H, 104
  Suzanne J, 34
  Sylvanus, 104
  Sylvanus T, 104
  Sylvia Mae, 54
  Thomas A, 104
  Thomas Edward, 34
  Walter, 166
  Wm, 34,35,69,104,135,198
  Wm Elwood, 104
  Wm G, 104
  Zerelda M, 166
  see also **JOHNSTON**
JOHNSTON, Alice Caroline (Wiggs), 35
  Asa Dillwyn, 35
  Elizabeth (Shoaf), 35
  Oscar B, 35
  Sarah R, 33
  see also **JOHNSON**
JOLLY, Lurana, 7
JONES, Alfred, 35
  Alice A, 35
  Amelia, 105
  Anna/Anne, 86,104
  Anna M, 50,51,105
  Bateman, 104,105
  Betsy/Betty, 23
  Byron, 105
  Charity, 44
  Charles Rollin, 105
  Claborn L, 105
  Clarkson, 105
  Clayborne/Clayburn S, 35,105
  Clayburn Everett, 35
  Clyde O, 35
  Cynthia (McWhinney), 35
  Daniel, 198,207
  Daniel H, 105
  David, 166,198
  Dona C, 35
  Edith Emma, 35
  Eli, 35,104
  Elihu, 35,104

JONES, Elizabeth, 35,57,166,171
  Emma, 198
  Emma J, 41
  Ephraim M, 166
  Esther, 9,13,78,104,198
  Esther (Jenkins), 198
  Eunice, 166,198
  Eunice (Macy), 198
  Francis, 198
  Franklin, 105
  George, 41
  Geula Elma, 198
  Gladys, 35
  Gulielma (Hunnicutt), 166
  Hannah, 4,13,57,58,78,86,104,133, 166,169
  Hannah B, 104,105
  Howard Kenworthy, 35
  Isaac E, 104,105
  Ivan, 125
  James, 35,104
  James Branson, 105
  Jane, 35,38,104,105
  Jemima, 166,198,207
  Jesse, 13,35,78,86,104,122,169,198
  Jesse Raymond, 35
  Jesse Silvenus, 104
  John, 23
  John D, 166
  John M, 104
  John V, 35
  Keziah, 198
  Keziah K (Wiles), 198
  Louis T, 35
  Louisa K (King), 35
  Lucinda, 198
  Luvena, 105
  Luvenia E, 105
  Lydia, 104,166,198
  Lydia Jane (Prickett), 41
  Margaret, 41,178
  Margaret Jessie (Kenworthy), 35,105
  Maria, 35,105
  Martha, 104,169,170
  Martha L, 93
  Martha L (Mather), 51
  Mary, 35,39,41,105,125,166,198
  Mary (Northcutt), 166
  Mary A, 105
  Mary E, 41
  Mary Frances (Lunscomb), 35
  Mary H, 35
  Mary J, 35
  Mary P, 25,93,105
  Mattie, 38,105
  Maud, 105
  Micajah, 35,104
  Minerva, 41
  Morgan, 35,39,58,104,105,133
  Morris, 105
  Morris Evans, 35
  Moses, 166,198
  Nancy M, 33
  Nellie, 166
  Newton, 105
  Newton S, 105
  Octavia, 105
  Paul, 35
  Percy, 35
  Pleasant, 198
  Priscilla, 105
  R, 198

JONES, Rachel, 168
    Rachel B, 104
    Rachel B Jr, 105
    Richard, 198
    Richard Mack, 35
    Robert D, 105
    Rollin, 105
    Ruth, 35,104
    Ruth (Bailey), 198
    Ruthanna, 104
    Sally Ann, 198
    Samuel, 35,38,41,51,93,105
    Samuel N, 105
    Sarah, 19,35,104
    Sarah E (Parker), 35
    Simpson, 198
    Sina A (Harvey), 35
    Stephen, 198
    Susanna/Susannah, 104,105,114,125, 166
    Sylvanus, 35,104
    Sylvester, 105,198
    Sylvester H, 105,166,198
    Thomas, 35
    Thomas Carlton, 166
    Walter, 35
    Wm, 198
    Wm C, 104,105,166
JORDAN, Elisabeth, 198
    Elizabeth (Dennis), 166
    John R, 35
    Martha, 41
    Olinda/Olive B (Thomas), 35
    Polly (Morris), 41
    Samuel S, 41
    W D, 166
JUDD, Sarah, 180
JULEN, Isaac, 105
    see also **JEWLIN, JULIAN**
JULIAN, Barbara, 100,105
    Behan/Bohan T, 166,172
    Charity, 198
    Charity L (Baldwin), 198
    Clella L, 166,172
    Clemma Nellie, 166
    Elizabeth (Hodson), 148
    Frank, 166
    Frank C, 198
JULIAN, Isaac, 80
    Joseph P, 148
    Josie Goldie, 166
    Josie Pearl, 198
    Keziah, 105
    Mary E, 198
    Mary Elizabeth (Baldwin), 166,172
    Mary J, 198
    Mary Jane (Baldwin), 198
    Maud, 166
    Nellie Maud, 198
    Pearl, 166
    Perry S, 198
    Perry Sherman, 166
    Rebecca (Hoover), 105
    Sarah, 105
    Sarah, 80
    Sarah E, 148,175
    Stella Rosalia/Rosalie, 166,198
    see also **JEWLIN, JULEN, JULIN**
JULIN, Rebecca, 105
    see also **JEWLIN, JULEN, JULIAN**
JUSTICE, Anna, 105
    Benjamin, 105
    Elisabeth, 105

JUSTICE, John, 105
    Jonathan, 105
    Mary, 105
    Sarah, 105

KAIN, Albert F, 105
    Albert H, 105
    Albert W, 35
    Elizabeth L, 105
    Elizabeth L (Brown), 35
    Henry C, 105
    Henry E, 105
    Henry F, 35
    Mary Ann/Anna (Mather), 35,105
    Rachel Mamorah/Manorah, 35,105
    Raymond, 35
    Rebecca, 105
    Ruth Anna, 35
    Salt, 35,105
    Wm, 35
    Wm E, 105
    see also **CAIN**
KALE, Anna Mabel, 35
    Martha (Mendenhall), 35
    Martha M, 105
    Wm, 35
    Wm H, 105
KAMINSKY, Anna (Lewis), 51
    Anna E, 105
    Anna E (Lewis), 35
    Charles E, 35,51
    Lillian V, 35,105
    Olive M, 35,51,105
KANNADA, Robert, 105
    see also **CANADA, CANADAY, KENADA, KENNADA, KENNADY**
KATES, Gertrude, 45
    see also **CATES**
KAUCHER, Katherine (Stump), 4
    Marillia C, 4
    Sena, 4
KEATES, Catherine Clibborn, 35
    Elizabeth (Robinson), 35
    Ellen Carruthers, 35
    Frank Tabor, 35
    Harry Rowland, 35
    Harry Swift, 35
    John, 35
    Lydia Ackers, 35
    Minnie Carruthers, 35
    Sarah (Rawson), 35
    Stonehill, 35
    see also **KATES**
KEEVER, Clara B, 175
    Fanny, 198
    John Carver, 166
    Mary, 166
    Moses, 166
    Romana (Lamb), 166
    Sarah (Bales), 166
KEISTER, May, 105
KEITH, Elizabeth, 50
KELLEY, Carl, 105
    Edmond J, 105
    Elizabeth, 5,59
    Hannah, 105
    Myrtle W, 105
    Oliver, 105
    Wm B, 105
    see also **KELLY**

KELLY, Agnes Rifner, 35
    Amy (Underwood), 105
    Anna, 56
    Anna P (Pearson), 35
    Benjamin Wade, 35
    Caroline (Potter), 35
    Cecilia R (Rifner), 35
    Charity, 105
    Donna Martha, 57
    Henrietta, 35
    Lois Anna, 35
    Mary V, 35
    Nicholas, 35
    Oliver J, 105
    Rebecca, 105
    Rebecca (Coffin), 105
    Robert, 35
    Robert Lincoln, 35
    Rose May, 35
    Wm Westley, 35
    see also **KELLEY**
KEMP, James P, 55
    Jane (Johnson), 55
    Othelia P, 55
    Sally, 198
KEMPTON, Alice G, 35
    Jane, 35
    John, 35
    Joseph Marshall, 35
    Sarah J, 35
KENADA, Joshua, 105
    Robert, 105
    Thomas, 105
    see also **CANADA, CANADAY, KANNADA, KENNADA, KENNADY**
KENDAL, Amy, 35
    Cyrus, 35,105
    David, 35
    Dennis, 35
    Elizabeth, 35
    Hannah, 35
    Lydia, 105
    Lydia, 35
    Margaret/Margaretta, 35,75
    Nancy, 35
    Thomas, 35
    Wm, 35,105
    see also **KENDALL**
KENDALL, Abigail, 35,105
    Albert, 105
    Alsie, 35
    Amy, 97
    Cyrus, 105
    David, 105
    Dennis, 35,105
    Elisabeth/Elizabeth, 35,90,97,105, 118,123
    Enos, 35,105
    Hannah, 90
    Lydia, 105
    Mahlon, 35,105
    Margaret/Margaretta/Margretta/ Marguretta, 35,105,123
    Martha R, 35
    Mary Elizabeth, 105
    Mary Elizabeth (Hill), 105
    Michael, 35
    Nancy, 105
    Rebecca Jane, 35,105
    Rebecca Jane (Hill), 105
    Thomas, 90,97,105,118,123

KENDALL, Williford, 105
    Wm, 35,105
    see also **KENDAL**
KENNADA, Robert, 105
    see also **CANADA, CANADAY,**
        KENADA, KENNADY
KENNADY, Wm, 105
    see also **KENNADA, KENNEDY**
KENNARD, Grace, 48
KENNEDY, Boater, 105
    Cassius R, 105
    Charles L, 105
    Clara, 105
    Clara R, 105
    Elizabeth, 57
    Ella V, 105
    Hannah, 3,35,105
    Jeanette/Jenette/Jennette, 3,35,105
    John, 105
    Louisa, 105
    Louisa, 35
    Omar R, 105
    Roxie/Roxy F, 105
    Russel, 105
    Walter, 105
    Wm, 105
KENSLER, Ann, 36,106
KENWORTHY, Abigail, 36
    Alice, 71
    Alice Caroline, 36
    Amos, 37,105,198
    Ann/Anna, 36,106
    Anna Edna, 36
    Caroline, 106
    Catharine, 36
    Charles, 106
    Charles Frederic, 36
    David, 36,105
    Dinah, 36
    Eli, 36,54,106
    Eliza Ellen (Bell), 166
    Elizabeth, 84,106
    Ella (Edgar), 36
    Elmira, 106
    Eunice Edna, 36
    Frank Edgar, 36
    Hannah, 36,105
    Harriet, 106
    Harriet K, 36,54
    Helen T, 36
    Isaac F, 36
    Isabel, 166
    Jesse, 35
    Jesse Henry, 36
    Jesse J, 36,45,65,105
    John B, 36
    John R, 106
    Joseph, 36,106
    Levi, 36,105
    Lina, 106
    Lizzie Alice, 106
    Lizzie Olive, 36
    Lydia Matilda, 36,45
    Margaret, 36,54
    Margaret Jesse/Jessie, 35,36,105
    Marianna (Thomas), 36
    Martha, 105
    Mary, 37,71,105,106
    Mary (Evans), 45
    Mary (Langston), 36
    Mary Alice, 36,65,106
    Mary E, 106

KENWORTHY, Mary E (Evans), 35
    Mary Grace Lillian, 36
    Mary P (Evans), 36,65
    Oliver N, 166
    Phebe, 198
    Rachel, 106
    Rachel (Puckett), 36
    Rebecca J, 36,106
    Richard P, 36
    Robert, 106
    Susan, 51
    Susannah, 36,105
    Thomas E, 106
    Thomas Evans, 36
    Truman C, 36
    Walter C, 166
    Wm, 36,71,105,106
    see also **KINWORTHY**
KENYON, Addison G, 106
    Albert M, 106
    Asenath/Asenith, 36,106
    Asenith W, 106
    Beriah, 106
    Charles, 106
    Charles G, 106
    Eunice Ann, 106
    Hoxie, 106
    Hoxie G, 106
    Isaac L, 106
    Isaac Lindley, 106
    Jane, 106
    Jane S (Brown), 106
    John, 36,106
    John, 36
    Martha, 106
    Mary, 106
    Mary H, 106
    Rebecca W, 36,106
    Rhoda J, 106
    Rodah Jane, 36
    Sarah, 106
KEPLER, Mary A, 8
KEPLINGER, Carrie R, 106
    Carrie Ruby, 36,53
    Edward T, 106
    Leslie Martin, 36
    Rosa/Rose, 36,53,106
    Theodore, 36,53,106
KEPPER, Anna, 4
KERN, Lucinda (Anthony), 6
    Martha, 6
    Seth, 6
KERR, Elvira, 41
    James G, 36
    Jennie Agnes, 36
    Mary S, 36
    Thomas, 198
KERSEY, Ann/Anna, 4,106
    Charity Williams, 3,22
    Charles, 36
    Charles A, 36,106
    Charles S, 106
    John, 106
    Margaret, 106
    Margaret H, 36
    Margaret W, 106
    Mary, 106
    Pliny Earl, 36,106
    Rachel (Hiatt), 3
    Richard, 106
    Richard M, 36
    Richard W, 106

KERSEY, Ruth (Morris), 36
    Thomas, 106
    Verling, 36
    Vierling, 106
    Wm, 3
KESSLER, Clifford O, 36
    Hannah B, 106
    Harry Nathan, 106
    Jenus, 36
    Kathlyn (Collins), 36
    Samuel, 36
KIDD, Francis A, 106
KIDWELL, James, 166
    Martin, 166,198
    Mary (Keever), 166
    Rosa (Howell), 166
KIMBALL, David N, 198
    Elmira, 198
    Elmira (Matthews), 166
    Josiah, 166
    Malinda Ella (Johnson), 166
    Malinda Ellen, 198
    Mary E, 166,198
    Melinda E, 198
    Wm, 198
    see also **KIMBLE**
KIMBLE, Emma D (Dennison), 36
    Wm, 36
    see also **KIMBALL**
KING, Abner, 106
    Almira, 106
    Anna, 106
    Anna E, 106
    Anna Gertude (Mote), 36
    Bertha Elizabeth, 36
    Calvin, 106
    Dean, 35,106
    Edward, 36
    Eliza, 179
    Ellen, 106
    Emery, 106
    Estella, 106
    Esther, 106
    Esther (Carpenter), 35
    Frances, 106
    Francis Ann, 36
    G Sherman, 106
    Hannah Ann, 15
    Harry E, 36
    Henry, 36
    Henry D, 106
    Isaac, 106
    John, 106
    John L, 106
    Joseph A, 36,106
    Joseph A, 36
    Lewis, 36
    Louisa K, 35
    Mary, 24,106
    Mary (Evans), 36
    Mary (Whiteman), 36
    Mary E, 106
    Mercy Ann, 106
    Phebe, 106,128
    Rebecca (Clark), 36
    Richard, 36
    Rose, 106
    Ruth, 106
    Sally, 106
    Sarah E, 36,106
    Thomas, 36
    Thomas W, 106
    Zeno, 106

KINLEY, Alpheus C, 166
    Barnabas C, 166
    Betty, 198
    Charles, 166,198
    Charles W, 198
    Eliza, 166
    Eliza (Mendenhall), 198
    Joel, 166,198
    Joseph, 166,198
    Lydia, 166,198
    Margaret, 166,198
    Rachel, 166,198
    Rebecca, 198
    Rebecca E, 166
KINSEY, Abram, 106
    Ann E, 106
    Chloe C, 55
    Frank, 36
    Fremont, 36
    Isaac, 106
    Isabella Louise (Bracken), 36
    J Fremont, 106
    Jacob, 51
    Julia, 55
    Maggie, 106
    Margaret, 106
    Margaret (Shoemaker/Showalter), 36, 49,106
    Margaret S, 106
    Mary, 50
    Mary A, 51,55
    Mary A (Randle), 51
    Mary Alice, 36,49
    Mary Ann (Wright), 36
    Oliver, 106
    Sarah, 106
    Susan (Candler), 36
    Thomas B, 36,49,106
    Thomas W, 106
    Thomas W, 106
    Wm, 55
    Wm C, 36,106
    Wm E, 106
    see also **KINZEY, KINZIE**
KINSINGER, Edward A, 166
    Ernest Clifford, 166
    Lillian (Ashbaugh), 166
KINWORTHY, Agnes, 106
    David Jr, 106
    Martha, 106
KINZEY, Oliver, 106
    Sarah, 106
    see also **KINSEY, KINZIE**
KINZIE, Mary, 50
    see also **KINSEY, KINZEY**
KIRBY, Ann, 106
    Edward, 106
    Elizabeth, 106
    Elizabeth P, 97
    Mark, 106
    Mary, 106
    Mary H, 106
    Wm, 106
KIRK, Ann/Anne/Annie Ethel, 76,106
    Benjamin, 36,106
    Charles, 76,106
    Charles W, 76,106
    Elizabeth, 36
    Hannah Jane, 106
    Isaiah/Isiah, 106
    Israel E, 106
    Mahlon, 106

KIRK, Rachel, 76,106
    Rebecca, 106
    Samuel T, 106
    Sarah, 106
    Sarah Jr, 106
    Sarah (Test), 70
    Sarah W, 106
    Sarah W (Kirk), 106
    Wm, 36,106
KIRKMAN, Alonzo, 107
    Alva, 36,107
    Bessie Evaline, 36,107
    Cyrus Edward, 36
    Elizabeth, 107
    Ella, 107
    Ella May, 36,107
    Flora, 107
    Flora (Werts), 36
    Henry, 36
    James M, 36,107
    Lela H (Hadley), 36
    Lelia, 107
    Lula/Lule, 36,107
    M L, 36
    Mattie, 36,107
    Murel, 36
    Nannie, 87
    Nannie E, 107
    Rebecca (Werts), 36
    Sarah Elizabeth, 36
    Wm H, 107
    Wm R, 36
KIRKPATRICK, Audra J, 107
    Earl M, 107
    Ellen H, 107
    Ellen M, 107
    George, 107
    George H, 107
    Sarah E, 107
    Vernie H, 107
KISER, James, 198
    Minnie, 198
KISKADDEN, Sarah J (White), 107
KITSELMAN, Albert Leroy, 36,107
    Alfred W, 36,107
    Franklin E, 36,107
    John, 36
    Margaret M, 36,107
    Margaret M (Burns), 107
    Marietta, 36,107
KITTERAL, Henrietta, 107
KIZER, James, 198
    Minnie, 198
KLEMMANS, Charles, 37
    Grace (Wolfe), 37
    see also **CLEMENS, CLEMENTS, CLEMONS**
KNIGHT, Absalom, 166
    Benajah/Benejah, 166,198
    Benjamin, 107
    Betsy Rachel, 107
    Charity, 155,198
    Christian, 107
    Delilah, 166
    Delilah M (Dennis), 198
    Edward S, 15
    Emma S, 15
    James, 107
    John, 107
    Lydia, 15
    Lydia (Burcham), 15
    Nathan, 198

KNIGHT, Nathan D, 166
    Phebe, 198
    Phebe Ellen, 166
    Sarah, 107
    Solomon, 107
    Sylvania, 155
    Thomas, 107
KNOTT, Arthur, 107
    Isabel/Isabella/Isabell, 37,107
    Wm, 37,107
KNOX, Charlotte, 30
    Esther, 166
    James, 166
    Lena (Berkhart), 166
KOON, Benjamin, 107
    Margaret E, 157
    see also **COONS, KOONS**
KOONS, Abigail, 2,37
    Elizabeth, 150
    Elmer, 199
    Fannie T, 107
    Francis, 107
    Gasper/Ghasper, 2,37,107
    Gasper Jr, 107
    Hannah, 2,107
    Henry, 2,107
    Jasper, 1
    Jeremiah, 2,37,107
    Jesse, 37
    John, 2
    Joseph, 107,199
    Nathan, 2,107
    Nevada, 199
    Nevada (Conley), 166
    Samuel, 2,107,199
    Sherman, 107
    Susannah, 111
    Thomas Benton, 166
    Wm, 2,37
    see also **COONS, KOON, KOONTZ**
KOONSMAN, Alice Vestina (Disinger), 166
    Mary J, 168
KOONTZ, Mildred Ellen, 199
    see also **COONS, KOONS**
KRAMER, Charles G, 37
    Charles T, 107
    Katherine (Ashinger), 49
    Laura M, 49
    Lillian Elizabeth, 37
    Mary J, 37,107
    Wm, 49
    see also **CRAMER**
KRICK, Elizabeth May (Lunsford), 37
KROSHER, Susannah (Baldwin), 107
KUTH, Jennie, 107
    Nicholas, 107

LABCYTAUX, Mary J, 152
LACEY, Margaret (Morris), 107
    Pearson, 107
    Peter, 107
    Susanna, 107
    see also **LACY**
LACKEY, Gerold, 37
    John, 37
LACY, John, 107
    Josiah, 107
    Margaret, 107
    Pearson, 107
    Penina (Hill), 107
    Peter, 107

LACY, Ruth, 107
    Sarah Ann, 107
    Susanna, 107
    Susannah, 107
    see also **LACEY**
LADD, Amanda C, 178
    Benjamin W, 107
    Caroline E (Coffin), 107
    Caroline Elizabeth, 107
    Elizabeth, 107
    Margaret (Jones), 178
    Wm H, 107
    Wm Thomas, 178
LAFLESH, Anna, 168
LAFLIN, Agatha, 37
    Wm, 37
LAIRD, G Andrew, 107
    George, 107
    George Andrew, 37,107
    Margery (Smith), 37
    Mildred Elizabeth, 37,107
    Sadie (Brown), 37
LAKE, Levine, 157
LAMAR, Alice, 199
    Alice (Billheimer), 37,167
    Anna Lenora, 166,199
    Effie L, 199
    Effie Luella, 167
    Elizabeth H, 199
    Elizabeth H (Haslam), 166
    Eunice, 184
    Eunice (Coffin), 148,167
    Eunice W (Coffin), 199
    Everett Wayne, 167
    Frank/Franklin, 37,107
    Frank/Franklin S, 167,199
    Fred, 199
    Fred C, 167
    Freddie Clyde, 199
    Hannah, 158,166,192,199
    Irena, 199
    Irena (Chamness), 161,166
    Isaac, 158,166,192,199
    Jesse, 161,166,167,199
    John Haslam, 167
    John Milton, 167
    Judith (Baldwin), 166,167,199
    Luther, 167
    Margaret E, 199
    Mary, 158,159,160,166,167
    Mary Elizabeth, 161,166
    Mary F, 199
    Mary Florence, 167
    Miles W, 166,167,199
    Nathan, 37,199
    Nathan S, 167
    Nathan Samuel, 167
    Nellie/Nelly Maud, 167,199
    Osborn, 167
    Paul Vernon, 166
    Ruth, 166,192
    Samuel, 148,166,167,199
    Thomas Levi, 166, 199
    Wm, 167
    Zetelia (Lemon), 37
    Zitella, 107
LAMB, ——, 45
    Absalom, 199
    Absalom H, 167
    Absalom R, 199
    Absalom/Absolom T, 167,199
    Albert, 107

LAMB, Albert Bernard, 107
    Albert S, 107
    Albert Smith, 37
    Alonzo F, 167
    Amanda (Hammer), 167
    Amassa, 167
    Amassa (Adamson), 151
    Angia (Connaway), 37
    Ann Rebecca, 37
    Anna, 37,107,167,199
    Avis, 167
    Barna/Barnaba/Barnabas, 107
    Benjamin, 199
    Benjamin F, 167,199
    Caleb, 107,166
    Carlista/Carlistie, 161,167,199
    Caroline, 199
    Caroline (Allen), 167
    Caroline (Grills), 167
    Catherine M, 108
    Cecilia (Locke), 166
    Charity, 167,199
    Charley E, 167
    Charlie, 167
    Clarkey Jane, 107
    Daniel, 167
    Dora, 199
    Dora Ellen (Merryweather), 167
    Dora V (Mills), 167
    Dorotha, 37,107
    Edgar A, 167,199
    Edgar H, 108
    Eli, 107
    Elias, 167
    Elisabeth/Elizabeth, 37,107,136,167, 199
    Eliza E, 107
    Elizabeth (Fres), 21
    Elvira, 199
    Elvira (Finch), 167
    Emily, 199
    Emily J (Starbuck), 167
    Emily Jane, 199
    Esau/Esaw, 2,107
    Flora Mary/May, 167,199
    Frances, 199
    Francy, 167
    George, 167
    George W, 167,199
    Glennie A (Gwin), 167
    Hannah, 2,107
    Hannah C, 107
    Hannah L, 167,199
    Harriet C (Woody), 167
    Harriett (Woody), 199
    Harrison, 167
    Harvey, 167
    Helena, 167,199
    Henry, 37
    Henry M, 199
    Henry Milton, 167
    Hiram, 199
    Hosea, 37,107
    Ira C, 167
    Isaac, 19,37,107
    Isaac Newton, 37,107
    Isaiah, 154,167
    Jacob, 20
    Jane C, 37
    Jane Caroline, 167
    Jesse M, 167
    Joab Lewis, 167

LAMB, John, 2,37,107,167
    John E, 108
    John H, 161,167,199
    John W, 199
    Jonathan, 2,107
    Joseph, 167
    Josh C, 199
    Josiah, 2,37,107
    Julia, 161
    Julia Ann (Gwin), 167
    Julia C, 161,181
    Katherine, 20,47
    Kendal, 199
    Keziah (Allen), 199
    Lannah/Leanna/Leannah, 161,167,199
    Laura Alice, 154,167
    Laura Frances, 167
    Leanna/Leannah (Lamb), 161,167
    Lenora, 167
    Leonna, 108
    Letty C, 167
    Lincoln, 199
    Lincoln E, 167
    Lousia, 197,199
    Louisa (Dennis), 167
    Lucinda, 172
    Lula, 167
    Lydia, 37
    Lydia (Mendenhall), 107
    Mahala, 188
    Marcelia (Woody), 167
    Marcella, 199
    Margaret, 37
    Margaret A, 107
    Martin, 167,199
    Martin E, 199
    Mary, ix,37,107,199
    Mary Alice, 180,206
    Mary Emily, 167
    Massa (Beeson), 167,199
    Massey, 199
    Miles/Milo, 107,154,167
    Miriam, 167
    Moody Raymond, 167
    Nancy, 2,107
    Nancy (Modlin), 154
    Naomi, 2,107
    Nellie R (Bond), 37
    Nelson Ulysses, 167
    Olinda, 150,151,178
    Olive Afton, 107
    Paul Alonzo, 167
    Phenias/Phineas, 19,37,107
    Rachel (Chamness), 154,199
    Rachel P, 167,199
    Rachel R (Chamness), 167
    Raymond, 108
    Rebecca, 19,107,151,156,167,172,176
    Rebecca (Healton), 167
    Rebecca (Jarrett), 37
    Restor/Restore, 37,107
    Reuben/Rueben, 2,107
    Rhoda, 37
    Romana, 166
    Rosa, 19,37
    Rosanna, 85,107
    Ruhama, 148
    Ruth, 2,107,154
    Ruth A, 19
    Samuel, 21,167,199
    Sarah, 5,20,37,107
    Sarah (Jones), 19

LAMB, Sarah (Smith), 37,107
    Sarah Emeline (Hockett), 167
    Sarah I, 21
    Susan, 167
    Susannah, 167
    Thomas, 37,107,151,167,199
    Thomas Jr, 199
    Thomas C, 167,199
    Thomas Clarkson, 199
    Thomas J, 107
    Ulysses, 199
    Vashti, 37,107
    Vashti (Lamb), 107
    Willis, 107
    Wm, 167
    Wm C, 167
    Wm M, 167
    see also **LAMM**
LAMBERT, Carrie (Burroughs), 159
LAMM, Flossie L, 37
    Iris L, 37
    Israel, 37
    Martha J (Livengood), 37
    Sarah, 37
    Ulin/Ullan, 37
    see also **LAMB**
LAMOTT, Emma, 37
    Gertie P, 37
    Jacob, 37
LANCASTER, Hannah, 108
    Hannah (Rue), 108
    Hannah N, 112
    Harriet, 66
    Rachel S, 112
    Wm, 112
LANDERS, Belle, 199
LANDICK, Dora, 181
LANE, Charles, 37
    Corilla M (Hadley), 37
    Isabella (Trueblood), 108
    Lydia, 18,37,108
    Phebe, 18,37,84,108
    Sarah, 37
    Sarah Ann (Bower), 37
    Theodore, 37
LANGDEN, Frank Warren, 108
    Jane D, 108
    Oliver O, 108
    Rhoda Alice (Fletcher), 108
    see also **LANGDON**
LANGDON, Rhoda Alice (Fletcher), 37
    see also **LANGDEN**
LANGSTON, Hannah, 167
    Jonathan, 167,199
    Luke, 36
    Margaret Ann, 167
    Mary, 36
    Mary Eliza, 167
    Rachel H, 167
    Rebecca (Roberts), 36
    Rebecca R, 167
    Wm L, 167
    see also **LANGSTOWN, LANSTON**
LANGSTOWN, Emily, 108
    see also **LANGSTON, LANSTON**
LANNING, Ann M, 37
    Edwin, 37
    Jenny M, 37
LANSTON, Hannah, 199
    Jonathan, 199
    Mary Eliza, 199
    Rachel, 199

LANSTON, Wm, 199
    see also **LANGSTON, LANGSTOWN**
LAPSHELEY, Angelina, 54
    Isadore Bell, 54
    Joseph, 54
LARROWE, Andrew H, 153
    Anna, 167
    Elnathan, 167,174,199
    Hannah, 167,202
    Janney, 167,202
    Joel, 167,195,199
    Jonathan, 167,199
    Lucy (Fogle), 153
    Matilda, 167
    Sally Jane, 153
    Sarah Etta, 174
    Susanna (Finch), 174
    Susannah, 167,195,199
    Wm, 167,199
    see also **LARUE**
LARUE, Matilda, 196
    see also **LARROWE**
LATIMER, Sarah Catharine/Catherine, 45,54
LAVIN, Maria M, 17
LAW, Jennie (Marquis), 108
    see also **LAWS**
LAWRENCE, Alice M, 108
    Alvin Leroy, 37,108
    Anna Leota, 37,108
    Benjamin Otho, 37,108
    Bertha Mary, 37
    Christopher, 108
    Christopher E, 37
    Dan, 108
    Dan K, 108
    Daniel W, 37
    Eli Verlin, 108
    Elizabeth (Windle), 37
    Hannah, 37,108
    Henry J, 37
    Inez Maria, 108
    Jesse, 108
    Lillian M, 108
    Lottie (Conner), 37
    Lucy A, 108
    Mary E, 108
    Mary E (Woolman), 37
    Mary Jane, 108
    Mary W, 37
    Nancy, 10
    Peter, 47
    Robert, 37
    Sarah, 47
    Sarah (Hinshaw), 47
    Thomas Everett, 108
    Wm E, 37
LAWS, Clement, 108
    Cornelia, 108
    Joanna, 108
    Joanna (Plummer), 108
    John M, 108
    Mary, 108
    Melson, 108
    see also LAW
LAWSON, A J, 16
    Eva A, 16
    Everett, 37
    Frank, 37
    Maggie, 37
    Maria, 16

LAYMAN, Aaron, 108
    Abraham, 108
    see also **LEHMAN, LEIGHMAN**
LEBO, Elmer, 37
    Mary E (Hodgin), 37
    Willard, 37
LEDBEATER, Wm, 108
    see also **LEDBETTER**
LEDBETTER, Elizabeth Jane, 167,168
    Hannah H, 168
    Hannah H C, 148,199
    Henry, 199
    Henry B, 199
    Henry W, 199
    Lydia, 199
    Lydia (Baldwin), 199
    Phebe, 108
    Phebe (Coffin), 148,161,167,168
    Rhoda J, 199
    Rhoda Roxana/Roxanna/Roxanne, 161,168,199
    Wesley Stark, 148,161,167,168
    Westley S, 199
    see also **LEADBETTER**
LEE, Ada E (Elliott), 37
    Alonzo, 168
    Anderson, 168,199
    Ann/Anna/Anne, 37,86,108,168,185
    Charles F, 37
    Charlotte, 37,108
    Clifton, 108
    Cora, 14
    David, 37
    Diana, 199
    Elizabeth, 4,168,200
    Elizabeth Jane, 200
    Elizabeth Jane (Ledbetter), 168
    Ellen, 152,158,162
    Ephraim, 168,199,200
    Ezra, 168,175,199,204
    Hannah, 37,108,168,199,211
    Henry, 37,108
    Hiram, 37,108,168
    Ishmael, 37,108
    Jane, 200
    Jesse, 168,199
    John, 168,185,194,199,200
    John Jr, 199
    Jonathan B, 168,199
    Margaret, 108,168
    Margaret (Hubler), 42
    Margaret E (Hubler), 37
    Mary, 108
    Mary Jane, 204
    Melva, 108
    Melva D, 37,42
    Minnie, 168
    Nathan, 37,108,199
    Nathan Jr, 37
    Pearl, 108
    Rachel, 185,194,199,203
    Rebecca, 199
    Ruth, 160,168,194
    Ruth (Allen), 37
    Samuel, 160,168,199
    Susan (Paine), 37
    Susanna, 175
    T Riley, 37
    Wm, 108,168,199
    Wm P, 37,42
    Zarilda/Zerilda Ann (Thornburg), 175,199
    Zerilda, 204

LEEDS, Ann/Anna/Annie, 30,71,108
    Ann C, 108
    Catharine, 108
    Elisabeth/Elizabeth B, 108
    Eliza J (Ireton), 38
    Elizabeth, 108
    George Elsworth, 38
    Holly R, 30
    Noah, 108
    Noah L, 108
    Noah S, 108
    Rebecca (Green), 30
    Ruby, 38
    Vencent Augustus, 108
    Vincent, 38,108
    Warner M, 108
    Wm, 108
    Wm B, 108
LEEDY, Anna, 32
LEFEVER, Alfred, 108
    Alfred Henry, 38
    Ellen Maria, 38,49
    Frederic Smith, 38
    Rachel, 108
    Rebecca C, 38,49
    Wm M, 38,49
    see also **LEFEVERE, LEFEVRE**
LEFEVERE, Alfred Henry, 108
    Ellen Maria, 108
    Frederick Smith, 108
    Rebecca, 108
    Wm M, 108
    see also **LEFEVER, LEFEVRE**
LEFEVRE, Alfred H, 108
    Frederick S, 108
    Rachel, 108
    Rebecca, 108
    see also **LEFEVER, LEFEVERE**
LEFFINGWELL, Amos Newton, 168
    Frank, 168
    Lucinda (Rhodes), 168
LEGGETT, Sarah B, 200
    Sarah E, 206
    Sarah E (Riggle), 168
    Wm, 168
LEHMAN, David, 38
    David E, 108
    Harriett B, 108
    Harriett B, 38
    see also **LAYMAN, LEIGHMAN**
LEIGHMAN, Marie, 52
    see also **LAYMAN, LEHMAN**
LEMON, Ida (Morgan), 37
    Orange V, 37
    Zetelia, 37
LENTZ, Emanuel, 168
    Mary (Heiney), 168
    Sarah Josephine, 168
LEONARD, Joseph, 211
    Pheobe, 211
    Sarah L, 211
LESH, Elizabeth (Baldwin), 200
LESTER, Louise, 28
LEVELL, Sarah Ann, 200
LEVERING, Annie, 36
LEWALLEN, Meshack, 108
    see also **LEWALLIN, LEWELLEN, LEWELLIN, LEWELLING, LEWELLYN, LLEWELYN, LUELLEN, LUELLING**

LEWALLIN, Henderson, 108
    Henry, 108
    John, 108
    Meshack, 108
    Seth, 108
    Wm, 108
    see also **LEWALLEN, LEWELLEN, LEWELLIN, LEWELLING, LEWELLYN, LLEWELYN, LUELLEN, LUELLING**
LEWELLEN, Jabez, 200
    see also **LEWALLEN, LEWALLIN, LEWELLIN, LEWELLING, LEWELLYN, LLEWELYN, LUELLEN, LUELLING**
LEWELLIN, Meshack, 108
    see also **LEWALLEN, LEWALLIN, LEWELLEN, LEWELLING, LEWELLYN, LLEWELYN, LUELLEN, LUELLING**
LEWELLING, Henry, 30
    Martha, 30
    Rachel, 30
    Rachel E, 30
    see also **LEWALLEN, LEWALLIN, LEWELLEN, LEWELLIN, LEWELLYN, LLEWELYN, LUELLEN, LUELLING**
LEWELLYN, Jabez, 200
    Mary, 200
    see also **LEWALLEN, LEWALLIN, LEWELLEN, LEWELLIN, LEWELLING, LLEWELYN, LUELLEN, LUELLING**
LEWIS, Alvah M, 168,200
    Ann L, 108
    Ann S, 38
    Anna, 51,168
    Anna E, 35
    Caroline (Davenport), 38
    Charles, 38
    Clark B, 16
    Clark E, 38,108, 109
    Cora (Clark), 168
    David, 94,108
    Delila/Delilah, 168,200
    Douglas J, 38
    Elisabeth/Elizabeth, 94,108
    Eliza Anna (Ong), 35
    Ellen C, 108
    Emaline/Emeline/Emmaline, 34,38, 108
    Emma B, 109
    Emma E (Brown), 16,38
    Emma E B, 109
    Esther A, 38
    Esther B, 109
    Eva, 161
    Hannah, 168
    Hannah (Hussey), 38
    Isaac, 108
    Isabella M, 38
    James W, 168
    Jesse, 38
    Jesse B, 38
    Jesse E, 109
    John Milton, 38,108
    Joseph E, 38
    Joseph T, 108
    Josiah, 108
    Josiah T, 38,108
    Katturah/Keturah, 94,108

LEWIS, Louisa, 180
    Lucinda, 168,200
    Lucy J, 38,108
    Margaret/Margret Ann, 38,108,168, 200
    Martha, 38,108,168,200
    Martha C, 108
    Martha Rachel, 108
    Mary, 168
    Mary A, 200
    Mary Ann, 168
    Mary Elizabeth, 38
    Nathan, 38,108
    Phebe, 41
    Phebe (Blue), 38
    Rachael/Rachel M, 38,108
    Rachel, 38,108
    Rachel (Cook) 94
    Roxa J (Minor), 38
    Ruth, 168
    Sally, 108
    Samuel, 168,200
    Sarah, 38,85,108
    Sarah L, 16
    Sarah T, 38,109
    Seth B, 38,109
    Stephen, 38,108
    Susanna/Susannah, 38,108,162,192
    Tennison, 38
    Thomas, 94,108,168,200
    Wm, 38,108,168,200
    Wm H, 168
    Zimri, 108
LINDAMOOD, Catharine, 162
    see also **LINDEMOTH, LINDEMUTH**
LINDEMOTH, John, 109
    see also **LINDAMOOD, LINDEMUATH**
LINDEMUTH, Elenora (Hoffman), 38
    John, 38
    Victoria, 38
    Victoria E, 109
    see also **LINDAMOOD, LINDEMOTH**
LINDLEY, Abraham, 109
    Amey/Amy, 109
    Aron, 109
    Catherine, 109
    David, 109
    Deborah, 109
    Elizabeth, 109
    Emmy, 109
    Esther, 109
    Grace, 109
    Hannah, 109
    Harlow, 38
    Henry, 109
    Hezekiah, 109
    Jacob, 109
    James, 109
    Jane, 109
    John, 109
    Jonathan, 109
    Joseph, 109
    Mahlon, 38
    Margery, 109
    Martha, 109
    Martha (Newlin), 38
    Mary, 109
    Owen, 109
    Rebecca (Hobson), 200

LINDLEY, Rebeckah Henley, 109
   Samuel, 109
   Sarah, 109
   Thomas, 109
   Wm, 109
LINES, Elijah, 168
   Elizabeth (Beabout), 168
   Sarah Josephine (Lentz), 168
   Thomas E, 168
LIPPENCOTT, Samuel R, 109
   see also **LIPPINCOT**,
      LIPPINCOTT
LIPPINCOT, Samuel R, 109
   see also **LIPPENCOTT**,
      LIPPINCOTT
LIPPINCOTT, Benjamin R, 109
   see also **LIPPENCOTT**,
      LIPPINCOT
LIPSEY, J Herbert, 38
LISTER, Ellen B, 38
   Ethel L, 38
   Josephine, 38
   Wm L, 38
LISTON, James, 109
   James Thomas, 109
   Jane, 109
   Jane Reese, 109
   Jonathan Allee, 109
   Margaret, 109
   Wm, 109
   Wm Maurice/Morris, 109
LITTLE, Anna, 109
   David, 38,109,133
   Jane, 109
   Jennette (Bond), 38
   Lora A, 8
   Mahlon, 8
   Martha, 7,57,59
   Martha (Fulghum) Bond, 38,109,133
   Mary, 109
   Mary Jane (Thornburg), 200
   Miriam, 8,109
   Orlando H, 38
   Sarah E, 57
LIVENGOOD, Martha J, 37
LLEWELLYN, Jabez, 168
   Mary, 168
   see also **LEWALLEN, LEWALLIN,**
      LEWELLEN, LEWELLIN,
      LEWELLING, LEWELLYN,
      LUELLEN, LUELLING
LLOYD, Elizabeth Anna, 62
LOCK, Wm, 200
   see also **LOCKE**
LOCKE, Cecilia, 166
   Charity, 168
   Chester Paul, 168
   Damaris/Demaris M, 168,178
   Demaris, 168,178,200,209
   Dora Alice (Burrows), 168
   Edgar R, 168
   Edith Marie, 168
   Elizabeth, 168
   Hannah, 168
   John Aaron, 168,200
   John Albert, 168
   Judith, 168,200
   Judith F, 200
   Levi, 168
   Lucretia, 168
   Luna D, 168
   Martha E (Thornburg), 168

LOCKE, Mary A, 175
   Mary Ann/Maryan, 150,168,179,208
   Mary E (Holiday), 168
   Orlanda E, 168
   Rachel, 168
   Wm, 168,178,200
   Wm M, 200
   Wm Milton, 168
LOCKWOOD, Fred, 38
   Isaac, 4
   Jane, 147
   Ruth, 4,38
   Ruth A, 4
LOER, Clara, 152
   Mary E, 152
   see also **LOHR**
LOGAN, Charles L, 168
   Florence Elizabeth, 168
   Mary J (Koonsman), 168
LOHR, Alma, 38
   Ida L, 38
   Mason, 38
   Viretta (Mendenhall), 38
   see also **LOER**
LONG, Eliza, 38
   Frank J, 38
   Ida M, 43
   John, 38
   Joseph, 38,43
   Lily J, 38
   Lucy, 38
   Mary, 43
LONGSHORE, Elenor, 132
LONGSTREET, Josephine, 109
LOSEY, J S, 38
   Phebe (Hunt), 109
   Phebe Ann (Hunt), 38
LOTT, Harriet, 38
   Louis Everett, 38
   Samuel, 38
LOUDEN, Pearl Adele, 26
LOVE, Charity, 200
LOVELL, John, 160
   Mary, 160
   Susan, 160
   Nelson, 200
LUCAS, Laura Bell, 157,176
   Levi F, 168
   Minnie (Lee), 168
   Sarah (Cox), 200
   Sherilee Cordelia, 168
LUCKER, Mary B, 16
LUELLEN, Clara (Conner), 168
   Della Anna, 168
   Jonathan M, 168
   Loring W, 168
   Margaret (Huffman), 168
   Rebecca M (Current), 168
   Wm Newton, 168
   see also **LEWALLEN, LEWALLIN,**
      LEWELLEN, LEWELLIN,
      LEWELLING, LEWELLYN,
      LLEWELLYN, LUELLING
LUELLING, Mary, 200
   see also **LEWALLEN, LEWALLIN,**
      LEWELLEN, LEWELLIN,
      LEWELLING, LEWELLYN,
      LLEWELLYN, LUELLEN
LUMPKIN, America, 155
   Cynthia Ella, 171
   Dempsey O, 168
   Edith, 168

LUMPKIN, Rebbecca, 200
   Rebecca (Dennis), 168
   Sarah (Maulsby), 200
LUNCHFORD, Adeline (Elmore), 109
   see **LUNSFORD**
LUNDY, Elizabeth, 200
   Elizabeth R, 200
   Ira S, 200
   James G, 200
   Lot, 200
   Martha, 61,109
   Martin L, 200
   Martin S, 200
   Mary Elwood, 168
   Mordecai, 200
   Mordecai E, 200
   Rachel, 168
   Wm, 168
LUNSCOMB, Mary Frances, 35
LUNSFORD, Adaline (Elmore), 18,23,37, 38
   Benjamin, 18,23,37,109
   Benjamin F, 38
   Charles M, 38
   Cora Mead, 18,38
   Elizabeth May, 37,38
   Flora Eva, 38
   Martha Pearl, 23,38
   Mattie (Jones), 38,109
   Nellie H, 38
   Wm W, 38
   see also **LUNCHFORD**
LYLE, Amy (Cox), 109
LYNDE, Belle, 50
   Sarah (Dugdale), 109
LYNN, Josie, 158
LYONS, Lavine (Mills), 200

McADAMS, Bertha, 109
   Maggie, 109
McALISTER, Samuel, 200
   see also **McALLISTER**
McALLISTER, Mary E, 168,200
   Samuel, 200
   see also **McALISTER**
McBETH, Beth Margaret (Fye), 38
   Donald, 38
McCALL, Dorcas, 109
   James, 109
   Joel, 109
   John, 109
   Margaret, 109
   Martha Jane, 109
   Mary, 109
   Susannah, 109
   Wm, 109
   see also **McCOLL**
McCALUM, Levi, 25
   Mary Ann, 25
   Melinda C, 25
   see also **MACALLIM, McCOLLUM**
McCARTY, Addie R, 25,44
   Jasper N, 25
   Mary A, 25
   Minerva, 60,63
McCAY, Joanna (McFerran), 109
   see also **McKAY**
McCLANE, Amanda, 147
   John, 147
   Mary, 147
   see also **McLAIN, McLANE**

McCLUER, David N, 38
  Eunice, 38
  George F, 38
  Melissa J, 38
  Rebecca (Roberts), 38
  Samuel, 38
  see also **McCLURE**
McCLURE, Eunice, 109
  George, 109
  Joseph, 109
  Letitia, 109
  Nathaniel D, 109
  see also **McCLUER**
McCLURG, Andrew, 38
  Jack, 38
  Rilda, 38
  Jesse, 168
McCOLL, Doracas, 109
  Margaret, 109
  Mary, 109
  Susanna, 109
  see also **McCALL**
McCOLLUM, John E, 168,200
  Martha, 200
  Martha (Mendenhall), 168
  Mary E, 200
  Mary Ellen, 168
  Miles, 168,200
  see also **MACOLLIM, McCALUM**
McCOMB, Anna, 49
McCOSKEY, Minnie, 14
McCOWN, Grace L, 48
  John H, 48
  Mary C, 48
McCOY, Alice, 25
  Eliza (Brown), 25
  James W, 25
  Minnie (Nabb), 38
McCRACKEN, David, 200
  Mary Jane, 109
  Nathan, 109
  Robert, 200
  Thomas Clarkson, 200
  see also **McCRAKEN**
McCRAKEN, Nathan, 109
  see also **McCRACKEN**
McCULLOUGH, Carrie M, 9
  Christiann, 9
  Ella R (Smith), 38
  J M, 9
McDEVITT, Claude H, 109
  Cocoa Blanche, 109
  Francis G, 109
  James H, 109
  Mary J, 109
  Rosoe C, 109
  see also **McDIVITT**
McDIVITT, Claude H, 109
  Cocoa Blanche, 109
  Francis G, 109
  Mary J, 109
  Rosco C, 109
  see also **McDEVITT**
McDONALD, Anna (Edwards), 52
  Caroline (Burns), 38,51
  Carrie, 109
  Dorcas (Elleman), 38
  Enos, 38
  Jennie, 52
  Michael, 52
  Orissa, 38,51,109
  Wm, 38,51,109

McDOWELL, Andrew, 109
  Andrew J, 109
McFADDEN, Martha (Wiggins), 168
  Wm H H, 168
McFERRAN, Joanna, 109
McGEE, Emma E, 38
  Minnie, 38
  Wm, 38
McGRAW, Anna J (Baldwin), 168
  Anna Jane, 200
  Anna/Annie M, 38,110
  Charles F/T, 38,110
  Charles Thomas, 110
  Elizabeth, 168
  Flora Alice, 38,110
  George, 110
  George M, 110
  George W, 38
  John, 200
  John W, 168,200
  Manerva Jane, 200
  Margaret Elmina, 168,200
  Martha E, 38,110
  Martha Ellen, 110
  Minerva Jane, 168
  Orpha Elizabeth, 168,200
  Steward/Stewart M, 38,110
  Stewart Maddison, 110
  Thomas, 168
  Violetta, 168,200
McGUNNIGILL, Abraham, 168
  Daisy, 168
  Mary (Retz), 168
McINTYRE, Adeline, 51
  Anna (Laflesh), 168
  Gussie M, 168
  Robert, 168
McKEE, Catharine, 38
  Margaret Ellen, 38
  Martha J, 48
  Wm, 38,110
McKINNEY, Jane (Underhill), 200
McKISSON, J D, 38
  Lydia (Threewits), 38
  Wm Douglas, 38
McLAIN, Catherine, 110
  James, 110
  John, 110
  Margaret, 110
  Samuel, 110
  see also **McCLANE, McLANE**
McLANE, Catherine, 110
  see also **McCLANE, McLAIN**
McLAUGHLIN, Asenath, 110
  Philip, 110
McLUCAS, Emily (Haworth), 110
McMATH, Anna, 38
  D H, 38
  Guy, 38
McMEANS, Fannie, 22
McMILLAN, Jane, 110
  Joshua F, 38
  Mary Elizabeth (Lewis), 38
  Viola Hanna, 38
  see also **McMILLEN, McMILLIN**
McMILLEN, Andrew, 39
  Jane, 39
  Joseph, 39
  see also **McMILLAN, McMILLIN**
McMILLIN, Minnie (Thay), 39
  see also **McMILLAN, McMILLEN**
McMULLEN, Ada, 110
  Nancy, 166

McNUTT, Lemuel C, 39
McPHERSON, Adrian, 39
  John, 110
  John H, 110
  John, T, 110
  John W, 110
  Louisa, 39
  Mary Edith, 39
McTAGGART, Alpheus, 110
  Caroline, 110
  Caroline (Richardson), 110
  Emma, 110
  see also **McTAGGERT**
McTAGGERT, Alpheus, 39
  Anna, 39
  Caroline, 39
  Clara, 39
  Emma, 39
  James R, 39
  see also **McTAGGART**
McWHINNEY, Cynthia, 35
  John, 110
  Sarah, 40

MABIE, Elizabeth (Avery), 11
  John, 11
  Susan, 11,39
  Susan, 39,65
MACE, Alice, 17
  see also **MACY**
MACKIE, Edith, 39
  George, 39,110
  Grace, 39,110
  James, 39,110
  Rebecca, 39,110
MACOLLIM, Jesse, 200
  John, 200
  Mary Ellen, 200
  Miles, 200
  see also **McCALUM, McCOLLUM**
MACY, Aaron, 169
  Achsah, 201
  Achsah (Johnson), 201
  Albert, 168
  Albert W, 169
  Alice, 169
  Alva, 200
  Alvah J, 168,169,178
  Alvah P, 200
  Alvy, 201
  Ann/Anna, 39,110,131,169
  Anna Lula (Wiggins), 169
  Asenith (Baldwin), 201
  Azra, 169
  Barachia/Barachiah/Barakiah, 169, 200,209
  Betsy Ann, 110
  Beulah, 110
  Bryan, 169
  Catharine/Catherine, 39,56,110
  Catherine (Parker), 110
  Charity, 169,201
  Charlotte, 161,169
  David, 169,200,201
  Delila, 200
  Earl L, 201
  Edward Earl, 201
  Eleanor, 201
  Eleanor (Thornburg), 169,170
  Eli, 39,110
  Elihu, 200
  Elihu C, 169

MACY, Elizabeth, 40,150,157
Ellen, 164
Elvira, 169,170,172,201
Elza, 169
Emma Bertha, 201
Enoch, 39
Eunice, 169,198
Eunice B, 39,110
Eustacia Ann, 169
Evie G, 201
Exaline, 169
Ezra, 200
Forrest, 169
Francis, 110
Francis B, 39,110
Frank, 169
Frank W, 201
Hannah, 168,169,190,198
Hannah M, 169
Harry B, 169,201
Henrietta Maria, 110
Henry, 169,200
Howard W, 201
Huldah, 169
Huldah B, 110
Huldah B (Hunt), 110
Huldah M, 205
Ira, 169,201
Ira C, 201
Irena, 169
Irwin, 169
Isaac, 169,170,186,200
Jesse, 169,201
Jethro, 164,169
John, 110,169,172,200,201
John G, 39
John H, 169
John Henry, 169
John M, 110
Jonathan, 110,169,198,200
Jonathan Jr, 200
Jonathan B, 150,161,169,200
Joseph, 150,169
Joseph R, 169
Julia Ann, 169,201
Julia E (Hendrix), 169
Julian (Mills), 201
Larkin, 169,201
Laurence G, 201
Lawrence, 169
Lewis, 169,201
Lillian (Parker), 169
Lucinda, 150,161,169,181,185,209
Lula, 201
Lydia, 169,179,201,209
Lydia Ann, 169,193
Malinda/Melinda, 78,169,189
Margaret, 169
Margaret (White), 110
Margaret Melinda, 169
Mary, 33,150,169,178
Mary (Charles), 110
Mary (Lewis), 168
Mary Ann, 169,194,201
Mary E, 172
Mary Elizabeth, 33
Mary Jane, 169
Mary Louise, 169
Matilda, 161,169,193,201
Matilda (Pierce), 150,169
Miles, 169
Minerva, 169,178

MACY, Mira/Myra, 169,194
Miriam C, 201
Miriam C (Pidgeon), 201
Murry H, 201
Nancy, 169,181
Nathan, 110,200
Nathan H, 169
Nathaniel, 201
Nellie M, 201
Obed, 110,201
Oliver, 201
Oliver Clinton, 169
Pamela, 200
Perry, 169,201
Phebe, 18,110
Phebe Ann, 100,110
Priscilla M, 18
Rachel, 186
Rebecca, 110,131
Rebecca/Rebekah (Barnard), 39,56
Reuben, 110,161,169,181
Rhoda H (Farmer), 201
Ruth, 169,194
Sarah, 110,169
Sarah (Hobson), 169
Stephen, 39,56,110,131
Stephen Jr, 39,110
Susan, 201
Susannah L, 169
Sylvanus, 169
Thomas, 110
Thomas Colman, 169
Tristram, 110
Wayne C, 169,201
Wm, 18,110,168,169,200,201
Wm Jr, 201
Wm Allen, 110
Wm Lewis, 169
Wm M, 169,201
Wm T, 169,201
Zackeus, 110
see also **MACE**
MADDEN, Solomon, 110
Susannah, 110
see also **MADEN**
MADDOCK, Alma, 110
Anna B, 39,110
Francis, 39,110
John C, 39,110
Martha Ellen, 39,110
Mildred Elizabeth, 39
Rachel H, 39,110
MAHARRY, Mary, 29
MADEN, Elizabeth, 110
George, 110
Hiram, 110
Solomon, 110
Susanna (Stuart), 110
see also **MADDEN**
MAHEW, Catherine, 110
see also **MAYHEW**
MAHONEY, Sarah (Hodson), 201
MAIN, Alexander, 154
Amos, 158
Magdalene, 154
Mary (Covalt), 154
Nancy (Bales), 158
Susanna, 158
MALES, Jane, 11
Jennie, 11,39,110
Maud Bertha/Bertie, 11,39,110
Samuel R, 11,39,110

MALOTT, James, 110
James A, 110
MALSBY, Ellen, 201
Mary Elisabeth, 201
Oliver E, 201
Richard J, 201
Thomas Monroe, 201
see also **MAULSBY**
MANFORD, Carl Monroe, 39
MANIFOLD, Alice, 150
Susannah, 110
Susannah (Butler), 110
MANLEY, Ernest, 110
Ernest G, 39,110
Estella/Estelle, 39,110
Esther, 39
Herbert, 110
Herbert H, 39
Hettie, 110
Lydia, 39,110
Lydia (Gordon), 39
Lydia G, 110
Pearl C, 39
Pearl Charlotte, 110
Ruth, 10
Ruth A, 39
Wm, 110
Wm F, 39,110
MANN, Earl H, 39
Mary Stuart (Hill), 39
MANNING, Elizabeth, 34
Elizabeth, 34
Lura, 34
Wm, 34
MARCHANT, Mary J, 10
MARCHARD, Fred, 39
Mary (Jones), 39
MARCUS, Mary (Cockayne), 110
MARDECK, Ann, 110
Elisabeth, 110
Susannah, 110
MARDOCK, Isaac, 110
James, 110
MARINDALE, Amanda, 111
see also **MARTINDALE**
MARINE, Asa, 111
Hanna, 39
John, 39,111
Jonathan, 111
Laura, 39
MARIS, Ann, 111
Benjamin L, 201
Eli, 111
Elinor, 111
Jane, 111
John, 111
Mary, 111
Sarah, 111
Thomas, 111
see also **MARRIS**
MARK, Charlotte, 58
MARKLE, Anna (Hart), 169
Gideon, 169
John, 169,201
MARKLEY, F Clindore, 39
Mae (Neff), 39
Ralph Herbert, 39
Russel, 39
MARLOTT, Laura B, 111
MARMON, Ann, 111
Anna (Hawkins), 39
Benjamin, 39

MARMON, Benjamin F, 39
  Benjamin Franklin, 111
  Betsy, 111
  Charles M, 39,111
  Charles Moffitt, 111
  Daniel, 111
  Daniel H, 39
  Daniel W, 39,111
  David, 39,111
  Elizabeth (Carpenter), 111
  Elizabeth C, 111
  Hannah (Moffitt) Craig, 111
  Hannah C, 39,111
  Hannah C Elizabeth (Carpenter), 39
  Harriet, 68, 111
  Howard C, 39,111
  James, 111
  James D, 39
  James N, 111
  James W, 39,111
  Lydia, 39,116
  Martin, 111
  Mary, 68,111
  Mary Townsend, 39
  Melinda, 39
  Pricilla/Priscilla, 39,103
  Rachel, 39,78,111
  Rebecca, 39,137
  Susanna, 111
  Walter C, 111
  Walter Carpenter, 39
  Wm, 39,111
MAROT, Bessie L, 39
  Henry, 39
  Jennie M, 39
  Lucy A, 39
MARQUIS, Charles,Charley, 39,111
  Harry, 39,111
  Mary (Cockayne), 39
  Jennie, 108,111
  Mary, 111
  Olive, 39,111
MARRIS, Ann, 39
  Elias H, 39
  John, 39
  Sarah M, 201
  see also **MARIS**
MARSH, Palemia, 11
MARSHAL, Susannah, 111
  see also **MARSHALL, MARSHILL**
MARSHALL, Aaron, 169,181,201
  Abbie, 39,111
  Abigail, 6
  Alonzo, 39,170
  Amelia H, 170
  Ann/Anna/Anne, 53,169,170,187,196, 201
  Anna Jane, 7,187,201
  Betsey, 170
  Calvin, 169,201
  Clayton, 170
  Collin/Collins, 169,201
  Cynthia, 201
  Cynthia (Swain), 169,170
  Cynthia Ellen, 170
  Elam, 201
  Elizabeth, 169,170,196
  Elmer Ellsworth, 170
  Elsie M, 39
  Elvira (Macy), 170,201
  Evan, 7,39,169,187,201
  Florene, 174

MARSHALL, Gulana/Gulielma, 7,169,187
  Gulielma (Bond), 201
  Hannah, 111
  Hannah (Elliott), 170
  Harry Swain, 170
  Jacob, 111,170,201
  John, 111,169,170,187,196,201
  John Elliott, 170
  Joshua, 169
  Keziah, 201
  Keziah (Davis), 170,201
  Lucinda (Swain), 170
  Luella, 169,171
  Mabin, 201
  Maggie E, 201
  Mahon, 169
  Margaret, 111
  Margaret (Wright), 39
  Margaret Ann, 169,201
  Martha, 111
  Martha (Jones), 169,170
  Martha Jane, 169,201
  Mary, 170,201
  Mary Ann, 170
  Matilda, 171
  Matilda (Macy), 169
  Miles, 111,169,170,201
  Miles C, 169
  Minerva, 169
  Mitchel/Mitchell, 111,169,201
  Myra, 169
  Nancy (Macy), 169,181
  Orlando, 169,170,171
  Osce/Osee Ann, 166,170
  Rachel, 169,187
  Rachel (Tolbert), 39
  Rebeckah, 170
  Reuben/Rueben, 170,201
  Rhoda, 170
  Stephen, 169,201
  Susannah, 111,170
  Swain, 170
  Thomas, 111,169,170,201
  Thomas III, 201
  Thomas Worth, 170
  Vernon, 169
  Wm, 111,169,170,201
  see also **MARSHAL, MARSHILL**
MARSHILL, Hannah, 201
  Miles, 201
  Osee Ann, 201
  Susannah, 201
  Thomas, 201
  Thomas Jr, 201
  see also **MARSHAL, MARSHALL**
MARTIN, Alice, 39,111
  Alpheus, 39,111
  Angus, 111
  Arthur, 201
  Benjamin LeRoy, 39,111
  Elihu, 201
  Elizabeth L (Reed), 111
  Elizabeth S, 39
  Elmina/Elmira B, 39,111
  Elmira, 201
  Eva, 201
  Isaac N, 39,111
  James, 39,111
  John, 111
  John L, 39
  Joseph C, 170,201
  Lot W, 22,39

MARTIN, Malinda (Hodgin), 170
  Malinda/Melinda, 201
  Mary, 50
  Mary (Crow), 170
  Mary R, 50
  Matilda, 22,39
  Minerva, 201
  Minnie, 22
  Ruth, 111
  Ruth A, 111
  Sarah, 111
  Ruth Anna, 39
  Sarah J, 39
  Squire, 170
  Susannah (Koons), 111
  Thomas Caldwell/Colwell, 39,111
MARTINDALE, Amanda, 39
  Emma, 5,39
  James, 5,39
  John, 39,110
  Lydia (White), 5,39
MARVEL, Charles, 40,111
  Elizabeth Johnson, 40
  Harriet A, 111
  Harriett (Pepper), 40
  Josiah P, 40,111
  Josiah Philip/Phillip, 40,111
  Mary Amy (Johnson), 40,111
MASON, Anna Mary (Brown), 40
  Edith, 111
  Grazil/Grizzel, 111
  Mandus E, 40
  Mary, 111
  Thomas, 111
  Thomas Jr, 111
MASSEY, Betsey Ann, 170,201
  James, 201
  Jane, 1,111
  Mary Ann, 201
  Murrel/Murrell, 201
  Rachel (Beeson), 201
MATHER, David, 33
  David L, 40
  Elizabeth, 31,100,111
  Elizabeth C, 26,40,111
  Ella (Hough), 40
  Emma R, 111
  Hannah, 111
  Henry, 111
  Irene, 40
  John P, 40,111
  Lillian, 40
  Louisa A, 40,111
  Lurena (Steddom), 33,40
  Martha L, 51
  Mary Ann/Anna, 35,40,105
  Phineas, 26,35,40
  Phineas R, 100,105,111
  Richard, 31,111
  Ruth Ann/Anna, 26,35,40,100,105, 111
  Ruth Ann (Pool), 111
  Samuel, 40
  Sarah B, 100
  Susan M, 40
  Susanna L, 31
  Susanna S, 40
  Susannah M, 33
  see also **MATHERS**
MATHERS, Mary Grace, 111
MATHEWS, Ann, 31
  Mary, 186
  see also **MATTHEWS**

MATIX, Alexander Alfred, 40
    Caroline, 40
    John Sr, 40
    John E, 40
    Laura Arminta, 40
    Mary, 40
    Mary A, 40
    see also **MATTOX**
MATTHEWS, Amos, 40
    Anna, 40,111
    Clarissa, 166
    Eliza, 18
    Elmira, 166
    Hannah, 111
    John, 166
    Marie L, 40
    Mary, 40,111
    Mary Grace, 40,111
    Priscilla R, 173
    Susannah (Wright), 40
    see also **MATHEWS**
MATTOX, Carolina, 40
    John, 40
    Mabel, 40
    see also **MATIX**
MAUDLIN, Abraham, 111
    Ana/Ann/Anne, 8,74,111
    Benjamin, 2,40,111
    Betsy, 111
    Betty, 111
    Charles, 111
    Delilah (Denny), 202
    Delilah S (Denny), 202
    Dillon, 111
    Eliza, 9,111
    Enoch, 111
    George, 111
    Hannah, 8,74,111
    Henry, 111
    John, 2,8,40,74,111
    Leah, 2,40,111
    Levi, 111
    Mary (Wickersham), 111
    Miriam, 111
    Miriam (Peacock), 111
    Nancy, 111
    Nathan, 111
    Peninah/Peninnah, 2,40
    Rachel, 40
    Rhoda A, 111
    Richard, 111
    Rueben, 111
    Samuel, 2,40
    Sarah, 40
    Strah, 111
    Susaner, 40
    Thomas, 2,40
    Wm, 111
    Wright, 2,40,111
    see also **MODLIN**
MAUL, Benjamin, 111
    Isaac, 111
    John, 111
    see also **MAULE**
MAULE, Ann, 100
    Benjamin, 40,111
    Isaac, 40,111
    John, 40,111
    Priscilla, 40,111
    Thomas, 40,111
    Thomas Benjamin, 111
    Wm, 40,111
    see also **MAUL**

MAULSBY, Benjamin, 170,202
    Cynthia, 205
    David, 170,178,200,202,208
    David Jr, 202
    Delphina, 170
    Elizabeth, 170,202,205
    Ellen E (Hunt), 170
    Ezra, 170,202
    Ira, 170,202
    James, 170,202
    John, 170,202,205
    John Jr, 202
    Keziah (Bales), 202
    Lemuel, 202
    Lucinda, 170,178,202,208
    Lydia, 170,190
    Macy, 202
    Macy B, 170,202
    Malinda/Melinda, 170,202
    Mary, 170,178,202,208
    Mary E, 170
    Mary Eliza, 202
    Matilda, 170,202
    Milton, 170
    Minerva, 202
    Nancy, 169
    Oliver E, 170
    Rachel (Patty), 202
    Rachel M (Beeson), 202
    Rachel Melvina, 170
    Rhoda, 170
    Richard J, 170,202
    Ruth, 170,202
    Ruth (Beeson), 202
    Ruth (Reynolds), 202
    Sally F, 202
    Sally P, 170
    Sarah, 200
    Silas, 202
    Silas B, 170
    Thomas, 170
    Thomas M, 170
    Wm, 170,202
MAULSBY, Wm O, 170
    Zerilda, 202
    see also **MALSBY**
MAXWELL, Albert D, 40,112
    Amanda, 40
    Ann/Anna/Anne, 34,40,112
    Ann Elizabeth, 112
    Ann Elizabeth (Moore), 112
    Benjamin F, 112
    Caroline, 40,112,135
    Charity (Wright), 112
    Elizabeth, 112
    Emeline Ann, 112
    Emiline, 40
    Emily, 112
    Emily P, 40
    Hannah, 111,112
    Hannah (Whitlock), 40
    Hugh, 112
    Hugh W, 40,112
    Jacob, 111,112
    Jemima, 112
    Jemima (Clark), 112
    John, 40,111,112
    John M, 40
    John S, 40
    Lindley H, 40,112
    Lydia, 112,202
    Margaret (Heavenridge), 112

MAXWELL, Mary, 40,112,135
    Mary Anna (Moore), 40,112
    Matilda, 112
    Miriam A, 112
    Miriam A (Coffin) Rambo, 112
    Miriam Allinson (Coffin), 40
    Nancy Jane, 40
    Rachel, 112
    Robert Moore, 40
    Ruth, 112
    Ruth Ann, 112
    Ruth Ann (James), 40
    Samuel, 40
    Sarah, 40,57,58,112
    Sarah (Clark), 112
    Sarah H, 40
    Sarah S (Rambo), 112
    Sarah Sylvania, 112
    Thomas, 112
    Wm, 112
MAY, Edward Franklin, 40
    John S, 40
    Sarah E, 40
    see also **MAYE**, **MAYS**
MAYE, Wm, 112
    see also **MAY**, **MAYS**
MAYHEW, Catherine L, 112
    Elizabeth, 40,112
    John M, 40
    Leah/Leslie C, 40
    Lorenzo, 40
    Margaret M, 112
    Margery, 40
    Maria G (Gooch), 40
    see also **MAHEW**
MAYS, Wm, 112
    see also **MAY**, **MAYE**
MEDLER, Joshua, 170
    Mary (Howell), 170
    Ruth, 170
MEEK, Elizabeth, 40
    Gulielma (Smith), 112
    Susan (Thornburg), 202
    see also **MEEKS**
MEEKER, Agusta, 54
    Benjamin, 112
    Davis, 112
    Emeline, 112
MEEKER, Harriet, 112
    Kate, 65
    Louisa, 112
    Mary, 112
    Robert B, 112
MEEKS, John Wesley, 112
    see also **MEEK**
MELBERT, Anna, 170,175,179,202
    Blanche, 170,202
    Catherine, 170
    Charles, 170,202
    Edgar, 170,202
    John, 170
    Michael, 170,275,179,202
    Philapena /Philipena/Phillipena
      (Cramer), 170,175,179
    Philipena/Phillippina, 202
MENDENHALL, A G, 170,171
    Aaron, 41,107,168,170,171,202
    Abigail, 6
    Adaline, 171
    Addison, 171
    Adella G, 112
    Adella Gardner, 40

MENDENHALL, Albert, 41
Albert J, 171
Alfred, 113
Alice, 48
Alice (Vining), 41
Alice A, 71
Alice Ann, 9,41
Alice Cary, 113
Alice F, 112
Alice Thayer, 40
Allen H, 40,112
Allen Harvey, 113
Alma, 170,202
Anderson/Anderton, 112,170
Ann, 112
Ann (Phillips), ix
Anna M, 113
Anna Mary, 51
Barnabas C, 170
Bentley/Bently, 40,112
Bertha E, 40,113
Betty (Walton), 55
Brooks, 202
Brooks J, 170
Caleb, 40,112
Caleb Jr, 112
Caleb S, 40,112
Carrie, 112
Charles, 112,170
Charles D, 112
Charles H, 41
Charles W, 112
Christiana, 171
Clara, 170,202
Clyde, 170,202
Cora E, 112
Cora Elisabeth, 40
Cynthia, 202
Cynthia (Dennis), 161,170,171,202
Cyrus, 170,202
Daniel, 40,112,170,171,202
David, 112
Davis F, 112
Davis Thayer, 40
Deborah, 171
Deborah (Horney), 40
Deborah M, 55
Delphina, 6
Dinah, 112
Edmund, 40
Edward, 112
Edwin, 40
Edwin H, 40,41,112
Elam, 202
Elijah, 112,170,202
Eliza, 141,171,198
Eliza (Hadley) Doan, 113
Eliza A, 112
Eliza Ann, 170,202
Elizabeth, ix,35,112
Elizabeth (Ary) Swindler, 112
Elizabeth (Swindle), 40,112
Elizabeth (Thayer),40
Elizabeth H, 41,113
Elizabeth M, 112
Ella, 202
Ellis G, 41,113
Emaline/Emilene/Emmeline, 202
Emaline (Bond), 171
Emma R, 41
Enos, 112
Esther, 171

MENDENHALL, Esther B, 188
Esther Carter, 171
Esther Jane, 112,113
Esther Jane (Irish), 40
Esther L Carter, 171
Eunice (Clark), 202
Eunice R, 171
Everet/Everett F, 40,112
Findley H, 40
Flora, 113
Flora Estella, 41
Freddy, 40
Gardner, 40
George L, 112
George LaFonte, 40
Georgia L, 22,41
Grace (Brown), 40
Griffith, 35,40,41,112
H, 100
Hannah, 112,202
Hannah (Larrowe), 202
Hannah (Milhous), 31,112,113
Hannah B, 41,112,127
Hannah C, 170
Hannah M (Hough), 113
Hannah N (Lancaster), 112
Hazel Ellen, 171
Henry, 6,40,113
Henry W, 41,112
Herbert, 41
Huldah, 159,171,112,202
Huldah (Coffin), 170
Isaac, 64,112,170,202
Isaiah, 171
J Edwin, 112
James, 40,41,51,111,170,171,202
James Carver, 41,112
Janetta/Jeannete (Richie), 41,112
Jeanette J (Richie), 40
Jesse Carpenter, 41
Jesse W, 170,171,202
John, 41,112,113,202
John A, 40,41,112
John B, 112
John C, 202
John R, 41
Jonathan, ix
Jonathan C, 170
Joseph, ix,152,202
Joseph C, 112,170
Joseph Coffin, 41,112
Joseph Edwin, 41
Julia (Stubbs), 41
Kirk, 41
Leora, 171
Lewis, 112
Lindley, 112
Lindley H, 170,171,202
Linus, 112
Lucy A, 202
Lucy Ann (Conley), 170
Luella, 170,202
Luella (Marshall), 171
Lydia, 9,41,93,107,112
Lydia (Richardson), 41
Lydia A, 41,112
Lydia J, 112
Lydia J (Hayworth), 112
Margaret, 112,202
Margaret C, 171
Mariam/Miriam, 44,108
Marietta, 46

MENDENHALL, Mark, 40
Martha, 35,40,41,168,178
Martha A, 202
Martha Ann, 112,113
Martha Ann (Reynolds), 171
Martha E, 161,171
Marticia C, 188
Martitia, 171
Mary, 112,152,153,170,171,202
Mary (Hockett), 168,170,171
Mary Ann, 159,171,180,210
Mary E, 112,202
Mary E (Jones), 41
Mary E (Young), 170
Mary Esther, 112
Maurice, 112
Melinda, 158,163,171,195
Milacent/Milicent,Millicent, 112,171,187
Millicent (Coffin), 41,112
Mildred, 23
Miles, 161,170,171,202
Mordecai, 112
Morris H, 41
Moses, 133
Myra, 202
Myra R, 171
Naomi J (Allen), 112
Naomi Jane (Allen), 112
Nathan, 46,170,202
Newman S, 170,171,202
Olinda, 41,125
Olinda B, 51,112
Olive, 24
Olive Jane, 41
Oliver, 171,202
Oliver L, 112
Olivia S, 85
Olivia Stevens, 19,41
Paris, 112,170
Pearl C, 40
Phebe, ix,112
Phebe (Oler), 170,171
Rachel, 139,152,202
Rachel (Brown), 64,170,202
Rachel A, 75
Rachel A (Johnson), 19,112
Ralph, 171
Rebecca/Rebekah, 133,198,202,210
Rebecca (Coffin), 163,171,180
Rebecca Ann, 41
Reese, 112,113
Reese J, 9,40,41,112
Rhoda, 37,46
Rhoda E, 112,139
Rhoda Elma, 41
Romania, 173
Rufus, 202
Rufus A, 171,202
S C, 85
Samuel, 112
Sarah, 7
Sarah (Williams), 112
Sarah Ann, 112
Sarah E, 41,112
Schuyler, 171
Silas, 170,202
Stephen, 85,112,139
Stephen C, 19,41,112
Susan, 31
Susan B, 41
Susannah, 112

MENDENHALL, Susannah (Gardner), 40
    Susannah (Pierce), 202
    Tabitha Jane, 113
    Valentine M, 170,202
    Viretta, 39,170,202
    Walter, 112
    Walter L, 41,112
    Wilson D, 171,202
    Wm, 41,55,112,113,163,171,180,198, 202,210
    Wm D, 171
    Wm Edwin, 41
    Wm G, 40
    Wm H, 170,171,202
    Wm O, 22,112
    Wm O'Neil, 41
    Wm White, 112
MENKE, Bessie Pormelia (Endsley), 41
    Frank H, 41
    Glenn Wilson, 41
    Sarah Ruth, 41
MERADETH, James H, 113
    see also **MEREDITH, MERIDITH**
MEREDITH, Abigail, 113
    Andrew, 113
    Basil F, 171
    Beulah Anna (Aydelott), 113
    David, 113
    Edith L, 171
    Elizabeth (Jones), 171
    Elwood, 171
    Esther, 113
    Harvey, 113
    Isaac H, 171
    Ithamar, 113
    Jabez, 113
    Jefferson, 113
    Joanna, 113
    John, 13
    Jonathan, 27
    Martha, 21
    Mary, 113
    Nancy (Purdue), 27
    Rachel, 113
    Rosanna/Roseanna, 113
    Sarah Bell (Frazier), 171
    Susanna, 113
    Tabitha C, 113
    Tabitha Jane, 113
    Tabitha Jane (Clawson), 113
    Tacy Ann, 6,18,27,32,48,64,95
    Temple, 113
    Thomas Jefferson, 113
    Wm, 113
    see also **MERADETH, MERIDETH**
MERIDETH, Susan, 41
    see also **MERADETH, MEREDITH**
MERRYWEATHER, Dora Ellen, 167
    George E, 167
    Susanna (Thornton), 167
METSKER, Mary A (Elwood), 41
    Rachel A, 175
METTERT, Elizabeth, 177
    George G, 177
    Mattie A, 177
METTLER, Eli, 55
    Rachel, 55
    Susan Hannah, 55
MICHOLLAND, Melissa J, 41
MIDDLETON, Elihu, 113
    Jeremiah, 113
    Samuel, 113

MIDDLETON, Sarah, 202
    Sarah L, 202
    Sidney, 113,202
MIKESELL, Catharine, 59
    Elizabeth, 59
    Lorene, 49
    Samuel, 59
MILBY, Anna M, 113
    Anna M (Mendenhall), 113
    Anna Mary (Mendenhall), 41
MILES, Anna, 131
    Anna (Kelly), 56
    Benjamin, 43
    Charles, 113
    Charles Homer, 41
    Cornelius, 41,129
    Cornelius V, 41,113
    Elizabeth (Bean), 43
    Elizabeth (Neal), 41
    Elvira (Kerr), 41
    Frances C, 17
    Jesse Clark, 41
    Joanna, 21,22,31,49
    Joanna/Johanna M, 57
    John, 57
    Lindley, 46,53
    Lydia (Willets), 46
    Lydia G (Willets), 53
    Margaret, 41,113,129
    Martha, 53
    Mary B (Lucker/Tucker), 13,16
    Mary E, 43
    Melissa, 56,113
    Melissa E, 46,131
    Rachel E, 41,113
    Rebecca (Jay), 57
    Rhoda M, 46
    Samuel, 41,56,131
    Vashti, 63
    Vashti E, 16
    Vashti H, 13
    Wade, 13,16
MILHOUS, Hannah, 31,41,100
    Martha, 100
    Martha (Vickers), 31,41
    Wm, 31,41,100
MILICAN, Eli, 202
    Mary Melinda, 202
    Wm, 202
    See also **MILIKAN, MILLICAN, MILLIKAN, MILLIKEN**
MILIKAN, Eli F, 202
    Mary, 113
    see also **MILICAN, MILLICAN, MILLIKAN, MILLIKEN**
MILLER, Alida C, 134
    Andrew, 41
    Anna/Annie M, 11,41,154
    Annie Mary (Newman), 41
    Barbara, 11,41,154
    Bertha, 113
    Catharine/Catherine, 134,154
    David, 41,113
    Elizabeth (Woodhurst), 52
    Emma J (Jones), 41
    Esther (Wright), 41
    Fred, 11,41
    Frederick, 154
    Grace A, 41
    Ida, 179
    Indiana, 59
    J C, 41

MILLER, J Newton, 113
    James, 41
    Jennie, 41
    John, 52
    John G, 41,113
    Jonathan, 113
    Kate C, 52
    Lydia, 113
    Lydia H (Rue), 113
    Margaret (Jones), 41
    Martin M, 113
    Mary, 113
    Maud, 41
    Minnie, 41
    Nancy (Harris), 41
    Parmelia, 41
    Paul D, 41
    Raymond, 113
    Rebecca (Cockayne), 41,113
    Rebecca (Gilpin), 113
    Robert, 134
    Sarah, 50
    Truman, 113
    Vernon, 113
    Viola, 41
MILLESON, Leon B, 113
MILLICAN, Eli, 203
    Jane, 25
    Mary Malinda, 203
    see also **MILICAN, MILIKAN, MILLIKAN, MILLIKEN**
MILLIKAN, Charles, 203
    Eli, 113,163
    Eli F, 203
    Ellen, 203
    Esther, 203
    John, 203
    Lewis , 203
    Mary E, 163,172
    Mary M (Holiday), 163
    Oliver E, 203
    Rebecca, 193
    Rebecca Jane, 203
    Richard J, 203
    Thomas K, 203
    Thomas Monroe, 203
    Wm, 203
    Wm M, 203
    see also **MILICAN, MILIKAN, MILLIKAN, MILLIKEN**
MILLIKEN, Almeda, 171,196
    Charity, 171
    Charles, 171
    Eli F, 171
    Esther, 171
    John, 171
    Mary E, 162,171
    Permelia A, 203
    Rebecca Jane, 171
    Sarah E, 171
    Thomas K, 171
    Wm, 171
    Wm M, 171
    see also **MILICAN, MILIKAN, MILLICAN, MILLIKAN, MILLIKEN**
MILLS, Aaron, 113,161,171,203
    Aaron L, 172
    Abner, 41
    Achsah, 206
    Adila, 172
    Alonzo, 172,203

MILLS, Amos, 41,113
    Ann/Anna, 113,172,186,203
    Anna M, 171
    Anne Maria/Annamariah, 113,171
    Annis, 171,186
    Arthur B, 172
    Asa, 113,203
    Austin, 171
    Benoni, 171,203,206
    Betsey/Betsy Ann, 171,172,188
    Betsey Jane, 171
    Betsy/Betty, 69,97,185
    Betty (Compton), 28,42
    Cassius C, 171,203
    Charity, 113,161,167,171,172,178, 203
    Cynthia Ella (Lumpkin), 171
    Cyrus, 203
    Daniel, 171,203
    David, 203
    Dora V, 167
    Dorinda Abigail, 172
    Eli, 113
    Elihu/Elihue, 171,172,203
    Elijah, 171,203
    Elisabeth/Elizabeth, 41,91,113,171, 172,203
    Elizabeth Jr, 203
    Elizabeth (Hoover), 113
    Elma Millicent, 17
    Emily, 171
    Emily (Wanzer), 41
    Enos, 172
    Flora P, 113
    Flora P (Pickett), 41
    Garelda, 113
    George, 41,113
    Gertrude, 41,113
    Gertrude Emily, 113
    Hannah, 113,171,178
    Hannah (Furnas), 41
    Hannah (Ratcliff), 203
    Henry, 113,171,172,178,203
    Henry F, 41
    Henry Irwin, 171
    Henry J, 113
    Hester Ann, 172,190
    Hezekiah, 113, 203
    Hugh, 41,171,203
    Huldah, 17,203
    Huldah (Mendenhall), 159,171
    Ira, 171
    Isaac, 203
    Jacob, 172
    James, 203
    Jamima/Jemima, 171,172,203,207
    Jane, 158,159,171,175,178,179,302
    Jemima (Hodson), 203
    Jesse, 203
    Joel, 167,171
    Joel T, 113
    John, 28,41,47,97,113,171,177,178, 180,188,203
    John B, 171,203
    John D, 17,159,171,203
    John Kindley, 172
    Jonathan, 113
    Joseph, 41,113
    Joseph John, 41,113
    Josiah, 113,171
    Julian, 201
    Juliann, 171

MILLS, Karenhappock, 171
    Kinsey, 113
    Kinsey M, 172
    Larinda/Lorinda, 171,203
    Lavine/Lavinia, 171,200
    Lettice/Lettie, 113,172
    Levi, 113
    Louisa A (Cain), 167
    Lucinda, 172
    Lydia (Hasket), 41
    Mahlon, 113
    Maritita/Maratitia, 171,203
    Martha E, 171
    Mary, 15,47,113,171,178,188,203,206
    Mary (Ellis), 171,203
    Mary Ann, 113
    Mary Elizabeth (Cook), 41
    Mary Jane, 172
    Millicent M, 159,172
    Milton, 113,203
    Moses, 113,172,203
    Moses Albert, 171
    Nancy, 172,185,190,203,207
    Nancy M, 172,185
    Noah, 113
    Oliver, 172,203
    Osom, 203
    Phebe, 171
    Polly, 172
    Rachel, 113,172,180
    Rebecca, 97
    Rebecca M, 28,41
    Rebeccah (Canaday), 203
    Richard, 172,185,190,207
    Rosa, 130
    Rosetta, 55,113
    Rowlan/Rowland R, 113
    Rufus, 203
    Ruth, 113,172,190
    Sally, 172
    Samuel, 113
    Sarah/Sarrah, 47,113,171,172,173, 177,178,180,184,191
    Seth, 113,171,172,203
    Susan, 113
    Susan (Merideth), 41
    Susanna/Susannah, 55, 113
    Thomas, 113,171,203
    Thomas H, 41,113
    Walter, 203
    Wm, 113,172,203
    Wm C, 41,171
    Zimri, 113
MINOR, Roxa J, 38
MIRZA, Moshie, 41
    Rachel (Nweeya), 41
MITCHELL, Alson E, 203
    Andrew F, 41
    Frances H, 41
    Martha (Jordan), 41
    Martha M, 41
    Parley, 41
    Phebe (Lewis), 41
MODLIN, Ann, 113
    Benjamin, 1
    Calvin, 203
    Calvin W, 172
    Clara Viola, 172,203
    Eliza Jane, 172,203
    Hannah, 172
    Hannah J, 183
    Jehu, 172

MODLIN, John Sherman, 172
    Jonathan, 172
    Joseph, 203
    Laura E, 172
    Laura Etta, 203
    Louisa, 172,203
    Lydia B, 172
    Mahlon, 172,203
    Margaret, 203
    Margaret (Crull), 172
    Martha, 11
    Martha Ann, 154,155,172,188
    Mildred, 188,203
    Mildred (Beeson), 155,203
    Mildred B (Beeson), 172
    Nancy, 154
    Nathan, 113
    Nathan H, 172
    Nathan L, 172,203
    Rachel N, 172
    Sarah E, 172
    Violet, 203
    Wm, 155,172,188,203
    see also **MAUDLIN**
MOFFAT, Hugh, 113
    see also **MOFETT**, **MOFFIT**, **MOFFITT**
MOFFETT, Anna F, 56,59
    see also **MOFFAT**, **MOFFIT**, **MOFFITT**
MOFFIT, Charles, 111
    Cynthia, 114
    David, 77
    Elizabeth, 111
    Hannah, 77,111
    Hugh, 114,135
    Jeremiah, 114
    Mary Barker, 114
    Ruth, 114
    Sally, 114
    Sarah, 135
    see also **MOFFAT**, **MOFFETT**, **MOFFITT**
MOFFITT, Abijah, 42,114
    Ann Elizabeth, 42,43
    Anna, 28,42
    Anna F, 42,131
    Arthur Clyde, 42,114
    Charles, 6,13,42,48,57,79,82,114,133
    Charles F, 42,114
    Chester, 114
    Cynthia Ann (Cook), 114
    David, 42
    Edward C, 114
    Elizabeth, 24,42,48,57,79,82,114,131, 133
    Elizabeth A, 133
    Emma Estelle, 42
    Estell/Estelle, 114
    Eunice, 42,114
    Eunice Estell, 6
    Hannah, 42,114,115
    Herschell P, 42,114
    Hugh, 42,43,82,114,115,116
    Hugh C, 42,114
    Hugh Charles, 42
    Jeremiah, 42,114
    John, 42,114
    Lucinda, 6,114
    Lydia (Townsend), 42
    Lydia L, 114
    Margery, 12, 42

MOFFITT, Margery (Cox), 77,114
    Mary, 42,81,114
    Mary Elisabeth, 42
    Nathan, 42
    Oliver Chester, 42,114
    Paul Appleton, 42
    Ruth, 42,48,114,115
    Sally (Childre), 114
    Sarah, 42,43
    Sarah (Baxter), 88
    Sarah May, 42,114
    Tacy, 42,79,114
    see also **MOFFAT**, **MOFFETT**, **MOFFIT**
MONDON, Millicent, 114
    Peninah, 114
    see also **MUNDEN**, **MUNDIN**
MONEY, Ann, 156
    Elizabeth, 156
    James, 156
    Sinia Esther, 156,172
MOON, Almina/Almira, 42,114
    Ann Elizabeth (Moffitt), 42
    Anna Elizabeth, 42
    Eleanor T, 42
    Elizabeth, 42,114,151
    Hannah, 114
    Hiram, 114
    Hiram E, 42,114
    Jane, 29
    John, 114
    Joseph, 114
    Larken, 42
    Louisa, 114
    Malinda, 42
    Margaret, 42,152
    Margery, 114
    Mary, 42,114
    Mary L, 42
    Mary T, 114
    Oscian, 114
    Ossian C, 42
    Riley, 114
    Sibbinah, 114
    Simon, 114
    Thomas H, 42
    Winfield Garfield, 42
    Winfred, 114
    Wm, 114
MOOR, Elisabeth, 114
    Hannah, 114
    Isabel Anne, 114
    Joshua, 114
    Lydia, 114
    Marcia Frances, 5
    Phebe, 114
    Susanna, 114
    see also **MOORE**, **MORE**
MOORE, Abigail, 77,114,127
    Abraham, 114
    Achasa/Achsah, 43,114
    Alexander/Elexander, 114
    Alice, 172,203
    Alice (Beeson), 172
    Amanda, 43,114
    Anderson, 172,203
    Andrew, 43
    Ann/Anna/Anne, 42,43,56,73,114,115
    Ann (Rambo), 40
    Ann (Small), 114
    Ann E, 42
    Ann Elizabeth, 43,112,114

MOORE, Ann Jane, 115
    Ann R (Rambo), 42,43
    Anna M, 115
    Anna Mary, 42
    Benajah/Benejah, 114
    Benjamin, 42,114,115
    Benjamin B, 42,114
    Carolina/Caroline, 42,114
    Catharine G, 42
    Chalkley, 42,114
    Charles, 132
    Charles H, 56,70
    Charles W, 42
    Christina, 43
    Cloyd, 114
    David, 114
    Deborah A, 114
    Deborah Ann (Stanton), 42
    Edith, 114
    Edna, 57
    Eli, 172,203
    Elias, 42,114
    Elizabeth, 12,42,114,153
    Elizabeth A (Binford), 42,43
    Elizabeth W, 87
    Ella, 115
    Ellen, 115
    Esther (Hiatt), 114
    Eunice (Moffitt), 114
    Evangeline, 103,115
    Exelina, 172
    Fannie (Campbell), 43
    George, 114
    George S, 114
    Grace, 115
    Grace Ella, 42
    Gulielma, 42
    Hannah, 42,114,115,157
    Hannah (Hiatt), 114
    Hannah (Shinn), 114
    Hannah P, 72
    Harriet, 42
    Hattie Elliott, 42
    Henry W, 114
    Herbert N, 42
    Hibbard T, 115
    Ida M (Long), 43
    Ira, 42,114
    Isaac, 57
    Isabel/Isabella, 42,114
    Jacob, 42,43,114
    James, 42,114
    Jane, 42,127
    Jane (Elliott), 42,114
    Jennie (Haisley), 42
    Jennie H, 115
    Jesse, 42
    John, 114
    John F, 42,43,114
    John G, 114
    John Parker, 42
    Jonathan, 42,114
    Jonathan M, 114
    Joseph, 42,114,115
    Joseph Edward, 42
    Joshua, 42,114
    Josiah, 42,114
    Katherine, 11
    Leah, 42
    Leah Jean, 114
    Lily (Hill), 47
    Lineas A, 42,114

MOORE, Louisa (Beeson), 172
    Lucy H, 42,115
    Lydia, 42,114,172
    Lydia B (Stanton), 11
    Lydia P, 43,114
    Marcia, 70,132
    Marcia (White), 56
    Marcia Frances/Francis, 70,115
    Margaret, 114,132
    Margaret (Steele), 42
    Margaret H, 114
    Martha, 81,114
    Martha (Cadwalader), 42
    Martha A (Bunger), 42
    Martha Ann, 172,203
    Martha Evangeline, 33,42,203
    Martha J, 42,114
    Mary, 56,114,115,132
    Mary (Thorn), 114
    Mary Anna/Maryann, 40,43,112,114
    Mary E, 42
    Mary F, 114
    Mary J, 42
    Mary T, 115
    Mary T (Thorne), 42
    Matilda, 42,114
    Melva D (Lee), 42
    Miles, 42,103
    Miriam, 42,77
    Mordacai, 12
    Nathan, 114
    Nathan Andrew, 42,43
    Otis J, 42,114
    Phebe, 114
    Rachel, 12,42,114.203
    Rachel (Bain), 33,42
    Richard, 114
    Richard W, 114
    Robert, 42,43
    Robert Jr, 114
    Robert C, 40
    Ruth, 42
    Samuel, 43,114,132
    Samuel A, 42
    Sarah, 43
    Sarah (Stokes), 114
    Squire, 172
    Susanna/Susannah, 42,114,159
    Susannah (Jones), 114
    Susannah F, 114
    Tacy (Butler), 42
    Thomas, 43,77,127,114
    Thomas Jr, 114
    Thomas Sr, 114
    Thomas E, 42
    Truman, 43,114
    Walter, 11
    Willard E, 115
    Willard Embree, 42
    Willis, 42,43,114
    Willis E, 115
    Wm, 43,114
    Wm A, 43,114
    Wm E, 43
    see also **MOOR**, **MORE**
MOORMAN, Ann/Anna, 115
    Betty, 115
    Enoch, 115
    Frank H, 115
    Hannah, 115
    Hannah C, 115
    Harriett, 43,115

MOORMAN, Henry T, 115
    Joel H, 43
    John, 115
    Levi, 43,115
    Lulu, 115
    Luzena, 17
    Lydia, 115
    Margaret J, 17
    Maria, 115
    Martha, 115
    Martha C (Coggeshall), 43
    Mary, 115
    Mary (Morris), 43
    Mary Alice, 43,115
    Nancy Hannah, 43,115
    Peninah, 43,115
    Priscilla, 115
    Rachel, 115
    Rebecca, 115
    Richmond, 43,115
    Robert, 17
    Sarah, 43,115
    Susannah, 115
    Uriah, 115
    see also **MORMAN**
MORAN, Bertha M (Healton), 172
    Michael, 172
MORE, Alice (Beeson), 203
    Joseph, 115
    Sarah, 83
    see also **MOOR**, **MOORE**
MORFIELD, Alice A (Jenkins), 43
    Francis, 43
MORGAN, Alluria F, 20
    Anna H, 43
    Anna W, 115
    Benjamin, 1,43,115
    Benjamin F, 43,115
    Beulah, 43,115
    Beulah (Beetle/Butte), 43
    Catherine/Katherine, 2,43
    Charles, 2,26,29,33,43,115
    Charles O, 43
    David Bransen, 115
    Elizabeth, 115
    Elizabeth (Johnson), 43,115
    George F, 43,115
    Gertrude, 43
    Hannah, 43,115
    Hannah (Hill), 115
    Hugh, 115
    Ida, 37
    Isaac, 2,43
    Jesse Henley, 43,115
    John, 23,115
    John Watkins, 115
    Lucina, 23
    Margaret, 115
    Margaret (Holloway), 115
    Mary, 115
    Micajah, 2, 43,115
    Michael/Michel (Butler), 26,33,43
    Minnie, 23
    Naomi, 2,43,115
    Naomi Harrison, 33
    Naomi W, 25,26,34,43,59
    Naomi W Harrison, 43
    Nathan, 43,115
    Nina, 43
    Rebecca (Small), 20
    Rebecca Shinn, 43
    Robert, 20

MORGAN, Rueben, 172
    Ruth, 115
    Ruth (Moffitt), 115
    Sarah, 115
    Sarah H, 43,115
    Susanna/Susannah, 22,28,29,43,115
    Thomas B, 43
    Thomas Evans, 43
    Wm B, 43,115
    Wm Earl/Earle, 43,115
MORMAN, Eli, 115
    Zachariah, 115
    see also **MOORMAN**
MORRILL, Harriett A, 60
MORRIS, Aaron, 115
    Abigail, 115
    Abigail (Charles), 115
    Abigail (Symons), 115
    Albert C, 43,115
    Ann/Anna, 18,43,104,115
    Ann E, 43
    Ann Elizabeth (Moffitt), 43
    Benjamin, 115
    Benoni, 43
    Charles E, 43
    Christopher, 115
    David, 43,115
    Dempsey, 115
    Dorian C, 43
    Edith, 43,115
    Elias H, 43
    Elisabeth/Elizabeth, 43,115
    Ellwood, 43
    Emily, 43
    Ernestine J (Paulus), 43
    Ernestine P, 115
    Esther W (Hunt), 43
    George, 115
    Gulielma, 115
    Hannah, 115,199
    Howard Clayton, 43
    Isac, 115
    Jabez W, 43
    Jehosaphat/Jehoshophat, 43, 115
    Jemima, 115
    Jess/Jesse, 5,43,74,107,115
    Job, 115
    John, 43,104,115,203
    Jonathan, 43,115
    Joseph, 43,115
    Joshua, 115
    Josiah, 115
    Levina, 115
    Levina (Cox), 36,43
    Margaret, 43,107,115
    Mariam/Miriam, 43,115,203
    Martha M, 5
    Mary, 43,74,115
    Mary (Symons) Charles, 115
    Mary Ann, 161
    Mary C, 115
    Mary C (Charles), 115
    Mary Charles, 43
    Mary Jane, 43,104
    Nathan, 43
    Nelly, 115
    Nelly (Osborn), 115
    Peggy, 115
    Penelope/Pennelope, 43,115
    Peninah, 115
    Peninah (Bundy) Symons, 115
    Penninnah (Bundy), 43

MORRIS, Phebe, 115
    Polly, 41
    Priscilla, 115
    Rachel, 203
    Rachel (Chamness), 203
    Rachel (Ward), 203
    Ralph Waldo, 43
    Reuben, 115,203
    Ruth, 36,43,115
    Samuel, 115
    Samuel Emlen, 43
    Samuel M, 115
    Samuel M H, 36
    Samuel Moore, 43
    Sarah, 43,74,115
    Sarah (Hill), 43,115
    Sarah (Lamb), 5
    Sarah (Townsend), 115
    Sarah M, 203
    Thomas E, 43
    Wm, 115,203
    Wm H, 115
MORRISON, Charles A, 172
    Edwin, 43
    Eli, 43
    Garrett, 163
    Hannah, 116
    James, 1,116
    James L, 116
    Jane, 116
    Joseph, 172
    Louis A, 43
    Margaret, 163
    Margaret (Oler), 172
    Mary E (Miles), 43
    Robert, 116
    S Elizabeth, 43
    Samantha E, 163
    Sarah Jane, 43
    see also **MORRISSON**
MORRISSON, Hannah, 116
    James, 116
    Mary (Hough), 116
    see also **MORRISON**
MORROW, ——, 39
    Albert Theodore, 44
    Alice (Holmes), 44
    Andrew, 2,44
    Anna H, 44
    Anna H (Brown), 116
    C L, 44
    D Kenneth, 44
    Elihu, 44,116
    Elisabeth/Elizabeth, 44,59,116,135
    Hannah, 2,44,59,96,135
    James W, 116
    James Wm, 44
    Jane, 44
    John, 1,2,44,116,130,135
    John Edward, 44
    Joseph, 2,44,116
    Martha Eliza, 44
    Mary, 2,44,95,96,116,130
    Mary (Stout), 44
    Melissa, 5
    Nancy, 44,130
    Rachel, 44
    Ruth, 2,44,95
    Sarah, 44
    Wm, 44
    see also **MURROW**

MORSE, Kent, 44
    N S, 44
    Nellie (Worth), 44
MOSS, Pearl M (Hale), 44
MOSSMAN, Alexander, 44
    Emma, 44
    Sarah (Charles), 44
MOTE, Anna Gertrude, 36, 44
    Annie E (Wallas), 116
    Charity (Jones), 44
    Charles Albert, 44
    Clara E, 116
    Clarence D, 44
    Clarence Leslie, 44, 116
    Cora May (Conley), 44
    Daisy B, 116
    Daisy Belle, 44
    David, 44, 116
    Deborah, 116
    Edgar Smith, 44
    Elbert, 116
    Elbert Linden, 44
    Emma, 116
    Emma Alice, 44
    Enos, 116
    George H, 116
    Gertrude, 116
    Hannah (Dickinson), 44
    Hannah L, 116
    Hannah L (Grave), 116
    Henry D, 44, 116
    Jennie S, 32, 44
    Jesse E, 116
    John, 44
    John Edgar, 44
    Kirk L, 44, 116
    L Albert, 116
    Linus, 116
    Luke Smith, 44
    Mabel, 44
    Marcus, 32, 44, 116
    Martha (Tyler), 36
    Martha Ann, 116
    Martha Ann (Reed), 116
    Martha J (Tyler), 44, 116
    Mary, 116
    Mary Alice, 116
    Minnie C, 44
    Minnie L, 116
    Miriam, 116
    Miriam (Mendenhall), 44
    Olive, 44
    Orrin S, 36, 44
    Orvan/Orvin S, 116
    Rhoda (Stiddom), 32
    Rhoda S, 116
    Rhoda S (Steddom), 44
    Samuel S, 116
    Samuel Steddom, 116
    Susanna/Susannah J, 44, 116
    Susanna Jane, 102
    Wm C, 44
    Zeno, 116
MOTT, Alvaretta (Stubbs), 116
MOYER, Daniel, 44
    Edith Estella, 44
    Martha, 44
MOYSTNER, Bertha, 172
    Clella L (Julian), 172
    Daniel, 172
    Gladis Maud, 172
    Jeremiah, 172
    Maria (Arnold), 172

MULFORD, Margaret, 162, 178
MULHOLLAND, Charles, 44
    John, 44
    Marjorie, 44
    Rasel, 44
MULLEN, Ada, 110, 116
    Elizabeth, 203
    Elizabeth (Baldwin), 172
    John, 116
    Josiah, 172
    Mary C, 203
    Mary C (Johnson), 172
    Merrit/Merritt B, 172, 203
    Priscilla, 161
    Rebecca, 8
    see also **MULLINS**
MULLENIX, Elizabeth, 203
MULLINS, John, 116
    see also **MULLEN**
MUMBOWER, Cora, 204
    Eunice, 204
    James, 204
    Thomas, 204
MUNDANE, Jesse, 44, 116
    Mary, 44
    Ruth Eliza, 44
    Sarah, 44
    Wm, 44
MUNDEN, Joseph, 116
    Margaret, 116
    Mary, 116
    Millicent, 116
    Peninnah, 116
    Ruth Alice, 116
    Thomas, 116
    see also **MONDON**, **MUNDIN**
MUNDIN, Joseph, 116
    see also **MONDON**, **MUNDEN**
MUNSON, Claud, 44
    Louis O, 44
    Luella, 44
MUNTZ, Lydia (Marmon), 116
MURDICK, Rachel, 116
    see also **MURDOCK**
MURDOCK, Rachel, 116
    Rachel (Jessup), 116
    see also **MURDICK**
MURFREY, Elizabeth, 116
    Lydia, 73
MURPHEY, Anna, 209
    Lydia, 73
    Miles, 116
    Martha, 204
    see also **MURPHY**
MURPHY, Anna, 172, 204
    Betsy (Cox), 204
    Clement, 116
    David, 204
    Della, 4
    Joshua, 204
    Margaret, 116, 204
    Mary, 4, 172
    Miles, 116
    Rachel, 172
    Robert, 116
    Sarah, 12
    Wm, 172, 204
    see also **MURPHEY**
MURRAY, Cornelious/Cornelius, 151, 172
    John B, 7
    Julia A, 151, 172
    Lucinda, 151, 172

MURRAY, Martha, 151, 172
    Mary Hortense, 7
    Rachel (Green), 7
    see also **MURRY**
MURROW, Phebe, 116
    see also **MORROW**
MURRY, James, 116
    John, 116
    Wm Jr, 116
    see also **MURRAY**
MUSTARD, Alpha R, 44
    Amanda Alice, 44
    Clude, 44
    James, 44
    Joseph, 44
    Minnie, 44
MYERS, Adam, 44, 116
    Catharine, 153
    Delphina, 10
    Elizabeth (Deering), 204
    Fred, 44
    Helen, 44
    Mary, 103, 166
    Nancy Ann, 47
    Nellie, 44
    Prudence, 103
    Ralph, 103
    Robert, 44
    Wm T, 44
    see also **MYRES**
MYRES, Elizabeth (Deering), 204
    Mary, 125
    see also **MYERS**
MYRICK, ——, 34
    Alabama (Hawton/Houston), 44
    Reuben, 44
    Stephen Stanton, 44

NABB, John, 38
    Melinda, 38
    Minnie, 38
NANCE, Hannah (Osborn), 116
NAPIER, Charlotte, 44
    Jennie (Paddock), 44
    R Aaron, 44
    Wm, 44
NEAL, Anna, 116
    Elizabeth, 41
NEFF, Edw, 39
    Ella, 39
    Mae, 39
    Sarah, 162
    Tressa, 44
NEGUS, Albert G, 116
    Anna, 123
    Charles, 116
    Eliza A, 22
    Hannah, 116
    Joseph, 22
    Lillian, 116
    Martha B, 116
    Mary E, 22
NELSON, Clara, 44
    Daniel, 10
    Dinah (Hinshaw), 176
    Freeman, 176
    John, 116
    Leslie W, 44
    Louisa, 36
    Martha A, 10
    Mary E, 176
    Sarah, 10
    Wayne, 44

NEWBERN, Effie, 9,25
  Eliza (Horn), 9,25
  Paul, 9,25
NEWBLIN, Viola, 44
NEWBY, Albert, 44
  Alfred, 116
  Alice, 44,117
  Anna F, 33
  Anna Grace, 44
  Benjamin, 116
  Benoni, 44,116,117
  Cassius Albert, 44
  Cyrus, 116
  Daniel, 44,117
  Elias, 116
  Elizabeth, 116
  Exum, 117
  Hannah M, 46
  Jane, 44,116
  Jemima, 46
  John, 116
  Jonathan D, 44,117
  Karen, 25,46
  Mary, 59,117
  Miriam, 44,117
  Miriam (Ratliff), 33
  Phebe, 117
  Rebecca (Hill), 117
  Rebecca H, 117
  Richard P, 44
  Robert, 46
  Seth, 116
  Susannah, 44,117
  Susannah W, 117
  Thomas, 33,44,116,117
  Wm, 44,116,117
  Wm Hurtley, 44,117
NEWCOMB, Carrie, 60,117
  see also **NEWCOMBE**
NEWCOMBE, Carrie D, 137
  see also **NEWCOMB**
NEWLAND, Herman, 44
  Mary, 44
NEWLIN, Charles, 44,117
  Edgar, 44,117
  Edgar S, 117
  Edward, 44,117
  Eli, 44
  Elizabeth, 11,29
  Elizabeth A, 77
  Emma, 117
  Emma (Mossman), 44
  FindleyFinley, 44,117
  Hannah, 44,117
  James M, 11,44
  Martha, 38
  Matilda (Ong), 11,44
  Viola, 117
NEWMAN, Alice E, 45
  Annie Mary/May, 41,45
  Charles, 41
  Charles E, 45,117
  Elizabeth, 117
  Fannie E, 41
  Frances E (Doan), 45
  Fredrick, 159
  Lisetta, 159
  Mary, 117
  Millicent, 117
  Millicent (Albertson), 117
  Sarah, 173
  Sophia, 159
  Walter H, 45

NEWSOM, Martha P, 45
  Luke, 117
NICCUM, Louisa, 151
  Sophia, 151,176
NICELY, Minnie, 45
  Ora Warren, 45
  Thomas, 45
NICHOLDSON, John, 117
  Samuel, 117
  see also **NICHOLSON, NICKLESON**
NICHOLLS, George D, 45
  Lydia Matilda (Kenworthy), 45
  see also **NICHOLS, NICKLES**
NICHOLS, Abijah, 45
  Andrew, 162
  Catherine, 162
  Chester, 45
  Elijah, 117
  Elijah V, 117
  Esther, 45
  James W, 45,117
  Joseph W, 117
  Kathleen, 45
  Luke, 45
  Lydia Ann, 162
  Malinda/Melinda, 45,117
  Malinda J, 117
  Mark, 45,117
  Mary A, 45,117
  Mary Ann, 117
  Mary H, 117
  Nate, 45
  Noah, 117
  Sarah, 45,117
  Simeon/Simon L, 45,117
  Simon D, 117
  see also **NICHOLLS, NICKLES**
NICHOLSON, —— (Lamb), 45
  Alma, 204
  Anna, 117
  Anna (Robinson), 45
  Edith (Bonnell), 45
  Edward W, 45,117
  Eliza, 34,45,104
  Elizabeth Marie (Peacock), 45
  Ellen, 45
  Ellen A, 117
  Elmer, 45
  Esther, 23,117
  F C, 45
  Fannie (Davis), 45
  Florence C, 45
  George, 50,161,166,172,173,175,177,197,204,205
  Gertrude (Brahell), 45
  Gertrude (Kates), 45
  Hannah C, 23
  Harry, 45
  Henry, 204
  Henry P, 172
  John, 23,45,117
  John H, 45
  John W, 45,117
  Josiah, 45,117
  Josiah H, 45
  Josiah W, 117
  Leah, 33,102,117
  Leora E, 204
  Leora Estella, 172
  Lucinda, 197,204,205
  Lucinda (Dennis), 50,161,166,172,173,175,177,204

NICHOLSON, Lucinda (Lamb), 172
  Macy, 172
  Macy, 204
  Marianna, 10,45,75,117
  Mary, 45,204
  Mary (White), 14,34,45
  Mary Alma, 172
  Mary B, 117
  Mary B (Winslow), 45
  Mary E, 161,166,172,173,197,204,205
  Mary E (Macy), 172
  Mary S (White), 117
  Mary W, 80,204
  Nathan, 172,204
  Olinda C, 172,204
  Oliver, 172,204
  Penina (Parker), 172
  Peninah/Penninah, 172,177,204,208
  Sarah, 14,45,80,117
  Sarah Ellen, 45
  Sarah N (White), 45
  Sarah N W, 117
  Sarah W, 75
  Tamer Hawkins, 50
  Thomas, 117,204
  Thomas D, 172
  Timothy, 10,14,34,75,80,104,117
  Walter J, 45
  see also **NICHOLDSON, NICKLESON**
NICKLES, Caroline C (Stanton), 45
  see also **NICHOLLS, NICHOLS**
NICKLESON, Peninnah, 208
  see also **NICHOLDSON, NICHOLSON**
NIXON, Amos, 117
  Ann, 117
  Asenath, 117
  Asenath H, 117
  Caleb, 117
  Christiana, 117
  Dorothy, 22
  Elisabeth, 117
  Emily, 117
  Foster, 117
  Gabriel, 117
  Gulielma, 117
  Gulielma (Pool), 117
  James, 117
  Jane, 22,117
  John, 22,45,117
  John Jr, 117
  Joseph, 117,140
  Josiah, 45,117
  Louisa, 117
  Lydia, 45
  Margaret J, 117
  Margaret Jane, 117
  Martha, 117
  Martha A, 117
  Martha Ann, 139
  Martha N (Pleas), 117
  Mary, 45,117,140
  Mary Emily, 117
  Miriam, 117,140
  Miriam (Nixon), 140
  Peninah, 69,117
  Pheriba, 117
  Rhoda, 117
  Samuel R, 117
  Sarah, 117

284

NIXON, Sarah Ann, 112
   Thomas, 117
   Wm, 45,117
   Zachariah, 117
NOBLETT, John, 172
   Marcella (Cook), 172
   Thomas Monroe, 172
   Zilpha, 172
NORADYKE, Clayton B, 117
   Elizabeth A, 117
   Mary Isabel, 117
   see also **NORDYKE**
NORDYKE, Alice, 45,54
   Alice Eliza, 45
   Charity, 117
   Charity (Ellis), 45
   Clara (Compton), 45
   Clayton B, 117
   David, 19,54,117
   David J, 45
   David John, 45
   Edith Mabel, 45
   Edward Samuel, 45
   Elizabeth A (Gifford), 117
   Ella, 45
   Elwood S, 117
   Eva, 45
   Frank Wm, 45
   Franklin David, 45,117
   Harry Edward, 45
   Henrietta, 45
   Henry, 117
   John, 204
   Joseph T, 117
   Joseph Thornburgh, 45
   Lillian, 45
   Lillian May, 117
   Louella/Luella E, 117
   Lydia J, 54,117
   Lydia J (Thornburg/Thornbury), 19, 45,117
   Lydia Mary, 45,54
   Martha, 29,204
   Micajah, 45,117
   Micajah Thomas, 45,54
   Phebe, 117
   Sarah Catharine/Catherine (Latimer), 45,54
   Sarah Catherine, 117
   Sarah Elma, 45
   Susan Bernice, 19,45
   Sylvanus A, 117
   Sylvanus Arthur, 45
   Sylvanus L, 117
   Thomas, 204
   Thomas R, 117
   Wm Byron, 45
   Wm Ellis, 45
   see also **NORADYKE**
NORRIS, Cora, 117
   Elizabeth Ann, 16
   Hannah, 16
   James, 117
   Jehu, 16
   Rebeckah, 117
   Sarah, 181
NORTH, Catharine (Allen), 45
   Daniel, 45,119,204
   David, 45
   Ellen, 204
   Keziah, 45,119

NORTHCUTT, Marticia, 166
   Mary, 166
   Wm, 166
NORTHERN, Henry J, 16
   Isadora, 16
   Isom Ray, 45
   Melissa (Allison), 16,45
NORTON, Dennis R, 118
   Edward, 118
   Elizabeth, 118
   Nancy, 118
   Nancy (Kendall), 118
   Richard, 118
NUBBELL, H Warren, 45
   Isaac, 45
   Mary E, 45
NUSS, Bertha Jane (Daulin), 45
   Elizabeth (Humphrey), 45
   Elvira, 45
   Jonathan C, 45
   Wilford, 45
NWEEYA, Rachel, 41

OAELSCHLAGEL, Josephine,118
   see also **OELSCHLEGER**
O'CONNELL, Ethel, 45
   Eugene, 45
   Melinda, 45
   Alpha Grace, 46,63
   Edwin Lee, 46
   Eliza J, 46
   Eliza J (Graham), 63
   Eliza Jane, 120
   Isaac Graham, 46
   John, 46,63
ODDIE, Jane, 120
   John, 120
   Mary Ann, 118
ODEL, Daniel, 118
   see also **ODELL**, **ODLE**
ODELL, Amelia Jane, 45
   Betty, 45
   Daniel, 45
   Enos, 45
   Mary J, 45
   Peter, 45
   Polly, 45
   Sarah, 45
   see also **ODEL**, **ODLE**
ODLE, Betty, 118
   Daniel, 118
   Daniel D, 118
   Elizabeth, 118
   Enos C, 118
   Polly, 118
   Sarah, 118
   Wm L, 118
   see also **ODEL**, **ODELL**
OELSCHLEGER, Josephine (Bogue), 45
   see also **OAELSCHLAGEL**
OFTERDENGER, Hannah, 172
OGBORN, Ann, 118
   Ann E, 118
   Cornelia, 118
   Eliza, 18
   Eliza B (Thornberry), 118
   Elizabeth, 118
   Elizabeth A, 118
   Elizabeth B, 118
   Hannah, 118,130
   Henry M, 118
   Isaac, 118

OGBORN, Isaac A, 118
   Isaac F, 118
   Joseph, 118
   Joseph, 45
   Joseph L, 118
   Joseph P, 118
   Lydia (Foulke), 118
   Rebecca, 118
   Samuel, 118
   Samuel F, 118
   Sarah (Foulke), 118
   Sarah B, 118
   see also **OGBURN**
OGBURN, Cornelia, 118
   Joseph P, 45
   Rebecca A, 45
   see also **OGBORN**
OGLE, Elisha, 176
   Mariam, 176
   Sarah, 176
O'HARA, Alpha Grace, 118
   Edwin Lee, 118
   Eliza Jane, 118
   Isaac Graham, 118
   John, 118
   see also **O'HARRA**
O'HARRA, Betsy (Van Horn), 118
   see also **O'HARA**
OHLER, Carrie, 46
   Reuben, 46
   Rhoda, 46
   see also **OLER**
OLER, John, 161
   Lillie, 161
   Margaret, 172
   Phebe, 170,171
   Priscilla (Mullen), 161
   see also **OHLER**
OLET, Lydia Ann, 180
   Sarah (Judd), 180
   Thomas, 180
OLIPHANT, Elizabeth, 118
   Horace M, 118
   Mahlon, 118
   Rachel B, 118
OLIVER, John, 46
   Russell M, 46
   Urry, 46
   Emma, 13
O'NEAL, Clara, 46,118
   Mary, 118
   Mary P, 24,46
ONG, Eliza Anna, 35
   Matilda, 11,44
ORON, Aaron, 16
   Martha, 16
   Mary L, 16
OSBORN, Abigail, 118,126
   Achsah, 204
   Achsah C (Cain), 173
   Agnes, 204
   Agnes (Patterson), 173
   Agnes B, 46
   Agnes B (Patterson), 46
   Alice May, 25
   Ambrose, 118
   Anna/Anne, 118,159,173
   Arthur W, 204
   Arthur Wendell, 173,204
   Asenath, 204
   Asenath/Aseniath W, 204
   Asenath W (Wood), 173

OSBORN, Benjamin, 173,204
    Caroline, 173,192
    Charles, 152,159,173,176,204
    Charles Austin, 173
    Charles N, 173,204
    Charles Newman, 204
    Charles W, 173,204
    Cynthia, 173,176,207
    Daisy, 204
    Daisy Mabel, 173
    Daniel, 118,173
    Daniel Worth, 173,204
    David, 118,204
    E, 46
    Edgar C, 173
    Edith, 118
    Edmund B, 173
    Elam/Elim, 173,204
    Eldora Lydia, 173
    Eli, 118
    Elihu, 173
    Elijah, 173,204
    Elisabeth/Elizabeth, 118,204
    Elison, 173
    Ethel, 173,204
    Eugene Field, 173
    Eunice, 173
    Frank, 173,204
    Gideon S, 173,204
    Hannah, 116,118
    Hannah (Swain), 152,159,173,176
    Isaiah, 173,204
    J Opal, 46
    James, 173,204
    Jefferson, 173
    Jehu, 173
    Jemima, 118
    Jesse, 118,204
    John, 173,204
    John S, 46
    Jonathan, 204
    Jordan, 173,204
    Josiah, 173,204
    Laura C, 173
    Laurinda, 173,204
    Leander, 173
    Louisa, 173
    Lydia, 118,173,204
    Lydia (Worth), 173,204
    Manda, 25
    Margaret (Stout), 173
    Martha, 118
    Martha A, 173
    Martha W, 173
    Mary, 118,173
    Mary (Barnard), 204
    Mary E (Rinehart), 173
    Mary M, 204
    Miriam, 204
    Narcissa, 173,204
    Nelly, 118
    Obed, 173
    Owen, 118,204
    Parker B, 173
    Parker Jordan, 204
    Rachel, 118,204
    Rachel (Hodson), 204
    Rachel (Johnson), 173
    Rebecca, 118
    Rhoda, 173
    Richard, 204
    Romania (Mendenhall), 173

OSBORN, Ruth, 6
    Sarah, 173,204
    Sarah (Newman), 173
    Sarah S, 152,173
    Susan, 118
    Susan (Williams), 118
    Susannah, 118
    Tamer, 118
    Theo, 25
    Thomas, 118,204
    Wm, 118,204
    Wm E, 173
    Worth, 204
    see also **OSBORNE OSBUN, OSBURN, OZBORN, OZBUN**
OSBORNE, Ellen, 118
    Frank, 46
    Gordon, 46
    Narcissa, 189
    Olive M (Vincent), 46
    see also **OSBORN, OSBUN, OSBURN, OZBORN, OZBUN**
OSBUN, Jesse, 204
    see also **OSBORN, OSBORNE, OSBURN, OZBORN, OZBUN**
OSBURN, Ambrose, 118
    Jesse, 118
    Wm, 118
    see also **OSBORN, OSBORNE, OSBUN, OZBORN, OZBUN**
OUTLAND, David, 46,118
    David Amos, 46
    Elizabeth, 204
    Elizabeth (Pidgeon), 173
    Henry L, 46
    Jennie Marie, 46,118
    Jesse, 173,204
    Leona B, 46
    Lydia Grace, 46,118
    Margaret, 46
    Mary L, 46
    Mildred, 46
    Rachel, 173
    Rhoda M, 118
    Rhoda M (Miles), 46
    Sopha M, 46
    Verona May, 46
    Wm, 173
OVERHOLTZ, Mary A, 51
OVERMAN, Albert, 118
    Albert J, 46
    Anna Mary (Johnson), 46
    Charles, 118
    Charles J, 46
    Clementine, 46
    Cornelius, 46,118
    Cyrus, 46
    Eli, 2,118
    Eliza Jane, 118
    Eliza Jane (Wright), 118
    Elizabeth, 46,118
    Elizabeth (Sawyer) Small, 118
    Ephraim, 1,2,46,53,118
    Ephraim Jr, 118
    Henry, 118
    Huldah, 118
    Isaac, 46,118
    Jennie, 46
    Jesse, 2,118
    Jonathan J, 46
    Keziah, 36,118
    Keziah K, 24
    L F, 46

OVERMAN, Lydia, 2,118
    Lydia (Rue), 118
    Lydia A, 127
    Lydia Ann, 46,53,61,118
    Marietta (Mendenhall), 46
    Mary, 118
    Mildred Edwards, 46
    Nathan, 1,118
    Nathan Jr, 118
    Nellie F, 46
    Polly (Thomas), 118
    Rachel, 2,118
    Reuben, 2
    Sarah, 46,118
    Silas, 2
    Susanna (Rue), 118
    Susannah, 118
    Zebulon, 118
OWEN, Benjamin F, 118, 120
    Benjamin Franklin Stockton, 46
    Charles, 118, 120
    Eddie, 173
    Hannah W, 46,118
    Malina, 53
    Nathan, 173
    Parker, 118, 120
    Pearl C, 70,119
    Samuel S, 118,119
    Samuel Stockton/Stocton, 46,118,119
    Sarah (Parker), 173
    Thomas, 46,118
    Thomas Jr, 118
    Thomas M, 118
    Thomas Mathews, 46,118
    see also **OWENS**
OWENS, Edward, 204
    Elijah, 204
    Mary, 119
    Pearl C, 119
    Pearl Constance, 119
    S Emily (Comer), 46
    Wilbur W, 119
    see also **OWEN**
OWSLEY, Charles S, 46
    Mary (Thistlethwaite), 119
    Mary E (Thistlethwaite), 46
OXLEY, Rachel, 161
OZBORN, Lydia, 119
    Martha, 119
    Mary, 119
    Rebecca, 119
    Susannah, 119
    see also **OSBORN, OSBORNE, OSBUN, OSBURN, OZBUN**
OZBUN, Elkanah H, 204
    Isaac, 204
    Jane, 20
    Jesse/Jessie, 20,204
    John, 204
    Mary, 204
    Mary (Davis), 204
    Mary Ann (Adams), 20
    Mary Jane, 204
    Mary Jane (Lee), 204
    Mary M (Adams), 204
    Rebecca, 204
    see also **OSBORN, OSBORNE, OSBUN, OSBURN, OZBORN**

PADDOCK, Clarence G, 46
    Jennie, 44
    John, 44
    Mamie, 44

PAGE, Anna Josephine, 119
    Betsey, 119
    Elias, 119
    Elias H, 119
    Elizabeth, 119
    George, 119
    Hance N, 119
    John, 119
    John C, 119
    Joseph C, 119
    Josephine, 119
    Margaret, 119
    Mary A, 119
    Mary Ann, 119, 120
    Sarah, 119
    Sarah (Votaw), 119
    Wm, 119
    see also **PAIGE**
PAIGE, Anna Josephine, 46
    Elisabeth, 46
    George, 46
    John, 46
    see also **PAGE**
PAINE, Susan, 37
    see also **PAYNE**
PAINTER, Edith (Dean), 58
    Elva B (Hinshaw), 46
    Imelda A, 58
    John H, 58
PALIN, Axiom, 119
    Henry, 119
    Mary, 119
    Myrtle J, 46
    Nixon, 119
    Sarah, 119
PALMER, Louis Clarent, 46
    Mary Elizabeth (Crawford), 46
    Sarah, 119
    Sarah (Pearson), 119
PANES, Morgan, 119
PARK, Adelaide, 55
    see also **PARKE**, **PARKS**
PARKE, Alma (Bowerman), 46
    Royden Edwin, 46
    Wm A, 46
    see also **PARK**
PARKER, Addie (Catey), 169,173
    Alvanus, 119
    Amanda J, 119
    Anna, 119
    Anna M (Wildman), 46
    Caren, 119
    Catharine/Catherine, 46,110,119
    Celia, 119
    Charles O, 119
    Charles T, 46
    Earl. 194
    Edith Lyle, 173
    Edna, 46
    Edward F, 46
    Edward W, 119
    Edward Winslow, 46
    Elisha, 46,119,173,205
    Eliza Jane (Bond), 173
    Elmina, 173,105
    Elmira Ann, 119
    Elwood, 46
    Emiline C, 119
    Esther, 59
    Evaline, 46,119
    Fidelia Coan, 46
    Frances, 205

PARKER, Francis T, 173
    George F, 46,119
    George Irvin, 173
    Hannah M (Newby), 46
    Henry J, 173,205
    Homer H, 46
    Horace G, 46,119
    Ida (Thorne), 46
    Ira C, 119
    Irvin, 194
    Isaac, 46,119
    James, 119
    James W, 46
    Jemima/Jemime, 119,129
    Jeremiah, 25,46,110,119,129
    Jesse, 119
    Jesse F, 119
    John, 46,119,173,205
    John E, 46
    John Oscar, 46,119
    John P, 46,119
    Jonathan, 119
    Joseph, 46
    Karen, 119,129
    Karen (Newby), 25,46
    Keren, 110
    Leroy, 119
    Lillian, 169,173
    Lindley Hoag, 46
    Lydia, 62
    Margaret Ruth, 46
    Martha, 119
    Martha D, 46,119
    Mary, 119, 205
    Mary A, 119
    Mary Alice, 46
    Mary E, 205
    Mary E (Nicholson), 173
    Mary E (Nicholson) Jessup, 205
    Mary G, 205
    Matilda, 17
    Milla A, 119
    Milley E, 205
    Milly, 197
    Miriam, 46,119
    Miriam J, 119
    Nancy Jane, 119
    Nathan, 169,173,197,205
    Nathan Earl, 173
    Ollie M (Horner), 46
    Oran K, 46
    Penina, 172
    Piety, 7,22,38
    Priscella, 46
    Rachel, 119
    Rachel (Johnson), 46
    Rebecca, 119
    Richard, 46,119
    Robert, 46,119
    Russell, 46
    Samuel, 119
    Samuel J, 173
    Samuel M, 173
    Sarah, 25,46,119,173,197,205
    Sarah E, 35
    Silas, 119
    Thomas, 119
    Ulysses, 173
    Walter B, 46
    Wm, 119
    Wm A, 119
    Wm B, 46,119

PARKER, Wm Francis, 46
    Wm M, 46,119
    Wm N, 120
PARKS, Clarence E, 47
    Elizabeth, 46
    Ernest E, 47
    Flora J, 47
    Gertrude, 27
    Jennie F (Randolph), 46
    Leonides L, 46
    Mary L, 47
    Wm, 46
    see also **PARK**
PARRISH, Frank Jarret, 119, 120
    Madge M, 119
    Maud, 119
    Susan J, 54
PARRY, Annie, 47
    Charles M, 47,119
    Elma, 119
    George, 119
    Grace, 119,136
    Gulielma, 27,47
    Isaac, 119
    Joseph, 119
    Joseph E, 119
    Joseph Edwin, 47
    Laura E, 119
    Martha, 27,47,95
    Mary, 47
    Mary (Hill), 119
    Mordecai, 27,47,119
    Rhoda E (Green), 47
    Robert, 119
    Ruth (Moffit), 119
    Samuel, 47
    Sarah, 47,119
    Sarah B, 119
    Sarah Belle, 47
    Thomas, 47
    Webster, 47
    Wm, 47,119
    see also **PERRY**
PARSHALL, Alva, 119
    Alva A, 47
    Catharine/Catherine, 119
    Catharine G, 47
    Elmer, 119
    Elmer E, 47
    Gussie J, 47,119
    Gussie Jane, 119
    Henry, 119
    Henry Alva, 119
    Jesse, 119
    Jesse A, 47
    Jessie O, 119
    John, 119
    John W, 47
    Roy, 47
    Roy J, 119
    Wm Elmer, 119
PARSON, Elmira M, 53
    see also **PARSONS**
PARSONS, Amos Walter, 173
    Benjamin F, 173
    Elizabeth, 205
    Florence Gertrude, 173
    George W, 173
    Priscilla R (Matthews), 173
    see also **PARSON**
PATON, Blanch Anna, 53
    Emily, 53

PATON, Margaret, 53
    Oliver, 53
    see also **PATTEN**
PATTEE, Clarkson W, 205
    see also **PATTY**
PATTEN, Ethel, 47
    see also **PATON**
PATTERSON, Agnes, 173
    Agnes B, 46
    Della, 119
    Electa, 178
    Jane (Turner), 173
    Mary M, 119
    Samuel F, 119
    Samuel R, 173
    Sarah E, 205
PATTY, Anna, 119
    Arthur A, 173
    Clarkson, 173,105
    Davis, 119
    Ellen, 173,205
    Erwin, 119
    Harvey, 119
    Lot, 119
    Mary, 119
    Mary E, 173
    Nancy, 185,205
    Oliver L, 173
    Rachel, 202,205
    Rachel Ella, 119
    Rebecca, 119
    Rhoda (Swain), 205
    Seth, 119
PAUL, Mary Etta (Davis), 173
    Nancy, 157
    Samuel, 173
PAULSON, Anna, 47
    Anna (Davenport), 14,119
    Anna A (Davenport), 47
    George, 14,119
    George Fiske, 47
    Lillian, 119
    Lillie, 47
    Margaret, 14,47,119
    Richard Adams, 47
PAULUS, Ernestine J, 43,120
PAYNE, Charlotte, 5
    Simeon,120
    see also **PAINE**
PEACOCK, Aaron, 120
    Abraham, 25,120,122
    Alice, 47
    Amos, 120
    Anne, 120
    Asa, 47
    Bernice, 47
    Cynthia A (Fries), 47
    Daniel L, 47,120
    Dinah (Rich), 47
    Elizabeth Marie, 45
    Elvy, 12
    Hannah, 120
    John, 120
    John J, 120
    John Randolph, 47
    Jonah, 120
    Levi, ix,47,120
    Levi C, 47,120
    Margaret, 12,28,120
    Martha, ix
    Martha (Haisley), 47
    Mary C, 47
    Mary H, 120

PEACOCK, Miriam, 111,120
    Rachel, 120
    Ruth, ix
    Sarah, 120
    Sarah (Lawrence), 47
    T C, 47
    Willis D, 47
    Wm, 120
PEAK, Charles, 173
    Mary E, 205
    Mary E (Woody), 173
PEAL, Mark, 120
    see also **PEEL, PEELE, PEELLE**
PEARCE, John, 205
    see also **PEIRCE, PIERCE**
PEARSON, Abigail (Bradway), 120
    Ann/Anna, 33,47,75,120
    Anna P, 35
    Bailey, 47,120
    Calvin W, 47,120
    Carrie, 173
    Cassius M, 47
    Catharine/Catherine/Katharine, 47,120
    Catherine (Price), 120
    Charles, 47
    Charles M, 173
    Clinton M, 47
    Edwin Arthur, 47
    Elisabeth, 120
    Elvira M, 53,120,128
    Enoch, 120
    Esther, 173
    Florence Irena, 47
    Hannah, 120
    Henry, 120
    Huldah, 120
    Isaac, 47,128
    Isabel, 150
    Jesse, 120
    John, 47,120
    Jonathan, 120
    Katie Rachel (Stubbs), 173
    Levi, 47,120
    Mahala/Mahalah, 5,33
    Martha, 33,102,120
    Marthanna (Taylor), 47
    Mary, 47,120
    Mary Ann, 120
    Mary Ann (Oddie), 120
    Mary E (Elliott), 47
    Moses, 33,35
    Nancy Ann (Myers), 47
    Nathan, 1,47,120
    Peter, 47,120
    Polly, 120
    Rachel, 47,120,128
    Rebecca, 120
    Rhoda, 120
    Robert, 120
    Sarah, 33,35,120
    Sarah (Pearson), 33,35
    Sarah J, 120
    Sarah Jane (Davenport), 47
    Solomon, 120
    Stanton, 47
    Susannah, 120
    Thomas, 120
    Thomas B, 47
    Thomas V, 120
    Walter Melville, 47
    Wm, 47,120
    Wm S C, 120
    see also **PEIRSON, PIERSON**

PECKINPAUGH, Clara Lula, 173
    Laverna, 173
    Madison, 173
    Maggie, 162
    Mathew, 162
    Sarah L (Fleming), 162
PEDRICK, Ann/Anna, 47,92
    Ann P, 24
    Catharine, 120
    Elizabeth, 120
    Hannah, 10,15,20,36
    Hannah E, 47
    Isaac, 47,120
    Isaac H, 47
    Joseph, 120
    Joseph B, 47,20
    Mary, 47
    Mary C, 47,120
    Mary Cox, 48
    Phillip, 120
    Richard, 24,47,48,92,120
    Richard R, 47
    Susanna/Susannah B, 24,47,92,120
    Susannah, 48
    Wm, 47
    Wm C/H, 120
PEEBLES, Deborah, 120
    Elijah, 120
    Emily, 191
    John, 159
    Lucy, 120
    Lucy Ann, 159,191
    Michel (Bailey), 159
    Samuel, 120
    Sarah, 120
PEEL, Rueben, 120
    see also **PEAL, PEELE, PEELLE**
PEELE, Bertha (Burken), 47
    Charles A, 47
    Charles F, 120
    Cynthia (Hendershott), 47
    Deborah, 120
    Dorcas, 47
    Edmond, 205
    Frances May, 47
    Hardin H, 47
    Harley, 47
    Henry, 47
    Henry E, 47,120
    Jeanette (Hartley), 47
    John, 47
    Josephine (Ullrick), 47
    Josephine E, 120, 120
    Lillian Ruth Urilla, 47
    Mark, 47,120
    Mary, 47,120
    Mary Jane, 205
    Mary Olive, 120
    Rebekah, 120
    Wm John, 47
    Zilpah, 120
    Zilpah (Elliott), 47
    see also **PEAL, PEEL, PEELLE**
PEELLE, Edmund, 173
    Elizabeth Dix, 21
    Henry, 21
    James R, 173
    Margaret, 120
    Mary, 21
    Mary Jane (Ellis), 173
    Phariba, 173
    Robert, 173
    see also **PEAL, PEEL, PEELE**

PEGG, David Sanders. 13,47
   Davis, 47,120
   Elisabeth, 120
   Elisabeth (Horney), 47
   Eva Elnora, 13,47
   James, 47,120
   Jane, 47
   John, 120
   Leah, 120
   Leah (Moore), 120
   Lydia, 15,47,81,120
   Lydia F (Fulghum), 13,47
   Margaret, 47,120
   Mary, 14,81,120
   Mary (Mills), 15,47
   Mary Catherine, 120
   Olive A, 120
   Rachel E, 120
   Rachel Ellen, 120
   Ruth, 120
   Sarah, 120
   Sarah Small, 120
   Valentine, 15,47,81,120
   Wm, 47
PEIRCE, Ann, 47
   Esther, 47
   John, 47
   Milly, 47
   Milly (Iddings), 47
   Samuel, 47
   see also PEARCE, PIERCE
PEIRSON, Aaron, 120
   Axium, 120
   George, 120
   Jane Ann, 120
   John, 120
   Joseph, 120
   Mary, 120
   Nathan, 120
   Wm, 120
   Wm Jr, 120
   Zeno, 120
   see also PEARSON, PIERSON
PEMBERTON, Beulah, 9
   Elizabeth, 17
   Henry, 9
   Ruth P, 9
PENNINGTON, Bertha (Walters), 48
   Jonah, 120
   Josiah, 48
   Levi T, 48
   Mary (Cook), 48
   Mary Esther, 48
PENNY, Sarah, 120
PEPPER, Harriett, 40
   Otis, 120
PERCIFIELD, Ira Otis, 48
   Sampson S, 48
   Sarah, 120
   Sarah A, 48
PERDUE, Elizabeth (Spronger), 120
PERISHO, Elizabeth, 120
   Joshua, 120
   Nathan, 120
   Sarah M (Chappell), 120
PERKINS, Anna (Jessup), 6
   Isaac H, 6
   Joseph, 205
   Laura Jennie. 6
PERRY, Albert Hockett, 173
   Almeda, 48
   Anna, 21
   Anna Elizabeth, 88

PERRY, Benjamin, 88
   Charles Coffin, 48,120
   Chester, 48
   Clarence, 48
   Elizabeth (Howell), 48
   Elizabeth E R, 88
   John, 173
   Joseph James, 48
   Mary, 120
   Mary Elizabeth, 48
   Monroe, 48
   Ruth (Moffitt), 48,120
   Susan, 173
   Susannah, 48
   Thomas, 120
   see also PARRY
PERSON, Solomon, 120
PERSONETT, Charles, 120
   Charles H, 120
   Elizabeth, 120
PERVIS, Ann, 120
   Rachel, 120
   see also PURVIS
PETERSON, Eliza, 120
   Eliza (Hunt), 120
PETRY, John, 120
   Lydia, 17
PETTIBONE, Elizabeth, 48
   Francis C, 48
   Frederick, 48
   Leota, 48
   Matilda C (York), 48
PETTY, Anna/Annie, 173,205
   Elizabeth, 205
   James, 205
PHILABAUM, Alonzo, 174,205
   Daniel, 48,174
   James, 48,205
   James B, 174
   James B, 205
   Lura, 205
   Maria/Mariah, 48,174
   Sarah, 205
   Sarah E, 205
   Sarah E (Staher), 174
   Sarah E (Stoker), 48
PHILIPS, Alida, 143
   Elvira, 120
   Elvira R, 120
   Nancy, 152
   see also PHILLIPS
PHILLIPS, Alta, 174,205
   Ann, ix
   Anna R, 48
   Charles/Charley, 174,205
   Earl, 48
   Elizabeth, 148
   Elvira (Roberts), 48
   Freddie A, 174
   Grace J, 120
   Hannah, 160
   Ida (Brown), 48
   J O, 48
   John, ix
   Josiah, 48
   Lucinda (Bogue), 48
   Martha, 205
   Martha Ann (Baldwin), 174
   Sophia, 174
   Wm, 174
   see also PHILIPS

PHOUTS, Levi, 120
   see also FOUTS, FOUTZ
PICKERALL, Mahlon, 48
   Sarah B (Horney), 48
   see also PICKERELL, PICKRELL
PICKERELL, Achsah, 120
   Henry, 120
   Mahlon, 120
   Sarah B Horney, 120
   see also PICKERALL, PICKRELL
PICKERING, Alice (Mendenhall), 48
   Benjamin, 205
   Bertha H (Snyder), 48
   Burrill A, 48
   Cynthia, 174,205
   Cynthia (Maulsby), 205
   Elisha, 205
   Enos, 205
   Erma R, 48
   Henry, 205
   Jonas, 205
   Macy, 174,205
   Martha, 78
   Miles, 205
   Nathan, 205
   Phebe, 173
   Ruth, 205
   Samuel, 174,205
   Sarah, 205
PICKET, Anne, 120
   Huldah M, 205
   Joseph, 120
   Lydia, 120
   Mary, 120
   Priscilla, 120
   Sarah, 120
   Thamer, 120
   Wm, 120
   see also PICKETT
PICKETT, Albert, 48,120
   Alice C, 48
   Alice Carrie, 120
   Asenath (Canaday), 41
   Benjamin E, 120
   Benjamin Everett, 48
   Benjamin M, 120
   Benjamin N, 120
   Clara Alice, 120
   Clemy Alice, 120
   Deborah, 48,120
   Elma (Bond), 48
   Emerson, 48
   Flora P, 41
   Florence, 48,120
   Florence E, 4
   Gail Marie, 48
   Hannah E, 48,120
   Harriet, 33,48
   Hattie, 120
   Huldah M (Macy), 205
   Ida (Study), 48
   Iowa Lilly, 48
   John, 120
   John D, 120
   John F, 48,120
   John Francis, 48
   Joshua, 1
   Katie, 48
   Lena P, 48
   Lilly E, 48
   Lot, 41
   Mary, 48,120

PICKETT, Minnie M, 120
    Minnie May, 48
    Myrtle, 48,120
    Nancy A, 48,120
    Oliver, 48
    Sarah, 70,120
    Susannah, 70,120
    Willie E, 120
    Willie Elmer, 48
    Wm, 120
    Wm F, 120
    Wm H, 48,120
    see also **PICKET, PICKITT, PIGGOTT**
PICKITT, Fannie (Coffin), 3
    John H, 3
    Susie R, 3
    see also **PICKET, PICKETT, PIGGOTT**
PICKRELL, Sarah B, 120
    see also **PICKERALL, PICKERELL**
PIDGEON, Albert Lindley, 174
    Benjamin Harrison, 174
    Carrie (Benedict), 174
    Carrie J, 205
    Charles, 153
    Charles C, 174
    David, 150,173,205
    David L, 174
    Edna Theresa, 174
    Elizabeth, 153,173,174,205
    Ellen, 152,174
    Emeline, 205
    Emeline (Howell), 174
    Florene (Marshall), 174
    Hannah, 205
    Hannah (Stanley), 174
    Isaac W, 174,205
    Isabel, 178
    Isabel C, 174
    Jane, 153
    Jesse, 159,178,205
    Jesse W, 152,174
    John Henry, 174
    Levine (Davis), 174
    Lizzie, 205
    Lizzie (Hardman), 174
    Lucinda, 150,174,181,185
    Lydia Ethel, 174
    Margaret (Gable), 174
    Martha Ann, 159,174
    Mary (Chamness), 152,159,174,178, 205
    Mary Alice, 174
    Miriam C, 174,201
    Rachel, 205
    Rachel (Wilson), 150,173,174
    Wilson, 174
    Wm, 205
    Wm C, 174,205
    Wm Harlan, 174
PIEHE, Wm, 120
PIERCE, Abigail Amanda, 120
    Alexander R, 120
    Ann/Anna, 120,174,185
    Armina, 174,193
    Casper G, 120
    Charles E, 120
    Charlotte D, 174
    Daniel, 174

PIERCE, Delila, 174
    Elizabeth, 174
    Elmer E, 120
    Esther, 120
    Exalina, 174
    Flora B, 160
    George R, 120
    Hannah, 176
    Isaac M, 120
    Jamima, 174
    John, 120,174,205
    John Wilson, 174
    Jonathan Lewis, 174
    Joseph J, 120
    Lewis, 205
    Lydia, 174
    Martha A, 120
    Mary, 162
    Matilda, 150,169
    Matilda Osborn, 174
    Milley, 120
    Moses, 174
    Nathan R, 120
    Pheraby, 157,162
    Rachel, 180
    Rebecca, 160,163
    Ruth, 174
    Samuel, 120,176
    Sarah E, 120
    Stephen J, 174
    Susannah, 174,202
    Wilson, 205
    Wm, 120
    Wm E, 120
    see also **PEARCE, PEIRCE**
PIERSON, Aaron, 120
    Elizabeth, 120
    Elizabeth (Blizzard), 120
    Exum, 120
    George, 120
    Jane Ann, 120
    John, 120
    Joseph, 120
    Marthana T, 120
    Mary, 120
    Nathan, 120
    Thomas, 120
    Wm, 120
    Zeno, 120
    see also **PEARSON, PEIRSON**
PIGGOTT, Benjamin, 2,120
    Deborah (Clark), 120
    Joshua, 2,69
    Mary, 69
    Sarah, 69,120
    see also **PICKET, PICKETT, PICKITT**
PIKE, Anna, 205
    Anna (Reynolds), 205
    Elam, 205
    Mary, 205
    Nathan, 205
    Rachel, 1
PILCHER, Clarence E, 48
    Lottie, 48
    Orlando, 48
PINKHAM, Arthur E, 120
    Bertha, 120
    Charles H, 120
    Charles Heber, 120
    Emma C, 120
    Gertrude H, 120

PINKHAM, Gertrude Harriett, 120
    Mary C, 120
    Mary Cornelia, 120
    Wm P, 120
PIPER, George M, 48
    Grace (Kennard), 48
    Marion K, 48
PITMAN, Elizabeth, 53
    Frank A, 174
    Hannah, 9
    Morris, 174
    Nancy J (Smith), 174
PITTS, Benjamin, 48
    Cadwaladar/Calwalender/Kadwalader, 120,205
    Elizabeth, 205
    Ellen (Baldwin), 48
    Harmon, 48
    Harriett E, 21
    Martha, 98
    Martha (Meredith), 21
    Mary, 205
    Mary (Chamness), 174,205
    Polly Emily, 176
    Ruth, 48
    Samuel, 21,205
    Sarah Ann, 59, 205
PLACE, Aaron L, 122
    Eliza, 121
    Elwood, 122
    Hannah, 121
    Isaac, 121
    Isaac, 122
    Jane, 122
    Lydia, 122
    Maurice/Morris, 121
    Naomi, 48,122
    Priscilla, 48,122
    Priscilla (Coffin), 122
    Wm, 48,121,122
    see also **PLEAS**
PLATT, Sarah E, 48
PLEAS, Aaron, 122
    Isaac, 83,117,122
    Jane, 83,117,122,128
    Jane Smith, 122
    Martha N, 117,122,128
    Maurice, 122
    Wm, 122
    see also **PLACE**
PLUMMER, Jane, 183
    Joann H, 122
    Joanna, 108
    John, 122
    John L, 122
    Joseph, 108
    Joseph P, 122
    Lydia, 122
    Mary M, 122
    Sarah C, 122
    Susanna, 108
POARCH, Catherine (Cain), 205
    Catherine C, 205
POER, Rebecca Ellen, 175
    Elizabeth, 4,5
    Samuel, 5
    Sarah, 5
POLLARD, Elizabeth, 5
    Samuel, 5
    Sarah, 5
POMEROY, Caroline, 33

POOL, Charles, 2,48,122
    Clarkey/Clarky, 48,84
    Elisabeth/Elizabeth, 2,48,84,111,117, 122,141
    Eliza Ann, 122
    Elizabeth Ann, 78,138
    Gulielma, 48,117
    Jane Ann (Hadley), 48,122
    John, 2,48,84,117,122,141,
    John R, 111
    Joseph, 48,78,122
    Joshua, 122
    Lillian, 122
    Louisa, 96,122
    Louisa M (Woodard) Hiatt, 122
    Rebecca/Rebekah, 78,122,138
    Rebecca (Towel), 13
    Rebecca C, 48,141
    Rebecca H, 122
    Ruth Ann/Ruthanna, 48,111
    Sarah, 48,84
    Thomas, 48,122
    Wm, 13,48,122,138
    see also **POOLE**
POOLE, Gertrude (Jenks), 47
    Jane Ann, 122
    Lillian, 122
    Lily, 122
    see also **POOL**
POPE, Ruth, 122
    Ruth Ann, 77
POSEGATE, Ellen, 122
    Isaac, 122
POSTHER, Henrietta (Heitland), 48
    Henry, 48,122
    Henry H, 48
    Lila H , 48
    Loran E, 48,122
    Minnie, 48,122
    Paul C, 122
    Paul S, 48
POTTENGER, Elmina, 122
    see also **POTTINGER**
POTTER, Benjamin F, 205
    Benjamin P, 174
    Caroline, 35
    Elizabeth, 174
    Elizabeth (Green), 163
    Emma, 163
    Hezekiah, 174
    Isaac B, 174
    Jehiel, 122
    Jehiel W, 174
    John C, 163
    Keziah, 174
    Martha, 174
    Mary Cox (Pedrick), 48
    Phebe, 174
    Rebecca (Branson), 122
    Rebecca (Hobson), 205
    Stephen, 122,174,205
    T M, 48
POTTINGER, Elmina, 122
    see also **POTTENGER**
POTTS, Edward, 122
    Edward G, 122
    John, 122
    Lindley, 122
    Mary, 122,138
    Rebecca, 122
    Ruthanna, 122,138
    Samuel, 122,138

POWEL, John, 85
    see also **POWELL**
POWELL, John, 85
    Mary, 85
    Sally, 122
    see also **POWEL**
POWER, Mate, 33
    see also **POWERS**
POWERS, Bertha B (Schlotte), 48
    George Clarkson, 48
    see also **POWER**
PRAY, Elivana (Townsend), 58
    Elizabeth M, 58,133
    Enos, 122
    Enos G, 58
    Joseph, 122
    Mary, 122
    Mary H, 122
    Rachel, 122
PRESNALL, Anna, 205
    Anna (Brown), 205
    Daniel, 122
    Hannah, 205
    James, 205
    Jehu, 122
    Jeremiah, 122
    John, 122
    Stephen, 205
    see also **PRESNELL**
PRESNELL, Benony, 122
    Daniel, 122
    John, 122
    Nathan, 122
    see also **PRESNALL**
PRETLOW, Elizabeth Ann, 122
    Julietta, 122,124
PRICE, Anna, 12,78
    Catharine/Catherine, 4,78,82,97,122
    Charles, 48
    Emma Jane, 122
    Exelina, 122
    Francis, 122
    James, 2,122
    Joseph A, 48
    Lydia, 122
    Lydia (Jones), 122
    Martha J (McKee), 48
    Mary, 82,111,122
    Rice, 1,2,4,78,82,97,122
    Robert, 2,122
    Sarah, 2,4,5,22
    Theodore, 122
    Theodore T, 122
    W Eleanor, 122
    Willimpe Eleanor, 122
    Zilpha, 97
PRICHARD, Samuel, 122
    see also **PRITCHARD**
PRICKET, John, 122
    see also **PRICKETT**
PRICKETT, Lydia Jane, 41
    see also **PRICKET**
PRIDDY, Sarah, 155
PRITCHARD, Anna O Unthank, 33
    Anna Unthank, 48
    Harriet (Pickett), 33,48
    Louisa, 59
    Samuel, 3,48
    Sarah Jane, 33,48
    see also **PRICHARD**
PROPST, J A, 48
    J Franklin, 48

PROVIANCE, Gulielma (Henley), 48
    Leroy, 48
PRYFOGLE, Alexander, 52,122
    Alice, 52,122
    Everet, 122
    Grace, 11,122
    Grace L (McCown), 48
    Laura, 52,122
    Lawrence, 122
    Sherman, 48,122
PUCKET, Beulah, 122
    Cyrus, 122
    Daniel, 122
    Greenlie, 122
    Levina, 122
    Mary Catharine, 122
    Thomas, 122
    see also **PUCKETT**
PUCKETT, Celia, 175
    Cyrus, 122,206
    Daniel,122,175,206
    Lavina, 171
    Levi C, 206
    Levina H, 158,175
    Rachel, 36,54
    Susannah, 123
    see also **PUCKET**
PUGH, Elizabeth, 33,102
    Melinda, 49
    Robert, 49
    Wm, 49
PURCELL, Myrtle (Teague), 49
PURDUE, Nancy, 27
PURDY, Gulielma, 123
    Samuel A, 123
    Benjamin, 123
    Jessie, 123
    Lizzie, 123
    Lizzie S, 123
    Wm McGriffin, 123
PURSLEY, Emma J (Gray), 161
    Grace, 161
    Willard F, 161
PURVIANCE, Gulielma, 123
PURVIS, Ann, 123
    Rachel, 123
    see also **PERVIS**
PYLE, Abijah H, 123
    Charles C, 123
    Cora (Spinning), 49
    David, 15,49,123
    Edna B, 20
    Elizabeth B, 123
    Elizabeth B (Bulla), 49
    Esther, 123
    Esther (Steddom), 15,49
    Joseph, 49
    Joseph C, 123
    Joseph S, 49
    Marietta, 123
    Mary C, 15,49,123
    Mary T, 123
    Olive S, 49
    Wm L, 123

QUAINTANCE, Charles C, 49
    Ethel, 49
    Greensburg P, 49
    Sarah, 49
    Vera, 49

QUIGG, Belle (Hawkins), 49,123
   Eugene K, 49
   Ira E, 49
   Katherine, 49
   Laura M (Kramer), 49
   Nancy (Frazier), 49
   Wm H, 49

RAGAN, Mary S, 81
   see also **REAGAN**
RAILSBACK, Isabella Louise (Conkle), 49
   Jehiel, 123
   Otho, 49
RAKESTRAW, Samuel A, 174
RAMBO, Ann, 40
   Ann R, 42,43,49
   Edward B, 49,123
   Elizabeth, 123
   Elizabeth, 43,49,132
   Elizabeth Jr, 123
   Francis H, 49,123
   Mariam A (Coffin), 123
   Miriam, 49,123
   Miriam (Coffin), 112
   Miriam A, 123
   Naomi C, 49,123
   Nathan, 49,123
   Sarah M, 49,112,123
   Sarah S, 112,123
   Sarah Sylvania, 49,123
   Wm, 49,123
   Wm A, 49,112,123
RAMSEY, Jennie M, 123
RANDALL, Bertha (Evans), 49
   Charles E, 49
   Dewitt, 49
   Elizabeth (Conoro), 66
   Frank T, 49
   Gulielma (Baily), 49
   Lucy A, 49
   Martha (Hockett), 49
   Mary, 41
   Mary Ann, 65,66
   Mary Madalin, 49
   Mildred Lucile, 49
   Robert W, 49
   Rowena M (Hearn), 49
   Wm, 49,66
   see also **RANDLE**
RANDLE, Mary A, 51
   Robert W, 123
   Rowena E, 123
   see also **RANDALL**
RANDOLPH, Jennie F, 46
   Moore S, 46
   Sarah, 46
RANKER, Sophia, 49,123
RAPER, Clarence, 49
   Oliver, 49
RASH, Elizabeth, 58
RATCLIFF, Achsah (Mills), 206
   Amelia, 123
   Cornelius, 123
   Elias, 206
   Elisabeth/Elizabeth, 123,195
   Enos, 206
   Hannah, 203
   Isaac, 206
   Jesse, 206
   Job, 195,203,206
   Joel, 206

RATCLIFF, John, 206
   Joseph, 123
   Letitia, 123
   Mary, 123
   Ruth, 96,123
   Sarah, 123
   Susanna (Ward), 206
   Susannah, 206
   Tamer/Thamar/Thamer, 195,203,206
   Thomas, 206
   see also **RATLIF**, **RATLIFF**
RATLIF, Achsah, 123
   Hannah, 123
   Margaret, 123
   see also **RATCLIFF**, **RATLIFF**
RATLIFF, Abigail, 49,67,123
   Achsah, 123,174
   Amelia, 123
   Anna, 123
   Benjamin, 123
   Carolina/Caroline, 123,176
   Caroline (Baily), 123
   Cornelias/Cornelius, 30,49,67,99,123,127
   Cornelius Jr, 49
   Cornelius S, 49
   Edward, 49
   Eli, 49,123,174
   Elias, 123,174,206
   Elizabeth, 49,67,99,123,127,174
   Elizabeth (Saint), 30,49
   Enos, 123
   Ephraim, 123
   Gabriel, 123
   George, 49,174
   Gulielma, 30,49,99,123
   Hannah, 123,174
   Isaac, 174
   Isom, 174
   Jane, 123
   Jemima, 174
   Jesse, 123
   Job, 174
   John, 49,123,174
   Jonathan, 123
   Joseph, 49,123
   Joseph Branson, 123
   Joshua, 123
   Letitia, 123
   Margaret, 49,107,123
   Margaret (Kendall), 123
   Margaret K, 142
   Mary, 49,123,174
   Mary Ann, 174
   Mary E, 13
   Mary Elizabeth, 174
   Milicent/Millicent, 49,67,123
   Miriam (Bogue), 174
   Miriam, 33
   Phineas/Phinehas, 123
   Rebecca/Rebekah, 123
   Richard, 123
   Rueben, 123
   Ruth, 49
   Samuel, 123
   Sarah, 46,49,123,127,174
   Sarah (Shugard), 49
   Sarah Etta (Larrowe), 174
   Stephen T, 174
   Susannah, 174

RATLIFF, Tamar, 174
   Thomas, 123,174
   Wm, 174
   Wm Elias, 174
   see also **RATCLIFF**, **RATLIF**
RAVALREE, Katharine, 123
   see also **REVELEE**
RAWSON, Sarah, 35
   Albertice C, 49
   Christian, 49,53
   Elizabeth C, 49,53
   Florence E, 53
   Golden Myrtle, 49
   James, 123
   James Monroe, 49
   Lorene (Mikesell), 49
   Lusena, 123
   Mary, 123
   Monroe, 123
   Myrtle, 123
RAYMOND, Isaac, 49
   Lovey M, 49
   Opal C, 49
RAZOR, Benjamin, 15
   Mary A, 15
   Nellie, 15
READ, Anna Hadley, 123
   see also **REED**, **REID**
REAGAN, Mary S, 15
   see also **RAGAN**
REECE, Charles, 123
   Charles, 49
   Christiana, 26
   Daniel, 194
   Delilah, 162,194,206
   Edwin, 49,123
   Emma Cora, 49
   Eunice, 40,123
   John, 123
   Oliver, 49
   Sarah, 194
   see also **REES**, **REESE**
REED, Albert, 49,123
   Albert S, 123
   Alice (Templar), 49
   Ann/Anna, 49,50,123
   Anna (Boswell), 123
   Anna (McComb), 49
   Anna (Negus), 123
   Anna M (Hadley), 49
   Charlotte, 49
   Deborah, 124
   Drucilla/Drusilla A (Unthank), 50,123
   Drusella/Drusilla A, 123
   Elizabeth, 49
   Elizabeth L, 111
   Ellen, 123
   Ellen M, 123
   Ellen Maria (Lefever), 49
   Frank L, 49
   Frank LeFever, 123
   Franklin, 123
   Hugh, 49,123
   Ida Florence, 50
   Jerome W, 49
   John, 33,49,50,103,123
   John G, 49,116,123
   John L, 111
   Lucinda, 49
   Margaret, 59
   Martha Ann, 49,116
   Mary, 49

REED, Mary Alice (Kinsey), 49
   Mary Ann, 124
   Mary Anna (Allen), 50
   Philander, 49
   Priscilla, 33,49,103
   Rowland T, 49,50,123
   Samuel Albert, 50
   Sarah, 103,111,116
   Sarah (Grave), 33,49,50,123
   Sarah Ada Evaline, 50
   Susan B, 136
   Susanna B, 49
   Walter, 123
   Walter Clarence, 49
   Wm H, 50
   Wm Maston, 49
   Wm Zedru, 50
   see also **READ, REID**
REEDER, Charles, 124
   Clara, 124
   Clara A, 124
   Joseph, 124
   Joseph H, 124
   Mary, 124
   Mary Alice, 124
   Mary Ellen, 124
   Samuel, 124
REES, Enos, 124
   Henry P, 124
   Hiram, 124
   John, 124
   Leonard D, 124
   Mary, 124
   Minetta, 124
   Rachel, 124
   Zachariah, 124
   see also **REECE, REESE**
REESE, Charles, 124
   Charles P, 124
   see also **REECE, REES**
REEVE, Sarah, 5
   see also **REEVES**
REEVES, A W, 50
   Ann, 124
   Charles P, 50,124
   Eva N (Compton), 50
   Harry B, 50
   Julietta, 124
   Julietta (Pretlow), 124
   LaBelle (Blair), 50
   Manassa, 50
   Mark, 50
   Mark E, 124
REICE, James, 124
   Joseph, 124
   Needham, 124
   see also **RICE**
REID, Alice, 124
   Anna, 124
   Emily Myrtle, 124
   George Andrew, 124
   James P, 124
   Nettie, 124
   Raleigh Newton, 124
   see also **READ, REED**
REIGLE, Clayton G, 50
   George W, 50
   Nancy J, 50
   Nancy J (Harland), 50
   see also **RIGGLE**

REIKER, Dixon, 50
   Laura, 50
   Wm C, 50
   see also **RICKER**
REIMAN, Louisa, 124
REMINGTON, Jacob, 157
   Martha Ellen, 157,181
   Sarah, 157
REPLOGLE, Lucinda, 176
   Phillip, 176
   Rachel (Cox), 176
RETZ, Ann Marie, 50
   Emma Florence (Harter), 174
   Frank, 174
   Margarett (Bailey), 50
   Mary, 168
   Mikel, 50
REVELEE, Anna, 27
   Flora B, 27
   Isaac, 27
   see also **RAVALREE**
REYNARD, Adam, 165,181
   Catharine (Stover) Wrightsman, 165
   Catherine (Stover), 181
   Rachel, 165,175,181
   see also **RINARD**
REYNOLDS, Albert, 175,206
   Amos, 175
   Ann/Anna, 155,175,205
   Anthony, 124,175,202,206,209
   Asenath C, 149,175
   Azariah, 175
   Bertha F, 175
   Charles C, 124
   Charles Earnest, 124
   Clarkson, 175,206
   Cynthia, 206
   Cynthia E (Baldwin), 175
   Cyrus Lindley, 175
   Daniel W, 175
   Deborah, 175
   Deborah (Williams), 206
   Delilah, 206
   Delmer M, 124
   Ebenezer, 155,175,206
   Edwin, 175,206
   Elijah, 175,206
   Elizabeth, 124,175,183,202,206,209
   Elizabeth D, 206
   Elizabeth D (Nicholson), 50,175
   Ellen, 206
   Elma, 147,150,158,159,178,191
   Elmira (Star), 175
   Eric L, 50
   Ezra, 149,154,175,206
   Francis, 175,206
   George, 124
   George L, 124
   Hannah, 124,175
   Hannah (Underhill), 206
   Harvey, 175,206
   Henry, 206
   Henry L, 206
   Henry Lindley, 175
   Herbert G, 124
   Isaac, 50,124,158,159,171,175,191,
      205,206
   Isaac Herbert, 175
   Isobel, 175
   Jane, 149,175,184
   Jesse, 175,206
   Jesse W, 175

REYNOLDS, Job, 158
   John, 175,206
   Josie (Hockett), 175
   Julia Ann, 158,175
   Lavina, 206
   Lavina (Puckett), 171
   Levi, 175,206
   Levina H (Puckett), 158,175
   Lillian Hayden (Brown), 50
   Lindley, 206
   Lovina, 206
   Lydia, 158,159,175,191
   Margaret/Margaretta, 10,25,124,135
   Maria Jane, 175
   Martha A, 175
   Martha Ann, 171,175,206
   Mary, 149,154,175,188,197
   Mary (Chamness), 149,175,206
   Mary (Wrightsman), 154,175
   Mary Cornelia, 124
   Mary E, 124
   Mary Ellen, 175
   Milo, 149,175,206
   Milton, 175,206
   Nancy Ann, 175
   Nellie, 175
   Othello E, 124
   Phebe (Hockett), 158
   Phebe Jane, 175,206
   Rachel, 155,175,184,206
   Rachel A (Metsker), 175
   Rachel Demaris, 175
   Rebecca E, 206
   Rebecca Ellen (Poer), 175
   Ruth, 149,175,202
   Samuel Clarkson, 124
   Sarah, 124,175,209
   Sarah (Hinshaw), 175
   Sarah B, 124
   Sarrah Jane, 175
   Susanna (Lee), 175
   Susannah, 154,155,175,206
   Tamar, 124,191,205
   Tamar/Tamer (Hawkins), 124,159,175
   Tamer Hawkins (Nicholson), 50
   Thomas C, 175
   Wenlock, 175,206
   Wilson, 50,175,206
   Wm, 124
   Zimri, 175, 206
RHATCHAMEL, Mary, 38
RHOADES, Emma, 124
   see also **RHODES**
RHODES, Alex, 50
   David, 124
   Eleanor, 124
   Lucinda, 168
   Mary Ann, 50
   Moses, 124
   Oscar M, 50
   Susannah, 124
   see also **RHOADES**
RHULE, Alfred, 50
   Annie (Hapner), 50
   John K, 50
   Sarah (Miller), 50
   see also **RUHLE**
RICE, Arthur A, 124
   Eva M, 124
   Fidella S, 124
   Howard S, 124
   Lillie C, 124
   Rachel A, 124
   see also **REICE**

RICH, Dinah, 47
    Emma, 50
    Esther A (Gram), 50
    Everett, 175
    Francis, 50
    Howell A T, 50
    Judith, 124
    Judith Ann, 50,92
    Lucetta H, 124
    Mary, 124
    Mary (Crampton), 124
    Nathan, 50,124
    Nellie (Thornburg), 175
    Ruby, 50
    Samuel, 124
    Susanna/Susannah, 92,140
RICHARDS, Burk/Burke, 50,124
    Caroline C, 50,124
    Carrie C, 124
    Ethan, 124
    Ethel, 50
    Isaac H, 50,124
    Jane Lydia, 50,124
    Lydia, 124
    Margaret J, 206
    Maria M, 124
    Maria Moffatt/Moffett, 50,124
    Mary, 124
    Mary Griffith, 50,124
    Mary J, 124
    Mary J (Burke), 50
    Mary Jane, 124
RICHARDSON, Caroline, 57,110
    Deborah, 124
    James, 50,124
    Lydia, 41
    Malinda, 124
RICHEY, Anna Mary, 79
    Anna S, 79
    S S, 79
    Samuel, 79
    see also **RICHIE**
RICHIE, Anna (Davenport), 40
    Anna (Shoemaker), 5,50,62
    Anna Mary, 50,124
    Anna/Annie S, 112,124
    Anne/Annie, 70,124,139
    Arthur C, 124
    Arthur Coffin, 50
    Belle (Lynde), 50
    Benjamin M, 124
    E Russel, 124
    Edward Russell, 50
    Elisabeth/Elizabeth S, 50,62,124
    Elizabeth, 138
    Grace L, 124
    Grace S, 50
    Hannah, 6,32,62
    Hannah H, 18,32,50,53
    Henry E, 124
    Janetta/Jeanette, 41,112
    Jeanette J, 40,50,124
    John S, 50,62,124,139
    Margaret H, 5
    Margaret W, 50,70,124
    Mary A (Brown), 50,62
    Mary B, 124,139
    Mary H (Hinckley), 50
    Robert, 18,50
    Robert A, 124
    Robert Annesley, 50,124
    Robert Clinton, 50

RICHIE, Rosalie/Rosaline Anna, 50,64,139
    Samuel, 70
    Samuel Charles, 50,124
    Samuel S, 5,40,50,62,112,124
    Sarah, 18,50
    Sarah M, 50,124
    see also **RICHEY**
RICHWINE, Anna (Melbert), 175
    Wesley, 175
RICKER, Charles, 50
    Laura (Childers), 50
    Orian/Owen, 50
    Pearl Parry, 50
    Sadie, 50
    Wm, 50
    Wm C, 50
    see also **REIKER**
RIDGEWAY, Lewvera, 16
    see also **RIDGWAY**
RIDGWAY, Mary R (Martin), 50
    see also **RIDGEWAY**
RIFNER, Cecilia R, 35
    James, 35
    Martha (Cilley), 35
RIGGIN, Herschel M, 50
    Melissa, 50
    Sanford L, 50
RIGGLE, Alvis, 175
    Elizabeth, 175
    Lucy A, 168,175,206
    Sarah E, 168,175
    see also **REIGLE, RIGGLES**
RIGGLES, Lucy D, 206
    see also **RIGGLE**
RIGHT, Frank, 50
    Gertrude, 50
    Margaret, 50
    see also **WRIGHT**
RIGHTSMAN, Rachel, 196
    see also **WRIGHTSMAN**
RILEY, Ellen (Fleming), 206
RINARD, James W, 206
    Nancy A, 156
    see also **REYNARD**
RINEHART, Mary E, 173
RISSEBRON, Emma, 19
    see also **RISSEBROW**
RISSEBROW, Emma, 60
    see also **RISSEBRON**
RITCLIF, Amelia, 124
    Letitia, 124
    Mary, 124
    Ruth, 124
RITTENHOUSE, Levi, 175
    Marietta, 206
    Marietta (Baldwin), 175
    Nancy, 175
    Wm W, 206
    Wm Walter, 175
    see also **WRITTENHOUSE**
ROBARDS, Thomas, 124
    see also **ROBERDS, ROBERTS**
ROBBINS, Marticia (Coffin), 206
ROBERDS, Ann, 95,124,138
    Anna M (Jones), 50
    Bethula, 138
    Elisabeth, 124
    Esther, 124
    Freeman, 124
    Hannah, 124
    Hannah (Johnson), 124
    Henry, 50

ROBERDS, Martha, 124
    Mary, 50
    Mary (Myers), 103
    Nathan, 50
    Phebe/Phoebe, 50,95
    Phenias, 124
    Ruth (Cox), 124
    Sarah, 138
    Solomon Whitson, 124
    Thomas, 95,138
    Thomas Jr, 50
    Walter, 124
    Willis W, 50
    Wm, 50
ROBERT, Jonathan, 124
    see also **ROBERTS**
ROBERTS, —— (Johnson), 50
    Abigail, 58
    Adeline (McIntyre), 51
    Albert, 50,51
    Albert B, 125
    Alice (Edgerton), 125
    Alice E, 125
    Alice J (Edgerton), 51
    Amy, 124
    Ann/Anna, 51,72,124
    Ann (Whitson), 51
    Anna M (Jones), 51
    Anna Mary, 51
    Annie M, 125
    Avis Jane, 51,102
    Belle, 51
    Belle R, 15
    Catherine/Katherine, 50,51
    Daniel, 51,125
    David, 50,124
    David Edward, 50
    Edward, 125
    Eli, 50,51,55
    Elijah, 51
    Elizabeth, 50,51,125
    Elizabeth (Rue), 125
    Elvira, 48,51
    Emma L, 51,125
    Esther, 51
    Ethel B, 125
    Evaline/Eveline, 50,51
    Flora, 14
    Frank C, 50,51
    Fred C, 50
    Frederic/Frederick, 125
    Frederic/Frederick Warner/Warren, 51,125
    Grace, 50,55
    Henry, 51,125
    Henry S, 15,50,51
    India Lizzie, 51
    Inez (Armstrong), 51
    Iona Lee, 51
    Ione, 125
    James, 50
    James G, 51
    Jane Lee, 125
    John, 79,124
    John H, 51,125
    Jonathan, 48,50,102,124,125
    Jordan, 125
    Levi J, 51
    Lindley H, 51,125
    Louis M, 51
    Lucretia, 50
    Lydia, 14

ROBERTS, Lydia C, 125
   Martha, 51
   Martha (Charles), 15,50,51,125
   Martha E, 20
   Mary, 51,75,102,124,125
   Mary (Kinzie/Kinsey), 50
   Mary (Smith), 48,50,51
   Mary A, 79
   Mary A (Kinsey), 51,55
   Mary Anna/Annie, 51,125
   Mary E, 125
   Mary E (Hockett), 50
   Milton, 51
   Phebe, 75,124
   Phinehas, 51,124
   Polly, 51
   Rebecca, 36,38
   Robert, 50
   Samuel, 51,125
   Sarah, 51,124,125
   Sarah E, 125
   Sarah E (Barton/Burton), 51
   Solomon W, 125
   Solomon Whitson, 51,124
   Thomas, 51,72,75,124,125
   Thomas Jr, 125
   Verona S R (Stubbs), 50
   Walter, 51,124
   Wm, 50,51,125
ROBERTSON, James, 206
   James C, 206
   Levine (Jenkins), 206
   Sarah, 125
ROBINETT, Dean, 56
   Luvica, 56
   Sarah Ruth, 56
ROBINSON, Anna, 45
   Charles, 125
   Charles H, 51
   Eleanora, 125
   Elizabeth, 35,125
   Elizabeth E, 51,125
   Ella May (Woodard), 51
   Elwood, 51
   Emma C, 24,51,125
   Fanny, 125
   Gertrude, 51,125
   Harmon, 125
   Irene, 125
   Isaac, 51,125
   Isaac King, 125
   Jane (Taylor), 125
   Jessie B, 51
   John, 35
   Lemuel, 51,125
   Lorenzo Dow, 125
   Lorrie E, 125
   Lydia Marine, 51
   Maggie, 206
   Martha (Carruthers), 35
   Martha Ann, 125
   Mary, 51
   Mary Woodard, 125
   Olive M (Kaminsky), 51
   Rebecca, 24,51,125
   Samuel, 125
   Sina T, 206
   Thomas, 24,51,125
   Wm, 51
   Wm H, 51,125
   Wm Henry, 51
   see also ROBISON

ROBISON, Mary Emily (Ross), 51
   see also ROBINSON
ROBOSON, Ida Jane, 175
   James C, 175
   John Franklin, 175
   Margaret Ellen, 175
   Sina, 175
   Wm Lewis, 175
ROCKHILL, Albert, 51
   Calvin, 51
   Ernest, 51
   Jane, 125
   Louanna, 51
   Lydia H (Hollingsworth), 51
RODAMMEL, Wm, 125
   see also RODEARMEL, ROTHEMERAL
RODEARMEL, Wm, 125
   see also RODAMMEL, ROTHEMERAL
RODEFELD, Lena E, 125
   Lina, 125
ROE, Ellen, 152
   Grace B, 51
   Mary Ann (Lamb), 206
   Rebecca, 125
   Sarah Cassie (Bogue), 51
   Sarah E, 125
   Sarah Elizabeth, 96,125
   Thurman, 51
   Wm, 51
   see also ROHE, ROWE
ROGERS, Alonzo, 125
   Anna, 51
   Anna /Annie (Valentine), 125
   Anna L, 51
   Ansel, 125
   Arthur C, 125
   Charles H, 51,125
   Charles R, 206
   Christiana, 125
   Cynthia, 125
   Daniel T, 125
   Eddie, 125
   Esta, 125
   Eunice, 51,125
   Eva (Coates), 175
   Eva H, 206
   Frank, 125
   Franz, 175
   George, 175,206
   Gertie, 125
   Jacob, 125
   John O, 206
   John Ores, 175
   Jonathan, 51
   Jonathan C, 125
   M C, 51
   Mary (Bryant), 51
   Nancy J, 125
   Olinda (Mendenhall), 125
   Olinda B, 125
   Olinda B (Mendenhall), 51
   Olive, 51
   Oliver, 51
   Orissa (McDonald), 51
   Paul, 175
   Paul D, 206
   Roscoe, 175
   Ruth A, 19
   Sally (Clay), 51
   Sarah L, 125
   Walter, 51

ROHE, Esther (Coate), 51
   see also ROE, ROWE
ROHRER, Ruth A, 22
ROLLINS, Ellen E, 10
ROOT, Clara B (Keever), 175
   Everett E, 175
   John Carl, 175
   Wm M, 175
ROPER, Oliver, 51,125
ROSE, Hester, 125
ROSECRANS, Maud/Maude (Wolfe/Wolf), 51, 125
ROSS, Bertha Omelia, 51
   Charles, 51
   Everett John, 51
   Hannah J, 15,125
   Ida, 125
   Ida E (Howard), 51
   John A, 51,125
   Mary Emily, 51
   Maryann, 51
   Susan (Kenworthy), 51
   Susanna, 125
   Timothy, 51
ROTHEMERAL, Asa, 125
   se also RODAMMEL, RODEARMEL
ROUTH, Alvis, 175
   Anna Miller, 175
   Cynthia E, 175,106
   Cynthia Emmiline, 197
   Elizabeth, 148
   Joseph E, 158,175
   Laura (Bobo), 175
   Lizzie Etta/Ettie, 158,175,107,206
   Malinda A, 177
   Marticia, 206
   Wesley, 206
   Zarilda/Zerelda Ann (Thornburg), 158,175
ROWE, Deryl Edward, 51
   Edward, 51
   Laura (Hinshaw), 51
   see also ROE, ROHE
ROWNTREE, Wm, 125
RUBY, Francis, 51
   Frank, 51
   Lula E, 51
RUE, Ada, 125
   Ada B, 51
   Alice/Allice, 51,125
   Edgar, 125
   Elizabeth, 125
   Eva, 51,125,130
   Hannah, 108,125
   Henry, 51,118,125
   Horace G, 52
   Ida Rebecca, 52
   John, 51,125
   Lewis, 52,125
   Lizzie Martha, 52
   Lydia, 118,125
   Lydia H, 51,113,125
   Maud Emma, 52
   Rachel, 113,125
   Rachel J, 51
   Rebecca, 84,118,125
   Rebecca/Rebekah (Talbot), 51,125
   Richard, 51,113,125
   Richard Edgar, 52
   Susanna/Susannah, 118,125

RUGG, Albert, 52
    Anna, 52
    Sadie, 52
RUHLE, Anna, 125
    John R, 125,
    see also **RHULE**
RULON, Eliza Ann (Atkinson), 125
    Sarah, 125
RUNNELS, Delilah, 192
RUSH, A Luella, 22
RUSSEL, George, 125
    Judith, 125
    Linetta, 125
    Ruth, 64,125
    Sarah, 64
    Susannah, 125
    Timothy, 64
    see also **RUSSELL**
RUSSELL, Bertram B, 52
    Elbert, 52,126
    Eliza (Sanders), 52
    Eliza Ellen (Hagerty), 18
    Esther, 164
    Franklin, 18
    George, 52,125
    Henry, 125,126
    James, 125
    Josiah, 52,125
    Judith, 52,125
    Lienetta (Cox), 52
    Lizzie Hunt, 52
    Lizzie Loretta, 18
    Marinda, 52
    Ruth, 52,125
    Sarah, 52,125
    Sina/Sinah, 52,125
    Susanna (Jones), 125
    Timothy, 52,125
    Wm, 52
    Wm E, 52
    see also **RUSSEL**
RUSSEY, Mary, 126
    Mary, 52
    Wm, 52
    see also **RUSSY**
RUSSY, Charity (Williams), 126
    see also **RUSSEY**
RYAN, Clyde, 52
    Daniel, 126
    Emily Jane (Wickett), 52
    Joseph, 52
    Viola, 52

SACKETT, Emily (Cole), 52
    Lemuel M, 52
    Mary Lyon (Coggeshall), 52
    Ralph Lemuel, 52
    Robert Lemuel, 52
    Robert S, 126
SAINT, Achsah M, 126
    Alpheus, 126
    Daniel, 49,52,126
    Elizabeth, 30,49
    Escum, 126
    Gulielma, 126
    Janette, 126
    Mary, 126
    Richard, 126
    Sarah, 126
    Thomas, 126
    Wm, 126

SAMMS, Elizabeth, 126
    Joseph, 126
    Lewis, 126
    Sarah, 126
    Sarah P, 126
    W E, 126
    see also **SAMS**
SAMPSON, George, 52
    Marie, 52
SAMS, Sarah, 52
    Sarah P, 126
    Wm, 52,126
    see also **SAMS**
SANDER, Martha, 25
    see also **SANDERS**
SANDERS, Abigail, 126
    Abigail (Osborn), 126
    Althea, 176
    Carolina (Ratliff), 176
    David, 31,126
    Eliza, 52
    Elizabeth, 31
    Ellen, 126
    Emma, 206
    Emma J, 176
    Frank, 206
    Frankie L, 176
    Gulielma, 27,60
    Hannah, 57
    Jacob, 126
    John, 126
    Joseph M, 176,206
    Martha, 8,20
    Mary, 52,53,126,206
    Mary C, 126
    Mary Caroline, 126
    Mary H (Baldwin), 176
    Milley, 126
    Sarah, 31,126
    Sarah Sr, 126
    Sarah (Ham), 126
    Sarah (Hoover), 126
    Seth, 206
    Seth O, 176
    Thomas M, 126
    Wright, 176
    see also **SANDER, SAUNDERS**
SANDS, Sarah, 126
SANSBURY, Nellie, 162
SARIEFT, Mary, 55
SAUNDERS, Jacob, 126
    see also **SANDERS**
SAVERY, Nellie (Goodrich) Clark, 206
    Sarah Pim, 206
    Thomas H, 206
    Wm H, 206
SAWYER, Elizabeth, 118
    Mary, 118
    Stephen, 118
SCANTLAND, Anna (Hollingsworth), 161, 164,176
    Aurie, 165,176
    Catherine (Burdett), 176
    Cecil H, 52
    E Josephine, 161,167,176
    Edith May, 176
    Elmer, 176
    George W, 161,165,176
    Mary Jane (Hunnicutt), 176
    Oliver H, 52
    see also **SCANTLIN**

SCANTLIN, Ann (Hollingsworth), 206
    Edith May, 206
    Jannie, 206
    see also **SCANTLAND**
SCARCE, Alice, 53,126
    Alice A, 127
    Caroline, 52,126
    Dorcas, 127
    Dorcas (Edwards), 18
    Earl, 52,126
    Edward, 52,126
    Howard, 52
    Jonathan, 18,127
    Sarah, 18
    Sarah E, 126
SCHAFFER, Urilla/Urillia, 18,59
    see also **SHAFER, SHAFFER**
SCHANCK, Herman F, 126
    see also **SHANK**
SCHEIBLE, Hannah B, 52
    James Mendenhall, 52
    Millicent (Coffin), 52
    see also **SHIBELY**
SCHELL, Clarkson E, 176
    David R, 176
    Hannah (Pierce), 176
    Harry Morton, 176
    Henry Alvador, 176
    John Franklin, 176
    Wm, 176
    Wm H, 176
    see also **SHELL**
SCHENCK, Cordelia (Test), 176,206
    Herman F, 126
    Murray, 176
SCHENEMON, Wm, 126
    see also **SCHINNAMON, SCHINNEMAN, SHINAMAN**
SCHEPMAN, Arl McDonald, 52
    Homer J, 52
    Jennie (McDonald), 52
    John H, 52
    LaVerne, 52
    Mary (Verregge), 52
SCHINNAMON, Rachel, 126
    see also **SCHENEMON, SCHINNEMAN, SHINAMAN**
SCHINNEMAN, Rachel, 126
    Wm, 126
    see also **SCHENEMON, SCHINNAMON, SHINAMAN**
SCHISSLER, Laura, 126
    Louise M (Spangler), 52
SCHLERETH, Dorothy, 52
SCHLOTTE, Bertha B, 48
SCHNEIDER, Alice A, 48,52
    Anna (Werner), 52
    Elizabeth, 52
    Elizabeth C, 6,52
    Elizabeth J, 70
    Elizabeth Jane, 72
    Fred, 52
    Jacob, 52
    Kate, 72
    Kate/Katie C, 52,126
    Kate C (Miller), 52
    Katherine, 52
    Lizzie J, 126
    Martha C, 52
    Mattie C, 126
    Philip/Phillip, 6,48,52,72,126
    Rhoda A, 48,52

SCHNEIDER, Susan, 52,126
    Susan, 6
    see also **SNYDER**
SCHOOLEY, Elizabeth, 126
    Hershel, 52
    Omri, 126
    Sadie, 52
    Wm, 52
    Wm H, 126
    see also **SHUELY**
SCHULTZ, Martha, 153
    see also **SHULTZ**
SCHUMAKER, Caroline, 30
    see also **SHOEMAKER**
SCHURMAN, Florence (Unthank), 52
    Henry, 52
    see also **SHERMAN**
SCHWENNESSON, Jacob, 176
    Lucinda (Replogle), 176
    see also **SCHWENNESUN**
SCHWENNESUN, Lucinda, 206
    see also **SCHWENNESON**
SCHWING, Sophia, 126
SCOTT, Agrippa, 52,126
    Ann/Anna/Anne, 52,126
    Ann Eliza, 126
    David, 25
    Eddie, 52,126
    Eddie D, 126
    Edith Bell (Wickett), 52
    Edwin, 126
    Eleanor (Dilhorn), 126
    Eliza, 25
    Eliza Ann, 126
    Ellsworth/Elsworth, 52,126
    Ellsworth/Elsworth G, 126
    Eva, 52,126
    Eva B, 126
    John L, 126
    Louisa, 126
    Mattie, 25
    Susanna, 52,126
    Willie H, 52,126
SEAGRAVE, Hannah M, 162
    Luther, 176
    Margaret (Mulford), 162,176
    Tarver, 162,176
SEAL, Angeline (Cook), 52
    Sarah, 52
    Thomas, 52
SEAMAN, Charles I, 52
    Elizabeth, 52
    John, 52
    Julia, 12
    Nellie G, 126
SEDGEWICK, Marcia S, 126
    see also **SEDGWICK**
SEDGWICK, Deborah W, 52
    Marcia E (Sutton), 52,126
    Richard, 52
    Richard S, 126
    see also **SEDGEWICK**
SELL, Elizabeth Ann (Dingley), 52
SETTLES, Francis (Wilson), 52
    John W, 52
    John Wesley, 126
    Ollie May, 52
SEWELL, Hannah, 52
    Henry, 52
    Jack, 52
    Phebe, 52
    Ruby, 52
    Turner, 52

SHAFER, Luzena (Beeson), 207
    see also **SCHAFFER**, **SHAFFER**
SHAFFER, Charley G, 176
    Cynthia (Chamness), 207
    Daniel, 176
    Elisha, 157,176,207
    Flossie L, 176
    Frances/Francis C, 176,207
    Guy M, 176,207
    James, 52
    James M, 126
    Laura (Pryfogle), 52
    Laura B, 207
    Laura Bell (Lucas), 157,176
    Lorinda, 207
    Louis, 126
    Mary A, 126
    Maud/Maude E, 157,176,207
    Olive, 126
    Sarah, 207
    Sarah (Ogle), 176
    Urilla, 47
    see also **SCHAFFER**, **SHAFER**
SHALLEY, Patience Ann, 160
SHANK, Rachel, 126
    Rachel (Clarke), 126
    see also **SCHANK**
SHARON, Elizabeth, 52
    Elizabeth C, 90
SHAW, Aaron, 126
    Alice, 160
    Cicely, 126
    Noble, 126
    Sarah, 126
    Sarah (Cox), 126
SHAWLEY, Daniel C, 176,207
    George, 176
    Patience Ann, 176
    Rachel (Bunnell), 176
SHEARON, Caleb, 52,127
    Elizabeth, 22,127
    Elizabeth Chaffin, 52
    Mary, 52
    Rachel Linetta/Lunetta, 22,52,127
    Ruth Ann, 127,139
    Warner, 22,52,127
SHEDLTNECK, Mary (Adams), 207
SHELEY, Blanch Anna (Paton), 53
    Emily (Paton), 53
    Granville Louis, 53
    Henry, 53
SHELL, Clarkson E, 207
    Hannah, 207
    Harry Merton, 207
    John Franklin, 207
    Wm, 207
    Wm H, 207
    see also **SCHELL**
SHEPARD, Alpha M, 176
    Alvah C, 176
    Rachel, 176
    Rachel A, 64
    Sidney E, 64
    Wm L, 64
    see also **SHEPHERD**, **SHEPPERD**
SHEPHERD, Alice (Scarce), 53
    Flora B, 176
    Isaac N, 53
    Phebe, 53
    Rachel, 207
    Rena, 53
    see also **SHEPARD**, **SHEPPERD**

SHEPPERD, Martha, 34
    see also **SHEPARD**, **SHEPHERD**
SHERBER, James, 127
SHERIDAN, Hannah (Wright), 127
    John, 127
    Margaret, 127
    Mary, 208
    Thomas, 127
SHERMAN, Edith, 4
    see also **SCHURMAN**
SHIBELY, Hannah B (Mendenhall), 127
    see also **SCHEIBLE**
SHIELDS, Abraham L, 207
    Abraham Lincoln, 176
    Abram, 207
    Andrew L, 207
    Benjamin, 176
    Gladys Merritt, 176
    Isaac F, 176,207
    Joanna, 207
    Joanna (Daniels), 176
    John B, 176,207
    Julia F, 176,207
    Lenora A, 176
    Leo Winston, 176
    Levi L, 176
    Martha J, 207
    Martha Jane, 176
    Mary, 176
    Olephia Troy (Dowell), 176
    Ophelia Troy, 176
    Phebe (Hunt), 207
    Rachel C, 176
    Rachel K, 207
    Sarah, 127
    Sarah E, 176
    Susanna (Hunt), 207
    Wilbur Branson, 176
    Wm B, 176,207
    Wm H, 176
SHINAMAN, Wm, 127
    see also **SCHENEMON**,
        SCHINNAMON, **SCHINNEMAN**
SHINN, Alice, 127
    Alice A (Scarce), 127
    Anna, 127
    Anna C, 53,127
    David, 127
    Hannah, 114,127
    James Eddie/Eddy, 53,127
    Miles J, 127
    Newman H, 53,127
    Susan, 127
SHIRLEY, Florence, 21
SHIVELY, Jacob, 154
    Lillie E, 154
    Nancy (Barekott), 154
    Sarah (Thornburg), 207
SHOAF, Elizabeth, 35
SHOEMAKER, Anna, 5,50,62
    Anna B, 18,53,84,127
    Charles, 18,36,84,127,176,207
    Charles H, 24,53,106
    Elijah, 176,207
    Elinor, 53
    Ezekiel, 176,207
    Hannah, 53,127
    Hannah B, 24,91
    Howard, 53
    Isaac, 127
    Isaac J, 53
    Margaret, 36,49,53,106,127

SHOEMAKER, Margaret Ann, 207
    Margaret Ann (Ellis), 176
    Martha E, 207
    Martha Ellen, 176
    Mary (Boone), 18,24,36,53
    Mary S, 84,106
    Rachel, 127
    Rachel J (Dilks), 53,127
    Sidney/Sydney D, 53,127
    Sophia, 176,207
    Tacy, 176,207
    Thomas Ellis, 176
    Wm, 127
    Wm C, 53,127
    see also **SCHUMAKER**
SHORT, Charles M, 127
    Eva, 127
    T Edward, 127
SHOWALTER, Anna J, 19
    Christopher, 19
    Frances M, 61
    Louise, 19
    Margaret, 36
    Mary K, 61
    Rosella, 61
SHOWAN, Henry C, 127
    Henry Clay, 53
    Jennie, 127
    Lydia Ann, 127,137
    Lydia Ann (Overman), 53,61
    Mary Elizabeth, 53
    see also **SHOWEN**
SHOWEN, Lydia A (Overman), 127
    see also **SHOWAN**
SHRIVER, Helen (Horney), 53, 127
SHROYER, John, 53
    Nellie Barnard (Conner), 53
SHUELY, Anna (Swain), 207
    see also **SCHOOLEY**
SHUGARD, George, 49
    Mary, 49
    Sarah, 49
    see also **SHUGARDS**, **SHUGART**
SHUGARDS, Mary, 127
    Sarah, 127
    Tamar, 127
    see also **SHUGARD**
SHUGART, Angelina, 15
    George, 127
    John, 127
    Mary, 127
    Sarah (Ratliff), 127
    see also **SHUGARD**
SHULTZ, C Irvin, 127
    Carlin/Corlin H, 53,127
    Eunice C, 127
    Eunice C (Hastings), 53
    Eva, 127
    Eva L, 53
    Irvin T, 53
    Jacob, 53
    Joseph, 127
    Joseph D, 53
    Martha Jane, 152
    Mary, 53
    Samuel F, 53
    Samuel T, 127
    see also **SCHULTZ**
SHUMAN, Lila, 127
    Sabina, 60
SHUMARD, Sarah (Burgess), 53
    Warren, 53

SHUNKWILER, Mae, 53
    Oliver, 53
SHUTE, Aaron, 53,127
    Alice, 53,131
    Amos H, 53
    Ann H, 89,127
    Charles, 33,53,127
    Edward F, 53
    Elizabeth, 127
    Elizabeth (Hill), 33,127
    Elizabeth H, 53
    Harriet/Harriett, 53,131
    Harriet H, 127
    Hiram, 53
    James P, 53
    Jane, 53,89
    Jane M, 33
    Lydia, 53,127
    Martha, 127
    Martha (Miles), 53
    Martha A, 127
    Miles L, 53
    Nancy H, 53
    Rebeckah, 53
    Robert, 53,127
    Samuel, 53,89,127,131
    Samuel Jr, 127
    Siby/Sibyl/Sybal, 53,127
SHUTT, Emma, 163
SICKLES, Cornelius, 176
    Peter E, 176
    Sophia (Niccum), 176
SIDDALL, Albert A, 127
    Albert P, 127
    Atticus, 127
    David, 127
    David J, 127
    Jesse P, 127
    Philemon F, 127
    Sarah, 127
    see also **SIDDLE**
SIDDLE, Albert, 127
    Atticus, 127
    David, 127
    Jesse, 127
    Philemon, 127
    see also **SIDDALL**
SIDWELL, David, 127
    Esther, 127
SIGERFOUSE, Cynthia (Osborn), 207
    see also **SIGGERFOOSE**
SIGGERFOOSE, Cynthia (Osborn), 176
    see also **SIGERFOUSE**
SILVERS, Ruth Ann (Cox), 127
SIMERSON, Elizabeth, 161
SIMMON, Abigail, 127
SIMMS, Ann (Marshall), 53
    Edward G, 53
    Estella, 53
    Florence E (Ray), 53
    Gertrude Elizabeth, 53
    Richard, 53
    Ruthanna Mary, 53
SIMONS, Alfred H, 207
    Elma, 207
    Lydia, 207
    Elizabeth (Graham), 12
    John, iii
    Margaret, 32
    Margaret S, 12
    Robert, 12
    see also **SYMONDS**, **SYMONS**

SINGLETON, Arthur B, 53,127
    Flora E, 53,127
SKINNER, Deiduma (Elliott), 127
SLEAP, Caroline Louise, 53
    Henry F, 53
    Lula Dunster, 53
    Lula R (Colgrove), 53
    Silas Frederick, 53
SLEEPER, Buddel, 33
    Elizabeth (Welsh), 33
    Martha Ann, 33
SLORP, Elizabeth (Pitman), 53
    Frank, 53
    Henry, 53
SMALL, Aaron, 2,53
    Abigail, 53,74
    Abigail (Stafford), 128
    Abner, 2,53,128
    Abraham, 127
    Amos, 127,128
    Ann, 114
    Ann Ruth, 127
    Benjamin, 1,2,53,128
    Clarky, 207
    Elizabeth, 53,57,127,128
    Elizabeth (Sawyer), 118
    Ephraim, 53,128
    Gideon, 114,120,127
    Isabel/Isabella, 127
    Jane, 57
    Jane (Moore), 127
    Jemima, 207
    Jemima (Cain), 207
    Jemima (Jones) Cain, 207
    Jesse, 2,53,127,128,207
    Jonathan, 127
    Joseph, 207
    Joshua, 127
    Josiah, 127
    Lydia, 2
    Mary, 2,53,92
    Miriam/Mirion, 2,53,88
    Miriam (Bundy), 127
    Nathan, 127,128
    Nathaniel, 127
    Obadiah, 57,127
    Peninah/Penninah, 2,53,89
    Rachel (Hawkins), 128
    Rebecca, 20
    Samuel, 127
    Sarah, 2,53,114,120,127,128
SMELSER, Frank, 128
SMILEY, George, 176
    Mary Hannah (Beeson), 176
SMITH, Abigail, 128
    Abraham, 176
    Adam, 207
    Adam Rinard, 176
    Agnes Lucile, 53
    Albert, 53,128
    Albert E, 54
    Albina Jane, 154
    Alice, 128
    Alice (Erwin), 128
    Alice (Nordyke), 54
    Alice W, 128
    Aloha B, 54
    Amanda, 128
    Amy Amanda (Cox), 128
    Andrew J, 54
    Ann/Anna/Anne/Annie, 15,16,54,82,
        128,136,207

SMITH, Ann (Adams), 207
   Ann Eliza (Thomas), 15
   Anna L, 176
   Arthur, 176
   Arthur D, 53,128
   Avis, 96,128
   Benjamin, 53,128
   Bertha (Hill), 53
   Bertha M, 176,207
   Caleb, 128
   Caroline, 53,54,128
   Caroline (Chamness), 176
   Caroline M (Hicks), 53
   Carrie, 128
   Carrie Ruby (Keplinger), 53
   Catharine/Catherine, 54,128
   Charles C, 153
   Charles Curtis, 53
   Charles G, 53,128
   Charlotte (Mark), 58
   Charlotte A, 54,128
   Clarence, 207
   Clarence A, 176
   Cornelius, 128
   Elisha, 54,128
   Eliz, 79
   Eliza, 28
   Eliza Ann, 128
   Eliza Willan, 28,54
   Elizabeth, 2,30,54,99,128,176
   Elizabeth (Abott), 153
   Elizabeth (Dickinson), 54
   Elizabeth (Hobbick), 54
   Elizabeth W (Barnes), 128
   Ella, 128
   Ella R, 38
   Ellen S, 25
   Elmira M (Parson/Pearson), 53,128
   Elvira P, 128
   Emily (Horney), 128
   Esther, 53,91
   Ethel L, 53
   Eunice/Unice, 136,179,207
   Eunice (Coffin), 176
   Ezra, 54,128
   Flora, 207
   Flora B (Shepherd), 176
   Gulielma, 2,54,112,128
   Hannah, 53,59,128
   Hannah (Whital/Whitall), 128
   Henry, 128
   Ina, 53
   Ira, 128
   Isabel/Isabelle, 53,128
   Jackson, 176,179
   Jacob, 54,82,128
   James, 28,54,128,154
   James L, 15
   Jane, 53,54,91,128
   Jarah, 128
   Jenettie, 176
   Jennettie E, 181
   John, iii,1,2,30,37,53,54,57,91,99,
      107,128,132,176
   John Jr, 128
   John C, 54
   John E, 128
   John Everett, 53
   John H, 38
   John R, 25
   John W, 53
   Jonah, 96
   Joseph, 53,54,128

SMITH, Joseph P, 53
   Katie, 128
   L Mary, 128
   Letitia, 37,54,57,99,107,116,128,132
   Lottie, 128
   Lurianna, 53
   Lydia, 53,207
   Lydia Mary (Nordyke), 54
   Mahlon T, 128
   Malina (Owen), 53
   Margaret (Foulke), 128
   Margery, 37,128
   Martha, 54,128,156,160
   Martha J, 38
   Mary, 3,48,50,51,53,54,63,124,128,
      140,154,207
   Mary Jr, 128
   Mary Sr, 128
   Mary (Barr), 176,181
   Mary (Smith), 54
   Mary (Taylor), 54
   Mary A, 128
   Mary Ann, 128
   Mary E, 58,128
   Mary E (Nelson), 176
   Mary Esther, 53
   Mary Evaline (Dennis), 176
   Mercy, 3
   Millicent, 128
   Minnie, 54,128
   Myrtle, 15
   Nancy, 155
   Nancy A (Rinard), 156
   Nancy J, 174
   Nathan, 2,54,128,207
   Nellie J, 176
   Nettie A, 153
   Nettie E, 181
   Omer F, 176,207
   Oriana/Orianna/Orina, 128
   Peninah/Penninah, 2,54,57,132
   Percy B, 54
   Peter, 156
   Phebe, 15,54,128
   Phebe (King), 128
   Polly Emily (Pitts), 176
   Rachel, 2,6
   Rebecca, 27
   Rebecca Ann, 176,179,207
   Richard, 176
   Robert, 1,128
   Robert B, 128
   Rosanna, 59
   Samuel, 54,128
   Samuel S, 128
   Samuel W, 128
   Sarah, 2,37,53,54,82,96,107,128
   Sarah (Frame), 25
   Sarah (Willan), 28
   Sarah J, 128
   Sarah J (Willan), 54
   Sarah Jane (Edgerton), 128
   Seth, 54,63,128,140
   Susan J (Parrish), 54
   Sylvia Mae (Johnson), 54
   Tamar, 128
   Tamar (Hawkins), 53
   Tiche/Tishe, 2,30,54,128
   Walter, 128
   Webster, 58
   Willis J, 54
   Wm, 53,54,128,207
   Wm B, 128
   Wm M, 128
   see also **SMYTH, SMYTHE**

SMITHSON, Carlista (Barnes), 176
   Clayton M, 176
   Michael, 176
SMITHY, Mary, 207
   Rebecca Ann, 207
SMOOT, Nancy J, 18
SMYTH, Martha, 128
   see also **SMITH, SMYTHE**
SMYTHE, Martha (Baldwin), 128
   see also **SMITH, SMYTH**
SNIPES, Mary, 128
SNODGRASS, Cora Alma, 149
   Hannah (Burroughs), 149
   Malvina, 147
   Pharaby, 147
   Wm, 147,149
SNYDER, Aaron, 16
   Agatha, 128
   Agatha (Teagle), 16
   Amy C, 54
   Anna B, 48
   Bertha H, 48
   Della May, 54
   Emily Catherine, 16
   George, 54
   John W, 54
   Philip, 128
   Rhoda Ann (Nordyke), 128
   Wm, 48
   see also **SCHNEIDER**
SOFRAIN, Eleanor, 32
   John, 32
   Marinetta, 32
SOLEMA, Blanch, 54
   Jennie, 54
   John, 54
SOMMERS, Mary A (Harvey), 54
SOWERWINE, George Albert, 176
   Isaac, 176
   Susanna (Clevenger), 176
SPAHR, Cora S, 54
   John R, 54
   Mamie/Marie (Gentry), 54
SPAIN, Clary, 165
   Milly, 165
   Thomas, 165
SPANGLER, John, 52
   Louise M, 52
   Marie (Leighman), 52
   Gertrude, 27
SPAULDING, Charles H, 54
   Mary E, 54
   Wm W, 54
SPEAR, Caroline, 55
   see also **SPEER**
SPECKENHIER, Harriet K (Kenworthy), 54
   Margaret (Kenworthy), 54
SPEER, Caroline, 55
   Gracie, 54
   James, 54
   John F, 54
   Mary, 54
   Mary E (Hunnicutt), 54
   Orisey, 54
   see also **SPEAR**
SPENCER, Alice H, 128
   Elisha, 128
   Elizabeth, 128
   Mary Emma, 128
SPINNING, Cora, 49
   Lida P, 54

SPIVAH, Axiom, 128
    Ephraim, 128
    see also **SPIVY**
SPIVY, Aba, 128
    Abigail, 74,128
    Becca, 128
    see also **SPIVAH**
SPONSLER, Sarah (Boswell), 128
SPOTTS, Adaline A (Winters), 54
    Alpha Charlotte, 54
    Elizabeth (Brown), 54
    Ida Marie, 54
    Wm, 54
SPRADLIN, Elizabeth Mary, 147,179,180
    Elwood H, 177
    Ethalinda, 177
    Fanny, 179
    Irena J, 177
    Lewis W, 177
    Lilly B, 177
    Louis, 207
    Lucy Jane, 150
    Mary Jane, 177,207
    Mary Jane (Thornburg), 207
    Susan Alwilda, 177
    Wright, 179
SPRAY, Phebe, 128
SPRINGER, Abigail, 129
    Barnabas, 129
    Daniel, 54
    Elizabeth, 129
    George, 129
    Margaret, 54
    Mathew/Matthew, 129
    Nettie Clara, 54
    Sally, 103,129
    Sarah, 129
    Stephen, 129
    Wm, 129
    Wm L, 129
SPRONG, Agusta (Meeker), 54
    Alex M, 54
    Otto, 54,129
SPRONGER, Elizabeth, 121
SQUIRES, Isadore Bell (Lapsheley), 54
    Rebecca, 207
STAFFORD, Abigail, 54,128,129
    Brantley/Brantly, 129
    Celia, 129
    Elam, 129
    Eli, 129
    Elias, 129
    Elizabeth, 129
    Henry, 129
    Martha, 129
    Nancy (Hastings), 54,129
    Philany, 129
    Samuel, 54,129
    Thomas, 129
    Wm, 129
STAHER, Ann, 174
    Sarah E, 174
    Urias, 174
    see also **STAYER**
STALKER, Alice, 30
    Deborah, 129
    Eli, 129
    Elizabeth, 129
    George, 129
    John, 129
    Rachel, 129

STANCOMB, Addie Myrtle, 54
    Charlotte, 54
    John, 54
STANLEY, Abel, 129
    Abigail/Abigial, 72,129,177
    Abraham/Abram, 54,129
    Ada, 129
    Ada F, 54
    Agatha, 207
    Agnes, 177
    Alva, 129
    Alva L, 54,129
    Anna, 129,177
    Anna Mary (Cook), 54
    Archelas/Archelaus/Archolas, 207
    Barclay, 129
    Belle (Iredell), 54
    Bertha A, 54
    Charles Asa, 54
    Clarkanna, 177
    Cyrus, 129
    Eliza, 129
    Elizabeth, 60,129,177
    Elmina, 72,129,177,209
    Elwood, 129
    Emmet, 129
    Franklin E, 129
    Franklin Emmet, 54
    George, 129
    Gere, 129
    Gulielma (Jessup), 54
    Gulielma J, 129
    Hannah, 129,174,205
    Hannah (Watson), 54
    Harvey, 129
    Huldah, 177
    Irena, 177
    Isaac, 54,129,207
    Isaac Orlo/Orlow, 54,129
    Jacob, 129
    James, 129,177,207
    Jane, 129
    Jemima, 129,177,207
    Jemima (Mills), 207
    Jemime (Parker), 129
    Jesse, 54,129,177,207
    Jonathan, 207
    Joseph, 177,207
    Joseph M, 208
    Joshua, 129
    Joshua F, 129
    Levi, 54
    Lewis, 177
    Lucinda, 54
    Lucinda E, 129
    Margaret, 207
    Margaret M, 54
    Margaret Maria, 129
    Marina Loan, 54
    Martha, 177
    Martin, 129
    Mary, 129,174,177
    Mary Ellen, 207
    Mary Ethel, 54
    Mary R, 129
    Matthew, 129
    Mauna Loa, 129
    Mertie, 129
    Michael, 154,174
    Millicent, 129
    Nancy, 177
    Nancy Ann, 177,207

STANLEY, Naomi, 177,207
    Naomi (Hodson), 207
    Naomi H, 129
    Naomy (Beeson), 207
    Nathan, 129
    Nathan D, 129
    Nathan Dix, 129
    Ota Mitchell, 54
    Rachel, 129,177
    Rebecca/Rebekah, 23,54,60,129,131, 177
    Richard, 72,129
    Samuel, 129
    Sarah, 129,177,207
    Sarah Etta, 54
    Sarah Jane, 207
    Solomon, 177
    Strangeman, 177,207
    Susan (Butler), 54
    Susanna, 129
    Temple, 129
    Thomas, 177
    Thomas E, 177
    Wm, 54,60,110,129,177,207
    Zebidee, 177
STANTON, Aaron/Aron, 129,177,208
    Ada Esther, 55
    Alfred, 129
    Almedia, 129
    Amos, 129
    Anna (Coffin), 129
    Anne, 129
    Caroline C, 45,54
    Carrie, 15,55
    Carrie C, 129
    Catharine/Catherine, 42,55,129
    Catharine/Catherine (Stanton), 42,55
    Charles F, 129
    Charles T, 129
    Daniel, 129
    David, 129,177,208
    Deborah, 114
    Deborah Ann, 42,55
    Edna Elizabeth, 54,129
    Edward, 15,55,129
    Edwin M, 177,208
    Edwin Murray, 208
    Elijah, 129
    Elizabeth, 129
    Elizabeth (Coffin), 129
    Elizabeth M, 28
    Elwood, 129
    Emily H (Hadley), 55
    Emma, 129
    Etta (Conner), 55
    Frederick, 55,129
    Geraldine A, 129
    Geraldine O, 55
    Guilelma, 129
    Hannah, 55,129
    Henrietta, 129
    Henry, 129
    Henry A, 55
    Henry F, 177
    Hepzibah, 129
    James, 129
    Jane (Beard), 55
    Jemima, 129
    Jemime (Coffin), 129
    Jennie Opal, 177,208
    John, 129
    John Milton, 45,54

STANTON, John T, 55
  Joseph, 42,55,129
  Joseph Fleming, 129
  Joshua, 55
  Latham, 129
  Lillie A, 177,208
  Louisa, 55
  Lucinda A, 177
  Lydia, 129,177,208
  Lydia B, 11
  Mahala, 55,129
  Mariella, 55
  Mary, 129
  Mary Emma, 55,129
  Mattie, 208
  Mattie A (Mettert), 177
  Maurice, 55
  Nathan, 208
  Oliver Henry, 129
  Penina/Peninah, 208
  Peninah/Penninah (Nicholson/
    Nickleson), 177,208
  Phebe, 57
  Phebe Ann, 15,55,129
  Phebe Ann (Williams), 129
  Rachel, 10
  Rachel (Hollingsworth), 129
  Rosilla, 129
  Ruth, 129
  Samuel, 129
  Sarah A, 10
  Stephen Butler, 129
  Susanna/Susannah, 79,129
  Thomas W, 177,208
  Wm, 10,129
  Wm A, 177,208
  Wm Edward, 55
  Wm Ellis, 177
STANTZ, Fanny, 165,170,181
STAR, Elmira, 175
  see also **STARR**
STARBUCK, Abigial, 129
  Andrew, 167
  Anna (Diller), 55
  Arthur Diller, 55
  Asa, 129
  Avis (Lamb), 167
  Edwin, 55
  Elihu Coffin, 129
  Emily J, 167
  Esther, 129
  Luzena (Jessup), 55
  Mahala, 129
  Mary, 129
  Samuel, 55
  Wm, 129
STARR, Anna, 130
  Anna/Annie E, 55,130
  Charles, 129,130
  Charles W, 129,130
  Deborah Ann, 31
  Elizabeth, 32,43,101,129
  Esther, 55,129,130
  Esther E, 55,130
  Henry, 55,129,130
  James, 55,129,130
  Jeremiah, 129,130
  Jesse, 129,130
  John, 32,55,101,129
  John Jr, 130
  Joshua, 55,129
  Mary, 32,55,101,129

STARR, Phebe, 55,129
  Sarah, 55,129
  Willets, 129,130
  Wm, 55,129
  see also **STAR**
STATE, Charlotte (Carr), 208
STATON, Martha J, 154,164
STAYER, Catherine, 130
  John, 130
  see also **STAHER**
STEADHAM, Elizabeth (Wright), 130
  Jonas L, 130
  see also **STEDDOM, STEDHAM,
    STIDDOM, STIDHAM**
STEARNS, Exalina, 208
  Exalina C (Hinshaw), 208
STEDDOM, Abijah, 55,130
  Alice (Teague), 49,55,62
  Anna T, 55,62
  Cornelia A, 130
  Cornelia Adelaide (Cammack), 55
  Deborah M, 130
  Deborah M (Mendenhall), 55
  Edward K, 55,130
  Ella C, 55,130
  Esther, 15,49,55
  Henry, 33,102
  John, 49,55,62
  Lurena, 33,40
  Martha, 130
  Martha (Pearson), 33,102
  Martha L, 55,130
  Mary, 28,33,102,103
  Rhoda S, 44
  Samuel, 44
  Susannah (Teague), 44
  see also **STEADHAM, STEDHAM,
    STIDDOM, STIDHAM**
STEDHAM, Elizabeth, 55
  Jonas, 55
  see also **STEADHAM, STEDDOM,
    STIDDOM, STIDHAM**
STEELE, Margaret, 42
STEER, Amos, 100
  Ann, 100
  Ann (Maule), 100
  Deborah, 100
  Deborah A, 100
  Deborah Ann, 130
STEGALL, Clara F, 55
  Curtis, 55
  Hilda M, 55
  Irvin Delbert, 55
  Isaiah/Ervin C, 55
  Milo, 55
  Milo C, 55
  Noah T, 55
  Susan H, 55
  Susan Hannah (Mettler), 55
  Viola, 55
  see also **STEGLE**
STEGLE, Sarah E, 55
  see also **STEGALL**
STEPHENS, Albertha, 6
  Alice, 130
  Caroline (Spear/Speer), 55
  Elizabeth, 179
  Eva (Rue), 130
  Francis W, 55
  Frank M/W, 130
  Henry, 55
  Jacob, 55

STEPHENS, Lavina, 6
  Moses C, 130
  Myra C, 55
  Peter, 6
  Pharaba (White), 55
  Phebe Alice (Hodgin), 5
  see also **STEVENS**
STEPHENSON, Elizabeth (Allen), 208
  Elza, 208
  Lizzie, 208
  Reuben, 208
  see also **STEVENSON**
STETLER, Hannah, 160
  Jesse, 160
  Margaret, 160
STEVENS, Eliza (King), 179
  Jesse C, 179
  Maggie, 148
  Olive Jane, 179
  see also **STEPHENS**
STEVENSON, Charles, 55
  Charles Ernest, 55
  Chloe C (Kinsey), 55
  Elmer P, 55
  Elzie D, 177
  Emily, 55
  Francis Charles, 55
  J Elmer, 55
  James, 177
  Lizzie, 208
  Rebecca, 130
  see also **STEPHENSON**
STEWARD, Hannah, 130
STEWART, Absalom, 130
  Albert W, 55,130
  Alice E, 55
  Anna/Annie (Young), 21,161
  Edgar, 55
  Edwin, 21,161
  Elizabeth, 30
  Elton, 177
  Esther, 208
  Florence, 55
  Jehu/Jehue, 4,68,130
  John, 55,130
  John Sidney, 130
  Jonathan, 130
  Laura Ann, 130
  Laura E, 21,161
  Lizzie, 130
  Margaret (Chamness), 177
  Margaret B, 208
  Mary, 4,55,68
  Robert, 55
  Rosa/Rosetta (Mills), 55,130
  Rose, 130
  Samuel W, 130
  Sarah, 4,68
  Sidney, 55,130
  Temple, 130
  see also **STUART**
STIDDOM, Rhoda, 32
  see also **STEADHAM, STEDDOM,
    STEDHAM, STIDHAM**
STIDHAM, Jesse Lois, 55
  Lillie F (Tucker), 55
  Mary E, 130
  Mary Emma, 130
  Nora A (Hampton), 55
  Wm A, 55
  see also **STEADHAM, STEDDOM,
    STEDHAM, STIDDOM**

STIGGLEMAN, Caroline, 139
    Carrie Alma, 130
    Corwin H, 55,130
    Henry, 139
    L H, 13
    Leo Charles, 55
    Leona Coreen (Winder), 55
    Leona H, 130
    Luella, 13
    Nellie Irene, 55,130
    Olive, 130,139
    Sallie E, 130
    Sarah, 13
    Wm G, 130
    see also **STIGLEMAN**
STIGLEMAN, Henry, 63
    Olive, 63
    see also **STIGGLEMAN**
STILLMAN, Juanita (Garza), 55
    Ralph, 55
STILLWELL, Ella E, 62,63
    see also **STILWELL**
STILWELL, Eliz, 21
    see also **STILLWELL**
STIMMEL, Anna E, 55
    John A, 55
    Samuel C, 55
STINGLEY, Gilead, 59
    Nancy Jane, 59
    Nettie B, 59
STOKER, Ann, 48
    Sarah E, 48
    Urias, 48
STOKES, Albert, 130
    Alexander, 130
    Ann, 130,141
    Benjamin, 130,141
    Edwin, 130
    Edwin Henry, 130
    Elizabeth, 130
    Hannah R, 130
    Isabell/Isabella, 130
    Jane, 130
    Martha, 130
    Samuel, 130
    Sarah, 114,130
    Susan, 130
    Thomas, 114
STONE, Adelaide (Conner), 16
    Elizabeth (Binford), 55
    Jesse Marvin, 55
    Rena Harriett, 55
STONEMAN, Mark D, 208
STOREY, Wm R, 130
STORMS, Mary Ann (Locke), 208
STOUT, Anna, 177
    Charles, 177,208
    Elias, 177,208
    Enoch, 177
    Ephraim, 177,208
    Hannah, 44
    Irena (Chamness), 177
    Irena/Irene, 8,208
    James, 177,208
    Jesse, 208
    Joseph, 44
    Levi, 130
    Lorenzo, 8
    Margaret, 173
    Mary, 44,148,149,164,165
    Noah, 208

STOUT, Rachel, 198
    Rebecca (Mullen), 8
    Robert, 177,208
    Ruth, 177
STOVER, Catharine/Catherine, 165,181
STRADER, Grace (Roberts), 55
STRADLIN, Mary, 36
STRANAHAN, Edgar, 130
    Edgar H, 55,130
    John Henry, 55
    Mary (Sarieft), 55
    Othelia P (Kemp), 55
    Wm, 55
STRATE, Anna, 55
    Francis Wesley, 55
    Harry, 55
STRATTEN, Joseph P, 130
    see also **STRATTON**
STRATTON, Abigail, 19,26
    Abram, 131
    Albert, 130
    Albert W, 131
    Amy, 130
    Benjamin, 130
    Caroline E, 130,131
    Charles, 131
    Charles W, 56,130,131
    Daniel, 130
    Edward D, 130,131
    Eli, 130
    Eliz, 130
    Ella Maria, 56,130
    Emily, 56
    Ephraim, 130
    Eunice, 130
    Hannah, 56,130
    Hannah (Ogborn), 130
    Henry H, 56,131
    Isaac, 56
    Jerusha, 130
    Job, 19
    John, 130
    Jonathan D, 130
    Joseph, 130
    Joseph Jr, 130
    Joseph D, 130
    Joseph E, 56,130,131
    Joseph I, 130
    Joseph J, 56
    Joseph Samuel, 130
    Katherine Mildred, 56
    Laura, 131
    Laura Amelia, 131
    Letitia, 19
    Levainy, 130
    Levi, 130
    Lucinda, 130
    Martha, 130
    Martha (Henley), 130
    Martha H, 56,130,131
    Mary, 130
    Micajah, 131
    Micajah H, 56
    Milicent Ann, 130
    Nancy (Morrow), 130
    Nancy M, 130
    Naomi/Naomy, 102,130
    Prudence, 130
    Ruth, 130
    Ruth (Crew), 130
    Samuel, 56,130
    Samuel F, 130

STRATTON, Samuel T, 131
    Sarah Elizabeth, 56
    Zimri, 56,130
    see also **STRATTEN**
STRAWBRIDGE, Benjamin, 62,131
    Elizabeth, 33,90,102,131,134
    Hannah (Gladdin), 62
    Jesse, 131
    Joseph, 33,90,102
    Joseph B, 131
    Mary, 90,131
    Sarah, 7,33,102,131
    Sarah H, 62
    Thomas, 131
    Thomas Clarkson, 131
STREET, Aaron, 88,131
    Anna, 56,131
    Anna (Macy), 131
    Charles F, 56,131
    Charles Fawcett, 131
    Charles T, 131
    Dorothy, 131
    Dorothy Jr (Gilbert), 131
    Edgar L, 56
    Edgar Louis, 131
    Eunice, 131
    Jane, 56,131
    John, 56,131
    John Jr, 131
    Lewis/Louis, 56,131
    Mary, 88,131
    Samuel, 56,131
    Samuel S, 131
    Sarah, 131
    Sarah T, 56,131
    see also **STREETE**
STREETE, Samuel S, 131
    see also **STREET**
STRETCH, Ann, 56,131
    Elizabeth, 56,131
    Hannah, 131
    Hannah Ann, 56
    James, 56,131
    James A, 56,131
    Sarah, 131
    Sarah G, 56
    Sarah J, 131
STRICKLER, Elnora, 177
STRIEDEL, Margaret, 57
STRODE, Deborah, 151
    Essie May, 177
    Malinda A (Routh), 177
    Thomas J, 177
STRONG, Corlis H, 56
    Henry, 56
    Louisa, 56
STROUD, Mary Ellen, 65,66
STUARD, Anna, 131
    Bauly, 131
    Mary, 131
    Sarah, 131
    Susannah, 131
    see also **STEWART**, **STUART**
STUART, Absalom/Absolum, 56,131
    Alice E, 131
    Amos, 56,57,131
    Ann/Anna, 56,68,131
    Beauly/Beulah, 56,131
    Benjamin, 56
    Charles, 131
    Cyrus, 56,131
    Edgar, 131

STUART, Eliza, 28,39
    Elizabeth, 56,131
    Florence, 131
    Hannah, 131
    Henry S, 56
    Ithamer, 56,131
    James, 131
    Jehu/Jehue, 56,110,131
    Jehu Jr, 131
    John, 25,56,131
    Jonathan, 131
    Lornhama, 131
    Lula (Crandall), 56
    Mary, 56,131
    Mary (Fulghum), 131
    Mary A, 56,131
    Matilda (Hadley), 57
    Melissa E, 131
    Melissa E (Miles), 56,131
    Ova Grace, 56
    Rachel, 52
    Robert, 56,31
    Samuel, 131
    Sarah, 25,27,56,110,131
    Sarah (Cook), 56
    Sarah (Guyer), 56
    Sarah A, 57
    Sidney/Sydney, 131
    Susanna, 56,110
    Temple, 56,131
    see also **STEWART**, **STUARD**
STUBBS, Albert, 131
    Alden, 56
    Alvan, 131
    Alvaretta/Alveretta, 116,131
    Alvin, 131
    Amy E, 56
    Ann, 131
    Ann (Harvey), 131
    Anna F, 131
    Anna F (Moffett/Moffitt), 56,59,131
    Bessie, 131
    Charlotte, 131
    Della M, 56
    Eli, 56,59,131
    Elisha, 56,131
    Elizabeth, 56,131
    Elizabeth (Townsend), 131
    Elizabeth Ann, 131
    Elvira, 131
    Enoch, 131
    Esther, 56,131
    Esther (Townsend), 131
    Ethel, 131
    Ethel B, 131
    Herbert, 131
    Isaac, 131
    Jesse, 41,131
    John, 131
    John F, 56
    Jonathan, 56,131
    Joseph, 56,131,178
    Joseph H, 131
    Julia, 41
    Katie Rachel, 173
    Kiziah, 14
    Lindley H, 131
    Lydia A, 131
    Lydia H (Grave), 131
    Margaret, 56,57,176
    Margaret M, 133,178
    Maria, 56,131

STUBBS, Maria C, 131
    Mary, 56,95,131
    Mary (Conarre), 56
    Mary (Jones), 41
    Mary Ann/Anna, 56,131
    Mary Emily, 56
    Mary Emma, 131
    Nathan, 131
    Rachel, 50,56,131
    Rachel C, 56
    Rebecca, 131
    Rosanna/Rosannah, 131
    Ruth Emma, 56,59,131
    Samuel, 95
    Sarah, 95,31
    Sarah (Townsend), 131,178
    Susannah, 131
    Thomas, 50
    Verona S R, 50
    Wm, 131
STUDY, A Emma, 155
    Addison, 56
    Alice J (Doan), 56
    David, 208
    Elizabeth, 29
    Ida, 48
    John, 155
    Mahala Ann (Ward), 208
    Martha, 29
    Nancy (Smith), 155
    Nellie, 148
    Wm, 29
    Wm A, 56
STUMP, Katherine, 4
STUPP, Katherine A (Garrison), 56
STYLES, Aaron, 56
    Alfred, 56
    Ernest Wm, 56
    Frona Elizabeth, 56
    George Kermeth, 56
    Luella May, 56
    Sarah, 56
    Sarah Ruth (Robinett), 56
SUFFRINS, Charles, 131
    David, 131
    Deborah, 131
    Harriet, 131
    Harriet (Shute), 131
    John, 131
    John, 56
    Samuel, 131
SUGART, George, 131
    George Zachariah, 131
    Isaiah, 131
    John, 131
SUMNER, Sarah, 131,132,153
SUTON, Helena B, 56
    see also **SUTTON**
SUTTON, Aaron, 56
    Aaron F, 132
    Aaron Franklin, 56
    Ann, 132
    Anna M, 132
    Anne (Moore), 56
    Caroline, 56,132
    Caroline H, 132
    Charles G, 56
    Charles J, 56
    David, 52,56,70,126,132
    Deborah A (White), 52,56
    Deborah W, 126,132
    Elizabeth M, 56

SUTTON, Emeline, 56
    Emeline (Sutton), 56
    Howard, 56,132
    Isaac, 56,132
    John G, 56,132
    Marcia E, 52,56,126,132
    Maria E, 132
    Mary, 70
    Mary (Moore), 56,132
    Mary B, 56,132
    Mary Ellen (Baxter), 56
    Sarah, 132
    Sarah (Underhill), 56
    see also **SUTON**
SWAIN, Alida, 56
    Almira, 177
    Ann E, 23
    Anna, 177,207
    Asenath/Asenith, 161,177,194
    Bethiah, 177
    Charles, 132,208
    Cynthia, 169,170,177
    Cynthia W, 177
    Elihu, 157,161,170,173,177,189,208, 209
    Elihu Jr, 208
    Eliza B, 132
    Eliza Bell, 132
    Eliza M, 177
    Elizabeth, 177,208
    Elizabeth (Rambo), 132
    Ellen, 56
    Ellen S, 46
    Elza/Elzy, 177,208
    Elzena, 56
    Elzena (Williams), 178
    Eunice, 132,189
    Eunice W, 155,177
    George, 177,208
    Hannah, 52,159,173,176,177,210
    Hepsabeth, 101,132
    Ira, 208
    Jethro, 177
    Job, 132,177,208
    John, 177,198,208
    Judith, 132
    Julia, 177,189
    Lindley, 178
    Lorenzo, 177
    Lucinda, 170,177,208
    Lucinda (Maulsby), 178,208
    Lydia, 132,208
    Margret, 177
    Mary, 132,177,208
    Mary (Worth), 161,170,177,208
    Minerva, 184
    Minerva M, 177
    Minnie, 56
    Nathaniel, 177
    Obed, 132,208
    Rachel, 157,177,178,209
    Rachel (Way), 132
    Rebekah, 132
    Rhoda, 155,177,198,205
    Rhoda (Worth), 170
    Rhoda Jane, 178
    Samuel, 177,208
    Sarah, 157,177,194,209
    Sarah (Mills), 173,177,178
    Sarah L, 208
    Sarah L (Leonard), 211
    Silvanus, 155,170,177

SWAIN, Thomas, 132,177,178,208
    Thomas F, 56
    Timothy, 132
    Useba, 177
    Wm F, 178
    Zeno, 132,178,208
    see also **SWAINE**
SWAINE, Francis, 132
    Paul, 132
    see also **SWAIN**
SWALLOW, Lydia, 132
SWARTS, Elizabeth, 132
    see also **SWARTZ**
SWARTZ, Elizabeth, 82
    see also **SWARTS**
SWEARENGEN, Cassie B, 14
    Elenor, 14
    George, 14
SWEET, Ann/Anna, 56,132
    Anna M, 132
    Catharine (Macy), 56
    Catherine, 132
    Charles M, 56
    Eli, 110
    Eli M, 56
    Judith, 56
    Louisa/Louiza Amelia/Emilia, 56,132
    Rebecca/Rebekah, 56,110,132
    Sarah, 56,132
    Solomon, 56,132
SWINDLE, Elizabeth, 40,41
SWINDLER, Elizabeth, 132
    Elizabeth (Ary), 112
SYDELL, Esther, 132
SYKES, Jesse, 179
    Lydia (Elliott), 179
    Sarah, 179
SYMONDS, Samuel, 132
    see also **SIMONS**, **SYMONS**
SYMONS, Abel, 132
    Abigail/Abigial, 115,132
    Abraham, 57,115,132
    Alfred, 57,132
    Alfred H, 178,208
    Anderson, 57,132
    Andrew, 132
    Ann, 57,132
    Ann (Bonine), 132
    Caleb, 56,57
    Eleanor, 132
    Elenor (Longshore), 132
    Elijah, 132
    Elizabeth, 57,132,133
    Elma, 178
    Gulielma, 132
    Hannah, 57,132
    Henry, 57,132
    James, 57,132
    Jane, 132
    Jane (Small), 57
    Jehosaphat, 57
    Jehu, 178
    Jemima H, 132
    Jemimah, 132
    Jesse, 57,132
    Jesse Sr, 132
    John, 57,132
    John M, 57
    Josiah, 57
    Letitia, 57,132
    Lucinda, 57,132
    Lydia, 56,57,132
    Lydia (Hall), 178

SYMONS, Lydia H, 208
    Lydia M, 57
    Margaret, 57,132
    Margaret (Moore), 132
    Mary, 12,29,52,66,77,115,132
    Mathew/Matthew, 115,132
    Nathan, 57,132
    Peninah/Peninnah, 56,132
    Peninah (Bundy), 115
    Peninah (Smith), 57,132
    Phebe, 132
    Rebecca, 132
    Rebecca W, 133
    Samuel, 57
    Sarah, 56,57,115,132
    Thomas, 57,132
    Thomas Jr, 132
    see also **SIMONS**, **SYMONDS**
TAGGART, Alpheus M, 57
    Caroline (Richardson), 57
    Alice, 208
    Earnest L, 57
    India Ora, 57
    Jesse/Jessie, 57,132
    Lydia E, 57,132
    Lydia Ellen, 132
    Melva/Melvia E, 132
    Melvin E, 57
    Miriam, 132
    Phebe, 57,132
    Phebe H, 133
    Samuel, 132
    Samuel A, 57
    Sarah, 132
    Wm, 132
TALBOT, Edward, 132
    Jacob, 8,51,57,132
    Rebecca/Rebeckah/Rebekah, 51,57, 125,132
    Sarah, 6,57
    Susanna/Susannah, 8,51,57
    see also **TALBOTT**
TALBOTT, Ann, 132
    Elisha, 132
    Hannah, 132
    Pamelia, 29
    Phebe, 132
    Susannah, 132
    see also **TALBOT**
TATE, Charlotte, 178,181
    Cynthia Ellen (Beeson), 208
    Elizabeth, 157
    Mariah Louisa, 208
    Octa, 178,208
TAYLOR, Alonzo, 178,208
    Amanda, 132
    Amanda E, 132
    Angeline, 57
    Anna M, 104
    Archibald, 178
    Archie, 208
    Barnabas C, 178
    Benjamin Willard, 178
    Beulah W, 57
    Calvin H, 132
    Charles A, 132
    Charlotte, 57,132
    Clarence J, 132
    David, 11
    Deborah, 18
    Deborah E, 18
    Elisabeth, 57,132,178,208

TAYLOR, Elizabeth B, 132
    Ella, 64
    Elwood, 178
    Frank, 57
    Genetta, 193
    George, 132
    Henry, 178
    Isaac, 57
    Isabelle (Greene), 57
    James, 57,132
    James C, 178
    Jane, 125,132
    Jesse, 18
    Jinnetha, 178
    John, 178,208
    John C, 132
    Joseph, 57
    Joshua, 47
    Laura, 155
    Laura M, 132
    Ledante, 178
    Lewis, 17
    Lewis A, 57,132
    Lillie May (Wolfe), 57
    Lucinda, 178
    Lydia, 208
    Mabel Odell, 178
    Macy M, 178
    Malinda, 178
    Mareb, 178
    Mareb (Beeson), 208
    Martha Ann/Marthanna, 17,47
    Mary, 54,57,133
    Mary Annie, 132
    Mary F, 57
    Mary Lenora (Beeson), 178
    Melissa Jane, 11,63
    Minerva (Hall), 11
    Minerva (Macy), 178
    Naomi, 17,75
    Nathan, 178
    Phebe (Stanton), 57
    Rebecca, 17,178,208
    Rebecca (Covalt), 178
    Sarah E, 132
    Wilson, 178,208
    Wm, 132,208
    Wm E, 132
TEAFORD, George Henry, 57
    Margaret, 57
    Orville J, 57
TEAGLE, Agatha, 16
TEAGUE, Alice, 49,55,62
    Edward Davis/Edwin Dawes, 133
    Edwin, 57,133
    Emma (Rissebron/Rissebrow), 19,60
    Isaac C, 88,133
    Isaac Cooper, 21,22,31,49,57
    Joanna, 88,133
    Joanna (Miles), 31,49
    Joanna M, 133
    Joanna/Johanna M (Miles), 21,22,57
    Laura P, 31,57,133
    Luella/Lula Webb, 133
    Lula, 19,60
    Martha E, 21,57,133
    Martha Elizabeth, 88
    Myrtle, 49,57,133
    Pearl, 57,133
    Prudence, 133
    Prudence (Cooper), 57
    Samuel, 57
    Susannah, 44
    Webster W, 19,60

TEAS, Ann, 133
　Charles, 57,133
　Edward, 133
　Edward S, 57
　Edward Y, 133
　Ellen M, 133
　Frederic, 57
　Gibson, 57,133
　John, 133
　Joseph, 133
　Lizzie Stewart, 133
　Martha, 133
　Mary, 57,133
　Mary M, 57
　Mary Rachel, 133
　Rebecca (Grave), 57,133
　Rebecca J, 133
　Sallie A, 133
　Sarah, 133
　Sarah A (Stuart), 57
　Sarah C, 57,133
　Sarah L, 133
　Sarah S (Hartley), 133
　Thomas A, 133
　Thomas L, 133
　Thomas S, 133
　Vestal H, 57
　Willie S, 57
　Wm S, 133
　see also **TEASE**
TEASE, Edward Y, 133
　Ellen, 133
　Frederick, 133
　Mary, 133
　Sarah, 133
　Thomas, 133
　Wm, 133
　see also **TEAS**
TEGAL, Isabell, 11
TEMPLAR, Alice, 49
　George W, 49
　Hannah (Berriman), 49
TEMPLIN, Elizabeth, 163
TEST, Alice, 133
　Alice, 58
　Almira, 178
　Alpheus, 24,32,57,91,101,144,133
　Anna, 101
　Anna M, 133
　Anna Maria, 32,57
　Annabel (Choclane), 57
　Bertha (Grace), 57
　Carrie, 58
　Charles D, 133
　Charles E, 133
　Charles Sumner, 58
　Chas Darwin, 57
　Cordelia, 176,178,189,206
　Donna M, 133
　Donna Martha (Kelly), 57
　Edna (Moore), 57
　Edward, 57
　Eliza Jane (Baldwin), 178
　Elizabeth, 70,106,133
　Elizabeth (Moffitt), 24,57
　Elizabeth A, 91,101
　Elizabeth A (Moffitt), 133
　Elizabeth M, 133
　Elizabeth M (Pray), 58
　Emily, 133,208
　Emily (Woodard), 58,78
　Emma, 24,57,78,91,194
　Erastus, 57,58,133

TEST, Frederick C, 133
　Frederick Cleveland, 57
　Hanna/Hannah, 133,178,208
　Hannah (Jones), 57,58,133
　Hannah Amelia, 57
　Hannah Mary, 58,133
　Herbert E, 57
　Herbert Erastus, 133
　Irvin, 57,178
　James W, 58,133
　John, 133
　Josiah, 133,178,208
　Lewis A, 133
　Lina E, 57
　Lina Estella, 133
　Lindley M, 57,58
　Louis A, 133
　Louis Agissiz, 57
　Lucile Clemens, 57
　Lydia, 133
　Lydia (Hall), 178
　Lydia H, 133,156,208
　Lydia Symons (Hall), 57
　Margaret (Striedel), 57
　Margaret (Stubbs), 57,176
　Margaret M, 133,208
　Margaret M (Stubbs), 178
　Martha, 58,133
　Martha (Fulghum) Bond Little, 133
　Martha (Little) Bond, 57
　Mary, 133
　Mary (Andrew), 133
　Mary (Taylor), 57,133
　Mary E, 34
　Mary Elisabeth, 57
　Mary Ellen, 178,208
　Mary Lenora, 57,103
　Mary W, 82
　Mattie, 133
　Miriam, 208
　Miriam (Dennis), 57
　Miriam C, 133,178,208
　Miriam C (Dennis), 208
　Oliver, 34,57,58,103,133,178,208
　Phebe, 32
　Phebe (Talbert), 57
　Phebe H, 133
　Rufus, 57,58,133,176,178,208
　Samuel, 57,70,82,106,133,178,208
　Samuel Jr, 57,58,133
　Samuel Sr, 58
　Samuel Edwin, 178,208
　Samuel Francis, 57
　Sarah, 70,82,103,133,208
　Sarah (Dennis), 34,57,178,208
　Sarah (Maxwell), 57,58
　Sarah E (Little) Bond, 57
　Sarah Elma, 57
　Sarah M, 133
　Sarah P (Anthony), 58
　Wilhelmina/Williamenah, 58,133,178
　Wilhelmina Lois, 133
　Will H, 133
　Wm, 58,133,178,208
　Wm H, 58
　Zaccheus/Zacheus, 53,133,178,208
THALLS, Isabel (Pidgeon), 178
　John, 178
THATCHER, Elizaberth (Symons), 133
　Elizabeth, 133
THAY, Minnie, 39
THAYER, David, 40
　Elizabeth, 40
　Elizabeth (Macy), 40

THEIS, Mary, 133
THISTLETHWAITE, Mary, 119
　Mary E, 46
　Rebecca W (Symons), 133
　Sarah (Ratliff), 46
　Timothy, 46
THOMAS, Achsa, 133
　Agnes M, 134
　Agnes Maria (Wickett), 58
　Albert, 134
　Albert Clarence, 58
　Albert R, 58
　Albert W, 178
　Alice, 74,134
　Alice Maud, 134
　Alida C, 134
　Alida C (Miller) Harned Clark, 134
　Amanda C (Ladd), 178
　Ann/Anna, ix,133,134
　Asenath, ix,134
　Benjamin, 133,134
　Benjamin F, 134
　Benjamin Franklin, 58
　Bertha (Elliott), 58
　Bessie, 58,134
　Bessie May, 134
　Betty, 133
　Blanche Elsie, 134
　Carlton, 58
　Charity, 209
　Charity (Mills), 178
　Charles, 133
　Charles E, 58
　Charles W, 134
　Clara E, 17
　Clara M (Chapin), 58
　Clarence, 134
　Cora E, 8,58
　Cynthia, 14,58
　Cyrus, 134
　Daisy May, 134
　Daniel, 133
　Effie M (Zeek), 58
　Elias, 134
　Elihu, 134
　Elijah, 133
　Eliza, 15
　Elizabeth, 62,134
　Elizabeth (Rash), 58
　Elizabeth (Pemberton), 17
　Elizabeth (Strawbridge), 134
　Elizabeth M, 134
　Ellsworth, 58,134
　Elmina (Stanley), 209
　Elmira, 134
　Elsie, 134
　Elvira, ix
　Esther Ann, 52,62,209
　Eva M, 58
　Everett E, 178
　Forest F, 58
　Francis, 133
　Franklin M, 58,134
　George, ix
　Gilbert, 178
　Grace, 134
　Guly, 133
　Hannah, 58,133,134
　Hannah (Cox), 134
　Hendley/Henley/Henly, 58,133
　Herbert, 58,134
　Herbert C, 134
　Herschell E, 58

305

THOMAS, Hiram, 134
    Howard, 134
    Howard D, 134
    Huldah, 58,133
    Isaac, 133
    Isaac H, 134
    James, 58,133
    James P, 134
    Jane, 134
    Jane R, 134
    Jeanette, 58
    Jennie, 58
    Jesse, 58,118,133,134,178
    John, 58,133,134
    Joseph, 17
    Joshua, 134
    Laura A, 58
    Laura Alice, 134
    Lenna M, 58
    Letitia, 134
    Letitia C (Crampton), 58
    Letitia Crampton, 134
    Lewis, 133
    Lincoln, 134
    Luke, 33,133
    Lydia, 58,118,133,134
    Maggie May, 134
    Manlove, 134
    Margaret Jane, 134
    Maria, 58
    Marquis, 58
    Martha, 134
    Martha C, 134
    Martha E, 58
    Martin M, 58
    Mary, 58,113,133,134,141,195
    Mary (Arnold), 178
    Mary (Witchell), 134
    Mary Ann/Maryann/Marianna, 33,36,
      43,133
    Mary Ruth, 178
    Mary T, 36
    Mary T (Green), 58
    Maud, 134
    Mildred (Fulghum), 33
    Milton, 133
    Minerva, 134
    Minerva (Elliott), 58
    Minerva C, 58
    Miriam, 134
    Molly, 133
    Myrtle, 134
    Myrtle Rebecca, 58
    N, 3
    Nancy, 133,134
    Nancy D, 58
    Nanney/Nanny, 58,133
    Nathan H, 178
    Olinda/Olive B, 35,58,134
    Paul, 178
    Peter, 8,14,35,58
    Peter C, 36
    Phebe Ann, 58
    Phebe Ann (Jenkins), 134
    Phebe Ellen (Hewit), 178
    Polley/Polly, 58,118,133
    Priscilla, 8,14,134
    Priscilla E (Cox), 35,58
    Rachel, 133
    Rebecca H, 134
    Richard W, 58
    Robert, 58,134
    Robison, 134

THOMAS, Ross B, 178
    Ruth, 58,209
    Samuel, 133
    Sarah, 133
    Sarah Ann, 134
    Sarah C, 134
    Sarah J (Allen), 178
    Sarah M, 58,134
    Selah, 133
    Sherman, 178
    Simeon, 133,178
    Solomon, 133
    Stephen, 133
    Stephen F, 134
    Susannah, 133
    Uriah, 134
    Wm, 58,134
    Wm Anderson, 58
    Wm B, 58
    Wm Esker, 134
    Wm L, 134
    Wm P, 134
    Wm Pen/Penn, 58,134
    Zephaniah, 58,134
THOMPSON, Abraham, 134
    Ada, 58
    Bessie V, 58
    Charles, 58,134
    Charles W, 134
    Elizabeth, 134
    Francis, 8
    Goldie, 58
    Hannah, 158
    Hannah (Wilson), 58
    James M, 58,134
    John B, 58
    John W, 58
    Joseph Henry, 158
    Louisa M, 89
    Luella Bond, 134
    Luella J, 58
    Mary, 8
    Mary E (Smith), 58
    Melissa, 147
    Minerva, 134
    Minerva W, 134
    Naomi, 8
    Viola, 158,192
    Warren, 58
    see also **THOMSON**
THOMSON, Cora, 134
    James, 134
    Luella, 134
    see also **THOMPSON**
THORN, Anna, 46
    Anna Rosella, 134
    Benjamin, 134
    Edwin J, 134
    Ella A, 134
    Ezra, 134
    see also **THORNE**
THORNBERG, Annetta, 58
    India, 58
    Restore, 58
    see also **THORNBERRY, THORN-
      BOROUGH, THORNBROUGH,
      THORNBURG, THORNBURGH,
      THORNBUROUGH, THORN-
      BURY**
THORNBERRY, Abel, 118,134
    Eliza B, 118
    Joseph, 1

THORNBERRY, Mary Ann, 134
    Rachel, 134
    Rhoda, 118,134
    Susanna, 134
    Wm Johnson, 134
    see also **THORNBERG, THORN-
      BOROUGH, THORNBROUGH,
      THORNBURG, THORNBURGH,
      THORNBUROUGH, THORN-
      BURY**
THORNBOROUGH, Abel, 134
    Elizabeth, 134
    Margaret, 134
    Sarah, 134
    see also **THORNBERG, THORN-
      BERRY, THORNBROUGH,
      THORNBURG, THORNBURGH,
      THORNBUROUGH, THORN-
      BURY**
THORNBROUGH, Elizabeth, 138
    Joseph, 138
    Margaret, 138
    see also **THORNBERG, THORN-
      BERRY, THORNBOROUGH,
      THORNBURG, THORNBURGH,
      THORNBUROUGH, THORN-
      BURY**
THORNBURG, Abbie B (Botkin), 178
    Abel, 58,134
    Ann, 178
    Ann, 187,209
    Anna (Baldwin), 209
    Bertha Lillian, 58
    Coleman, 179,209
    Crozier B, 178
    Cynthia E, 178,183
    Damaris M (Locke), 178
    Demaris (Locke), 209
    Dempsey/Dempsy, 158,159,175,178,
      179,191,209
    Dempsey C, 209
    Dempsey Carver, 178
    Edward, 209
    Effie, 209
    Effie May, 178
    Eleanor, 169,170
    Electa, 209
    Electa (Patterson), 178
    Elihu S, 178
    Eliza, 58
    Elizabeth, 155,179
    Elizabeth (Hunt), 178,209
    Elizabeth M, 209
    Elizabeth Mary (Spradlin), 179,180
    Ella, 209
    Ellen N, 179
    Elmarinda, 179
    Elsie, 179
    Elvin, 178
    Elvin P, 209
    Elvin Pleasant, 178,179,209
    Elwood, 178
    Emily R, 179
    Emma, 209
    Emma Florence, 150,179
    Emma J, 179,180
    Ethalinda L (Williams), 178
    Ethalinda T, 209
    Frank V, 178,209
    George G, 209
    George L, 178
    Harry C, 178
    Henry, 169,178,179,185,187,209
    Henry Jr, 209
    Ida May, 179

THORNBURG, Irena/Irene, 8,152,156,158,
    161,178,191,209
  James Riley, 178
  Jane, 191
  Jane (Mills), 158,159,175,178,179
  Janetta/Jeanette, 134
  Jesse, 179,209
  Joab, 209
  Job, 209
  John, 157,175,178,179,209
  John H, 209
  John Henry, 150,179,209
  John M, 58
  John R, 179
  Jonathan, 179
  Joseph, 134,179
  Joseph W, 179,209
  Julia (Gwin), 178
  Julia Ann, 209
  Julia Ann (Gwin), 179
  Larkin, 179,209
  Larkin W, 179
  Laurence D, 179
  Lenora F, 179
  Lewis, 179,209
  Lewis Marion, 179
  Lillian, 134
  Lindon H, 209
  Lorenzo, 179,209
  Lucinda Ann, 179
  Lydia, 58,134,209
  Lydia (Howell), 209
  Lydia (Macy), 179,209
  Lydia Ellen, 209
  Lydia J, 19,45
  Macy M, 179
  Madison, 179,209
  Margaret (Beeson), 209
  Martha Ann, 209
  Martha E, 168,178
  Martha Ellen, 189
  Mary, 178,179,209
  Mary A (Foutz), 179
  Mary A (Locke), 175
  Mary Ann/Maryann, 58,184
  Mary Ann (Locke), 150,179
  Mary Eliza, 178
  Mary Jane, 178,179,200,207,209
  Milton, 209
  Milton Erwin, 178
  Nancy (Maulsby), 169
  Nathan, 209
  Nellie, 175,179
  Orlando, 179,209
  Orlistus Winston, 178
  Ottawa, 178
  Peggy, 209
  Phebe, 209
  Rachel, 32,58,159,178,185,187,190,
    191,209
  Rachel (Swain), 157,158,209
  Rachel E, 209
  Rachel R, 179,180
  Rebecca, 134,179
  Rebecca Ann, 134
  Rhoda, 58
  Richard, 134
  Sarah, 134,178,207
  Sarah (Foland), 58
  Sarah (Reynolds), 209
  Sarah Bernice 19
  Sarah E, 10,17,191
  Sarah Emeline, 178
  Sarah/Sarrah Jane, 178,192

THORNBURG, Seth, 178,179,209
  Sophia, 185
  Sophia B, 179
  Surelda (Harris), 179
  Susan, 202,209
  Thomas, 209
  Thomas E, 209
  Thomas Elwood, 179
  Walter, 134,178,179,209
  Walter M, 179,209
  Walter R, 178
  Wilson, 209
  Wilson H, 178
  Wm, 58,134,209
  Wm R, 178,179,180,209
  Zarilda/Zerelda/Zerilda Ann, 158,175,
    178,199
  see also **THORNBERG, THORN-
    BERRY, THORNBOROUGH,
    THORNBROUGH, THORN-
    BURGH, THORNBUROUGH,
    THORNBURY**
THORNBURGH, Electa, 209
  Elizabeth, 134
  Elizabeth Mary (Spradlin), 147
  Ellen N, 147
  Elvin Pleasant, 209
  Hannah, 134
  Henry, 134
  John, 134
  Joseph, 134
  Lydia, 134
  Milton, 134
  Ottie, 209
  Rachel, 166
  Rebecca, 134
  Rebecca Ann, 134
  Rhoda, 134
  Richard, 134
  Sarah, 134
  Sarah (Charles), 134
  Unice, 134
  Walter, 134
  Walter R, 209
  Wm, 134
  Wm R, 147
  see also **THORNBERG, THORN-
    BERRY,THORNBOROUGH,
    THORNBROUGH, THORN-
    BURG, THORNBUROUGH,
    THORNBURY**
THORNBUROUGH, Lydia, 134
  Rhoda, 134
  see also **THORNBERG, THORN-
    BERRY, THORNBOROUGH,
    THORNBROUGH, THORN-
    BURG, THORNBURGH,
    THORNBURY**
THORNBURY, Abel, 117
  Lydia J, 117
  Rhoda, 117
  see also **THORNBERG, THORNB-
    ERRY, THORNBOROUGH,
    THORNBROUGH, THORN-
    BURG, THORNBURGH,
    THORNBUROUGH**
THORNE, Allen Haines, 46,58
  Anna Mary, 46
  Benjamin, 134
  Edwin J, 134
  Elizabeth, 34
  Ezra, 134
  Hannah, 30

THORNE, Ida, 46,58
  John, 34
  Josephine, 134
  Levi, 134
  Levi E, 134
  Mary, 114,134
  Mary T, 42
  Minnia, 58
  Ollie M, 58
  Rachel, 10
  Ruth, 134
  Ruth (Greene), 42
  Ruth H, 46,58
  Thos, 42
  Wm C, 134
  Wm G, 134
  see also **THORN**
THORNTON, Abiah, 134
  Anna E, 20
  Caturah, 134
  Eleanor, 134
  Eli, 134,135
  Elizabeth, 134
  Jane S (Beard), 135
  John, 20
  Mary, 134
  Rebecca, 134
  Rosa E, 20
  Sarah, 134
  Susanna, 167
  Uriah, 134
THREEWITS, Lydia, 38
THURSTON, Catherine, 12
TIBBETTS, Abigail (Roberts), 58
  Charles Albert, 58
  Charles Edwin, 58
  Edith Mary, 58
  Herbert Edwin, 58
  Imelda A (Painter), 58
  J Walter, 58
  Mary H (Dean), 58
  Philip, 58
TICE, Margaretta (Reynolds), 135
TILSON, Anna (Melbert), 179
  Isaac F, 179
  Luther, 135
TIMBERLAKE, Alfred, 7,135
  Amelia, 135
  Ann Eliza, 135
  Anna E, 7,135
  Aquilla, 12
  Arthur, 135
  Benjamin B, 58,59
  Catherine, 135
  Edward, 58,59,135
  Eliza D, 12,78
  Jonathan, 135
  Martha, 135
  Martha (Brown), 58
  Martha N (Brown), 59,135
  Mary, 135
  Mary O (Floyd), 58
  Matilda, 135
  Phebe, 7,135
  Phebe (Dean), 12
  Rebecca, 135
  Sarah Matilda, 135
  Susannah E, 135
TIMONS, Emanuel, 135
  John, 135

TINKLE, Blanch Amy, 179
    Catharine (Hughes), 179
    Clifford, 209
    Cordelia Maud, 179
    Eunice Marie, 179
    Harvey, 209
    Jesse Luther, 179
    Rebecca Ann (Smith), 179
    Samuel, 179
    Samuel Clifford, 179
    Sarah, 154,155
    Wm Harvey, 179
TITSWORTH, A D, 135
    Abraham, 59
    Abraham D, 59,135
    Frederic F/H, 59
    Hellen Bills, 59
    Marey/Mary E, 59,135
    Mary E (Harrison), 135
    Mary Elizabeth/Emily (Harrison), 26,93
    Mary R, 135
TODD, Louise, 32
TOLBERT, Rachel, 39
TOMS, Elizabeth (Henby), 59
    Elizabeth W, 135
    Elmira, 59
    John, 59
    Joseph, 59,135
    Linville, 59
    Maud, 59,135
    Wm Henry, 59,135
TONEY, Alice (Davenport), 59
    Sarah Jane, 135
TOOKER, Emily H, 59
TOWEL, Caleb Harvey, 13
    Henry, 135
    Rebecca, 13
    Sarah, 13
TOWNSEND, Amos, 59,135
    Anna (French), 59
    Barbara, 2,135
    Catherine, 135
    Celah, 59
    Charlotte, 59
    Cicily, 135
    Cicily (Johnson), 135
    Daniel, 59,135
    Elcy, 80
    Eli, 59,135
    Elivana, 58
    Eliza Ann, 59
    Elizabeth, 2,131,135
    Elizabeth (Edgerton), 179
    Elizabeth (Morrow), 59,135
    Elvira, 3,59,65,131,135,181
    Emily Jane, 27
    Emma Spencer, 135
    Esther, 59,131
    Francis, 59
    Harvey, 59,179
    Hester, 2
    James, 1,59
    Jesse C, 59
    John, 1,2,3,59,80,131,135,179
    John C, 63
    John Jr, 135
    John M, 59
    Johnathan/Jonathan, 2,59,135
    Josiah, 135
    Laura J, 63
    Lydia, 42,59,114
    Mahlon, 59,135
    Marietta, 63

TOWNSEND, Mary, 2,14,59,80,135
    Mary A, 59
    Nancy, 135
    Olive, 59
    Olive Jane (Stevens)
    Rachel, 59
    Rebecca, 59,135
    Rosanna (Smith), 59
    Sarah, 2,59,115,131,135,178
    Selah, 3
    Sina, 135
    Stephen, 59,135
    Thomas, 59
    Wm, 59,135
    Wm Sr, 135
    Wm John, 2
TRACY, Catharine (Mikesell), 59
    John, 59
TREFFINGER, Ada B (Williams), 59
    John F, 59
TROGGETT, Sarah M (Bond), 59
TRUBLOOD, Abigail, 135
    Betsy, 135
    Elizabeth, 135
    Isabel, 135
    Margaret, 135
    Miriam, 135
    Mourning, 135
    Peggy, 135
    see also **TRUEBLOOD**
TRUEBLOOD, Almeda (Baldwin), 59
    Almeda F, 135
    Almeda P (Finney), 59
    Alpheus, 59
    Alva, 59
    Amy L, 59
    Benjamin, 135
    Bessie, 135
    Betty, 93
    Caleb, 135
    Charles Kingsley, 59
    Edwin P, 59,135
    Elias, 59
    Elizabeth (Kelley), 59
    Ephraim, 135
    Ephraim Overman, 135
    Esther (Parker), 59
    Francis, 59
    Herschel J, 59
    Howard Moffitt, 59
    Inez, 59
    Isabella, 108
    James, 135
    Jehu, 59
    Jonathan, 135
    Joseph, 135
    Joshua, 59
    Josiah, 135
    Lancaster, 135
    Laura Bessie, 59
    Louisa (Pritchard), 59
    Miriam, 135
    Peggy, 135
    Penina (Henley), 59
    Pennina H, 135
    Ralph Waldo, 59
    Ruth Emma (Stubbs), 59
    Virgil, 59,135
    Walter L, 59,135
    Wilford S, 59
    Wm, 135
    Wm Josiah, 135
    Wm N, 59,135
    see also **TRUBLOOD**

TRUCKNESS, Ann/Anna, 3
    Fred, 3
TUCKER, Caroline, 135
    Caroline (Maxwell), 135
    Caroline M, 135
    Eva Estella, 135
    Lillie F, 55
    Mary B, 13
    Mary (Maxwell), 135
    Orville Hugh, 135
    Roland/Rollin, 135
    Ruth Elizabeth, 135
TURNER, Caroline, 59
    Elijah H, 59
    Elmer, 59
    Estella, 59
    Harry E, 59
    Jane, 173
    John, 59
    Margaret E, 59
    Nettie B (Stingley), 59
    Noble E, 59
    Orville Hugh, 59
    Rollin, 59
    Ruth Elizabeth, 59
TUTTLE, Dorothy, 59
    Henry F, 59
    Nellie (Clark), 59
TYLER, Ann Elizabeth, 114
    Charles Henry, 59,135
    John, 44,116
    Joseph, 59,135
    Joseph S, 135
    Joseph Sparkes, 135
    Martha, 36
    Martha J, 44,114,116,135
    Phebe M, 44,116
    Sally, 135
    Sarah (Ennis), 59,135

ULLRICK, Frederick/Fredrick, 18,47,59
    Josephine, 47,59
    Laura F, 17,18,59
    Urilla (Schaffer/Shaffer), 18,47,59
    see also **ULRICH**
ULRICH, Elizabeth, 162
    see also **ULLRICK**
UMBERHOWER, Cora, 135
    John, 135
UNDERHILL, Alexander E, 59
    Alfred, 179,209
    Alfred C, 179,209
    Alfred M, 135
    Anna, 179,209
    Anna (Murphey), 209
    Anna Jane, 179,209
    Armina, 179
    Belinda, 179
    Clarkson, 179,209
    Edward D, 209
    Edward F, 59,179
    Elvira, 179
    Emily, 179
    Emma, 135,209
    Emma Arminta, 179
    Hannah, 179,106
    Ida (Miller), 179
    Indiana (Miller), 59
    Jane, 179,200,206
    Jane W, 16,59
    Jennie, 190
    Jesse B, 16,59,135,209

UNDERHILL, Jesse Butlar/Butler, 179
    John, 135,179,206,209
    John E, 179
    John M, 59,179,209
    Juliana, 179
    Lemuel, 179,209
    Mary, 179
    Olive Sylphia, 59
    Sarah, 56,135,209
    Susan (Bowers), 16,59,179
UNDERWOOD, Amy, 105,136
    Barclay, 136
    Deborah, 136
    Eliza, 136
    Harriet, 136
    Israel, 136
    John, 136
    Mary, 136
    Naomi, 136
UNTHANK, Albert, 60
    Alice, 136
    Anna, 60,136
    Annie E, 60
    Betsy, 60,136
    Beulah, 17,60,61,63,66
    Charles B, 136
    Charles R, 52,59
    Drucilla/Drusilla A, 50,123
    Elizabeth, 13,41,60,79,136
    Florence, 52,60,136
    Frank, 60
    James, 41
    John, 60,39,136
    John Allen, 60,136
    Jonathan, 60,136
    Joseph, 13,23,60,63,79,90,91,136,140
    Leveicy/Levicy, 60,136
    Mahala/Mahalah, 91,136
    Mary, 60,136
    Mary E, 136
    Mary E (Whitacre), 52,59
    Pleasant, 59,60,136
    Rachel, 136
    Rachel (Williams), 136
    Rebecca/Rebeckah/Rebekah, 41,60, 63,79,90,91,136
    Rebecca (Hiatt), 50
    Rebecca (Stanley), 13,23,60
    Sally, 60,136
    Sarah, 23,60,90,136
    Sarah Ann, 136
    Sarah Ann (Pitts), 59
    Susan B (Reed), 136
    Wm, 50,136
    Wm A, 60
    Wm H, 136
    Wm S, 136
UPTON, Samuel, 209
    Samuel G, 209
UTTER, Dora, 60
    George, 60
    Glen, 60
    Mattie E (Allison), 60
    Minnie, 60
    Phebe, 60
    Walter F, 60

VALE, Caroline, 83
VALENTINE, Ann/Anna/Annie, 60,125,136
    Cornelia, 60,136
    Edward J, 60

VALENTINE, Fletcher E, 60
    George, 136
    Georgiana/Georgianna, 60,136
    Gulielma, 60,136
    Harriett A (Morrill), 60
    John, 60,125,136
    Joseph Edward, 60
    Martha, 60,125,136
    Warren P, 60
    Wm H, 60,136
    Wm Henry, 60,136
VANCE, B H, 30
    Elizabeth, 4,30
    Jennie C, 30
VAN ETTAN, Bertha, 136
    Daniel, 136
    Daniel Jr, 136
    Earl, 136
    Edward, 136
    Florence, 136
    Wm, 136
    see also **VAN ETTEN**
VAN ETTEN, Bertha A, 136
    Daniel J, 136
    Daniel L, 136
    Edward C, 136
    Florence, 136
    Herbert, 136
    Herbert H, 136
    Wm W, 136
    see also **VAN ETTAN**
VAN HORN, Betsy, 112,118
    James, 210
VAN MATRE, Sarah, 162
VANSANT, Mary, 136
    see also **VAN ZANT**
VANSCHOIACH, Leonard, 136
    see also **VANSCHOICK**
VANSCHOICK, Isaac, 136
    see also **VANSCHOIACH**
VAN ZANT, Biba, 12
    Catherine (Thurston), 12
    Elizabeth, 12
    Mary M, 136
    see also **VANSANT**
VARDAMAN, Mary (Davis), 179
    Mollie Elnora, 179
    Wm, 179
VARNEY, Rachel, 4
    Wm H, 136
VAZEY, Mary E (Williams), 60
VEAL, Cynthia, 210
    Cynthia (Cox), 179
    Emma Bell, 152
VENARD, Ruth, 136
VERE, Mary, 72
VEREGEE, Dora, 60
    Frank, 60
    Dora, 136
    Frank H, 136
    see also **VEREGGEE**
VEREGGEE, Anna, 61
    Mary, 52
    see also **VEREGEE**
VESTAL, Betty, 84
    Elisabeth/Elizabeth, 99
    Ira, 99
    Jemima, 84
    John, 99
    Mary, 84,99
    Rachel, 84,99
    Samuel, 136

VICKERS, Christine, 136
    Edwin, 136
    Edwin Nixon, 136
    Isaac M, 136
    Martha, 31,41
    Matilda, 136
    Thomas, 136
    Victor, 136
VINCENT, Christene (Carter), 46
    Germaine, 46
    Grace (Parry), 136
    Olive M, 46
VINING, Alice, 41
VORE, Albert, 136
    Alice, 60
    Ann/Anne, 136
    Azel, 60,136
    Bell E, 60
    Deborah (Underwood), 136
    Eliza, 136
    Elizabeth, 60,136
    Elizabeth (Lamb), 136
    Elmer E, 60
    Eva J, 60
    Gilbert, 136
    Inez, 60
    Isaac, 136
    Isaac L, 60
    Israel C, 136
    Jacob, 136
    Jacob Jr, 136
    John, 60,136
    Martha Jane, 60
    Mary, 136
    Mary Jr, 136
    Mary Jane, 60,136
    Nellie S, 60
    Othello, 60
    Phinehas, 136
    Ruth, 136
    Sadie (Hodgin), 60
    Sarah, 136
    Sarah Ann, 60
    Tacy, 60,136
    Thomas, 136
    Vernon W, 60
    see also **VORES**
VORES, James, 179
    James M, 179
    Mary J (Davis), 179
    see also **VORE**, **VORIS**
VORIS, James, 210
    see also **VORES**
VOSS, Anna A, 60
    Annie K, 136
    Blanch/Blanche, 60,136
    Carl L, 60,136
    Clarence S, 60,136
    Michael F, 136
    Michael T, 60
    Pearl A, 60,136
VALENTINE, Anna M, 136
    Anna Maria (Hiatt), 60
    Clarence G, 60
    Daniel, 136
    Elizabeth, 136
    Elizabeth (Hampton), 60
    Ida, 136
    Ida M, 60
    Isaac, 60,136
    Jonathan, 60,136
    Mary, 136
    Sarah, 6,119

WADE, Belle H, 136
WADMAN, Charles, 179
    Elizabeth, 159
    Hannah (Swain), 210
    Jane (Elliott), 179
    Sarah (Sykes), 179
    Wm H, 179
WAGGONER, Martha, 65
    see also **WAGNER**
WAGNER, Hannah, 136
    Mary E (Charles), 179
    Robert, 179
    see also **WAGNER**
WAKEFIELD, Charlotte W, 136
    Jennie, 60,136
    Jennie C, 136
    Joseph J, 60,136
    Mary A, 136
    Mary Ann, 60
WALDO, Henry Clay, 60
    Nancy Ann (Bell), 60
    Ruth, 60
WALKER, Agustus, 18
    Calvin B, 60,136
    Cornelia, 136
    Elisabeth P, 136
    Eliza, 18
    Eliza (Walker), 18
    Eliza A, 136
    Eliza Ann, 60,136
    Elizabeth, 60,136
    James C, 60
    John S, 60
    Josephine, 18
    Lewis/Louis C, 60,136
    Martha J, 136
    Martha Jane, 60,136
    Naomi C, 136
    Sarah, 136
    Sarah (Clawson), 60
    Sarah C, 60
WALL, Charles, 60
    Jane E, 60
    Mabel, 60
WALLACK, David, 60,136
    Sarah, 60,136
WALLAS, Annie E, 116
    Elizabeth, 116
    Samuel, 116
WALLON, Henry, 136
    James, 136
WALTER, Daisy Dale, 179
    Elizabeth (Stephens), 179
    Ida M (Abshire), 179
    Roscoe S, 179
    Samuel, 179
    Venus A, 179
    see also **WALTERS**
WALTERS, Belle, 60,137
    Bertha, 48
    Laura M (Bolender), 60
    Mary, 137
    Wm, 60,137
    see also **WALTER**
WALTHALL, Jane, 165
WALTON, Betty, 55
    George Franklin, 137
    Opal, 137
    Phebe, 130
    Rebecca (Wright), 137
WALTZ, Edward, 179
    Elmer, 179
    Lena, 210
    Mary Ann (Heller), 179

WAMPLER, Jacob B, 60
    Joshua M, 60
    Rachel E, 60
WAND, Ellen J D, 60
    Florence E, 60
    Patrick, 60
WANZER, Emily, 41
    Michael, 41
WARD, Almina/Almira Jane, 60,137
    Bell, 19
    Christena M (Brown), 179
    Cyrus, 179
    Deborah, 137
    Edgar J, 19,60
    Elizabeth, 137
    Elizabeth (Edgerton), 137
    Elizabeth A, 60,137
    Elizabeth N, 60
    Enos, 137
    Eunice (Howes), 19
    Florence E, 137
    Florence G, 60
    Grace, 60
    George, 210
    George F, 179,210
    Hannah, 137
    Hattie, 179
    Isaac, 137
    Isaiah, 137
    Jacob M, 60
    James, 19
    Joshua, 180
    Josiah, 137
    Keziah, 12,13,27
    Laura A, 150,179
    Laura Ann, 210
    Leona A, 179
    Lida A, 210
    Lida Alice, 179
    Lizzie N, 137
    Lula (Teague), 19,60
    Lula W, 137
    Mahala Ann, 208
    Mahala Ann (Wright), 180,210
    Manual, 180
    Margaret C, 19,20,210
    Martha C, 60
    Mary, 8,179,203,206,210
    Mary T, 60,137
    Obed, 180,203,206,210
    Orvill/Orville P, 60,137
    Patience, 210
    Rachel, 203
    Richard G, 137
    Sapphira, 137
    Sophia, 137
    Susanna, 12,206
    Timothy, 180,210
    Triall, 180
    Wm, 180
WARDER, Carrie D (Newcomb/
    Newcombe), 60,137
    James, 60
WARE, Lucia, 62
WAREHAM, Eliza, 33
WARING, Emma, 60,137
    Gertrude, 61
    Gertrude L, 137
    Percival, 61,137
    Semira H, 61,137
    Wm P, 60,137
    see also **WHARING**

WARNER, Ella, 61,137
    Faircomb H, 137
    Fairlamb Harrison, 61
    Harrison, 137
    Harvey, 137
    Rebecca, 137
    Rebecca P, 61,137
WARREN, Andrew L, 137
    Azariah, 137,210
    Daniel, 137
    David, 137
    Henry, 137,210
    Hoover, 137
    James, 137,210
    James Jr, 137
    John, 137
    Margaret, 137
    Mary, 137
    Rachel, 137
    Sarah, 137,210
    Seth, 210
    Susanna, 137
    Tabitha, 89,137
    Wm Stewart, 137
    Zina, 137
    see also **WARRIN**
WARRIN, May, 137
    Rachel, 137
    Susan, 137
    see also **WARREN**
WASBURN, Helena, 137
    see also **WASHBURN**,
        WASHBURNE
WASHBURN, Esther, 137
    John, 137
    Maria D, 137
    Paul, 137
    Paul V, 137
    Winifred, 137
    see also **WASBURN, WASHBURNE**
WASHBURNE, Esther, 61
    Florence, 61
    John, 61
    Maria (Dickinson), 61
    Paul Valens, 61
    Winefred, 61
    see also **WASBURN, WASHBURN**
WASHUM, Rebecca (Marmon), 137
WASON, Asenath, 137
    Charlotte, 137
    Jehiel, 137
    Jesse, 137
    Nancy, 137
    see also **WASSON**
WASSON, Abigail, 61
    Ansalem/Anselm, 61,137
    Archibald, 61,137
    Asenath, 137
    Calvin, 61,37
    Charlotte, 137
    Elisabeth, 137
    Eliza, 61,137
    Elizabeth, 137
    Elizabeth, 61,137
    Jehiel, 61,137
    Jesse, 137
    Joseph, 61
    Lydia (Bond), 137
    Macamey/Macamy, 61,137
    Mary, 61
    Mary (Bond), 137
    Nancy, 137
    Nathan, 61

WASSON, Ruth (Clark), 137
    Sally, 61
    Sarah, 61
    Wm, 61
    see also **WASON**
WATKINS, Rachel, 137
    Sarah (Antrum), 210
WATSON, Arthur, 61
    Arthur Lewis, 137
    Catherine (Hoover), 137
    Charles C, 61
    David A, 137
    Edgar, 137
    Edna, 61
    Elizabeth, 54,61,137
    Emily, 61
    Frank E, 61
    Franklin L, 61
    Franklin S, 137
    Hannah, 54,61,137
    Harmon C, 61,137
    Ho, 137
    Ida, 137
    Ida Ho, 61
    Idell, 61,137
    James, 54,61,137
    Jane, 61,137
    Josephine, 61
    Lake, 137
    Lake/Late G, 61,137
    Leah, 61
    Lewis, 61
    Lizzie B, 137
    Lizzie Bell, 61
    Lydia A, 137
    Lydia Ann (Overman) Showan, 61
    Lydia Ann (Showan), 137
    Mary, 61
    Mary Joseph, 137
    Wm, 61,137
WATT, Irene, 137
    see also **WATTS**
WATTER, Betty, 61
    Draper, 61
    Mary, 61
WATTS, Ann P, 37
    Leotha, 61
    Martha (Lundy), 61
    Newton, 61
    Tilly, 61
    see also **WATT**
WAY, Alice (Hiatt), 137
    Anna Louisa, 137
    Anthony, 137
    Charlotta/Charlotte, 137
    David L, 137
    Esther, 137
    Hannah, 137
    Henry, 15,137
    Henry H, 137
    Hiram, 137
    Huldah, 61,137
    Joel, 137
    Jonathan, 137
    Joseph, 137
    Lydia, 137
    Manlove, 137
    Martha, 137
    Mary, 74,137
    Mary Ann/Maryann, 137
    Millicent, 137
    Narcissa, 15,137

WAY, Obed, 137
    Rachel, 132,137
    Rebecca, 137
    Rhoda/Rodah, 61,137
    Robert, 137
    Sarah, 137
    Seth, 137
    Thomas, 137
    Wm, 137
WEAKS, Benjamin, 137
    James, 137
    John, 137
    Ralph, 137
    Wm, 137
    see also **WEEKS**
WEATHERALD, Henry, 137
    see also **WEATHERALL**,
        WETHERALD
WEATHERALL, Henry, 137
    see also **WEATHERALD**,
        WETHERALD
WEAVER, Emma J, 210
    Emma J (Thornburg), 180
    Fannie, 64
    George, 180
    John, 180
    Rachel, 210
    Rachel R (Thornburg), 180
WEBB, Alice C, 61,137
    Anna (Vereggee), 61
    Benjamin, 61,137
    Elizabeth A (Hodgson), 61
    John Richard, 61
    Lewis, 61
    Mary Edith, 61
    Rena, 61
    Robert W, 137
    Robert Williams, 61
    Sarah (Williams), 61,137
    Sarah W, 137
    Wm, 61
WEBER, Bessie, 180
    Charles, 180
    Sarah (Hoover), 180
WEBSTER, Ella/Allen M, 61,138
    Hubert, 138
    James, 4
    Joseph, 210
    Linda Myra, 210
    Myra, 210
    Rachel (Varney), 4
    Rilla, 4
    Taylor, 138
WEEKLY, A V, 61
    Charles Luther, 61
    Mary L, 61
WEEKS, Ann/Anna/Anne, 61,91,138
    Benjamin, 61,138
    Caroline M, 138
    Caroline M (Clark), 19,61
    Casandra/Cassandra, 61,138
    Cassandra/Cassie M, 138,140
    Charles L, 61,138
    Cora M, 61,138
    Frank W, 61,138
    George F, 138
    Hanna E, 138
    Hannah Eliza, 138
    Harry D, 138
    James, 61,138,140
    Jane, 61,91,138
    John, 61,91,138

WEEKS, John W, 19,61
    John Wesley, 61,138
    Lois, 61
    Louisa, 19,61,138
    Lydia, 61,93,138
    Margaret, 138
    Margaret (Thornbrough), 138
    Mary E, 61,138
    Merrick C, 61,138
    Minnie C, 61
    Minnie E, 138
    Nathan, 61
    Rachel, 61
    Rachel H, 138
    Ralph, 61,138
    Ray, 138
    Ray C, 61
    Reuben, 61
    Ruth Anna, 61,140
    Samuel, 61
    Susan G, 138
    Susanna/Susannah, 61,138
    Wm, 61,138
    see also **WEEKS**
WEHR, Anna, 61
    Chris, 61
    Lilian, 61
WEISNOR, Abigail, 105
WELLER, Grace R (Dilks), 61
WELSH, John, 138
    John H, 138
    Martha, 138
WERKING, Hannah, 158,181
WERNER, Anna, 52,138
    Dorothy (Schlereth), 52
    Joseph, 52
WERTS, Flora, 36
    Jacob, 36
    Louisa (Nelson), 36
    Rebecca, 36
WEST, Gladys, 61
    Mary, 61,138
    Mary (Benbow), 138
    Raymond, 61
    Wm, 61,138
WESTCOMBE, Charles F, 61
    Charles Trusted, 138
    Elizabeth, 138
    Priscilla, 61
    Priscilla (White), 138
    Samuel Thompson, 138
WETHERALD, Hannah J, 138
    Hannah Jane, 138
    see also **WEATHERALD**,
        WETHERALL
WEYL, Jemima, 210
    Martha, 173
WHARING, Semira H, 138
    see also **WARING**
WHEAT, Jane, 49
WHEELER, Keziah, 138
    Lela, 20
    Mary P, 138
WHETZEL, Rosella (Showalter), 61
WHINERY, Adelaide, 62
    Alpheus, 61
    Enos, 61
    Henry, 61
    James, 61
    Mary, 61
    Oliver M, 62
    Thomas, 210
    see also **WHINNERY**

WHINNERY, Adelaide, 138
    Adeline, 138
    Alpheus, 138
    Arthur, 138
    Enos, 138
    Eva, 138
    Henry, 138
    James, 138
    Mary, 138
    Oliver M, 138
    see also **WHINERY**
WHITACRE, ——, 42
    Aquilla, 138
    Bethele/Bethula/Bethulah/Bethuly, 62,138
    Christopher, 138
    Dora (Brumfield), 62
    Elizabeth, 138
    Ellen, 24
    Ephraim, 138
    James, 62
    James M, 62
    Jess/Jesse, 62
    John, 62,138
    John M, 6
    Jonathan, 138
    Jonathan R, 62
    Joseph, 24,138
    Joseph Jonathan, 138
    Levi, 138
    Lilian H, 24
    Louis, 138
    Louisa, 62
    Mamie, 62
    Margaret, 62
    Margaret H, 6
    Martha, 62,138
    Martha (White), 62
    Mary, 138
    Mary A, 31
    Mary Ann, 62,138
    Mary E, 52,59
    Milton, 59
    Milton H, 62,138
    Patience, 138
    Phebe, 62
    Philip, 62
    Rachel, 138
    Rachel (Smith), 6
    Rebecca, 87,138
    Robert, 138
    Ruth, 62
    Rhoda, 32
    Ruth Anna, 138
    Ruthanna (Potts), 138
    Samuel, 138
    Sarah, 62,138
    Sarah (Bakehorn), 59
    Sarah (Roberds), 138
    Susannah, 138
    Wm, 62,138
    see also **WHITAKER**
WHITAKER, John, 138
    Jonathan, 138
    Jonathan R, 138
    Joseph, 138
    Lewis, 138
    Louisa, 138
    Mary Ann, 103,138
    Milton H, 138
    Samuel, 138
    Sarah, 103,138

WHITAKER, Wm, 103,103
    Wm, 138
    see also **WHITACRE**
WHITAL, Hannah, 128
    see also **WHITALL**
WHITALL, Alice, 128
    Hannah, 128
    see also **WHITAL**
WHITE, ——, 64
    Aaron, 56
    Albert F, 62
    Alice, 62,138,139
    Alice (Clawson), 62
    Angelina, 62
    Angeline H, 139
    Anna, 138
    Anna C, 138
    Anna T, 139
    Anna T (Steddom), 62
    Annie (Richie), 139
    Benjamin, 138
    Benjamin M, 62,139
    Caroline, 139
    Charles, 62,138
    Charles A, 139
    Charles S, 62,138,139
    Daisy (Barnet), 62
    David, 62
    David F, 62,139
    David Francis, 62
    Davis, 180
    Deborah A, 52,56
    Dililah (Boswell), 138
    Ed, 62
    Edgar F, 139
    Edgar T, 180
    Edith, 62,139
    Edmund, 138
    Edwin J, 139
    Eliza, 70,138
    Eliza W, 139
    Elizabeth, 13,17,27,28,50,61,138
    Elizabeth (Hough), 62
    Elizabeth (Richie), 138
    Elizabeth (White), 62
    Elizabeth (Wilson), 55,62
    Elizabeth Ann, 138
    Elizabeth Ann (Pool), 138
    Elizabeth Anna (Lloyd), 62
    Elizabeth H, 62,139
    Elizabeth S (Richie), 62
    Ellen Alice, 62
    Ellen S, 139
    Ellis C, 139
    Ellis Clinton, 62
    Esther G, 139
    Esther Griffin, 62
    Esther M, 139
    Esther Mary, 62,139
    Eynone, 62
    George, 62
    George Alexander, 62
    Hannah, 70,138
    Hannah Amelia, 138
    Hannah Amelia (Coffin), 138
    Hannah D, 139
    Hannah H (Dilks), 139
    Hannah H Jr (Dilks), 62
    Hannah J, 30
    Harriet/Harriett, 20,89
    Harry B, 62,139
    Hattie P, 62

WHITE, Helen D, 139
    Helen Dora, 62,139
    Henry E, 62,139
    J Edwin, 62,139
    J Seldon, 139
    James Smith, 139
    James T, 138
    Jane (Boswell), 138
    Jesse, 5,138
    Joel, 138
    John, 45,70,117,138
    John T, 138
    Joseph, 62,139
    Joseph Jr, 139
    Joseph C, 62,139
    Joseph Selden, 62
    Josiah T, 55,62,139
    Josiah T Jr, 62,139
    K T, 64
    Lettisha, 138
    Lewis, 138
    Louisa Gazzeal, 180
    Louise/Louisa Winifred, 20,62
    Lucia (Ware), 62
    Lucinda, 52
    Lydia, 5,39
    Lydia (Parker), 62
    Lydia F, 139
    Lydia Florence, 62,139
    M Caroline, 139
    Madison, 62
    Marcia, 56
    Margaret, 56,138
    Margaret Susan, 95
    Marian/Marion E, 62,139
    Martha, 62
    Mary, 14,34,45,62,64,117,138
    Mary (Albertson), 5
    Mary (White), 45
    Mary A, 62,139
    Mary A (White), 62
    Mary Abigail, 139
    Mary Alice, 62
    Mary B (Johnson), 62
    Mary B J, 139
    Mary Caroline, 139
    Mary Caroline (Cotton), 20,62
    Mary I, 139
    Mary J (Jarrett), 62
    Mary Jarrett, 139
    Mary S, 117,138
    Mary U, 139
    Maurice W, 62
    Millicent H, 5
    Milton, 138
    Miriam, 139
    Miriam (Chamness), 180
    Miriam E, 139
    Miriam T (Chamness), 210
    Mordecai Morris, 138
    Nathan, 138
    Oliver, 20,62,138,139
    Ora M, 62,139
    Orpha A, 30
    Pharaba/Phariba, 55,139
    Pharaba/Phariba W, 62,139
    Priscilla, 138
    Rachel M, 104
    Ray, 62
    Raymond P, 62,139
    Reaborn, 139
    Rebecca, 138

WHITE, Richard, 139
  Robert F, 62,139
  Robert Fisher, 62
  Robeson Taylor, 62
  Rosa/Rose Elma, 62,139
  Rosalie/Rosaline Annie/Anne
    (Richie), 62,139
  Rose Elma, 62
  Roy, 139
  Samuel Richie, 62
  Sarah, 138,139
  Sarah H, 10
  Sarah H (Strawbridge), 62
  Sarah J, 107
  Sarah Josephine, 62,138
  Sarah N, 45
  Silas, 180,210
  Susanna, 138
  Thomas, 139
  Thomas N, 62
  Thomas P, 30
  Thomas Rayburn, 62
  Winifred, 139
  Winnie L, 139
  Wm, 138
  Wm D, 139
  Wm Dilks, 62
  Wm H, 62
  Wm Irvin, 62,162
  Wm J, 139
  Wm W, 139
WHITELY, Charles O, 139
WHITEMAN, Mary, 36
WHITLOCK, Hannah, 40
WHITSON, Amos, 139
  Ann, 51
  Joshua Compton, 139
  Nathan, 139
  Rebeckah, 139
  Ruth, 21,161
  Willis, 139
WHITTER, Levi, 210
  see also **WHITTIER**
WHITTIER, Amanda M, 149,180
  Eliza (Anderson), 149,161,180
  Levi, 180
  Nettie Ann, 161,180
  Thomas, 149,161,180
  see also **WHITTER**
WICKER, Albert Elmore, 180
  Louisa Gazzeal (White), 180
  Noland, 180
WICKERSHAM, Abel, 139
  Ann/Anna/Anne, 30,51,81,139
  Ann Eliza, 139
  Ann Eliza (Dilhorn), 139
  Caleb, 139
  Catherine, 139
  Jehu, 81,111,139
  John, 139
  Lydia, 139
  Mary, 81,111,139
  Miriam, 139
  Rachel, 139
  Rhoda, 139
  Ruth Anna, 15
  Sarah, 139
  Wm, 139
WICKETT, Agnes Maria, 58,62
  Benjamin, 11,28,58,62,63,97,139
  Benjamin C, 52,62
  Benjamin F, 63
  Benjamin L, 139

WICKETT, Charles Henry, 62
  Clarinda (Crampton), 63
  Edgar S, 63
  Edith Bell/Belle, 52,62,139
  Ella E, 139
  Ella E (Stillwell), 62,63
  Emily Jane, 53,62,139
  Esther, 62,139
  Esther Ann, 139
  Esther Ann (Thomas), 52,62
  Fred S, 139
  Frederic, 63
  Frederick S, 62,63
  Herbert A, 63,139
  John Emmett, 62
  Leroy, 62,139
  Mabel E, 63,139
  Margaret Ann, 62
  Mary, 53
  Mary Esther, 28,62,97,139
  Mary S, 63
  Maude (Akin), 62
  Nathan Clem, 62
  Nellie S, 63,139
  Ora D, 63
  Samuel H, 63
  Sarah E, 76
  Sarah Elizabeth, 11,36,62,139
  Susan, 97,139
  Susan (Collins), 11,28,58,62,63
  Thomas Wm, 62,63,139
  Wm F, 62,139
WIDENER, Margaret J, 166
WIDOWS, Sarah, 139
WIGGINS, Anna Lula, 169
  Daniel P, 63
  Emma, 63
  Ernest, 63
  Frederick D, 63,139
  George, 63,139
  Horace, 139
  J L, 63
  Jessie, 63
  John, 63
  John D, 63,139
  John T, 168
  Laura, 139
  Martha, 168
  Mary (Burr), 169
  Mary Almeda (Elmore), 63
  Mary Eva (Henley), 63
  Nancy, 168
  Philemon, 169
  Phoebe, 63
  Rebecca (Boswell), 139
  Ruth A, 139
  Ruth Ann, 63
  Ruth Ann (Shearon), 139
  Ruth E, 63,139
WIGGS, Alice Caroline, 35
  Anne E (Hartman), 35
  Windsor, 35
WILCOX, Amos, 63
  George, 152
  Martha, 63
  Martha Ann (Nixon), 139
  Mary, 152
  Mary Ann, 152
  Sarah, 63
WILCUTS, Jonathan, 139
  Mary, 139
  Rhoda E (Mendenhall), 139
  see also **WILLCUTS, WILLCUTTS**

WILDIG, Minnie, 63
  Raymond Lowe, 63
  Wm B, 63
WILDMAN, Almeda M, 63
  Anna M, 46
  Edward, 30
  Hannah (Thorne), 30
  John, 139
  Marion/Martin, 63
  Mary T, 139
  Murray Shipley, 63,139
  Olive (Stiggleman/Stigleman), 63,139
  Olive M, 63
  Olive S, 139
  Rachel W, 30
WILES, Amelia, 153
  Anna Maria, 180
  Daniel, 210
  Daniel H, 180
  Deborah J, 210
  Elizabeth, 152
  Elizabeth, 157,162,165,180
  Elizabeth D, 180,197
  Esther G, 180
  Frances/Francis, 152,180,210
  Frances C, 197
  Frances/Francis Clanton, 165,180
  Isaac, 180
  Jane D, 210
  Keziah, 198
  Keziah K, 180,198
  Lenora, 210
  Luke, 152,165,180,197,198,210
  Luke Jr, 210
  Luke Sr, 210
  Martha Ann, 180
  Nancy, 180
  Nancy E, 180
  Nathan, 210
  Nathan H, 180
  Orlando, 210
  Rachel, 180
  Rebeckah, 180
  Rhoda, 165,180,197
  Rhoda H, 198
  Rhoda Jane, 180
  Stephen, 180
  Susannah, 210
  Thomas, 180,210
  Wm, 180,210
  Wm D, 210
  Wm Davis, 180
WILKINS, Amos, 139
WILKINSON, Alice (Jessup), 63
  Alva, 63
  Anna, 63,139
  Edward, 139
  Edwin, 139
  Edwin F, 63,139
  Hannah, 162
  Henry, 139
  Henry F, 63,139
  Hettie W, 147
  Jane (Lockwood), 147
  Lanson, 147
  Martha (Wood), 180
  Mary J, 139
  Mary Jane, 63,139
  Myrtle Loretta, 180
  Orville A, 63
  Wm, 180

WILLAN, Elizabeth (Fossett), 54
    James, 54
    Sarah, 28
    Sarah J, 54
WILLCUTS, Levi M, 139
    Milly, 139
    Rachel, 139
    see also **WILCUTS, WILLCUTTS**
WILLCUTTS, David, 139
    Jonathan, 139
    Thomas, 139
    see also **WILCUTS, WILLCUTS**
WILLETS, Ann, 139
    Ann (Brown), 139
    Belinda, 139
    Charity P, 139
    Harriet, 139
    Isaac, 139
    Joseph, 139
    Joshua, 139
    Levi, 112
    Lydia, 46
    Lydia G, 53
    Maria, 139
    Martha, 139
    Rhoda E, 112
    Ruben, 210
    see also **WILLETT, WILLETTS, WILLITS**
WILLETT, Isaac, 139
    see also **WILLETS, WILLETTS, WILLITS**
WILLETTS, Charity P, 140
    Isaac, 139,140
    Isaiah, 140
    Joshua, 139
    Lewis, 140
    Martha Ellen, 140
    Miriam (Nixon) Nixon, 140
    Newton, 139
    Rueben, 139
    Susannah, 140
    see also **WILLETS, WILLETT, WILLITS**
WILLIAMS, Abigail, 153
    Abraham, 180,120
    Achilles, 17,61,63,66,118,140,143
    Achsa, 63,140
    Ada B, 59,140
    Ada Florence, 63,140
    Adda, 27
    Albert, 140
    Alexander, 210
    Alfred, 63,140,180
    Alfred H, 63
    Alfred K, 140
    Almisa, 64
    Almyra, 141
    Alonzo, 140
    Alonzo P, 140
    Alpha Grace (O'Hara), 63
    Alpheus, 64
    Ann/Anna, 63,140,141,163,178
    Ann (Hobson), 210
    Ann L, 77
    Anna J, 63
    Anna Lynce, 140
    Asenath/Aseneth, 63,140
    Azariah, 180,206,210
    Azariah Jr, 210
    Barbara, 141
    Barbara J, 141

WILLIAMS, Barbara J (Greenbrier), 63
    Benjamin F, 63,140
    Bertha Minnie, 63
    Bertie, 140
    Beulah/Bulah, 118,140,143
    Beulah (Unthank), 17,61,63,66
    Billey/Billy, 140
    Boaz, 210
    Boyd, 140
    Caleb, 140,180,210
    Caroline, 17,63,84,100,140,180,211
    Casandra/Cassandra, 140
    Charity, 20,126,140
    Charles, 210
    Charles A, 180
    Chester, 63
    Christena, 211
    Christena (Covalt), 180
    Christopher, 140
    Clark, 140
    Clarkson, 180
    Cyrus M, 140
    Cyrus S, 140
    Daniel, 63,180,210
    Daniel B, 180,211
    Daniel W, 141
    Daniel Walter, 63,140
    David, 180,210
    David W, 64
    Deborah, 180,206,210
    Deborah Ann, 180
    Dora A, 63
    Earl, 63,141
    Edgar A, 140
    Edward, 63
    Edwin, 59
    Elim, 180
    Elisha, 63
    Eliza Ann, 140
    Elizabeth, 63,140
    Elizabeth (Crampton), 140
    Elizabeth (Haxton), 63
    Elizabeth A, 63,140
    Elizabeth D, 140
    Elmer C, 63
    Elzena, 178
    Emily, 140
    Emma, 63
    Emsley, 180
    Emsley T, 210
    Estella, 141
    Esther, 63,140
    Ethalinda L, 178
    Evaline, 63
    Exalina, 159,180
    Freddie, 140
    Frederick Wm, 140
    George, 140,210
    George W, 63,140
    George Walker, 63,140
    Goldie M, 64
    Granville, 63,140
    Granville F/T, 140
    Hannah, 140
    Hannah J, 140
    Harvey A, 211
    Harvey Alonzo, 180,211
    Harvy, 140
    Henry, 140,180,210
    Henry B, 64
    Henry C, 211
    Henry D, 64,140

WILLIAMS, Herbert P, 64,141
    Hezekiah, 63,140
    Howard E, 64
    Ida, 140
    Ida Mae Pearl, 63
    Ida Mary (Dennis), 63
    Ida Pearl, 141
    Isaac, 140,210,211
    Isaac C, 210
    Ithamer H, 64
    James, 210
    James Earl, 63,140
    Jane, 180
    Jared, 210
    Jason, 153
    Jehiel, 140
    Jennie, 180,211
    Jesse, 63,64,77,100,140,178
    Jesse Jr, 140
    Jesse B, 159,180,210,211
    Jesse L, 140
    Jesse O, 140
    Jesse T, 64,140
    Jesse Turner, 140
    John, 63,140,180,210
    John Boyd, 140
    John F C, 64,140
    John H, 141
    John H, 63
    John M, 60,63,210
    John Mills, 180
    John P, 63,140
    John W, 140
    John Wm, 63,140
    Jonathan, 140,180,210
    Joseph, 63,140,149,180,210
    Joseph C, 180,211
    Joshua, 140
    Josiah, 140
    King R, 63,140
    Laura, 185
    Laura J (Townsend), 63
    Lerton, 140
    Lester, 180,211
    Lezene/Luzena/Luzene, 140,180,210
    Liddia/Lydia, 140,156
    Lillie, 140
    Lillie C, 64,140
    Louie Pearl, 211
    Lula, 63,140
    Luther Converse, 140
    Lydia, 7
    Lydia A, 211
    Lydia Ann (Olet), 180
    Mable, 63
    Mae E, 63
    Malinda/Melinda, 63,140
    Marchant/Merchant, 140,180,210
    Margaret, 180,210
    Margaret K (Higgenbotham), 63
    Margaret M, 64
    Marilla, 211
    Marilla C (Craner), 180
    Martha, 64,140
    Martha (Demine), 59
    Martha Ann, 63,66
    Martha J, 149
    Martha Jane, 163
    Martin, 210
    Mary, 63,140,180
    Mary (Cook), 140
    Mary (Smith), 63,140

WILLIAMS, Mary Alice, 63,140
    Mary Alice (Lamb), 180
    Mary Ann/Maryann, 211
    Mary Ann (Mendenhall), 159,180,210
    Mary Anne (Browne), 3
    Mary E, 60,141
    Mary Elizabeth, 140
    Mary Ellen, 153
    Mary Evalina (Coats), 63
    Mary Evelina, 63
    Mary S, 140
    Mathew/Matthew, 180,210,211
    Matilda, 140,180,210
    Matilda (Baldwin), 140
    Mattie M, 63,140
    May, 140
    Melissa Jane (Taylor), 63
    Micajah T, 140
    Mildred V, 63
    Millican, 180
    Milton, 63,140
    Minerva, 63,141
    Minerva (McCarty), 60,63
    Minnie, 140
    Minnie F, 63
    Nancy, 149
    Nancy (Biggs), 180
    Nancy E (Beeson), 210
    Narcissa, 140
    Nathan, 63,140,141
    Nathan S, 64
    Nellie, 64,140
    Nelly A, 140
    Obed, 180,211
    Oliver, 63,180,210
    Ora Chalfant, 63
    Owen, 140
    Pearl, 211
    Pheba (Bonine), 140
    Phebe Ann, 129,140
    Polly, 140
    Polly Ann, 180
    Prudence, 64
    Rachel, 63,136,140,180,210
    Rachel (Atkinson), 210
    Rachel (Mills), 180
    Rachel A (Shepard), 64
    Rebecca/Rebekah, 63,66,140,143
    Rebecca L, 63,140
    Rhoda, 180
    Richard, 31,64,140,180,210
    Robert, 63,64,140,156
    Robert T, 64,141
    Rosa, 63,140
    Rosetta, 140
    Rufus, 180
    Ruth, 140,210
    Ruth Ann/Ruthanne, 64,140
    Ruth Anna (Weeks), 140
    Salina, 140,180,210
    Sally, 140,180
    Sarah, 61,63,77,100,112,136,140,156,
      180,206
    Sarah (Russel), 64
    Sarah Elizabeth, 3
    Sarah T, 140
    Serton Converse, 63
    Sophia/Sophiah, 180,185,211
    Sophia (Cates), 180
    Sophia (Thornburg), 185
    Stella, 63
    Stephen/Steven, 64

WILLIAMS, Susan, 118,140
    Susanna/Susannah, 31,63,140
    Susannah (Rich), 140
    Thomas Patten, 180
    W H, 63
    Walter C, 64
    Wesley, 63
    Willie D, 140
    Wm, 63,64,140,180,210
    Wm Albert, 140
    Wm D, 63
    Wm S, 140
    Zalinda/Zelinda, 63,140
WILLIAMSON, Anna, 64,141
    Augusta/Augustie, 64,141
    Augustine M, 141
    Sarah, 64,141
    Silas, 64,141
WILLIS, Anna, 181
    Bertha, 211
    Cora V, 211
    Cora Violet, 181
    Cynthia Ellen, 181
    David, 141,181,211
    David Jr, 211
    Dollie Robertha, 181
    Dottie R, 211
    Eliza Ann, 181,211
    Hanah, 181
    Hannah (Lee), 211
    Harvey, 181
    Henry, 181,211
    Isaac, 181,211
    Jesse, 181,211
    John, 181,211
    Jonathan, 181,211
    Lindsey, 181
    Loucinda/Lucinda, 141,211
    Lydia, 141,181,186,211
    Maggie, 211
    Marcus, 211
    Margaret J, 211
    Margaret J (Wright), 181
    Mark R, 181,211
    Mary, 181
    Metilda, 141
    Rachel, 181,211
    Ruth, 211
    Sarah, 181
    Sarah Lavine, 211
    Viola, 211
    Waldo, 211
    Wm, 181,211
WILLITS, Ann, 141
    Isaac, 211
    Mary (Harris), 211
    Rachel, 211
    Rueben, 211
    Wm, 141
    see also **WILLETS**, **WILLETT**,
      WILLETTS
WILLMET, Charles, 141
    Joseph, 141
    Thomas, 141
WILLMORE, Jesse W, 211
    Martha Jane, 211
    see also **WILMORE**
WILLMOT, Elizabeth, 141
    Lydia, 141
    Polly, 141
    Rebecca, 141
    see also **WILLMOT**, **WILMOT**,
      WILMOTT

WILLMOTT, Thomas, 141
    see also **WILLMOT**, **WILMOT**,
      WILMOTT
WILLOUGHBY, Leosa 10
WILLS, Mary (Thomas), 141
WILLSON, Jesse, 211
    see also **WILSON**
WILMORE, Jesse, 211
    Jesse W, 181
    Martha Jane, 181
    Mary A, 181
    see also **WILLMORE**
WILMOT, Thomas, 141
    see also **WILLMOT**, **WILLMOTT**,
      WILMOTT
WILMOTT, A A, 64
    Edward Stanbrook, 64
    Elinor, 64
    Ella Mary, 64
    Joseph, 141
    R K, 64
    Robert Renison, 64
    Winifred Emily, 64
    see also **WILLMOT**, **WILLMOTT**,
      WILMOT
WILSON, —— (White), 64
    Abigail, 64,141
    Ada M, 141
    Alice Lillian, 141
    Asenath (Dennis), 211
    Benezetti/Benizette, 64,141
    Benjamin, 141
    Catharine/Catherine, 141
    Charles, 141
    Christian, 211
    Christopher, 14
    David, 141
    Eleazar/Eliazar, 64,141
    Eli, 141
    Eliza (Mendenhall), 141
    Eliza A (Mendenhall), 64
    Elizabeth, 4,25,55,62,64,141,142,154,
      158,159,171,172,181,186,211
    Elizabeth B, 141
    Elizabeth C, 141
    Ella (Taylor), 64,141
    Ella T, 141
    Ellis G, 141
    Elmina H, 141
    Esther J, 141
    Esther Mariah, 141
    Ethel, 64,141
    Eva, 141
    Eva E, 141
    Ezekiah Lassiter, 64
    Ezekiel, 141
    Ezekiel L, 64
    Fannie (Weaver), 64
    Fannie/Fanny J, 64,141
    Folger, 141
    Folger Pope, 64
    Francis, 52
    Hannah, 58,141,164,181,190
    Hannah (Baldwin), 181,211
    Harmon, 141
    Harmon C, 64,141
    Harvey, 141
    Harvey T, 64
    Henry, 64,141
    Hester Mariah, 141
    Homer, 64,141
    Huldah J, 141

WILSON, Ida, 64,141
    Irena, 141
    Isaac, 64,141
    Isabel, 181,211
    Isabel (Beason), 211
    J Mark, 64
    Jabez, 181
    James, 64,141
    James C, 141
    Jeffries, 141
    Jesse, 181,211
    John, 64,141
    John Charles, 64
    John S, 64
    Joseph, 25,64,141
    Joseph R, 141
    Joseph Thomas, 141
    Josephine, 64
    Kezia/Keziah, 141
    Letta, 64
    Lincoln, 64,141
    Louella, 141
    Luetta, 141
    Lydia, 141
    M Elizabeth, 141
    M Peninah (Hill), 141
    Manliff, 181
    Manlove, 211
    Margaret (Butler), 14
    Maria, 141
    Martha, 141
    Martha Ellen, 141
    Mary, 64,141
    Mary (White), 64
    Mary Elizabeth, 179
    Mary W, 141
    Maurice/Morris E, 141
    Melissa E, 14
    Milicent/Millicent, 141
    Miriam Penninah (Hill), 64
    Morris Edward, 141
    Nathan, 141
    Nathan E, 181
    Nathan L, 211
    Newby, 206,211
    Olive, 64,141
    Rachel, 27,150,173,174
    Rebecca C, 141
    Ruth, 64,141
    Ruthanna, 25
    Samuel, 64,141
    Sarah, 14,64,141
    Sarah (Clawson), 141
    Sarah (Stokes), 141
    Sarah P, 141
    Sarah W, 141
    Theodate P, 141
    Theodore Pope, 64
    Thomas, 141
    Thomas Jefferson, 141
    Thomas T, 141
    Thomas Thornburgh, 64
    Timothy, 64,141
    Virgil, 141
    W R, 64
    Wm B, 141
    Wm N, 141
    Wm Nicholson, 64
    Wm Penn, 141
    Wm Poole, 141
    Wm Taylor, 64,141
    Zeruah (Beeson), 181
    see also **WILLSON**

WILT, Dora S, 141
    Frank, 141
WIMMER, Hannah, 161
WINCHESTER, Cora Ann (Henley), 64
    Irwin, 64
WINDER, Abner, 64,141
    Cora (Zimmer), 55,64
    Cora E, 141
    Elmina H (Foster), 64
    Esther Ann, 101,141
    Hope, 141
    Joseph, 84
    Joseph E, 64
    Joseph John, 141
    Leona C, 141
    Leona Coreen, 55,64
    Mary J, 17,18
    Mary Jane, 84,141
    Rebecca, 64
    Rebecca C, 141
    Rebecca C (Pool), 141
    Ross Raymond, 64
    Samuel C, 141
    Samuel Charles, 55,64,141
    Susan, 64,141
    Wayne H, 64
WINDLE, Deborah, 64,141
    Elizabeth, 37
    Emilie, 64
    Emily, 141
    Job, 64
    Mary (Evans), 64
    Mary E, 141
    Rebecca, 64,141
WINDSOR, Alfred, 181,211
    Charlotte (Tate), 181
    China, 181
    Ned, 181
    Nettie E (Smith), 181
    see also **WINSER**
WINSER, Octie, 211
    see also **WINDSOR**
WINSLOW, Ed, 45
    Henry, 142
    John, 64,142
    John H, 142
    John Hubbard, 142
    John M, 142
    John Milton, 142
    Mary, 45,142
    Mary Amy, 142
    Mary Amy (Barker), 101
    Mary B, 45,117,142
    Mary Barker, 142
    Robert B, 101,142
WINSTON, Seth, 142
WINTERS, Adaline A, 54
WINTROW, Rachel (Draper), 64
    Ross, 64
    Wm, 64
WIRTS, Adam, 64
    Charles I, 64
    Cora M (Bennett), 64
    Dorris L, 64
    Jacob C, 64
    Mary F, 64
    Sarah, 64
WISE, Charles, 211
    Charles B, 181
    David, 181
    Joseph, 181
    Malvina (Adams), 181

WISE, Mary (Wright), 181
    Viretta (Davis), 181
WISENER, Jacob, 2
    Isaac, 2
    Mary, 2
    Sarah, 2
    Thomas, 2
WISHARD, Lucinda B J, 142
    Lucinda P (Jessup), 64
WITCHEL, Isaac, 142
    Mary, 142
    see also **WITCHELL**
WITCHELL, Isaac, 142
    Mary, 134,142
    see also **WITCHEL**
WOLF, Ella, 64
    George, 64
    Georgia Edith, 64
    Lilly, 13
    Wm, 64
    see also **WOLFE**
WOLFE, Clayton B, 64,142
    Daisy Pearl, 64
    David, 64,142
    David W, 57,64
    Elfleela R, 142
    Elfreda A, 64
    Elijah, 142
    Elijah B, 142
    Elizabeth, 37
    Grace, 37,65
    Harry, 142
    Harry P F, 64,142
    Indiana, 64
    James A Garfield, 64
    John E, 37,51,65,142
    Lillie May, 57,64
    Lizzie, 142
    Martha, 142
    Mary, 37,142
    Mary Adaline/Adeline, 51,65,142
    Mary Elizabeth (Jenkinson), 65
    Mattie E, 57,64,142
    Maud, 51,65
    Nellie J, 64
    Wm, 142
    Wm Clement, 65
WOLFORD, Anna, 142
    Asenath/Asenith, 211
    Asenath C (Baldwin), 181
    Charles C, 142
    Della May, 181,211
    Dora (Landick), 181
    Harry, 142
    John/Johnie, 181,211
    John H, 211
    John W, 181
    Milton, 211
WOOD, Asenath W, 173
    Bertha, 142
    Cora Bertha (Hill), 65
    Elizabeth (Wilson), 142
    Elizabeth A (Crew), 65
    Elva, 181
    Emmaline (Featherling), 181
    George, 65
    Jacob, 142,173
    John, 181
    Joseph, 211
    Joseph L, 181,211
    Louanna H (Haughton), 65
    Luanna, 142

WOOD, Margaret, 211
　Margaret J, 181
　Margaret K (Ratliff), 142
　Martha, 180
　Mary Alice (Kenworthy), 65
　Mary Ann, 211
　Mary Ann (Davis), 181
　N S, 65
　Phebe (Pickering), 173
　Ruth Evyline, 65
　Sarah E, 181,211
　Simeon, 142
　Stephen Albert, 181
　Thomas, 65
　Wm T, 65
　Wyatt Sumner, 65
　see also **WOODS**
WOODARD, Adaline, 211
　Albert M, 65,142
　Alice, 65,142,211
　Alice J, 181
　Alpheus Lindley, 211
　Alta, 102
　Annie B (Evans), 18,65,142
　Bertha, 65
　Cadan, 142
　Catharine Mayhew, 142
　Cornelius J, 142
　Edward, 32
　Ella, 65
　Ella M, 142
　Ella May, 51,65,142
　Elvira, 142
　Elvira (Townsend), 65,181
　Elvira F, 142
　Emily, 58,133,178
　Emily Jane, 211
　Ethel, 18,65
　Isaac Evans, 65
　Isaac P, 32,65,142
　Jesse, 200,211
　Laura Alice (Hodgin), 65
　Laura H, 142
　Leander J, 18,65,142
　Lena Lucile, 142
　Lois, 65
　Lona Lucile, 65
　Louisa, 96,142
　Louisa M, 122
　Luke, 65,142,181
　Lydia, 32,65,142
　Lydia Alta, 32,65,142
　Martha Jane, 65,142
　Mary Ann, 211
　Mary C, 142
　Miriam, 96
　Nathan D, 142
　Oliver C, 65,142
　Rachel, 142
　Rebecca, 65,142
　Sarah, 47
　Sarah B, 142
　Sarah (Burgess), 142
　Thomas, 96,122,211
　Vera Chandler, 65
　Vestal, 211
WOODHURST, Cora, 8
　Elizabeth, 52
WOODS, Angelina, 142
　see also **WOOD**
WOODY, Alanson G, 173
　Alanson Gray, 181
　Alson, 211

WOODY, Anthony, 211
　Anthony C, 181
　Elizabeth (Chamness), 167,181
　Genetta, 211
　George, 211
　George L, 181
　Hannah, 147,148,167
　Harriet C, 167
　Harriett, 181,199,211
　Hugh, 154,167,181,211
　James, 181
　Jennettie E (Smith), 181
　Joshua, 167,181,211
　Laura Alice, 211
　Lavia A, 181
　Malinda/Melinda (Chamness), 167,
　　181,211
　Marcelia, 167,181
　Mary, 181,211
　Mary (Atkinson), 154,181
　Mary C, 187
　Mary E, 173,181
　Polly C, 181
　Ruth, 154,155,175,181
　Sarah (Brown), 173,181
WOOLAN, Emma S, 65
　Hiram S, 65
　Ruby Francis, 65
WOOLARD, Aaron, 158,181
　Edith, 181
　Hannah (Werking), 158,181
　Jennie, 158,181
WOOLLEY, Anna B (Brower), 65
　Ashen D, 65
　Harry Herbert, 65
　Martha (Waggoner), 65
　Mary, 65
　Mary Helen, 65
　Milton, 65
　R H, 65
　Wm Herbert, 65
WOOLMAN, Anna, 65
　Elizabeth A, 65
　Mary E, 37
　Uriah, 65
WOOTEN, Abijah, 142
　Addie T, 142
　Andrew, 142
　Charles Welden, 142
　Docia, 142
　Docia S, 65
　Elmer O, 65
　Lydia, 142
　Martha, 65
　Mary, 65
　Naomi T, 142
　Wm S, 65,142
　see also **WOOTON**
WOOTON, Abijah, 65,142
　Addie F/T, 65,142
　Charles Welden, 65,142
　Docia S, 142
　Elmer O, 142
　Martha, 142
　Mary, 142
　Naomi, 65
　Waldo Emerson, 65,142
　Wm S, 142
　see also **WOOTEN**
WORLEY, Mary/May, 11
　Ellen, 11
　John, 11

WORTH, David, 155,158,181,191
　Eunice, 191
　Eunice (Gardner), 155,158,181
　Evalina/Evelina/Eveline, 17,158,181,
　　191
　Job, 166,177,181,204,211
　Joseph Clinton, 211
　Joseph Dewit Clinton, 142
　Keziah, 142
　Laura Ann, 142,143
　Louisa, 153,155,181
　Lydia, 142,143,173,204
　Mary, 161,170,177,181,208
　Miriam, 156
　Nancy (Macy) Marshall, 181
　Nellie, 44
　Obed, 211
　Obed B, 211
　Reuben, 211
　Reuben M, 65,142,211
　Reuben W, 143
　Rhoda, 166,170,177
　Rhoda, 181,204,211
　Sarah L (Leonard) Swain, 211
　Thomas, 181,211
　Wm, 211
WORTHINGTON, Elizabeth, 142
　Elizabeth Farnam, 142
　Elizabeth W, 142
　Henry, 142
　Henry W, 142
　Jeremiah Willits, 142
　Samuel, 142
　Sarah, 142
WRIGHT, Aaron, 142,143
　Abel, 65
　Abegail, 212
　Absolom, 39
　Allen, 65,211
　Andrew, 65
　Ann/Annie, 11,65,77,112,143
　Anna C, 66
　Aquilla, 143
　Benjamin C, 65
　Benjamin Corrydon/Corydon, 143
　Benjamin F, 65
　Benjamin Franklin, 143
　Betsey, 211
　Caroline (Carpenter), 65
　Caroline M, 143
　Caroline M (Carpenter), 143
　Charity, 112,142,143
　Charles, 65
　Charles Evan, 66
　Charles S, 143
　Cyrus, 65,66,118,142
　David, 2,65,66,142,211
　Deborah, 65,143
　E D, 66
　Edmund, 65,143
　Edward, 65,142,143
　Edwin C, 143
　Eli, 65
　Elijah, 1,65,66,90,127
　Elijah Sr, 11,65
　Elisabeth/Elizabeth, 65,130,142,143,
　　157,210,211,212
　Eliza, 143,212
　Eliza (Clark), 66,143
　Eliza Jane, 65,118,143
　Eliza Jennie (Chapman), 66
　Eliza M, 212

WRIGHT, Eliza S, 11
    Elizabeth F, 66
    Ellen Florence, 65,143
    Emily, 143
    Emma C, 66
    Ena, 66
    Enoch, 65
    Esther, 41,142
    Esther G, 65
    Evan, 65,143
    Francis, 143
    Francis M, 66,143
    Frank, 34,143
    Fremont, 143
    George, 211,212
    Gertrude, 34
    Granville L, 143
    Granville S, 65,143
    Hannah, 2,65,66,127,142,143,181
    Hannah P, 143
    Harriet (Lancaster), 66
    Hatfield, 142
    Henry, 66
    Henry C, 65,143
    Hepsa (Coffin), 65,142
    Ida Jessamine, 65
    Isaac, 41,65,112,142,143
    Jabez, 66,143
    Jacob, 143
    Jacob L, 143
    Jacob S, 65
    Jacob T, 143
    James, 65,66,142,143,211,212
    James Jr, 143
    James H, 142
    Jane, 23,65,66,90
    Jemima W (Hunnicutt), 212
    Jesse, 65,211,212
    Joel, 143,211
    Joel Kindley/Lindley, 66,143
    John, 66,142,143
    John E, 212
    John H, 142
    John Prior, 142
    Jonathan, 65,66,142,143
    Jonathan J, 143
    Joshua, 210
    Judith, 212
    Juliet, 10
    Kate, 143
    Katherine, 65
    Laura, 8
    Laura Ann, 66,143
    Laura Ann (Worth), 143
    Lewis, 66
    Lucinda, 212
    Lucretia, 142
    Luke, 211,212
    Lydia, 66,81,142,143
    Lydia (Hawkins), 142
    Macaijah/Micajah, 143
    Mahala, 212
    Mahala Ann, 180,210
    Margaret, 34,39
    Margaret J, 181
    Martha, 5
    Martin, 65
    Mary, 65,66,74,142,143,181
    Mary (Randall), 41

WRIGHT, Mary (Wright), 142
    Mary Amanda, 66,143
    Mary Ann, 36,142,143
    Mary Ann (Randall), 65,66
    Mary B, 143
    Mary C, 66
    Mary Catharine, 143
    Mary E, 66
    Mary Ellen (Stroud), 65,66
    Mary Emily, 143
    Mary Emily (Hawkins), 65
    Mary H, 142
    Mary Josephine, 65,143
    Mary K, 143
    Mary Kinsey, 143
    Mary L, 66
    Mary S, 212
    Mary S (Beeson), 212
    Matilda/Matildah Ann, 65,143
    Millicent, 142
    Miriam, 65,66,118,142
    Morris P, 66,143
    Moses, 143
    Naomi, 142
    Nathan, 65,66,143
    Nathan C, 65,66
    O H, 66
    Oliver, 65
    Orlena, 143
    Parvin, 65,66,143
    Pearl M, 66
    Ralph, 1,2,65,66,142
    Ralph Jr, 142
    Rebecca, 66,137,142,143
    Rebecca (Charles), 66,143
    Rebecca (Williams), 66,143
    Reuben Worth, 143
    Rhoda, 65,74,142
    Richardson, 66
    Ruth, 65,66
    Samuel, 65
    Sarah, 65,78,95,142,143,212
    Sarah (Norris), 181
    Susan, 86,143
    Susan (Baldwin), 39
    Susan B, 5
    Susan C, 143
    Susan Carpenter, 65
    Susan Jane, 143
    Susan Jane (Grave), 66
    Susanna/Susannah, 11,40,65,66,90,
      112,127,142,143
    Thaddeus/Thadeus, 66,143
    Theodore, 66
    Theodore F, 143
    Thomas, 66
    Thomas W, 143
    Walter B, 66,143
    Walter G, 143
    Wilbur S, 143
    Wilson, 65
    Wm, 65,66,142,143,181,211
    Wm Arthur, 66
    see also **RIGHT**
WRIGHTSMAN, Abraham, 150,165,175,
    181
    James, 181
    Mary, 154,175,181
    Nancy, 150,181

WRIGHTSMAN, Rachel (Reynard), 150,
    165,175,181
    Rachel Elizabeth (Bales), 181
    see also **RIGHTSMAN**
WRITTENHOUSE, Mary Etta, 212
    Walter, 212
    see also **RITTENHOUSE**
WYATT, Audry J, 143
    Barton, 66,143
    Mary, 66,143
    Mary C, 143
    Pearl, 66

YAGER, Rose Anna, 143
    Thomas, 143
    see also **YEAGER**
YATES, Eliza, 143
    see also **YEATES**
YATKINS, Hiram, 66
    Marcus, 66
    Sarah, 66
    Wm, 66
YEAGER, Anna, 143
    Thomas, 143
    see also **YAGER**
YEARYAN, George, 66
    I/J Chester, 66
    Phenette, 66
YEATS, Clarke, 143
    Elizabeth, 143
    Enoch, 143
    Mary, 143
    Patrick, 143
    see also **YATES**
YEO, Martha Ann, 143
    Martha Ann (Williams), 66
    Milton J, 66
    Wm H, 143
YORK, Amy, 48
    Matilda C, 48
    Thomas, 48
YOUNG, Abner, 66
    Anna/Annie, 21,161
    Edward C, 143
    Emma Bell, 165,181
    Eustace Sherman, 206
    Fanny (Stantz), 165,170,181
    Hiram, 143
    Marie, 28
    Mary E, 170,181
    Rebecca, 66,143
    Robert W, 143
    Susan, 66
    Wm, 165,170,181
YOUNT, Henry, 30
    Katherine, 30
    Mary Ann, 30
    see also **YOUNTS**
YOUNTS, Edith Bell (Gray), 181
    Oliver U, 181
    see also **YOUNT**

ZEEK, Effie M, 58
ZIMMER, Cora, 55,64
ZIMMERMAN, David E, 181
    Elta, 181
    Levine, 181
    Wm, 181